AIA

Professional 2 Level
FINANCIAL ACCOUNTING AND REPORTING 2
LEARNING & PRACTICE WORKBOOK

In this 2025 edition

- A **user-friendly format** for easy navigation
- **Exam-centred topic coverage**, directly linked to AIA's syllabus
- **Exam focus points** showing you what the examiner will want you to do
- Regular **fast forward** summaries emphasising the key points in each chapter
- **Questions** and **quick quizzes** to test your understanding
- **Practice question bank** containing exam standard questions with answers
- **Exam question bank** containing recent exam standard questions with answers
- **Mock exam** for real exam practice
- A full index

FOR EXAMS FROM MAY 2025

Second edition November 2024

ISBN 9781 0355 2583 6

eISBN 9781 0355 2611 6

British Library Cataloguing-in-Publication Data
A catalogue record for this book is available from the British Library

Published by

BPP Learning Media Ltd
BPP House, Aldine Place
142-144 Uxbridge Road
London W12 8AA

learningmedia.bpp.com

Printed in the United Kingdom

> Your learning materials, published by BPP Learning Media Ltd, are printed on paper obtained from traceable sustainable sources.

All rights reserved. No part of this publication may be reproduced, stored in a retrieval system or transmitted in any form or by any means, electronic, mechanical, photocopying, recording or otherwise, without the prior written permission of BPP Learning Media.

The contents of this book are intended as a guide and not professional advice. Although every effort has been made to ensure that the contents of this book are correct at the time of going to press, BPP Learning Media makes no warranty that the information in this book is accurate or complete and accept no liability for any loss or damage suffered by any person acting or refraining from acting as a result of the material in this book.

We are grateful to the Association of International Accountants for permission to reproduce past examination questions. The suggested solutions in the exam answer bank have been prepared by BPP Learning Media Ltd.

BPP Learning Media is grateful to the IASB for permission to reproduce extracts from the International Financial Reporting Standards including all International Accounting Standards, SIC and IFRIC Interpretations (the Standards). The Standards together with their accompanying documents are issued by:

The International Accounting Standards Board (IASB) 30 Cannon Street, London, EC4M 6XH, United Kingdom. Email: info@ifrs.org Web: www.ifrs.org

Disclaimer: The IASB, the International Financial Reporting Standards (IFRS) Foundation, the authors and the publishers do not accept responsibility for any loss caused by acting or refraining from acting in reliance on the material in this publication, whether such loss is caused by negligence or otherwise to the maximum extent permitted by law.

©
BPP Learning Media Ltd
2024

A note about copyright

Dear Customer

What does the little © mean and why does it matter?

Your market-leading BPP books, course materials and e-learning materials do not write and update themselves. People write them on their own behalf or as employees of an organisation that invests in this activity. Copyright law protects their livelihoods. It does so by creating rights over the use of the content.

Breach of copyright is a form of theft – as well as being a criminal offence in some jurisdictions, it is potentially a serious breach of professional ethics.

With current technology, things might seem a bit hazy but, basically, without the express permission of BPP Learning Media:

- Photocopying our materials is a breach of copyright
- Scanning, ripcasting or conversion of our digital materials into different file formats, uploading them to facebook or e-mailing them to your friends is a breach of copyright

You can, of course, sell your books, in the form in which you have bought them – once you have finished with them. (Is this fair to your fellow students? We update for a reason.) Please note the e-products are sold on a single user licence basis: we do not supply 'unlock' codes to people who have bought them secondhand.

And what about outside the UK? BPP Learning Media strives to make our materials available at prices students can afford by local printing arrangements, pricing policies and partnerships which are clearly listed on our website. A tiny minority ignore this and indulge in criminal activity by illegally photocopying our material or supporting organisations that do. If they act illegally and unethically in one area, can you really trust them?

Copyright © IFRS Foundation

All rights reserved. Reproduction and use rights are strictly limited. No part of this publication may be translated, reprinted or reproduced or utilised in any form either in whole or in part or by any electronic, mechanical or other means, now known or hereafter invented, including photocopying and recording, or in any information storage and retrieval system, without prior permission in writing from the IFRS Foundation. Contact the IFRS Foundation for further details.

The IFRS Foundation logo, the IASB logo, the IFRS for SMEs logo, the "Hexagon Device", "IFRS Foundation", "eIFRS", "IAS", "IASB", "IFRS for SMEs", "IASs", "IFRS", "IFRSs", "International Accounting Standards" and "International Financial Reporting Standards", "IFRIC" "SIC" and "IFRS Taxonomy" are **Trade Marks** of the IFRS Foundation.

Further details of the Trade Marks including details of countries where the Trade Marks are registered or applied for are available from the Licensor on request.

Contents

Page

Introduction

The introduction pages contain lots of valuable advice and information. They include tips on studying for and passing the exam, also the content of the syllabus and what has been examined.

How the BPP Learning Media Learning & Practice Workbook can help you pass – Help yourself study for your AIA exams – Syllabus – AIA List of examinable Standards – Command words and learning outcomes – The exam paper

Part A Contemporary issues

1	Current thought and practice	3
2	Presentation of published financial statements	27
3	Sustainability reporting	59
4	Ethics and regulation of corporate financial reporting	79
5	Reporting for specialised entities	93

Part B Business combinations and group financial statements

6	Revision of basic groups	109
7	Complex groups	155
8	Changes in group structures	183
9	Foreign currency translation	209
10	Group statements of cash flows	233

Part C Accounting and reporting techniques

11	Interim reporting, first-time adoption and fair values	261
12	Tangible non-current assets and inventory	283
13	Intangible non-current assets	319
14	Financial instruments	337
15	Leases	379
16	Employee benefits	401
17	Taxation	425
18	Reporting financial performance	459
19	Provisions, contingencies and events after the reporting period	497
20	Related parties and share-based payment	511
21	Revenue recognition and off balance	533
22	IFRS for SMEs	561
23	Ratio and trend analysis	585

Answers to end of chapter questions 607
Practice question bank 643
Practice answer bank 671
New Section – Exam question bank 717
New Section – Exam answer bank 749
Mock exam 813
Index 835

How the BPP Learning Media Learning & Practice Workbook can help you pass

> It provides you with the knowledge and understanding, skills and application techniques that you need to be successful in your exams

This Learning & Practice Workbook has been targeted at the **Financial Accounting and Reporting 2** syllabus.

- It is **comprehensive**. It covers the syllabus content. No more, no less.
- It is written at the **right level**. Each chapter is written with AIA's syllabus in mind.
- It is aimed at the **exam**. We have taken account of recent exams, guidance the examiner has given and the assessment methodology.

> It allows you to study in the way that best suits your learning style and the time you have available, by following your personal Study Plan (see page v)

You may be studying at home on your own or you may be attending a course. You may like to read every word, or you may prefer to do a fast read through and learn through doing practise questions the rest of the time. However, you study, you will find the BPP Learning Media Learning & Practice Workbook meets your needs in designing and following your personal Study Plan.

Help yourself study for your AIA exams

Exams for professional bodies such as AIA are very different from those you have taken at college or university. You will be under **greater time pressure before** the exam – as you may be combining your study with work. Here are some hints and tips.

The right approach

1 **Develop the right attitude**

Believe in yourself	Yes, there is a lot to learn. But thousands have succeeded before and you can too.
Remember why you're doing it	You are studying for a good reason: to advance your career.

2 **Focus on the exam**

Read through the Syllabus	This tells you what you are expected to know and is supplemented by **Exam focus points** in the text.
Study the Exam paper section	Past papers are likely to be good guides to what you should expect in the exam.

3 **The right method**

See the whole picture	Keeping in mind how all the detail you need to know fits into the whole picture will help you understand it better. • The **Introduction** of each chapter puts the material in context. • The **Syllabus content** and **Exam focus points** show you what you need to **grasp**.
Use your own words	To absorb the information (and to practise your written communication skills), you need to **put it into your own words**. • **Take notes.** • Answer the **questions** in each chapter. • Draw **mindmaps**. • Try **'teaching' a subject** to a colleague or friend.
Give yourself cues to jog your memory	The Learning & Practice Workbook uses **bold** to **highlight key points**. • Try **colour coding** with a highlighter pen. • Write **key points** on cards.

4 **The right recap**

Review, review, review	Regularly reviewing a topic in summary form can **fix it in your memory**. The Learning & Practice Workbook helps you review in many ways. • **Chapter roundups** summarise the 'Fast forward' key points in each chapter. Use them to recap each study session. • The **Quick quiz** actively tests your grasp of the essentials. • Go through the **Examples** in each chapter a second or third time.

INTRODUCTION

Developing your personal Study Plan

BPP recommends you follow a study plan. Planning and sticking to the plan are key elements of learning successfully.

There are five steps you should work through.

Step 1   How do you learn?

What types of intelligence do you display when learning? You might be advised to brush up on certain study skills before launching into this Learning & Practice Workbook, but refer to the 'tackling your studies' section below which will help.

Step 2   What do you prefer to do first?

If you prefer to get to grips with a theory before seeing how it is applied, we suggest you concentrate first on the explanations we give in each chapter before looking at the examples and case studies. If you prefer to see first how things work in practice, read through the detail in each chapter, and concentrate on the examples and case studies, before supplementing your understanding by reading the detail.

Step 3   How much time do you have?

Work out the time you have available per week, given the following.

- The standard you have set yourself
- The other exam(s) you are sitting
- Practical matters such as work, travel, exercise, sleep and social life

Note your time available in box A.   A [   ] Hours

Step 4   Allocate your time

- Take the time you have available per week for this Learning & Practice Workbook shown in box A, multiply it by the number of weeks available and insert the result in box B.   B [   ]
- Divide the figure in box B by the number of chapters in this text and insert the result in box C.   C [   ]

Remember that this is only a rough guide. Some of the chapters in this book are longer and more complicated than others, and you will find some subjects easier to understand than others.

Step 5   Implement

Set about studying each chapter in the time shown in box C, following the key study steps in the order suggested by your particular learning style.

This is your personal **Study Plan**. You should try to combine it with the study sequence outlined below. You may want to modify the sequence to adapt it to your **personal style**.

Tackling your studies

The best way to approach this Learning & Practice Workbook is to tackle the chapters in order. Taking into account your individual learning style, you could follow this sequence for each chapter.

Key study steps	Activity
Step 1 **Topic list**	This topic list helps you navigate each chapter; each numbered topic is a numbered section in the chapter.
Step 2 **Introduction**	This sets your objectives for study by giving you the big picture in terms of the context of the chapter. The content is referenced to the syllabus, and Exam guidance shows how the topic is likely to be examined. The Introduction tells you **why** the topics covered in the chapter need to be studied.
Step 3 **Knowledge brought forward boxes**	These highlight information and techniques that it is assumed you have 'brought forward' with you from your earlier studies. Remember that you may be tested on these areas in the exam. If you are unsure of these areas, you should consider revising your more detailed study material from earlier papers.
Step 4 **Fast forward**	Fast forward boxes give you a quick summary of the content of each of the main chapter sections. They are listed together in the roundup at the end of each chapter to help you review each chapter quickly.
Step 5 **Explanations**	Proceed methodically through each chapter, particularly focusing on areas highlighted as significant in the chapter introduction, or areas that are frequently examined.
Step 6 **Key terms and Exam focus points**	- Key terms can often earn you **easy marks** if you state them clearly and correctly in an exam answer. They are highlighted in the index at the back of this text. - Exam focus points state how the topic has been or may be examined, difficulties that can occur in questions about the topic, and examiner feedback on common weaknesses in answers.
Step 7 **Note taking**	Take brief notes, if you wish. Don't copy out too much. Remember that being able to record something yourself is a sign of being able to understand it. Your notes can be in whatever format you find most helpful; lists, diagrams, mindmaps.
Step 8 **Examples**	Work through the examples very carefully as they illustrate key knowledge and techniques.
Step 9 **Case studies**	Study each one, and try to add flesh to them from your own experience. They are designed to show how the topics you are studying come alive in the real world.
Step 10 **Questions**	Attempt each one, as they will illustrate how well you've understood what you've read.
Step 11 **Answers**	Check yours against ours, and make sure you understand any discrepancies.
Step 12 **Chapter roundup**	Review it carefully, to make sure you have grasped the significance of all the important points in the chapter.
Step 13 **Quick quiz**	Use the Quick quiz to check how much you have remembered of the topics covered and to practise questions in a variety of formats.
Step 14 **Question practice**	Attempt the Question suggested at the very end of the chapter. These are all AIA past exam questions, so provide an excellent indication of the type and standard of question that you can expect in your real exam. Some of these questions cover more than one subject area, which is a common feature of exam questions.

INTRODUCTION

AIA Achieve Academy

AIA provides an interactive course of study, AIA Achieve Academy, which offers students the tools, resources and learning environment to study for the exams. The study tools include a course of study e-book, marked practice questions, marked mock exam paper and feedback and technical advice via an e-Tutor. Contact the Study Support team at: Achieve@aiaworldwide.com.

Moving on...

When you are ready to start revising, you should still refer back to this Learning & Practice Workbook.

- As a source of **reference** (you should find the index particularly helpful for this)
- As a way to **review** (the Fast forwards, Exam focus points, Chapter roundups and Quick quizzes help you here)

Syllabus

Financial Accounting 2 builds upon the knowledge required for the preceding Financial Accounting papers in the Professional 1 and Foundation level examination. The paper addresses the need for qualified accountants both to have an awareness of current thought, debates and developments affecting the financial reporting, and the ability to apply relevant financial reporting standards to advanced accounting topics. Extant International Financial Reporting/International Accounting Standards and relevant aspects of International Standards in Auditing, as stated in Sections 3.4.and 3.5, are examinable within this paper.

The paper reflects learning outcomes which are consistent with proficiency at the Advanced level under IES 2 for Financial Accounting and Reporting, relating to work situations that are characterised by high levels of ambiguity, complexity and uncertainty.

Relationship to the Qualification Structure

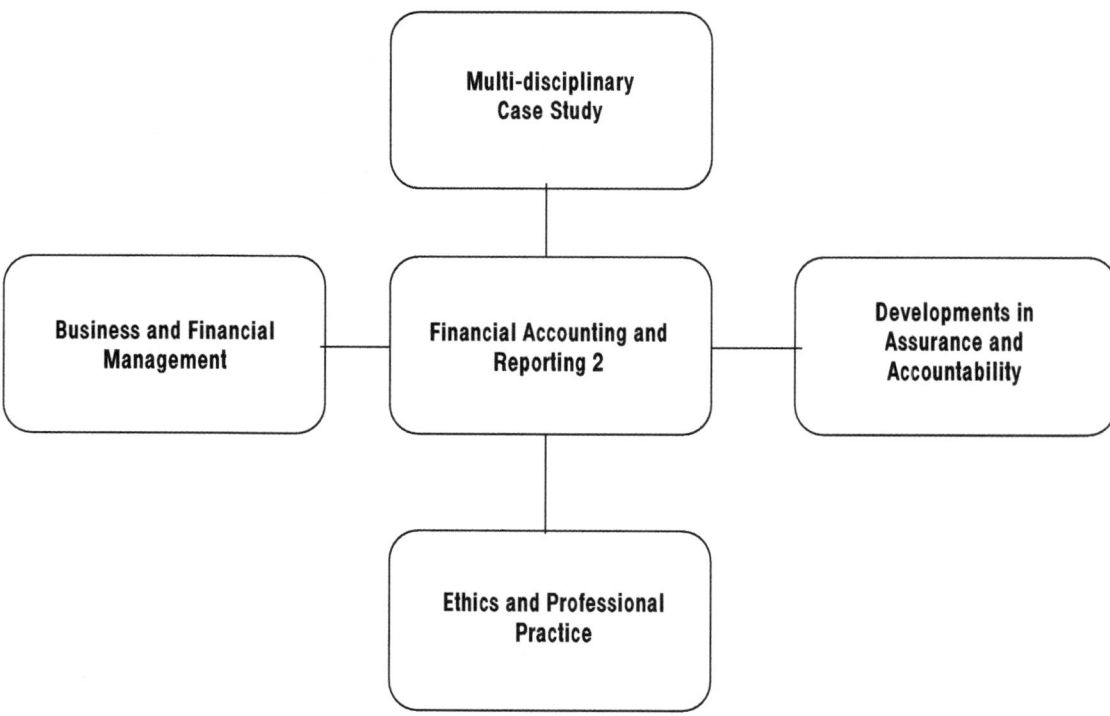

INTRODUCTION

Aims

The aim of this paper is to develop and examine the candidate's ability:

1. To critically evaluate current thought and developments in international financial accounting and reporting
2. To apply knowledge and professional judgement in an assessment of the requirements of International Financial Reporting Standards and other reporting requirements
3. To prepare and assess a wide variety of accounting and financial statements in a range of business contexts

Learning Outcomes

In order to successfully complete this paper, candidates will demonstrate that they be able to:

1. Discuss and/or apply of knowledge, critically evaluating current thought and developments in international financial accounting and reporting, including the conceptual framework, accounting regulation and specialised entities, sustainability reporting and the ethical and professional responsibilities of an accountant
2. Use judgment in applying current international reporting requirements and regulations to complex problems
3. Prepare and interpret a wide variety of corporate accounting and reporting statements including the financial statements of groups in accordance with appropriate international financial reporting standards
4. Prepare and assess reports and other communications which aim to offer to users professional advice on a group entity's financial performance and position

Structure of Paper

Assessment is by a three-hour 15-minute examination (including 15 minutes reading time) consisting of four questions.

Question 1 will be a compulsory scenario-based question worth 40 marks which will involve the preparation of consolidated financial statements and the consideration of related financial reporting issues.

Questions 2, 3 and 4 will be primarily case study-based question and could concern any part of the syllabus. Each question will be worth 20 marks and students must attempt all questions.

Normally approximately 70% of the paper will be computational. The remainder (approximately 30%) will be narrative discussion based. Individual questions may have both computational and discussion elements.

Overall, the paper examines a candidate's ability to act in a professional capacity in the area of international financial accounting and reporting.

INTRODUCTION

Syllabus

1: Current Thought and Developments (Learning Outcome 1)

Topic Weighting 15%

- The development and application of international reporting practice, including:
    - the development and application of international financial reporting standards including first-time adoption of IFRS and implications for an entity's accounting systems
    - the Conceptual Framework for Financial Reporting published by IASB, including:
    - its contribution in helping financial statements to meet the needs of users, including its role in the IASB's promulgation of the 'balance sheet method of income determination' and 'fair value'.
- Measurement bases, as outlined in the Conceptual Framework, asset valuation and income measurement,
- Concepts of capital and capital maintenance - as outlined in the Conceptual Framework
- The development and application of sustainability reporting and its significance as an effective communication tool within the annual report including:
    - Sustainability reporting and its usefulness to a wide range of stakeholder groups.
    - International Sustainability Disclosure Standards issued by the International Sustainability Standards Board (ISSB).
    - Appraisal of an entity's sustainability disclosures in the annual report.

Exposure Drafts (EDs), Discussion Papers (DPs) and interpretations by the IFRS Interpretations Committee (IFRICs) as notified by AIA through its student newsletter.

The ethical and professional responsibilities of accountants in a business context.

2: Business Combinations and the Financial Statements of Groups (Learning Outcomes 2, 3, 4)

Topic Weighting 50%

This section covers IAS 1, 7, 27, 29, and IFRS 5, 10, 11, 12 and 13

- Specific accounting and corporate reporting issues relating to business combinations, and reconstructions including:
    - conceptual differences, including identification of control
    - acquisition accounting, including the determination of cost of acquisition and the recognition and measurement of identifiable net assets and goodwill and non-controlling interests
    - equity accounting versus proportional consolidation
    - assessment of an entity's going concern status, including accounting for a reconstruction
    - separate financial statements
    - joint arrangements.
- The preparation, presentation and assessment of financial statements of groups, including:
    - statements of comprehensive income, financial position, cash flow and changes in equity
    - the identification and treatment of subsidiaries, associated companies, joint arrangements, foreign entities, and multi-entity structures.
    - acquisitions and disposals, including piecemeal acquisitions and disposals and conversion of passive investments and/or associates into subsidiaries and vice versa; and measurement of goodwill and non-controlling interests using the fair value method

INTRODUCTION

- exclusion of subsidiaries from group accounts and exemptions from preparing group accounts
- continuing and discontinued operations
- reporting within hyperinflationary economies
- assessment of particular consolidation techniques and strategies including their impact on key performance indicators (KPIs). Impact on KPIs could include an assessment of ratios relevant to profit, profitability, liquidity, funds management and investment (including trend analysis) and could include consideration of the difficulties of international financial analysis.

3: Accounting and Reporting Techniques (Learning Outcomes 2, 3, 4)

Topic Weighting 35%

- Particular accounting and reporting issues involving the reporting of financial performance within the context of all types of proprietorship organisations, including:
    - accounting policies, changes in accounting estimates and errors (IAS 8)
    - accounting for non-current assets, including investment properties, and intangible assets, use of fair values, impairment, revaluations and non-current assets held for sale (IAS 16, 36, 38, 40 and IFRS 13)
    - events after the reporting period (IAS 10)
    - income taxes (IAS 12)
    - revenue recognition (IFRS 15)
    - borrowing costs (IAS 23)
    - related party disclosures (IAS 24)
    - financial instruments including hedge accounting (IAS 32, IFRS 9)
    - earnings per share (IAS 33)
    - effects of changes in foreign exchange rates (IAS 21)
    - interim financial reporting (IAS 34)
    - provisions, contingent liabilities and contingent assets IAS 37)
    - operating segments (IFRS 8)
    - leases (IFRS 16)
    - employee benefits (IAS 19)
    - share based payments (IFRS 2)
    - inventories (IAS 2)
    - accounting for government grants (IAS 20)
    - presentation and Disclosure in Financial Statements (IFRS 18)
- The application of knowledge from all parts of the syllabus to the financial reporting needs of small to medium-sized entities (SMEs).

Extant International Standards on Auditing and all International Financial Reporting Standards/International Accounting Standards; as stated in Sections 3.4 and 3.5, are examinable, subject to the rule defined under New Legislation (Refer to Section 3.3). For RPQ (statutory auditor qualification) students the relevant UK standards are Financial Reporting Standards (FRS) issued by the FRC. In respect of auditing, the relevant UK standards are all current Auditing Standards (ISAs (UK and Ireland)) issued by the FRC.

Relationship to Qualification Structure

Financial Accounting and Reporting 2 builds upon the knowledge required for the preceding Financial Accounting papers in the Professional 1 level and the Foundation Unit level examinations. Candidates will also be expected to relate the topics covered in this paper to those in Developments in Assurance and Accountability.

Ethics

Students are advised that the standards outlined in The Code of Ethics for Professional Accountants issued by the International Ethics Standards Board for Accountants (IESBA Code) are implicit in, and examinable throughout, the AIA syllabus. In this paper a brief question relating to ethics could be included in any of the five questions but will typically be included as part of the compulsory question 1 and the coverage of the paper is consistent with the relevant learning outcomes in IES 4 *Professional Values, Ethics and Attitudes*.

The Code can be accessed via the AIA website at: www.aiaworldwide.com

Recommended Reading Lists

AIA Magazine – International Accountant

ISSN: 1465 – 5144

AIA Learning and Practice Workbooks

Financial Accounting and Reporting 2

Publisher: BPP Learning Media

ISBN: 9781035525836

The e-Book is available at: exams@aiaworldwide.com

Contact AIA for information on purchasing a hard copy of the textbook at: membership@aiaworldwide.com

You can purchase any of the books listed below quickly and easily through the publisher's website or link stated below. The following is a list of suggested readings which students may consult to supplement the above text.

International GAAP 2024
Publisher: Ernst & Young
 Link: https://www.ey.com/en_nl/ifrs-technical-resources/international-gaap-2024-global-perspective-on-ifrs

Financial Accounting and Reporting (20th Edition)
Authors: Elliot, B. and Elliot, J
Publisher: Pearson Education Limited
ISBN: 9781292399805

International Financial Reporting and Analysis (9th Edition)
Authors: Alexander, D, Van Mourik, C, Hoogendoom, M and Jorissen, A
Publisher: Cengage Learning
ISBN: 9781473792005

Free website providing comprehensive information about IFRS: www.iasplus.com/en

INTRODUCTION

Examinable standards

IFRS Accounting Standards and IFRS Sustainability Disclosure Standards

In the Financial Accounting component of the Foundation Unit candidates are required to have studied a limited number of IFRS Accounting Standards, however in Financial Accounting and Reporting 1 (FAR 1) and Financial Accounting and Reporting 2 (FAR 2) the bulk of IFRS Accounting Standards and IFRS Sustainability Disclosure Standards are examinable. Refer to the syllabi. A list of currently examinable standards is presented in the Tables below.

Note. Students following the Audit Qualification (AQ) are expected to be aware of the FRC accounting standards. The relevant accounting standards issued by the FRC are Financial Reporting Standards 100 to 105 including FRC 105 The Financial Reporting Standard applicable to The Micro-entities Regime. Accounting standards apply to all companies, and other entities that prepare accounts that are intended to provide a true and fair view. The Foreword to Accounting Standards explains the authority, scope and application of accounting standards. Audit candidates should refer to the FRC website site to view the relevant standards.

Key

FA   Financial Accounting (Foundation Unit)

MA   Management Accounting (Foundation Unit)

CGA   Corporate Governance and Audit (Foundation Unit)

PGA   Principles of Governance and Audit (Professional 1 Level)

FAR 1   Financial Accounting and Reporting 1 (Professional 1 Level)

FAR 2   Financial Accounting and Reporting 2 (Professional 2 Level)

DAA   Developments in Assurance and Accountability (Professional 2 Level)

International Accounting Standards (IASs)		Examinable in Paper						
No	Title	FA	MA(F)	CGA (F)	PGA	FAR1	FAR2	DAA
1	Presentation of Financial Statements	✓		✓	✓	✓	✓	✓
2	Inventories	✓	✓	✓	✓	✓	✓	✓
7	Statements of Cash Flows	✓		✓	✓	✓	✓	✓
8	Accounting Policies, Changes in Accounting Estimates and Errors					✓	✓	✓
10	Events After the Reporting Period	✓		✓	✓	✓	✓	✓
12	Income Taxes					✓	✓	✓
16	Property, Plant and Equipment	✓		✓	✓	✓	✓	✓
19	Employee Benefits						✓	✓
20	Accounting for Governments Grants and Disclosure of Government Assistance					✓	✓	✓
21	The Effects of Changes in Foreign Exchange Rates						✓	✓
23	Borrowing Costs					✓	✓	✓
24	Related Party Disclosures					✓	✓	✓
27	Separate Financial Statements					✓	✓	✓

INTRODUCTION

	International Accounting Standards (IASs)	Examinable in Paper						
28	Investment in Associates and Joint Ventures					✓	✓	✓
29	Financial Reporting in Hyperinflationary Economies						✓	✓
32	Financial Instruments: Presentation					✓	✓	✓
33	Earnings per Share					✓	✓	✓
34	Interim Financial Reporting					✓	✓	✓
36	Impairment of Assets					✓	✓	✓
37	Provisions, Contingent Liabilities and Contingent Assets	✓		✓	✓	✓	✓	✓
38	Intangible Assets	✓		✓	✓	✓	✓	✓
40	Investment Property					✓	✓	✓

International Financial Reporting Standards (IFRS)		Examinable in Paper					
No	Title	FA	MA (F)	CGA	PGA	FAR 1	FAR2
1	First-time Adoption of International Financial Reporting Standards				✓	✓	✓
2	Share-based Payment						✓
3	Business Combinations				✓	✓	✓
5	Non-current Assets Held for Sale and Discontinued Operations				✓	✓	✓
7	Financial Instruments: Disclosures					✓	✓
8	Operating Segments				✓	✓	✓
9	Financial Instruments					✓	✓
10	Consolidated Financial Statements				✓	✓	✓
11	Joint Arrangements					✓	✓
12	Disclosure of Interests in Other Entities				✓		✓
13	Fair Value Measurement						✓
15	Revenue from Contracts with Customers			✓	✓	✓	✓
16	Leases				✓	✓	✓
18	Presentation and Disclosure in Financial Statements					✓	✓
IFRS for SMEs	IFRS for Small and Medium-sized Entities					✓	✓

Note. Free website providing comprehensive information about IFRS: www.iasplus.com

IFRS Sustainability Disclosure Standards		Examinable in Paper					
No	Title	FA	MA (F)	CGA	PGA	FAR 1	FAR2
S1	General requirements for disclosure of sustainability-related information					✓	✓
S2	Climate-related disclosures					✓	✓

Other useful reading includes:

IFRS in Your Pocket – latest edition

https://www.iasplus.com/en-gb/publications/global/ifrs-in-your-pocket/ifrs-in-your-pocket-2023

New supporting materials for the IFRS for SMEs Standard available:

https://www.ifrs.org/issued-standards/ifrs-for-smes/

https://www.ifrs.org/supporting-implementation/supporting-materials-for-the-ifrs-for-smes/

Exposure drafts, discussion papers and IFRIC's are not examinable in the Foundation Unit or Financial Accounting and Reporting 1. Those still current (ie they have not been superseded by other publications) are examinable in Financial Accounting and Reporting 2 but only an understanding of their basic principles is required.

Command words

The following list contains active command words appropriate for use at the Professional 2 level of the AIA qualification. Reference to the command words is essential to understanding how the assessment is applied in AIA exams.

Cognitive Levels of Learning	Command Words	Definitions
Professional 2 Synthesis and Evaluation 20% Application and Analysis 70% Knowledge and Comprehension 10%	Appraise	Assess the worth, value, or quality of
	Assess	Determine the strength, weakness and significance
	Calculate/Compute	Select the appropriate method and techniques and apply your knowledge and understandings to work out and show how figures were arrived at
	Critically Analyse	Examine in detail using arguments for and against, and develop a view
	Develop	Elaborate or expand in detail
	Evaluate	Determine the value in light of arguments for and against
	Integrate	Combine information and/or standards and theory from different accounting disciplines or different parts of the case study to provide holistic professional recommendations or conclusions
	Justify	Demonstrate the correctness of an action, claim or conduct
	Prepare	To make or get ready for use
	Recommend	Advise the appropriate action in terms the recipient will understand
	Report	Give an account of the results of the investigation

Past exam paper analysis

The analysis below shows the topics which were examined in recent past papers included in the Exam Question Bank.

November 2021 (see Exam Question Bank)

Question 1: Aguila covers the following standards

- IFRS 5: Non-current Assets Held for Sale and Discontinued Operations
  This standard provides guidance on how to classify and account for discontinued operations, which is essential for assessing the sale of Dion.
- IFRS 10: Consolidated Financial Statements
  Relevant for determining control over subsidiaries and the requirements for presenting consolidated financial statements, including non-controlling interests.
- IFRS 3: Business Combinations
  This standard governs the accounting for business combinations, including the acquisition method and the treatment of goodwill and non-controlling interests.
- IAS 36: Impairment of Assets
  This standard is applicable for evaluating any impairment losses related to goodwill or other assets, particularly concerning Nabis.

Question 2: Diablo covers the following standards

- IAS 36: Impairment of Assets
  This standard outlines the requirements for impairment testing of cash-generating units (CGUs), including calculating the recoverable amounts for Navajo's divisions.
- IFRS 2: Share-based Payment
  Relevant for understanding how to account for share-based payments, including the treatment of share appreciation rights (SARs).
- IAS 16: Property, Plant and Equipment
  This standard applies to the accounting treatment of revalued properties and impairment losses on assets.

Question 3: Roca covers the following standards

- IFRS 2: Share-based Payment
  This standard governs the recognition and measurement of share-based payment transactions, including the accounting treatment of share appreciation rights (SARs).
- IAS 19: Employee Benefits
  Relevant for accounting for pension obligations and determining the treatment of employment benefits, including contributions and bonuses.
- IFRS 16: Leases
  This standard applies to lease accounting, including the recognition of lease liabilities and right-of-use assets.

Question 4: Gila covers the following standards

- IFRS 10: Consolidated Financial Statements
  This standard addresses the preparation and presentation of consolidated financial statements, including the treatment of subsidiaries and associates.
- IFRS 12: Disclosure of Interests in Other Entities
  Relevant for the disclosure requirements related to interests in subsidiaries and associates.

INTRODUCTION

- IAS 7: Statement of Cash Flows
  This standard provides the framework for preparing the cash flow statement, including the indirect method for operating activities.

- IFRS Practice Statement 2: Making Materiality Judgements
  Important for evaluating the need for disclosures, particularly in light of transactions that may not seem significant at first glance.

May 2022 (see Exam Question Bank)

Question 1: Amyklas covers the following standards

- IFRS 5: Non-current Assets Held for Sale and Discontinued Operations
  This standard outlines the classification, measurement, and presentation of non-current assets held for sale and discontinued operations, crucial for evaluating the disposal of Dion.

- IFRS 10: Consolidated Financial Statements
  This standard addresses the requirements for the preparation and presentation of consolidated financial statements, including control and the treatment of subsidiaries.

- IFRS 3: Business Combinations
  Relevant for the acquisition of Nabis and the measurement of goodwill, including how it is impaired and presented.

- IAS 36: Impairment of Assets
  This standard applies to the assessment of impairment losses related to the recoverable amount of Nabis.

Question 2: Spartan covers the following standards

- **IFRS** 15: Revenue from Contracts with Customers
  This standard governs the recognition of revenue from contracts, relevant for the treatment of commercial contracts and non-refundable deposits.

- IFRS 9: Financial Instruments
  This standard is relevant for assessing financial instruments, including how to account for convertible loan stock.

- IAS 1: Presentation of Financial Statements
  This standard addresses how to present financial information, including correcting accounting errors and providing proper disclosures.

Question 3: Mesoa covers the following standards

- IAS 19: Employee Benefits
  This standard outlines the accounting treatment for defined benefit pension plans, including recognition of pension costs, actuarial gains and losses, and the treatment of pension deficits.

- IFRS 2: Share-based Payment
  Relevant for accounting for employee share options and their impact on the financial statements, including deferred tax considerations.

- IAS 12: Income Taxes
  This standard addresses deferred tax assets and liabilities, especially in the context of trading losses and their carryforward.

Question 4: Prytanis covers the following standards

- IFRS 10: Consolidated Financial Statements
  This standard applies to the preparation and presentation of consolidated financial statements, relevant for accounting for associates and subsidiaries.

INTRODUCTION

- IFRS 12: Disclosure of Interests in Other Entities
  This standard is relevant for the disclosure of interests in associates and how their performance affects the consolidated financial statements.

- IAS 7: Statement of Cash Flows
  Relevant for preparing the cash flow statement using the indirect method, including adjustments for operating activities.

- IFRS Practice Statement 2: Making Materiality Judgements
  Important for discussing the need for comprehensive disclosures and evaluating the usefulness of financial statement information.

November 2022 (see Exam Question Bank)

Question 1: Argon covers the following standards

- IFRS 10: Consolidated Financial Statements
  This standard governs the preparation of consolidated financial statements, including how to determine control over subsidiaries and the implications for consolidating their results.

- IFRS 3: Business Combinations
  Relevant for accounting for the acquisition of Zinc, including the measurement of goodwill and the treatment of non-controlling interests.

- IAS 21: The Effects of Changes in Foreign Exchange Rates
  This standard is crucial for determining the functional currency of Zinc and accounting for foreign currency transactions, particularly given that Zinc operates in Zloty (ZL).

- IAS 36: Impairment of Assets
  This standard applies to the assessment of goodwill and any impairment losses that should be recognised, particularly concerning the impairment test performed on Zinc.

Question 2: Neon covers the following standards

- IFRS 16: Leases
  This standard governs the accounting for leases, including the sale and leaseback transaction and the treatment of lease liabilities and right-of-use assets.

- IAS 40: Investment Property
  Relevant for accounting for investment properties, including the recognition of rental income and the treatment of initial rent-free periods.

- IFRS 15: Revenue from Contracts with Customers
  This standard may apply when assessing the recognition of revenue related to utility contracts, depending on their structure.

Question 3: Krypton covers the following standards

- IAS 16: Property, Plant and Equipment
  This standard provides guidance on the recognition and measurement of tangible assets, including the treatment of decommissioning costs related to the biotech plant.

- IFRS 2: Share-based Payment
  Relevant for accounting for share appreciation rights (SARs), including recognition of expenses and the estimation of expected forfeitures.

- IAS 12: Income Taxes
  This standard addresses the treatment of deferred tax assets and liabilities, which is relevant when calculating the revised gearing ratio and assessing tax implications.

Question 4: Xenon covers the following standards

INTRODUCTION

- **IFRS 10: Consolidated Financial Statements**
  This standard applies to the consolidation of subsidiaries and the treatment of non-controlling interests, particularly following the sale of shares in Radon.
- **IFRS 3: Business Combinations**
  Relevant for accounting for the initial acquisition of Radon and subsequent disposals, including any impact on goodwill.
- **IFRS 13: Fair Value Measurement**
  This standard may apply when measuring the fair value of the non-controlling interest and the valuation of shares during the disposal.

May 2023 (see Exam Question Bank)

Question 1: Nysa covers the following standards

- **IFRS 11: Joint Arrangements**
  This standard provides guidance on how to account for joint arrangements, including determining whether a joint arrangement is a joint operation or a joint venture, and how to consolidate the results of Nbu.
- **IFRS 3: Business Combinations**
  Relevant for accounting for acquisitions, including the acquisition of Xanadu and Eden, and how to measure goodwill and non-controlling interests.
- **IAS 36: Impairment of Assets**
  This standard applies when assessing whether any impairment losses need to be recognised on the goodwill or net assets related to the acquisitions.
- **IFRS 13: Fair Value Measurement**
  This standard is important for determining fair values, especially in the context of measuring the non-controlling interest and other valuations at the time of acquisition.

Question 2: Nirvana covers the following standards

- **IFRS 9: Financial Instruments**
  This standard governs the recognition and measurement of financial instruments, including the accounting treatment for the issuance of sterling bonds.
- **IFRS 16: Leases**
  Relevant for accounting for leasing transactions, including the sale and leaseback transaction and the treatment of any lease liabilities.
- **IAS 19: Employee Benefits**
  This standard is applicable when accounting for defined benefit pension plans, particularly in calculating pension obligations and expenses.

Question 3: Nibiru covers the following standards

- **IFRS 13: Fair Value Measurement**
  This standard outlines how to measure fair value for readily traded assets and how to determine fair values for the land based on its intended use.
- **IAS 16: Property, Plant and Equipment**
  Relevant for accounting for property, plant, and equipment, including how to account for interest-free loans and decommissioning costs.
- **IFRS 2: Share-based Payment**
  This standard applies to the accounting treatment of share options, including the calculation of expenses related to share-based payments.

Question 4: Elysium covers the following standards

INTRODUCTION

- **IFRS 10: Consolidated Financial Statements**
  This standard governs the consolidation of subsidiaries and the treatment of non-controlling interests, particularly in the context of Elysium's acquisition of Avalon.

- **IFRS 3: Business Combinations**
  Relevant for accounting for acquisitions, including the measurement of goodwill and how to account for changes in ownership stakes in subsidiaries.

- **IAS 1: Presentation of Financial Statements**
  This standard provides guidance on how to prepare the statement of changes in equity, including the disclosure of transactions affecting equity.

- **IFRS Practice Statement 2: Making Materiality Judgements**
  Important for evaluating the ethical implications of the bond disclosures and the need for transparency in financial reporting.

November 2023 (see Exam Question Bank)

Question 1: Uno covers the following standards

- **IFRS 3: Business Combinations**
  This standard provides guidance on accounting for business combinations, including the acquisition of Dos and how to measure goodwill and non-controlling interests.

- **IFRS 11: Joint Arrangements**
  Relevant for accounting for the investment in Nbu, including how to classify and account for joint ventures.

- **IAS 36: Impairment of Assets**
  This standard is important for testing goodwill for impairment, particularly in relation to the acquisition of Tres.

- **IFRS 13: Fair Value Measurement**
  Used to determine fair values for financial reporting purposes, especially when calculating non-controlling interests and potential impairments.

Question 2: Cuatro covers the following standards

- **IFRS 16: Leases**
  This standard governs the accounting treatment of lease contracts, including how to account for lease liabilities and any related assets.

- **IFRS 2: Share-based Payment**
  Relevant for the accounting treatment of share options, including the recognition of share-based payment expenses and their implications for deferred tax.

- **IFRS 15: Revenue from Contracts with Customers**
  This standard applies when assessing whether Cuatro is acting as a principal or an agent in the contract for specialised equipment.

Question 3: Cinco covers the following standards

- **IAS 40: Investment Properties**
  This standard governs the accounting for investment properties, including how to transition from a cost model to a fair value model and how to account for gains and losses on revaluation.

- **IFRS 9: Financial Instruments**
  This standard covers the recognition and measurement of financial instruments, including how to account for loans and investments in bonds.

Question 4: Elysium covers the following standards

INTRODUCTION

- **IFRS 10: Consolidated Financial Statements**
  This standard provides guidance on how to prepare consolidated financial statements, including the treatment of acquisitions and non-controlling interests.

- **IFRS 3: Business Combinations**
  Relevant for the accounting treatment of the acquisition of Avalon and how to calculate goodwill and control changes.

- **IFRS Practice Statement 2: Making Materiality Judgements**
  Important for assessing the disclosures related to the bond covenant and the ethical implications surrounding them.

Contemporary issues

Current thought and practice

Introduction

Welcome to the Financial Accounting and Reporting 2 paper using International Financial Reporting Standards (IFRS Accounting Standards). This paper builds on the knowledge gained in your earlier studies so you should recognise most of the standards ad topics covered. However, at this level, you need to think critically about them and show an understanding of topical issues. In the exam, you will need to put yourself in the role of an adviser to a business entity, using your knowledge to give practical advice.

1 The regulatory system of accounting

> **FAST FORWARD** — Various national factors will affect the regulatory framework of entities, but our concern in this text is with international matters, particularly the **IASB** and **IFRS Accounting Standards**.

1.1 Introduction

This section revises material from your earlier studies. If necessary, refer back to your Financial Accounting and Reporting 1 studies.

1.1.1 Factors which have shaped financial accounting

- National/local legislation
- Accounting concepts and individual judgement
- Accounting standards
- Other international influences
- Generally accepted accounting principles (GAAP)
- True and fair view (or fair presentation)

1.2 National/local legislation

Limited liability companies may be **required by law** to prepare and publish financial statements annually. The form and content of the statements may be regulated primarily by national legislation, but must also comply with financial reporting standards such as the International Financial Reporting Standards (IFRS Accounting Standards).

1.3 Accounting concepts and individual judgement

Financial statements are prepared on the basis of a number of **fundamental accounting assumptions and conventions**. However, accountants still have to use judgement in putting these assumptions into practice.

Using the same data, different accountants are likely to produce very different financial statements. If the exercise of judgement is completely unfettered, any **comparability** between the financial statements of different organisations will disappear. In addition, deliberate manipulation can occur in order to present statements in the most favourable light.

1.4 Accounting standards

1.4.1 Financial reporting standards

Financial reporting standards attempt to deal with some of the subjectivity, and to achieve comparability between different organisations. Standards are developed at both a **national level** (in most countries) and an **international level**.

1.4.2 IFRS Accounting Standards

The **International Accounting Standards Board (IASB)** is responsible for developing global accounting standards. It issues International Financial Reporting Standards (IFRS Accounting Standards). The IASB also adopted those International Accounting Standards (IASs) and Standards Interpretation Committee (SIC) interpretations that were already in issue. The term IFRS Accounting Standards will be used throughout this Learning & Practice Workbook to refer to all financial reporting standards in issue.

1.4.3 Interpretations

The IFRS Interpretations Committee (IFRSIC) is responsible for preparing interpretations of IFRS Accounting Standards. Once these have been approved by the IASB, they have the same standing as IFRS Accounting Standards.

The IFRSIC deals with issues of reasonably widespread importance, not issues of concern to only a small number of entities.

The interpretations cover both:

- Mature issues (areas where there is unsatisfactory practice within the scope of existing IFRS Accounting Standards)
- Emerging issues (new topics relating to an existing IFRS Accounting Standards but not considered when the Standard was developed).

The IASB publishes a report on IFRSIC recommendations immediately after each IFRSIC meeting. This report is made available (in electronic format) as soon as possible to subscribers and, subsequently, posted to the IFRS website (https://www.ifrs.org/).

1.5 Sustainability Disclosure Standards

1.5.1 International Sustainability Standards Board

The International Sustainability Standards Board (ISSB) was established by the IFRS Foundation in November 2021 following strong market demand for its establishment. It develops and issues IFRS Sustainability Disclosure Standards.

There is increasing demand from users of corporate reporting for information about sustainability factors and the ISSB was established to develop high quality disclosure standards in this area.

Sustainability reporting will be considered in more detail in Chapter 3.

1.6 Other international influences

These include the EC (EU), the UN, and IFAC.

1.6.1 European Commission (EC)

The EC is an arm of the European Union (EU) which is responsible for new legislation. The regulations form one part of a broader programme for the harmonisation of company law in member states. The Commission is uniquely the only organisation to produce international standards of accounting practice which are legally enforceable, in the form of **directives** which must be included in the national legislation of member states.

However, the EC has also **acknowledged the role of the IASB** in harmonising world-wide accounting rules and it promotes the use of IFRS Accounting Standards worldwide.

Since 2005, the EC has required all listed companies in member states to use those IFRS Accounting Standards, as endorsed by the European Financial Reporting Advisory Group (EFRAG) for their consolidated financial statements. There are occasionally differences between IFRS Accounting Standards as issued by the IASB and IFRS Accounting Standards as endorsed by EFRAG (and used within the EU). These differences are either (i) arising from the timing of implementation of new and revised IFRS Accounting Standards (for example, when there is a delay, even if short, between the issue of a new IFRS Accounting Standard and its endorsement by EFRAG or (ii) a refusal by EFRAG to endorse fully a new IFRS Accounting Standard (for example, it took a number of years for EFRAG to endorse IFRS 9 due to concerns about its impact on the insurance industry).

PART A CONTEMPORARY ISSUES

1.6.2 United Nations (UN)

Various bodies working under the umbrella United Nations Conference on Trade and Development (UNCTAD) gather information concerning the activities and reporting of multinational companies. The UN processes are highly **political** and probably reflect the attitudes of the governments of developing countries to multinationals.

1.6.3 International Federation of Accountants (IFAC)

IFAC is the global organisation for the accountancy profession. IFAC identifies its objective as serving the public interest by strengthening the profession and contributing to the development of strong international economies. IFAC has over 180 members and associates in 135 countries and jurisdictions, representing almost 3 million accountants. (Source: http:www.ifac.org)

1.7 Generally Accepted Accounting Principles (GAAP)

We also need to consider some important terms which you will meet in your financial accounting studies. GAAP, as a term, has sprung up in recent years and may or may not have statutory or legal authority or definition, depending on the country involved. GAAP is in fact a **dynamic concept** and changes constantly as circumstances alter through new legislation, standards and practice It signifies **all the rules, from whatever source, which govern accounting**.

- Local (national) company legislation
- National and international accounting standards
- Statutory requirements in other countries (particularly the US)
- Stock exchange requirements

1.8 True and fair view (faithful representation/ fair presentation)

It is a requirement of both national legislation (in some countries eg the UK) and International Standards on Auditing (ISAs) that the financial statements should give a true and fair view of (or present fairly) the assets, liabilities, financial position and profit or loss of the entity.

1.8.1 Faithful representation and compliance with IFRS Accounting Standards

The terms 'present fairly' and 'true and fair view' are not defined in accounting or auditing standards. The IASB's *Conceptual Framework for Financial Reporting* includes 'faithful representation' as one of the fundamental qualitative characteristics, making it clear that the financial statements must represent the substance of the economic phenomena that it purports to represent (Conceptual Framework, para 2.12). The Conceptual Framework will be covered in more detail in section 4 of this chapter. Under IAS 1 *Presentation of Financial Statements,* the application of IFRS Accounting Standards is presumed to result in fair presentation. Non-compliance with IFRS Accounting Standards is only permitted when compliance would be so misleading as to conflict with the objective of financial statements set out in the *Conceptual Framework* (IAS 1, paras. 19 – 23).

2 The IFRS Foundation and the International Accounting Standards Board (IASB)

FAST FORWARD You should be able to describe the **organisation of the IFRS Foundation and the IASB** and their relationships with intergovernmental bodies, professional accountancy bodies, national standard-setting bodies and IOSCO.

2.1 Background

The IFRS Foundation is an oversight body of both the IASB and ISSB and includes governance, oversight and support operations.

The primary mission of the IFRS Foundation is to develop high-quality IFRS Standards that bring transparency, accountability and efficiency to capital markets around the world. IFRS Standards include IFRS Accounting Standards and IFRS Sustainability Disclosure Standards.

The principal objectives of the IFRS Foundation are:

- To develop, in the public interest, high-quality, understandable, enforceable and globally accepted standards for general purpose financial reporting based on clearly articulated principles. The International Accounting Standards Board (IASB) is responsible for developing a set of accounting standards (IFRS Accounting Standards) and the International Sustainability Standards Boards (ISSB) is responsible for developing a set of sustainability disclosure standards (IFRS Sustainability Disclosure Standards);
- To promote the use and rigorous application of IFRS Standards;
- To take account of the needs a range of sizes and types of entities in diverse economic settings; and
- To promote and facilitate adoption of IFRS Standards through the convergence of national and regional accounting standards and IFRS Standards.

(Source: http://www.ifrs.org)

2.2 Scope and authority of IFRS Accounting Standards

The IASB is the independent financial reporting standard-setting body of the IFRS Foundation, including technical staff and experts advisors.

The IASB achieves its objectives primarily by developing and publishing IFRS Accounting Standards and promoting the use of those standards in **general purpose financial statements** and other financial reporting.

IFRS Accounting Standards set out the **recognition, measurement, presentation** and **disclosure requirements** dealing with transactions and events that are important in general purpose financial statements. IFRS Accounting Standards are based on the IASB's *Conceptual Framework for Financial Reporting,* which:

- Addresses the **concepts** underlying the information presented in general purpose financial statements
- Facilitates the **consistent** and logical formulation of IFRS Accounting Standards
- Provides a **basis for the use of judgement** in resolving accounting issues

IFRS Accounting Standards are designed to apply to the general purpose financial statements and other financial reporting of all profit-oriented entities. Profit-oriented entities include those engaged in commercial, industrial, financial and similar activities, whether organised in **corporate or in other forms**.

General purpose financial statements provide information about the reporting entity that is useful to existing and potential investors, lenders and other creditors in making decisions about providing resources to the reporting entity (Conceptual Framework, para 1.2). However other stakeholders may also find them useful, for example employees, regulators and the public at large. To provide the information required by the users, the financial statements must provide information about an entity's economic resources and claims and changes in those resources and claims and information about how effectively management have discharged their responsibilities to use the entity's resources (Conceptual Framework, para 1.4)

A complete set of financial statements comprises:

- A statement of financial position
- A statement of profit or loss and other comprehensive income
- A statement of changes in equity
- A statement of cash flows
- Notes, comprising a summary of significant accounting policies and other explanatory information

- Comparative information

The term 'financial statements' includes a complete set of financial statements prepared for an interim or annual period, and condensed financial statements for an interim period.

In the interest of timeliness and cost considerations and to avoid repeating information previously reported, an entity may provide less information in its **interim financial statements** than in its annual financial statements. **IAS 34** *Interim Financial Reporting* **prescribes** the **minimum content** of complete or condensed financial statements for an interim period.

The **IASB's objective** is to require **like transactions** and events to be accounted for and **reported in a like way** and unlike transactions and events to be accounted for and reported differently, both within an entity over time and among entities. Consequently, the **IASB**, with very few exceptions, **does not permit choices in accounting treatment.**

2.3 IASB due process

IFRS Accounting Standards and Interpretations are developed through an international **due process** that involves accountants, financial analysts and other users of financial statements, the business community, stock exchanges, regulatory and legal authorities, academics and other interested individuals and organisations from around the world. The IASB consults the IFRS Advisory Council in public meetings on major projects, agenda decisions and work priorities, and discusses technical matters in meetings that are open to public observation.

The steps in the IASB standard-setting process are:

Agenda Consultation

The IASB develops a new project work plan every five years after comprehensive review and consultation. The work plan can be updated between agenda consultations if required.

Research programme

The first stage of most projects is research to determine with standard-setting is required. A discussion paper is sometimes issued for public comment.

If a post-implementation review of an issued standard has raised any issues, this might also be an area for research.

Standard-setting programme

If research indicates that a new or amended standards is required, the process for this is:

- Exposure draft of proposed changes issued for public consultation
- IASB / IFRSIC review exposure draft responses responses
- New/updated IFRS Accounting Standard / IFRIC Interpretation issued

Maintenance programme

The IASB monitor application of all issued standards and if there are any issues with implementation or application of a standard then an IFRIC Interpretation or IFRS Accounting Standard narrow-scope amendment might be recommended.

2.4 Comment periods

The IASB issues each Exposure Draft of a Standard and discussion documents for public comment, with a normal comment period of **120 days**. For a major project, or one that is controversial, this period may be

extended. In certain circumstances, the IASB may expose proposals for a much shorter period. However, such limited periods would be used only in extreme circumstances.

2.5 The consultation process

The development of an IFRS Accounting Standard involves an **open, public process of debating technical issues** and evaluating input sought through several mechanisms. Opportunities for interested parties to participate in the development of IFRS Standard would include, depending on the nature of the project:

(a) Participation in the development of views as a member of the **IFRS Advisory Council**
(b) Participation in **advisory groups**
(c) Submission of a **comment letter** in response to a **discussion document**
(d) Submission of a **comment letter** in response to an **Exposure Draft**
(e) Participation in **public hearings**
(f) Participation **in field visits and field tests**

The IASB publishes an annual report on its activities during the past year and priorities for next year. This report provides a basis and opportunity for comment by interested parties.

IASB reports on its technical projects on its website. IASB publishes a report on IASB decisions immediately after each IASB meeting in its newsletter *IASB Update*. Do visit the IFRS website on a regular basis.

2.6 Current position

The IASB has now been in existence for some years and has issued 19 IFRS Accounting Standards, as well as revising many of the standards previously issued (IASs).

The most recent accounting standard that will be covered in FAR 2 is IFRS 18 *Presentation and Disclosure in Financial Statements* which will replace IAS 1 *Presentation of Financial Statements*.

An understanding of the basic principles of the Exposure Drafts, Discussion Papers and IFRIC Interpretations listed on page x of the Introduction to this Learning & Practice Workbook is also required in the Financial Accounting and Reporting 2 paper.

Exam focus point

> Remember that the examiner is likely to concentrate on emerging or controversial areas in the exam. This means you are likely to see questions covering new standards or standards that the IASB is currently working on.

In addition, the IASB has an extensive work plan for the continued development and improvement of international accounting standards. The following are the issues that are being dealt with by the IASB. In addition the IASB operates an annual improvements process through which minor changes and enhancements are made to existing IFRS Accounting Standards.

Hot topic	Where to find it
Recent changes	
Presentation of financial statements	Chapter 2
Sustainability Reporting	Chapter 3
Narrow scope amendments and other projects	see below

Other projects are covered in the relevant chapters of the Learning & Practice Workbook.

2.3.1 IFRS Accounting Projects

The IFRS Foundation work plan sets out all current projects. The work plan is updated after each IASB, Interpretations Committee and ISSB meeting.

There are seven project categories:

- Application question

- Standard-setting project
- Maintenance project
- Governance project
- Research project
- Taxonomy project
- SME Q&A

Some of the key projects as at July 2024 are:

Climate-related and Other Uncertainties in Financial Statements – An exposure draft is due to be issued providing examples to illustrate how the effects of climate-related and other uncertainties should be applied when preparing financial statements.

Practice Statement 1 *Management Commentary* – a revised Practice Statement is due to be issued in 2025 following the issue of an exposure draft in collaboration with the ISSB to include more guidance around management commentary on sustainability matters.

Post-implementation review of both IFRS 15 *Revenue from Contract with Customers* and IFRS 16 *Leases* are both underway.

Details of all current projects can be found on the IFRS website www.ifrs.org and you are expected to have an awareness of these as current issues, but do not need to understand the detail of the projects.

3 *Conceptual Framework*

FAST FORWARD

IFRS Accounting Standards are based on the IASB's *Conceptual Framework for Financial Reporting*.

3.1 The principle of a *Conceptual Framework*

Key term

A *Conceptual Framework*, in the field we are concerned with, is a statement of generally accepted theoretical principles which form the frame of reference for financial reporting. These theoretical principles provide the basis for the development of new accounting standards and the evaluation of those already in existence.

The financial reporting process is concerned with providing information that is useful in the business and economic decision-making process. Therefore, a *Conceptual Framework* will form the **theoretical basis** for determining which events should be accounted for, how they should be measured and how they should be communicated to the user. Although it is theoretical in nature, a *Conceptual Framework* for financial reporting has highly practical final aims.

The **danger of not having a Conceptual Framework** is demonstrated in the way some countries' standards have developed over recent years; standards tend to be produced in a **haphazard and fire-fighting approach**. Where an agreed framework exists, the standard-setting body act as an architect or designer, rather than a fire-fighter, building accounting rules on the foundation of sound, agreed basic principles.

The lack of a *Conceptual Framework* also means that fundamental principles are tackled more than once in different standards, thereby producing contradictions and inconsistencies in basic concepts. This leads to ambiguity and this affects the true and fair concept of financial reporting.

Another problem with the lack of a *Conceptual Framework* has become apparent in the USA. The large number of **highly detailed standards** produced by the Financial Accounting Standards Board (FASB) has created a financial reporting environment governed by specific rules rather than general principles. This would be avoided if a cohesive set of principles were in place.

A *Conceptual Framework* can also bolster standard setters against political pressure from various 'lobby groups' and interested parties. Such pressure would only prevail if it was acceptable under the *Conceptual Framework*.

3.2 Advantages of a *Conceptual Framework*

The **advantages** arising from using a *Conceptual Framework* may be summarised as follows:

(a) The situation is **avoided** whereby standards are developed on a **patchwork** basis, where a particular accounting problem is recognised as having emerged, and resources are then channelled into **standardising accounting practice** in that area, without regard to whether that particular issue is necessarily the most important issue remaining at that time without standardisation. It facilitates consistency of standards.

(b) As stated above, the development of certain standards (particularly national standards) have been subject to considerable political interference from interested parties. Where there is a conflict of interest between user groups on which policies to choose, policies deriving from a *Conceptual Framework* will be **less open to criticism** that the standard-setter buckled to **external pressure**.

3.3 Counter-argument

A counter-argument might be as follows:

(a) Financial statements are intended for a **variety of users**, and it is not certain that a single *Conceptual Framework* can be devised which will suit all users.

(b) Given the diversity of user requirements, there may be a need for a variety of accounting standards, each produced for a **different purpose** (and with different concepts as a basis).

(c) It is not clear that a *Conceptual Framework* makes the task of **preparing and then implementing** standards any easier than without a framework.

Before we look at the IASB's attempt to produce a *Conceptual Framework*, we need to consider another term of importance to this debate: Generally Accepted Accounting Principles, or GAAP.

3.4 Generally Accepted Accounting Principles (GAAP)

The term GAAP signifies all the rules, from whatever source, which govern accounting in a country. This is seen primarily as a combination of:

- National corporate law
- National accounting standards
- Local stock exchange requirements

Although those sources are the basis for the GAAP of individual countries, the concept also includes the effects of **non-mandatory sources** such as:

- International financial reporting standards
- Statutory requirements in other countries

In many countries, like the UK, GAAP does not have any statutory or regulatory authority or definition, unlike other countries, such as the USA. The term is mentioned rarely in legislation, and only then in fairly limited terms.

3.5 The IASB'S *Conceptual Framework*

The latest version of the *Conceptual Framework* was issued in March 2018. The *Conceptual Framework* has been covered in detail in your earlier studies. Included below are the key issues which are relevant for this paper. Reference will be made to the *Conceptual Framework* where relevant throughout the course.

3.5.1 Purpose and status

The purpose of the *Conceptual Framework* is to:

(a) Assist the International Accounting Standards Board (Board) to develop IFRS Accounting Standards that are based on consistent concepts;

(b) Assist preparers to develop consistent accounting policies when no standard applies to a particular transaction or other event, or when a standard allows a choice of accounting policy; and

(c) Assist all parties to understand and interpret the standards.

(*Conceptual Framework*, para. SP1)

The *Conceptual Framework* is not a standard and so does not overrule any individual IFRS Accounting Standard. In the (rare) case of conflict between an IFRS Accounting Standard and the *Conceptual Framework*, the **IFRS Accounting Standard will prevail**.

3.5.2 The objective of general purpose financial reporting

The objective of general purpose financial reporting is to provide financial information about the reporting entity that is useful to existing and potential **investors, lenders and other creditors** in making **decisions relating to providing resources** to the entity.

Those decisions involve decisions about:

(a) Buying, selling or holding equity and debt instruments;

(b) Providing or settling loans and other forms of credit; or

(c) Exercising rights to vote on, or otherwise influence, management's actions that affect the use of the entity's resources.

(*Conceptual Framework*, para.1.2)

For example, providers of capital need to make decisions about whether to buy, sell or hold equity and debt instruments, or whether to provide or settle loans and other forms of credit.

The **focus therefore is on capital providers** (investors in the form of equity capital and lenders, and other creditors in the form of debt capital) as the primary users of financial statements. Financial reporting is aimed at users who provide resources to an entity but are not able to compel the entity to provide them with the information that they need in order to make decisions. Although the *Conceptual Framework* acknowledges that other parties, such as regulators and members of the public, may also find general purpose financial reports useful, it states that those reports are not primarily directed to these other groups.

The revised *Conceptual Framework* explains that existing and potential investors, lenders and other creditors may make decisions about buying, selling or holding shares or debt instruments, or providing or settling loans (Conceptual Framework, para. 1.2).

To make these decisions, the primary users need information about:

(a) The **economic resources of the entity**;

(b) **Claims against the entity**;

(c) Changes in the entity's **economic resources and claims**; and

(d) How efficiently and effectively the entity's management and governing board have discharged their responsibilities to use the entity's economic resources.

(*Conceptual Framework*, para. 1.4)

The *Conceptual Framework* requires that financial performance is reflected by the application of **accrual accounting**. Accrual accounting is important because information about a reporting entity's economic resources and claims and changes in its economic resources and claims during a period provides a better basis for assessing the entity's past and future performance than information solely about cash receipts and payments during that period.

Question

Useful information

On 30 November 20X8, Sykes failed to make an interest payment to SB Bank and consequently breached the conditions of a long-term loan agreement. Under the terms of the loan agreement, the loan became immediately repayable. On 3 December 20X8, SB Bank agreed that provided Sykes made the interest payment by 30 April 20X9, it would not demand immediate repayment of the loan.

At the reporting date of 31 December 20X8, Sykes classified the loan as a non-current liability. The loan is for a large sum of money that is material to the financial statements of Sykes.

Required

Discuss whether the classification of the loan as a non-current liability provides useful information to investors.

Answer

According to the *Conceptual Framework*, the objective of financial reporting is to provide financial information about the entity that is useful to investors (and certain other stakeholders) in making decisions about providing resources to the entity.

Reporting the loan as non-current is not useful to investors as it is misleading. If Sykes does not make the interest payment by 30 April 20X9, the loan would become repayable immediately. Given the size of the loan, this could affect Sykes's ability to continue as a going concern.

3.5.3 Qualitative characteristics of useful financial information

Chapter 3 considers the qualities that make financial information useful. It distinguishes between fundamental qualitative characteristics and enhancing qualitative characteristics.

The **fundamental qualitative characteristics** are:

(a) **Relevance**: Information is relevant if it is capable of **making a difference** in the decisions made by users. Information may be capable of making a difference in a decision even if some users choose not to take advantage of it or are already aware of it. Financial information is capable of making a difference in decisions if it has predictive value, confirmatory value, or both.

Materiality is an entity specific **aspect of relevance**. Information is material if omitting, misstating, or obscuring it could be reasonably expected to influence the decisions that users make on the basis of financial information about a specific reporting entity. Information can be material by its nature, magnitude or both.

(b) **Faithful representation**: To be useful, financial information must not only represent relevant phenomena but it must also **faithfully represent** the phenomena that it purports to represent. A perfectly faithful representation is **complete, neutral** and **free from error**.

Information must be both relevant and faithfully represented if it is to be useful. In practice there must be a balance between the two.

The **enhancing qualitative characteristics** are:

(a) **Comparability**: This enables users to identify and understand similarities in, and differences among, items. **Consistency** (use of the same methods for the same items) is not the same as comparability, although it helps to achieve comparability.

(b) **Verifiability**: This helps assure users that information faithfully represents the economic phenomena it purports to represent. It means that different knowledgeable and independent observers could reach consensus, although not necessarily complete agreement, that a particular depiction is a faithful representation.

(c) **Timeliness**: This means having information available to decision-makers in time to be capable of influencing their decisions.

(d) **Understandability**: For users who have a reasonable knowledge of business and economic activities and who review and analyse the information diligently.

Cost is a pervasive **constraint** on the reporting entity's ability to provide useful financial information. It is important that the costs of reporting financial information are justified by the benefits.

3.5.4 Key points relating to the elements of the financial statements and recognition/derecognition

The main points are revised below.

> Knowledge brought forward from earlier studies

Underlying assumption

- The financial statements are normally prepared on the assumption that the entity is a going concern.

The elements of financial statements

- **Asset**. A present economic resource controlled by the entity as a result of past events. An economic resource is a right that has the potential to produce economic benefits.
- **Liability**. A present obligation of the entity to transfer an economic resource as a result of past events.
- **Equity**. The residual interest in the assets of the entity after deducting all its liabilities.
- **Income**. Increases in assets, or decreases in liabilities, that result in increases in equity, other than those relating to contributions from equity participants.
- **Expenses**. Decreases in assets, or increases in liabilities, that result in decreases in equity, other than those relating to distributions to equity participants.

Recognition of the elements of financial statements

- Items which meet the definition of assets or liabilities may still not be recognised in financial statements because they must also meet certain recognition criteria.

Definition

Recognition. Recognition is the process of capturing for inclusion in the statement of financial position, or the statement(s) of financial performance, an item that meets the definition of one of the elements of financial statements.

An item should be recognised in the financial statements if:

(a) The item meets the definition of an **element** (asset, liability, income, expense or equity); and

(b) Recognition of that element provides users of the financial statements with information that is **useful**, ie with:

- **Relevant** information about the element
- A **faithful representation** of the element

Items may still qualify for recognition at a later date due to changes in circumstances or subsequent events.

3.5.5 Measurement

The *Conceptual Framework* describes the different measurement bases used in IFRS Accounting Standards and the factors to consider in selecting a measurement basis. IFRS Accounting Standards use a mixed measurement approach, which means that different measurement bases are used for different classes of elements. This is opposed to a single measurement basis in which all items are measured using the same basis, eg all items are measured at fair value. The IASB believes that a mixed measurement approach provides the most useful information to primary users of financial statements.

Individual IFRS Accounting Standards specify which particular measurement basis should be used in most circumstances. The measurement principles in the *Conceptual Framework* will therefore mainly be used by the IASB to develop IFRS Accounting Standards. However, preparers of financial statements can use the measurement principles to help them choose a measurement basis where a choice is offered in an IFRS Accounting Standard.

> **FAST FORWARD**
>
> The Conceptual Framework considers two measurement bases:
> - Historical cost
> - Current value

Key terms

> **Historical cost.** Historical cost measures provide monetary information about assets, liabilities and related income and expenses, using information derived, at least in part, from the price of the transaction or other event that gave rise to them. (Conceptual Framework, para 6.4)
>
> **Current value.** Current value measures provide monetary information about assets, liabilities and related income and expenses, using information updated to reflect conditions at the measurement date. (Conceptual Framework, para.6.10)

3.5.6 Historical cost

Historical cost is the most commonly adopted measurement basis. The use of historical cost means transactions and balances are recorded at the date of the original transaction which is not updated to reflect current prices. Historical cost is usually combined with other bases, eg inventory is carried at the lower of cost and net realisable value.

Advantages of historical cost

(a) Amounts used are objective, as it is more difficult to manipulate cost-based figures.

(b) Amounts are reliable, they can always be verified, they exist on invoices and documents.

(c) The statement of financial position and statement of cash flows figures are consistent with each other.

(d) There is less possibility for manipulation by using 'creative accounting' in asset valuation.

(e) Cost is a measure which is **readily understood**

Disadvantages of historical cost

(a) Overstatement of profit – it shows current revenues less out of date costs. During periods where price inflation is low, profit overstatement will be marginal. The disadvantages of historical cost accounting become most apparent in periods of inflation.

(b) Out of date asset values – based on their historical values.

(c) Return on assets/capital employed is **distorted** by both (a) and (b).

(d) Holding gains/losses (ie the fact that something is worth more or costs more over time simply due to price rises) are not measured separately from operating results.

(e) Historical cost does not measure any gain/loss on monetary items arising from the impact of inflation (ie the fact that savers lose because the purchasing power of their savings is eroded, while borrowers gain because they still owe the same nominal amount while earnings have risen due to inflation).

(f) Historical cost gives a **misleading trend of results** since comparative figures are not restated for the effects of inflation.

3.5.7 Current value

Current value accounting attempts to address some of the problems of HCA by using information updated to reflect conditions at the measurement date. The Conceptual Framework recognises four current value measurement bases:

- Fair value
- Value in use for assets / fulfilment value for liabilities
- Current cost

3.5.8 Fair value

> **Fair value**: Fair value is the price that would be received to sell an asset, or paid to transfer a liability, in an orderly transaction between market participants at the measurement date (*Conceptual Framework:* para. 6.12 and IFRS 13: Appendix A).

Fair value is measured in accordance with IFRS 13 Fair Value Measurement

Fair value is most commonly calculated by taking the open market value. Where there is no active market for the asset or liability, then the following should be used as a basis:

- Estimates of future cash flows
- Time value of money (discounting the future cash flows)

3.5.9 Value in use and fulfilment value

Key term

> **Value in use**: Value in use is the present value of the cash flows, or other economic benefits, that an entity expects to derive from the use of an asset and from its ultimate disposal
>
> **Fulfilment value**: Fulfilment value is the present value of the cash, or other economic resources, that an entity expects to be obliged to transfer as it fulfils a liability. (Conceptual Framework: para. 6.17).

Value in use looks at the likely future value to the entity of using the asset and fulfilment value considers the future payments to third parties.

Value in use and fulfilment value both consider entity-specific factors, whereas fair value is market specific.

3.5.10 Current cost

Key term

> **Current cost of an asset:** The current cost of an asset is the cost of an equivalent asset at the measurement date, comprising the consideration that would be paid at the measurement date plus the transaction costs that would be incurred at that date (Conceptual Framework: para. 6.21).
>
> **Current cost of a liability**: The current cost of a liability is the consideration that would be received for an equivalent liability at the measurement date minus the transaction costs that would be incurred at that date (Conceptual Framework: para. 6.21).

Current cost differs from historical cost as current cost assesses the price to purchase at the reporting date, rather than the date the asset was acquired or liability assumed.

Where the current cost cannot be obtained from information in the market, then the entity can adjust for condition and age to buy a similar model.

Advantages of using current value

(a) Assets are valued after management has considered the expected benefits from their future use. Value in use is therefore a useful guide for management in deciding whether to hold or sell assets.

(b) It is relevant to the needs of information users in:

    (i) Assessing the stability of the business entity

    (ii) Assessing the vulnerability of the business (eg to a takeover), or the liquidity of the business

    (iii) Evaluating the performance of management in maintaining and increasing the business substance

    (iv) Judging future prospects

Limitations of using current value

(a) The discount factor used to calculate the present value of future cash flows requires subjective judgements by management. Also, the expected benefits from cash flows from the asset will be upon management's best estimates and judgements.

(b) There may be problems in deciding how to provide an estimate of current costs for non-current assets which can only be purchased new, such as a bespoke or specialist piece of machinery.

(c) As the *Conceptual Framework* allows different groups of assets and liabilities to be valued on different bases (which are the most useful to users of the financial statements), this can mean that some assets will be valued at current cost, but others will be valued at value in use or fair value.

Summary of information about assets provided by particular measurement bases:

Measurement basis	Carrying amount of an asset in the statement of financial position	Value changes of the same asset in the statement of profit or loss
Historical cost	Historical cost (including transaction costs), to the extent unconsumed or uncollected, and recoverable	Not recognised, except to reflect an impairment (for financial assets—income and expenses from changes in estimated cash flows)
Fair value	Price that would be received to sell the asset (without deducting transaction costs on disposal)	Reflected in income and expenses from changes in fair value
Value in use	Present value of future cash flows from the use of the asset and from its ultimate disposal (after deducting present value of transaction costs on disposal)	Reflected in income and expenses from changes in value in use
Current cost	Current cost (including transaction costs), to the extent unconsumed or uncollected, and recoverable	Income and expenses reflecting the effect of changes in prices (holding gains and holding losses)

3.5.11 Factors to consider in selecting a measurement basis

(1) Nature of information provided (paras. 6.23–6.42)

Different information is produced by applying a different measurement basis to the same asset (or other element). It is important to consider what information is produced by a measurement basis in both the statement of financial position and the statement of profit or loss. Which one is more important will depend on the particular circumstances.

(2) Usefulness of information provided

To be useful, the information provided by a measurement basis must be **relevant** and a **faithful representation.**

Relevance of information is affected by:

- How the asset/liability contributes to future cash flows, eg current cost is likely to provide relevant information for assets (eg property, plant and equipment) which indirectly contribute to future cash flows when used in combination with other assets.
- The characteristics of the asset or liability (and related income/expense), eg if the value of an asset is subject to market fluctuations then fair value may be more relevant than historical cost. (para. 6.49)

(3) Other factors

- Cost constraint: do the benefits of the information provided by the selected measurement basis justify the costs? (para. 6.64)
- Enhancing qualitative characteristics: eg consistently using the same measurement basis aids comparability, verifiability is enhanced by using measures that can be independently corroborated (paras. 6.65, 6.68).

3.0.7 Concepts of capital and capital maintenance

Most entities use a **financial concept of capital** when preparing their financial statements.

We need to define the different concepts of capital.

Key term

> **Capital.** Under a **financial** concept of capital, such as invested money or invested purchasing power, capital is the net assets or equity of the entity. The financial concept of capital is adopted by most entities.
>
> Under a **physical concept** of capital, such as operating capability, capital is the productive capacity of the entity based on, for example, units of output per day.

The definition of profit is also important.

Key term

> **Profit.** Profit is earned if the capital (either financial or physical) at the end of the period is greater than the capital at the start pf the period, excluding distributions to and contributions from owners during the period. *(Conceptual Framework, para 8.3)*

The main difference between the two concepts of capital maintenance is the treatment of the **effects of changes in the prices of assets and liabilities** of the entity. In general terms, an entity has maintained its capital if it has as much capital at the end of the period as it had at the beginning of the period.

4 Harmonisation and international differences

Before we look at any countries in particular, we must consider what barriers there are to international harmonisation of financial reporting standards and why harmonisation is considered so desirable, before looking at comparative accounting systems.

4.1 Barriers to harmonisation

There are undoubtedly many barriers to international harmonisation. If there were not, then greater progress would probably have been made by now. The main problems are as follows:

(a) **Different purposes of financial reporting**. In some countries the purpose is solely for tax assessment, while in others it is for investor decision making.

(b) **Different legal systems**. These prevent the development of certain accounting practices and restrict the options available.

(c) **Different user groups**. Countries have different ideas about who the relevant user groups are and their respective importance. In the USA and UK investor and creditor groups are given prominence, while in continental Europe employees enjoy a higher profile.

(d) **Needs of developing countries**. Developing countries are obviously behind in the standard-setting process and they need to develop the basic standards and principles already in place in most developed countries.

(e) **Nationalism** is demonstrated in an unwillingness to accept another country's standard.

(f) **Cultural differences** result in objectives for accounting systems differing from country to country.

(g) **Unique circumstances**. Some countries may be experiencing unusual circumstances which affect all aspects of everyday life, including the ability of companies to produce proper reports, eg hyperinflation, civil war, currency restriction.

(h) **The lack of strong accountancy bodies**. Many countries do not have strong independent accountancy or business bodies, which would press for better standards and greater harmonisation.

(i) **Inertia and cost**. There is often a national resistance to change reinforced by cost considerations.

4.2 Advantages of global harmonisation

In spite of all these difficulties, why is harmonisation perceived as so desirable? The advantages are based on the benefits to users and preparers of financial statements.

Question — Globalisation

Suggest reasons why harmonisation is seen as desirable on a global basis.

Answer

(a) **Investors**, both individual and corporate, would like to be able to compare the financial results of different companies internationally (as well as nationally) in making investment decisions. Differences in accounting practice and reporting can be a barrier to such cross-border analysis. There is a growing amount of international investment across borders, but there are few financial analysts experienced in international markets. For example, an analyst familiar with UK accounting principles finds it difficult to analyse the financial statements of a Dutch or German company. Harmonisation would aid these analysts.

(b) **Multinational companies** would benefit from harmonisation for many reasons.

- Better access to foreign investor funds
- Aid internal communication of financial information
- Easier appraisal of foreign entities for take-overs and mergers
- Easier to comply with reporting requirements of overseas stock exchanges
- Easier consolidation of foreign subsidiaries and associated companies
- Possible reduction in audit costs
- Easier to transfer of accounting staff across national borders

(c) **Governments of developing countries** would save time and money by adopting international standards. If these were used internally, governments of developing countries could control the activities of foreign multinational companies within their own country, as these companies could not 'hide' behind foreign accounting practices which are difficult to understand.

(d) **Tax authorities**. It would be easier to calculate the tax liability of investors, including multinationals who receive income from overseas sources.

(e) **Regional economic groups** usually promote trade within a specific geographical region. This would be aided by common accounting practices within the region.

(f) **Large international accounting firms** would benefit as accounting and auditing would be much easier if similar accounting practices existed throughout the world.

4.3 Progress with harmonisation to date

The IASB publishes data about the use of IFRS Accounting Standards globally. As at September 2023, 147 jurisdictions require the use of IFRS Accounting Standards for all or most publicly accountable entities. A further 12 countries permitted the use of IFRS Accounting Standards.

However, significant global economies such as China and USA do not currently permit the use of IFRS Accounting Standards. Some of the key global economies are discussed in the following sections.

The barriers to harmonisation may be daunting but some progress has been made. There are various bodies which are working on different aspects of harmonisation and these are discussed below. The most important of these bodies, in the light of recent developments, are the IASB and the UK Financial Reporting Council (FRC).

4.4 European Union (EU)

> **FAST FORWARD**
>
> The EC has required that **since 2005** consolidated financial statements of all listed companies should comply with IFRS.

As we have already seen, the EC regulations form one part of a broader programme for the harmonisation of company law in EU member states. The commission is uniquely the only organisation to produce **international** standards of accounting practice which are legally enforceable, in the form of directives which must be included in the national legislation of member states. The directives have been criticised as they might become constraints on the application of world-wide standards and bring accounting standardisation and harmonisation into the political arena.

The EC adopted a regulation stating that **from 2005 consolidated financial statements of listed companies have been required to comply with international accounting standards.** The implications of this proposal are far reaching.

Many commentators believe that, in the light of the above, it is only a matter of time before national standard setting bodies like the UK Financial Reporting Council are, in effect, replaced by the IASB and national standards fall into disuse.

4.5 United Kingdom

The UK left the Europe Union, but IFRS Accounting Standards have continued to be required for UK listed companies. All IFRS Accounting Standards that were endorsed by the EU have become UK-endorsed from 1 January 2021. Any new IFRS Accounting Standards will need to be adopted by the UK.

4.5.1 UK Financial Reporting Council (FRC)

The UK FRC considers the development of international standards of **fundamental importance**. In addition, the UK FRC meets on a formal and regular basis with standard-setters around the world.

The FRC issued FRS 100 *Application of Financial Reporting Requirements* in November 2012 which lays out the future of UK GAAP and provides rules and guidance on how to select the appropriate accounting framework for a particular entity or group.

From January 2015, UK companies will be required to follow one of four sets of accounting requirements, depending on factors such as their size and whether they are listed:

- Full IFRS Accounting Standards
- IFRS Accounting Standards together with FRS 101 *Reduced Disclosure Framework*. FRS 101 makes minor amendments to IFRS in order to achieve compliance with the UK Companies Act and reduces IFRS Accounting Standard disclosures significantly for qualifying entities, such as subsidiaries of groups reporting their individual entity financial statements under EU adopted IFRS Accounting Standards.
- FRS 102 *The Financial Reporting Standard Applicable in the UK and Republic of Ireland*, a new single UK standard based on the *IFRS for Small and Medium-sized Entities*, which will replace existing UK accounting standards. FRS 102 adopts an IFRS-based framework, amended to ensure compliance with company law and improves accounting for financial instruments. It is intended for all UK entities other than those applying the FRSSE, or listed companies preparing group financial statements, who are already required to report under full IFRS Accounting Standards. Such companies will still be allowed to apply FRS 101 or FRS 102 in preparing their individual entity financial statements.
- FRS 105 - Financial Reporting Standard applicable to the Micro-entities Regim.

The issue of FRS 101 ensures that IFRS Accounting Standards become more accessible to unlisted companies in the UK which have, to date, been allowed to adopt full IFRS Accounting Standards, but are, in many cases reluctant to do so due to the onerous disclosure requirements.

The UK FRC is going to be replaced with the establishment of the Audit, Reporting and Governance Authority (ARGA).

4.6 IFRS Accounting Standard convergence with US GAAP

FAST FORWARD

> The IASB has worked with the US FASB for a number of years and some convergence was achieved. However progress has halted, and there are still **significant differences between IFRS Accounting Standards and US GAAP.**

4.6.1 Norwalk agreement

In October 2002, the IASB reached an agreement with the US FASB (Financial Accounting Standards Board) (the **'Norwalk' agreement**) to undertake a short-term convergence project aimed at removing a variety of individual differences between US GAAP and IFRS Accounting Standards. The first standard resulting from this project was IFRS 5 *Non-current Assets Held for Sale and Discontinued Operations* (published March 2004).

4.6.2 Principles-based approach

In March 2003, an 'identical style and wording' approach was agreed for standards issued by FASB and the IASB on joint projects. Revised business combinations standards were issued as a result of this approach in January 2008, and most recently, IFRS 10–13 in May 2011.

The FASB also recognised the need to follow a **'principles-based' approach** to standard-setting (as the IASB has always done) in the light of corporate failures and scandals which led to criticism of the 'rules-based' approach.

4.6.3 Common *Conceptual Framework*

In October 2004 the IASB and FASB agreed to develop a **common *Conceptual Framework*** which would be a significant step towards harmonisation of future standards (discussed earlier in this chapter). Together the IASB and FASB worked on the objective and qualitative characteristics of financial reporting; however, the remainder of the project was completed by the IASB working alone.

4.6.4 Memorandum of understanding

In February 2006, the two Boards signed a **'Memorandum of Understanding' (MoU)**. This laid down a 'roadmap of convergence' between IFRS and US GAAP in the period 2006-2008, identifying short-term and longer-term convergence projects that would bring the most significant improvements to IFRS and US GAAP.

In June 2010 the convergence strategy documented in the Memorandum of Understanding was modified. The modified work plan retained a target completion date of June 2011 or earlier for the MoU projects for which 'the need for improvement of both IFRS and US GAAP is the most urgent'. However it deferred less important work until after this date.

In April 2012, the IASB and FASB issued an update note stating that:

- Most short-term projects were now complete or close to completion
- Several longer-term projects were complete, with three – those on leases, revenue recognition and financial instruments – yet to be finalised.

A final standard on revenue recognition was issued in May 2014 and IFRS 9 *Financial Instruments* was issued in July 2014.

4.6.5 IASB and FASB

After 2014, the two boards continued to meet, but no further projects were completed. In 2017, the SEC issued a statement that both sets of accounting standards were expected to continue for the foreseeable future implying that any further convergence was unlikely.

The two boards do still meet on a regular basis and publish the minutes of the meetings.

4.7 Dialogue with other key standard setters

The IASB maintains a policy of dialogue with other key standard-setters around the world, in the interest of harmonising standards across the globe.

National standard-setters are often involved in the development of Discussion Papers and Exposure Drafts on new areas.

4.7.1 Asia and Oceania

The national standards of China are substantially converged with IFRS Accounting Standards. China has committed to adopting IFRS Accounting Standards for some Chinese companies but a timetable for this has yet to be put in place.

IFRS Accounting Standards are permitted in Japan along with US GAAP and Japanese accounting standards.

Australia and New Zealand both require IFRS Accounting Standards to be used for listed companies.

4.7.2 Russia

The Russian Federation requires all listed companies to use IFRS Accounting Standards.

4.7.3 South America

IFRS Accounting Standards are required in most South American companies for listed companies, including Brazil.

4.7.4 Africa

Almost all African countries have adopted IFRS Accounting Standards.

4.8 The situation today and in the future

Many organisations committed to global harmonisation have done a great deal of work towards this goal. It is the case at present, however, that fundamental disagreements exist between countries and organisations about the way forward. One of the major gulfs is between the reporting requirements in developed countries and those in non-developed countries. The IFRS Foundation and the World Bank announced a cooperation agreement in 2017 to work together to assist emerging economies to consider the adoption of IFRS Accounting Standards.

Chapter roundup

- Various national factors will affect the regulatory framework of entities, but our concern in this text is with international matters, particularly the **IASB** and **IFRS Accounting Standards**.
- You should be able to describe the **organisation of the IFRS Foundation and the IASB** and its relationships with intergovernmental bodies, professional accountancy bodies, national standard-setting bodies and IOSCO.
- IFRS Accounting Standards are based on the IASB's *Conceptual Framework for Financial Reporting*.
- The Conceptual Framework considers two measurement bases:
  - Historical cost
  - Current value
- The EC has required that **since 2005** consolidated financial statements of all listed companies should **comply with IFRS**.
- IFRS Accounting Standards are used widely around the world. However, **several large economies have not adopted** IFRS Accounting Standards, notably China and the USA.

Quick quiz

1. Which of the following factors govern the regulatory system of accounting over entities? Circle all that apply.

    (a) National legislation
    (b) Local legislation
    (c) IAS
    (d) Accounting systems
    (e) IFRS
    (f) Auditing systems
    (g) FBI

2. What are the objectives of the IFRS Foundation and the IASB?

3. Which is the most recent IFRS Accounting Standard applicable to FAR 2?

Answers to quick quiz

1. (a), (b), (c) and (e)
2. See Section 2.1
3. IFRS 18 *Presentation and Disclosure in Financial Statements*

   is the most recent standard applicable to the FAR 2 course.

End of chapter question

IASB

'A major achievement of the IASB has been the development of its *Conceptual Framework*. However, it is too theoretical to be applied to accounting standards.'

Critically analyse this statement, considering what the merits of the *Conceptual Framework* are and whether you agree with the criticism that it is too theoretical.

(10 marks)

PART A: CONTEMPORARY ISSUES

Presentation of published financial statements

Topic list	Syllabus reference
1 Limited liability	LO1
2 IAS 1 *Presentation of Financial Statements*	LO1
3 Statement of financial position	LO1
4 The current/non-current distinction	LO1
5 Statement of profit or loss and other comprehensive income	LO1
6 Statement of changes in equity	LO1
7 Notes to the financial statements	LO1
8 IFRS 18 *Presentation and Disclosure of Financial Statements*	LO1

Introduction

The bulk of this Learning & Practice Workbook looks at the accounts of limited liability companies, either single companies or groups of companies.

In this chapter we look at the overall **content and format** of company financial statements. These are governed by IAS 1 *Presentation of Financial Statements*.

A new accounting standard, IFRS 18 *Presentation and Disclosure of Financial Statements* has been issued by the IASB. Although it is only mandatory from 2027, early adoption is possible.

1 Limited liability

FAST FORWARD: Limited liability offers various advantages to companies, although there are disadvantages as well.

1.1 Fundamental differences

There are some fundamental differences in the financial statements of limited liability companies **compared to sole-traders or partnerships**, of which the following are perhaps the most significant.

(a) The **national legislation** governing the activities of limited liability companies tends to be very extensive. Among other things such legislation may define certain minimum accounting records which must be maintained by companies; it may specify that the annual financial statements of a company must be filed with a government bureau and so available for public inspection; and often contains detailed requirements on the minimum information which must be disclosed in a company's financial statements. Businesses which are not limited liability companies (non-incorporated businesses) often enjoy comparative freedom from statutory regulation.

(b) The **owners of a company** (its members or shareholders) may be very numerous. Their capital is shown differently from that of a sole trader; and similarly the 'appropriation account' of a company is different.

1.2 Limited liability

You may be able to recognise the relative **advantages and disadvantages** of limited liability.

Limited liability companies offer **limited liability to their owners**. This means that the maximum amount that an owner stands to lose in the event that the company becomes insolvent and cannot pay off its debts is his share of the capital in the business. Thus limited liability is a major advantage of turning a business into a limited liability company. However, in practice, banks or other lenders will normally seek personal guarantees from shareholders before making loans or granting an overdraft facility and so the advantage of limited liability is lost to a small owner managed business.

As a business grows, it needs **more capital** to finance its operations, and significantly more than the people currently managing the business can provide themselves. One way of obtaining more capital is to invite investors from outside the business to invest in the ownership or equity of the business. These new co-owners would not usually be expected to help with managing the business. To such investors, limited liability is very attractive.

Investments are always risky undertakings, but with limited liability the investor knows the maximum amount that he stands to lose when he puts some capital into a company.

There are however additional requirements placed on limited liability companies:

(a) Compliance with national legislation
(b) Compliance with national accounting standards and/or IFRS Accounting Standards
(c) Any formation and annual registration costs

1.3 The accounting records of limited liability companies

There is almost always a **national legal requirement** for companies to keep accounting records which are sufficient to show and explain the company's transactions. The records will probably:

(a) Disclose the company's current financial position at any time
(b) Contain:
   (i) Day-to-day entries of money received and spent
   (ii) A record of the company's assets and liabilities

(iii) Where the company deals in goods:

(1) A statement of inventories held at the year end, and supporting inventory count records

(2) With the exception of retail sales, statements of goods bought and sold which identify the sellers and buyers of those goods

(c) Enable the managers of the company to ensure that the **final financial statements** of the company give a true and fair view of the company's profit or loss and statement of financial position.

The detailed requirements of accounting records which must be maintained will vary from country to country.

Question — Regulation

How are limited liability companies regulated in your country?

2 IAS 1 *Presentation of Financial Statements*

FAST FORWARD

IAS 1 covers the **form and content** of financial statements, which comprise:

- Statement of financial position
- Statement of profit or loss and other comprehensive income
- Statement of changes in equity
- Statement of cash flows
- Notes to the financial statements, comprising significant accounting policies and other explanatory information
- Comparative information in respect of the preceding period

IAS 1 *Presentation of Financial Statements* gives substantial guidance on the form and content of published financial statements. Central to understanding how items should be presented in the financial statements is the notion of fair presentation.

A new standard, IFRS 18 *Presentation and Disclosure of Financial Statements* has been issued and will replace IAS 1 for financial periods beginning on or after 1 January 2027. This new standard is discussed later in the chapter.

2.1 Fair presentation

IAS 1 provides guidance is provided on the meaning of present fairly: '[represent faithfully] …the effects of transactions and other events…in accordance with the definitions and recognition criteria for assets, liabilities, income and expenses as set out in the [Conceptual] Framework' (IAS 1: para. 15).

Fair presentation is achieved if IFRS Accounting Standards are appropriately applied and additional disclosure is given when it is necessary (IAS 1: para. 15). However, very rarely, management may come to the conclusion that complying with an IFRS requirement would be 'so misleading that it would conflict with the objective of financial statements set out in the Framework' (IAS 1: para. 19). If so, and if local laws and regulations permit, the entity can depart from that IFRS requirement, as long as it 'discloses:

(a) That management has concluded that the financial statements present fairly the entity's financial position, financial performance and cash flows;

(b) That it has complied with applicable IFRS Accounting Standards except that it has departed from a particular requirement to achieve a fair presentation;

(c) Full details of the departure; and

(d) The financial effect of the departure on each item in the financial statements that would have been reported in complying with the requirement.' (IAS 1: para. 20)

However, when local law prohibits departure from the requirement, then the entity should make disclosures which will reduce the perceived misleading effects of complying. These include the details of why management believe it to be misleading and adjustments showing what they believe is necessary to fairly present the information (IAS 1: para. 23).

2.2 Profit or loss for the period

The statement of profit or loss and other comprehensive income is the most significant indicator of a company's financial performance. So it is important to ensure that it is not misleading.

IAS 1 stipulates that all items of income and expense recognised in a period shall be included in profit or loss unless an **IFRS Accounting Standard** or an **Interpretation** requires otherwise.

Circumstances where items may be excluded from profit or loss for the current year include the correction of errors and the effect of changes in accounting policies. These are covered in IAS 8 *Accounting Policies, Changes in Accounting Estimates and Errors*.

2.3 Disclosure and materiality

IAS 1 specifies disclosures of certain items in certain ways.

- Some items must appear in the statement of financial position or statement of profit or loss and other comprehensive income
- Other items can appear in a **note to the financial statements** instead
- **Recommended formats** are given which entities may or may not follow, depending on their circumstances

Obviously, disclosures specified by **other standards** must also be made, and we will mention the necessary disclosures when we cover each standard in turn. Disclosures in both IAS 1 and other standards must be made either in the statement or in the notes unless otherwise stated, ie disclosures cannot be made in an accompanying commentary or report.

Disclosures are subject to materiality judgements.

2.3.1 Materiality

Material: 'Information is material if omitting, misstating or obscuring it could reasonably be expected to influence decisions that the primary users of general purpose financial reports make on the basis of those reports, which provide financial information about a specific reporting entity. In other words, materiality is an entity-specific aspect of relevance based on the nature or magnitude, or both, of the items to which the information relates in the context of an individual entity's financial report.' (IAS 1: para. 7, emphasis added)

The IASB has amended the definition of 'material' to make it clear that obscuring information has the same effect as omitting or misstating it. Obscuring information means making the information so difficult to find or so difficult to understand, that it may as well have been omitted.

2.3.2 Making materiality judgements

Preparers of financial statements make **materiality judgements** when applying IFRS Accounting Standards.

Recognition and measurement	• The recognition and measurement criteria only need to be applied when **the effect** of applying them is **material**. • For example, an entity may choose to capitalise items of property, plant and equipment only when the cost of an individual item exceeds, say $1,000, on the basis that capitalising items below this amount will not have a material effect on the financial statements.
Presentation and disclosure	• Disclosure criteria: if the information provided by a certain disclosure requirement is **not material**, the **entity does not need to make that disclosure**, even if that disclosure is part of a list of minimum required disclosures in an IFRS Accounting Standard. • However, the entity should consider whether it also needs to disclose information not specifically required by an IFRS Accounting Standard if that information is needed to understand the financial statements.

Four-step process to making materiality judgements (paras. 29–65)

One way of making materiality judgements when preparing the financial statements is to apply the following four-step process:

Step 1: Identify information that is potentially material	
Consider requirements of IFRS Accounting Standards	Consider common information needs of primary users

Step 2: Assess whether that information is material	
Could information reasonably be expected to influence primary users?	Consider qualitative and quantitative factors

Step 3: Organise information into draft financial statements	
Apply judgment to determine best way to communicate clearly and concisely	Eg: emphasise material matters, explain simply, minimise duplication

Step 4: Review complete set of draft financial statements	
On the basis of complete set of financial statements: has all material information been identified?	On the basis of complete set of financial statements: has materiality been considered from a wide perspective and in aggregate?

Both quantitative factors and qualitative factors should be considered.

Qualitative factors	Quantitative factors
These are characteristics that make information more likely to influence the decisions of primary users, they can be internal or external: • Internal include: involvement of related parties, uncommon features, unexpected changes in trends • External include: geographic location, industry section, state of the economy	• Consider the size of the effect of the transaction/event against measures of the entity's financial position, performance and cash flows • Consider any unrecognised items (eg contingent liabilities) that could affect primary users' perception • Can be assessed with the help of a threshold – such as 5% of profit

Illustration 1 – Material related party transaction

Red has identified measures of profitability as of great interest to the primary users of its financial statements. During the year, Red agreed a five year contract in which Green (a related party), will perform maintenance services for Red for an annual fee of $1.5 million.

Red first assessed whether the information about the transaction was material from a quantitative perspective. A threshold of $2.5 million (3% of net profit) was used. From a purely quantitative perspective, Red assessed that the effect of the contract was not material.

Red then considered the transaction from a qualitative perspective. Having considered that the transaction was with a related party, Red concluded that the impact of the transaction was large enough to reasonably be expected to influence primary users' decisions (eg the presence of a qualitative factor lowered the quantitative threshold).

Red assessed information about the transaction with Green as material and disclosed that information in its financial statements.

Illustration 2 – Immaterial related party transaction

During the year Red sold an almost fully depreciated machine to Blue (a related party) at an amount consistent with the machine's market value.

Red assessed whether the information about the transaction was material. From a purely quantitative perspective, Red initially concluded that the impact of the related party transaction was not material. However, a qualitative factor exists: the fact that the machine was sold to a related party makes the information more likely to influence the decisions of primary users. Therefore Red further assessed the transaction from a quantitative perspective, but concluded that its impact was too small to reasonably be expected to influence primary users' decisions, even though the transaction was with a related party.

Red assessed information about the transaction with Blue to be immaterial and did not disclose it in its financial statements.

(Based on IFRS Practice Statement 2, Examples I and J)

2.4 Identification of financial statements

As a result of the above point, it is most important that entities **distinguish the financial statements** very clearly from any other information published with them. This is because all IFRS Accounting Standards apply **only** to the financial statements (ie the main statements and related notes), so readers of the annual report must be able to differentiate between the parts of the report which are prepared under IFRS Accounting Standards, and other parts which are not.

The entity should **identify each** financial statement and the notes very clearly. IAS 1 also requires disclosure of the following information in a prominent position. If necessary it should be repeated wherever it is felt to be of use to the reader in his understanding of the information presented.

• **Name** of the reporting entity (or other means of identification)

- Whether the financial statements cover the **single entity** only or a group of entities
- The **date of the end of the reporting period** or the period covered by the financial statements (as appropriate)
- The **presentation currency**
- The **level of rounding** used in presenting amounts in the financial statements

Judgement must be used to determine the best method of presenting this information. In particular, the standard suggests that the approach to this will be very different when the financial statements are communicated electronically.

The **level of rounding** is important, as presenting figures in thousands or millions of units makes the figures more understandable. The level of rounding must be disclosed, however, and it should not obscure necessary details or make the information less relevant.

2.5 Reporting period

It is normal for entities to present financial statements **annually** and IAS 1 states that they should be prepared at least as often as this. If (unusually) the end of an entity's reporting period is changed, for whatever reason, the period for which the statements are presented will be less or more than one year. In such cases the entity should also disclose:

(a) The **reason(s) why** a period other than one year is used; and
(b) The fact that the comparative figures given **are not in fact comparable**.

For practical purposes, some entities prefer to use a period which **approximates to a year**, eg 52 weeks, and the IAS allows this approach as it will produce statements not materially different from those produced on an annual basis.

3 Statement of financial position

> **FAST FORWARD**
>
> IAS 1 suggests a **format** for the statement of financial position. Certain items are specified for **disclosure in the financial statements**.

IAS 1 discusses the distinction between current and non-current items in some detail, as we shall see in the next section. First of all we can look at the **suggested format** of the statement of financial position (given in an appendix to the standard) and then look at further disclosures required.

3.1 Example: Statement of financial position

The example given by IAS 1 revised is as follows:

XYZ GROUP – STATEMENT OF FINANCIAL POSITION AT 31 DECEMBER

	20X7 $'000	20X6 $'000
Assets		
Non-current assets		
Property, plant and equipment	350,700	360,020
Goodwill	80,800	91,200
Other intangible assets	227,470	227,470
Investments in associates	100,150	110,770
Financial assets	142,500	156,000
	901,620	945,460
Current assets		
Inventories	135,230	132,500
Trade receivables	91,600	110,800
Other current assets	25,650	12,540

PART A CONTEMPORARY ISSUES

	20X7 $'000	20X6 $'000
Cash and cash equivalents	312,400	322,900
	564,880	578,740
Total assets	1,466,500	1,524,200
Equity and liabilities		
Equity attributable to owners of the parent		
Share capital	650,000	600,000
Retained earnings	243,500	161,700
Other components of equity	10,200	21,200
	903,700	782,900
Non-controlling interest	70,050	48,600
Total equity	973,750	831,500
Non-current liabilities		
Long-term borrowings	120,000	160,000
Deferred tax	28,800	26,040
Long-term provisions	28,850	52,240
Total non-current liabilities	117,650	238,280
Current liabilities		
Trade and other payables	115,100	187,620
Short-term borrowings	150,000	200,000
Current portion of long-term borrowings	10,000	20,000
Current tax payable	35,000	42,000
Short-term provisions	5,000	4,800
Total current liabilities	315,100	454,420
Total liabilities	492,750	92,700
Total equity and liabilities	1,466,500	1,524,200

IAS 1 (revised) specifies various items which must appear in the **statement of financial position**.

(a) Property, plant and equipment
(b) Investment property
(c) Intangible assets
(d) Financial assets (excluding amounts shown under (e), (h) and (i))
(e) Investments accounted for using the equity method
(f) Biological assets
(g) Inventories
(h) Trade and other receivables
(i) Cash and cash equivalents
(j) Assets classified as held for sale under IFRS 5
(k) Trade and other payables
(l) Provisions
(m) Financial liabilities (other than (j) and (k))
(n) Current tax liabilities and assets as in IAS 12
(o) Deferred tax liabilities and assets
(p) Liabilities included in disposal groups under IFRS 5
(q) Non-controlling interests
(r) Issued capital and reserves

Any **other line items**, headings or sub-totals should be shown in the statement of financial position when it is necessary for an understanding of the entity's financial position.

The example shown above is for illustration only (although we will follow the format in this Learning & Practice Workbook). The IAS, however, does not prescribe the order or format in which the items listed should be presented. It simply states that they **must be presented separately** because they are so different in nature or function from each other.

Whether additional items are presented separately depends on judgements based on the assessment of the following factors:

(a) **Nature and liquidity of assets and their materiality**. Thus goodwill and assets arising from development expenditure will be presented separately, as will monetary/non-monetary assets and current/non-current assets.

(b) **Function within the entity**. Operating and financial assets, inventories, receivables and cash and cash equivalents are therefore shown separately.

(c) **Amounts, nature and timing of liabilities**. Interest-bearing and non-interest-bearing liabilities and provisions will be shown separately, classified as current or non-current as appropriate.

The standard also requires separate presentation where **different measurement bases** are used for assets and liabilities which differ in nature or function. According to IAS 16, for example, it is permitted to measure certain items of property, plant and equipment at cost or at a revalued amount.

3.2 Information presented in the statement of financial position or the notes

Further **sub-classification** of the line items listed above should be disclosed either in the statement of financial position or in the notes. The classification will depend upon the nature of the entity's operations. As well as each item being sub-classified by its nature, any amounts payable to or receivable from any **group company or other related party** should also be disclosed separately.

The sub-classification details will in part depend on the requirements of IFRS Accounting Standards. The size, nature and function of the amounts involved will also be important and the factors listed above should be considered. **Disclosures** will vary from item to item and IAS 1 gives the following examples.

(a) **Property, plant and equipment** are classified by class as described in IAS 16, *Property, Plant and Equipment*

(b) **Receivables** are analysed between amounts receivable from trade customers, other members of the group, receivables from related parties, prepayments and other amounts

(c) **Inventories** are sub-classified, in accordance with IAS 2 *Inventories,* into classifications such as merchandise, production supplies, materials, work in progress and finished goods

(d) **Provisions** are analysed showing separately provisions for employee benefit costs and any other items classified in a manner appropriate to the entity's operations

(e) **Equity capital and reserves** are analysed showing separately the various classes of paid in capital, share premium and reserves

The standard then lists some **specific disclosures** which must be made, either in the statement of financial position or in the related notes.

(a) **Share capital disclosures** (for each class of share capital)

(i) Number of shares authorised

(ii) Number of shares issued and fully paid, and issued but not fully paid

(iii) Par value per share, or that the shares have no par value

(iv) Reconciliation of the number of shares outstanding at the beginning and at the end of the year

(v) Rights, preferences and restrictions attaching to that class including restrictions on the distribution of dividends and the repayment of capital

(vi) Shares in the entity held by the entity itself or by related group companies

(vii) Shares reserved for issuance under options and sales contracts, including the terms and amounts

(b) Description of the nature and purpose of **each reserve** within owners' equity

Some types of entity have no share capital, eg partnerships. Such entities should disclose information which is **equivalent** to that listed above. This means disclosing the movement during the period in each category of equity interest and any rights, preferences or restrictions attached to each category of equity interest.

4 The current/non-current distinction

> **FAST FORWARD**
>
> You should appreciate the distinction between **current** and **non-current** assets and liabilities and their different treatments.

4.1 The current/non-current distinction

An entity must present **current** and **non-current** assets as separate classifications in the statement of financial position. A presentation based on liquidity should only be used where it provides more relevant and reliable information, in which case all assets and liabilities must be presented broadly **in order of liquidity**.

In either case, the entity should disclose any portion of an asset or liability which is expected to be recovered or settled **after more than 12 months**. For example, for an amount receivable which is due in instalments over 18 months, the portion due after more than 12 months must be disclosed.

The IAS emphasises how helpful information on the **operating cycle** is to users of financial statements. Where there is a clearly defined operating cycle within which the entity supplies goods or services, then information disclosing those net assets that are continuously circulating as **working capital** is useful.

This distinguishes them from those net assets used in the long-term operations of the entity. Assets that are expected to be realised and liabilities that are due for settlement within the operating cycle are therefore highlighted.

The liquidity and solvency of an entity is also indicated by information about the **maturity dates** of assets and liabilities. As we will see later, IFRS 7 *Financial Instruments: Disclosures* requires disclosure of maturity dates of both financial assets and financial liabilities. (Financial assets include trade and other receivables; financial liabilities include trade and other payables.) In the case of non-monetary assets, eg inventories, such information is also useful.

4.2 Current assets

Key term

> An asset should be classified as a **current asset** when it:
>
> - The entity expects to realise the asset, or intends to sell or consume it, in its normal operating cycle; or
> - The asset is held primarily for trading purposes; or
> - The asset is expected to be realised within 12 months of the end of the reporting period; or
> - The asset is cash or a cash equivalent asset which is not restricted in its use.
>
> All other assets should be classified as non-current assets.   (IAS 1)

Non-current assets includes tangible, intangible, operating and financial assets of a long-term nature. Other terms with the same meaning can be used (eg 'fixed', 'long-term').

The term 'operating cycle' has been used several times above and the standard defines it as follows.

Key term

> The **operating cycle** of an entity is the time between the acquisition of assets for processing and their realisation in cash or cash equivalents.   (IAS 1)

Current assets therefore include inventories and trade receivables that are sold, consumed and realised as part of the normal operating cycle. **This is the case even where they are not expected to be realised within 12 months**.

Current assets will also include **marketable securities** if they are expected to be realised within 12 months after the reporting period. If expected to be realised later, they should be included in non-current assets.

4.3 Current liabilities

Key term

A liability should be classified as a **current liability** when it:

- The entity expects to settle the liability in its normal operating cycle; or
- The liability is held primarily for the purpose of trading; or
- The liability is due to be settled within 12 months after the reporting period; or
- The entity does not have an unconditional right to defer settlement of the liability for at least 12 months after the reporting period.

All other liabilities should be classified as non-current liabilities. (IAS 1)

The categorisation of current liabilities is very similar to that of current assets. Thus, some current liabilities are part of the **working capital** used in the normal operating cycle of the business (ie trade payables and accruals for employee and other operating costs). Such items will be classed as current liabilities **even where they are due to be settled more than 12 months after the end of the reporting period**.

There are also current liabilities which are not settled as part of the normal operating cycle, but which are due to be settled within 12 months of the end of the reporting period. These include bank overdrafts, income taxes, other non-trade payables and the current portion of interest-bearing liabilities. Any interest-bearing liabilities that are used to finance working capital on a long-term basis, and that are not due for settlement within 12 months, should be classed as **non-current liabilities**.

A **non-current financial liability** due to be **settled within 12 months** of the end of the reporting period should be classified as a **current liability**, even if an agreement to refinance, or to reschedule payments, on a long-term basis is completed after the end of the reporting period and before the financial statements are authorised for issue.

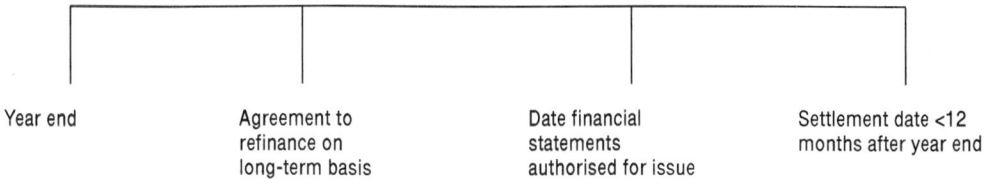

Year end | Agreement to refinance on long-term basis | Date financial statements authorised for issue | Settlement date <12 months after year end

A **non-current financial liability** that is payable on **demand** because the entity **breached** a **condition** of its loan agreement should be classified as **current** at the end of the reporting period even if the **lender** has agreed **after the end of the reporting period**, and **before** the financial statements are **authorised for issue**, **not** to **demand payment** as a consequence of the breach.

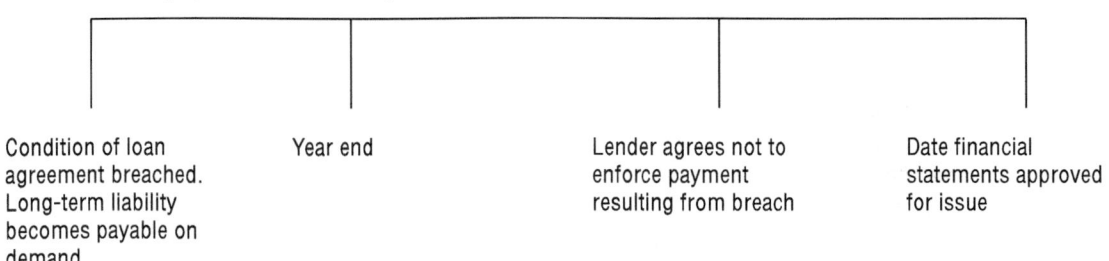

Condition of loan agreement breached. Long-term liability becomes payable on demand | Year end | Lender agrees not to enforce payment resulting from breach | Date financial statements approved for issue

However, if the **lender** has **agreed** by the **end of the reporting period** to provide a **period of grace** ending **at least 12 months after the end of the reporting period** within which the entity can rectify the breach and during that time the lender cannot demand immediate repayment, the liability is classified as **non-current**.

PART A CONTEMPORARY ISSUES

5 Statement of profit or loss and other comprehensive income

FAST FORWARD

IAS 1 requires all items of income and expense in a period to be shown in a **statement of profit or loss and other comprehensive income.**

5.1 Statement of profit or loss and other comprehensive income – format

IAS 1 allows income and expense items to be presented either:

(a) In a single statement of profit or loss and other comprehensive income; or
(b) In two statements: a separate statement of profit and loss and a statement of profit or loss and other comprehensive income.

Exam focus point

In the examinations, generally 'Statement of profit or loss and other comprehensive income' will be referred to and this will usually relate to the single statement format. If 'Statements of Profit or Loss' is referred to, this is the statement from 'Revenue' to 'Profit for the year'. Where we have used 'statement of profit or loss' in this text, this can be taken to refer to the section of the statement of profit or loss and other comprehensive income as far as profit, or separate statement or profit or loss.

XYZ GROUP – STATEMENT OF PROFIT OR LOSS AND OTHER COMPREHENSIVE INCOME FOR THE YEAR ENDED 31 DECEMBER 20X7

	20X7	20X6
	$'000	$'000
Revenue	39,000	355,000
Cost of sales	(245,000)	(230,000)
Gross profit	145,000	125,000
Other income	20,667	11,300
Distribution costs	(9,000)	(8,700)
Administrative expenses	(20,000)	(21,000)
Other expenses	(2,100)	(1,200)
Finance costs	(8,000)	(7,500)
Share of profit of associates	35,100	30,100
Profit before tax	161,667	128,000
Income tax expense	(40,417)	(32,000)
Profit for the year from continuing operations	121,250	96,000
Loss for the year from discontinued operations	–	(30,500)
Profit for the year	121,250	65,500
Other comprehensive income:		
Items that will not be reclassified to profit or loss:		
Gains on property revaluation	933	3,367
Remeasurements of defined benefit pension plans	(667)	1,333
Share of gain on property revaluation of associates	400	(700)
Income tax relating to items that will not be reclassified	(166)	(1,000)
	500	3,000
Items that may be reclassified subsequently to profit or loss		
Exchange differences on translating foreign operations	5,334	10,667
Financial assets held at fair value through other comprehensive income	(24,000)	26,667
Cash flow hedges	(667)	(4,000)
Income tax relating to items that may be reclassified	4,833	(8,334)
	(14,500)	25,000

	20X7	20X6
	$'000	$'000
Other comprehensive income for the year, net of tax	(14,000)	28,000
Total comprehensive income for the year	107,250	93,500
Profit attributable to:		
Owners of the parent	97,000	52,400
Non-controlling interest	24,250	13,100
	121,250	65,500
Total comprehensive income attributable to		
Owners of the parent	85,800	74,800
Non-controlling interest	21,450	18,700
	107,250	93,500
Earnings per share (in currency units)	0.46	0.30

Companies are given the option of presenting this information in two statements as follows:

XYZ GROUP – STATEMENT OF PROFIT OR LOSS AND OTHER COMPREHENSIVE INCOME FOR THE YEAR ENDED 31 DECEMBER 20X7:

	20X7	20X6
	$'000	$'000
Revenue	39,000	355,000
Cost of sales	(245,000)	(230,000)
Gross profit	145,000	125,000
Other income	20,667	11,300
Distribution costs	(9,000)	(8,700)
Administrative expenses	(20,000)	(21,000)
Other expenses	(2,100)	(1,200)
Finance costs	(8,000)	(7,500)
Share of profit of associates	35,100	30,100
Profit before tax	161,667	128,000
Income tax expense	(40,417)	(32,000)
Profit for the year from continuing operations	121,250	96,000
Loss for the year from discontinued operations	–	(30,500)
Profit for the year	121,250	65,500
Profit attributable to:		
Owners of the parent	97,000	52,400
Non-controlling interest	24,250	13,100
	121,250	65,500

XYZ GROUP STATEMENT OF PROFIT OR LOSS AND OTHER COMPREHENSIVE INCOME FOR THE YEAR ENDED 31 DECEMBER 20X7

	20X7	20X6
	$'000	$'000
Profit for the year	121,250	65,500
Other comprehensive income:		
Items that will not be reclassified to profit or loss		
Gains on property revaluation	933	3,367
Remeasurements of defined benefit pension plans	(667)	1,333
Share of gain on property revaluation of associates	400	(700)
Income tax relating to items that will not be reclassified	(166)	(1,000)
	500	3,000
Items that may be reclassified subsequently to profit or loss		
Exchange differences on translating foreign operations	5,334	10,667
Financial assets at fair value through other comprehensive income	(24,000)	26,667

	20X7 $'000	20X6 $'000
Cash flow hedges	(667)	(4,000)
Income tax relating to items that may be reclassified	4,833	(8,334)
	(14,500)	25,000
Other comprehensive income for the year, net of tax	(14,000)	28,000
Total comprehensive income for the year	107,250	93,500
Total comprehensive income attributable to		
Owners of the parent	85,800	74,800
Non-controlling interest	21,450	18,700
	107,250	93,500

5.2 Presentation of other comprehensive income

IAS 1 requires that regardless of whether a one or two statement presentation is adopted, other comprehensive income must be grouped into amounts which, in accordance with other IFRS Accounting Standards:

(a) Will not be reclassified subsequently to profit or loss; and
(b) May be reclassified subsequently to profit or loss if specific conditions are met.

A similar disclosure must be made for the share of the comprehensive income of associates and joint ventures that are accounted for using the equity method. Items of other comprehensive income may be presented either net of related tax effects or before related tax effects. If the second approach is adopted, the aggregate amount of income tax relating to items of other comprehensive income must be disclosed and this must be split according to whether the other comprehensive income may be reclassified to profit or loss.

The blurring of distinctions between different items in OCI is the result of an underlying general lack of agreement among users and preparers about which items should be presented in OCI and which should be part of the profit or loss section. For instance, a common misunderstanding is that the split between profit or loss and OCI is on the basis of realised versus unrealised gains. This is not, and has never been, the case.

This lack of a consistent basis for determining how items should be presented has led to the somewhat inconsistent use of OCI in financial statements.

This method of presentation is shown in the examples in Section 5.1 above.

5.3 Statement of profit or loss formats

FAST FORWARD

> IAS 1 offers **two** possible formats for the statement of profit or loss section or separate statement of profit or loss – by function or by nature. Classification by function is more common.

5.3.1 Statement of profit or loss by function

XYZ GROUP
STATEMENT OF PROFIT OR LOSS FOR THE YEAR ENDED 31 DECEMBER 20X8

Illustrating the classification of expenses by **function**

	20X8 $'000	20X7 $'000
Revenue	X	X
Cost of sales	(X)	(X)
Gross profit	X	X
Other income	X	X
Distribution costs	(X)	(X)
Administrative expenses	(X)	(X)
Other expenses	(X)	(X)
Finance costs	(X)	(X)

	20X8 $'000	20X7 $'000
Share of profit of associates	X	X
Profit before tax	X	X
Income tax expense	(X)	(X)
Profit for the year	X	X
Attributable to:		
Owners of the parent	X	X
Non-controlling interest	X	X
	X	X

5.3.2 Statement of profit or loss nature

Illustrating the classification of expenses by **nature**

	20X8 $'000	20X7 $'000
Revenue	X	X
Other operating income	X	X
Changes in inventories of finished goods and work in progress	(X)	X
Work performed by the entity and capitalised	X	X
Raw material and consumables used	(X)	(X)
Employee benefits expense	(X)	(X)
Depreciation and amortisation expense	(X)	(X)
Impairment of property, plant and equipment	(X)	(X)
Other expenses	(X)	(X)
Finance costs	(X)	(X)
Share of profit of associates	X	X
Profit before tax	X	X
Income tax expense	(X)	(X)
Profit for the year	X	X
Attributable to:		
Owners of the parent	X	X
Non-controlling interest	X	X
	X	X

Note. The usual method of presentation is expenses by function and this is the format likely to appear in your exam.

5.4 Information presented in the profit or loss section or separate statement of profit or loss

The standard lists the following as the **minimum** to be disclosed in the statement of profit or loss:

(a) Revenue
(b) Finance costs
(c) Share of profits and losses of associates and joint ventures accounted for using the equity method
(d) Tax expense
(e) A single amount for the total of discontinued operations

The following items must be disclosed in the statement of profit or loss as allocations of profit or loss for the period.

(a) Profit or loss attributable to non-controlling interest
(b) Profit or loss attributable to owners of the parent

The allocated amounts must not be presented as items of income or expense. (These relate to group financial statements, covered later in this text.)

Income and expense items can only be **offset** when, and only when:

(a) It is permitted or required by an IFRS Accounting Standard; or

(b) Gains, losses and related expenses arising from the same or similar transactions and events are immaterial, in which case they can be aggregated.

5.5 Information presented either in the statement or in the notes

An analysis of expenses must be shown either in the statement of profit or loss section (as above, which is encouraged by the standard) or by note, using a classification based on **either** the nature of the expenses or their function. This **sub-classification of expenses** indicates a range of components of financial performance; these may differ in terms of stability, potential for gain or loss and predictability.

5.5.1 Nature of expense method

Expenses are not reallocated amongst various functions within the entity, but are aggregated in the statement of profit or loss **according to their nature** (eg purchase of materials, depreciation, wages and salaries, transport costs). This is by far the easiest method, especially for smaller entities.

5.5.2 Function of expense/cost of sales method

You are likely to be more familiar with this method. Expenses are classified according to their function as part of cost of sales, distribution or administrative activities. This method often gives **more relevant information** for users, but the allocation of expenses by function requires the use of judgement and can be arbitrary. Consequently, perhaps, when this method is used, entities should disclose **additional information** on the nature of expenses, including staff costs, and depreciation and amortisation expenses.

Which of the above methods is chosen by an entity will depend on **historical and industry factors**, and also the **nature of the organisation**. Under each method, there should be given an indication of costs which are likely to vary (directly or indirectly) with the level of sales or production. The choice of method should fairly reflect the main elements of the entity's performance.

5.6 Further points

(a) IAS 1 also requires disclosure of the amount of **dividends** (both in total and per share) recognised in the period covered by the financial statements. This may be shown either in the statement of changes in equity or in the notes. Dividends are not disclosed in the statement of profit or loss and other comprehensive income.

(b) An entity must disclose, in its significant accounting policies and/or other notes, the **judgements** made by management in **applying** the **accounting policies** that have the **most significant effect** on the amounts of items recognised in the financial statements.

(c) An entity must disclose in the notes information regarding **key assumptions** about the **future**, and other sources of **measurement uncertainty**, that have a significant **risk of** causing a **material adjustment** to the carrying amounts of assets and liabilities within the **next financial year**.

The figure in the statement of financial position for capital and reserves therefore bears **no relationship** to the market value of shares. Market values are the product of a large number of factors, including general economic conditions, alternative investment returns (eg interest rates), likely future profits and dividends and, not least, market sentiment.

6 Statement of changes in equity

FAST FORWARD

IAS 1 requires a statement of changes in equity. This shows the movement in the equity section of the statement of financial position.

6.1 Format

This is the format of the statement of changes in equity as per IAS 1 (revised).

XYZ GROUP – STATEMENT OF CHANGES IN EQUITY FOR THE YEAR ENDED 31 DECEMBER 20X7

	Share capital $'000	Retained earnings $'000	Equity instruments at FVTOCI $'000	Revaluation surplus $'000	Total $'000	Non-controlling interest $'000	Total equity $'000
Balance at 1 January 20X6	600,000	118,100	1,600	–	719,700	29,800	749,500
Changes in accounting policy	–	400	–	–	400	100	500
Restated balance	600,000	118,500	1,600	–	720,100	29,900	750,000
Changes in equity							
Dividends	–	(10,000)	–	–	(10,000)	–	(10,000)
Total comprehensive income for the year	–	53,200	16,000	1,600	70,800	18,700	89,500
Balance at 31 December	600,000	161,700	17,600	1,600	780,900	48,600	829,500
Changes in equity for 20X7							
Issue of share capital	50,000	–	–	–	50,000	–	50,000
Dividends	–	(15,000)	–	–	(15,000)	–	(15,000)
Total comprehensive income for the year	–	96,600	(14,400)	800	83,000	21,450	104,450
Transfer to retained earnings	–	200	–	(200)	–	–	–
Bal at 31 December 20X7	650,000	243,500	3,200	2,200	898,900	70,050	968,950

Note that where there has been a change of accounting policy necessitating a retrospective restatement, the adjustment is disclosed for each period. So, rather than just showing an adjustment to the balance b/f on 1.1.X7, the balances for 20X6 are restated.

7 Notes to the financial statements

FAST FORWARD

Some items need to be disclosed by way of note.

7.1 Contents of notes

The notes to the financial statements will **amplify** the information given in the statement of financial position, statement of profit or loss and other comprehensive income and statement of changes in equity. To some extent, then, the contents of the notes will be determined by the level of detail shown in **the statements**.

7.2 Structure

The notes to the financial statements should perform the following functions:

(a) Provide information about the **basis on which the financial statements were prepared** and which **specific accounting policies** were chosen and applied to significant transactions/events

(b) Disclose any information, not shown elsewhere in the financial statements, which is **required by IFRS Accounting Standards**

(c) Show any additional information that is relevant to understanding which is not shown elsewhere in the financial statements

The way the notes are presented is important. They should be given in a **systematic manner** and **cross referenced** back to the related figure(s) in the statement of financial position, statement of profit or loss and other comprehensive income or statement of cash flows.

A systematic manner may be achieved by giving prominence to the most important items, grouping together information about similar items, or following the order of the items in the primary statements.

Notes to the financial statements will amplify the information shown therein by giving the following:

(a) More **detailed analysis** or breakdowns of figures in the statements
(b) **Narrative information** explaining figures in the statements
(c) **Additional information**, eg contingent liabilities and commitments

IAS 1 suggests a **certain order** for notes to the financial statements. This will assist users when comparing the statements of different entities.

(a) Statement of **compliance** with IFRS Accounting Standards
(b) Statement of the **measurement basis** (bases) and accounting policies applied
(c) **Supporting information** for items presented in each financial statement in the same order as each line item and each financial statement is presented
(d) Other disclosures, eg:
  (i) Contingent liabilities, commitments and other financial disclosures
  (ii) Non-financial disclosures

The order of specific items may have to be varied occasionally, but a systematic structure is still required.

7.3 Presentation of accounting policies

The accounting policies section should describe the following:

(a) The **measurement basis** (or bases) used in preparing the financial statements
(b) The **other accounting policies** used, as required for a proper understanding of the financial statements

This information may be shown in the notes or sometimes as a **separate component** of the financial statements.

The information on measurement bases used is obviously fundamental to an understanding of the financial statements. Where **more than one basis is used**, it should be stated to which assets or liabilities each basis has been applied.

7.4 Other disclosures

An entity must disclose in the notes:

(a) The amount of dividends proposed or declared before the financial statements were authorised for issue but not recognised as a distribution to owners during the period, and the amount per share
(b) The amount of any cumulative preference dividends not recognised

IAS 1 ends by listing some **specific disclosures** which will always be required if they are not shown elsewhere in the financial statements:

(a) The domicile and legal form of the entity, its country of incorporation and the address of the registered office (or, if different, principal place of business)
(b) A description of the nature of the entity's operations and its principal activities
(c) The name of the parent entity and the ultimate parent entity of the group

Financial statements

The accountant of Wislon Co has prepared the following list of account balances as at 31 December 20X7.

	$'000
50c ordinary shares (fully paid)	450
10% debentures (secured)	200
Retained earnings 1.1.X7	242
General reserve 1.1.X7	171
Land and buildings 1.1.X7 (cost)	430
Plant and machinery 1.1.X7 (cost)	830
Accumulated depreciation	
Buildings 1.1.X7	20
Plant and machinery 1.1.X7	222
Inventory 1.1.X7	190
Sales	2,695
Purchases	2,152
Ordinary dividend	15
Debenture interest	10
Wages and salaries	254
Light and heat	31
Sundry expenses	113
Suspense account	135
Trade receivables	179
Trade payables	195
Cash	126

Notes.

(a) Sundry expenses include $9,000 paid in respect of insurance for the year ending 1 September 20X8. Light and heat does not include an invoice of $3,000 for electricity for the three months ending 2 January 20X8, which was paid in February 20X8. Light and heat also includes $20,000 relating to salesmen's commission.

(b) The suspense account is in respect of the following items.

	$'000
Proceeds from the issue of 100,000 ordinary shares	120
Proceeds from the sale of plant	300
	420
Less consideration for the acquisition of Mary & Co	285
	135

(c) The net assets of Mary & Co were purchased on 3 March 20X7. Assets were valued as follows:

	$'000
Financial assets	231
Inventory	34
	265

All the inventory acquired was sold during 20X7. The financial assets are held at fair value and this remains unchanged at 31.12.X7. Goodwill has not been impaired in value.

(d) The property was acquired some years ago. The buildings element of the cost was estimated at $100,000 and the estimated useful life of the assets was 50 years at the time of purchase. As at 31 December 20X7 the property is to be revalued at $800,000.

(e) The plant was sold on 1.1.X7. It had cost $350,000 and had a carrying amount of $274,000 at the date of disposal. $36,000 depreciation is to be charged on plant and machinery for 20X7.

PART A   CONTEMPORARY ISSUES

(f) The management wish to provide for:
  (i) Debenture interest due
  (ii) A transfer to general reserve of $16,000
  (iii) Audit fees of $4,000

(g) Inventory as at 31 December 20X7 was valued at $220,000 (cost).

(h) Taxation is to be ignored.

Required

Prepare the financial statements of Wislon Co as at 31 December 20X7. You do not need to produce notes to the statements.

Answer

(a) Normal adjustments are needed for accruals and prepayments (insurance, light and heat, debenture interest and audit fees). The debenture interest accrued is calculated as follows.

	$'000
Charge needed in profit or loss (10% × $200,000)	20
Amount paid so far, as shown in list of account balances	10
Accrual: presumably six months' interest now payable	10

The accrued expenses shown in the statement of financial position comprise:

	$'000
Debenture interest	10
Light and heat	3
Audit fee	4
	17

(b) The mis-posting of $20,000 to light and heat is also adjusted, by reducing the light and heat expense, but charging $20,000 to salesmen's commission.

(c) Depreciation on the building is calculated as $\frac{\$100,000}{50} = \$2,000$.

The carrying amount of the property is then $430,000 − $20,000 − $2,000 = $408,000 at the end of the year. When the property is revalued a revaluation surplus of $800,000 − $408,000 = $392,000 should be recognised.

(d) The profit on disposal of plant is calculated as proceeds $300,000 (per suspense account) less carrying amount $274,000, ie $26,000. The cost of the remaining plant is calculated at $830,000 − $350,000 = $480,000. The depreciation provision at the year end is:

	$'000
Balance 1.1.X7	222
Charge for 20X7	36
Less depreciation on disposals (350 − 274)	(76)
	182

(e) Goodwill arising on the purchase of Mary & Co is:

	$'000
Consideration (per suspense account)	285
Assets at valuation	265
Goodwill	20

This is shown as an asset in the statement of financial position. The financial assets, being owned by Wislon at the year end, are also shown on the statement of financial position, whereas Mary's inventory, acquired and then sold, is added to the purchases figure for the year.

(f) The other item in the suspense account is dealt with as follows:

	$'000
Proceeds of issue of 100,000 ordinary shares	120
Less nominal value 100,000 × 50c	50
Excess of consideration over par value (= share premium)	70

(g) The transfer to general reserve increases it to $171,000 + $16,000 = $187,000.

We can now prepare the financial statements.

WISLON CO
STATEMENT OF PROFIT OR LOSS AND OTHER COMPREHENSIVE INCOME FOR THE YEAR ENDED 31 DECEMBER 20X7

	$'000
Revenue	2,695
Cost of sales (W1)	(2,156)
Gross profit	539
Other income (profit on disposal of plant)	26
Administrative expenses (W2)	(437)
Finance costs	(20)
Profit for the year	108
Items which will not be reclassified to profit or loss	
Gain on property revaluation	392
Total comprehensive income for the year	500

Note.
The only item of 'other comprehensive income' for the year was the revaluation gain. If there had been no revaluation gain, a statement of profit or loss only would have been required.

Workings

1   Cost of sales

	$'000
Opening inventory	190
Purchases (2,152 + 34 re Mary)	2,186
Closing inventory	(220)
	2,156

2   Administrative expenses

	$'000
Wages, salaries and commission (254 + 20)	274
Sundry expenses (113 – (9 × 9/12))	107
Light and heat (31 – 20 + 3)	14
Depreciation: buildings	2
Plant	36
Audit fees	4
	437

PART A CONTEMPORARY ISSUES

WISLON CO
STATEMENT OF FINANCIAL POSITION AS AT 31 DECEMBER 20X7

	$'000	$'000
Assets		
Non-current assets		
Property, plant and equipment		
Property at valuation		800
Plant: Cost	480	
Accumulated depreciation	(182)	
		298
Goodwill		20
Financial assets		231
		1,349
Current assets		
Inventory	220	
Trade receivables	179	
Prepayments	6	
Cash	126	
		531
Total assets		1,880
Equity and liabilities		
Equity		
50c ordinary shares	500	
Share premium	70	
Revaluation surplus	392	
General reserve	187	
Retained earnings	319	
		1,468
Non-current liabilities		
10% loan stock (secured)		200
Current liabilities		
Trade payables	195	
Accrued expenses	17	
		212
Total equity and liabilities		1,880

WISLON CO
STATEMENT OF CHANGES IN EQUITY
FOR THE YEAR ENDED 31 DECEMBER 20X7

	Share capital $'000	Share premium $'000	Retained earnings $'000	General reserve $'000	Revaluation surplus $'000	Total $'000
Balance at 1.1.X7	450	–	242	171	–	863
Issue of share capital	50	70				120
Dividends			(15)			(15)
Total comprehensive income for the year			108		392	500
Transfer to reserve			(16)	16		–
Balance at 31.12.X7	500	70	319	187	392	1,468

Note. that the total comprehensive income is analysed into its components.

8 IFRS 18 Presentation and Disclosure of Financial Statements

> **FAST FORWARD**
>
> IFRS 18 *Presentation and Disclosure of Financial Statements* is a new standard which will replace IAS 1 from 2027.

8.1 Improvements to primary financial statements

The IASB began a project in 2016 to look at improvements to primary financial statements to improve communication. An exposure draft was published in 2019, and finally, in 2024 a new standard was issued, IFRS 18.

The project was initiated as a result of differences in companies' presentations of the statement of profit or loss. IAS 1 only required the profit, or loss, for the period. There was no requirement to present any other subtotals. In practice, companies were including subtotals such as operating profit which were not defined in the standards. This resulted in a lack of comparability between entities as the subtotals were not always calculated in the same way.

The project also identified a lack of guidance about what information to present in the primary financial statements and what to present in the notes.

Many companies were also found to define their own performance measures. While investors often found these useful in analysing performance, the lack of transparency as to how the measures were calculated, or linked to the primary financial statements was noted as an area of concern.

The benefits of the new standard are improvement to the quality of financial reporting that will:

- Provide investors with additional useful information about financial performance
- Improve the ability of investors to compare performance between companies and between reporting periods
- Improve transparency to help investors understand performance measures used by management and how these compare to measures defined by IFRS Accounting Standards

8.2 IFRS 18 requirements

IFRS 18 was published in April 2024. The standard is expected to improve the quality of financial reporting by:

- Requiring defined subtotals in the statement of profit or loss;
- Requiring disclosure about management-defined performance measures; and
- Adding new principles for aggregation and disaggregation of information.

These improvements are expected to enable users of financial reporting, particularly investors, to make more informed decisions.

8.3 Subtotals and categories in the statement of profit or loss

IFRS 18 requires an entity to classify income and expenses in the statement of profit or loss into the following categories:

- Operating
- Investing
- Financing

There are two required subtotals that must be included:

- Operating profit

- Profit before financing and income taxes

Additional subtotals are also permitted as required e.g. gross profit. The profit or loss for the reporting period must also be presented.

The income tax expenses and any profit or loss from discontinued operations are also included on the face of the statement.

An example of the structure of the statement of profit or loss under IFRS 18 would be:

Statement of profit or loss	20X2	20X1	Categories
Revenue	367,000	353,100	
Cost of sales	(241,600)	(224,100)	
Gross profit	**125,400**	**129,000**	Operating
Other operating income	12,200	4,100	
Selling expenses	(28,900)	(27,400)	
Research and development expenses	(25,100)	(25,900)	
General and administrative expenses	(20,900)	(22,400)	
Goodwill impairment loss	(4,500)	–	
Other operating expenses	(1,200)	(5,600)	
Operating profit	**57,000**	**51,800**	
Share of profit and gains on disposal of associates and joint ventures	5,300	7,300	Investing
Profit before financing and income taxes	**62,300**	**59,100**	
Interest expenses on borrowings and lease liabilities	(13,000)	(13,200)	Financing
Interest expenses on pension liabilities and provisions	(6,500)	(6,000)	
Profit before income taxes	**42,800**	**39,900**	
Income tax expense	(10,700)	(9,975)	Income taxes
Profit from continuing operations	**32,100**	**29,925**	
Loss from discontinued operations	–	(5,500)	Discontinued operations
Profit	**32,100**	**24,425**	

8.3.1 Operating category

The **operating category** will include all income and expenses from a company's operations including those from its main business activities. It is the default category for any income and expenses that do not fall into the investing or financing categories.

8.3.2 Investing category

The **investing category** will include income and expenses from assets that generate a return individually, and largely independently of other resources held. It includes any income generated by the assets, income and expenses that arise from initial and subsequent measurement of the assets including derecognition and incremental expenses relating to acquisition or disposal of assets. It includes income and expenses from cash and cash equivalents.

Some examples of income and expenditure classified in the investing category are:

- Rental income and remeasurements of investment property
- Finance income from investments in debt
- Dividends from equity investments

8.3.3 Financing category

The **financing category** will include all income and expenses from liabilities that arise from transactions that involve only the raising of finance. It also includes interest expenses and the effects of changes in interest rates from other liabilities such as lease liabilities and defined benefit pension liabilities.

Some examples of income and expenditure classified in the financing category are:

- Expenses relating to a bond issue
- Interest expenses relating to a lease contract

IFRS 18 includes requirements for bank and insurers who have financing and investing activities as their main business activity.

8.4 Management-defined performance measures

Many companies include alternative performance measures in their annual reports or financial statements such as adjusted operating profit, free cash flow, adjusted EBITDA (earnings before interest, tax, depreciation and amortisation). Investors often find these useful but there is a lack of transparency about how they are calculated.

IFRS 18 defines management-defined performance measures (MPMs) as:

- Subtotals of income and expenses not listed in IFRS 18 or required by IFRS Accounting Standards
- Included in public communications outside financial statements such as management commentary or press releases
- Measures that communicate management's view of a company's financial performance

8.4.1 Disclosure requirements of MPMs

IFRS 18 requires all MPMs to be reconciled back to an IFRS-defined subtotal in a single disclosure note to the financial statements. The reconciliation must include the income tax effect and the effect on any non-controlling interest.

As well as the reconciliation, explanations are required for each MPM about:

- Why the MPM is reported
- How the MPM is calculated including how the tax effect was determined
- Any changes to the MPM (if relevant)

The note must include a statement to confirm that the MPMs provide management's view of an aspect of the financial performance of the entity as a whole and are not necessarily comparable with MPMs in other entities.

8.5 Grouping of information

The review project identified that investors have concerns about the amount of detailed information provided by companies in their financial statements. Some companies provide too much detailed information and some don't provide enough.

IFRS 18 provides guidance as to whether information should be included in the primary financial statements or in the notes.

It sets out the role of the primary financial statements to provide **useful structured summaries** of a company's assets, liability, equity, income, expenses and cash flows. To be useful the structure summaries should allow investors to:

- Obtain an understandable overview;
- Make comparisons; and
- Identify items or areas about which they may wish to seek additional information in the notes.

A company should use the role of the primary financial statements to determine what is **material** and needs to be presented in the primary financial statements.

The notes to the financial statements provide **material** information that enables investors to understand items in the primary financial statements and supplement the primary financial statements to achieve the objective of the financial statements.

8.5.1 Principles for grouping

Items should be aggregated based on shared characteristics and disaggregated based on characteristics which are not shared in both the primary financial statements and notes.

The aggregation and disaggregation of items must not obscure material information.

Companies will need to consider whether they need to present all of the line items listed in IFRS 18 in the statement of profit or loss and statement of financial position, or whether some items should be aggregated. They will also need to consider if any additional subtotals and line items are necessary to provide a useful structure summary of the financial statements.

IFRS 18 requires the use of meaningful labels and that 'other' should only be used when there is no alternative.

8.5.2 Presentation of operating expenses

IFRS 18 requires companies to classify and present operating expenses in a way that provides the most useful structured summary of expenses. Operating expenses might be presented by nature or by function or a mixture of both.

8.5.3 Disclosure of expenses by nature

Where company presents one or more line items for operating expenses classified by function e.g. cost of sales or administrative expenses, IFRS 18 requires a note to be included that specifies how five expenses by nature relating to each line item of operating expenses in the statement of profit or loss.

These five specified expenses are:

- Depreciation
- Amortisation
- Employee benefits
- Impairment losses and reversals of impairment losses
- Write-downs and reversals of write-downs of inventories

An example of a specified expenses by nature note is:

	20X2	20X1
Depreciation		
Cost of sales	23,710	21,990
Research and development expenses	2,515	2,590
General and administrative expenses	4,975	4,750
Total depreciation	**31,200**	**29,330**
Amortisation		
Research and development expenses	13,840	12,690
Total amortisation	**13,840**	**12,690**
Employee benefits		
Cost of sales	61,640	57,175
Selling expenses	7,515	7,110
Research and development expenses	6,545	6,750
General and administrative expenses	8,920	5,825
Total employee benefits	**84,620**	**76,860**
Impairment losses[a]		
Research and development expenses	1,600	1,500
Goodwill impairment loss	4,500	—
Total impairment losses	**6,100**	**1,500**
Write-down of inventories[a]		
Cost of sales	2,775	2,625
Total write-down of inventories	**2,775**	**2,625**

(a) The amounts disclosed represent the total of impairment losses and reversals of impairment losses and the total of write-down of inventories and reversals of write-down of inventories.

8.6 Impact on other financial statements

IFRS 18 makes very limited changes to specific requirements in the statement of cash flows and the statement of financial position. There are no changes to the specific requirements in IAS 1 relating to the statement of comprehensive income and the statement of changes in equity.

The disclosure requirements in IAS 1 relating to material accounting policies, sources of estimation uncertainty, capital management and debt covenants are unchanged.

8.7 Impact on other IFRS Accounting Standards

IFRS 18 requires slight amendments to IAS 7 and IAS 33. These amendments apply as soon as a company adopts IFRS 18.

8.7.1 IAS 7 Statement of cash flows

IFRS 18 requires companies to classify and present operating expenses in a way that provides the most The operating profit or loss subtotal will be the starting point for the indirect method of reporting cash flows from operating activities under IAS 7.

The presentation alternatives for cash flows related to interest and dividends paid and received are removed. Interest and dividends received are investing cash flows and interest and dividends paid are financing cash flows.

8.7.2 IAS 33 Earning per share

Currently, entities can include in the notes, additional EPS calculations based on any component of the statement of profit or loss and other comprehensive income.

The amendment to IAS 33 permits the disclosure of an additional EPS only if the numerator is a total or subtotal identified in IFRS 18, or is an MPM.

8.7.3 IAS 8 Accounting Policies, Changes in Accounting Estimates and Errors

Some of the current requirements of IAS 1 will move to IAS 8 once IFRS 18 is effective. These include:

- Fair presentation and compliance with IFRS Accounting Standards
- Going concern
- Disclosure of selection and application of accounting policies

The title of IAS 8 will become *Basis of Preparation of Financial Statements* to reflect the extended content.

8.8 Effective date and transition

An entity is required to apply IFRS 18 for reporting period beginning on or after 1 January 2027. Earlier application is permitted.

IFRS 18 must be applied **retrospectively**, with a specific requirement for comparative figures in the statement of profit or loss. A reconciliation is required for these figures between the restated amounts presented under IFRS 18 and the amounts previously presented under IAS 1.

If a company applies IAS 34 *Interim Financial Reporting*, then the condensed interim financial statements should be prepared following IFRS 18 in the first year in which the company is applying IFRS 18.

The IASB expect that companies will incur some costs implementing IFRS 18, mostly in relation to changes to internal systems and processes.

Chapter roundup

- **Limited liability** offers various advantages to companies, although there are disadvantages as well.
- IAS 1 covers the **form and content of** financial statements, which comprise:
  - Statement of financial position
  - Statement of profit or loss and other comprehensive income
  - Statement of changes in equity
  - Statement of cash flows
  - Notes to the financial statements, comprising significant accounting policies and other explanatory information
  - Comparative information in respect of the preceding period
- IAS 1 suggests a **format** for the statement of financial position. Certain items are specified for **disclosure in the financial statements**.
- You should appreciate the distinction between **current and non-current** assets and liabilities and their different treatments.
- IAS 1 requires all items of income and expense in a period to be shown in a **statement of profit or loss and other comprehensive income**.
- IAS 1 offers **two** possible formats for the statement of profit or loss section or separate statement of profit or loss – by function or by nature. Classification by function is more common.
- IAS 1 requires a statement of changes in equity. This shows the movement in the equity section of the statement of financial position.
- Some items need to be disclosed by way of note.
- IFRS 18 will replace IAS 1 from 2027. As well as changes to the presentation of the statement of profit or loss, it will also impact the information reported on the face of the primary financial statements and in the notes.

Quick quiz

1. Limited liability means that the shareholders of a company are not legally accountable.

    True ☐   False ☐

2. Which of the following are examples of current assets?

    (a) Property, plant and equipment
    (b) Prepayments
    (c) Cash equivalents
    (d) Manufacturing licences
    (e) Retained earnings

3. Provisions must be disclosed in the statement of financial position.

    True ☐   False ☐

4. Which of the following must be disclosed in the statement of profit or loss?

    (a) Tax expense
    (b) Analysis of expenses
    (c) Profit or loss for the period.

PART A CONTEMPORARY ISSUES

5   *Fill in the blanks.*

The accounting policies section of the notes describes:

The .... used in preparing the financial statements and...................................... required for a proper understanding of the financial statements.

Answers to quick quiz

1   False. It means that if the company becomes insolvent, the maximum that an owner stands to lose is his share capital in the business.
2   (b) and (c) only
3   True
4   (a) only
5   Measurement basis (or bases)
    Specific accounting policies

End of chapter question

Polymer

The following list of account balances has been prepared by Polymer Co, plastics manufacturers, on 31 May 20X8, which is the end of the company's accounting period.

	$	$
Authorised and issued 300,000 ordinary shares of $1 each		300,000
100,000 8.4% cumulative redeemable preference shares of $1 each		100,000
Revaluation surplus		50,000
Share premium		100,000
Other components of equity		50,000
Retained earnings – 31 May 20X7		283,500
Patents and trademarks	215,500	
Freehold land at cost	250,000	
Right-of-use asset - property at initial measurement	75,000	
Amortisation of right-of-use asset property – 31 May 20X7		15,000
Factory plant and equipment at cost	150,000	
Accumulated depreciation – plant and equipment – 31 May 20X7		68,500
Furniture and fixtures at cost	50,000	
Accumulated depreciation – furniture and fixtures – 31 May 20X7		15,750
Motor vehicles at cost	75,000	
Accumulated depreciation – motor vehicles – 31 May 20X7		25,000
10% loan notes (20Y0 – 20Y5)		100,000
Trade receivables/ trade payables	177,630	97,500
Bank overdraft		51,250
Inventories – raw materials at cost – 31 May 20X7	108,400	
Purchases – raw materials	750,600	
Carriage inwards – raw materials	10,500	
Manufacturing wages	250,000	
Manufacturing overheads	125,000	
Cash	5,120	
Work in progress – 31 May 20X7	32,750	
Sales		1,526,750
Administrative expenses	158,100	
Selling and distribution expenses	116,800	
Legal and professional expenses	54,100	
Allowance for receivables – 31 May 20X8		5,750
Inventories – finished goods – 31 May 20X7	184,500	
	2,789,000	2,789,000

Additional information:

(1) Inventories at 31 May 20X8 were:

	$
Raw materials	112,600
Finished goods	275,350
Work in progress	37,800

(2) Depreciation for the year is to be charged as follows:
Plant and equipment 8% on cost – charged to production
Furniture and fixtures 10% on cost – charged to admin
Motor vehicles 20% on reducing value – 25% admin
– 75% selling and distribution

(3) Financial, legal and professional expenses include:

	$
Solicitors' fees for purchase of freehold land during year	5,000

(4) An accrual should be recognised for a full year's interest on the loan notes.

(5) Income tax on the profits for the year is estimated at $40,000 and is due for payment on 28 February 20X9.

(6) The directors recommended on 30 June 20X8 that a dividend of 3.5c per share be paid on the ordinary share capital. No ordinary dividend was paid during the year ended 31 May 20X7.

(7) The right-of-use asset - property relates toe right-of-use assets held under lease contracts. The contracts commenced ten years ago. The lease term and useful life of the property were both 50 years on commencement of the lease.

Required

From the information given above, prepare the statement of profit or loss of Polymer Co for the year to 31 May 20X8 and a statement of financial position at that date for publication in accordance with IFRS Accounting Standards.

Notes to the financial statements are not required. **(25 marks)**

Sustainability reporting

Topic list	Syllabus reference
1 Sustainability	LO1
2 Sustainable development	LO1
3 Sustainability reporting frameworks	LO1
4 IFRS Sustainability Disclosure Standards	LO1
5 Sustainability and stakeholders	LO1

Introduction

The sustainability reporting landscape is changing rapidly. Companies are under increasing pressure to demonstrate that they contribute positively to society. Existing frameworks, such as the Global Reporting Initiative Standards have been joined by the new IFRS Sustainability Disclosure Standards and the European Sustainability Reporting Standards. Corporate reporting on sustainability issues is very topical and relevant to accountants today.

PART A   CONTEMPORARY ISSUES

1 Sustainability

Sustainability is a multifaceted concept aimed at improving people's lives and safeguarding the planet for future generations. Stemming from the 1987 Brundtland report, sustainable development is defined as 'development that meets the needs of the present without compromising the ability of future generations to meet their own needs.'

The scope of sustainability has evolved beyond environmental concerns to encompass a wide range of issues, including increasing disparities in wealth, population growth, biodiversity loss, deteriorating air and water quality, climate change, human rights, and bribery and corruption.

In recent years, heightened awareness of environmental, social, and governance (ESG) issues has prompted global stock exchanges to mandate sustainability reporting for listed companies. Consequently, board directors are now expected to integrate ESG considerations into their business strategies and decision-making processes.

Sustainability issues can have an impact on a business, but businesses also have an impact on sustainability matters which can create both opportunities and risks for businesses and stakeholders need information about these opportunities and risks to make informed decisions.

2 Sustainable development

> **FAST FORWARD**
>
> Businesses are increasingly focussed on communicating their sustainability impact to investors and can do this by linking to the United National Sustainable Development Goals.

Sustainable development encompasses the idea of balancing economic growth, environmental protection, and social equity to ensure a prosperous and harmonious future for all, across the world.

Sustainable development acknowledges the interconnectedness of economic, environmental, and social factors, emphasising the importance of long-term thinking and responsible stewardship of resources. It seeks to address current challenges while safeguarding the well-being of future generations.

2.1 United Nations Sustainable Development Goals

The 2030 Agenda for Sustainable Development, adopted by all United Nations Member States in 2015, is a comprehensive blueprint for achieving a better and more sustainable future for all. At its heart are the 17 Sustainable Development Goals (SDGs), which are an urgent call for action by all countries in a global partnership. The 2030 Agenda recognises that eradicating poverty in all its forms and dimensions, accelerating sustainable development, and ensuring that no one is left behind are among the greatest global challenges and priorities.

The UN Sustainable Development Goals ('UN SDGs'), also known as the Global Goals, are a universal call to action to end poverty, protect the planet, and ensure that all people enjoy peace and prosperity by 2030.

The seventeen UN SDGs address a wide range of interconnected issues, including poverty, inequality, climate change, environmental degradation, peace, and justice. Each goal has specific targets to be achieved over the next decade, with the aim of addressing the root causes of global challenges and promoting sustainable development in all its dimensions.

The 17 UN SDG's are as follows: (**Source:** https://www.un.org/sustainabledevelopment/sustainable-development-goals/)

SUSTAINABLE DEVELOPMENT GOALS

The Sustainable Development Goals can help businesses understand how they can create social, environmental and economic value for both investors and other stakeholders. Reporting information on the Sustainable Development Goals can help investors and other stakeholders to make decisions about whether the resources they provide to an entity are being used in a responsible way.

3 Sustainability reporting frameworks

FAST FORWARD

> There are a number of different sustainabiltiy reporting frameworks in place, include the GRI Standards which have been in place for a number of years. Different frameworks focus on sustainability **impacts** or **dependencies**, or both. The IFRS Foundation is working to harmonise global sustainability reporting.

Sustainability reporting has become a key part of annual corporate reporting due to an increasing expectation of this information from stakeholders, particularly investors. It is one of the biggest issues in corporate reporting currently.

A number of different sustainability reporting frameworks have evolved for companies to follow, leading to some confusion for preparers and users of corporate reporting.

The IFRS Foundation formed the International Sustainability Standards Board (ISSB) in 2021 to bring some of the existing frameworks together but there are still a number of different reporting frameworks available.

Sustainability reporting can contain information from two different perspectives known as **impacts** and **dependencies**:

Key term

> **Impacts** are defined as the impact of a business on the environment and society
>
> **Dependencies** are defined as the impact of government, regulations, environmental and other sustainability matters on a business

The IFRS Sustainability Disclosure Standards issued by the ISSB have a focus on dependencies when determining matters to include in sustainability reporting. Information on dependencies is generally considered to be more useful for investors and creditors as the impact on the business might impact future performance.

Other frameworks, such as the Global Reporting Initiative (GRI) Standards takes an impacts approach to reporting. This impacts approach is useful to a wider range of stakeholders who want to know the sustainable impact of the business.

This Chapter will look at the IFRS Sustainability Disclosure Standards in detail. However, it is useful to have knowledge of some of the other key sustainability reporting frameworks in place.

Sustainability Reporting Framework	Description
GRI Standards	The GRI Standards taken an Impacts approach to sustainability reporting, focussing on the impact of the business on society and the environment.
Task Force on Climate-related Financial Disclosure (TCFD)	TCFD was established in 2015 to develop recommendations for voluntary climate-related financial disclosures, aiding stakeholders in assessing climate-related risks and opportunities.
Task-Force on Nature-related Financial Disclosure (TFND)	TNFD was launched in 2021 to provide guidance for businesses on how to consider and report on nature-related impacts and dependencies.
European Sustainability Reporting Standards (ESRS)	The European Union has adopted the ESRS which are applicable from 2024. These standards adopt an impact and dependencies approach.
Integrated Reporting Framework	This framework is designed to the value impact of business on financial and non-financial areas including environmental and social matters.

3.1 GRI Standards

GRI Standards enable an organisation to understand and report on its impacts on the economy, environment and society. GRI Standards take an impacts approach – material topics are identified based on the impact of the organisation on the environment and society.

There are three types of GRI Standards as follows:

Type of GRI Standard	Description
Universal Standards	These standards apply to all organisations. The standards cover the concepts and principles of GRI Standard reporting, general disclosures and how to identify material topics for reporting.
Sector Standards	These standards enable more consistent reporting on sector-specific impacts. Standards in issue include oil and gas, agriculture but the intention is to have standards in 40 different sectors.
Topic Standards	Topic standards work alongside universal standards. Once material topics have been identified, the topic standard provides guidance on measuring and reporting topics such as waste, health and safety.

Organisation can report 'in accordance with' GRI Standards if they comply with specific requirement in the standards including explaining all omitted disclosures and publishing a GRI content index.

Alternatively, organisations can report 'with reference to' GRI Standards.

Case Study

Shell plc began producing sustainability reports in 1997. Its 2023 Sustainability Report was the 27th such report. Shell prepares its report with reference to GRI Standards and the disclosures are indexed to the GRI Standards. Shell's sustainability reporting is going to be incorporated into the annual report from 2024 onwards.

Shell's 2023 Sustainabiltiy Report can be review here https://reports.shell.com/sustainability-report/2023/

3: SUSTAINABILITY REPORTING

In May 2024, the GRI and IFRS Foundation announced that they will work together to jointly identify and identify common disclosures. They will continue to make decisions separately, but with a focus on working towards a global and comprehensive system of sustainability reporting. One of the first areas to be considered for collaboration is Biodiversity.

3.2 Task Force on Climate-related Financial Disclosures (TCFD)

The Paris Agreement, an international treaty on Climate Change, was signed by nearly 200 countries at the United Nations Framework Convention on Climate Change in 2015. This agreement is generally regarded as the framework for international action towards mitigating climate change and its impacts through a global commitment to collective action on climate change, with the goal of achieving a sustainable and resilient future for all. The Paris Agreement set the ambition to reduce greenhouse gas emissions to attempt to restrict global temperature increases. The term 'net Zero' refers to the global reduction of greenhouse gas emissions to net Zero by 2050 and is the action required to limit temperature rises.

Although the Paris Agreement was a treaty between countries, organisations and individuals within individual countries must work together to reduce greenhouse gas emissions.

Following the Paris Agreement, the TCFD was set up in 2015 to improve and increase the reporting of climate-related financial information.

The recommendations of the TCFD required organisations disclose the financial impact of climate-related risks and opportunities and to assess how resilient the organisation in relation to future climate changes. The four core elements of TCFD disclosures were:

- Governance
- Strategy
- Risks
- Metrics and targets

The TCFD recommendations were used by the ISSB to develop IFRS S2 *Climate-related Disclosures* and the TCFD was disbanded in October 2023, having met its intended remit and purpose.

3.3 Task Force on Nature-related Financial Disclosures (TNFD)

The TNFD was set up in 2021 with the aim of providing decision-useful information about nature-related impact, dependencies, risks and opportunities.

The TNFD defines nature as the environment and society. The four realms of nature are land, ocean, freshwater and atmosphere and these realms encompass many different ecosystems. The ecosystems are assets on which society and business depend and also impact.

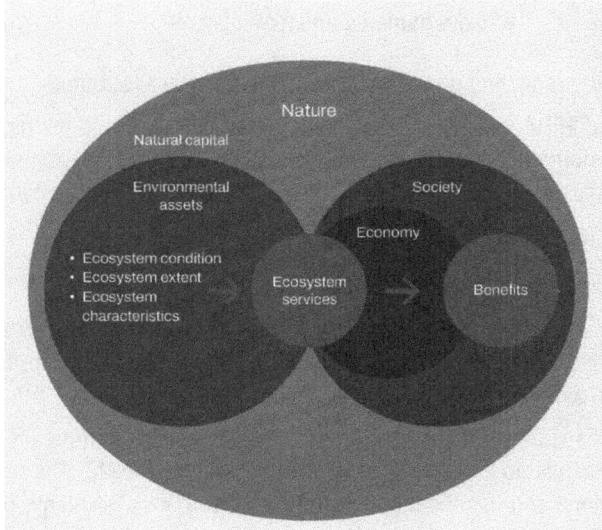

(Source: https://tnfd.global/about/why-nature-matters/)

The World Economic Forum has identified climate and environmental risks as the most significant risks to global business over the next decade, but also the risks for which we are the least prepared. Businesses often do not understand the impact of nature on their business of the impact on their business on nature.

The TNFD issued recommendations and guidance in September 2023 to enable businesses to integrate nature into decision making. The four core elements are consistent with the TCFD disclosures – governance, strategy, risks and metrics & targets.

These recommendations are voluntary but in April 2024, the ISSB announced that it was starting research projects about the risks and opportunities associated with biodiversity, ecosystems, ecosystem services and human capital and would consider the recommendation of the TNFD as part of this research.

3.4 European Sustainability Reporting Standards (ESRS)

Following the Paris Agreement, the European Union (EU)

The EU Corporate Sustainability Reporting Directive cam into force in 2023 and will have an impact on sustainability reporting for accounting period commencing in 2024, reporting in 2025. Implementation is being phased in over a three-year period.

The Directive requires large EU companies, and some listed SMEs to report on sustainability. Some non-EU companies that operate in the EU will also need to comply with the reporting requirements.

The sustainability reporting requirements are set out in the ESRS. ESRS are published by the European Financial Reporting Advisory Group (EFRAG). These standards adopt an impacts and dependencies approach to materiality, requiring companies to report on both their impact on society and the environment, and the impact of society and the environment on the company. This is known as a **double materiality** approach.

ESRS reporting focusses on four areas, similar to the other frameworks:

- Governance
- Strategy
- Impact, risk and opportunity management
- Metrics and targets

The ESRS are still being developed but the structure is as follows:

Type of ESRS	Description
Cross-cutting Standards	These standards apply to all organisations. The standards cover the general requirements and general disclosures for ESRS.
Topical Standards	Topical standards are split into: • Environment standards • Social standards • Governance standard

There is a requirement for sustainability reporting under ESRS to have external assurance.

In May 2024, the IFRS Foundation and EFRAG published guidance material to illustrate the high level of alignment achieved between IFRS Sustainability Disclosure Standards ESRS. This guidance sets out how a company can apply both sets of standards, including detailed analysis of the alignment in climate-related disclosures.

3.5 Strategic Report

UK companies are required prepare a strategic report, unless they meet the definition of a small company. The strategic report provides a narrative overview of the business and a description of the principal risks and uncertainties facing the business, which is likely to include sustainability matters.

In 2022, mandatory climate-related financial disclosures were introduced for large companies in the Companies (Strategic Report) (Climate-related Financial Disclosure) Regulations 2022. The requirements are based on the TCFD recommendations and use the same structure: governance, strategy, risk management, metrics and targets (which is the structure used by IFRS Sustainability Disclosure Standards as well).

The disclosures should be included in a Non-Financial and Sustainability Information (NFSI) statement within their strategic report. The NFSI statement provides information about the principal risks and uncertainties relating to environmental matters, employee matters, social matters, respect for human rights and anti-corruption and anti-bribery matters.

3.6 Integrated reporting

Integrating financial and non-financial reporting to provide a more holistic view of the value of a company was given a framework in 2013 when the International Integrated Reporting Council (IIRC) published the International Integrated Reporting Framework.

The Framework refers to an organisation's resources as 'capitals'. Capitals are used to assess value creation. Increases or decreases in these capitals indicate the level of value created or lost over a period. Capitals cover various types of resources found in a standard organisation. These may include financial capitals, such as the entity's financial reserves through to its intellectual capital which is concerned with intellectual property and staff knowledge.

The Integrated Reporting Framework is now the responsibility of the IFRS Foundation and was revised in 2021 to make it more useful for stakeholders. The concepts of integrated reporting are embedded into ISSB Standards. The chairs of the IASB and ISSB have made a long-term commitment to developing a corporate reporting framework including the principles and concepts from the current integrated reporting framework.

The Framework takes a principles-based approach and is based on three fundamental concepts:

Value creation
- Value is created when there are **increases, decreases or transformations of an entity's capitals** cause by its business activities and outputs
- Value may be created **for the entity itself** (which) in turn should lead to returns for investors) or **for other external stakeholders**.

The capitals
- The capitals are **stocks of value** that are increased, decreased or transformed through the activities and outputs of the organisation.
- The capitals comprise financial, manufactured, intellectual, human, social and relationship and natural.

The value creation process
- The value creation process is the process by which an entity **uses its capitals as inputs and converts them to outputs**.
- An entity's outputs include its products, services, by-products and waste.

3.6.1 Types of capital

The integrated reporting framework classifies the capitals as:

Capital	Description
Financial capital	The source of funds available to an entity such as share capital, loans and other sources of finance.
Manufactured capital	The equipment and tools used in an entity's production process. Manufactured capital is man-made and does not include natural resources.
Intellectual capital	Includes an entity's formal research and development and the less formal knowledge that is gather, used and managed by the entity.
Human capital	Refers to an entity's management and its employees and the skills they have developed through education, training and experience.
Natural	Includes water, fish, trees and timber and other similar resources that occur in nature.
Social and relationship capital	Refers to the relationships in place within an entity and between an entity and its external stakeholders such as suppliers, customers, governments and the community in which the entity operates.

Source: *The Integrated Reporting Framework*, https://integratedreporting.ifrs.org/

3.6.2 Interaction of capitals

Capitals continually interact with one another, an increase in one will result in a decrease another. For example, a decision to purchase a new IT system would improve an entity's 'manufactured' capital while decreasing its financial capital in the form of its cash reserves.

At present adopting integrated reporting is voluntary, as a result organisations are free to report only on those 'capitals' felt to be most relevant in communicating performance.

3.6.3 Short term v long term

Integrated reporting forces management to balance the organisation's short term objectives against its longer term plans. Business decisions which are solely dedicated to the pursuit of increasing profit (financial capital) at the expense of building good relations with key stakeholders such as customers (social capital) is likely to hinder value creation in the longer term. It is thought that by producing a holistic view of organisational performance that this will lead to improved management decision making, ensuring that decisions are not taken in isolation.

3.6.4 Monetary values

Integrated reporting is not aimed at attaching a monetary value to every aspect of the organisations operations. It is fundamentally concerned with evaluating value creation through the communication of qualitative and quantitative performance measures. Key performance indicators are effective in communicating performance.

For example when providing detail on customer satisfaction this can be communicated as the number of customers retained compared to the previous year. Best practice in integrated reporting requires organisations to report on both positive and negative movements in 'capital' to avoid only providing half the story.

3.6.5 Materiality

When preparing an integrated report management should disclose matters which are likely to impact on an organisations ability to create value. The inclusion of both internal and external threats regarded as being materially important are evaluated and quantified. This provides users with an indication of how management intend to combat risks should they materialise.

4 IFRS Sustainability Disclosure Standards

IFRS Sustainability Disclosure Standards are published by the International Sustainability Standards Board (ISSB). As the need demand for sustainability reporting has increased, a number of different bodies and organisations were issuing standards and guidance.

This result in confusion for both preparers and users of sustainability reporting.

4.1 International Sustainability Standards Board (ISSB)

The International Sustainability Standards Board (ISSB) was established in response to investors' demand for high-quality, transparent, reliable, and comparable reporting on climate and other Environmental, Social, and Governance (ESG) issues. Announced by the IFRS Foundation Trustees on 3 November 2021, the ISSB aims to develop sustainability reporting requirements under the IFRS umbrella.

IFRS Sustainability Disclosure Standards will complement conventional financial reporting, providing non-financial information on company performance, risk profiles, and economic decisions within sustainable business development contexts. By doing so, they will facilitate sustainability disclosure to investors and stakeholders.

The formation of the ISSB included the consolidation of the Climate Disclosure Standards Board and the Value Reporting Foundation which was responsible for the Integrated Reporting Framework and SASB Standards.

3: SUSTAINABILITY REPORTING

The ISSB has four key objectives:

(a) To develop standards for a global baseline of sustainability disclosures;

(b) To meet the information needs of investors;

(c) To enable companies to provide comprehensive sustainability information to global capital markets; and

(d) To facility interoperability with disclosures that are jurisdiction-specific and/or aimed at broader stakeholder groups.

To meet that final objective, the ISSB works closely with the GRI, EFRAG, TNFD and other bodies operating in the sustainability reporting sector.

The ISSB also works in close cooperation with the IASB ensuring connections between IFRS Accounting Standards and IFRS Sustainability Disclosure Standards. However, other financial reporting standards can also be used along with the IFRS Sustainability Disclosure Standards.

4.2 IFRS Sustainability Disclosure Standards

The ISSB published its first two standards in June 2023:

- IFRS S1 *General Requirements for Disclosure of Sustainability-related Financial Information*
- IFRS S2 *Climate-related Disclosures*

The ISSB's priority is now to support the implementation of these standards while commencing research projects on biodiversity, ecosystems and ecosystem services, and human capital working alongside the GRI and TNFD.

IFRS Sustainability Disclosure Standards apply a **financial approach** to materiality. Financial materiality considers the importance of information which affects the financial position or performance of the reporting entity. IFRS Sustainability Disclosure Standards refer to 'risks and opportunities that could reasonably be expected to affect the entity's prospects'.

For a company to state that it complies with IFRS Sustainability Disclosure Standards, it must comply with both IFRS S1 and S2.

IFRS Sustainability Disclosure Standards were endorsed by the International Organisation of Securities Commissions (IOSCO) in July 2023. The standards are not mandatory, but national regulations may make them mandatory.

The standards are applicable for accounting periods beginning on or after 1 January 2024. There are some transition provisions relating to IFRS S2

4.3 IFRS S1 General Requirements for Disclosure of Sustainability-related Financial Information

The first standards issued by the ISSB was IFRS S1 *General Requirements for Disclosure of Sustainability-related Financial Information*. This standard sets out the core content for a complete set of sustainability-related financial disclosures to meet the needs of global capital markets.

4.3.1 Objective and scope

IFRS S1 states that the objective of the standard is to 'require an entity to disclose information about its **sustainability-related risks and opportunities** that is useful to **primary users** of general purpose financial reports in making decisions relating to providing resources to the entity'. (IFRS S1, para 1)

Key term

> IFRS S1 states that the objective of the standard is to 'require an entity to disclose information about its **sustainability-related risks and opportunities** that is useful to **primary users** of general purpose financial reports in making decisions relating to providing resources to the entity'. (IFRS S1, para 1)

The primary users of general purpose financial reports are existing and potential investors, lenders and other creditors. (IFRS S1, Appx A) Other stakeholders such as customers and employees are not considered to be primary users.

Information about sustainability-related risks and opportunities are considered to be useful to the primary users because the cash-generating capability of an entity comes from the necessary interactions between its stakeholders, society, the economy and the natural environment through the entities **value chain**. (IFRS S1, para 2, 3)

The value chain is defined in IFRS S1 as 'the full range of interactions, resources and relationships related to a reporting entity's business model and the external environment in which it operates'. (IFRS S1. Appx A). This includes the product/services of the entity, human resources, marketing and distribution, procurement, sales and delivery, financing, legal etc.

The standard requires the disclosure of all material sustainability-related risks and opportunities that could reasonably be expected to affect the cash flows, access to finance or cost of capital over the short, medium and long term.

IFRS Sustainability Disclosure Standards focus on climate-related **impacts**, that is, the impact of climate-related risks and opportunities on the cash-generating capability of the entity.

4.3.2 Conceptual foundations

IFRS S1 covers the conceptual foundations for sustainability-related financial information.

Foundation	Description
Fair presentation	The disclosures must include all material sustainability-related risks and opportunities that could reasonably be expected to affect any entity's prospects. Information should be complete, neutral and accurate.
Materiality	Only material information should be disclosed. Information is material if omitting, misstating or obscuring the information could reasonably be expected to influence the decision-making of the primary users.
Reporting entity	Sustainability-related financial disclosures should be for the same entity as the related financial statements.
Connecting disclosures	Information should be provided to allow the primary users to understand the connections between the sustainability-related risks and opportunities and the financial performance of the entity. This includes data and assumptions used in preparing sustainability and financial reporting disclosures.

These conceptual foundations are in alignment with the qualitative characteristics of financial information the IFRS *Conceptual Framework for Financial Reporting*.

4.3.3 Core content

IFRS S1 requires a company to prepare disclosures about how it manages its sustainability related risks and opportunities (SROs) under four headings: governance, strategy, risk management and metrics and targets (IFRS S1, para 25). These headings are those originally set out in the TCFD recommendations, but are intended for all sustainability-related disclosures, not just climate-related matters.

Governance (para 26-27)	Strategy (para 28-42)
The governance process, controls and procedures used to monitor and manage SROs e.g. • Who has responsibility for SORs overall, and in practice?	The approach used to manage SORs, including information that enables investors to understand the current and anticipated financial effects of SORs on the company's financial position, performance and cashflows over the short, medium and long term e.g.

• Who oversees the setting of targets and metrics?	• The effects of SORs on the business and value chain • The resilience of the entity to SORs
Risk management (para 43-44)	**Metrics and Targets (para 45-53)**
The process to identify, evaluate, prioritise and monitor SORs e.g. • How risks are assessed and prioritised • How SORs are integrated into the overall risk management of the entity	Performance in relation to SORs including progress towards any targets required by law or regulation e.g. • The metric used and any target • The base period from which progress is measured

4.3.4 General requirements

Currently the only other standard which includes metrics to disclose is IFRS S2 *Climate-related Disclosures*. IFRS S1 acknowledges that there are other sources of guidance and requires entities to specifically consider whether any of the disclosure topics in the Sustainability Accounting Standards Board (SASB) Standards are applicable.

The SASB was a separate body, but is now consolidated under the IFRS Foundation. SASB Standards are overseen by the ISSB and all open SASB projects were transferred to the ISSB as well. SASB Standards consist of industry-specific guidance for 77 sectors and can be found here. https://sasb.ifrs.org/standards/

IFRS S1 also requires companies to consider the most recent requirements of other sustainability-related standard setting bodies as well as the SORs identified by other entities that operating in the same industry or geographic region.

The sustainability-related reporting should be made at the same time, and for the same reporting period, as the related financial statements. Comparative information should be disclosed for numerical and narrative information.

A number of transition arrangement are in place:

- Comparative information is not required in the first year of application
- In the first year, the sustainability report does not need to be published at the same time as the annual financial statements, allowing some extra time for preparation
- In the first year of reporting, an entity is permitted to only disclose information on climate-related SORs in accordance with IFRS S2

4.4 IFRS S2 Climate-related Disclosures

IFRS S2 *Climate-related disclosures* is the first subject-specific ISSB Standard. It requires disclosure of the climate-related risks and opportunities that could reasonably be expected to affect the entity's financial prospects.

The standard drew from the recommendations of the TCFD as well as incorporating industry-based disclosure requirements from the SASB Standards.

4.4.1 Scope

IFRS S2 applies to:

- Climate-related risks to which the entity is exposed, which are:
  - **Climate-related physical risks**
  - **Climate-related transition risks**
- **Climate-related opportunities** available to the entity

(IFRS S2, para 3)

Many companies and economic sectors face risks from both climate change and from the transition to a lower-carbon economy. Climate-related physical risks can be event-driven (acute physical risk) or from longer-term shifts in climactic patterns (chronic physical risk). Acute physical risks come from severe weather events such as hurricanes, drought, floods. There has been an increase in the frequency and severity of such events as a result of global temperature increases. Chronic physical risks exist due to longer-term climate impacts such as increasing sea levels or biodiversity loss. Both acute and chronic physical risks can have financial implications for an entity on all aspects of the value chain e.g. increase supplier prices, property damage, employee health and safety.

Transition risks arise from different influences such as:

- Policy and legal risks e.g. carbon emission legislation
- Technology risk e.g. unsuccessful investment in new technology
- Market risk e.g. change in demand
- Reputation risk e.g. loss of customers

IFRS S2 also requires an entity to consider the climate-related opportunities, that is, the potential positive effects arising from climate change.

4.4.2 Core content

The core content of IFRS S2 follows the same format as set out in S1: governance, strategy, risks management and metrics and targets.

The governance requirements for IFRS S2 are similar to IFRS S1, but with an emphasis on *climate-related* risks and opportunities.

Many of the IFRS S2 strategy disclosures are also similar to IFRS S1, but there are a number of additional climate-specific disclosures including:

- The climate resilience of the strategy and business model
- Each climate-related risk but be identified as either a physical or a transition risk
- Information about the climate-related transition plan of the business
- Howe the entity plans to achieve climate-related targets

4.4.3 Metrics and targets

IFRS S2 requires a number of cross-industry metrics, industry-based metrics and legal/entity specific targets to be disclosed.

Greenhouse gas (GHG) emissions form a significant part of the disclosures. GHG emissions are split into three categories as follows:

Category	Description
Scope 1 GHG emissions	Direct GHG emissions that occur from sources that are owned or controlled by an entity
Scope 2 GHG emissions	Indirect GHG emissions from the generation of purchased or acquired electricity, steam, heating or cooling consumed by an entity.
Scope 3 GHG emissions	Indirect GHG emissions (not including Scope 2 GHG emissions) that occur in the value chain of an entity, including both upstream and downstream emissions.

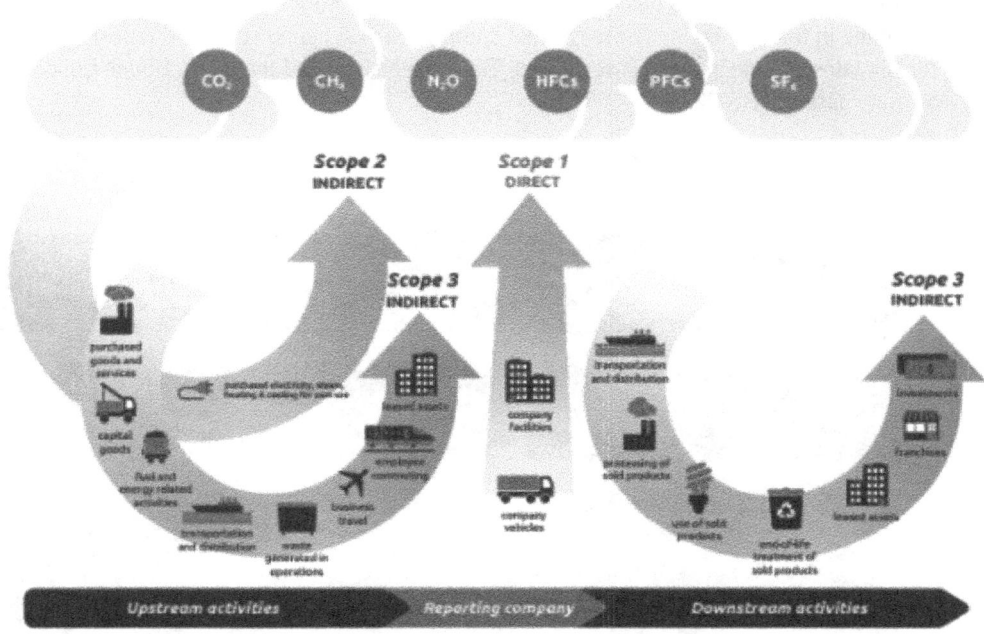

Source: https://ghgprotocol.org/blog/you-too-can-master-value-chain-emissions

IFRS S2 requires the following cross-industry metrics to be disclosed (para 29)

- Greenhouse gas emissions – Scope 1, 2 and 3
- The amount and percentage of assets or business activities:
    - Vulnerable to climate-related transition risks and climate-related physical risks
    - Aligned with climate-related opportunities
- Capital deployment – the amount of capital expenditure, financing or investment deployed towards climate-related risks and opportunities
- Internal carbon pricing – the price per metric tonne and whether/how it is being used in decision making
- Remuneration – linkage of executive management remuneration with climate-related factors

There is industry-based guidance with metrics for 68 industry sectors which can be viewed here https://www.ifrs.org/issued-standards/ifrs-sustainability-standards-navigator/ifrs-s2-climate-related-disclosures.html/content/dam/ifrs/publications/html-standards-issb/english/2023/issued/ibg/. These metrics are the relevant climate-related metrics from the equivalent SASB standard.

IFRS S2 also requires the disclosure of any climate-related targets set to monitor progress towards achieving climate-related strategic goals, and any targets required by law or regulation. This includes information such as the metric used to measure progress, the objective of the target, the period to which it applies, the base period and any milestones or interim targets.

4.4.4 Example disclosure

The IFRS Sustainability Disclosure Standards S1 and S2 were issued in 2023 only come into force for reporting periods starting on 1 January 2024, although earlier adoption was permitted. As such, the first corporate reports prepared under IFRS S1 and S2 will be published in 2025.

A number of companies have considered the requirements of the IFRS Sustainability Disclosure Standards when preparing their 2023 annual reporting, published in 2024 such as Taylor Wimpey plc.

Below are some extracts from the Taylor Wimpey plc 2023 Annual Report and Sustainability Summary relating to climate-related disclosures in each of the four core content areas. As a premium listed company in the UK, Taylor Wimpey must comply the FCA listing rules and report against the Task Force for Climate-related Financial Disclosures. They have also used the SASB House Builders standard as well as considering IFRS S2.

Governance

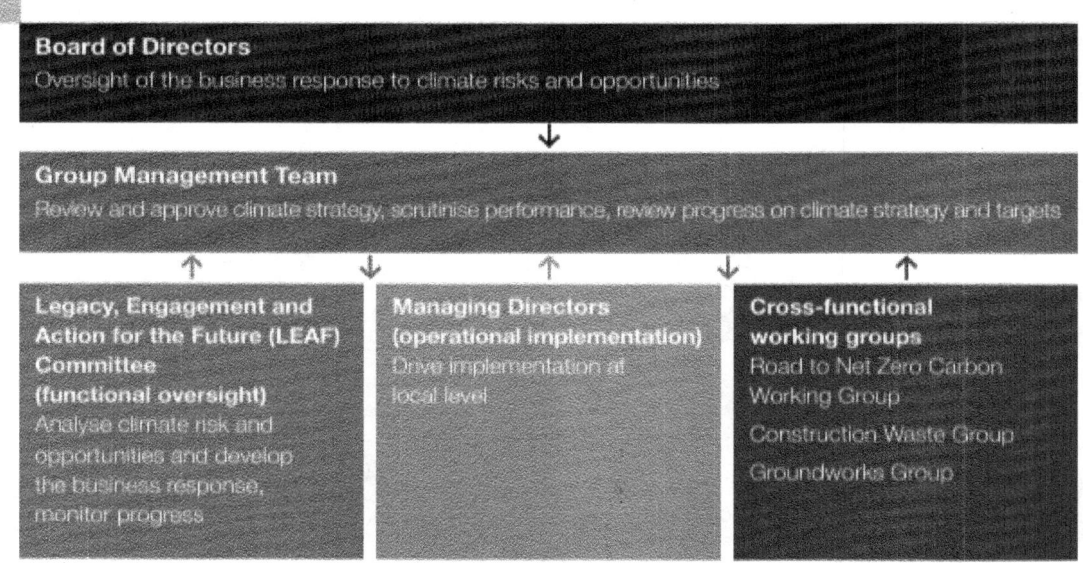

Strategy

Strategy

Climate change presents risks and opportunities for our business, including those related to the transition to a lower carbon economy and those associated with the physical impacts of climate change. Sustainability is one of our four strategic cornerstones, reflecting the importance of climate change and other environmental matters to our business and stakeholders.

We assess climate risks and opportunities using short term (to 2025), medium term (to 2030) and long term (beyond 2030) horizons, looking at their potential impacts on our business, strategy and financial planning. Our approach is informed by our materiality assessment and climate scenario analysis. We also refer to industry-based guidance such as criteria set by the SASB Standard for the Home Builders sector, the Next Generation benchmark and the work of the Future Homes Hub, a collaboration for the UK new homes sector.

3: SUSTAINABILITY REPORTING

Risk management

	Description	Example risks / opportunities	Our mitigations	Residual risk after mitigation (1.5°C scenario unless stated)
	Market and reputation (stakeholder)			
	Residual risks or opportunities (moderate to high):		Risk type: Transition (market, reputation)	
	Time frame analysed: Short term (up to 2025), Medium term (up to 2030)		Opportunity type: Products, markets	
	Changing customer demands in relation to low carbon homes as sustainability awareness grows, green mortgages evolve, and existing building stock becomes comparatively more expensive to run	Opportunity if more efficient and lower emission homes become more attractive to customers than secondhand market.	• We conduct regular research to monitor and understand changing customer attitudes to sustainability issues, including low carbon homes • We engage customer, sales and marketing teams and marketing agencies to ensure the benefits of new low carbon homes are communicated effectively • We partner with peers through the Future Homes Hub and engage with government to ensure the benefits of low carbon homes are communicated, and to support further development of green mortgages	Short term minor opportunity and considered likely with impact on financial statements potentially reflected in increased revenue which could be material, but is not possible to quantify reliably. Medium term major opportunity and considered balanced likelihood with impact on financial statements potentially reflected in increased revenue which could be material, but is not possible to quantify reliably.
	Changing customer demands in relation to low carbon homes	Risk that customers may resist installation of new low carbon technologies or be dissatisfied with their performance. Risk of reputational damage if low carbon homes are not delivered to customers in line with changing expectations.	• We will be communicating with customers and training customer, sales and marketing teams to ensure customers are supported to use new technologies • We take a 'Fabric-first' approach to home energy efficiency to minimise complexity and maintenance for customers where possible • We invest in research and product trials to ensure quality, performance and ease of use, e.g. our FHS trial homes	Short term minor risk exposure, likely with impact on financial statements expected to be immaterial based on current regulatory changes. Medium term major risk exposure, unlikely with impact on financial statements dependent on extent customer demands change, which is not possible to reliably estimate.

Metrics and targets

How did we perform in 2023?

Climate change

- Total carbon footprint (scopes 1, 2 and 3) of 1.94 million tonnes CO_2e (2022: 2.54 million tonnes). Total intensity was 187.0 tonnes per 100 sqm of build (2022: 190.0 tonnes per 100 sqm).

- Operational emissions intensity (scopes 1 and 2), has decreased by 5% against our 2019 baseline, with absolute operational emissions falling by 35% over the same period.

- Operational emissions intensity and site energy intensity increased year on year, reflecting challenging economic conditions. While we completed fewer homes, there was only a small reduction in the number of outlets which meant we continued to use energy for site compounds, street lighting and pumping stations and fixed facilities such as offices, IT systems and our logistics warehouse.

- REGO-backed renewable electricity accounted for around 79% of total Group electricity consumption (2022: 70%).

- 21.1% reduction in company car fleet emissions (including grey fleet) since 2019 and 72% of vehicles now electric or hybrid (2022: 55%).

- Installed 1,385 EV charging points on our developments.

- Included on the Financial Times European Climate Leaders list and our Net Zero Transition Plan was shortlisted in the Edie Awards for 2024.

- We have been recognised by the CDP as a Supplier Engagement Leader and received a Supplier Engagement score of A for our approach to engaging suppliers on climate change (2022: A).

Greenhouse gas emissions intensity
(scope 1 and 2 emissions per 100 sqm of completed homes)

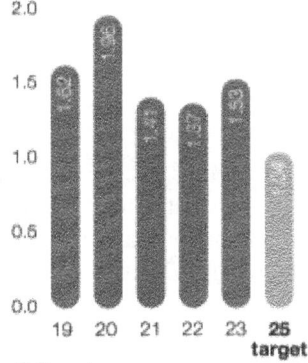

● Target
● Tonnes CO_2e/100 sqm

79%
electricity from renewable sources

5 Sustainability and stakeholders

The sustainability reporting landscape is evolving rapidly. GRI Standards and Integrated Reporting are established frameworks which companies have been using for a number of years. The first sustainability disclosures prepared under IFRS Sustainability Disclosure Standards and European Sustainability Reporting Standards will probably be issued in 2025.

Although there has been some harmonisation between the different sustainability reporting frameworks, stakeholders will still be faced with reporting differences. The ISSB has been actively working with all the key sustainability reporting standard setters to meet its objective of facilitating interoperability between the various standards.

The most fundamental difference between IFRS Sustainability Disclosure Standards, GRI Standards and ESRS is how materiality is determined, summarised in the following table.

	IFRS Sustainability Disclosure Standards	**GRI Standards**	**ESRS**
Materiality	Financial materiality	Impact materiality	Double materiality
Key users of sustainability-related disclosures	Existing and potential investors and lenders	All stakeholders	All stakeholders
Disclosures	Material sustainability-related risks and opportunities that are expected to impact the entity's financial prospects	Significant positive or negative sustainability impacts on the economy, environment, and people, including their human rights as a result of the entites activities or business relationships along the value chain.	Sustainability matters that are material from an impact and financial perspective. These can be environment, social or governance matters that have an actual or pential positive or negative material impact.

5.1 Adoption of sustainability reporting frameworks

A number of countries are considering the adoption of the IFRS Sustainability Disclosure Standards. As of July 2024, some countries have committed to adopting the standards, some are in the process of consulting about the adoption. Some countries plan to make the standard mandatory for listed or public interest entities and other countries will make them optional. Large economies such as China and India have held consultations on the use of the standards with adoption expected from 2026 onwards.

In the UK, the IFRS Sustainability Disclosure standards are being reviewed by the UK Sustainability Disclosure Technical Advisory Committee with a recommendation on whether or not to adopt expected in Q4 2024. If the recommendation is do adopt the standards will be issued as UK-endorsed Sustainability Disclosure Standards. It is expected that these will be mandatory for UK listed companies with further public consultation for the impact on other UK companies.

ESRS are mandatory for all large and all listed companies in the EU. Large, listed companies and large financial services companies. Non-EU companies who list in the EU will also need to comply. There is a phased introduction over 3 years with large, listed companies applying ESRS from 2024, but listed SMEs only have to apply from 2026.

Chapter roundup

- Although not compulsory, **sustainability reporting** is becoming increasingly important as stakeholders are increasing relying on information about the sustainable practices of businesses to make decisions.
- There are a number of different sustainability reporting frameworks including GRI Standards, TCFD/TNFD, Integrated Reporting, ESRS and IFRS Sustainability Reporting Standards
- The **International Sustainability Standards Boards** was established by the IFRS Foundation and has published two sustainability disclosure standards.
- **IFRS S1** describes the concept of sustainability and the required disclosures for general sustainability reports.
- IFRS S2 sets out the requirements for a company to disclose material information about **climate-related risks and opportunities**.
- The sustainability landscape is rapidly changing, with more standards expected to be introduced over the next few years. The ISSB is working with all of the other major bodies to try to reduce the reporting burden and increase the interoperability between the various sustainability reporting frameworks.

Quick quiz

1. Name the four areas of core content set out in IFRS S1.
2. A company can only apply IFRS Sustainability Disclosure Standards if it already applies IFRS Accounting Standards.

    True ☐
    False ☐

3. Describe Scope 1, 2 and 3 greenhouse gas emissions.
4. Under IFRS Sustainabiltiy Disclosure Standards, who are the primary users of sustainability reporting?
5. Which sustainability standards apply double materiality?
6. How are SASB Standards most frequently used in sustainability reporting?
7. Give three examples of capitals set out when applying Integrated Reporting?

Answers to quick quiz

1. Governance
   Strategy
   Risk management
   Metrics and targets

2. False. Although the IASB and the ISSB work closely together, IFRS Sustainability Disclosure Standards can be applied without also applying IFRS Accounting Standards.

3.

Category	Description
Scope 1 GHG emissions	Direct GHG emissions that occur from sources that are owned or controlled by an entity
Scope 2 GHG emissions	Indirect GHG emissions from the generation of purchased or acquired electricity, steam, heating or cooling consumed by an entity.
Scope 3 GHG emissions	Indirect GHG emissions (not including Scope 2 GHG emissions) that occur in the value chain of an entity, including both upstream and downstream emissions.

4. Potential and actual investors, lenders and creditors

5. European Sustainability Reporting Standards

6. SASB Standards are overseen by the ISSB and the sector-specific standards should be considered and applied by companies applying IFRS Sustainability Disclosure Standards

7. Financial capital

   Manufactured capital

   Intellectual capital

   Human capital

   Natural

   Social and relationship capital

End of chapter question

Schrodenfischer

You are a trainee accountant working for Schrodenfischer AG which produces financial statements in accordance with IFRS Accounting Standards. Schrodenfischer AG is an owner-managed business with a wide range of customers and suppliers, and 150 employees.

The managing director of Schrodenfischer AG is proud of the fact that the company operates ethically. The company has adopted environmentally friendly operating procedures making an effort to reduce carbon emissions throughout operations. It also contributes resources to local, national, and international arts and charity organisations.

The managing director does not feel the conventional financial statements of the company adequately inform stakeholders about these activities and would like to know how best to quantify and present this information in the company's corporate report.

Required

Advise the managing director of the various frameworks in place for sustainability reporting and why these might be beneficial for Schrodenfischer.

PART A CONTEMPORARY ISSUES

Ethics and regulation of corporate financial reporting

Topic list	Syllabus reference
1 The case for regulation	LO1
2 Impact of changes in accounting standards and policies	LO1
3 Accounting theory and practice	LO1
4 Principles and guidance on professional ethics	LO1
5 Ethics relating to sustainability	LO1
6 Practical situations	LO1

Introduction

This chapter looks at two important issues which are related: regulation of financial reporting; and professional ethics.

The first part of the chapter focuses on changes in accounting standards and accounting policies and the implications for reporting entities.

The second part of the chapter introduces the IESBA Code which you will be required to observe when you become a member of the AIA. Ethics are an important aspect of the AIA qualification. They need to be applied in all aspects of managerial behaviour. An attempt to massage profit figures, or non-disclosure of a close relationship may amount to unethical behaviour.

PART A   CONTEMPORARY ISSUES

1 The case for regulation

1.1 Introduction

The regulatory framework is the most important element in ensuring relevant and reliable financial reporting and thus meeting the needs of shareholders and other users.

Without a single body overall responsible for producing financial reporting standards (the IASB) and a framework of general principles within which they can be produced (the *Conceptual Framework*), there would be no means of enforcing compliance with GAAP. Also, GAAP would be unable to evolve in any structured way in response to changes in economic conditions.

1.2 Principles-based versus rules-based systems

> **FAST FORWARD**
>
> A principles-based system works within a set of laid down principles. A rules-based system regulates for issues as they arise. Both of these have advantages and disadvantages.

The *Conceptual Framework* provides the background of principles within which standards can be developed. This system is intended to ensure that standards are not produced which are in conflict with each other and also that any departure from a standard can be judged on the basis of whether or not it is in keeping with the principles set out in the *Conceptual Framework*. This is a **principles-based** system.

In the absence of a reporting framework, a more **rules-based** approach has to be adopted. This leads to a large mass of regulation designed to cover every eventuality, as in the US. As we have seen over the past few years, a large volume of regulatory measures does not always detect or prevent financial irregularity. Rules can be evaded by means of 'creative accounting'. This is the deliberate manipulation of figures in the financial statements to give a biased impression of an entity's performance while still complying with accounting standards.

However, management may need to use judgement in applying principles. It can be argued that principles-based standards are also open to abuse.

In practice, current IFRS Accounting Standards are a mixture of rules and principles. For example, most of the standards relating to non-current assets are based on the fundamental principles in the *Conceptual Framework*, although the definition of assets and the recognition criteria under the revised *Conceptual Framework* 2018 has resulted in some differences between the terminology and criteria used in the standards and that in the *Conceptual Framework*. In contrast, the standards on financial instruments have been influenced by US reporting practice and are extremely detailed, with many definitions and rules.

1.3 The 'free market' versus accounting regulation

> **FAST FORWARD**
>
> There are many convincing arguments in favour of regulation of corporate financial reporting.

Some economists advocate a 'free market' approach to accounting regulation. Supporters of the 'free market' approach argue that accounting information is like any other good. If there is a demand for that information it will be supplied. Regulation of the market (by means of accounting standards) leads to the supply of non-optimal information.

However, the absence of effective regulation has been blamed for many failures in accounting; such as the Wall Street Crash in 1929, the GEC/AEI debacle of the 1960s, the WorldCom and Enron catastrophes and more recently the 2008 financial crisis.

There are many convincing arguments in favour of regulation:

(a)   Regulation leads to uniformity (or at least standardisation) which in turn provides for greater comparability between entities.

(b)   A 'free' market for information cannot be efficient and such inefficiencies lead to the provision of information which may therefore not be the best available.

(c) Without adequate regulation there is no way of knowing whether the information investors are using is in any way fraudulent. Investors and other users need to be able to have faith in the information.

(d) Regulation is needed to protect those who have less power (to demand information) than others.

2 Impact of changes in accounting standards and policies

FAST FORWARD

Accounting policies may be adopted for the purpose of **manipulation**.

Changes in accounting standards can have a significant impact on the financial statements.

We discussed the disclosure of accounting policies in your earlier studies. The choice of accounting policy and the effect of its implementation are almost as important as its disclosure in that the results of a company can be altered significantly by the choice of accounting policy.

2.1 The effect of choice of accounting policies

Where accounting standards allow alternative treatment of items in the financial statements, then the accounting policy note should declare which policy has been chosen. It should then be applied consistently.

Consider, though, the **effects produced by the different treatment of some items**.

An example is the treatment of investment properties, which may be measured under either the cost model or the fair value model. Under the cost model, investment properties are measured at historic cost less depreciation, in accordance with IAS 16 *Property, Plant and Equipment*. Under the fair value model, investment properties are measured at fair value with gains or losses arising from a change in fair value recognised in profit or loss. (We will be covering investment properties in Chapter 12.)

The choice of accounting policy will impact on the calculation of ratios used as the starting point in the interpretation of financial statements. For example, a company that chooses to revalue its non-current assets will have a higher asset value and higher capital employed than a company that holds its assets at historical cost. The company that chooses to revalue may therefore report a lower return on capital employed (ROCE), despite otherwise outperforming an equivalent company that chooses to hold at historical cost. You should be able to think of other examples of how the choice of accounting policy can affect the financial statements.

2.2 Changes in accounting policy

The effect of a change of accounting policy is treated as a retrospective adjustment to the opening balance of each affected component of equity, as if the accounting policy had always applied.

IAS 8 *Accounting Policies, Changes in Accounting Estimates and Errors* states that changes in accounting policies are rare, and only allowed if **required by statute** or if the change results in **relevant and more reliable information.**

There is still some scope for directors to **manipulate the results** through change(s) of accounting policies. This would be done to avoid the effect of an old accounting policy or gain the effect of a new one. It is likely to be done in a sensitive period, perhaps when the company's profits are low or the company is about to announce a rights issue. The management would have to convince the auditors that the new policy was more appropriate, but it is not difficult to produce reasons in such cases.

The effect of such a change is **very short-term**. Most analysts and sophisticated users will discount its effect immediately, except to the extent that it will affect any dividend (because of the effect on distributable profits). It may help to avoid breaches of banking covenants because of the effect on certain ratios.

Obviously, the accounting policy for any item in the financial statements could only be changed once in quite a long period of time. No auditors would allow another change, even back to the old policy, unless there was a wholly exceptional reason.

The managers of a company can choose accounting policies **initially** to suit the company or the type of results they want to get. Any changes in accounting policy must be justified, but some managers might try to change accounting policies just to manipulate the results.

2.3 Changes in accounting standards

> **FAST FORWARD**
>
> You may be asked to **advise the directors** on the implication of a change in accounting standards, or on the effect of using the correct accounting treatment.

The effect of a change of accounting standard can be far reaching. For example IFRS 16 *Leases* was brought in to replace IAS 17, companies with lease arrangements that would previously been 'off balance sheet' now require right of use assets and associated lease liabilities to be recognised. The introduction of IFRS 16 has had a huge impact on the financial statements of companies in many industries, such as retail companies which rely heavily on rented retail space.

While IFRS 16 has benefits for the users of financial statements in terms of transparency and comparability, it has had a significant impact on the most commonly used financial ratios, such as:

- Gearing, because debt has increased
- Asset turnover, because assets have increased
- Profit margin ratios, because rent expenses are removed and replaced with depreciation and finance costs.

This in turn affects the way in which users interpret and analyse the financial statements. For example, banks often impose loan covenants when making loans to companies. These covenants may need renegotiating if applying IFRS 16 causes a company's liabilities to increase significantly.

Exam focus point

The Examiner has said that this topic is likely to be examined by a written question, possibly including a small calculation.

Usually you will be in the position of advising the directors. You are very likely to be asked to explain the significance of a proposed change in accounting standards. The Examiner has also said that you may be asked to consider ethics. If the directors, in adopting certain accounting treatments, are acting unethically, you may need to discuss this.

3 Accounting theory and practice

3.1 The nature of profit

During your earlier studies you have seen that accounting 'profit' is an arbitrary figure, subject to the whims and biases of accountants and the variety of treatments in accounting standards. We will be covering individual IFRS Standards in detail in later chapters, but you can probably remember the examples that we give below.

3.1.1 IAS 2 *Inventories*

Companies are allowed to use different methods of valuing inventory under IAS 2, which means that the final inventory figure in the statement of financial position will be different under each method. Profit, and therefore ratios such as gross profit margin, operating profit margin and return on capital employed will all be affected by the closing inventory valuation, particularly where the level of inventory fluctuates to a great extent.

3.1.2 IAS 16 *Property, plant and equipment*

IAS 16 allows different accounting bases for depreciation. Choosing to use the reducing balance method rather than the straight-line method can front-load the depreciation charge for assets. It is also the case that the subjectivity surrounding the estimated economic lives of assets can lead to manipulation of profits.

The accounting policy choice relating to historic cost or the revaluation model has been discussed above.

3.2 Other problems with financial statement information

You will have already studied ratio analysis and possibly other techniques used in analysing financial statements. So you will already know that while these techniques are useful, they have some serious limitations.

Two frequent problems affecting financial analysis (the interpretation of financial statements) are discussed here.

- Seasonal fluctuations
- Window dressing

3.2.1 Seasonal fluctuations

Many companies are located in industries where trade is seasonal. For example:

- Swimwear manufacturers
- Ice cream makers
- Umbrella manufacturers
- Gas companies
- Travel agents

Year on year the seasonal fluctuations affecting such companies does not matter; a year end has to be chosen and as long as the fluctuations are at roughly the same time every year, then there should be no problem.

A major difficulty can arise if companies affected by seasonal fluctuations change their accounting date. A shorter period (normally) may encompass part, all or none of the busy season. Whatever happens, the figures will be distorted and the comparatives will be meaningless. Analysts would not know how to extrapolate the figures from the shorter period to produce a comparison for the previous year. Weightings could be used, but these are likely to be inaccurate.

Case Study

An example of the problems this can cause occurred when the UK company British Gas plc changed its accounting period to 31 December from 31 March. The company published two reports and financial statements.

- For the year to 31 March 1991
- For the year to 31 December 1991

Thus including the first three months of the calendar year in both reports. As a note to the later financial statements, the company produced a profit and loss account for the last nine months of the calendar year.

Although the British Gas auditors did not qualify the audit report, the Review Panel was not very happy about this double counting of results. The nine month profit and loss account did not meet the provisions of the Companies Act 1985, which then applied, 'either as to its location or its contents, nor did it contain the relevant earnings per share figure'. British Gas had to promise that, in their 1992 results, the 1991 comparative would be for the nine months period only.

The effect here is obvious. The first three months of the calendar year are when British Gas earns a high proportion of its profits (winter!). If the 1991 results had covered the period from 1 April only, then the profits would have been reduced by more than an average loss of three months' profit. By using a 12 month period, British Gas avoided the risk of the period's results looking too bad.

3.2.2 Window dressing

Window dressing transactions were made largely redundant by IAS 10 *Events After the Reporting Period*. Note that window dressing transactions were not outlawed, but full disclosure would render such transactions useless.

One example of window dressing is a situation where a large cheque is written against one group company's positive bank balance in favour of another group company with a large overdraft. The cheque is put through at the year end and then cancelled at the beginning of the next year, thus concealing the overdraft in the consolidated statement of financial position (where positive and negative bank balances cannot be netted off).

You may be able to think of other examples of window dressing and you should look for any potential examples which come up in examination questions.

Further discussion is included in Chapter 23 Interpretation of Financial Statements.

4 Principles and guidance on professional ethics

> **FAST FORWARD**
>
> The AIA has adopted the *Code of Ethics for Professional Accountants issued by IESBA (the IESBA Code).*

4.1 The public interest

> **FAST FORWARD**
>
> Organisations sometimes issue **codes of conduct** to employees. Many employees are bound by professional codes of conduct.

The International Federation of Accountants (IFAC) sets international standards of ethics through the International Ethics Standards Board for Accountants (IESBA). Its *Code of Ethics for Professional Accountants (the IESBA Code)* gives the key reason why accountancy bodies produce ethical guidance: the public interest.

> 'A distinguishing mark of the accountancy profession is its acceptance of the responsibility to act in the public interest. Therefore, a professional accountant's responsibility is not exclusively to satisfy the needs of an individual client or employer.
>
> **The public interest** is considered to be the collective well-being of the community of people and institutions the professional accountant serves, including clients, lenders, governments, employers, employees, investors, the business and financial community and others who rely on the work of professional accountants.'

The **key reason** that **accountants need** to have an **ethical code** is that **people rely on them and their expertise**.

Accountants deal with a range of issues on behalf of clients. They often have access to confidential and sensitive information. Auditors claim to give an independent view. It is therefore critical that accountants, and particularly auditors, are, and are seen to be, independent.

The AIA has adopted the IESBA Code. All AIA members are bound by the AIA's Constitution to observe this Code.

The Code consists of fundamental principles, specific guidance and explanatory notes. It can be downloaded from the AIA website: www.aiaworldwide.com/Ethics.

4.2 The fundamental principles

IESBA
• **Integrity**. A professional accountant should be **straightforward** and **honest** in all professional and business relationships.
• **Objectivity**. A professional accountant **should not allow bias, conflict of interest or undue influence of others** to override professional or business judgements.
• **Professional Competence and Due Care**. A professional accountant has a continuing duty to maintain professional knowledge and skill at a level required to ensure that a client or employer receives the advantage of competent professional service based on current developments in practice, legislation and techniques. A professional accountant should act diligently and in accordance with applicable technical and professional standards when providing professional services.
• **Confidentiality**. A professional accountant should respect the confidentiality of information acquired as a result of professional or business relationships **and should not disclose** any such information to third parties without proper and specific authority **unless there is a legal or professional right or duty to disclose**. Confidential information acquired as a result of professional and business relationships should not be used for the personal advantage of the professional accountant or third parties.
• **Professional Behaviour**. A professional accountant should **comply with relevant laws and regulations and should avoid any action that discredits the profession**.

4.3 Ethical framework

The ethical guidance discussed above is in the form of a **framework, rather than a set of rules**. There are a number of advantages of a framework over a system of ethical rules. These are outlined in the table below.

Advantages of an ethical framework over a rules based system
A framework of guidance places the onus on the accountant to **actively consider** independence for every given situation, rather than just agreeing a checklist of forbidden items. It also requires him or her to **demonstrate** that a responsible conclusion has been reached about ethical issues.
The framework **prevents accountants interpreting legalistic requirements narrowly** to get around the ethical requirements. There is an extent to which rules engender deception, whereas principles encourage compliance.
A framework **allows for** the variations that are found in every **individual situation**. Each situation is likely to be different.
A framework can accommodate a **rapidly changing environment**, such as the one that auditors are constantly in.
A **framework can contain prohibitions** where these are necessary because safeguards are not feasible.

5 Ethics relating to sustainability

FAST FORWARD

The increasing focus on sustainability reporting adds new ethical challenges for accountants. There is a risk of **greenwashing** through reporting.

5.1 Greenwashing

Greenwashing is a deceptive practice that involves making misleading or false statements about a company's environmental impact or sustainability practices.

With the increasing importance placed in sustainability reporting by stakeholders, the veracity of the reporting is very important. Greenwashing includes false or exaggerated information and information that is unsubstantiated. It might be included in sustainability reporting disclosures or in company marketing materials.

6 Practical situations

FAST FORWARD

Exam questions may ask you to think about what should be done if breaches of laws, regulations or ethical guidelines occur. **Close relationships** between the parties or other **conflicts of interest** are often a complication.

Exam focus point

Ethics is most likely to be tested as part of a larger question. The examiner has said that it could be included in any of the exam questions but will typically be included as part of Question 4.

6.1 The problem

Examination questions will expect you to be able to apply your understanding of ethical issues to practical problems arising in organisations. The exam may present you with a scenario, typically containing an array of detail much of which is potentially relevant. The problem, however, will be one or other of two basic types.

(a) A wishes B to do C which is in breach of D

where

    A = a situation, person, group of people, institution or the like

    B = you/a management accountant, the person with the ethical dilemma

    C = acting, or refraining from acting, in a certain way

    D = an ethical principle, quite possibly one of the IESBA Code fundamental principles

(b) Alternatively, the problem may be that A has done C, B has become aware of it and D requires some kind of response from B.

6.2 Example: The problem

An accountant joined a manufacturing company as its Finance Director. The company had acquired land on which it built industrial units. Before he had started at the company, the Finance Director discovered that one of the units had been sold and the selling price was significantly larger than the amount which appeared in the company's records. The difference had been siphoned off to another company – one in which his boss, the Managing Director, was a major shareholder. Furthermore, the Managing Director had kept his relationship with the second company a secret from the rest of the board.

The Finance Director confronted the Managing Director and asked him to reveal his position to the board. However, the Managing Director refused to disclose his position to anyone else. The secret profits on the sale of the unit had been used, he said, to reward the people who had secured the sale. Without their help, he added, the manufacturing company would be in a worse position financially.

The Finance Director then told the Managing Director that unless he reported to the board he would have to inform the board members himself. The Managing Director still refused. The Finance Director disclosed the full position to the board.

The problem is of the **second basic type**. B is of course the easiest party to identify. Here it is the **Finance Director**. A is clear, as well: it is the **Managing Director**. C is the **MD's breach of his directorial duties** regarding related party transactions not to obtain any personal advantage from his position of director without the consent of the company for whatever gain or profit he has obtained. D is the **principle that requires B not to be a party to an illegal act**. (Note that we distinguish between ethical and legal

obligations. B has legal obligations as a director of the company. He has ethical obligations not to ignore his legal obligations. In **this** case the two amount to the same thing.)

6.3 Relationships

You may have a feeling that the resolution of the problem described above is just too easy, and you would be right. This is because A, B, C and D are either people, or else situations involving people, who stand in certain relationships to each other.

- A may be B's boss, B's subordinate, B's equal in the organisational hierarchy, B's husband, B's friend.

- B may be new to the organisation, or well-established and waiting for promotion, or ignorant of some knowledge relevant to the situation that A possesses or that the people affected by C possess.

- C or D, as already indicated, may involve some person(s) with whom B or A have a relationship – for example the action may be to misrepresent something to a senior manager who controls the fate of B or A (or both) in the organisation.

Question — Relationships

Identify the relationships in the scenario above. What are the possible problems arising from these relationships?

Answer

The MD is the Finance Director's boss. He is also a member of the board and is longer established as such than B the Finance Director.

In outline the problems arising are that **by acting ethically the Finance Director will alienate the MD**. Even if the problem were to be resolved the episode would sour all future dealings between these two parties. Also, **the board may not be sympathetic to the accusations of a newcomer**. The Finance Director may find that he is ignored or even dismissed.

Relationships should never be permitted to affect ethical judgement. If you knew that your best friend at work had committed a major fraud, for example, **integrity** would demand that **in the last resort** you would have to bring it to the attention of somebody in authority. But note that this is only in the last resort. Try to imagine what you would do in practice in this situation.

Surely your **first course** would be to try to **persuade your friend** that what he or she had done was wrong, and that he or she had an ethical responsibility to own up. Your **second option**, if this failed, might be to try to get **somebody** (perhaps somebody outside the organisation) that you knew could **exert pressure** on your friend to persuade him or her to own up.

There is obviously a limit to how far you can take this. The important point is that just because you are dealing with a situation that involves ethical issues, this **does not mean that all the normal principles of good human relations and good management have to be suspended**. In fact this is the time when such business principles are most important.

6.4 Consequences

Actions have consequences and the consequences themselves are quite likely to have their own ethical implications.

In the example given above, we can identify the following further issues:

(a) The MD's secret transaction appears to have been made in order to secure the sale of an asset the proceeds of which are helping to prop up the company financially. Disclosure of the truth behind the sale may mean that the company is pursued for compensation by the buyer of the site. The **survival of the company** as a whole may be jeopardised.

(b) If the truth behind the transaction becomes public knowledge this could be highly damaging for the company's **reputation**, even if it can show that only one black sheep was involved.

(c) The board may simply rubber stamp the MD's actions and so the Finance Director may still find that he is expected to be party to dishonesty. (This assumes that the **company as a whole is amoral** in its approach to ethical issues. In fact the MD's refusal to disclose the matter to the board suggests otherwise.)

In the last case we are back to square one. In the first two cases, the Finance Director has to consider the ethicality or otherwise of taking action that could lead to the collapse of the company, extensive redundancies, unpaid creditors and shareholders and so on.

6.5 Actions

In spite of the difficulties, your aim will usually be to reach a satisfactory resolution to the problem. **The actions that you recommend** will often include the following.

- **Informal discussions** with the parties involved.
- **Further investigation** to establish the full facts of the matter. What extra information is needed?
- The **tightening up of controls or the introduction of new ones**, if the situation arose due to laxity in this area. This will often be the case and the principles of professional competence and due care and of technical standards will usually be relevant.
- **Attention to organisational matters** such as changes in the management structure, improving communication channels, attempting to change attitudes.

Question — Cunning plan

Your finance director has asked you to join a team planning a takeover of one of your company's suppliers. An old school friend works as an accountant for the company concerned, the finance director knows this, and has asked you to try and find out 'anything that might help the takeover succeed, but it must remain secret'.

Answer

There are three issues here. Firstly you have a **conflict of interest** as the finance director wants you to keep the takeover a secret, but you probably feel that you should tell your friend what is happening as it may affect their job.

Second, the finance director is asking you to deceive your friend. Deception is unprofessional behaviour and will break your ethical guidelines. Therefore the situation is presenting you with **two conflicting demands**. It is worth remembering that no employer should ask you to break your ethical rules.

Finally, the request to break your own ethical guidelines constitutes **unprofessional behaviour** by the finance director. You should consider reporting him to their relevant body.

Question — Manipulation

Carrow's directors are concerned about the results for the year in the statement of profit or loss and other comprehensive income and the subsequent effect on the statement of cash flows. During the year the company has sold several items of property, plant and equipment and the directors have suggested that the sale proceeds should be included in 'cash generated from operations'. They are afraid of an adverse market reaction to their results and are very aware of the importance of meeting targets in order to ensure job security, and feel that the adjustments for the proceeds would enhance the 'cash health' of the business.

Discuss the ethical responsibility of the company accountant in ensuring that manipulation of the statement of cash flows, such as that suggested by the directors, does not occur.

Answer

Directors may, particularly in times of falling profit and cash flow, wish to **present a company's results in a favourable light.** This may involve manipulation by creative accounting techniques such as window dressing, or, as is proposed here, an **inaccurate classification.**

If the proceeds of the sale of property, plant and equipment are presented in the cash flow statement as part of 'cash generated from operations', the picture is **misleading**. Operating cash flow is crucial, in the long term, for the survival of the company, because it derives from trading activities, which is what the company is there to do. **Sales of non-current assets generate short term cash flow,** and cannot be repeated year-on-year, unless there are to be no assets left to generate trading profits with.

As **a professional, the accountant has a duty** not only to the company he works for, but to his professional body, stakeholders in the company, and to **the principles of independence and fair presentation of financial statements.**

It is essential that the accountant **tries to persuade the directors not to proceed with the adjustments**, which he or she must know violates IFRS and may well go against the requirements of local legislation. If, despite his protests, the directors insist on the misleading presentation, then the accountant has a duty to **bring this to the attention of the auditors.**

Exam focus point

In an internal company role, ethical problems could be in the following forms.

- Discovering an illegal act or fraud perpetrated by the company (ie its directors)
- Discovering a fraud or illegal act perpetrated by another employee
- Pressure from superiors to take certain viewpoints, for example towards budgets (pessimistic/optimistic etc) or not to report unfavourable findings
- Breaches or potential breaches of confidentiality

PART A CONTEMPORARY ISSUES

Chapter roundup

- A principles-based system works within a set of laid down principles. A rules-based system regulates for issues as they arise. Both of these have advantages and disadvantages.
- There are many convincing arguments in favour of regulation of corporate financial reporting.
- Accounting policies may be adopted for the purposes of **manipulation**.

  Changes in accounting standards can have a significant impact on the financial statements.
- You may be asked to **advise the directors** on the implication of a change in accounting standards, or on the effect of using the correct accounting treatment.
- The AIA has adopted the *Code of Ethics for Professional Accountants issued by IESBA (The IESBA Code)*.
- Organisations sometimes issue **codes of conduct** to employees. Many employees are bound by professional codes of conduct.
- Exam questions may ask you to think about what should be done if breaches of laws, regulations or ethical guidelines occur. **Close relationships** between the parties or other **conflicts of interest** are often a complication.

Quick quiz

1. Give an example of a recent change to IFRS which will have a significant impact on the financial statements.

2. Match the fundamental principle to the characteristic.

   Fundamental principle: (a) Integrity
   (b) Objectivity

   Characteristic: (i) Members should be straightforward and honest in all professional and business relationships.
   (ii) Members should not allow bias, conflict or interest or undue influence of others to override professional or business judgements.

3. Jenny has been put under significant pressure by her manager to change the conclusion of a report she has written which reflects badly on the manager's performance. Which ethical threat is Jenny facing?

4. Which ethical threat is described as 'A financial or other interest will inappropriately influence the accountant's judgement or behaviour'.

5. An accountant who does not meet their continuing professional development (CPD) requirements is most at risk of breaching which ethical principle.

Answers to quick quiz

1. The issue of IFRS 16 which replaced IAS 17 and effectively removed off balance sheet finance in respect of leasing arrangements.

2. (a) (i)
   (b) (ii)

3. Jenny is facing an intimidation threat, as indicated by 'significant pressure'

4. This is a self-interest threat.

5. An accountant not completing CPD is most at risk of breaching the principle of professional competence and due care

End of chapter question

Mancroft

Mancroft is considering selling its subsidiary, Hungate. Just prior to the year end, Hungate sold inventory to Mancroft at a price of $3 million. The carrying amount of the inventory in the financial records of Hungate was $1 million. The cash was received before the year end, and as a result the bank overdraft of Hungate was virtually eliminated. After the year end the transaction was reversed, and it was agreed that this type of transaction would be carried out again when the interim financial statements were produced for Hungate, if the company had not been sold by that date.

Required

Explore how the manipulation of financial statements by company accountants is inconsistent with their responsibilities as members of the accounting profession, setting out the distinguishing features of a profession and the privileges that society gives to a profession. (Your answer should include reference to the sale of the inventory and should suggest the correct treatment of this transaction.)

PART A CONTEMPORARY ISSUES

Reporting for specialised entities

Topic list	Syllabus reference
1 The not-for-profit sector: Primary aims	LO1
2 The not-for-profit sector: Regulatory framework	LO1
3 The not-for-profit sector: Performance measurement	LO1
4 Smaller entities	LO1
5 Other specialised entities	LO1

Introduction

You should be aware that not-for-profit entities and smaller entities may have different accounting needs from the larger profit-making entities that you are used to. This chapter gives you the background you need to set you thinking about whether a one-size-fits-all set of standards is adequate.

PART A   CONTEMPORARY ISSUES

1 The not-for-profit sector: Primary aims

Exam focus point

A question could feature a not-for-profit organisation, a small or medium-sized entity (SME) or (possibly) some other kind of specialised entity. You might be asked to apply your knowledge of IFRS Accounting Standards to a transaction or event or to discuss more theoretical issues, such as the information needs of the users of the financial statements of (say) a charity or a local authority.

FAST FORWARD

The not-for-profit sector includes **public sector entities** and **private** not-for-profit entities such as charities.

Not-for-profit entities have **different goals** from profit making entities, but they still need to be **properly managed** and their financial statements need to present the information fairly.

What organisations do we have in mind when we refer to **not-for-profit and public sector entities**? These are the most obvious examples:

(a) Central government departments and agencies
(b) Local or federal government departments
(c) Publicly funded bodies providing healthcare (in the UK this would be the NHS) and social housing
(d) Further and higher education institutions
(e) Charitable bodies

The first four are **public sector entities**. Charities are **private** not-for-profit entities.

Not-for-profit entities have different goals and purposes to profit-making entities and are responsible to different stakeholders. However, they may be dealing in very large sums of money and it is important that they are properly managed and that their financial statements present fairly the results of their operations.

Traditionally, public sector organisations have used a cash-based accounting system. This system does not, however, provide information necessary for efficient and effective financial operations and a growing number of countries are moving to some form of accruals-based accounting within the public sector.

1.1 *Conceptual Framework* for not-for-profit entities

The *Conceptual Framework* focuses only on business entities in the private sector. There was an earlier monitoring group in respect of the development of the *Conceptual Framework* which made the following points:

(a) Not-for-profit entities have different objectives, different operating environments and other different characteristics to private sector businesses.

(b) The following issues exist regarding application of the proposals to not-for-profit entities:

- Insufficient emphasis on accountability/stewardship
- A need to broaden the definition of users and user groups
- The emphasis on future cash flows is inappropriate to not-for-profit entities
- Insufficient emphasis on budgeting

1.2 Accountability/stewardship

Not-for-profit entities are not reporting to shareholders, but it is very important that they can account for funds received and show how they have been spent. In some cases, resources may be contributed for specific purposes and management is required to show that they have been utilised for that purpose. Perhaps most importantly, taxpayers are entitled to see how the government is spending their money.

1.3 Users and user groups

The primary user group for not-for-profit entities is the providers of funds. In the case of public bodies, such as government departments, this primary group will consist of taxpayers. In the case of private

bodies such as charities it will be financial supporters, and also potential future financial supporters. There is also a case for saying that a second primary user group should be recognised, being the recipients of the goods and services provided by the not-for-profit entity.

1.4 Cash flow focus

Not-for-profit entities need to generate cash flows, but other aspects of financial information are generally more significant – for instance, the resources the entity has available to deliver future goods and services, the cost and effectiveness of those it has delivered in the past and the degree to which it is meeting its objectives.

1.5 Budgeting

Budgets and variance analyses are very important to not-for-profit entities. In some cases, funding is supplied on the basis of a formal, published budget.

2 The not-for-profit sector: Regulatory framework

FAST FORWARD

The International Public Sector Accounting Standards Board (IPSASB) is developing a set of **International Public Sector Accounting Standards** based on IFRS. In the UK, public benefit entities are considered in FRS 102, the single standard which has replaced other UK accounting standards for unlisted companies.

Regulation of public not-for-profit entities, principally local and national governments and governmental agencies is by the International Public Sector Accounting Standards Board (IPSASB), which comes under the International Federation of Accountants (IFAC).

2.1 International public sector accounting standards

The IPSASB is developing a set of International Public Sector Accounting Standards (IPSASs), based on IFRS Accounting Standards. To date 42 IPSASs have been issued. The IPSAS are mainly based on the accrual method of accounting and one of the aims of the IPSASB is to move public sector organisations from the cash to the accruals basis of accounting. You don't need to know the standards for the exam.

2.1.1 Regulatory framework in the UK

In the UK, central government and the health sector have been preparing their financial statements under IFRS Accounting Standards from 2009/2010 onwards. The change was extended to local government in 2010/2011.

The governance framework for UK government entities formalises a common accounting standards setting hierarchy. IFRS Accounting Standards are at the top of the hierarchy; next, in a supportive role and providing additional public-sector specific guidance, are IPSAS, and finally UK standards.

FRS 102 is applicable to public sector entities, not just companies. It incorporates the special considerations for public benefit entities (PBEs) and certain paragraphs that apply solely to PBEs are identified by the prefix 'PBE'.

2.2 Characteristics of not-for-profit entities

2.2.1 Private Sector

Not-for-profit entities in the private sector have the following characteristics:

- Their objective is to provide goods and services to various recipients and not to make a profit
- They are generally characterised by the absence of defined ownership interests (shares) that can be sold, transferred or redeemed

- They may have a wide group of stakeholders to consider (including the public at large in some cases)
- Their revenues generally arise from contributions (donations or membership dues) rather than sales
- Their capital assets are typically acquired and held to deliver services without the intention of earning a return on them

2.2.2 Public Sector

Not-for-profit entities in the public sector have similar key characteristics to those in the private sector. They are typically established by legislation and:

- Their objective is to provide goods and services to various recipients or to develop or implement policy on behalf of governments and not to make a profit
- They are characterised by the absence of defined ownership interests that can be sold, transferred or redeemed
- They typically have a wide group of stakeholders to consider (including the public at large)
- Their revenues are generally derived from taxes or other similar contributions obtained through the exercise of coercive powers
- Their capital assets are typically acquired and held to deliver services without the intention of earning a return on them

2.3 Not-for-profit entities – specific issues

While the general trend is to get not-for-profit entities producing financial statements which are based as far as possible on accrual accounting and the provisions of IFRS Standards, and which are generally comparable to those produced for profit-making entities, there are two issues which have yet to be resolved.

2.3.1 Cost of transition

While there has been a general assumption that for public sector entities the move to the accruals basis will result in more relevant and better quality financial reporting, no actual cost-benefit analysis has been undertaken on this.

One of the arguments in favour of the adoption of the accruals basis is that it will be possible to compare the cost of providing a service against the same cost in the private sector. It will then be possible to see how goods and services can be most cheaply sourced.

However, it is questionable whether governments get a good deal anyway when they involve themselves with the private sector and the move to accruals accounting has not gained universal acceptance. The main issue is the huge cost involved in terms of the number of qualified accountants required. For developing countries this cost is considered to be prohibitive.

2.3.2 Definition of a liability

The IASB's *Conceptual Framework* defines a liability as 'a present obligation of the entity to transfer an economic resource as a result of past events' (Conceptual Framework, para 4.26). A liability is recognised when the transaction meets the definition of an element and its recognition provides information that is useful to the primary users of financial information.

Public benefit entities are subject to a commitment to provide public benefits, but there is an issue to be resolved over whether this commitment meets the definition of a liability. It may be the case that the provision of public benefits does not result in the transfer of **economic** benefits A distinction must also be drawn between 'general commitments to provide public benefits' and 'specific commitments to provide public benefits'. The specific commitment can be regarded as a 'present obligation', but it can be argued that the obligation only arises when the entity formally undertakes to provide something such as a non-performance-related grant. (If the grant were performance-related, the entity would be able to withdraw from the agreement if the performance targets were not reached.)

The issue is of major importance in the financial reporting of the social policies of governments.

2.4 Charities

Charities are regulated by accounting standards, charity law, relevant company law and best practice. This will vary from country to country. Here we are taking the UK as a typical example.

2.4.1 Statement of financial activities

In addition to a statement of financial position, charities also produce a Statement of Financial Activities (SoFA), an Annual Report to the Charity Commission and sometimes an income and expenditure account. The SoFA is the primary statement showing the results of the charity's activities for the period.

The SoFA shows incoming resources, resources expended, and the resultant net movement in funds. Under incoming resources, income from all sources of funds are listed. These can include:

- Subscription or membership fees
- Public donations
- Donations from patrons
- Government grants
- Income from sale of goods
- Investment income
- Publication sales
- Royalties

The resources expended will show the amount spent directly in furtherance of the charity's objects. It will also show items which form part of any statement of profit or loss (income statement), such as salaries, depreciation, travelling and entertaining, audit and other professional fees. These items can be very substantial.

Charities, especially the larger charities, now operate very much in the way that profit-making entities do. They run high-profile campaigns which cost money and they employ professional people who have to be paid. At the same time, their stakeholders will want to see that most of their donation is going towards achieving the aims for which funds were donated, not on the running of the business.

One of the problems charities experience is that, even although the accruals basis is being applied, they will still have income and expenditure recognised in different periods, due to the difficulty of correlating them. The extreme example is a campaign to persuade people to leave money to the charity in their will. The costs will have to be recognised, but there is no way to predict when the income will arise. The

Exam focus point Examiner has said that candidates need to have only a basic awareness of the special requirements of not-for-profit organisations. Candidates also need to be aware of the issues concerning the appropriateness of applying IFRS Accounting Standards to their performance measures and statements of financial position. This topic will almost certainly be tested by means of an essay question.

Question — *Conceptual Framework* and not-for-profit organisations

Should the *Conceptual Framework* apply equally to profit-oriented and non profit-oriented entities or just to profit-oriented entities?

Answer

Arguments for applying the *Conceptual Framework* to not-for-profit organisations:

- There is evidence that some national standard setters consider non profit-oriented entities to be just as important as profit-oriented entities as their *Conceptual Frameworks* cater for both. So the idea is not totally without support around the world.

PART A CONTEMPORARY ISSUES

- One of the main features of the last 20 years or so has been the introduction of performance based accountability into both profit-oriented and non profit-oriented sectors. The financial position of both sectors is also of growing concern. It would follow from this that common concepts and principles could be developed.

- Many public sector bodies use IFRS Accounting Standards for reporting purposes; eg concerning the recognition of liabilities.

- If the above development continues then it may be best to develop a framework that applies to both sectors from the beginning. If a framework develops which concentrates on one rather than the other then costly and disruptive changes may have to be made in future.

Arguments against applying the *Conceptual Framework* to not-for-profit organisations:

- The performance of a non profit-oriented entity is likely to be measured in terms of the quality of its contribution to society. The performance of a profit-oriented entity is not measured in this way. It is measured in terms of the returns it makes and in an assessment of its future cash flow potential. This focus on returns and the future cash flows therefore colours the type of information it produces. Concepts and principles to reflect this will therefore be very different to that for a non profit-oriented entity.

- Risk is assessed in very different ways. A profit-oriented entity has shareholders whose risk is assessed and measured in a different way to those interested in the affairs of a non profit-oriented entity whose stakeholders may be interested more in environmental or employment risk than in financial risk. Objectives of financial reporting would therefore vary greatly.

- The IASB's activities are in accordance with the constitution of its overseeing body, the IFRS Foundation, which seeks to develop financial statements and other financial reporting to aid economic decision making in the world's capital markets. This is a major statement which focuses on, although undefined, profit-oriented entities.

3 The not-for-profit sector: Performance measurement

Not-for-profit and public sector entities produce financial statements in the same way as profit-making entities do but, while they are expected to remain solvent, their performance cannot be measured simply by the bottom line.

A public sector entity is not expected to show a profit or to underspend its budget. In practice, central government and local government departments know that if they underspend the budget, next year's allocation will be correspondingly reduced. This leads to a rash of digging up the roads and other expenditure just before the end of the financial year as councils strive to spend any remaining funds.

Private and public sector entities are judged principally on the basis of what they have achieved, not how much or how little they have spent in achieving it. So how is performance measured?

3.1 Public sector entities

These will have performance measures laid down by government. The emphasis is on economy, efficiency and effectiveness. Departments and local councils have to show how they have spent public money and what level of service they have achieved. Performance measurement will be based on Key Performance Indicators (KPIs). Examples of these for a local council could be:

- Number of homeless people rehoused
- % of rubbish collections made on time
- Number of children in care adopted

Public sector entities use the services of outside contractors for a variety of functions. They then have to be able to show that they have obtained the best possible value for what they have spent on outside services. This principle is usually referred to as Value For Money (VFM). In the UK, local authorities are

5: REPORTING FOR SPECIALISED ENTITIES

required to report under a system known as Best Value. They have to show that they applied 'fair competition' in awarding contracts.

Best Value is based on the principle of the 'four Cs':

1   **Challenging** why, how and by whom a service is provided
2   **Comparing** performance against other local authorities
3   **Consulting** service users, the local community etc
4   Using fair **Competition** to secure efficient and effective services

3.2 Charities

While charities must demonstrate that they have made proper use of whatever funds they have received, their stakeholders will be more interested in what they have achieved in terms of their stated mission. People who donate money to a relief fund for earthquake victims will want to know what help has been given to survivors, before enquiring how well the organisation has managed its funds. Although it must be said that any mismanagement of funds by a charity is taken very seriously by the donating public.

Some charities produce 'impact reports' which highlight what the charity set out to achieve, what it has achieved and what it has yet to do. Stakeholders should know what the organisation is aiming to achieve and how it is succeeding. Each charity will have its own performance indicators which enable it to measure this.

| Question | Charity performance indicators |

Choose a charity with which you are familiar and produce a possible set of performance indicators for it.

4 Smaller entities

FAST FORWARD The IASB has addressed the **Big GAAP/Little GAAP** debate by issuing an *IFRS for SMEs*.

4.1 Background

Within each individual country **local regulations** govern, to a greater or lesser degree, the issue of financial statements. These local regulations include accounting standards issued by the national regulatory bodies and/or professional accountancy bodies in the country concerned. In some cases they also include IFRS Standards.

IFRS Accounting Standards do not override local regulations on financial statements. Entities should simply disclose the fact where IFRS Accounting Standards are complied with in all material respects. Members of the IASB in individual counties will attempt to persuade local authorities, where current regulations deviate from IFRS Accounting Standards, that the benefits of harmonisation make local change worthwhile.

4.2 Application of IFRS Accounting Standards to smaller entities

Exam focus point The Examiner has said that candidates need to be aware of the 'Big GAAP vs. Little GAAP' debate.

In most countries the majority of companies or other types of entity are **very small**. They are generally owned and managed by one person or a family. The owners have invested their own money in the business and there are no outside shareholders to protect.

Large entities, by contrast, particularly companies listed on a stock exchange, may have shareholders who have invested their money, possibly through a pension fund, with no knowledge whatever of the company. These shareholders need protection and the regulations for such companies need to be more stringent.

It could therefore be argued that company financial statements should be of two types:

(a) 'Simple' ones for small companies with fewer regulations and disclosure requirements
(b) 'Complicated' ones for larger companies with extensive and detailed requirements

This is sometimes called the **big GAAP/little GAAP divide**.

Some standards may simply not apply to a smaller entity. For example, a company with equity not quoted on a stock exchange has no need to comply with IAS 33 *Earnings per Share*. Also an entity with a small local market may find IFRS 8 *Operating Segments* to be superfluous.

It is certainly the case that there are several IFRS Accounting Standards which very rarely have any bearing on small company financial statements, whereas others almost always have an impact. In particular, almost all small companies will be affected by the standards on:

- Property, plant and equipment
- Impairment
- Inventories
- Presentation of financial statements
- Events after the reporting period
- Taxes on income
- Revenue
- Provisions and contingencies

Although these standards are relevant, their application can cause small entities problems and burden them with additional costs. For example, impairment reviews can be time consuming and a smaller entity may not have sufficient staff to spare to carry out these reviews.

These problems historically resulted in calls to take one of two approaches to the issue of small entity reporting:

- Exclude small entities from the scope of certain more complex IFRS Accounting Standards, such that only 'core' standards remain applicable; or

- Provide smaller entities with a new IFRS Accounting Standard containing all requirements relevant to them.

The IASB has taken the second of these approaches, and in 2009 issued the IFRS for SMEs.

4.3 IFRS for small and medium-sized entities

In July 2009, the IASB published an International Financial Reporting Standard for small and medium-sized entities (IFRS for SMEs). The standard consists of the fundamental requirements drawn from existing full IFRS Accounting Standards, organised by topic. Topics not relevant to SMEs (for example, segment reporting and earnings per share) have been omitted. The requirements regarding recognition and measurement have been simplified in certain cases (for example, those relating to financial instruments and intangible assets). Disclosure requirements have also been simplified.

The accounting requirements of the IFRS for SMEs are covered in detail in Chapter 22.

4.4 Small Business Enterprise and Employment Act

The Act was passed in 2015 and applies to businesses in the UK. The Act is designed to make the United Kingdom a more attractive place to start, finance and grow a business and reduce the barriers faced by many small businesses. It deals with a number of issues including access to finance, regulatory reform, company filing requirements, insolvency and employment regulations.

The main provisions dealing with company reporting and qualification of directors are:

- Companies need to keep a register of people with significant control (PSCs). These are people to whom one or more of the following apply:

- Hold more than 25% of shares
- Hold more than 25% of voting rights
- Can appoint or remove a majority of directors
- Are able to, or do, exercise significant influence or control.

- The statement of capital is simplified – no need to set it out in full if there have been no changes during the year.
- An accelerated strike-off procedure for companies no longer trading – reduced from three months to two months.
- The date of birth of directors will no longer appear on the public record.
- Newly-appointed officers must have consented to act – if they did not consent they can apply to have the notification of their appointment removed.
- Directors can now be disqualified for certain convictions obtained abroad and for instructing another unfit director.
- Bearer shares are abolished.
- A procedure is set out for dealing with registered office disputes.
- The annual return filed with Companies House is replaced with a 'confirmation statement' to be submitted at least once a year. This statement contains information relating to the company's registered office, directors and shareholders.

5 Other specialised entities

Exam focus point

You may be asked to apply current accounting standards to a particular transaction or event in an 'unusual' entity.

5.1 Approaching specialised entity questions

Examiners use unusual situations in order to test whether you are flexible enough to apply your knowledge and understanding of accounting standards in a fresh context. Below are some typical questions.

5.1.1 An agricultural college

An agricultural college is not the kind of setting you are used to encountering in your accountancy studies. It doesn't manufacture or trade in goods. But there are issues that it will have in common with companies that do.

Question — Agricultural college

Swindale Agricultural College derives its income from a variety of sources. It receives a grant from central government, further subsidies from the European Union and money from the local council tax. In addition, students pay fees.

The Diploma in Agriculture course lasts nine months – from October till the end of June. The College's accounting year end is 31 December 20X8. Students pay $3,000 subsidised tuition fees. As at 1 October 20X8, twenty students have enrolled, each paying a non-refundable deposit of $1,200. The balance of $1,800 per student is to be paid in nine monthly instalments of $200.

The College Bursar argues that because the deposit is non-refundable, the fee income should be recognised on a cash receipt basis.

Required

Advise the College Bursar on the correct accounting treatment for the fee income. Show the journal entries for this treatment.

Answer

This question deals with revenue recognition, specifically in the context of the provision of a service.

Total fee income from students for this course (deposits and instalments) will be:

(20 × $1,200) + (20 × $200 × 9) = $60,000

Currently it is proposed to recognise revenue on the basis of cash received, which, as at 31 December 20X8, is the deposit plus three monthly instalments:

(20 × $1,200) + (20 × $200 × 3) = $36,000

This is wrong, as it does not take account of the accrual concept. As at 31 December 20X8, only one third of the course (three out of nine months) has been delivered, so only one third of the total fee income should be recognised. Income recognised should be $20,000.

There is an element of deferred income. As this is over months, rather than years, it will not be necessary to discount to arrive at the fair value of the consideration. The excess of the $36,000 cash received over the $20,000 revenue recognised should be regarded as deferred income. These deposits are non-refundable, but they create an obligation to complete the contract. Accordingly they should be a liability in the statement of financial position.

The journal entries are as follows:

DEBIT	Cash	$36,000
CREDIT	Fee income (recognised)	$20,000
CREDIT	Deferred income (received in advance of delivery of services)	$16,000

5.1.2 A football club

You do not need any specialist knowledge of the football club finance sector to answer this question, which is basically about accounting for assets. The principles are exactly the same as when accounting for assets held by any other entity.

We will be revising the relevant accounting standards later in the text, but you should be able to remember enough of your earlier studies to make a reasonable attempt at this question.

Question
Football club

United Wanderers is a famous football club but has significant cash flow problems. The directors and shareholders wish to take steps to improve the club's financial position. The following proposals had been drafted in an attempt to improve the cash flow of the club. However, the directors need advice upon their implications.

(a) **Player registrations**

The club capitalises the unconditional amounts (transfer fees) paid to acquire players.

The club proposes to amortise the cost of the transfer fees over ten years instead of the current practice which is to amortise the cost over the duration of the player's contract. The club has sold most of its valuable players during the current financial year but still has two valuable players under contract.

Player	Transfer fee capitalised $m	Amortisation to 31 December 20X6 $m	Contract commenced	Contract expires
Headham	20	4	1 January 20X6	31 December 20Y0
Meadows	15	10	1 January 20X5	31 December 20X7

If United Wanderers wins the national football league, then a further $5 million will be payable to the two players' former clubs. United Wanderers is currently performing very poorly in the league.

(b) **Player trading**

Another proposal is for the club to sell its two valuable players, Headham and Meadows. It is thought that it will receive a total of $16 million for both players. The players are to be offered for sale at the end of the current football season on 1 May 20X7.

Required

Discuss how the above proposals would be dealt with in the financial statement of United Wanderers for the year ending 31 December 20X6, setting out their accounting treatment and appropriateness in helping the football club's cash flow problems.

Answer

(a) **Player registrations**

The player registrations are **capitalised** by the club as intangible non-current assets under IAS 38 *Intangible Assets*. This is an **acceptable** accounting treatment; the transfer fees should be classified as assets as it is probable that expected future benefits will flow to the club as a result of the contracts and the cost can be measured reliably at the amount of the transfer fees actually paid.

According to IAS 38, intangible non-current assets which are capitalised should be **amortised over their useful life**. Therefore on the face of it claiming a useful life of 10 years might be acceptable. However IAS 38 recommends that amortisation reflects the useful life of the assets and the pattern of economic benefits. Therefore the proposal to amortise the transfer fees over a period of **10 years is not acceptable as the contracts are only for 5 years and 3 years**.

In terms of **cash flow** this proposal regarding the amortisation would have **no effect** at all. It would simply be a bookkeeping entry which would reduce the amortisation charge to the statement of profit or loss and other comprehensive income.

The potential payment to the two players' former clubs of $5 million would **not** appear to be **probable** due to the current form of the club. Therefore under IAS 37 *Provisions, Contingent Liabilities and Contingent Assets* no provision would be recognised for this amount. However, the possible payment does fall within the IAS 37 definition of a contingent liability which is a possible obligation arising out of past events whose existence will be confirmed only by the occurrence or non-occurrence of one or more uncertain future events not wholly within the control of the entity. Therefore as a contingent liability the amount and details would be **disclosed** in the notes to the financial statements.

(b) **Player trading**

In accounting terms there is no issue to deal with at 31 December 20X6 as the potential sale of the players will not fall to be classified as 'held for sale' non-current assets under IFRS 5 *Non-current Assets Held for Sale and Discontinued Operations*. In order for these players to be classified as held for sale they would need to be available for immediate sale which they are not.

However, the club must consider carrying out an **impairment review** of these assets at 31 December 20X6. If the players are sold for the anticipated figure of $16 million then the following loss will be incurred:

	$m
Carrying amount at 1 May 20X7	
Headham ($20m – ($4m + (4/12 × $4m))	14.7
Meadows ($15m – ($10 + (4/12 × $5))	3.3
	18.0
Potential sales value	16.0
Potential loss	2.0

This potential loss of $2 million on the sale of these players may be evidence of impairment and a review should be carried out at 31 December 20X6 and the **players' value written down to recoverable amount** if necessary.

In terms of cash flow, the sale of the players would **provide much needed cash**. However, as the club is performing poorly currently the sale of the two best players **may lead to even worse performance** which is likely to have a detrimental affect on ticket sales and the liquidity of the club in future.

5.2 Other possibilities

The possibilities are wide ranging, and you need to apply common sense. Suppose, for example, the question relates to a property dealer, who was trying to classify his properties as investment properties? This would not be permitted, because the properties are for sale and not held for investment potential.

Chapter roundup

- The not-for-profit sector includes **public sector entities** and **private** not-for-profit entities such as charities.

  Not-for-profit entities have **different goals** from profit making entities, but they still need to be **properly managed** and their financial statements need to present the information fairly.

- The International Public Sector Accounting Standards Board (IPSASB) is developing a set of **International Public Sector Accounting Standards** based on IFRS Accounting Standards. In the UK, public benefit entities are considered in FRS 102, the single standard which has replaced other UK accounting standards for unlisted companies.

- The IASB has addressed the **Big GAAP/Little GAAP debate** by issuing an *IFRS for SMEs*.

Quick quiz

1 Charities are public sector entities. True or false?

2 Why do not-for-profit entities need to prepare financial statements if they are not reporting to shareholders?

3 Are there any special reporting standards for the public sector?

4 Are there any special IFRS Accounting Standards for small companies?

Answers to quick quiz

1 False. Charities are private not-for-profit profit entities.

2 They often deal in large sums of money.

3 Yes, the IPSASB is developing a set of International Public Sector Accounting Standards; in the UK public benefit entities are considered within FRS 102.

4 Yes, the *IFRS for Small and Medium-sized Entities (SMEs)* was published in 2009.

End of chapter question

Small and medium-sized entities

In July 2009, the IASB issued the *International Financial Reporting Standard for Small and Medium-sized Entities* (IFRS for SMEs). The aim of the new standard is to provide a simplified, self-contained set of accounting principles for smaller companies. The resulting standard reduces the volume of accounting guidance applicable to SMEs by more than 85% when compared to a full set of IFRS.

Required

Assess the advantages and disadvantages of having a separate IFRS for SMEs as opposed to requiring compliance with full IFRS Accounting Standards. **(10 marks)**

Business combinations and group financial statements

Revision of basic groups

Topic list	Syllabus reference
1 Introduction	LO2
2 Types of investment	LO2, LO3
3 IFRS 3 *Business Combinations*	LO2, LO3
4 IFRS 10 *Consolidated Financial Statements*	LO2, LO3
5 IFRS 3 – further issues	LO2, LO3
6 Associates	LO2, LO3
7 Joint arrangements	LO2, LO3
8 Disclosure of interests in other entities	LO2, LO3
9 Separate financial statements of investor	LO2, LO3

Introduction

Basic groups were covered in your earlier studies. In this paper, the emphasis is likely to be on the **more complex** aspects of consolidation. This chapter is mainly revision of the accounting treatment required for subsidiaries, associates and joint arrangements.

Note. The term 'statement of profit or loss and other comprehensive income' is used. Examiners will normally use this term or may use 'statement of profit or loss' where the last line of the statement is 'profit for the year'.

PART B BUSINESS COMBINATIONS AND GROUP FINANCIAL STATEMENTS

1 Introduction

Exam focus point

You are unlikely to be examined just on the basic principles. However, you will gain marks for knowing the basic principles in a more complex consolidation.

In traditional accounting terminology, a **group of companies** consists of a **parent company** and one or more **subsidiary companies** which are controlled by the parent company. A group may also have investments in associates and joint arrangements.

The guidance in respect of group accounting is found in six accounting standards:

FAST FORWARD

- IAS 27 *Separate Financial Statements*
- IAS 28 *Investments in Associates and Joint Ventures*
- IFRS 3 *Business Combinations*
- IFRS 10 *Consolidated Financial Statements*
- IFRS 11 *Joint Arrangements*
- IFRS 12 *Disclosure of Interests in Other Entities*

1.1 Definitions

Exam focus point

All the definitions relating to group financial statements are extremely important. You must **learn them** and **understand** their meaning and application.

Definitions are very important when looking at group financial statements.

The definitions listed below include some which you have met before in your previous studies. Other, definitions are new and will be explained in the relevant sections of the chapter.

Key terms

Consolidated financial statements. The financial statements of a group in which the assets, liabilities, equity, income, expenses and cash flows of the parent and its subsidiaries are presented as those of a single economic entity. (IAS 27, IAS 28, IFRS 10)

Subsidiary. An entity that is controlled by another entity. (IFRS 3, IFRS 10)

Parent. An entity that controls one or more entities. (IFRS 3, IFRS 10)

Group. A parent and its subsidiaries. (IFRS 10)

Control. An investor controls an investee when the investor is exposed to, or has rights to, variable returns from its involvement with the investee and has the ability to affect those returns through its power over the investee. (IFRS 10)

Power. Existing rights that give the current ability to direct the relevant activities (IFRS 10)

Relevant activities. Activities of the investee that significantly affect the investee's return (IFRS 10)

Associate. An entity, over which the investor has significant influence (IAS 28)

Significant influence is the power to participate in the financial and operating policy decisions of an investee or an economic activity but is not control or joint control over those policies. (IAS 28)

Joint arrangement. An arrangement of which two or more parties have joint control. (IFRS 11)

Joint control. The contractually agreed sharing of control of an arrangement, which exists only when decisions about the relevant activities require the unanimous consent of the parties sharing control (IFRS 11)

> **Key terms (cont'd)**
>
> **Joint operation.** A joint arrangement whereby the parties that have joint control of the arrangement have rights to the assets and obligations for the liabilities relating to the arrangement. (IFRS 11)
>
> **Joint venture.** A joint arrangement whereby the parties that have joint control of the arrangement have rights to the net assets of the arrangement. (IFRS 11)
>
> **The Equity method** is a method of accounting whereby the investment is initially recognised at cost and adjusted thereafter for the post-acquisition change in the investor's share of the investee's net assets. The investor's profit or loss includes its share of the investee's profit or loss and the investor's other comprehensive income includes its share of the investee's other comprehensive income. (IAS 28)
>
> **Acquiree.** The business or businesses that the **acquirer** obtains control of in a **business combination**. (IFRS 3)
>
> **Acquirer.** The entity that obtains control of the **acquiree**. (IFRS 3)
>
> **Business combination.** A transaction or other event in which an **acquirer** obtains control of one or more **businesses**. (IFRS 3)
>
> **Contingent consideration.** Usually, an obligation of the **acquirer** to transfer additional assets or **equity interests** to the former owners of an **acquiree** as part of the exchange for **control** of the **acquiree** if specified future events occur or conditions are met. (IFRS 3)
>
> **Fair value.** The price that would be received to sell an asset or paid to transfer a liability in an orderly transaction between market participants at the measurement date. (IFRS 3)
>
> **Non-controlling interest.** The equity in a subsidiary not attributable, directly or indirectly, to a parent. (IFRS 3, IFRS 10)

2 Types of investment

> **FAST FORWARD**
>
> Investments can be in subsidiaries, associates, joint arrangements or be financial asset investments. The accounting treatment applied differs depending on the type of investment.

2.1 Investment in subsidiaries

One entity is a subsidiary of another where it is **controlled** by that entity.

IFRS 10 identifies three separate elements of control. It states that an investor controls an investee if and only if it has all of the following:

Power over the investee to direct the **relevant activities**	+	Exposure or rights to **variable returns** from its involvement with the investee	+	The **ability** to use its power over the investee to affect the amount of the investor's returns

Examples of power (IFRS 10: para. B15):
- Voting rights
- Rights to appoint, reassign or remove key management personnel
- Rights to appoint or remove another entity that directs relevant activities
- Management contract

Examples of **relevant activities**:
- Sell and purchase goods/services
- Select, acquire, dispose of assets
- Research and develop new products/processes
- Determine funding structure/obtain funding

Examples of variable returns (IFRS 10: paras. 15, B57):
- Dividends
- Interest from debt
- Changes in value of investment
- Remuneration for servicing investee's assets or liabilities
- Fees/exposure to loss from providing credit/liquidity support
- Residual interest in assets and liabilities on liquidation
- Tax benefits
- Access to future liquidity
- Returns not available to other interest holders, eg cost savings

An investor can have the current **ability** to direct the activities of an investee even **if it does not actively direct the activities** of the investee

Only the principal (not on agent) may control an investee when exercising it decision-making powers

> **Exam focus point**
>
> You should learn the definition of control as you may be asked to apply it in the exam.

2.1.1 Accounting treatment in group financial statements

IFRS 10 requires a parent to present consolidated financial statements, in which the financial statements of the parent and subsidiary (or subsidiaries) are combined and presented **as a single entity**. This process is **consolidation.** We shall cover the detailed accounting requirements in Sections 3–5 of this chapter.

2.2 Investments in associates

This type of investment is something less than a subsidiary, but more than a simple investment (nor is it a joint venture). The key criterion here is **significant influence**. This is defined as the 'power to participate', but **not** to 'control' (which would make the investment a subsidiary).

Significant influence can be determined by the holding of voting rights (usually attached to shares) in the entity. IAS 28 states that if an investor holds **20% or more** of the voting power of the investee, it is presumed that the investor has significant influence over the investee, **unless** it can be clearly shown that this is not the case.

Significant influence is presumed **not** to exist if the investor holds **less than 20%** of the voting power of the investee, unless it can be demonstrated otherwise.

The **existence of significant influence** is evidenced in one or more of the following ways.

(a) Representation on the **board of directors** (or equivalent) of the investee
(b) Participation in the **policy making process**
(c) **Material transactions** between investor and investee
(d) Interchange of **management personnel**
(e) Provision of **essential technical information**

2.2.1 Accounting treatment in group financial statements

IAS 28 requires the use of the **equity method** of accounting for investments in associates in consolidated financial statements. This method will be explained in detail in Section 6 of this chapter.

2.3 Investments in joint arrangements

IFRS 11 defines a joint arrangement as an arrangement of which two or more parties have joint control. The joint arrangement may be either a joint operation or a joint venture depending on the rights of the parties with joint control.

2.3.1 Accounting treatment in group financial statements

IFRS 11 requires that:

- Equity accounting is applied in the case of joint ventures
- The parties with joint control recognise their share of joint items

The identification and classification of joint arrangements and relevant accounting treatment is discussed in more detail in Section 7 of this chapter.

2.4 Other investments

Investments which do not meet the definitions of any of the above are financial assets and should be accounted in accordance with IFRS 9 *Financial Instruments*. Financial instruments are covered in Chapter 14.

2.5 Summary of types of investments

We can summarise the different levels of investment **and** the required accounting treatment as follows.

Investment	Criteria	Required treatment in group financial statements
Subsidiary	Control	Full consolidation
Associate	Significant influence	Equity accounting
Joint venture	Joint control	Equity accounting
Joint operation	Joint control	Recognise share of joint items
Investment which is none of the above	Asset held for accretion of wealth	Financial asset accounting per IFRS 9

The remainder of the chapter will consider each of these levels of investment in more detail. Firstly, however, we shall recap the basic requirements of IFRS 3 *Business Combinations*. A business combination is a transaction where an acquirer obtains **control** of one or more businesses. It is therefore relevant to accounting for **subsidiaries.**

3 IFRS 3 *Business Combinations*

You should be familiar with IFRS 3 *Business Combinations* from your previous studies. Here is a recap of the basic calculation of goodwill.

3.1 Objective of IFRS 3

The objective of IFRS 3 is to improve the relevance, reliability and comparability of the information that a reporting entity provides in its financial statements about a business combination and its effects. To accomplish that, IFRS 3 establishes principles and requirements for how the acquirer:

(a) Recognises and measures in its financial statements the identifiable assets acquired, the liabilities assumed and any non-controlling interest in the acquiree.

(b) Recognises and measures the goodwill acquired in the business combination or a gain from a bargain purchase.

(c) Determines what information to disclose to enable users of the financial statements to evaluate the nature and financial effects of the business combination.

3.2 Identifying a business combination

IFRS 3 requires entities to determine whether a transaction or other event is a business combination by applying the definition in the IFRS. As we saw earlier, a business combination is defined as 'a transaction or other event in which an acquirer obtains control of one or more businesses'.

3.3 The acquisition method

Entities must account for each business combination by applying the **acquisition method.** This requires:

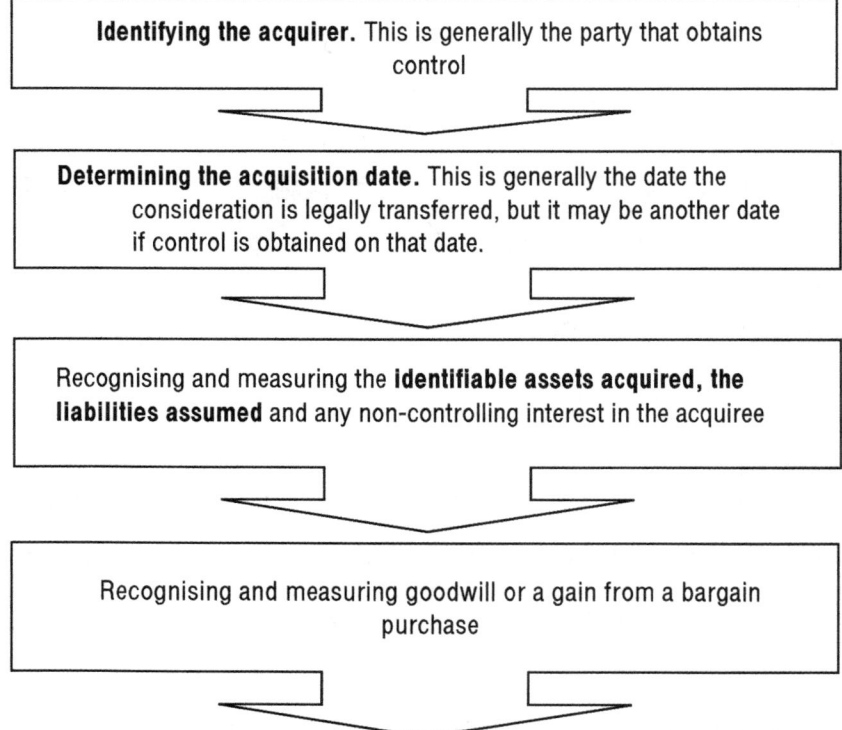

The recognition and measurement of identifiable assets acquired and liabilities assumed other than the non-controlling interest is dealt with in Section 3. Below we deal with the cost of the acquisition, the consideration transferred, the goodwill and the non-controlling interest, as these treatments have recently changed.

3.4 Acquisition-related costs

Under IFRS 3, **costs relating to the acquisition must be recognised as an expense** at the time of the acquisition. They are not regarded as an asset. (Costs of issuing debt or equity are to be accounted for under the rules of IFRS 9.)

3.5 Consideration

The consideration transferred is measured at fair value (in accordance with IFRS 13), calculated as the acquisition date fair values of:

- The assets transferred by the acquirer;
- The liabilities incurred by the acquirer (to former owners of the acquiree); and
- Equity interests issued by the acquirer (IFRS 3: paras. 37–40).

3.5.1 Deferred and contingent consideration

Deferred consideration is not defined in IFRS 3, but can be considered as any consideration transferred after the date of acquisition.

Contingent consideration is defined in IFRS 3 as 'usually, an obligation of the acquirer to transfer additional assets or equity interests to the former owners of an acquiree as part of the exchange for control of the acquiree if specified future events occur or conditions are met. However, contingent consideration also may give the acquirer the right to the return of previously transferred consideration if specified conditions are met.' (IFRS 3, Defined terms)

Deferred and contingent consideration should be accounted for as follows:

Item	Treatment
Deferred consideration	Discounted to present value to measure its fair value

Contingent consideration (to be settled in cash or shares)	Measured at fair value at the acquisition date Subsequent measurement (IFRS 3: para. 58):
	(a) If the change is due to additional information obtained that affects the position at the acquisition date, goodwill should be remeasured (if within the measurement period)
	(b) If the change is due to any other change, eg meeting earnings targets:
	  (i) Consideration is equity instruments - not remeasured
	  (ii) Consideration is cash - remeasure to fair value with gains or losses through profit or loss
	  (iii) Consideration is a financial instrument - account for under IFRS 9

3.6 Goodwill and the non-controlling interest

IFRS 3 views the group as an economic entity. This means that it treats all providers of equity – including non-controlling interests – as shareholders in the group, even if they are not shareholders of the parent. Thus goodwill attributable to the non-controlling interest may be recognised.

We will come back to this point below, but first we need to consider how IFRS 3 sets out the calculation for goodwill.

3.6.1 IFRS 3 goodwill calculation

In words, IFRS 3 states:

> Fair value of consideration paid by parent + non-controlling interest – fair value of the subsidiary's net identifiable assets = consolidated goodwill

3.6.2 BPP proforma goodwill calculation

The proforma goodwill calculation could be set out like this:

	$
Consideration transferred	X
Amount of any non-controlling interests	X
	X
Less net acquisition-date fair value of identifiable assets acquired and liabilities assumed	(X)
	X

While the above layout reflects the wording of the standard, for the purposes of your workings in the examination, the following layout is recommended:

		Group	NCI
	$	$	$
Consideration transferred/Fair value of non-controlling interests		X	X
Less: net fair value of identifiable assets acquired and liabilities assumed	X		
× Group/NCI %		(X)	(X)
		X	X
		X	

PART B BUSINESS COMBINATIONS AND GROUP FINANCIAL STATEMENTS

The NCI (non-controlling interest) column is only needed if the NCI interest is to be measured at fair value (see below). When the NCI is measured at fair value, goodwill arises that is attributable to the NCI.

3.6.3 Measuring non-controlling interest at acquisition

FAST FORWARD

The non-controlling interest may be measured **either at fair value or at the non-controlling interest's proportionate share of the acquiree's identifiable net assets.**

The non-controlling interest now forms part of the calculation of goodwill. The question now arises as to how it should be measured.

The 'economic entity' principle (see 1.7.2) suggests that the non-controlling interest should be measured at fair value. In fact, IFRS 3 gives a **choice**:

> 'For each business combination, the acquirer shall measure any non-controlling interest in the acquiree **either at fair value or at the non-controlling interest's proportionate share of the acquiree's identifiable net assets.**' *(IFRS 3)*

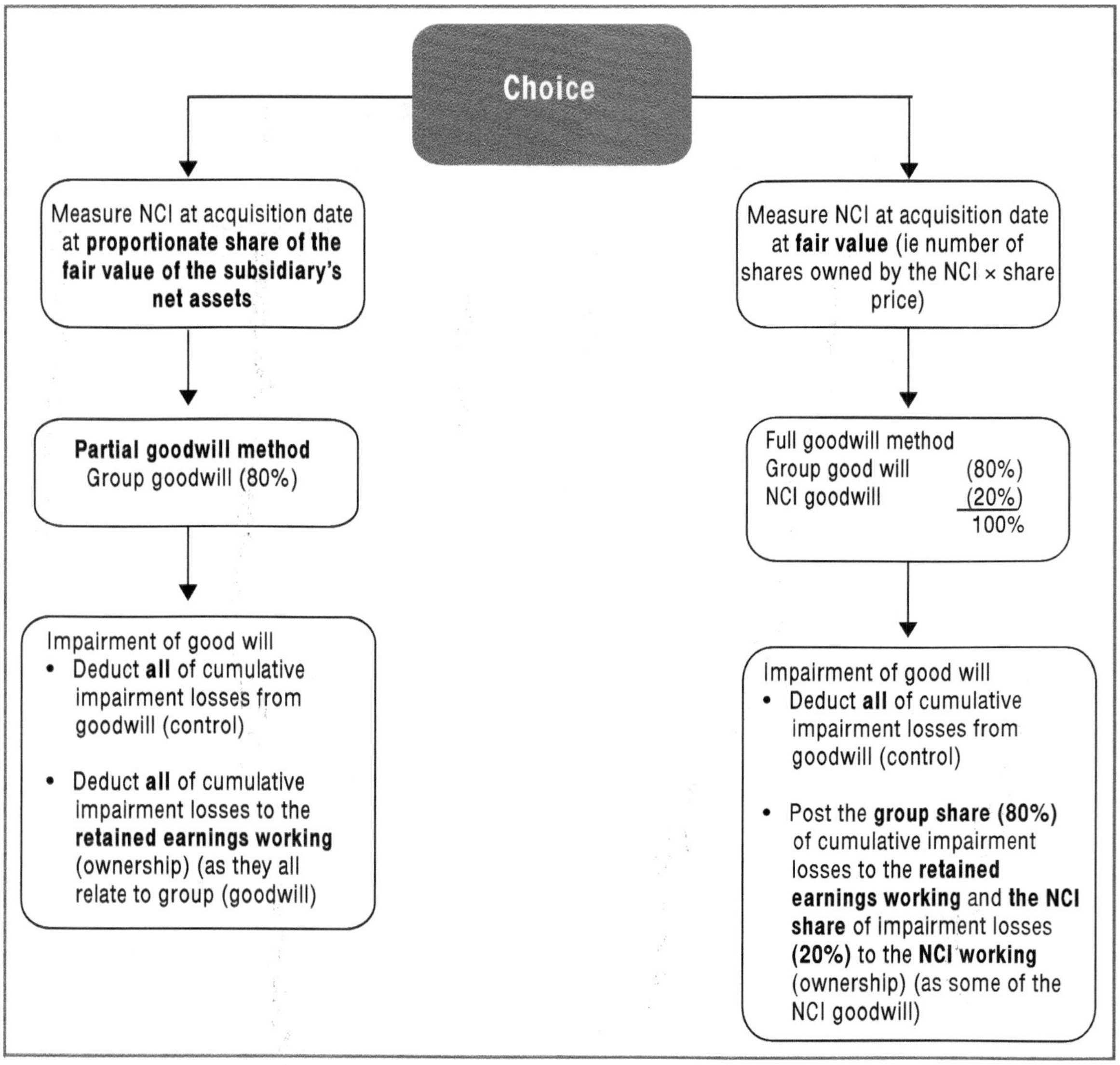

```
                                    Choice
                    ┌──────────────────┴──────────────────┐
                    ▼                                     ▼
        Measure NCI at acquisition date         Measure NCI at acquisition date
        at proportionate share of the           at fair value (ie number of
        fair value of the subsidiary's          shares owned by the NCI × share
                 net assets                                 price)
                    │                                     │
                    ▼                                     ▼
           Partial goodwill method              Full goodwill method
           Group goodwill (80%)                 Group good will      (80%)
                                                NCI goodwill         (20%)
                                                                     100%
                    │                                     │
                    ▼                                     ▼
        Impairment of good will                 Impairment of good will
        • Deduct all of cumulative              • Deduct all of cumulative
          impairment losses from                  impairment losses from
          goodwill (control)                      goodwill (control)

        • Deduct all of cumulative              • Post the group share (80%)
          impairment losses to the                of cumulative impairment
          retained earnings working               losses to the retained
          (ownership) (as they all                earnings working and the NCI
          relate to group (goodwill))             share of impairment losses
                                                  (20%) to the NCI working
                                                  (ownership) (as some of the
                                                  NCI goodwill)
```

Exam focus point

The examiner may refer to valuation at (full) fair value as the 'full goodwill' method.

3.6.4 Goodwill calculation: Simple examples

Now we will look at goodwill calculations on the two bases: the IFRS 3 proportion of net assets method and the IFRS 3 fair value method.

(a) **IFRS 3 proportion of net assets method**

On 31 December 20X8, Penn acquired 4 million of the 5 million $1 ordinary shares of Sylvania, paying $10m in cash. On that date, the fair value of Sylvania's net assets was $7.5m.

It is the group's policy to value the non-controlling interest at its proportionate share of the fair value of the subsidiary's identifiable net assets.

Calculate goodwill on the acquisition.

Answer

	$'000	$'000
Consideration transferred	10,000	
Non-controlling interest: 20% × $7.5m		1,500
Fair value of net assets acquired: 80%/20% × $7.5m	(6,000)	(1,500)
Goodwill	4,000	–

BPP note. You will see that the NCI column is not needed because the figures cancel each other out.

(b) **IFRS 3 fair value method**

On 31 December 20X8, Penn acquired 4 million of the 5 million $1 ordinary shares of Sylvania, paying $10m in cash. On that date, the fair value of Sylvania's net assets was $7.5m.

It is the group's policy to value the non-controlling interest at fair value. The market price of the shares held by the non-controlling shareholders just before the acquisition was $2.00

Calculate goodwill on the acquisition.

Answer

	$'000	$'000
Consideration transferred/FV NCI	10,000	2,000
Fair value of net assets acquired: 80%/20% × $7.5m	(6,000)	(1,500)
Goodwill	4,000	500

Goodwill attributable to non-controlling interest is $500,000

Total goodwill on the acquisition (parent + NCI) is $4m + $0.5m = $4.5m.

> **BPP note.** The goodwill attributable to the non-controlling interest is not in proportion to that attributable to the parent. If it were in proportion, the total goodwill would be $4m × 100%/80% = $5m, and so the goodwill attributable to the NCI would be $1m.

3.6.5 Why is the goodwill attributable to the NCI not always proportionate?

In Example (b) above, the goodwill attributable to the non-controlling interest is not in proportion to that attributable to the parent. Generally, this is because owners of the parent have paid a higher price in order to obtain control. You can calculate the share price the owners of the parent must have paid – it is $10m/4m, that is $2.50 per share. The premium to acquire control may reflect the value of synergies between the parent and subsidiary.

3.6.6 Subsequent measurement of the non-controlling interest

Subsequent to acquisition the non-controlling interest will increase (or decrease) by the NCI share of any post-acquisition movement in the subsidiary's reserves. IFRS 10 *Consolidated Financial Statements* requires that this is the case even if it results in the non-controlling interests having a deficit balance due to the allocation of losses.

Your calculation of non-controlling interest at the year-end will look like this:

	$'000	$'000
Share capital	X	
Retained earnings	X	
Provision for unrealised profit	X	
NCI share of identifiable net assets (a × NCI %)		X
NCI share of goodwill (FV method only)		X
Non-controlling interest		X

Note that the NCI share of goodwill is added on only where the parent has opted to measure the NCI at the acquisition date at fair value.

An alternative calculation involves increasing the acquisition date fair value of the non-controlling interest by the NCI share of post-acquisition profits:

	$'000
FV of the NCI at acquisition	X
NCI share of post-acquisition profits	X
Non-controlling interest	X

Because the NCI share of goodwill is included in both the top half of the statement of financial position (within total goodwill), and in the bottom half (within the NCI), the statement of financial position will balance.

3.6.7 Goodwill impairment under the full goodwill method

Where the full goodwill method is used, IAS 36 *Impairment of Assets* requires a subsidiary's goodwill impairment loss to be allocated between the parent and the non-controlling interest on the same basis as the subsidiary's profits and losses are allocated. Thus if there is an impairment loss of $1 million in respect of a subsidiary in which the parent holds a 75% stake, $750,000 would be allocated to the parent (and debited to group retained earnings) and $250,000 would be allocated to the NCI.

It could be argued that this requirement represents an anomaly; looking back to the calculation in Section 1.7.5 (b) above, of the recognised goodwill of $4.5 million only $500,000 (ie 11%) relates to the NCI, but it will suffer 25% of any goodwill impairment.

In other words, **the impairment of the goodwill is allocated proportionately, even if the goodwill on the non-controlling interest is not itself proportionate.**

> **Exam focus point**
>
> You are required to know **both** methods of measuring the NCI in FAR 2. Questions will normally ask specifically for one or other method.
>
> There are a number of ways of presenting the information to test the fair value method:
>
> (i) As above, the subsidiary's share price just before the acquisition could be given and then used to value the non-controlling interest. It would then be a matter of multiplying the share price by the number of shares held by the non-controlling interests. (**Note.** the parent is likely to have paid more than the subsidiary's pre acquisition share price in order to gain control.)
>
> (ii) The question could simply state that the directors valued the non-controlling interest at the date of acquisition at $2 million.
>
> (iii) An alternative approach would be to give (in the question) the value of the goodwill attributable to the non-controlling interest. In this case the NCI's goodwill would be added to the parent's goodwill and to the carrying amount of the non-controlling interest itself.

4 IFRS 10 *Consolidated Financial Statements*

> **FAST FORWARD**
>
> **IFRS 10** *Consolidated Financial Statements* provides accounting guidance on the consolidation procedures to be applied when preparing the combined financial statements of a parent and its subsidiaries

Consolidated financial statements are prepared for a parent and its subsidiaries. We have already seen that an entity is a subsidiary when it is **controlled** by another entity.

Where a parent controls one or more subsidiaries, IFRS 10 requires, with limited exemptions, that consolidated financial statements are prepared to include **all subsidiaries, both foreign and domestic** other than:

- Those held for sale in accordance with IFRS 5
- Those held under such long-term restrictions that control cannot be operated.

The rules on exclusion of subsidiaries from consolidation are necessarily strict, because this is a common method used by entities to manipulate their results. If a subsidiary which carries a large amount of debt can be excluded, then the gearing of the group as a whole will be improved. In other words, this is a way of taking debt **off the statement of financial position**.

It has been argued that subsidiaries should be excluded from consolidation on the grounds of **dissimilar activities**, ie the activities of the subsidiary are so different to the activities of the other companies within the group that to include its results in the consolidation would be misleading. IFRS 10 rejects this argument: exclusion on these grounds is not justified because better (relevant) information can be provided about such subsidiaries by consolidating their results and then giving additional information about the different business activities of the subsidiary, eg under IFRS 8 *Operating Segments*.

4.1 Exemption from preparing group financial statements

A parent **need not present** consolidated financial statements if and only if:

(a) It is a **wholly owned subsidiary** or it is a **partially owned subsidiary** of another entity and its other owners, including those not otherwise entitled to vote, have been informed about, and do not object to, the parent not presenting consolidated financial statements;

(b) Its securities are **not publicly traded;**

(c) It is **not in the process of issuing securities** in public securities markets; **and**

(d) The **ultimate or intermediate parent** publishes financial statements that are available for public use and comply with IFRSs, in which subsidiaries are consolidated or are measured at fair value through profit or loss in accordance with this IFRS.

A parent that does not present consolidated financial statements must comply with the IAS 27 (2011) rules on separate financial statements (discussed later in the chapter).

4.1.1 Investment Entities

An investment entity is defined as an entity that:

(a) Obtains funds from one or more investors for the purpose of providing those investors with investment management services;

(b) Commits to its investors that its business purpose is to invest funds solely for returns from capital appreciation, investment income, or both; and

(c) Measures and evaluates the performance of substantially all of its investments on a fair value basis.

IFRS 10 excludes investment entities from applying IFRS 3 and preparing consolidated accounts and instead requires that such investments are financial assets measured at fair value through profit or loss in accordance with IFRS 9 (see Chapter 14).

4.2 Consolidation procedures

4.2.1 Preparation of consolidated financial statements

In order to prepare consolidated financial statements, the following procedures are applied:

1. Assets, liabilities, income and expenses are combined on a line by line basis.
2. The carrying amount of the parent's investment in each subsidiary and the parent's proportion of equity in each subsidiary are eliminated.
3. Non-controlling interests representing the equity of subsidiaries which does not belong to the parent are recognised.

4.2.2 Intragroup transactions

As the consolidated financial statements are prepared for a group as a single economic entity, intra-group balances and transactions should be eliminated as part of the consolidation process. You should be familiar with the common intragroup transactions from your previous studies. Here is a reminder of the key adjustments:

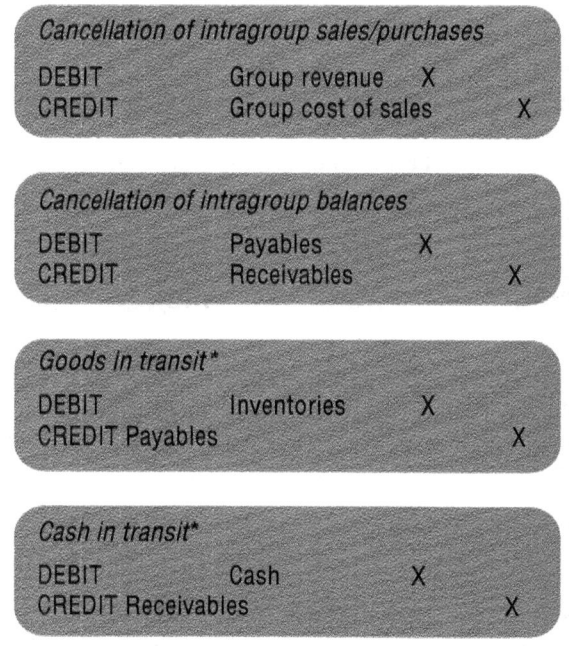

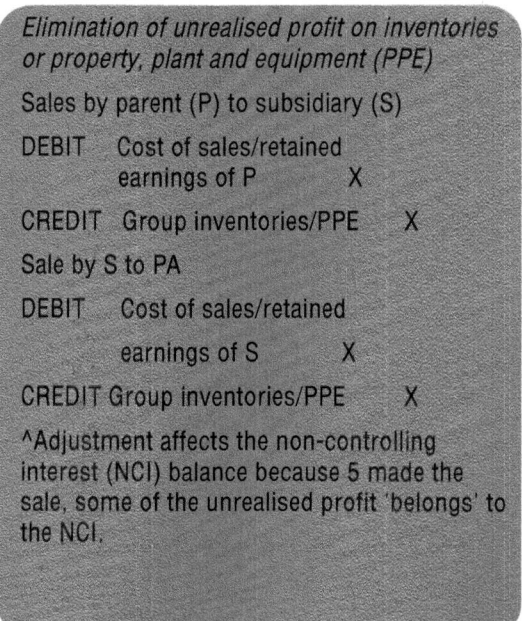

4.2.3 Different reporting dates

In most cases, all group companies will prepare financial statements to the same reporting date. One or more subsidiaries may, however, prepare financial statements to a different reporting date from the parent and the bulk of other subsidiaries in the group.

In such cases the subsidiary may prepare additional statements to the reporting date of the rest of the group, for consolidation purposes. If this is not possible, the subsidiary's financial statements may still be used for the consolidation, **provided that** the gap between the reporting dates is **three months or less**.

Where a subsidiary's financial statements are drawn up to a different accounting date, **adjustments should be made** for the effects of significant transactions or other events that occur between that date and the parent's reporting date.

4.2.4 Uniform accounting policies

Consolidated financial statements should be prepared using **the same accounting policies** for like transactions and other events in similar circumstances.

Adjustments must be made where members of a group use different accounting policies, so that their financial statements are suitable for consolidation.

4.2.5 Date of inclusion/exclusion

The results of subsidiary undertakings are included in the consolidated financial statements from:

(a) The date of 'acquisition', ie the **date control passes to the parent**; to
(b) The date of 'disposal', ie the **date control passes from the parent**

Once an investment is no longer a subsidiary, it should be treated as an associate under IAS 28 (2003) (if applicable) or as a financial asset investment under IFRS 9.

4.3 Revision: Summary of techniques

The summary given below is very brief but it encompasses all the major, but basic, rules of consolidation for, firstly, the consolidated statement of financial position.

> Knowledge brought forward from earlier studies

Summary of technique: Consolidated statement of financial position

- **Net assets**: 100% P plus 100% S.
- **Share capital**: P only.
- **Reserves**: 100% P plus group share of post-acquisition retained reserves of S less consolidation adjustments.
- **Non-controlling interest**: NCI share of S's consolidated net assets (**proportion of net assets method**).
  NCI share of S's consolidated net assets plus NCI share of goodwill (**fair value method**).

The method of consolidation is as follows:

- Determine the **group structure**. Draw chart showing the percentages holdings and dates of acquisition.

- Consider **adjustments** for:
  - Dividends
  - Provisions for unrealised profits (PUP)
  - Revaluations to fair value
  - Intragroup inventory and cash in transit

- Combine **net assets**, cancelling any **intra-group balances**.
  - Current accounts
  - Debentures

- **Share capital** of P only

- Calculate the **non-controlling interest** in net assets

NCI % of share capital	X
NCI % of reserves	X
NCI % of revaluations to fair value	X
NCI goodwill (if NCI measured at FV at acquisition)	X
NCI % of unrealised profit	(X)
	X

  Or

NCI at acquisition date (either a proportion of net assets or FV)	X
NCI % of post-acquisition movement in reserves	X/(X)
	X

PART B BUSINESS COMBINATIONS AND GROUP FINANCIAL STATEMENTS

- Calculate the **goodwill (positive or negative)**

Consideration transferred	X
NCI (proportion of net assets or FV)	X
Assets acquired	
Share capital	(X)
Pre-acquisition reserves	(X)
Revaluation to fair value	(X)
Goodwill	X

- If cost is **greater than** the share of net assets acquired, then the difference is **goodwill**, which should be capitalised and retained in the statement of financial position, subject to annual impairment reviews (see Chapter 13).

- If cost is **less than** the share of net assets acquired, then the difference is a **gain on bargain purchase** (sometimes termed **negative** goodwill). The treatment of this is also discussed in Chapter 13.

- **Calculate retained earnings reserve**

	P	S	A
Per question	X	X	X
Adjustments	X(X)	X(X)	X(X)
Fair value adjustment (% × adj)		X/(X)	X/(X)
Accumulated profits at acquisition	–	(X)	(X)
	X	X	X
Share of post acquisition profits of subsidiary (% × X)	X		
	X		

The technique for the preparation of a **consolidated statement of profit or loss and other comprehensive income** is given below

---

Summary of technique: Consolidated statement of profit or loss and other comprehensive income

Adjustments required for consolidation of a subsidiary are as follows.

- Eliminate **intra-group sales and purchases**.
- Eliminate any **unrealised profits** on intra-group purchases still in inventory at the year end.
- Eliminate any **intra-group** interest receivable/payable dividends receivable.
- Analyse profit for the year between owners of the parent and NCI.

For the inclusion of a subsidiary carry out the following:

- **Combine all P and S results** from turnover to profit for the year (where the acquisition is mid-year, use a time-apportioned basis).

- **Calculate NCI**:
  - Where there are no preference shares: NCI = % × profit for the year
  - Where there are preference shares an additional working is required

Unrealised profits/losses

Only where **S sells to P**, allocate the unrealised profit between NCI and P: *Debit* Group reserves, *Debit* non-controlling interest, *Credit* Inventory.

Now try the following questions to refresh your memory on the topics listed above.

Question

Revision of basic groups

Boo Co has owned 80% of Goose Co's equity since its incorporation. On 31 December 20X8 it despatched goods which cost $80,000 to Goose, at an invoiced cost of $100,000. Goose received the goods on 2 January 20X9 and recorded the transaction then. The two companies' draft financial statements as at 31 December 20X8 are shown below.

STATEMENTS OF PROFIT OR LOSS AND OTHER COMPREHENSIVE INCOME

	Boo $'000	Goose $'000
Revenue	5,000	1,000
Cost of sales	2,900	600
Gross profit	2,100	400
Other expenses	1,700	320
Profit before tax	400	80
Income tax	130	25
Profit for the year	270	55

STATEMENTS OF CHANGES IN EQUITY (SUMMARY)

	$'000	$'000
Opening balance	2,260	285
Total comprehensive income (profit) for the year	270	55
Dividends paid	(130)	–
Closing balance	2,400	340

STATEMENTS OF FINANCIAL POSITION

	Boo $'000	Boo $'000	Goose $'000	Goose $'000
Assets				
Non-current assets				
Property, plant and equipment		1,920		200
Investment in Goose		80		–
		2,000		200
Current assets				
Inventory	500		120	
Trade receivables	650		40	
Bank and cash	390		35	
		1,540		195
		3,540		395
Equity and liabilities				
Equity				
Share capital		2,000		100
Retained earnings		400		240
		2,400		340
Current liabilities				
Trade payables	1,010		30	
Tax	130		25	
		1,140		55
		3,540		395

Required

Prepare draft consolidated financial statements.

Answer

BOO GROUP
CONSOLIDATED STATEMENT OF PROFIT OR LOSS AND OTHER COMPREHENSIVE INCOME FOR THE YEAR ENDED 31 DECEMBER 20X8

	$'000
Revenue (5,000 + 1,000 – 100)	5,900
Cost of sales (2,900 + 600 – 80)	3,420
Gross profit	2,480
Other expenses (1,700 + 320)	2,020
Profit before tax	460
Income tax (130 + 25)	155
Profit for the year	305
Profit attributable to:	
Owners of the parent	294
Non-controlling interest (20% × 55)	11
	305

CONSOLIDATED STATEMENT OF CHANGES IN EQUITY (SUMMARY)
FOR THE YEAR ENDED 31 DECEMBER 20X8

	Group $'000	NCI $'000
Opening balance (balancing figure)	2,408	57
Group profit for the year (as above)	294	11
Dividends paid	(130)	–
Closing balance (per statement of financial position)	2,572	68

CONSOLIDATED STATEMENT OF FINANCIAL POSITION AS AT 31 DECEMBER 20X8

	$'000	$'000
Assets		
Non-current assets (1,920 + 200)		2,120
Current assets		
Inventory (500 + 120 + 80)	700	
Trade receivables (650 – 100 + 40)	590	
Bank and cash (390 + 35)	425	
		1,715
		3,835
Equity and liabilities		
Equity		
Share capital (Boo only)		2,000
Retained earnings (W)		572
Shareholders' funds		2,572
Non-controlling interest (20% × 340)		68
		2,640
Current liabilities		
Trade payables (1,010 + 30)	1,040	
Income tax (130 + 25)	155	
		1,195
		3,835

Working: Group retained earnings

	Boo $'000	Goose $'000
Per question	400	200
Closing inventory in transit (at cost)	80	
Intercompany sale	(100)	
Share of Goose ($240 × 80%)	192	
Group net owned profits	572	

This working is, of course, only necessary when you are not required to prepare the consolidated income statement. Here, it serves as a proof of the consolidated income statement as well as of the reserves figure in the statement of financial position.

Question — NCI at proportion of net assets

The draft statements of financial position of Oak and its subsidiary Chestnut at 30 September 20X8 are as follows:

	Oak $	Oak $	Chestnut $	Chestnut $
Non-current assets				
Land and buildings		225,000		270,000
Plant		202,500		157,500
		427,500		427,500
Investment				
Shares in Chestnut at cost		562,500		
Current assets				
Inventory	255,000		180,000	
Receivables	375,000		90,000	
Bank	112,500		22,500	
		742,500		292,500
		1,732,500		720,000
Equity				
Called up share capital – issued and fully paid				
$1 ordinary shares		1,125,000		450,000
Retained earnings		450,000		202,500
		1,575,000		652,500
Current liabilities		157,500		67,500
		1,732,500		720,000

The following information is also available:

(a) Oak purchased 360,000 shares in Chestnut some years ago when that company had a credit balance of $105,000 in retained earnings. The goodwill had been impaired and was fully written off in profit or loss by 30 September 20X7.

(b) For the purpose of the takeover, the land of Chestnut was revalued at $120,000 in excess of its carrying amount. This was not reflected in the financial statements of Chestnut. Land is not depreciated.

(c) At 30 September 20X8 Chestnut owed Oak $15,000 for goods purchased.

(d) The inventory of Chestnut includes goods purchased from Oak at a price which includes a profit to Oak of $10,500.

(e) It is the group's policy to value the non-controlling interest at its proportionate share of the fair value of the subsidiary's identifiable net assets.

PART B BUSINESS COMBINATIONS AND GROUP FINANCIAL STATEMENTS

Required

Prepare the consolidated statement of financial position for Oak as at 30 September 20X8.

BPP hint. You don't need a separate column for non-controlling interest in the goodwill working.

Answer

OAK
CONSOLIDATED STATEMENT OF FINANCIAL POSITION AS AT 30 SEPTEMBER 20X8

	$	$
Non-current assets		
Land and buildings (W5)		615,000
Plant (202,500 + 157,500)		360,000
		975,000
Current assets		
Inventory (W6)	424,500	
Receivables (W7)	450,000	
Bank (112,500 + 22,500)	135,000	
		1,009,500
		1,984,500
Equity		
Ordinary $1 shares		1,125,000
Retained earnings (W3)		495,000
		1,620,000
Non-controlling interest (W4)		154,500
Total equity		
Current liabilities one year (W8)		210,000
		1,984,500

Workings

1. Group structure: $\frac{360,000}{450,000} = 80\%$

2. Goodwill

	$	$
Consideration transferred		562,500
Net assets acquired		
Share capital	450,000	
Reserves	105,000	
Revaluation surplus	120,000	
	675,000	
Group share: 80%		540,000
Goodwill – fully impaired (see W3)		22,500

3. Retained earnings

	Oak $	Chestnut $
Oak	450,000	202,500
Goodwill written off as impaired (W2)	(22,500)	
Unrealised profit	(10,500)	
Retained earnings at acquisition		(105,000)
	417,000	97,500
Chestnut × 80%	78,000	
	495,000	

4 Non-controlling interests

	$
Share capital	450,000
Retained earnings	202,500
Revaluation surplus	120,000
	772,500
20% × $772,500 =	$154,500

5 Land and buildings

	$	$
Oak		225,000
Chestnut:		
Carrying amount	270,000	
Revaluation surplus	120,000	
		390,000
		615,000

6 Inventory

	$
Oak	255,000
Chestnut	180,000
Less unrealised profit	(10,500)
	424,500

7 Receivables

	$
Oak	375,000
Chestnut	90,000
Less intragroup	(15,000)
	450,000

8 Current liabilities

	$
Oak	157,500
Chestnut	67,500
Less intragroup	(15,000)
	210,000

Question — Non-controlling interest at fair value

You are provided with the following statements of financial position for Shark and Minnow.

STATEMENTS OF FINANCIAL POSITION AS AT 31 OCTOBER 20X0

	Shark		Minnow	
	$'000	$'000	$'000	$'000
Non-current assets, at book value				
Plant		325		70
Fixtures		200		50
		525		120
Investment				
Shares in Minnow at cost		200		
Current assets				
Inventory at cost	220		70	
Receivables	145		105	
Bank	100		0	
		465		175
		1,190		295

PART B BUSINESS COMBINATIONS AND GROUP FINANCIAL STATEMENTS

	Shark		Minnow	
	$'000	$'000	$'000	$'000
Equity				
$1 Ordinary shares		700		170
Retained earnings		215		50
		915		220
Current liabilities				
Payables	275		55	
Bank overdraft	0		20	
		275		75
		1,190		295

The following information is also available:

(a) Shark purchased 70% of the issued ordinary share capital of Minnow four years ago, when the retained earnings of Minnow were $20,000. There has been no impairment of goodwill.

(b) For the purposes of the acquisition, plant in Minnow with a book value of $50,000 was revalued to its fair value of $60,000. The revaluation was not recorded in the financial statements of Minnow. Depreciation is charged at 20% using the straight-line method.

(c) Shark sells goods to Minnow at a mark-up of 25%. At 31 October 20X0, the inventories of Minnow included $45,000 of goods purchased from Shark.

(d) Minnow owes Shark $35,000 for goods purchased and Shark owes Minnow $15,000.

(e) It is the group's policy to value the non-controlling interest at fair value.

(f) The market price of the shares of the non-controlling shareholders just before the acquisition was $1.50.

Required

Prepare the consolidated statement of financial position of Shark as at 31 October 20X0.

Answer

SHARK
CONSOLIDATED STATEMENT OF FINANCIAL POSITION AS AT 31 OCTOBER 20X0

	$'000	$'000
Non-current assets		
Plant (W4)	397	
Fixtures (200 + 50)	250	
		647
Intangible asset: Goodwill (W1)		77
		724
Current assets		
Inventory (W5)	281	
Receivables (W6)	200	
Bank	100	
		581
		1,305
Capital and reserves		
Share capital		700
Retained earnings (W2)		221
		921

	$'000	$'000
Non-controlling interests (W3)		84
Total equity		1,005
Current liabilities		
Payables (W7)	280	
Bank overdraft	20	
		300
		1,305

Workings

1   Goodwill

		Group	NCI
	$'000	$'000	$'000
Consideration transferred/FV NCI		200	76.5
(30% × 170,000 × $1.50)			
Net assets acquired			
Share capital	170		
Retained earnings	20		
Revaluation surplus (60 – 50)	10		
	200		
Group/NCI share: 70%/30%		140	60.0
Goodwill in parent		60	16.5

$76.5m

2   Retained earnings

	Shark $'000	Minnow $'000
Shark	215.0	50.0
PUP (W5)	(9.0)	
Excess depn on plant (W4)		(8.0)
Retained earnings at acquisition		(20.0)
	206.0	22.0
Minnow (22 × 70%)	15.4	
	221.4	

3   Non-controlling interests

	$'000	$'000
Share capital		170
Revaluation surplus	10	
Less excess depreciation (W4)	(8)	
		2
Retained earnings		50
		222
NCI in sub's identifiable net assets: 30% × $222,000		67
Goodwill attributable to NCI (W1)		17
Non-controlling interest		84

4   Plant

	$'000	$'000
Shark		325
Minnow		
Per question	70	
Revaluation surplus (60 – 50)	10	
Depreciation thereon (10 × 20% × 4)	(8)	
		72
		397

5   Inventory

	$'000	$'000
Shark		220
Minnow	70	
Less PUP (45 × $^{25}/_{125}$)	(9)	
		61
		281

6   Receivables

	$'000	$'000
Shark		145
Less intragroup		(35)
		110
Minnow	105	
Less intragroup	(15)	
		90
		200

7   Payables

	$'000	$'000
Shark		275
Less intragroup		(15)
		260
Minnow	55	
Less intragroup	(35)	
		20
		280

5 IFRS 3 – further issues

FAST FORWARD

Goodwill arising on consolidation is the excess of the fair value of the consideration transferred plus the non-controlling interest over the fair value of the identifiable assets and liabilities acquired.

We have already considered the basic requirements of IFRS 3, and considered the calculation of goodwill:

	$
Consideration transferred	X
Amount of any non-controlling interests	X
	X
Less net acquisition-date fair value of identifiable assets acquired and liabilities assumed	(X)
	X

Goodwill is specifically calculated as the difference between the consideration transferred plus the non-controlling interest and the **fair value** of the **identifiable** net assets of the acquiree.

Consideration must therefore be given to the fair value of the identifiable net assets of the acquiree, and in particular:

1   The meaning of identifiable and the recognition principles applied to the assets and liabilities of the acquiree, and

2   The measurement principle and establishing the fair value of the identifiable assets and liabilities of the acquiree.

5.1 Recognition principles

An asset or liability is identifiable if it is either:

- Separable ie capable of being separated from the entity and sold or transferred either individually or with a related contract or
- Arises from contractual or other legal rights, regardless of whether those rights are transferable from the entity.

Identifiable assets and liabilities are recognised as net assets of the acquiree within the goodwill calculation where:

- They meet the definition of assets and liabilities in the *Conceptual Framework;* and
- Are part of the business combination transaction rather than the result of separate transactions.

There are limited exceptions to the recognition principles and these are considered later in this section.

5.1.1 Recognition of intangible assets

It is important to note that as a result of the recognition principles, an acquirer must recognise acquired identifiable intangible assets (such as internally generated brand names, patents or customer relationships), even if the acquiree did not recognise the assets in its own financial statements).

5.1.2 Restructuring costs and future losses

An acquirer should not recognise liabilities for future losses or other costs expected to be incurred as a result of the business combination.

IFRS 3 explains that a plan to restructure a subsidiary following an acquisition is not a present obligation of the acquiree at the acquisition date. Neither does it meet the definition of a contingent liability. Therefore an acquirer **should not recognise a liability for** such **a restructuring plan** as part of allocating the cost of the combination unless the subsidiary was already committed to the plan before the acquisition.

This **prevents creative accounting**. An acquirer cannot set up a provision for restructuring or future losses of a subsidiary and then release this to profit or loss in subsequent periods in order to reduce losses or smooth profits.

5.2 Measurement principles

IFRS 3 requires that the identifiable assets and liabilities of an acquiree are measured at their acquisition date fair value. Fair value is defined by IFRS 13 *Fair Value Measurement.*

Key term

> **Fair value**. The price that would be received to sell an asset or paid to transfer a liability in an orderly transaction between market participants at the measurement date.

The IFRS 13 guidance with regard to establishing fair value is applicable to business combinations. This is covered in Chapter 11.

Again, there are some exceptions listed within IFRS 3 to the measurement principles.

5.3 Exceptions to the recognition and measurement principles

IFRS 3 provides limited exceptions to the recognition and measurement principles discussed above.

5.3.1 Contingent liabilities

Contingent liabilities of the acquirer are **recognised** if their **fair value can be measured reliably**. A **contingent liability** must be recognised even if the outflow is not probable, provided there is a present obligation.

This is a departure from the normal rules in IAS 37; contingent liabilities are not normally recognised, but only disclosed.

After their initial recognition, the acquirer should measure contingent liabilities that are recognised separately at the higher of:

(a) The amount that would be recognised in accordance with IAS 37
(b) The amount initially recognised

5.3.2 Income taxes

A deferred tax asset or liability arising from the assets acquired and liabilities assumed in a business combination is recognised and measured in accordance with IAS 12 *Income Taxes*.

5.3.3 Employee benefits

A liability (or asset) related to the acquiree's employee benefit arrangements is recognised in accordance with IAS 19 *Employee Benefits*.

5.3.4 Share-based payment transactions

A liability or an equity instrument related to the share-based payment transactions of the acquiree is measured in accordance with the method in IFRS 2 *Share-based Payment*.

5.3.5 Assets held for sale

An acquired non-current asset or disposal group that is classified as held for sale at the acquisition date is measured in accordance with IFRS 5 *Non-current Assets Held for Sale and Discontinued Operations*.

5.3.6 Indemnification assets

The measurement of an indemnification asset should be consistent with the measurement of the indemnified item, for example an employee benefit or a contingent liability.

5.3.7 Reacquired rights

Reacquired rights are valued on the basis of the remaining contractual term of the related contract regardless of whether market participants would consider potential contractual renewals in determining its fair value.

5.4 Consolidation adjustments

In order to comply with IFRS 3, we must ensure that the subsidiary's identifiable net assets are all included in the goodwill calculation at their **fair value**. They will also be recognised in the consolidated statement of financial position at this amount.

In the case of items which are recognised by the acquiree in its own financial statements but not held at fair value, there are two possible ways of achieving this.

(a) The **subsidiary company** might **incorporate any necessary revaluations** in its own books of account. In this case, we can proceed directly to the consolidation, taking asset values and reserves figures straight from the subsidiary company's statement of financial position.

(b) The **revaluations** may be made as a **consolidation adjustment without being incorporated** in the subsidiary company's books. In this case, we must make the necessary adjustments to the subsidiary's statement of financial position as a working. Only then can we proceed to the consolidation.

Note. Remember that when depreciating assets are revalued, there may be a corresponding alteration in the amount of depreciation charged and accumulated.

Where an asset is not recognised by the acquiree, however is identifiable and meets the recognition principles of IFRS 3, the second approach must be used ie a consolidation adjustment is required.

5.5 Example: Fair value adjustments

P Co acquired 75% of the ordinary shares of S Co on 1 September 20X5. At that date the fair value of S Co's non-current assets was $23,000 greater than their carrying amount, and the balance of retained earnings was $21,000. The statements of financial position of both companies at 31 August 20X6 are given below. S Co has not incorporated any revaluation in its books of account.

P CO
STATEMENT OF FINANCIAL POSITION AS AT 31 AUGUST 20X6

	$	$
Assets		
Non-current assets		
Property, plant and equipment	63,000	
Investment in S Co at cost	51,000	
		114,000
Current assets		82,000
Total assets		196,000
Equity and liabilities		
Equity		
Ordinary shares of $1 each	80,000	
Retained earnings	96,000	
		176,000
Current liabilities		20,000
Total equity and liabilities		196,000

S CO
STATEMENT OF FINANCIAL POSITION AS AT 31 AUGUST 20X6

	$	$
Assets		
Property, plant and equipment		28,000
Current assets		43,000
Total assets		71,000
Equity and liabilities		
Equity		
Ordinary shares of $1 each	20,000	
Retained earnings	41,000	
		61,000
Current liabilities		10,000
Total equity and liabilities		71,000

If S Co had revalued its non-current assets at 1 September 20X5, an addition of $3,000 would have been made to the depreciation charged to profit or loss for 20X5/X6. It is the group's policy to value the non-controlling interest at acquisition at its proportionate share of the fair value of the subsidiary's net assets.

Required

Prepare P Co's consolidated statement of financial position as at 31 August 20X6.

Solution

S Co has not incorporated the revaluation in its draft statement of financial position. Before beginning the consolidation workings we must therefore adjust the company's balance of profits at the date of acquisition and at the year end.

S Co adjusted balance of retained earnings

	$	$
Balance per financial statements at 1 September 20X5		21,000
Consolidation adjustment: revaluation surplus		23,000
∴ Pre-acquisition profits for consolidation purposes		44,000
Profit for year ended 31 August 20X6		
Per draft financial statements $(41,000 – 21,000)	20,000	
Consolidation adjustment: increase in depreciation charge	(3,000)	
		17,000
Adjusted balance of retained earnings at 31 August 20X6		61,000

In the consolidated statement of financial position, S Co's non-current assets will appear at their revalued amount: $(28,000 + 23,000 – 3,000) = $48,000. The consolidation workings can now be drawn up.

1 *Goodwill*

	$	$
Consideration transferred		51,000
Non-controlling interest (64,000 × 25%)		16,000
		67,000
Share of net assets acquired as represented by		
Ordinary share capital	20,000	
Retained earnings		
$(21,000 + 23,000)	44,000	
		(64,000)
Goodwill		3,000

2 *Retained earnings*

	P Co $	S Co $
Per question	96,000	41,000
Pre-acquisition profits		(21,000)
Depreciation adjustment		(3,000)
Post-acquisition S Co		17,000
Group share in S Co		
($17,000 × 75%)	12,750	
Group retained earnings	108,750	

3 *Non-controlling interest*

	$
Share capital (25% × $20,000)	5,000
Retained earnings (25% × $61,000)	15,250
	20,250

P CO CONSOLIDATED STATEMENT OF FINANCIAL POSITION AS AT 31 AUGUST 20X6

	$	$
Assets		
Property, plant and equipment $(63,000 + 48,000)	111,000	
Goodwill	3,000	
		114,000
Current assets $(82,000 + 43,000)		125,000
		239,000

6: REVISION OF BASIC GROUPS

	$	$
Equity and liabilities		
Equity		
Ordinary shares of $1 each	80,000	
Retained earnings	108,750	
		188,750
Non-controlling interest		20,250
		209,000
Current liabilities $(20,000 + 10,000)		30,000
		239,000

Question — Fair value

An asset is recorded in S Co's books at its historical cost of $4,000. On 1 January 20X5 P Co bought 80% of S Co's equity and attributed a fair value of $3,000 to the asset. At that date it had been depreciated for two years out of an expected life of four years on the straight line basis. There was no expected residual value. On 30 June 20X5 the asset was sold for $2,600. What is the profit or loss on disposal of this asset to be recorded in S Co's financial statements and in P Co's consolidated financial statements for the year ended 31 December 20X5?

Answer

S Co: Carrying amount at disposal (at historical cost) = $4,000 × (4 − 2½)/4 = $1,500
∴ Profit on disposal = $1,100 (depreciation charge for the year = $500)

P Co: Carrying amount at disposal (at fair value) = $3,000 × (2 − ½)/2 = $2,250
∴ Profit on disposal for consolidation = $350 (depreciation for the year = $750)

The non-controlling interest would be credited with 20% of both items as part of the one line entry in the income statement.

Question — More fair values

Tyzo Co prepares financial statements to 31 December. On 1 September 20X7 Tyzo Co acquired 6 million $1 shares in Kono Co at $2.00 per share. At that date Kono Co produced the following interim financial statements.

	$m		$m
Property, plant and equipment		Trade payables	3.2
(note 1)	16.0	Taxation	0.6
Inventories (note 2)	4.0	Bank overdraft	3.9
Receivables	2.9	Non-current loans	4.0
Cash in hand	1.2	Share capital ($1 shares)	8.0
		Reserves	4.4
	24.1		24.1

Notes.

1. The property, plant and equipment of Kono Co had a fair value of $16.8 million at 1 September 20X7.

2. The inventories of Kono Co which were shown in the interim financial statements are raw materials at cost. They would have cost $4.2 million to replace at 1 September 20X7.

3. On 1 September 20X7 Tyzo Co took a decision to rationalise the group so as to integrate Kono Co. The costs of the rationalisation were estimated to total $3.0 million and the process was due to start on 1 March 20X8. No provision for these costs has been made in the financial statements given above.

4 Kono Co has disclosed a contingent liability relating to litigation of $200,000 in its interim financial statements.

5 Tyzo Group values the non-controlling interest using the full goodwill method. The market value of the shares not purchased by Tyzo Co on 1 September 20X7 was $1.75.

Required

Compute the goodwill on consolidation of Kono Co that will be included in the consolidated financial statements of the Tyzo Co group for the year ended 31 December 20X7, explaining your treatment of the items mentioned above. You should refer to the provisions of relevant accounting standards.

Answer

Goodwill on consolidation of Kono Co

		Group $m	NCI $m
Consideration ($2.00 × 6m)		12.0	
Non-controlling interest (2m × $1.75)			3.5
Group share of fair value of net assets acquired			
Share capital	8.0		
Pre-acquisition reserves	4.4		
Fair value adjustments			
Property, plant and equipment (16.8 – 16.0)	0.8		
Inventories (4.2 – 4.0)	0.2		
Contingent liability	(0.2)		
	(13.2)		
Group share/NCI share		(9.9)	(3.3)
Goodwill		2.1	0.2
Total Goodwill			2.3

Notes on treatment

(a) Share capital and pre-acquisition profits represent the carrying amount (book value) of the net assets of Kono Co at the date of acquisition. Adjustments are then required to this carrying amount in order to give the fair value of the net assets at the date of acquisition. For short-term monetary items, fair value is their carrying amount on acquisition.

(b) The fair value of the property, plant and equipment is $0.8m in excess of book value.

(c) The fair value of the raw materials is their replacement cost. In this case that amount is $4.2m.

(d) The rationalisation costs cannot be reported in pre-acquisition results under IFRS 3 as they are not a liability of Kono Co at the acquisition date.

(e) The contingent liability should be included as part of the acquisition net assets of Kono even though it is recognised in Kono's individual financial statements. However, the amount at which it is disclosed is not necessarily the fair value at which a third party would assume the liability. If the probability of an outflow of resources is low, then the fair value will be lower than $200,000.

5.6 Goodwill arising on acquisition

Goodwill should be carried in the statement of financial position at **cost less any accumulated impairment losses**. The treatment of goodwill is covered in detail in Chapter 13.

5.7 Adjustments after the initial accounting is complete

Sometimes the fair values of the acquiree's identifiable assets and liabilities and/or of the consideration transferred can only be determined **provisionally** by the **end of the period in which the combination** takes place. In this situation, the acquirer **should account for the combination using those provisional values**. The acquirer should **recognise any adjustments** to those provisional values as a result of completing the initial accounting:

(a) **Within the measurement period** (a maximum of 12 months from the acquisition date), and
(b) **From** the acquisition date (ie retrospectively)

This means that:

(a) The **carrying amount** of an item that is recognised or adjusted as a result of completing the initial accounting shall be calculated **as if its fair value** at the acquisition date **had been recognised from that date.**

(b) **Goodwill should be adjusted** from the acquisition date by an amount equal to the adjustment to the fair value of the item being recognised or adjusted.

Any further adjustments after the initial accounting is complete should be **recognised only to correct an error** in accordance with IAS 8 *Accounting Policies, Changes in Accounting Estimates and Errors*. Any subsequent changes in estimates are dealt with in accordance with IAS 8 (ie the effect is recognised in the current and future periods). IAS 8 requires an entity to account for an error correction retrospectively, and to present financial statements as if the error had never occurred by restating the comparative information for the prior period(s) in which the error occurred.

6 Associates

> **FAST FORWARD**
>
> IAS 28 deals with identifying and accounting for associates.

IAS 28 *Investments in Associates and Joint Ventures* provides accounting guidance on identifying and accounting for an associate.

In Section 2 we established that an associate is an entity over which the investor has significant influence. We also saw that significant influence is defined as 'the power to participate in the financial and operating policy decisions of the investee but is not control or joint control of those policies'.

This section of the chapter therefore concentrates on accounting for associates.

6.1 The equity method

IAS 28 requires all investments in associates to be accounted for using the equity method, **unless** the investment is classified as 'held for sale' in accordance with IFRS 5 in which case it should be accounted for under IFRS 5 (see Chapter 18).

6.1.1 Exemptions from applying the equity method

An investor is exempt from applying the equity method if:

(a) It is a parent exempt from preparing consolidated financial statements under IFRS 10; or
(b) All of the following apply:
   (i) The investor is a **wholly-owned subsidiary** or it is a **partially owned subsidiary** of another entity and its other owners, including those not otherwise entitled to vote, have been informed about, and do not object to, the investor not applying the equity method;
   (ii) Its securities are **not publicly traded**;
   (iii) It is **not in the process of issuing securities** in public securities markets; and
   (iv) The **ultimate or intermediate parent** publishes financial statements available for public use that comply with IFRSs, in which subsidiaries are consolidated or are measured at fair value through profit or loss in accordance with IFRS 10.

The use of the equity method should be **discontinued** from the date that the investor **ceases to have significant influence.**

From that date, the investor shall account for the investment in accordance with IFRS 9 *Financial Instruments*. The fair value of the investment at the date that it ceases to be an associate shall be regarded as its fair value on initial measurement as a financial asset under IFRS 9.

6.2 Consolidated financial statements

> **FAST FORWARD**
>
> The **equity method** should be applied in the consolidated financial statements:
>
> - **Statement of financial position**: investment in associate measured at cost plus (or minus) the group's share of the associate's post-acquisition retained profits (or losses)
> - **Statement of profit or loss and other comprehensive income**: group share of associate's profit for the year.

Many of the procedures required to apply the equity method are the same as are required for full consolidation. In particular, **intra-group unrealised profits** must be excluded.

Even if the investor pays more than asset value for its investment in its associate, there is no separate presentation of any goodwill. It is subsumed within the cost figure.

6.2.1 Consolidated statement of profit or loss and other comprehensive income

The basic principle is that the investing company (X Co) should take account of its **share of the earnings** of the associate, Y Co, whether or not Y Co distributes the earnings as dividends. X Co achieves this by adding to consolidated profit the group's share of Y Co's profit after tax (and where relevant, adding to consolidated other comprehensive income the group's share of other comprehensive income).

Notice the difference between this treatment and the **consolidation** of a subsidiary company's results. If Y Co were a subsidiary X Co would take credit for the whole of its sales revenue, cost of sales etc and would then make adjustments to allocate any profit or loss (and other comprehensive income) attributable to the non-controlling interest.

Under equity accounting, the associate's sales revenue, cost of sales and so on are **not amalgamated** with those of the group. Instead the group share of the associate's profit after tax for the year is presented as a separate line item in arriving at consolidated profit before tax. Where relevant the group share of the associate's other comprehensive income is presented as a separate line item in arriving at consolidated total comprehensive income.

6.2.2 Consolidated statement of financial position

A figure for **investment in associates** is shown which, at the time of the acquisition, must be stated at cost. This amount will increase (decrease) each year by the amount of the group's share of the associate's profit (loss) and, where relevant, other comprehensive income for the year.

6.3 Example: Associate

P Co, a company with subsidiaries, acquires 25,000 of the 100,000 $1 ordinary shares in A Co for $60,000 on 1 January 20X8. In the year to 31 December 20X8, A Co earns profits for the year of $24,000, from which it declares a dividend of $6,000.

How will A Co's results be accounted for in the individual and consolidated financial statements of P Co for the year ended 31 December 20X8?

Solution

In the **individual financial statements** of P Co, the investment will be recorded on 1 January 20X8 at cost. Unless there is an impairment in the value of the investment (see below), this amount will remain in the individual statement of financial position of P Co permanently. The only entry in P Co's individual statement of profit or loss and other comprehensive income will be to record the dividends received. For the year ended 31 December 20X8, P Co will:

DEBIT	Cash	$1,500	
CREDIT	Profit or loss: income from shares in associated companies		$1,500

In the **consolidated financial statements** of P Co equity accounting principles will be used to account for the investment in A Co. Consolidated profit after tax will include the group's share of A Co's profit for the year (25% × $24,000 = $6,000). To the extent that this has been distributed as dividend, it is already included in P Co's individual financial statements and will automatically be brought into the consolidated results. That part of the group's profit share which has not been distributed as dividend ($6,000 − $1,500 = $4,500) will be brought into consolidation by the following adjustment.

DEBIT	Investment in associates	$4,500	
CREDIT	Profit or loss: income from shares in associates		$4,500

The asset 'Investment in associates' is then stated at $64,500, being cost plus the group share of post-acquisition retained profits.

6.4 Consolidated statement of profit or loss and other comprehensive income

The treatment of associates' profits in the following proforma should be studied carefully.

6.4.1 Pro-forma consolidated statement of profit or loss and other comprehensive income

The following is a **suggested layout** (using the figures given in the illustration above) for an income statement for a company having subsidiaries as well as associates.

	$'000
Revenue	1,400
Cost of sales	770
Gross profit	630
Distribution costs and administrative expenses	290
	340
Interest and similar income receivable	30
	370
Finance costs	(20)
	350
Share of associates profit for the year	17
Profit before taxation	367
Income tax expense	
Parent company and subsidiaries	145
Profit for the year	222
Profit attributable to:	
Owners of the parent	200
Non-controlling interest	22
	222

6.4.2 Statement of profit or loss and other comprehensive income: Investor with no subsidiaries

The treatment required by the standard is given above. The following layout is suggested.

	$
Revenue	X
Cost of sales	(X)
Gross profit	X
Distribution costs/administrative expenses	(X)
	X
Finance costs	X
Share of profit for the year of associate	X
Profit before taxation	(X)
	X
Taxation	X
Profit for the year	X

6.5 Consolidated statement of financial position

As explained earlier, the consolidated statement of financial position will contain an **asset 'Investment in associates'**. The amount at which this asset is stated will be its original cost plus the group's share of any **profits earned since acquisition** which have not been distributed as dividends.

6.6 Example: Consolidated statement of financial position

On 1 January 20X6 the net identifiable assets of A Co amount to $220,000, financed by 100,000 $1 ordinary shares and retained earnings of $120,000. P Co, a company with subsidiaries, acquires 30,000 of the shares in A Co for $75,000. During the year ended 31 December 20X6 A Co's profit for the year is $30,000, from which dividends of $12,000 are paid.

Show how P Co's investment in A Co would appear in its consolidated statement of financial position at 31 December 20X6.

Solution

CONSOLIDATED STATEMENT OF FINANCIAL POSITION
AS AT 31 DECEMBER 20X6 (extract)

	$
Non-current assets	
Investment in associate	
Cost	75,000
Group share of post-acquisition retained earnings (30% × $18,000)	5,400
	80,400

Question — Associate 1

Set out below are the draft financial statements of Parent Co and its subsidiaries and of Associate Co. Parent Co acquired 40% of the equity capital of Associate Co three years ago when the latter's retained earnings stood at $40,000.

SUMMARISED STATEMENT OF FINANCIAL POSITION

	Parent Co & subsidiaries $'000	Associate Co $'000
Property, plant and equipment	220	170
Investment in Associate at cost	60	–
Loan to Associate Co	20	–
Current assets	100	50
Loan from Parent Co	–	(20)
	400	200
Share capital ($1 shares)	250	100
Retained earnings	150	100
	400	200

SUMMARISED STATEMENTS OF PROFIT OR LOSS AND OTHER COMPREHENSIVE INCOME

	Parent Co & subsidiaries $'000	Associate Co $'000
Profit before tax	95	80
Tax	35	30
Profit for the period	60	50

You are required to prepare the summarised consolidated financial statements of Parent Co.

Answer

PARENT CO
CONSOLIDATED STATEMENT OF PROFIT OR LOSS AND OTHER COMPREHENSIVE INCOME

	$'000
Profit from operations	95
Share of profits of associate (50 × 40%)	20
Profit before tax	115
Income tax expense	35
Profit attributable to the owners of Parent Co	80

PARENT CO
CONSOLIDATED STATEMENT OF FINANCIAL POSITION

	$'000
Assets	
Property, plant and equipment	220
Interest in associate (see note)	104
Current assets	100
Total assets	424
Equity and liabilities	
Share capital	250
Retained earnings (W)	174
Total equity and liabilities	424

	Note	$'000
	Interest in associate	
	Cost	60
	Share of post-acquisition retained earnings 40% × (100 – 40)	24
		84
	Loan to associate	20
		104

Workings: retained earnings

	Parent & subsidiaries $'000	Associate $'000
Per question	150	100
Pre-acquisition		40
Post-acquisition		60
Group share in associate ($60 × 40%)	24	
Group retained earnings	174	

Question — Associate 2

Alfred Co bought 25,000 ordinary shares on 31 December 20X8 in Grimbald Co at a cost of $38,000. Grimbald Co has 100,000 ordinary shares in issue.

During the year to 31 December 20X9 Grimbald Co made a profit for the year of $82,000 and the taxation charge on the year's profits was $32,000. A dividend of $20,000 was paid on 31 December out of these profits.

Calculate the amount in respect of the associate which should be presented in the 20X8 and 20X9 consolidated financial statements of the Alfred group.

Answer

At 31 December 20X8 (the date the investment was made), the investment in the associate should be presented in the consolidated statement of financial position at its cost of $38,000.

The amounts in the 20X9 consolidated financial statements are as follows.

CONSOLIDATED STATEMENT OF PROFIT OR LOSS AND OTHER COMPREHENSIVE INCOME

	$
Group share of associate's profit for the year (25% × (82,000 – 32,000))	12,500

CONSOLIDATED STATEMENT OF FINANCIAL POSITION

	$
Interest in associate	45,500
The asset 'interest in associate' comprises:	
Cost	38,000
Share of post-acquisition retained earnings (12,500 – (25% × 20,000 dividend paid))	7,500
	45,500

The following points are also relevant and are similar to a parent-subsidiary consolidation situation:

(a) Use financial statements drawn up to the **same reporting date.**

(b) If this is impracticable, adjust the financial statements for **significant transactions/ events** in the intervening period. The difference between the reporting date of the associate and that of the investor must be no more than three months.

(c) Use **uniform accounting policies** for like transactions and events in similar circumstances, adjusting the associate's statements to reflect group policies if necessary.

(d) If an associate has **cumulative preferred shares** held by outside interests, calculate the share of the investor's profits/losses after adjusting for the preferred dividends (whether or not declared).

6.7 'Upstream' and 'downstream' transactions

'Upstream' transactions are, for example, sales of assets from an associate to the investor. 'Downstream' transactions are, for example, sales of assets from the investor to an associate.

Profits and losses resulting from 'upstream' and 'downstream' transactions between an investor (including its consolidated subsidiaries) and an associate are eliminated to the extent of the investor's interest in the associate. This is very similar to the procedure for eliminating intra-group transactions between a parent and a subsidiary. The important thing to remember is that **only the group's share is eliminated**.

The double entry is as follows, where A% is the parent's holding in the associate, and PUP is the provision for unrealised profit.

DEBIT	Retained earnings of parent	PUP × A%
CREDIT	Group inventories	PUP × A%

For upstream transactions (associate sells to parent/subsidiary) where the parent holds the inventories.

OR

DEBIT	Retained earnings of parent/subsidiary	PUP × A%
CREDIT	Investment in associate	PUP × A%

For downstream transactions, (parent/subsidiary sells to associate) where the associate holds the inventory.

6.8 Example: Downstream transaction

A Co, a parent with subsidiaries, holds 25% of the equity shares in B Co. During the year, A Co makes sales of $1,000,000 to B Co at cost plus a 25% mark-up. At the year-end, B Co has all these goods still in inventories.

Solution

A Co has made an unrealised profit of $200,000 (1,000,000 × 25/125) on its sales to the associate. The group's share of this is 25%, ie $50,000. This must be eliminated.

The double entry is:

DEBIT	A Co: Retained earnings	$50,000	
CREDIT	Investment in associate (B Co)		$50,000

Because the sale was made to the associate, the group's share of the unsold inventories forms part of the investment in associate at the year end. If the sale had been from the associate B to A, ie an upstream transaction, the double entry would have been.

DEBIT	A Co: Retained earnings	$50,000	
CREDIT	A Co: Inventories		$50,000

If preparing the consolidated statement of profit or loss and other comprehensive income, you would deduct the $50,000 from the group share of the associate's profit.

6.9 Associate's losses

When the equity method is being used and the investor's share of losses of the associate equals or exceeds its interest in the associate, the investor should **discontinue** including its share of further losses. The investment is reported at nil value. The interest in the associate is normally the carrying amount of the investment in the associate, but it also includes any other non-current interests, for example, preference shares or long term receivables or loans.

After the investor's interest is reduced to nil, **additional losses** should only be recognised where the investor has incurred obligations or made payments on behalf of the associate (for example, if it has guaranteed amounts owed to third parties by the associate).

6.10 Impairment losses

IFRS 9 *Financial Instruments* sets out a list of indications that a financial asset (including an investment in an associate) may have become impaired. Any impairment loss is recognised in accordance with IAS 36 *Impairment of Assets* for each associate individually, reducing the carrying amount of any associate affected. Any reversal of that impairment loss is recognised in accordance with IAS 36 to the extent that the recoverable amount of the investment subsequently increases.

6.11 Section summary

Statement of profit or loss and OCI	Profit before tax: Parent and subsidiary + associate's profit after tax	
	Tax: Parent and subsidiary only	
Statement of financial position	Interests in associated companies should be stated at:	$
	Cost	X
	Share of post-acquisition retained earnings	X
		X
	Also disclose group's share of post-acquisition reserves of associated companies and movements therein.	

7 Joint arrangements

FAST FORWARD

> IFRS 11 *Joint Arrangements* provides guidance on identifying, classifying and accounting for joint arrangements. A joint arrangement is classified as either a joint operation or a joint venture.

Two or more persons may decide to enter into a business arrangement together without wishing to form a long-term partnership. Usually the parties agree to place limitations on their activities, for example, a joint arrangement to manufacture and sell 'total eclipse of the sun' souvenirs could be limited by time, while a joint arrangement to buy and sell a bankrupt's inventory (a fairly common occurrence in practice) comes to an end when all the inventory has been sold.

Joint arrangements are often found when each party can **contribute in different ways** to the venture. For example, one party may provide finance, another purchases or manufactures goods, while a third offers marketing skills.

7.1 Definition of a joint arrangement

A joint arrangement is an arrangement of which two or more parties have **joint control**.

7.1.1 Joint control

Joint control is defined as 'the contractually agreed sharing of control of an arrangement which exists only when decisions about the relevant activities require the unanimous consent of the parties sharing control.'

Therefore:

- Where there is no contractual arrangement to establish joint control, then there is no joint control;
- Where unanimous consent is not required to make decisions then there is no joint control.

IFRS 11 makes additional points about joint arrangements and joint control:

- No single party controls the arrangement on its own.
- A party with joint control of an arrangement can prevent any of the other parties from controlling the arrangement.
- An arrangement can be a joint arrangement even if not all parties have joint control; some parties to a joint arrangement may participate but not have joint control.
- Judgement should be applied when assessing whether a party has joint control of an arrangement.

Example: Joint control

Three parties establish an arrangement. Adam has 50% of the voting rights in the arrangement, Brent has 30% and Cranberry has 20%. The contractual arrangement between the parties specifies that at least 75% of votes are required to make decisions about relevant activities of the arrangement.

In this case, Adam can block a decision, however, does not control the arrangement alone as it needs the agreement of Brent. Therefore, Adam and Brent have joint control of the arrangement as decisions about relevant activities cannot be made without them agreeing. Cranberry is a participating party to the arrangement, however, does not have joint control.

7.1.2 Contractual arrangement

IFRS 11 states that the contractual arrangement required to establish joint control may be evidenced in a number of ways including:

- A written contract between the controlling parties
- Minutes of discussions between controlling parties
- Incorporation of the arrangement in the articles or by-laws of the joint arrangement

The contractual arrangement will deal with issues such as:

(a) The purpose, activity and duration of the joint venture

(b) The appointment of the board of directors and voting rights of the controlling parties

(c) Capital contributions by the controlling parties

(d) The sharing by the controlling parties of the output, income, expenses or results of the joint venture

One party may be identified in the contractual arrangement as the operator or manager of the joint venture. This does not indicate that that party controls the joint arrangement, simply that they are acting within the financial and operating policies agreed by the controlling parties in accordance with the contractual arrangement.

If it is evident that the operator does have control of the activity then the arrangement is a subsidiary of the operator rather than a joint operation or venture.

7.2 Types of joint arrangement

IFRS 11 classes joint arrangements as either **joint operations** or **joint ventures**. The classification of a joint arrangement as a joint operation or a joint venture depends upon the rights and obligations of the parties to the arrangement.

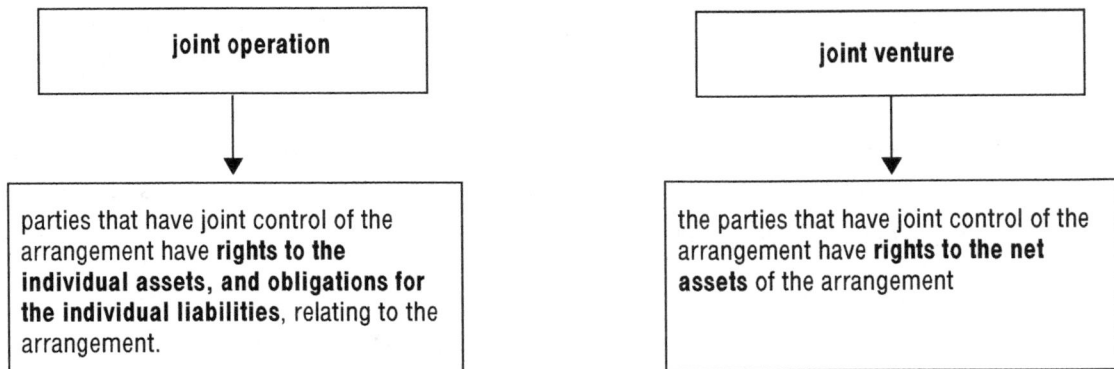

Under these definitions, the accounting treatment is determined based on the **substance** of the joint arrangement. If no separate entity has been created, the investor should separately recognise in its financial statements the direct rights it has to the assets and the obligation it has for liabilities under that arrangement. If a separate vehicle (entity) is created, the venturer accounts for its share of that entity using equity accounting.

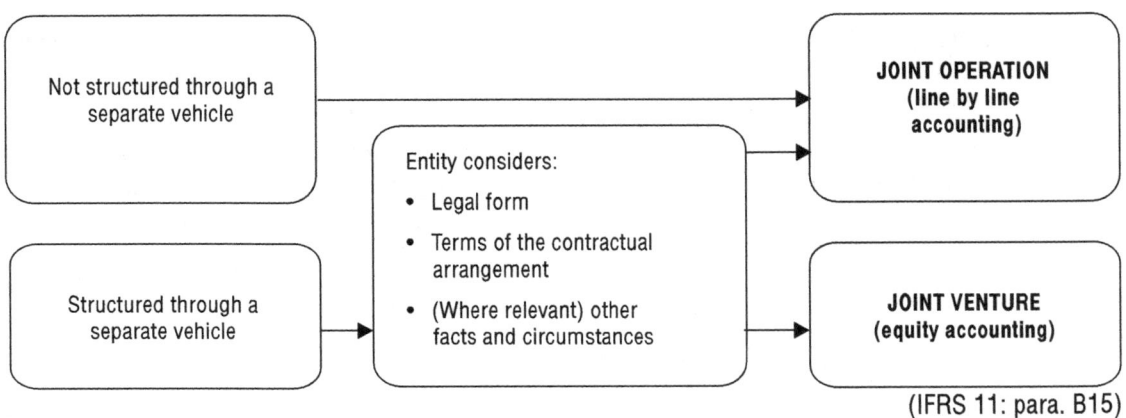

(IFRS 11: para. B15)

7.3 Accounting for joint arrangements

7.3.1 Joint operations

IFRS 11 requires that a joint operator recognises line-by-line the following in relation to its interest in a joint operation:

(a) Its assets, including its share of any jointly held assets;
(b) Its liabilities, including its share of any jointly incurred liabilities;
(c) Its revenue from the sale of its share of the output arising from the joint operation;
(d) Its share of the revenue from the sale of the output by the joint operation; and
(e) Its expenses, including its share of any expenses incurred jointly.

This treatment is applicable in both the separate and consolidated financial statements of the joint operator.

7.3.2 Joint ventures

In its consolidated financial statements, IFRS 11 requires that a joint venturer recognises its interest in a joint venture as an investment and accounts for that investment using the equity method in accordance with IAS 28 *Investments in Associates and Joint Ventures* unless the entity is exempted from applying the equity method (see Section 6.1.1 which is also applicable to joint ventures).

In its separate financial statements, a joint venturer should account for its interest in a joint venture in accordance with IAS 27 *Separate Financial Statements* (see Section 9).

7.4 Applying IAS 28 to joint ventures

The consolidated statement of financial position is prepared by:

- Including the interest in the joint venture at cost plus share of post-acquisition total comprehensive income
- Including the group share of the post-acquisition total comprehensive income in group reserves

The consolidated statement of profit or loss and other comprehensive income will include:

- The group share of the joint venture's profit or loss
- The group share of the joint venture's other comprehensive income.

The use of the equity method should be **discontinued** from the date on which the joint venturer ceases to have joint control over, or have significant influence on, a joint venture.

7.4.1 Transactions between a joint venture and a joint venture

Upstream transactions

A joint venturer may **sell or contribute assets** to a joint venture so making a profit or loss. Any such gain or loss should, however, only be recognised to the extent that it reflects the substance of the transaction.

Therefore:

- Only the **gain** attributable to the interest of the other joint venturers should be recognised in the financial statements.
- The full amount of any **loss** should be recognised when the transaction shows evidence that the net realisable value of current assets is less than cost, or that there is an impairment loss.

Downstream transactions

When a joint venturer purchases assets from a joint venture, the joint venturer should not recognise its share of the profit made by the joint venture on the transaction in question until it resells the assets to an independent third party, ie until the profit is realised.

Losses should be treated in the same way, **except** losses should be recognised immediately if they represent a reduction in the net realisable value of current assets, or a permanent decline in the carrying amount of non-current assets.

Question
Inventories

Kirstan Co contributes inventories to a 50:50 joint venture it has undertaken with Pirstan Co. The recorded historical cost of the inventories is $2m.

What gain or loss should Kirstan Co recognise in its financial statements when the fair value (net realisable value) of the inventories is estimated at the date of transfer and recorded by the joint venture as:

(a) $2.2m?
(b) $1.8m?

Answer

(a) Kirstan Co has made a profit of $0.2m, but only 50% of this can be considered as realised, ie that part attributable to the other venturer. Kirstan Co should therefore recognise a gain of $0.1m.

(b) A loss of $0.2m has been made on the inventories, the entire amount of which should be recognised by Kirstan Co. It is known that the loss will be made, even though the inventories have not yet been sold, and so prudence requires that the full loss should be recognised.

7.4.2 Acquisition of an interest in a joint operation

A joint operator which acquires an interest in a joint operation which meets the definition of a business will be required to apply the relevant principles for accounting for a business combination in IFRS 3 and other standards, and to disclose the relevant information required by those standards.

8 Disclosure of interests in other entities

> **FAST FORWARD**
>
> IFRS 12 requires disclosures in respect of the significant judgements and assumptions made when determining type of investment, interests in subsidiaries, interests in associates and interests in joint ventures.

IFRS 12 *Disclosure of Interests in Other Entities* was issued in 2011 collating the consolidated financial statement disclosure requirements in respect of subsidiaries, associates and joint arrangements into one standard.

The standard does not apply to the separate financial statements of the investor, which are instead covered by IAS 27 *Separate Financial Statements*.

The following sections list the disclosures required by IFRS 12.

8.1 Significant judgements and assumptions

An entity should disclose information about significant judgements and assumptions that it has made in determining:

1. That it has control of another entity.
2. That it has joint control over an arrangement.
3. That it has significant influence over another entity.
4. That a joint arrangement structured through a separate entity is either a joint operation or a joint venture.
5. That it is an investment entity.

8.2 Interests in subsidiaries

Information must be disclosed which enables users of the consolidated financial statements

(a) To understand the composition of the group and the interest that non-controlling interests have in the group's activities and cash flows

(b) To evaluate:

  (i) The nature and extent of significant restrictions on an entity's ability to access or use assets and settle liabilities of the group

  (ii) The nature of and changes in the risks associated with an entity's interests in consolidated structured entities

  (iii) The consequences of changes in an entity's ownership interest in a subsidiary that do not result in a loss of control (see Chapter 8)

  (iv) The consequences of losing control in a subsidiary during the reporting period (see Chapter 8)

8.3 Interests in joint arrangements and associates

An entity shall disclose information that enables users of the financial statements to evaluate:

(a) The nature, extent and financial effects of its interests in joint arrangements and associates, including the nature and effects of its contractual relationship with the other investors with joint control of, or significant influence over, joint arrangements and associates

(b) The nature of, and changes in, the risks associated with its interests in joint ventures and associates.

9 Separate financial statements of investor

FAST FORWARD

IAS 27 is applied when accounting for subsidiaries, associates and joint ventures in the separate financial statements of the investor. It requires that these investments are accounted for either at cost or in accordance with IFRS 9.

As part of the 'package' of consolidation standards issued in 2011, the IASB revised and renamed IAS 27 as *Separate Financial Statements*.

The revised standard is applied when accounting for investments in subsidiaries, associates and joint ventures when an entity elects, or is required to present separate financial statements.

Note that an investment entity which is required to account for all subsidiaries in accordance with IFRS 9 presents separate financial statements as its only financial statements.

9.1 Accounting treatment in separate statement of financial position

When separate financial statements are prepared by an investor, investments in subsidiaries, joint ventures and associates are accounted for either:

(a) At cost;
(b) In accordance with IFRS 9; or
(c) Using the equity method as described in IAS 28.

The same accounting must be applied to each category of investments.

Where investments are accounted for at cost, should they become classified as held for sale, they are accounted for in accordance with IFRS 5 *Non-current Assets Held for Sale and Discontinued Operations*.

An amendment to IAS 27 was issued in August 2014 which allows parent companies to use the equity method to value subsidiaries, joint ventures and associates in their own (separate) financial statements. The use of the equity method in this way was formerly permissible, but in 2003 the option was removed and all investments had to be accounted in accordance with financial asset rules (ie at cost or fair value).

9.2 Accounting treatment in separate statement of profit or loss and other comprehensive income

The investor should recognise a dividend from a subsidiary, associate or joint venture in profit or loss when its right to receive a dividend is established.

9.3 Disclosure requirements

IAS 27 requires the following disclosures in separate financial statements:

1. When an investor elects not to prepare consolidated financial statements and instead prepares separate financial statements, it must disclose:

    (i) The fact that the financial statements are separate financial statements and details of the exemption from consolidation

    (ii) A detailed list of investments in subsidiaries, associates and joint ventures

2. When consolidated financial statements are also prepared:

    (i) Details of the related consolidated financial statements

    (ii) The fact that the statements are separate financial statements and the reason why they are prepared if not required by law

    (iii) A detailed list of investments in subsidiaries, associates and joint ventures

    (iv) A description of the method used to account for the investments

3. When an investment entity prepares separate financial statements as its only financial statements, that fact is disclosed and IFRS 12 disclosures are also required.

Chapter roundup

- The following statements are relevant:
    - IAS 27 *Separate Financial Statements*
    - IAS 28 *Investments in Associates and Joint Ventures*
    - IFRS 3 *Business Combinations*
    - IFRS 10 *Consolidated Financial Statements*
    - IFRS 11 *Joint Arrangements*
    - IFRS 12 *Disclosure of Interests in Other Entities*

- Investments are classified as subsidiaries, associates, joint arrangements or financial asset investments. The accounting treatment applied differs depending on the type of investment.

- The non-controlling interest may be measured **either at fair value or at the non-controlling interest's proportionate share of the acquiree's identifiable net assets**.

- **IFRS 10 *Consolidated Financial Statements*** provides accounting guidance on the consolidation procedures to be applied when preparing the combined financial statements of a parent and its subsidiaries.

- **Goodwill arising on consolidation** is the excess of the fair value of the consideration transferred plus the non-controlling interest over the fair value of the identifiable assets and liabilities acquired.

- **IAS 28** deals with identifying and accounting for associates.

- The **equity method** should be applied in the consolidated financial statements:

    - **Statement of financial position**: investment in associate measured at cost plus (or minus) the group's share of the associate's post-acquisition retained profits (or losses)

    - **Statement of profit or loss and other comprehensive income**: group share of associate's profit after tax.

- IFRS 11 *Joint Arrangements* provides guidance on identifying, classifying and accounting for joint arrangements. A joint arrangement is classified as either a joint operation or a joint venture.

- IFRS 12 requires disclosures in respect of the significant judgements and assumptions made when determining type of investment, interests in subsidiaries, interests in associates and interests in joint ventures.

- IAS 27 is applied when accounting for subsidiaries, associates and joint ventures in the separate financial statements of the investor. It requires that these investments are accounted for either at cost or in accordance with IFRS 9.

Quick quiz

1. What are the three elements of control within the definition of control as defined within IFRS 10 *Consolidated Financial Statements*?

2. If a company holds 20% or more of the voting shares of another company, it is presumed to have significant influence. True or false?

3. What is significant influence?

4. What is a non-controlling interest?

5. How is the non-controlling interest on acquisition to be valued?

6. How should an investment in a subsidiary be accounted for in the separate financial statements of the parent?

7. Describe the requirement of IFRS 3 in relation to the remeasurement of a subsidiary company's assets.

8. When land and buildings are acquired in a business combination, how should they normally be measured?

9. Which party to a business combination is the acquirer?

10. An associate is a _____ in which an investor has _____, but which is not a subsidiary or a joint venture of the investor. *Complete the blanks.*

11. What is the effect of the equity method on the statement of profit or loss and other comprehensive income and the statement of financial position?

12. Joint control exists where shared control is established in a _____. It exists only where decisions about the relevant activities require the _____ of the parties sharing control.

13. What forms of evidence of a contractual agreement might exist?

14. How should a joint venturer account for its share of a joint venture?

Answers to quick quiz

1. An investor controls an investee if the investor has:

   (i) Power over the investee
   (ii) Exposure, or rights, to variable returns from its involvement with the investee
   (iii) The ability to use its power over the investee to affect the amount of the investor's returns.

2. True.

3. The power to participate in, but not to control, the financial and operating decisions of the investee.

4. The part of the profit or loss and the net assets attributable to interests not owned by the parent.

5. Either at fair value or at the non-controlling interest's proportionate share of the acquiree's identifiable net assets.

6. (a) At cost or
   (b) Under IFRS 9 or
   (c) Using the equity method as described in IAS 28.

7. Fair value is not affected by the acquirer's intentions. Therefore only intentions after acquisition are reflected in the statement of comprehensive income after acquisition.

8. At fair value, by reference to their market value.

9. The acquirer is the entity that obtains control of the other combining entities or businesses.

10. An associates is an **entity** in which an investor has **significant influence**, but which is not a subsidiary or a joint venture of the investor.

11. (a) *Statement of profit or loss and other comprehensive income.* Investing entity includes its share of the earnings of the associate, by adding its share of profit for the year.

    (b) *Statement of financial position.* Investment in associates is included in assets at cost adjusted by the relevant share of post-acquisition retained profits/losses.

12. Joint control exists where shared control is established in a contractual agreement. It exists only where decisions about the relevant activities require the unanimous consent of the parties sharing control.

13.
    - Written contract between the parties
    - Minutes of discussions between the venturers
    - incorporation of the arrangement in the articles or by-laws of the joint arrangement

14. Equity accounting should be applied in accordance with IAS 28 (2011).

PART B BUSINESS COMBINATIONS AND GROUP FINANCIAL STATEMENTS

End of chapter question

Akkeal (AIA May 2004 – amended)

The following are the income statements for four limited liability companies for the financial year ended 31 March 20X4.

STATEMENTS OF PROFIT OR LOSS AND OTHER COMPREHENSIVE INCOME FOR THE YEAR ENDED 31 MARCH 20X4

	Akkeal $'000	Belloan $'000	Curtyn $'000	Dojin $'000
Revenue	16,400	8,870	13,800	11,300
Cost of sales	(5,600)	(4,200)	(5,900)	(8,100)
Gross profit	10,800	4,670	7,900	3,200
Operating expenses	(5,780)	(3,370)	(4,700)	(1,540)
Profit from operations	5,020	1,300	3,200	1,660
Dividends receivable	1,247	600	0	0
Investment income	233	97	140	0
Finance cost	(333)	(240)	(350)	0
Profit before taxation	6,167	1,757	2,990	1,660
Tax	(1,800)	(500)	(700)	(400)
Profit for the period	4,367	1,257	2,290	1,260

The following additional information is available:

- Belloan is a subsidiary of Akkeal. Akkeal owns 60% of the ordinary shares in Belloan.

- Curtyn is an associate of Akkeal. Akkeal owns 30% of the ordinary shares in Curtyn.

- Dojin is a joint venture between Akkeal and three other companies which each own 25% of the ordinary shares in Dojin and have established joint control via written agreement.

- During the financial year ended 31 March 20X4 Belloan made sales to Akkeal. The invoice value of these sales to Akkeal was $1,500,000. This represented cost to Belloan plus a mark-up of 20%. 10% of these goods remained unsold at 31 March 2004.

- All goodwill acquired in business combinations had been fully written off by 1 April 20X3.

- In each company each ordinary share carries one vote and there are no voting rights other than those attaching to the ordinary shares.

- Akkeal is a publicly listed company and its issued ordinary share capital throughout the year was 20 million shares.

- Dividends paid by the four companies during the year ended 31 March 20X4 were:

    Akkeal: Ordinary dividends paid $2,000,000
    Belloan: Ordinary dividends paid $700,000
    Curtyn: Ordinary dividends $1,500,000
    Dojin: Ordinary dividends $880,000

Required

Prepare the consolidated statement of profit or loss and other comprehensive income of Akkeal in accordance with IFRS 10 *Consolidated Financial Statements*, IAS 28 (2011) *Investments in Associates and Joint Ventures*. You should

- Include a figure for earnings per share calculated and disclosed in accordance with IAS 33 *Earnings per Share*.

(25 marks)

Complex groups

Topic list	Syllabus reference
1 Multi-entity structures	LO2
2 Consolidating sub-subsidiaries	LO2
3 Direct holdings in sub-subsidiaries	LO2
4 Associates held by subsidiaries	LO2

Introduction

This chapter introduces the first of several more complicated consolidation topics. The best way to tackle these questions is to be logical and to carry out the consolidation on a **step by step** basis.

In questions of this nature, it is very helpful to sketch a **diagram of the group structure**, as we have done. This clarifies the situation and it should point you in the right direction: always sketch the group structure as your first working and double check it against the information in the question.

1 Multi-entity structures

> **FAST FORWARD**
>
> When a holding company has **several subsidiaries**, the consolidated statement of financial position shows a single figure for non-controlling interests and for goodwill arising on consolidation. In cases where there are several subsidiary companies, the technique is to open up a single non-controlling interest working and a columnar goodwill working.

1.1 Introduction

In this section we shall consider how the principles of the preparation of the statement of financial position may be applied to more complex structures of companies within a group.

(a) Several subsidiary companies

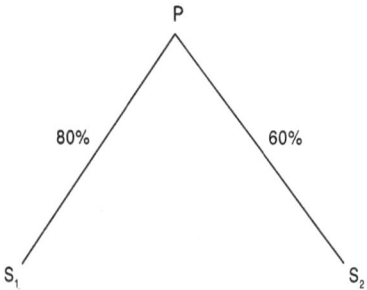

You have already seen this type of structure in your previous studies.

(b) Sub-subsidiaries

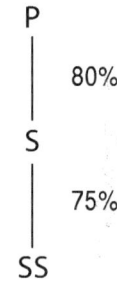

P holds a controlling interest in S which in turn holds a controlling interest in SS. SS is therefore a subsidiary of a subsidiary of P, in other words, a **sub-subsidiary** of P.

(c) **Direct holdings in sub-subsidiaries: 'D' shaped groups**

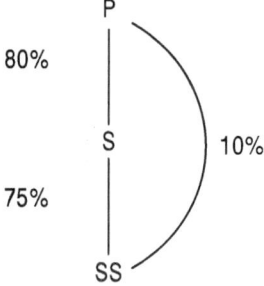

In this example, SS is a sub-subsidiary of P with additional shares held directly by P.

In practice, groups are usually larger, and therefore more complex, but the procedures for consolidation of large groups will not differ from those we shall now describe for smaller ones.

1.2 A parent company which has several subsidiaries

Where a company P has several subsidiaries S_1, S_2, S_3 and so on, the technique for consolidation is exactly as previously described. **Cancellation** is from the holding company, which has assets of investments in subsidiaries S_1, S_2, S_3, to each of the several subsidiaries.

The consolidated statement of financial position will show:

(a) A single figure for **non-controlling interest**; and
(b) A single figure for **goodwill** arising.

A single working should be used for each of the constituents of the consolidated statement of financial position: one working for goodwill, one for non-controlling interest, one for retained earnings (reserves), and so on.

1.3 Sub-subsidiaries

A slightly different problem arises when there are sub-subsidiaries in the group, which is how should we **identify the non-controlling interest** in the retained earnings of the group? Suppose P owns 80% of the equity of S, and that S in turn owns 60% of the equity of SS.

It would appear that in this situation:

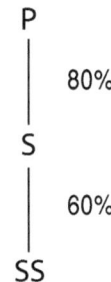

(a) P owns 80% of 60% = 48% of SS
(b) The non-controlling interest in S owns 20% of 60% = 12% of SS
(c) The non-controlling interest in SS itself owns the remaining 40% of the SS equity

SS is nevertheless a **sub-subsidiary** of P, because it is a subsidiary of S which in turn is a subsidiary of P. The chain of control thus makes SS a sub-subsidiary of P which owns only 48% of its equity.

The total non-controlling interest in SS may be checked by considering a **dividend** of $100 paid by SS where S then distributes its share of this dividend in full to its own shareholders.

		$
S will receive	$60	
P will receive	80% × $60 =	48
Leaving for the total non-controlling interest in SS		52
		100

Question
Effective interest

Top owns 60% of the equity of Middle Co, which owns 75% of the equity of Bottom Co. Calculate Top Co's effective holding in Bottom Co.

Answer

Top owns 60% of 75% of Bottom Co = 45%.

1.4 Date of effective control

The date the sub-subsidiary comes under the **control of the holding company** needs to be determined:

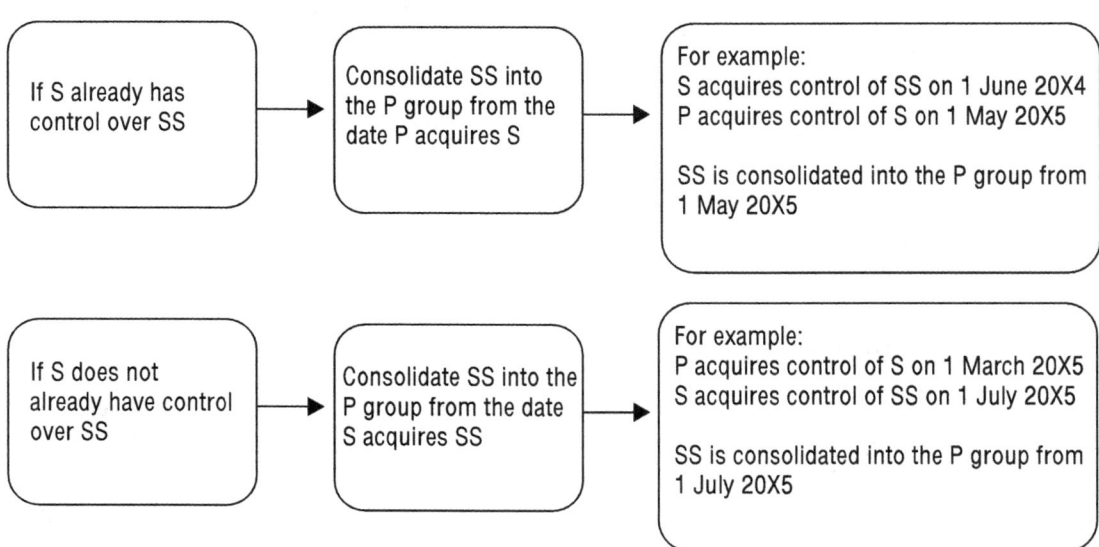

The dates of acquisition and the order in which the group is built up will make a difference to how we calculate goodwill and non-controlling interest.

1.5 Pro-forma goodwill calculation

Before we progress to the complex group calculations, here is a reminder of how IFRS 3 *Business Combinations* requires goodwill to be measured.

	$
Consideration transferred	X
Amount of any non-controlling interests	X
Fair value of acquirer's previously held equity interest	X
Less net acquisition-date fair value of identifiable assets acquired and liabilities assumed	X
	X

While the above layout reflects the wording of the standard, for the purposes of your workings in the examination, the following layout is recommended.

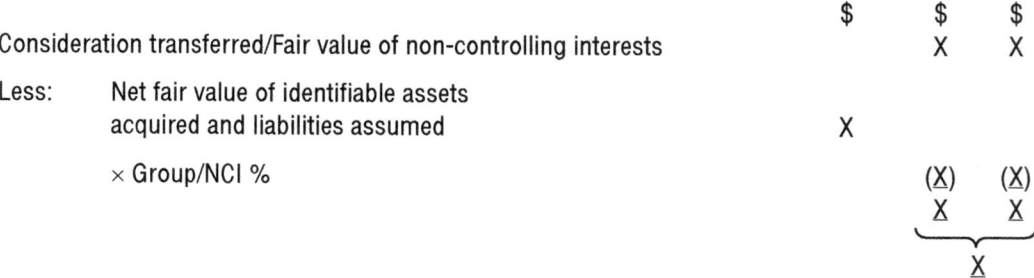

The NCI (non-controlling interest) column is only needed if the NCI interest is to be measured at fair value. As we saw in Chapter 6, when the NCI is measured at fair value, goodwill arises that is attributable to the NCI.

2 Consolidating sub-subsidiaries

FAST FORWARD

When dealing with **sub-subsidiaries,** you will need to calculate effective interest owned by the group and by the non-controlling interest.

The **date of acquisition** is important when dealing with sub-subsidiaries.

Remember that it is the post-acquisition reserves from a **group perspective** which are relevant.

Exam focus point

Don't panic when a question seems very complicated – sketch the group structure and analyse the information in the question methodically.

The basic consolidation method is as follows:

(a) **Net assets**: show what the group controls.

(b) **Equity (capital and reserves)**: show who owns the net assets included elsewhere in the statement of financial position. Reserves (retained earnings), therefore, are based on **effective holdings**.

As indicated earlier, the major problem on consolidation is to identify the non-controlling interest share of the retained earnings of S and (especially) SS.

As we have already covered the consolidation procedure for simple groups in your previous studies and earlier chapters, the approach to consolidating sub-subsidiaries is best demonstrated by examples.

2.1 Example: Subsidiary acquired first

The draft statements of financial position of P Co, S Co and SS Co on 30 June 20X7 were as follows:

	P Co $	S Co $	SS Co $
Assets			
Non-current assets			
Property, plant and equipment	105,000	125,000	180,000
Investments, at cost			
80,000 shares in S Co	120,000	–	–
60,000 shares in SS Co	–	110,000	–
Current assets	80,000	70,000	60,000
	305,000	305,000	240,000
Equity and liabilities			
Equity			
Ordinary shares of $1 each	80,000	100,000	100,000
Retained earnings	195,000	170,000	115,000
	275,000	270,000	215,000
Payables	30,000	35,000	25,000
	305,000	305,000	240,000

P Co acquired its shares in S Co on 1 July 20X4 when the reserves of S Co stood at $40,000; and

S Co acquired its shares in SS Co on 1 July 20X5 when the reserves of SS Co stood at $50,000.

It is the group's policy to measure the non-controlling interest at acquisition at its proportionate share of the fair value of the subsidiary's net assets.

Required

Prepare the draft consolidated statement of financial position of P Group at 30 June 20X7.

Note. Assume no impairment of goodwill.

Solution

This is **two acquisitions** from the point of view of the P group. In 20X4, the group buys 80% of S. Then in 20X5 S (which is now part of the P group) buys 60% of SS.

P buys 80% of S, then S (80% of S from the group's point of view) buys 60% of SS.

Having calculated the non-controlling interest and the P group interest (see working 1 below), the workings can be constructed. You should, however, note the following.

(a) Group structure working (see working 1).

(b) **Goodwill working**: compare the costs of investments with the effective group interests acquired (80% of S Co and 48% of SS Co).

(c) **Non-controlling interest working**: bring in the total non-controlling interests in S Co's share capital and retained earnings (20%), and the total non-controlling interests in SS Co's share capital and retained earnings (52%).

(d) **Retained earnings working**: bring in the share of S Co's and SS Co's post-acquisition retained earnings in the normal way.

1 Group structure

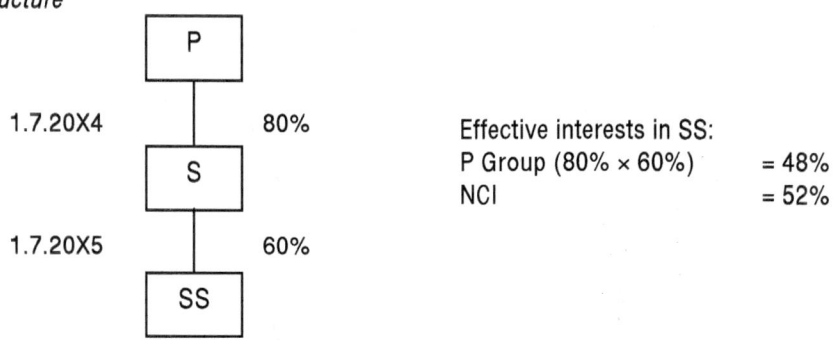

Effective interests in SS:
P Group (80% × 60%) = 48%
NCI = 52%

2 Goodwill

	P in S		S in SS	
	$	$	$	$
Consideration transferred		120,000	(80% ×110,000)	88,000
Fair value of identifiable NA acquired:				
Share capital	100,000		100,000	
Retained earnings	40,000		50,000	
	140,000		150,000	
Group share	80%		48%	
		(112,000)		(72,000)
		8,000		16,000
				24,000

3 Non-controlling interests

	S $	SS $
Net assets per Q	270,000	215,000
Less investment in SS	(110,000)	-
	160,000	215,000
	× 20%	× 52%
	32,000	111,800

$ 143,800

Note. The cost of the investment in SS Co must be split between the non-controlling interest and the parent company. Only the latter is shown in the goodwill workings to ensure that we have only P Co's share of the goodwill arising in the S Co subgroup appearing in the consolidated statement of financial position. This is done by taking the group share of the subsidiary's 'cost' in the goodwill working and by deducting the cost from the net assets allocated to the non-controlling interests.

4 Retained earnings

	P Co $	S Co $	SS Co $
Per question	195,000	170,000	115,000
Pre-acquisition		(40,000)	(50,000)
Post-acquisition		130,000	65,000
Group share:			
In S Co ($130,000 × 80%)	104,000		
In SS Co ($65,000 × 48%)	31,200		
Group retained earnings	330,200		

P CO
CONSOLIDATED STATEMENT OF FINANCIAL POSITION AT 30 JUNE 20X7

	$
Assets	
Non-current assets	
Property, plant and equipment ($105,000 + $125,000 + $180,000)	410,000
Goodwill (W2)	24,000
Current assets ($80,000 + $70,000 + $60,000)	210,000
	644,000
Equity	
Ordinary shares of $1 each fully paid	80,000
Retained earnings (W4)	330,200
	410,200
Non-controlling interest (W3)	143,800
	554,000
Payables ($30,000 + $35,000 + $25,000)	90,000
	644,000

2.2 Example: Subsidiary acquired first: Non-controlling interest at fair value

Now let us consider the impact on the calculations if the full goodwill method is applied.

The draft statements of financial position of P Co, S Co and SS Co on 30 June 20X7 were as follows.

	P Co $	S Co $	SS Co $
Assets			
Non-current assets			
Property, plant and equipment	105,000	125,000	180,000
Investments, at cost			
80,000 shares in S Co	120,000	–	–
60,000 shares in SS Co	–	110,000	–
Current assets	80,000	70,000	60,000
	305,000	305,000	240,000
Equity and liabilities			
Equity			
Ordinary shares of $1 each	80,000	100,000	100,000
Retained earnings	195,000	170,000	115,000
	275,000	270,000	215,000
Payables	30,000	35,000	25,000
	305,000	305,000	240,000

P Co acquired its shares in S Co on 1 July 20X4 when the reserves of S Co stood at $40,000; and S Co acquired its shares in SS Co on 1 July 20X5 when the reserves of SS Co stood at $50,000.

It is the group's policy to measure the non-controlling interest at fair value at the date of acquisition. The fair value of the non-controlling interest in S on 1 July 20X4 was $29,000. The fair value of the 52% non-controlling interest in SS on 1 July 20X5 was $80,000.

Required

Prepare the draft consolidated statement of financial position of P Group at 30 June 20X7.

Note. Assume no impairment of goodwill.

Solution

The main difference from the example in 2.1 above is that extra columns are needed in the goodwill calculation for the goodwill attributable to the non-controlling interest. As explained in Chapter 6, the goodwill attributable to the non-controlling interest is also added to the NCI figure at the year end.

P CO
CONSOLIDATED STATEMENT OF FINANCIAL POSITION AT 30 JUNE 20X7

	$
Assets	
Non-current assets	
Property, plant and equipment (as before)	410,000
Goodwill (W2)	27,000
Current assets (as before)	210,000
	647,000
Equity	
Ordinary shares of $1 each fully paid	80,000
Retained earnings (W4)	330,200
	410,200
Non-controlling interest (W3)	146,800
	557,000
Payables (as before)	90,000
	647,000

7: COMPLEX GROUPS

1 Group structure

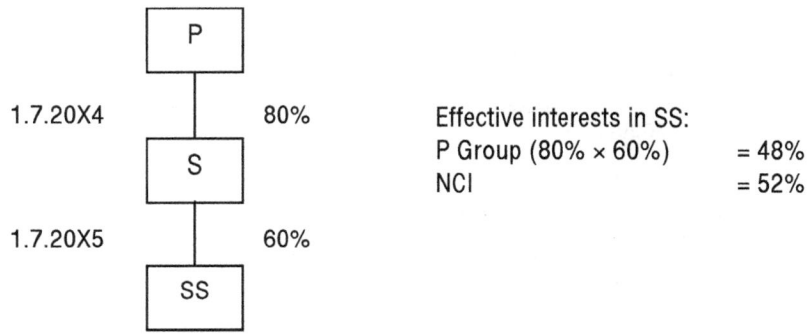

Effective interests in SS:
P Group (80% × 60%) = 48%
NCI = 52%

2 Goodwill

	P in S				S in SS	
	Group		NCI		Group	NCI
	$	$	$	$	$	$
Consideration transferred/ FV NCI		120,000	29,000	(80% × 110,000) 88,000	80,000
Fair value of identifiable net assets acquired						
Share capital	100,000				100,000	
Retained earnings	40,000				50,000	
	140,000				150,000	
Group/NCI Share	(80%)		(20%)	(48%)		(52%)
		(112,000)	(28,000)		(72,000)	(78,000)
		8,000	1,000		16,000	2,000

$27,000

3 Non-controlling interests

The non-controlling interest working in this example has one extra step: adding on the non-controlling interest in goodwill as calculated in working 2. The cost of investment in SS is again deducted as the NCI is being calculated on the net assets that have been consolidated (see note above).

	S	SS
	$	$
Net assets per Q	270,000	215,000
Less investment in SS	(110,000)	-
	160,000	215,000
	× 20%	× 52%
	32,000	111,800
Non-controlling interests in goodwill (W2)	1,000	2,000
	33,000	113,800

146,800

PART B   BUSINESS COMBINATIONS AND GROUP FINANCIAL STATEMENTS

4   Retained earnings

	P Co $	S Co $	SS Co $
Per question	195,000	170,000	115,000
Pre-acquisition		(40,000)	(50,000)
Post-acquisition		130,000	65,000
Group share:			
In S Co ($130,000 × 80%)	104,000		
In SS Co ($65,000 × 48%)	31,200		
Group retained earnings	330,200		

2.3 Example: Sub-subsidiary acquired first

Using the figures in Section 2.1, assume that:

(a)   S Co purchased its holding in SS Co on 1 July 20X4
(b)   P Co purchased its holding in S Co on 1 July 20X5

The retained earnings figures on the respective dates of acquisition are the same, but on the date P Co purchased its holding in S Co, the retained earnings of SS Co were $60,000.

In this version, there is only **one** acquisition from the perspective of P group: ie on 1 July 20X5 it acquires S and SS as a 'job lot'. Putting it another way, it acquires a **pre-existing group**.

So we do **one** calculation of goodwill looking at what P paid – ie the $120,000, versus what it acquired – ie 80% of the **consolidated** net assets of S and 48% of the **consolidated** net assets of SS.

Solution

The point here is that SS Co only became part of the P group on 1 July 20X5, **not** on 1 July 20X4. This means that only the retained earnings of SS Co arising **after** 1 July 20X5 can be included in the post-acquisition reserves of P Co group. Goodwill arising on the acquisition will be calculated by comparing the cost of the investment to the consolidated separable net assets of S (as represented by share capital and consolidated retained earnings, net of all goodwill).

P CO
CONSOLIDATED STATEMENT OF FINANCIAL POSITION AS AT 30 JUNE 20X7

	$
Non-current assets	
Property, plant and equipment (as before)	410,000
Goodwill (W2)	19,200
	429,200
Current assets (as before)	210,000
	639,200
Equity and liabilities	
Ordinary shares $1 each, fully paid	80,000
Retained earnings (W4)	325,400
	405,400
Non-controlling interest (W3)	143,800
	549,200
Payables (as before)	90,000
	639,200

Workings

1   Group structure

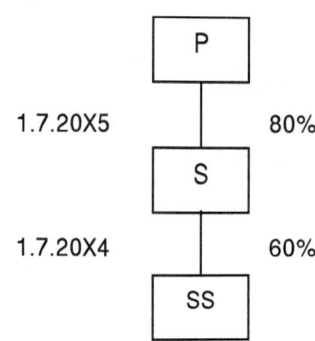

P owns an effective interest of 48% in SS. NCI in SS is 52%.

2   Goodwill

Note. Cost of investment in sub-sub is always deducted because we are looking at the net assets that would actually appear in the consolidated SOFP

The working should be set out as:

			$	$
Consideration transferred				120,000
Less:				
Fair value of identifiable assets and liabilities acquired				
S	Share capital		100,000	
	Pre-acquisition retained earnings		40,000	
	Less investment in SS		(110,000)	
			30,000	
		80%		(24,000)
SS	Share capital		100,000	
	Pre-acquisition retained earnings		60,000	
			160,000	
		48%		(76,800)
				19,200

3   *Non-controlling interests*

The cost of investment in SS is again deducted as the NCI is being calculated on the net assets that have been consolidated (see note above).

	S	SS
	$	$
Net assets per Q	270,000	215,000
Less investment in SS	(110,000)	–
	160,000	215,000
	× 20%	× 52%
	32,000	111,800

$ 143,800

4   *Retained earnings*

	$
P Co (as before)	195,000
S Co (as before)	104,000
SS Co (115 – 60) × 48%	26,400
	325,400

2.4 Example: Sub-subsidiary acquired first: Non-controlling interest at fair value

Now we shall reconsider the example in Section 2.4 above, but this time assume that the group measures the non-controlling interest at a fair value of $95,000 on the date of acquisition.

The revised goodwill and non-controlling interest workings are as follows:

Goodwill

The working should be set out as:

			$	Group $	NCI $
Consideration transferred/FV of the NCI				120,000	95,000
Less:					
Fair value of identifiable assets and liabilities acquired					
S	Share capital		100,000		
	Pre-acquisition retained earnings		40,000		
	Less investment in SS		(110,000)		
			30,000		
		80%/20%		(24,000)	(6,000)
SS	Share capital		100,000		
	Pre-acquisition retained earnings		60,000		
			160,000		
		48%/52%		(76,800)	(83,200)
				9,200	5,800
Total goodwill					25,000

Non-controlling interests

	S $	SS $
Net assets per Q	270,000	215,000
Less investment in SS	(110,000)	–
	160,000	215,000
	× 20%	× 52%
	32,000	111,800

	143,800
Goodwill	5,800
NCI	149,600

7: COMPLEX GROUPS

Remember – the rest of the balances in the consolidated statement of financial position are the same, regardless of which method is used to measure the non-controlling interest.

Question — Sub-subsidiary

The statements of financial position of Antelope Co, Yak Co and Zebra Co at 31 March 20X4 are summarised as follows.

	Antelope Co $	Antelope Co $	Yak Co $	Yak Co $	Zebra Co $	Zebra Co $
Assets						
Non-current assets						
Freehold property		100,000		100,000		–
Plant and machinery		210,000		80,000		3,000
		310,000		180,000		3,000
Investments in subsidiaries						
Shares, at cost	110,000		6,200		–	
Loan account	–		3,800		–	
Current accounts	10,000		12,200		–	
		120,000		22,200		3,000
Current assets						
Inventories	170,000		20,500		15,000	
Receivables	140,000		50,000		1,000	
Cash at bank	60,000		16,500		4,000	
		370,000		87,000		20,000
		800,000		289,200		23,000
Equity and liabilities						
Equity						
$1 Ordinary share capital	200,000		100,000		10,000	
Retained earnings	379,600		129,200		(1,000)	
		579,600		229,200		9,000
Current liabilities						
Trade payables	160,400		40,200		800	
Due to Antelope Co	–		12,800		600	
Due to Yak Co	–				12,600	
Taxation	60,000		7,000		–	
		220,400		60,000		14,000
		800,000		289,200		23,000

Antelope Co acquired 75% of the shares of Yak Co in 20X1 when the credit balance on the retained earnings of that company was $40,000. No dividends have been paid since that date. Yak Co acquired 80% of the shares in Zebra Co in 20X3 when there was a debit balance on the retained earnings of that company of $3,000. Subsequently $500 was received by Zebra Co and credited to its retained earnings, representing the recovery of a bad debt written off before the acquisition of Zebra's shares by Yak Co.

During the year to 31 March 20X4 Yak Co purchased inventory from Antelope Co for $20,000 which included a profit mark-up of $4,000 for Antelope Co. At 31 March 20X4 one half of this amount was still held in the inventories of Yak Co. Group accounting policies are to make a full allowance for unrealised intra-group profits.

It is the group's policy to measure the non-controlling interest at its proportionate share of the fair value of the subsidiary's net assets.

Prepare the draft consolidated statement of financial position of Antelope Co at 31 March 20X4. (Assume no impairment of goodwill.)

State how your answer would differ if the non-controlling interest were measured at fair value given the following information:

PART B BUSINESS COMBINATIONS AND GROUP FINANCIAL STATEMENTS

- The fair value of a share in Y immediately prior to its acquisition by A was $1.50
- The fair value of a share in Z immediately prior to its acquisition by Y was 75c

Answer

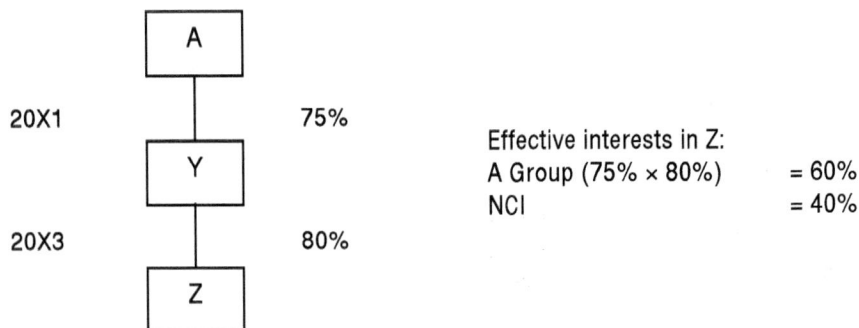

Effective interests in Z:
A Group (75% × 80%) = 60%
NCI = 40%

Workings

1 Goodwill

	A in Y		Y in Z	
	$	$	$	$
			(75% ×	
Consideration transferred		110,000	6,200)	4,650
Fair value of identifiable NA acquired:				
Share capital	100,000		10,000	
Retained earnings: ($3,000) + $500	40,000		(2,500)	
	140,000		7,500	
Group share	75%		60%	
		(105,000)		(4,500)
		5,000		150

$ 5,150

2 Non-controlling interests

	Yak	Zebra
	$	$
Net assets per Q	229,200	9,000
Less investment in Zebra	(6,200)	–
	223,000	9,000
	× 25%	× 40%
	55,750	3,600

59,350

3   Retained earnings

	Antelope $	Yak $	Zebra $
Per question	379,600	129,200	(1,000)
Adjustment bad debt recovery			(500)
Pre-acquisition profit/losses		(40,000)	3,000
Post-acquisition profits		89,200	1,500

Group share
In Yak ($89,200 × 75%)   66,900
In Zebra ($1,500 × 60%)   900

Unrealised profit in inventories
Sitting in parent
($4,000) × ½)   (2,000)
Group retained earnings   445,400

ANTELOPE CO
CONSOLIDATED STATEMENT OF FINANCIAL POSITION AS AT 31 MARCH 20X4

	$	$
Assets		
Non-current assets		
Freehold property ($100,000 + $100,000)		200,000
Plant and machinery ($210,000 + $80,000 + $3,000)		293,000
		493,000
Goodwill (W1)		5,150
		498,150
Current assets		
Inventories (($170,000 + $20,500 + $15,000 – 2,000)	203,500	
Receivables ($140,000 + $50,000 + $1,000)	191,000	
Cash at bank ($60,000 + $16,500 + $4,000)	80,500	
		475,000
		973,150
Equity and liabilities		
Equity		
Ordinary share capital		200,000
Retained earnings (W3)		445,400
Shareholders' funds		645,400
Non-controlling interests (W2)		59,350
		704,750
Current liabilities		
Trade payables ($160,400 + $40,200 + $800)	201,400	
Taxation ($60,000 + $7,000)	67,000	
		268,400
		973,150

PART B BUSINESS COMBINATIONS AND GROUP FINANCIAL STATEMENTS

If Antelope adopted a policy of measuring the non-controlling interest at fair value, workings 1 and 2 would change as follows:

1 Goodwill

	A in Y		Y in Z		
	$	$	$	$	$
Consideration transferred		110,000	(75% × 6,200)	4,650	
Fair value of NCI					
25,000 shares × $1.50		37,500			
4,000 shares × 75c					3,000
Fair value of identifiable NA acquired:					
Share capital	100,000		10,000		
Retained earnings:	40,000		(2,500)		
($3,000) + $500					
	140,000		7,500		
Group share 75%/25%	(105,000)	(35,000)	60%/40% (4,500)	(3,000)	
	5,000	2,500		150	—

{ 7,650 }

2 Non-controlling interests

	Yak $	Zebra $
Net assets per Q	229,200	9,000
Less investment in Zebra	(6,200)	–
	223,000	9,000
	× 25%	× 40%
	55,750	3,600
NCI goodwill	2,500	–
	58,250	3,600

{ 61,850 }

Therefore reported goodwill would be $7,650 and the non-controlling interest would be $61,850. All other amounts in the consolidated statement of financial position would remain the same.

2.5 Section summary

You should follow this **step by step approach** in all questions using the single-stage method. This applies to Section 3 below as well.

Step 1 Sketch the **group structure** and check it to the question.

Step 2 **Add details** to the sketch of dates of acquisition, holdings acquired (percentage and nominal values) and cost.

Step 3 **Goodwill working**: compare costs of investment with the **effective** group interests acquired.

Step 4 **Non-controlling interest working**: total NCI in subsidiary plus total NCI in sub-subsidiary.

Step 5 **Reserves working**: include the group share of subsidiary and sub-subsidiary post-acquisition retained earnings (effective holdings again).

Step 6 Prepare the **consolidated statement of financial position** (and statement of profit or loss and other comprehensive income if required).

3 Direct holdings in sub-subsidiaries

Consider the following structure, sometimes called a **'D-shaped' group**.

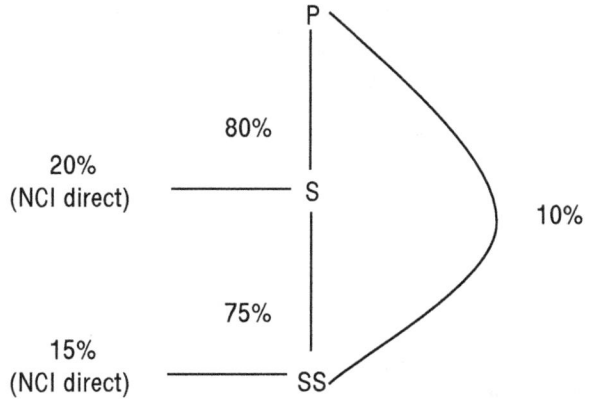

In the structure above, there is:

(a)	A **direct** non-controlling share in S of		20%
(b)	A **direct** non-controlling share in SS of	15%	
(c)	An **indirect** non-controlling share in SS of 20% × 75% =	15%	
			30%

The effective interest in SS is:

Group 80% × 75% indirect	=	60%
Direct		10%
		70%
∴ NCI		30%
		100%

Having ascertained the structure and non-controlling interests, proceed as for a typical sub-subsidiary situation.

Question   'D' shaped group

The draft statements of financial position of Hulk Co, Molehill Co and Pimple Co as at 31 May 20X5 are as follows.

	Hulk Co		Molehill Co		Pimple Co	
	$	$	$	$	$	$
Assets						
Non-current assets						
Property, plant and equipment		90,000		60,000		60,000
Investments in subsidiaries (cost)						
Shares in Molehill Co	90,000		–		–	
Shares in Pimple Co	25,000		42,000		–	
		115,000		42,000		–
		205,000		102,000		60,000
Current assets		40,000		50,000		40,000
		245,000		152,000		100,000

PART B BUSINESS COMBINATIONS AND GROUP FINANCIAL STATEMENTS

	Hulk Co		Molehill Co		Pimple Co	
	$	$	$	$	$	$
Equity and liabilities						
Equity						
Ordinary shares $1	100,000		50,000		50,000	
Retained earnings	45,000		32,000		25,000	
Other reserves	50,000		20,000		–	
		195,000		102,000		75,000
Non-current liabilities						
12% loan		–		10,000		–
		195,000		112,000		75,000
Current liabilities						
Payables		50,000		40,000		25,000
		245,000		152,000		100,000

(a) Hulk Co acquired 60% of the shares in Molehill on 1 January 20X3 when the balance on that company's retained earnings was $8,000 (credit) and there were no other reserves.

(b) On 1 January 20X4 Hulk acquired 20% of the shares of Pimple Co and Molehill acquired 60% of the shares of Pimple Co when that company's retained earnings stood at $15,000.

(c) There has been no payment of dividends by either Molehill or Pimple since they became subsidiaries.

(d) There was no impairment of goodwill.

(e) It is the group's policy to measure the non-controlling interest at acquisition at fair value. The fair value of the non-controlling interest in Molehill at acquisition was $45,000; the fair value of a share in Pimple immediately prior to the acquisition date was $1.75.

Required

Prepare the consolidated statement of financial position of Hulk Co as at 31 May 20X5.

Answer

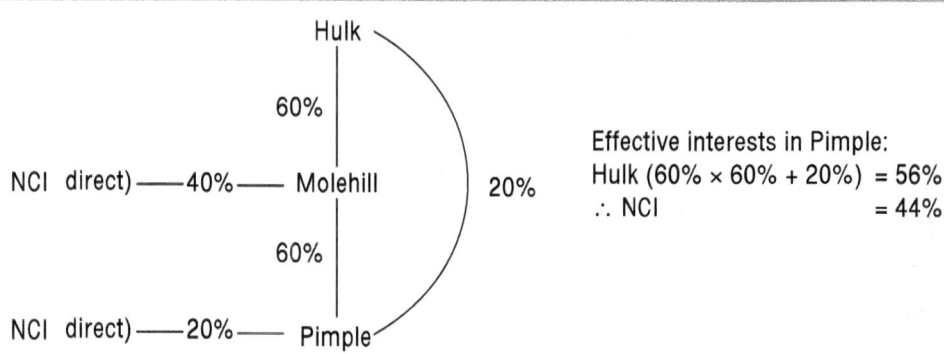

Effective interests in Pimple:
Hulk (60% × 60% + 20%) = 56%
∴ NCI = 44%

The direct non-controlling interest in Molehill Co is	40%
The direct non-controlling interest in Pimple Co is	20%
The indirect non-controlling interest in Pimple Co is (40% of 60%)	24%
The total non-controlling interest in Pimple Co is	44%

The group share of Molehill Co is 60% and of Pimple Co is (100 – 44)% = 56%

Workings

1 **Goodwill**

Hulk in Molehill

		Group $	NCI $
Consideration transferred/fair value of NCI		90,000	45,000
Fair value of net assets acquired			
share capital	50,000		
Retained earnings	8,000		
	58,000 × 60% /40%	(34,800)	(23,200)
		55,200	21,800

Molehill/Hulk in Pimple

		Group $	NCI $
Consideration transferred by Molehill (60% × 42,000)		25,200	
Consideration transferred by Hulk		25,000	
Fair value of NCI (44% × 50,000 × $1.75)			38,500
		50,200	
Fair value of net assets acquired			
Share capital	50,000		
Retained earnings	15,000		
	65,000	(36,400)	(28,600)
	× 56% / 44%		
		13,800	9,900

Total goodwill: 55,200 + 21,800 + 13,800 + 9,900 = 100,700

2 **Non-controlling interests**

	Molehill $	Pimple $
Net assets per question	102,000	75,000
Investment in Pimple	(42,000)	–
	60,000	75,000
	× 40%	× 44%
	24,000	33,000
Goodwill	21,800	9,900
	45,800	42,900
	$88,700	

3 **Retained earnings**

	Hulk $	Molehill $	Pimple $
Per question	45,000	32,000	25,000
Pre-acquisition profits		(8,000)	(15,000)
Post-acquisition retained earnings		24,000	10,000

Group share:

In Molehill ($24,000 × 60%)	14,400
In Pimple ($10,000 × 56%)	5,600
Group retained earnings	65,000

4   Other reserves

	$
Hulk Co	50,000
Molehill Co: all post-acquisition ($20,000 × 60%)	12,000
	62,000

HULK CO
CONSOLIDATED STATEMENT OF FINANCIAL POSITION AS AT 31 MAY 20X8

	$	$
Assets		
Non-current assets		
Property, plant and equipment ($90,000 + $60,000 + $60,000)	210,000	
Goodwill (W1)	100,700	
		310,700
Current assets ($40,000 + $50,000 + $40,000)		130,000
		440,700
Equity and liabilities		
Equity		
Ordinary shares $1	100,000	
Retained earnings (W3)	65,000	
Other reserves (W4)	62,000	
Shareholders' funds	227,000	
Non-controlling interests (W2)	88,700	
		315,700
Non-current liabilities		
12% loan		10,000
		325,700
Current liabilities		
Payables ($50,000 + $40,000 + $25,000)		115,000
		440,700

4 Associates held by subsidiaries

Now let us consider a vertical group where the subsidiary holds an associate rather than a sub-subsidiary:

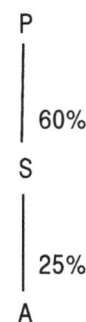

Here, P controls S which has a significant influence in A and therefore A is an associate of P by virtue of the fact that P has indirect significant influence over it. P's effective holding in A is 15% (60% × 25%)

There is also a 40% non-controlling interest in the subsidiary and that non-controlling interest has a 10% (40% × 25%) interest in the associate. Therefore the non-controlling interest shown in the consolidated financial statements of the group should include the **non-controlling interest of the subsidiary's interest** in the results and net assets of the associated company.

This means that the group financial statements must include the 'gross' share of net assets, pre-tax profits and tax, in accounting for the **non-controlling interest separately**. The relevant amounts for inclusion in the consolidated financial statements based on the above illustration would be as follows.

CONSOLIDATED STATEMENT OF PROFIT OR LOSS AND OTHER COMPREHENSIVE INCOME

Operating profit	(P 100% + S 100%)
Share of profit for the year of associate	(A 25%)
Tax	(P 100% + S 100%)
Non-controlling interest	(S 40% + A 10%)
Retained profits	(P 100% + S 60% + A 15%)

CONSOLIDATED STATEMENT OF FINANCIAL POSITION

Investment in associate company	(figures based on 25% holding)
Non-controlling interest	((40% × shareholders' funds of S) + (10 × post-acquisition retained earnings of A))
Unrealised reserves	(15% × post-acquisition reserves of A)
Group retained earnings	((100% × P) + (60% × post-acquisition of S))

4.1 Example

Parker Co has held an 80% investment in Swiffen Co for a number of years, acquired when the retained earnings of Swiffen were $50,000. Swiffen recently acquired a 40% holding in Aspin Co when the reserves of that company were $40,000. The summarised statements of financial position of the three companies at 31 December 20X9 were as follows:

	Parker $'000	Swiffen $'000	Aspin $'000
Non-current assets	320	220	105
Investment in S/A	80	22	
Current assets	15	40	18
	415	282	123
Share capital	50	30	15
Retained earnings	240	170	95
	290	200	110
Liabilities	125	82	13
	415	282	123

Other relevant information is as follows:

- Parker Co measures the non-controlling interest as a proportion of the fair value of net assets acquired.

- At the date of acquisition, Swiffen's statement of financial position included land with a market value $10,000 in excess of its carrying amount.

- During the year Parker has sold goods to Swiffen. Current account balances at the year end agree at $2,000. At the year end Swiffen is holding inventory purchased from Parker at a cost of $2,000. The original cost of this inventory to Parker was $1,000.

- There has been no impairment of the goodwill in Swiffen or investment in Aspin.

Prepare the consolidated statement of financial position of the Swiffen group at 31 December 20X9.

Solution

CONSOLIDATED STATEMENT OF FINANCIAL POSITION OF THE SWIFFEN GROUP AT 31 DECEMBER 20X9

	$'000
Non-current assets (320 + 220 + 10)	550
Investment in associate (W2)	44
Goodwill (W3)	8
Current assets (15 + 40 – 2 – 1 (PUP))	52
	654
Share capital	50
Retained earnings (W5)	352.6
Non-controlling interest (W6)	46.4
Liabilities (125 + 82 – 2)	205
	654

Workings

1 Group structure

```
        P
        |
        |  80%
        S
        |
        |  40%
        A
```

2 Investment in Associate

	$'000
Cost	22
Group share of post-acquisition profits (95 – 40) × 40%	22
	44

3 Goodwill

	$'000
Consideration transferred	80
NCI (90 × 20%)	18
Net assets acquired	98
Share capital	(30)
Reserves	(50)
FV adjustment	(10)
Goodwill	8

4   Retained earnings

	P	S	A
	$	$	$
At 31.12.X9	240	170	95
At acquisition		(50)	(40)
		120	55
PUP	(1)		
S × 80%	96.0		
A × 32%	17.6		
	352.6		

5   Non-controlling interest

	$'000
S: 20% × (200 + 10)	42.0
A: 8% × (95 − 40)	4.4
	46.4

PART B BUSINESS COMBINATIONS AND GROUP FINANCIAL STATEMENTS

Chapter roundup

- When a holding company has **several subsidiaries**, the consolidated statement of financial position shows a single figure for non-controlling interests and for goodwill arising on consolidation. In cases where there are several subsidiary companies, the technique is to open up a single non-controlling interest working and a columnar goodwill working.
- When dealing with **sub-subsidiaries,** you will need to calculate effective interest owned by the group and by the non-controlling interest.
- The **date of acquisition** is important when dealing with sub-subsidiaries.
- Remember that it is the post-acquisition reserves from a **group perspective** which are relevant

Quick quiz

1. B Co owns 60% of the equity of C Co which owns 75% of the equity of D Co. What is the total non-controlling interest percentage ownership in D Co?
2. What is the basic consolidation method for sub-subsidiaries?
3. L Co acquired a controlling interest in M Co on 1 October 20X4. M Co already had a controlling interest in N Co, which was acquired on 1 May 20X3. From which date should N Co be consolidated into the L Co group?
4. What is meant by the term 'D-shaped group'?
5. P Co owns 25% of R Co's equity and 75% of Q Co's equity. Q Co owns 40% of R Co's equity. What is the total non-controlling interest percentage ownership in R Co?

Answers to quick quiz

1   B
    | 60%
    C
    | 75%
    D

    Non-controlling interest = 25% + (40% of 75%) = 55%

2   - Net assets: show what the group controls
    - Equity (capital and reserves): show who owns the net assets

3   N Co should be consolidated into the L Co group from 1 October 20X4, which is the earliest date at which N Co is under the control of the L Co group.

4. A D-shaped group arises when a parent company has an indirect interest in a sub-subsidiary and also a direct non-controlling interest in that sub-subsidiary.

5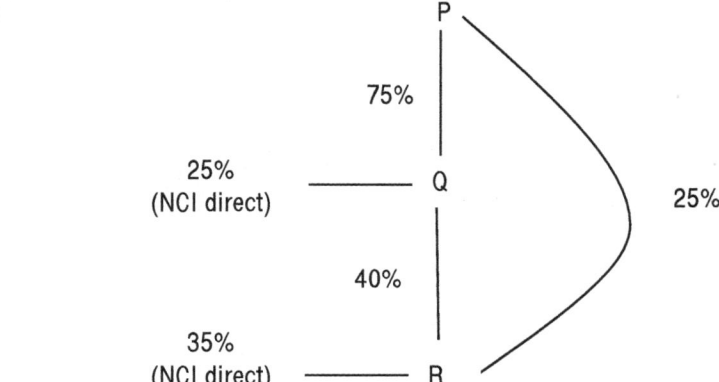

Total non-controlling interest in R is 35% + (25% × 40%) = 45%

End of chapter question

Insolo (AIA November 2007)

The following are the summarised statements of financial position of Insolo, Vanior and Transbuy, three limited liability companies, as at 31 October 20X7, the end of the companies' most recent financial year:

STATEMENTS OF FINANCIAL POSITION AS AT 31 OCTOBER 20X7

ASSETS	Insolo	Vanior	Transbuy
Non-current assets	$	$	$
Property, plant and equipment	4,568,900	3,556,000	4,280,700
Investments, at cost	3,869,500	2,801,600	34,200
	8,438,400	6,357,600	4,314,900
Current assets			
Inventories, at cost	440,000	186,500	230,800
Trade receivables	539,080	306,750	401,200
Other receivables	87,090	34,000	16,500
Cash and cash equivalents	236,700	186,300	207,530
	1,302,870	713,550	856,030
Total assets	9,741,270	7,071,150	5,170,930
LIABILITIES AND EQUITY			
Non-current liabilities	500,000	420,000	320,800
Current liabilities			
Trade payables	539,080	345,620	412,090
Other payables	66,900	18,700	14,500
Taxation	164,200	88,600	65,400
	770,180	452,920	491,990
Equity			
Share capital			
Ordinary shares of $1	2,000,000	2,250,000	1,800,000
Preference shares of $1	400,000	200,000	300,000
Retained earnings	6,071,090	3,748,230	2,258,140
	9,741,270	7,071,150	5,170,930

The following additional information is available:

(i) Insolo purchased 1,350,000 ordinary shares in Vanior paying $2.85 per share on 1 November 2004 when Vanior's reserves were $1,262,500. For the purposes of the acquisition some land owned by Vanior was agreed to have a fair value $400,000 higher than its carrying value. The land is not depreciated and the acquisition valuation was not recorded in the financial statements of Vanior. All other assets and liabilities were recorded in the statement of financial position of Vanior at their fair values.

(ii) Vanior purchased 1,260,000 ordinary shares paying $2.15 per share and 60,000 preference shares paying $1.25 per share in Transbuy on 1 November 2005 when Transbuy's reserves were $662,857. All assets and liabilities of Transbuy were recorded in its statement of financial position at their fair values as at 1 November 20X5. During the year ended 31 October 20X6 the goodwill arising on the acquisition of Transbuy was impaired by $220,000.

(iii) Included in the inventory of Vanior as at 31 October 20X7 were items valued at $100,000. These items had been purchased from Insolo and the original cost of the items to Insolo was $68,200. Vanior had invoices totalling $41,200 payable to Insolo as at 31 October 20X7.

(iv) Included in the inventory of Transbuy as at 31 October 20X7 were items valued at $80,000. These items had been purchased from Vanior which purchased them from a non-related company for $55,700. Transbuy had invoices totalling $53,200 payable to Vanior as at 31 October 20X7.

(v) It is the group's policy to measure the non-controlling interest at acquisition at its proportionate share of the fair value of the subsidiary's net assets.

Required

(a) Calculate the goodwill paid by each holding company on the acquisition of its subsidiary.

(6 marks)

(b) Prepare the consolidated statement of financial position of Insolo as at 31 October 20X7 showing all supportive workings clearly. **(19 marks)**

(Total 25 marks)

PART B BUSINESS COMBINATIONS AND GROUP FINANCIAL STATEMENTS

Changes in group structures

Topic list	Syllabus reference
1 Disposals	LO2 + LO3
2 Business combinations achieved in stages	LO2 + LO3
3 Bonus issues and capital reductions	LO2 + LO3

Introduction

Controlling interest in a company is rarely gained in a single purchase transaction. It is more likely that control is gained through a series of smaller acquisitions. Parent companies can, of course, also decide to dispose of some or all of their controlling interests in a subsidiary or associate. These purchase and disposal transactions are common in practise and are likely to come up in the exam. Your approach should be the same as for more simple consolidation questions: **methodical and logical**. If you understand the basic principles of consolidation, you should be able to tackle these complicated questions.

PART B BUSINESS COMBINATIONS AND GROUP FINANCIAL STATEMENTS

1 Disposals

FAST FORWARD

Disposals can drop a subsidiary holding to associate status, non-current asset investment status or to zero, or a parent might still retain a subsidiary with a reduced holding. You should be able to deal with all these situations. Remember particularly how to deal with **goodwill**.

1.1 Types of disposal

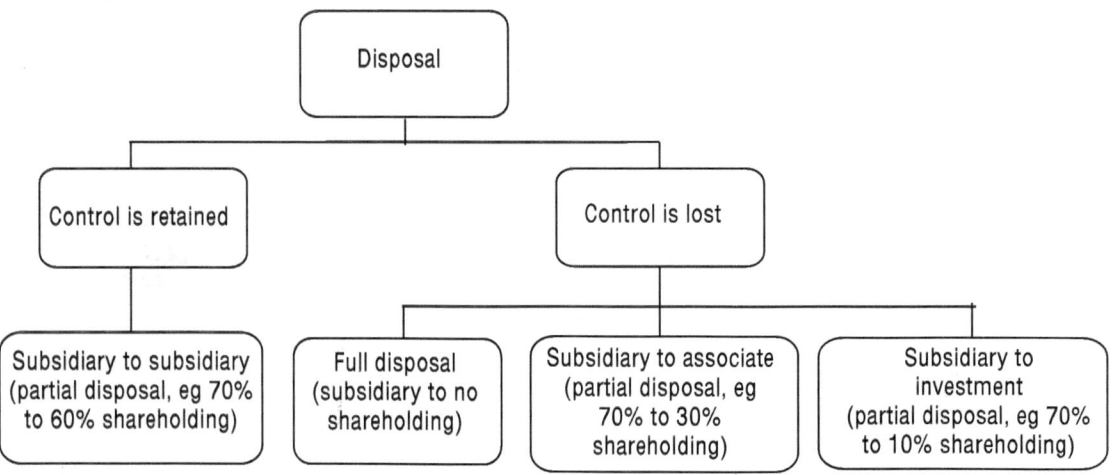

1.2 General principle: 'crossing an accounting boundary'

Under IFRS 3 *Business Combinations* disposal occurs only when one entity loses control over another, which is generally when its holding is decreased to less than 50%. The Deloitte guide: *Business Combinations and Changes in Ownership Interests* calls this **'crossing an accounting boundary'**. For illustration purposes, the Deloitte guide assumes that percentage holding is key when determining whether control is lost. You should be aware of the indicators of control, as covered in Chapter 6, and be able to apply those to determine whether control is lost.

On disposal of a controlling interest, any retained interest (an associate or financial asset investment) is measured at fair value on the date that control is lost. This fair value is used in the calculation of the gain or loss on disposal, and also becomes the carrying amount for subsequent accounting for the retained interest.

If the **50%** boundary is **not crossed** or control is not lost, such as when the interest in a subsidiary is reduced, the event is treated as a **transaction between owners**.

Whenever control is lost, calculate a gain or loss on disposal, revalue any retained investment to fair value, and report a gain or loss in profit or loss for the year. If there is a disposal in which control is retained, no gain or loss is reported; instead there is an adjustment to the parent's equity.

The following diagram, from the *Deloitte* guide, may help you visualise the boundary.

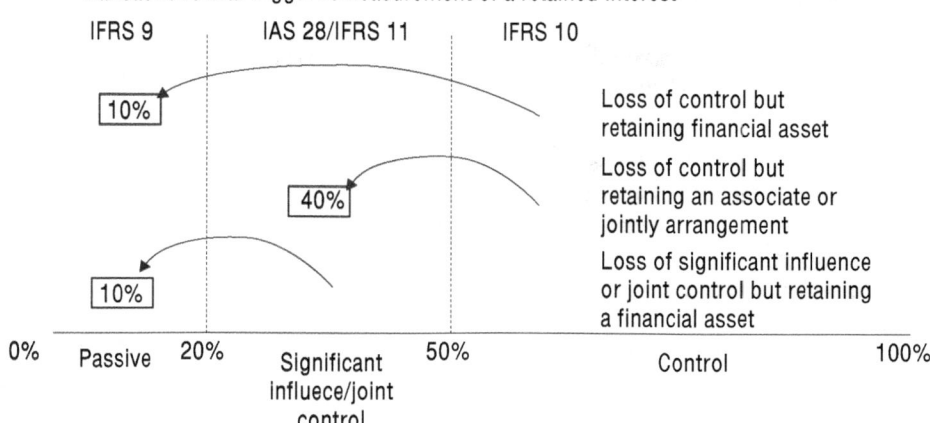

1.3 Effective date of disposal

The effective date of disposal is **when control passes**: the date for accounting for an entity ceasing to be a subsidiary is the date on which its former parent relinquishes its control over that entity. The consolidated statement of profit or loss and other comprehensive income should include the results of a subsidiary up to the date of its disposal. IFRS 5 on disclosure of discontinued operations (see Chapter 18) will have an impact here.

1.4 Control lost: calculation of group gain on disposal

A proforma calculation is shown below. This needs to be adapted for the circumstances in the question, in particular whether it is a full or partial disposal.

		$
Fair value of consideration received		X
Fair value of any interest retained		X
Less:	net assets × share (%) held at date control lost	(X)
	goodwill less any NCI in goodwill at date control lost	(X)
Add/less:	gains/(losses) previously recognised in OCI	X/(X)
Group profit/(loss)		X/(X)

Following IAS 1 *Presentation of Financial Statements*, this gain may need to be disclosed separately if it is material.

1.4.1 Analogy: trading in a large car for a smaller one

It may seem counter-intuitive that the investment retained is now part of the 'proceeds' for the purposes of calculating the gain. One way of looking at it is to imagine that you are selling a larger car and putting part of the proceeds towards a smaller one. If the larger car you are selling cost you less than the smaller car and cash combined, you have made a profit. Likewise, the company making the disposal sold a larger stake to gain, at fair value, a smaller stake and some cash on top, which is the 'consideration received'.

This analogy is not exact, but may help.

1.5 Control lost: Calculation of gain in parent's separate financial statements

This calculation is more straightforward: the proceeds are compared with the carrying amount of the investment sold. The investment will be held at cost or in accordance with IFRS 9 *Financial Instruments*.

	$
Fair value of consideration received	X
Less carrying amount of investment disposed	(X)
Add/(less) fair value changes previously recognised in OCI (if designated as FV through OCI)	X/(X)
Profit/(loss) on disposal	X/(X)

The profit on disposal is generally taxable, and the **tax charge based on the parent's gain** rather than the group's.

1.6 Disposals where control is lost: Accounting treatment

1.6.1 Full disposal

For a **full disposal**, apply the following treatment:

(a) **Statement of profit or loss and other comprehensive income**

  (i) Consolidate results and non-controlling interest to the date of disposal.
  (ii) Show the group profit or loss on disposal.

(b) **Statement of financial position**

  There will be no non-controlling interest and no consolidation as there is no subsidiary at the date the statement of financial position is being prepared.

1.6.2 Partial disposal

For **partial disposals**, use the following treatments:

(a) **Subsidiary to associate**

  (i) **Statement of profit or loss and other comprehensive income**

    (1) Treat the investment as a subsidiary up to the date of disposal, ie consolidate for the correct number of months and show the non-controlling interest in that amount.
    (2) Show the profit or loss on disposal.
    (3) Treat as an associate thereafter.

  (ii) **Statement of financial position**

    (1) The investment remaining is at its fair value at the date of disposal (to calculate the gain).
    (2) Equity account (as an associate) thereafter, using the fair value as the new 'cost'. (Post-'acquisition' retained earnings are added to this cost in future years to arrive at the carrying value of the investment in the associate in the statement of financial position.)

(b) **Subsidiary to financial asset investment**

  (i) **Statement of profit or loss and other comprehensive income**

    (1) Treat the investment as a subsidiary up to the date of disposal, ie consolidate.
    (2) Show profit or loss on disposal.
    (3) Show dividend income only thereafter.

(ii) **Statement of financial position**

(1) The investment remaining is at its fair value at the date of disposal (to calculate the gain).

(2) Thereafter, treat as a financial asset under IFRS 9.

1.7 Disposals where control is retained

Control is retained where the disposal is from **subsidiary to subsidiary**. The accounting treatment is treatment is as follows.

1.7.1 Statement of profit or loss and other comprehensive income

(a) The subsidiary is **consolidated in full** for the whole period.

(b) The **non-controlling interest in the statement of profit or loss and other comprehensive income** will be based on the percentages before and after disposal, ie time apportion.

(c) There is no profit or loss on disposal.

1.7.2 Statement of financial position

(a) The non-controlling interest in the statement of financial position is based on the year end percentage.

(b) The change (increase) in non-controlling interests is shown as an adjustment to the parent's equity.

(c) Goodwill on acquisition is unchanged in the consolidated statement of financial position.

1.7.3 Adjustment to the parent's equity

This reflects the fact that the non-controlling share has increased (as the parent's share has reduced). A subsidiary to subsidiary disposal is, in effect, **a transaction between owners**. Specifically, it is a reallocation of ownership between parent and non-controlling equity holders. **The goodwill is unchanged**, because it is a historical figure, unaffected by the reallocation. The adjustment to the parent's equity is calculated as follows.

	$
Fair value of consideration received	X
Increase in NCI in net assets at disposal	(X)
Increase in NCI in goodwill at disposal *	(X)
Adjustment to parent's equity	X

*Note. This line is only required where non-controlling interests are measured at fair value at the date of acquisition (ie where there is an increase in the non-controlling interest share of goodwill already recognised).

If you are wondering why the decrease in shareholding is treated as a transaction between owners, look back to Chapter 6. IFRS 3 views **the group as an economic entity**, and views **all providers of equity**, including non-controlling interests, as **owners of the group**. Non-controlling shareholders are not outsiders, they are owners of the group just like the parent.

You can practise the adjustment to parent's equity in the example and question below.

1.7.4 Gain in the parent's separate financial statements

This is calculated as for disposals where control is lost: see Section 1.5 above.

PART B BUSINESS COMBINATIONS AND GROUP FINANCIAL STATEMENTS

1.8 Example: Partial disposals

Chalk Co bought 100% of the voting share capital of Cheese Co on its incorporation on 1 January 20X2 for $160,000. Cheese Co earned and retained $240,000 from that date until 31 December 20X7. At that date the statements of financial position of the companies and the group were as follows.

	Chalk Co $'000	Cheese Co $'000	Consolidated $'000
Investment in Cheese	160	–	–
Other net assets	1,000	500	1,500
	1,160	500	1,500
Share capital	400	160	400
Retained earnings	560	240	800
Current liabilities	200	100	300
	1,160	500	1,500

It is the group's policy to value the non-controlling interest at its proportionate share of the fair value of the subsidiary's identifiable net assets.

On 1 January 20X8 Chalk Co sold 40% of its shareholding in Cheese Co for $280,000 in cash. The profit on disposal (ignoring tax) in the financial statements of the parent company is calculated as follows.

	Chalk $'000
Fair value of consideration received	280
Carrying amount of investment (40% × 160)	64
Profit on sale	216

We now move on to calculate the adjustment to equity for the group financial statements.

Because only 40% of the 100% subsidiary has been sold, leaving a 60% subsidiary, **control is retained**. This means that there is **no group profit on disposal in profit or loss for the year**. Instead, there is an **adjustment to the parent's equity**, which affects group retained earnings.

Point to note

> Remember that, when control is retained, the disposal is just a transaction between owners. The non-controlling shareholders are owners of the group, just like the parent.

The adjustment to parent's equity is calculated as follows.

	$'000
Fair value of consideration received	280
Increase in non-controlling interest in net assets at the date of disposal (40% × (160 + 240))	160
Adjustment to parent's equity	120

This increases group retained earnings and does not go through group profit or loss for the year. (Note that there is no goodwill in this example, or non-controlling interest in goodwill, as the subsidiary was acquired on incorporation.)

Solution 1

The statements of financial position immediately after the sale will appear as follows:

	Chalk Co $'000	Cheese Co $'000	Consolidated $'000
Investment in Cheese (160 – 64)	96		
Other net assets (Chalk 1,000 + 280)	1,280	500	1,780
	1,376	500	1,780
Share capital	400	160	400
Retained earnings*	776	240	920
Non-controlling interest	–	–	160

	Chalk Co $'000	Cheese Co $'000	Consolidated $'000
Equity	1,176		1,480
Current liabilities	200	100	300
	1,376	500	1,780

*Chalk's retained earnings are $560,000 + $216,000 profit on disposal. Group retained earnings are increased by the adjustment above: $800,000 + $120,000 = $920,000.

Solution 2

Using the above example, assume that Chalk Co sold 60% of its holding in Cheese Co for $440,000 in cash. The fair value of the 40% holding retained was $200,000. The gain or loss on disposal in the books of the parent company would be calculated as follows:

	Parent company $'000
Fair value of consideration received	440
Carrying value of investment (60 × 160)	96
Profit on sale	344

This time control is lost, so there will be a gain in group profit or loss, calculated as follows:

	$'000
Fair value of consideration received	440
Fair value of investment retained	200
Less Chalk's share of consolidated carrying value at date control lost (100% × (160 + 240))	(400)
Group profit on sale	240

Note that there was no goodwill arising on the acquisition of Cheese, otherwise this too would be deducted in the calculation.

The statements of financial position would now appear as follows:

	Chalk Co $'000	Cheese Co $'000	Consolidated $'000
Investment in Cheese (Note 1)	64		200
Other net assets (Chalk 1,000 + 440)	1,440	500	1,440
	1,504	500	1,640
Share capital	400	160	400
Retained earnings (Note 2)	904	240	1,040
Current liabilities	200	100	200
	1,504	500	1,640

Notes.

1 The investment in Cheese is measured at prorata cost (40% × 160) in Chalk's SOFP but at fair value in the group SOFP. In fact it is equity accounted at fair value at date control lost plus share of post-'acquisition' retained earnings. But there are no retained earnings yet because control has only just been lost.

2 Chalk's retained earnings are $560,000 (per question) plus parent's profit on the sale of $344,000, ie $904,000. Group retained earnings are $800,000 (per question) plus group profit on the sale of $240,000, ie $1,040,000.

The following comprehensive question should help you get to grips with disposal problems. Try to complete the whole question without looking at the solution, and then check your answer very carefully. **Give yourself at least two hours**. This is a very difficult question.

Exam focus point | Questions may involve part-disposals leaving investments with both subsidiary and associate status.

PART B BUSINESS COMBINATIONS AND GROUP FINANCIAL STATEMENTS

Question — Disposal

Smith Co bought 80% of the share capital of Jones Co for $324,000 on 1 October 20X5. At that date Jones Co's retained earnings balance stood at $180,000. The statements of financial position at 30 September 20X8 and the summarised statements of profit or loss and other comprehensive income to that date are given below.

	Smith Co $'000	Jones Co $'000
Non-current assets	360	270
Investment in Jones Co	324	–
Current assets	370	370
	1,054	640
Equity		
$1 ordinary shares	540	180
Retained earnings	414	360
Current liabilities	100	100
	1,054	640
Profit before tax	153	126
Tax	(45)	(36)
Profit for the year	108	90

No entries have been made in the financial statements for any of the following transactions.

Assume that profits accrue evenly throughout the year.

It is the group's policy to value the non-controlling interest at its proportionate share of the fair value of the subsidiary's identifiable net assets.

Ignore taxation.

Required

Prepare the consolidated statement of financial position and statement of profit or loss and other comprehensive income at 30 September 20X8 in each of the following circumstances. (Assume no impairment of goodwill.)

(a) Smith Co sells its entire holding in Jones Co for $650,000 on 30 September 20X8.

(b) Smith Co sells one quarter of its holding in Jones Co for $160,000 on 30 June 20X8.

(c) Smith Co sells one half of its holding in Jones Co for $340,000 on 30 June 20X8, and the remaining holding (fair value $250,000) is to be dealt with as an associate.

(d) Smith Co sells one half of its holding in Jones Co for $340,000 on 30 June 20X8, and the remaining holding (fair value $250,000) is to be dealt with as a financial asset.

Answer

(a) *Complete disposal at year end (80% to 0%)*

CONSOLIDATED STATEMENT OF FINANCIAL POSITION
AS AT 30 SEPTEMBER 20X8

	$'000
Non-current assets	360
Current assets (370 + 650)	1,020
	1,380
Equity	
$1 ordinary shares	540
Retained earnings (W2)	740
Current liabilities	100
	1,380

CONSOLIDATED STATEMENT OF PROFIT OR LOSS AND OTHER COMPREHENSIVE INCOME FOR THE YEAR ENDED 30 SEPTEMBER 20X8

	$'000
Profit before tax (153 + 126)	279
Profit on disposal (W1)	182
Tax (45 + 36)	(81)
	380
Profit attributable to:	
Owners of the parent	362
Non-controlling interest (20% × 90)	18
	380

Workings

1 *Profit on disposal of Jones Co*

	$'000	$'000
Fair value of consideration received		650
Less share of consolidated carrying value when control lost:		
net assets (540 × 80%)	432	
Goodwill (see Note)	36	
		(468)
		182

Note: goodwill

	$'000
Consideration transferred	324
Acquired: 80% × (180 + 180)	(288)
	36

2 *Retained earnings carried forward*

	$'000
Smith per question	414
Jones: 80% × (360 − 180)	144
Profit on disposal (W1)	182
	740

Or:

	$'000
Brought forward Smith (414 − 108 profit for year)	306
Jones: 80% × (360 − (180 + 90 profit for year))	72
Profit for year attributable to owners (per statement of profit or loss and other comprehensive income)	362
	740

(b) *Partial disposal: subsidiary to subsidiary (80% to 60%)*

CONSOLIDATED STATEMENT OF FINANCIAL POSITION AS AT 30 SEPTEMBER 20X8

	$'000
Non-current assets (360 + 270)	630
Goodwill (part (a))	36
Current assets (370 + 160 + 370)	900
	1,566
Equity	
$1 ordinary shares	540
Retained earnings (W2)	610
	1,150
Non-controlling interest (40% × 540)	216
Current liabilities (100 + 100)	200
	1,566

PART B BUSINESS COMBINATIONS AND GROUP FINANCIAL STATEMENTS

CONSOLIDATED STATEMENT OF PROFIT OR LOSS AND OTHER COMPREHENSIVE INCOME
FOR THE YEAR ENDED 30 SEPTEMBER 20X8

	$'000	$'000
Profit before tax (153 + 126)		279
Tax (45 + 36)		(81)
Profit for the period		198
Profit attributable to:		
Owners of the parent		175.5
Non-controlling interest		
20% × 90 × 9/12	13.5	
40% × 90 × 3/12	9.0	
		22.5
		198.0

Workings

1 *Adjustment to parent's equity on disposal of 20% of Jones*

	$'000	$'000
Fair value of consideration received		160.0
Less increase in NCI in net assets at disposal		
20% × (540 − (3/12 × 90))		(103.5)
		56.5

2 *Group retained earnings*

	Smith $'000	Jones 60% $'000	Jones 20% sold $'000
Per question/at date of disposal (360 − (90 × 3/12))	414.0	360	337.5
Adjustment to parent's equity on disposal (W1)	56.5		
Retained earnings at acquisition		(180)	(180.0)
		180	157.5
Jones: share of post acq'n. earnings (180 × 60%)	108.0		
Smith: share of post acq'n. earnings (157.5 × 20%)	31.5		
	610.0		

Or:

	$'000
Brought forward As before (306 + 72)	378.0
Adjustment on disposal (W1)	56.5
Profit for year attributable to owners (per statement of profit or loss and other comprehensive income)	175.5
	610.0

(c) (i) *Partial disposal: subsidiary to associate (80% to 40%)*

CONSOLIDATED STATEMENT OF FINANCIAL POSITION AS AT 30 SEPTEMBER 20X8

	$'000
Non-current assets	360
Investment in associate (W3)	259
Current assets (370 + 340)	710
	1,329
Equity	
$1 ordinary shares	540
Retained earnings (W2)	689
Current liabilities	100
	1,329

CONSOLIDATED STATEMENT OF PROFIT OR LOSS AND OTHER COMPREHENSIVE INCOME FOR THE YEAR ENDED 30 SEPTEMBER 20X8

	$'000
Profit before tax (153 + 9/12 × 126)	247.5
Profit on disposal (W1)	140.0
Share of profit of associate (90 × 3/12 × 40%)	9.0
Tax 45 + (9/12 × 36)	(72.0)
Profit for the period	324.5
Profit attributable to:	
Owners of the parent	311.0
Non-controlling interest (20% × 90 × 9/12)	13.5
	324.5

Workings

1 Profit on disposal in Smith Co

	$'000	$'000
Fair value of consideration received		340
Fair value of 40% investment retained		250
Less share of consolidated carrying value when control lost		
80% × ((540 − (90 × 3/12))	414	
Goodwill (part (a))	36	
		(450)
		140

2 Group retained earnings

	Smith $'000	Jones 40% $'000	Jones 40% sold $'000
Per question/at date of disposal (360 − (90 × 3/12))	414	360	337.5
Group profit on disposal (W1)	140		
Retained earnings at acquisition		(180)	(180.0)
		180	157.5
Jones: share of post acq'n. earnings (180 × 40%)	72		
Jones: share of post acq'n. earnings (157.5 × 40%)	63		
	689		

Or:

	$'000
Brought forward as before (306 + 72)	378
Profit for year attributable to owners (per statement of profit or loss and other comprehensive income)	311
	689

3 Investment in associate

	$'000
Fair value at date control lost (new 'cost')	250
Share of post 'acq'n' retained reserves (90 × 3/12 × 40%)	9
	259

(d) *Partial disposal: subsidiary to financial asset (80% to 40%)*

CONSOLIDATED STATEMENT OF FINANCIAL POSITION
AS AT 30 SEPTEMBER 20X8

	$'000
Non-current assets	360
Investment (fair value at date of disposal)	250
Current assets (370 + 340)	710
	1,320
Equity	
$1 ordinary shares	540
Retained earnings (W)	680
Current liabilities	100
	1,320

CONSOLIDATED STATEMENT OF PROFIT OR LOSS AND OTHER COMPREHENSIVE INCOME
FOR THE YEAR ENDED 30 SEPTEMBER 20X8

	$'000
Profit before tax (153 + (9/12 × 126)	247.5
Profit on disposal (See (c) above)	140.0
Tax (45 + (9/12 × 36))	(72.0)
Profit for the period	315.5
Profit attributable to:	
Owners of the parent	302.0
Non-controlling interest	13.5
	315.5

Working: retained earnings

	Smith $'000	Jones $'000
Per question/at date of disposal (360 – (90 × 3/12))	414	337.5
Group profit on disposal (W1)	140	
Retained earnings at acquisition		(180.0)
		157.5
Smith: share of post acq'n. earnings (157.5 × 80%)	126	
	680	

Or:

	$'000
Brought forward as before (306 + 72)	378
Profit for year attributable to owners (per statement of profit or loss)	302
	680

1.9 Section summary

Disposals occur frequently in Financial Accounting and Reporting 2 consolidation questions.

- The effective date of disposal is when **control is lost**.
- Treatment of **goodwill** is according to IFRS 3.
- Disposals may be **full** or **partial** to subsidiary, associate or investment status.
    - **If control is lost,** the interest retained is **fair valued** and becomes part of the calculation of the gain on disposal.
    - **If control is retained**, the change in non-controlling interests is shown as **an adjustment to parent's equity**.
- **Gain or loss** on disposal is calculated for the parent company and the group.

2 Business combinations achieved in stages

FAST FORWARD

Transactions of the type described in this chapter can be very complicated and certainly look rather daunting. Remember and apply the **basic techniques** and you should find such questions easier than you expected.

Business combinations achieved in stages (step acquisitions) can lead to a company becoming a non-current asset investment, an associate and then a subsidiary over time. Make sure you can deal with each of these situations.

A parent company may acquire a controlling interest in the shares of a subsidiary as a result of **several successive share purchases**, rather than by purchasing the shares all on the same day. Business combinations achieved in stages may also be known as 'step acquisitions' or 'piecemeal acquisitions'.

Point to note

Business combinations achieved in stages are in many ways a mirror image of disposals. The same principles underly both.

2.1 Types of business combination achieved in stages

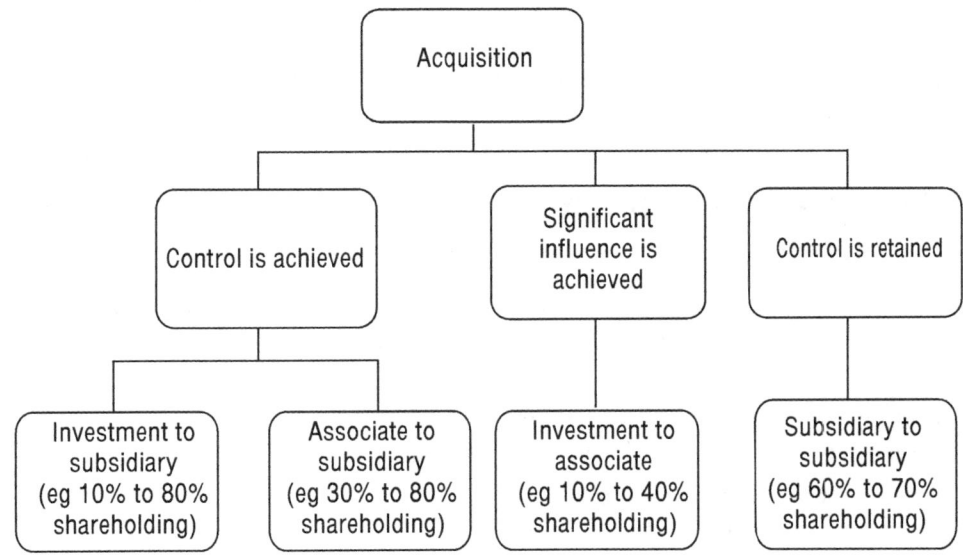

2.2 General principle

Under IFRS 3 a business combination occurs only when one entity **obtains control over another**, which is generally when 51% or more has been acquired. The Deloitte guide: *Business Combinations and Changes in Ownership Interests* calls this '**crossing an accounting boundary**'. As was discussed re: disposals, you should not rely solely on percentage holding to determine whether control exists, however the illustrations provide a useful visual as to the stages of investment.

When control is obtained, the original investment – whether an investment under IFRS 9 with no significant influence, or an associate – is **remeasured at fair value at the acquisition date**. This **previously held interest** at fair value, together with any consideration transferred, is the **'cost' of the combination** used in calculating the goodwill.

If control already exists but the percentage holding increases, such as when the interest in a subsidiary is increased, the event is treated as a **transaction between owners**.

Whenever you control is obtained, the original investment is revalued to fair value, and a gain or loss is reported in profit or loss for the year. If a controlling interest already exists, no gain or loss is reported; instead there is an adjustment to the parent's equity.

The following diagram, from the *Deloitte* guide may help you visualise the boundary.

Transactions that trigger remeasurement of an existing interest

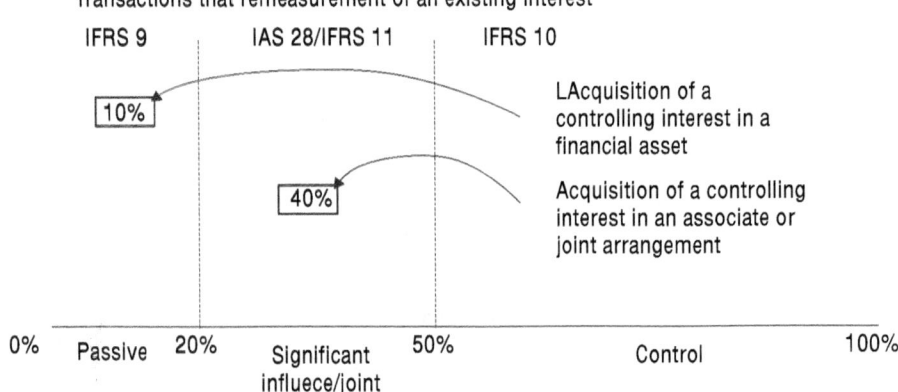

As you will see from the diagram, the third situation (c) in Section 2.1, where an interest in a subsidiary is increased from, say, 60% to 80%, does not involve crossing that all-important 50% threshold. Likewise, purchases of stakes of up to 50% do not involve crossing the boundary, and therefore do not trigger a calculation of goodwill.

Exam focus point

> In an exam, if you get a question with a business combination achieved in stages, ignore all purchases made before control is achieved, that is purchases bringing the total holding to less than 50%.

2.3 Investment or associate becomes a subsidiary: calculation of goodwill

The previously held investment is remeasured to fair value, with any gain being reported in profit and loss, and the goodwill calculated as follows.

		Group	NCI
Consideration transferred/Fair value of NCI		X	X
Fair value of acquirer's previously held equity interest		X	
Less: Net fair value of identifiable assets acquired and liabilities assumed	X		
× Group/NCI %		(X)	(X)
		X	X

Note. You only need the NCI column if NCI at acquisition is measured at fair value.

2.3.1 Analogy: Trading in a small car for a larger one

It may seem counter-intuitive that the previous investment is now part of the 'cost' for the purposes of calculating the goodwill. One way of looking at it is to imagine that you are part-exchanging a small car for a larger one. The value of the car you trade in is put towards the cost of the new vehicle, together with your cash (the 'consideration transferred'). Likewise, the company making the acquisition has part-exchanged its smaller investment – at fair value – for a larger one, and must naturally pay on top of that to obtain the larger investment.

This analogy is not exact, but may help.

Try the following question to get the hang of the calculation of goodwill and profit on de-recognition of the investment.

Question
Piecemeal acquisition 1

Good, whose year end is 30 June 20X9 has a subsidiary, Will, which it acquired in stages. The details of the acquisition are as follows:

Date of acquisition	Holding acquired %	Retained earnings at acquisition $m	Purchase consideration $m
1 July 20X7	20	270	120
1 July 20X8	60	450	480

The share capital of Will has remained unchanged since its incorporation at $300m. The fair values of the net assets of Will were the same as their carrying amounts at the date of the acquisition. Good did not have significant influence over Will at any time before gaining control of Will. The group policy is to measure non-controlling interest at its proportionate share of the fair value of the subsidiary's identifiable net assets. The fair value at 1 July 20X8 of Good's original 20% holding in Will is $160m.

Required

(a) Calculate the goodwill on the acquisition of Will that will appear in the consolidated statement of financial position at 30 June 20X9.

(b) Calculate the profit on the remeasurement of the previously held investment in Will to be reported in group profit or loss for the year ended 30 June 20X9.

Answer

(a) *Goodwill (at date control obtained)*

	$m	$m
Consideration transferred		480
Fair value of previously held equity interest		160
Fair value of identifiable assets acquired and liabilities assumed		
Share capital	300	
Retained earnings	450	
	750	
× 80%		(600)
		40

(b) *Profit on remeasurement of previously held equity interest*

	$m
Fair value at date control obtained	160
Cost	(120)
	40

In this short example, the figures for goodwill and profit on derecognition are the same. In the more complicated examples, such as the one in Section 2.5 below, they may different because the investment (a financial asset) may be revalued before or after control was obtained.

2.4 Increase in previously held controlling interest: adjustment to parent's equity

An example of this would be where an investment goes from a 60% subsidiary to an 80% subsidiary. The 50% threshold has not been crossed, so there is no re-measurement to fair value and no gain or loss to profit or loss for the year. The increase is treated as a **transaction between owners**. As with disposals, ownership has been **reallocated** between parent and non-controlling shareholders.

Accordingly the parent's equity is adjusted. The required adjustment is calculated by comparing the consideration paid with the decrease in non-controlling interest. (As the parent's share has increased, the NCI share has decreased.) The **calculation is as follows**:

	$
Fair value of consideration paid	(X)
Decrease in NCI in net assets at date of transaction	X
Decrease in NCI in goodwill at date of transaction *	X
Adjustment to parent's equity	(X)

*****Note.** This line is only required where non-controlling interests are measured at fair value at the date of acquisition (ie where there is an decrease in the non-controlling interest share of goodwill already recognised).

Remember that IFRS 3 views **the group as an economic entity,** and **views all providers of equity**, including non-controlling interests, as **owners of the group**.

You can practise this adjustment in the example below.

2.5 Comprehensive Example: Step acquisition of a subsidiary

Peace acquired 25% of Miel on 1.1.20X1 for $2,020,000 (equivalent to the fair value of $10.10 per share acquired on that date) when Miel's reserves were standing at $5,800,000. The fair value of Miel's identifiable assets and liabilities at that date was $7,200,000. Both Peace and Miel are stock market listed entities.

A further 35% stake in Miel was acquired on 30 September 20X2 for $4,025,000 (equivalent to the fair value of $14.375 per share acquired on that date) giving Peace control over Miel. The fair value of Miel's identifiable assets and liabilities at that date was $9,400,000, and Miel's reserves stood at $7,800,000.

Summarised statements of financial position of the two companies at 31 December 20X2 show:

	Peace $'000	Miel $'000
Non-current assets		
Property, plant and equipment	38,650	7,600
Investment in Miel	7,020	–
	45,670	7,600
Current assets	12,700	2,200
	58,370	9,800
Equity		
Share capital ($1)	10,200	800
Reserves	40,720	7,900
	50,920	8,700
Liabilities	7,450	1,100
	58,370	9,800

The difference between the fair value of the identifiable assets and liabilities of Miel and their book value relates to the value of a plot of land. The land had not been sold by 31 December 20X2.

For consistency with the measurement of other shares, Peace applies IFRS 9 and holds all investments in subsidiaries and associates as financial assets at fair value through OCI in its separate financial statements as permitted by IAS 27.

At 31 December 20X2, the fair value of Peace's 60% holding in Miel was $7,020,000 (equivalent to $14.625 per share).

The investment in Miel figure at 31.12.20X2 is therefore made up of:

	$'000
Purchase of 25% stake at cost	2,020
Fair value adjustments on 25% stake to 30.9.X2 [($14.375 – $10.10) × 200,000 shares]	855
	2,875
Purchase of 35% stake at cost	4,025
	6,900
Fair value adjustments on 60% stake to 31.12.X2 [($14.625 – $14.375) × 480,000 shares]	120
Fair value of 60% stake at 31.12.X2	7,020

Group policy is to measure non-controlling interests at the date of acquisition at their proportionate share of the net fair value of the identifiable assets acquired and liabilities assumed.

No impairment losses on recognised goodwill have been necessary to date.

Required

(a) Prepare the consolidated statement of financial position of Peace Group as at 31 December 20X2 in the following circumstances:

   (i) The 25% interest in Miel allowed Peace significant influence over the financial and operating policy decisions of Miel.

   (ii) The other 75% of shares were held by a single shareholder and Peace was allowed no influence in the running of Miel until acquiring control.

(b) Show the consolidated current assets, non-controlling interests and reserves figures if Peace acquired an **additional** 10% interest in Miel on 1 January 20X3 for $1,200,000 in cash.

Solution

Parts (a)(i) and (a)(ii) to the example would generate the same overall answer.

(a) PEACE GROUP
CONSOLIDATED STATEMENT OF FINANCIAL POSITION AS AT 31 DECEMBER 20X2

	$'000
Non-current assets	
Property, plant and equipment (38,650 + 7,600 + (W2) 800)	47,050
Goodwill (W3)	1,260
	48,310
Current assets (12,700 + 2,200)	14,900
	63,210
Equity attributable to owners of the parent	
Share capital	10,200
Reserves (W5)/(W6)	40,660
	50,860
Non-controlling interests (W4)	3,800
	54,660
Liabilities (7,450 + 1,100)	8,550
	63,210

Workings

1 *Group structure*

```
              Peace
                |
         1.1.X1    30.9.X2
          25%   +   35%   =  60%
                        ∴ Non-controlling interests = 40%
               Miel
```

PART B BUSINESS COMBINATIONS AND GROUP FINANCIAL STATEMENTS

2 Fair value adjustments

Measured at date control achieved (only)

	At acquisition 30.9.X2 $'000	Movement $'000	At year end 31.12.X2 $'000
Land (9,400 – (800 + 7,800))	800	–	800

3 Goodwill

	$'000	$'000
Consideration transferred		4,025
FV of P's previously held equity interest		2,875
Fair value of identifiable assets acq'd & liabilities assumed:		
Share capital	800	
Reserves	7,800	
Fair value adjustments (W2)	800	
	9,400	
× 60%		(5,640)
		1,260

4 Non-controlling interests

	$'000	$'000
Net assets at year end per question	8,700	
Fair value adjustment (W2)	800	
	9,500	
× 40%		3,800

5 Consolidated reserves (if previously held as an associate) (a)(i)

	$'000 Peace	$'000 Miel 35%	$'000 Miel 25%
Per question	40,720	7,900	7,900
Profit on derecognition of investment *	355		
Fair value movement (W2)			(0)
Reserves at acquisition		(7,800)	(5,800)
		100	2,100
Share of post acquisition reserves			
Miel 35% (100 × 35%)	35		
Miel 25% (2,100 × 25%)	525		
Less: Fair value gain recognised in Peace's separate FS (855 + 120)	(975)		
	40,660		

* Profit on derecognition of 25% associate

	$'000
Fair value at date control obtained	2,875
P's share of carrying value (2,020 + ((7,800 – 5,800) × 25%))	(2,520)
	355

6   *Consolidated reserves (if previously held as a financial asset) (a)(ii)*

	$'000 Peace	$'000 Miel
Per question	40,720	7,900
Profit on derecognition of investment*	855	
Fair value movement (W2)		(0)
Reserves at acquisition		(7,800)
		100
Miel - Share of post-acquisition reserves (100 × 60%)	60	
Less: Fair value gain recognised in Peace's separate FS (855 + 120)	(975)	
	40,660	

*   *Profit on derecognition of 25% investment*

	$'000
Fair value at date control obtained	2,875
Cost	(2,020)
	855

The profit would be the same whether the financial asset had been revalued or not, as any revaluation above original cost previously recognised in other comprehensive income is transferred to profit or loss.

(b)   *Current assets (14,900 – 1,200)*   13,700

Non-controlling interests

	$'000	$'000
Net assets at year end per question	8,700	
Fair value adjustment (W2)	800	
	9,500	
× (40% – 10%)		2,850

Consolidated reserves

	$'000
Per part (a)	40,660
Adjustment to parent's equity on acq'n of 10% (W)	(250)
	40,410

Note. No other figures in the statement of financial position are affected.

Working: Adjustment to parent's equity on acquisition of additional 10% of Miel

	$'000
Fair value of consideration paid	(1,200)
Decrease in NCI in net assets at acq'n (9,500 × 10%)	950
	(250)

2.6 Comprehensive example: Step acquisition of a subsidiary with non-controlling interest at fair value

The facts are the same as in Section 2.5 above, except that group policy is to measure non-controlling interests at the date of acquisition at fair value.

PART B BUSINESS COMBINATIONS AND GROUP FINANCIAL STATEMENTS

Solution

Parts (a)(i) and (a)(ii) to the example would generate the same overall answer.

(a) PEACE GROUP
CONSOLIDATED STATEMENT OF FINANCIAL POSITION AS AT 31 DECEMBER 20X2

	$'000
Non-current assets	
Property, plant and equipment (38,650 + 7,600 + (W2) 800)	47,050
Goodwill (W3)	2,100
	49,150
Current assets (12,700 + 2,200)	14,900
	64,050
Equity attributable to owners of the parent	
Share capital	10,200
Reserves (W5)/(W6)	40,660
	50,860
Non-controlling interests (W4)	4,640
	55,500
Liabilities (7,450 + 1,100)	8,550
	64,050

Workings

1 *Group structure*

```
      Peace
        |
        | 1.1.X1    30.9.X2
        |  25%  +   35%   =  60%
        |                    ∴ Non-controlling interests = 40%
       Miel
```

2 *Fair value adjustments*
Measured at date control achieved (only)

	At acquisition 30.9.X2 $'000	Movement $'000	At year end 31.12.X2 $'000
Land (9,400 – (800 + 7,800))	800	–	800

3 *Goodwill*

		Group $'000	NCI $'000
	$'000		
Consideration transferred		4,025	
FV NCI (800 × $14.375 × 40%)			4,600
FV P's previously held equity interest		2,875	
Fair value of identifiable assets acq'd & liabilities assumed:			
Share capital	800		
Reserves	7,800		
Fair value adjustments (W2)	800		
	9,400		
× 60%/40%		(5,640)	(3,760)
		1,260	840
		2,100	

8: CHANGES IN GROUP STRUCTURES

4 **Non-controlling interests**

	$'000	$'000
Net assets at year end per question	8,700	
Fair value adjustment (W2)	800	
	9,500	
× 40%		3,800
NCI in goodwill (W3)		840
		4,640

5 **Consolidated reserves (if previously held as an associate) (a)(i)**

	$'000 Peace	$'000 Miel 35%	$'000 Miel 25%
Per question	40,720	7,900	7,900
Profit on derecognition of investment *	355		
Fair value movement (W2)			(0)
Reserves at acquisition		(7,800)	(5,800)
		100	2,100
Share of post-acquisition reserves			
Miel 35% (100 × 35%)	35		
Miel 25% (2,100 × 25%)	525		
Less: Fair value gain recognised in Peace's separate FS (855 + 120)	(975)		
	40,660		

* **Profit on derecognition of 25% associate**

	$'000
Fair value at date control obtained	2,875
P's share of carrying amount (2,020 + (7,800 − 5,800) × 25%)	(2,520)
	355

6 **Consolidated reserves (if previously held as a financial asset) (a)(ii)**

	$'000 Peace	$'000 Miel
Per question	40,720	7,900
Profit on derecognition of investment*	855	
Fair value movement (W2)		(0)
Reserves at acquisition		(7,800)
		100
Miel – Share of post-acquisition reserves (100 × 60%)	60	
Less: Fair value gain recognised in Peace's separate FS (855 + 120)	(975)	
	40,660	

* **Profit on derecognition of 25% investment**

	$'000
Fair value at date control obtained	2,875
Cost	(2,020)
	855

The profit would be the same whether the financial asset had been revalued or not, as any revaluation above original cost previously recognised in other comprehensive income is transferred to profit or loss.

2.7 Section summary

Where control is **achieved in stages:**

- **Remeasure** any previously held equity interest to **fair value at the date control is achieved**.
- Report any **gain in profit or loss**.
- Where a **controlling interest is increased**, treat as a transaction between owners and **adjust parent's equity**.

3 Bonus issues and capital reductions

> **Exam focus point**
>
> You may be asked to deal with a capital reorganisation, such as a bonus issue or a capital reduction. These are both straightforward.

3.1 Bonus issues

A bonus issue is simply a **capitalisation of retained earnings** and therefore there is no alteration in the percentage holding of any party. When calculating goodwill, it is easiest to ignore the effect of the bonus issue and simply use the retained earnings and share capital as at acquisition.

3.2 Capital reductions

A capital reduction will involve a **reduction in the par (nominal) value of shares in issue**. In acquisition accounting, we are using calculations which show the net assets acquired (as represented by pre-acquisition retained earnings and share capital), so any change in the nominal value of the shares at a later date is irrelevant and should be ignored.

8: CHANGES IN GROUP STRUCTURES

Chapter roundup

- **Disposals** can drop a subsidiary holding to associate status, financial asset investment status or to zero, or a parent might still retain a subsidiary with a reduced holding. You should be able to deal with all these situations. Remember particularly how to deal with **goodwill**.

- Transactions of the type described in this chapter can be very complicated and certainly look rather daunting. Remember and apply the **basic techniques** and you should find such questions easier than you expected.

- **Business combinations achieved in stages (step acquisitions)** can lead to a company becoming a financial asset investment, an associate and then a subsidiary over time. Make sure you can deal with each of these situations.

Quick quiz

1. Control is always lost when there is a disposal of shares in a subsidiary. True or false?

2. Why is the fair value of the interest retained used in the calculation of a gain on disposal where control is lost?

3. When is the effective date of disposal of shares in a subsidiary?

4. Subside owns 60% of Diary at 31 December 20X8. On 1 July 20X9, it buys a further 20% of Diary. How should this transaction be treated in the group financial statements at 31 December 20X9.

5. Ditch had a 75% subsidiary, Dodge, at 30 June 20X8. On 1 January 20X9, it sold two thirds of this investment, leaving it with a 25% holding, over which it retained significant influence. How will the remaining investment in Dodge appear in the group financial statements for the year ended 30 June 20X9?

Answers to quick quiz

1 False. Control may be retained if the investee is still a subsidiary after the disposal, even though the parent owns less and the non-controlling interest owns more.

2 It is viewed as part of the consideration received.

3 When control passes

4 As a transaction between owners, with an adjustment to the parent's equity to reflect the difference between the consideration paid and the decrease in non-controlling interest.

5 At its fair value at the date of disposal plus a 25% share of the profits accrued between the date of disposal and the year end, less any impairment at the year end.

End of chapter question

Mozart, Constanza and Salzburg (AIA May 2006)

The following are the summarised statements of profit or loss of Mozart, Constanza and Salzburg (three limited liability companies) for the year ended 31 December 20X5.

	Mozart $	Constanza $	Salzburg $
Revenue	9,850,000	7,684,000	5,464,500
Cost of sales	(6,402,500)	(4,610,400)	(4,371,600)
Gross profit	3,447,500	3,073,600	1,092,900
Operating expenses	(1,419,900)	(565,200)	(362,170)
Profit from operations	2,027,600	2,508,400	730,730
Proceeds from sale of shares in Salzburg	1,050,000		
Income from shares in group companies	360,000	–	–
Profit before tax	3,437,600	2,508,400	730,730
Income tax	(608,280)	(752,520)	(219,219)
Profit for the year	2,829,320	1,755,880	511,511

The summarised statements of financial position of the three companies as at 31 December 20X5 were:

	Mozart $	Constanza $	Salzburg $
Assets			
Non-current assets			
Property, plant and equipment	5,548,450	3,370,400	2,374,200
Investments, at cost	3,660,000	–	–
	9,208,450	3,370,400	2,374,200
Current assets	1,133,000	724,000	430,000
Total assets	10,341,450	4,094,400	2,804,200
Liabilities			
Current liabilities	767,950	434,400	318,200
Equity			
Ordinary shares of $1	5,000,000	2,000,000	1,500,000
Reserves	4,573,500	1,660,000	986,000
	9,573,500	3,660,000	2,486,000
	10,341,450	4,094,400	2,804,200

Mozart purchased 60% of the equity of Constanza for $1.40 a share in 20X2 when Constanza's reserves were $455,000. Mozart also purchased 60% of the equity of Salzburg for $2.20 a share in 20X3 when Salzburg's reserves were $785,000.

On 30 June 20X5 Mozart sold 525,000 of its shares in Salzburg for $2.00 a share. After the sale there were four shareholders in Salzburg – all limited liability companies. The shareholders put in place a contractual agreement to run Salzburg as a joint venture as from 1 July 20X5. The fair value of the group's interest in the joint venture was equal to its proportionate share of Salzburg's net assets at that date. At the date of disposal, the goodwill relating to the acquisition of Salzburg had been written down to zero.

During the year ended 31 December 20X5 Constanza paid dividends totalling $600,000. Salzburg did not pay any dividends.

The statement of profit or loss of Mozart does not include the profit or loss on the sale of the shares in Salzburg because the company accountant is not sure how this should be calculated or reported. Nor does he know how to report the tax effects of the sale of the shares. The rate of income tax is 30%. The accountant has reported the sales proceeds as income for the year.

It is the group's policy to value the non-controlling interest at its proportionate share of the fair value of the subsidiary's identifiable net assets.

Required

(a) Advise, with appropriate calculations, how the profit or loss on the disposal of the shares in Salzburg would be reported in:

  (i) Mozart's individual statement of profit or loss and other comprehensive income; and

  (ii) Mozart's consolidated statement of profit or loss and other comprehensive income for the year ended 31 December 20X5. **(6 marks)**

(b) Prepare the consolidated statement of financial position of Mozart as at 31 December 20X5. Show full supportive workings. **(19 marks)**

(Total 25 marks)

PART B BUSINESS COMBINATIONS AND GROUP FINANCIAL STATEMENTS

Foreign currency translation

Topic list	Syllabus reference
1 Foreign currency translation	LO2
2 IAS 21: Individual company	LO2
3 IAS 21: Consolidated financial statements	LO2
4 Hyperinflation	LO1

Introduction

Many of the largest companies in any country, while based there, have subsidiaries and other interests all over the world: they are truly **global companies** and so foreign currency consolidations take place frequently in practice.

1 Foreign currency translation

FAST FORWARD

Questions on foreign currency translation have always been popular with examiners. In general you are required to prepare **consolidated financial statements** for a group which includes a foreign subsidiary.

If a company trades overseas, it will buy or sell assets in foreign currencies. For example, an Indian company might buy materials from Canada, and pay for them in US dollars, and then sell its finished goods in Germany, receiving payment in Euros, or perhaps in some other currency. If the company owes money in a foreign currency at the end of the accounting year, or holds assets which were bought in a foreign currency, those liabilities or assets must be translated into the local currency (in this text $), in order to be shown in the books of account.

A company might have a subsidiary abroad (ie a foreign entity that it owns), and the subsidiary will trade in its own local currency. The subsidiary will keep books of account and prepare its annual financial statements in its own currency. However, at the year end, the holding company must consolidate the results of the overseas subsidiary into its group financial statements, a process which requires the assets and liabilities and the profits of the subsidiary to be translated from the foreign currency into $.

If foreign currency exchange rates remained constant, there would be no accounting problem. As you will be aware, however, foreign exchange rates are continually changing, and it is not inconceivable for example, that the rate of exchange between the Polish zloty (Z) and sterling (£) might be Z6.2 to £1 at the start of the accounting year, and Z5.6 to £1 at the end of the year (in this example, a 10% increase in the relative strength of the zloty).

There are two distinct types of foreign currency transaction, conversion and translation.

1.1 Conversion gains and losses

Conversion is the process of exchanging amounts of one foreign currency for another. For example, suppose a local company buys a large consignment of goods from a supplier in Germany. The order is placed on 1 May and the agreed price is €124,250. At the time of delivery the rate of foreign exchange was €3.50 to $1. The local company would record the amount owed in its books as follows:

DEBIT	Inventory account (124,250 ÷ 3.5)	$35,500	
CREDIT	Payables account		$35,500

When the local company comes to pay the supplier, it needs to obtain some foreign currency. By this time, however, if the rate of exchange has altered to €3.55 to $1, the cost of raising €124,250 would be (÷ 3.55) $35,000. The company would need to spend only $35,000 to settle a debt for inventories 'costing' $35,500. Since it would be administratively difficult to alter the value of the inventories in the company's books of account, it is more appropriate to record a profit on conversion of $500.

DEBIT	Payables account	$35,500	
CREDIT	Cash		$35,000
CREDIT	Profit or loss		$500

Profits (or losses) on conversion would be included in profit or loss for the year in which conversion (whether payment or receipt) takes place.

Suppose that another home company sells goods to a Chinese company, and it is agreed that payment should be made in Chinese Yuan (Y) at a price of Y116,000. We will further assume that the exchange rate at the time of sale is Y10.75 to $1, but when the debt is eventually paid, the rate has altered to Y10.8 to $1. The company would record the sale as follows:

DEBIT	Receivables account (116,000 ÷ 10.75)	$10,800	
CREDIT	Sales account		$10,800

When the Y116,000 are paid, the local company will convert them into $, to obtain (÷ 10.8) $10,750. In this example, there has been a loss on conversion of $50 which will be written off to profit of loss for the year:

DEBIT	Cash	$10,750	
DEBIT	Profit or loss	$50	
CREDIT	Payables account		$10,800

There are **no accounting difficulties** concerned with foreign currency conversion gains or losses, and the procedures described above are uncontroversial.

1.2 Translation

Foreign currency translation, as distinct from conversion, does not involve the act of exchanging one currency for another. **Translation is required at the end of an accounting period when a company still holds assets or liabilities in its statement of financial position which were obtained or incurred in a foreign currency.**

These assets or liabilities might consist of any of the following:

(a) An individual home company holding individual **assets** or **liabilities** originating in a foreign currency 'deal'.

(b) An individual home company with a separate **branch** of the business operating abroad which keeps its own books of account in the local currency.

(c) A home company which wishes to consolidate the **results of a foreign subsidiary**.

Suppose, for example, that a Belgian subsidiary purchases a piece of property for €2,100,000 on 31 December 20X7. The rate of exchange at this time was €70 to $1. During 20X8, the subsidiary charged depreciation on the building of €16,800, so that at 31 December 20X8, the subsidiary recorded the asset as follows:

	€
Property at cost	2,100,000
Less accumulated depreciation	16,800
Carrying amount	2,083,200

At this date, the rate of exchange has changed to €60 to $1.

The local holding company must translate the asset's value into $, but there is a **choice of exchange rates**.

(a) Should the rate of exchange for translation be the rate which existed at the date of purchase, which would give a carrying amount of 2,083,200 ÷ 70 = $29,760?

(b) Should the rate of exchange for translation be the rate existing at the end of 20X8 (the closing rate of €60 to $1)? This would give a carrying amount of $34,720.

Similarly, should depreciation be charged to group profit or loss at the rate of €70 to $1 (the historical rate), €60 to $1 (the closing rate), or at an average rate for the year (say, €64 to $1)?

1.3 Consolidated financial statements

If a parent has a subsidiary whose financial statements are presented in a foreign currency, those financial statements must be translated into the local currency before they can be included in the consolidated financial statements.

Where the affairs of a foreign operation are very closely interlinked with those of the investing company, it should be included in the consolidated financial statements as if the transactions had been entered into by the investing company in its own currency. Non-monetary assets and depreciation are translated at **historic rate** and sales, purchase and expenses at **average rate**. **Exchange differences** arising on retranslation are reported as part of **profit or loss** on ordinary activities.

Where a foreign operation is effectively a separate business, the **closing rate** is used for most items in the financial statements. **Exchange differences** are taken **directly** to **equity** (and reported in other comprehensive income).

We will look at the consolidation of foreign subsidiaries in much more detail in Section 3 of this chapter.

2 IAS 21: Individual company

The questions discussed above are addressed by IAS 21 *The Effects of Changes in Foreign Exchange Rates*. We will examine those matters which affect single company financial statements here.

2.1 Definitions

These are some of the definitions given by IAS 21.

Key terms

> **Foreign currency.** A currency other than the functional currency of the entity.
>
> **Functional currency.** The currency of the primary economic environment in which the entity operates.
>
> **Presentation currency.** The currency in which the financial statements are presented.
>
> **Exchange rate.** The ratio of exchange for two currencies.
>
> **Exchange difference.** The difference resulting from translating a given number of units of one currency into another currency at different exchange rates.
>
> **Closing rate.** The spot exchange rate at the year end date.
>
> **Spot exchange rate.** The exchange rate for immediate delivery.
>
> **Monetary items.** Units of currency held and assets and liabilities to be received or paid in a fixed or determinable number of units of currency.
>
> (IAS 21)

Each entity – whether an individual company, a parent of a group, or an operation within a group (such as a subsidiary, associate or branch) – should determine its **functional currency** presentation currency.

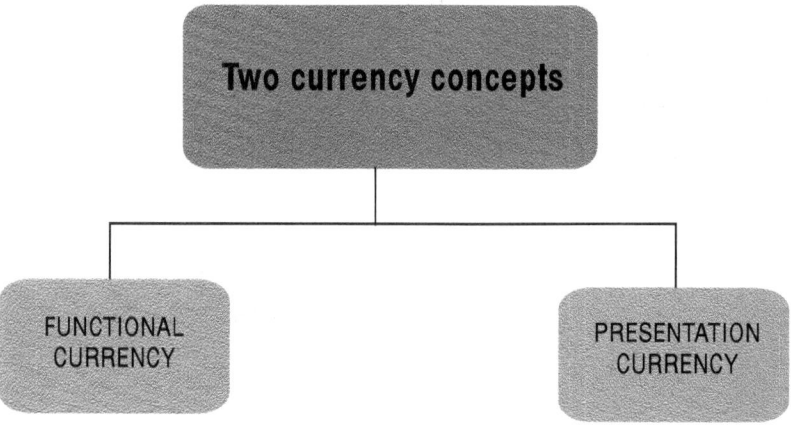

FUNCTIONAL CURRENCY
- Currency of the **primary economic environment** in which the entity operates (IAS 21: para. 8)
- The currency used for **measurement** in the financial statements
- Other currencies treated as a foreign currency

PRESENTATION CURRENCY
- Currency in which the financial statements **are presented** (IAS 21: para. 8)
- Can be **any currency**
- Special rules apply to translation from functional currency to presentation currency
- Same rules used for translating foreign operations

2.2 Foreign currency transactions: initial recognition

IAS 21 states that a foreign currency transaction should be recorded, on initial recognition in the functional currency, by applying the exchange rate between the reporting currency and the foreign currency **at the date of the transaction** to the foreign currency amount.

An **average rate** for a period may be used if exchange rates do not fluctuate significantly.

2.3 Reporting at subsequent year ends

The following rules apply at each subsequent year end

Item	Retranslation	Presentation of gain or loss
Monetary items	Retranslated at the closing rate	Gain or loss on translation to profit or loss
Non-monetary items carried at historical cost	Not retranslated. Retain at historical rate.	No gain or loss arises.
Non-monetary items carried at fair value	Translated at the rate on which the valuation was determined.	Gain or loss follows the presentation of the revaluation gain or loss. For example, an exchange gain on the a revalued property would be presented in OCI.

Question — Entries

White Cliffs Co, whose year end is 31 December, buys some goods from Rinka SA of France on 30 September. The invoice value is €40,000 and is due for settlement in equal instalments on 30 November and 31 January.

The exchange rate moved as follows:

	€ = $1
30 September	1.60
30 November	1.80
31 December	1.90
31 January	1.85

Required

State the accounting entries in the books of White Cliffs Co.

Answer

The purchase will be recorded in the books of White Cliffs Co using the rate of exchange ruling on 30 September.

DEBIT	Purchases	$25,000	
CREDIT	Trade payables		$25,000

Being the $ cost of goods purchased for €40,000 (€40,000 ÷ €1.60/$1)

On 30 November, White Cliffs must pay €20,000. This will cost €20,000 ÷ €1.80/$1 = $11,111 and the company has therefore made an exchange gain of $12,500 − $11,111 = $1,389.

DEBIT	Trade payables	$12,500	
CREDIT	Profit or loss: exchange gains		$1,389
CREDIT	Cash		$11,111

On 31 December, the year end, the outstanding liability will be recalculated using the rate applicable to that date: €20,000 ÷ €1.90/$1 = $10,526. A further exchange gain of $1,974 has been made and will be recorded as follows:

DEBIT	Trade payables	$1,974	
CREDIT	Profit or loss: exchange gains		$1,974

The total exchange gain of $3,363 will be included in the operating profit for the year ending 31 December.

On 31 January, White Cliffs must pay the second instalment of €20,000. This will cost them $10,811 (€20,000 ÷ €1.85/$1).

DEBIT	Trade payables	$10,526	
	Profit or loss: exchange losses	$285	
CREDIT	Cash		$10,811

When a gain or loss on a non-monetary item is recognised in other comprehensive income, any **related exchange differences** should also be **recognised in other comprehensive income**. This might happen, for example, where property is revalued.

3 IAS 21: Consolidated financial statements

3.1 Definitions

The following definitions are relevant here.

Key terms

Foreign operation. A subsidiary, associate, joint venture or branch of a reporting entity, the activities of which are based or conducted in a country or currency other than those of the reporting entity.

Net investment in a foreign operation. The amount of the reporting entity's interest in the net assets of that operation. (IAS 21)

3.2 Determining functional currency

FAST FORWARD

You may have to make the decision yourself as to whether the subsidiary has the same functional currency as the parent or a different functional currency from the parent. This determines whether the subsidiary is treated as an **extension of the parent** or as a **net investment.**

A holding or parent company with foreign operations must **translate the financial statements** of those operations into its own reporting currency before they can be consolidated into the group financial statements. In theory there are two methods: **the method used depends** upon **whether** the foreign operation has the **same functional currency as the parent**.

IAS 21 states that an entity should consider the following factors in determining its functional currency:

(a) The currency that mainly **influences sales prices** for goods and services (often the currency in which prices are denominated and settled)

(b) The currency of the **country whose competitive forces and regulations** mainly determine the sales prices of its goods and services

(c) The currency that mainly **influences labour, material and other costs** of providing goods or services (often the currency in which prices are denominated and settled)

Sometimes the functional currency of an entity is not immediately obvious. Management must then exercise judgement and may also need to consider:

(a) The currency in which **funds from financing activities** (raising loans and issuing equity) are generated

(b) The currency in which **receipts from operating activities** are usually retained

Where a parent has a foreign operation a number of factors are considered:

(a) Whether the activities of the foreign operation are carried out as an **extension of the parent**, rather than being carried out with a **significant degree of autonomy**

(b) Whether **transactions with the parent** are a high or a low proportion of the foreign operation's activities

(c) Whether **cash flows** from the activities of the foreign operation **directly affect the cash flows of the parent** and are readily available for remittance to it

(d) Whether the activities of the foreign operation are **financed from its own cash flows** or by **borrowing from the parent**

To sum up: in order to determine the functional currency of a foreign operation it is necessary to consider the **relationship** between the foreign operation and its parent:

- If the foreign operation carries out its business as though it were an **extension of the parent's operations**, it almost certainly has the **same functional currency** as the parent.

- If the foreign operation is **semi-autonomous** it almost certainly has **a different functional currency** from the parent.

The translation method used has to reflect the economic reality of the relationship between the reporting entity (the parent) and the foreign operation.

3.2.1 Same functional currency as the reporting entity

In this situation, the foreign operation normally carries on its business as though it were an **extension of the reporting entity's operations**. For example, it may only sell goods imported from, and remit the proceeds directly to, the reporting entity.

Any **movement in the exchange rate** between the reporting currency and the foreign operation's currency will have an **immediate impact** on the reporting entity's cash flows from the foreign operations. In other words, changes in the exchange rate affect the **individual monetary items** held by the foreign operation, **not** the reporting entity's net investment in that operation.

3.2.2 Different functional currency from the reporting entity

Exam focus point

Many exam questions include of a foreign operation consolidation.

In this situation, although the reporting entity may be able to exercise control, the foreign operation normally operates in a **semi-autonomous** way. It accumulates cash and other monetary items, generates income and incurs expenses, and may also arrange borrowings, all **in its own local currency**.

A change in the exchange rate will produce **little or no direct effect on the present and future cash flows** from operations of either the foreign operation or the reporting entity. Rather, the change in exchange rate affects the reporting entity's **net investment** in the foreign operation, not the individual monetary and non-monetary items held by the foreign operation.

Exam focus point

Where the foreign operation's functional currency is different from the parent's, the financial statements need to be translated before consolidation.

3.3 Accounting treatment: Same functional currency as the reporting entity

Where a foreign operation has the same functional currency as its parent, it will almost certainly keep its accounting records in its functional currency, even if this is not the same as the local currency. This means that the financial statements of the foreign operation **do not need to be translated**.

In theory, the foreign operation could keep its accounting records and prepare individual financial statements in the local currency. In this situation, the foreign operation's transactions should be translated **as if they had been those of the parent**. The same procedures used for individual company financial statements should be applied (see Section 2 above).

We can summarise the treatment here:

(a) **Statement of profit or loss and other comprehensive income:** translate using actual rates. An average for a period may be used, but not where there is significant fluctuation and the average is therefore unreliable.

(b) **Non-monetary items**: translate using an historical rate at the date of purchase (or revaluation to fair value, or reduction to realisable/recoverable amount). This includes inventories and non-current assets (and their depreciation).

(c) **Monetary items**: translate at the closing rate.

(d) **Exchange differences**: report as part of profit or loss for the year.

IAS 21 does not directly cover this situation or this method of translation as it assumes that where a foreign operation has the same functional currency as the parent the foreign operation always prepares financial statements in the functional currency.

3.4 Accounting treatment: Different functional currency from the reporting entity

The financial statements of the foreign operation must be translated to the functional currency of the parent. Different procedures must be followed here, because the functional currency of the parent is the **presentation currency** of the foreign operation.

(a) The **assets and liabilities** shown in the foreign operation's statement of financial position are translated at the **closing rate** at the year end, regardless of the date on which those items originated. The balancing figure in the translated statement of financial position represents the reporting entity's net investment in the foreign operation.

(b) Amounts in the **statement of profit or loss and other comprehensive income** should be translated at the rate ruling at the date of the transaction (an **average rate** will usually be used for practical purposes).

(c) **Exchange differences** arising from the re-translation at the end of each year of the parent's net investment should be **reported in other comprehensive income and taken to equity**, not included in profit or loss for the year, until the disposal of the net investment.

3.5 Example: Different functional currency from the reporting entity

A dollar-based company, Stone Co, set up a foreign subsidiary on 30 June 20X7. Stone subscribed €24,000 for share capital when the exchange rate was €2 = $1. The subsidiary, Brick Inc, borrowed €72,000 and bought a non-monetary asset for €96,000. Stone Co prepared its financial statements on 31 December 20X7 and by that time the exchange rate had moved to €3 = $1. As a result of highly unusual circumstances, Brick Inc sold its asset early in 20X8 for €96,000. It repaid its loan and was liquidated. Stone's capital of €24,000 was repaid in February 20X8 when the exchange rate was €3 = $1.

Required

Account for the above transactions as if the entity has a different functional currency from the parent.

Solution

From the above it can be seen that Stone Co will record its initial investment at $12,000 (€24,000 ÷ €2/$1) which is the starting cost of its shares. The statement of financial position of Brick Inc at 31 December 20X7 is summarised below.

	€'000
Non-monetary asset	96
Share capital	24
Loan	72
	96

This may be translated as follows.

	$'000
Non-monetary asset (€3 = $1)	32
Share capital and reserves (retained earnings) (balancing figure)	8
Loan (€3 = $1)	24
	32
Exchange gain/(loss) for 20X7	(4)

The exchange loss is the differences between the value of the original investment ($12,000) and the total of share capital and reserves (retained earnings) as disclosed by the above statements of financial position.

On liquidation, Stone Co will receive $8,000 (€24,000 converted at €3 = $1). No gain or loss will arise in 20X8.

3.6 Some practical points

The following points apply:

(a) For consolidation purposes calculations are simpler if a subsidiary's share capital is translated at the **historical rate** (the rate when the investing company acquired its interest) and reserves are found as a balancing figure.

(b) **Dividends declared** by a subsidiary should always be translated at the actual rate on the dates of payment. This is because the investing company will record the items at these rates in its own books.

> **FAST FORWARD**
>
> You must be able to calculate **exchange differences**.
>
> **Practising** examination questions is the best way of learning this topic.

3.7 Summary of method

A summary of the translation method is given below, which shows the main steps to follow in the consolidation process.

Exam focus point: You should learn this summary.

Step	Translation
Step 1 Translate the **closing statement of financial position** (net assets/shareholders' funds) and use this for preparing the consolidated statement of financial position in the normal way.	Use the **closing rate** at the year end for all items (see note).

PART B BUSINESS COMBINATIONS AND GROUP FINANCIAL STATEMENTS

Step	Translation
Step 2 Translate the **statement of profit or loss and other comprehensive income**. (In all cases, dividends should be translated at the rate ruling when the dividend was paid.)	Use the **average rate** for the year for all items (but see comment on dividends). The figures obtained can then be used in preparing the consolidated statement of profit or loss and other comprehensive income.
Step 3 Translate the **shareholders' funds** (net assets) at the beginning of the year.	Use the **closing rate** at the beginning of the year (the opening rate for the current year).
Step 4 Calculate the **total exchange difference** for the year as follows. 　　　　　　　　　　　　　　　　　　　$ Closing net assets at closing rate (Step 1)　　　　　　　　　　　　　　X Less opening net Assets at opening rate (Step 3)　　　　　　　　　　　　　　X 　　　　　　　　　　　　　　　　　　X Less retained profit per translated statement of profit or loss and other comprehensive income (Step 2)　　 X Exchange differences　　　　　　　 X Group share (%)　　　　　　　　　　X It may be necessary to adjust for any profits or losses taken direct to reserves during the year.	This stage will be **unnecessary** unless you are asked to state the total exchange differences or are asked to prepare a statement of the movement on reserves, where the exchange difference will be shown. For **exam purposes** you can translate the closing shareholders' funds as follows. (a) Share capital + pre-acquisition reserves at historical rate. (b) Post-acquisition reserves as a balancing figure.

Note. As mentioned above, the share capital may be translated at the historical rate. The reserves will then be the balancing figure. The advantage of this method is that it simplifies the 'cancellation' of the share capital on consolidation.

Question — Consolidated financial statements

The abridged statements of financial position and statements of profit or loss and other comprehensive income of Darius Co and its foreign subsidiary, Xerxes Inc, appear below.

DRAFT STATEMENT OF FINANCIAL POSITION AS AT 31 DECEMBER 20X9

	Darius Co		Xerxes Inc	
	$	$	€	€
Assets				
Non-current assets				
Plant at cost	600		500	
Less depreciation	(250)		(200)	
		350		300
Investment in Xerxes				
100 €1 shares		25		–
		375		300

9: FOREIGN CURRENCY TRANSLATION

	Darius Co		Xerxes Inc	
	$	$	€	€
Current assets				
Inventories	225		200	
Receivables	150		100	
		375		300
		750		600
Equity and liabilities				
Equity				
Ordinary $1/€1 shares	300		100	
Retained earnings	300		280	
		600		380
Non-current loans		50		110
Current liabilities		100		110
		750		600

STATEMENTS OF PROFIT OR LOSS AND OTHER COMPREHENSIVE INCOME
FOR THE YEAR ENDED 31 DECEMBER 20X9

	Darius Co	Xerxes Inc
	$	€
Profit before tax	200	160
Tax	100	80
Profit after tax, retained	100	80

The following further information is given.

(a) Darius Co has had its interest in Xerxes Inc since the incorporation of the company.

(b) Depreciation is 8% per annum on cost.

(c) There have been no loan repayments or movements in the cost of non-current assets during the year. The opening inventory of Xerxes Inc was €120. Assume that inventory turnover times are very short.

(d) Exchange rates: €4 to $1 when Xerxes Inc was incorporated
€2.5 to $1 when Xerxes Inc acquired its non-current assets
€2 to $1 on 31 December 20X8
€1.6 to $1 average rate of exchange year ending 31 December 20X9
€1 to $1 on 31 December 20X9.

Required

Prepare the summarised consolidated financial statements of Darius Co.

Answer

Step 1 The statement of financial position of Xerxes Inc at 31 December 20X9, other than share capital and retained earnings, should be translated at €1 = $1.

SUMMARISED STATEMENT OF FINANCIAL POSITION AT 31 DECEMBER 20X9

	$	$
Non-current assets (CA)		300
Current assets		
Inventories	200	
Receivables	100	
		300
		600
Non-current liabilities		110
Current liabilities		110

∴ Shareholders' funds = 600 – 110 – 110 = $380

PART B BUSINESS COMBINATIONS AND GROUP FINANCIAL STATEMENTS

Since Darius Co acquired the whole of the issued share capital on incorporation, the post-acquisition retained earnings including exchange differences will be the value of shareholders' funds arrived at above, less the original cost to Darius Co of $25. Post-acquisition retained earnings = $380 – $25 = $355.

SUMMARISED CONSOLIDATED STATEMENT OF FINANCIAL POSITION AS AT 31 DECEMBER 20X9

		$	$
Assets			
Non-current assets (net carrying amount)	$(350 + 300)		650
Current assets			
Inventories	$(225 + 200)	425	
Receivables	$(150 + 100)	250	
			675
			1,325
Equity and liabilities			
Equity			
Ordinary $1 shares (Darius only)			300
Retained earnings	$(300 + 355)		655
			955
Non-current liabilities: loans	$(50 + 110)		160
Current liabilities	$(100 + 110)		210
			1,325

Note. It is quite unnecessary to know the amount of the exchange differences when preparing the consolidated statement of financial position.

Step 2 The statement of profit or loss and other comprehensive income should be translated at average rate (€1.6 = $1).

SUMMARISED STATEMENT OF PROFIT OR LOSS AND OTHER COMPREHENSIVE INCOME OF XERXES INC FOR THE YEAR ENDED 31 DECEMBER 20X9

	$
Profit before tax	100
Tax	50
Profit after tax, retained	50

SUMMARISED CONSOLIDATED STATEMENT OF PROFIT OR LOSS AND OTHER COMPREHENSIVE INCOME FOR THE YEAR ENDED 31 DECEMBER 20X9

		$
Profit before tax	$(200 + 100)	300
Tax	$(100 + 50)	150
Profit after tax, retained	$(100 + 50)	150

Step 3 The equity interest at the beginning of the year can be found as follows.

	€
Equity value at 31 December 20X9	380
Retained profit for year	80
Equity value at 31 December 20X8	300
Translated at € 2 = $1, this gives	$150

Step 4 The exchange difference can now be calculated.

	$
Equity interest at 31 December 20X9 (stage 1)	380
Equity interest at 1 January 20X9 (stage 3)	150
	230
Less retained profit (stage 2)	50
Exchange gain	180

CONSOLIDATED STATEMENT OF MOVEMENTS ON RESERVES
FOR THE YEAR ENDED 31 DECEMBER 20X9

	$
Consolidated reserves at 31 December 20X8	325
Exchange gains arising on consolidation	180
Retained profit for the year	150
Consolidated reserves at 31 December 20X9	655

Notes.

1. The post-acquisition reserves of Xerxes Inc at the beginning of the year must have been $150 – $25 = $125 and the reserves of Darius Co must have been $300 – $100 = $200. The consolidated reserves must therefore have been $325.

2. The exchange gains arising on consolidation are reported as a separate line item in 'other comprehensive income'.

3.8 Analysis of exchange differences

The exchange differences in the above exercise could be reconciled by splitting them into their component parts.

Exam focus point

Such a split is not required by IAS 21, but it may help your understanding of the subject.

The exchange difference consists of those exchange gains/losses arising from:

- Translating **income/expense items** at the exchange rates at the date of transactions, whereas **assets/liabilities** are translated at the closing rate.
- Translating the **opening net investment** (opening net assets) in the foreign entity at a closing rate different from the closing rate at which it was previously reported.

This can be demonstrated using the above question.

Using the opening statement of financial position and translating at €2 = $1 and €1 = $1 gives the following.

	€2 = $1 $	€1 = $1 $	Difference $
Non-current assets at net carrying amount (€300 + (depreciation of 8% of €500) = €340)	170	340	170
Inventories (€120)	60	120	60
Net current monetary liabilities (balancing figure)	(25)	(50)	(25)
Total = €410 (see below)	205	410	205
Shareholders' funds (€380 – €80 = €300)	150	300	150
Loans (€110)	55	110	55
Total = €410	205	410	205

Translating the statement of profit or loss and other comprehensive income using €1.60 = $1 and €1 = $1 gives the following results.

	€1.60 = $1 $	€1 = $1 $	Difference $
Profit before tax, depreciation and increase in inventory values	75	120	45
Increase in inventory values	50	80	30
	125	200	75
Depreciation	(25)	(40)	(15)
	100	160	60
Tax	(50)	(80)	(30)
Profit for the year, retained	50	80	30

The overall position is then:

	$	$
Gain on non-current assets ($170 – $15)		155
Loss on loan		(55)
Gain on inventories ($60 + $30)	90	
Loss on net monetary current assets/		
Liabilities (all other differences)		
($45 – $30 – $25)	(10)	
		80
Net exchange gain: as above		180

3.9 Non-controlling interest

In problems involving non-controlling interest the following points should be noted.

(a) The figure for **non-controlling interest in the statement of financial position** will be the appropriate proportion of the translated share capital and reserves of the subsidiary. In addition, it may be necessary to show any dividend payable to the NCI as a liability. Dividends payable should be translated at the closing rate for this purpose.

(b) The **non-controlling interest in the statement of profit or loss and other comprehensive income** will be the appropriate proportion of dollar profits available for distribution. If the functional currency of the subsidiary is the same as that of the parent, this profit will be arrived at **after** charging or crediting the exchange differences.

3.10 Example: Non-controlling interest

The summarised financial statements of Camrumite Inc are shown below.

STATEMENT OF FINANCIAL POSITION AS AT 31 DECEMBER 20X3

	€
Non-current assets	10,000
Net monetary assets	5,000
	15,000
Equity (share capital and reserves)	15,000

STATEMENT OF CHANGES IN EQUITY FOR THE YEAR ENDED 31 DECEMBER 20X3

	€
Profit for the year	3,080
Dividends payable	1,680
Retained profit	1,400

60% of the issued capital of Camrumite Inc is owned by Bates Co, a company based in another country.

There have been no movements in non-current assets during the year. The depreciation charge for the year was €560.

The exchange rate has moved as follows:

Date on which non-current assets were acquired	€8 = $1
1 January 20X3	€5 = $1
Average for the year ended 31.12.X3	€7 = $1
31 December 20X3	€8 = $1

You are required to calculate the figures for non-controlling interest to be included in the consolidated financial statements of Bates Co.

Show the movements on the non-controlling interest account during the year.

9: FOREIGN CURRENCY TRANSLATION

Solution

Translating the shareholders' funds using the closing rate as at 31 December 20X3 gives €15,000 ÷ 8 = $1,875. The non-controlling interest in the statement of financial position will be 40% × $1,875 = $750.

The dividend payable translated at the closing rate is €1,680 ÷ 8 = $210. The amount payable to the non-controlling shareholders is 40% × $210 = $84.

The profit for the year translated at the average rate is €3,080 ÷ 7 = $440. The non-controlling interest in the statement of profit or loss and other comprehensive income is therefore 40% × $440 = $176.

At the beginning of the year the share capital and reserves must have been €15,000 − €1,400 = €13,600. Translating this at the rate ruling on 1 January 20X3 gives €13,600 ÷ 5 = $2,720. The non-controlling interest at 1 January 20X3 was 40% × $2,720 = $1,088.

	$	$
Shareholders' funds as at 1 January 20X3		2,720
Add: profit for year	440	
less dividends	210	
		230
		2,950
Less shareholders' funds at 31 December 20X3		1,875
Exchange loss		1,075
Non-controlling interest therein $1,075 × 40%		430

The non-controlling interest can be summarised as follows:

	$
Balance at 1 January 20X3	1,088
Non-controlling interest in profit for the year	176
Non-controlling interest in exchange losses	(430)
	834
Balance at 31 December 20X3	750
Dividend payable to non-controlling shareholders	84
	834

3.11 Further matters relating to foreign operations

3.11.1 Goodwill and fair value adjustments

Goodwill and fair value adjustments arising on the acquisition of a foreign operation should be treated as assets and liabilities of the acquired entity. This means that they should be expressed in the functional currency of the foreign operation and translated at the **closing rate**.

Here is a layout for calculating goodwill and the exchange gain or loss. The parent holds 90% of the shares. NCI is valued as the proportionate share of the fair value of the subsidiary's identifiable net assets.

Goodwill

	F'000	F'000	Rate	$'000
Consideration transferred (12,000 × 6)		72,000		
Non-controlling interest		6,600		
66,000 × 10%		78,600		
Less:				
Less share capital	40,000			
Pre acquisition retained earnings	26,000			
		(66,000)		
At 1.4.X1		12,600	6**	2,100
Foreign exchange gain		–	Balance	420
At 31.3.X7		12,600	5***	2,520

** Historic rate
*** Closing rate

3.11.2 Consolidation procedures

Follow normal consolidation procedures, except that where an exchange difference arises on **long or short-term intra-group monetary items**, these cannot be offset against other intra-group balances. This is because these are commitments to convert one currency into another, thus exposing the reporting entity to a gain or loss through currency fluctuations.

If the foreign operation's **reporting date** is different from that of the parent, it is acceptable to use the financial statements made up to that date for consolidation, as long as adjustments are made for any significant changes in rates in the interim.

3.11.3 Disposal of foreign entity

When a parent disposes of a foreign entity, the cumulative amount of deemed exchange differences relating to that foreign entity should be **reclassified from equity to profit or loss** (ie recognised as **income** or **expense**) in the same period in which the gain or loss on disposal is recognised. Effectively, this means that these exchange differences are recognised once by taking them to reserves and then are recognised for a second time ('recycled') by transferring them to profit or loss (the statement of profit or loss and other comprehensive income) on disposal of the foreign operation.

3.11.4 In the parent's financial statements

In the parent company's own financial statements, exchange differences arising on a **monetary item** that is effectively part of the parent's net investment in the foreign entity should be recognised **in profit or loss** in the separate financial statements of the reporting entity or the individual financial statements of the foreign operation, as appropriate.

3.12 Change in functional currency

The functional currency of an entity can be changed only if there is a change to the underlying transactions, events and conditions that are relevant to the entity. For example, an entity's functional currency may change if there is a change in the currency that mainly influences the sales price of goods and services.

Where there is a change in an entity's functional currency, the entity translates all items into the new functional currency **prospectively** (ie from the date of the change) using the exchange rate at the date of the change.

3.13 Tax effects of exchange differences

IAS 12 *Income Taxes* should be applied when there are tax effects arising from gains or losses on foreign currency transactions and exchange differences arising on the translation of the financial statements of foreign operations.

3.14 Foreign associates

Foreign associates will be companies with substantial autonomy from the group and so their **functional currency will be different** from that of the parent.

3.15 Section summary

- Where the functional currency of a foreign operation is **different** from that of the parent/reporting entity, they need to be translated before consolidation
    - Operation is semi-autonomous
    - Translate assets and liabilities at **closing rate**
    - Translate statement of profit or loss and other comprehensive income at **average rate**
    - Exchange differences through **reserves/equity**

4 Hyperinflation

> **FAST FORWARD**
>
> IAS 29 *Financial Reporting in Hyperinflationary Economies* requires financial statements of entities operating within a hyperinflationary economy to be restated in terms of measuring units current at the year end.

In a hyperinflationary economy, **money loses its purchasing power very quickly**. Comparisons of transactions at different points in time, even within the same accounting period, are misleading. It is therefore considered inappropriate for entities to prepare financial statements without making adjustments for the **fall in the purchasing power of money over time**. Ensure you understand the concept of purchasing power as covered in Chapter 1.

IAS 29 *Financial Reporting in Hyperinflationary Economies* applies to the **primary financial statements** of entities (including consolidated financial statements and statements of cash flows) whose functional currency is the currency of a hyperinflationary economy. In this section, we will identify the hyperinflationary currency as $H.

The standard does not define a **hyperinflationary economy** in exact terms, although it indicates the characteristics of such an economy, for example, where the cumulative inflation rate over three years approaches or exceeds 100%.

Question — Hyperinflation

What other factors might indicate a hyperinflationary economy?

Answer

These are examples, but the list is not exhaustive.

(a) The population prefers to retain its wealth in non-monetary assets or in a relatively stable foreign currency. Amounts of local currency held are immediately invested to maintain purchasing power.

(b) The population regards monetary amounts not in terms of the local currency but in terms of a relatively stable foreign currency. Prices may be quoted in that currency.

(c) Sales/purchases on credit take place at prices that compensate for the expected loss of purchasing power during the credit period, even if that period is short.

(d) Interest rates, wages and prices are linked to a price index.

The reported value of **non-monetary assets**, in terms of current measuring units, increases over time. For example, if a non-current asset is purchased for $H1,000 when the price index is 100, and the price index subsequently rises to 200, the value of the asset in terms of current measuring units (ignoring accumulated depreciation) will rise to $H2,000.

In contrast, the value of **monetary assets and liabilities**, such as a debt for 300 units, is unaffected by changes in the prices index, because it is an actual money amount payable or receivable. If a customer owes $H300 when the price index is 100, and the debt is still unpaid when the price index has risen to 150, the customer still owes just $H300. The purchasing power of monetary assets, however, will decline over time as the general level of prices goes up.

4.1 Requirement to restate financial statements in terms of measuring units current at the year end

In most countries, financial statements are produced on the basis of either:

(a) **Historical cost**, except to the extent that some assets (eg property and investments) may be revalued, or

(b) **Current cost**, which reflects the changes in the values of specific assets held by the entity.

In a hyperinflationary economy, neither of these methods of financial reporting are meaningful unless adjustments are made for the fall in the purchasing power of money. IAS 29 therefore requires that the **primary financial statements** of entities in a hyperinflationary economy should be produced by restating the figures prepared on either a historical cost basis or a current cost basis in terms of **measuring units current at the year end**.

Key term

> **Measuring unit current at the year end date.** This is a unit of local currency with a purchasing power as at the date of the statement of financial position, measured by reference to a general prices index.

Financial statements that are not restated (ie that are prepared on a historical cost basis or current cost basis without adjustments) may be presented as **additional statements** by the entity, but this is discouraged. The primary financial statements are those that have been restated.

After the assets, liabilities, equity and statement of profit or loss and other comprehensive income of the entity have been restated, there will be a **net gain or loss on monetary assets and liabilities (the 'net monetary position')** and this should be recognised separately in profit or loss for the period.

4.2 Statement of financial position: Historical cost

Where the entity produces its financial statements on a historical cost basis, the following procedures should be applied:

(a) Items that are not already expressed in terms of measuring units current at the year end should be restated, using a **general prices index**, so that they are valued in measuring units current at the year end.

(b) **Monetary assets and liabilities** are not restated, because they are already expressed in terms of measuring units current at the year end.

(c) Assets that are **already stated at market value or net realisable value** need not be restated, because they too are already valued in measuring units current at the year end.

(d) Any assets or liabilities **linked by agreement to changes in the general level of prices**, such as indexed-linked loans or bonds, should be adjusted in accordance with the terms of the agreement to establish the amount outstanding as at the year end.

(e) All **other non-monetary assets**, eg tangible non-current assets, intangible non-current assets (including accumulated depreciation/amortisation) investments and inventories, should be restated in terms of measuring units as at the year end, by applying a general prices index.

The **method of restating** these assets should normally be to multiply the original cost of the assets by a factor: (prices index at year end /prices index at date of acquisition of the asset).

4.3 Statement of profit or loss and other comprehensive income: historical cost

In the statement of profit or loss and other comprehensive income, all amounts of income and expense should be **restated in terms of measuring units current at the year end**. All amounts therefore need to be restated by a factor that allows for the change in the prices index since the item of income or expense was first recorded.

4.4 Gain or loss on net monetary position

In a period of inflation, an entity that holds monetary assets (cash, receivables) will suffer a fall in the purchasing power of these assets. By the same token, in a period of inflation, the value of monetary liabilities, such as a bank overdraft or bank loan, declines in terms of current purchasing power.

(a) If an entity has an **excess of monetary assets over monetary liabilities**, it will suffer a loss over time on its net monetary position, in a period of inflation, in terms of measuring units as at 'today's date'.

(b) If an entity has an **excess of monetary liabilities over monetary assets**, it will make a gain on its net monetary position, in a period of inflation.

4.5 Example: Hyperinflationary financial statements

An entity maintains an unchanged position over time. At 1 January, when the general prices index was 100, its statement of financial position was as follows:

	$H
Assets	
Non-monetary assets	2,000
Monetary assets	2,000
	4,000
Liabilities and equity	
Monetary liabilities	1,000
Equity	3,000
	4,000

Suppose that the general prices index rises to 150 at 31 December.

Required

Show the adjustments required in the statement of financial position.

Solution

Restating this statement of financial position in terms of measuring units when the prices index is 50% higher gives the following.

	$H
Assets	
Non-monetary assets (× 150/100)	3,000
Monetary assets	2,000
	5,000
Liabilities and equity	
Monetary liabilities	1,000
Equity (× 150/100)	4,500
	5,500

The entity has suffered a loss on its net monetary position of $H500, in terms of measuring units at the current date $H(5,500 − 5,000). This is because it has held net monetary assets of $H1,000 during the period.

In the financial statements of an entity reporting in the currency of a hyperinflationary economy, the gain or loss on the net monetary position:

(a) May be derived as the **difference between total assets and total equity and liabilities**, after restating the non-monetary assets, owners' equity, statement of profit or loss and other comprehensive income items and index-linked items; **or**

(b) May be estimated by **applying the change in the general prices index** for the period to the weighted average of the net monetary position of the entity in the period.

The gain or loss on the net monetary position should be **included in net income** and disclosed separately. (Any adjustment that was made to index-linked items can be set off against this net monetary gain or loss.)

4.6 Current cost financial statements: Restating the financial statements

A similar procedure is required to restate the financial statements of an entity that prepares its financial statements using a current cost basis.

(a) Items stated in the statement of financial position at current cost do not need to be restated. Other items should be restated in the same way as for adjusting financial statements prepared on a historical cost basis.

(b) In the **statement of profit or loss and other comprehensive income**, cost of sales and depreciation are generally reported at current costs at the time of consumption and sales and other expenses at money amounts at the time they occurred. These items will need to be restated in terms of measuring units as at the year end by making a prices index adjustment.

(c) There will be a **gain or loss on the net monetary position**, which will be established in the same way as for financial statements based on historical cost.

4.7 Economies ceasing to be hyperinflationary economies

When an economy ceases to be a hyperinflation economy, entities reporting in the currency of the economy are no longer required to produce financial statements in compliance with IAS 29.

Suppose for example that in 20X4 an entity reports in compliance with IAS 29, but in 20X5 it reverts to historical cost accounting because the economy is no longer a hyperinflationary economy. As a starting point for reverting to historical cost reporting, the entity should use the amounts expressed in terms of measuring units as at the end of 20X4 as the basis for its carrying amounts in 20X5 and subsequent years.

4.8 Disclosures

IAS 29 calls for the following disclosures:

- The fact that the **financial statements have been restated** for the changes in general purchasing power.
- Whether the financial statements as shown are based on **historical cost or current cost**.
- The **identity of the prices index** used to make the restatements, its level at the year end the movement in the index during the current and the previous reporting periods.

In financial statements prepared under IAS 29, corresponding figures for the previous year should be **restated using the general prices index**.

4.9 Hyperinflation and changes in foreign exchange rates

IAS 21 *The Effects of Changes in Foreign Exchange Rates* was covered earlier in this chapter. A parent may have a foreign operation whose functional currency is the currency of a hyperinflationary economy. When the parent prepares consolidated financial statements it should:

(a) **Restate the financial statements** of the foreign operation in accordance with IAS 29; **before**

(b) **Translating all amounts** from the foreign operation's functional currency to the presentation currency **at the closing rate**.

The following example is a simple illustration of the problems that can arise where a foreign subsidiary operates in a hyperinflationary economy.

4.10 Section summary

- IAS 29 does not define **hyperinflationary economies**, but they have various characteristics.
- Financial statements should be **restated based on a measuring unit current** at the year end
    - **Monetary assets/liabilities** do not need to be restated
    - **Non-monetary assets/liabilities** must be restated by applying a general prices index
    - **Items of income/expense** must be restated
    - **Gain/loss on net monetary items** must be reported in profit or loss for the year

Chapter roundup

- Questions on foreign currency translation have always been popular with examiners. In general you are required to prepare **consolidated financial statements** for a group which includes a foreign subsidiary.

- You may have to make the decision yourself as to whether the subsidiary has the same functional currency as the parent or a different functional currency from the parent. This determines whether the subsidiary is treated as an **extension of the parent** or as a **net investment**.

- You must be able to calculate **exchange differences**.
  Practising examination questions is the best way of learning this topic.

- **IAS 29** *Financial Reporting in Hyperinflationary Economies* requires financial statements of entities operating within a hyperinflationary economy to be restated in terms of measuring units current at the year end.

Quick quiz

1. What is the difference between conversion and translation?
2. Define 'monetary' items according to IAS 21.
3. How should foreign currency transactions be recognised initially in an individual entity's financial statements?
4. What factors must management take into account when determining the functional currency of a foreign operation?
5. How should goodwill and fair value adjustments be treated on consolidation of a foreign operation?
6. When can an entity's functional currency be changed?

Answers to quick quiz

1. (a) Conversion is the process of exchanging one currency for another.
   (b) Translation is the restatement of the value of one currency in another currency.

2. Money held and assets and liabilities to be received or paid in fixed or determinable amounts of money.

3. Use the exchange rate at the date of the transaction. An average rate for a period can be used if the exchange rates did not fluctuate significantly.

4. See Section 3.2

5. Treat as assets/liabilities of the foreign operation and translate at the closing rate.

6. Only if there is a change to the underlying transactions relevant to the entity.

End of chapter question

Eufonion (AIA November 2008)

(a) According to IAS 21 *The Effects of Changes in Foreign Exchange Rates*, how should a company decide what its functional currency is? **(5 marks)**

(b) Until recently Eufonion, a UK limited liability company, reported using the euro (€) as its functional currency. However, on 1 November 20X7 the company decided that its functional currency should now be the dollar ($).

The summarised statement of financial position of Eufonion as at 31 October 20X8 in € million was as follows:

	€m
ASSETS	
Non-current assets	420
Current assets	
Inventories	26
Trade and other receivables	42
Cash and cash equivalents	8
	76
Total assets	496
EQUITY AND LIABILITIES	
Equity	
Share capital	200
Retained earnings	107
	307
Non-current liabilities	85
Current liabilities	
Trade and other payables	63
Current taxation	41
	104
Total liabilities	189
Total equity and liabilities	496

Non-current liabilities includes a loan of $70 million which was raised in dollars ($) and translated at the closing rate of $1 = €0.72425.

Trade receivables includes an amount of $20 million invoiced in dollars ($) to an American customer which has been translated at the closing rate of $1 = €0.72425.

PART B BUSINESS COMBINATIONS AND GROUP FINANCIAL STATEMENTS

All items of property, plant and equipment were purchased in euros (€) except for plant which was purchased in British pounds (£) in 2007 and which cost £150 million. This was translated at the exchange rate of £1 = €1.46015 as at the date of purchase. The carrying value of the equipment was £90 million as at 31 October 20X8.

Required

Translate the statement of financial position of Eufonion as at 31 October 20X8 into dollars ($m), the company's new functional currency. **(5 marks)**

(c) The directors of Eufonion (as in (b) above) are now considering using the British pound (£) as the company's presentation currency for the financial statements for the year ended 31 October 20X9.

Required

Advise the directors how they should translate the company's statement of profit or loss and other comprehensive income for the year ended 31 October 20X9 and its statement of financial position as at 31 October 20X9 into the new presentation currency. **(6 marks)**

(d) Discuss whether or not a reporting entity should be allowed to present its financial statements in a currency which is different to its functional currency.

(4 marks)

(Total 20 marks)

Group statements of cash flows

Topic list	Syllabus reference
1 Cash flows and funds flows	LO2
2 IAS 7 *Statement of Cash Flows:* Single company	LO2, LO3
3 Group statements of cash flows	LO2, LO3
4 Foreign currency translation and the statement of cash flows	LO2, LO3
5 Examiner's guide to approaching an exam question	LO3

Introduction

A statement of cash flows is an additional primary statement of **great value** to users of financial statements for the extra information it provides.

You should be familiar with the basic principles, techniques and definitions relating to statements of cash flows from your earlier studies. This chapter develops the principles and preparation techniques to include **consolidated financial statements**.

1 Cash flows and funds flows

> **FAST FORWARD**
>
> **Statements of cash flows** are a useful addition to the financial statements of companies because it is recognised that accounting profit is not the only indicator of a company's performance.
>
> Statements of cash flows concentrate on the sources and uses of cash and are a useful indicator of a company's **liquidity and solvency**.

1.1 Users of the Statement of cash flows

Management
- Cash flow provides **more relevant information** on which decisions should be taken.
- Cash flow accounting can be both **retrospective** and iclude a **forecast** for the future. This is of great information value to all users of accounting information.
- Forecasts can subsequently be monitored by the use of **variance statements** which compare actual cash flows against the forecast.

Users of cash flow information

Shareholders
- **Survival** of a company depends on its ability to generate cash. Cash flow accounting directs attention towards this critical issue.
- Cash flow accounting can be better for **stewardship** as cash flows are objective and not subject to manipulation.
- Cash flow reporting provides a better means of comparing the results of different companies than traditional profit reporting.
- It helps manage expectations about potential dividend payments. Shareholders might believe that a company could pay all its profits as a **dividend**. The statement of cash flows helps them understand the impact of cash flows helps them understand the impact of cash payments.

Creditors (long- and short-term) are more interested in an entity's ability to repay them than in its profitablity.
- Coul be misled by profit accounting; eg creditors might consider tha a profitable company is a **going concern**
For example, if a company builds up large amounts of unsold inventories of goods, their cost would not be chargeable against profits, but cash would have been used up in making them, thus weakening the company's liquid resources.

2 IAS 7 *Statement of Cash Flows:* Single company

> **FAST FORWARD**
>
> You need to be aware of the **format** of the statement as laid out in **IAS 7**. Setting out the format is an essential first stage in preparing the statement, so this format must be learnt.

The aim of IAS 7 is to provide information to users of financial statements about the cash flows of an entity's **ability to generate cash and cash equivalents**, as well as indicating the cash needs of the entity. The statement of cash flows provides **historical** information about cash and cash equivalents, classifying cash flows between operating, investing and financing activities.

2.1 Scope

A statement of cash flows should be presented as an **integral part** of an entity's financial statements. All types of entity can provide useful information about cash flows as the need for cash is universal, whatever the nature of their revenue-producing activities. Therefore **all entities are required by the standard to produce a statement of cash flows**.

2.2 Definitions

The standard gives the following definitions, the most important of which are **cash** and **cash equivalents**.

Key terms

> **Cash** comprises cash on hand and demand deposits.
>
> **Cash equivalents** are short-term, highly liquid investments that are readily convertible to known amounts of cash and which are subject to an insignificant risk of changes in value.
>
> **Cash flows** are inflows and outflows of cash and cash equivalents.
>
> **Operating activities** are the principal revenue-producing activities of the entity and other activities that are not investing or financing activities.
>
> **Investing activities** are the acquisition and disposal of non-current assets and other investments not included in cash equivalents.
>
> **Financing activities** are activities that result in changes in the size and composition of the equity capital and borrowings of the entity. (IAS 7)

2.3 Cash and cash equivalents

The standard expands on the definition of cash equivalents: they are not held for investment or other long-term purposes, but rather to meet short-term cash commitments. To fulfil the above definition, an investment's **maturity date should normally be three months from its acquisition date**. It would usually be the case then that equity investments (ie shares in other companies) are **not** cash equivalents. An exception would be where preferred shares were acquired with a very close maturity date.

Loans and other borrowings from banks are classified as investing activities. In some countries, however, **bank overdrafts** are repayable on demand and are treated as part of an entity's total cash management system. In these circumstances an overdrawn balance will be included in cash and cash equivalents. Such banking arrangements are characterised by a balance which fluctuates between overdrawn and credit.

Movements between different types of cash and cash equivalent are not included in cash flows. The investment of surplus cash in cash equivalents is part of cash management, not part of operating, investing or financing activities.

2.4 Presentation of a statement of cash flows

IAS 7 requires statements of cash flows to report cash flows during the period classified by **operating, investing and financing activities**.

The manner of presentation of cash flows from operating, investing and financing activities **depends on the nature of the entity**. By classifying cash flows between different activities in this way users can see the impact on cash and cash equivalents of each one, and their relationships with each other. We can look at each in more detail.

2.4.1 Operating activities

This is perhaps the key part of the statement of cash flows because it shows whether, and to what extent, companies can **generate cash from their operations**. It is these operating cash flows which must, in the end, pay for all cash outflows relating to other activities, ie paying loan interest, dividends and so on.

Most of the components of cash flows from operating activities will be those items which **determine the profit or loss of the entity**, ie they relate to the main revenue-producing activities of the entity. The standard gives the following as examples of cash flows from operating activities:

- Cash receipts from the sale of goods and the rendering of services
- Cash receipts from royalties, fees, commissions and other revenue
- Cash payments to suppliers for goods and services
- Cash payments to and on behalf of employees
- Cash payments/refunds of income taxes unless they can be specifically identified with financing or investing activities
- Cash receipts and payments from contracts held for dealing or trading purposes

Certain items may be included in the profit or loss for the period which do *not* relate to operational cash flows. For example the profit or loss on the sale of a piece of plant will be included in profit or loss, but the cash flows will be classed as from **investing activities**.

2.4.2 Investing activities

The cash flows classified under this heading show the extent of new investment in **assets which will generate future profit and cash flows**. The standard gives the following examples of cash flows arising from investing activities.

- Cash payments to acquire property, plant and equipment, intangibles and other non-current assets, including those relating to capitalised development costs and self-constructed property, plant and equipment
- Cash receipts from sales of property, plant and equipment, intangibles and other non-current assets
- Cash payments to acquire shares or debentures of other entities
- Cash receipts from sales of shares or debentures of other entities
- Cash advances and loans made to other parties
- Cash receipts from the repayment of advances and loans made to other parties
- Cash payments for or receipts from futures/forward/option/swap contracts except where the contracts are held for dealing purposes, or the payments/receipts are classified as financing activities

2.4.3 Financing activities

This section of the statement of cash flows shows the share of cash which the entity's capital providers have claimed during the period. This is an indicator of **likely future interest and dividend payments**. The standard gives the following examples of cash flows which might arise under these headings.

- Cash proceeds from issuing shares
- Cash payments to owners to acquire or redeem the entity's shares
- Cash proceeds from issuing debentures, loans, notes, bonds, mortgages and other short or non-current borrowings
- Cash repayments of amounts borrowed
- Cash payments by a lessee for the reduction of the outstanding liability relating to a lease

2.5 Reporting cash flows from operating activities

The standard offers a choice of method for this part of the statement of cash flows.

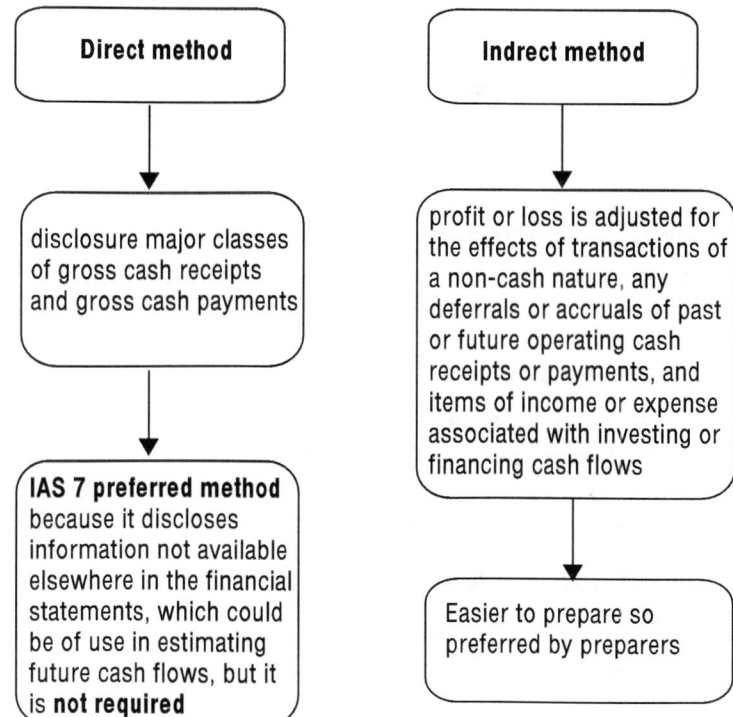

2.5.1 Using the direct method

There are different ways in which the **information about gross cash receipts and payments** can be obtained. The most obvious way is simply to extract the information from the accounting records. This may be a laborious task, however, and the indirect method below may be easier.

2.5.2 Using the indirect method

The profit or loss for the period is adjusted for the following.

(a) Changes during the period in inventories, operating receivables and payables
(b) Non-cash items, eg depreciation, provisions, profits/losses on the sales of assets
(c) Other items, the cash flows from which should be classified under investing or financing activities.

A **proforma** of such a calculation is as follows and this method may be more common in the exam.

	$
Profit before taxation (statement of profit or loss and OCI)	X
Add depreciation	X
Loss (profit) on sale of non-current assets	X
(Increase)/decrease in inventories	(X)/X
(Increase)/decrease in receivables	(X)/X
Increase/(decrease) in payables	X/(X)
Cash generated from operations	X
Interest (paid)/received	(X)
Income taxes paid	(X)
Net cash flows from operating activities	X

It is important to understand why **certain items are added and others subtracted**. Note the following points.

(a) Depreciation is not a cash expense, but is deducted in arriving at the profit figure in the statement of profit or loss and other comprehensive income. It makes sense, therefore, to eliminate it by adding it back.

(b) By the same logic, a loss on a disposal of a non-current asset (arising through under provision of depreciation) needs to be added back and a profit deducted.

(c) An increase in inventories means less cash – you have spent cash on buying inventory.

(d) An increase in receivables means the company's debtors have not paid as much, and therefore there is less cash.

(e) If we pay off payables, causing the figure to decrease, again we have less cash.

2.5.3 Indirect versus direct

The direct method **is encouraged** where the necessary information is not too costly to obtain, but IAS 7 does not require it. In practice, therefore, the direct method is rarely used. It could be argued that companies ought to monitor their cash flows carefully enough on an ongoing basis to be able to use the direct method at minimal extra cost.

2.6 Interest and dividends

Cash flows from interest and dividends received and paid should each be **disclosed separately**. Each should be classified in a consistent manner from period to period as either operating, investing or financing activities.

Dividends paid by the entity can be classified in **one of two ways**:

(a) As a **financing cash flow**, showing the cost of obtaining financial resources.

(b) As a component of **cash flows from operating activities** so that users can assess the entity's ability to pay dividends out of operating cash flows.

2.7 Taxes on income

Cash flows arising from taxes on income should be **separately disclosed** and should be classified as cash flows from operating activities **unless** they can be specifically identified with financing and investing activities.

Taxation cash flows are often **difficult to match** to the originating underlying transaction, so most of the time all tax cash flows are classified as arising from operating activities.

2.8 Components of cash and cash equivalents

The components of cash and cash equivalents should be disclosed and a **reconciliation** should be presented, showing the amounts in the statement of cash flows reconciled with the equivalent items reported in the statement of financial position.

It is also necessary to disclose the **accounting policy** used in deciding the items included in cash and cash equivalents, in accordance with IAS 1 *Presentation of Financial Statements*, but also because of the wide range of cash management practices worldwide.

2.9 Other disclosures

All entities should disclose, together with a **commentary by management**, any other information likely to be of importance. Disclosure is required of restrictions on the use of or access to any part of cash equivalents. Disclosure is encouraged of:

(a) The amount of undrawn borrowing facilities which are available.

(b) Cash flows which increased operating capacity compared to cash flows which merely maintained operating capacity.

2.10 Example: Statement of cash flows

In the next section we will look at the procedures for preparing a statement of cash flows. First, look at this **example**, adapted from the example given in the standard.

2.10.1 Direct method

STATEMENT OF CASH FLOWS (DIRECT METHOD)
YEAR ENDED 20X7

	$m	$m
Cash flows from operating activities		
Cash receipts from customers	30,150	
Cash paid to suppliers and employees	(27,600)	
Cash generated from operations	2,550	
Interest paid	(270)	
Income taxes paid	(900)	
Net cash from operating activities		1,380
Cash flows from investing activities		
Purchase of property, plant and equipment	(900)	
Proceeds from sale of equipment	20	
Interest received	200	
Dividends received	200	
Net cash used in investing activities		(480)
Cash flows from financing activities		
Proceeds from issue of share capital	250	
Proceeds from non-current borrowings	250	
Payment of lease liabilities	(90)	
Dividends paid*	(1,200)	
Net cash used in financing activities		(790)
Net increase in cash and cash equivalents		110
Cash and cash equivalents at beginning of period (Note)		120
Cash and cash equivalents at end of period (Note)		230

* This could also be shown as an operating cash flow

2.10.2 Indirect method

STATEMENT OF CASH FLOWS (INDIRECT METHOD)
YEAR ENDED 20X7

	$m	$m
Cash flows from operating activities		
Profit before taxation	3,390	
Adjustments for:		
Depreciation	450	
Investment income	(500)	
Interest expense	400	
	3,740	
Increase in trade and other receivables	(500)	
Decrease in inventories	1,050	
Decrease in trade payables	(1,740)	
Cash generated from operations	2,550	
Interest paid	(270)	
Income taxes paid	(900)	

Net cash from operating activities		1,380
Cash flows from investing activities		
Purchase of property, plant and equipment	(900)	
Proceeds from sale of equipment	20	
Interest received	200	
Dividends received	200	
Net cash used in investing activities		(480)
Cash flows from financing activities		
Proceeds from issue of share capital	250	
Proceeds from non-current borrowings	250	
Payment of lease liabilities	(90)	
Dividends paid*	(1,200)	
Net cash used in financing activities		(790)
Net increase in cash and cash equivalents		110
Cash and cash equivalents at beginning of period (Note)		120
Cash and cash equivalents at end of period (Note)		230

	20X7 $m	20X6 $m
Cash on hand and balances with banks	40	25
Short-term investments	190	95
Cash and cash equivalents	230	120

*Note. This could also be shown as an operating cash flow

2.11 Disclosures

Amendments to IAS 7 were issued in 2016 as a result of *Disclosure Initiative* (Amendments to IAS 7) which seek to improve information provided to the users of financial statements regarding an entity's financing and liquidity:

Area	Disclosure required
Information about an entity's financing activities, excluding equity items	An entity should disclose a reconciliation of the amounts in the opening and closing statements of financial position for each item for which cash flows have been, or would be, classified as financing activities in the statement of cash flows, excluding equity items. This will result in improved disclosures about an entity's debt and movements in debt during the reporting period.
Disclosures that help those users to understand the liquidity of an entity.	Extended disclosures previously required by IAS 7 about an entity's liquidity and introduces disclosures about the restrictions that affect the decisions of an entity to use cash and cash equivalent balances, including tax liabilities that would arise on the repatriation of foreign cash and cash equivalent balances.

2.12 Section summary

FAST FORWARD

Remember the **step-by-step preparation procedure** and use it for all the questions you practise.

Remember the steps involved in preparation of a statement of cash flows.

Step 1 Set out the proforma leaving plenty of space.

Step 2 Complete the reconciliation of profit before tax to net cash flow from operating activities, as far as possible.

Step 3 Calculate the following where appropriate.

- Tax paid
- Dividends paid
- Purchase and sale of non-current assets
- Issues of shares
- Repayment of loans
- Repayment of lease liabilities (the interest and capital elements need to be presented separately)

Step 4 Work out the profit if not already given using: opening and closing balances, tax charge and dividends.

Step 5 Slot the figures into the statement and any notes required.

Question — Single company

Kane Co's statement of profit or loss and other comprehensive income for the year ended 31 December 20X8 and statements of financial position at 31 December 20X7 and 31 December 20X8 were as follows.

KANE CO

STATEMENT OF PROFIT AND LOSS AND OTHER COMPREHENSIVE INCOME FOR THE YEAR ENDED 31 DECEMBER 20X8

	$'000	$'000
Sales		720
Raw materials consumed	70	
Staff costs	94	
Depreciation	118	
Loss on disposal of non-current asset	18	
		300
		420
Interest payable		28
Profit before tax		392
Income tax expense		124
Profit for the year		268

KANE CO
STATEMENT OF FINANCIAL POSITION AS AT 31 DECEMBER

	20X8		20X7	
	$'000	$'000	$'000	$'000
Assets				
Non-current assets				
Cost	1,596		1,560	
Depreciation	318		224	
		1,278		1,336

PART B BUSINESS COMBINATIONS AND GROUP FINANCIAL STATEMENTS

	20X8		20X7	
	$'000	$'000	$'000	$'000
Current assets				
Inventory	24		20	
Trade receivables	76		58	
Bank	48		56	
		148		134
Total assets		1,426		1,470
Equity and liabilities				
Equity				
Share capital	360		340	
Share premium	36		24	
Retained earnings	686		490	
		1,082		854
Non-current liabilities				
Non-current loans		200		500
Current liabilities				
Trade payables	42		30	
Taxation	102		86	
		144		116
		1,426		1,470

During the year, the company paid $90,000 for a new piece of machinery.

Required

Prepare a statement of cash flows for Kane Co for the year ended 31 December 20X8 in accordance with the requirements of IAS 7, using the indirect method.

Answer

KANE CO
STATEMENT OF CASH FLOWS FOR THE YEAR ENDED 31 DECEMBER 20X8

	$'000	$'000
Net cash flow from operating activities		
Operating profit	420	
Depreciation charges (W)	118	
Loss on sale of tangible non-current assets	18	
Increase in inventories (24 – 20)	(4)	
Increase in receivables (76 – 58)	(18)	
Increase in payables (42 – 30)	12	
Cash generated from operations	546	
Interest paid	(28)	
Dividends paid (268 + 490 – 686)	(72)	
Tax paid (86 + 124 – 102)	(108)	
Net cash flow from operating activities		338
Cash flows from investing activities		
Payments to acquire tangible non-current assets	(90)	
Receipts from sales of tangible non-current assets (W)	12	
Net cash outflow from investing activities		(78)
Cash flows from financing activities		
Issues of share capital (360 + 36 – 340 – 24)	32	
Non-current loans repaid (500 – 200)	(300)	
Net cash flows from financing		(268)
Decrease in cash and cash equivalents		(8)
Cash and cash equivalents at 1.1.X8		56
Cash and cash equivalents at 31.12.X8		48

Working: non-current asset disposals

COST

	$'000		$'000
At 1.1.X8	1,560	At 31.12.X8	1,596
Purchases	90	Disposals (balance)	54
	1,650		1,650

ACCUMULATED DEPRECIATION

	$'000		$'000
At 31.1.X8	318	At 1.1.X8	224
Depreciation on disposals (balance)	24	Charge for year	118
	342		342
Carrying amount of disposals			30
Net loss reported			(18)
Proceeds of disposals			12

3 Group statements of cash flows

FAST FORWARD

Group cash flows should not present a great problem if you understand how to deal with acquisitions and disposals of subsidiaries, non-controlling interest and dividends.

Group statements of cash flows follow the same principles as for single company statements, with some additional complications.

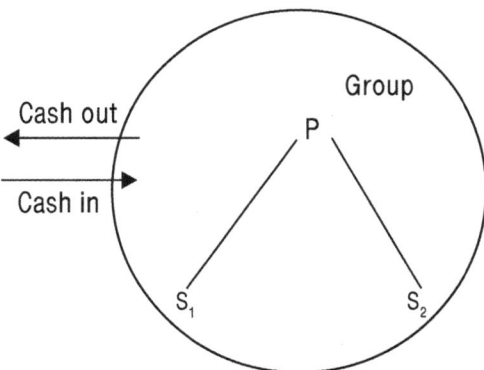

Cash flows that are **internal to the group** should be eliminated in the preparation of a consolidated statement of cash flows. Where a subsidiary **joins or leaves** a group during a financial year the cash flows of the group should include the cash flows of the subsidiary concerned for the same period as that for which the group's statement of profit or loss and other comprehensive income includes the results of the subsidiary.

3.1 Acquisitions and disposals of subsidiaries and other business units

An entity should present separately the aggregate cash flows arising from acquisitions and from disposals of subsidiaries or other business units and classify them as **investing activities**.

Disclosure is required of the following, in aggregate, in respect of both acquisitions and disposals of subsidiaries or other business units during the period.

- Total purchase/disposal consideration
- Portion of purchase/disposal consideration discharged by means of cash/cash equivalents

- Amount of cash/cash equivalents in the subsidiary or business unit disposed of
- Amount of assets and liabilities other than cash/cash equivalents in the subsidiary or business unit acquired or disposed of, summarised by major category

The amounts shown in the statements of cash flows for purchase or disposal of subsidiaries or business units will be the amounts paid or received **net** of cash/cash equivalents acquired or disposed of.

3.2 Consolidation adjustments and non-controlling interest

The group statement of cash flows should only deal with flows of cash and cash equivalents external to the group, so all intra-group cash flows should be eliminated. **Dividends paid to non-controlling interest** should be included under the heading 'cash flow from financing' and disclosed separately.

3.3 Example: Non-controlling interest

The following are extracts of the consolidated results for Jarvis Co for the year ended 31 December 20X8.

CONSOLIDATED STATEMENT OF PROFIT OR LOSS AND OTHER COMPREHENSIVE INCOME (EXTRACT)

	$'000
Group profit before tax	90
Income tax expense	(30)
Profit for the year	60
Profit attributable to:	
Owners of the parent	45
Non-controlling interest	15
	60

CONSOLIDATED STATEMENT OF FINANCIAL POSITION (EXTRACT)

	20X1 $'000	20X2 $'000
Non-controlling interest	300	306

Calculate the dividends paid to the non-controlling interest during the year.

Solution

The non-controlling interest share of profit after tax represents retained profit plus dividends paid.

NON-CONTROLLING INTEREST

	$'000		$'000
Dividend paid	9	Balance b/fwd	300
Balance c/fwd	306	Profit for period (I/S)	15
	315		315

3.4 Associates and joint ventures

In respect of associates and joint ventures accounted for using the equity method, only the actual cash flows from sales or purchases between the group and the associate/joint venture, and investments in and dividends from the entity should be included in the consolidated statement of cash flows. Dividends should be included in **operating cash flows**, where they are shown within operating profit in the statement of profit or loss and other comprehensive income.

3.5 Example: Associate

The following are extracts of the consolidated results of Pripon Co for the year ended 31 December 20X8.

CONSOLIDATED STATEMENT OF PROFIT OR LOSS AND OTHER COMPREHENSIVE INCOME (EXTRACT)

	$'000
Group profit before tax	150
Share of associate's profit after tax	30
	180
Tax	75
Profit after tax	105

CONSOLIDATED STATEMENT OF FINANCIAL POSITION (EXTRACTS)

	20X1 $'000	20X2 $'000
Investment in associate	264	276

Calculate the dividend received from the associate.

Solution

ASSOCIATE

	$'000		$'000
Balance b/fwd	264	Dividend from associate	18
Profit after tax	30	Balance c/fwd	276
	294		294

3.6 Section summary

The preparation of consolidated statements of cash flows will, in many respects, be the same as those for single companies, with the following **additional complications**:

- Acquisitions and disposals of subsidiary
- Cancellation of intra-group transactions
- Non-controlling interest
- Associates and joint ventures

Question — Consolidated cash flow

Topiary Co is a 40 year old company producing garden statues carved from marble. Twenty-two years ago it acquired a 100% interest in a marble importing company, Hardstuff Co. In 20W9 it acquired a 40% interest in a competitor, Landscapes Co and on 1 January 20X7 it acquired a 75% interest in Garden Furniture Designs. The draft consolidated financial statements for the Topiary Group are as follows:

DRAFT CONSOLIDATED STATEMENT OF PROFIT OR LOSS AND OTHER COMPREHENSIVE INCOME

FOR THE YEAR ENDED 31 DECEMBER 20X7

	$'000	$'000
Operating profit		4,455
Share of profits after tax of associates		1,050
Income from non-current investments		600
Interest payable		(450)
Profit before taxation		5,655
Tax on profit		
Income tax	1,173	
Deferred taxation	312	
Tax attributable to investment income	135	
		(1,620)
Profit for the year		4,035

PART B BUSINESS COMBINATIONS AND GROUP FINANCIAL STATEMENTS

	$'000	$'000
Attributable to:		
Owners of the parent		3,735
Non-controlling interest		300
		4,035

DRAFT CONSOLIDATED STATEMENT OF FINANCIAL POSITION AS AT 31 DECEMBER

	20X6		20X7	
	$'000	$'000	$'000	$'000
Assets				
Non-current assets				
Property, plant and equipment				
Buildings at carrying amount		6,600		6,225
Machinery: cost	4,200		9,000	
aggregate depreciation	(3,300)		(3,600)	
carrying amount		900		5,400
		7,500		11,625
Goodwill				300
Investments in associates		3,000		3,300
Other investments		1,230		1,230
		11,730		16,455
Current assets				
Inventories	3,000		5,925	
Receivables	3,825		5,550	
Cash	5,460		13,545	
		12,285		25,020
		24,015		41,475
Equity and liabilities				
Equity				
Share capital: 25c shares	6,000		11,820	
Share premium account	6,285		8,649	
Retained earnings	7,500		10,335	
	19,785		30,804	
Non-controlling interest	–		345	
Total equity		19,785		31,149
Non-current liabilities				
Obligations under leases	510		2,130	
Loans	1,500		4,380	
Deferred tax	39		90	
		2,049		6,600
Current liabilities				
Trade payables	840		1,500	
Obligations under leases	600		720	
Income tax	651		1,386	
Accrued interest and finance charges	90		120	
		2,181		3,726
		24,015		41,475

Notes

1 There had been no acquisitions or disposals of buildings during the year.

 Machinery costing $1.5m was sold for $1.5m resulting in a profit of $300,000. New machinery was acquired in 20X7 including additions of $2.55m acquired under leases.

2   Information relating to the acquisition of Garden Furniture Designs

	$'000
Machinery	495
Inventories	96
Trade receivables	84
Cash	336
Trade payables	(204)
Income tax	(51)
	756
Non-controlling interest	(189)
	567
Goodwill	300
	867
2,640,000 shares issued as part consideration	825
Balance of consideration paid in cash	42
	867

3   Loans were issued at a discount in 20X7 and the carrying amount of the loans at 31 December 20X7 included $120,000 representing the finance cost attributable to the discount and allocated in respect of the current reporting period.

Required

Prepare a consolidated statement of cash flows for the Topiary Group for the year ended 31 December 20X7 as required by IAS 7, using the indirect method. There is no need to provide notes to the statement of cash flows.

Answer

TOPIARY CO
CONSOLIDATED STATEMENT OF CASH FLOWS
FOR THE YEAR ENDED 31 DECEMBER 20X7

	$'000	$'000
Cash flows from operating activities		
Profit before tax	6,090	
Adjustments for:		
Depreciation (W1)	975	
Profit on sale of plant	(300)	
Share of associate's profits	(1,485)	
Investment income	(600)	
Interest payable	450	
Operating profit before working capital changes	5,130	
Increase in trade and other receivables (5,500 – 3,825 – 84)	(1,641)	
Increase in inventories (5,925 – 3,000 – 96)	(2,829)	
Increase in trade payables (1,500 – 840 – 204)	456	
Cash generated from operations	1,116	
Interest paid (W2)	(300)	
Income taxes paid (W3)	(750)	
Net cash from operating activities		66
Cash flows from investing activities		
Purchase of subsidiary (W4)	294	
Purchase of property, plant and equipment (W5)	(3,255)	
Proceeds from sale of plant	1,500	
Dividends from investment (600 – 135)	465	
Dividends from associate (W6)	750	
Net cash used in investing activities		(246)

PART B BUSINESS COMBINATIONS AND GROUP FINANCIAL STATEMENTS

	$'000	$'000
Cash flows from financing activities		
Issue of ordinary share capital (W8)	7,359	
Issue of loan notes (W9)	2,760	
Capital payments under leases (W10)	(810)	
Dividends paid to owners (3,735 + 7,500 – 10,335)	(900)	
Dividends paid to non-controlling interest (W7)	(144)	
Net cash flows from financing activities		8,265
Net increase in cash and cash equivalents		8,085
Cash and cash equivalents at 1.1.X7		5,460
Cash and cash equivalents at 31.12.X7		13,545

Workings

1 Depreciation charges

	$'000	$'000
Freehold buildings (6,600 – 6,225)		375
Plant		
Closing balance	3,600	
Opening balance	3,300	
	300	
Depreciation on disposal	300	
		600
		975

2 Interest

	$'000
Accrued interest b/f	90
Expense	450
Discount	(120)
Less accrued interest c/f	(120)
	300

3 Taxation

	$'000	$'000
Opening balance		
Income tax	651	
Deferred tax	39	
		690
Statement of profit or loss and OCI (1,173 + 312)		1,485
Closing balances		
Income tax	1,386	
Deferred tax	90	
		(1,476)
		699
On acquisition		51
Cash outflow		750

4 Purchase of subsidiary

	$'000
Cash received on acquisition	336
Less cash consideration	(42)
Cash inflow	294

5 Purchase of tangible non-current assets: machinery

	$'000	$'000
Cost at 31 December 20X7		9,000
Cost at 1 January 20X7		4,200
		4,800
Disposal		1,500
		6,300
On acquisition	495	
Leased	2,550	
		(3,045)
Cash outflow		3,255

6 Dividends from associate

	$'000
Opening balance	3,000
Share of profit after tax	1,050
	4,050
Closing balance	3,300
	750

7 Non-controlling interest

	$'000
Opening balance	
Profit for year	300
On acquisition	189
	489
Closing balance	(345)
Cash outflow	144

8 Issue of ordinary share capital

	$'000	$'000
Closing balance		
Shares	11,820	
Premium	8,649	
		20,469
Non-cash consideration		
Shares	660	
Premium	165	
		(825)
Opening balance		
Shares	6,000	
Premium	6,285	
		(12,285)
Cash inflow		7,359

9 Issue of loan notes

	$'000
Closing balance	4,380
Opening balance	1,500
	2,880
Finance cost	120
Cash inflow	2,760

10 Capital payments under leases	$'000	$'000
Opening balances		
Current		600
Non-current		510
		1,110
New lease commitment		2,550
Closing balances		
Current	720	
Non-current	2,130	
		(2,850)
Cash outflow		810

4 Foreign currency translation and the statement of cash flows

FAST FORWARD

A **foreign exchange difference** in a group statement of cash flows must be analysed into its constituent parts.

Exam focus point

Questions on this topic are possible. They normally feature cash flows from an individual transaction but you may be asked to deal with a foreign subsidiary.

4.1 Individual companies

Receipts and payments should be translated into the reporting currency at the **rate ruling** at the date on which the receipt or payment is made.

Exchange differences **do not give rise to cash flows** and therefore they would not be reflected in the statement of cash flows.

4.2 Group companies

The main problems relating to foreign exchange differences are when dealing with the cash flows of an overseas subsidiary. IAS 7 requires that all cash flows relating to an overseas subsidiary be translated at the exchange rates between the functional currency and the foreign currency at the date of the cash flows. Where the average rate is used to translate the subsidiary's statement of profit and loss and other comprehensive income then the subsidiary's cash flows will also be translated using this rate.

If the **average rate** is used, then merely using the statement of financial position to derive the figures would not be appropriate as the resulting statement of cash flows would not comply with IAS 7, some items being translated at the closing rate. The practical answer to this problem is to use the following method (which would be time consuming in practice).

Step 1 Produce a statement of cash flows for each subsidiary.

Step 2 Translate each into dollars using the average rate.

Step 3 Consolidate them into the group statement of cash flows (after eliminating intra-group items).

The other main point to note is that the exchange differences on translation must be **analysed into their constituent parts**, namely long-term assets, receivables, cash, payables and non-controlling interests. In the example shown below, the split is given.

4.3 Example: Foreign currency translation

The draft statements of financial position and statements of profit or loss and other comprehensive income of Guinevere Co are as follows.

CONSOLIDATED STATEMENTS OF FINANCIAL POSITION
AS AT 31 DECEMBER

	20X8 $'000	20X8 $'000	20X7 $'000	20X7 $'000
Assets				
Non-current assets				
Property, plant and equipment	32,907		22,926	
Financial assets	6,300		6,300	
		39,207		29,226
Current assets				
Inventories	21,735		18,300	
Receivables	19,230		21,633	
Cash and cash equivalents	2,859		495	
		43,824		40,428
		83,031		69,654
Equity and liabilities				
Equity				
Share capital	15,000		15,000	
Share premium	9,000		9,000	
Reserves	34,476		21,909	
	58,476		45,909	
Non-controlling interests	7,557		5,991	
		66,033		51,900
Non-current liabilities				
Loans		3,006		4,230
Current liabilities				
Trade payables	5,760		5,070	
Income taxes	8,232		8,454	
		13,992		13,524
		83,031		69,654

There were no non-current asset disposals during the year. The depreciation charge for the year was $5,931,000. There were no non-current asset payables at either year end.

Receivables as at 31 December 20X8 include called up share capital not paid of $3,705,000 (20X7: $8,238,000).

CONSOLIDATED STATEMENT OF PROFIT OR LOSS AND OTHER COMPREHENSIVE INCOME
FOR THE YEAR ENDED 31 DECEMBER 20X8

	$'000
Group operating profit	20,865
Income from financial assets	144
Interest payable	(522)
Group profit before tax	20,487
Income tax expense	(8,490)
Group profit for the year	11,997
Attributable to:	
Owners of the parent	11,319
Non-controlling interest	678
	11,997

Note reserves

PART B BUSINESS COMBINATIONS AND GROUP FINANCIAL STATEMENTS

	$'000
Reserves as at 1 January 20X8	21,909
Profit for the year	11,319
Dividends	(1,674)
Exchange gain on translation (Note 1)	4,068
Exchange loss on loan	(1,146)
Reserves as at 31 December 20X8	34,476

Note 1: Exchange gain
The exchange gain on translation is made up as follows.

	$'000
Non-current assets	3,684
Inventories	1,179
Receivables	633
Cash	117
Payables	(189)
Non-controlling interest	(1,356)
	4,068

Required

Prepare the group statement of cash flows for Guinevere Co for the year ended 31 December 20X8, in accordance with IAS 7.

Solution

STATEMENT OF CASH FLOWS FOR THE YEAR ENDED 31 DECEMBER 20X8

	$'000	$'000
Cash flows from operating activities		
Net profit before tax	20,487	
Adjustments for:		
Depreciation	5,931	
Investment income	(144)	
Interest expense	522	
Operating profit before working capital changes	26,796	
Increase in trade and other receivables		
(19,230 – 3,705 – 21,633 + 8,238 – 633)	(1,497)	
Increase in inventories (21,735 – 18,300 – 1,179)	(2,256)	
Increase in trade payables (5,760 – 5,070 – 189)	501	
Cash generated from operations	23,544	
Interest paid	(522)	
Income taxes paid (8,454 + 8,490 – 8,232)	(8,712)	
Net cash from operating activities		14,310
Cash flows from investing activities		
Dividends received	144	
Dividends paid to non-controlling interest		
(5,991 + 678 + 1,356 – 7,557)	(468)	
Payments to acquire long-term assets		
(5,931 + 32,907 – 22,926 – 3,684)	(12,228)	
Net cash used in investing activities		(12,552)
Cash flows from financing activities		
Proceeds of share issue (8,238 – 3,705)	4,533	
Repayment of loans (3,006 – 4,230 – 1,146)	(2,370)	
Dividends paid	(1,674)	
Net cash from financing activities		489
Increase in cash and cash equivalents		2,247
Cash and cash equivalents at 1.1.X8		495
Effect of exchange rate changes		117
Cash and cash equivalents at 31.12.X8		2,859

5 Examiner's guide to approaching an exam question

The FAR2 examiner has produced the following guidance with regard to approaching a statement of cash flows exam question.

The first point to note is that the IAS 7 **principles** are the same whether you are preparing a statement of cash flows for a group or for an individual company. These are as follows:

- *Cash and cash equivalents*. IAS 7 requires the presentation of information about the historical changes in cash and cash equivalents.

- Cash flows **must** be analysed between:
    - *Operating activities*. Operating cash flows may be presented using the direct method (which is preferred by the IASB) or the indirect method (which is preferred by entities in practice and by examiners in examinations).
    - *Investing activities*
    - *Financing activities*

It is important to learn the definitions of all the above headings. You may be asked to use your judgement to decide where an item should be presented or whether an item is a 'cash or cash equivalent' or should be included elsewhere on the statement. With respect to this, cash flows concerning interest and dividends received and paid may be classified as operating, investing or financing, provided the classification is consistent from one period to the next. Cash flows arising from income taxes are **normally** to be classified as operating **unless** they can be specifically identified as referring to investing or financing activities.

Steps in the preparation of a group statement of cash flows:

1. Draft out a pro forma group statement of cash flows with the headings required by IAS 7.

    This means that your statement would look something like this:

    XYZ Group
    Consolidated statement of cash flows
    for the year ended...........

	$m
Cash flows from operating activities	
	–
	=
Cash generated from operations	X
Interest paid	
Income taxes paid	
Net cash used in/generated by operating activities	X
Cash flows from investing activities	
Net cash used in/generated by investing activities	X
Cash flows from financing activities	
Net cash used in/generated by financing activities	X
Net increase/decrease in cash and cash equivalents	X
Cash and cash equivalents at the beginning of the year	X
Effects of exchange rates changes on the balance of cash held in foreign currencies	X
Cash and cash equivalents at the end of the year	X

Leave plenty of space between the headings so that you can fill in the missing information as you go through the question. If the question asks you to use the indirect method there will usually be much more space required between 'cash flows from operating activities' and 'cash generated from operations' than if it asks you to use the direct method. This is because when using the direct method there is no need to present all the accrual adjustments such as depreciation, gain on disposal of plant and equipment, impairment losses, net foreign exchange gains/losses etc.

2 Begin with the 'cash flows from operating activities' section and complete the statement as far as you can. If you are using the indirect method (as is likely at Paper 13 level), this must begin with 'profit for the year'. This is normally taken directly from the statement of profit or loss and other comprehensive income. However the examiner may require you to make adjustments to this figure before you include it in the group statement of cash flows if, for example, there have been errors in its calculation (as in the May 2010 exam). Next, read through the question and include on the statement of cash flows any adjustments necessary to the 'profit for the year' figure for accrual items which have been included in its calculation but which have not resulted in cash flows.

Note above comment concerning the importance of learning the definitions and the possible inclusion of interest, dividends and income taxes in operating, investing or financing cash flows. If the question has given you information concerning company policy in this respect, then include those cash flows as directed. That is, include any interest, dividends or tax cash flows in operating activities if so directed by the question.

3 Read through the question and calculate cash flows with respect to investing activities; for example, proceeds from disposal of property, payments for intangible assets etc. Insert the figures onto the group statement of cash flows.

4 Read through the question and calculate cash flows with respect to financing activities; for example, payments to buy back shares, proceeds from borrowings, repayment of borrowings etc. Insert the figures onto the group statement of cash flows.

5 Make sure you have correctly dealt with the group implications of a cash flow statement. This will normally involve:

(a) Include dividends received from associates and net cash flows from acquiring and disposing of subsidiaries and associates in investing activities.

(b) Include proceeds from disposal of partial interest in subsidiaries in financing activities.

6 Complete the group statement of cash flows by inserting figures for cash equivalents.

Remember that the FAR 2 exam questions are more advanced than the FAR 1 questions and will be more complex. Note therefore that, as mentioned in point 2 above, when you get to step 2 and before beginning to enter figures onto the group statement of cash flows, check to see whether the question requires you to make any amendments to any of the figures as a result, for example, of a finance director misunderstanding an IFRS's requirements.

Chapter roundup

- **Statements of cash flows** are a useful addition to the financial statements of companies because it is recognised that accounting profit is not the only indicator of a company's performance.
- Statements of cash flows concentrate on the sources and uses of cash and are a useful indicator of a company's **liquidity and solvency**.
- You need to be aware of the **format** of the statement as laid out in **IAS 7**. Setting out the format is an essential first stage in preparing the statement, so this format must be learnt.
- Remember the **step-by-step preparation procedure** and use it for all the questions you practise.
- **Group cash flows** should not present a great problem if you understand how to deal with acquisitions and disposals of subsidiaries, non-controlling interest and dividends.
- **A foreign exchange difference** in a group statement of cash flows must be analysed into its constituent parts.

Quick quiz

1. What is the objective of IAS 7?
2. What are the benefits of cash flow information according to IAS 7?
3. What are the standard headings required by IAS 7 to be included in a statement of cash flows?
4. What is the 'indirect method' of preparing a statement of cash flows?
5. How should an acquisition or disposal of a subsidiary be shown in the statement of cash flows?

Answers to quick quiz

1. To provide users of financial statements with information about the entity's ability to generate cash and cash equivalents, and the entity's cash needs.
2. See Section 2.2
3. Operating, investing and financing activities.
4. The profit or loss for the period is adjusted for non-cash items; changes in inventories, receivables and payables from operations; and other items resulting from investing or financing activities.
5. Cash flows from acquisitions and disposal, net of cash acquired/disposed of, are disclosed separately under investing activities.

End of chapter question

Porter

The following consolidated financial statements relate to Porter, a public limited company:

PORTER GROUP: STATEMENT OF FINANCIAL POSITION AS AT 31 MAY 20X6

	20X6 $m	20X5 $m
Non-current assets		
Property, plant and equipment	958	812
Goodwill	15	10
Investment in associate	48	39
	1,021	861
Current assets		
Inventories	154	168
Trade receivables	132	112
Financial assets measured at fair value	16	0
Cash and cash equivalents	158	48
	460	328
	1,481	1,189
Equity attributable to owners of the parent		
Share capital ($1 ordinary shares)	332	300
Share premium account	212	172
Retained earnings	188	165
Revaluation surplus	101	54
	833	691
Non-controlling interests	84	28
	917	719
Non-current liabilities		
Non-current borrowings	380	320
Deferred tax liability	38	26
	418	346
Current liabilities		
Trade and other payables	110	98
Interest payable	8	4
Current tax payable	28	22
	146	124
	1,481	1,189

PORTER GROUP: STATEMENT OF PROFIT OR LOSS AND OTHER COMPREHENSIVE INCOME
FOR THE YEAR ENDED 31 MAY 20X6

	$m
Revenue	956
Cost of sales	(634)
Gross profit	322
Other income	6
Distribution costs	(97)
Administrative expenses	(115)
Finance costs	(16)
Share of profit of associate	12
Profit before tax	112
Income tax expense	(34)
PROFIT FOR THE YEAR	78
Other comprehensive income:	
Gains on property revaluation	58
Share of other comprehensive income of associate	8
Income tax relating to components of other comprehensive income	(17)
Other comprehensive income for the year, net of tax	49
TOTAL COMPREHENSIVE INCOME FOR THE YEAR	127
Profit attributable to:	
Owners of the parent	68
Non-controlling interests	10
	78
Total comprehensive income attributable to:	
Owners of the parent	115
Non-controlling interests	12
	127

The following information relates to the consolidated financial statements of Porter:

(a) During the period, Porter acquired 60% of a subsidiary. The purchase was effected by issuing shares of Porter on a 1 for 2 basis, at their market value on that date of $2.25 per share, plus $26m in cash.

A statement of financial position of the subsidiary, prepared at the acquisition date for consolidation purposes, showed the following position:

	$m
Property, plant and equipment	92
Inventories	20
Trade receivables	16
Cash and cash equivalents	8
	136
Share capital ($1 shares)	80
Reserves	40
	120
Trade payables	12
Income taxes payable	4
	136

An impairment test conducted at the year end, resulted in a write-down of goodwill relating to another wholly owned subsidiary. This was charged to cost of sales.

Group policy is to value non-controlling interests at the date of acquisition at the proportionate share of the fair value of the acquiree's identifiable assets acquired and liabilities assumed.

(b) Depreciation charged to the consolidated profit or loss amounted to $44m. There were no disposals of property, plant and equipment during the year.

(c) Other income represents gains on financial assets measured at fair value. The financial assets represent investments in quoted shares were purchased shortly before the year end with surplus cash, and are expected to be sold after the year end. No dividends have yet been received.

(d) Included in 'trade and other payables' is the $ equivalent of an invoice for 102m shillings for some equipment purchased from a foreign supplier. The asset was invoiced on 5 March 20X6, but had not been paid for at the year end, 31 May 20X6.

Exchange gains or losses on the transaction have been included in administrative expenses. Relevant exchange rates were as follows:

	Shillings to $1
5 March 20X6	6.8
31 May 20X6	6.0

(e) Movement on retained earnings was as follows:

	$m
At 31 May 20X5	165
Total comprehensive income	68
Dividends paid	(45)
At 31 May 20X6	188

Required

Prepare a consolidated statement of cash flows for Porter for the year ended 31 May 20X6 in accordance with IAS 7 *Statement of Cash Flows*, using the indirect method.

Notes to the statement of cash flows are not required.

(Total 25 marks)

PART C

Accounting and reporting techniques

Interim reporting, first-time adoption and fair values

Topic list	Syllabus reference
1 IAS 34 *Interim Financial Reporting*	LO2, LO3, LO4
2 IFRS 1 *First-time Adoption of International Financial Reporting Standards*	LO2, LO3, LO4
3 IFRS 13 *Fair Value Measurement*	LO2, LO3, LO4

Introduction

This chapter deals with three accounting standards:

- IAS 34 *Interim Financial Reporting*, which provides guidance on the content of interim financial reports for those companies which produce them;
- IFRS 1 *First-time Adoption of IFRS*, which explains the procedures which companies adopting IFRS Standards for the first time should follow, and
- IFRS 13 *Fair Value Measurement*, which provides guidance on establishing the fair value of items, when other IFRS Standards permit or require measurement at fair value.

1 IAS 34 *Interim Financial Reporting*

FAST FORWARD

IAS 34 complements stock exchange rules on interim financial reporting in many countries, but it may provide a blueprint for developing markets.

IAS 34 recommends that **entities should produce interim financial reports** and, for entities that do publish such reports, it lays down principles and guidelines for their production.

The following definitions are used in IAS 34.

Key terms

- **Interim period** is a financial reporting period shorter than a full financial year.
- **Interim financial report** means a financial report containing either a complete set of financial statements (as described in IAS 1) or a set of condensed financial statements (as described in this standard) for an interim period. (IAS 34, para 4)

1.1 Scope

The standard does not make the preparation of interim financial reports **mandatory**, taking the view that this is a matter for governments, securities regulators, stock exchanges or professional accountancy bodies within each country to decide. The IASB does, however, strongly recommend to governments etc. that interim financial reporting should be a requirement for companies whose equity or debt securities are **publicly traded**.

(a) An interim financial report should be produced by such companies for **at least the first six months of their financial year** (ie a half year financial report).

(b) The report should be **available no later than 60 days** after the end of the interim period.

(IAS 34, para 1)

Thus, a company with a year ending 31 December would be required as a minimum to prepare an interim report for the half year to 30 June, and this report should be available before the end of August.

1.2 Minimum components

The proposed standard specifies the **minimum component elements** of an interim financial report:

- Condensed statement of financial position
- Condensed statement of profit or loss and other comprehensive income
- Condensed statement of changes in equity
- Condensed statement of cash flows
- Selected note disclosures

(IAS 34, para 8)

The rationale for requiring only condensed statements and selected note disclosures is that entities need not duplicate information in their interim report that is contained in their report for the previous financial year. Interim statements should **focus more on new events, activities and circumstances**.

1.3 Form and content

Where **full financial statements** are given as interim financial statements, they should comply with IAS 1 *Presentation of Financial Statements*, otherwise IAS 34 specifies minimum contents.

If **condensed financial statements are published, the condensed financial statements** should include, as a minimum, each of the headings and sub-totals that were presented in the most recent published financial statements, and additional notes as required by the standard. Additional notes should be presented if their omission would make the condensed interim financial statements misleading (IAS 34, para 10)

Basic earnings per share and diluted earnings per share should also be disclosed. (IAS 34, para 11)

1.3.1 Significant events and transactions and selected explanatory notes

IAS 34 states that the interim financial report should include an explanation of events and transactions that are significant in providing an understanding of the changes in financial position and performance of the entity since the end of the last annual reporting period (IAS 34, para 15).

In addition to disclosing significant events and transactions, the notes to the interim report should include the following (unless the information is contained elsewhere in the report).

- A statement that the **same accounting policies and methods of computation** have been used for the interim statements as were used for the most recent annual financial statements. If not, the nature of the differences and their effect should be described. (The accounting policies for preparing the interim report should only differ from those used for the previous annual financial statements in a situation where there has been a change in accounting policy since the end of the previous financial year, and the new policy will be applied for the annual financial statements of the current financial period.)

- Explanatory comments on the **seasonality or 'cyclicality'** of operations in the interim period. For example, if a company earns most of its annual profits in the first half of the year, because sales are much higher in the first six months, the interim report for the first half of the year should explain this fact.

- The **nature and amount** of items during the interim period affecting assets, liabilities, capital, net income or cash flows, that are unusual, due to their nature, incidence or size.

- The **issue or repurchase** of equity or debt securities.

- Nature and amount of any **changes in estimates** of amounts reported in an earlier interim report during the financial year, or in prior financial years if these affect the current interim period.

- **Dividends paid** on ordinary shares and the dividends paid on other shares.

- **Segmental results** for the operating segments of the entity (see IFRS 8).

- Any **significant events since the end of the interim period**.

- Effect of the acquisition or disposal of subsidiaries during the interim period.

- Any significant change in a **contingent liability or a contingent asset** since the end of the reporting period. (IAS 34, para 16A)

The entity should also disclose the fact that the interim report has been produced **in compliance with** IAS 34 on interim financial reporting.

Question
Disclosures

Give some examples of the type of events or transactions which require disclosure if significant.

Answer

The following are examples from IAS 34, para 15B. The list is not exhaustive.

(a) The write-down of inventories or reversal of a write-down

(b) Recognition of an impairment loss or its reversal

(c) The reversal of provisions for restructuring costs

(d) Acquisitions and disposals of property, plant and equipment

(e) Commitments for the purchase of property, plant and equipment

(f) Litigation settlements

(g) Correction of prior period errors

(h) Changes in the business or economic circumstances that affect the fair value of financial instruments

(i) Any loan default or breach of loan agreement not remedied by the end of the reporting period

(j) Related party transactions

(k) Changes in the classification of financial assets due to a change in the purpose or use of those assets

(l) Changes in contingent liabilities and assets.

1.4 Periods covered

The standard requires that interim financial reports should provide financial information for the following periods or as at the following dates:

- **Statement of financial position data** as at the end of the current interim period, and comparative data as at the end of the most recent financial year.
- **Statement of profit or loss and other comprehensive income data** for the current interim period and cumulative data for the current year to date, together with comparative data for the corresponding interim period and cumulative figures for the previous financial year.
- **Statement of cash flow data** should be cumulative for the current year to date, with comparative cumulative data for the corresponding interim period in the previous financial year.
- **Data for the statement of changes in equity** should be for both the current interim period and for the year to date, together with comparative data for the corresponding interim period, and cumulative figures, for the previous financial year. (IAS 34, para 20)

1.5 Materiality

Materiality should be assessed in relation to the interim period financial data. It should be recognised that interim measurements **rely to a greater extent on estimates** than annual financial data.

(IAS 34, para 23)

1.6 Recognition and measurement principles

A large part of IAS 34 deals with recognition and measurement principles, and guidelines as to their practical application. The **guiding principle** is that an entity should use the **same recognition and measurement principles in its interim statements as it does in its annual financial statements**. (IAS 34, para 28)

This means, for example, that a cost that would not be regarded as an asset in the year-end statement of financial position should not be regarded as an asset in the statement of financial position for an interim period. Similarly, an accrual for an item of income or expense for a transaction that has not yet occurred (or a deferral of an item of income or expense for a transaction that has already occurred) is inappropriate for interim reporting, just as it is for year-end reporting.

Applying this principle of recognition and measurement may result, in a subsequent interim period or at the year-end, in a **remeasurement** of amounts that were reported in a financial statement for a previous interim period. **The nature and amount of any significant remeasurements should be disclosed**.

1.7 Example: Interim measurement

Williamswood prepares annual financial statements to 31 May each year and half-yearly interim financial statements to 30 November.

On 1 June 20X1, Williamswood acquired a property for $5 million. The property is held at historic cost. On 1 October 20X3, as a consequence of a proposed move to new premises, the property was classified as held for sale. At the time of classification as held for sale, the carrying amount of the property was $3.5 million after adjusting for impairment of $150,000, the fair value less costs to sell was $3.4 million.

At the date of the published interim financial statements, 30 November 20X3, the property market had improved and the fair value less costs to sell was reassessed at $3.52 million. At the year end on 31 May 20X4, the market had improved even further, so that the fair value less costs to sell was $3.95 million. The property was sold on 5 June 20X4 for $4 million.

Required

Discuss how the above items should be dealt with in the interim financial statements of Williamswood at 30 November 20X3 and the annual financial statements at 31 May 20X4

Solution

Interim financial statements at 30 November 20X3

In accordance with IAS 34 Interim Financial Reporting, an entity must apply the same accounting policies in its interim financial statements as in its annual financial statements. Measurements should be made on a 'year to date' basis. Williamswood's interim financial statements for the six months to 30 November 20X3 must apply the provisions of IFRS 5 Non-Current Assets Held for Sale and Discontinued Operations to the valuation of the property.

Application of IFRS 5

Immediately before classification of the asset as held for sale, the entity must recognise an impairment in accordance with IAS 36. The impairment loss is of $150,000 is recognised in profit or loss as the property is held at historical cost. The carrying amount of $3.5 million provided in the question is after recognising impairment losses and therefore does not require any further adjustment before being used in calculating the initial value of the held for sale asset.

In accordance with IFRS 5, an asset held for sale should be measured at the lower of its carrying amount ($3.5 million) and fair value less costs to sell ($3.4 million). An additional write-down of $100,000 is charged to profit or loss at the date of classification as held for sale. Depreciation ceases from this date.

Once the asset has been classified as held for sale, there may be an additional impairment loss or a subsequent increase based on the difference between the revised carrying amount and the fair value less cost to sell.

At the interim date, the information provided indicates a subsequent increase of $120,000 as the fair value less costs to sell ($3.52 million) exceed the revised carrying amount of the asset ($3.4 million). This increase may be recognised in profit or loss as it is less than the previous cumulative impairment losses relating to the asset of $250,000 ($150,000 + $100,000).

At the year end date, there is a further increase of $430,000 ($3.95 million fair value less costs to sell - $3.52 million revised carrying amount). This exceeds the total amount of the impairment loss and therefore cannot all be recognised. The increase is restricted to give a revised carrying amount of $3.65 million ($3.52 million carrying amount + $130,000 unused impairment loss reversal).

On 5 June 20X4, the property is sold for $4 million, at which point a gain of $350,000 is recognised. If material, this sale would be disclosed a non-adjusting event under IAS 10 Events After the Reporting Period.

1.7.1 Revenues received occasionally, seasonally or cyclically

Revenue that is received as an occasional item, or within a seasonal or cyclical pattern, should not be anticipated or deferred in interim financial statements, if it would be inappropriate to anticipate or defer the revenue for the annual financial statements. In other words, the principles of revenue recognition should be applied consistently to the interim reports and year-end reports.

(IAS 34, para 37)

1.7.2 Costs incurred unevenly during the financial year

These should only be anticipated or deferred (ie treated as accruals or prepayments) if it would be appropriate to anticipate or defer the expense in the annual financial statements. For example, it would be appropriate to anticipate a cost for property rental where the rental is paid in arrears, but it would be inappropriate to anticipate part of the cost of a major advertising campaign later in the year, for which no expenses have yet been incurred.

1.7.3 Payroll taxes or insurance contributions paid by employers

In some countries these are assessed on an annual basis, but paid at an uneven rate during the course of the year, with a large proportion of the taxes being paid in the early part of the year, and a much smaller proportion paid later on in the year. In this situation, it would be appropriate to use an estimated average annual tax rate for the year in an interim statement, not the actual tax paid. This treatment is appropriate because it reflects the fact that the taxes are assessed on an annual basis, even though the payment pattern is uneven.

1.7.4 Cost of a planned major periodic maintenance or overhaul

The cost of such an event later in the year must not be anticipated in an interim financial statement **unless** there is a legal or constructive obligation to carry out this work. The fact that a maintenance or overhaul is planned and is carried out annually is not of itself sufficient to justify anticipating the cost in an interim financial report.

1.7.5 Other planned but irregularly-occurring costs

Similarly, these costs such as charitable donations or employee training costs, should not be accrued in an interim report. These costs, even if they occur regularly and are planned, are nevertheless discretionary.

1.7.6 Year-end bonus

A year end bonus should not be provided for in an interim financial statement *unless* there is a constructive obligation to pay a year end bonus (eg a contractual obligation, or a regular past practice) and the size of the bonus can be reliably measured.

1.7.7 Holiday pay

The same principle applies here. If holiday pay is an enforceable obligation on the employer, then any unpaid accumulated holiday pay may be accrued in the interim financial report.

1.7.8 Non-monetary intangible assets

The entity might incur expenses during an interim period on items that might or will generate non-monetary intangible assets. IAS 38 *Intangible Assets* requires that costs to generate non-monetary intangible assets (eg development expenses) should be recognised as an expense when incurred **unless** the costs form part of an identifiable intangible asset. Costs that were initially recognised as an expense cannot subsequently be treated instead as part of the cost of an intangible asset. IAS 34 states that interim financial statements should adopt the same approach. This means that it would be inappropriate in an interim financial statement to 'defer' a cost in the expectation that it will eventually be part of a non-monetary intangible asset that has not yet been recognised: such costs should be treated as an expense in the interim statement.

1.7.9 Depreciation

Depreciation should only be charged in an interim statement on non-current assets that have been acquired, not on non-current assets that will be acquired later in the financial year.

1.7.10 Foreign currency translation gains and losses

These should be calculated by the same principles as at the financial year end, in accordance with IAS 21 *The Effects of Changes in Foreign Exchange Rates*.

1.7.11 Tax on income

An entity will include an expense for income tax (tax on profits) in its interim statements. The **tax rate** to use should be the estimated average annual tax rate for the year. For example, suppose that in a particular jurisdiction, the rate of tax on company profits is 30% on the first $200,000 of profit and 40% on profits above $200,000. Now suppose that a company makes a profit of $200,000 in its first half year, and expects to make $200,000 in the second half year. The rate of tax to be applied in the interim financial report should be 35%, not 30%, ie the expected average rate of tax for the year as a whole. This approach is appropriate because income tax on company profits is charged on an annual basis, and an effective annual rate should therefore be applied to each interim period.

As another illustration, suppose a company earns pre-tax income in the first quarter of the year of $30,000, but expects to make a loss of $10,000 in each of the next three quarters, so that net income before tax for the year is zero. Suppose also that the rate of tax is 30%. In this case, it would be inappropriate to anticipate the losses, and the tax charge should be $9,000 for the first quarter of the year (30% of $30,000) and a negative tax charge of $3,000 for each of the next three quarters if actual losses are the same as anticipated.

Where the tax year for a company does not coincide with its financial year, a separate estimated weighted average tax rate should be applied for each tax year, to the interim periods that fall within that tax year.

Some countries give entities tax credits against the tax payable, based on amounts of capital expenditure or research and development, etc. Under most tax regimes, these credits are calculated and granted on an annual basis; therefore it is appropriate to include anticipated tax credits within the calculation of the estimated average tax rate for the year, and apply this rate to calculate the tax on income for interim periods. However, if a tax benefit relates to a specific one-time event, it should be recognised within the tax expense for the interim period in which the event occurs.

1.7.12 Inventory valuations

Within interim reports, inventories should be valued in the same way as for year-end financial statements. It is recognised, however, that it will be necessary to rely more heavily on estimates for interim reporting than for year-end reporting.

In addition, it will normally be the case that the net realisable value of inventories should be estimated from selling prices and related costs to complete and dispose at interim dates.

1.8 Use of estimates

Although accounting information must be reliable and free from material error, it may be necessary to sacrifice some accuracy and reliability for the sake of timeliness and cost-benefits. This is particularly the case with interim financial reporting, where there will be much less time to produce reports than at the financial year end. The standard therefore recognises that estimates will have to be used to a greater extent in interim reporting, to assess values or even some costs, than in year-end reporting.

An appendix to IAS 34 gives some examples of the use of estimates.

(a) **Inventories**. An entity might not need to carry out a full inventory count at the end of each interim period. Instead, it may be sufficient to estimate inventory values using sales margins.

(b) **Provisions**. An entity might employ outside experts or consultants to advise on the appropriate amount of a provision as at the year end. It will probably be inappropriate to employ an expert to make a similar assessment at each interim date. Similarly, an entity might employ a professional valuer to revalue fixed assets at the year end, whereas at the interim date(s) the entity will not rely on such experts.

(c) **Income taxes**. The rate of income tax (tax on profits) will be calculated at the year end by applying the tax rate in each country/jurisdiction to the profits earned there. At the interim stage, it may be sufficient to estimate the rate of income tax by applying the same 'blended' estimated weighted average tax rate to the income earned in all countries/jurisdictions.

The principle of **materiality** applies to interim financial reporting, as it does to year-end reporting. As already noted the assessment of materiality in interim financial reports will rely more heavily on estimates than in year-end reports. Materiality should be assessed in relation to the interim financial statements themselves, and should be independent of 'annual materiality' considerations.

1.9 Section summary

- IAS 34 in concept makes **straightforward proposals** for the production of interim financial reports by entities.
- It is essential to apply **principles of recognition and measurement** that will prevent entities from 'massaging' the interim figures.
- The **detail** in the guidelines is therefore very important, and the application of the recognition and measurement principles to particular valuations and measurements needs to be understood.

2 IFRS 1 *First-time Adoption Of International Financial Reporting Standards*

FAST FORWARD

IFRS 1 sets out the precise way in which an entity should implement a change from local accounting standards to IFRS Accounting Standards.

The standard is intended to ensure that an entity's **first financial statements using IFRS Accounting Standards** contain **high quality information** that is transparent for users and comparable over all periods presented; provides a suitable starting point for accounting under IFRS Accounting Standards; and can be generated at a cost that does not exceed the benefits to users.

Key terms

Date of transition to IFRS Accounting Standards. The beginning of the earliest period for which an entity presents full comparative information under IFRS in its first IFRS financial statements.

Deemed cost. An amount used as a surrogate for cost or depreciated cost at a given date.

Fair value. The price that would be received to sell an asset or paid to transfer a liability in an orderly transaction between market participants at the measurement date.

First IFRS financial statements. The first annual financial statements in which an entity adopts IFRS by an explicit and unreserved statement of compliance with IFRS.

Opening IFRS statement of financial position. An entity's statement of financial position (published or unpublished) at the date of transition to IFRS.

Previous GAAP. The basis of accounting that a first time adopter used immediately before adopting IFRS.

Reporting date. The end of the latest period covered by financial statements or by an interim financial report.

(IFRS 1, Appendix A)

IFRS 1 **only applies** where an entity prepares IFRS financial statements **for the first time**. Changes in accounting policies made by an entity that already applies IFRS Accounting Standards should be dealt with by applying either IAS 8 *Accounting Policies, Changes in Accounting Estimates and Errors* or specific transitional requirements in other standards.

2.1 Making the transition to IFRS

An entity should:

(a) Select accounting policies that comply with IFRS Accounting Standards **at the reporting date** for the entity's first IFRS financial statements.

(b) Prepare an **opening IFRS statement of financial position** at the **date of transition to IFRS**. This is the starting point for subsequent accounting under IFRS Standards. The date of transition to IFRS Accounting Standards is the beginning of the earliest comparative period presented in an entity's first IFRS financial statements.

(c) **Disclose the effect** of the change in the financial statements.

2.2 Example: Reporting date and opening IFRS statement of financial position

An listed company has a 31 December year end and will be required to comply with IFRS Accounting Standards from 1 January 20X5.

Required

What is the date of transition to IFRS?

Solution

The company's first IFRS financial statements will be for the **year ended 31 December 20X5**.

IFRS 1 requires that at least one year's comparative figures are presented in the first IFRS financial statements. The comparative figures will be for the year ended 31 December 20X4.

Therefore the date of transition to IFRS is **1 January 20X4** and the company prepares an opening IFRS statement of financial position at this date.

2.3 Preparing the opening IFRS statement of financial position

IFRS 1 states that in its opening IFRS statement of financial position an entity shall:

(a) **Recognise all assets and liabilities** whose recognition is required by IFRS Accounting Standards

(b) Not recognise items as assets or liabilities if IFRS Accounting Standards do not permit such recognition

(c) **Reclassify items** that it recognised under previous GAAP as one type of asset, liability or component of equity, but are a different type of asset liability or component of equity under IFRS Accounting Standards

(d) **Apply IFRS Accounting Standards in measuring** all recognised assets and liabilities

This involves restating the statement of financial position prepared at the same date under the entity's previous GAAP so that it complies with IFRS Accounting Standards in force **at the first reporting date**. In our example above, the company prepares its opening IFRS statement of financial position at **1 January 20X4**, following accounting policies that comply with IFRS Accounting Standards in force at **31 December 20X5**.

The accounting policies that an entity uses in its opening IFRS statement of financial position may differ from those it used for the same date using its previous GAAP. The resulting adjustments are recognised directly **in retained earnings** (in equity) **at the date of transition**. (This is because the adjustments arise from events and transactions before the date of transition to IFRS.)

An entity's **estimates** under IFRS Accounting Standards at the date of transition must be **consistent** with those made at the same date under previous GAAP, (after adjustments to reflect any difference in accounting policies), unless there is **objective evidence** that those estimates were **in error**.

2.4 Exemptions from other IFRS Accounting Standards

IFRS 1 contains a number of exemptions. Some of these exemptions relate to retrospective application of other IFRS Accounting Standards, and some relate to recognition and measurement of items when preparing the first financial statements under IFRS Accounting Standards and the opening IFRS statement of financial position. The purpose is to ensure that the cost of producing IFRS financial statements does not exceed the benefits to users. Some of the exemptions are detailed below.

2.4.1 Business combinations

IFRS 3 *Business Combinations* need not be applied retrospectively to business combinations that occurred before the date of the opening IFRS statement of financial position. This has the following consequences:

(a) Combinations keep the **same classification** (eg acquisition, uniting of interests) as in the previous GAAP financial statements.

(b) **All acquired assets and liabilities are recognised** other than:

- Some financial assets and financial liabilities derecognised under the previous GAAP (derivatives and special purpose entities must be recognised);
- Assets (including goodwill) and liabilities that were not recognised under previous GAAP and would not qualify for recognition under IFRS.

Any resulting change is recognised by **adjusting retained earnings** (ie equity) unless the change results from the recognition of an intangible asset that was previously subsumed within goodwill.

(c) **Items which do not qualify for recognition** as an asset or liability under IFRS must be excluded from the opening IFRS statement of financial position. For example, intangible assets that do not qualify for separate recognition under IAS 38 must be reclassified as part of goodwill.

(d) The carrying amount of **goodwill** in the opening IFRS statement of financial position is the same as its carrying amount **under previous GAAP**. However, goodwill must be tested for impairment at the transition date.

2.4.2 Property, plant and equipment

An entity may measure an item of property, plant and equipment at its **fair value at the transition** date and then use the fair value as its **deemed** cost at that date.

An entity may use a **previous GAAP revaluation**, or a valuation for the purpose of a privatisation or initial public offering, as the deemed cost at the transition date, so long as the revaluation was **broadly comparable** to fair value or depreciated replacement cost at the date of the valuation.

These exemptions are also available for:

(a) Investment properties measured under the cost model in IAS 40 *Investment Property*
(b) Intangible assets that meet the recognition criteria and the criteria for revaluation in IAS 38

2.4.3 Cumulative translation differences

IAS 21 requires some exchange differences is to be classified as a separate component of equity, for example, differences arising when a the financial statements of a foreign operation are translated. The cumulative translation differences must be included in the gain or loss on disposal of the foreign operation. Under the exemption, the **cumulative translation differences for all foreign operations are deemed to be zero at the transition date**. The gain or loss on a subsequent disposal of a foreign operation will exclude translation differences that arose before the transition date. Later translation differences will be included.

2.4.4 Compound financial instruments

IAS 32 *Financial Instruments: Presentation* requires compound financial instruments to be split at inception into separate liability and equity components. If the liability component is no longer outstanding at the date of the translation to IFRS, the split is not required.

2.4.5 Designation of previously recognised financial instruments

When financial assets are first recognised, they may be designated as financial assets measured at fair value in accordance with IFRS 9 *Financial Instruments*. Financial liabilities may be designated as fair value through profit or loss in accordance with IFRS 9.

Note. An entity may make such a designation at the date of transition to IFRS.

2.4.6 Share-based payment transactions

An entity is encouraged, but not required, to apply IFRS 2 *Share-based Payment* to:

(a) Equity instruments that were granted and vested before the date of transition to IFRS or 1 January 2005 (whichever is the later)

(b) Liabilities arising from share-based payment transactions that were settled before the date of transition to IFRS

Question — IFRS 1

Russell Co will adopt International Financial Reporting Standards (IFRS) for the first time in its financial statements for the year ended 31 December 20X4.

In its previous financial statements for 31 December 20X2 and 20X3, which were prepared under local GAAP, the company made a number of routine accounting estimates, including accrued expenses. It also recognised a general provision for liabilities, calculated at a fixed percentage of its retained profits for the year. This is required under its local GAAP.

Subsequently, some of the accruals were found to be overestimates and some were found to be underestimates.

Required

Discuss how the matters above should be dealt with in the IFRS financial statements of Russell Co for the year ended 31 December 20X4.

Answer

Provided that the routine accounting estimates have been made in a manner consistent with IFRS no adjustments are made in the first IFRS financial statements. The only exception to this is if the company has subsequently discovered that these estimates were in error. Although there were some overestimates and some underestimates, this is probably not the case here.

The general provision is a different matter. This provision would definitely not have met the criteria for recognition under IAS 37 *Provisions, Contingent Liabilities and Contingent Assets* and therefore it will not be recognised in the opening IFRS statement of financial position (1 January 20X3) or at subsequent year ends.

2.5 Presentation and disclosure

An entity's first IFRS financial statements must include **at least**:

(a) Three statements of financial position;
(b) Two statements of profit or loss and other comprehensive income;
(c) Two separate statements of profit or loss (if presented);
(d) Two statements of cash flows; and
(e) Two statements of changes in equity and related notes.

An entity must also **explain the effect** of the transition from previous GAAP to IFRS Accounting Standards on its financial position, financial performance and cash flows by providing **reconciliations**:

(a) Of **equity** reported under previous GAAP to equity under IFRS Accounting Standards at the **date of transition** and at the **end of the last period presented in accordance with previous GAAP**.

(b) Of **total comprehensive income** reported under previous GAAP to total comprehensive income reported under IFRS Accounting Standards for the latest period in the entity's most recent financial statements.

The reconciliations must give sufficient detail to enable users to understand the material adjustments to the statement of financial position and statement of profit or loss and other comprehensive income.

If an entity presented a statement of cash flows under its previous GAAP, it should also explain the material **adjustments to the statement of cash flows**.

If an entity recognised or reversed any **impairment losses** for the first time in preparing its opening IFRS statement of financial position, it must provide the disclosures that IAS 36 *Impairment of Assets* would have required if the entity had recognised those impairment losses or reversals in the period beginning with the date of transition to IFRS Accounting Standards.

If an entity corrects **errors made under previous GAAP**, the reconciliations must distinguish the correction of errors from changes in accounting policies.

Where **fair value has been used as deemed cost** for a non-current asset in the opening IFRS statement of financial position, the financial statements must disclose the aggregate of fair values and the aggregate adjustments to the carrying amounts reported under previous GAAP for each line in the opening IFRS statement of financial position.

2.5.1 Change in accounting policy

IAS 8 does not apply to the changes in accounting policies that occur when an entity first adopts IFRS or to changes in those policies until after the first IFRS financial statements are presented.

Therefore IAS 8's disclosure requirements do not apply to the first IFRS financial statements.

If, after the issue of its first IFRS interim report but before the issue of its first IFRS financial statements, an entity changes its accounting policies or use of IFRS 1 exemptions, it must update its reconciliations between IFRS and the previous GAAP accordingly.

2.6 Interim financial reports

IFRS 1 applies to any interim financial report that an entity presents under IAS 34 *Interim Financial Reporting* for part of the period covered by the first IFRS financial statements.

Where interim financial reports are presented, an entity should provide the same reconciliations required for full financial statements and described above. Material adjustments to the statement of cash flows, if any, should also be disclosed.

2.7 Managing the change to IFRS Accounting Standards

The implementation of the above technical aspects is likely to entail careful management in most companies. Here are some of the **change management considerations** that should be addressed:

(a) **Accurate assessment of the task involved.** Underestimation or wishful thinking may hamper the effectiveness of the conversion and may ultimately prove inefficient.

(b) **Proper planning.** This should take place at the overall project level, but a **detailed** task **analysis** could be drawn up to **control work performed**.

(c) **Human resource management.** The project must be properly structured and staffed.

(d) **Training.** Where there are **skills gaps**, remedial training should be provided.

(e) **Monitoring and accountability**. A relaxed 'it will be alright on the night' attitude could spell danger. Implementation **progress** should be **monitored** and **regular meetings** set up so that participants can **personally account for what they are doing** as well as **flag up any problems** as early as possible. **Project drift should be avoided**.

(f) **Achieving milestones**. Successful completion of key steps and tasks should be appropriately acknowledged, ie what managers call 'celebrating success', so as to **sustain motivation and performance**.

(g) **Physical resourcing**. The need for IT **equipment** and **office space** should be properly assessed.

(h) **Process review**. Care should be taken not to perceive the change as a one-off quick fix. Any charge in **future systems** and processes should be assessed and properly implemented.

(i) **Follow-up procedures**. As with general good management practice, the **follow up procedures** should be planned in to **make sure that the changes stick** and that any further changes are identified and addressed.

2.8 Section summary

You need to be able to advise an entity making the change from previous GAAP to IFRS on:

- The **general rules** (including the date of the **opening IFRS statement of financial position**)
- The **exemptions** available
- How to deal with **estimates** in previous financial statements
- **Explaining the effects** of the change on the financial statements (preparing reconciliations)
- The **practical aspects** of managing the change

3 IFRS 13 *Fair Value Measurement*

FAST FORWARD

IFRS 13 *Fair Value Measurement* establishes a single source of guidance for fair value measurement under IFRS Accounting Standards.

Exam focus point

Fair value is an important issue. As well as explaining and applying the requirements of IFRS 13, you could be asked to explain the advantages and disadvantages of measuring assets and liabilities at fair value.

IFRS 13 *Fair Value Measurement* is applicable to most areas of accounting. Fair value is one of the current value measurement bases as defined in the *Conceptual Framework*. The standard defines fair value, provides guidance on its determination and introduces consistent requirements for disclosures on fair value measurements. The standard does not include requirements on when fair value measurement is required, but instead prescribes how fair value is to be measured if another standard requires it.

3.1 Scope

IFRS 13 will apply where another IFRS Accounting Standard requires or allows fair value measurements or related disclosures, with the following exceptions:

- Share-based payments (Chapter 20)
- Leasing transactions (Chapter 15)
- Other standards where measurement is similar to fair value but not fair value eg net realisable value in IAS 2 *Inventories* and value in use in IAS 36 *Impairment of Assets*.

IFRS 13 also gives relief from its disclosure requirements in respect of:

- Plan assets measured at fair value in accordance with IAS 19 *Employee Benefits*.
- Assets for which the recoverable amount is fair value less costs of disposal in accordance with IAS 36.

- Retirement benefit plan investments measured at fair value under IAS 26 *Accounting and Reporting by Retirement Benefit Plans*. This standard is outside the scope of Paper 13.

3.2 Definitions

Key terms

> Fair value is defined by IFRS 13 as **'the price that would be received to sell an asset or paid to transfer a liability in an orderly transaction between market participants at the measurement date.'**

Other important definitions are given below:

Key terms

> **Transaction costs** The costs to sell an asset or transfer a liability in the principal (or most advantageous) market for the asset or liability that are directly attributable to the disposal of an asset or transfer of a liability and that:
>
> (i) Result directly from and are essential to that transaction
> (ii) Would not have been incurred had the decision to sell the asset or transfer the liability not been made.
>
> **Market participants** are buyers and sellers in the principal (or most advantageous) market for the asset or liability.
>
> **Principal market** is the market with the greatest volume and level of activity for the asset or liability.
>
> **Most advantageous market** is the market that maximises the amount that would be received to sell the asset or minimises the amount that would be paid to transfer the liability after taking into account transport and transaction costs.
>
> **Active market** is a market in which transactions for the asset or liability take place with sufficient frequency and volume to provide pricing information on an ongoing basis.
>
> **Entry price** The price paid to acquire an asset or received to assume a liability in an exchange transaction.
>
> **Exit price** The price that would be received to sell an asset or paid to transfer a liability.
>
> **Inputs** The assumptions that market participants would use when pricing as asset or liability.

3.3 General considerations in measuring fair value

IFRS 13 stipulates the following factors that should be considered in fair value measurement:

(a) The asset or liability
(b) The market
(c) Market participants
(d) The price

3.3.1 The asset or liability

A fair value measurement relates to a particular asset or liability and should therefore take into account the specific characteristics of the asset or liability, if market participants consider these when pricing the item.

Such characteristics may include the condition and location of the item and any restrictions on sale or use at the measurement date.

IFRS 13 may be applied to an individual asset or liability or a group of related assets and liabilities eg a business.

3.3.2 Example: Characteristics of the asset or liability

A donor contributes land in a residential area to a not-for-profit neighbourhood association. The land is currently used as a playground and the donor specifies that as long as the association owns the land, it must continue to be used as a playground. There is, however, no restriction on the further sale of the land. The land is sought after by a number of residential property developers.

In this case, the donor restriction on use of the land is specific to the association, and the restriction would not be transferred to market participants. Therefore the fair value of the land is the higher of its fair value used as a playground and its fair value as a site for residential development, regardless of the restriction of use of the land by the association.

3.3.3 The market

Under IFRS 13, fair value is determined based on a transaction in the principal market. The **principal market** is the market with the greatest volume and level of activity for the asset or liability.

If there is no principal market, the **most advantageous market** is used. This is the market in which the entity could achieve the most beneficial price.

The principal market (or most advantageous market if there is no principal market) is assumed to be the market in which the entity normally transacts unless there is evidence to the contrary.

IFRS 13 prohibits the adjustment of fair value for transaction costs, but it does require that these are considered in the determination of the most advantageous market. IFRS 13 does, however allow fair value to be adjusted for transport costs, where location is a characteristic of the asset.

3.3.4 Example: Most advantageous market

An asset is sold in two different markets as follows:

	Market A	Market B
	$	$
Price	27	25
Transport costs	(3)	(2)
	24	23
Transaction costs	(3)	(1)
	21	22

There is no principal market for the asset. What is its fair value?

Solution

As a principal market for the asset does not exist, its fair value is measured using the price in the most advantageous market.

Transaction costs are considered in the determination of the most advantageous markets, but are not taken into consideration in determining fair value.

The most advantageous market is Market B where the net price achieved is $22.

The transaction price of the asset (before transaction costs) in this market is $23, and therefore this is fair value.

3.3.5 Market participants

IFRS 13 emphasises that a fair value measurement is based on the assumptions of market participants who are:

- Independent (not a related party)
- Knowledgeable (have a reasonable understanding of the asset or liability and the transaction)
- Able to transact in the asset or liability
- Willing to transact in the asset or liability (motivated but not forced to transact).

Market participants seek to maximise the fair value of an asset or minimise the fair value of a liability in a transaction to sell the asset or transfer the liability.

IFRS 13 does not require that specific market participants are identified, but instead that a profile of potential market participants is developed.

3.3.6 The price

Under IFRS 13, fair value is based on **exit price** (the price that would be received to sell an asset or paid to transfer a liability) rather than transaction price or entry price (the price that was paid to acquire an asset or received to assume a liability). The exit price concept is based on current expectations about the sale or transfer price from the perspective of market participants.

3.4 Specific considerations in measuring fair value

As well as the general considerations listed above, IFRS 13 stipulates specific factors that should be considered when measuring:

(a) Non-financial assets
(b) Liabilities and equity
(c) Financial instruments

3.4.1 Non-financial assets

The fair value of a non-financial asset is measured based on its **highest and best use** from a market participant's perspective, taking into account whether a particular use is:

- Physically possible (eg it may not be physically possible to use marshland for residential development)
- Legally permissible (eg it is not legally permissible to build on green belt land)
- Financially feasible (eg the costs of using a property in a particular way may not produce the investment return required by market participants).

The **highest and best use** of an asset is assumed to be an entity's current use of a non-financial asset, unless market or other factors suggest otherwise. Some entities will not use an asset at its highest and best use, for example if they are holding an asset defensively in order to restrict availability to others. In this case, measurement is still based on the highest and best use and disclosure is made of the fact that the asset is not used in that way.

3.4.2 Example: Highest and best use

An entity acquires control of another entity which owns land. The land is currently used as a factory site. The local government zoning rules also now permit construction of residential properties in this area, subject to planning permission being granted. Apartment buildings have recently been constructed in the area with the support of the local government.

Market values are as follows:

	$
Value in its current use	20
Value as a potential development site (including uncertainty over whether planning permission would be granted)	30
Demolition costs to convert the land to a vacant site	2

The fair value of the land is $28 million ($30m – $2m) as this is its highest and best use because market participants would take into account the site's development potential when pricing the land

3.4.3 Liabilities and equity

IFRS 13 makes several points relevant in the fair value measurement of liabilities and equity:

Fair value measurement assumes a liability or an entity's own equity instrument is transferred to a market participant at the measurement date, In particular it is assumed that:

(a) A liability remains outstanding and the market participant would be required to fulfil the obligation

(b) An entity's own equity instrument would remain outstanding and the market participant would take on the rights and responsibilities associated with the instrument.

(i) Where liabilities and equity instruments are held by other parties as assets, and a quoted price is unavailable for the transfer of such an instrument, the fair value of the liability/equity to the issuer is measured from the perspective of the market participant that holds the asset.

(ii) Where liabilities and equity instruments are **not** held by other parties as assets, and a quoted price is unavailable for the transfer of such an instrument, the fair value of the liability/equity is measured using a valuation technique from the perspective of the market participant that owes the liability or has a claim on the equity.

(iii) The fair value of a liability should reflect the effect of non-performance risk (the risk that an entity will not fulfil an obligation).

3.4.4 Example: Fair value of a liability

Fair value of a liability

Energy Co assumed a contractual decommissioning liability when it acquired a power plant from a competitor.

The plant will be decommissioned in ten years' time.

Assumptions made by Energy Co equivalent to those that would be used by market participants, assuming Energy Co was allowed to transfer the liability, are:

Estimated labour, material and overhead cost	Estimated probability
$6m	40%
$8m	50%
$10m	10%

Third party contractors typically add a 20% mark-up in the industry and expect a premium of 5% of the expected cash flows (after including the effect of inflation) to take into account risk that cash flows may be more than expected.

Inflation is expected to be 3% annually on average over the ten years.

The risk-free interest rate for a ten year maturity is 4%.

An appropriate adjustment to the risk-free rate for Energy Co's non-performance risk is 2% (giving an entity-specific discount rate of 4% + 2% = 6%).

	$m
Expected cash flow $[(6 \times 40\%) + (8 \times 50\%) + (10 \times 10\%)]$	7.400
Third party contractor mark-up $(7.4 \times 20\%)$	1.480
	8.880
Inflation adjustment $((8.88 \times 1.03^{10}) - 8.88)$	3.054
	11.934
Risk premium $(11.934 \times 5\%)$	0.597
	12.531
Fair value (present value of expected cash flow adjusted for market risk $12.531 \times 1/1.06^{10}$)	6.997

3.4.5 Financial instruments

In markets for securities, financial instruments and commodities, dealers generally buy at the bid price and sell at the ask price. Where this is relevant, the price within the bid-ask spread that is most representative of fair value in the circumstances is used to measure fair value.

IFRS 13 does not, however disallow the use of other pricing conventions that are used by market participants, such as mid-market pricing. Once management has established which convention it is using, this must be applied consistently.

3.5 Valuation techniques

Unless transactions are directly observable in a market (in which case the determination of fair value can be relatively straightforward), a valuation technique is used. IFRS 13 identifies 3 valuation techniques that may be used to determine fair value:

(a) The **market approach**, in which an entity uses prices and other relevant information generated by market transactions involving identical or comparable assets, liabilities or groups of assets and liabilities.

(b) The **income approach**, in which an entity converts future amounts (eg cash flows, income and expenses) to a single discounted (ie current) amount.

(c) The **cost approach** in which an entity determines a value which reflects the amount that would be required currently to replace the service capacity of an asset (often referred to as current replacement cost).

A valuation technique should be selected which maximises the use of relevant observable inputs, such as closing prices on a stock exchange, and minimises the use of unobservable inputs. Once selected the technique should be applied consistently unless alternative techniques provide a more representative measure of fair value. Any changes are regarded as changes in accounting estimate, although the IAS 8 disclosures are not required.

3.6 Fair value at initial recognition

When an asset is acquired or a liability assumed in an exchange transaction, the transaction price is the price paid to acquire the asset or received to assume the liability. This is the **entry price**. Fair value is, however, determined by reference to the **exit price**. This may be the same as the transaction price/entry price in some instances (eg when the transaction to buy an asset takes place in the market in which it would be sold). It may not be the same, if the entry price transaction:

(a) Is between related parties
(b) Takes place under duress eg if the seller is in financial difficulty
(c) Takes place in a market other than the principal (or most advantageous market)

3.7 Fair value hierarchy

A fair value measurement is ranked according to the IFRS 13 fair value hierarchy in order to increase consistency and comparability of fair value measurements. This ranking is **based on the type of inputs** rather than the valuation technique used. A fair value measurement is classified as the same level of the fair value hierarchy as the lowest level input that is significant to the measurement.

The levels are:

Level 1 inputs	Quoted prices (unadjusted) in active markets for identical assets or liabilities that the entity can access at the measurement date (IFRS 13: para. 76).	For example, share prices quoted on a stock exchange
Level 2 inputs	Inputs other than quoted prices included within Level 1 that are observable for the asset or liability, either directly (ie prices) or indirectly (ie derived from prices). For example quoted prices for similar assets in active markets or for identical or similar assets in non-active markets or use of quoted interest rates for valuation purposes (IFRS 13: para. 81–82).	For example, share prices recently determined in a market that is not active

Level 3 inputs	Unobservable inputs for the asset or liability, eg discounting estimates of future cash flows (IFRS 13: para. 86). Level 3 inputs are only used where relevant observable inputs are not available or where the entity determines that transaction price or quoted price does not represent fair value.	For example, discounted cash flows.

3.8 Disclosure

Extensive disclosures are required in order to help users of the financial statements assess:

- For both recurring and non-recurring fair value measurements, valuation techniques and inputs used to measure fair values.
- For recurring fair value measurements which use significant level 3 (unobservable) inputs, the effect of the measurements on profit or loss and other comprehensive income for the period.

Recurring fair value measurements are those which require regular updating eg those in relation to investment properties; non-recurring fair value measurements are those which are required only in particular circumstances eg when an asset becomes held for sale and is measured at fair value less costs to sell.

The minimum disclosures for each class of asset and liability measured at fair value after initial recognition are as follows:

(a) The fair value measurement at the end of the reporting period (for both recurring and non-recurring fair value measurements).

(b) For non-recurring fair value measurements, the reasons for measurement.

(c) For recurring and non-recurring fair value measurements, the level in which they are categorised in the fair value hierarchy.

(d) For assets and liabilities that are measured at fair value on a recurring basis, details of any transfers between level 1 and level 2.

(e) For recurring and non-recurring level 2 and 3 fair value measurements, a description of the valuation technique and inputs used.

(f) Changes in valuation technique and reasons for the change.

(g) Quantitative information about significant unobservable inputs used in level 3 fair values unless those inputs are not developed by the reporting entity when measuring fair value.

3.9 Fair value: advantages and problems

IFRS 9 requires that some types of financial instrument are measured at fair value. Other IFRS Accounting Standards allow the use of fair value (for example, for non-current assets). Fair value is believed to provide more relevant information than historical cost because:

(a) For some types of financial asset, historical cost can be zero, which does not reflect the underlying reality.

(b) Fair values should have more predictive value.

(c) Some assets are traded on an active market or held for their investment potential (rather than being held to be used in the business).

(d) Fair value often reflects the way risks are managed (for financial instruments).

(e) For assets such as property fair value provides information on the resources actually available to an entity.

However, **fair value is not without problems**:

(a) Some of the changes in fair value will never be realised, which makes the figure reported in the statement of profit or loss and other comprehensive income misleading (particularly if changes in value are recognised in profit or loss).

(b) Fair value may not be reliable, and in a non-active market it may be irrelevant.

(c) Fair valuing investment properties and financial assets can result in volatile profits (as gains and losses impact profit or loss).

(d) Fair value is irrelevant where management does not intend to sell an asset.

In an economic downturn, fair value measurement means that many companies suffer significant losses and many assets lose their value. Financial instruments, property, intangibles (such as goodwill and development costs) and defined benefit pension plans can all be affected, as has been seen recently, particularly in the case of a number of financial institutions.

11: INTERIM REPORTING, FIRST-TIME ADOPTION AND FAIR VALUES

Chapter roundup

- IAS 34 complements stock exchange rules on interim financial reporting in many countries, but it may provide a blueprint for developing markets.
- IFRS 1 sets out the precise way in which an entity should implement a change from local accounting standards to IFRS Accounting Standards.
- IFRS 13 *Fair Value Measurement* establishes a single source of guidance for fair value measurement under IFRS Accounting Standards.

Quick quiz

1. Under IAS 34 depreciation should only be charged on non-current assets ……………………… …………………… (complete the blanks).

2. IFRS 1 permits a previous GAAP revaluation to be used as deemed cost at the date of transition.

    True ☐
    False ☐

3. How is fair value defined in IFRS 13?

4. What valuation techniques are suggested by IFRS 13 to establish fair value?

5. What type of inputs are classified as Level 1 in the IFRS 13 fair value hierarchy?

Answers to quick quiz

1 That have been acquired.

2 True. This is a specific 'exception'.

3 Fair value is the price that would be received to sell an asset or paid to transfer a liability in an orderly transaction between market participants at the measurement date.

4 The market approach, the income approach and the cost approach.

5 Unadjusted, quoted prices in active markets for identical assets or liabilities that the entity can access at the measurement date.

End of chapter question

Tollirene (AIA May 2004) (amended)

Tollirene is a publicly quoted limited liability company operating in a country which is to adopt international accounting standards as from 1 January 20X5. Tollirene currently uses a variety of domestic accounting standards and tax rules to prepare its financial statements and is therefore subject to the requirements of IFRS 1 *First-time Adoption of International Financial Reporting Standards*.

Tollirene has six subsidiaries. Three of the subsidiaries are also holding companies – but none are listed. All the subsidiaries have a financial year end of 31 December. The companies comprising the group have prepared their financial statements for the year ended 31 December 20X3 and Tollirene is currently finalising the consolidated financial statements for the year ended 31 December 20X3.

The chief executive officer of Tollirene would like to know how the move to IFRS Accounting Standards will affect the group and has asked for your help.

Required

Report to the chief executive officer of Tollirene explaining:

- The impact of IFRS 1 on the group of companies, and
- The impact (if any) on the preparation of the financial statements for the years ended 31 December 20X3, 20X4 and 20X5.

(25 marks)

Tangible non-current assets and inventory

Topic list	Syllabus reference
1 The definition of an asset	LO2
2 Revision of IASs 16, 20 and 23	LO2
3 IAS 36 *Impairment of Assets*	LO2
4 Impairment: Cash-generating units	LO2
5 IAS 40 *Investment Property*	LO2
6 IAS 2 *Inventories*	LO2

Introduction

We look again here at the **IASB definition of an asset**, as given in the *Conceptual Framework*, and consider how it can be applied to tangible non-current assets.

You have covered several of the relevant standards relating to non-current assets in your earlier studies. These are straightforward and are revised briefly in Section 2, with some questions for you to try. If you have any problems, **go back to your earlier study material**.

IAS 36 covers the **impairment of assets**. This is a topical area, is concerned with ensuring that non-current assets are not overvalued in the financial statements.

Investment properties are discussed in detail in Section 5.

The topic of **inventories** is revised in Section 6.

1 The definition of an asset

> **FAST FORWARD**
>
> You must learn the IASB *Conceptual Framework* **definition of an asset**: a present economic resource controlled by the entity as a result of past events. An economic resource is a right that has the potential to produce economic benefits. (Conceptual Framework, para 4.3-4.4)
>
> This definition was changed when the *Conceptual Framework* was revised in 2018. It still ties in closely with the definitions produced by **other standard-setters**, particularly FASB (USA) and FRC (UK).

Assets have been defined in many different ways and for many purposes. The definition of an asset is important because it directly affects the **treatment** of such items. A good definition will prevent abuse or error in the accounting treatment: otherwise some assets might be treated as expenses, and some expenses might be treated as assets.

1.1 IASB definition

> **FAST FORWARD**
>
> The definition has three important characteristics:
> - **Right**
> - **Potential to produce economic benefits**
> - **Control**

Remember the definition of an asset in the IASB's *Conceptual Framework*.

Key term

> **Asset**: A present economic resource controlled by the entity as a result of past events. An economic resource is a right that has the potential to produce economic benefits. (Conceptual Framework, para 4.3-4.4)

1.1.1 Rights

Rights can take several forms

Rights that correspond to an obligation of another party, such as the right to receive cash or other benefits (hence for example, trade receivables and prepayments) or to exchange resources on favourable terms (financial assets).

Rights that do not correspond to an obligation of another party, such as rights over physical assets such as property, plant and equipment and inventory and rights to use intellectual property (intangible assets). (Conceptual Framework, para. 4.6)

Rights can arise from legislation (for example holding the legal title to a property) or be contractual (for example, obtaining a right of use asset through a lease arrangement) but may also arise by acquiring or creating know-how that is not in the public domain (capitalising development costs) or by creating a constructive obligation on a third party.

In this chapter we are concerned with rights over physical assets.

1.1.2 Potential to produce economic benefits

This is the part of the definition of an asset that has changed most in the 2018 version of the Conceptual Framework. It does not need to be certain, or even likely, that the right will produce economic benefits. It just needs to be possible that the rights exists and could generate economic benefits for the entity in at least one circumstance. (Conceptual Framework, para. 4.14)

1.2 Definition of a non-current asset

Non-current assets may be defined as follows:

> A **non-current asset** is one intended for use on a continuing basis in the company's activities, ie it is not intended for resale or consumption in its normal operating cycle.

Essentially, an asset is classified as non-current when it does not meet the criteria to be classified as current. IAS 1 paragraph 66 specifies the following criteria for making the distinction between current and non-current assets.

An entity shall classify an asset as current when:

(a) It expects to realise the asset, or intends to sell or consume it, in its normal operating cycle;

(b) It holds the asset primarily for the purpose of trading;

(c) It expects to realise the asset within 12 months after the reporting period; or

(d) The asset is cash or a cash equivalent (as defined in IAS 7) unless the asset is restricted from being exchanged or used to settle a liability for at least 12 months after the reporting period.

An entity shall classify all other assets as non-current.

2 Revision of IASs 16, 20 and 23

FAST FORWARD

> You should already be familiar with many standards relating to **non-current assets** from Papers 1 and 11. If not, go back to your earlier study material.
> - IAS 16 *Property, Plant and Equipment*
> - IAS 20 *Accounting for Government Grants and Disclosure of Government Assistance*
> - IAS 23 *Borrowing Costs*

You have studied these standards for earlier papers, but they are fairly straightforward. Read the summary of knowledge brought forward and try the relevant questions. If you have any difficulty, go back to your earlier study material and re-read it.

2.1 IAS 16 *Property, Plant and Equipment*

Knowledge brought forward from earlier studies

IAS 16 *Property, Plant and Equipment*

Definitions

- **Property, plant and equipment** are tangible items with the following properties:
    - Held by an entity for use in the production or supply of goods or services, for rental to others, or for administrative purposes; and
    - Expected to be used during more than one period
- **Cost** is the amount of cash or cash equivalents paid or the fair value of the other consideration given to acquire an asset at the time of its acquisition or construction.
- **Residual value** is the estimated amount that an entity would currently obtain from disposal of the asset, after deducting the estimated costs of disposal, if the asset were already of the age and in the condition expected at the end of its useful life.
- **Fair value** is the price that would be received to sell an asset or paid to transfer a liability in an orderly transaction between market participants at the measurement date.

- **Carrying amount** is the amount at which an asset is recognised after deducting any accumulated depreciation and accumulated impairment losses.

Recognition

As with all assets, **recognition** depends on two criteria:

- It is probable that future economic benefits associated with the item will flow to the entity
- The cost of the item can be measured reliably

These recognition criteria apply to **subsequent expenditure** as well as costs incurred initially (ie, there are no longer separate criteria for recognising subsequent expenditure).

Initial measurement

Once recognised as an asset, items should **initially be measured at cost,** including:

- **Purchase price**, plus import duties less trade discount/rebate
- **Directly attributable costs** of bringing the asset to working condition for intended use
- **Initial estimate** of the **costs of dismantling and removing the item** and **restoring the site** on which it is located.

IAS 16 also provides additional guidance on **directly attributable costs** included in the cost of an item of property, plant and equipment.

(a) These costs bring the asset to the location and condition necessary for it to be capable of operating in the manner intended by management, including those costs to test whether the asset is functioning properly.

(b) These are determined after deducting the net proceeds from selling any items produced when bringing the asset to its location and condition.

The standard also states that **income and related expenses** of operations that are incidental to the construction or development of an item of property, plant and equipment should be recognised in profit or loss.

IAS 16 specifies that **exchanges of items of property, plant and equipment**, regardless of whether the assets are similar, are measured at **fair value**, unless the exchange transaction lacks commercial substance or the fair value of neither of the assets exchanged can be measured reliably. If the acquired item is not measured at fair value, its cost is measured at the carrying amount of the asset given up.

Expenditure incurred in replacing or renewing a component of an item of property, plant and equipment shall be **recognised in the carrying amount of the item**. The carrying amount of the replaced or renewed component asset shall be derecognised. A similar approach is also applied when a separate component of an item of property, plant and equipment is identified in respect of a major inspection to enable the continued use of the item.

Measurement subsequent to initial recognition.

IAS 16 allows a choice between measurement models:

- **Cost model**: carry asset at cost less accumulated depreciation and any accumulated impairment losses
- **Revaluation model**: carry asset at revalued amount, ie fair value less subsequent accumulated depreciation and any subsequent accumulated impairment losses. (IAS 16 makes clear that the revaluation model is available only if the fair value of the item can be measured reliably).

Where the revaluation model is adopted certain rules apply:

1. When an item of property, plant and equipment is revalued, the whole class of assets to which it belongs should be revalued.
2. Revaluations must be kept up to date; the frequency of valuation depends on the volatility of fair values of individual assets. Where the current fair value is significantly different from carrying value then a revaluation should be carried out.
3. All items within a class should be revalued at the same time to prevent selective revaluation and to avoid disclosing a mixture of costs and values from different dates in the financial statements. A rolling basis of revaluation is allowed if the revaluations are kept up to date and the revaluation of a class of assets is completed in a short period of time.

Fair value is measured in accordance with IFRS 13 (see Chapter 11)

A revaluation is accounted for as follows:

- An increase in value is recognised in other comprehensive income and carried in a revaluation surplus
- A decrease is an expense in profit or loss after cancelling a previous revaluation surplus
- Additional disclosure required

Depreciation

- Depreciation is based on the carrying amount in the statement of financial position. It must be determined separately for each significant part of an item.
- Where an asset has been revalued the excess of the depreciation charge over historical cost depreciation can be transferred to realised earnings in the statement of changes in equity.
- The residual value and useful life of an asset, as well as the depreciation method, must be reviewed at least at each financial year end. Changes are changes in accounting estimates and are accounted for prospectively as adjustments to future depreciation.
- Depreciation of an asset ceases when the asset is derecognised or reclassified as held for sale (IFRS 5).

  Depreciation does not cease when the asset becomes idle or is retired from active use unless the asset is fully depreciated. However, under usage methods of depreciation the depreciation charge can be zero while there is no production.

Derecognition

An asset is derecognised either on disposal or when no future economic benefits are expected from its use.

Any gain or loss arising at derecognition (such as a gain on disposal) is included in profit or loss in the accounting period in which when the asset is derecognised (unless required otherwise by IFRS).

The recognition criteria for property, plant and equipment reflect the criteria given in the 2010 *Conceptual Framework*. The revised Conceptual Framework sets out principles for recognition which are less prescriptive: assets should be recognised if they meet the definition of an asset and recognition provides users with information that is useful (ie relevant and a faithful representation). The recognition criteria in IAS 16 are arguably an application of these principles. No changes to the criteria in IAS 16 were proposed when the revised Conceptual Framework was issued and the IASB has not stated whether it plans to amend them in the future.

A further point worth emphasising here is the relationship between the accounting treatment of **impairments and revaluations**.

(a) An **impairment loss** should be treated in the same way as a **revaluation decrease**, ie the decrease should be charged directly against any related revaluation surplus to the extent that the decrease does not exceed the amount held in the revaluation surplus in respect of that same asset. Any excess decrease is recognised as an expense

(b) A **reversal of an impairment** loss should be treated in the same way as a **revaluation increase**, ie a revaluation increase should be recognised as income to the extent that it reverses a revaluation decrease or an impairment loss of the same asset previously recognised as an expense.

Question
Depreciation

What are the purposes of providing for depreciation?

Answer

The financial statements of a business try to recognise that the cost of a non-current asset is gradually consumed as the asset wears out. This is done by gradually writing off the asset's cost in profit or loss over several accounting periods. This process is known as depreciation, and is an example of the accrual assumption. Depreciation should be allocated on a systematic basis to each accounting period during the useful life of the asset.

With regard to the accrual principle, it is fair that the profits should be reduced by the depreciation charge, this is not an arbitrary exercise. Depreciation is not, as is sometimes supposed, an attempt to set aside funds to purchase new non-current assets when required. Depreciation is not generally provided on freehold land because it does not 'wear out' (unless it is held for mining).

2.1.1 Example: Revaluation surplus

Binkie Co has an item of land carried in its books at $13,000. Two years ago a slump in land values led the company to reduce the carrying amount from $15,000. This was recognised as an expense in profit or loss. There has been a surge in land prices in the current year, however, and the land now has a fair value measured in accordance with IFRS 13 of $20,000.

Account for the revaluation in the current year.

Solution

The double entry is:

DEBIT	Asset value (statement of financial position)	$7,000	
CREDIT	Profit or loss		$2,000
	Other comprehensive income (revaluation surplus)		$5,000

The case is similar for a **decrease in value** on revaluation. Any decrease should be recognised as an expense, except where it offsets a previous increase taken as a revaluation surplus in equity. Any decrease greater than the previous upwards increase in value must be taken as an expense in profit or loss.

2.1.2 Example: Revaluation decrease

Let us simply swap round the example given above. The original cost was $15,000, revalued upwards to $20,000 two years ago. The fair value has now fallen to $13,000.

Account for the decrease in value.

Solution

The double entry is:

DEBIT	Other comprehensive income (revaluation surplus)	$5,000	
DEBIT	Profit or loss	$2,000	
CREDIT	Asset value (statement of financial position)		$7,000

There is a further complication when a **revalued asset is being depreciated**. As we have seen, an upward revaluation means that the depreciation charge will increase. Normally, a revaluation surplus is only realised when the asset is sold, but when it is being depreciated, part of that surplus is being realised as

the asset is used. The amount of the surplus realised is the difference between depreciation charged on the revalued amount and the depreciation which would have been charged on the asset's original cost. **This amount can be transferred to retained (ie realised) earnings in the statement of changes in equity, NOT through the profit or loss.**

2.1.3 Example: revaluation and depreciation

Crinckle Co bought an asset for $10,000 at the beginning of 20X6. It had a useful life of five years. On 1 January 20X8 the asset was revalued to $12,000. The expected useful life has remained unchanged (ie three years remain).

Account for the revaluation and state the treatment for depreciation from 20X8 onwards.

Solution

On 1 January 20X8 the carrying amount of the asset is $10,000 − (2 × $10,000 ÷ 5) = $6,000. For the revaluation:

DEBIT	Asset value (statement of financial position)	$6,000	
CREDIT	Other comprehensive income (revaluation surplus)		$6,000

The depreciation for the next three years will be $12,000 ÷ 3 = $4,000, compared to depreciation on cost of $10,000 ÷ 5 = $2,000. So each year, the extra $2,000 can be treated as part of the surplus which has become realised:

DEBIT	Statement of changes in equity (revaluation surplus)	$2,000	
CREDIT	Statement of changes in equity (retained earnings)		$2,000

This is a movement on equity only, not an item in total comprehensive income.

2.2 Government grants

IAS 20 is very straightforward. The question after the following summary covers the accounting problem it tackled.

> **Knowledge brought forward from earlier studies**
>
> **IAS 20** *Accounting for Government Grants And Disclosure Of Government Assistance*
>
> *Definitions*
>
> - **Government assistance.** Action by government designed to provide an economic benefit specific to an entity or range of entities qualifying under certain criteria. This does not include benefits provided only indirectly through action affecting general trading conditions.
> - **Government grants.** Assistance by government in the form of transfers of resources to an entity in return for past or future compliance with certain conditions relating to the operating activities of the entity. They exclude those forms of government assistance which cannot reasonably have a value placed upon them and transactions with government which cannot be distinguished from the normal trading transactions of the entity.
> - **Grants related to assets.** Government grants whose primary condition is that an entity qualifying for them should purchase, construct or otherwise acquire non-current assets. Subsidiary conditions may also be attached, restricting the type or location of the assets or the periods during which they are to be acquired or held.
> - **Grants related to income.** Government grants other than those related to assets.
> - **Forgivable loans.** Loans which the lender undertakes to waive repayment of under certain prescribed conditions.
>
> *Accounting treatment*
>
> - **Recognise government grants and forgivable loans** once compliance with conditions and receipt/waiver are both reasonably assured.

- Grants are recognised under the **income approach**: recognise grants as income to match them with related costs that they have been received to compensate.
- Use a **systematic basis** of matching over the relevant periods.
- Grants for **depreciable assets** should be recognised as income on the same basis as the asset is depreciated.
- Grants for **non-depreciable assets** should be recognised as income over the periods in which the cost of meeting the obligation is incurred.
- A grant may be **split into parts** and allocated on different bases where there are a series of conditions attached.
- Where **related costs have already been incurred**, the grant may be recognised as income in full immediately.
- A grant in the form of a **non-monetary asset** may be valued at fair value or a nominal value.
- **Grants related to assets** may be presented in the statement of financial position *either* as **deferred income** *or* deducted in arriving at the carrying amount of the asset.
- **Grants related to income** may be presented in the statement of profit or loss *either* as a **separate credit** *or* **deducted** from the related expense.
- Repayment of government grants should be accounted for as a **revision of an accounting estimate**.

Disclosure

- **Accounting policy** note.
- **Nature and extent** of government grants and other forms of assistance received.
- **Unfulfilled conditions** and other contingencies attached to recognised government assistance.

Question: Government grants

IAS 20 suggests that there are two approaches to recognising government grants: a capital approach (credit directly to owners' interests) and an income approach. IAS 20 requires the use of the income approach, but what are the arguments in support of each method?

Answer

IAS 20 gives the following arguments in support of each method.

Capital approach

(a) The grants are a **financing device**, so should go through the statement of financial position. In the statement of profit or loss they would simply offset the expenses which they are financing. No repayment is expected by the Government, so the grants should be credited directly to owners' interests (equity).

(b) Grants are **not earned**, they are incentives without related costs, so it would be wrong to take them to profit or loss.

Income approach

(a) The grants are **not received from owners** so should not be credited directly to owners' interests (equity).

(b) Grants are **not given or received for nothing**. They are earned by compliance with conditions and by meeting obligations. There are therefore associated costs with which the grant can be matched in the statement of profit or loss as these costs are being compensated by the grant.

(c) Grants are an extension of **fiscal policies** and so as income and other taxes are charged against income, so grants should be credited to income.

2.3 IAS 23 *Borrowing Costs*

This is another standard you should be familiar with. Read the following section carefully.

> **Knowledge brought forward from earlier studies**

Key term

IAS 23 *Borrowing Costs*

- IAS 23 deals with the treatment of borrowing costs, often associated with the construction of **self-constructed assets**, but which can also be applied to an asset purchased that takes time to get ready for use/sale.

Definitions

- **Borrowing costs**: Interest and other costs incurred by an entity in connection with the borrowing of funds.
- **Qualifying asset**: An asset that necessarily takes a substantial period of time to get ready for its intended use or sale.

Accounting treatment

- **Recognition**: Borrowing costs that are directly attributable to the acquisition, construction or production of a qualifying asset should be capitalised (where it is probable they will result in future economic benefit and the costs can be measured reliably). All other borrowing costs should be recognised as an expense in the period in which they are incurred.
- **Borrowing costs eligible for capitalisation** are those that would have been avoided otherwise. Use judgement where a range of debt instruments is held for general finance.
- **Amount of borrowing costs available for capitalisation** is actual borrowing costs incurred less any investment income from temporary investment of those borrowings.
- For borrowings obtained generally, apply the **capitalisation rate** to the expenditure on the asset (weighted average borrowing cost). It must not exceed actual borrowing costs.
- Capitalisation of borrowing costs **commences** when the entity first meets all the following conditions:
    - (a) it incurs expenditure on the asset
    - (b) it incurs borrowing costs
    - (c) it undertakes activities necessary to prepare the asset for use or sale
- **Capitalisation is suspended** if active development is interrupted for extended periods. (Necessary temporary delays or technical/administrative work will not cause suspension).
- **Capitalisation ceases** (normally) when physical construction of the asset is substantially completed, capitalisation should cease when each stage or part that is capable of being used separately is completed.

Disclosure

- **Accounting policy** note.
- Amount of **borrowing costs capitalised** during the period.
- **Capitalisation rate** used to determine borrowing costs eligible for capitalisation.

Question — Borrowing costs 1

Rechno borrowed $15m to finance the construction of two assets, both of which were expected to take a year to build. Construction started 1 January 20X8. The loan facility was drawn down on 1 January 20X8, and was utilised as follows, with the remaining funds invested temporarily.

	Asset X $m	Asset Y $m
1 January 20X8	2.5	5.0
1 July 20X8	2.5	5.0

The loan rate was 10% and Rechno can invest surplus funds at 8%.

Required

Ignoring compound interest, calculate the borrowing costs which may be capitalised for each of the assets and consequently the cost of each asset as at 31 December 20X8.

Answer

		Asset X $'000	Asset Y $'000
Borrowing costs			
To 30 June 20X8	$2.5m/$5.0m × 10% × 6/12	125	250
To 31 December 20X8	$5.0m/$10m × 10% × 6/12	250	500
		375	750
Less investment income			
To 30 June 20X8	$2.5m/$5.0m × 8% × 6/12	(100)	(200)
		275	550

	$'000	$'000
Cost of assets		
Expenditure incurred	5,000	10,000
Borrowing costs	275	550
	5,275	10,550

Question

Borrowing costs 2

Zenzi had the following loans in place at the beginning and end of 20X8.

	1 January 20X8 $m	31 December 20X8 $m
10.0% Bank loan repayable 20Y3	120	120
9.5% Bank loan repayable 20Y1	80	80
8.9% debenture repayable 20Y8	–	150

The 8.9% debenture was issued to fund the construction of a qualifying asset (a piece of mining equipment), construction of which began on 1 July 20X8.

On 1 January 20X8, Zenzi began construction of another qualifying asset, a piece of machinery for a hydro-electric plant, using existing borrowings. Expenditure drawn down for the construction was: $30m on 1 January 20X8, $20m on 1 October 20X8.

Required

Calculate the borrowing costs to be capitalised for the hydro-electric plant machine.

Answer

Capitalisation rate = weighted average rate = $(10\% \times \frac{120}{120+80}) + (9.5\% \times \frac{80}{120+80}) = 9.8\%$

Borrowing costs = ($30m × 9.8%) + ($20m × 9.8% × 3/12)
= $3.43m

2.4 Sustainability and IAS 16

Sustainability issues can have a variety of impacts on tangible non-current assets such as:
- The useful life of existing assets and any residual value might decrease if these asset need to be replaced with more sustainable options. This will impact the depreciation charge.
- Companies may need to invest in more environmental assets. Economic benefits from these assets may arise directly e.g. constructing a wind turbine to generate electricity for a factory or indirectly e.g. electric vehicle charging stations.
- Decommissioning costs changing e.g. increased costs to rectify contamination.

3 IAS 36 *Impairment of Assets*

FAST FORWARD

> IAS 36 *Impairment of Assets* is a topical area and it affects both intangible and tangible non-current assets.

There is an established principle that assets should not be carried above their recoverable amount. IAS 36 describes the procedures which should be followed in order to ensure that this is the case. This has been a very relevant standard in recent years as a result of the global economic downturn and continues as to be a topical area as a result of economic uncertainty surrounding, for example in relation to climate-related issues.

3.1 Scope

IAS 36 applies to all tangible, intangible and financial assets except for:

1. Inventories (IAS 2)
2. Assets arising from contracts (IFRS 15)
3. Deferred tax assets (IAS 12)
4. Assets arising from employee benefits (IAS 19)
5. Financial assets within the scope of IFRS 9
6. Investment property measured at fair value (IAS 40)
7. Non-current assets classified as held for sale in accordance with IFRS 5

Other assets are excluded from the scope of IAS 36. However, these relate to IAS 41 *Agriculture* and IFRS 4 *Insurance Contracts* and these standards do not form part of the Paper 13 syllabus.

These assets are excluded from IAS 36 because rules for recognising and measuring impairment are already included in the relevant standard.

3.2 The basic principle

Key terms

> **Impairment**: a fall in the value of an asset or cash-generating unit, so that its 'recoverable amount' is now less than its carrying amount in the statement of financial position.
>
> **Carrying amount**: is the amount at which an asset is recognised in the statement of financial position after deducting accumulated depreciation (amortisation) and any impairment losses thereon.
>
> (See IAS 16 and IAS 36)

The basic principle underlying IAS 36 is relatively straightforward. If an asset's value in the financial statements is higher than its realistic value, measured as its 'recoverable amount', the asset is judged to have suffered an impairment loss. It should therefore be reduced in value, by the amount of the **impairment loss**. The amount of the impairment loss should be **recognised as an expense in profit or loss** immediately.

The main accounting issues to consider are therefore as follows:

(a) When should an asset be tested for impairment?
(b) How should the **recoverable amount** of the asset be measured?
(c) How should an 'impairment loss' be **reported in the financial statements**?

3.3 Frequency of impairment testing

An asset must be tested for impairment when there is an indication of impairment at the reporting date. In addition IAS 36 requires certain assets to be tested for impairment annually. These are:

- Goodwill acquired in a business combination
- Intangible assets with an indefinite useful life
- Intangible assets which are not yet available for use.

3.3.1 Indications of impairment

An entity should carry out a **review of its assets at the end of each reporting period**, to assess whether there are any indications of impairment. The concept of **materiality** applies, and only material impairment needs to be identified.

IAS 36 suggests how **indications of a possible impairment** of assets might be recognised. The following must be considered as a minimum:

External	Internal
(a) Observable indications that the asset's value has declined during the period significantly more than expected due to the passage of time or normal use	(a) Evidence of obsolescence or physical damage
(b) Significant changes with an adverse effect on the entity in the technological or market environment, or in the economic or legal environment	(b) Significant changes with an adverse effect on the entity*: (i) The asset becomes idle (ii) Plans to discontinue/restructure the operation to which the asset belongs (iii) Plans to dispose of an asset before the previously expected date (iv) Reassessing an asset's useful life as finite rather than indefinite
(c) Increased market interest rates or other market rates of return affecting discount rates and thus reducing value in use	
(d) Carrying amount of net assets of the entity exceeds market capitalisation.	(c) Internal evidence available that asset performance will be worse than expected

3.4 Performing an impairment test: Measuring the recoverable amount of the asset

FAST FORWARD

Impairment is determined by comparing the carrying amount of the asset with its **recoverable amount**.

The recoverable amount of an asset is the higher of the asset's **fair value less costs of disposal** and its **value in use**.

Where there are indications of impairment or the asset in question requires annual testing, an impairment test must be performed. This involves comparing its carrying amount with its recoverable amount. An asset is impaired when its carrying amount exceeds its recoverable amount.

12: TANGIBLE NON-CURRENT ASSETS AND INVENTORY

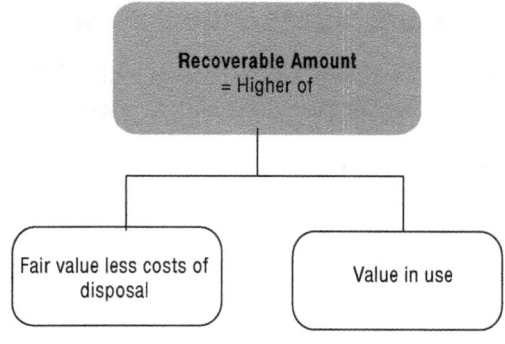

(IAS 36: para. 6)

3.4.1 Fair value less costs of disposal

An asset's fair value less costs of disposal is fair value established in accordance with IFRS 13 *Fair Value Measurement* (see Chapter 11) less any selling costs. Selling costs include sales transaction costs, such as legal expenses, other than those that have been recognised as liabilities.

3.4.2 Value in use

The concept of 'value in use' is very important. It is defined as the present value of future cash flows expected to be derived from an asset or cash-generating unit.

Key term

> The **value in use** of an asset is measured by:
>
> – Estimating cash inflows and outflows from the use and eventual disposal of the asset
> – Discounting those cash flows to present value

There are therefore two elements to the calculation of value in use: cash flows and an appropriate discount rate.

Cash flows

The cash flows which must be taken into consideration include all future cash inflows and outflows from the continuing use and ultimate disposal of the asset. They should:

- Be based on reasonable and supportable assumptions
- Be based on the most **recent budgets or financial forecasts** up to a maximum period of five years ahead, unless a longer period can be justified
- Exclude the effects of future restructurings or improving / enhancing the asset's performance (including servicing the asset)
- Not include income tax receipts or payments or cash flows from financing activities
- Assume disposal at arm's length

Cash flows beyond the period covered by the most recent forecasts should be estimated by extrapolating projections based on the budgets using a steady or declining growth rate for subsequent years unless an increasing rate can be justified. The growth rate should not exceed the long-term average growth rate for the products, industries or country in which the entity is based or market in which the asset is used unless a higher rate can be justified.

Foreign currency future cash flows should be forecast in the currency in which they will arise and discounted using a rate appropriate for that currency. The resulting figure should then be translated into the reporting currency at the spot rate at the date of the calculation ie year end.

Discount rate

The **discount rate** should be a pre-tax rate (or rates) that reflects the current assessment of the time value of money and the risks specific to the asset. The discount rate should not include a risk weighting if the underlying cash flows have already been adjusted for risk.

3.5 Recognition and measurement of an impairment loss

Where the carrying amount of an asset exceeds its recoverable amount, the asset must be written down to the recoverable amount. The amount written off the asset is referred to as an impairment loss.

The accounting entries will depend on whether the impaired asset is held at historic cost or a revalued amount.

The rule for assets at **historic cost** is:

Rule to learn

> The impairment loss is recognised as an expense in profit or loss.

The rule for assets held at a **revalued amount** (such as property revalued under IAS 16) is:

Rule to learn

> The impairment loss is to be treated as a revaluation decrease under the relevant IFRS. In other words:
> - To the extent that there is a revaluation surplus held in respect of the asset, the impairment loss should be charged to that revaluation surplus
> - Any excess should be recognised in profit or loss

3.5.1 Example: recognition of impairment loss 1

At 31 December 20X9, Kilnsey Co identified a possible indication of impairment relating to one of its properties. The property was purchased on 1 January 20X4 at a cost of $400,000 and depreciation on a 2% straight-line basis commenced immediately. On 1 January 20X9 the company adopted a policy of revaluing all properties and the property was revalued to $405,000. Its total useful life remained unchanged and the company made an annual reserve transfer in respect of the excess depreciation. At 31 December 20X9 the impairment test revealed a value in use of $330,000 and fair value less costs of disposal of $320,000.

How should the impairment be recognised?

Solution

	$
Cost of property on 1.1.X4	400,000
Depreciation to 1.1.X9 2% × $400,000 × 5 years	(40,000)
	360,000
Revaluation surplus	45,000
Valuation at 1.1.X9	405,000
Depreciation for y/e 31.12.X9 ($405,000/45 years)	(9,000)
Carrying amount at 31.12.X9	396,000
Impairment loss	(66,000)
Recoverable amount	330,000

The revaluation surplus at the date of the impairment is $44,000 (the $45,000 surplus on revaluation less one year's transfer of excess depreciation to retained earnings). Therefore $44,000 of the impairment loss reduces the revaluation surplus to $nil and the remaining $22,000 is charged to profit or loss.

3.5.2 Example: Recognition of an impairment loss 2

A company that extracts natural gas and oil has a drilling platform in the Caspian Sea. It is required by legislation of the country concerned to remove and dismantle the platform at the end of its useful life. Accordingly, the company has included an amount in its financial statements for removal and dismantling costs, and is depreciating this amount over the platform's expected life.

The company is carrying out an exercise to establish whether there has been an impairment of the platform.

(a) Its carrying amount in the statement of financial position is $3m.

(b) The company has received an offer of $2.8m for the platform from another oil company. The bidder would take over the responsibility (and costs) for dismantling and removing the platform at the end of its life.

(c) The present value of the estimated cash flows from the platform's continued use is $3.3m.

(d) The carrying amount in the statement of financial position for the provision for dismantling and removal is currently $0.6m.

What should be the carrying amount of the drilling platform in the statement of financial position, and what, if anything, is the impairment loss?

Solution

Fair value less costs of disposal	=	$2.8m
Value in use	=	PV of cash flows from use less the carrying amount of the provision/liability = $3.3m – $0.6m = $2.7m
Recoverable amount	=	Higher of these two amounts, ie $2.8m
Carrying amount	=	$3m
Impairment loss	=	$0.2m

The carrying amount should be reduced to $2.8m.

3.6 Depreciating an impaired asset

After an impairment loss is recorded, the new carrying amount of the impaired asset, less any residual value should be spread over its remaining useful life.

Both the residual value and useful life may need to be reassessed in the light of the impairment.

3.7 Reversal of an impairment loss

An impairment loss on an individual asset can be reversed should recoverable amount exceed carrying amount subsequent to the initial loss (with the exception of goodwill, which we shall see in the next section).

Rule to learn

> An impairment loss recognised for an asset in prior years should be reversed if, and only if, there has been a change in the estimates used to determine the asset's recoverable amount since the last impairment loss was recognised.

Indicators that an impairment loss may have reversed mirror those indicators that an impairment loss has occurred. Even where no reversal of impairment loss is recognised, these indicators may indicate that the useful life, residual value or depreciation method applied to an asset may require reassessment.

The impairment loss can be reversed to the extent that the increased carrying amount of an individual asset does not exceed the amount that the asset would have been carried at had there been no initial impairment.

3.7.1 Recognising the reversal of an impairment loss

The accounting entries for the reversal of an impairment loss depend on whether the reversal relates to an asset held at historic cost or revalued amount:

- An impairment reversal is recognised in profit or loss when it relates to an asset held at historic cost

- In relation to a revalued asset, the reversal is recognised in profit or loss to the extent that the original impairment loss was recognised in profit or loss and as a revaluation surplus thereafter.

3.7.2 Example: Reversal of an impairment loss

Continuing with the example in Section 3.5.1 above, let's now assume that the estimates used to determine recoverable amount have been revised and the recoverable amount at 31 December 20Y0 is calculated as $370,000.

At 31 December 20Y0 the carrying amount of the property is:

	$
Carrying amount at 31.12.X9 after impairment	330,000
Depreciation in year (330,000/44 years)	(7,500)
Carrying amount at 31.12.Y0	322,500

The recoverable amount of the property is assessed as $370,000, meaning a potential reversal of $47,500 ($370,000 − $322,500) of the impairment loss. The reversal cannot, however, increase the value of the asset above the value that it would have had, had the impairment loss not occurred. Therefore a check is required:

	$
Carrying amount at 31.12.X9 before impairment	396,000
Depreciation in year (as in y/e 31.12.X9) (405,000/45 years)	(9,000)
Carrying amount at 31.12.Y0 had impairment not occurred	387,000

In this case the reversal will not increase the carrying amount above $387,000 and therefore the full $47,500 reversal can be recognised as follows:

- $22,000 in profit or loss to reverse the impairment loss recognised in profit or loss, and
- $25,500 as a revaluation surplus.

4 Impairment: Cash-generating units

FAST FORWARD

> Where the recoverable amount of a single asset can not be estimated, the impairment test must be performed for the cash-generating unit (CGU) to which that asset belongs.

IAS 36 goes into quite a large amount of detail about the important concept of cash-generating units. As a basic rule, the recoverable amount of an asset should be calculated for the **asset individually** as we saw in the last section of the chapter. However, there will be occasions when it is not possible to estimate such a value for an individual asset, particularly in the calculation of value in use. This is because cash inflows and outflows cannot be attributed to the individual asset.

If it is not possible to calculate the recoverable amount for an individual asset, the recoverable amount of the asset's cash-generating unit should be measured instead.

Key term

> A **cash-generating unit** is the smallest identifiable group of assets that generates cash inflows that are largely independent of the cash inflows of other assets or groups of assets.
>
> (IAS 36)

Question — Cash generating unit 1

Can you think of some examples of how a cash-generating unit would be identified?

Answer

Here are two possibilities.

(a) A mining company owns a private railway that it uses to transport output from one of its mines. The railway now has no market value other than as scrap, and it is impossible to identify any separate cash inflows from the use of the railway itself. Consequently, if the mining company suspects an impairment in the value of the railway, it should treat the mine as a whole as a cash-generating unit, and measure the recoverable amount of the mine as a whole.

(b) A bus company has an arrangement with a town's authorities to run a bus service on four routes in the town. Separately identifiable assets are allocated to each of the bus routes, and cash inflows and outflows can be attributed to each individual route. Three routes are running at a profit and one is running at a loss. The bus company suspects that there is an impairment of assets on the loss-making route. However, the company will be unable to close the loss-making route because it is under an obligation to operate all four routes, as part of its contract with the local authority. Consequently, the company should treat all four bus routes together as a cash-generating unit, and calculate the recoverable amount for the unit as a whole.

Question — Cash generating unit 2

Minimart belongs to a retail store chain Maximart. Minimart makes all its retail purchases through Maximart's purchasing centre. Pricing, marketing, advertising and human resources policies (except for hiring Minimart's cashiers and sales force) are decided by Maximart. Maximart also owns five other stores in the same city as Minimart (although in different neighbourhoods) and 20 other stores in other cities. All stores are managed in the same way as Minimart. Minimart and four other stores were purchased five years ago and goodwill was recognised.

What is the cash-generating unit for Minimart?

Answer

In identifying Minimart's cash-generating unit, an entity considers whether, for example:

(a) Internal management reporting is organised to measure performance on a store-by-store basis.
(b) The business is run on a store-by-store profit basis or on a region/city basis.

All Maximart's stores are in different neighbourhoods and probably have different customer bases. So, although Minimart is managed at a corporate level, Minimart generates cash inflows that are largely independent from those of Maximart's other stores. Therefore, it is likely that Minimart is a cash-generating unit.

Question — Cash generating unit 3

Mighty Mag Publishing Co owns 150 magazine titles of which 70 were purchased and 80 were self-created. The price paid for a purchased magazine title is recognised as an intangible asset. The costs of creating magazine titles and maintaining the existing titles are recognised as an expense when incurred. Cash inflows from direct sales and advertising are identifiable for each magazine title. Titles are managed by customer segments. The level of advertising income for a magazine title depends on the range of titles in the customer segment to which the magazine title relates. Management has a policy to abandon old titles before the end of their useful lives and replace them immediately with new titles for the same customer segment.

What is the cash-generating unit for an individual magazine title?

Answer

It is likely that the recoverable amount of an individual magazine title can be assessed. Even though the level of advertising income for a title is influenced, to a certain extent, by the other titles in the customer segment, cash inflows from direct sales and advertising are identifiable for each title. In addition, although titles are managed by customer segments, decisions to abandon titles are made on an individual title basis.

Therefore, it is likely that individual magazine titles generate cash inflows that are largely independent one from another and that each magazine title is a separate cash-generating unit.

If an active market exists for the output produced by the asset or a group of assets, this asset or group of assets should be identified as a cash-generating unit, even if some or all of the output is used internally.

Cash-generating units should be identified consistently from period to period for the same type of asset unless a change is justified.

4.1 Testing a CGU for impairment

When performing an impairment test on a cash-generating unit (CGU), the carrying amount of the CGU's assets should be compared with the recoverable amount of the same assets.

In some cases identifying the assets of a cash-generating unit is not straightforward. This is particularly true when one asset is shared between a number of CGUs or goodwill can be attributed to a number of CGUs.

We shall deal with these 'corporate assets' (shared assets) and goodwill in the next sections, but first let's consider a simple example of allocating assets to CGUs.

4.1.1 Example: Cash-generating units

Fourways Co is made up of four cash-generating units. All four units are being tested for impairment.

(a) Property, plant and equipment and separate intangibles would be allocated to cash-generating units as far as possible.

(b) Current assets such as inventories, receivables and prepayments would be allocated to the relevant cash-generating units.

(c) The figure for each cash-generating unit resulting from this exercise would be compared to the relevant recoverable amount, computed on the same basis.

4.2 Corporate assets

Corporate assets are group or divisional assets such as a head office building, IT equipment or a research centre. Essentially, corporate assets are assets that do not generate cash inflows independently from other assets, and their carrying amount cannot be fully attributed to a cash-generating unit under review.

IAS 36 requires that these corporate assets are allocated to CGUs on a 'reasonable and consistent' basis before an impairment test takes place.

Where such an allocation is not possible, the entity should:

(i) Compare the carrying amount of the CGU (excluding the corporate asset) with its recoverable amount and recognise any impairment loss

(ii) Identify the smallest group of cash-generating units that includes the cash-generating unit to which the corporate asset belongs and to which a portion of the carrying amount of the asset can be allocated on a reasonable and consistent basis

(iii) Compare the carrying amount of that group of cash-generating units (including the portion of the corporate asset allocated to the group of units) with the recoverable amount of the group of units and recognise any impairment loss

4.2.1 Example: Allocation of a corporate asset to CGUs

Rombald Co has four divisions which are also cash-generating units: 1, 2, 3 and 4. The carrying amounts of these divisions are $150,000, $600,000, $300,000 and $250,000 respectively.

The divisions are managed from a head office with a carrying amount of $650,000. What is the carrying amount of each division after this corporate asset has been allocated to the divisions for the purpose of impairment testing?

Solution

	Division A	Division B	Division C	Division D	Total
Carrying amount	150,000	600,000	300,000	250,000	1,300,000
Allocation of corporate asset	150/1,300 × $650 = 75,000	600/1,300 × $650 = 300,000	300/1,300 × $650 = 150,000	250/1,300 × $650 = 125,000	
Total carrying amount of each CGU	225,000	900,000	450,000	375,000	

4.3 Goodwill

For the purpose of impairment testing, goodwill acquired in a business combination must be **allocated** to each of the **cash-generating units** that are expected to benefit from the synergies of the combination.

Where goodwill cannot be allocated on a non-arbitrary basis to individual cash-generating units, it should be allocated to groups of cash-generating units

Each unit (or group of units) to which the goodwill is so allocated should:

(a) Represent the **lowest level** within the entity at which the goodwill is monitored for internal management purposes.

(b) Not be **larger than a reporting segment** determined in accordance with IFRS 8 *Operating Segments*.

It may be impractical to complete the allocation of goodwill before the first reporting date after a business combination, particularly if the acquirer is accounting for the combination for the first time using provisional values. The initial allocation of goodwill must be completed before the end of the first reporting period beginning after the acquisition date.

4.3.1 Impairment testing and goodwill

Where goodwill has been allocated to individual CGUs, those CGUs should be tested annually for impairment by comparing their carrying amount (including the allocated goodwill) with their recoverable amount (including goodwill).

Where goodwill is attributable to a number of CGUs but cannot be allocated to those CGUs on an individual basis:

1. Each individual CGU to which goodwill is attributable and for which indications of impairment have been identified should be tested for impairment by comparing their carrying amount (excluding goodwill) with their recoverable amount (excluding goodwill); and then

2. The CGUs to which the goodwill is attributable should be tested for impairment on an aggregate basis by comparing their aggregate carrying amount (including goodwill) with their aggregate recoverable amount (including goodwill).

Consider the following:

Allocating goodwill to CGUs

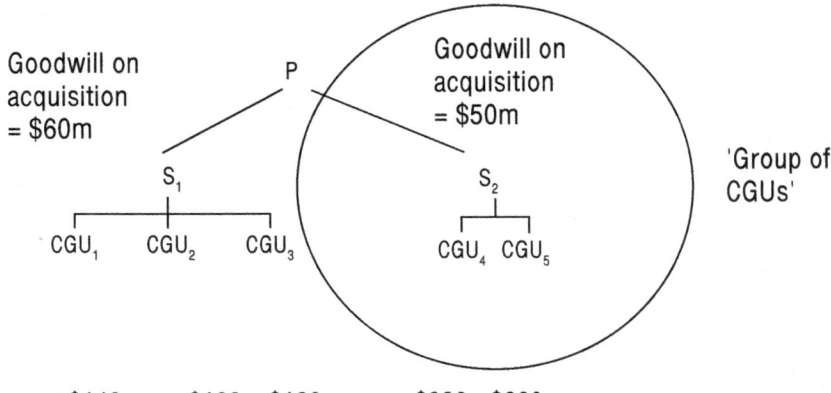

Carrying amount $140m $160m $180m $220m $260m

Allocated $17.5m $20m $22.5m
goodwill at
acquisition

On acquisition of S, the goodwill can be allocated on a non-arbitrary basis to the three acquired CGUs (in this case based on carrying amount of the acquired assets). Each CGU is tested for impairment including the allocated goodwill.

On acquisition of S2, the nature of the CGUs and their risks is different such that the goodwill cannot be allocated on a non-arbitrary basis. Instead, it is allocated to the group of CGUs to which it relates and is tested for impairment as part of that group of CGUs (here, S2).

4.3.2 Example: Impairment testing and goodwill

Skipton Co has identified 6 CGUs within its organisation. Goodwill arising on a business combination is attributable to four of these. Explain the requirements of IAS 36 with regard to impairment testing if:

(a) The goodwill can be allocated to the four CGUs to which it is attributed
(b) The goodwill cannot be allocated to the four CGUs to which it is attributed.

Solution

(a) The two CGUs to which no goodwill is attributed are tested for impairment only if there are indications of impairment by comparing their carrying amount with their recoverable amount.

The four CGUs to which goodwill is attributed and allocated must be tested for impairment annually, since it is a requirement of IAS 36 that goodwill is tested annually. The carrying amount of each CGU (including the allocation of goodwill) must be compared with its recoverable amount (including goodwill) in turn.

(b) Again, the two CGUs to which no goodwill is attributed are tested for impairment only if there are indications of impairment by comparing their carrying amount with their recoverable amount.

The four CGUs to which goodwill is attributed are tested on an individual basis for impairment only if there are indications of impairment by comparing their carrying amount (excluding goodwill) with their recoverable amount (excluding goodwill).

The four CGUs to which goodwill is attributed are tested annually on an aggregate basis (due to the IAS 36 requirement to test goodwill for impairment annually) by comparing their aggregate carrying amount (including goodwill) with their aggregate recoverable amount (including goodwill).

4.3.3 Goodwill and non-controlling interests

In addition to the problem of allocating goodwill to CGUs, there may be a further problem where there is a non-controlling interest in the business combination which created the goodwill.

Chapter 6 explained that IFRS 3 allows two methods of measuring non-controlling interests in a subsidiary:

(a) As the non-controlling interest's proportionate share of the acquiree's identifiable net assets; or
(b) At the **fair value** of the non-controlling interest.

Where the non-controlling interest is measured at fair value, the reported goodwill is 'full' goodwill. This includes the goodwill 'belonging' to the non-controlling interest as well as the goodwill 'belonging' to the parent.

Where the non-controlling interest is measured as a proportion of net assets, the reported goodwill is the parent's goodwill only.

When performing an impairment test, we must ensure that we are comparing like with like. The recoverable amount of a CGU (or group of CGUs) includes all of its goodwill, and therefore it is important that the carrying amount of the CGU (or group of CGUs) does as well.

Therefore where the non-controlling interest is measured as a proportion of net assets and the reported goodwill is the parent goodwill only, an adjustment should be made to notionally gross up the reported goodwill to include the goodwill attributable to the non-controlling interest.

The goodwill is grossed up in proportion to ownership.

4.3.4 Example: Non-controlling interests

On 1 January 20X4 a parent acquires an 80% interest in a subsidiary for $1,600,000, when the identifiable net assets of the subsidiary are $1,500,000. The subsidiary is a cash-generating unit.

The non-controlling interest is measured as the proportionate share of the acquiree's net assets.

At 31 December 20X4, the recoverable amount of the subsidiary is $1,000,000. The carrying amount of the subsidiary's identifiable net assets is $1,350,000.

Calculate the impairment loss at 31 December 20X4.

Solution

At 31 December 20X4 the cash-generating unit consists of the subsidiary's identifiable net assets (carrying amount $1,350,000) and goodwill of $400,000 ($1,600,000 − (80% × $1,500,000)). For the purposes of the impairment test goodwill is grossed up to reflect the 20% non-controlling interest.

	Goodwill $'000	Identifiable net assets $'000	Total $'000
Carrying amount	400	1,350	1,750
Unrecognised non-controlling interest	100	–	100
	500	1,350	1,850
Recoverable amount			(1,000)
Impairment loss			850

We shall come back to this example in a moment to see how the impairment loss is allocated between the assets of the cash-generating unit.

4.4 Recognising an impairment loss in a CGU

An impairment loss should be recognised for a **cash-generating unit** if (and only if) the recoverable amount for the cash-generating unit is less than the carrying amount in the statement of financial position for all the assets in the unit.

When an impairment loss is recognised for a cash-generating unit (or group of CGUs), the loss should be allocated between the assets in the unit in the following order:

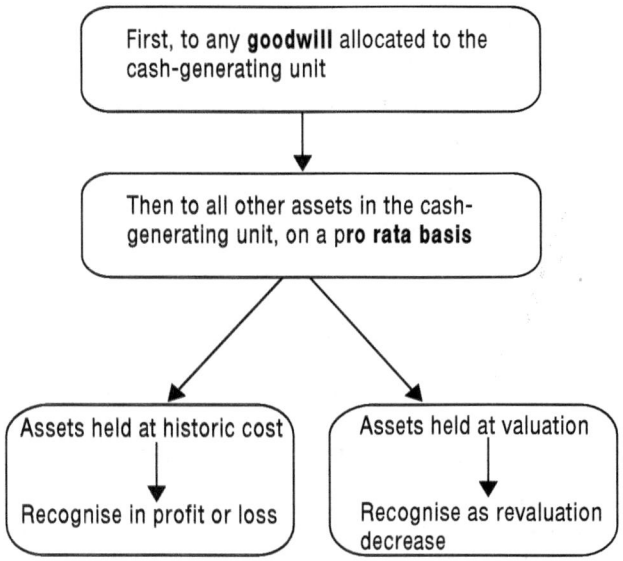

In allocating an impairment loss, the carrying amount of an asset should not be reduced below the **highest** of:

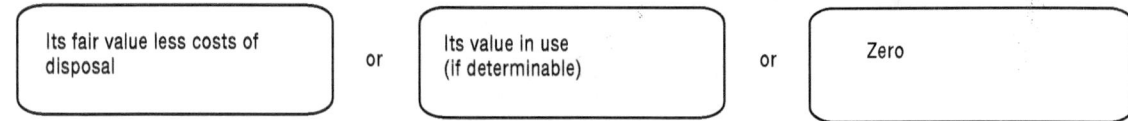

Any remaining amount of an impairment loss should be recognised as a liability if required by another IFRS.

4.4.1 Example: Allocation of impairment loss to CGU

Now let's revisit the example in Section 4.3.2 above.

The impairment loss of $850,000 should be allocated between the parent and the non-controlling interest goodwill in the first instance and then to the other assets of the CGU as follows.

	Goodwill (80%) $'000	Goodwill (NCI) $'000	Identifiable net assets $'000	Total $'000
Carrying amounts	400	100	1,350	1,850
Impairment	(400)	(100)	(350)	(850)
	–	–	1,000	1,000

The NCI goodwill is a notional amount and the $100,000 impairment loss allocated against it is also notional. It is therefore not recognised in profit or loss.

The entity does, however, recognise an impairment of $750,000 ($400,000 + $350,000) in its financial statements, all of it allocated to the owners of the parent.

Now let's assume that the recoverable amount of the cash-generating unit was $1,400,000 and therefore the impairment loss was $450,000 ($1,850,000 – $1,400,000).

This loss is allocated in its entirety to the $500,000 goodwill balance. It must be split between the parent and NCI on the same basis as that which profit or loss is allocated:

	Goodwill (80%) $'000	Goodwill (NC1) $'000
Carrying amounts	400	100
Impairment (80%/20% × $450,000)	(360)	(90)
	40	10

As before, only the impairment in relation to the parent's goodwill is recognised.

4.4.2 Example: Allocation of impairment loss to CGU 2 (non-controlling interest at fair value)

On 1 January 20X4 a parent acquires an 80% interest in a subsidiary for $1,600,000, when the identifiable net assets of the subsidiary are $1,500,000. The subsidiary is a cash-generating unit.

The non-controlling interest is measured at its fair value of $350,000.

At 31 December 20X4, the recoverable amount of the subsidiary is $1,000,000. The carrying amount of the subsidiary's identifiable net assets is $1,350,000.

Calculate the impairment loss at 31 December 20X4 and allocate it to the assets of the CGU.

Solution

At 31 December 20X4 the cash-generating unit consists of the subsidiary's identifiable net assets (carrying amount $1,350,000) and goodwill of $450,000 ($1,600,000 + $350,000 − $1,500,000)). Goodwill includes the amount attributable to the 20% non-controlling interest.

	Goodwill $'000	Identifiable net assets $'000	Total $'000
Carrying amount	450	1,350	1,800
Recoverable amount			(1,000)
Impairment loss			800

The impairment loss should be allocated as follows.

	Goodwill $'000	Identifiable net assets $'000	Total $'000
Carrying amounts	450	1,350	1,800
Impairment	(450)	(350)	(800)
Recoverable amount	–	1,000	1,000

The whole of the impairment loss is recognised in profit or loss.

4.4.3 Example: Impairment loss

A company has acquired another business for $4.5m: identifiable net assets are valued at $4.0m and goodwill at $0.5m.

An asset with a carrying amount of $1.0m is destroyed in a terrorist attack. The asset was not insured and has no scrap value. The loss of the asset, without insurance, has prompted the company to estimate whether there has been an impairment of assets in the acquired business and what the amount of any such loss is. The recoverable amount of the acquired business has been estimated at $3.1m.

Solution

The destroyed asset should be derecognised and a loss on abandonment of $1.0m recognised as an expense in profit or loss.

After this, the carrying amount of the business is $3.5m ($4.0m + $0.5m − $1.0m). The recoverable amount is measured as $3.1m and therefore there is an impairment loss of $0.4m. The impairment loss will be recognised in profit or loss. The loss will all be allocated to goodwill.

The carrying amount of the assets will now be $3.0m for identifiable assets and $0.1m for goodwill.

4.5 Reversal of an impairment loss

As with an individual asset, an impairment loss in relation to a cash-generating unit can be reversed, with one exception: any loss recognised for goodwill.

The reversal is allocated pro rata to the assets (other than goodwill) of the CGU, however the increased carrying amount of each asset **cannot exceed the lower of**:

- Its recoverable amount; and
- The amount that the asset would have been carried at had there been no initial impairment.

The reversal is recognised in profit or loss to the extent that it relates to a non-revalued asset and treated as a revaluation increase to the extent that it relates to a revalued asset.

Rule to learn

> An impairment loss recognised for an asset (other than goodwill) in prior years should be reversed if, and only if, there has been a change in the estimates used to determine the asset's recoverable amount since the last impairment loss was recognised.

Question — Reversal of impairment loss

A cash-generating unit comprising a factory, plant and equipment etc and associated goodwill becomes impaired because the product it makes is overtaken by a technologically more advanced model produced by a competitor. The recoverable amount of the cash-generating unit falls to $60m, resulting in an impairment loss of $80m, allocated as follows.

	Carrying amounts before impairment $m	Carrying amounts after impairment $m
Goodwill	40	–
Patent (with no market value)	20	–
Tangible non-current assets	80	60
Total	140	60

After three years, the entity makes a technological breakthrough of its own, and the recoverable amount of the cash-generating unit increases to $90m. The carrying amount of the tangible non-current assets had the impairment not occurred would have been $70m.

Required

Calculate the reversal of the impairment loss.

Answer

The reversal of the impairment loss is recognised to the extent that it increases the carrying amount of the tangible non-current assets to what it would have been had the impairment not taken place, ie a reversal of the impairment loss of $10m is recognised and the tangible non-current assets written back to $70m. Reversal of the impairment is not recognised in relation to the goodwill and patent because the effect of the external event that caused the original impairment has not reversed – the original product is still overtaken by a more advanced model.

4.6 Disclosure

IAS 36 calls for substantial disclosure about impairment of assets. The information to be disclosed includes the following:

- For each class of assets, the amount of **impairment losses recognised** and the amount of any **impairment losses reversed** split between profit or loss and other comprehensive income.

- For each impairment loss recognised or reversed, a description of the circumstances, the amount, a description of the nature of the asset or CGU, the recoverable amount and whether it reflects fair value less costs or disposal or value in use.

A narrow scope amendment to IAS 36 was issued in May 2013. This clarified the disclosure requirements, which had become unclear since the issue of IFRS 13. The standard now states that for each asset (including goodwill) or cash-generating unit for which an impairment loss has been recognised/reversed during the period, the following should be disclosed:

- The recoverable amount of the asset/CGU and whether it is based on (i) value in use or (ii) fair value less cost to sell.
- If based on (ii), the basis on which on which it was determined, including:
    - The level of the fair value hierarchy (see IFRS 13) within which the measurement of the asset/CGU is categorised.
    - For those categorised within Levels 2 or 3 of the fair value hierarchy:
        - A description of the valuation techniques used, and whether/why that technique has changed
        - Each key assumption used

In addition, the basis on which recoverable amount has been determined shall be disclosed for each CGU for which carrying amount of goodwill/intangible assets with indefinite useful life is significant, even if no impairment has taken place.

4.7 Sustainability and IAS 36

Environmental factors, such as climate-related emissions regulations are having an increasing impact on the impairment of assets. Companies are having to make decisions about the future use and viability of assets to meet legal and regulatory sustainability targets which might result in an impairment review.

The estimation of future cashflows to calculate value in use might be impacted by climate-related or other sustainability matters. Climate-related matters might also need to be disclosed in any impairment disclosure note.

4.8 Section summary

The main aspects of IAS 36 to consider are:

- **Indications** of impairment of assets
- **Measuring recoverable amount**, as the higher of fair value less costs of disposal and value in use
- **Measuring value in use**
- **Cash-generating units**
- **Accounting treatment** of an impairment loss, for individual assets and cash-generating units
- **Reversal** of an impairment loss

5 IAS 40 *Investment Property*

FAST FORWARD

IAS 40 *Investment Property* defines investment property as property **held to earn rentals or for capital appreciation** or both, rather than for:
- Use in production or supply of goods or services
- Sale in the ordinary course of business

An entity may own, or lease, land or a building **as an investment** rather than for use in the business. It may therefore generate cash flows largely independently of other assets which the entity holds.

Consider the following definitions.

Key terms

> **Investment property** is property (land or a building – or part of a building – or both) held (by the owner or by the lessee as a right-of-use asset) to earn rentals or for capital appreciation or both, rather than for:
>
> (a) Use in the production or supply of goods or services or for administrative purposes, or
> (b) Sale in the ordinary course of business
>
> **Owner-occupied property** is property held by the owner (or by the lessee as a right-of-use asset) for use in the production or supply of goods or services or for administrative purposes.
>
> **Fair value** is the price that would be received to sell an asset or paid to transfer a liability in an orderly transaction between market participants at the measurement date.
>
> **Cost** is the amount of cash or cash equivalents paid or the fair value of other consideration given to acquire an asset at the time of its acquisition or construction.
>
> **Carrying amount** is the amount at which an asset is recognised in the statement of financial position.

Examples of investment property include:

(a) **Land held for non-current capital appreciation** rather than for short-term sale in the ordinary course of business
(b) Land held for a currently undetermined future use
(c) A **building** owned by the reporting entity (or a right-of-use asset relating to a building held by the entity) and **leased out under an operating lease**
(d) A building that is vacant but is held to be leased out under an operating lease
(e) Property that is being constructed or developed for future use as investment property

Question — Investment property

Rich Co owns a piece of land. The directors have not yet decided whether to build a factory on it for use in its business or to keep it and sell it when its value has risen.

Would this be classified as an investment property under IAS 40?

Answer

Yes. If an entity has not yet determined whether it will use the land as an owner-occupied property or for short-term sale in the ordinary course of business, the land is considered to be held for capital appreciation and classified as investment property.

5.1 Recognition

Investment property should be recognised as an asset when **two conditions** are met.

| It is **probable** that the **future economic benefits** that are associated with the investment property will **flow to the entity**. | and | The **cost** of the investment property can be **measured reliably** |

5.2 Initial measurement

An investment property should be measured initially at its **cost**, including transaction costs.

A property interest held as a right-of use asset and classified as an investment property shall be measured initially at its cost in accordance with IFRS 16. The right of use asset is measured at the total of the initial measurement of the lease liability, plus any payments made before commencement, less any initial direct costs incurred by the lessee, plus any expected dismantling/restoration costs.

5.3 Measurement subsequent to initial recognition

FAST FORWARD

Entities can choose between:

- A **fair value model**, with fair value measured in accordance with IFRS 13 and changes in fair value being recognised in profit or loss
- A **cost model** – the treatment most commonly used under IAS 16

IAS 40 requires an entity to **choose between two models**.

Fair value model	Any change in fair value reported in profit or loss, not depreciated
Cost model	As cost model of IAS 16 – unless held for sale (IFRS 5) or leased (IFRS 16)

Whatever policy it chooses should be applied to **all of its investment property**.

5.3.1 Fair value model

Under the fair value model **all changes in fair value are recognised in profit or loss**.

Fair value is established in accordance with IFRS 13, taking into account rental income from current leases and other assumptions that market participants would use when pricing investment property under current market conditions.

An entity that chooses the fair value model should measure all of its investment property at fair value unless fair value cannot be measured reliably. In this case, the IAS 16 cost model should be applied going forward. Where investment property is under construction and fair value cannot be reliably measured, but it is expected that the fair value will be measurable when the property is complete, the cost model is applied during construction until fair value becomes measurable or construction is complete, if earlier.

5.3.2 Cost model

The cost model is the **cost model in IAS 16**. Investment property should be measured at **depreciated cost, less any accumulated impairment losses**. An entity that chooses the cost model should **disclose the fair value of its investment property**.

5.3.3 Changing models

Once the entity has chosen the fair value or cost model, it should apply it to all its investment property. It **should not change from one model to the other unless the change results in the financial statements providing reliable and more relevant information**. IAS 40 states that it is highly unlikely that a change from the fair value model to the cost model will result in a more relevant presentation.

5.4 Transfers

Transfers to or from investment property should **only** be made **when there is a change in use**. For example, owner occupation commences so the investment property will be treated under IAS 16 as an owner-occupied property.

Transfer from investment property to owner-occupied or inventories
- Cost for subsequent accounting is fair value at date of change of use
- Apply IAS 16, IAS 2 or IFRS 16 as appropriate after date of change of use

Transfer from owner-occupied to investment property
- Apply IAS 16 or IFRS 16 (for property held by a lessee as right-of-use asset) up to date of change of use
- At date of change, property revalued to fair value
- At date of change, any difference between the carrying amount under IAS 16 or IFRS 16 and its fair value is treated as a revaluation under IAS 16

5.5 Disposals

Derecognise (eliminate from the statement of financial position) an investment property on disposal or when it is permanently withdrawn from use and no future economic benefits are expected from its disposal.

Any **gain or loss** on disposal is the difference between the net disposal proceeds and the carrying amount of the asset. It should generally be **recognised as income or expense in profit or loss**.

Compensation from third parties for investment property that was impaired, lost or given up shall be recognised in profit or loss when the compensation becomes receivable.

5.6 Disclosure requirements

These relate to:

- Choice of fair value model or cost model
- Criteria for classification as investment property
- Assumptions in determining fair value
- Use of independent professional valuer (encouraged but not required)
- Rental income and expenses
- Any restrictions or obligations

5.6.1 Fair value model – additional disclosures

An entity that adopts this model must also disclose a **reconciliation** of the carrying amount of the investment property at the beginning and end of the period.

IFRS 13 *Fair Value Measurement* disclosures are also relevant where the fair value model is used.

5.6.2 Cost model – additional disclosures

These relate mainly to the depreciation method as well as a **reconciliation** of the carrying amount of the investment property at the beginning and end of the period. In addition, an entity which adopts the cost model **must disclose the fair value** of the investment property.

5.7 Decision tree

The decision tree below summarises which IFRSs apply to various kinds of property.

Exam focus point

Learn this decision tree – it will help you tackle most of the problems you are likely to meet in the exam!

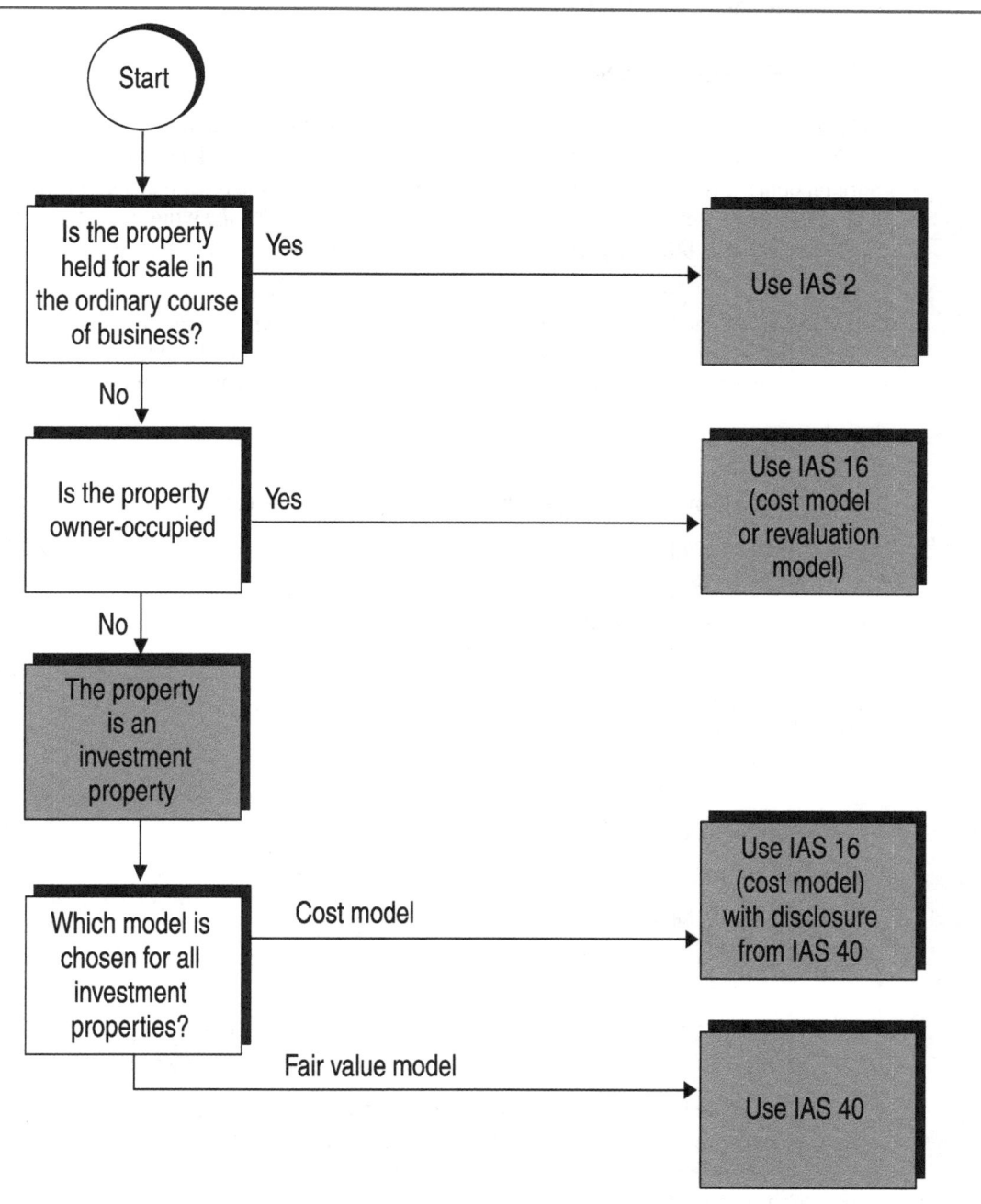

6 IAS 2 *Inventories*

You have studied inventories in your earlier studies, so this section is a quick revision of that.

> **FAST FORWARD**
>
> IAS 2 requires that inventories are measured at the lower of cost and net realisable value

6.1 Introduction

In most businesses the value put on inventory is an important factor in the determination of profit. Inventory valuation is, however, a highly subjective exercise and consequently there is a wide variety of different methods used in practice.

6.2 IAS 2 *Inventories*

IAS 2 lays out the required accounting treatment for inventories. The major area of contention is the cost **value of inventory** to be recorded. This is recognised as an asset of the entity until the related revenues are recognised (ie the item is sold) at which point the inventory is recognised as an expense (ie cost of sales). Part or all of the cost of inventories may also be expensed if a write-down to **net realisable value** is necessary. The IAS also provides guidance on the cost formulas that are used to assign costs to inventories.

In other words, the fundamental accounting assumption of **accruals** requires costs to be matched with associated revenues. In order to achieve this, costs incurred for goods which remain unsold at the year end must be carried forward in the statement of financial position and matched against future revenues.

6.3 Scope

The following items are **excluded** from the scope of the standard.

- Work in progress under **long-term contracts** (covered by IFRS 15 *Revenue from Contracts with Customers*, see Chapter 21)
- **Financial instruments** (ie shares, bonds)
- **Biological assets**

6.4 Definitions

The following definitions are important.

Key terms

- **Inventories** are assets:
    - Held for sale in the ordinary course of business;
    - In the process of production for such sale; or
    - In the form of materials or supplies to be consumed in the production process or in the rendering of services.
- **Net realisable value** is the estimated selling price in the ordinary course of business less the estimated costs of completion and the estimated costs necessary to make the sale. (IAS 2)
- **Fair value** is the price that would be received to sell an asset or paid to transfer a liability in an orderly transaction between market participants at the measurement date. (IFRS 13)

Inventories can **include** any of the following:

- **Goods purchased and held for resale**, eg goods held for sale by a retailer, or land and buildings held for resale
- **Finished goods** produced

- **Work in progress** being produced
- Materials and supplies awaiting use in the production process (**raw materials**)

6.5 Measurement of inventories

The standard states that '**Inventories should be measured at the lower of cost and net realisable value.**'

> **Exam focus point**
>
> This is a very important rule and you will be expected to apply it in the exam.

6.6 Cost of inventories

The cost of inventories will consist of all costs of:

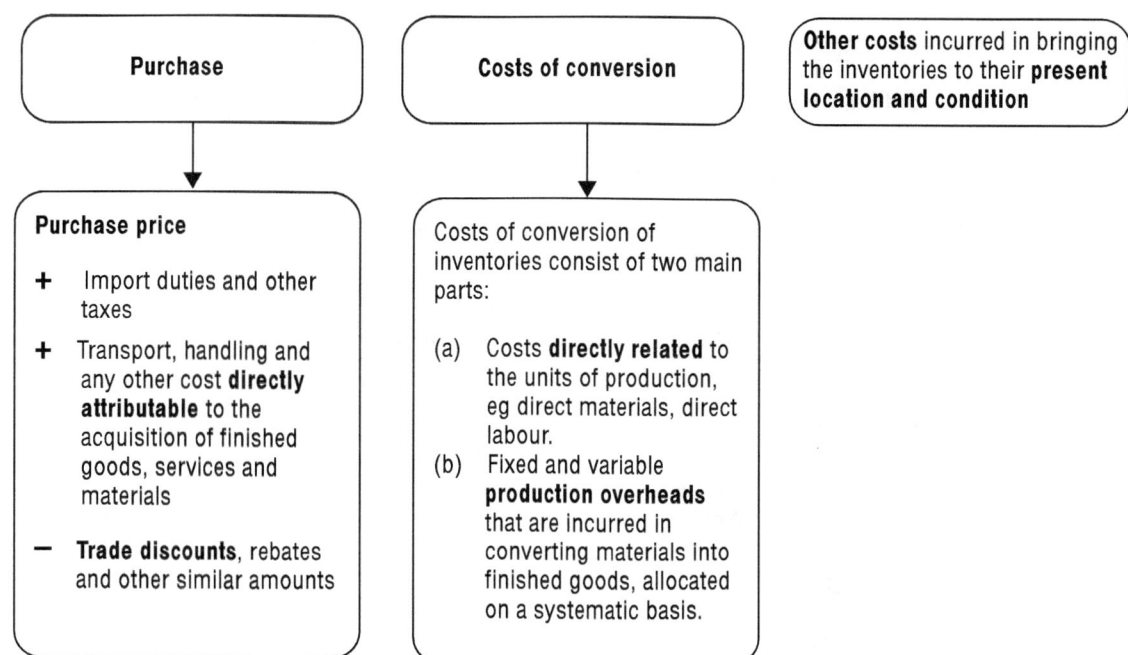

You may have come across the terms 'fixed production overheads' or 'variable production overheads' elsewhere in your studies. The standard defines them as follows.

> **Key terms**
>
> - **Fixed production overheads** are those indirect costs of production that remain relatively constant regardless of the volume of production, eg the cost of factory management and administration.
> - **Variable production overheads** are those indirect costs of production that vary directly, or nearly directly, with the volume of production, eg indirect materials and labour. (IAS 2)

The standard emphasises that fixed production overheads must be allocated to items of inventory on the basis of the **normal capacity of the production facilities**. This is an important point.

(a) **Normal capacity** is the expected achievable production based on the average over several periods/seasons, under normal circumstances.

(b) The above figure should take account of the capacity lost through **planned maintenance**.

(c) If it approximates to the normal level of activity then the **actual level of production** can be used.

(d) **Low production** or **idle plant** will **not** result in a higher fixed overhead allocation to each unit.

(e) **Unallocated overheads** must be recognised as an expense in the period in which they were incurred.

(f) When production is **abnormally high**, the fixed production overhead allocated to each unit will be reduced, so avoiding inventories being stated at more than cost.

(g) The allocation of variable production overheads to each unit is based on the **actual use** of production facilities.

6.6.1 Costs not included

The standard lists types of cost which **would not be included** in cost of inventories. Instead, they should be recognised as an **expense** in the period they are incurred.

(a) **Abnormal amounts** of wasted materials, labour or other production costs

(b) **Storage costs** (except costs which are necessary in the production process before a further production stage)

(c) **Administrative overheads** not incurred to bring inventories to their present location and conditions

(d) **Selling costs**

6.6.2 Techniques for the measurement of cost

Two techniques are mentioned by the standard, both of which produce results which **approximate to cost**, and so both of which may be used for convenience.

(a) **Standard costs** are set up to take account of normal production values: amount of raw materials used, labour time etc. They are reviewed and revised on a regular basis.

(b) **Retail method** is often used in the retail industry where there is a large turnover of inventory items, which nevertheless have similar profit margins. The only practical method of inventory valuation may be to take the total selling price of inventories and deduct an overall average profit margin, thus reducing the value to an approximation of cost. The percentage will take account of reduced price lines. Sometimes different percentages are applied on a department basis.

6.7 Cost formulae

Cost of inventories should be assigned by **specific identification** of their individual costs for:

(a) Items that are **not ordinarily interchangeable**
(b) Goods or services produced and segregated for **specific projects**

Specific costs should be attributed to individual items of inventory when they are segregated for a specific project, but not where inventories consist of a large number of interchangeable (ie identical or very similar) items. In the latter case the rule is as specified below.

6.7.1 Interchangeable items

Rule to learn

> The cost of inventories should be assigned by using the **first-in, first-out (FIFO)** or **weighted average** cost formulas. The LIFO formula (last in, first out) is **not permitted** by IAS 2.

You should be familiar with these methods from your earlier studies. Under the weighted average cost method, a recalculation can be made after each purchase, **or alternatively only at the period end**.

6.8 Net realisable value (NRV)

As a general rule assets should not be carried at amounts greater than those expected to be realised from their sale or use. In the case of inventories this amount could fall below cost when items are **damaged or become obsolete**, or where the **costs to completion have increased** in order to make the sale.

In fact we can identify the principal situations in which **NRV is likely to be less than cost**, ie where there has been:

(a) An **increase in costs** or a **fall in selling price**
(b) A **physical deterioration** in the condition of inventory
(c) **Obsolescence** of products
(d) A decision as part of the company's marketing strategy to manufacture and sell products at a **loss**
(e) **Errors in production or purchasing**

A write down of inventories would normally take place on an item by item basis, but similar or related items may be **grouped together**. This grouping together is acceptable for, say, items in the same product line, but it is not acceptable to write down inventories based on a whole classification (eg finished goods) or a whole business.

The assessment of NRV should take place **at the same time** as estimates are made of selling price, using the most reliable information available. Fluctuations of price or cost should be taken into account if they relate directly to **events after the reporting period,** which confirm conditions existing at the end of the period.

The reasons why inventory is held must also be taken into account. Some inventory, for example, may be held to satisfy a firm contract and its NRV will therefore be the **contract price**. Any additional inventory of the same type held at the period end will, in contrast, be assessed according to general sales prices when NRV is estimated.

Net realisable value must be reassessed at the end of each period and compared again with cost. If the NRV has risen for inventories held over the end of more than one period, then the previous write down must be **reversed** to the extent that the inventory is then valued at the lower of cost and the new NRV. This may be possible when selling prices have fallen in the past and then risen again.

On occasion a write down to NRV may be of such size, incidence or nature that it must be **disclosed separately**.

6.9 Recognition as an expense

The following treatment is required **when inventories are sold**:

(a) The **carrying amount** is recognised as an expense in the period in which the related revenue is recognised.
(b) The amount of any **write-down of inventories** to NRV and all losses of inventories are recognised as an expense in the period the write-down or loss occurs.
(c) The amount of any **reversal of any write-down of inventories**, arising from an increase in NRV, is recognised as a reduction in the amount of inventories recognised as an expense in the period in which the reversal occurs.

6.10 Consistency – different cost formulas for inventories

IAS 2 allows two cost formulas (FIFO or weighted average cost) for inventories that are ordinarily interchangeable or are not produced and segregated for specific projects. The issue is whether an entity may use different cost formulas for different types of inventories.

IAS 2 provides that an entity should use **the same cost formula for all inventories having similar nature and use to the entity.** For inventories with different nature or use (for example, certain commodities used in one business segment and the same type of commodities used in another business segment), different cost formulas may be justified. A difference in geographical location of inventories (and in the respective tax rules), by itself, is not sufficient to justify the use of different cost formulas.

6.11 Sustainability and IAS 2

Changes to environmental legislation may result in obsolescence or changes to existing products which may impact inventory valuation.

PART C ACCOUNTING AND REPORTING TECHNIQUES

Chapter roundup

- You must learn the IASB *Conceptual Framework* **definition of an asset**: a present economic resource controlled by the entity as a result of past events. An economic resource is a right that has the potential to produce economic benefits.
- This definition was changed when the *Conceptual Framework* was revised in 2018. It still ties in closely with the definitions produced by **other standard-setters**, particularly FASB (USA) and FRC (UK).
- The definition has three important characteristics:
  - **Right**
  - **Potential to produce economic benefits**
  - **Control**
- You should already be familiar with many standards relating to **non-current assets** from Papers 1 and 11. If not, go back to your earlier study material.
  - IAS 16 *Property, Plant and Equipment*
  - IAS 20 *Accounting for Government Grants and Disclosure of Government Assistance*
  - IAS 23 *Borrowing Costs*
- **IAS 36 *Impairment of Assets*** is a topical area and it affects both intangible and tangible non-current assets.
- Impairment is determined by comparing the carrying amount of the asset with its **recoverable amount**.
- The recoverable amount of an asset is the higher of the asset's **fair value less costs of disposal** and **its value in use**.
- Where the recoverable amount of a single asset cannot be estimated, the impairment test must be performed for the cash-generating unit to which that asset belongs.
- IAS 40 *Investment Property* defines investment property as property **held to earn rentals or for capital appreciation** or both, rather than for:
  - Use in production or supply of goods or services
  - Sale in the ordinary course of business.
- Entities can choose between:
  - A **fair value model**, with fair value measured in accordance with IFRS 13 and changes in fair value being recognised in profit or loss
  - A **cost model** – the treatment most commonly used under IAS 16
- IAS 2 requires that inventories are measured at the lower of cost and net realisable value.

Quick quiz

1. How does the IASB *Conceptual Framework* define an asset?
2. How might a non-current asset be defined?
3. Define an impairment.
4. How is value in use calculated?
5. What is a cash-generating unit?
6. Investment property **must** be valued at fair value. True or false?

Answers to quick quiz

1. An asset is a present economic resource controlled by the entity as a result of past event
2. One intended for use on a continuing basis in the company's activities.
3. A fall in the value of an asset, so that its recoverable amount is now less than its carrying amount.
4. The present value of estimated future cash flows generated by the asset, including its estimated net disposal value (if any).
5. The smallest identifiable group of assets for which independent cash flows can be identified and measured.
6. False, it can be valued at cost or fair value.

PART C   ACCOUNTING AND REPORTING TECHNIQUES

End of chapter question

NCH (AIA May 2006)

NCH is a pharmaceutical company which has a factory in Ireland the sole activity of which is the manufacture of a popular drug. NCH has patents which ensure that it has been the sole manufacturer of this drug and the company has priced the drug accordingly and has enjoyed high levels of profit.

However, NCH's sole manufacturing rights are currently being challenged in the courts, and it now looks probable that the company will lose its protection which was due to run until the end of 20X8. This will reduce not only the number of units of this drug the company will be able to sell but also the selling price it will be able to charge.

The net assets employed in the Irish factory as at 31 March 20X6 were:

	Carrying amount €	Fair Value less costs of disposal €
Net assets	131,500,000	115,144,500
Apportioned head office assets	850,000	150,000
	132,350,000	115,294,500

The scrap value of the net assets employed in the manufacturing unit is estimated to be €1,000,000 as at 31 March 20X9.

The following figures come from the company's internal budgets for the drug:

Budgets for the year ended 31 March	20X7	20X8	20X9
Sales in units			
– estimated as at end of 20X4	1,500,000	1,650,000	1,700,000
– estimated as at end of 20X5	1,500,000	500,000	500,000
Unit costs and revenues	€	€	€
– estimated as at end of 20X4	40.00	40.00	40.00
– estimated as at end of 20X5	40.00	35.00	30.00
Materials	(18.00)	(18.00)	(18.00)
Other production costs	(4.20)	(4.20)	(4.20)
Apportioned head office costs	(1.80)	(1.80)	(1.80)
Income per unit (20X4 estimates)	16.00	11.00	6.00
Income per unit (20X5 estimates)	16.00	6.00	1.00
Discount rate for equivalent level of risk	5%	5%	5%
Expected rate of inflation	3%	3%	4%
Real cost of capital	8.15%	8.15%	9.20%

Required

(a) Calculate the values necessary for the impairment review as at 31 March 20X6 for the Irish factory.
(14 marks)

(b) Advise as to whether the carrying value of the factory should be revised, the new carrying amount and the amount of any impairment loss. **(3 marks)**

(c) Advise on the way in which an impairment loss should be treated in the following circumstances:

   (i) The asset was previously revalued; and **(3 marks)**
   (ii) The impairment loss cannot be allocated to a particular non-current asset. **(5 marks)**

(Total 25 marks)

Intangible non-current assets

Topic list	Syllabus reference
1 IAS 38 *Intangible Assets*	LO3
2 Goodwill and IFRS 3	LO2 and LO3

Introduction

We begin our examination of intangible non-current assets with a discussion of IAS 38.

Goodwill and its treatment is a controversial area, as is the accounting for items similar to goodwill, such as brands. Goodwill is very important in **group financial statements**.

PART C   ACCOUNTING AND REPORTING TECHNIQUES

1 IAS 38 *Intangible Assets*

The objectives of the standard are:

(a) To establish the criteria for when an intangible asset may or should be **recognised**
(b) To specify how intangible assets should be **measured**
(c) To specify the **disclosure requirements** for intangible assets

It applies to all intangible assets with certain **exceptions**: deferred tax assets (IAS 12 *Income Taxes*), leases that fall within the scope of IFRS 16 *Leases*, financial assets, insurance contracts, assets arising from employee benefits (IAS 19 *Employee Benefits*), non-current assets held for sale and mineral rights and exploration and extraction costs for minerals etc (although intangible assets used to develop or maintain these rights are covered by the standard). Also, it does **not** apply to goodwill acquired in a business combination, which is dealt with under IFRS 3 *Business Combinations*.

1.1 Definition and recognition of an intangible asset

FAST FORWARD

> **Intangible assets** are defined by **IAS 38** as non-monetary assets without physical substance. They must be:
>
> – **Identifiable**
> – **Controlled** as a result of a past event
> – Expected to provide **future economic benefits**
>
> An intangible asset is recognised in the financial statements where:
>
> – It is probable that future economic benefits attributable to the asset will flow to the entity; and
> – The cost can be measured reliably.

The definition of an intangible asset is a key aspect of the standard because the rules for deciding whether or not an intangible asset is **recognised** in the financial statements of an entity are based on the definition of what an intangible asset is.

Key term

> An **intangible asset** is an identifiable non-monetary asset without physical substance. The asset must be a resource:
>
> (a) Controlled by the entity as a result of events in the past
> (b) From which future economic benefits are expected to flow

Examples of items that might be considered as intangible assets include computer software, patents, copyrights, motion picture films, customer lists, franchises and fishing rights. An item should not be recognised as an intangible asset, however, unless it **fully meets the definition** in the standard. The guidelines go into great detail on this matter.

You should note that the definitions used in IAS 38 are not consistent with the generally definition of an asset provided by the *Conceptual Framework*. The *Conceptual Framework* only requires that there is a 'potential to produce' economic benefits, whereas IAS 38 requires 'expected future economic benefits'. The criterial under IAS 38 is therefore stricter than that in the *Conceptual Framework*.

1.1.1 Intangible asset: Must be identifiable

An intangible asset must be identifiable (in order to distinguish it from goodwill).

(a) It must be separable, ie capable of being sold separately from the entity's other operations; or
(b) It must arise from contractual or other legal rights, even if those legal rights cannot be sold separately from the entity owning them.

1.1.2 Intangible asset: Control by the entity

Another element of the definition of an intangible asset is that it must be under the control of the entity as a result of a past event. The entity must therefore be able to enjoy the future economic benefits from the asset, and prevent the access of others to those benefits. A **legally enforceable right** is evidence of such control, but is not always a **necessary** condition.

(a) Control over **technical knowledge or know-how** only exists if it is protected by a **legal right**.

(b) The skill of employees, arising out of the benefits of **training costs**, are most unlikely to be recognisable as an intangible asset, because an entity does not control the future actions of its staff.

(c) Similarly, **market share and customer loyalty** cannot normally be intangible assets since an entity cannot control the actions of its customers.

1.1.3 Intangible asset: Future economic benefits

The requirement to provide future economic benefits forms part of the definition of an intangible asset and is also one of the recognition criteria relevant to an intangible asset.

Rule to learn

> An intangible asset should be recognised if, and only if **both** the following are true:
>
> (a) It is probable that the **future economic benefits** that are attributable to the asset will **flow to the entity**.
>
> (b) The **cost can be measured reliably**

Economic benefits may come from the **sale** of products or services, or from a **reduction in expenditures** (cost savings).

Management has to exercise its judgement in assessing the degree of certainty attached to the flow of economic benefits to the entity. External evidence is best.

1.2 Application of definition and recognition criteria to internally generated assets

FAST FORWARD

> **Internally generated goodwill** cannot be recognised as an asset but other internally generated assets may be, eg R & D.

Before we go on to consider the 'reliable measurement' of the cost of an intangible asset, we shall apply the above definition and the first of the recognition criteria to some specific (and commonly examined) internally generated intangible assets.

1.2.1 Internally generated goodwill

Rule to learn

> Internally generated goodwill may **not** be recognised as an **asset**.

The standard deliberately precludes recognition of internally generated goodwill because it is not an identifiable resource that can be measured reliably at cost.

1.2.2 Research

Research activities by definition do not meet the criteria for recognition under IAS 38. This is because, at the research stage of a project, it cannot be certain that future economic benefits will probably flow to the entity from the project. There is too much uncertainty about the likely success or otherwise of the project. **Research costs should therefore be recognised as an expense in profit or loss as they are incurred.**

Examples of research costs

(a) Activities aimed at obtaining new knowledge

(b) The search for, evaluation and final selection of, applications of research findings or other knowledge

(c) The search for alternatives for materials, devices, products, processes, systems or services

(d) The formulation, design evaluation and final selection of possible alternatives for new or improved materials, devices, products, systems or services

1.2.3 Development

Development costs **should be recognised** as intangible assets provided that all the following 'PIRATE' criteria can be demonstrated.

- **P**robable future economic benefits
- **I**ntention to complete and use/sell asset
- **R**esources adequate and available to complete and use/sell asset
- **A**bility to use/sell the asset
- **T**echnical feasibility of completing asset for use/sale
- **E**xpenditure can be measured reliably

In contrast with research costs, development costs are incurred at a later stage in a project, and the probability of success should be more apparent. Examples of development costs include the following.

(a) The design, construction and testing of pre-production or pre-use prototypes and models

(b) The design of tools, jigs, moulds and dies involving new technology

(c) The design, construction and operation of a pilot plant that is not of a scale economically feasible for commercial production

(d) The design, construction and testing of a chosen alternative for new or improved materials, devices, products, processes, systems or services

1.2.4 Other internally generated assets

The standard **prohibits** the recognition of **internally generated brands, mastheads, publishing titles and customer lists** and similar items as intangible assets. These all fail to meet one or more (in some cases all) the definition and recognition criteria and in some cases are probably indistinguishable from internally generated goodwill.

13: INTANGIBLE NON-CURRENT ASSETS

1.3 Initial measurement

FAST FORWARD

Intangible assets should initially be measured at cost, but subsequently they can be carried at **cost or at a fair value** measured in accordance with IFRS 13 *Fair Value Measurement*.

An intangible asset is initially measured at cost. The application of this depends on how the asset was acquired or generated:

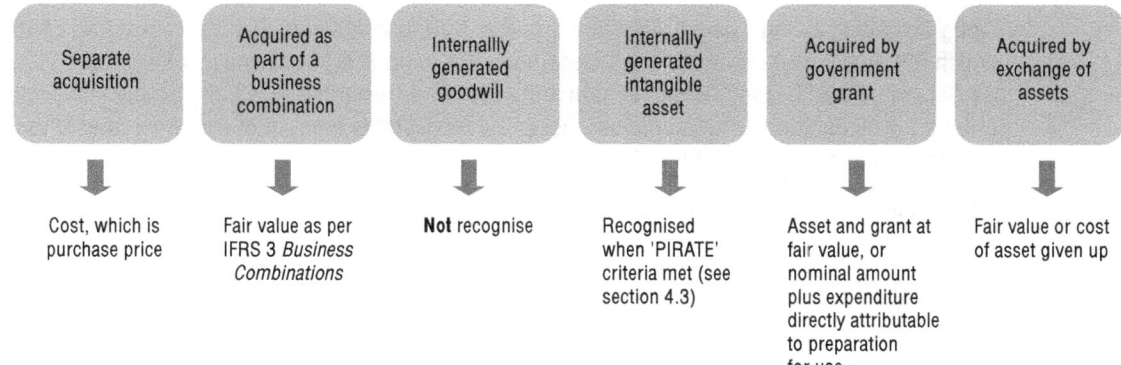

1.3.1 Separately acquired assets

If an intangible asset is **acquired separately**, its cost can usually be measured reliably as its purchase price (including incidental costs of purchase such as legal fees, and any costs incurred in getting the asset ready for use).

1.3.2 Assets acquired as part of a business combination

When an intangible asset is acquired as **part of a business combination** (ie an acquisition or takeover), the cost of the intangible asset is its fair value at the date of the acquisition.

IFRS 3 explains that the fair value of intangible assets acquired in business combinations can normally be measured with sufficient reliability to be **recognised separately** from goodwill.

IFRS 13 should be applied in establishing the fair value of assets acquired as part of a business combination (see Chapter 11).

1.3.3 Internally generated intangible assets

The cost of an internally generated intangible asset should comprise only those costs that can be **directly attributed** or allocated on a reasonable and consistent basis to creating, producing or preparing the asset for its intended use. The principles underlying the costs which may or may not be included are similar to those for other than non-current assets and inventory.

The cost of an internally operated intangible asset is the sum of the **expenditure incurred from the date when** the intangible asset first **meets the recognition criteria**. If, as often happens, considerable costs have already been recognised as expenses before management could demonstrate that the criteria have been met, this earlier expenditure should not be retrospectively recognised at a later date as part of the cost of an intangible asset.

1.3.4 Exchange of assets

If one intangible asset is exchanged for another, the cost of the intangible asset is measured at fair value unless:

(a) The exchange transaction lacks commercial substance; or
(b) The fair value of neither the asset received nor the asset given up can be measured reliably.

Otherwise, its cost is measured at the carrying amount of the asset given up.

1.3.5 Acquired by government grant

In accordance with IAS 20 *Accounting for Government Grants and Disclosure of Government Assistance*, intangible assets acquired by way of government grant and the grant itself may be recorded initially either at cost (which may be zero) or fair value.

| Question | Recognition criteria |

Doug Co is developing a new production process. During 20X3, expenditure incurred was $100,000, of which $90,000 was incurred before 1 December 20X3 and $10,000 between 1 December 20X3 and 31 December 20X3. Doug Co can demonstrate that, at 1 December 20X3, the production process met the criteria for recognition as an intangible asset. The recoverable amount of the know-how embodied in the process is estimated to be $50,000.

How should the expenditure be treated?

Answer

At the end of 20X3, the production process is recognised as an intangible asset at a cost of $10,000. This is the expenditure incurred since the date when the recognition criteria were met, that is 1 December 20X3. As the estimated recoverable amount of at $50,000 is greater than cost, no impairment loss need be recognised. The $90,000 expenditure incurred before 1 December 20X3 is expensed, because the recognition criteria were not met. It will never form part of the cost of the production process recognised in the statement of financial position.

1.4 Recognition of an expense

All expenditure related to an intangible which does not meet the criteria for recognition either as an identifiable intangible asset or as goodwill arising on an acquisition should be **expensed as incurred**. IAS 38 gives examples of such expenditure.

- Start up costs
- Training costs
- Advertising costs
- Business relocation costs

Prepaid costs for services, for example advertising or marketing costs for campaigns that have been prepared but not launched, can still be recognised as a **prepayment**.

If costs have been recognised as an expense in profit or loss in previous financial statements, they may not subsequently be recognised as part of the cost of the asset.

1.5 Subsequent measurement of intangible assets

The standard allows two methods of valuation for intangible assets after they have been first recognised.

Cost model	Carry asset at cost less accumulated amortisation and impairment losses (IAS 38, para. 74)
Revaluation model	Carry asset at revalued amount, fair value amount less subsequent accumulated amortisation and impairment losses (IAS 38, para. 75)

A number of rules apply where the revaluation model is applied:

(a) The fair value must be able to be measured reliably with reference to an **active market** in that type of asset.

(b) The **entire class** of intangible assets of that type must be revalued at the same time (to prevent selective revaluations).

(c) If an intangible asset in a class of revalued intangible assets cannot be revalued because there is **no active market** for this asset, the asset should be carried at its **cost less any accumulated amortisation and impairment losses**.

(d) Revaluations should be made with such **regularity** that the carrying amount does not differ from that which would be determined using fair value at the year end.

Point to note

> This treatment is **not** available for the **initial recognition** of intangible assets. This is because the cost of the asset must be reliably measured.

The guidelines state that it is **uncommon for an active market** to exist for an intangible asset; therefore the revaluation model will usually not be available. For example, although copyrights, publishing rights and film right can be sold, each has a unique sale value. In such cases, revaluation to fair value would be inappropriate. A fair value might be obtainable however for assets such as fishing rights or quotas or taxi cab licences.

1.5.1 Accounting for a revaluation

Where an intangible asset is revalued upwards to a fair value, the amount of the revaluation should be recognised in other comprehensive income and carried in equity under the heading of a **revaluation surplus**.

However, if a revaluation surplus is a **reversal of a revaluation decrease** that was previously recognised as an expense in profit or loss, the increase is recognised in profit or loss.

Where the carrying amount of an intangible asset is revalued downwards, the amount of the **downward revaluation** should be charged as an expense against income, unless the asset has previously been revalued upwards. A revaluation decrease should be first charged against any previous revaluation surplus in respect of that asset.

Question — Downward valuation

An intangible asset is measured by a company at fair value. The asset was revalued by $400 in 20X3, and there is a revaluation surplus of $400 in the statement of financial position. At the end of 20X4, the asset is valued again, and a downward valuation of $500 is required.

Required

State the accounting treatment for the downward revaluation.

Answer

In this example, the downward valuation of $500 is first set against the revaluation surplus of $400. The revaluation surplus will be reduced to 0 and a charge of $100 made as an expense in 20X4.

When the revaluation model is used, and an intangible asset is revalued upwards, the cumulative revaluation **surplus may be transferred to retained earnings** when the surplus is eventually realised. The surplus would be realised when the asset is disposed of. However, the surplus may also be realised over time as the **asset is used** by the entity. The amount of the surplus realised each year is the difference between the amortisation charge for the asset based on the revalued amount of the asset, and the amortisation that would be charged on the basis of the asset's historical cost. The realised surplus in such case should be transferred from revaluation surplus directly to retained earnings in the statement of changes in equity, and should not be recognised in profit or loss.

1.6 Amortisation of intangible assets

An entity should **assess** the useful life of an intangible asset, which may be **finite or indefinite**. An intangible asset with a finite useful life should be amortised over its **expected useful life**, with the amortisation charge recognised in profit or loss.

1.6.1 Assessment of useful life

An intangible asset has an indefinite useful life when there is **no foreseeable limit** to the period over which the asset is expected to generate net cash inflows for the entity.

Many factors are considered in determining the useful life of an intangible asset, including: expected usage; typical product life cycles; technical, technological, commercial or other types of obsolescence; the stability of the industry; expected actions by competitors; the level of maintenance expenditure required; and legal or similar limits on the use of the asset, such as the expiry dates of related leases. Computer software and many other intangible assets normally have short lives because they are susceptible to technological obsolescence. However, uncertainty does not justify choosing a life that is unrealistically short.

The useful life of an intangible asset that arises from **contractual or other legal rights** should not exceed the period of the rights, but may be shorter depending on the period over which the entity expects to use the asset.

1.6.2 Residual value

The **residual value** of an intangible asset with a finite useful life is **assumed to be zero** unless a third party is committed to buying the intangible asset at the end of its useful life or unless there is an active market for that type of asset (so that its expected residual value can be measured) and it is probable that there will be a market for the asset at the end of its useful life.

1.6.3 Amortisation period and amortisation method

Amortisation should start when the asset is **available for use**. It should cease at the earlier of the date that the asset is classified **as held for sale** in accordance with IFRS 5 *Non-current Assets Held for Sale and Discontinued Operations* and the date that the asset is **derecognised**.

The amortisation method used should reflect the **pattern in which the asset's future economic benefits are consumed**. If such a pattern cannot be predicted reliably, the straight-line method should be used.

The amortisation period and the amortisation method used for an intangible asset with a finite useful life should be **reviewed at each financial year end**.

1.7 Intangible assets with indefinite useful lives

FAST FORWARD

> **Impairment** rules follow **IAS 36**. There are substantial disclosure requirements.

An intangible asset with an indefinite useful life **should not be amortised**, but in accordance with IAS 36 *Impairment of Assets* should be tested for impairment at least annually.

The useful life of an intangible asset that is not being amortised should be **reviewed each year** to determine whether it is still appropriate to assess its useful life as indefinite. Reassessing the useful life of an intangible asset as finite rather than indefinite is an indicator that the asset may be impaired and therefore it should be tested for impairment.

Question — Useful life

It may be difficult to establish the useful life of an intangible asset, and judgement will be needed. Consider how to determine the useful life of a **purchased** brand name and how to provide evidence that its useful life might in fact exceed 20 years.

Answer

Factors to consider would include the following:

(a) Legal protection of the brand name and the control of the entity over the (illegal) use by others of the brand name (ie control over pirating)
(b) Age of the brand name
(c) Status or position of the brand in its particular market
(d) Ability of the management of the entity to manage the brand name and to measure activities that support the brand name (eg advertising and PR activities)
(e) Stability and geographical spread of the market in which the branded products are sold
(f) Pattern of benefits that the brand name is expected to generate over time
(g) Intention of the entity to use and promote the brand name over time (as evidenced perhaps by a business plan in which there will be substantial expenditure to promote the brand name)

1.8 Disposals/retirements of intangible assets

An intangible asset should be eliminated from the statement of financial position when it is disposed of or when there is no further expected economic benefit from its future use. On disposal the gain or loss arising from the **difference between the net disposal proceeds and the carrying amount** of the asset should be taken to the statement of profit or loss and other comprehensive income as a gain or loss on disposal (ie treated as income or expense).

1.9 Disclosure requirements

The standard has fairly extensive disclosure requirements for intangible assets. The financial statements should disclose the **accounting policies** for intangible assets that have been adopted.

For **each class of intangible assets**, disclosure is required of the following:

- The **method of amortisation** used
- The **useful life** of the assets or the amortisation rate used
- The **gross carrying amount**, the **accumulated amortisation** and the **accumulated impairment losses** as at the beginning and the end of the period
- A **reconciliation of the carrying amount** as at the beginning and at the end of the period (additions, retirements/disposals, revaluations, impairment losses, impairment losses reversed, amortisation charge for the period, net exchange differences, other movements)
- The carrying amount of **internally generated intangible assets**

The financial statements should also disclose the following:

- In the case of intangible assets that are assessed as having a indefinite useful life, the carrying amounts and the reasons supporting that assessment
- For intangible assets acquired by way of a **government grant** and initially recognised at fair value, the **fair value initially recognised**, the **carrying amount** and whether they are subsequently measured under the cost model or the revaluation model

- The carrying amount, nature and remaining amortisation period of any intangible asset that is **material to the financial statements of the entity as a whole**
- The existence (if any) and amounts of intangible assets whose **title is restricted** and of intangible assets that have been **pledged as security** for liabilities
- The amount of any **commitments for the future acquisition of intangible assets**

Where intangible assets are accounted for at revalued amounts, disclosure is required of the following:

- The **effective date of the revaluation** (by class of intangible assets)
- The **carrying amount** of revalued intangible assets
- The carrying amount that would have been shown (by class of assets) **if the cost model had been used**, and the amount of amortisation that would have been charged
- The amount of any **revaluation surplus** on intangible assets, as at the beginning and end of the period, and movements in the surplus during the year (and any restrictions on the distribution of the balance to shareholders)

The financial statements should also disclose the amount of research and development expenditure that have been charged as expenses of the period.

IFRS 13 disclosures are also relevant where intangible assets are measured at fair value in accordance with that standard (see Chapter 11).

1.10 Sustainability and IAS 38

Intangible assets may be impacted by climate-related matters. The useful life of intangible assets may be impacted by strategic or regulatory changes which might result in increased amortisation or impairment. There may be additional research and development expenditures.

1.11 Section summary

- An intangible asset must be identifiable, ie separable or arising from contractual or other legal rights.
- An intangible asset should be recognised if, and only if, it is probable that future economic benefits will flow to the entity and the cost of the asset can be measured reliably.
- An asset is initially recognised at cost and subsequently carried either at cost or revalued amount.
- Costs that do not meet the recognition criteria should be expensed as incurred.
- An intangible asset with a finite useful life should be amortised over its useful life. An intangible asset with an indefinite useful life should not be amortised.

Question — List

As an aid to your revision, list the examples given in IAS 38 of activities that might be included in either research or development.

Answer

IAS 38 gives these examples.

Research

- Activities aimed at obtaining new knowledge
- The search for applications of research findings or other knowledge
- The search for product or process alternatives
- The formulation and design of possible new or improved product or process alternatives

Development

- The evaluation of product or process alternatives
- The design, construction and testing of pre-production prototypes and models
- The design of tools, jigs, moulds and dies involving new technology
- The design, construction and operation of a pilot plant that is not of a scale economically feasible for commercial production

Question — Project

Forkbender Co develops and manufactures exotic cutlery and has the following projects in hand.

	Project 1 $'000	Project 2 $'000	Project 3 $'000	Project 4 $'000
Deferred development Expenditure b/f 1.1.X8	280	450	–	–
Development expenditure Incurred during the year				
Salaries, wages and so on	35	29	60	20
Overhead costs	2	5	–	3
Materials and services	3	13	11	4
Patents and licences	1	2	–	–
Market research	–	10	2	–

Project 1 was originally expected to be highly profitable but this is now in doubt, since the scientist in charge of the project is now behind schedule, with the result that competitors are gaining ground.

Project 2: commercial production started during the year. Sales were 20,000 units in 20X8 and future sales are expected to be: 20X8 30,000 units; 20X9 60,000 units; 20Y0 40,000 units; 20Y1 30,000 units. There are no sales expected after 20Y1.

Project 3: these costs relate to a new project, which meets the criteria for deferral of expenditure and which is expected to last for three years.

Project 4 is another new project, involving the development of a 'loss leader', expected to raise the level of future sales.

The company's policy is to defer development costs, where permitted by IAS 38. Expenditure carried forward is written off evenly over the expected sales life of projects, starting in the first year of sale.

Required

Show how the above projects should be treated in the accounting statements of Forkbender Co for the year ended 31 December 20X8 in accordance with best accounting practice. Justify your treatment of each project.

Answer

Project 1 expenditure, including that relating to previous years, should all be written off in 20X8, as there is now considerable doubt as to the profitability of the project.

Since commercial production has started under Project 2 the expenditure previously deferred should now be amortised. This will be done over the estimated life of the product, as stated in the question.

Project 3: the development costs should be deferred.

Since *Project 4* is not expected to be profitable; its development costs should not be deferred.

STATEMENT OF FINANCIAL POSITION AS AT 31 DECEMBER 20X8 (extract)

	$'000
NON-CURRENT ASSETS	
Intangible assets	
Development costs (Note 2)	480

NOTES TO THE FINANCIAL STATEMENTS

1   Accounting policies

   Research and development

   Research and development expenditure is written off as incurred, except that development costs incurred on an individual project are carried forward when their future recoverability can be foreseen with reasonable assurance. Any expenditure carried forward is amortised over the period of sales from the related project.

2   Development costs

	$'000	$'000
Balance brought forward 1 January 20X8		730
Development expenditure incurred during 20X8	188	
Development expenditure amortised during 20X8	438	
		(250)
Balance carried forward 31 December 20X8		480

Note. IAS 38 would not permit the inclusion of market research in deferred development costs. Market research costs might, however, be carried forward separately under the accruals principle.

Workings

	1	2	3	4	Total
	$'000	$'000	$'000	$'000	$'000
B/F	280	450			730
Salaries etc.	35		60	20	115
Overheads	2			3	5
Materials etc.	3		11	4	18
Patents etc.	1				1
C/F	0	(360)	(71)	–	(431)
Written off	321	*90	–	27	438

* **Note.** Calculated as 1/5 of carrying amount of the asset.

2 Goodwill and IFRS 3

FAST FORWARD

If a business has **goodwill**, it means that the value of the business is greater than the fair value of its identifiable net assets. The valuation of goodwill is extremely subjective and fluctuates constantly. For this reason, goodwill other than that acquired in a business combination is **not** shown as an asset in the statement of financial position.

Goodwill can be created in a number of different ways:

(a) By building up a **reputation** (by word of mouth perhaps) for high quality products or high standards of service

(b) By **responding promptly and helpfully** to queries and complaints from customers

(c) Through the **personality of the staff** and their attitudes to customers

13: INTANGIBLE NON-CURRENT ASSETS

The value of goodwill to a business might be **extremely significant**. However, goodwill is not usually recognised in the financial statements of a business at all, and we should not normally expect to find an amount for goodwill in its statement of financial position

2.1 Goodwill acquired in a business combination

FAST FORWARD

> When one entity **purchases another entity**, the purchaser and vendor will fix an agreed price which may include an element in respect of goodwill. The way in which goodwill is then valued is not an accounting problem, but a matter of agreement between the two parties.
>
> **Goodwill acquired in a business combination** is then carried in the statement of financial position as an intangible asset under the requirements of **IFRS 3**. It must be reviewed for impairment annually.

There is one exception to the general rule that goodwill has no objective valuation. This is **when a business is sold**.

When an entity purchases another entity, it will have to purchase not only its net assets, but is also likely to pay an additional amount which reflects the goodwill attributable to the business.

Exam focus point

> Goodwill acquired in a business combination is shown in the statement of financial position because its measurement results from a market transaction. It has no tangible substance, and so it is an **intangible non-current asset**.

2.2 How is goodwill measured?

When an entity is purchased, any goodwill acquired in the business combination must be recognised in the consolidated financial statements of the group. The goodwill recognised in the financial statements of the group will be initially measured as **the difference between the consideration transferred and the fair value of the identifiable net assets acquired**.

2.2.1 IFRS 3 Business Combinations

IFRS 3 covers the accounting treatment of goodwill acquired in a business combination.

Key term

> **Goodwill**. An asset representing future economic benefits arising from other assets acquired in a business combination that are not individually identified and separately recognised. (IFRS 3)

Goodwill acquired in a business combination is **recognised as an asset** and is initially measured at **cost**. Cost is the excess of the consideration paid to acquire the entity, plus the non-controlling interest less the net fair value of the acquiree's identifiable assets and liabilities.

Goodwill is subsequently measured **at cost less any accumulated impairment losses**. It is **not amortised**. Instead it is tested for impairment at least annually, in accordance with IAS 36 *Impairment of Assets*.

2.2.2 Goodwill and non-controlling interests

IFRS 3 views the **group as an economic entity**. This means that it treats **all provides of equity including non-controlling interests as shareholders in the group**, even if they re not shareholders in the parent.

Thus goodwill attributable to the non-controlling interest may be recognised. (See also Chapter 6.)

2.2.3 Bargain purchase

A bargain purchase arises when the fair value of the net assets acquired exceeds the consideration transferred plus non-controlling interest (see Chapter 6). This difference is sometimes called **negative goodwill**.

A bargain purchase might arise, for example, in a business combination that is a forced sale in which the seller is acting under compulsion. However, the recognition or measurement exceptions for particular items may also result in recognising a gain (or change the amount of a recognised gain) on a bargain purchase.

Before recognising a bargain purchase, the acquirer must reassess whether it has correctly identified all of the assets acquired and all of the liabilities assumed and must recognise any additional assets or liabilities that are identified in that review. The acquirer must then review the procedures used to measure the amounts this IFRS requires to be recognised at the acquisition date for all of the following:

(a) The identifiable assets acquired and liabilities assumed

(b) The non-controlling interest in the accquiree, if any

(c) For a business combination achieved in stages, the acquirer's previously held interest in the acquiree

(d) The consideration transferred

The purpose of this review is to ensure that the measurements appropriately reflect all the available information as at the acquisition date.

Any excess (ie, negative goodwill) remaining should be **recognised immediately in profit or loss**.

IFRS 3 requires extensive **disclosures** about goodwill acquired in business combinations. These include a **reconciliation** of the carrying amount of goodwill at the beginning and end of the period, showing separately:

(a) The gross amount and accumulated impairment losses at the beginning of the period
(b) Additional goodwill recognised during the period
(c) Impairment losses recognised during the period
(d) Net exchange differences arising during the period, and
(e) The gross amount and accumulated impairment losses at the end of the period

Question — Characteristics of goodwill

What are the main characteristics of goodwill which distinguish it from other intangible non-current assets? To what extent do you consider that these characteristics should affect the accounting treatment of goodwill? State your reasons.

Answer

Goodwill may be distinguished from other intangible non-current assets by reference to the following characteristics.

(a) It is incapable of realisation separately from the business as a whole.

(b) Its value has no reliable or predictable relationship to any costs which may have been incurred.

(c) Its value arises from various intangible factors such as skilled employees, effective advertising or a strategic location. These indirect factors cannot be valued.

(d) The value of goodwill may fluctuate widely according to internal and external circumstances over relatively short periods of time.

(e) The assessment of the value of goodwill is highly subjective.

It could be argued that, because goodwill is so different from other intangible non-current assets, it does not make sense to account for it in the same way. Thus the capitalisation and amortisation treatment would not be acceptable. Furthermore, because goodwill is so difficult to value, any valuation may be misleading, and it is best eliminated from the statement of financial position altogether. However, there are strong arguments for treating it like any other intangible non-current asset. This issue remains controversial.

13: INTANGIBLE NON-CURRENT ASSETS

Chapter roundup

- **Intangible assets** are defined by **IAS 38** as non-monetary assets without physical substance. They must be:
    - **Identifiable**
    - **Controlled** as a result of a past event
    - Expected to provide **future economic benefits**
- An intangible asset is recognised in the financial statements where:
    - It is probable that future economic benefits attributable to the asset will flow to the entity; and
    - The cost can be measured reliably.
- **Internally generated goodwill** cannot be recognised as an asset but other internally generated assets may be, eg R & D.
- Intangible assets should initially be measured at cost, but subsequently they can be carried at **cost or at a fair value** measured in accordance with IFRS 13 *Fair Value Measurement*.
- **Impairment** rules follow **IAS 36**. There are substantial disclosure requirements.
- If a business has **goodwill**, it means that the value of the business is greater than the fair value of its identifiable net assets. The valuation of goodwill is extremely subjective and fluctuates constantly. For this reason, goodwill other than that acquired in a business combination is **not** shown as an asset in the statement of financial position.
- When one entity **purchases another entity**, the purchaser and vendor will fix an agreed price which may include an element in respect of goodwill. The way in which goodwill is then valued is not an accounting problem, but a matter of agreement between the two parties.
- **Goodwill acquired in a business combination** is then carried in the statement of financial position as an intangible asset under the requirements of **IFRS 3**. It must be reviewed for impairment annually.

Quick quiz

1. Internally generated goodwill can be recognised. True or false?
2. How should research and development costs be treated under IAS 38?
3. When can a revaluation surplus on intangible assets be transferred to retained earnings?
4. Over what period should an intangible asset normally be amortised?
5. How should the gain or loss on the disposal of an intangible asset be calculated?
6. Why is it unusual to record goodwill as an asset in the financial statements?
7. What is goodwill acquired in a business combination?
8. What method of accounting for goodwill acquired in a business combination is required by IFRS 3?
9. Over what period should goodwill be amortised?
10. What treatment does IFRS 3 prescribe for a gain on a bargain purchase?

PART C   ACCOUNTING AND REPORTING TECHNIQUES

Answers to quick quiz

1. False
2.
   - Research costs are recognised as an expense in profit or loss as they are incurred
   - Development costs should be recognised as intangible assets if the criteria in Section 1.7.2 are met
3. When the surplus is eventually realised
4. Over its useful life, which may be finite or indefinite
5. The difference between the net disposal proceeds and the carrying value
6. The value of goodwill is usually inherent in the business but does not have an 'objective' value
7. The excess of the consideration transferred plus the non-controlling interest over the identifiable net assets acquired
8. Cost less accumulated impairment losses
9. Goodwill should not be amortised
10. Before recognising a gain, measurement procedures for assets and liabilities and for consideration must be reviewed. Any gain remaining is recognised in profit or loss immediately

End of chapter question

Grimsel (AIA November 2007)

(a) Explain what is meant by 'component depreciation' and its status under International Accounting Standards. **(3 marks)**

(b) Trin, a limited liability company, owns its business premises. It has just installed extensive specialised machinery and fittings in the premises. The estimated remaining useful life is ten years for the building and six years for the machinery and fittings. Trin knows that decommissioning the machinery and fittings in six years' time will cost around $910,000 at current prices.

Required

Explain and justify how Trin should account for the costs of decommissioning its machinery and fittings. **(3 marks)**

(c) Cozz, a limited liability company, has an asset, purchased on 1 November 20X2, which was reported in its statement of financial position as at 1 November 20X6 as follows:

	$
Cost	240,000
Accumulated depreciation	118,000
	122,000

The accumulated depreciation figure is made up as follows:

	$
Four years' depreciation based on the asset's estimated life of 12 years	80,000
Impairment recognised during the year ended 31 October 20X5	20,000
Impairment recognised during the year ended 31 October 20X6	18,000
	118,000

As at 31 October 20X7 there was no change to the estimate of this asset's economic life or residual value. The asset's recoverable amount was estimated to be $125,000 as at 31 October 20X7. Cozz reports this class of assets at historical cost.

13: INTANGIBLE NON-CURRENT ASSETS

Required

What charge will Cozz make in its statement of profit or loss and other comprehensive income for the year ended 31 October 20X7 for this asset and how will the asset be reported in the statement of financial position as at 31 October 20X7? **(6 marks)**

(d) The following is the summarised statement of financial position of Grimsel, a limited liability company, as at 31 October 20X7:

	$'000	$'000
ASSETS		
Non-current assets		
Property, plant and equipment		7,540
Current assets		
Inventory	2,230	
Receivables	4,120	
Cash	430	
		6,780
		14,320
LIABILITIES AND EQUITY		
Current liabilities		3,775
Non-current liabilities		12,500
Equity		
Issued share capital	5,000	
Accumulated losses	6,955	
		(1,955)
		14,320

Grimsel has been a very successful company in its time. However, a series of losses due to a declining share in the market and demands from its bankers for repayment of significant bank debt included in current and non-current liabilities have left its shareholders keen to sell.

Brenner, another limited liability company, operates in the same line of business as Grimsel. Brenner has been very successful and sees an opportunity to acquire Grimsel at a bargain price.

Brenner has successfully concluded negotiations with Grimsel and has agreed a price of $2,000,000 for all the issued share capital of Grimsel.

The following additional information is available:

(i) The values of all the assets and liabilities identified in Grimsel's statement of financial position were agreed as fair values for the purposes of the purchase with the exception of the following assets:

Fair values	$'000
Property, plant and equipment	8,000
Inventory	2,000
Receivables	3,710

(ii) Grimsel has a deferred income tax asset of $2,200,000. This is not shown in Grimsel's statement of financial position because it was unlikely that Grimsel would be able to recover this amount because of its continuing losses. Brenner is trading profitably in the same type of business and will be able to realise this benefit.

(iii) Grimsel has significant patents which were internally developed. These patents are still useful and a fair value of $1,000,000 has been established in accordance with IFRS 13.

PART C ACCOUNTING AND REPORTING TECHNIQUES

(iv) Brenner will also take over Grimsel's customer list. This is a sensitive area. While the customer list was not of much value to Grimsel, the directors of Brenner feel that it could be of significant value but wish to continue keeping it off the statement of financial position. The fair value of the customer list to Brenner has been measured at $1,500,000 in accordance with IFRS 13.

Required

Applying the rules in IFRS 3 calculate the amount of goodwill arising on the acquisition of Grimsel by Brenner. **(8 marks)**

(e) Summarise the guidance in IFRS 3 when goodwill turns out to be a negative. **(5 marks)**

(Total 25 marks)

Financial instruments

Topic list	Syllabus reference
1 Financial instruments	LO3
2 Presentation of financial instruments	LO3
3 Recognition and measurement of financial instruments	LO3
4 Impairment and uncollectability of financial assets	LO3
5 Embedded derivatives	LO3
6 Hedge accounting	LO3
7 Disclosure of financial instruments	LO3

Introduction

Financial instruments is a complex and controversial area. The numbers involved in financial instruments are often huge, but don't let this put you off. In this chapter we aim to simplify the topic as much as possible and to focus on the important issues.

The debate over **measurement and recognition** of financial instruments is very closely connected to the '**off balance sheet finance,** although the introduction of IFRS 9 has largely removed this issue.

1 Financial instruments

> **FAST FORWARD**
>
> Financial instruments can be very complex, particularly **derivative instruments**, although **primary instruments** are more straightforward.

1.1 Background

The dynamic nature of international financial markets has resulted in the widespread use of a variety of financial instruments. Prior to the issue of IAS 32 and IAS 39 (the forerunner of IFRS 9), many financial instruments were 'off balance sheet', being neither recognised nor disclosed in the financial statements while still exposing the shareholders to significant risks.

The IASB has developed the following standards in relation to financial instruments:

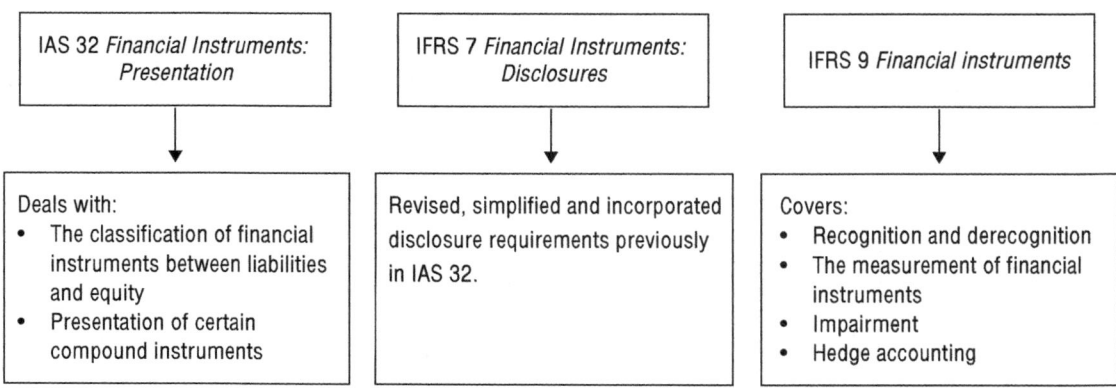

IAS 32 *Financial Instruments: Presentation*	IFRS 7 *Financial Instruments: Disclosures*	IFRS 9 *Financial instruments*
Deals with: • The classification of financial instruments between liabilities and equity • Presentation of certain compound instruments	Revised, simplified and incorporated disclosure requirements previously in IAS 32.	Covers: • Recognition and derecognition • The measurement of financial instruments • Impairment • Hedge accounting

1.2 Definitions

The most important definitions are relevant to all the standards.

> **FAST FORWARD**
>
> The important definitions to learn are:
> - **Financial asset**
> - **Financial liability**
> - **Equity instrument**

Key terms

Financial instrument. Any contract that gives rise to both a financial asset of one entity and a financial liability or equity instrument of another entity.

Financial asset. Any asset that is:

(a) Cash;

(b) An equity instrument of another entity;

(c) A contractual right to receive cash or another financial asset from another entity; or to exchange financial instruments with another entity under conditions that are potentially favourable to the entity; or

(d) A contract that will or may be settled in the entity's own equity instruments and is:

    (i) A non-derivative for which the entity is or may be obliged to receive a variable number of the entity's own equity instruments; or

    (ii) A derivative that will or may be settled other than by the exchange of a fixed amount of cash or another financial asset for a fixed number of the entity's own equity instruments.

Financial liability. Any liability that is:

(a) A contractual obligation:

    (i) To deliver cash or another financial asset to another entity; or

    (ii) To exchange financial instruments with another entity under conditions that are potentially unfavourable to the entity; or

(b) A contract that will or may be settled in the entity's own equity instruments and is:

    (i) A non-derivative for which the entity is or may be obliged to deliver a variable number of the entity's own equity instruments; or

    (ii) A derivative that will or may be settled other than by the exchange of a fixed amount of cash or another financial asset for a fixed number of the entity's own equity instruments.

Equity instrument. Any contract that evidences a residual interest in the assets of an entity after deducting all of its liabilities.

Fair value. The price that would be received to sell an asset or paid to transfer a liability in an orderly transaction between market participants at the measurement date.

Derivative. A financial instrument or other contract with all three of the following characteristics:

(a) Its value changes in response to the change in a specified interest rate, financial instrument price, commodity price, foreign exchange rate, index of prices or rates, credit rating or credit index, or other variable (sometimes called the 'underlying');

(b) It requires no initial net investment or an initial net investment that is smaller than would be required for other types of contracts that would be expected to have a similar response to changes in market factors; and

(c) It is settled at a future date.   (IAS 32, IFRS 9 and IFRS 13)

We should clarify some points arising from these definitions:

(a) A '**contract**' need not be in writing, but it must comprise an agreement that has 'clear economic consequences' and which the parties to it cannot avoid, usually because the agreement is enforceable in law.

(b) An '**entity**' here could be an individual, partnership, incorporated body or government agency.

1.2.1 Financial assets and liabilities

The definitions of **financial assets and financial liabilities** may seem rather circular, referring as they do to the terms financial asset and financial instrument. The point is that there may be a chain of contractual rights and obligations, but it will lead ultimately to the receipt or payment of cash **or** the acquisition or issue of an equity instrument.

Examples of **financial assets** include:	Examples of **financial liabilities** include
• Trade receivables	• Trade payables
• Options	• Debentures
• Investment in shares in another entity	• Redeemable preference shares
• Investment in debt	• Forward contracts standing at a loss

Financial instruments include both of the following.

(a) **Primary instruments**: eg receivables, payables and equity securities

(b) **Derivative (or secondary) instruments**: eg financial options, futures and forwards, interest rate swaps and currency swaps, **whether recognised or unrecognised**.

IAS 32 makes it clear that the following items are **not** financial instruments:

- **Physical assets**, eg inventories, property, plant and equipment, leased assets and intangible assets (patents, trademarks etc). Where a contract is expected to be satisfied by **physical** delivery (eg of wheat or gold), it is **not** a financial instrument. This is known as the 'normal purchase/sale exemption'.
- **Prepaid expenses**, deferred revenue and most warranty obligations
- Liabilities or assets that are **not contractual** in nature
- Contractual rights/obligations that **do not involve transfer of a financial asset**, eg commodity futures contracts, operating leases

Question — Why not?

Why do physical assets and prepaid expenses not qualify as financial instruments?

Answer

Refer to the definitions of financial assets and liabilities given above.

(a) **Physical assets**: control of these creates an opportunity to generate an inflow of cash or other assets, but it does not give rise to a present right to receive cash or other financial assets.

(b) **Prepaid expenses, etc**: the future economic benefit is the receipt of goods/services rather than the right to receive cash or other financial assets.

1.3 Derivatives

A **derivative** is a financial instrument that **derives** its value from the price or rate of an underlying item. Common **examples** of derivatives include the following:

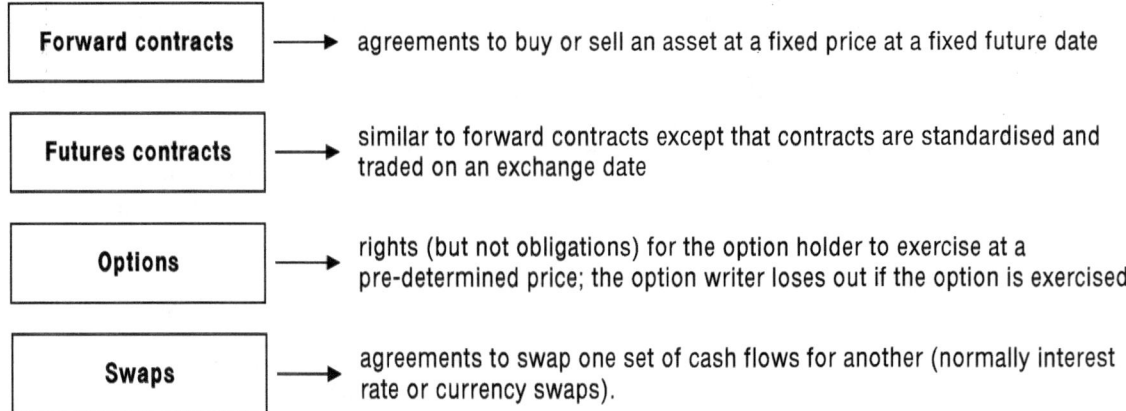

Forward contracts	agreements to buy or sell an asset at a fixed price at a fixed future date
Futures contracts	similar to forward contracts except that contracts are standardised and traded on an exchange date
Options	rights (but not obligations) for the option holder to exercise at a pre-determined price; the option writer loses out if the option is exercised
Swaps	agreements to swap one set of cash flows for another (normally interest rate or currency swaps).

The nature of derivatives often gives rise to **particular problems**:

The **value** of a derivative (and the amount at which it is eventually settled) depends on **movements** in an underlying item (such as an exchange rate). This means that settlement of a derivative can lead to a very different result from the one originally envisaged. A company which has derivatives is exposed to **uncertainty and risk** (potential for gain or loss) and this can have a very material effect on its financial performance, financial position and cash flows. Derivative contracts normally have **little or no initial cost**, although they are required to be recognised under IFRS 9.

1.4 Section summary

- Three accounting standards are relevant:
    - **IFRS 9** *Financial Instruments*
    - **IAS 32** *Financial Instruments: Presentation*
    - **IFRS 7** *Financial Instruments: Disclosures*
- The definitions of **financial asset, financial liability** and **equity instrument** are fundamental to the standards.
- Financial instruments include:
    - **Primary** instruments
    - **Derivative** instruments

2 Presentation of financial instruments

2.1 Objective

The objective of IAS 32 is to establish principles for presenting financial instruments as liabilities or equity and for offsetting financial assets and financial liabilities. It applies to the classification of financial instruments, from the perspective of the issuer, into financial assets, financial liabilities and equity instruments; the classification of related interest, dividends, losses and gains; and the circumstances in which financial assets and financial liabilities should be offset.

2.1.1 Scope

IAS 32 should be applied in the presentation and disclosure of **all types of financial instruments**, with the following exclusions:.

- Interests in subsidiaries (IFRS 10)
- Interests in associates (IAS 28)
- Interests in joint ventures (IAS 28, IFRS 11)
- Pensions and other post-retirement benefits (IAS 19)
- Insurance contracts (IFRS 4)
- Financial instruments, contracts and obligations under share-based payment transactions (IFRS 2)

2.2 Liabilities and equity

> **FAST FORWARD**
>
> A financial instrument must be classified as a **financial asset**, a **financial liability** or **equity** according to its **substance**.
>
> The critical feature of a financial liability is the **contractual obligation to deliver cash** or another financial asset.

The main principle of IAS 32 here is that financial instruments should be presented according to their **substance, not merely their legal form**.

In particular, entities which issue financial instruments should classify them (or their component parts) as **either financial liabilities or equity**, which depends on the following:

- The **substance of the contractual arrangement** on initial recognition
- The definitions of a **financial liability** and an **equity instrument**

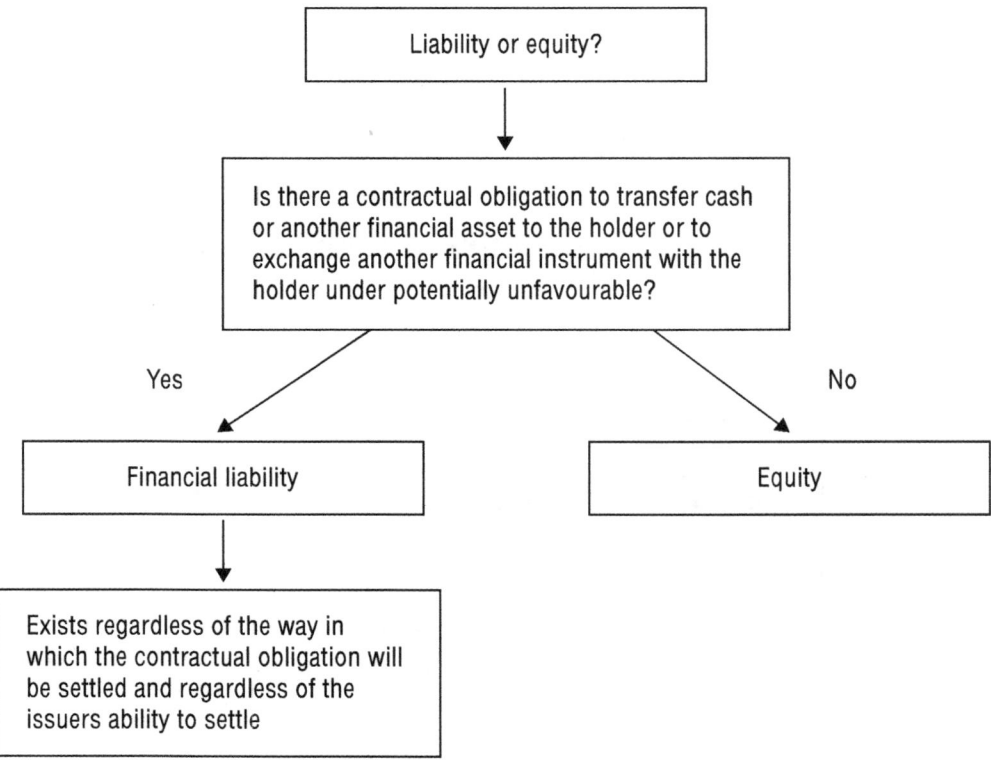

Although substance and legal form are often **consistent with each other**, this is not always the case. In particular, a financial instrument may have the legal form of equity, but in substance it is in fact a liability. Other instruments may combine features of both equity instruments and financial liabilities.

For example, many entities issue **preference shares** which must be **redeemed** by the issuer for a fixed (or determinable) amount at a fixed (or determinable) future date. Alternatively, the holder may have the right to require the issuer to redeem the shares at or after a certain date for a fixed amount. In such cases, the issuer has an **obligation**. Therefore, the instrument is a **financial liability** and should be classified as such.

The classification of the financial instrument is made when it is **first recognised** and this classification will continue until the financial instrument is removed from the entity's statement of financial position.

2.3 Contingent settlement provisions

An entity may issue a financial instrument where the way in which it is settled depends on:

(a) The occurrence or non-occurrence of uncertain future events; or
(b) The outcome of uncertain circumstances;

that are beyond the control of both the holder and the issuer of the instrument. For example, an entity might have to deliver cash instead of issuing equity shares. In this situation it is not immediately clear whether the entity has an equity instrument or a financial liability.

Such financial instruments should be classified as **financial liabilities** because the issuer does not have an unconditional right to avoid settlement by delivery of cash or another financial asset, unless the possibility of settlement is remote.

2.4 Settlement options

When a derivative financial instrument gives one party a **choice** over how it is settled (eg the issuer can choose whether to settle in cash or by issuing shares) the instrument is a **financial asset** or a **financial liability** unless **all the alternative choices** would result in it being an equity instrument.

2.5 Compound financial instruments

FAST FORWARD

> Compound instruments are split into equity and liability components and presented in the statement of financial position accordingly.

Some financial instruments contain both a liability and an equity element. In such cases, IAS 32 requires the component parts of the instrument to be **classified separately**, according to the substance of the contractual arrangement and the definitions of a financial liability and an equity instrument.

One of the most common types of compound instrument is **convertible debt**. This creates a primary financial liability of the issuer and grants an option to the holder of the instrument to convert it into an equity instrument (usually ordinary shares) of the issuer. This is the economic equivalent of the issue of conventional debt plus a warrant to acquire shares in the future.

The following approach should be adopted to calculate the initial carrying amount of the liability and equity elements

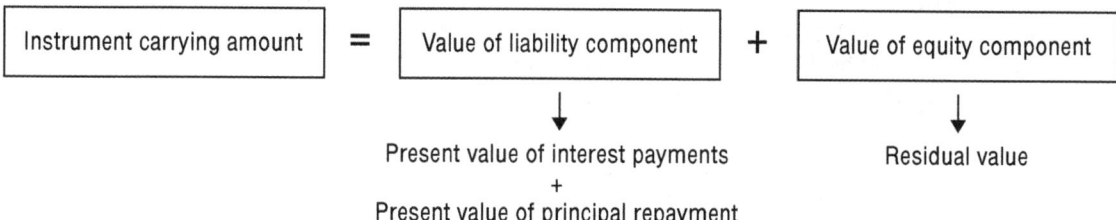

2.6 Example: Valuation of compound instruments

Rathbone Co issues 2,000 convertible bonds at the start of 20X2. The bonds have a three-year term, and are issued at par with a face value of $1,000 per bond, giving total proceeds of $2,000,000. Interest is payable annually in arrears at a nominal annual interest rate of 6%. Each bond is convertible at any time up to maturity into 250 common shares.

When the bonds are issued, the prevailing market interest rate for similar debt without conversion options is 9%. At the issue date, the market price of one common share is $3. The dividends expected over the three-year term of the bonds amount to 14c per share at the end of each year. The risk-free annual interest rate for a three-year term is 5%.

Required

What is the value of the equity component in the bond?

Solution

The liability component is valued first, and the difference between the proceeds of the bond issue and the fair value of the liability is assigned to the equity component. The present value of the liability component is calculated using a discount rate of 9%, the market interest rate for similar bonds having no conversion rights, as shown.

	$
Present value of the principal: $2,000,000 payable at the end of three years ($2m × 0.772)*	1,544,000
Present value of the interest: $120,000 payable annually in arrears for three years ($120,000 × 2.531)*	303,725
Total liability component	1,847,720
Equity component (balancing figure)	152,280
Proceeds of the bond issue	2,000,000

* These figures can be obtained from discount and annuity tables.

The split between the liability and equity components remains the same throughout the term of the instrument, even if there are changes in the **likelihood of the option being exercised**. This is because it is not always possible to predict how a holder will behave. The issuer continues to have an obligation to make future payments until conversion, maturity of the instrument or some other relevant transaction takes place.

Question

Definite variables

On 1 January 20X1, EFG issued 10,000 5% convertible bonds at their par value of $50 each. The bonds will be redeemed on 1 January 20X6. Each bond is convertible at the option of the holder at any time during the five year period. Interest on the bond will be paid annually in arrears.

The prevailing market interest rate for similar debt without conversion options at the date of issue was 6%.

At what value should the equity element of the financial instrument be recognised in the financial statements of EFG at the date of issue?

Answer

Top tip. The method to use here is to find the present value of the principal value of the bond, $500,000 (10,000 × $50) and the interest payments of $25,000 annually (5% × $500,000) at the market rate for non-convertible bonds of 6%, using discount factor tables. The difference between this total and the principal amount of $500,000 is the equity element.

	$
Present value of principal $500,000 × 0.747	373,500
Present value of interest $25,000 × 4.212	105,300
Liability value	478,800
Principal amount	500,000
Equity element	21,200

2.7 Treasury shares

If an entity **reacquires its own equity instruments**, those instruments ('treasury shares') shall be **deducted from equity**. No gain or loss shall be recognised in profit or loss on the purchase, sale, issue or cancellation of an entity's own equity instruments. Consideration paid or received shall be recognised directly in equity.

2.8 Interest, dividends, losses and gains

As well as looking at statement of financial position presentation, IAS 32 considers how financial instruments affect the statement of profit or loss and other comprehensive income (and movements in equity). The treatment varies according to whether interest, dividends, losses or gains relate to a financial liability or an equity instrument.

(a) Interest, dividends, losses and gains relating to a financial instrument (or component part) classified as a **financial liability** should be recognised as **income or expense** in profit or loss.

(b) Distributions to holders of a financial instrument classified as an **equity instrument** should be **debited directly to equity** by the issuer.

(c) **Transaction costs** of an equity transaction (when an entity issues or acquires its own equity) shall be accounted for as a **deduction from equity** (unless they are directly attributable to the acquisition of a business, in which case they are accounted for under IFRS 3).

You should look at the requirements of IAS 1 *Presentation of Financial Statements* for further details of disclosure.

2.9 Offsetting a financial asset and a financial liability

A financial asset and financial liability should **only** be **offset**, with the net amount reported in the statement of financial position, when an entity:

(a) Has a **legally enforceable right of set off**; and

(b) Intends to settle on a **net basis**, or to realise the asset and settle the liability simultaneously, ie at the same moment.

This will reflect the expected **future cash flows** of the entity in these specific circumstances. In all other cases, financial assets and financial liabilities are presented separately.

2.10 Section summary

- Financial instruments issued to raise capital must be classified as **liabilities** or **equity**.
- The **substance** of the financial instrument is more important than its **legal form**.
- The **critical feature of a financial liability** is the contractual obligation to deliver cash or another financial instrument.
- **Compound instruments** are split into equity and liability parts and presented accordingly.
- **Interest, dividends, losses and gains** are treated according to whether they relate to an equity instrument or a financial liability.

Question — Classification

During the financial year ended 28 February 20X5, MN issued the two financial instruments described below. For **each** of the instruments, identify whether it should be classified as a financial liability or equity, **explaining in not more than 40 words each** the reason for your choice. In each case you should refer to the relevant International Accounting Standard or International Financial Reporting Standard.

(i) Redeemable preferred shares with a coupon rate 8%; the shares are redeemable on 28 February 20X9 at premium of 10%.

(ii) A grant of share options to senior executives; the options may be exercised from 28 February 20X8.

Answer

(i) **Financial liability**. The preference shares require regular distributions to the holders but more importantly have the debt characteristic of being redeemable. Therefore according to IAS 32 *Financial Instruments: Presentation* they must be classified as debt.

(ii) **Equity**. According to IFRS 2 *Share-based Payment* the grant of share options must be recorded as equity in the statement of financial position. It is an alternative to cash as a method of payment for the provision of services by the directors.

Note. IAS 32 requires that if the holder of a financial instrument can require the issuer to redeem it for cash or another financial asset ('puttable instrument') it should be classified as a liability. Some ordinary shares and partnership interests allow the holder to 'put' the instrument (that is to require the issuer to redeem it in cash). Such shares might more usually be considered as equity, but application of IAS 32 results in their being classified as liabilities.

However, IAS 32 allows entities to classify such instruments as equity, so long as they meet certain conditions, ie because they represent a residual interest in the net assets of the entity. It further requires that instruments imposing an obligation on an entity to deliver to another party a pro rata share of the net assets only on liquidation should be classified as equity.

3 Recognition and measurement of financial instruments

> **FAST FORWARD**
>
> IFRS 9 states that **all financial assets and liabilities** should be **recognised in the statement of financial position, including derivatives**.

IFRS 9 *Financial Instruments* establishes principles for recognising and measuring financial assets and liabilities.

3.1 Scope

IFRS 9 applies to **all entities** and to **all types of financial instruments except** those specifically excluded, as listed below.

(a) Investments in **subsidiaries, associates, and joint ventures** that are accounted for under IFRS 10, IAS 27 or IAS 28.

(b) **Leases** covered in IFRS 16

(c) **Employee benefit plans** covered in IAS 19

(d) Equity instruments **issued by the entity** eg ordinary shares issued, or options and warrants

(e) **Insurance contracts** covered in IFRS 4

(f) Any **forward contracts between an acquirer and a selling shareholder** to buy or sell an acquiree **that will result in a business combination at a future acquisition date** covered under IFRS 3.

(g) **Loan commitments** that cannot be settled net in cash or another financial instrument

(h) Financial instruments, contracts and obligations under **share-based payment transactions**, covered in IFRS 2

(i) Rights to payments to reimburse the entity for expenditure it is required to make to settle a liability recognised as a provision under IAS 37

(j) Rights and obligations within the scope of IFRS 15.

3.2 Initial recognition

IFRS 9 requires that financial instruments are recognised in the statement of financial position when the entity becomes a party to the **contractual provisions of the instrument**.

Point to note

> An important consequence of this is that all derivatives should be included in the statement of financial position.

Notice that this is **different** from the recognition criteria in the *Conceptual Framework* and in most other standards. Items are normally recognised when there is a probable inflow or outflow of resources and the item has a cost or value that can be measured reliably.

3.2.1 Example: Initial recognition

An entity has entered into two separate contracts.

(a) A firm commitment (an order) to buy a specific quantity of iron.

(b) A forward contract to buy a specific quantity of iron at a specified price on a specified date, provided delivery of the iron is not taken.

Contract (a) is a **normal trading contract**. The entity does not recognise a liability for the iron until the goods have actually been delivered. (Note that this contract is not a financial instrument because it involves a physical asset, rather than a financial asset.)

Contract (b) is a **financial instrument**. Under IFRS 9, the entity recognises a financial liability (an obligation to deliver cash) on the **commitment date**, rather than waiting for the closing date on which the exchange takes place.

Note that planned future transactions, no matter how likely, are not assets and liabilities of an entity – the entity has not yet become a party to the contract.

3.2.2 Classification and measurement of financial assets

IFRS 9 requires that on recognition financial assets are classified as measured at either:

- **Amortised cost**;
- **Fair value through other comprehensive income**; or
- **Fair value through profit or loss**

This classification is made on the basis of both:

(a) The **entity's business model** for managing the financial assets; and
(b) The **contractual cash flow** characteristics of the financial asset.

		Initial measurement (IFRS 9: para. 5.1.1)	Subsequent measurement (IFRS 9: paras. 4.1.2 – 4.1.5, 5.7.5)
1	**Investments in debt instruments** Business model approach (Note 1):		
	(a) Held to collect contractual cash flows; and cash flows are solely principal and interest	Fair value + transaction costs	Amortised cost
	(b) Held to collect contractual cash flows **and to sell**; and cash flows are solely principal and interest	Fair value + transaction costs	Fair value through other comprehensive income (with reclassification to profit or loss (P/L) on derecognition) NB: interest revenue calculated on amortised cost basis recognised in P/L
2	**Investments in equity instruments not 'held for trading'** (optional irrevocable election on initial recognition)	Fair value + transaction costs	Fair value through other comprehensive income (no reclassification to P/L on derecognition) NB: dividend income recognised in P/L
3	**All other financial assets** (and any financial asset if this would eliminate or significantly reduce an 'accounting mismatch' (Note 2))	Fair value (transaction costs expensed in P/L)	Fair value through profit or loss

1 The business model approach relates to groups of debt instrument assets and the accounting treatment depends on the entity's intention for that group of assets.

   (a) If the intention is to hold the group of debt instruments until they are redeemed, ie receive ('collect') the interest and capital ('principal') cash flows, then changes in fair value are not relevant, and the difference between initial and maturity value is recognised using the amortised cost method.

   (b) If the intention is principally to hold the group of debt instruments until they are redeemed, but they may be sold if certain criteria are met (eg to meet regulatory solvency requirements), then their fair value is now relevant as they may be sold and so they are measured at fair value. Changes in fair value are recognised in other comprehensive income, but interest is still recognised in profit or loss on the same basis as if the intention was not to sell if certain criteria are met.

2 An 'accounting mismatch' is a measurement or recognition inconsistency that would otherwise arise from measuring assets or liabilities or recognising gains or losses on them on different bases. Any financial asset can be designated at fair value through profit or loss if this would eliminate the mismatch.

An application of these rules means that:

- **Equity investments** may not be classified as measured at amortised cost and must be measured at measured at **fair value through profit and loss**. This is because contractual cash flows on specified dates are not a characteristic of equity instruments. However, if an equity investment is **not held for trading**, an entity can make an irrevocable election at initial recognition to measure it at **fair value through other comprehensive income** with only dividend income recognised in profit or loss.

- **Derivatives** are measured at fair value.

- **Debt instruments** may be classified as measured at either amortised cost or fair value depending on whether they meet the criteria above. For example, a debt instrument that is held for trading would be measured at fair value through profit or loss. The objective of holding the asset is to realise a short-term gain (a change in fair value), not to receive payments of interest and principal (the contractual cash flows).

Even where the criteria are met at initial recognition, a debt instrument may be classified (irrevocably) as measured at fair value through profit or loss if doing so eliminates or significantly reduces a **measurement or recognition inconsistency** (sometimes referred to as an 'accounting mismatch') that would otherwise arise from measuring assets or liabilities or recognising the gains and losses on them on different bases.

3.2.3 Example: Financial asset at amortised cost

On 1 January 20X1 Abacus Co purchases a debt instrument for its fair value of $1,000. The debt instrument is due to mature on 31 December 20X5 and will be redeemed at par. The instrument has a principal amount of $1,250 and the instrument carries fixed interest at 4.72% that is paid annually. The effective interest rate is 10%.

How should Abacus Co account for the debt instrument over its five year term?

Solution

Abacus Co will receive interest of $59 ($1,250 × 4.72%) each year and $1,250 when the instrument matures.

Abacus must allocate the discount of $250 and the interest receivable over the five year term at a constant rate on the carrying amount of the debt. To do this, it must apply the effective interest rate of 10%.

The following table shows the allocation over the years.

Year	Amortised cost at beginning of year $	Statement of profit or loss: Interest income for year (@10%) $	Interest received during year (cash inflow) $	Amortised cost at end of year $
20X1	1,000	100	(59)	1,041
20X2	1,041	104	(59)	1,086
20X3	1,086	109	(59)	1,136
20X4	1,136	113	(59)	1,190
20X5	1,190	119	(1,250 + 59)	–

Each year the carrying amount of the financial asset is increased by the interest income for the year and reduced by the interest actually received during the year.

Question — Financial Assets: Measurement

Wharton, a public limited company, has requested your advice on accounting for the following financial instrument transactions:

(a) On 1 January 20X1, Wharton made a $10,000 interest-free loan to an employee to be paid back on 31 December 20X2. The market rate on an equivalent loan would have been 5%.

(b) Wharton anticipates capital expenditure in a few years and so invests its excess cash into short- and long-term financial assets so it can fund the expenditure when the need arises. Wharton will hold these assets to collect the contractual cash flows, and, when an opportunity arises, the entity will sell financial assets to re-invest the cash in financial assets with a higher return. The managers responsible for this portfolio are remunerated on the overall return generated by the portfolio.

As part of this policy, Wharton purchased $50,000 par value of loan notes at a 10% discount on their issue on 1 January 20X1. The redemption date of these loan notes is 31 December 20X4. An interest coupon of 3% of par value is paid annually on 31 December. Transaction costs of $450 were incurred on the purchase. The annual internal rate of return on the loan notes is 5.6%. At 31 December 20X1, due to a decrease in market interest rates, the fair value of these loan notes increased to $51,000.

Required

Discuss, with suitable calculations, how the above financial instruments should be accounted for in the financial statements of Wharton for the year ended 31 December 20X1.

Answer

(a) **Loan to employee**

This is an investment in debt where the business model is to collect the contractual cash flows. It should be initially measured at fair value plus transaction costs (none here). However, as this is an interest free loan, the cash paid is not equivalent to the initial fair value. Therefore, the initial fair value is calculated as the present value of future cash flows discounted at the market rate on interest of an equivalent loan:

$$\$10{,}000 \times \frac{1}{1.05^2} = \$9{,}070$$

The loan should be subsequently measured at amortised cost:

	$
Fair value on 1 January 20X1	9,070
Effective interest income (9,070 × 5%)	454
Coupon received (10,000 × 0%)	(0)
Amortised cost at 31 December 20X1	9,524

Finance income of $454 should be recorded in profit or loss for the year ended 31 December 20X1 and the amortised cost of $9,524 in the statement of financial position as at 31 December 20X1.

(b) **Loan notes**

These loan notes are an investment in debt instruments where the business model is to collect the contractual cash flows (which are solely principal and interest) and to sell financial assets. This is because Wharton will make decisions on an ongoing basis about whether collecting contractual cash flows or selling financial assets will maximise the return on the portfolio until the need arises for the invested cash.

Therefore, they should be measured initially at fair value plus transaction costs: $45,450 ([$50,000 × 90%] + $450).

Subsequently, the loan notes should be held at fair value through other comprehensive income under IFRS 9. However, the interest revenue must still be shown in profit or loss.

	$
Fair value on 1 January 20X1 ((50,000 × 90%) + 450))	45,450
Effective interest income (45,450 × 5.6%)	2,545
Coupon received (50,000 × 3%)	(1,500)
	46,495
Revaluation gain (to other comprehensive income) [bal. figure]	4,505
Fair value at 31 December 20X1	51,000

Consequently, $2,545 of finance income will be recognised in profit or loss for the year, $4,505 revaluation gain recognised in other comprehensive income and there will be a $51,000 loan note asset in the statement of financial position.

3.2.4 Classification and measurement of financial liabilities

On initial **recognition**, IFRS 9 requires that financial liabilities are **classified as measured at** either:

1 **Most financial liabilities** are measured at amortised cost.

   However, some financial liabilities are measured at **fair value through profit or loss** if fair value information is relevant to the user of the financial statements. This includes where a company is 'trading' in financial liabilities, ie taking on liabilities hoping to settle them for less in the short term to make a profit, and derivatives standing at a loss which are financial liabilities rather than financial assets.

2 As with financial assets, financial liabilities can be designated at fair value through profit or loss if doing so would eliminate an '**accounting mismatch**', ie a measurement or recognition inconsistency that would otherwise arise from measuring assets or liabilities or recognising gains or losses on them on different bases.

	Initial measurement (IFRS 9: para. 5.1.1)	Subsequent measurement (IFRS 9: para. 4.2.1)
1 **Most financial liabilities** (eg trade payables, loans, preference shares classified as a liability)	Fair value less transaction costs	Amortised cost
2 **Financial liabilities at fair value through profit or loss** (Note 1) – 'Held for trading' (short-term profit making) – Derivatives that are liabilities – Designated on initial recognition at 'fair value through profit or loss' to eliminate/significantly reduce an 'accounting mismatch' (Note 2) – A group of financial liabilities (or financial assets and financial liabilities) managed and performance evaluated on a fair value basis in accordance with a documented risk management or investment strategy	Fair value (transaction costs expensed in P/L)	Fair value through profit or loss *

Question — Financial liabilities measured at amortised cost 1

Galaxy Co issues a bond for $503,778 on 1 January 20X2. No interest is payable on the bond, but it will be redeemed on 31 December 20X4 for $600,000. The bond has **not** been designated as at fair value through profit or loss.

Required

Calculate the charge to the statement of profit or loss of Galaxy Co for the year ended 31 December 20X2 and the balance outstanding at 31 December 20X2.

Answer

The bond is a 'deep discount' bond and is a financial liability of Galaxy Co. It is measured at amortised cost. Although there is no interest as such, the difference between the initial cost of the bond and the price at which it will be redeemed is a finance cost. This must be allocated over the term of the bond at a constant rate on the carrying amount.

To calculate amortised cost we need to calculate the effective interest rate of the bond:

$$\frac{600,000}{503,778} = 1.191 \text{ over three years}$$

To calculate an annual rate, we take the cube root, $(1.191)^{1/3} = 1.06$, so the annual interest rate is 6%.

The charge to profit or loss for the year ended 31 December 20X2 is $30,226 ($503,778 × 6%).

The balance outstanding at 31 December 20X2 is $534,004 ($503,778 + $30,226).

Question: Financial liabilities measured at amortised cost 2

On 1 January 20X3 Deferred issued $600,000 loan notes. Issue costs were $200. The loan notes do not carry interest, but are redeemable at a premium of $152,389 on 31 December 20X4. The effective finance cost of the debentures is 12%.

What is the finance cost in respect of the loan notes for the year ended 31 December 20X4?

Answer

The premium on redemption of the preferred shares represents a finance cost. The effective rate of interest must be applied so that the debt is measured at amortised cost (IFRS 9).

At the time of issue, the loan notes are recognised at their net proceeds of $599,800 ($600,000 − $200).

The finance cost for the year ended 31 December 20X4 is $80,613, calculated as follows:

	B/f $	Interest @ 12% $	C/f $
20X3	599,800	71,976	671,776
20X4	671,776	80,613	752,389

3.2.5 Re-classification of financial instruments

On initial recognition, financial assets must be classified in accordance with IFRS 9. In some cases they may be subsequently reclassified.

IFRS 9 requires that when an entity changes its business model for managing financial assets, it should reclassify all affected financial assets. This reclassification applies only to debt instruments, as equity instruments must be classified as measured at fair value.

IFRS 9 prohibits the reclassification of financial liabilities.

The Application guidance to IFRS 9 includes examples of circumstances when a reclassification is required or is not permitted.

3.3 Derecognition

Derecognition is the removal of a previously recognised financial instrument from an entity's statement of financial position. IFRS 9 provides the rules relating to the derecognition of both financial assets and financial liabilities.

3.3.1 Derecognition of financial assets

An entity should derecognise a **financial asset** when:

(a) The **contractual rights** to the cash flows from the financial asset **expire**; or

(b) The entity **transfers substantially all the risks and rewards of ownership** of the financial asset to another party.

Question: Risks and rewards

Can you think of an example of a situation in which:

(a) An entity has transferred substantially all the risks and rewards of ownership?
(b) An entity has retained substantially all the risks and rewards of ownership?

Answer

IFRS 9 includes the following examples:

(a) (i) An unconditional sale of a financial asset
(ii) A sale of a financial asset together with an option to repurchase the financial asset at its fair value at the time of repurchase

(b) (i) A sale and repurchase transaction where the repurchase price is a fixed price or at the sale price plus a lender's return
(ii) A sale of a financial asset together with a total return swap that transfers the market risk exposure back to the entity

---

Exam focus point

The principle here is that of **substance over form**.

3.3.2 Derecognition of financial liabilities

An entity should derecognise a **financial liability** when it is **extinguished** – ie, when the obligation specified in the contract is discharged or cancelled or expires.

Where an existing borrower and lender exchange one financial liability for another with substantially different terms, this is accounted for as an extinguishment of the original financial liability and recognition of a new financial liability.

Equally a substantial modification of the terms of an existing financial liability (or part of it) is accounted for as an extinguishment of the original financial liability and recognition of a new financial liability.

A modification is substantial where the discounted present value of cash flows under the new terms, discounted using the original effective interest rate, is at least 10% different from the discounted present value of the cash flows of the original financial liability.

3.3.3 Partial derecognition

It is possible for only **part** of a financial asset or liability to be derecognised. This is allowed if the part comprises:

(a) Only specifically identified cash flows; or
(b) Only a fully proportionate (*pro rata*) share of the total cash flows.

For example, if an entity holds a bond it has the right to two separate sets of cash inflows: those relating to the principal and those relating to the interest. It could sell the right to receive the interest to another party while retaining the right to receive the principal.

3.3.4 Gain or loss on derecognition

On derecognition, the amount to be included in profit or loss for the period is calculated as follows:

Formula to learn

	$	$
Carrying amount of asset/liability (or the portion of asset/liability) transferred	X	
Less: Proceeds received/paid	X	
Any cumulative gain or loss reported as other comprehensive income	X	
		(X)
Difference to profit or loss		X

Where only part of a financial asset is derecognised, the carrying amount of the asset should be allocated between the part retained and the part transferred based on their relative fair values on the date of transfer. A gain or loss should be recognised based on the proceeds for the portion transferred.

Question: Derecognition

(a) AB sells an investment in shares, but retains a call option to repurchase those shares at any time at a price equal to their current market value at the date of repurchase.

(b) EF enters into a stocklending agreement where an investment is lent to a third party for a fixed period of time for a fee. At the end of the period of time the investment (or an identical one) is returned to EF.

Required

Discuss whether the following financial instruments would be derecognised.

Answer

(a) AB should derecognise the asset as it only has an option (rather than an obligation) to purchase.

(b) EF should not derecognise the asset as it has retained substantially all the risks and rewards of ownership. The inventory should be retained in its books even though the legal title is temporarily transferred.

3.3.5 Credit risk

IFRS 9 requires that financial liabilities which are **designated as measured at fair value through profit or loss are treated differently**. In this case the gain or loss in a period must be classified into:

- Gain or loss **resulting from credit risk**; and
- **Other** gain or loss.

This provision of IFRS 9 was in response to an anomaly regarding changes in the credit risk of a financial liability.

Changes in a financial liability's credit risk affect the fair value of that financial liability. This means that when an entity's creditworthiness deteriorates, the fair value of its issued debt will decrease (and *vice versa*). For financial liabilities measured using the fair value option, this causes **a gain (or loss) to be recognised in profit or loss for the year**. For example:

STATEMENT OF PROFIT OR LOSS AND OTHER COMPREHENSIVE INCOME (EXTRACT)
PROFIT OR LOSS FOR THE YEAR

	$'000
Liabilities at fair value (except derivatives and liabilities held for trading)	
Change in fair value	100
Profit (loss) for the year	100

Many users of financial statements found this result to be **counter-intuitive** and confusing. Accordingly, IFRS 9 requires the gain or loss as a result of credit risk to be recognised in other comprehensive income, unless it creates or enlarges an **accounting mismatch**, in which case it is recognised in profit or loss. The other gain or loss (not the result of credit risk) is recognised in profit or loss.

On derecognition any gains or losses recognised in other comprehensive income are **not** transferred to **profit or loss**, although the cumulative gain or loss may be transferred within equity.

3.3.6 Example

On 1 July 20X3 Bravo plc issued 8% 10 year redeemable bonds at their par value of $10,000,000. LIBOR is used as a benchmark rate by Bravo and the coupon rate for these bonds was based on LIBOR plus 7%. LIBOR was 1% at 1 July 2013 and was 0.75% at 30 June 20X4. At 30 June 2014, the market value of the bonds was $10,254,000, implying an interest rate of 7.6%.

Required

Calculate and explain the amounts to be shown in the financial statements of Bravo plc for the year ended 30 June 20X4 in respect of the bonds issued.

Solution

(1) Compute the liability's internal rate of return at the start of the period using the observed market price of the liability and the liability's contractual cash flows at the start of the period. Deduct from this rate of return the observed (benchmark) interest rate at the start of the period, to arrive at an instrument-specific component of the internal rate of return.

(2) Calculate the present value of the cash flows associated with the liability using the liability's contractual cash flows at the end of the period and a discount rate equal to the sum of (i) the observed (benchmark) interest rate at the end of the period and (ii) the instrument-specific component of the internal rate of return.

(3) The difference between the observed market price of the liability at the end of the period and the amount determined above is the change in fair value that is not attributable to changes in the observed (benchmark) interest rate. This is the amount to be presented in other comprehensive income.

At 1 July 20X3 the interest rate offered by the bonds is 8%. This consists of LIBOR – 1% – plus an instrument-specific component of 7%. The market value at 30 June 20X4 implies an interest rate of 7.6% (this can be calculated as the internal rate of return of the cash flows). This reflects a decrease of 0.25 percentage points in LIBOR and an increase in credit risk (assuming no other changes), as explained below.

Interest rate at 1 July 20X3	8.00%
Decrease in LIBOR	–0.25%
Implied change in credit risk (balancing figure)	–0.15%
Interest rate at 30 June 20X4	7.60%

	$'000	$'000
Market value at 30 June 20X4	10,254	
PV of future cashflows at instrument specific rate (W1)	10,160	
Increase in liability to be presented in OCI		94
Market value at 1 July 20X3	10,000	
Increase in liability to be presented in profit or loss		160
Total increase		254

(W1) The discount rate to be used is equal to the sum of (i) the observed (benchmark) interest rate at the end of the period ie 0.75% and (ii) the instrument-specific component of the internal rate of return. This gives a discount rate of 0.75% plus 7.00% = 7.75%. The present value of contractual cashflows is as follows:

Time	Cash $'000	DR 7.75%	PV $'000
1 – 9	800	6.312	5,050
9	10,000	0.511	5,110
			10,160

PART C ACCOUNTING AND REPORTING TECHNIQUES

3.4 Section summary

- **All financial assets** and **liabilities** should be **recognised in the statement of financial position**, including derivatives.
- Financial instruments are initially measured at fair value. Where financial instruments are classified as measured at amortised cost, transaction costs increase this amount for financial assets and decrease this amount for financial liabilities.
- Financial assets are subsequently measured at:
    - Fair value with changes in value recognised in other comprehensive income
    - Fair value with changes in value recognised in profit or loss, or
    - Amortised cost with interest recognised in profit or loss
- Financial liabilities are subsequently measured at fair value or amortised cost with gains and losses recognised in profit or loss
- In limited circumstances reclassifications of financial assets can be made.
- Financial assets should be derecognised when the rights to the cash flows from the asset expire or where substantially all the risks and rewards of ownership are transferred to another party.
- Financial liabilities should be derecognised when they are extinguished.

(IFRS 9)

4 Impairment and uncollectability of financial assets

> **FAST FORWARD**
>
> IFRS 9 requires companies to recognise future expected credit losses in respect of certain financial assets

IFRS 9 uses a forward-looking impairment model. Under this model future expected credit losses are recognised. This is different to the impairment model used in IAS 36 Impairment of Assets in which an impairment loss is only recognised when objective evidence of impairment exists.

IFRS 9's impairment rules apply primarily to certain financial assets (IFRS 9: paras. 5.5.1–5.5.2):

- Financial assets measured at amortised cost (business model: objective – to collect contractual cash flows of principal and interest)
- Investments in debt instruments measured at fair value through other comprehensive income (OCI) (business model: objective – to collect contractual cash flows of principal and interest and to sell financial assets)

The impairment rules do not apply to financial assets measured at fair value through profit or loss as subsequent measurement at fair value will already take into account any impairment.

4.1 Recognition of credit losses

On initial recognition of a financial asset and at each subsequent reporting date, a loss allowance for expected credit losses must be recognised.

> Loss allowance: The allowance for expected credit losses on financial assets.
>
> Expected credit losses: The weighted average of credit losses with the respective risks of a default occurring as the weights.
>
> Credit loss: The difference between all contractual cash flows that are due to an entity...and all the cash flows that the entity expects to receive, discounted.

(IFRS 9: Appendix A)

4.1.1 At initial recognition

At initial recognition of a financial asset, a loss allowance equal to 12-month expected credit losses must be recognised.

12-month expected credit losses are defined as 'the portion of lifetime expected credit losses that result from default events on a financial instrument that are possible within the 12 months after the reporting date' (IFRS 9: Appendix A). They are calculated by multiplying the probability of default in the next 12 months by the present value of the lifetime expected credit losses that would result from the default (IFRS 9: para. B5.5.43).

Lifetime expected credit losses are defined as 'the expected credit losses that result from all possible default events over the expected life of the financial instrument' (IFRS 9: Appendix A).

4.1.2 At subsequent reporting dates (IFRS 9: paras. 5.5.3–5.5.8)

At each subsequent reporting date, the loss allowance required depends on whether there has been a significant increase in credit risk of that financial instrument since initial recognition.

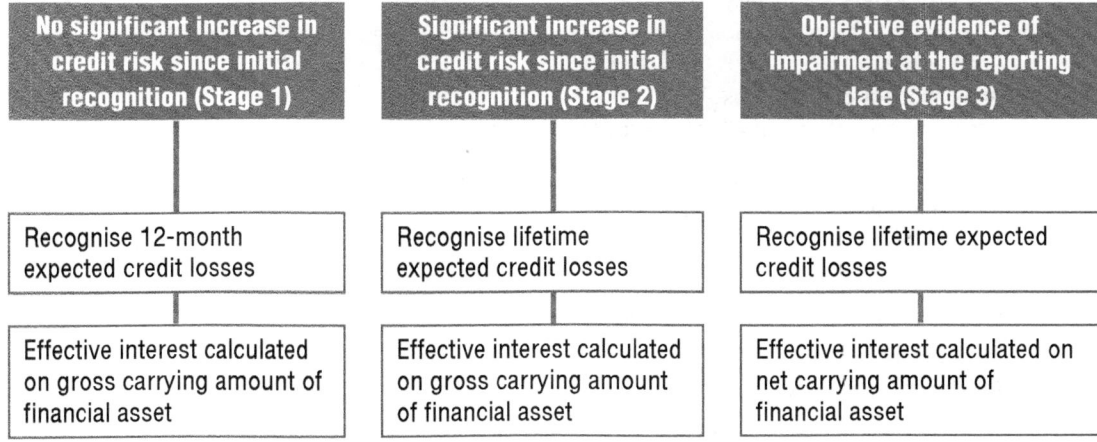

4.1.3 Significant increase in credit risk

To determine whether credit risk has increased significantly, management should assess whether there has been a significant increase in the risk of default.

There is a rebuttable presumption that the credit risk has increased significantly when contractual payments are more than 30 days past due. (IFRS 9: paras. 5.5.9–5.5.11)

Credit losses are treated as follows.

Type of financial asset	Treatment of credit loss
Investments in debt instruments measured at amortised cost	- Recognised in profit or loss - Credit losses held in a separate allowance account offset against the carrying amount of the asset: Financial asset X Allowance for credit losses (X) Carrying amount (net of allowance for credit losses) X
Investments in debt instruments measured at fair value through other comprehensive income	- Portion of the fall in fair value relating to credit losses recognised in profit or loss - Remainder recognised in other comprehensive income - No allowance account necessary because already carried at fair value (which is automatically reduced for any fall in value, including credit losses)

(IFRS 9: paras. 5.5.8 and 5.5.2)

4.1.4 Example

A company has a portfolio of loan assets. Its business model is to collect the contractual cash flows of interest and principal only. All loan assets have an effective interest rate of 7.5%. The portfolio was initially recognised at $840,000 on 1 January 20X1 with a separate allowance of $5,000 for 12-month expected credit losses (present value of lifetime expected credit losses of $100,000 × 5% chance of default within 12 months). A discount factor of 7.5% has been applied in calculating the loss allowance. No repayments are due in the first year.

At 31 December 20X1, the credit risk of the loan assets has increased significantly. The expectation of lifetime expected credit losses remains the same.

Required

Explain the accounting treatment of the portfolio of loan assets, with suitable calculations.

Solution

The loan assets are initially recognised on 1 January 20X1 as follows:

	$
Loan assets	840,000
Allowance for credit losses	(5,000)
Carrying amount (net of allowance for credit losses)	835,000

As the business model for the loan assets is to collect the contractual cash flows of interest and principal only, they should be measured at amortised cost:

	$
At 1 January 20X1	840,000
Effective interest income (7.5% × $840,000)	63,000
Cash received	(0)
At 31 December 20X1	903,000

The discount on the allowance must be unwound by one year resulting in a finance cost of $375 (7.5% × $5,000). At 31 December 20X1, as there has been a significant increase in credit risk, the allowance for credit losses is adjusted to the present value of lifetime expected credit losses (measured at the end of the first year) of $107,500 ($100,000 × 1.075):

	$
At 1 January 20X1	5,000
Unwind discount	375
Increase in allowance	102,125
At 31 December 20X1	107,500

A total finance cost relating to the allowance of $102,500 ($375 + $102,125) should be recognised in profit or loss for the year ended 31 December 20X1.

At 31 December 20X1, the amount to recognise in the statement of financial position is therefore:

	$
Loan assets	903,000
Allowance for credit losses	(107,500)
Carrying amount (net of allowance for credit losses)	795,500

In the year ended 31 December 20X2, effective interest income and finance cost will be calculated on the gross figures of $903,000 and $107,500 respectively, or (if there is objective evidence of actual impairment) on the net figure of $795,500.

The measurement of expected credit losses should reflect (IFRS 9: para. 5.5.17):

(a) An unbiased and probability-weighted amount that is determined by evaluating a range of possible outcomes;

(b) The time value of money; and

(c) Reasonable and supportable information that is available without undue cost and effort at the reporting date about past events, current conditions and forecasts of future economic conditions.

4.1.5 Impairment loss reversal

If an entity has measured the loss allowance at an amount equal to lifetime expected credit losses in the previous reporting period, but determines that the conditions are no longer met, it should revert to measuring the loss allowance at an amount equal to 12-month expected credit losses (IFRS 9: para. 5.5.7).

The resulting impairment gain is recognised in profit or loss (IFRS 9: para. 5.5.8).

4.1.6 Sustainability impact

Climate-related matters may effect credit losses. Weather events such as fires or floods, or regulatory changes could impact the ability of a borrower to repay debt and increase the credit risk and possible impairment of financial assets.

4.2 Trade receivables, contract assets and lease receivables

A simplified approach is permitted for trade receivables, contract assets and lease receivables. For trade receivables or contract assets that do not have a significant IFRS 15 financing element, the loss allowance is measured at the lifetime expected credit losses, from initial recognition (IFRS 9: para. 5.5.15).

For other trade receivables and contract assets and for lease receivables, the entity can choose (as a separate accounting policy for trade receivables, contract assets and for lease receivables) to apply the three stage approach or to recognise an allowance for lifetime expected credit losses from initial recognition (IFRS 9: para. 5.5.15).

4.3 Purchased or originated credit-impaired financial assets

A financial asset may already be credit-impaired when it is purchased. In this case it is originally recognised as a single figure with no separate allowance for credit losses. However, any subsequent changes in lifetime expected credit losses are recognised as a separate allowance (IFRS 9: para. 5.5.13).

Question — Impairment of financial assets

On 1 January 20X5, ABC Bank made loans of $10 million to a group of customers with similar credit risk. The business model for these loan assets is to collect the contractual cash flows of interest and principal only. Interest payable by the customers on these loans is LIBOR + 2%, reset annually. On 1 January 20X5, the initial present value of expected losses over the life of the loans was $500,000 (using a discount factor of 3%). The probability of default over the next 12 months was estimated at 1 January 20X5 to be 15%. Customers pay instalments annually in arrears. Cash of $400,000 (including interest) was received from customers during the year ended 31 December 20X5. The LIBOR rate for the year ended 31 December 20X5 was 1.8%.

After the loans were advanced, the country entered into an economic recession. By 31 December 20X5, the directors believed that there was objective evidence of impairment due to the late payment of some of the customers. The present value of lifetime expected credit losses was revised to $800,000.

Required

Discuss, with suitable calculations, the accounting treatment of the loans for the year ended 31 December 20X5.

Answer

On 1 January 20X5, ABC Bank should recognise an allowance for credit losses of $75,000 (15% × $500,000), being the 12 month expected credit losses. Per IFRS 9, this is calculated by multiplying the probability of default in the next 12 months (15%) by the lifetime credit losses that would result from the default ($500,000). A corresponding expense of $75,000 should be recognised in profit or loss. The allowance will be presented set off against the loan assets in the statement of financial position.

During the year ended 31 December 20X5, an interest cost of $2,250 ($75,000 × 3%) must be recognised on the brought forward allowance with a corresponding increase in the allowance to unwind one year of discounting.

Interest revenue of $380,000 ($10,000,000 × 3.8%) should also be recognised in profit or loss for the year ended 31 December 20X5. This is calculated on the gross carrying amount of $10,000,000. The interest rate of 3.8% is the LIBOR of 1.8% plus 2% per the loan agreement.

The gross carrying amount of the loans at 31 December 20X5 is:

	$
1 January 20X5	10,000,000
Interest revenue (3.8% × $10,000,000)	380,000
Cash received	(400,000)
31 December 20X5 gross carrying amount	9,980,00

However, by 31 December 20X5, due to the economic recession and the existence of objective evidence of impairment in the form of late payment by customers, Stage 3 has now been reached. Therefore, the revised lifetime expected credit losses of $800,000 should now be recognised in full. The allowance must be increased from $77,250 ($75,000 + interest of $2,250) to $800,000 which will result in an extra charge of $722,750 to profit or loss:

	$
1 January 20X5 (12-month expected credit losses) (15% × $500,000)	75,000
Unwind discount (3% × $75,000)	2,250
Increase in allowance	722,750
31 December 20X5 (lifetime expected credit losses)	800,000

The following amounts will be presented in the statement of financial position at 31 December 20X5:

	$
Loan assets	9,980,000
Allowance for credit losses	(800,000)
Net carrying amount	9,180,000

In the year ended 31 December 20X6, as Stage 3 has been reached, interest revenue will be calculated on the carrying amount net of the allowance for credit losses of $9,180,000 ($9,980,000 − $800,000). Conversely, if the loans were still at Stage 1 or Stage 2, interest income and interest cost would have been calculated on the gross carrying amounts of $9,980,000 and $800,000 respectively.

4.4 Section summary

Financial assets accounted for at amortised cost should be adjusted for expected credit losses.

Expected credit losses are required to be estimated on initial recognition of the asset and at subsequent measurement dates.

IFRS 9 provided a three-stage impairment loss model:

- Stage 1 – on initial recognition and at subsequent measurement dates if no significant increase in credit risk. 12 month expected credit losses recognised.

- Stage 2 – at subsequent measurement if there is a significant increase in credit risk. Lifetime expected credit losses recognised. Effective interest rate subsequently applied to gross carrying amount.

- Stage 3 – at subsequent measurement if there is objective evidence of impairment. Lifetime expected credit losses recognised. Effective interest rate subsequently applied to net carrying amount.

5 Embedded derivatives

FAST FORWARD

An **embedded derivative** is a derivative instrument that is combined with a non-derivate **host contract** to form a single hybrid instrument.

Certain contracts that are not themselves derivatives (and may not be financial instruments) include derivative contracts that are 'embedded' within them. These non-derivatives are called **host contracts**.

Key term

An **embedded derivative** is a derivative instrument that is combined with a non-derivative host contract to form a single hybrid instrument.

5.1 Examples of host contracts

Possible examples include:

(a) A lease
(b) A debt or equity instrument
(c) An insurance contract
(d) A sale or purchase contract
(e) A long term contract

5.2 Examples of embedded derivatives

Possible examples include:

(a) A bond which is redeemable in five years' time with part of the redemption price being based on the increase in the FTSE 100 Index.

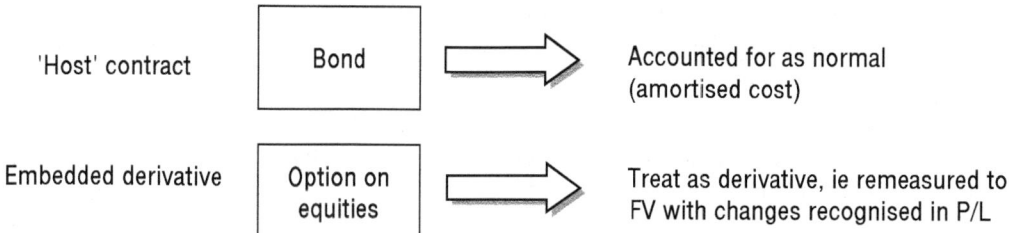

(b) A construction contract priced in a foreign currency. The construction contract is a non-derivative contract, but the changes in foreign exchange rate is the embedded derivative.

5.3 Accounting treatment of embedded derivatives

5.3.1 Financial asset host contract

Where the host contract is a financial asset within the scope of the standard, the classification and **measurement rules of the standard are applied to the entire hybrid contract**.

This is a simplification of the IAS 39 rules, and different from the treatment of financial liability host contracts (see below).

5.3.2 Other host contracts

Where the host contract is not a financial asset within the scope of IFRS 9, the standard requires that an embedded derivative be **separated from its host contract** and accounted for as a derivative when the following conditions are met:

(a) The economic characteristics and risks of the embedded derivative are not closely related to the economic characteristics and risks of the host contract.

(b) A separate instrument with the same terms as the embedded derivative would meet the definition of a derivative.

(c) The hybrid (combined) instrument is not measured at fair value with changes in fair value recognised in the profit or loss (a derivative embedded in a financial liability need not be separated out if the entity holds the combined instrument at fair value through profit or loss).

6 Hedge accounting

FAST FORWARD

Hedge accounting is allowed in certain strictly defined circumstances.

6.1 Introduction

IFRS 9 **requires hedge accounting** where there is a **designated hedging relationship** between a hedging instrument and a hedged item. It is **prohibited otherwise**.

Key terms

Hedging, for accounting purposes, means designating one or more hedging instruments so that their change in fair value is an offset, in whole or in part, to the change in fair value or cash flows of a hedged item.

A **hedged item** is an asset, liability, firm commitment, or forecasted future transaction that:

(a) Exposes the entity to risk of changes in fair value or changes in future cash flows, and that
(b) Is designated as being hedged.

A **hedging instrument** is a designated derivative or (in limited circumstances) another financial asset or liability whose fair value or cash flows are expected to offset changes in the fair value or cash flows of a designated hedged item. (A non-derivative financial asset or liability may be designated as a hedging instrument for hedge accounting purposes only if it hedges the risk of changes in foreign currency exchange rates.)

Hedge effectiveness is the degree to which changes in the fair value or cash flows of the hedged item attributable to a hedged risk are offset by changes in the fair value or cash flows of the hedging instrument. (IFRS 9)

In simple terms, entities hedge to reduce their exposure to risk and uncertainty, such as changes in prices, interest rates or foreign exchange rates. Hedge accounting recognises hedging relationships by allowing (for example) losses on a hedged item to be offset against gains on a hedging instrument.

Generally only assets, liabilities etc that involve external parties can be designated as hedged items. The foreign currency risk of an intragroup monetary item (eg payable/receivable between two subsidiaries) may qualify as a hedged item in the group financial statements if it results in an exposure to foreign exchange rate gains or losses that are not fully eliminated on consolidation. This can happen (per IAS 21) when the transaction is between entities with different functional currencies.

In addition, the foreign currency risk of a highly probable group transaction may qualify as a hedged item if it is in a currency other than the functional currency of the entity and the foreign currency risk will affect profit or loss.

6.2 IFRS 9 principles-based model

IFRS 9 contains a **principles based model** for hedge accounting that aims to **align accounting with risk management activities**. This will combine the following.

(a) A **management view**, that aims to use information produced internally for risk management purposes,

(b) An **accounting view** that seeks to address the risk management issue of the timing of recognition of gains and losses.

(c) An **objective-based assessment** for hedge effectiveness.

6.3 Conditions for hedge accounting

Before a hedging relationship qualifies for hedge accounting, **all** of the following **conditions** must be met.

(a) The hedging relationship **consists only of eligible hedging instruments and eligible hedged items**.

(b) There must **be formal documentation** (including identification of the hedged item, the hedging instrument, the nature of the risk that is to be hedged and how the entity will assess the hedging instrument's effectiveness in offsetting the exposure to changes in the hedged item's fair value or cash flows attributable to the hedged risk).

(c) The hedging relationship meets all of the following hedge effectiveness criteria

   (i) There is an **economic relationship** between the hedged item and the hedging instrument, ie the hedging instrument and the hedged item have values that generally move in the opposite direction because of the same risk, which is the hedged risk;

   (ii) The **effect of credit risk does not dominate the value** changes that result from that economic relationship, ie the gain or loss from credit risk does not frustrate the effect of changes in the underlyings on the value of the hedging instrument or the hedged item, even if those changes were significant; and

   (iii) The **hedge ratio of the hedging relationship** (quantity of hedging instrument vs quantity of hedged item) is the same as that resulting from the quantity of the hedged item that the entity **actually hedges** and the quantity of the hedging instrument that the entity **actually uses** to hedge that quantity of hedged item.

6.4 Example: Hedging

A company owns inventories of 20,000 gallons of oil which cost $400,000 on 1 December 20X3.

In order to hedge the fluctuation in the market value of the oil the company signs a futures contract to deliver 20,000 gallons of oil on 31 March 20X4 at the futures price of $22 per gallon.

The market price of oil on 31 December 20X3 is $23 per gallon and the futures price for delivery on 31 March 20X4 is $24 per gallon.

Required

Explain the impact of the transactions on the financial statements of the company:

(a) Without hedge accounting
(b) With hedge accounting

Solution

The futures contract was intended to protect the company from a fall in oil prices (which would have reduced the profit when the oil was eventually sold). However, oil prices have actually risen, so that the company has made a loss on the contract.

Without hedge accounting:

The futures contract is a derivative and therefore must be re-measured to fair value under IFRS 9. The loss on the futures contract is recognised in profit or loss:

DEBIT	Profit or loss (20,000 × 24 – 22)	$40,000	
CREDIT	Financial liability		$40,000

With hedge accounting:

The loss on the futures contract is recognised in the profit or loss as before.

The inventories are revalued to fair value:

	$
Fair value at 31 December 20X3 (20,000 × 23)	460,000
Cost	(400,000)
Gain	60,000

The gain is also recognised in profit or loss:

DEBIT	Inventory	$60,000	
CREDIT	Profit or loss		$60,000

The net effect on the profit or loss is a gain of $20,000 compared with a loss of $40,000 without hedging.

The **standard** identifies three types of **hedging relationship**.

> **Key terms**
>
> **Fair value hedge**: a hedge of the exposure to changes in fair value of a recognised asset or liability or an unrecognised firm commitment, or a component of any such item, that is attributable to a particular risk and could affect profit or loss.
>
> **Cash flow hedge**: a hedge of the exposure to variability in cash flows that
>
> (a) Is attributable to a particular risk associated with all, or a component of, a recognised asset or liability (such as all or some future interest payments on variable-rate debt) or a highly probable forecast transaction; and
>
> (b) Could affect profit or loss.
>
> **Hedge of a net investment in a foreign operation**: IAS 21 defines a net investment in a foreign operation as the amount of the reporting entity's interest in the net assets of that operation. (IFRS 9)

The hedge in the example above is a **fair value hedge** (it hedges exposure to changes in the fair value of a recognised asset: the oil).

This is a highly controversial topic and therefore, likely to be examined, probably in Section B.

6.5 Accounting treatment

6.5.1 Fair value hedges

Hedging instrument

The **gain or loss** resulting from **re-measuring** the hedging instrument at fair value is **recognised in profit or loss**. However, **if** the hedging instrument hedges **an equity instrument** for which an entity has **elected** to present **changes in fair value in other comprehensive income**, then the **gain or loss** on the hedging instrument must be recognised in **other comprehensive income.**

Hedged item

The gain or loss on the hedged item attributable to the **hedged risk** should **adjust the carrying amount** of the hedged item and be **recognised in profit or loss**. If the hedged item is a **financial asset through other comprehensive income** (mandatory), the **gain or loss** on the hedged item is also **recognised through profit or loss.**

However, if the hedged item is an **investment in an equity instrument held at fair value through other comprehensive income**, the **gains and losses on both** the hedged investment and the hedging instrument will be **recognised in other comprehensive income**.

This ensures that hedges of investments of equity instruments held at fair value through other comprehensive income can be accounted for as hedges.

6.5.2 Example: fair value hedge

On 1 July 20X6 Joules acquired 10,000 ounces of a material which it held in its inventory. This cost $200 per ounce, so a total of $2 million. Joules was concerned that the price of this inventory would fall, so on 1 July 20X6 he sold 10,000 ounces in the futures market for $210 per ounce for delivery on 30 June 20X7. On 1 July 20X6 the conditions for hedge accounting were all met.

At 31 December 20X6, the end of Joules' reporting period, the fair value of the inventory was $220 per ounce while the futures price for 30 June 20X7 delivery was $227 per ounce. On 30 June 20X7 the trader sold the inventory and closed out the futures position at the then spot price of $230 per ounce.

The IFRS 9 hedging criteria have been met.

Required

Set out the accounting entries in respect of the above transactions.

Solution

At 31 December 20X6 the increase in the fair value of the inventory was $200,000 (10,000 × ($220 – $200)) and the increase in the forward contract liability was $170,000 (10,000 × ($227 – $210)). The IFRS 9 hedge accounting criteria have been met, so hedge accounting was permitted.

31 December 20X6	Debit $	Credit $
Profit or loss	170,000	
Financial liability		170,000
(To record the loss on the forward contract)		
Inventories	200,000	
Profit or loss		200,000
(To record the increase in the fair value of the inventories)		

At 30 June 20X7 the increase in the fair value of the inventory was another $100,000 (10,000 × ($230 – $220)) and the increase in the forward contract liability was another $30,000 (10,000 × ($230 – $227)).

30 June 20X7	Debit $	Credit $
Profit or loss	30,000	
Financial liability		30,000
(To record the loss on the forward contract)		
Inventories	100,000	
Profit or loss		100,000
(To record the increase in the fair value of the inventories)		
Profit or loss	2,300,000	
Inventories		2,300,000
(To record the inventories now sold)		
Cash	2,300,000	
Profit or loss – revenue		2,300,000
(To record the revenue from the sale of inventories)		
Financial liability	200,000	
Cash		200,000
(To record the settlement of the net balance due on closing the financial liability)		

Note that because the fair value of the material rose, Joules made a profit of only £100,000 on the sale of inventories. Without the forward contract, the profit would have been £300,000 (2,300,000 – 2,000,000). In the light of the rising fair value the trader might in practice have closed out the futures position earlier, rather than waiting until the settlement date.

6.5.3 Cash flow hedges

These hedge the risk of change in value of future cash flows from a recognised asset or liability (or highly probable forecast transaction) that could affect profit or loss, eg hedging a variable rate interest income stream. The hedging instrument is accounted for as follows:

(a) The portion of the gain or loss on the hedging instrument that is effective (ie up to the value of the loss or gain on cash flow hedged) is recognised in other comprehensive income ('items that may be reclassified subsequently to profit or loss') and the cash flow hedge reserve.

(b) Any excess is recognised immediately in profit or loss.

The amount that has been accumulated in the cash flow hedge reserve is then accounted for as follows:

(a) If a hedged forecast transaction subsequently results in the recognition of a non-financial asset or non-financial liability, the amount shall be removed from the cash flow reserve and be included directly in the initial cost or carrying amount of the asset or liability;

(b) For all other cash flow hedges, the amount shall be reclassified from other comprehensive income to profit or loss in the same period(s) that the hedged expected future cash flows affect profit or loss.

6.5.4 Example: Cash flow hedge

Bets Co signs a contract on 1 November 20X1 to purchase an asset on 1 November 20X2 for €60,000,000. Bets reports in US$ and hedges this transaction by entering into a forward contract to buy €60,000,000 on 1 November 20X2 at US$1: €1.5.

Spot and forward exchange rates at the following dates are:

	Spot	Forward (for delivery on 1.11.X2)
1.11.X1	US$1: €1.45	US$1: €1.5
31.12.X1	US$1: €1.20	US$1: €1.24
1.11.X2	US$1: €1.0	US$1: €1.0 (actual)

The IFRS 9 hedging criteria have been met.

Required

Show the double entries relating to these transactions at 1 November 20X1, 31 December 20X1 and 1 November 20X2.

Solution

Entries at 1 November 20X1

The value of the forward contract at inception is zero so no entries recorded (other than any transaction costs), but risk disclosures will be made.

The contractual commitment to buy the asset would be disclosed if material (IAS 16).

Entries at 31 December 20X1

Gain on forward contract:

	$
Value of contract at 31.12.X1 (€60,000,000/1.24)	48,387,096
Value of contract at 1.11.X1 (€60,000,000/1.5)	40,000,000
Gain on contract	8,387,096

Compare to movement in value of asset (unrecognised):

Increase in $ cost of asset

(€60,000,000/1.20 – €60,000,000/1.45) $8,620,690

As this is higher, the hedge is deemed fully effective at this point:

DEBIT Financial asset (Forward a/c)	$8,387,096	
CREDIT Equity		$8,387,096

Entries at 1 November 20X2

Additional gain on forward contract

	$
Value of contract at 1.11.X2 (€60,000,000/1.0)	60,000,000
Value of contract at 31.12.X1 (€60,000,000/1.24)	48,387,096
Gain on contract	11,612,904

Compare to movement in value of asset (unrecognised):

Increase in $ cost of asset

(€60,000,000/1.0 – €60,000,000/1.2) $10,000,000

Therefore, the hedge is not fully effective during this period, but it still meets the IFRS 9 hedging criteria (and hence hedge accounting can be used):

DEBIT Financial asset (Forward a/c)	$11,612,904	
CREDIT Equity		$10,000,000
CREDIT Profit or loss		$1,612,904

Purchase of asset at market price

DEBIT Asset (€60,000,000/1.0)	$60,000,000	
CREDIT Cash		$60,000,000

Settlement of forward contract

DEBIT Cash	$20,000,000	
CREDIT Financial asset (Forward a/c)		$20,000,000

Realisation of gain on hedging instrument

The cumulative gain of $18,387,096 recognised in equity is removed from equity (the cash flow hedge reserve) and included directly in the initial cost of the asset.

6.5.5 Rebalancing hedging relationships

Rebalancing denotes adjustments to the designated quantities of the hedged item or the hedging instrument of an already existing hedging relationship for the purpose of maintaining a hedge ratio that complies with the hedge.

IFRS 9 requires rebalancing to be undertaken if the risk management objective remains the same, but the hedge effectiveness requirements are no longer met. Where the risk management objective for a hedging relationship has changed, rebalancing does not apply and the hedging relationship must be discontinued.

6.5.6 Discontinuing

An entity cannot voluntarily discontinue hedge accounting as it could under the old IAS 39. Under IFRS 9, an entity is **not allowed to discontinue hedge accounting where the hedging relationship still meets the risk management objective and continues to meet all other qualifying criteria.**

Hedge accounting should be discontinued only when the hedging relationship ceases to meet the qualifying criteria. This includes instances when the hedging instrument expires or is sold, terminated or exercised. Discontinuing hedge accounting can either affect a hedging relationship in its entirety, or only a part of it. If only part of the hedging relationship is affected, hedge accounting continues for the remainder of the hedging relationship.

6.5.7 Premium paid for options

Under IFRS 9, **the part of an option that reflects time value premium should be treated as a cost of hedging**, which will be presented in other comprehensive income. This is intended to decrease inappropriate volatility in profit or loss and it should be more consistent with risk management practices.

6.5.8 Forward element of forward contracts and foreign currency basis spreads

When an entity separates the forward element and the spot element of a forward contract and designates as the hedging instrument only the change in the value of the spot element, or when an entity excludes the foreign currency basis spread from a hedge the entity may recognise the change in value of the excluded portion in other comprehensive income. The change in value of the excluded portion will later be removed or reclassified from equity as a single amount or on an amortised cost basis (depending on the nature of the hedged item) and ultimately **recognised in profit or loss.**

6.5.9 Hedges of a group of items

IFRS 9 **permits** the designation of a group of assets as a hedged item provided that the following **three conditions** are met.

(a) It consist of items that are eligible individually for hedging

(b) The items in the group are managed together on a group basis for the purposes of risk management.

6.5.10 Accounting for hedges of credit risk using credit derivatives

IFRS 9 **permits certain credit exposures to be designated at fair value through profit or loss** if a credit derivative that is measured at fair value through profit or loss is used to manage the credit risk of all, or a part of, the exposure on a fair value basis.

A credit exposure may be a financial instrument within or outside the scope of IFRS 9, for example, loan commitments, that is managed for credit risk. The designation would be permitted if both of the following apply.

(a) The name of the credit exposure matches the reference entity of the credit derivative.

(b) The seniority of the financial instrument matches that of the instruments that can be delivered in accordance with the credit derivative.

If the qualifying criteria are no longer met and the instrument is not otherwise required to be measured at fair value through profit or loss, the entity must discontinue measuring the financial instrument that gave rise to the credit risk at fair value through profit or loss.

6.5.11 Disclosures

IFRS 7 *Financial Instruments: Disclosures* is revised by IFRS 9.

Disclosures relating to hedging must be presented in a **single note** (or alternatively a **separate section**) of the financial statements. In that way, all the effects of hedging are seen together in detail in this note.

6.6 Section summary

- **Hedge accounting** means designating one or more instruments so that their change in fair value is **offset** by the change in fair value or cash flows of another item.
- **Hedge accounting** is permitted in certain circumstances, provided **the qualifying criteria are met.**
- There are three types of hedge: **fair value** hedge; **cash flow** hedge; hedge of a **net investment in a foreign operation**. Only the first two are examinable.
- The accounting treatment of a hedge **depends on its type**.

7 Disclosure of financial instruments

FAST FORWARD

IFRS 7 specifies the **disclosures** required for financial instruments. The standard requires qualitative and quantitative disclosures about exposure to risks arising from financial instruments and specifies minimum disclosures about credit risk, liquidity risk and market risk. IFRS 13 disclosure requirements are also relevant where financial instruments are measured at fair value.

The IASB maintains that users of financial instruments need information about an entity's exposures to risks and how those risks are managed, as this information can **influence a user's assessment of the financial position and financial performance of an entity** or of the amount, timing and uncertainty of its **future cash flows**.

There have been new techniques and approaches to measuring risk management, which highlighted the need for guidance.

7.1 General requirements

The extent of disclosure required depends on the extent of the entity's use of financial instruments and on its exposure to risk. IFRS 7 **adds to the requirements previously in IAS 32** by requiring:

- Enhanced statement of financial position and statement of profit or loss and other comprehensive income disclosures
- Disclosures about an allowance account when one is used to reduce the carrying amount of impaired financial instruments.

The standard requires **qualitative and quantitative disclosures about exposure to risks** arising from financial instruments, and specifies minimum disclosures about **credit risk**, **liquidity risk** and **market risk**.

7.2 Objective

The objective of the IFRS is to require entities to provide disclosures in their financial statements that enable users to evaluate:

(a) The significance of financial instruments for the entity's financial position and performance
(b) The nature and extent of risks arising from financial instruments to which the entity is exposed during the period and at the reporting date, and how the entity manages those risks.

The principles in IFRS 7 complement the principles for recognising, measuring and presenting financial assets and financial liabilities in IAS 32 *Financial Instruments: Presentation*, IAS 39 *Financial Instruments: Recognition and Measurement* and IFRS 9 *Financial Instruments*.

7.3 Classes of financial instruments and levels of disclosure

The entity must group financial instruments into classes **appropriate to the nature of the information disclosed**. An entity must decide in the light of its circumstances how much detail it provides. Sufficient information must be provided to permit reconciliation to the line items presented in the statement of financial position.

7.3.1 Statement of financial position

The following must be disclosed:

(a) **Carrying amount** of financial assets and liabilities by IFRS 9 category
(b) **Reason for any reclassification** of a financial asset between fair value and amortised cost (and *vice versa*)

(c) Information to enable users of financial statements to evaluate the effect of netting arrangements on financial position (ie rights of set off). In order to achieve this, disclosure must be made of the gross amounts of recognised financial assets and liabilities, the amounts that are set off and the net amounts presented in the statement of financial position.

(d) The **carrying amount** of financial assets the entity has **pledged as collateral** for liabilities or contingent liabilities and the associated terms and conditions.

(e) When financial assets are impaired by credit losses and the entity records the impairment in a separate account (eg an **allowance account** used to record individual impairments or a similar account used to record a collective impairment of assets) rather than directly reducing the carrying amount of the asset, it must disclose a **reconciliation** of changes in that account during the period for each class of financial assets.

(f) The **existence of multiple embedded derivatives**, where compound instruments contain these.

(g) Defaults and breaches.

(h) **Details** of the assets and exposure to risk where the entity has made a **transfer** such that part or all of the financial assets do not qualify for derecognition.

7.3.2 Statement of profit or loss and other comprehensive income

The entity must disclose the following **items of income, expense, gains or losses**, either on the face of the financial statements or in the notes:

(a) Net gains/losses by IFRS 9 category (broken down as appropriate: eg interest, fair value changes, dividend income)

(b) Interest income/expense

(c) Impairment losses by class of financial asset.

7.3.3 Other disclosures

(1) Entities must disclose in the summary of **significant accounting policies** the measurement basis used in preparing the financial statements and the other accounting policies that are relevant to an understanding of the financial statements, as per IAS 1.

(2) Disclosures must be made relating to hedge accounting so as to provide information about:

   (a) An entity's risk management strategy and how it is applied to manage risk;

   (b) How the entity's hedging activities may affect the amount, timing and uncertainty of its future cash flows; and

   (c) The effect that hedge accounting has had on the entity's statement of financial position, statement of comprehensive income and statement of changes in equity.

   Disclosures relating to hedging must be presented in a **single note** or **separate section** of the financial statements.

(3) Disclosures must be made relating to **fair value by class** in a way that allows comparison with carrying amount for those financial instruments **measured at amortised cost**. (Financial assets and liabilities may only be offset to the extent that their carrying amounts are offset in the statement of financial position).

   Disclosures of fair value are not required when the carrying amount is a reasonable approximation of fair value (eg receivables).

   The disclosure requirements of IFRS 13 *Fair Value Measurement* are also relevant where financial instruments are held at fair value (see Chapter 11).

7.3.4 Example: Fair value disclosures required by IFRS 7

Background

On 1 January 20X1 an entity purchases for $15 million financial assets that are not traded in an active market. The entity has only one class of such financial assets.

The transaction price of $15 million is the fair value at initial recognition.

After initial recognition, the entity will apply a valuation technique to establish the financial assets' fair value. This valuation technique includes variables other than data from observable markets.

At initial recognition, the same valuation technique would have resulted in an amount of $14 million, which differs from fair value by $1 million.

The entity has cumulative existing differences of $5 million at 1 January 20X1.

Application of requirements

The entity's 20X2 disclosure would include the following:

Accounting policies

The entity uses the following valuation technique to determine the fair value of financial instruments that are not traded in an active market: [description of technique, not included in this example]. Differences may arise between the fair value at initial recognition (which, in accordance with IFRS 9, is generally the transaction price) and the amount determined at initial recognition using the valuation technique. Any such differences are [description of the entity's accounting policy].

In the notes to the financial statements

As discussed in note X, the entity uses [name of valuation technique] to measure the fair value of the following financial instruments that are not traded in an active market. However, in accordance with IFRS 9, the fair value of an instrument at inception is generally the transaction price. If the transaction price differs from the amount determined at inception using the valuation technique, that difference is [description of the entity's accounting policy].

The differences yet to be recognised in profit or loss are as follows:

	31 Dec 20X2 $m	31 Dec 20X1 $m
Balance at beginning of year	5.3	5.0
New transactions	–	1.0
Amounts recognised in profit or loss during the year	(0.7)	(0.8)
Other increases	–	0.2
Other decreases	(0.1)	(0.1)
Balance at end of year	4.5	5.3

Disclosures of fair value are **not required** if carrying value is a reasonable approximation to fair value, or if fair value cannot be measured reliably.

7.4 Nature and extent of risks arising from financial instruments

In undertaking transactions in financial instruments, an entity may assume or transfer to another party one or more of **different types of financial risk** as defined below. The disclosures required by the standard show the extent to which an entity is exposed to these different types of risk, relating to both recognised and unrecognised financial instruments.

Type of risk	Description
Credit risk	The risk that one party to a financial instrument will cause a financial loss for the other party by failing to discharge an obligation.
Currency risk	The risk that the fair value or future cash flows of a financial instrument will fluctuate because of changes in foreign exchange rates.

Type of risk	Description
Interest rate risk	The risk that the fair value or future cash flows of a financial instrument will fluctuate because of changes in market interest rates.
Liquidity risk	The risk that an entity will encounter difficulty in meeting obligations associated with financial liabilities.
Market risk	The risk that the fair value or future cash flows of a financial instrument will fluctuate because of changes in market prices. Market risk comprises three types of risk: currency risk, interest rate risk and other price risk.
Other price risk	The risk that the fair value or future cash flows of a financial instrument will fluctuate because of changes in market prices (other than those arising from interest rate risk or currency risk), whether those changes are caused by factors specific to the individual financial instrument or its issuer, or factors affecting all similar financial instruments traded in the market.

7.4.1 Qualitative disclosures

For each type of risk arising from financial instruments, an entity must disclose:

(a) The **exposures to risk** and how they arise

(b) Its objectives, policies and processes for managing the risk and the methods used to measure the risk

(c) Any **changes** in (a) or (b) from the previous period.

7.4.2 Quantitative disclosures

For each financial instrument risk, **summary quantitative data** about risk exposure at the end of the reporting period must be disclosed. This should be based on the information provided internally to key management personnel. More information should be provided if this is unrepresentative of risk exposure during the reporting period.

Information about **credit risk** must be disclosed by class of financial instrument:

(a) Maximum exposure at the reporting date, ie without deduction of collateral

(b) A description of collateral held as security and of other credit enhancements and their financial effect

(c) Information about the credit quality of financial assets that are neither **past due** nor impaired

(d) An age analysis for financial assets that are either past due or impaired

(e) Collateral taken possession of and other credit enhancements obtained, including the nature and carrying amount of the assets and policy for disposing of or using assets not readily convertible into cash.

For **liquidity risk** entities must disclose:

(a) A maturity analysis of financial liabilities
(b) A description of the way risk is managed

Disclosures required in connection with **market risk** are:

(a) Sensitivity analysis, showing the effects on profit or loss and equity of changes in each market risk and the method and assumptions used.

(b) If the sensitivity analysis reflects interdependencies between risk variables, such as interest rates and exchange rates, an explanation of the method used, its objective and its **limitations** must also be disclosed.

7.5 Capital disclosures

Certain disclosures about managing **capital** are required. An entity's capital does not relate solely to financial instruments, but has more general relevance. Accordingly, those disclosures are included in IAS 1, rather than in IFRS 7.

Chapter roundup

- Financial instruments can be very complex, particularly **derivative instruments**, although **primary instruments** are more straightforward.
- The important definitions to learn are:
  - **Financial asset**
  - **Financial liability**
  - **Equity instrument**
- A financial instrument must be classified as a **financial asset**, a **financial liability** or **equity** according to its **substance**.
- The critical feature of a financial liability is the **contractual obligation to deliver cash** or another financial asset.
- **Compound instruments** are split into **equity** and **liability** components and presented in the statement of financial position accordingly.
- IFRS 9 states that **all financial assets and liabilities** should be **recognised in the statement of financial position, including derivatives**.
- IFRS 9 requires companies to recognise **future expected credit losses** in respect of financial assets.
- An **embedded derivative** is a derivative instrument that is combined with a non-derivate **host contract** to form a single hybrid instrument.
- **Hedge accounting** is allowed in certain strictly defined circumstances.
- **IFRS 7** specifies the **disclosures** required for financial instruments. The standard requires qualitative and quantitative disclosures about exposure to risks arising from financial instruments and specifies minimum disclosures about credit risk, liquidity risk and market risk. IFRS 13 disclosure requirements are also relevant where financial instruments are measured at fair value.

Quick quiz

1. Which issues are dealt with by IAS 32?
2. Define the following:
   (a) Financial asset
   (b) Financial liability
   (c) Equity instrument
3. What items are **not** financial instruments according to IAS 32?
4. What is the critical feature used to identify a financial liability?
5. How should compound instruments be presented in the statement of financial position?
6. Define interest rate risk and credit risk.
7. When should a financial asset be derecognised?
8. How are financial instruments initially measured?
9. What is hedging?
10. Name the three types of hedging relationship identified by IFRS 9.

Answers to quick quiz

1. Classification; presentation; offsetting
2. See Key Terms, Section 1.2
3. Physical assets; prepaid expenses; non-contractual assets or liabilities; contractual rights not involving transfer of financial assets
4. The contractual obligation to deliver cash or another financial asset to the holder
5. By calculating the present value of the liability component and then deducting this from the instrument as a whole to leave a residual value for the equity component
6. See table, under Section 6.4
7. Financial assets should be derecognised when the rights to the cash flows from the asset expire or where substantially all the risks and rewards of ownership are transferred to another party
8. At the fair value of the consideration given or received ie cost
9. See Key Terms, Section 5.1
10. Fair value hedge; cash flow hedge; hedge of a net investment in a foreign operation

End of chapter question

Financial instruments (AIA May 2004)

This question should be answered applying the provisions of IAS 32 *Financial Instruments: Presentation* and IFRS 9 *Financial Instruments*.

(a) Alpha, a non-listed company, has issued 2,400,000 ordinary shares with a face value of $1. The company incurred costs of $49,880 in connection with the issue. These have been analysed as follows.

	$
Feasibility study	6,480
Publicity and printing costs	11,500
Management time spent negotiating the issue	8,500
Legal fees and costs	23,400

Required

Advise the directors of Alpha how these issue costs should be treated in the financial statements.

(4 marks)

(b) Gamma issues $10,000,000 bonds at par at the start of Year 1. The bonds bear interest at 9% per annum and are redeemable in 15 years at par. Gamma has the option to redeem the bonds after four years at a premium of 25%.

Required

Advise how the above should be treated in Gamma's Statements of profit or loss and other comprehensive income for Years 1 to 4 if Gamma decides to redeem the bonds at the end of Year 4. **(4 marks)**

(c) Theta issues $800,000 debt at the start of Year 1. The debt is repayable after five years at a premium of $250,000. The debt bears interest at 5.5% per year for the first year. The interest is to be paid annually just after the end of the financial year. The rate of interest will increase by 0.5% each year after the first so that by Year 5 it will be 7.5%. The rate of interest implicit in the cash flows associated with this debt issue is 11.37351% per year.

Required

Advise how:

(i) The interest; and
(ii) The debt

Should be reported in the financial statements for the first two years. **(7 marks)**

(Total 15 marks)

PART C ACCOUNTING AND REPORTING TECHNIQUES

15: Leasing contracts

Topic list	Syllabus reference
1 Introduction to leases	LO3
2 Lessee accounting	LO3
3 Lessor accounting	LO3
4 Sale and leaseback transactions	LO3
5 Disclosure	LO3

Introduction

Leasing transactions are extremely common in business and you will often come across them in both your business and personal capacity. You should be familiar with the more straightforward aspects of this topic from your earlier studies, but we will go through these aspects in full as leasing can be very complicated. The first section of this chapter goes over some of that basic groundwork, before the chapter moves on to more complicated aspects.

1 Introduction to leases

FAST FORWARD

IFRS 16 *Leases* covers accounting for lease transactions by both lessees and lessors.

1.1 Identifying a lease

A **lease** is a contract that conveys to the customer ('lessee') the right to use an asset for a period of time in exchange for consideration. A contract contains a lease if the customer has the **right to control the use of an identified asset** for a period of time.

1.1.1 Right to control an asset

A lessee (customer) controls an asset if both of the following conditions are met (IFRS 16, para. B9):

The customer has right to obtain substantially all of the economic benefits from use of the identified asset.	and	The customer has the right to direct the use of the identified asset
A customer can **obtain substantially all of the economic benefits from use** of the asset either directly by using or holding the asset or indirectly by sub-leasing the asset. Economic benefits include the primary output of the asset (for example, goods produced by a machine) and any other economic benefits from using the asset (such as rental income from a tenant).		A customer has the right to **direct the use** of an identified asset throughout the period of use if one of the following applies: (a) The customer has the right to direct how and for what purpose the asset is used; or (b) Decisions about how and for what purpose the asset is used are predetermined (for example because of the way that the asset was designed and constructed) and the customer has the right to determine how to operate the asset (operating the asset itself or directing others to operate the asset) without the supplier having the right to change those operating instructions; or (c) Decisions about how and for what purpose the asset is used are predetermined and the customer designed the asset.

Legal ownership of the asset does not indicate which party controls the asset.

The accounting treatment in the lessee's books is driven by the *Conceptual Framework's* definitions of assets and liabilities rather than the legal form of the lease. The legal form of a lease is that the title to the underlying asset remains with the lessor during the period of the lease.

1.1.2 Identified asset

The identified asset is typically explicitly specified in a contract. However, an asset can also be identified by being implicitly specified at the time that the asset is made available for use by the customer (IFRS 16: para. B13).

Even if an asset is specified, a customer does not have the right to use an identified asset if the supplier has the substantive right to substitute the asset throughout the period of use (IFRS 16: para. B14).

15: LEASING CONTRACTS

The following flowchart from IFRS can be used to determine whether a **contract** contains a **lease**.

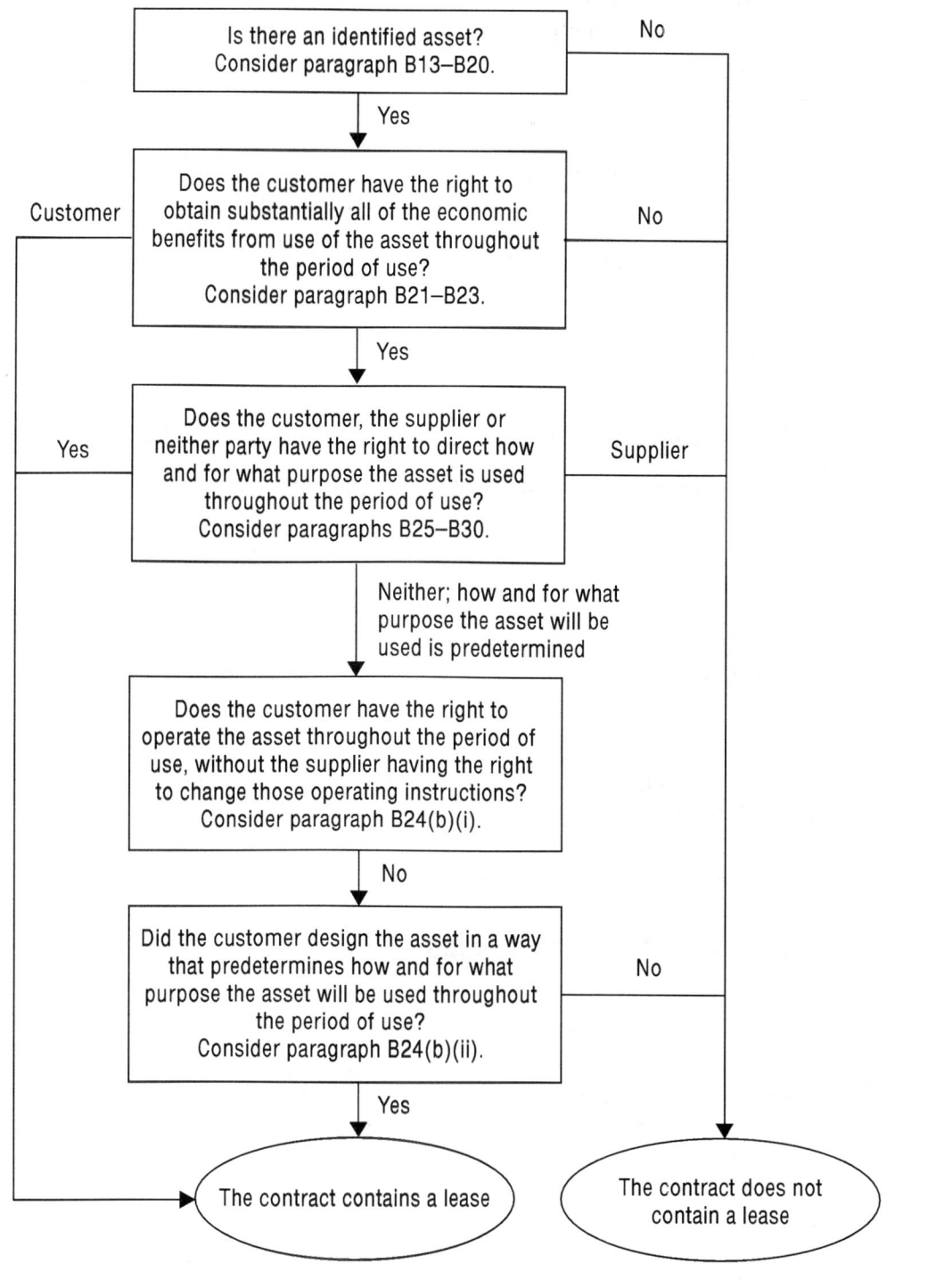

(IFRS 16)

1.2 Separating multiple components of a lease

A contract may contain both a lease component and a non-lease component. In other words it may include an amount payable by the lessee for activities and costs that do not transfer goods or services to the lessee (IFRS 16: para. B33). These activities and costs might, for example, include maintenance, repairs or cleaning.

IFRS 16 requires entities to account for the lease component of the contract separately from the non-lease component. The entity must split the rental or lease payment and:

- Account for the lease component under IFRS 16; and
- Account for the service element separately, generally as an expense in profit or loss.

The consideration in the contract is allocated on the basis of the stand-alone prices of the lease component(s) and the non-lease component(s).

1.3 Example: Separating multiple components of a lease

Livery Co leases a delivery van from Bettalease Co for three years at $12,000 per year. This payment includes servicing costs.

Livery could lease the same make and model of van for $11,000 per year and would need to pay $2,000 a year for servicing.

Required:

Allocate the payments into their lease and non-lease components

Solution

Livery Co would allocate $10,154 ($12,000 × $11,000 ÷ $(11,000 + 2,000)) to the lease component and account for that as a lease under IFRS 16.

Livery Co would allocate $1,846 ($12,000 × $2,000 ÷ $(11,000 + 2,000)) to the servicing component and recognise it in profit or loss as an expense.

1.4 Impact of IFRS 16 *Leases*

IFRS 16 *Leases* is a relatively new standard which aims to ensure that the financial statements faithfully represent the leasing arrangements that the entity has entered into.

The previous standard, IAS 17 Leases, had two categories of lease - finance leases, which required leased assets and associated lease liabilities to be recognised on the financial statements; and operating leases which did not result in recognition of assets or liabilities: such leases were referred to as 'off balance sheet leases'. Off balance sheet leases were accounted for by simply reporting a rental expense in the statement of profit or loss.

IFRS 16 recognises that companies generally use leasing arrangements as a means of obtaining assets and therefore requires the majority of leased assets and the associated obligations to be recognised in the financial statements. This helps to improve comparability between companies that choose to lease rather than buy assets and ensures that the financial statements more faithfully represent the underlying substance of an entity's transactions.

While IFRS 16 has benefits for the users of financial statements in terms of transparency and comparability, it has had a significant impact on the most commonly used financial ratios, such as:

Ratio	Impact
Gearing	Debt will increase therefore gearing ratio increase
Asset turnover	Assets will increase therefore asset turnover will decrease
Return on capital employed	Capital employed will increase and therefore ROCE will decrease

Ratio	Impact
Profit margins	Operating profit is likely to increase (as lease costs have been replaced by depreciation costs), net profit may also increase (finance costs also need to be included). The impact depends on the size of the lease.
Interest cover	Finance costs will increase, but operating profit is also likely to increase.

This table will make more sense as we work through the lessee accounting in section 2 below.

The impact on ratios will in turn affect the way in which users interpret and analyse the financial statements. For example, banks often impose loan covenants when making loans to companies. These covenants may need renegotiating if applying IFRS 16 causes a company's liabilities to increase significantly.

1.4.1 Accounting treatment by lessees

IFRS 16 requires all contracts containing leases to result in the recognition of an asset - in respect of the resource being used - and a liability – in respect of the obligation to make payments to the supplier over the life of the contract

The most significant effect of the new requirements in IFRS 16 will be an increase in lease assets and financial liabilities. Accordingly, for companies with material 'off balance sheet leases', there will be a change to the assets and liabilities included in the statement of financial position and this will result in changes to key financial ratios such as leverage.

IFRS 16 also changes the nature of expenses related to 'off balance sheet leases'. Applying IAS 17 companies would record an operating expense in respect of the payments made to use the resource, typically on a straight-line basis over the life of the contract. Applying IFRS 16 will result in a depreciation expense in respect of the leased asset and (included within operating expenses) and an interest expense on lease liabilities (included within finance expenses). Although the depreciation charge may be calculated on a straight-line basis the interest expense reduces over the life of the lease as lease payments are made (thus reducing the outstanding liability over time). This results in a gradual year on year reduction total expense as an individual lease matures. However, as many companies hold a portfolio of leases that start and end in different reporting periods this difference is unlikely to be significant.

(IFRS *Project Summary*)

1.4.2 Accounting treatment by lessors

Under IFRS 16 lessors continue to distinguish between finance leases and operating leases.

To address concerns about the lack of information about a lessor's risk exposure, IFRS 16 requires lessors to make additional disclosures, including information about assets subject to operating leases and residual value risk.

Question

Identifying a lease

Which of the following transactions, taken from the IFRS 16 Illustrative Examples, would result in recognising a lease?

Scenario 1

A utility company (the customer) enters into a contract with a power company (the supplier) to purchase all of the electricity produced by a new solar farm for 20 years. The solar farm is explicitly specified in the contract and the supplier cannot substitute electricity from a different source. The customer specified the location and design of farm; the supplier is responsible for building the solar farm to specifications, and then operating and maintaining it. The supplier will retain ownership of the farm. There are no decisions to be made about whether, when or how much electricity will be produced because the design of the asset has predetermined those decisions. The supplier will receive tax credits relating to the construction and ownership of the solar farm, while the customer will receive renewable energy credits that accrue from the use of the farm to generate power.

Scenario 2

A utility company (the customer) enters into a contract with a power company (the supplier) to purchase all of the electricity produced by a single specified power plant for three years. The power plant is explicitly specified in the contract and the supplier cannot substitute electricity from a different source. The contract sets out the quantity and timing of power that the power plant will produce throughout the period of use, which cannot be changed in the absence of extraordinary circumstances (for example, emergency situations). The supplier designed the power plant when it was constructed some years before entering into the contract with customer (the customer had no involvement in that design). The power plant is owned by the supplier and is operated by the supplier on a day-to-day basis in accordance with industry-approved operating practices.

Answer

Scenario 1

The contract contains a lease.

There is an identified asset because the solar farm is explicitly specified in the contract, and the supplier does not have the right to substitute the specified solar farm.

The customer has the right to control the use of the solar farm throughout the 20-year period of use because:

(i) **The customer has the right to obtain substantially all of the economic benefits** from use of the solar farm over the 20-year period of use. The customer has exclusive use of the solar farm; it takes all of the electricity produced by the farm over the 20-year period of use as well as the renewable energy credits that are a by-product from use of the solar farm. Although the supplier will receive economic benefits from the solar farm in the form of tax credits, those economic benefits relate to the ownership of the solar farm rather than the use of the solar farm and, thus, are not considered in this assessment.

(ii) **The customer has the right to direct the use of the solar farm.** Neither the customer, nor the supplier, decides how and for what purpose the solar farm is used during the period of use because those decisions are predetermined by the design of the asset (ie the design of the solar farm has, in effect, programmed into the asset any relevant decision-making rights about how and for what purpose the solar farm is used throughout the period of use). The customer does not operate the solar farm; the supplier makes the decisions about the operation of the solar farm. However, the customer's design of the solar farm has given it the right to direct the use of the farm. Because the design of the solar farm has predetermined how and for what purpose the asset will be used throughout the period of use, the customer's control over that design is substantively no different from the customer controlling those decisions.

Scenario 2

The contract does not contain a lease.

There is an identified asset because the power plant is explicitly specified in the contract, and the supplier does not have the right to substitute the specified plant.

The customer has the right to obtain substantially all of the economic benefits from use of the power plant over the three years of the contract. The customer will take all of the electricity produced by the plant during those three years.

However, **the customer does not have the right to direct the use of the power plant.** How and for what purpose the plant is used (ie whether, when and how much power the plant will produce) is predetermined in the contract. The customer has no right to change how and for what purpose the plant is used during the period of use. The customer has no other decision-making rights about the use of the power plant during the period of use (for example, it does not operate the power plant) and did not design the plant.

The supplier is the only party that can make decisions about the plant during the period of use by making the decisions about how the plant is operated and maintained. The customer has the same rights regarding the use of the plant as if it were one of many customers obtaining power from the plant.

(IFRS *16 Illustrative example 9*)

2 Lessee accounting

FAST FORWARD

If a contract contains a lease the customer recognises an asset and a liability in the statement of financial position.

2.1 Accounting treatment

When an entity enters into a contract that contains a lease, the lessee recognises

- A **right-of-use asset** in respect of the resource that is controlled by the customer; and
- A **liability** in respect of the obligation to make future payments

(IFRS 16, para 24)

Key terms

Lease. A contract, or part of a contract, that conveys the right to use an asset, **the underlying asset**, for a period of time in exchange for consideration.

Underlying asset. An asset that is the subject of a lease, for which the right to use that asset has been provided by a **lessor** to a **lessee**.

Right-of-use asset. An asset that represents a lessee's right to use an **underlying asset** for the **lease term**.

Lease payments. Payments made by a **lessee** to a **lessor** relating to the right to use an **underlying asset** during the **lease term**, comprising:

(a) Fixed payments, less any **lease incentives**

(b) **Variable lease payments** that depend on an index or rate

(c) The exercise price of a purchase option if the lessee is reasonably certain to exercise that option

(d) Payment of lease termination penalties if applicable

Interest rate implicit in the lease.

The discount rate that, at the inception of the lease, causes the aggregate present value of:

(a) The lease payments; and
(b) The **unguaranteed residual value**

to be equal to the sum of:

(a) The fair value of the **underlying asset**; and
(b) Any initial direct costs.

Lessee's incremental borrowing rate. The rate of interest that a **lessee** would have to pay to borrow over a similar term, and with a similar security, the funds necessary to obtain an asset of similar value to the **right of use asset** in a similar economic environment.

Unguaranteed residual value. That portion of the residual value of the underlying asset, the realisation of which by the lessor is not assured. **Variable lease payments.** The portion of payments made by a **lessee** to a **lessor** for the right to use an **underlying asset** during the **lease term** that varies because of changes in facts or circumstances occurring after the commencement date, other than the passage of time.

> **Lease term.** The non-cancellable period for which the lessee has contracted to lease the asset together with any further terms for which the lessee has the option to continue to lease the asset, with or without further payment, when at the inception of the lease it is reasonably certain that the lessee will exercise the option and any periods covered by an option to terminate the lease if the lessee is reasonably certain not to exercise that option (IFRS 16: para.18)
>
> - **Short-term lease.** A lease that at the commencement date has a term of 12 months or less and does not contain a purchase option.
> - **Lease incentives.** Payments made by the **lessor** to the **lessee**, or the reimbursement or assumption by the lessor of costs of the lessee. (IFRS 16: Appendix A)

2.1.1 Initial measurement of the right of use asset

The **asset** is **initially measured** at the amount of the lease liability plus any initial direct costs incurred by the lessee. Such costs are often incurred in connection with securing or negotiating a lease. Only those costs which are directly attributable to activities performed by the lessee to obtain a finance lease should be added to the amount recognised as an asset.

	$
Initial measurement of lease liability (present value of future lease payments)	X
Lease payments made at/before commencement date	X
Initial direct costs incurred by lessee	X
Estimated dismantling and restoration costs (where an obligation exists)	X
Lease incentives received	(X)
Cost of right-of-use asset	**X**

2.1.2 Subsequent measurement of the right of use asset

In **subsequent periods** the **asset** is measured using a cost model ie at cost less accumulated depreciation and impairment losses.

The asset is measured at fair value if

(i) the asset is an investment property and the lessee measures its investment property at fair value under IAS 40 or

(ii) the asset relates to a class of PPE to which the lessee applies IAS 16's revaluation model.

2.1.3 Initial measurement of the lease liability

The **liability** is **initially measured** at the present value of the **future** lease payments (PVFLP) payable over the lease term, discounted at the **rate implicit in the lease**. (If that rate cannot be readily determined the lessee uses their **incremental borrowing rate**.)

The lease liability cash flows to be discounted include the following (IFRS 16: para. 27):

- Fixed payments (including variable payments that are fixed in substance, such as when there is no genuine variability)
- Variable payments that depend on an index (eg CPI) or rate (eg market rent)
- Amounts expected to be payable under residual value guarantees (eg where a lessee guarantees to the lessor that an asset will be worth a specified amount at the end of the lease)
- Purchase options (if reasonably certain to be exercised).

Other variable payments (eg payments that arise due to level of use of the asset) are accounted for as period costs in profit or loss as incurred (IFRS 16: para. 38).

You should note that if lease payments are made in advance or on the commencement date, the PVFLP will NOT include the first instalment paid (as by its nature, it is not a future lease payment if it is paid on or before the first day of the lease). If payments are made in arrears, the PVFLP will include all lease payments due.

2.1.4 Subsequent measurement of the lease liability

In **subsequent periods** the liability is remeasured to reflect the unwinding of the discount and any payments made to reduce the outstanding finance.

Remeasurement of the liability also reflects any reassessments or modifications (for example, changes in the lease term, changes in future variable payments).

2.1.5 Amounts recognised in the statement of profit or loss

The statement of profit or loss and other comprehensive income will include:

- the **depreciation charge** associated with the leased asset (as well as any impairment losses and, possibly, revaluation gains and losses on leased assets classified as investment property); and
- the **finance expense** associated with the financing element of the lease contract.

The depreciation charge will reduce operating profit and the finance expense will reduce net profit.

2.2 Allocating the finance charge

When the lessee makes a rental payment it will comprise two elements:

(a) An **interest charge** on the finance provided by the lessor. This proportion of each payment is interest payable in the statement of profit or loss of the lessee.

(b) A repayment of part of the **capital cost** of the asset. In the lessee's books this proportion of each rental payment must be debited to the lessor's account to reduce the outstanding liability.

The accounting problem is to decide what proportion of each instalment paid by the lessee represents interest, and what proportion represents a repayment of the capital advanced by the lessor. This is done by the actuarial method, using the interest rate implicit in the lease.

2.3 Example: Apportionment of rental payments

(This is based on IFRS 16 Illustrative example 13)

A lessee enters into a five-year lease of a building which has a remaining useful life of 10 years. Lease payments are $50,000 per annum, payable at the beginning of each year.

The lessee incurs initial direct costs of $20,000 and receives lease incentives of $5,000. There is no transfer of the asset at the end of the lease and no purchase option.

The interest rate implicit in the lease is not immediately determinable but the lessee's incremental borrowing rate is 5%.

At the commencement date the lessee pays the initial $50,000, incurs the direct costs and receives the lease incentives.

The lease liability is measured at the present value of the future lease payments (note that as the payments are in advance, the payment in the first year is excluded:

	$
$50,000/1.05	47,619
$50,000/1.05^2	45,351
$50,000/1.05^3	43,192
$50,000/1.05^4	41,135
	177,297

Assets and liabilities will initially be recognised as follows:

	Debit $	Credit $
Right-of-use asset:		
Initial payment	50,000	
Discounted liability	177,297	

PART C ACCOUNTING AND REPORTING TECHNIQUES

Initial direct costs	20,000		
Incentives received	(5,000)		
		242,297	
Lease liability			177,297
Cash	(50,000 + 20,000 – 5,000)		65,000
		242,297	242,297

At the end of Year 1 the liability will be measured as:

	$
Opening balance	177,297
Interest 5%	8,865
	186,162
Current liability	50,000
Non-current liability	136,162
	186,162

The right of use asset will be depreciated over five years, being the shorter of the lease term and the useful life of the underlying asset.

Now we will see how this would work out if the lease payments were made **in arrears**.

At the commencement date the lessee would incur the direct costs and receive the lease incentives.

The lease would be measured at the present value of the **five** payments, as all of them represent future lease payments on the commencement of the lease:

	$
$50,000/1.05$	47,619
$50,000/1.05^2$	45,351
$50,000/1.05^3$	43,192
$50,000/1.05^4$	41,135
$50,000/1.05^5$	39,176
	216,473

Assets and liabilities would be recognised as follows:

	Debit $	Credit $
Right-of-use asset:		
Discounted liability	216,473	
Direct costs	20,000	
Lease incentives	(5,000)	
	231,473	
Lease liability		216,473
Cash (20,000 – 5,000)		15,000
	231,473	231,473

At the end of Year 1 the liability will be measured as:

	$
Opening balance	216,473
Interest 5%	10,824
Lease payment Year 1	(50,000)
Year-end balance	177,297

In order to ascertain the split between non-current and current liabilities, we work out the balance at the end of Year 2:

	$
Opening balance	177,297
Interest 5%	8,865

Lease payment Year 2	(50,000)
Year-end balance	136,162

The statement of financial position will show:

	$
Non-current liability	136,162
Current liability (177,297 – 136,162)	41,135
	177,297

Note that when payments are made in arrears the next instalment due will contain interest, so this is effectively deducted to arrive at the capital repayment.

2.4 Exemptions

For practical purposes IFRS 16 allows the following exemptions from the requirements to recognise lease assets and liabilities:

- Short-term leases (12 months or less)
- Leases for which the underlying asset is of low value

The assessment of whether an underlying asset is of low value is performed on an absolute basis. Leases of low-value assets qualify for the exemption regardless of whether those leases are material to the lessee.

The assessment is not affected by the size, nature or circumstances of the lessee. Accordingly, different lessees are expected to reach the same conclusions about whether a particular underlying asset is of low value.

An underlying asset can be of low value only if:

(a) The lessee can benefit from use of the underlying asset on its own or together with other resources that are readily available to the lessee; and

(b) The underlying asset is not highly dependent on, or highly interrelated with, other assets for which the underlying asset is of low value

Examples of low value items given in the standard are tablet and personal computers, small items of office furniture and telephones.

3 Lessor accounting

> **FAST FORWARD**
>
> Under IFRS 16 lessors continue to distinguish between finance leases and operating leases.

3.1 Key definitions – lessor accounting

> **FAST FORWARD**
>
> Make sure you learn these **important definitions which are applicable to lessor accounting**:
> - Finance lease
> - Operating lease
> - Minimum lease payments
> - Interest rate implicit in the lease
> - Guaranteed and unguaranteed residual value
> - Gross and net investment in the lease

Key terms

Finance lease. A lease that transfers substantially all the risks and rewards incidental to ownership of an asset. Title may or may not eventually be transferred.

Operating lease. A lease other than a finance lease.

Minimum lease payments. The payments over the lease term that the lessee is or can be required to make, excluding contingent rent, costs for services and taxes to be paid by and be reimbursable to the lessor, together with:

(a) For a lessee, any amounts guaranteed by the lessee or by a party related to the lessee

(b) For a lessor, any residual value guaranteed to the lessor by one of the following.

    (i) The lessee

    (ii) A party related to the lessee

    (iii) An independent third party financially capable of meeting this guarantee

However, if the lessee has the option to purchase the asset at a price which is expected to be sufficiently lower than fair value at the date the option becomes exercisable for it to be reasonably certain, at the inception of the lease, that the option will be exercised, the minimum lease payments comprise the minimum payments payable over the lease term to the expected date of exercise of this purchase option and the payment required to exercise it

Interest rate implicit in the lease.

The discount rate that, at the inception of the lease, causes the aggregate present value of

(a) The minimum lease payments; and
(b) The unguaranteed residual value

to be equal to the sum of

(a) The fair value of the leased asset; and
(b) Any initial direct costs.

Initial direct costs are **incremental costs** that are directly attributable to **negotiating** and **arranging** a lease, except for such costs incurred by manufacturer or dealer lessors. Examples of initial direct costs include amounts such as **commissions, legal fees** and relevant internal costs.

Lease term. The non-cancellable period for which the lessee has contracted to lease the asset together with any further terms for which the lessee has the option to continue to lease the asset, with or without further payment, when at the inception of the lease it is reasonably certain that the lessee will exercise the option.

A **non-cancellable lease** is a lease that is cancellable only in one of the following situations.

(a) Upon the occurrence of some remote contingency

(b) With the permission of the lessor

(c) If the lessee enters into a new lease for the same or an equivalent asset with the same lessor

(d) Upon payment by the lessee of an additional amount such that, at inception, continuation of the lease is reasonably certain

The **inception of the lease** is the earlier of the date of the lease agreement and the date of commitment by the parties to the principal provisions of the lease. As at this date:

(a) A lease is classified as either an operating lease or a finance lease; and

(b) In the case of a finance lease, the amounts to be recognised at the commencement of the lease term are determined.

Economic life is either:

(a) The period over which an asset is expected to be economically usable by one or more users; or

(b) The number of production or similar units expected to be obtained from the asset by one or more users.

Useful life is the estimated remaining period, from the beginning of the lease term, without limitation by the lease term, over which the economic benefits embodied in the asset are expected to be consumed by the entity.

Fair value is the amount for which an asset could be exchanged, or a liability settled, between knowledgeable, willing parties in an arm's length transaction.

Guaranteed residual value is:

(a) For a lessee, that part of the residual value which is guaranteed by the lessee or by a party related to the lessee (the amount of the guarantee being the maximum amount that could, in any event, become payable).

(b) For a lessor, that part of the residual value which is guaranteed by the lessee or by a third party unrelated to the lessor who is financially capable of discharging the obligations under the guarantee.

Unguaranteed residual value is that portion of the residual value of the leased asset, the realisation of which by the lessor is not assured or is guaranteed solely by a party related to the lessor.

Gross investment in the lease is the aggregate of:

(a) The minimum lease payments receivable by the lessor under a finance lease; and
(b) Any unguaranteed residual value accruing to the lessor.

Net investment in the lease is the gross investment in the lease discounted at the interest rate implicit in the lease.

Unearned finance income is the difference between:

(a) The gross investment in the lease; and
(b) The net investment in the lease.

The **lessee's incremental borrowing rate of interest** is the rate of interest the lessee would have to pay on a similar lease or, if that is not determinable, the rate that, at the inception of the lease, the lessee would incur to borrow over a similar term, and with a similar security, the funds necessary to purchase the asset.

Variable lease payments are payments made by a lessee to a lessor that vary because of changes in facts or circumstances occurring after the commencement date, other than the passage of time (eg percentage of sales, amount of usage, price indices, market rates of interest). (IFRS 16 Appendix A)

3.2 Finance lease or operating lease?

The following diagram can be used to determine whether a lease is a **finance lease** or an **operating lease**.

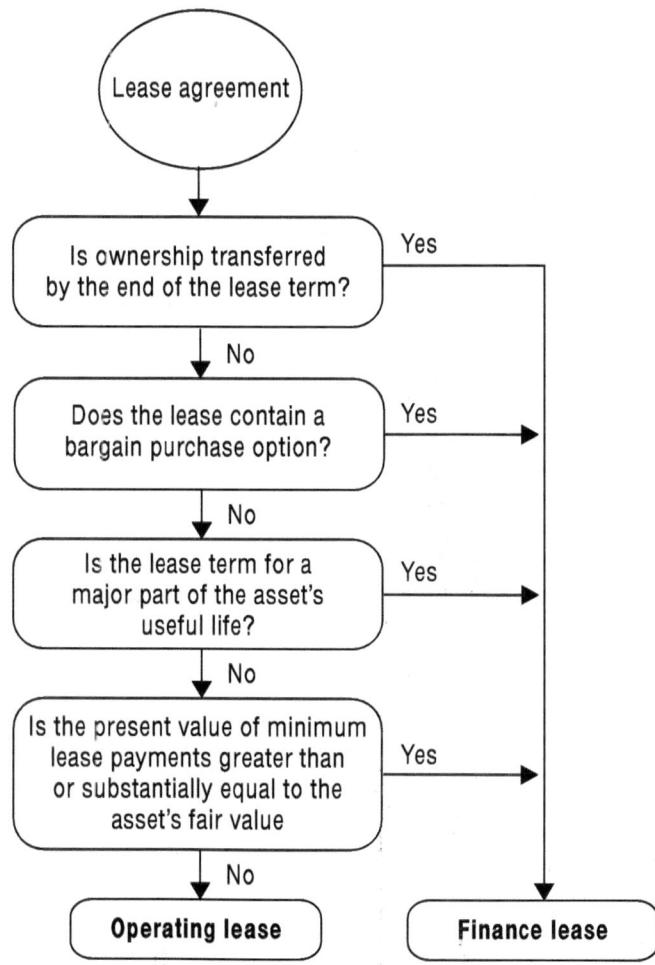

3.3 Example: Gross investment

Willco Co has just purchased a lorry from Drogon Trucks Co for $50,000. The lorry has been leased to Newton Freight Co on a two-year lease requiring annual payments in arrears of $13,500. Drogon Trucks have agreed to buy the truck back at open market value at the end of the lease.

Newton Freight Co have guaranteed that the value of the lorry after two years will be not less than $30,000. A realistic estimate of its value at that time is $33,000, ie the unguaranteed residual value is $3,000.

What is the gross investment in the lease at the start of the lease?

Solution

At the start of the lease the 'minimum lease payments' will be the rentals due of $27,000 plus the guaranteed residual of $30,000 giving $57,000. The gross investment in the lease will be the minimum lease payments of $57,000 plus the unguaranteed residual of $3,000 ($33,000 – $30,000) giving $60,000.

3.4 Example: Net investment

It will be apparent from the definition of net investment above that when any residual amount receivable by the lessor is insignificant (as is usually the case in normal full payout leases), the net investment in the lease will be equal to the cash selling price of the leased asset.

Consider again the example given in Section 2.2, this time from the point of view of the lessor.

Solution

	Years ending 31 December			
	20X0	20X1	20X2	20X3
	$	$	$	$
Net investment in the lease	7,710			
Less deposit	(2,000)			
Balance outstanding	5,710	4,566	3,251	1,739
Finance income at 15%	856	685	488	261
Instalment received	(2,000)	(2,000)	(2,000)	(2,000)
Balance outstanding at period end	4,566	3,251	1,739	–

The lessor's statement of financial position and notes will include the following amounts for each year.

	As at 31 December		
	20X3	20X4	20X5
	$	$	$
Finance lease receivables	4,566	3,251	1,739
Of which: due in one year (2,000 – 685) and (2,000 – 488)	1,315	1,512	1,739
due in more than one year	3,251	1,739	–

Note that under the assumptions of this question the total net investments shown above are the same as the obligations shown in the lessee's statement of financial position. This would not have been the case had the lessee based its disclosure on a present value found using its cost of borrowing rather than the implied rate in the lease.

3.5 Operating leases

An **asset** held for use in operating leases by a lessor should be recorded as a non-current asset and depreciated over its useful life. The basis for depreciation should be consistent with the lessor's policy on similar non-lease assets and follow the guidance in IAS 16.

Income from an operating lease, excluding charges for services such as insurance and maintenance, should be recognised on **a straight-line basis** over the period of the lease (even if the receipts are not on such a basis), unless another systematic and rational basis is more representative of the time pattern in which the benefit from the leased asset is receivable.

Initial direct costs incurred by lessors in negotiating and arranging an operating lease should be **added to the carrying amount** of the leased asset and recognised as an expense over the lease term on the same basis as lease income, ie capitalised and amortised over the lease term.

Lessors should refer to IAS 36 in order to determine whether a leased asset has become impaired.

A lessor who is a **manufacturer or dealer** should not recognise any selling profit on entering into an operating lease because it is not the equivalent of a sale.

3.6 Example: Operating lease

Martin Co has supplied an asset to a customer for a period of 12 months commencing 1 July 20X1 and has correctly classified the contract as an operating lease. The customer receives the first three months rent free and pays $12,000 per month starting in the fourth month.

What income should Martin Co recognise in its statement f profit or loss for the year ended 31 December 20X1?

Solution

The income will be recognised on a straight line basis over the life of the contract. Total income is $12,000 × 9 = $108,000. Income for the six months ended 31 December 20X1 should therefore be $108,000 × 6/12 = $54,000.

4 Sale and leaseback transactions

FAST FORWARD

In a sale and leaseback transaction, an asset is sold by a vendor and then the same asset is **leased back** to the same vendor. The lease payment and sale price are normally interdependent because they are negotiated as part of the same package.

4.1 Sale or not?

To determine whether the transfer of an asset is accounted for as a sale an entity applies the requirements of IFRS 15 *Revenue from Contracts with Customers* for determining when a performance obligation is satisfied.

4.1.1 Transfer is a sale

If the transfer satisfies the IFRS 15 requirement to be accounted for as a sale:

- The seller/lessee measures the right-of-use asset arising from the leaseback at the proportion of the previous carrying amount of the asset that relates to the **right-of use retained** by the seller/lessee.
- The seller/lessee only recognises the amount of any gain or loss on the sale that relates to the **rights transferred** to the buyer (IFRS 16: para. 100).

If the fair value of the consideration for the sale does not equal the fair value of the asset, or if the lease payments are not at market rates, the following adjustments should be made:

- Any **below-market terms** should be accounted for as a prepayment of lease payments (the shortfall in consideration received from the lessor is treated as a lease payment made by the lessee).
- Any **above-market terms** are accounted for as additional financing provided by the buyer/lessor (the additional amount paid by the lessor is treated as additional liability, **not** as gain on the sale) (IFRS 16: para. 101).

4.1.2 Transfer is not a sale

If the transfer does not satisfy the IFRS 15 requirements to be accounted for as a sale, the seller continues to recognise the transferred asset and the transfer proceeds are treated as a financial liability, accounted for in accordance with IFRS 9. The transaction is more in the nature of a secured loan.

4.2 Example: sale and leaseback

[Adapted from IFRS 16 Illustrative example 24]

The seller/lessee sells a building to the buyer/lessor for $800,000 cash. The carrying amount of the building prior to the sale was $600,000. The seller/lessee arranges to lease the building back for five years at $120,000 per annum, payable in arrears. The remaining useful life is 15 years.

The transaction satisfies the performance obligations in IFRS 15, so will be accounted for as a sale and leaseback.

At the date of sale the fair value of the building was $750,000, so the excess $50,000 paid by the buyer is recognised as additional financing provided by the buyer/lessor.

The interest rate implicit in the lease is 4.5% and the present value of the annual payments is:

	$
$120,000/1.045$	114,833
$120,000/1.045^2$	109,888
$120,000/1.045^3$	105,155
$120,000/1.045^4$	100,627
$120,000/1.045^5$	96,294
	526,797

Of this, $476,797 relates to the lease and $50,000 relates to the additional financing.

At the commencement date, the seller/lessee measures the right-of-use asset arising from the leaseback of the building at the proportion of the previous carrying amount of the building that relates to the right-of-use retained. This is calculated as carrying amount × discounted lease payments/fair value.

In our example: $600,000 × 476,797/750,000 = $381,437

The seller/lessee only recognises the amount of gain that relates to the rights transferred. The gain on sale of the building is $150,000 (750,000 – 600,000), of which:

(a) 150,000 × 476,797/750,000 = $95,360 – relates to the rights retained
(b) The balance – 150,000 – 95,360 = $54,640 – relates to the rights transferred to the buyer

At the commencement date the lessee accounts for the transaction as follows:

	Debit $	Credit $
Cash	800,000	
Right-of-use asset	381,437	
Building		600,000
Financial liability		526,797
Gain on rights transferred		54,640
	1,181,437	1,181,437

The right-of-use asset will be depreciated over five years, the gain will be recognised in profit or loss and the financial liability will be increased each year by the interest charge and reduced by the lease payments.

5 Disclosures

FAST FORWARD

There are separate disclosure requirements for lessees and lessors under IFRS 16.

5.1 Lessees

A lessee is required to disclose:

- Depreciation charge for right-of-use assets by class of underlying asset
- Interest expense on lease liabilities
- Expenses relating to short-term leases and leases of low-value assets
- Expense relating to variable lease payments
- Income from subleasing right-of-use assets
- Total cash outflow for leases
- Additions to right-of-use assets
- Gains or losses arising from sale and leaseback transactions
- Carrying amount of right-of-use assets at the end of the period.

5.2 Lessors

A lessor is required to disclose:

For finance leases:

- Selling profit or loss;
- Finance income on net investment in the lease; and
- Income relating to variable lease payments not included in the net investment in the lease

Also:

- Information in respect of significant changes in the carrying amount of the net investment in finance leases
- Maturity analysis of lease payments receivable

PART C ACCOUNTING AND REPORTING TECHNIQUES

For **operating leases**:

Lease income, separately disclosing income relating to variable lease payments that do not depend on an index or rate.

IAS 16 requirements in relation to assets subject to an operating lease

Lessors should also disclose information in respect of the nature of leasing activities and how associated risk is managed.

Exam focus point

The **disclosure requirements** for both lessees and lessors should force disclosure of sale and leaseback transactions. IAS 1 *Presentation of Financial Statements* should be considered.

Chapter roundup

- IFRS 16 *Leases* covers accounting for lease transactions by both lessees and lessors.
- If a contract contains a lease the customer recognises an asset and a liability in the statement of financial position.
- **Under IFRS 16 lessors continue to distinguish between finance leases and operating leases**.
- Make sure you learn these **important definitions which are applicable to lessor accounting**:
    - Finance lease
    - Operating lease
    - Minimum lease payments
    - Interest rate implicit in the lease
    - Guaranteed and unguaranteed residual value
    - Gross and net investment in the lease
- **In** a sale and leaseback transaction, an asset is sold by a vendor and then the same asset is **leased back** to the same vendor. The lease payment and sale price are normally interdependent because they are negotiated as part of the same package.
- **There are separate disclosure requirements for lessees and lessors under IFRS 16**.

Quick quiz

1. What are the conditions for determining that a customer controls an identified asset?
2. How are right of use assets initially measured?
3. What is the present value of future lease payments?
4. Distinguish between a finance lease and an operating lease from the perspective of a lessor.
5. The full extent of the gain on a sale and leaseback transaction can be recognised in profit or loss. True or False?
6. List the disclosure requirements for lessees under leases.

Answers to quick quiz

1 The customer controls an asset if both of the following conditions are met.

- The customer has right to obtain substantially all of the economic benefits from use of the identified asset.
- The customer has the right to direct the use of the identified asset.

2 A right of use asset is initially measured as:

	$
Initial measurement of lease liability (present value of future lease payments)	X
Lease payments made at/before commencement date	X
Initial direct costs incurred by lessee	X
Estimated dismantling and restoration costs (where an obligation exists)	X
Lease incentives received	(X)
Cost of right-of-use asset	**X**

3 The present value of future lease payments (PVFLP) is calculated as all lease payments not paid at the commencement date of the lease (ie it excludes any deposits or payments in advance) discounted at the discount rate implicit in the lease. The PVFLP is the initial amount of the lease liability.

4 (a) A finance lease transfers substantially all the risks and rewards incident to ownership of an asset. Title may or may not be transferred eventually

   (b) An operating lease is a lease other than a finance lease

5 False. Only the gain in respect of the rights transferred to the buyer/lessor can be recognised in the statement of profit or loss. No gain can be recognised in respect of the rights retained.

6 (a) Depreciation charge for right-of-use assets by class of underlying asset;

   (b) Interest expense on lease liabilities;

   (c) The expense relating to short-term leases

   (d) The expense relating to leases of low-value assets

   (e) The expense relating to variable lease payments not included in the measurement of lease liabilities;

   (f) Income from subleasing right-of-use assets;

   (g) Total cash outflow for leases;

   (h) Additions to right-of-use assets;

   (i) Gains or losses arising from sale and leaseback transactions; and

   (j) The carrying amount of right-of-use assets at the end of the reporting period by class of underlying asset

15: LEASING CONTRACTS

End of chapter question

Trench Quarries (AIA May 2010 amended)

(Trench Quarries is a public liability company and an independent quarry operator. The company provides ready-mixed concrete to major building contractors. At 31 March 2010 the company has a lease of a machine in operation at one of its quarries and wishes to know how this contract should be accounted for in the company's financial statements.

On 1 October 2009 the company entered into a five year agreement to lease a machine used to crush rock. Trench Quarries and the lessor became committed to the main provisions of the lease at that date. The machine was delivered on 1 October 2009, at which date its estimated useful life was six years. The following information concerns the lease agreement:

Initial direct costs paid by Trench Quarries	$0.2 million
Present value of the future lease payments	$7.3 million
Lease payments payable in advance	$0.8 million per month

The machine was due to commence commercial production on 1 October 2009 but, due to difficulties in training Trench Quarry operators, did not do so until 1 January 2010. As a result the lessor allowed the lease payments to begin on 1 January 2010.

Required

(a) Advise the appropriate accounting treatment of the above lease agreement to comply with IFRS 16 *Leases*. **(10 marks)**

(b) Explain the reasons for the introduction of IFRS 16 *Leases* and analyse the likely effect on companies that had previously accounted for some leases as expenses. **(10 marks)**

(Total 20 marks)

PART C ACCOUNTING AND REPORTING TECHNIQUES

Employee benefits

Topic list	Syllabus reference
1 IAS 19 *Employee Benefits*	LO3
2 Short-term employee benefits	LO3
3 Post-employment benefits	LO3
4 Defined contribution plans	LO3
5 Defined benefit plans: Recognition and measurement	LO3
6 The asset ceiling	Lo3
7 Approach to defined benefits questions	LO3
8 Other long-term benefits	LO3
9 Termination benefits	LO3

Introduction

An increasing number of companies and other entities now provide a **pension and other employee benefits** as part of their employees' remuneration package. In view of this trend, it is important that there is standard best practice for the way in which employee benefit costs are **recognised, measured, presented and disclosed** in the sponsoring entities' financial statements.

1 IAS 19 *Employee Benefits*

FAST FORWARD

IAS 19 *Employee Benefits* is a long and complex standard covering both short-term and long-term (post-employment) benefits. The complications arise when dealing with **post-employment benefits**.

IAS 19 covers **all employee benefit costs**, except share-based payment, not only retirement benefit (pension) costs. Before we look at IAS 19, we should consider the nature of employee benefit costs and why there is an accounting problem which must be addressed by a standard.

1.1 The conceptual nature of employee benefit costs

When a company or other entity employs a new worker, that worker will be offered a **package of pay and benefits**. Some of these will be short-term and the employee will receive the benefit at about the same time as he or she earns it, for example basic pay, overtime etc. Other employee benefits are **deferred**, however, the main example being retirement benefits (ie a pension).

The cost of these deferred employee benefits to the employer can be viewed in various ways. They could be described as **deferred salary** to the employee. Alternatively, they are a **deduction** from the employee's true gross salary, used as a tax-efficient means of saving. In some countries, tax efficiency arises on retirement benefit contributions because they are not taxed on the employee, but they are allowed as a deduction from taxable profits of the employer.

1.2 Accounting for employee benefit costs

Short-term employee benefit costs	• tends to be quite straightforward
	• simply recognised as an expense in the employer's financial statements of the current period
Deferred employee benefits	• much more difficult
	• large amounts involved, long time scale, complicated estimates and uncertainties

1.3 IAS 19 *Employee Benefits*

IAS 19 prescribes the following:

(a) When the cost of employee benefits should be **recognised as a liability or an expense**
(b) The **amount** of the liability or expense that should be recognised

As a basic rule, the standard states the following:

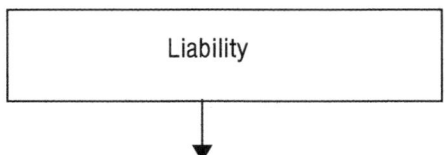

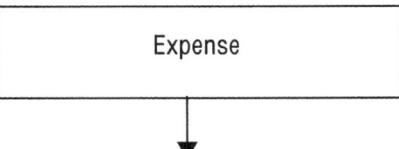

Recognised when an employee has provided a service in exchange for benefits to be received by the employee at some time in the future

Recognised when the entity enjoys the economic benefits from a service provided by an employee regardless of when the employee received or will receive the benefits from providing the service.

The basic problem is therefore fairly straightforward. An entity will often enjoy the **economic benefits** from the services provided by its employees in advance of the employees receiving all the employment benefits from the work they have done, for example they will not receive pension benefits until after they retire.

1.4 Categories of employee benefits

The standard recognises four categories of employee benefits, and proposes a different accounting treatment for each. These four categories are as follows:

Short-term benefits including: • Wages and salaries • Social security contributions • Paid annual / sick / maternity / paternity leave • Profit shares and bonuses paid within 12 months of the year end • Non-monetary benefits, eg medical care, cars, free goods	Post-employment benefits, eg pensions and post-employment medical care
Other long-term benefits, eg profit shares, bonuses or deferred compensation payable later than 12 months after the year end, sabbatical leave, long-service benefits	Termination benefits, eg early retirement payments and redundancy payments

Benefits under share-option schemes and the like are accounted for under IFRS 2 *Share-based Payment* (see Chapter 20).

1.5 Definitions

IAS 19 uses a great many important definitions. They are grouped together here, but you should refer back to them as necessary as you work through the rest of this chapter.

Key terms

Definitions of employee benefits

Employee benefits are all forms of consideration given by an entity in exchange for service rendered by employees or for the termination of employment.

Short-term employee benefits are employee benefits (other than termination benefits) that are expected to be settled wholly before 12 months after the end of the annual reporting period in which the employees render the related service.

Post-employment benefits are employee benefits (other than termination benefits and short-term employee benefits) which are payable after the completion of employment.

Other long-term employee benefits are all employee benefits other than short-term employee benefits, post-employment benefits and termination benefits.

Termination benefits are employee benefits provided in exchange for the termination of an employee's employment as a result of either:

(a) An entity's decision to terminate an employee's employment before the normal retirement date; or

(b) An employee's decision to accept an offer of benefits in exchange for the termination of employment.

Definitions relating to classification of plans

Post-employment benefit plans are formal or informal arrangements under which an entity provides post-employment benefits for one or more employees.

Defined contribution plans are post-employment benefit plans under which an entity pays fixed contributions into a separate entity (a fund) and will have no legal or constructive obligation to pay further contributions if the fund does not hold sufficient assets to pay all employee benefits relating to employee service in the current and prior periods.

Defined benefit plans are post-employment benefit plans other than defined contribution plans.

Multi-employer plans are defined contribution plans (other than state plans) or defined benefit plans (other than state plans) that:

PART C ACCOUNTING AND REPORTING TECHNIQUES

(a) Pool the assets contributed by various entities that are not under common control, and
(b) Use those assets to provide benefits to employees of more than one entity, on the basis that contribution and benefit levels are determined without regard to the identity of the entity that employs the employees concerned.

Definitions relating to the net defined benefit liability (asset)

The **net defined benefit liability (asset)** is the deficit or surplus, adjusted for any effect of limiting a net defined benefit asset to the asset ceiling.

The **deficit or surplus** is:

(a) The present value of the defined benefit obligation; less
(b) The fair value of plan assets (if any).

The **asset ceiling** is the present value of any economic benefits available in the form of refunds from the plan or reductions in future contributions to the plan.

The **present value of a defined benefit** obligation is the present value, without deducting any plan assets, of expected future payments required to settle the obligation resulting from employee service in the current and prior periods.

Plan assets comprise:

(a) Assets held by a long-term employee benefit fund; and
(b) Qualifying insurance policies

Asset held by a long-term employee benefit fund are assets (other than non-transferable financial instruments issued by the reporting entity) that:

(a) Are held by an entity (a fund) that is legally separate from the reporting entity and exists solely to pay or fund employee benefits; and
(b) Are available to be used only to pay or fund employee benefits, are not available to the reporting entity's own creditors (even in bankruptcy), and cannot be returned to the reporting entity, unless either:

   (i) The remaining assets of the fund are sufficient to meet all the related employee benefit obligations of the plan or the reporting entity; or
   (ii) The assets are returned to the reporting entity to reimburse it for employee benefits already paid

A **qualifying insurance policy** is an insurance policy issued by an insurer that is not a related party (as defined in IAS 24) of the reporting entity, if the proceeds of the policy:

(a) Can be used only to pay or fund employee benefits under a defined benefit plan; and
(b) Are not available to the reporting entity's own creditors (even in bankruptcy) and cannot be paid to the reporting entity, unless either:

   (i) The proceeds represent surplus assets that are not needed for the policy to meet all the related employee benefit obligations; or
   (ii) The proceeds are returned to the reporting entity to reimburse it for employee benefits already paid.

Fair value is the price that would be received to sell an asset or paid to transfer a liability in an orderly transaction between market participants at the measurement date.

Definitions relating to defined benefit cost

Service cost comprises:

(a) **Current service cost**, which is the increase in the present value of the defined benefit obligation resulting from employee service in the current period;
(b) **Past service cost**, which is the change in the present value of the defined benefit obligation for employee service in prior periods, resulting from a plan amendment (the introduction or

withdrawal of, or changes to, a defined benefit plan) or a curtailment (a significant reduction by the entity in the number of employees covered by a plan); and

(c) And gain or loss on settlement.

Net interest on the net defined benefit liability (asset) is the change during the period in the net defined benefit liability (asset) that arises from the passage of time.

Remeasurements of the net defined benefit liability (asset) comprise:

(a) Actuarial gains and losses;

(b) The return on plan assets, excluding amounts included in net interest on the net defined benefit liability (asset); and

(c) Any change in the effect of the asset ceiling, excluding amounts included in net interest on the net defined benefit liability (asset).

Actuarial gains and losses are changes in the present value of the defined benefit obligation resulting from:

(a) Experience adjustments (the effects of differences between the previous actuarial assumptions and what has actually occurred); and

(b) The effects of changes in actuarial assumptions.

The **return on plan assets** is interest, dividends and other income derived from the plan assets, together with realised and unrealised gains or losses on the plan assets, less:

(a) Any costs of managing plan assets; and

(b) Any tax payable by the plan itself, other than tax included in the actuarial assumptions used to measure the present value of the defined benefit obligation.

A **settlement** is a transaction that eliminates all further legal or constructive obligations for part or all of the benefits provided under a defined benefit plan, other than a payment of benefits to, or on behalf of, employees that is set out in the terms of the plan and included in the actuarial assumptions.

(IAS 19)

1.6 Section summary

There are **two key issues** or problems to consider.

- It may be necessary to rely on **actuarial assumptions** about what the future amount of benefits payable will be.
- If benefits are payable later than 12 months after the end of the accounting period, the future benefits payable should be **discounted** to a present value.

2 Short-term employee benefits

Accounting for short-term employee benefits is fairly straightforward, because there are **no actuarial assumptions** to be made, and there is **no requirement to discount** future benefits (because they are all, by definition, payable no later than 12 months after the end of the accounting period).

2.1 Recognition and measurement

The rules for short-term benefits are essentially an application of **basic accounting principles and practice**.

cost of short-term employee benefits should be recognised as an **expense** (or as part of the cost of an asset

→ **Unpaid amounts** recognised as a **liability** (accrued expense)

→ **Prepaid amounts** recognised as an **asset** (prepayment)

2.2 Short-term absences

Short-term accumulating paid absences	Absences for which an employee is paid, and if the employee's entitlement has not been used up at the end of the period, they are carried forward to the next period, for example paid holiday which, if unused, can be carried to future periods.
	Cost of the benefits of such absences should be **charged as an expense as the employees render service**
Short-term non-accumulating paid absences	Absences for which an employee is paid when they occur, but an **entitlement to the absences does not accumulate**. The employee can be absent, and be paid, but only if and when the circumstances arise, for example maternity/paternity pay, (in most cases) sick pay, and paid absence for jury service.
	The cost of these should be **recognised when the absences occur.**

2.3 Example: Unused holiday leave

A company gives its employees an annual entitlement to paid holiday leave. If there is any unused leave at the end of the year, employees are entitled to carry forward the unused leave for up to 12 months. At the end of 20X9, the company's employees carried forward in total 50 days of unused holiday leave. Employees are paid $100 per day.

Required

State the required accounting for the unused holiday carried forward.

Solution

The cost of $5,000 short-term accumulating compensated absences should be recognised as a liability and an expense in the year when the entitlement arises, ie in 20X9.

Question — Sick leave

Plyman Co has 100 employees. Each is entitled to five working days of paid sick leave for each year, and unused sick leave can be carried forward for one year. Sick leave is taken on a LIFO basis (ie firstly out of the current year's entitlement and then out of any balance brought forward).

As at 31 December 20X8, the average unused entitlement is two days per employee. Plyman Co expects (based on past experience which is expected to continue) that 92 employees will take five days or less sick leave in 20X9, the remaining eight employees will take an average of 6½ days each.

Required

State the required accounting for sick leave.

> **Answer**
>
> Plyman Co expects to pay an additional 12 days of sick pay as a result of the unused entitlement that has accumulated at 31 December 20X8, ie 1½ days × 8 employees. Plyman Co should recognise a liability equal to 12 days of sick pay.

2.4 Profit sharing or bonus plans

Profit shares or bonuses payable within 12 months after the end of the accounting period should be recognised as an expected cost when the entity has a **present obligation to pay it**, ie when the employer has no real option but to pay it. This will usually be when the employer recognises the profit or other performance achievement to which the profit share or bonus relates.

2.5 Example: Profit sharing plan

Mooro Co runs a profit sharing plan under which it pays 3% of its profit for the year to its employees if none have left during the year. Mooro Co estimates that this will be reduced by staff turnover to 2.5% in 20X9.

Required

Which costs should be recognised by Mooro Co for the profit share?

Solution

Mooro Co should recognise a liability and an expense of 2.5% of profit.

2.6 Disclosure

There are **no specific disclosure requirements for short-term employee benefits** in the standard.

3 Post-employment benefits

> **FAST FORWARD**
>
> There are **two types of post-employment benefit plan**:
> - Defined contribution plans
> - Defined benefit plans
>
> **Defined contribution plans** are simple to account for because it is the contributions payable which are promised and the eventual benefits depend on them.
>
> **Defined benefit plans** are much more difficult to account for because it is the eventual benefits which are promised and the total contributions depend on them.

Many employers provide post-employment benefits for their employees after they have stopped working. **Pension schemes** are the most obvious example, but an employer might provide post-employment death benefits to the dependants of former employees, or post-employment medical care.

Post-employment benefit schemes are often referred to as '**plans**'. The 'plan' receives regular contributions from the employer (and sometimes from current employees as well) and the money is invested in assets, such as stocks and shares and other investments. The post-employment benefits are paid out of the income from the plan assets (dividends, interest) or from money from the sale of some plan assets.

There are two types or categories of post-employment benefit plan, as given in the definitions in Section 1.5 above.

(a) **Defined contribution plans.** With such plans, the employer (and possibly current employees too) pay regular contributions into the plan of a given or 'defined' amount each year. The contributions are invested, and the size of the post-employment benefits paid to former employees depends on how well or how badly the plan's investments perform. If the investments perform well, the plan will be able to afford higher benefits than if the investments performed less well.

(b) **Defined benefit plans.** With these plans, the size of the post-employment benefits is determined in advance, ie the benefits are 'defined'. The employer (and possibly current employees too) pay contributions into the plan, and the contributions are invested. The size of the contributions is set at an amount that is expected to earn enough investment returns to meet the obligation to pay the post-employment benefits. If, however, it becomes apparent that the assets in the fund are insufficient, the employer will be required to make additional contributions into the plan to make up the expected shortfall. On the other hand, if the fund's assets appear to be larger than they need to be, and in excess of what is required to pay the post-employment benefits, the employer may be allowed to take a 'contribution holiday' (ie stop paying in contributions for a while).

3.1 Section summary

- There are two categories of **post-retirement benefits**:
    - Defined contribution schemes
    - Defined benefit schemes
- **Defined contribution schemes** provide benefits commensurate with the fund available to produce them.
- **Defined benefit schemes** provide promised benefits and so contributions are based on estimates of how the fund will perform.
- **Defined contribution scheme costs** are easy to account for and this is covered in the next section.
- The main part of the rest of this chapter deals with the more difficult question of how **defined benefit scheme costs** are accounted for.

4 Defined contribution plans

Accounting for payments into defined contribution plans is straightforward.

(a) The **obligation** is determined by the amount payable into the plan in each period.

(b) There are no actuarial assumptions to make.

(c) If the obligation is settled in the current period (or at least no later than 12 months after the end of the current period) there is **no requirement for discounting**.

IAS 19 requires the following, which is consistent with the required treatment for a short term employee benefit:

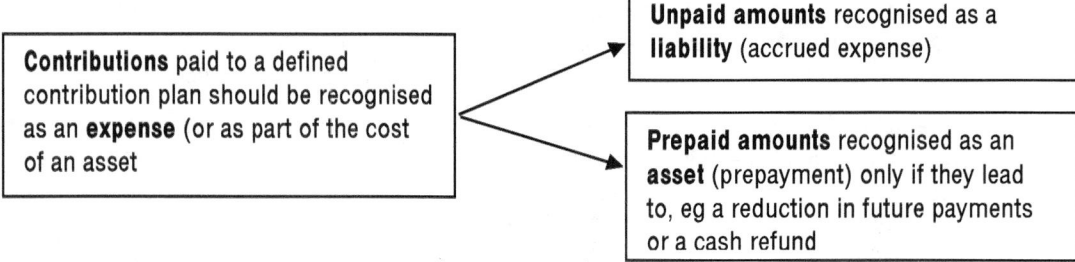

In the (unusual) situation where contributions to a defined contribution plan do not fall due entirely within 12 months after the end of the period in which the employees performed the related service, then these should be **discounted**. The discount rate to be used is discussed below.

Disclosure requirements

(a) A **description** of the plan
(b) The amount recognised as an **expense** in the period

5 Defined benefit plans: Recognition and measurement

Accounting for defined benefit plans is much more complex. The complexity of accounting for defined benefit plans stems largely from the following factors.

(a) The future benefits (arising from employee service in the current or prior years) **cannot be estimated exactly**, but whatever they are, the employer will have to pay them, and the liability should therefore be recognised now. To estimate these future obligations, it is necessary to use **actuarial assumptions**.

(b) The obligations payable in future years should be valued, by discounting, on a **present value** basis. This is because the obligations may be settled in many years' time.

(c) If actuarial assumptions change, the amount of required contributions to the fund will change, and there may be **remeasurements**. A contribution into a fund in any period is not necessarily the total for that period, due to remeasurements.

Most of the definitions given in the standard (shown in Section 1) are to do with defined benefit plans.

5.1 Outline of the method

FAST FORWARD | There is a **five-step method** for accounting for the expenses and liability of a defined benefit pension plan.

An outline of the method used for an employer to account for the expenses and obligation of a defined benefit plan is given below. The stages will be explained in more detail later.

Step 1
Section 5.3

Determining the deficit or surplus. This involves:

(i) Using an actuarial technique, the projected unit credit method, to make a reliable estimate of the ultimate cost to the entity of the benefit that employees have earned in return for their service in the current and prior periods. This requires an entity to consider **actuarial assumptions** ie estimates about variables such as employee turnover and future increases in salary that will affect the future benefit. (see **Section 5.3.1**)

(ii) Discounting the benefit in order to determine the present value of the defined benefit obligation and the current service cost. (see **Section 5.3.3**)

(iii) Deducting the fair value of the plan assets from the present value of the defined benefit obligation. (see **Section 5.3.4**)

Step 2
Section 5.4

Determining the amount of the net defined benefit liability (asset) as the amount of the deficit or surplus determined in (a), adjusted for any effect of limiting a net defined benefit asset to the asset ceiling.

Step 3
Section 5.5

Account for contributions to the pension plan (which increase plan assets) and benefits paid from the pension plan (which decrease both plan assets and plan obligations)

Step 4 Determining amounts to be recognised in profit or loss:

Section 5.6
(i) Current service cost (calculated using the projected unit credit method – see **Section 5.3)**
(ii) Any past service cost and gain or loss on settlement
(iii) Net interest on the defined benefit liability (asset)

Step 5 Determining the remeasurements of the net defined benefit liability (asset) to be recognised in other comprehensive income, comprising:

Section 5.6
(i) Actuarial gains and losses
(ii) Return on plan assets excluding amounts included in net interest on the defined benefit liability (asset)
(iii) Any change in the effect of the asset ceiling, excluding amounts included in net interest on the net defined benefit liability (asset).

5.2 Constructive obligation

IAS 19 makes it very clear that it is not only its legal obligation under the formal terms of a defined benefit plan that an entity must account for, but also for any **constructive obligation** that it may have. A constructive obligation, which will arise from the entity's informal practices, exist when the entity has no realistic alternative but to pay employee benefits, for example if any change in the informal practices would cause unacceptable damage to employee relationships.

5.3 Step 1 – Determining the deficit or surplus

5.3.1 The Projected Unit Credit Method

FAST FORWARD

> Future benefits are attributed to services performed by employees using the **Projected Unit Credit Method**.

With this method, it is assumed that each period of service by an employee gives rise to an **additional unit of future benefits**. The present value of that unit of future benefits can be calculated, and attributed to the period in which the service is given as the current service cost. The units, each measured separately, build up to the overall obligation. The accumulated present value of (discounted) future benefits will incur interest over time, and an interest expense should be recognised.

The method relies on a number of actuarial assumptions – some of which are non-financial such as employee turnover and mortality rates, and some of which are financial, such as expected future salaries. These are discussed in the next section.

In practice, the mathematics will be complex. Here is a simplified example, using figures rounded to whole numbers.

5.3.2 Example: Projected Unit Credit Method

An employer pays a lump sum to employees when they retire. The lump sum is equal to 1% of their salary in the final year of service, for every year of service they have given.

(a) An employee is expected to work for 5 years (actuarial assumption)
(b) His salary is expected to rise by 7% pa (actuarial assumption)
(c) His salary in 20X1 is $10,000
(d) The discount rate applied is 10% pa

Required

Calculate the amounts chargeable to each of years 20X1 to 20X5 and the closing obligation each year, assuming no change in actuarial assumptions.

16: EMPLOYEE BENEFITS

Solution

Since his salary in 20X1 is $10,000, his salary in 20X5 is expected to be $13,107 (£10,000 × 1.07^4). His lump sum entitlement is therefore expected to be 1% of $13,107 ie $131 for each year's service, giving $655 in total.

Using the Projected Unit Credit Method, and assuming that the actuarial assumptions do not change over the years 20X1 to 20X5, and that the employee does leave at the end of 20X5, the calculations are as follows:

Future benefit attributable to:	20X1 $	20X2 $	20X3 $	20X4 $	20X5 $
Prior years	0	131	262	393	524
Current year (1% of final salary)	131	131	131	131	131
Prior and current years total	131	262	393	524	655

The future benefit builds up to $655 over the five years, at the end of which the employee is expected to leave and the benefit is payable.

These figures, however, have not been discounted. The benefit attributable to the current year should be discounted, in this example at 10%, from the end of 20X5.

	20X1 $	20X2 $	20X3 $	20X4 $	20X5 $
Opening obligation (note 1)	–	89	196	324	476
Interest (note 2)	–	9	20	33	48
Current service cost (note 3)	89	98	108	119	131
Closing obligation (note 4)	89	196	324	476	655

Notes

1. The opening obligation is the closing obligation of the previous period, brought forward.
2. Interest is 10% of this opening obligation (rounded to the nearest $).
3. The current service cost is the future obligation attributed to the current period (in this example $131 in each year), discounted back by 10% for 4, 3, 2 and 1 years respectively.
4. The closing obligation is the total of the opening obligation brought forward, the interest charged on that amount and the current year service cost.
5. The calculations in the example above assume that actuarial forecasts are exactly correct. If these were to prove incorrect (which is likely in practice), there could be an adjustment to make, resulting in an actuarial gain or an actuarial loss.

5.3.3 Actuarial assumptions

FAST FORWARD

> Actuarial assumptions made should be unbiased and based on market expectations.

Actuarial assumptions are needed **to estimate the size of the future (post-employment) benefits** that will be payable under a defined benefit plan. The main categories of actuarial assumptions are as follows.

(a) **Demographic assumptions** are about mortality rates before and after retirement, the rate of employee turnover, early retirement, claim rates under medical plans for former employees, and so on.

(b) **Financial assumptions** are the expected return on plan assets, future salary levels (allowing for seniority and promotion as well as inflation) and the future rate of increase in medical costs (not just inflationary cost rises, but also cost rises specific to medical treatments and to medical treatments required given the expectations of longer average life expectancy).

The standard requires actuarial assumptions to be neither too cautious nor too imprudent: they should be **'unbiased'**. They should also be based on **'market expectations'** at the year end, over the period during which the obligations will be settled.

5.3.4 Discount rate

The example above shows how the post-employment benefit obligation estimated based on actuarial assumptions is discounted in order to determine the present value of the defined benefit obligation and current service cost in each year.

The **discount rate** adopted should be determined by reference to **market yields** (at the year end) on high quality fixed-rate corporate bonds. In the absence of a 'deep' market in such bonds, the yields on comparable government bonds should be used as reference instead. The maturity of the corporate bonds that are used to determine a discount rate should have a term to maturity that is consistent with the expected maturity of the post-employment benefit obligations, although a single weighted average discount rate is sufficient.

5.3.5 Fair value of plan assets

The fair value of plan assets are deducted from the present value of the defined benefit obligation or give the net deficit or surplus.

Plan assets are:

(a) Assets such as stocks and shares, held by a fund that is legally separate from the reporting entity, which exists solely to pay employee benefits.

(b) Insurance policies, issued by an insurer that is not a related party, the proceeds of which can only be used to pay employee benefits.

Investments which may be used for purposes other than to pay employee benefits are not plan assets.

The standard requires that the plan assets are measured at fair value, defined in accordance with IFRS 13 *Fair Value Measurement* as 'the price that would be received to sell an asset or paid to transfer a liability in an orderly transaction between market participants at the measurement date.'

IAS 19 includes the following **specific requirements:**

(a) The plan assets should exclude any contributions due from the employer but not yet paid.

(b) Plan assets are reduced by any liabilities of the fund that do not relate to employee benefits, such as trade and other payables.

5.4 Step 2 – Determining the net defined benefit (asset) in the statement of financial position

In the statement of financial position, the amount recognised as a **defined benefit liability** (which may be a negative amount, ie an asset) should be the following:

(a) The **present value of the defined obligation** at the year end, **minus**

(b) The **fair value of the assets of the plan** as at the year end (if there are any) out of which the future obligations to current and past employees will be directly settled.

Where there is a net defined benefit asset, the amount of this may be limited by the 'asset ceiling'. We shall discuss this in more detail later in the chapter.

5.5 Step 3 – Accounting for contributions and benefits

Contributions paid into the plan by the sponsoring employer and benefits paid out of the plan to its members (in the form of pension payments) are easy to account for:

Contributions		
• Into the plan by the company • As advised by actuary	DEBIT CREDIT	Plan assets (SOFP) Company cash
Benefits	DEBIT	PV defined benefit obligation (SOFP)
• Actual pension payments made	CREDIT	Plan assets (SOFP)

5.5.1 Employee contributions

In some entities, employees also make contributions to the retirement plan. These contributions reduce the cost to the entity of providing the benefits, and so are deducted from service cost.

- If the amounts of the contributions are independent of the numbers of years of service, the entity is permitted (but may choose not to) recognise them as reduction of service cost in the period in which the service is rendered, instead of attributing them to periods of service.

- If the amounts are dependent on the number of years of service, then those amounts must be attributed to periods of service using the same attribution method used to allocate service cost to periods of service.

5.6 Step 4 Amounts to be recognised in the statement of profit or loss and Step 5 Amounts to be recognised in other comprehensive income

Step three of the four step plan is determining amounts to be recognised in the statement of profit or loss and other comprehensive income.

All of the gains and losses that affect the plan obligation and plan asset must be recognised. The **components of defined benefit cost must be recognised as follows** in the statement of profit or loss and other comprehensive income:

Component	Recognised in
(a) **Service cost**	Profit or loss
(b) **Net interest on the net defined benefit liability**	Profit or loss
(c) **Remeasurements of the net defined benefit liability (asset)**	Other comprehensive income (not reclassified to profit or loss)

The revised *Conceptual Framework* (2018) does not define profit or loss or clarify the meaning or importance of other comprehensive income, or how the distinction between profit or loss and other comprehensive income should be made in practice. It does however assert that 'the statement of profit or loss is the primary source of information about an entity's performance for the reporting period' (CF: para. 7.16). It also states that all income and expenses in a period are, in principle, included in the statement of profit or loss. However when the IASB is developing standards, in exceptional circumstances, it may require a change in the current value of an asset or liability to be included in OCI if this results in the statement of profit or loss providing more useful information (Conceptual Framework: para. 7.17).

The IASB has not, at present, proposed any amendments to IAS 19 in light of the revised *Conceptual Framework*.

5.6.1 Service costs

These include current service costs, past services costs and gains/losses on settlement and curtailment

(a) Current service cost

This is the increase in the present value of the defined benefit obligation resulting from employee services during the period. The measurement and recognition of this cost arises from the Projected Unit Credit method covered in 5.3.2 above.

Current service cost		
• Increase in the present value of the obligation resulting from employee service in the current period		
• Calculated using actuarial assumptions at beginning of reporting period.	DEBIT	Current service cost (P/L)
	CREDIT	PV defined benefit obligation (SOFP)
• If plan amendment, curtailment or settlement in reporting period, current service cost for remainder of reporting period calculated using actuarial assumptions used to remeasure obligation/asset.		

(b) **Past service cost,** which is the change in the obligation relating to service in **prior periods.** This results from amendments or curtailments to the pension plan.

A plan **amendment** arises when an entity either introduces a defined benefits plan or **changes the benefits payable** under an existing plan. As a result, the entity has taken on additional obligations that it has not previously provided for. For example, an employer might decide to introduce a medical benefits scheme for former employees. This will create a new defined benefit obligation, that has not yet been provided for.

A **curtailment occurs when an entity significantly reduces the number of employees covered by a plan.** This could result from an isolated event, such as closing a plant, discontinuing an operation or the termination or suspension of a plan.

Past service costs can be either **positive** (if the changes increase the obligation) or **negative** (if the change reduces the obligation).

Past service cost		
	Increase in obligation:	
• Change in PV obligation for employee service in prior periods, resulting from a plan amendment or curtailment	DEBIT	Past service cost (P/L)
	CREDIT	PV defined benefit obligation (SOFP)
• Charged or credited immediately to profit or loss	Decrease in obligation:	
	DEBIT	PV defined benefit obligation (SOFP)
	CREDIT	Past service cost (P/L)

(c) Any **gain or loss on settlement**.

A **settlement** occurs either when an employer enters into a transaction to eliminate part or all of its post-employment benefit obligations (other than a payment of benefits to or on behalf of employees under the terms of the plan and included in the actuarial assumptions).

A curtailment and settlement might **happen together**, for example when an employer brings a defined benefit plan to an end by settling the obligation with a one-off lump sum payment and then scrapping the plan.

The gain or losses on a settlement is the difference between:

(a) The **present value of the defined benefit obligation** being settled, as valued on the date of the settlement; and

(b) The **settlement price**, including any plan assts transferred and any payments made by the entity directly in connection with the settlement.

Settlement / curtailment		
• Reduction in plan liabilities (and possibly plan assets) due to the ending of the plan	DEBIT	PV defined benefit obligation (SOFP)
	CREDIT	FV defined benefit assets (SOFP)
• Charged or credited immediately to profit or loss	DR/CR	Profit of loss (bal fig)

5.6.2 Net interest on the net defined benefit liability

IAS 19 requires that annual interest should be calculated on the **net defined benefit liability (asset)**. It therefore incorporates two elements:

(i) An interest charge arising on the unwinding of the discount on the defined benefit obligation as time passes; and

(ii) Interest income recognised on the plan assets.

The calculation is of net interest is:

The **net defined benefit liability/(asset)** should be determined as at the **start** of the accounting period, taking account of changes during the period as a result of contributions paid into the scheme, settlements, benefits paid out etc

Many exam questions include the assumption that all payments into and out of the scheme take place at the end of the year, so that the interest calculations can be based on the opening balances.

The **discount rate** is that determined by reference to **market yields** (at the year end) on high quality fixed-rate corporate bonds, as discussed in Section 5.3.4.

Net interest cost		
• Interest applied to b/d obligation and assets (and netted in profit or loss).	DEBIT	Net interest cost (P/L) (x% × b/d obligation)
• If plan amendment, curtailment or settlement in reporting period, interest for remaining period calculated on remeasured obligation/asset, using the discount rate used to remeasure obligation/asset.	CREDIT	PV defined benefit obligation (SOFP)
	and	
• The interest on assets is time apportioned for contributions less benefits paid in the period (if they occur throughout the year rather than at the start or end of the year). The interest on obligations is also time apportioned for benefits paid in the period.	DEBIT	Plan assets (SOFP) (x% × b/d assets)
	CREDIT	Net interest cost (P/L)

5.6.3 Remeasurements of the net defined benefit liability (asset)

Remeasurements of the net defined benefit liability/(asset) comprise:

(a) Actuarial gains and losses;

(b) The return on plan assets, (excluding amounts included in net interest on the net defined benefit liability/(asset); and

(c) Any change in the effect of the asset ceiling, (excluding amounts included in net interest on the net defined benefit liability/(asset).

The gains and losses relating to points (a) and (b) above will arise in every defined benefit scheme so we will look at these in this section. The asset ceiling is a complication that is not relevant in every case, so it is dealt with separately, later in the chapter.

Actuarial gains and losses

At the end of each accounting period, a new valuation, using updated assumptions, should be carried out on the obligation. Actuarial gains or losses arise because of the following.

- **Actual events** (eg employee turnover, salary increases) differ from the actuarial assumptions that were made to estimate the defined benefit obligations
- The effect of **changes to assumptions** concerning benefit payment options
- **Estimates are revised** (eg different assumptions are made about future employee turnover, salary rises, mortality rates, and so on)
- The effect of changes to the **discount rate.**

Actuarial gains and losses are recognised in other comprehensive income. They are **not reclassified to profit or loss.**

Return on plan assets

A new valuation of the plan assets is carried out at each period end, using current fair values. Any difference between the new value, and what has been recognised up to that date (normally the opening balance, interest, and any cash payments into or out of the plan) is treated as a 'remeasurement' and recognised in other comprehensive income.

Remeasurements	Recognise all changes due to remeasurements in other comprehensive income
• Arising from annual valuations of obligation and assets	DR/CR PV defined benefit obligation (SOFP)
• On obligation, differences between actuarial assumptions and actual experience during the period, or changes in actuarial assumptions	DR/CR Other comprehensive income
• On assets, differences between actual return on plan assets and amounts included in net interest	DR/CR FV defined benefit assets (SOFP) DR/CR Other comprehensive income

5.6.4 Example

At 1 January 20X2 the fair value of the assets of a defined benefit plan were valued at $1,100,000 and the present value of the defined benefit obligation was $1,250,000. On 31 December 20X2, the plan received contributions from the employer of $490,000 and paid out benefits of $190,000.

The current service cost for the year was $360,000 and a discount rate of 6% is to be applied to the net liability/(asset).

After these transactions, the fair value of the plan's assets at 31 December 20X2 was $1.5m. The present value of the defined benefit obligation was $1,553,600.

Required

Calculate the actuarial gains or losses and the return on plan assets and illustrate how this pension plan will be treated in the statement of profit or loss and other comprehensive income and statement of financial position for the year ended 31 December 20X2.

Solution

It is always useful to set up a working reconciling the assets and obligation:

	Assets $	Obligation $
Fair value/present value at 1/1/X2	1,100,000	1,250,000
Interest (1,100,000 × 6%)/(1,250,000 × 6%)	66,000	75,000
Current service cost		360,000
Contributions received	490,000	
Benefits paid	(190,000)	(190,000)
Return on plan assets (balancing figure)	34,000	–
Actuarial loss (balancing figure)	–	58,600
	1,500,000	1,553,600

The following accounting treatment is required.

(a) In the **statement of profit or loss and other comprehensive income**, the following amounts will be recognised:

In profit or loss	$
Current service cost	360,000
Net interest on net defined benefit liability (75,000 – 66,000)	9,000
In other comprehensive income	
Remeasurement losses on defined benefit liability	(24,600)

(b) In the **statement of financial position**, the net defined benefit liability of $53,600 (1,553,600 – 1,500,000) will be recognised.

5.7 Section summary

The recognition and measurement of defined benefit plan costs are complex issues.

- Learn and understand the definitions of the various elements of a defined benefit pension plan
- Learn the **outline method** of accounting (see Section 5.1)
- Learn the recognition method for the:
    - Statement of financial position
    - Statement of profit or loss and other comprehensive income

6 The asset ceiling

6.1 Asset ceiling test

When we looked at the recognition of the net defined benefit liability/(asset) in the statement of financial position at the beginning of Section 5 the term 'asset ceiling' was mentioned. This term relates to a threshold established by IAS 19 to ensure that any defined benefit asset (ie a pension surplus) is carried at no more than its recoverable amount. In simple terms, this means that any net asset is restricted to the amount of cash savings that will be available to the entity in future.

6.2 Net defined benefit assets

A net defined benefit asset may arise if the plan has been overfunded or if actuarial gains have arisen. This meets the definition of an asset (as stated in the *Conceptual Framework*) because **all** of the following apply:

(a) The entity **controls a resource** (the ability to use the surplus to generate future benefits).

(b) That control is the **result of past events** (contributions paid by the entity and service rendered by the employee).

(c) **Future benefits** are available to the entity in the form of a reduction in future contributions or a cash refund, either directly or indirectly to another plan in deficit.

The **asset ceiling** is the present value of those future benefits. The discount rate used is the same as that used to calculate the net interest on the net defined benefit liability/(asset). The net defined benefit asset would be reduced to the asset ceiling threshold. Any related write down would be treated as a **remeasurement** and recognised in **other comprehensive income.**

If the asset ceiling adjustment was needed in a subsequent year, the changes in its value would be treated as follows:

(a) **Interest** (as it is a discounted amount) recognised in profit or loss as part of the net interest amount

(b) **Other changes** recognised in profit or loss

6.3 Suggested approach and question

The suggested approach to defined benefit schemes is to deal with the change in the obligation and asset in the following order.

Step	Item	Recognition	
1	**Record opening figures:** • Asset • Obligation		
2	**Interest cost on obligation** • Based on discount rate and PV obligation at start of period. • Should also reflect any changes in obligation during period.	DEBIT CREDIT	*Interest cost (SPLOCI)* *(X% × b/d obligation)* *PV defined benefit obligation (SOFP)*
3	**Interest on plan assets** • Based on discount rate and asset value at start of period. • Technically, this interest is also time apportioned on contributions less benefits paid in the period.	DEBIT CREDIT	*Plan assets (SOFP)* *Interest cost (SPLOCI)* *(X% × b/d assets)*
4	**Current service cost** • Increase in the present value of the obligation resulting from employee service in the current period.	DEBIT CREDIT	*Current service cost (SPLOCI)* *PV defined benefit obligation (SOFP)*
5	**Contributions** • As advised by actuary.	DEBIT CREDIT	*Plan assets (SOFP)* *Company cash*

16: EMPLOYEE BENEFITS

Step	Item	Recognition	
6	**Benefits** • Actual pension payments made.	DEBIT CREDIT	*PV defined benefit obligation (SOFP)* *Plan assets (SOFP)*
7	**Past service cost** • Increase/decrease in PV obligation as a result of introduction or improvement of benefits.	**Positive (increase in obligation):** DEBIT *Past service cost (SPLOCI)* CREDIT *PV defined benefit obligation (SOFP)* **Negative (decrease in obligation):** DEBIT *PV defined benefit obligation (SOFP)* CREDIT *Past service cost (SPLOCI)*	
8	**Gains and losses on settlement** • Difference between the value of the obligation being settled and the settlement price	**Gain** DEBIT *PV defined benefit obligation (SOFP)* CREDIT *Service cost (SPLOCI)* **Loss** DEBIT *Service cost (SPLOCI)* CREDIT *PV defined benefit obligation (SOFP)*	
9	**Remeasurements: actuarial gains and losses** • Arising from annual valuations of obligation. • On obligation, differences between actuarial assumptions and actual experience during the period, or changes in actuarial assumptions.	**Gain** DEBIT *PV defined benefit obligation (SOFP)* CREDIT *Other comprehensive income (SPLOCI)* **Loss** DEBIT *Other comprehensive income (SPLOCI)* CREDIT *PV defined benefit obligation (SOFP)*	
10	**Remeasurements: return on assets** • Arising from annual valuations of plan assets	**Gain** DEBIT *FV plan assets (SOFP)* CREDIT *Other comprehensive income (SPLOCI)* **Loss** DEBIT *Other comprehensive income (SPLOCI)* CREDIT *FV plan assets (SOFP)*	
11	**Disclose in accordance with the standard**	See comprehensive question.	

Exam focus point

It would be useful for you to do one last question on accounting for post-employment defined benefit schemes.

Question — Comprehensive

For the sake of simplicity and clarity, all transactions are assumed to occur at the year end.

The following data applies to the post employment defined benefit compensation scheme of BCD Co.
Discount rate: 10% (each year)
Present value of obligation at start of 20X2: $1m
Market value of plan assets at start of 20X2: $1m

PART C ACCOUNTING AND REPORTING TECHNIQUES

The following figures are relevant:

	20X2 $'000	20X3 $'000	20X4 $'000
Current service cost	140	150	150
Benefits paid out	120	140	150
Contributions paid by entity	110	120	120
Present value of obligation at year end	1,200	1,650	1,700
Fair value of plan assets at year end	1,250	1,450	1,610

Additional information:

(1) At the end of 20X3, a division of the company was sold. As a result of this, a large number of the employees of that division opted to transfer their accumulated pension entitlement to their new employer's plan. Assets with a fair value of $48,000 were transferred to the other company's plan and the actuary has calculated that the reduction in BCD's defined benefit liability is $50,000. The year end valuations in the table above were carried out **before** this transfer was recorded.

(2) At the end of 20X4, a decision was taken to make a one-off additional payment to former employees currently receiving pensions from the plan. This was announced to the former employees before the year end. This payment was not allowed for in the original terms of the scheme. The actuarial valuation of the obligation in the table above **includes** the additional liability of $40,000 relating to this additional payment.

Required

Show how the reporting entity should account for this defined benefit plan in each of years 20X2, 20X3 and 20X4.

Answer

The actuarial gain or loss is established as a balancing figure in the calculations, as follows:

Present value of obligation

	20X2 $'000	20X3 $'000	20X4 $'000
PV of obligation at start of year	1,000	1,200	1,600
Interest cost (10%)	100	120	160
Current service cost	140	150	150
Past service cost			40
Benefits paid	(120)	(140)	(150)
Settlements		(50)	
Actuarial (gain)/loss on obligation: balancing figure	80	320	(100)
PV of obligation at end of year	1,200	1,600*	1,700

*(1,650 – 50)

Market value of plan assets

	20X2 $'000	20X3 $'000	20X4 $'000
Market value of plan assets at start of year	1,000	1,250	1,402
Interest on plan assets (10%)	100	125	140
Contributions	110	120	120
Benefits paid	(120)	(140)	(150)
Settlements	–	(48)	–
Return on plan assets: balancing figure	160	95	98
Market value of plan assets at year end	1,250	1,402*	1,610

*(1,450 – 48)

In the statement of financial position, the liability that is recognised is calculated as follows:

	20X2 $'000	20X3 $'000	20X4 $'000
Present value of obligation	1,200	1,600	1,700
Market value of plan assets	1,250	1,402	1,610
Liability/(asset) in statement of financial position	(50)	198	90

The following will be recognised in profit or loss for the year:

	20X2 $'000	20X3 $'000	20X4 $'000
Current service cost	140	150	150
Past service cost	–	–	40
Net interest on defined benefit liability (asset)	–	(5)	20
Gain on settlement of defined benefit liability		2	
Expense recognised in profit or loss	140	147	210

The following remeasurements will be recognised in other comprehensive income for the year:

	20X2 $'000	20X3 $'000	20X4 $'000
Actuarial (gain)/loss on obligation	80	320	(100)
Return on plan assets	(160)	(95)	(98)

7 Other long-term benefits

FAST FORWARD

Other long-term employment benefits are accounted for in the same way as defined benefit pension plans with the exception of remeasurements, which are recognised in profit or loss rather than other comprehensive income.

In Section 5.5.1 we identified that the total service cost may comprise not only the current service.

There may be other long-term employment benefits, in addition to post-employment benefits. These include **bonuses** and **profit shares** payable 12 months or more after the end of the reporting period, and **long-term sabbatical leave**.

The measurement of other long-term employee benefits is not usually subject to the same degree of uncertainty as the measurement of post-employment benefits. Therefore a simplified method of accounting is adopted in which remeasurements are not recognised in other comprehensive income.

(a) The surplus or deficit in an other long-term employee benefit plan is measured as for a defined benefit pension plan; and

(b) The net total of the following is recognised in profit or loss except to the extent that another IFRS permits their inclusion in the cost of an asset:

    (i) Service cost
    (ii) Net interest on the net defined benefit liability (asset)
    (iii) Remeasurements of the net defined benefit liability (asset)

There are no specific disclosure requirements with respect to these benefits.

8 Termination benefits

FAST FORWARD

Termination benefits are recognised as a liability and expense when an entity can no longer withdraw the offer of the termination benefit or recognises any related restructuring costs.

Termination benefits are benefits to employees arising as a consequence of **termination of their employment**; they arise from either:

(i) An entity's decision to terminate employment; or

(ii) An employee's decision to accept an entity's offer of benefits in exchange for termination of employment eg the payment of a lump sum to an employee who volunteers for early retirement.

8.1 Recognition of termination benefits

The standard requires that these costs should be recognised in full as a liability and an expense at the earlier of:

- The date on which the entity can no longer withdraw the offer of benefits; or
- When the entity recognises costs for a restructuring that is within the scope of IAS 37 and involves the payment of termination benefits.

8.2 Measurement of termination benefits

Termination benefits should be measured in accordance with the nature of the employee benefit:

- If the termination benefits are expected to be settled wholly before 12 months after the end of the accounting period in which the termination benefit is recognised, the requirements for short-term employment benefits are applied;
- If the termination benefits are not expected to be settled wholly before 12 months after the end of the annual reporting period, the requirements for other long-term employee benefits are applied.

Chapter roundup

- IAS 19 *Employee Benefits* is a long and complex standard covering both short-term and long-term (post-employment) benefits. The complications arise when dealing with **post-employment benefits**.
- There are **two types of post-employment benefit plan**:
    - Defined contribution plans
    - Defined benefit plans
- **Defined contribution plans** are simple to account for because it is the contributions payable which are promised and the eventual benefits depend on them.
- **Defined benefit plans** are much more difficult to account for because it is the eventual benefits which are promised and the total contributions depend on them.
- There is a **five-step method** for accounting for the expenses and liability of a defined benefit pension plan.
- Future benefits are attributed to services performed by employees using the **Projected Unit Credit Method**.
- **Actuarial assumptions** made should be unbiased and based on market expectations.
- You should know how to deal with **past service cost**.
- **Other long-term employment benefits** are accounted for in the same way as defined benefit pension plans with the exception of remeasurements, which are recognised in profit or loss rather than other comprehensive income.
- **Termination benefits** are recognised as a liability and expense when an entity can no longer withdraw the offer of the termination benefit or recognises any related restructuring costs.

Quick quiz

1. What are the four categories of employee benefits given by IAS 19?
2. What is the difference between defined contribution and defined benefit plans?
3. What is a 'constructive obligation' compared to a legal obligation?
4. Which gains and losses on a defined benefit liability (asset) should be recognised in profit or loss?
5. Which gains and losses on a defined benefit liability (asset) should be recognised in other comprehensive income?
6. How should termination benefits be recognised?

    A Provided for as part of the costs of employment when incurred
    B Part of a special provision for future liabilities
    C Recognised in full as a liability and expense when a future obligation is recognised
    D Amortised over the period of employment

PART C ACCOUNTING AND REPORTING TECHNIQUES

Answers to quick quiz

1.
   - Short-term
   - Post-employment
   - Other long-term
   - Termination

2. See Section 3

3. A constructive obligation exists when the entity has no realistic alternative than to pay employee benefits.

4. Current service cost + past service cost + gains or losses on settlement + net interest on the defined benefit liability (asset).

5. Actuarial gains and losses + return on plan assets other that that included in net interest + change in the effect of the asset ceiling other than that included in net interest.

6. C Recognised in full as a liability and an expense in the accounting period when the entity recognises a demonstrable obligation to pay the benefits in the future

End of chapter question

Employee benefits (AIA May 2008 – adapted)

The following information relates to the defined benefit employee compensation scheme of an entity:

Present value of obligation at start of 20X8 ($'000)	20,000
Market value of plan assets at start of 20X8 ($'000)	20,000
Discount rate per year	8%

	20X8 $'000	20X9 $'000
Current service cost	1,250	1,430
Benefits paid out	987	1,100
Contributions paid by entity	1,000	1,100
Present value of obligation at end of the year	23,000	25,500
Market value of plan assets at end of the year	21,500	22,300

Assume that all transactions occur at the end of the year.

Required

(i) Calculate the present value of the defined benefit plan obligation as at the start and end of 20X8 and 20X9 showing clearly any actuarial gain or loss on the plan obligation for each year. **(4 marks)**

(ii) Calculate the market value of the defined benefit plan assets as at the start and end of 20X8 and 20X9 showing clearly any remeasurement on the plan assets for each year. **(4 marks)**

(iii) Show the total charge in respect of this plan in the statement of profit or loss and other comprehensive income for 20X8 and the statement of profit or loss and other comprehensive income for 20X9.

(4 marks)

(Total 12 marks)

Taxation

Topic list	Syllabus reference
1 Current tax revised	LO3
2 Deferred tax	LO3
3 Taxable temporary differences	LO3
4 Deductible temporary differences	LO3
5 Measurement and recognition of deferred tax	LO3
6 Presentation and disclosure of taxation	LO3
7 Deferred taxation and business combinations	LO3

Introduction

In almost all countries entities are taxed on the basis of their trading income. In some countries this may be called corporation or corporate tax, but we will follow the terminology of IAS 12 *Income Taxes* and call it **income tax**.

There are two aspects of income tax which must be accounted for: **current tax** and **deferred tax**. Current tax is revised briefly in Section 1. The rest of this chapter is concerned with deferred tax, which students invariably find difficult.

Section 7 introduces a new aspect of deferred tax, relating to **business combinations**. This represents one of the most complex areas of deferred tax.

Note. Throughout this chapter we will assume a current corporate income tax rate of 30% and a current personal income tax rate of 20%, unless otherwise stated.

PART C ACCOUNTING AND REPORTING TECHNIQUES

1 Current tax revised

FAST FORWARD

Taxation consists of **two components**.
- Current tax
- Deferred tax

Current tax is the amount payable to the tax authorities in relation to the trading activities during the period. It is generally straightforward and is covered in Section 1.

Deferred tax is an accounting measure, used to match the tax effects of transactions with their accounting impact. It is quite complex, and is covered from Section 2.

These are some of the definitions given in IAS 12 *Income Taxes*. We will look at the rest later.

Key terms

Accounting profit. Profit or loss for a period before deducting tax expense.

Taxable profit (tax loss). The profit (loss) for a period, determined in accordance with the rules established by the taxation authorities, upon which income taxes are payable (recoverable).

Tax expense (tax income). The aggregate amount included in the determination of profit or loss for the period in respect of current tax and deferred tax.

Current tax. The amount of income taxes payable (recoverable) in respect of the taxable profit (tax loss) for a period.   (IAS 12)

IAS 12 *Income Taxes* covers both current tax and deferred tax.

> **Current tax** is the amount **actually payable** to the tax authorities in relation to the trading activities of the entity during the period.

> **Deferred tax** is an **accounting measure**, used to match the tax effects of transactions with their accounting effect.

1.1 Recognition of current tax liabilities and assets

IAS 12 requires any **unpaid tax** in respect of the current or prior periods to be recognised as a **liability**.

Conversely, any **excess tax** paid in respect of current or prior periods over what is due should be recognised as an asset.

Question — Current tax

In 20X8 Darton Co had taxable profits of $120,000 and the rate of tax is 30%. In the previous year (20X7) income tax on 20X7 profits had been estimated as $30,000.

Required

Calculate tax payable and the charge for 20X8 if the tax due on 20X7 profits was subsequently agreed with the tax authorities as:

(a) $35,000
(b) $25,000

Any under- or overpayments are not settled until the following year's tax payment is due.

Answer

(a)

	$
Tax due on 20X8 profits ($120,000 × 30%)	36,000
Underpayment for 20X7	5,000
Tax charge and liability	41,000

(b)

	$
Tax due on 20X8 profits (as above)	36,000
Overpayment for 20X7	(5,000)
Tax charge and liability	31,000

Taking this a stage further, IAS 12 also requires an asset to be recognised in respect of the benefit relating to any tax loss that can be **carried back** to recover current tax of a previous period. This is acceptable because it is probable that the benefit will flow to the entity **and** it can be reliably measured.

1.2 Example: Tax losses carried back

In 20X7 Eramu Co paid $50,000 in tax on its 20X7 profits. In 20X8 the company made tax losses of $24,000. The local tax authority rules allow losses to be carried back to offset against current tax of prior years. The rate of tax is 30%

Required

Show the double entry in 20X8.

Solution

Tax relief due on losses = 30% × $24,000 = $7,200.

The double entry will be:

DEBIT	Tax recoverable (statement of financial position)	$7,200	
CREDIT	Tax relief (statement of profit or loss and other comprehensive income)		$7,200

The tax receivable will be shown as an asset until the repayment is received from the tax authorities.

1.3 Measurement

Measurement of current tax liabilities (assets) for the current and prior periods is very simple. They are measured at the **amount expected to be paid to (recovered from) the tax authorities**. The tax rates (and tax laws) used should be those enacted (or substantively enacted) by the end of the reporting period.

1.4 Recognition of current tax

Normally, current tax is recognised as income or expense and included in the profit or loss for the period, except in two cases.

(a) Tax arising from a **business combination** which is an acquisition is treated differently (see Part B of this text and Section 7 of this chapter).

(b) Tax arising from a transaction or event which is recognised **directly in other comprehensive income or in equity** (in the same or a different period).

The rule in (b) is logical. If a transaction or event is charged or credited directly to other comprehensive income/equity, rather than to profit or loss, then the related tax should be also. An example of such a situation is where, under IAS 8 *Accounting Policies, Changes in Accounting Estimates and Errors*, an adjustment is made to the **opening balance of retained earnings** due to either a change in accounting policy that is applied retrospectively, or to the correction of a fundamental error.

1.5 Presentation

In the statement of financial position, **tax assets and liabilities** should be shown separately from other assets and liabilities.

Current tax assets and liabilities can be **offset**, but this should happen only when certain conditions apply.

(a) The entity has a **legally enforceable right** to set off the recognised amounts.

(b) The entity intends to settle the amounts on a **net basis**, or to realise the asset and settle the liability at the same time.

The **tax expense (income)** related to the profit or loss from ordinary activities should be shown in the statement of profit or loss and other comprehensive income.

The **disclosure requirements** of IAS 12 are extensive and we will look at these later in the chapter.

2 Deferred tax

FAST FORWARD

Deferred tax assets and liabilities arise from taxable and deductible temporary differences.

2.1 What is deferred tax?

When a company recognises an asset or liability, it expects to recover or settle the carrying amount of that asset or liability. In other words, it expects to sell or use up assets, and to pay off liabilities. What happens if that recovery or settlement is likely to make future tax payments larger (or smaller) than they would otherwise have been if the recovery or settlement had no tax consequences?

Similarly, some items of income or expense are included in accounting profit in one period, but included in taxable profit in a different period (IAS 12: para. 17). This is because the accounting profit is determined by applying the principles of IFRS, whereas taxable profit is determined by applying the tax rules established by the tax authorities. Without some form of adjustment, this difference may cause the tax charge in the statement of profit or loss and other comprehensive income to be misleading. In both of these circumstances, IAS 12 requires companies to recognise a deferred tax liability (or deferred tax asset) (IAS 12: paras. 15 and 24).

There is a long standing debate at to conceptual basis for recognising deferred tax.

Conceptual Framework – definition of asset and liability	As a result of past transaction or event, an entity has an obligation to pay tax or a right to future tax relief. Therefore, the entity has met the *Conceptual Framework* definition of a liability or asset and so needs to record a deferred tax liability or asset.
Conceptual Framework – accruals concept	To achieve 'matching' in the statement of profit or loss and other comprehensive income, the entity should record tax in the accounts in the same period as the item that the tax relates to is recorded. If the tax is paid in a different period to that in which the item is accounted for, a deferred tax adjustment is needed.

2.2 Definitions

Here are the definitions relating to deferred tax given in IAS 12.

Key terms

Deferred tax liabilities are the amounts of income taxes payable in future periods in respect of taxable temporary differences.

Deferred tax assets are the amounts of income taxes recoverable in future periods in respect of:

- Deductible temporary differences
- The carry forward of unused tax losses
- The carry forward of unused tax credits

Temporary differences are differences between the carrying amount of an asset or liability in the statement of financial position and its tax base. Temporary differences may be either:

(a) **Taxable temporary differences**, which are temporary differences that will result in taxable amounts in determining taxable profit (tax loss) of future periods when the carrying amount of the asset or liability is recovered or settled

(b) **Deductible temporary differences**, which are temporary differences that will result in amounts that are deductible in determining taxable profit (tax loss) of future periods when the carrying amount of the asset or liability is recovered or settled.

The **tax base** of an asset or liability is the amount attributed to that asset or liability for tax purposes.

(IAS 12, para 5)

2.3 Tax base

We can expand on the definition given above by stating that the **tax base of an asset** is the amount that will be deductible for tax purposes against any taxable economic benefits that will flow to the entity when it recovers the carrying value of the asset. Where those economic benefits are not taxable, the tax base of the asset is the same as its carrying amount.

Question
Tax base 1

State the tax base of each of the following assets.

(a) A machine cost $10,000. For tax purposes, depreciation of $3,000 has already been deducted in the current and prior periods and the remaining cost will be deductible in future periods, either as depreciation or through a deduction on disposal. Revenue generated by using the machine is taxable, any gain on disposal of the machine will be taxable and any loss on disposal will be deductible for tax purposes.

(b) Interest receivable has a carrying amount of $1,000. The related interest revenue will be taxed on a cash basis.

(c) Trade receivables have a carrying amount of $10,000. The related revenue has already been included in taxable profit (tax loss).

(d) A loan receivable has a carrying amount of $1m. The repayment of the loan will have no tax consequences.

(e) Dividends receivable from a subsidiary have a carrying amount of $5,000. The dividends are not taxable.

Answer

(a) The tax base of the machine is $7,000.
(b) The tax base of the interest receivable is nil.
(c) The tax base of the trade receivables is $10,000.
(d) The tax base of the loan is $1m.
(e) The tax base of the dividend is $5,000.

In the case of (e), in substance the entire carrying amount of the asset is deductible against the economic benefits. There is no taxable temporary difference. An alternative analysis is that the accrued dividends receivable have a tax base of nil and a tax rate of nil is applied to the resulting taxable temporary difference ($5,000). Under both analyses, there is no deferred tax liability.

In the case of a **liability**, the tax base will be its carrying amount, less any amount that will be deducted for tax purposes in relation to the liability in future periods. For revenue received in advance, the tax base of

Question

Tax base 2

State the tax base of each of the following liabilities.

(a) Current liabilities include accrued expenses with a carrying amount of $1,000. The related expense will be deducted for tax purposes on a cash basis.

(b) Current liabilities include interest revenue received in advance, with a carrying amount of $10,000. The related interest revenue was taxed on a cash basis.

(c) Current liabilities include accrued expenses with a carrying amount of $2,000. The related expense has already been deducted for tax purposes.

(d) Current liabilities include accrued fines and penalties with a carrying amount of $100. Fines and penalties are not deductible for tax purposes.

(e) A loan payable has a carrying amount of $1m. The repayment of the loan will have no tax consequences.

Answer

(a) The tax base of the accrued expenses is nil.
(b) The tax base of the interest received in advance is nil.
(c) The tax base of the accrued expenses is $2,000.
(d) The tax base of the accrued fines and penalties is $100.
(e) The tax base of the loan is $1m.

IAS 12 gives the following examples of circumstances in which the carrying amount of an asset or liability will be **equal to its tax base**.

- **Pre-paid expenses** which have already been deducted in determining an entity's current tax liability for the current or earlier periods.

- A **loan payable** which is measured at the amount originally received and this amount is the same as the amount repayable on final maturity of the loan.

- **Accrued expenses** which will never be deductible for tax purposes.

- **Accrued income** which will never be taxable.

2.4 Temporary differences

You may have found the definition of temporary differences somewhat confusing. Remember that accounting profits form the basis for computing **taxable profits**, on which the tax liability for the year is calculated. However, accounting profits and taxable profits are different. There are two reasons for the differences.

Permanent differences	Temporary differences
These occur when certain items of revenue or expense are excluded from the computation of taxable profits (for example, entertainment expenses may not be allowable for tax purposes).	These occur when items of revenue or expense are included in both accounting profits and taxable profits, but not for the same accounting period. For example, an expense which is allowable as a deduction in arriving at taxable profits for 20X7 might not be included in the financial statements until 20X8 or later. In the long run, the total taxable profits and total accounting profits will be the same (except for permanent differences) so that timing differences originate in one period and are capable of reversal in one or more subsequent periods. Deferred tax is the tax attributable to **temporary differences**.

The distinction made in the definition between **taxable temporary differences** and **deductible temporary differences** can be made clearer by looking at the explanations and examples given in the standard and its appendices.

2.4.1 Section summary

- Deferred tax is an **accounting measure**. It does **not** represent tax payable to the tax authorities.
- The **tax base** of an asset or liability is the value of that asset or liability for tax purposes.
- You should understand the difference between **permanent and temporary differences**.
- Deferred tax is the tax attributable to **temporary differences**.

3 Taxable temporary differences

Rule to learn

The rule to remember here is that:

'All taxable temporary differences give rise to a deferred tax liability.'

The following are examples of circumstances that give rise to taxable temporary differences.

3.1 Transactions that affect the statement of profit or loss and other comprehensive income

Transaction	Deferred tax implication
Interest revenue	**Accounting profit** – interest revenue is received in arrears and included in accounting profit on the basis of time apportionment. **Taxable profit** – it is included in taxable profit on a cash basis.
Sale of goods revenue	**Accounting profit** – revenue is included in accounting profit when the performance obligations are satisfied (per IFRS 15), **Taxable profit** – revenue is included in taxable profit when cash is received.
Depreciation	**Accounting profit** – depreciation is recognised based on the depreciation policy of the company. **Taxable profit** – depreciation is not recognised for tax purposes. It is replaced with tax depreciation (known as capital allowances in the UK). If tax depreciation exceeds accounting depreciation, a taxable TD arises. For example, when new assets are purchased, accelerated allowances may be available against taxable profits which exceed the amount of depreciation chargeable on the assets in the financial statements for the year of purchase.
Amortisation of development costs	**Accounting profit** – the amortisation of capitalised development costs will be recognised in profit or loss. **Taxable profit** – development costs are deducted in full from taxable profit in the period in which they were incurred.

3.2 Transactions that affect the statement of financial position

Transaction / balance	Deferred tax implication
Depreciation of an asset	**Depreciation of an asset** is not deductible for tax purposes. No deduction will be available for tax purposes when the asset is sold/scrapped.
Loans payable	A borrower records a **loan** at proceeds received (amount due at maturity) less transaction costs. The carrying amount of the loan is subsequently increased by amortisation of the transaction costs against accounting profit. The transaction costs were, however, deducted for tax purposes in the period when the loan was first recognised. A **loan** payable is measured on initial recognition at net proceeds (net of transaction costs). The transaction costs are amortised to accounting profit over the life of the loan. Those transaction costs are not deductible in determining the taxable profit of future, current or prior periods.

Transaction / balance	Deferred tax implication
Liability component of compound financial instrument (eg convertible bond)	The liability component of a **compound financial instrument** is measured at a discount to the amount repayable on maturity, after assigning a portion of the cash proceeds to the equity component (see IAS 32 *Financial Instruments: Presentation*). The discount is not deductible in determining taxable profit.

3.3 Fair value adjustments and revaluations

- **Current investments** or financial instruments are carried at fair value. This exceeds cost, but no equivalent adjustment is made for tax purposes.
- Property, plant and equipment is **revalued** by an entity (under IAS 16 *Property, Plant and Equipment*), but no equivalent adjustment is made for tax purposes. This also applies to non-current investments.

The standard also looks at the deferred tax implications of business combinations and consolidations. We will look at these in Section 7.

Remember the rule we gave you above, that all taxable temporary differences give rise to a deferred tax liability? There are **two circumstances** given in the standards where this does **not** apply.

(a) The deferred tax liability arises from the initial recognition of **goodwill**.

(b) The deferred tax liability arises from the **initial recognition** of an asset or liability in a transaction which:

    (i) Is **not** a business combination (see Section 7); **and**
    (ii) At the time of the transaction affects neither accounting profit nor taxable profit.

3.3.1 Example: Taxable temporary differences

A company purchased an asset costing $1,500. At the end of 20X8 the carrying amount is $1,000. The cumulative depreciation for tax purposes is $900 and the current tax rate is 25%.

Required

Calculate the deferred tax liability for the asset.

Solution

First, what is the tax base of the asset? It is $1,500 – $900 = $600.

In order to recover the carrying value of $1,000, the entity must earn taxable income of $1,000, but it will only be able to deduct $600 as a taxable expense. The entity must therefore pay income tax of $400 × 25% = $100 when the carrying value of the asset is recovered.

The entity must therefore recognise a deferred tax liability at the end of 20X8 of $400 × 25% = $100, recognising the difference between the carrying amount of $1,000 and the tax base of $600 as a taxable temporary difference.

3.4 Revalued assets

Under IAS 16 assets may be revalued. If this affects the taxable profit for the current period, the tax base of the asset changes and **no temporary difference** arises.

If, however (as in some countries), the revaluation does **not** affect current taxable profits, the tax base of the asset is not adjusted. Consequently, the taxable flow of economic benefits to the entity as the carrying value of the asset is recovered will differ from the amount that will be deductible for tax purposes. The difference between the carrying amount of a revalued asset and its tax base is a temporary difference and gives rise to a **deferred tax liability or asset**.

3.5 Initial recognition of an asset or liability

A temporary difference can arise on initial recognition of an asset or liability, eg if part or all of the cost of an asset will not be deductible for tax purposes. The **nature of the transaction** which led to the initial recognition of the asset is important in determining the method of accounting for such temporary differences.

If the transaction affects **either** accounting profit or taxable profit, an entity will **recognise any deferred tax liability or asset**. The resulting deferred tax expense or income will be recognised in the statement of profit or loss and other comprehensive income.

Where a transaction affects **neither accounting profit nor taxable profit** it would be normal for an entity to recognise a deferred tax liability or asset and adjust the carrying amount of the asset or liability by the same amount. However, IAS 12 does **not** permit this recognition of a deferred tax asset or liability as it would make the financial statements less transparent. This will be the case both on initial recognition and subsequently, nor should any subsequent changes in the unrecognised deferred tax liability or asset as the asset is depreciated be made.

3.6 Example: Initial recognition

As an example of the last paragraph, suppose Petros Co intends to use an asset which cost $10,000 in 20X7 through its useful life of five years. Its residual value will then be nil. The tax rate is 40%. Any capital gain on disposal would not be taxable (and any capital loss not deductible). Depreciation of the asset is not deductible for tax purposes.

Required

State the deferred tax consequences in each of years 20X7 and 20X8.

Solution

At the end of 20X7, as it recovers the carrying amount of the asset, Petros Co will earn taxable income of $10,000 and pay tax of $4,000. The resulting deferred tax liability of $4,000 would not be recognised because it results from the initial recognition of the asset.

At the end of 20X8, the carrying amount of the asset is now $8,000. In earning taxable income of $8,000, the entity will pay tax of $3,200. Again, the resulting deferred tax liability of $3,200 is not recognised, because it results from the initial recognition of the asset.

The following question on accelerated depreciation should clarify some of the issues and introduce you to the calculations which may be necessary in the exam.

Question — Deferred tax

Jonquil Co buys equipment for $50,000 and depreciates it on a straight-line basis over its expected useful life of five years. For tax purposes, the equipment is depreciated at 25% per annum on a straight-line basis. Tax losses may be carried back against taxable profit of the previous five years. In year 20X0, the entity's taxable profit was $25,000. The tax rate is 40%.

Required

Assuming nil profits/losses after depreciation in years 20X1 to 20X5 show the current and deferred tax impact in years 20X1 to 20X5 of the acquisition of the equipment.

Answer

Jonquil Co will recover the carrying amount of the equipment by using it to manufacture goods for resale. Therefore, the entity's current tax computation is as follows:

	20X1 $	20X2 $	Year 20X3 $	20X4 $	20X5 $
Taxable income*	10,000	10,000	10,000	10,000	10,000
Depreciation for tax purposes	12,500	12,500	12,500	12,500	0
Taxable profit (tax loss)	(2,500)	(2,500)	(2,500)	(2,500)	10,000
Current tax expense (income) at 40%	(1,000)	(1,000)	(1,000)	(1,000)	4,000

*ie nil profit plus ($50,000 ÷ 5) depreciation add-back.

The entity recognises a current tax asset at the end of years 20X1 to 20X4 because it recovers the benefit of the tax loss against the taxable profit of year 20X0.

The temporary differences associated with the equipment and the resulting deferred tax asset and liability and deferred tax expense and income are as follows:

	20X1 $	20X2 $	Year 20X3 $	20X4 $	20X5 $
Carrying amount	40,000	30,000	20,000	10,000	0
Tax base	37,500	25,000	12,500	0	0
Taxable temporary difference	2,500	5,000	7,500	10,000	0
Opening deferred tax liability	0	1,000	2,000	3,000	4,000
Deferred tax expense (income): bal fig	1,000	1,000	1,000	1,000	(4,000)
Closing deferred tax liability @ 40%	1,000	2,000	3,000	4,000	0

The entity recognises the deferred tax liability in years 20X1 to 20X4 because the reversal of the taxable temporary difference will create taxable income in subsequent years. The entity's statement of profit or loss and other comprehensive income is as follows:

	20X1 $	20X2 $	Year 20X3 $	20X4 $	20X5 $
Income	10,000	10,000	10,000	10,000	10,000
Depreciation	10,000	10,000	10,000	10,000	10,000
Profit before tax	0	0	0	0	0
Current tax expense (income)	(1,000)	(1,000)	(1,000)	(1,000)	4,000
Deferred tax expense (income)	1,000	1,000	1,000	1,000	(4,000)
Total tax expense (income)	0	0	0	0	0
Profit for the period	0	0	0	0	0

3.7 Section summary

- With one or two exceptions, all taxable temporary differences give rise to a **deferred tax liability**.
- Many taxable temporary differences are **timing differences**.
- Timing differences arise when income or an expense is included in accounting profit in one period, but in taxable profit in a **different period**.

4 Deductible temporary differences

Refer again to the definition given in Section 2 above.

Rule to learn

> The rule to remember here is that:
>
> 'All deductible temporary differences give rise to a deferred tax asset.'

There is a proviso, however. The deferred tax asset must also satisfy the **recognition criteria** given in IAS 12. This is that a deferred tax asset should be recognised for all deductible temporary differences to the extent that it is **probable that taxable profit will be available** against which it can be utilised. Before we look at this issue in more detail, let us consider the examples of deductible temporary differences given in the standard.

4.1 Transactions that affect the statement of profit or loss and other comprehensive income

Transaction	Deferred tax implication
Retirement benefit costs	**Accounting profit** – pension costs are a deduction from accounting profit as service is provided by the employee.
	Taxable profit – pension costs are not deducted in determining taxable profit until the entity pays either retirement benefits or contributions to a fund. (This may also apply to similar expenses.)
Depreciation	**Accounting profit** – depreciation is recognised based on the depreciation policy of the company.
	Taxable profit – depreciation is not recognised for tax purposes. It is replaced with tax depreciation (known as capital allowances in the UK).
	If tax depreciation is less than accounting depreciation, a deductible TD arises. For example, the depreciation policy of a company might be to depreciate equipment over 4 years on the straight line basis (effectively 25% per annum) whereas capital allowances might be 20% per annum on the reducing balance basis. In the first year, accumulated accounting depreciation would exceed the tax depreciation on the asset.
Cost of goods sold	**Accounting profit** – the cost of inventories sold before the end of the reporting period is recognised for accounting purposes when goods/services are delivered
	Taxable profit – the cost of but is deducted from taxable profit when the cash is received
Impairment	**Accounting profit** – An impairment loss due to, for example, the NRV of inventory falling below cost, or the recoverable amount of an item of property, plant and equipment falling below its carrying amount is recognised in accounting profit in the period in which the impairment occurs.
	Taxable profit – the fall in value is not recognised for tax purposes until the asset is sold.
Deferred income	**Accounting profit** – income received but not earned in a period is not recognised in accounting profit as it is deferred until future periods.
	Taxable profit – the income is taxed in the period in which it is received.

4.2 Fair value adjustments and revaluations

Current investments or **financial instruments** may be carried at fair value, which is less than cost, but no equivalent adjustment is made for tax purposes.

The IASB clarified **that unrealised losses on debt instruments measured at fair value and measured at cost for tax purposes give rise to a deductible temporary difference** regardless of whether the debt instrument's holder expects to recover the carrying amount of the debt instrument by sale or by use.

This may seem to contradict the key requirement that an entity recognises deferred tax assets only if it is probable that it will have future taxable profits. However, the amendment also addresses the issue of what constitutes future taxable profits, and clarifies that:

(a) Unrealised losses on debt instruments measured at fair value and measured at cost for tax purposes give rise to a deductible temporary difference regardless of whether the debt instrument's holder expects to recover the carrying amount of the debt instrument by sale or by use.

(b) The carrying amount of an asset does not limit the estimation of probable future taxable profits.

(c) Estimates for future taxable profits exclude tax deductions resulting from the reversal of deductible temporary differences.

(d) An entity assesses a deferred tax asset in combination with other deferred tax assets. Where tax law restricts the utilisation of tax losses, an entity would assess a deferred tax asset in combination with other deferred tax assets of the same type.

4.2.1 Example: Deferred tax asset and unrealised loss

(Adapted from IAS 12, Illustrative Example 7)

Humbert has a debt instrument with a nominal value of $2,000,000. The fair value of the financial instrument at the company's year end of 30 June 20X4 is $1,800,000. Humbert has determined that there is a deductible temporary difference of $200,000. Humbert intends to hold the instrument until maturity on 30 June 20X5, and expects that the $2,000,000 will be paid in full. This means that the deductible temporary difference will reverse in full.

Humbert has, in addition, $60,000 of taxable temporary differences that will also reverse in full in 20X5. The company expects the bottom line of its tax return to show a tax loss of $40,000.

Assume a tax rate of 20%.

Required

Discuss, with calculations, whether Humbert can recognise a deferred tax asset under IAS 12 *Income Taxes*.

Solution

The first stage is to use the reversal of the taxable temporary difference to arrive at the amount to be tested for recognition.

Under the current requirements of IAS 12 Humbert will consider whether it has a tax liability from a taxable temporary difference that will support the recognition of the tax asset:

	$'000
Deductible temporary difference	200
Reversing taxable temporary difference	(60)
Remaining amount (recognition to be determined)	140

At least $60,000 may be recognised as a deferred tax asset.

The next stage is to calculate the future taxable profit. Following the amendment, this is done using a formula, the aim of which is to derive the amount of tax profit or loss before the reversal of any temporary difference:

	$'000
Expected tax loss (per bottom line of tax return)	(40)
Less reversing taxable temporary difference	(60)
Add reversing deductible temporary difference	200
Taxable profit for recognition test	100

Finally, the results of the above two steps should be added, and the tax calculated:

Humbert would recognise a deferred tax asset of ($60,000 + $100,000) × 20% = $32,000. This deferred tax asset would be recognised even though the company has an expected loss on its tax return.

4.3 Leases and deferred tax

4.3.1 Issue

Under a lease, the lessee recognises a right-of-use asset and a corresponding lease liability. The net of these two amounts figure is the carrying amount of the right-of-use asset for deferred tax purposes.

If an entity is granted tax relief as lease rentals are paid, a temporary difference arises, as the tax base of the lease is zero.

This results in a deferred tax asset. Tax deductions are allowed on the lease rental payment made, which, at the beginning of the lease, is lower than the combined depreciation expense and finance cost recognised for accounting. Therefore, the future tax saving on the additional accounting deduction is recognised now in order to apply the accruals concept.

4.3.2 Measurement

The deferred tax asset temporary difference is measured as:

	$
Carrying amount RoU asset	X
Carrying amount of lease liability	(X)
	X/(X)
Tax base	0
Deferred tax (liability) / asset	(X)/X

Question — Deferred tax

On 1 January 20X1, Heggie leased a machine under a five year lease. The useful life of the asset to Heggie was four years and there is no residual value. The annual lease payments are $6 million payable in arrears each year on 31 December. The present value of the lease payments was $24 million using the interest rate implicit in the lease of approximately 8% per annum. At the end of the lease term legal title remains with the lessor. Heggie incurred $0.4 million of direct costs of setting up the lease. The directors have not leased an asset before and are unsure how to account for it and whether there are any deferred tax implications. The company can claim a tax deduction for the annual lease payments and lease set-up costs. Assume a tax rate of 20%.

Answer

Lease accounting

A right-of-use asset of $24.4 million should be recognised in Heggie's financial statements. This comprises the $24 million present value of lease payments not paid at the 1 January 20X1 commencement date plus the 'initial direct costs' incurred in setting up the lease of $0.4 million.

The asset should be depreciated from the commencement date (1 January 20X1) to the earlier of the end of the asset's useful life (4 years) and the end of the lease term (5 years) unless the legal title reverts to the lessee at the end of the lease term. Here, as the legal title remains with the lessor, the asset should be depreciated over four years, giving an annual depreciation charge of $6.1 million ($24.4m/4 years) and a carrying amount of $18.3 million at 31 December 20X1.

A lease liability should initially be recognised on 1 January 20X1 at the present value of lease payments not paid at the commencement date. This amounts to $24 million. An annual finance cost of 8% of the carrying amount should be recognised in profit or loss and added to the liability. The first lease instalment on 31 December 20X1 is then deducted from the liability, giving a carrying amount of $19.9 million (Working) at 31 December 20X1.

Deferred tax

The carrying amount in the financial statements will be the net of the right-of-use asset and lease liability.

As tax relief is granted on a cash basis, ie when lease payments and set-up costs are paid, the tax base is zero, giving rise to a temporary difference.

This results in a deferred tax asset and additional credit to tax in profit or loss of $0.3 million (see below). The tax deduction is based on the lease rental and set-up costs which is lower than the combined depreciation expense and finance cost. The future tax saving of $0.3 million on the additional accounting deduction is recognised now in order to apply the accruals concept.

Computation

	$m	$m
Carrying amount:		
Right-of-use asset ($24.4m – ($24.4m/4 years))	18.3	
Lease liability (W1)	(19.9)	
		(1.6)
Tax base		0.0
Temporary difference		(1.6)
Deferred tax asset (20%)		0.3

Working: Lease liability

	$m
b/d at 1 January 20X1	24.0
Interest (24 × 8%)	1.9
Instalment in arrears	(6.0)
c/d at 31 December 20X1	19.9

4.4 Recognition of deductible temporary differences

We looked earlier at the important recognition criteria above. As with temporary taxable differences, there are also circumstances where the overall rule for recognition of deferred tax asset is **not** allowed. This applies where the deferred tax asset arises from **initial recognition** of an asset or liability in a transaction which is not a business combination, **and** at the time of the transaction, affects neither accounting nor taxable profit/tax loss.

Let us lay out the reasoning behind the recognition of deferred tax assets arising from deductible temporary differences.

(a) When a **liability is recognised**, it is assumed that its carrying amount will be settled in the form of outflows of economic benefits from the entity in future periods.

(b) When these resources flow from the entity, part or all may be deductible in determining taxable profits of a **period later** than that in which the liability is recognised.

(c) A **temporary tax difference** then exists between the carrying amount of the liability and its tax base.

(d) A **deferred tax asset** therefore arises, representing the income taxes that will be recoverable in future periods when that part of the liability is allowed as a deduction from taxable profit.

(e) Similarly, when the carrying amount of an asset is **less than its tax base**, the difference gives rise to a deferred tax asset in respect of the income taxes that will be recoverable in future periods.

4.4.1 Example: Deductible temporary differences

Pargatha Co recognises a liability of $10,000 for accrued product warranty costs on 31 December 20X7. These product warranty costs will not be deductible for tax purposes until the entity pays claims. The tax rate is 25%.

Required

State the deferred tax implications of this situation.

Solution

What is the tax base of the liability? It is nil (carrying amount of $10,000 less the amount that will be deductible for tax purposes in respect of the liability in future periods).

When the liability is settled for its carrying amount, the entity's future taxable profit will be reduced by $10,000 and so its future tax payments by $10,000 × 25% = $2,500.

The difference of $10,000 between the carrying amount ($10,000) and the tax base (nil) is a deductible temporary difference. The entity should therefore recognise a deferred tax asset of $10,000 × 25% = $2,500 **provided that** it is probable that the entity will earn sufficient taxable profits in future periods to benefit from a reduction in tax payments.

4.5 Recognition of deferred tax assets

Deductible temporary differences can be recognised as deferred tax assets only when we can be sure that sufficient taxable profit will be available against which a deductible temporary difference can be utilised. IAS 12 states that this will be assumed when sufficient **taxable temporary differences** exist which relate to the same taxation authority and the same taxable entity. The following describes the matters that should be considered when determining whether a deferred tax asset can be recognised:

Recognition of deductible temporary differences

Sufficient taxable temporary differences?

- yes: Taxable temporary differences expected to reverse:
  (a) In the same period as the expected reversal of the deductible temporary difference.
  (b) In periods into which a tax loss arising from the deferred tax asset can be carried back or forward.

  → Recognise deductible temporary difference as a deferred tax asset

- no: May still be recognised if:
  (a) **Taxable profits** are sufficient in the same period as the reversal of the deductible temporary difference (or in the periods into which a tax loss arising from the deferred tax asset can be carried forward or backward), ignoring taxable amounts arising from deductible temporary differences arising in future periods.
  (b) **Tax planning opportunities** exist that will allow the entity to create taxable profit in the appropriate periods

With reference to **tax planning opportunities** are actions that an entity would take in order to create or increase taxable income in a particular period before the expiry of a tax loss or tax credit carry forward. For example, in some countries it may be possible to increase or create taxable profit by electing to have interest income taxed on either a received or receivable basis, or deferring the claim for certain deductions from taxable profit.

In any case, where tax planning opportunities **advance taxable profit** from a later period to an earlier period, the utilisation of a tax loss or a tax credit carry forward will still depend on the existence of future taxable profit from sources other than future originating temporary differences.

If an entity has a **history of recent losses**, then this is evidence that future taxable profit may not be available (see below).

4.6 Unused tax losses and unused tax credits

An entity may have unused tax losses or credits (ie which it can offset against taxable profits) at the end of a period. Should a deferred tax asset be recognised in relation to such amounts? IAS 12 states that a deferred tax asset may be recognised in such circumstances **to the extent that it is probable future taxable profit will be available against which the unused tax losses/credits can be utilised**.

The **criteria for recognition** of deferred tax assets here is the same as for recognising deferred tax assets arising from deductible differences, hence the flowchart in 4.4 above can be used when considering whether deferred tax assets arise from unused tax losses and credits.

The existence of **unused tax losses** is strong evidence, however, that future taxable profit may not be available. So where an entity has a history of recent tax losses, a deferred tax asset arising from unused tax losses or credits should be recognised only to the extent that the entity has sufficient taxable temporary differences or there is other convincing evidence that sufficient taxable profit will be available against which the unused losses/credits can be utilised by the entity.

In these circumstances, the following criteria should be considered when assessing the probability that taxable profit will be available against which unused tax losses/credits can be utilised.

- Existence of **sufficient taxable temporary differences** (same tax authority/taxable entity) against which unused tax losses/credits can be utilised before they expire
- Probability that the entity will have **taxable profits** before the unused tax losses/credits expire
- Whether the unused tax losses result from **identifiable causes**, unlikely to recur
- Availability of **tax planning opportunities** (see above)

To the extent that it is **not probable** that taxable profit will be available, the deferred tax asset is **not** recognised.

4.7 Reassessment of unrecognised deferred tax assets

For **all** unrecognised deferred tax assets, at each year end an entity should **reassess the availability of future taxable profits** and whether part or all of any unrecognised deferred tax assets should now be recognised. This may be due to an improvement in trading conditions which is expected to continue.

4.8 Section summary

- Deductible temporary differences give rise to a **deferred tax asset**.
- Deferred tax assets can only be recognised when **sufficient future taxable profits** exist against which they can be utilised.

5 Measurement and recognition of deferred tax

5.1 Basis of provision of deferred tax

IAS 12 adopts the full provision method of providing for deferred tax. The **full provision method** recognises that each timing difference at the year end has an effect on future tax payments. If a company claims an accelerated tax allowance on an item of plant, future tax assessments will be bigger than they would have been otherwise. Future transactions may well affect those assessments still further, but that is not relevant in assessing the position at the year end. The **disadvantage** of full provision is that, under certain types of tax system, it gives rise to large liabilities that may fall due only far in the future.

5.2 Example: Full provision

Suppose that Girdo Co begins trading on 1 January 20X7. In its first year it makes profits of $5m, the depreciation charge is $1m and the tax allowances on those assets is $1.5m. The rate of corporation tax is 30%.

Solution

The tax liability is $1.35m again, but the debit to profit or loss is increased by the deferred tax liability of 30% × $0.5m = $150,000. The total charge to profit or loss is therefore $1.5m which is an effective tax rate of 30% on accounting profits (ie 30% × $5.0m). Again, no judgement is involved in using this method.

5.3 Applicable tax rates

IAS 12 requires deferred tax assets and liabilities to be measured at the tax rates expected to apply in the period **when the asset is realised or liability settled**, based on tax rates and laws enacted (or substantively enacted) at the end of the reporting period.

5.4 Different rates of tax

In addition, in some countries different tax rates apply to different levels of taxable income. In such cases, deferred tax assets and liabilities should be measured using the **average rates** that are expected to apply to the taxable profit (loss) of the periods in which the temporary differences are expected to reverse.

5.5 Manner of recovery or settlement

In some countries, the way in which an entity **recovers or settles** the carrying amount of an asset or liability may affect the following.

(a) The tax rate applying when the entity recovers/settles the carrying amount of the asset/liability
(b) The tax base of the asset/liability

In such cases, the entity must consider the expected manner of recovery or settlement. Deferred tax liabilities and assets must be measured accordingly, using an **appropriate tax rate and tax base**.

5.6 Example: Manner of recovery/settlement

Richcard Co has an asset with a carrying amount of $10,000 and a tax base of $6,000. If the asset were sold, a tax rate of 20% would apply. A tax rate of 30% would apply to other income.

Required

State the deferred tax consequences if the entity:

(a) Sells the asset without further use.
(b) Expects to retain the asset and recover its carrying amount through use.

Solution

(a) A deferred tax liability is recognised of $(10,000 − 6,000) \times 20\% = \$800$.
(b) A deferred tax liability is recognised of $(10,000 − 6,000) \times 30\% = \$1,200$.

Question — Recovery 1

Emida Co has an asset which cost $100,000. At the end of 20X9 the carrying amount was $80,000 and the asset was revalued to $150,000. No equivalent adjustment was made for tax purposes. Cumulative depreciation for tax purposes is $30,000 and the tax rate is 30%. If the asset is sold for more than cost, the cumulative tax depreciation of $30,000 will be included in taxable income but sale proceeds in excess of cost will not be taxable.

Required

State the deferred tax consequences of the above. (**Hint.** Assume first that the entity expects to recover the carrying amount through use, and secondly that it will not and therefore will sell the asset instead.)

Answer

The tax base of the asset is $70,000 ($150,000 − $80,000).

If the entity expects to recover the revalued carrying amount by using the asset, it must generate taxable income of $150,000, but will only be able to deduct depreciation of $70,000. On this basis there is a deferred tax liability of $24,000 ($80,000 × 30%).

If the entity expects to recover the carrying amount by selling the asset immediately for proceeds of $150,000, the deferred tax liability will be computed as follows.

	Taxable temporary difference $	Tax rate	Deferred tax liability $
Cumulative tax depreciation	30,000	30%	9,000
Proceeds in excess of cost	50,000	Nil	–
Total	80,000		9,000

Note. The additional deferred tax that arises on the revaluation is charged to other comprehensive income: see below.

Question — Recovery 2

The facts are as in Recovery 1 above, except that if the asset is sold for more than cost, the cumulative tax depreciation will be included in taxable income (taxed at 30%) and the sale proceeds will be taxed at 40% after deducting an inflation-adjusted cost of $110,000.

Required

State the deferred tax consequences of the above (use the same hint as in Recovery 1).

Answer

If the entity expects to recover the carrying amount by using the asset, the situation is as in Recovery 1 above in the same circumstances.

If the entity expects to recover the carrying amount by selling the asset immediately for proceeds of $150,000, the entity will be able to deduct the indexed costs of $110,000. The profit of $40,000 will be taxed at 40%. In addition, the cumulative tax depreciation of $30,000 will be included in taxable income and taxed at 30%. On this basis, the tax base is $80,000 ($110,000 – $30,000), there is a taxable temporary difference of $70,000 and there is a deferred tax liability of $25,000 ($40,000 × 40% plus $30,000 × 30%).

Exam focus point

If the tax base is not immediately apparent in Recovery 2 above, it may be helpful to consider the fundamental principle of IAS 12: that an entity should recognise a deferred tax liability (asset) whenever recovery or settlement of the carrying amount of an asset or liability would make future tax payments larger (smaller) than they would be if such recovery or settlement would have no consequences.

5.7 Manner of recovery – Investment properties

IAS 12 includes a rebuttable presumption that deferred tax on investment properties carried at fair value under IAS 40 *Investment Property* should be measured based on recovery through sale.

The presumption is rebutted where the investment property is depreciable and is held with the intention of consuming substantially all of the economic benefits of the property through use rather than sale, in other words where the entity expects the asset's income-generating ability to wear out whilst the asset is still owned by the entity.

5.8 Manner of recovery – revalued non-depreciable assets

Where a non-depreciable asset (freehold land) is carried at revaluation under IAS 16, no part of the carrying amount of such an asset is considered to be recovered through use. Therefore, the deferred tax liability or asset that arises from revaluation must be measured based on the tax consequences that would follow from the sale of the asset rather than through use.

In some jurisdictions, this will result in the use of a capital gains tax rate rather than the rate applicable to corporate earnings.

5.9 Discounting

IAS 12 states that deferred tax assets and liabilities **should not be discounted** because the complexities and difficulties involved. Discounting would require detailed scheduling of the timing of the reversal of each temporary difference, but this is often impracticable. If discounting were permitted but not required, this would affect comparability, so it is barred completely. However, carrying amounts determine temporary differences even when such carrying amounts are discounted (eg retirement benefit obligations: see Chapter 16).

5.10 Carrying amount of deferred tax assets

The carrying amount of deferred tax assets should be **reviewed at the end of the reporting period** and reduced where appropriate (insufficient future taxable profits). Such a reduction may be reversed in future years.

5.11 Recognition

As with current tax, deferred tax should normally be recognised as income or an expense and included in the profit or loss for the period. The exceptions are where the tax arises from the events below.

(a) A transaction or event which is recognised (in the same or a different period) **in other comprehensive income or directly in equity**.

(b) A business combination that is an **acquisition**.

The figures shown for deferred tax in profit or loss will consist of **two components**.

(a) Deferred tax relating to **timing differences**.

(b) Adjustments relating to **changes in the carrying amount of deferred tax assets/liabilities** (where there is no change in timing differences), eg changes in tax rates/laws, reassessment of the recoverability of deferred tax assets, or a change in the expected recovery of an asset.

Items in (b) will be recognised in profit or loss, **unless** they relate to items previously recognised in other comprehensive income or charged/credited to equity.

Deferred tax (and current tax) should be recognised in other comprehensive income or charged/credited directly to equity if the tax relates to items also recognised in other comprehensive income or charged/credited directly to equity (in the same or a different period).

The following show examples of from IAS.

(a) **Revaluations** of property, plant and equipment recognised in other comprehensive income (IAS 16)

(b) The effect of a **change in accounting policy** (applied retrospectively) or correction of an **error** charged/credited directly to equity (IAS 8)

Where it is not possible to determine the amount of current/deferred tax that relates to items recognised in other comprehensive income or credited/charged to equity, such tax amounts should be based on a reasonable **prorata allocation** of the entity's current/deferred tax.

5.12 Section summary

- There are two methods of calculating deferred tax when **tax rates change**.
    - **Deferral method** (use tax rates current when differences **arise**)
    - **Liability method** (use tax rate expected when differences **reverse**: per IAS 12)

- Where different rates of tax apply to different rates of income, the **manner of recovery/settlement** of assets/liabilities is important.

- Deferred tax should normally be recognised as income or an expense and **included in profit or loss** for the period.

- Deferred tax should be recognised in other comprehensive income or **charged/credited directly to equity** if the tax relates to items also recognised in other comprehensive income or charged/credited directly to equity.

6 Presentation and disclosure of taxation

> **FAST FORWARD**
>
> IAS 12 *Income Taxes* covers both current and deferred tax. It has substantial presentation and disclosure requirements.

IAS 12 contains rules for comprehensive presentation and disclosure of taxation items, which are summarised here.

6.1 Presentation of tax assets and liabilities

These should be **presented separately** from other assets and liabilities in the statement of financial position. Deferred tax assets and liabilities should be distinguished from current tax assets and liabilities.

In addition, deferred tax assets/liabilities should **not** be classified as current assets/liabilities, where an entity makes such as distinction.

There are only limited circumstances where **current tax** assets and liabilities may be **offset**. This should only occur if the entity:

(a) Has a legally enforceable right to set off the recognised amounts; **and**
(b) Intends either to settle on a net basis, or to realise the asset and settle the liability simultaneously.

Similar criteria apply to the **offset of deferred tax assets and liabilities**.

6.2 Presentation of tax expense

The tax expense or income related to the profit or loss from ordinary activities should be presented in the statement of profit or loss and other comprehensive income.

6.3 Disclosure

As you would expect, the major components of tax expense or income should be disclosed separately. These will generally include the following.

- **Current tax expense** (income)
- Any adjustments recognised in the period for **current tax of prior periods** (ie for over/under statement in prior years)
- Amount of **deferred tax expense (income)** relating to the origination and reversal of **temporary differences**
- Amount of **deferred tax expense (income)** relating to changes in **tax rates** or the imposition of **new taxes**
- Amount of the benefit arising from a previously unrecognised tax loss, tax credit or temporary difference of a prior period that is used to **reduce current tax expense**
- Amount of the benefit from a previously unrecognised tax loss, tax credit or temporary difference of a prior period that is used to **reduce deferred tax expense**
- Deferred tax expense arising from the **write-down**, or reversal of a previous write-down, of a deferred tax asset

There are substantial additional disclosures required by the standard. All these items should be shown separately.

- Aggregate current and deferred tax relating to items that are charged or credited to **equity**
- The amount of income tax relating to each component of other comprehensive income
- An explanation of the relationship between **tax expense (income)** and **accounting profit** in either or both of the following forms
    - A numerical reconciliation between tax expense (income) and the product of accounting profit multiplied by the applicable tax rate(s), disclosing also the basis on which the applicable tax rate(s) is (are) computed
    - A numerical reconciliation between the average effective tax rate and the applicable tax rate, disclosing also the basis on which the applicable tax rate is computed
- An explanation of **changes in the applicable tax rate(s)** compared to the previous accounting period

- The amount (and expiry date, if any) of **deductible temporary differences, unused tax losses, and unused tax credits** for which no deferred tax is recognised in the statement of financial position
- In respect of each type of **temporary difference**, and in respect of each type of **unused tax loss** and **unused tax credit**:
  - The amount of the deferred tax assets and liabilities recognised in the statement of financial position for each period presented
  - The amount of the deferred tax income or expense recognised in profit or loss, if this is not apparent from the changes in the amounts recognised in the statement of financial position
- In respect of **discontinued operations**, the tax expense relating to:
  - The gain or loss on discontinuance; **and**
  - The profit or loss from the ordinary activities of the discontinued operation for the period, together with the corresponding amounts for each prior period presented
- **Temporary differences** arising from investments in subsidiaries, branches, associates or joint arrangements, where no deferred tax liabilities have been recognised (see Section 7.4)

In addition, an entity should disclose the amount of a deferred tax asset and the nature of the evidence supporting its recognition, when:

(a) The utilisation of the deferred tax asset is dependent on future taxable profits in excess of the profits arising from the reversal of existing taxable temporary differences; and

(b) The entity has suffered a loss in either the current or preceding period in the tax jurisdiction to which the deferred tax asset relates.

7 Deferred taxation and business combinations

FAST FORWARD

> You must appreciate the deferred tax aspects of **business combinations** as this aspect of deferred tax may appear in the exam.

Much of the above will be familiar to you from your earlier studies. You may be asked about the **group aspects of deferred taxation**. Everything that IAS 12 states in relation to deferred tax and business combinations is brought together in this section.

7.1 Tax bases

Remember the definition of the tax base of an asset or liability given in Section 2.3 above? In relation to business combinations and consolidations, IAS 12 gives (in an appendix) examples of circumstances that give rise to taxable temporary differences and to deductible temporary differences.

7.1.1 Circumstances that give rise to taxable temporary differences

The carrying amount of an asset is increased to **fair value** in a business combination that is an acquisition and no equivalent adjustment is made for tax purposes	**Unrealised losses resulting from intragroup transactions** are eliminated by inclusion in the carrying amount of inventory or property, plant and equipment	Investments in foreign subsidiaries, branches or associates or interests in foreign joint arrangements are affected by **changes in foreign exchange rates**
Retained earnings of subsidiaries, branches, associates and joint arrangements are included in consolidated retained earnings, but income taxes will be payable if the profits are distributed to the reporting parent	An entity financial statements in its own currency for the cost of the non-monetary assets of a foreign operation that is **integral to the reporting entity's operations** but the taxable profit or tax loss of the foreign operation is determined in the foreign currency	

Question: Deferred tax and business combinations 1

What are the consequences of the above situations?

Note. You may want to read through to the end of this section before you attempt this question.

Answer

(a) *Fair value adjustment*

On initial recognition, the resulting deferred tax liability increases goodwill or decreases the bargain purchase gain.

(b) *Unrealised losses*

The tax bases of the assets are unaltered.

(c) *Consolidated earnings*

IAS 12 does not allow recognition of the resulting deferred tax liability if the parent, investor or venturer is able to control the timing of the reversal of the temporary difference and it is probable that the temporary difference will not reverse in the foreseeable future.

(d) *Changes in exchange rates: investments*

There may be either a taxable temporary difference or a deductible temporary difference in this situation. IAS 12 does not allow recognition of the resulting deferred tax liability if the parent, investor or venturer is able to control the timing of the reversal of the temporary difference and it is probable that the temporary difference will not reverse in the foreseeable future.

(e) *Changes in exchange rates: use of own currency*

Again, there may be either a taxable temporary difference or a deductible temporary difference. Where there is a taxable temporary difference, the resulting deferred tax liability is recognised, because it relates to the foreign operation's own assets and liabilities, rather than to the reporting **entity**'s investment in that foreign operation. The deferred tax is charged to profit or loss.

7.1.2 Circumstances that give rise to deductible temporary differences

(a) **A liability is recognised at its fair value** in a business combination that is an acquisition, but none of the related expense is deducted in determining taxable profit until a later period.

(b) **Unrealised profits resulting from intragroup transactions** are eliminated from the carrying amount of assets, such as inventory or property, plant or equipment, but no equivalent adjustment is made for tax purposes.

(c) Investments in foreign subsidiaries, branches or associates or interests in foreign joint arrangements are affected by **changes in foreign exchange rates**.

(d) A foreign operation financial statements for its non-monetary assets in its own (functional) currency. If its taxable profit or loss is determined in a different currency (under the presentation currency method) changes in the exchange rate result in temporary differences. The resulting deferred tax is charged or credited to profit or loss.

Question: Deferred tax and business combinations 2

What are the consequences of the above situations?

Note. Again, you should read to the end of this section before you answer this question.

Answer

(a) *Fair value of liabilities*

The resulting deferred tax asset decreases goodwill or increases the bargain purchase gain.

(b) *Unrealised profits*

The tax bases of the liabilities are unaltered.

(c) *Changes in exchange rates: investments*

As noted in the prior question, there may be a taxable temporary difference or a deductible temporary difference. IAS 12 requires recognition of the resulting deferred tax asset to the extent, and only to the extent, that it is probable that:

(i) The temporary difference will reverse in the foreseeable future; and
(ii) Taxable profit will be available against which the temporary difference can be utilised.

(d) *Changes in exchange rates: use of own currency*

As noted in the prior question, there may be either a taxable temporary difference or a deductible temporary difference. Where there is a deductible temporary difference, the resulting deferred tax asset is recognised to the extent that it is probable that sufficient taxable profit will be available, because the deferred tax asset relates to the foreign operation's own assets and liabilities, rather than to the reporting **entity**'s investment in that foreign operation. The deferred tax is charged to profit or loss.

7.2 Taxable temporary differences

In a business combination, the cost of the acquisition must be allocated to the fair values of the identifiable assets and liabilities acquired as at the date of the transaction. Temporary differences will arise when the tax bases of the identifiable assets and liabilities acquired are not affected by the business combination or are affected differently. For example, the carrying amount of an asset is increased to fair value but the tax base of the asset remains at cost to the previous owner; a taxable temporary difference arises which results in a deferred tax liability and this will also affect goodwill.

7.3 Deductible temporary differences

In a business combination that is an acquisition, as in Section 7.2 above, when a **liability** is recognised on acquisition but the related costs are not deducted in determining taxable profits until a later period, a deductible temporary difference arises resulting in a deferred tax asset. A deferred tax asset will also arise when the fair value of an identifiable asset acquired is less than its tax base. In both these cases goodwill is affected (see below).

7.4 Investments in subsidiaries, branches and associates and interests in joint arrangements

When such investments are held, **temporary differences** may arise because the carrying amount of the investment (ie the parent's share of the net assets including goodwill) becomes different from the tax base (often the cost) of the investment. Why do these differences arise? These are some examples.

- There are **undistributable profits** held by subsidiaries, branches, associates and joint arrangements
- There are **changes in foreign exchange rates** when a parent and its subsidiary are based in different countries
- There is a **reduction in the carrying amount** of an investment in an associate to its recoverable amount

The **temporary difference in the consolidated financial statements** may be different from the temporary difference associated with that investment in the parent's separate financial statements when the parent carries the investment in its separate financial statements at cost or revalued amount.

IAS 12 requires entities to **recognise a deferred tax liability** for all taxable temporary differences associated with investments in subsidiaries, branches and associates, and interests in joint arrangements, **except** to the extent that both of these conditions are satisfied:

(a)   The parent/investor/venturer is able to **control the timing of the reversal** of the temporary difference; **and**

(b)   It is probable that the temporary difference **will not reverse** in the foreseeable future.

As well as the fact of parent control over reversal of temporary differences, it would often be **impracticable** to determine the amount of income taxes payable when the temporary differences reverses. So when the parent has determined that those profits will not be distributed in the foreseeable future, the parent does not recognise a deferred tax liability. The same applies to investments in branches.

Where a foreign operation's taxable profit or tax loss (and therefore the tax base of its non-monetary assets and liabilities) is determined in a **foreign currency**, changes in the exchange rate give rise to temporary differences. These relate to the foreign entity's own assets and liabilities, rather than to the reporting entity's investment in that foreign operation, and so the reporting entity should recognise the resulting deferred tax liability or asset. The resulting deferred tax is charged or credited to profit or loss.

An investor in an **associate** does not control that entity and so cannot determine its dividend policy. Without an agreement requiring that the profits of the associate should not be distributed in the foreseeable future, therefore, an investor should recognise a deferred tax liability arising from taxable temporary differences associated with its investment in the associate. Where an investor cannot determine the exact amount of tax, but only a minimum amount, then the deferred tax liability should be that amount.

In a **joint arrangement**, the agreement between the parties usually deals with profit sharing. When a venturer can control the sharing of profits and it is probable that the profits will not be distributed in the foreseeable future, a deferred liability is not recognised.

IAS 12 then states that a **deferred tax asset** should be recognised for all deductible temporary differences arising from investments in subsidiaries, branches and associates, and interests in joint arrangements, to the extent that (and **only** to the extent that) both these are probable:

(a)   That the temporary difference will **reverse** in the foreseeable future; **and**
(b)   That **taxable profit** will be available against which the temporary difference can be utilised.

The **prudence principles** discussed above for the recognition of deferred tax assets should be considered.

7.5 Recognition of deferred tax arising from business combinations

As noted above, temporary differences may arise in a business combination. IFRS 3 *Business Combinations* requires an entity to recognise any resulting deferred tax assets (to the extent that they meet the relevant recognition criteria) or deferred tax liabilities as identifiable assets and liabilities at the date of acquisition. These deferred tax assets and liabilities, consequently, will **affect goodwill or negative goodwill**. An entity will not, however, recognise deferred tax liabilities arising from the initial recognition of goodwill.

An acquirer may consider that, as a result of a business combination, it is probable that it will **recover its own deferred tax asset** that was not recognised prior to the business combination, eg by utilising unused tax losses against the future taxable profit of the acquiree. The acquirer should recognise a deferred tax asset but does not take it into account in calculating goodwill.

If deferred tax assets of an acquiree were not originally recognised as identifiable assets at the acquisition date but are **recognised subsequently**, the accounting is as follows:

(a)   **If the assets are recognised during the measurement period** (see Chapter 6), **adjust (reduce) the carrying amount of goodwill** to the amount that would have been recognised if the deferred tax assets had been recognised at acquisition and **recognise the reduction in the carrying amount** of goodwill as an expense in profit or loss (this expense will cancel out the deferred tax income, leaving a nil effect on profit or loss).

(b) **Otherwise, recognise the effect in profit or loss**

The acquirer cannot, however, create a bargain purchase gain by the type (a) adjustments.

Question — Recognition

In 20X2 Jacko acquired a subsidiary, Jilly, which had deductible temporary differences of $3m. The tax rate at the date of acquisition was 30%. The resulting deferred tax asset of $0.9m was not recognised as an identifiable asset in determining the goodwill of $5m resulting from the business combination. Two years after the acquisition, Jacko decided that future taxable profit would probably be sufficient for the entity to recover the benefit of all the deductible temporary differences.

Required

(a) Consider the accounting treatment of the subsequent recognition of the deferred tax asset in 20X4.
(b) What would happen if the tax rate had risen to 40% by 20X4 or decreased to 20%?

Answer

(a) The deferred tax asset is recognised two years after the acquisition, so outside the measurement period. Jacko should recognise a deferred tax asset of $0.9m ($3m × 30%) and deferred tax income of $0.9m in profit or loss.

(b) If the tax rate rises to 40%, Jacko should recognise a deferred tax asset of $1.2m ($3m × 40%) and deferred tax income of $0.12m in profit or loss.

If the tax rate falls to 20%, Jacko should recognise a deferred tax asset of $0.6m ($3m × 20%) and deferred tax income of $0.6m in profit or loss.

7.6 Example: Deferred tax adjustments (1)

Red is a private limited company and has two 100% owned subsidiaries, Blue and Green, both themselves private limited companies. Red acquired Green on 1 January 20X2 for $5 million when the fair value of its net assets was $4 million, and the tax base of the net assets was $3.5 million. The acquisition of Green and Blue was part of a business strategy whereby Red would build up the 'value' of the group over a three year period and then list its existing share capital on the stock exchange.

(a) The following details relate to the acquisition of Green, which manufactures electronic goods.

(i) Part of the purchase price has been allocated to intangible assets because it relates to the acquisition of a database of key customers from Green. The recognition and measurement criteria for an intangible asset under IFRS 3 *Business Combinations*/IAS 38 *Intangible Assets* do not appear to have been met but the directors feel that the intangible asset of $0.5 million will be allowed for tax purposes and have computed the tax provision accordingly. However, the tax authorities could possibly challenge this opinion.

(ii) Green has sold goods worth $3 million to Red since acquisition and made a profit of $1 million on the transaction. The inventory of these goods recorded in Red's statement of financial position at the year end of 31 May 20X2 was $1.8 million.

(iii) The balance on the retained earnings of Green at acquisition was $2 million. The directors of Red have decided that, during the three years to the date that they intend to list the shares of the company, they will realise earnings through future dividend payments from the subsidiary amounting to $500,000 per year. Tax is payable on any remittance or dividends and no dividends have been declared for the current year.

(b) Blue was acquired on 1 June 20X1 and is a company which undertakes various projects ranging from debt factoring to investing in property and commodities. The following details relate to Blue for the year ending 31 May 20X2.

(i) Blue has a portfolio of readily marketable government securities which are held as current assets. These investments are stated at market value in the statement of financial position with any gain or loss taken to profit or loss. These gains and losses are taxed when the investments are sold. Currently the accumulated unrealised gains are $4 million.

(ii) Blue has calculated that it requires a specific allowance of $2 million against loans in its portfolio. Tax relief is available when the specific loan is written off.

(iii) When Red acquired Blue it had unused tax losses brought forward. At 1 June 20X1, it appeared that Blue would have sufficient taxable profit to realise the deferred tax asset created by these losses but subsequent events have proved that the future taxable profit will not be sufficient to realise all of the unused tax loss.

The current tax rate for Red is 30% and for public companies is 35%.

Required

Write a note suitable for presentation to the partner of an accounting firm setting out the deferred tax implications of the above information for the Red Group of companies.

Solution

Acquisition of the subsidiaries – general

Fair value adjustments have been made in both cases and these will **affect the deferred tax charge for the year**. This is because the deferred tax position is viewed **from the perspective of the group as a whole**. For example, it may be possible to recognise deferred tax assets which previously could not be recognised by individual companies, because there are now sufficient tax profits available within the group to utilise unused tax losses. Therefore a **provision** should be made for **temporary differences between fair values of the identifiable net assets acquired and their carrying values** ($4 million less $3.5 million in respect of Green). **No provision should be made for the temporary difference** of $1 million arising on goodwill recognised as a result of the combination with Green.

Future listing

Red plans to seek a listing in three years' time. Therefore, it will become a **public company** and will be subject to a **higher rate of tax**. IAS 12 states that deferred tax should be measured at the **average tax rates expected to apply in the periods in which the timing differences are expected to reverse**, based on current enacted tax rates and laws. This means that Red may be paying tax at the higher rate when some of its timing differences reverse and this should be taken into account in the calculation.

Acquisition of Green

(a) The directors have calculated the tax provision on the assumption that the intangible asset of $0.5 million will be allowed for tax purposes. However, this is not certain and the directors **may eventually have to pay the additional tax**. If the directors cannot be persuaded to adjust their calculations, a **liability for the additional tax should be recognised**.

(b) The intra-group transaction has resulted in an **unrealised profit** of $0.6 million in the group financial statements and this will be **eliminated on consolidation**. The tax charge in the group statement of profit or loss and other comprehensive income includes the tax on this profit, for which **the group will not become liable to tax until the following period. From the perspective of the group, there is a temporary difference**. Because the temporary difference arises in the financial statements of Red, **deferred tax should be provided** on this difference (an asset) using the rate of tax payable by Red.

(c) **Deferred tax should be recognised on the unremitted earnings of subsidiaries** unless the parent is able to **control the timing of dividend payments** or it is **unlikely that dividends will be paid for the foreseeable future**. Red controls the dividend policy of Green and this means that there would normally be no need to make a provision in respect of unremitted profits.

However, the profits of Green **will be distributed** to Red over the next few years and **tax will be payable** on the dividends received. Therefore a **deferred tax liability should be shown**.

Acquisition of Blue

(a) A **temporary difference arises** where non-monetary assets are **revalued upwards** and the **tax treatment of the surplus is different from the accounting treatment**. In this case, the revaluation surplus has been **recognised in profit or loss** for the current period, rather than in other comprehensive income/equity but no corresponding adjustment has been made to the tax base of the investments because the gains will be taxed in future periods. Therefore the company **should recognise a deferred tax liability on the temporary difference of $4 million**.

(b) A temporary difference arises when the provision for the loss on the loan portfolio is first recognised. The general allowance is expected to increase and therefore it is unlikely that the temporary difference will reverse in the near future. However, a **deferred tax liability should still be recognised**. The temporary difference gives rise to a **deferred tax asset**. IAS 12 states that **deferred tax assets should not be recognised unless it is probable that taxable profits will be available** against which the taxable profits can be utilised. **This is affected by the situation in point (c) below**.

(c) In theory, unused tax losses give rise to a deferred tax asset. However, IAS 12 states that **deferred tax assets should only be recognised to the extent that they are regarded as recoverable**. They should be regarded as recoverable to the extent that on the basis of all the evidence available it is **probable that there will be suitable taxable profits against which the losses can be recovered**. The future taxable profit of Blue **will not be sufficient to realise all the unused tax loss. Therefore the deferred tax asset is reduced to the amount that is expected to be recovered**.

This reduction in the deferred tax asset implies that it was **overstated at 1 June 20X1**, when it was acquired by the group. As these are the first post-acquisition financial statements, **goodwill should also be adjusted**.

7.7 Example: Deferred tax adjustments 2

You are the accountant of Pay it. Your assistant is preparing the consolidated financial statements of the year ended 31 March 20X2. However, he is unsure how to account for the deferred tax effects of certain transactions as he has not studied IAS 12. These transactions are given below.

Transaction 1

During the year, Pay it sold goods to a subsidiary for $10 million, making a profit of 20% on selling price. 25% of these goods were still in the inventories of the subsidiary at 31 March 20X2. The subsidiary and Pay it are in the same tax jurisdiction and pay tax on profits at 30%.

Transaction 2

An overseas subsidiary made a loss adjusted for tax purposes of $8 million ($ equivalent). The only relief available for this tax loss is to carry it forward for offset against future taxable profits of the overseas subsidiary. Taxable profits of the oversees subsidiary suffer tax at a rate of 25%.

Required

Compute the effect of both the above transactions on the deferred tax amounts in the consolidated statement of financial position of Pay it at 31 March 20X2. You should provide a full explanation for your calculations and indicate any assumptions you make in formulating your answer.

Solution

Transaction 1

This intra-group sale will give rise to a **provision for unrealised profit** on the unsold inventory of $10,000,000 × 20% × 25% = $500,000. This provision must be made in the consolidated financial statements. However, this profit has already been taxed in the financial statements of Payit. In other words there is a **timing difference**.

In the following year when the inventory is sold outside the group, the provision will be released, but the profit will not be taxed. The timing difference therefore gives rise to a **deferred tax asset**. The asset is 30% × $500,000 = $150,000.

Deferred tax assets are recognised to the extent that they are **recoverable**. This will be the case if **it is more likely than not** that **suitable tax profits** will exist from which the reversal of the timing difference giving rise to the asset can be deducted. The asset is carried forward on this assumption.

Transaction 2

An unrelieved tax loss gives rise to a **timing difference** because the loss is recognised in the financial statements but not yet allowed for tax purposes. When the overseas subsidiary generates sufficient taxable profits, the loss will be offset against these in arriving at taxable profits.

The amount of the deferred tax asset to be carried forward is 25% × $8m = $2m.

As with Transaction 1, deferred tax assets are recognised to the extent that they are **recoverable**. This will be the case if **it is more likely than not** that **suitable tax profits** will exist from which the reversal of the timing difference giving rise to the asset can be deducted.

7.8 Presentation and disclosure

7.8.1 Offset

In consolidated financial statements, a **current** tax asset of one entity in a group is offset against a current tax liability of another entity in the group if, and only if, the entities concerned have a **legally enforceable** right to make/receive a single net payment **and** the entities intend to make/receive such a net payment or recover the asset and settle the liability simultaneously.

7.8.2 Tax expense: exchange differences

IAS 21 requires certain exchange differences to be recognised as income/expense without specifying where such differences should be presented in the statement of profit or loss and other comprehensive income. IAS 12 merely states that, where exchange differences on **deferred foreign tax liabilities or assets** are recognised in the statement of profit or loss and other comprehensive income, such differences may be classified as deferred tax expense/income if this presentation is considered most useful.

7.8.3 Disclosure

IAS 12 requires the aggregate amount of temporary differences associated with investments in subsidiaries, branches and associates and interests in joint arrangements, for which deferred tax liabilities **have not been recognised** to be disclosed separately.

7.9 Section summary

In relation to deferred tax and business combinations you should be familiar with:

- Circumstances that give rise to **taxable temporary differences**
- Circumstances that give rise to **deductible temporary differences**
- Their **treatment** once an acquisition takes place
- Reasons **why deferred tax arises** when investments are held
- **Recognition** of deferred tax on business combinations

Chapter roundup

- Taxation consists of **two components**.
    - Current tax
    - Deferred tax

- **Current tax** is the amount payable to the tax authorities in relation to the trading activities during the period. It is generally straightforward and is covered in Section 1.

- **Deferred tax** is an accounting measure, used to match the tax effects of transactions with their accounting impact. It is quite complex, and is covered in Section 2.

- **Deferred tax assets and liabilities** arise from taxable and deductible temporary differences.

- **IAS 12 *Income Taxes*** covers both current and deferred tax. It has substantial presentation and disclosure requirements.

- You must appreciate the deferred tax aspects of **business combinations** as this aspect of deferred tax may appear in the exam.

Quick quiz

1   What is the difference between 'current tax' and 'deferred tax'?

2   How should current tax be measured?

    A   The total liability, including deferred tax
    B   The amount expected to be paid to (or recovered from) the tax authorities
    C   The amount calculated on profit at current tax rates
    D   The amount calculated on profit at future tax rates

3   A taxable temporary difference does not give rise to a deferred tax liability. True or false?

4   What basis of provision for deferred tax is required by IAS 12?

5   What two methods can be used for calculating deferred tax when the tax rate changes?

6   Current tax assets and liabilities cannot be offset. True or false?

7   How do temporary differences arise when investments are held in subsidiaries, associates etc?

Answers to quick quiz

1   (a)   Current tax is the amount payable (recoverable) in respect of the taxable profit (tax loss) for a period.

    (b)   Deferred tax is used to match the tax effects of transactions with their accounting impact.

2   B   The amount expected to be paid to (or recovered from) the tax authorities.

3   False, except when the liability arises in a business combination or affects neither accounting nor tax profit or loss

4   Full provision

5
    - Deferral method
    - Liability method (required by IAS 12)

6   False. They can be offset only if the entity has a legally enforceable right to offset **and** it intends to actually carry out the offset.

7   When the carrying amounts of the investment become different to the tax base of the investment

End of chapter question

DT

DT, a public limited company, has decided to adopt the provisions of IFRS for the first time in its financial statements for the year ending 30 November 20X1. The amounts of deferred tax provided and unprovided as set out in the notes of the group financial statements for the year ending 30 November 20X0 were as follows.

	Provided $m	Unprovided $m
Tax depreciation in excess of accounting depreciation	38	12
Other temporary differences	11	14
Liabilities for health care benefits	(12)	
Losses available for offset against future taxable profits	(34)	(56)
Income tax on capital gains arising on the disposal of property which had been deferred	–	165
Tax that would arise if properties were disposed of at their revalued amounts	–	140
	3	275

The following notes are relevant to the calculation of the deferred tax liability as at 30 November 20X1.

(a)   DT acquired a 100% holding in a foreign company on 30 November 20X1. The subsidiary does not plan to pay any dividends for the financial year to 30 November 20X1 or in the foreseeable future. The carrying amount in DT's consolidated financial statements of its investment in the subsidiary at 30 November 20X1 is made up as follows.

	$m
Carrying value of net assets acquired excluding deferred tax	76
Goodwill (before deferred tax and impairment losses)	14
Carrying amount/cost of investment	90

The tax base of the net assets of the subsidiary at acquisition was $60 million. No deduction is available in the subsidiary's tax jurisdiction for the cost of the goodwill.

17: TAXATION

Immediately after acquisition on 30 November 20X1, DT had supplied the subsidiary with inventories amounting to $30 million at a profit of 20% on selling price. The inventories had not been sold by the year end and the tax rate applied to the subsidiary's profit is 25%. There was no significant difference between the fair values and carrying values on the acquisition of the subsidiary.

(b) The carrying amount of the property, plant and equipment (excluding that of the subsidiary) is $2,600 million and their tax base is $1,920 million. The tax arising on the revaluation of properties of $140 million, if disposed of at their revalued amounts, is the same at 30 November 20X1 as at the beginning of the year. The revaluation of the properties is included in the carrying amount above.

Other taxable temporary differences (excluding the subsidiary) amount to $90 million as at 30 November 20X1.

(c) The liability for health care benefits in the statement of financial position had risen to $100 million as at 30 November 20X1 and the tax base is zero. Health care benefits are deductible for tax purposes when payments are made to retirees. No payments were made during the year to 30 November 20X1.

(d) Under the tax law of the country, tax losses can be carried forward for three years only. The taxable profits for the years ending 30 November were anticipated to be as follows:

20X1	20X2	20X3
$m	$m	$m
110	100	130

The auditors are unsure about the availability of taxable profits in 20X3 as the amount is based upon the projected acquisition of a profitable company. It is anticipated that there will be no future reversals of existing taxable temporary differences until after 30 November 20X3.

(e) Income tax of $165 million on the property disposed of becomes payable on 30 November 20X4 under the deferral relief provisions of the tax laws of the country. There had been no sales or revaluations of property during the year to 30 November 20X1.

(f) Income tax is assumed to be 30% for the foreseeable future in DT's jurisdiction and the company wishes to discount any deferred tax liabilities at a rate of 4% if allowed by IAS 12.

(g) There are no other temporary differences other than those set out above. The directors of DT have calculated the opening balance of deferred tax using IAS 12 to be $280 million and not the total of the provided and unprovided amounts of $278 million at the beginning of the year.

Required

Calculate the liability for deferred tax required by the DT Group at 30 November 20X1 and the deferred tax expense in profit or loss for the year ending 30 November 20X1 using IAS 12, commenting on the effect that the application of IAS 12 will have on the financial statements of the DT Group.

PART C ACCOUNTING AND REPORTING TECHNIQUES

Reporting financial performance

Topic list	Syllabus reference
1 Reporting financial performance: IAS 1 and IAS 8	LO4
2 IFRS 5 *Non-Current Assets Held for Sale and Discontinued Operations*	LO4
3 IFRS 8 *Operating Segments*	LO4
4 IAS 33 *Earnings per Share*	LO4
5 Management commentary	LO4

Introduction

This chapter covers a great many standards, but you are very familiar with some of them.

IFRS 5 *Non-Current Assets Held for Sale and Discontinued Operations* requires separate reporting of information which relates to **discontinued operations** from that relating to continuing operations. It also requires the separate presentation of non-current assets held for sale.

IFRS 8 *Operating Segments* requires extensive disclosure about an entity's operating segments.

Earnings per share is important: it is used internationally as a comparative performance figure.

PART C ACCOUNTING AND REPORTING TECHNIQUES

1 Reporting financial performance: IAS 1 and IAS 8

> **FAST FORWARD**
>
> Go back to your earlier studies to revise **IAS 1** and **IAS 8**.

In Chapter 2 we looked at the format and content of financial statements, current assets and liabilities. In this chapter, we cover some of the other aspects of IAS 1 *Presentation of Financial Statements* and also revise IAS 8 *Accounting Policies, Changes in Accounting Estimates and Errors.* We also look at the impact of the implementation of IFRS 18 *Disclosure and Presentation of Financial Statements*.

1.1 Objectives and scope

The objective of IAS 1 is:

> 'to prescribe the basis for presentation of general purpose financial statements, in order to ensure comparability both with the entity's own financial statements of previous periods and with the financial statements of other entities.'

IAS 1 applies to all **general purpose financial statements** prepared in accordance with IFRS, ie those intended to meet the needs of users who are not in a position to demand reports tailored to their specific needs.

1.2 Purpose of financial statements

The **objective of financial statements** is to provide information about the financial position, performance and cash flows of an entity that is useful to a wide range of users in making economic decisions. They also show the result of **management stewardship** of the resources of the entity.

In order to fulfil this objective, financial statements must provide information about the following aspects of an entity's results:

- Assets
- Liabilities
- Equity
- Income and expenses (including gains and losses)
- Contributions by, and distributions to owners in their capacity as owners
- Cash flows

Along with other information in the notes and related documents, this information will assist users in predicting the entity's **future cash flows**.

1.3 Components of financial statements

As well as reporting a complete set of financial statements,

IAS 1 recognises that many entities wish to present, as part of the annual report, a **financial review** by management (which is **not** part of the financial statements), explaining the main features of the entity's performance and position, and the principal uncertainties it faces. The report may include a review of the following.

(a) **Factors/influences determining performance**: changes in the environment in which the entity operates, the entity's response to those changes and their effect, and the entity's policy for investment to maintain and enhance performance, including its dividend policy

(b) Entity's sources of funding, the policy on gearing and its risk management policies

(c) **Strengths and resources** of the entity whose value is not reflected in the statement of financial position under IFRS

> **Exam focus point**
>
> IFRS are only concerned with the financial statements, so IAS 1 has no mandatory rules concerning such a review.

18: REPORTING FINANCIAL PERFORMANCE

However, the IASB has issued an IFRS Practice Statement on Management Commentary. This is discussed later in this chapter.

1.4 Fair presentation and compliance with IFRS

Most importantly, financial statements should **present fairly** the financial position, financial performance and cash flows of an entity. **Compliance with IFRS** is presumed to result in financial statements that achieve a fair presentation.

The following points made by IAS 1 expand on this principle.

(a) **Compliance with IFRS** should be disclosed

(b) **All relevant IFRS** must be followed if compliance with IFRS is disclosed

(c) Use of an **inappropriate accounting treatment** cannot be rectified either by disclosure of accounting policies or notes/explanatory material

There may be (very rare) circumstances when management decides that compliance with a requirement of an IFRS would be so misleading that it would conflict with the *Conceptual Framework's* objective of financial statements. **Departure from the IFRS** is therefore required to achieve a fair presentation. The following should be disclosed in such an event.

(a) Management confirmation that the financial statements fairly present the entity's financial position, performance and cash flows

(b) Statement that all IFRS have been complied with **except** departure from one IFRS to achieve a fair presentation

(c) Details of the nature of the departure, why the IFRS treatment would be misleading, and the treatment adopted

(d) Financial impact of the departure

IAS 1 states what is required for a fair presentation:

Selection and application of **accounting policies**	**Presentation of information** in a manner which provides relevant, reliable, comparable and understandable information	**Additional disclosures** where required

The IAS then goes on to consider certain important assumptions which underpin the preparation and presentation of financial statements, which we might call **fundamental assumptions**.

1.5 Going concern

Key term

The entity is normally viewed as a **going concern**, that is, as continuing in operation for the foreseeable future. Hence, it is assumed that the entity has neither the intention nor the need to enter liquidation or to cease trading.

(Conceptual Framework, para. 3.9)

This assumption is based on the notion that, when preparing a normal set of financial statements, it is always expected that the business will **continue to operate** for the foreseeable future (at least the next 12 months should be considered). In particular, the entity will not go into liquidation or scale down its operations in a material way.

The main significance of the going concern assumption is that the assets of the business **should not be valued at their 'break-up' value**, which is the amount that they would sell for if they were sold off piecemeal and the business were thus broken up.

If the going concern assumption is not followed, that fact must be disclosed, together with:

- The **basis** on which the financial statements have been prepared
- The **reasons** why the entity is not considered to be a going concern

1.5.1 Assessing going concern

In assessing whether the going concern assumption is appropriate, management takes into account all available information about the future. When an entity has a history of profitable operations and ready access to financial resources, the entity may reach a conclusion that the going concern basis of accounting is appropriate without detailed analysis.

In other cases, management may need to consider a wide range of factors relating to current and expected profitability (ie consider profit forecasts), debt repayment schedules and potential sources of replacement financing (including considering cash flow forecasts) before it can satisfy itself that the going concern basis is appropriate.

1.6 Accrual accounting

Key term

> **Accrual accounting** depicts the effects of transactions and other events and circumstances on a reporting entity's economic resources and claims in the periods in which those effects occur, even if the resulting cash receipts and payments occur in a different period
>
> (Conceptual Framework, para 1.17)

Entities should prepare their financial statements on the basis that transactions are recorded in them, not as the cash is paid or received, but as the revenues or expenses are **earned or incurred** in the accounting period to which they relate.

1.7 Consistency of presentation

To maintain consistency, the presentation and classification of items in the financial statements should **stay the same from one period to the next. There are two exceptions**.

(a) There is a significant change in the **nature of the operations** or a review of the financial statements presentation indicates a **more appropriate presentation**.

(b) A change in presentation is **required by an IFRS**.

1.8 Materiality and aggregation

All material items should be presented separately in the financial statements.

Amounts which are **immaterial** should be aggregated with amounts of a similar nature or function and need not be presented separately.

Key term

> **Material**. Information is material if omitting, misstating or obscuring it could reasonably be expected to influence decisions that the primary users of general purpose financial reports make on the basis of those reports
>
> (Conceptual Framework, para 2.11)

An error which is too trivial to affect anyone's understanding of the financial statements is referred to as **immaterial**. In preparing financial statements it is important to assess what is material and what is not, so that time and money are not wasted in the pursuit of excessive detail. Determining whether or not an item is material is a very subjective exercise. There are common 'materiality factors' which can be used to help assess whether information is material. These are:

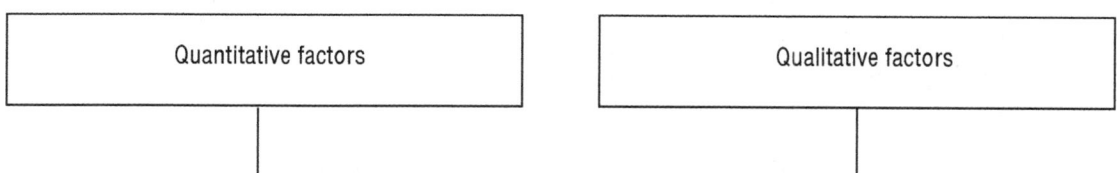

Quantitative factors:
- Consider the size of the effect of the transaction/event against measures of the entity's financial position, performance and cash flows
- Consider any unrecognised items (eg contingent liabilities) that could affect primary users' perception
- Can be assessed with the help of a threshold – such as 5% of profit.

Qualitative factors:
- These are characteristics that make information more likely to influence the decisions of primary users, they can be internal or external

  Internal include: involvement of related parties, uncommon features, unexpected changes in trends

  External include: geographic location, industry section, state of the economy

Both quantitative factors and qualitative factors should be considered.

It is usually more efficient to assess items from a quantitative perspective first: if an item exceeds the quantitative threshold, it is material and no further assessment is required.

1.8.1 Materiality and the Disclosure Initiative

The IASB has recognised in recent years that there has been excessive amounts of information reported in the financial statements, partially caused by misunderstanding or misapplication of the principle of materiality. This has compounded in a disclosure problem:

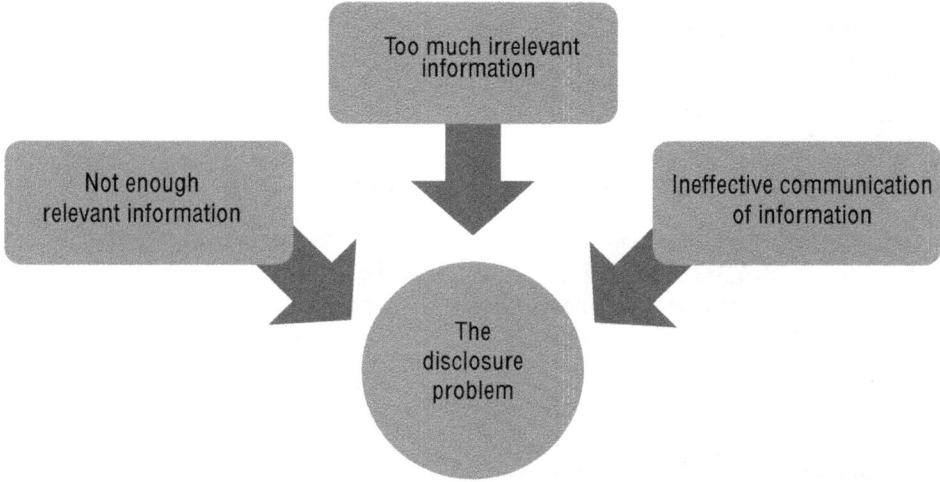

Materiality, as defined above and applied, was identified by the IASB as a contributing factor to the disclosure problem. In response the IASB:

Revised the definition of 'material'	The IASB has amended the definition of 'material' to make it clear that obscuring information has the same effect as omitting or misstating it. Obscuring information means making the information so difficult to find or so difficult to understand, that it may as well have been omitted.
Issued IFRS Practice Statement 2: Making Materiality Judgements	Aim is to encourage greater application of judgement in the preparation of financial statements. 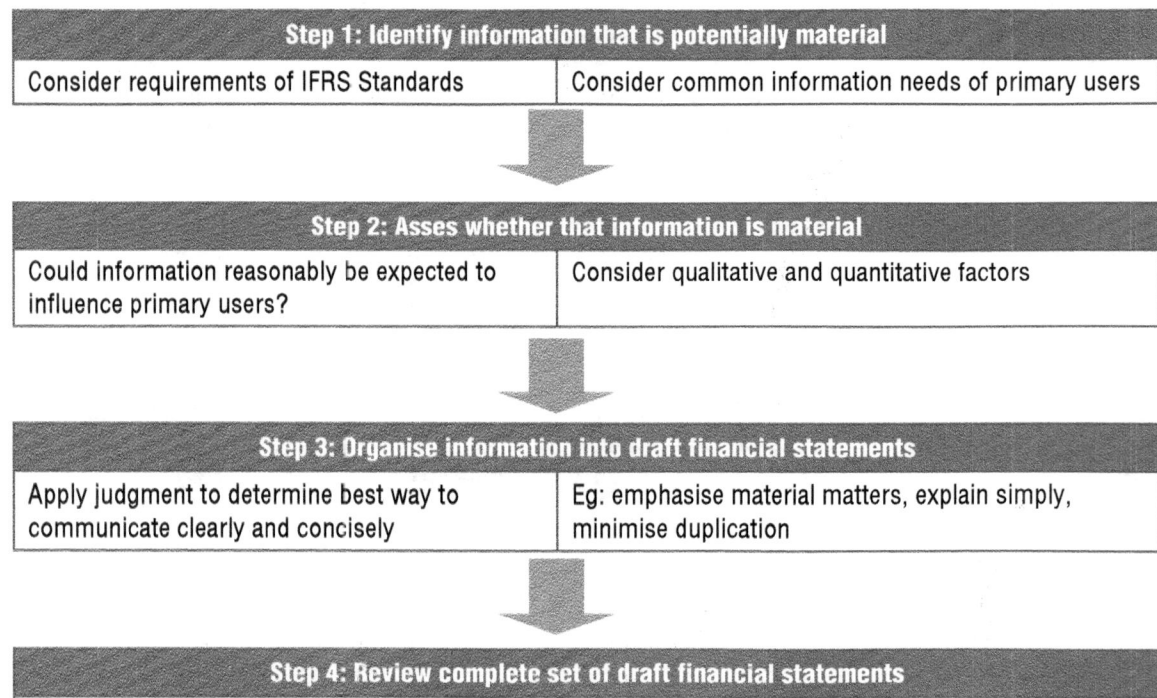

Recognition and measurement
- The recognition and measurement criteria only need to be applied when **the effect** of applying them is **material**.
- For example, an entity may choose to capitalise items of property, plant and equipment only when the cost of an capitalising items below this amount will not have a material effect on the financial statements.

Presentation and disclosure
- Disclosure criteria: If the information provided by a certain disclosure requirement is **not material**, the **entity does not need to make that disclosure**, even if that disclosure is part of a list of minimum required disclosures in an IFRS Standard.
- However, the entity should consider whether it also needs to disclose information not specifically required by an IFRS Standard if that information is needed to understand the financial statements.

One way of making materiality judgements when preparing the financial statements is to apply the following 4-step approach:

Step 1: Identify information that is potentially material	
Consider requirements of IFRS Standards	Consider common information needs of primary users

Step 2: Asses whether that information is material	
Could information reasonably be expected to influence primary users?	Consider qualitative and quantitative factors

Step 3: Organise information into draft financial statements	
Apply judgment to determine best way to communicate clearly and concisely	Eg: emphasise material matters, explain simply, minimise duplication

Step 4: Review complete set of draft financial statements	
On the basis of complete set of financial statements: has all material information been identified?	On the basis of complete set of financial statements: has materiality been considered from a wide perspective and in aggregate?

1.9 Offsetting

IAS 1 does not allow **assets and liabilities to be offset** against each other unless such a treatment is required or permitted by another IFRS.

Income and expenses can be offset only when:

(a) An IAS requires/permits it; **or**

(b) Gains, losses and related expenses arising from the same/similar transactions are not material (aggregate).

1.10 Comparative information

1.10.1 Minimum comparative information

Except where IFRS Standards permit or require otherwise, an entity should present comparative information in respect of the preceding period for all amounts reported in the current period's financial statements, hence a minimum of two years information must be reported. Comparative information for narrative and descriptive information should be presented if it is relevant to understanding the current period's financial statements.

1.10.2 Additional comparative information

Additional comparative information may be presented as long as it is prepared in accordance with IFRS Standards. For example, a third statement of profit or loss and other comprehensive income may be presented for an additional comparative period. Where a third statement is presented (regardless of whether it is a statement of profit or loss and other comprehensive income, a statement of financial position or any other statement):

(1) The relevant notes to that statement should be presented for the third period

(2) The other main financial statements are not required (ie a full third set of financial statements is not necessary).

1.11 Disclosure of accounting policies

There should be a specific section for accounting policies in the notes to the financial statements and the following should be disclosed (subject to materiality as discussed above) there.

(a) **Measurement bases** used in preparing the financial statements
(b) Each **specific accounting policy** necessary for a proper understanding of the financial statements

To be clear and understandable it is essential that financial statements should disclose the accounting policies used in their preparation. This is because **policies may vary**, not only from entity to entity, but also from country to country. As an aid to users, all the major accounting policies used should be disclosed in the same place.

1.11.1 Reclassification adjustments and related tax effects

Entities must present other comprehensive income split according to whether it may subsequently be reclassified to profit or loss or will not subsequently be classified to profit and loss. Where items of other comprehensive income are presented inclusive of tax and tax is disclosed separately, this must also be split according to whether it may be reclassified.

In addition to this requirement, entities must **disclose reclassification adjustments which have arisen in a period** relating to each item of other comprehensive income. These are amounts reclassified in the current period from other comprehensive income to profit and loss.

Entities should disclose **income tax relating to reclassification adjustments** for each component of other comprehensive income. This information will be useful, because often different tax rates are applied to these items than are applied to profit or loss.

1.12 Presentation of dividends

Dividends must be presented in the statement of changes in equity or in the notes. They cannot be presented in the statement of profit or loss and other comprehensive income

This reflects the fact that a dividend distribution is an owner change in equity, which must be presented separately from non-owner changes in equity.

1.13 Impact of IFRS 18

In Chapter 2, the new IFRS Accounting Standard IFRS 18 *Presentation and Disclosure in Financial Statements* was introduced. This standard is effective for accounting period starting on, or after, 1 January 2027 and will replace IAS 1.

Whilst many of the topics covered in this chapter are not substantially changed by the introduction of IFRS 18, the new standard will not include the material about general features of financial statements of the disclosure of accounting policies. This material will be moved to IAS 8, and IAS 8 will be renamed as *Basis of Preparation of Financial Statements* when IFRS 18 comes into effect.

1.14 Revision of IAS 8

You have studied this standard already but it is long and important. If you do not understand any of this or if you have problems with the revision question, go back and revise your earlier study material.

> Knowledge brought forward from earlier studies

Key terms

> **IAS 8** *Accounting Policies, Changes in Accounting Estimates and Errors*
>
> *Definitions*
>
> - **Accounting policies** are the specific principles, bases, conventions, rules and practices adopted by an entity in preparing and presenting financial statements.
>
> - A **change in accounting estimate** is an adjustment of the carrying amount of an asset or a liability or the amount of the periodic consumption of an asset, that results from the assessment of the present status of, and expected future benefits and obligations associated with, assets and liabilities. Changes in accounting estimates result from new information or new developments and, accordingly, are not corrections of errors.
>
> - **Material**: as defined in IAS 1 (see above)
>
> - **Prior period errors** are omissions from, and misstatements in, the entity's financial statements for one or more prior periods arising from a failure to use, or misuse of, reliable information that:
>
>   (a) Was available when financial statements for those periods were authorised for issue; and
>
>   (b) Could reasonably be expected to have been obtained and taken into account in the preparation and presentation of those financial statements.
>
>   Such errors include the effects of mathematical mistakes, mistakes in applying accounting policies, oversights or misinterpretations of facts, and fraud.
>
> - **Retrospective application** is applying a new accounting policy to transactions, other events and conditions as if that policy had always been applied.
>
> - **Retrospective restatement** is correcting the recognition, measurement and disclosure of amounts of elements of financial statements as if a prior period error had never occurred.
>
> - **Prospective application** of a change in accounting policy and of recognising the effect of a change in an accounting estimate, respectively, are:
>
>   (a) Applying the new accounting policy to transactions, other events and conditions occurring after the date as at which the policy is changes; and

(b) Recognising the effect of the change in the accounting estimate in the current and future periods affected by the change.

- **Impracticable**. Applying a requirement is impracticable when the entity cannot apply it after making every reasonable effort to do so. It is impracticable to apply a change in an accounting policy retrospectively or to make a retrospective restatement to correct an error if one of the following apply.

    (a) The effects or the retrospective application or retrospective restatement are not determinable.

    (b) The retrospective application or retrospective restatement requires assumptions about what management's intent would have been in that period.

    (c) The retrospective application or retrospective restatement requires significant estimates of amounts and it is impossible to distinguish objectively information about those estimates that: provides evidence of circumstances that existed on the date(s) at which those amounts are to be recognised, measured or disclosed; and would have been available when the financial statements for that prior period were authorised for issue from other information.

Accounting policies

- Accounting policies are determined by **applying the relevant IFRS**.
- Where there is no applicable IFRS or IFRIC management should use its **judgement** in developing and applying an accounting policy that results in information that is **relevant** and **reliable**. Management should refer to:

    (a) The requirements in IFRS and IFRICs dealing with **similar** and **related issues**.

    (b) The definitions, recognition criteria and measurement concepts for assets, liabilities and expenses in the *Conceptual Framework*.

    Management may also consider the most recent pronouncements of other standard-setting bodies that use a similar *Conceptual Framework* to develop standards, other accounting literature and accepted industry practices if these do not conflict with the sources above.

- An entity shall select and apply its accounting policies for a period **consistently** for similar transactions, other events and conditions, unless an IFRS specifically requires or permits categorisation of items for which different policies may be appropriate. If an IFRS requires or permits categorisation of items, an appropriate accounting policy shall be selected and applied consistently to each category.

Changes in Accounting Policies

- These are **rare**: only required by statute/standard-setting body/results in reliable and more relevant information.
- **Adoption of new IFRS**: follow transitional provisions of IFRS. If no transitional provisions: **retrospective** application.
- **Other changes in policy**: **retrospective** application. Adjust opening balance of each affected component of equity, ie as if new policy has always been applied.
- **Prospective** application is **no longer allowed** unless it is **impracticable** to determine the cumulative effect of the change. (See definition of impracticable above.)
- An entity should **disclose** information relevant to assessing the **impact of new IFRS** on the financial statements where these have been **issued but have not yet come into force**.

Changes in Accounting Estimates

- Estimates arise because of **uncertainties inherent within them**; judgement is required but this does not undermine reliability.

- Effect of a change in accounting estimate should be included in profit or loss in:
  - Period of change, if change affects only current period; or
  - Period of change and future periods, if change affects both.

Errors

(See definition of prior period error above.)

- **Prior period errors**: correct **retrospectively**.
- This involves:
  (a) Either restating the comparative amounts for the prior period(s) in which the error occurred; or
  (b) When the error occurred before the earliest prior period presented, restating the opening balances of assets, liabilities and equity for that period

  so that the financial statements are presented as if the error had never occurred.

- Only where it is **impracticable** to determine the cumulative effect of an error on prior periods can an entity correct an error **prospectively**.

The following question will allow you to revise IAS 8.

Question — Prior period error

During 20X7 Lubi Co discovered that certain items had been included in inventory at 31 December 20X6, valued at $4.2m, which had in fact been sold before the year end. The following figures for 20X6 (as reported) and 20X7 (draft) are available.

	20X6 $'000	20X7 (draft) $'000
Sales	47,400	67,200
Cost of goods sold	(34,570)	(55,800)
Profit before taxation	12,830	11,400
Income taxes	(3,880)	(3,400)
Profit	8,950	8,000

Retained earnings at 1 January 20X6 were $13m. The cost of goods sold for 20X7 includes the $4.2m error in opening inventory. The income tax rate was 30% for 20X6 and 20X7.

Required

Prepare the statement of profit or loss and other comprehensive income for 20X7, with the 20X6 comparative, and retained earnings.

Answer

STATEMENT OF PROFIT OR LOSS AND OTHER COMPREHENSIVE INCOME

	20X6 $'000	20X7 $'000
Sales	47,400	67,200
Cost of goods sold (W1)	(38,770)	(51,600)
Profit before tax	8,630	15,600
Income tax (W2)	(2,620)	(4,660)
Profit	6,010	10,940
RETAINED EARNINGS		
Opening retained earnings		
As previously reported	13,000	21,950
Correction of prior period error (4,200 – 1,260 tax)	–	(2,940)
As restated	13,000	19,010

	20X6	20X7
	$'000	$'000
Profit for year	6,010	10,940
Closing retained earnings	19,010	29,950

Workings

1 Cost of goods sold

	20X6	20X7
	$'000	$'000
As stated in question	34,570	55,800
inventory adjustment	4,200	(4,200)
	38,770	51,600

2 Income tax

	20X6	20X7
	$'000	$'000
As stated in question	3,880	3,400
Inventory adjustment (4,200 × 30%)	1,260	1,260
	2,620	4,660

2 IFRS 5 *Non-current Assets Held for Sale and Discontinued Operations*

FAST FORWARD

IFRS 5 requires non-current assets 'held-for-sale' to be presented separately in the statement of financial position.

2.1 Aim

IFRS 5 requires non-current assets and groups of assets that are 'held-for-sale' to be **presented separately** in the statement of financial position and the results of discontinued operations to be presented separately in the statement of profit or loss and other comprehensive income. This is required so that users of financial statements will be better able to make **projections** about the financial position, profits and cash flows of the entity.

Key term

Disposal group: a group of assets to be disposed of, by sale or otherwise, together as a group in a single transaction, and liabilities directly associated with those assets that will be transferred in the transaction. (In practice, a disposal group could be a subsidiary, a cash-generating unit or a single operation within an entity.) (IFRS 5)

IFRS 5 does not apply to certain assets covered by other accounting standards:

(a) Deferred tax assets (IAS 12 *Income Taxes*)

(b) Assets arising from employee benefits (IAS 19 *Employee Benefits*)

(c) Financial assets (IFRS 9 *Financial Instruments*)

(d) Investment properties accounted for in accordance with the fair value model (IAS 40 *Investment Property*)

(e) Agricultural and biological assets that are measured at fair value less costs to sell (IAS 41 *Agriculture*)*

(f) Insurance contracts (IFRS 4 *Insurance Contracts*)*

*IAS 41 and IFRS 4 are not examinable in this paper

2.2 Classification of assets held-for-sale

An asset (or disposal group) should be classified as **held for sale** if its carrying amount will be recovered **principally through a sale transaction** rather than **through continuing use**. A number of detailed criteria must be met:

The asset must be **available for immediate sale** in its present condition

Its sale must be **highly probable** (ie significantly more likely than not).

(a) Management must be **committed** to a plan to sell the asset.

(b) There must be an active programme to **locate a buyer**.

(c) The asset must be marketed for sale at a **price that is reasonable** in relation to its current fair value.

(d) The sale should be expected to take place **within one year** from the date of classification.

(e) It is unlikely that significant changes to the plan will be made or that the plan will be withdrawn.

A non-current asset (or disposal group) should still be classified as held-for-sale, even if the sale has not actually taken place within one year. However, the delay must have been **caused by events or circumstances beyond the entity's control** and there must be sufficient evidence that the entity is still committed to sell the asset or disposal group. Otherwise the entity must cease to classify the asset as held-for-sale.

If an entity acquires a disposal group (eg a subsidiary) exclusively with a view to its subsequent disposal, it should classify the asset as held-for-sale only if the sale is expected to take place within one year and it is highly probable that all the other criteria will be met within a short time (normally three months).

If an entity is committed to a sale plan involving loss of control of a subsidiary, it should classify all the assets and liabilities of the subsidiary as held-for-sale when the criteria above are met, even if the entity will retain a non-controlling interest in its former subsidiary after the sale.

A non-current asset that is to be **abandoned** should not be classified as held-for-sale. This is because its carrying amount will be recovered principally through continuing use. However, a disposal group to be abandoned may meet the definition of a discontinued operation (and therefore separate disclosure may be required) when it ceases to be used (see below).

Question — Held for sale?

On 1 December 20X3, a company became committed to a plan to sell a manufacturing facility and has already found a potential buyer. The company does not intend to discontinue the operations currently carried out in the facility. At 31 December 20X3 there is a backlog of uncompleted customer orders. The subsidiary will not be able to transfer the facility to the buyer until after it ceases to operate the facility and has eliminated the backlog of uncompleted customer orders. This is not expected to occur until spring 20X4.

Required

Should the manufacturing facility be classified as 'held for sale' at 31 December 20X3?

Answer

The facility will not be transferred until the backlog of orders is completed; this demonstrates that the facility is not available for immediate sale in its present condition. The facility cannot be classified as 'held for sale' at 31 December 20X3. It must be treated in the same way as other items of property, plant and equipment: it should continue to be depreciated and should not be separately disclosed.

2.3 Measurement of assets held-for-sale

Key terms

> **Fair value:** The price that would be received to sell an asset or paid to transfer a liability in an orderly transaction between market participants at the measurement date.
>
> **Costs to sell:** The incremental costs directly attributable to the disposal of an asset (or disposal group), excluding finance costs and income tax expense.
>
> **Recoverable amount:** The higher of an asset's fair value less costs to sell and its value in use.
>
> **Value in use:** The present value of estimated future cash flows expected to arise from the continuing use of an asset and from its disposal at the end of its useful life.

An asset (or disposal group) that is held for sale should be measured at the **lower of** its **carrying amount** and **fair value less costs to sell**. Fair value less costs to sell is equivalent to net realisable value. Fair value is measured in accordance with IFRS 13 *Fair Value Measurement* (see Chapter 11). The following approach should be adopted for measuring assets classified as held for sale:

Step 1 — Immediately before initial classification as held for sale, the asset (or disposal group) is **measured in accordance with the applicable IFRS** (eg property, plant and equipment held under the IAS 16 revaluation model is revalued).

Step 2 — On classification of the non-current asset (or disposal group) as held for sale, it is **written down to fair value less costs to sell** (if **less than** carrying amount).

Any impairment loss arising under IFRS 5 is **charged to profit or loss** (and the credit allocated to assets of a disposal group using the IAS 36 rules, ie first to goodwill then to other assets pro rata based on carrying amount).

Step 3 — Non-current assets/disposal groups classified as held for sale are **not depreciated/amortised**.

Step 4 — Any **subsequent changes in fair value less costs to sell** are recognised as a **further impairment loss (or reversal of an imapirment loss)**.

However, gains recognised cannot exceed cumulative impairment losses to date (whether under IAS 36 or IFRS 5).

Step 5 — Presented:
- As **single amounts** (of assets and liabilities);
- On the **face** of the statement of financial position;
- **Separately** from other assets and liabilities; and
- Normally as **current** assets and liabilities (not offset).

(IFRS 5, paras. 15, 18, 20–22, 25, 38)

An asset (or disposal group) that is **no longer classified as held for sale** (for example, because the sale has not taken place within one year) is measured at the **lower of**:

(a) Its **carrying amount** before it was classified as held for sale, adjusted for any depreciation that would have been charged had the asset not been held for sale

(b) Its **recoverable amount** at the date of the decision not to sell

2.4 Presenting discontinued operations

FAST FORWARD

The results of discontinued operations should be presented separately in the statement of profit or loss and other comprehensive income.

Key terms

Discontinued operation: a component of an entity that has either been disposed of, or is classified as held for sale, and:

(a) Represents a separate major line of business or geographical area of operations;

(b) Is part of a single co-ordinated plan to dispose of a separate major line of business or geographical area of operations; or

(c) Is a subsidiary acquired exclusively with a view to resale.

Component of an entity: operations and cash flows that can be clearly distinguished, operationally and for financial reporting purposes, from the rest of the entity.

An entity should **present and disclose information** that enables users of the financial statements to evaluate the financial effects of **discontinued operations** and disposals of non-current assets or disposal groups.

An entity should disclose a **single amount in the statement of profit or loss and other comprehensive income** comprising the total of:

(a) The **post-tax profit or loss** of discontinued operations; and

(b) The post-tax gain or loss recognised on the **measurement to fair value less costs to sell** or on the disposal of the assets or disposal group(s) constituting the discontinued operation.

An entity should also disclose an **analysis** of the single amount into:

(a) The revenue, expenses and pre-tax profit or loss of discontinued operations

(b) The related income tax expense

(c) The gain or loss recognised on the measurement to fair value less costs to sell or on the disposal of the assets or the discontinued operation

(d) The related income tax expense

This analysis may be presented either in the statement of profit or loss and other comprehensive income or in the notes. If it is presented in the statement of profit or loss and other comprehensive income, it should be presented in a section identified as relating to discontinued operations, ie separately from continuing operations. This analysis is not required where the discontinued operation is a newly acquired subsidiary that has been classified as held-for-sale.

An entity should disclose the **net cash flows** attributable to the operating, investing and financing activities of discontinued operations. These disclosures may be presented either in the statement of cash flows or in the notes.

The prior period amounts relating to the operations discontinued in the current period should be restated in the comparative figures in the statement of profit or loss and other comprehensive income and the statement of cash flows, but **not** in the statement of financial position.

Gains and losses on the remeasurement of a disposal group that is not a discontinued operation but is held for sale should be included in profit or loss from continuing operations.

2.5 Illustration

The following illustration is taken from the implementation guidance to IFRS 5. Profit for the period from discontinued operations would be analysed in the notes.

XYZ GROUP
STATEMENT OF PROFIT OR LOSS AND OTHER COMPREHENSIVE INCOME FOR THE YEAR ENDED 31 DECEMBER 20X2

	20X2 $'000	20X1 $'000
Continuing operations		
Revenue	X	X
Cost of sales	(X)	(X)
Gross profit	X	X
Other income	X	X
Distribution costs	(X)	(X)
Administrative expenses	(X)	(X)
Other expenses	(X)	(X)
Finance costs	(X)	(X)
Share of profit of associates	X	X
Profit before tax	X	X
Income tax expense	(X)	(X)
Profit for the period from continuing operations	X	X
Discontinued operations		
Profit for the period from discontinued operations	X	X
Profit for the period	X	X
Attributable to:		
Owners of the parent	X	X
Non-controlling interest	X	X
	X	X

An alternative to this presentation would be to analyse the profit from discontinued operations in a separate column in the statement of profit or loss and other comprehensive income.

Question — Treatment of closure

On 20 October 20X3 the directors of a parent company made a public announcement of plans to close a steel works. The closure means that the group will no longer carry out this type of operation, which until recently has represented about 10% of its total turnover. The works will be gradually shut down over a period of several months, with complete closure expected in July 20X4. At 31 December output had been significantly reduced and some redundancies had already taken place. The cash flows, revenues and expenses relating to the steel works can be clearly distinguished from those of the group's other operations.

Required

How should the closure be treated in the financial statements for the year ended 31 December 20X3?

Answer

Because the steel works is being closed, rather than sold, it cannot be classified as 'held-for-sale'. In addition, the steel works is not a discontinued operation. Although at 31 December 20X3 the group was firmly committed to the closure, this has not yet taken place and therefore the steel works must be included in continuing operations. Information about the planned closure could be disclosed in the notes to the financial statements and the steel works' results should be presented as from discontinued operations (with adjustments to the comparative figures) when it ceases to be used.

2.6 Presentation of a non-current asset or disposal group classified as held-for-sale

Non-current assets and disposal groups classified as held-for-sale should be **presented separately** from other assets in the statement of financial position. The liabilities of a disposal group should be presented separately from other liabilities in the statement of financial position.

(a) Assets and liabilities held for sale **should not be offset**.

(b) The **major classes** of assets and liabilities held for sale should be **separately disclosed** either in the statement of financial position or in the notes.

(c) IFRS 5 requires non-current assets or disposal groups held for sale to be shown as a separate component of current assets/current liabilities.

2.7 Additional disclosures

In the period in which a non-current asset (or disposal group) has been either classified as held-for-sale or sold the following should be disclosed.

(a) A **description** of the non-current asset (or disposal group)

(b) A description of the **facts and circumstances** of the disposal

(c) Any **gain or loss** recognised when the item was classified as held-for-sale

(d) If applicable, the **segment** in which the non-current asset (or disposal group) is presented in accordance with IFRS 8 *Operating Segments*

Where an asset previously classified as held for sale is **no longer held-for-sale**, the entity should disclose a description of the facts and circumstances leading to the decision and its effect on results. Its results should be included within those from continuing operations.

IFRS 13 *Fair Value Measurement* disclosures are also relevant to assets held-for-sale.

3 IFRS 8 *Operating Segments*

3.1 Introduction

Large entities produce a wide range of products and services, often in several different countries. Further information on how the overall results of entities are made up from each of these product or geographical areas will help the users of the financial statements. This is the reason for **segment reporting**:

- The entity's **past performance** will be better understood
- The entity's **risks and returns** may be better assessed
- More **informed judgements** may be made about the entity as a whole

Risks and returns of a **diversified, multi-national company** can only be assessed by looking at the individual risks and rewards attached to groups of products or services or in different groups of products or services or in different geographical areas. These are subject to differing rates of profitability, opportunities for growth, future prospects and risks.

Segment reporting is covered by IFRS 8 *Operating Segments*.

3.2 Objective

An entity must disclose information to enable users of its financial statements to evaluate the nature and financial effects of the business activities in which it engages and the economic environments in which it operates.

3.3 Scope

Only entities whose **equity or debt securities are publicly traded** (ie on a stock exchange) need disclose segment information. In group financial statements, only **consolidated** segmental information needs to be shown. (The statement also applies to entities filing or in the process of filing financial statements for the purpose of issuing instruments in a public market.)

3.4 Definition of operating segment

FAST FORWARD

> Reportable segments are **operating segments** or aggregations of operating segments that meet specified criteria.

You need to learn this definition, as it is crucial to the standard.

Key term

> **Operating segment**: This is a component of an entity:
>
> (a) That engages in business activities from which it may earn revenues and incur expenses (including revenues and expenses relating to transactions with other components of the same entity);
>
> (b) Whose operating results are regularly reviewed by the entity's chief operating decision maker to make decisions about resources to be allocated to the segment and assess its performance; and
>
> (c) For which discrete financial information is available.
>
> (IFRS 8)

The term 'chief operating decision maker' identifies a function, not necessarily a manager with a specific title. That function is to allocate resources and to assess the performance of the entity's operating segments.

3.5 Aggregation

Two or more operating segments may be **aggregated** if the segments have **similar economic characteristics**, and the segments are similar in **each** of the following respects:

- The **nature of the products or services**
- The **nature of the production process**
- The type or class of customer for their products or services
- The methods used to distribute their products or provide their services, and
- If applicable, the **nature of the regulatory environment**

3.6 Determining reportable segments

FAST FORWARD

> IFRS 8 adopts a **management approach** to identifying reportable segments.

An entity must report separate information about **each operating segment** that:

(a) Has been identified as meeting the **definition of an operating segment**; and

(b) Where the segment total is **10% or more of total**:

    (i) **Revenue** (internal and external);

    (ii) **Reported profit or loss of all segments not reporting a loss** (or all segments in loss if greater); or

    (iii) **Assets**.

In each case the 10% test is made against the total amount for all operating segments.

At least **75% of total external revenue** must be reported by operating segments. Where this is not the case, additional segments must be identified (even if they do not meet the 10% thresholds).

Two or more operating segments **below** the thresholds may be aggregated to produce a reportable segment if the segments have similar economic characteristics, and the segments are similar in a **majority** of the aggregation criteria above.

Operating segments that do not meet **any of the quantitative thresholds** should be reported separately if management believes that information about the segment would be useful to users of the financial statements.

3.6.1 Decision tree to assist in identifying reportable segments

The following decision tree will assist in identifying reportable segments.

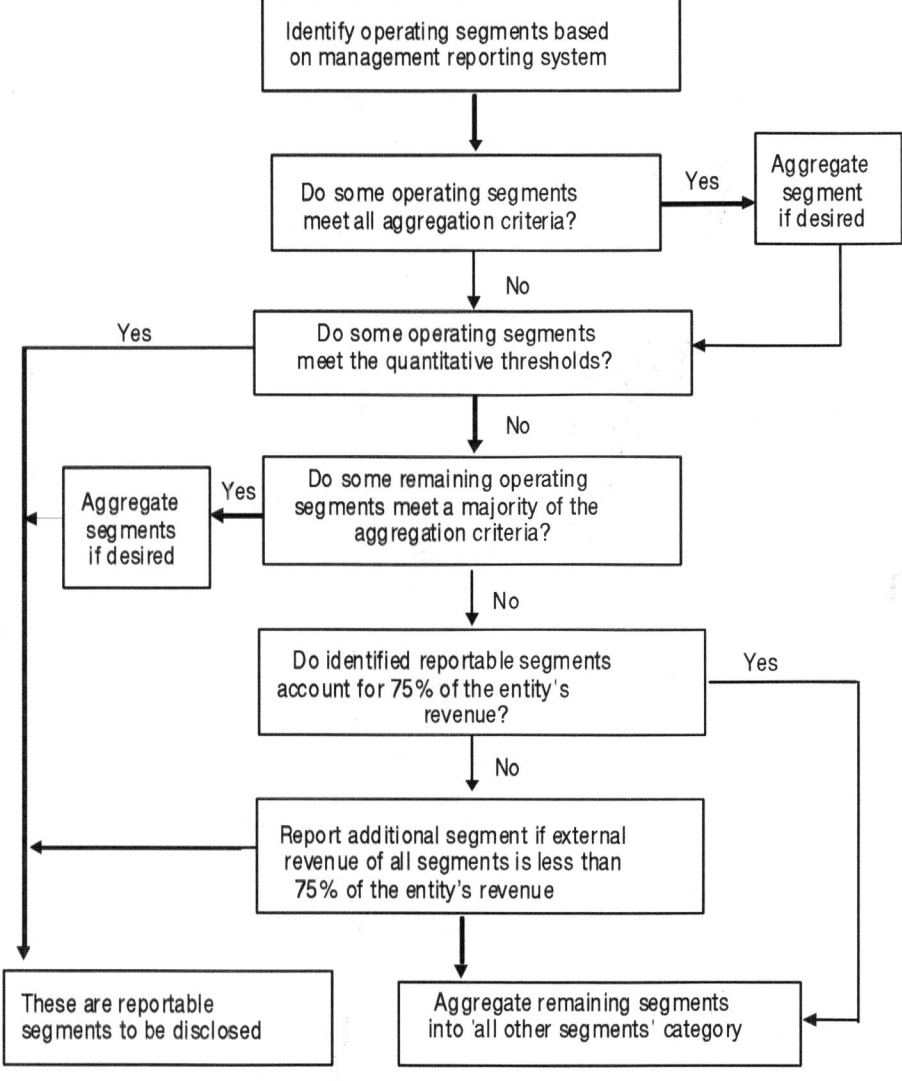

18: REPORTING FINANCIAL PERFORMANCE

3.7 Disclosures

FAST FORWARD

- IFRS 8 disclosures are of:
    - Operating segment profit or loss
    - Segment assets
    - Segment liabilities
    - Certain income and expense items

    Disclosure under the last two headings is only required if these amounts are regularly reported to the chief operating decision maker.

- Disclosures are also required about the revenues derived from products or services and about the countries in which revenues are earned or assets held, even if that information is not reported to management for decision making.

Disclosures required by the IFRS are extensive, and best learned by looking at the example and proforma, which follow the list.

(a) Factors used to identify the entity's reportable segments

(b) **Types of products and services** from which each reportable segment derives its revenues

(c) Reportable segment revenues, profit or loss, assets, liabilities and other material items:

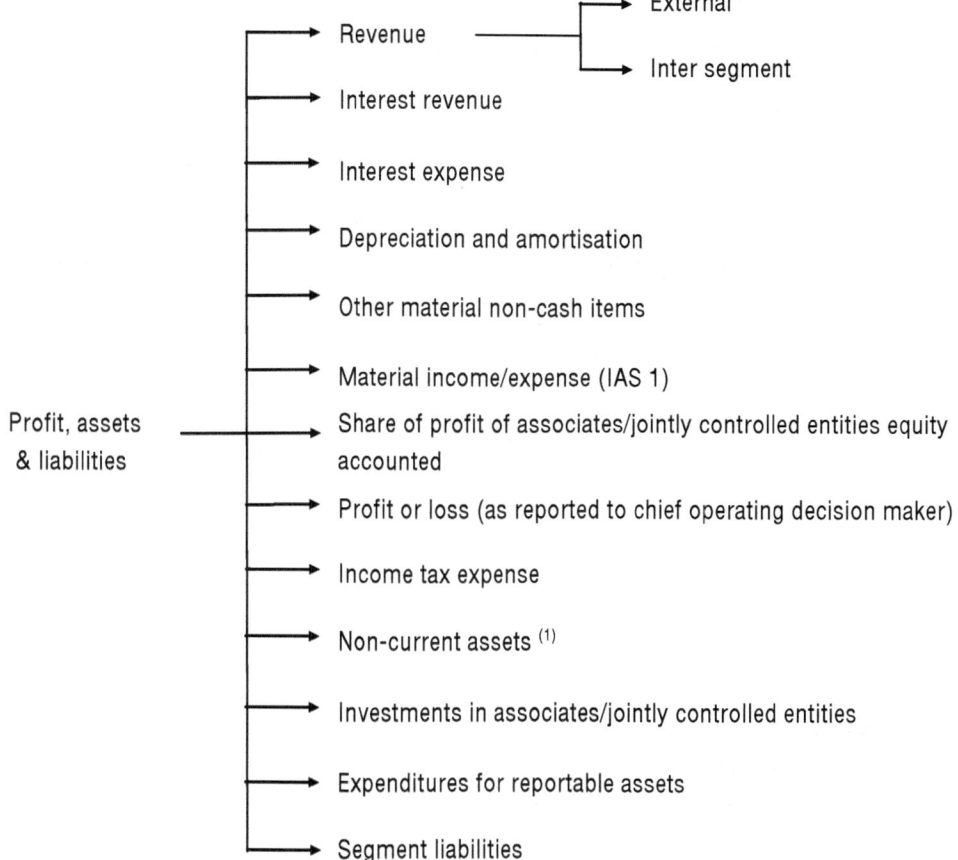

The amounts disclosed should be measured as they are reported to the chief operating decision maker, which is not necessarily the measurements required by IFRS.

A **reconciliation** is required of the total of each of the above items to the entity's total figures reported in its financial statements and measured under IFRS.

Reporting of a measure of **profit or loss** for each segment is compulsory. Other items are disclosed if included in the figures reviewed by or regularly provided to the chief operating decision maker.

(d) **External revenue** by each product and service (if reported basis is not products and services)

(e) Geographical information:

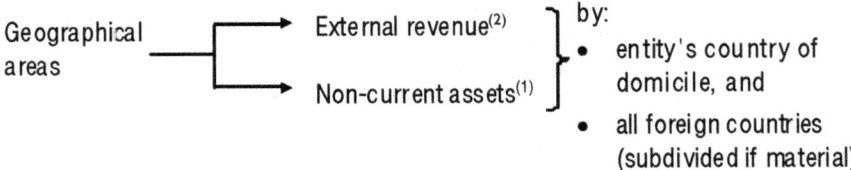

Notes

(1) Non-current assets excludes financial instruments, deferred tax assets, post-employment benefit assets, and rights under insurance contracts.

(2) External revenue is allocated based on the customer's location.

(f) Information about **reliance on major customers** (ie those who represent more than 10% of external revenue)

Note that amounts disclosed under (d), (e) and (f) above must be measured under IFRS.

3.7.1 Illustration

The following illustration is adapted from the IFRS 8 *Implementation Guidance*, which emphasises that this is for illustrative purposes only and that the information must be presented in the most understandable manner in the specific circumstances.

The hypothetical company does not allocate tax expense (tax income) or non-recurring gains and losses to reportable segments. In addition, not all reportable segments have material non-cash items other than depreciation and amortisation in profit or loss. The amounts in this illustration, denominated as dollars, are assumed to be the amounts in reports used by the chief operating decision-maker.

	Car parts $	Motor vessel $	Software $	Electronics $	Finance $	All other $	Totals $
Revenues from external customers	3,000	5,000	9,500	12,000	5,000	1,000[a]	35,500
Intersegment revenues	–	–	3,000	1,500	–	–	4,500
Interest revenue	450	800	1,000	1,500	–	–	3,750
Interest expense	350	600	700	1,100	–	–	2,750
Net interest revenue [b]	–	–	–	–	1,000	–	1,000
Depreciation and amortisation	200	100	50	1,500	1,100	–	2,950
Reportable segment profit	200	70	900	2,300	500	100	4,070
Other material non-cash items:							
Impairment of assets	–	200	–	–	–	–	200
Reportable segment assets	2,000	5,000	3,000	12,000	57,000	2,000	81,000
Expenditure for reportable segment non-current assets	300	700	500	800	600	–	2,900
Reportable segment liabilities	1,050	3,000	1,800	8,000	30,000	–	43,850

(a) Revenues from segments below the quantitative thresholds are attributable to four operating segments of the company. Those segments include a small property business, an electronics equipment rental business, a software consulting practice and a warehouse leasing operation. None of those segments has ever met any of the quantitative thresholds for determining reportable segments.

(b) The finance segment derives a majority of its revenue from interest. Management primarily relies on net interest revenue, not the gross revenue and expense amounts, in managing that segment. Therefore, as permitted by IFRS 8, only the net amount is disclosed.

3.7.2 Suggested proforma

Information about profit or loss, assets and liabilities

	Segment A	Segment B	Segment C	All other segments	Inter segment	Entity total
Revenue – external customers	X	X	X	X	–	X
Revenue – inter segment	X	X	X	X	X	–
	X	X	X	X	(X)	X
Interest revenue	X	X	X	X	(X)	X
Interest expense	(X)	(X)	(X)	(X)	X	(X)
Depreciation and amortisation	(X)	(X)	(X)	(X)	–	(X)
Other material non-cash items	X/(X)	X/(X)	X/(X)	X/(X)	X/(X)	X/(X)
Material income/expense (IAS 1)	X/(X)	X/(X)	X/(X)	X/(X)	X/(X)	X/(X)
Share of profit of associate/JVs	X	X	X	X	–	X
Segment profit before tax	X	X	X	X	(X)	X
Income tax expense	(X)	(X)	(X)	(X)	–	(X)
Unallocated items						X/(X)
Profit for the period						X
Segment assets	X	X	X	X	(X)	X
Investments in associate/JVs	X	X	X	X	–	X
Unallocated assets						X
Entity's assets						X
Expenditures for reportable assets	X	X	X	X	(X)	X
Segment liabilities	X	X	X	X	(X)	X
Unallocated liabilities						X
Entity's liabilities						X

Information about geographical areas

	Country of domicile	Foreign countries	Total
Revenue – external customers	X	X	X
Non-current assets	X	X	X

3.8 Critique of IFRS 8

IFRS 8 adopts a managerial approach. The published segment information is based on the way that the company or group is actually managed and an entity's reportable segments (called operating segments) are the ones used in its internal management reports. This approach has resulted in IFRS 8 being a controversial standard. Some users claim that the managerial approach to defining segments is too flexible and allows management to hide information, particularly the extent of their overseas operations. Some critics of IFRS 8 would like entities to be required to report all segment information by country.

3.9 Section summary

IFRS 8 is a **disclosure standard**.

- **Segment reporting** is necessary for a better understanding and assessment of:
  - Past performance
  - Risks and returns
  - Informed judgements
- IFRS 8 adopts the **managerial approach** to identifying segments
- The standard gives guidance on how segments should be **identified** and **what information should be disclosed** for each

It also sets out **requirements for related disclosures** about products and services, geographical areas and major customers.

4 IAS 33 *Earnings per Share*

FAST FORWARD

> **Earnings per share** is a measure of the amount of profits earned by a company for each ordinary share. Earnings are profits after tax and preferred dividends.

The objective of IAS 33 is to improve the **comparison** of the performance of different entities in the same period and of the same entity in different accounting periods.

4.1 Definitions

The following definitions are given in IAS 33.

Key terms

> **Ordinary share**: an equity instrument that is subordinate to all other classes of equity instruments.
>
> **Potential ordinary share**: a financial instrument or other contract that may entitle its holder to ordinary shares.
>
> **Options, warrants and their equivalents**: financial instruments that give the holder the right to purchase ordinary shares.
>
> **Contingently issuable ordinary shares** are ordinary shares issuable for little or no cash or other consideration upon the satisfaction of certain conditions in a contingent share agreement.
>
> **Contingent share agreement**: an agreement to issue shares that is dependent on the satisfaction of specified conditions.
>
> **Dilution** is a reduction in earnings per share or an increase in loss per share resulting from the assumption that convertible instruments are converted, that options or warrants are exercised, or that ordinary shares are issued upon the satisfaction of certain conditions.
>
> **Antidilution** is an increase in earnings per share or a reduction in loss per share resulting from the assumption that convertible instruments are converted, that options or warrants are exercised, or that ordinary shares are issued upon the satisfaction of certain conditions. (IAS 33)

4.1.1 Ordinary shares

There may be more than one class of ordinary shares, but ordinary shares of the same class will have the same rights to receive dividends. Ordinary shares participate in the profit for the period **only after other types of shares**, eg preference shares classified as equity.

4.1.2 Potential ordinary shares

IAS 33 identifies the following examples of financial instrument and other contracts generating potential ordinary shares.

(a) **Debts** (financial liabilities) **or equity instruments**, including preference shares, that are convertible into ordinary shares

(b) **Share warrants and options**

(c) Shares that would be issued upon the satisfaction of **certain conditions** resulting from contractual arrangements, such as the purchase of a business or other assets

4.2 Scope

IAS 33 has the following **scope restrictions**.

(a) Only companies with (potential) ordinary shares which are **publicly traded** need to present EPS (including companies in the process of being listed).

(b) EPS need only be presented on the basis of **consolidated results** where the parent's results are shown as well.

(c) Where companies **choose** to present EPS, even when they have no (potential) ordinary shares which are publicly traded, they must do so according to IAS 33.

4.3 Basic EPS

FAST FORWARD

> You should know how to calculate **basic EPS** and how to deal with related complications (issue of shares for cash, bonus issue, share splits/reverse share splits, rights issues).
>
> **Basic EPS** is calculated by dividing the profit or loss for the period attributable to ordinary equity holders by the weighted average number of ordinary shares outstanding during the period.

Basic EPS should be calculated for **profit or loss attributable to ordinary equity holders** of the parent entity and **profit or loss from continuing operations** attributable to those equity holders (if this is presented).

Basic EPS should be calculated by dividing the **profit** or loss for the period attributable to ordinary equity holders by the **weighted average number of ordinary shares** outstanding during the period.

$$\frac{\text{Profit/(loss attributable to ordinary shareholders}}{\text{Weighted average number of ordinary shares outstanding during the period}}$$

4.3.1 Earnings

Earnings includes **all items of income and expense** (including tax and non-controlling interests) **less** profit attributable to **holders of preference shares** classified as equity, including preference dividends.

The dividends on **preference shares** classified as equity to be deducted from profit consist of the following:

(a) Dividends on non-cumulative preference shares declared in respect of the period.

(b) Dividends on cumulative preference shares required for the period, **whether or not** they have been declared (**excluding** those paid/declared during the period in respect of previous periods).

If an entity purchases its own preference shares classified as equity for more than their carrying amount, the excess should be treated as a return to the preference shareholders and deducted from profit or loss attributable to ordinary equity holders.

4.3.2 Per share

The number of ordinary shares used should be the weighted average number of ordinary shares during the period. This figure (for all periods presented) should be **adjusted for events**, other than the conversion of potential ordinary shares, that have changed the number of shares outstanding without a corresponding change in resources.

The **time-weighting factor** is the number of days the shares were outstanding compared with the total number of days in the period. A reasonable approximation is usually adequate.

Shares are usually included in the weighted average number of shares from the **date consideration is receivable** which is usually the date of issue. In other cases consider the specific terms attached to their issue (consider the substance of any contract). The treatment for the issue of ordinary shares in different circumstances is as follows.

Consideration	Start date for inclusion
In exchange for cash	When cash is receivable
On the voluntary reinvestment of dividends on ordinary or preferred shares	The dividend payment date
As a result of the conversion of a debt instrument to ordinary shares	Date interest ceases accruing
In place of interest or principal on other financial instruments	Date interest ceases accruing
In exchange for the settlement of a liability of the entity	The settlement date
As consideration for the acquisition of an asset other than cash	The date on which the acquisition is recognised
For the rendering of services to the entity	As services are rendered

Ordinary shares issued as **purchase consideration** in an acquisition should be included as of the date of acquisition because the acquired entity's results will also be included from that date.

Ordinary shares that will be issued on the **conversion** of a mandatorily convertible instrument are included in the calculation from the **date the contract is entered into**.

If ordinary shares are **partly paid**, they are treated as a fraction of an ordinary share to the extent they are entitled to dividends relative to fully paid ordinary shares.

Contingently issuable shares (including those subject to recall) are included in the computation when all necessary conditions for issue have been satisfied.

4.4 Effect on basic EPS of changes in capital structure

4.4.1 New issues/buy backs

When there has been an issue of new shares or a buy-back of shares, the corresponding figures for EPS for the previous year will be comparable with the current year because, as the weighted average of shares has risen or fallen, there has been a **corresponding increase or decrease in resources**. Money has been received when shares were issued, and money has been paid out to repurchase shares. It is assumed that the sale or purchase has been made at full market price.

There are other events, however, which change the number of shares outstanding, **without a corresponding change in resources**. In these circumstances (four of which are considered by IAS 33) it is necessary to make adjustments so that the current and prior period EPS figures are comparable.

4.4.2 Capitalisation/bonus issue and share split/reverse share split

These two types of event can be considered together as they have a similar effect. In both cases, the number of ordinary shares held by equity holders changes, but for **no consideration is received or paid**. So there is no change in resources held by the entity.

This problem is solved by **adjusting the number of ordinary shares outstanding before the event** for the proportionate change in the number of shares outstanding as if the event had occurred at the beginning of the earliest period reported.

4.4.3 Rights issue

A rights issue of shares is an issue of new shares to existing equity holders **at a price below the current market value**. The offer of new shares is made on the basis of x new shares for every y shares currently held, eg a 1 for 3 rights issue is an offer of 1 new share at the offer price for every 3 shares currently held. Because the rights price is below the market price, there is a 'free', ie bonus, element in the issue.

To arrive at figures for EPS when a rights issue is made, we first calculate the **theoretical ex-rights price**. This is a weighted average value per share.

The procedures for calculating the EPS for the current year and a corresponding figure for the previous year are as follows.

(a) The **EPS for the corresponding previous period** should be multiplied by the following fraction. (**Note.** The market price on the last day of quotation is taken as the fair value immediately prior to exercise of the rights, as required by the standard.)

$$\frac{\text{Theoretical ex-rights price}}{\text{Market price on last day of quotation (with rights)}}$$

(b) To obtain the **EPS for the current year** you should:

(i) Multiply the number of shares before the rights issue by the fraction of the year before the date of issue and by the following fraction.

$$\frac{\text{Market price on last day of quotation with rights}}{\text{Theoretical ex-rights price}}$$

(ii) Multiply the number of shares after the rights issue by the fraction of the year after the date of issue and add to the figure arrived at in (i).

The total earnings should then be divided by the total number of shares so calculated.

Question

Basic EPS

Macarone Co has produced the following profit figures.

	$m
20X6	1.1
20X7	1.5
20X8	1.8

On 1 January 20X7 the number of shares outstanding was 500,000. During 20X7 the company announced a rights issue with the following details.

Rights: 1 new share for each 5 outstanding (100,000 new shares in total)

Exercise price: $5.00

Last date to exercise rights: 1 March 20X7

The market (fair) value of one share in Marcoli immediately prior to exercise on 1 March 20X7 = $11.00.

Required

Calculate the EPS for 20X6, 20X7 and 20X8.

Answer

Computation of theoretical ex-rights price

This computation uses the total fair value and number of shares.

$$\frac{\text{Fair value of all outstanding shares} + \text{total received from exercise of rights}}{\text{No shares outstanding prior to exercise} + \text{no shares issued in exercise}}$$

$$= \frac{(\$11.00 \times 500,000) + (\$5.00 \times 100,000)}{500,000 + 100,000} = \$10.00$$

Another method of calculation is:

20X6	Shares	Price	
		$	$
Initial holding	5	11.00	55.00
Rights issue	1	5.00	5.00
	6		60.00

so $10.00 per share.

Computation of EPS

			20X6	20X7	20X8
			$	$	$
20X6	EPS as originally reported				
	$\dfrac{\$1,100,000}{500,000}$		2.20		
20X6	EPS restated for rights issue =				
	$\dfrac{\$1,100,000}{500,000} \times \dfrac{10}{11}$		2.00		
20X7	EPS including effects of rights issue				
	$\dfrac{\$1,500,000}{(500,000 \times 2/12 \times 11/10) + (600,000 \times 10/12)}$			2.54	
20X8	EPS = $\dfrac{\$1,800,000}{600,000}$				3.00

4.5 Diluted EPS

FAST FORWARD

Diluted EPS is calculated by adjusting the profit attributable to ordinary equity holders and the weighted average number of shares outstanding for the effects of all dilutive potential ordinary shares.

At the end of an accounting period, a company may have in issue some **securities** which do not (at present) have any 'claim' to a share of equity earnings, but **may give rise to such a claim in the future**, for example.

(a) A **separate class of equity shares** which at present is not entitled to any dividend, but will be entitled after some future date.

(b) **Convertible loan stock** or **convertible preferred shares** which give their holders the right at some future date to exchange their securities for ordinary shares of the company, at a pre-determined conversion rate.

(c) **Options or warrants.**

In such circumstances, the future number of shares ranking for dividend might increase, which in turn results in a fall in the EPS. In other words, a **future increase** in the **number of equity shares will cause a dilution or 'watering down' of equity**, and it is possible to calculate a **diluted earnings per share** (ie the

EPS that would have been obtained during the financial period if the dilution had already taken place). This will indicate to investors the possible effects of a future dilution.

4.5.1 Earnings

The earnings calculated for basic EPS should be adjusted by the **post-tax** (including deferred tax) effect of the following.

| Any **dividends** on dilutive potential ordinary shares that were deducted to arrive at earnings for basic EPS. | **Interest recognised** in the period for the dilutive potential ordinary shares | Any **other changes in income or expenses** (fees and discount, premium accounted for as yield adjustments) that would result from the conversion of the dilutive potential ordinary shares |

Interest and other changes in income may have consequences for **other income or expenses not directly related to the dilutive potential ordinary shares**, for example the change in profit may impact on a staff bonus scheme. When calculating diluted EPS, the profit or loss for the period is adjusted for any such consequential changes in income or expense.

4.5.2 Per share

The number of ordinary shares is the weighted average number of ordinary shares calculated for basic EPS plus the weighted average number of ordinary shares that would be issued on the conversion of all the **dilutive potential ordinary shares** into ordinary shares.

It should be assumed that dilutive ordinary shares were converted into ordinary shares at the **beginning of the period** or, if later, at the actual date of issue. There are two other points.

(a) The computation assumes the most **advantageous conversion rate** or exercise rate from the standpoint of the holder of the potential ordinary shares.

(b) A **subsidiary, joint venture or associate** may issue potential ordinary shares that are convertible into either ordinary shares of the subsidiary, joint venture or associate, or ordinary shares of the reporting entity. If these potential ordinary shares have a dilutive effect on the consolidated basic EPS of the reporting entity, they are included in the calculation of diluted EPS.

4.6 Example: Diluted EPS

In 20X7 Farrah Co had a basic EPS of 105c based on earnings of $105,000 and 100,000 ordinary $1 shares. It also had in issue $40,000 15% Convertible Loan Stock which is convertible in two years' time at the rate of 4 ordinary shares for every $5 of stock. The rate of tax is 30%.

Required

Calculate the diluted EPS.

Solution

Diluted EPS is calculated as follows.

Step 1 **Number of shares**: the additional equity on conversion of the loan stock will be 40,000 × 4/5 = 32,000 shares

Step 2 **Earnings**: Farrah Co will save interest payments of $6,000 ($40,000 × 15%) but this increase in profits will be taxed. Hence the earnings figure may be recalculated:

	$
Gross profit $((105,000 ÷ (1 − 30%)) + 6,000)$	156,000
Tax (30%)	46,800
Profit after taxation	109,200

Step 3 **Calculation**: Diluted EPS = $\frac{\$109,200}{132,000}$ = 82.7c

Step 4 **Dilution**: the dilution in earnings would be 105c − 82.7c = 22.3c per share.

Question — EPS 1

Ardent Co has 5,000,000 ordinary shares of 25 cents each in issue. During 20X4 the company also had in issue $2,000,000 of 10% convertible loan stock, convertible in one year's time at the rate of 3 shares per $5 of stock.

The total earnings in 20X4 were $1,750,000.

The rate of tax is 35%.

Required

Calculate the EPS and diluted EPS.

Answer

(a) EPS = $\frac{\$1,750,000}{5 \text{ million}}$ = 35 cents

(b) On dilution, the (maximum) number of shares in issue would be:

	Shares
Current	5,000,000
On conversion of 10% stock (2 million × 3/5)	1,200,000
	6,200,000

	$	$
Current earnings		1,750,000
Add interest saved on 10% stock		120,000
Revised earnings		1,880,000

Fully diluted EPS = $\frac{\$1,880,000}{6.2 \text{ million}}$ = 30.3 cents

4.6.1 Treatment of options

FAST FORWARD — You must be able to deal with **options** and all other **dilutive potential ordinary shares**.

It should be assumed that options are exercised and that the assumed proceeds would have been received from the issue of shares at the average market price of the ordinary shares during the period.

Options and other share purchase arrangements are dilutive when they would result in the issue of ordinary shares for **less than the average market price of ordinary shares during the period**. The amount of the dilution is the average market price of ordinary shares during the period less the issue price. In order to calculate diluted EPS, each transaction of this type is treated as consisting of two parts.

(a) A contract to issue a certain number of ordinary shares at their **average market price** during the period. These shares are fairly priced and are assumed to be neither dilutive nor antidilutive. They are ignored in the computation of diluted earnings per share.

(b) A contract to issue the remaining ordinary shares for **no consideration**. Such ordinary shares generate no proceeds and have no effect on the profit attributable to ordinary shares outstanding. Therefore such shares are dilutive and they are added to the number of ordinary shares outstanding in the computation of diluted EPS.

To the extent that **partly paid shares** are not entitled to participate in dividends during the period, they are considered the equivalent of **warrants** or **options**.

Employee share options with fixed or determinable terms (ie **not performance based**) and outstanding shares are treated as **options** in the calculation of diluted earnings per share. **Performance based** employee share options are treated as **contingently issuable shares** because their issue is contingent upon satisfying specified conditions in addition to the passage of time.

Question   EPS 2

Brand Co has the following results for the year ended 31 December 20X7.

Profit for year	$1,200,000
Weighted average number of ordinary shares outstanding during year	500,000 shares
Average market value of one ordinary share during year	$20.00
Weighted average number of shares under option during year	100,000 shares
Exercise price for shares under option during year	$15.00

Required

Calculate both basic and diluted earnings per share.

Answer

	Per share	Earnings $	Shares
Profit for year		1,200,000	
Weighted average shares outstanding during 20X7			500,000
Basic earnings per share	2.40		
Number of shares under option			100,000
Number of shares that would have been issued at market value: (100,000 × $15.00/$20.00)			(75,000)*
Diluted earnings per share	2.29	1,200,000	525,000

*The earnings have not been increased as the total number of shares has been increased only by the number of shares (25,000) deemed for the purpose of the computation to have been issued for no consideration.

4.6.2 Interim financial reports

Where an entity issues interim financial reports, EPS is based on the earnings and weighted average number of shares for the 'year-to-date'.

IAS 33 states that dilutive potential ordinary shares must be determined **independently for each period presented**. The number of dilutive potential ordinary shares included in the year-to-date period is not a weighted average of the dilutive potential ordinary shares included in each interim computation.

4.6.3 Contingently issuable shares

Contingently issuable (potential) ordinary shares are treated **as for basic EPS**. If the conditions have not been met, the number of contingently issuable shares included in the computation is based on the number of shares **that would be issuable** if the end of the reporting period was the end of the contingency period. Restatement is not allowed if the conditions are not met when the contingency period expires.

4.6.4 Contracts that may be settled in ordinary shares or cash

Where an entity has issued a contract that may be settled either in ordinary shares or in cash at the **issuer's option**, the entity shall **presume** that the contract will be settled **in ordinary shares**, and the resulting potential ordinary shares should be included in diluted earnings per share if the effect is dilutive.

For contracts that may be settled in ordinary shares or cash at the **holder's option**, the **more dilutive** of cash settlement and share settlement should be used in the calculation.

4.7 Dilutive potential ordinary shares

According to IAS 33, potential ordinary shares should be treated as dilutive when, and only when, their conversion to ordinary shares would **decrease profit per share** from continuing ordinary operations. How is this determined?

The **profit from continuing ordinary activities** is 'the control number', used to establish whether potential ordinary shares are dilutive or antidilutive. The profit from continuing ordinary activities is the profit from ordinary activities **after deducting** dividends on preference shares classified as equity and after excluding items relating to discontinued operations. It also excludes the effects of changes in accounting policies and of corrections of prior period errors.

Potential ordinary shares are **antidilutive** when their conversion to ordinary shares would increase earnings per share from continuing ordinary operations or decrease loss per share from continuing ordinary operations. The effects of antidilutive potential ordinary shares are ignored in calculating diluted EPS.

In considering whether potential ordinary shares are dilutive or antidilutive, each issue or series of potential ordinary shares is **considered separately, not** in aggregate. The sequence in which potential ordinary shares are considered may affect whether or not they are dilutive. Therefore, in order to maximise the dilution of basic EPS, each issue or series of potential ordinary shares is considered in sequence from the most dilutive to the least dilutive. This may sound very confusing, but the following example may help.

4.8 Example: Dilutive potential ordinary shares

Carter plc has the following results for the year ended 31 December 20X7.

Earnings: profit attributable to ordinary equity holders	$10,000,000
Ordinary shares outstanding	2,000,000
Average market value of one ordinary share during the year	$75.00
Tax rate	40%

Potential ordinary shares are as follows.

(a) Options: 100,000 with exercise price of $60

(b) Convertible preference shares: 800,000 shares entitled to a cumulative dividend of $8 per share (each preference share is convertible to two ordinary shares)

(c) 5% Convertible bond: nominal amount $100,000,000, each 1,000 bond is convertible to 20 ordinary shares and there is no amortisation of premium or discount affecting the determination of interest expense

Required

Calculate the diluted EPS.

Solution

Step 1 Calculate the increase in earnings attributable to ordinary equity holders on conversion of the potential ordinary shares.

	Increase in earnings $	Increase in number of ordinary shares	Earnings per Incremental shares $
Options			
Increase in earnings	Nil		
Incremental shares issued for no Consideration 100,000 × $(75 – 60)/$75		20,000	Nil
Convertible preference shares			
Increase in profit $8 × 800,000	6,400,000		
Incremental shares 2 × 800,000		1,600,000	4.00
5% Convertible bonds			
Increase in profit ((100,000,000 × 0.05) × (1 – 40%))	3,000,000		
Incremental shares 100,000 × 20		2,000,000	1.50

Step 2 Now calculate the diluted EPS in order of most dilutive to least dilutive.

	Profit attributable $	Ordinary shares	Per share $	
As reported	10,000,000	2,000,000	5.00	
Options		20,000		
	10,000,000	2,020,000	4.95	Dilutive
5% Convertible bonds	3,000,000	2,000,000		
	13,000,000	4,020,000	3.23	Dilutive
Convertible preference shares	6,400,000	1,600,000		
	19,400,000	5,620,000	3.45	Antidilutive

Note. Since diluted EPS is increased when taking the convertible preference shares into account (from $3.23 to $3.45), the convertible preference shares are antidilutive and are ignored in the calculation of diluted EPS. Therefore, diluted EPS is $3.23.

Potential ordinary shares are **weighted** for the period they were outstanding. Any that were cancelled or allowed to lapse during the reporting period are included in the computation of diluted EPS only for the portion of the period during which they were outstanding. Potential ordinary shares that have been converted into ordinary shares **during the reporting period** are included in the calculation of diluted EPS from the beginning of the period to the date of conversion. From the date of conversion, the resulting ordinary shares are included in basic (and therefore in diluted) EPS.

4.9 Retrospective adjustment

If the number of ordinary or potential ordinary shares outstanding **increases** as a result of a capitalisation, bonus issue or share split, or decreases as a result of a reverse share split, the calculation of basic and diluted EPS for all periods presented should be **adjusted retrospectively**.

If these changes occur **after the year end** but before issue of the financial statements, the calculations per share for the financial statements and those of any prior period should be based on the **new number of shares** (and this should be disclosed).

In addition, basic and diluted EPS of all periods presented should be adjusted for the effects of **errors**, and adjustments resulting from **changes** in **accounting policies**, accounted for retrospectively (as required by IAS 8).

An entity **does not restate diluted EPS** of any prior period for changes in the assumptions used or for the conversion of potential ordinary shares into ordinary shares outstanding.

4.10 Presentation

A entity should present in the statement of profit or loss and other comprehensive income (or the statement of profit or loss where this is presented separately), basic and diluted EPS for:

(a) Profit or loss from continuing operations; and

(b) Profit or loss for the period for each class of ordinary share that has a different right to share in the profit for the period.

The basic and diluted EPS should be presented with **equal prominence** for all periods presented.

Basic and diluted EPS for any **discontinuing operations** must also be presented.

Disclosure must still be made where the EPS figures (basic and/or diluted) are **negative** (ie a loss per share).

4.11 Disclosure

An entity should disclose the following.

(a) The amounts used as the **numerators** in calculating basic and diluted EPS, and a **reconciliation** of those amounts to the profit or loss for the period.

(b) The weighted average number of ordinary shares used as the **denominator** in calculating basic and diluted EPS, and a **reconciliation** of these denominators to each other.

(c) Instruments that could potentially dilute basic EPS but which were **not included** in the calculation because they were **antidilutive** for the period presented.

An entity should also disclose a description of ordinary share transactions or potential ordinary share transactions, other than capitalisation issues and share splits, which occur **after the year end** when they are of such importance that non-disclosure would affect the ability of the users of the financial statements to make proper evaluations and decisions (see IAS 10 *Events After the Reporting Period*). Examples of such transactions include the following:

(a) Issue of shares for cash

(b) Issue of shares when the proceeds are used to repay debt or preferred shares outstanding at the year end

(c) Redemption of ordinary shares outstanding

(d) Conversion or exercise of potential ordinary shares, outstanding at the year end, into ordinary shares

(e) Issue of warrants, options or convertible securities

(f) Achievement of conditions that would result in the issue of contingently issuable shares

EPS amounts are not adjusted for such transactions occurring after the end of the reporting period because such transactions **do not affect the amount of capital used** to produce the profit or loss for the period.

4.12 Alternative EPS figures

An entity may present **alternative EPS figures if it wishes**. However, IAS 33 lays out certain rules where this takes place.

(a) The weighted average number of shares as calculated under IAS 33 **must** be used.

(b) A **reconciliation** must be given between the component of profit used in the alternative EPS (if it is not a line item in the statement of profit or loss and other comprehensive income) and the line item for profit reported in the statement of profit or loss and other comprehensive income.

(c) The entity must indicate the basis on which the **numerator** is determined.

(d) Basic and diluted EPS must be shown with **equal prominence**.

(e) The alternative EPS figure must be shown in the notes (not in the statement of profit or loss and other comprehensive income).

4.13 Significance of earnings per share

Earnings per share (EPS) is one of the most frequently quoted statistics in financial analysis. Because of the widespread use of the price earnings **(P/E) ratio** as a yardstick for investment decisions, it became increasingly important.

It seems that reported and forecast EPS can, through the P/E ratio, have a **significant effect on a company's share price**. Thus, a share price might fall if it looks as if EPS is going to be low. This is not very rational, as EPS can depend on many, often subjective, assumptions used in preparing a historical statement, namely the statement of profit or loss and other comprehensive income. It does not necessarily bear any relation to the value of a company, and of its shares. Nevertheless, the market is sensitive to EPS.

EPS has also served as a means of assessing the **stewardship and management** role performed by company directors and managers. Remuneration packages might be linked to EPS growth, thereby increasing the pressure on management to improve EPS. The danger of this, however, is that management effort may go into distorting results to produce a favourable EPS.

4.14 Section summary

EPS is an important measure for investors.

- **Basic EPS** is straightforward, although it may require adjustments for **changes in capital structure**
- **Diluted EPS** is more complex (and more likely in an exam question). You must be able to deal with:
    - Options
    - Dilutive potential ordinary shares
    - Retrospective adjustment

5 Management commentary

> **FAST FORWARD**
>
> The non-mandatory IFRS Practice Statement 1 *Management Commentary* provides guidance for those entities which publish management commentary. The IASB expects to issue a revised version of the Practice Statement in 2025.

The IASB believes that the **quality of financial reports** can be improved through management commentary and consequently it issued an IFRS Practice Statement 1 *Management Commentary* in 2010

This document provides a broad, non-binding framework for the presentation of narrative reporting to accompany financial statements prepared in accordance with IFRS Accounting Standards.

5.1 Definition of management commentary

The following definition is given in the Practice Statement:

Management commentary. A narrative report that provides a context within which to interpret the financial position, financial performance and cash flows of an entity. It also provides management with an opportunity to explain its objectives and its strategies for achieving those objectives.

5.2 Scope of the Practice Statement

The Practice Statement applies only to management commentary that relates to financial statements prepared in accordance with IFRS. It does not apply to any other information presented in the financial statements.

The Practice Statement does not prescribe:

- Which entities should publish management commentary
- How frequently entities should publish management commentary
- The level of assurance to which management commentary should be subjected

5.3 Identification of management commentary

The Practice Statement requires that:

- The financial statements to which management commentary relates are either be presented with the commentary or indentified within the commentary.
- Management commentary should be distinguished from other information.
- Management should explain the extent to which the Practice Statement has been followed.

5.4 Framework for management commentary

The Practice Statement provides a framework for the presentation of management commentary, which considers its purpose and the principles which underlie it.

5.4.1 Purpose

Management commentary should provide a context for the financial statements, explaining management's views about what has happened, why it has happened and what the implications are for the future. The views should be balanced to include both positive and negative circumstances.

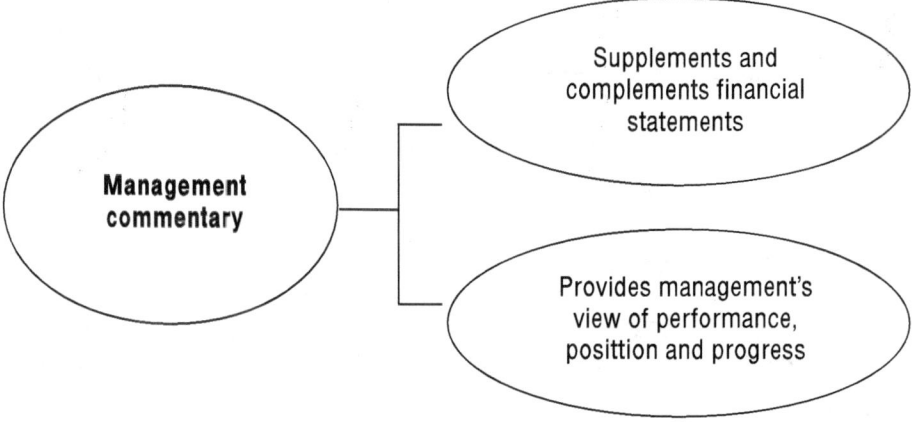

5.4.2 Principles

The following principles underlie a management commentary:

- Commentary should provide a **management's view** of an entity's performance, position and progress (and therefore it should derive from information that is important to management in managing the business).

- It should **supplement and complement information presented in the financial statements**, by providing explanations and background conditions in respect of amounts in the financial statements. It may also include other information that is not presented in the financial statements but which is important to management.

- It should include **forward looking information**. Such information does not predict the future, but instead sets out management's objectives for the entity and its strategies for achieving those objectives. Management should also explain how and why the performance of the entity is short of, meets or exceeds forward-looking disclosures made in the prior period management commentary.

- It should **include information which possesses the qualitative characteristics** described in the *Conceptual Framework*. The information presented should be material to the entity.

- It should provide information to help users to **assess the performance** of the entity **and actions of the management** relative to stated strategies and plans for progress.

5.5 Presentation

The Practice Statement accepts that the form of management commentary will vary from entity to entity, however, requires that in all cases it is clear and straightforward.

It should focus on the most important information and specifically should:

- Be consistent with the related financial statements
- Reflect any segment information contained within the financial statements
- Not duplicate disclosures made in the notes to the accounts without providing additional analysis
- Avoid generic disclosures which do not relate specifically to the entity in question

5.6 Elements of management commentary

The Practice Statement requires that management commentary includes information that is essential to an understanding of:

Element	User needs
Nature of the business	The knowledge of the business in which an entity is engaged and the external environment in which it operates.
Objectives and strategies	To assess the strategies adopted by the entity and the likelihood that those strategies will be successful in meeting management's stated objectives
Resources, risks and relationships	A basis for determining the resources available to the entity as well as obligations to transfer resources to others; the ability of the entity to generate long-term sustainable net inflows of resources; and the risks to which those resource-generating activities are exposed, both in the near term and in the long term
Results and prospects	The ability to understand whether an entity has delivered results in line with expectations and, implicitly, how well management has understood the entity's market, executed its strategy and managed the entity's resources, risks and relationships
Performance measures and indicators	The ability to focus on the critical performance measures and indicators that management uses to assess and manage the entity's performance against stated objectives and strategies

5.7 Management commentary project

In 2021, the IASB issued an exposure draft to revise the Practice Statement. Research had identified that management commentaries are not always providing useful and relevant information to users. The increase in reporting on sustainability issues is also changing the information that users are looking for.

The issues identified were:

- Failure to focus on material matters, by omission or opacity
- Too much generic information and not enough entity-specific information
- Too much focus on short-term matters
- Lack of information about intangible resources and relationship and the ESG (environmental, social and governance) matters affecting the entity
- Difficulty reconciling information in the management commentary to the financial statements or other company reporting
- Difficulty comparing information to prior periods / other entities
- Lack of balance and completeness

The exposure draft was broadly well received and in June 2024 the IASB decided to finalise the project and plans to publish a new Practice Statement in 2025 in collaboration with the ISSB.

Chapter roundup

- Go back to your earlier studies to revise **IAS 1** and **IAS 8**.
- **IFRS 5** requires non-current assets 'held for sale' to be presented separately in the statement of financial position.
- The results of discontinued operations should be presented separately in the statement of profit or loss and other comprehensive income.
- Reportable segments are **operating segments** or aggregations of operating segments that meet specified criteria.
- IFRS 8 adopts a **management approach** to identifying reportable segments.
- IFRS 8 disclosures are of:
    - Operating segment profit or loss
    - Segment assets
    - Segment liabilities
    - Certain income and expense items

    Disclosure under the last two headings is only required if these amounts are regularly reported to the chief operating decision maker.
- Disclosures are also required about the revenues derived from products or services and about the countries in which revenues are earned or assets held, even if that information is not reported to management for decision making.
- **Earnings per share** is a measure of the amount of profits earned by a company for each ordinary share. Earnings are profits after tax and preferred dividends.
- You should know how to calculate **basic EPS** and how to deal with related complications (issue of shares for cash, bonus issue, share splits/reverse share splits, rights issues).
- **Basic EPS** is calculated by dividing the profit or loss for the period attributable to ordinary equity holders by the weighted average number of ordinary shares outstanding during the period.
- **Diluted EPS** is calculated by adjusting the profit attributable to ordinary equity holders and the weighted average number of shares outstanding for the effects of all dilutive potential ordinary shares.
- You must be able to deal with **options** and all other **dilutive potential ordinary shares**.
- The non-mandatory IFRS Practice Statement *Management Commentary* provides guidance for those entities which publish management commentary.

Quick quiz

1. What is the full title of IAS 8? (*Fill in the blanks.*)

    Accounting……………, changes in accounting…………………… and ………………

2. For a non-current asset to be held for sale, a buyer must already have been found. True or false?
3. A non-current asset held for sale should be measured at the lower of …………..… and …………………………………………….(*Fill in the blanks.*)
4. All entities must disclose segment information. True or false?
5. Which numerator is used to rank dilutive shares?
6. Why is the numerator adjusted for convertible bonds when calculating diluted EPS?

Answers to quick quiz

1. Accounting **policies**, changes in accounting **estimates** and **errors**
2. False. There must be an **active programme** to locate a buyer.
3. The lower of **its carrying amount** and **fair value less costs to sell**.
4. False. Only entities whose equity or debt securities are publicly traded need disclose segment information.
5. Profit from continuing operations only
6. Because the issue of shares will affect earnings by the interest saving.

End of chapter question

Bartolo (AIA November 2004)

(a) Bartolo, a limited liability company, had an issued share capital as at 31 October 20X4 consisting of 20,000,000 ordinary shares of 50 cents each and 800,000 6.8% convertible preference shares of $1 each. The company also had in issue $5,500,000 of 12% convertible bonds.

Profit from continuing operations after tax for the year ended 31 October 20X4 was $880,000. The average market price of Bartolo plc's ordinary shares was $0.99 per share during the year ended 31 October 20X4.

Each convertible bond is convertible into 2.5 ordinary shares. Each convertible preference share is convertible into 1.25 ordinary shares. In addition, Bartolo plc's directors have options to purchase 460,000 ordinary shares at $0.85 per share in 20X6.

Income tax is 30%.

Required

Calculate Bartolo plc's diluted earnings per share for the year ended 31 October 20X4 in accordance with IAS 33 *Earnings per Share*. **(12 marks)**

(b) The issued share capital of Contessa, a limited liability company, as at 1 November 20X3 consisted of 25,000,000 ordinary shares of 60 cents each, fully paid. On 1 February 20X4 Contessa made a 1 for 10 rights issue at $1.15 per ordinary share.

Contessa's statement of profit or loss and other comprehensive income for the year ended 31 October 20X4 reports a profit on ordinary activities of $3,100,000. The statement of profit or loss and other comprehensive income for the year ended 31 October 20X3 reported a profit on ordinary activities after taxation of $2,200,000 and an earnings per share figure of 8.80 cents.

The market value of Contessa plc's ordinary shares immediately before the rights issue on 1 February 20X4 was $1.40 per share.

Required

Calculate earnings per share in accordance with IAS 33 *Earnings per Share* for the years ended 31 October 20X4 and 31 October 20X3 for disclosure in the published financial statements for the year ended 31 October 20X4. **(9 marks)**

(c) The draft statement of profit or loss and other comprehensive income of Figaro, a limited liability company, for the financial year ended 31 October 20X4 shows a profit before tax of $2,276,850, an income tax expense of $1,350,000 and a transfer from deferred taxation of $227,600. At 1 November 20X3 Figaro had in issue 4,000,000 equity shares of £1 each. On 1 July 20X4 Figaro split its share capital into 5,000,000 shares of 80 cents each. Figaro's reported earnings per share figure for the year ended 31 October 20X3 was 22.2 cents.

Required

Calculate the two earnings per share figures which will be reported in the statement of profit or loss and other comprehensive income for the year ended 31 October 20X4. **(4 marks)**

(Total 25 marks)

Provisions, contingencies and events after the reporting period

Topic list	Syllabus reference
1 IAS 10 *Events After the Reporting Period*	LO3
2 IAS 37 *Provisions, Contingent Liabilities and Contingent Assets*	LO3

Introduction

You should be very familiar with both of these topics from your earlier studies.

IAS 37 is a topical area with the IASB currently working on proposed amendments to the standard.

1 IAS 10 *Events After the Reporting Period*

FAST FORWARD

IAS 10 should be familiar from your earlier studies, but it still could come up in part of a question.

You have already studied IAS 10 *Events After the Reporting Period* extensively.

Knowledge brought forward from earlier studies

> **IAS 10 *Events After the Reporting Period***
>
> *Definition*
>
> **Events occurring after the reporting period** are those events, both favourable and unfavourable, that occur between the end of the reporting period and the date on which the financial statements are authorised for issue. Two types of events can be identified:
>
> - Those that provide further evidence of conditions that existed at the end of the reporting period, and
> - Those that are indicative of conditions that arose after the reporting period.
>
> *Accounting treatment*
>
> - **Adjust** assets and liabilities where events after the year end provide further evidence of conditions existing at the year end.
> - **Do not adjust**, but instead disclose, important events after the year end that do not affect condition of assets/liabilities at the year end.
> - **Dividends** for period proposed/declared after the year end but before financial statements are approved should not be recognised as a liability at the year end (no obligation exists at that time) but should be disclosed as required by IAS 1 *Presentation of Financial Statements*.
>
> *Disclosure*
>
> - Nature of event
> - Estimate of financial effect (or statement that estimate cannot be made)

Window dressing is the arranging of transactions, the substance of which is primarily to alter the appearance of the statement of financial performance: it is **not** falsification of financial statements. IAS 10 does allow window dressing but **disclosure** should be made of such transactions.

2 IAS 37 *Provisions, Contingent Liabilities and Contingent Assets*

FAST FORWARD

Under IAS 37, a **provision** should be recognised:

- When an entity has a **present obligation**, legal or constructive
- It is **probable** that a **transfer of economic benefits** will be required to settle it
- A reliable estimate can be made of its amount

As we have seen with regard to events after the reporting period, financial statements must include **all the information necessary for an understanding of the company's financial position**. Provisions, contingent liabilities and contingent assets are 'uncertainties' that must be accounted for consistently if are to achieve this understanding.

2.1 Objective

IAS 37 *Provisions, Contingent Liabilities and Contingent Assets* aims to ensure that appropriate **recognition criteria** and **measurement bases** are applied to provisions, contingent liabilities and contingent assets and that **sufficient information** is disclosed in the **notes** to the financial statements to enable users to understand their nature, timing and amount..

2.1.1 Provisions

Important

> The key aim of IAS 37 is to ensure that provisions are made only where there are valid grounds for them.

IAS 37 views a provision as a liability.

Key terms

> A **provision** is a **liability** of uncertain timing or amount.
>
> A **liability** is an obligation of an entity to transfer economic benefits as a result of past transactions or events. (IAS 37)

The IAS distinguishes provisions from other liabilities such as trade payables and accruals. This is on the basis that for a provision there is **uncertainty** about the timing or amount of the future expenditure. While uncertainty is clearly present in the case of certain accruals, the uncertainty is generally much less than for provisions.

IAS 37 requires recognition of a liability only if it is probable that the obligation will result in an outflow of resources from the entity. This reflects the recognition criteria in the previous (2010) version of the *Conceptual Framework*, which as discussed in Chapter 1, were applied inconsistently across IFRS Standards. The 'probable' criterion is not included in the definition of a liability or recognition criteria in the revised 2018 version of the *Conceptual Framework*. As the *Conceptual Framework* does not override the requirements of individual standards, the recognition requirements of IAS 37 will remain – for the moment at least. The IASB has acknowledged that there are issues with IAS 37. It is currently developing proposals improvements to IAS 37. The proposals include:

- aligning the definition of a liability and requirements for identifying liabilities with the Conceptual Framework and
- clarifying two aspects of the measurement requirements.

2.2 Recognition

IAS 37 states that a provision should be **recognised** as a liability in the financial statements when:

| An entity has a **present obligation** (legal or constructive) as a result of a past event | It is probable that a **transfer of economic benefits** will be required to settle the obligation | A **reliable estimate** can be made of the obligation |

(IAS 37, para. 14)

2.3 Meaning of obligation

It is fairly clear what a legal obligation is. However, you may not know what a **constructive obligation** is.

Key term

> IAS 37 defines a **constructive obligation** as:
>
> 'An obligation that derives from an entity's actions where:
>
> - By an established pattern of past practice, published policies or a sufficiently specific current statement the entity has indicated to other parties that it will accept certain responsibilities, and

Question — Recognise a provision

In which of the following circumstances might a provision be recognised?

(a) On 13 December 20X9 the board of an entity decided to close down a division. The accounting date of the company is 31 December. Before 31 December 20X9 the decision was not communicated to any of those affected and no other steps were taken to implement the decision.

(b) The board agreed a detailed closure plan on 20 December 20X9 and details were given to customers and employees.

(c) A company is obliged to incur clean up costs for environmental damage that has already been caused.

(d) A company intends to carry out future expenditure to operate in a particular way in the future.

Answer

(a) No provision would be recognised; the decision has not been communicated so there is no obligation.

(b) A provision would be made in the 20X9 financial statements; the decision has been communicated so there is a constructive obligation.

(c) A provision for such costs is appropriate.

(d) No present obligation exists and under IAS 37 no provision would be appropriate. This is because the entity could avoid the future expenditure by its future actions, maybe by changing its method of operation.

2.3.1 Probable transfer of economic benefits

For the purpose of the IAS, a transfer of economic benefits is regarded as **'probable'** if the event is **more likely than not** to occur. This appears to indicate a probability of more than 50%. However, the standard makes it clear that where there is a number of similar obligations the probability should be based on considering the population as a whole, rather than one single item.

2.4 Example: Transfer of economic benefits

If a company has entered into a warranty obligation, then the probability of transfer of economic benefits may well be extremely small in respect of one specific item. However, when considering the population as a whole the probability of some transfer of economic benefits is quite likely to be much higher. If there is a **greater than 50% probability** of some transfer of economic benefits then a **provision** should be made for the **expected amount**.

2.4.1 Measurement of provisions

Important

The amount recognised as a provision should be the best estimate of the expenditure required to settle the present obligation at the end of the reporting period.

The estimates will be determined by the **judgement** of the entity's management supplemented by the experience of similar transactions.

Allowance is made for **uncertainty**.

(a) Where the provision being measured involves a large population of items ⇒ Use expected values.

(b) Where a single obligation is being measured ⇒ The individual most likely outcome may be the best estimate

Question   Warranty

Parker Co sells goods with a standard warranty under which, at no extra cost to the customers, the cost of repairs of any manufacturing defect that becomes apparent within the first six months of purchase will be covered. The company's past experience and future expectations indicate the following pattern of likely repairs.

% of goods sold	Defects	Cost of repairs $m
75	None	–
20	Minor	1.0
5	Major	4.0

Required:

What is the expected cost of repairs?

Answer

The cost is found using 'expected values' (75% × $nil) + (20% × $1.0m) + (5% × $4.0m) = $400,000.

Where the effect of the **time value of money** is material, the amount of a provision should be the **present value** of the expenditure required to settle the obligation. An appropriate **discount** rate should be used.

The discount rate should be a **pre-tax rate** that reflects current market assessments of the time value of money and the risks specific to the liability. **The discount rate(s) should not reflect risks for which future cash flow estimates have been adjusted.**

2.4.2 Future events

Future events which are reasonably expected to occur (eg new legislation, changes in technology) may affect the amount required to settle the entity's obligation and should be taken into account, but only if there is objective evidence that the future events will occur.

2.4.3 Expected disposal of assets

Gains from the expected disposal of assets should not be taken into account in measuring a provision.

2.4.4 Reimbursements

Some or all of the expenditure needed to settle a provision may be expected to be recovered from a third party. If so, the **reimbursement should be recognised only when it is virtually certain that reimbursement will be received if the entity settles the obligation.**

- The reimbursement should be treated as a separate asset, and the amount recognised should not be greater than the provision itself.
- The provision and the amount recognised for reimbursement may be netted off in profit or loss.

2.4.5 Changes in provisions

Provisions should be reviewed at each year-end and adjusted to reflect the current best estimate. If it is no longer probable that a transfer of economic benefits will be required to settle the obligation, the provision should be reversed.

2.4.6 Use of provisions

A provision should be used only for expenditures for which the provision was originally recognised. Setting expenditures against a provision that was originally recognised for another purpose would conceal the impact of two different events and would not be in keeping with the fundamental characteristic of faithful representation.

2.4.7 Future operating losses

Provisions should not be recognised for future operating losses. They do not meet the definition of a liability and the general recognition criteria set out in the standard.

2.4.8 Onerous contacts

If an entity has a contract that is onerous, the present obligation under the contract **should be recognised and measured** as a provision.

Key term

> An **onerous contract** is a contract in which the unavoidable costs of meeting the obligations under the contract exceed the economic benefits expected to be received under it.

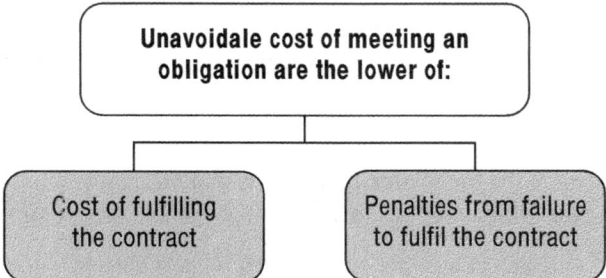

An example may be a fixed price supply contract related to a particular product that, due to inflation, now costs more to manufacture than the fixed sale price agreed in the contract. If an entity has a contract that is onerous, the present obligation under the contract must be recognised and measured as a provision (IAS 37: para. 66).

A lease agreement that becomes onerous is only within the scope of IAS 37, and therefore results in the creation of a provision, if simplified accounting is applied, so that no lease liability has been recognised. This is only the case where a lease is short-term or for an asset with a low value.

2.5 Examples of possible provisions

It is easier to see what IAS 37 is driving at if you look at examples of those items which are possible provisions under this standard. Some of these we have already touched on.

Issue	Discussion
Warranties	These are argued to be genuine provisions as on past experience it is probable, ie more likely than not, that some claims will emerge. The provision must be estimated, however, on the basis of the class as a whole and not on individual claims. There is a clear legal obligation in this case.
Major repairs	IAS 37 argues that the mere intention to carry out repairs is not an obligation. The entity can always sell the asset in the meantime. The only solution is to treat major assets such as aircraft, ships, furnaces etc as a series of smaller assets where each part is depreciated over shorter lives. Thus any major overhaul is a replacement and therefore capital rather than revenue expenditure.
Self insurance	Historically, companies sometimes created a provision for self insurance based on the expected cost of making good fire damage etc instead of paying premiums to an insurance company. Under IAS 37 such a provision is not justifiable as the entity has no obligation until a fire or accident occurs. No obligation exists until that time.

Issue	Discussion
Environmental contamination	If the company has an environment policy such that other parties would expect the company to clean up any contamination or if the company has broken current environmental legislation then a provision for environmental damage must be made.
Decommissioning or abandonment costs.	When an oil company initially purchases an oilfield, it may be put under a legal obligation to decommission the site at the end of its life. Prior to IAS 37 most oil companies built up the provision gradually over the life of the field so that no one year would be unduly burdened with the cost.
	Under IAS 37, however, a legal obligation exists as a result of the initial expenditure to prepare the field for oil extraction and therefore a liability exists immediately. This would appear to result in a large charge to profit and loss in the first year of operation of the field. However, IAS 16 *Property, Plant and Equipment* takes the view that the cost of purchasing the field in the first place is not only the cost of the field itself but also the costs of putting it right again. Thus all the costs of abandonment may be capitalised.
	Sustainability alert: As companies transition towards Net Zero and aim to reduce their emissions it may result in an increase in decommissioned or abandoned assets, or the speeding up of the decommissioning.
Restructuring	This is considered in detail below

2.5.1 Provisions for restructuring

One of the main purposes of IAS 37 was to target abuses of provisions for restructuring. Accordingly, IAS 37 lays down **strict criteria** to determine when such a provision can be made.

Key term

> IAS 37 defines a **restructuring** as:
>
> A programme that is planned and is controlled by management and materially changes either:
>
> - The scope of a business undertaken by an entity; or
> - The manner in which that business is conducted.
>
> (IAS 37, para 10)

The IAS gives the following **examples** of events that may fall under the definition of restructuring.

- The **sale or termination** of a line of business
- The **closure of business locations** in a country or region or the **relocation** of business activities from one country region to another
- **Changes in management structure**, for example, the elimination of a layer of management
- **Fundamental reorganisations** that have a material effect on the **nature and focus** of the entity's operations

(IAS 37, para 70)

The question is whether or not an entity has an obligation – legal or constructive – at the year-end.

- An entity must have a **detailed formal plan** for the restructuring.
- It must have **raised a valid expectation** in those affected that it will carry out the restructuring by starting to implement that plan or announcing its main features to those affected by it.

Important

> **A mere management decision is not normally sufficient**. Management decisions may sometimes trigger off recognition, but only if earlier events such as negotiations with employee representatives and other interested parties have been concluded subject only to management approval.

Where the restructuring involves the **sale of an operation** then IAS 37 states that no obligation arises until the entity has entered into a **binding sale agreement**. This is because until this has occurred the entity will be able to change its mind and withdraw from the sale even if its intentions have been announced publicly.

2.5.2 Costs to be included within a restructuring provision

The IAS states that a restructuring provision should include only the **direct expenditures** arising from the restructuring.

- **Necessarily entailed** by the restructuring
- Not associated with the **ongoing activities** of the entity

The following costs should specifically **not** be included within a restructuring provision.

- **Retraining** or relocating continuing staff
- **Marketing**
- **Investment in new systems** and distribution networks

Question — Restructuring

Trailer, a public limited company, operates in the manufacturing sector. During the year ended 31 May 20X5, Trailer announced two major restructuring plans. The first plan is to reduce its capacity by the closure of some of its smaller factories, which have already been identified. This will lead to the redundancy of 500 employees, who have all individually been selected and communicated with. The costs of this plan are $9 million in redundancy costs, $4 million in retraining costs and $5 million in lease termination costs.

The second plan is to re-organise the finance and information technology department over a one-year period but it does not commence for two years. The plan results in 20% of finance staff losing their jobs during the restructuring. The costs of this plan are $10 million in redundancy costs, $6 million in retraining costs and $7 million in equipment lease termination costs.

Required:

Discuss the treatment of each of the above restructuring plans in the financial statements of Trailer for the year ended 31 May 20X5.

Answer

Plan 1:

A provision for restructuring should be recognised in respect of the closure of the factories in accordance with IAS 37 Provisions, Contingent Liabilities and Contingent Assets. The plan has been communicated to the relevant employees (those who will be made redundant) and factories have already been identified. A provision should only be recognised for directly attributable costs that will not benefit ongoing activities of the entity. Thus, a provision should be recognised for the redundancy costs and the lease termination costs, but none for the retraining costs:

	$m
Redundancy costs	9
Retraining	-
Lease termination costs	5
Liability	14

DEBIT	Profit or loss (retained earnings)	$14m	
CREDIT		Current liabilities	$14m

Plan 2:

No provision should be recognised for the reorganisation of the finance and IT department. Since the reorganisation is not due to start for two years, the plan may change, and so a valid expectation that management is committed to the plan has not been raised. As regards any provision for redundancy, individuals have not been identified and communicated with, and so no provision should be made at 31 May 20X3 for redundancy costs.

2.5.3 Disclosure

Disclosures for provisions fall into two parts.

- Disclosure of details of the **change in carrying value** of a provision from the beginning to the end of the year
- Disclosure of the **background** to the making of the provision and the uncertainties affecting its outcome

2.6 Contingent liabilities

FAST FORWARD

An entity **should not recognise a contingent asset or liability**, but they **should be disclosed**.

Now that you understand provisions, it will be easier to understand contingent assets and liabilities.

Key term

IAS 37 defines a **contingent liability** as:

- A possible obligation that arises from past events and whose existence will be confirmed only by the occurrence or non-occurrence of one or more uncertain future events not wholly within the entity's control; or
- A present obligation that arises from past events but is not recognised because:
    - It is not probable that a transfer of economic benefits will be required to settle the obligation; or
    - The amount of the obligation cannot be measured with sufficient reliability.

IAS 37, para. 10

As a rule of thumb, probable means more than 50% likely. **If an obligation is probable, it is not a contingent liability** – instead, a **provision is needed**.

2.6.1 Treatment of contingent liabilities

Contingent liabilities **should not be recognised in financial statements** but they **should be disclosed**, unless the possibility of an outflow of resources is remote. The required disclosures are:

- A brief description of the nature of the contingent liability
- An estimate of its financial effect
- An indication of the uncertainties that exist in relation to the amount or timing of any outflow
- The possibility of any reimbursement

2.7 Contingent assets

Key term

IAS 37 defines a **contingent asset** as:

A possible asset that arises from past events and whose existence will be confirmed by the occurrence of one or more uncertain future events not wholly within the entity's control.

A contingent asset must not be recognised. Only when the realisation of the related economic benefits is **virtually certain** should recognition take place. At that point, **the asset is no longer a contingent asset!**

PART C ACCOUNTING AND REPORTING TECHNIQUES

2.7.1 Disclosure: Contingent assets

Contingent assets must only be disclosed in the notes if they are material and if an inflow of economic benefits is **probable**. In that case a brief description of the contingent asset should be provided along with an estimate of its likely financial effect.

2.7.2 'Let out'

IAS 37 permits reporting entities to avoid disclosure requirements relating to provisions, contingent liabilities and contingent assets if they would be expected to **seriously prejudice** the position of the entity in dispute with other parties. However, this 'let out' should only be employed in **extremely rare** cases. Details of the general nature of the provision/contingencies must still be provided, together with an explanation of why it has not been disclosed.

You must practise the questions below to get the hang of IAS 37. But first, study the flow chart, taken from IAS 37, which is a good summary of its requirements.

Exam focus point

If you learn this flowchart you should be able to deal with most tasks you are likely to meet in an exam.

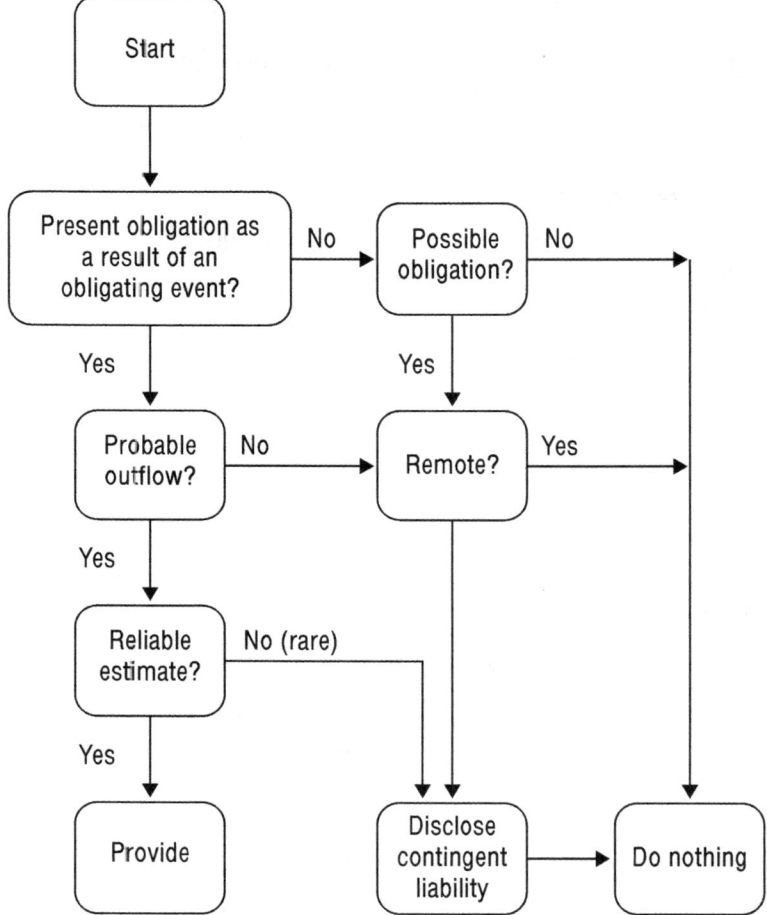

Question — Recognise or not 1?

Warren Co gives warranties at the time of sale to purchasers of its products. Under the terms of the warranty the manufacturer undertakes to make good, by repair or replacement, manufacturing defects that become apparent within a period of three years from the date of the sale. Should a provision be recognised?

Answer

Warren Co **cannot avoid** the cost of repairing or replacing all items of product that manifest manufacturing defects in respect of which warranties are given before the year end, and a provision for the cost of this should therefore be made.

Warren Co is obliged to repair or replace items that fail within the entire warranty period. Therefore, in respect of **this year's sales**, the obligation provided for at the year end should be the cost of making good items for which defects have been notified but not yet processed, **plus** an estimate of costs in respect of the other items sold for which there is sufficient evidence that manufacturing defects **will** manifest themselves during their remaining periods of warranty cover.

Question — Recognise or not 2?

After a wedding in 20X8 ten people fell ill, possibly as a result of food poisoning from products sold by Callow Co. Legal proceedings are started seeking damages from Callow but it disputes liability. Up to the date of approval of the financial statements for the year to 31 December 20X8, Callow's lawyers advise that it is probable that it will not be found liable. However, when Callow prepares the financial statements for the year to 31 December 20X9 its lawyers advise that, owing to developments in the case, it is probable that it will be found liable.

What is the required accounting treatment:

(a) At 31 December 20X8?
(b) At 31 December 20X9?

Answer

(a) *At 31 December 20X8*

On the basis of the evidence available when the financial statements were approved, there is no obligation as a result of past events. No provision is recognised. The matter is disclosed as a contingent liability unless the probability of any transfer of resources is regarded as remote.

(b) *At 31 December 20X9*

On the basis of the evidence available, there is a present obligation. A transfer of economic benefits in settlement is probable.

A provision is recognised for the best estimate of the amount needed to settle the present obligation.

2.8 Section summary

- The objective of IAS 37 is to ensure that appropriate recognition criteria and measurement bases are applied to provisions and contingencies and that sufficient information is disclosed.
- The IAS seeks to ensure that provisions are **only recognised** when a **measurable obligation** exists. It includes detailed rules that can be used to ascertain when an obligation exists and how to measure the obligation.
- The standard attempts to **eliminate** the **'profit smoothing'** which has gone on before it was issued.

Chapter roundup

- **IAS 10** should be familiar from your earlier studies, but it still could come up in part of a question.
- Under IAS 37, a **provision** should be recognised:
    - When an entity has a **present obligation**, legal or constructive
    - It is **probable** that a **transfer of economic benefits** will be required to settle it
    - A reliable estimate can be made of its amount
- An entity **should not recognise a contingent asset or liability**, but they **should be disclosed**.

Quick quiz

1   According to IAS 37 when, and only when, can a provision be recognised?

2   Provisions are always recognised as an expense in profit or loss. True or false?

3   A provision can be made for future operating losses. True or false?

4   When should a contingent liability be recognised under IAS 37?

5   A company intends to claim $10,000 from its insurance company in respect of inventory that was water-damaged. It expects to be awarded the full amount but has not yet submitted a claim to its insurance company received confirmation from the insurance company. Should a contingent asset be recognised for the $10,000 it expects to be awarded?

Answers to quick quiz

1. Three conditions are all met.
   - Present obligation
   - Probable transfer of economic benefits
   - Reliable estimate of value

2. False. Provisions may also be recognised as part of the cost of an asset, the most common being provisions for decommissioning.

3. False. Future operating losses do not meet the definition of a liability and cannot be provided for

4. Contingent liabilities are never recognised in the financial statements. However, if material, they should be disclosed in a note to the financial statements.

5. This would not meet the definition of a contingent asset as it is not yet probable that the amount the company intends to claim from the insurance company will be received. When confirmation is received from the insurance company, the amount will become a receivable.

End of chapter question

Tine Foods (AIA May 2007)

(a) Explain how IAS 37 defines a provision and identify what distinguishes a provision from other liabilities. **(2 marks)**

(b) Summarise the rules in IAS 37 for recognising a provision. **(3 marks)**

(c) Tine Foods, a limited liability company, has been sued over its use of its 'Geordie' brand name. The case has been held and the claim was dismissed in January 20X7. However, the appellant has appealed – but the appeal has yet to be heard. In February 20X7 Tine Foods sold the brand name to a large multinational company. Tine Foods has granted a warranty to the multinational company with regard to the validity of the trademark and a contractual liability would be triggered in the event that the 'Geordie' brand name was to be cancelled.

Advise the directors of Tine Foods how they should report this item in the financial statements for its financial year ended 31 March 20X7? **(3 marks)**

(d) During the year ended 31 March 20X6 Tanfield Trucks purchased an interest in an associated company. In its financial statements for the year ended 31 March 20X6 Tanfield Trucks disclosed that following the acquisition of the associated company it would reorganise its distribution functions. It set up a provision for $500,000 on its statement of financial position, charging the amount as exceptional selling and distribution expenses for the year ended 31 March 20X6. The reorganisation was completed during the year ended 31 March 20X7. The costs paid for the reorganisation amounted to $460,000 with a further $34,000 incurred but not yet paid as at 31 March 20X7.

Advise the directors of Tanfield Trucks how they should report this item in the financial statements for the year ended 31 March 20X7? **(3 marks)**

(Total 11 marks)

Related parties and share-based payment

20

Topic list	Syllabus reference
1 IAS 24 *Related Party Disclosures*	LO4
2 IFRS 2 *Share-Based Payment*	LO3 and LO4

Introduction

Section 1 deals with related party disclosures, which is important for the users understanding of the impact of related parties and related party transactions on an entity's business decisions and financial statements.

Section 2 deals with IFRS 2 on share-based payment, focusing on the different types of share based payment transaction, when to recognise the transactions and how to measure them.

1 IAS 24 *Related Party Disclosures*

> **IAS 24** is a disclosure standard. It is concerned with improving the quality of information provided by financial statements.

Related party relationships and transactions are a normal part of business. The users of financial statements, however, assume that transactions have been undertaken on an **arm's length basis**, ie on terms such as could have obtained in a transaction with an external party, in which each side bargained knowledgeably and freely, unaffected by any relationship between them.

These assumptions may not be justified when **related party relationships** exist, because the requisite conditions for competitive, free market dealings may not be present.

Related party relationships can lead an entity to undertake transactions that it would not normally enter into and transactions can have an effect on the profit or loss and financial position of an entity.

Consider the following effect of a related party relationship:

1.1 Example: The effect of related party relationships

Rigby manufactures smart watches and buys a specialist microchip from unrelated company Penny at a cost of $2.20 per unit and with 60 day credit terms. The microchip is also made by Jude, a member of the BTL Group, but it would cost Rigby $2.60 per unit to purchase it from Jude and payment would need to be made after 30 days. During the reporting period, the BTL Group purchases 100% of the equity of Rigby and obtains control over it, making Rigby a subsidiary. The members of the BTL Group are related parties of Rigby from that date. The BTL Group instructs Rigby to buy the microchip only from Jude. As a result, Rigby terminates its trading relationship with Penny.

Required

Consider the impact of the related party transaction from the perspective of the stakeholders of Rigby.

Solution

As a result of the related party relationship, Rigby pays an additional $0.40 per unit for the microchip and will therefore suffer reduced gross and net profits. It will have to pay for the purchases after 30 days rather than its current 60 days which will negatively impact its working capital cycle.

The above is a simple example which highlights why it is important that related party relationships and transactions are suitably disclosed in the financial statements in order to aid the users understanding of the entity. The disclosures support the fundamental qualitative characteristic of faithful representation as it helps to ensure the financial statements report the substance of the phenomena it purports to represent.

1.2 Objective of IAS 24

IAS 24 tackles the related parties issue by ensuring that financial statements contain the **disclosures necessary** to draw attention to the possibility that the reported financial position and results may have been affected by the existence of related parties and by material transactions with them.

1.3 Scope

The standard requires disclosure of related party transactions and outstanding balances in the **separate financial statements** of a parent, venturer or investor presented in accordance with IAS 27 *Separate Financial Statements* as well as in consolidated financial statements.

An entity's separate financial statements disclose related party transactions and outstanding balances with other entities in a group. **Intragroup** transactions and balances are **eliminated** in the preparation of consolidated financial statements.

1.4 Definitions

The following important definitions are given by the standard. Note that the definitions of **control** and **significant influence** are the same as those given in IFRS 10 *Consolidated Financial Statements*, IFRS 11 *Joint Arrangements* and IAS 28 *Investments in Associates and Joint Ventures*.

> **Key terms**
>
> **Related party.** A related party is a person or entity that is related to the entity that is preparing its financial statements ('the reporting entity')
>
> **(a) A person or a close member of that person's family is related to a reporting entity if that person:**
>
>   (i)   Has control or joint control over the reporting entity;
>
>   (ii)   Has significant influence over the reporting entity; or
>
>   (iii) Is a member of the key management personnel of the reporting entity or of a parent of the reporting entity.
>
> **(b) An entity is related to a reporting entity if any of the following conditions applies:**
>
>   (i)   The entity and the reporting entity are members of the same group (which means that each parent, subsidiary and fellow subsidiary is related to the others).
>
>   (ii)   One entity is an associate or joint venture of the other entity (or an associate or joint venture of a member of a group of which the other entity is a member).
>
>   (iii) Both entities are joint ventures of the same third party.
>
>   (iv) One entity is a joint venture of a third entity and the other entity is an associate of the third entity.
>
>   (v)   The entity is a post-employment benefit plan for the benefit of employees of either the reporting entity or an entity related to the reporting entity. If the reporting entity is itself such a plan, the sponsoring employers are also related to the reporting entity.
>
>   (vi) The entity is controlled or jointly controlled by a person identified in (a).
>
>   (vii) A person identified in (a) (i) has significant influence over the entity or is a member of the key management personnel of the entity (or of a parent of the entity).
>
> **Related party transaction.** A transfer of resources, services or obligations between a reporting entity and a related party, regardless of whether a price is charged.
>
> The terms **control, joint control and significant influence** are defined in IFRS 10, IFRS 11 and IAS 28 and are used in this standard with the meanings specified in those IFRSs.
>
> **Key management personnel** are those persons having authority and responsibility for planning, directing and controlling the activities of the entity, directly or indirectly, including any director (whether executive or otherwise) of that entity.
>
> **Close members of the family of an individual** are those family members who may be expected to influence, or be influenced by, that person in their dealings with the entity, and include:
>
> (a)   That person's children and spouse or domestic partner;
> (b)   Children of that person's spouse or domestic partner; and
> (c)   Dependants of that person or that person's spouse or domestic partner.
>
>   (IAS 24, para 9)

The most important point to remember here is that, when considering each possible related party relationship, attention must be paid to the **substance of the relationship, not merely the legal form**.

IAS 24 lists the following which are **not related parties**.

(a) **Two entities simply because they have a director or other member of key management personnel in common** or because a member of key management personnel of one entity has significant influence over the other entity.

(b) **Two venturers, simply because they share joint control over a joint venture.**

(c) (i) Providers of finance
 (ii) Trade unions
 (iii) Public utilities
 (iv) Government departments and agencies of a government that does not control, jointly control or significantly influence the reporting entity simply by virtue of their normal dealings with an entity.

(d) **A customer, supplier, franchisor, distributor, or general agent** with whom an entity transacts a significant volume of business, simply by virtue of the resulting economic dependence.

(IAS 24, para 11)

1.5 Disclosure

Relationships between **parents and subsidiaries** must be **disclosed irrespective** of **whether** any **transactions** have **taken place between** the related parties. An entity must disclose the **name** of its **parent** and, if different, the **ultimate controlling party**. This will enable a reader of the financial statements to be able to form a view about the effects of a related party relationship on the reporting entity. (IAS 24, para 13)

An entity should disclose **key management personnel compensation** in **total** and for **each** of the following **categories**:

(a) **Short-term employee benefits** (eg wages, salaries, social security contributions, paid annual leave and paid sick-leave, profit sharing and bonuses and non-monetary);

(b) **Post-employment benefits** (eg pensions, other retirement benefits, life insurance and medical care);

(c) **Other long-term benefits** (eg long-service leave, profit sharing, bonuses and deferred compensation);

(d) **Termination benefits; and**

(e) **Share based payments.**

Compensation includes amounts paid on behalf of a parent of the entity in respect of the entity. (IAS 24, para 17 and 17A)

Where **transactions have taken place** between related parties, the entity should disclose the **nature** of the related party relationships, as well as information about the **transactions and outstanding balances including commitments** necessary for an understanding of the potential effect of the relationship on the financial statements. As a minimum, disclosures must include:

(a) The **amount of the transactions**

(b) The **amount of outstanding balances including commitments**, and

 (i) Their terms and conditions, including whether they are secured, and the nature of the consideration to be provided in settlement

 (ii) Details of any guarantees given or received

(c) Provisions for **doubtful debts** related to the amount of outstanding balances

(d) The **expense** recognised during the period in respect of **bad or doubtful debts** due from related parties.

(IAS 24, para 18)

The disclosures required by IAS 24, para 18 shall be made separately for **each** of the following categories:

(a) The parent
(b) Entities with joint control or significant influence over the entity
(c) Subsidiaries
(d) Associates
(e) Joint ventures in which the entity is a joint venturer
(f) Key management personnel of the entity or its parent
(g) Other related parties

Examples of related party transactions include:

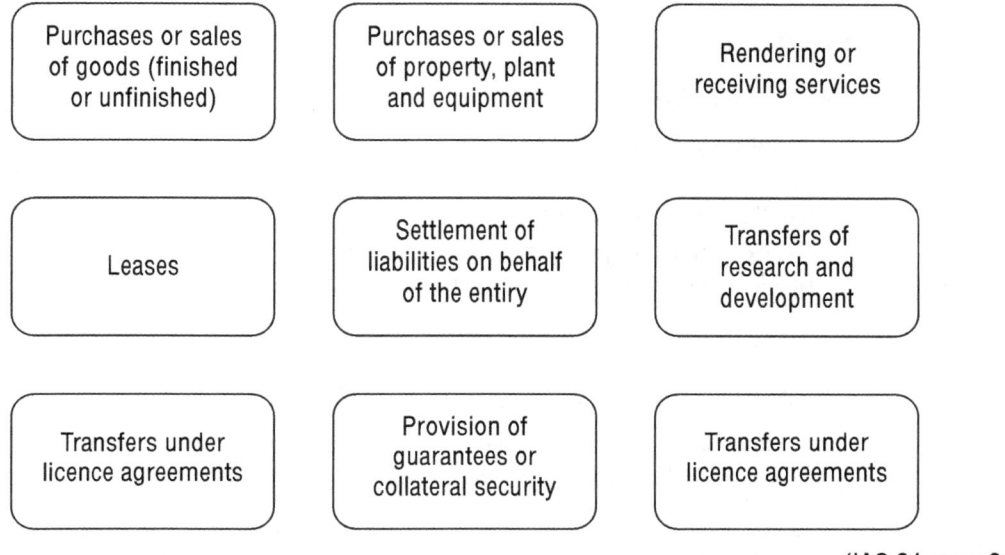

(IAS 24, para 21)

Items of a similar nature may be **disclosed in aggregate unless** separate disclosure is necessary for an understanding of the effect on the financial statements.

Disclosures that related party transactions were made on terms equivalent to those that prevail in arm's length transactions should only be made if such disclosures can be substantiated.

The IASB has recently made it clear that disclosure is not required if the information provided by that disclosure is not material. That is, it will not influence the decisions made by primary users on the basis of information provided in the financial statements.

1.5.1 Government-related entities

An entity is exempt from making disclosures in relation to the nature of relationships, transactions and outstanding balances with the following:

(a) A government that has control, joint control or significant influence over the reporting entity; and

(b) Another entity that is a related party because the same government has control, joint control or significant influence over both the reporting entity and the other entity.

Where an entity takes advantage of this exemption, it must disclose:

(a) The name of the government and the nature of its relationship with the reporting entity (control, joint control or significant influence)

(b) The following information in sufficient detail to enable an understanding of the effect of related party transactions on the entity's financial statements:

(i) The nature and amount of each individually significant transaction; and

(ii) For other transactions that are collectively but not individually significant, a qualitative or quantitative indication of their extent.

In order to determine whether a transaction is **individually significant**, the entity should consider whether it is:

(a) Significant in terms of size
(b) Carried out on non-market terms
(c) Outside normal day to day business operations such as the purchase and sale of businesses
(d) Disclosed to regulatory or supervisory authorities
(e) Reported to senior management
(f) Subject to shareholder approval

1.6 Section summary

IAS 24 is concerned with **disclosure**. You should learn the following.

- **Definitions**: these are very important
- Relationships covered
- Relationships that **are not** related parties
- The exemption for government-related entities
- **Disclosures**: again, very important, representing the whole purpose of the standard

Question — Related parties

The Rain Group has a number of subsidiaries, associates and joint ventures in its group structure. During the financial year to 31 October 20X9 the following events occurred:

(a) Drizzle is a major customer of Rain. During the year, Rain agreed to provide a loan of $1m to Drizzle at market interest rates in order to guarantee continuity of supply. Rain often provides loan finance to its customers and suppliers.

(b) On 1 July 20X9, Rain sold its wholly owned subsidiary, Shower. One of the directors of Rain continues to also be a director of Shower. Prior to the disposal, Rain supplied Shower with second-hand office equipment and after the disposal, Shower leased its factory from Rain. The transactions were all contracted for at market rates.

(c) Rain pays $6m per annum in contributions to its post-employment benefit plan.

Required

Discuss whether the above events would require disclosure in the financial statements of the Rain Group, a public limited company, under IAS 24 Related Party Disclosures.

Answer

(a) IAS 24 does not require disclosure of major customers, even where there is economic dependence between the companies. It also does not consider providers of finance in the ordinary course of business to be related parties. As Rain regularly provides loans to its customers and suppliers, the loan is considered to be in the ordinary course of business, supported by the fact that the transaction is at market interest rates. No disclosure is therefore needed in respect of the transaction between Rain and Drizzle.

(b) IAS 24 does not require intragroup transactions and balances eliminated on consolidation to be disclosed. IAS 24 does not deal with the situation where an undertaking becomes, or ceases to be, a subsidiary during the year. Despite the disposal, Rain and Shower continue to be related parties as they have key management personnel in common. Best practice indicates that related party transactions should be disclosed for the period when Shower was not part of the group and therefore the rental agreement should be disclosed.

(c) Post-employment benefit schemes of the reporting entity are included in the IAS 24 definition of related parties. The contributions paid must be disclosed.

2 IFRS 2 *Share-based Payment*

FAST FORWARD

Share-based payment transactions should be recognised in the financial statements. You need to understand and be able to advise on:

- Recognition
- Measurement
- Disclosure

of both equity-settled and cash-settled transactions.

2.1 Background

Transactions whereby entities purchase goods or services from other parties, such as suppliers and employees, by **issuing shares or share options** to those other parties are **increasingly common**. Share schemes are a common feature of director and executive remuneration and in some countries the authorities may offer tax incentives to encourage more companies to offer shares to employees. Companies whose shares or share options are regarded as a valuable 'currency' commonly use share-based payment to obtain employee and professional services.

The increasing use of share-based payment has raised questions about the accounting treatment of such transactions in company financial statements.

2.1.1 Arguments against recognition of share-based payment in the financial statements

There are a number of arguments against recognition. The IASB has considered and rejected the arguments below.

(a) **No cost therefore no charge**

There is no cost to the entity because the granting of shares or options does not require the entity to sacrifice cash or other assets. Therefore a charge should not be recognised.

This argument is unsound because it ignores the fact that a transaction has occurred. The employees have provided valuable services to the entity in return for valuable shares or options.

(b) **Earnings per share is hit twice**

It is argued that the charge to profit or loss for the employee services consumed reduces the entity's earnings, while at the same time there is an increase in the number of shares issued.

However, the dual impact on earnings per share simply reflects the two economic events that have occurred.

(i) The entity has issued shares or options, thus increasing the denominator of the earnings per share calculation.

(ii) It has also consumed the resources it received for those shares or options, thus reducing the numerator.

(c) **Adverse economic consequences**

It could be argued that entities might be discouraged from introducing or continuing employee share plans if they were required to recognise them on the financial statements. However, if this happened, it might be because the requirement for entities to account properly for employee share plans had revealed the economic consequences of such plans.

A situation where entities are able to obtain and consume resources by issuing valuable shares or options without having to account for such transactions could be perceived as a **distortion**.

2.2 Objective and scope

IFRS 2 requires an entity to **reflect the effects of share-based payment transactions** in its profit or loss and financial position.

IFRS 2 applies to all share-based payment transactions. There are three types.

Equity-settled share-based payment	The entity receives goods or services as consideration for **equity instruments** of the entity (including shares or share options).
Cash-settled share-based payment	The entity acquires goods or services by **incurring liabilities** to the supplier of those goods or services for amounts that are based on the price (or value) of the entity's shares or other equity instruments.
Transactions with a choice of settlement	The entity receives or acquires goods or services and the terms of the arrangement provide either the entity or the supplier with a choice of whether the entity settles the transaction in cash or by issuing equity instruments.

Certain transactions are **outside the scope** of the IFRS:

(a) Transactions with employees and others in their capacity as a holder of equity instruments of the entity (for example, where an employee receives additional shares in a rights issue to all shareholders)

(b) The issue of equity instruments in exchange for control of another entity in a business combination

(IFRS 2, para 2-6)

Key terms

Share-based payment transaction. A transaction in which the entity receives goods or services as consideration for equity instruments of the entity (including shares or share options), or acquires goods or services by incurring liabilities to the supplier of those goods or services for amounts that are based on the price of the entity's shares or other equity instruments of the entity.

Share-based payment arrangement. An agreement between the entity and another party (including an employee) to enter into a share-based payment transaction, which thereby entitles the other party to receive cash or other assets of the entity for amounts that are based on the price of the entity's shares or other equity instruments of the entity, or to receive equity instruments of the entity, provided the specified vesting conditions, if any, are met.

Equity instrument. A contract that evidences a residual interest in the assets of an entity after deducting all of its liabilities.

Equity instrument granted. The right (conditional or unconditional) to an equity instrument of the entity conferred by the entity on another party, under a share-based payment arrangement.

Share option. A contract that gives the holder the right, but not the obligation, to subscribe to the entity's shares at a fixed or determinable price for a specified period of time.

Fair value. The amount for which an asset could be exchanged, a liability settled, or an equity instrument granted could be exchanged, between knowledgeable, willing parties in an arm's length transaction.

Grant date. The date at which the entity and another party (including an employee) agree to a share-based payment arrangement, being when the entity and the other party have a shared understanding of the terms and conditions of the arrangement. At grant date the entity confers on the other party (the counterparty) the right to cash, other assets, or equity instruments of the entity, provided the specified vesting conditions, if any, are met. If that agreement is subject to an approval process (for example, by shareholders), grant date is the date when that approval is obtained.

Intrinsic value. The difference between the fair value of the shares to which the counterparty has the (conditional or unconditional) right to subscribe or which it has the right to receive, and the price (if any) the other party is (or will be) required to pay for those shares. For example, a share option with an exercise price of $15 on a share with a fair value of $20, has an intrinsic value of $5.

Measurement date. The date at which the fair value of the equity instruments granted is measured. For transactions with employees and others providing similar services, the measurement date is grant date. For transactions with parties other than employees (and those providing similar services), the measurement date is the date the entity obtains the goods or the counterparty renders service.

Vest. To become an entitlement. Under a share-based payment arrangement, a counterparty's right to receive cash, other assets, or equity instruments of the entity vests when the counterparty's entitlement is no longer conditional on the satisfaction of any vesting conditions.

Vesting conditions. The conditions that determine whether the entity receives the services that entitle the counterparty to receive cash, other assets or equity instruments of the entity, under a share-based payment arrangement. Vesting conditions are either service conditions or performance conditions. Service conditions require the counterparty to complete a specified period of service, and specified performance targets to be met (such as a specified increase in the entity's profit over a specified period of time).

Vesting period. The period during which all the specified vesting conditions of a share-based payment arrangement are to be satisfied.

(IFRS 2, Appendix A)

Note that the definition of fair value within IFRS 2 is not in line with that provided in IFRS 13 *Fair Value Measurement*. Share-based payments is one of the few areas of accounting where fair value is relevant to which IFRS 13 does **not** apply.

2.3 Recognition: The basic principle

An entity should **recognise goods or services received or acquired in a share-based payment transaction when it obtains the goods or as the services are received.**

Goods or services received or acquired in a share-based payment transaction **should be recognised as expenses unless they qualify for recognition as assets**. For example, services are normally recognised as expenses (because they are normally rendered immediately), while goods are recognised as assets.

If the goods or services were received or acquired in an **equity-settled** share-based payment transaction, the entity should recognise **a corresponding increase in equity** (reserves).

If the goods or services were received or acquired in a **cash-settled** share-based payment transaction, the entity should recognise a **liability**.

If **equity-settled**, recognise a corresponding **increase in equity**	If **cash-settled**, recognise a corresponding **liability**
DEBIT Expense X CREDIT Equity* X	DEBIT Expense X CREDIT Liability X

*IFRS 2 does not specify where in the equity section the credit entry should be presented. Some entities present a separate component of equity (eg 'Share-based payment reserve'); other entities may include the credit in retained earnings.

2.4 Equity-settled share-based payment transactions

2.4.1 Measurement

The issue here is how to measure the 'cost' of the goods and services received and the equity instruments (eg the share options) granted in return.

The general principle in IFRS 2 is that when an entity recognises the goods or services received and the corresponding increase in equity, it should measure these at the **fair value of the goods or services received – this is known as the direct method**. Where the transaction is with **parties other than employees**, there is a rebuttable presumption that the fair value of the goods or services received can be estimated reliably.

If the fair value of the goods or services received cannot be measured reliably, such as in transactions with employees, the entity should measure their value by reference to the **fair value of the equity instruments granted – this is the indirect method**.

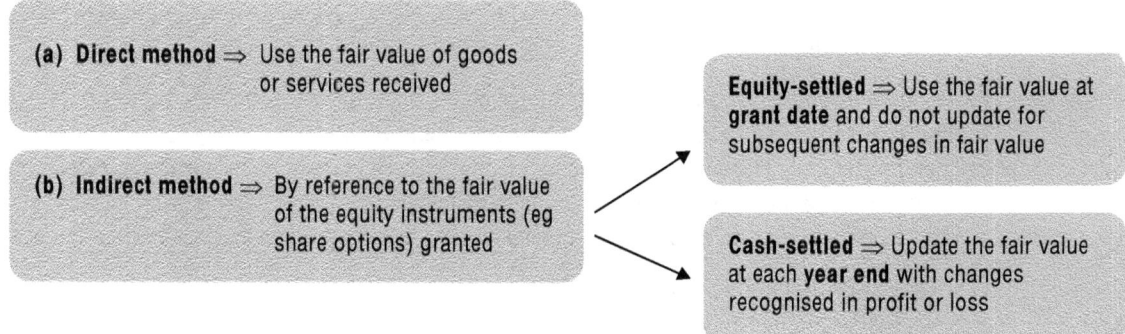

2.4.2 Determining the fair value of equity instruments granted

Where a transaction is measured by reference to the fair value of the equity instruments granted, fair value is based on **market prices** if available, taking into account the terms and conditions upon which those equity instruments were granted.

If market prices are not available, the entity should estimate the fair value of the equity instruments granted using a **valuation technique**. (These are beyond the scope of this exam.)

2.4.3 Recognition of transactions in which services are received

The issue here is **when** to recognise the transaction.

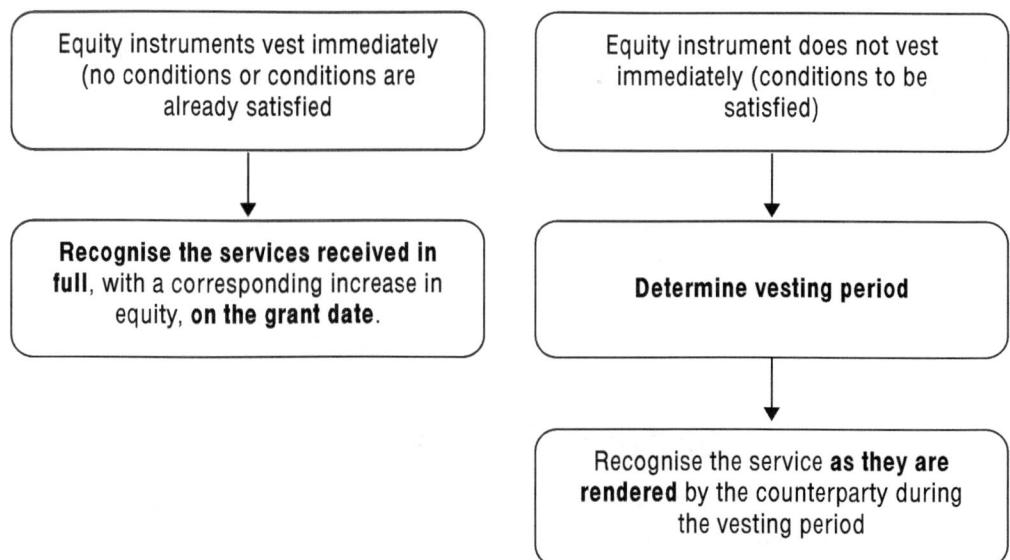

2.5 Example: Date of recognition

Consider the situation in which on 1 January 20X1, an entity grants its employees the right to each receive 1,000 share options provided they remain in employment until 31 December 20X3:

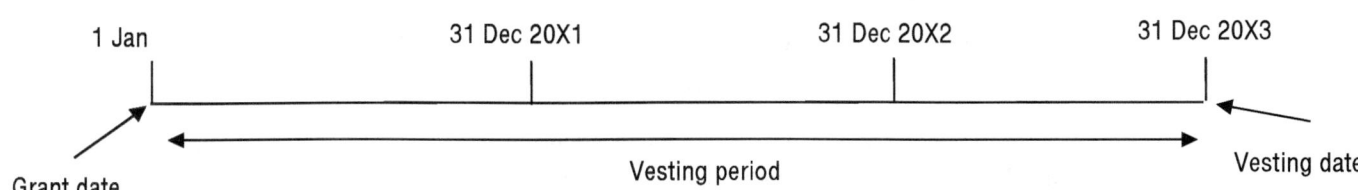

Required
Explain when the entity should recognise the share-based payment transaction

Solution

The entity should recognise the share based payment in the period in which the employees provide the service. In this case, the employees are required to provide their services for a three-year period from 1 January 20X1 to 31 December 20X3. The entity has received the benefits of the employees service across this period and should therefore also recognise the transaction across the period.

The entity should recognise an amount for the goods or services received during the vesting period based on the **best available estimate** of the **number of equity instruments expected to vest**. It should **revise** that estimate if subsequent information indicates that the number of equity instruments expected to vest differs from previous estimates. On **vesting date**, the entity should revise the estimate to **equal the number of equity instruments that actually vest**.

Once the goods and services received and the corresponding increase in equity have been recognised, the entity should make no subsequent adjustment to total equity after vesting date.

PART C ACCOUNTING AND REPORTING TECHNIQUES

The approach required is as follows:

In the first year of the share-based payment, the expense is equal to the equity or liability balance at the year end:

| Share-based payment equity or liability value at year end | = | Estimated number of employees entitled to benefits* | × | Number of instruments per employee | × | Fair value** per instrument | × | Proportion of vesting period elapsed at year end |

*Remove expected leavers over **whole** vesting period

Equity-settled: at **grant date
Cash-settled: at **year end**

For subsequent years, the expense is calculated as the **movement** in the equity or liability balance.

2.6 Example: Equity-settled share-based payment transaction

On 1 January 20X1 an entity grants 100 share options to each of its 400 employees. Each grant is conditional upon the employee working for the entity until 31 December 20X3. The fair value of each share option is $20.

During 20X1 20 employees leave and the entity estimates that a total of 20% of the 400 employees will leave during the three-year period.

During 20X2 a further 25 employees leave and the entity now estimates that a total of 25% of the 400 employees will leave during the three-year period.

During 20X3 a further 10 employees leave.

Required

Calculate the remuneration expense that will be recognised in respect of the share-based payment transaction for each of the three years ended 31 December 20X3.

Solution

IFRS 2 requires the entity to recognise the remuneration expense, based on the fair value of the share options granted, as the services are received during the three-year vesting period.

In 20X1 and 20X2 the entity estimates the number of options expected to vest (by estimating the number of employees likely to leave) and bases the amount that it recognises for the year on this estimate.

In 20X3 it recognises an amount based on the number of options that actually vest. A total of 55 employees left during the three-year period and therefore 34,500 options (400 − 55 × 100) vested.

The amount recognised as an expense for each of the three years is calculated as follows:

	Cumulative expense at year-end $	Expense for year $
20X1 (400 × 80%) × 100 × $20 × 1/3	213,333	213,333
20X2 (400 × 75%) × 100 × $20 × 2/3	400,000	186,667
20X3 (400 − 20 − 25 − 10) ×100 × $20 × 3/3	690,000	290,000

Question: Share-based payment

On 1 January 20X3 an entity grants 250 share options to each of its 200 employees. The only condition attached to the grant is that the employees should continue to work for the entity until 31 December 20X6. Five employees leave during the year to 31 December 20X3 and this pattern is expected to continue.

The market price of each option was $12 at 1 January 20X3 and $15 at 31 December 20X3.

Required

Show how this transaction will be reflected in the financial statements for the year ended 31 December 20X3.

Answer

The remuneration expense for the year is based on the fair value of the options granted at the grant date (1 January 20X3). As five of the 200 employees left during the year it is reasonable to assume that 20 employees will leave during the four-year vesting period and that therefore 45,000 options (180 employees × 250 options) will actually vest.

Therefore the entity recognises a remuneration expense of $135,000 (180 × 250 × $12 × ¼) in profit or loss and a corresponding increase in equity of the same amount.

2.7 Cash-settled share-based payment transactions

Examples of this type of transaction include:

(a) **Share appreciation rights** granted to employees: the employees become entitled to a future cash payment (rather than an equity instrument), based on the increase in the entity's share price from a specified level over a specified period of time; or

(b) An entity might grant to its employees a right to receive a future cash payment by granting to them a **right to shares that are redeemable**

The basic principle is that the entity measures the goods or services acquired and the liability incurred at the **fair value of the liability**.

The entity should **remeasure** the fair value of the liability **at each reporting date** until the liability is settled **and at the date of settlement**. Any **changes** in fair value are recognised in **profit or loss** for the period.

The entity should recognise the services received, and a liability to pay for those services, **as the employees render service**. For example, if share appreciation rights do not vest until the employees have completed a specified period of service, the entity should recognise the services received and the related liability, over that period.

2.8 Example: Cash-settled share-based payment transaction

On 1 January 20X1 an entity grants 100 cash share appreciation rights (SARS) to each of its 500 employees, on condition that the employees continue to work for the entity until 31 December 20X3.

During 20X1 35 employees leave. The entity estimates that a further 60 will leave during 20X2 and 20X3.

During 20X2 40 employees leave and the entity estimates that a further 25 will leave during 20X3.

During 20X3 22 employees leave.

At 31 December 20X3 150 employees exercise their SARs. Another 140 employees exercise their SARs at 31 December 20X4 and the remaining 113 employees exercise their SARs at the end of 20X5.

The fair values of the SARs for each year in which a liability exists are shown below, together with the intrinsic values at the dates of exercise.

	Fair value $	Intrinsic value $
20X1	14.40	
20X2	15.50	
20X3	18.20	15.00
20X4	21.40	20.00
20X5		25.00

Required

Calculate the amount to be recognised in the statement of profit or loss and other comprehensive income for each of the five years ended 31 December 20X5 and the liability to be recognised in the statement of financial position at 31 December for each of the five years.

Solution

For the three years to the vesting date of 31 December 20X3 the expense is based on the entity's estimate of the number of SARSs that will actually vest (as for an equity-settled transaction). However, the fair value of the liability is **remeasured** at each year-end.

The intrinsic value of the SARs at the date of exercise is the amount of cash actually paid.

		Liability at year-end $	$	Expense for year $
20X1	Expected to vest (500 – 35 – 60):			
	405 × 100 × $14.40 × 1/3	194,400		194,400
20X2	Expected to vest (500 – 35 – 40 – 25):			
	400 × 100 × $15.50 × 2/3	413,333		218,933
20X3	Exercised:			
	150 × 100 × $15.00		225,000	
	Not yet exercised (500 – 35 – 40 – 22 – 150):			
	253 × 100 × $18.20	460,460	47,127	
				272,127
20X4	Exercised:			
	140 × 100 × $20.00		280,000	
	Not yet exercised (253 – 140):			
	113 × 100 × $21.40	241,820	(218,640)	
				61,360
20X5	Exercised:			
	113 × 100 × $25.00		282,500	
		Nil	(241,820)	
				40,680
				787,500

Transactions in which either the entity or the other party has a choice of settling in cash or by issuing equity instruments:

(a) If the entity has incurred a liability to settle in cash or other assets, it should account for the transaction as a cash-settled share-based payment transaction

(b) If no such liability has been incurred, the entity should account for the transaction as an equity-settled share-based payment transaction.

2.9 Transactions with a choice of settlement

2.9.1 Entity has the choice

If the entity has the choice of whether to settle the share-based payment in cash or by issuing shares, the accounting treatment depends on whether there is a **present obligation** to settle the transaction in cash.

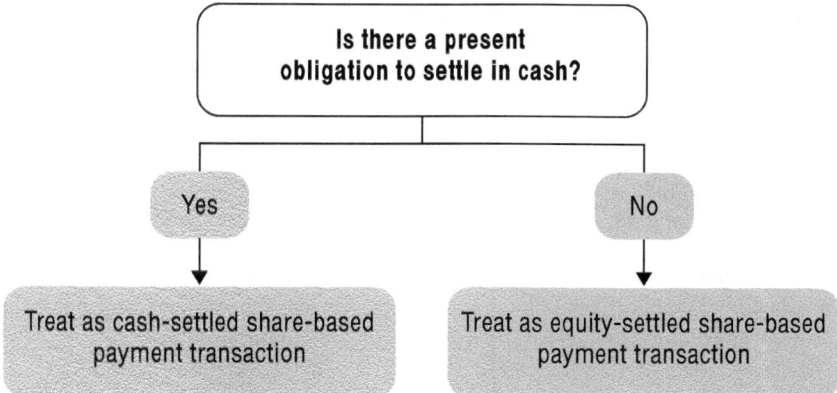

A present obligation exists if the entity has a stated policy of settling such transactions in cash or past practice of settling in cash, because this creates an expectation, and so a constructive obligation, to settle future such transactions in cash.

2.9.2 Counterparty has the choice

If instead the counterparty (eg employee or supplier) has the right to choose whether the share-based payment is settled in cash or shares, the entity has granted a compound financial instrument (IFRS 2: para. 34).

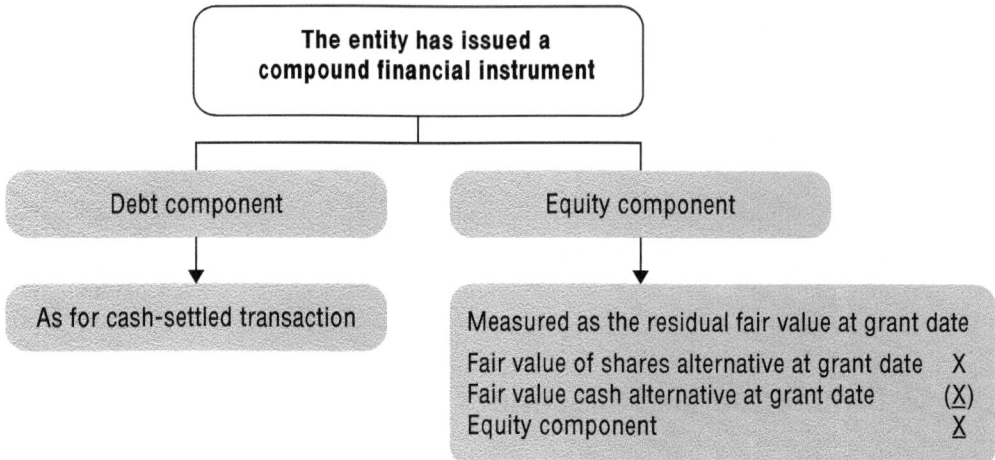

2.10 Example: Choice of settlement

On 30 September 20X3, Saddler granted one of its directors the right to choose either 24,000 shares in Saddler or a cash payment equal to the value of 20,000 shares on the settlement date, 30 September 20X4. This right is not conditional on future employment. The company estimates that the fair value of the share alternative is $4.50 per share at 30 September 20X3 (taking into account a condition that they must be held for 2 years). Saddler's market share price was $5.20 per share on 30 September 20X3, and this rose to $5.40 by the date the financial statements were authorised for issue.

Required

Explain the accounting treatment of the above transaction for the year ended 30 September 20X3.

Solution

The right granted to the director represents a share-based payment with a choice of settlement where the counterparty has the choice. Consequently, a compound financial instrument has in substance been issued and it needs to be broken down into its equity (equity-settled) and liability (cash-settled) components. The equity-settled component is measured as a residual, consistent with the definition of equity, by comparing, at grant date, the fair value of the shares alternative and the cash alternative.

The accounting entry on the grant date (30 September 20X3) would therefore be as follows (all figures from Working below):

DEBIT	Profit or loss – remuneration expense	$108,000	
CREDIT	Liability		$104,000
CREDIT	Equity		$4,000

The equity component is not subsequently revalued (consistent with the treatment of equity-settled share-based payment), but the liability component will need to be adjusted for any changes in the fair value of the cash alternative up to the settlement date (30 September 20X4).

The post-year end change in the share price (which will affect the cash-settled share-based payment) is a non-adjusting event after the reporting period, as it relates to conditions that arose after the year end. The liability is not therefore adjusted for this, but the difference (20,000 × $0.20 = $4,000) would be disclosed if considered material. This is unlikely here, but may be considered material due to the fact that it is a transaction with a member of key management personnel.

At the settlement date the liability element of the share-based payment will be re-measured to its fair value at that date and the method of settlement chosen by the director will then determine the accounting treatment (payment of the liability or transfer to share capital/share premium).

Working: Fair value of equity component	$
Fair value of the shares alternative at grant date	
(24,000 shares × $4.50)	108,000
Fair value of the cash alternative at grant date	
(20,000 phantom shares × $5.20)	(104,000)
∴ Fair value of the equity component of the compound instrument	4,000

It can be seen that where the right to the shares alternative is more valuable than the right to a cash alternative, at the grant date the equity component then has a value of the **residual** amount, not the full amount of the shares alternative, as the director must surrender the cash alternative in order to accept the shares alternative; he cannot accept both.

2.11 Deferred tax implications

2.11.1 Issue

An entity may receive a tax deduction that differs from related cumulative remuneration expense, and may arise in a later accounting period.

Exam focus point

> For example, an entity recognises an expense for share options granted under IFRS 2, but does not receive a tax deduction until the options are exercised and receives the tax deduction at the share price on the exercise date.

2.11.2 Measurement

The deferred tax asset temporary difference is measured as:

Carrying amount of share-based payment expense	0
Less: tax base of share-based payment expense	

(estimated amount tax authorities will permit as a deduction
in future periods, based on year end information) (X)
Temporary difference (X)
Deferred tax asset at X% X

If the amount of the tax deduction (or estimated future tax deduction) exceeds the amount of the related cumulative remuneration expense, this indicates that the tax deduction relates also to an equity item.

The excess is therefore recognised directly in equity.

2.11.3 Example: Deferred tax implications of share-based payment

On 1 January 20X2, Bruce granted 5,000 share options to an employee vesting two years later on 31 December 20X3. The fair value of each option measured at the grant date was $3.

Tax law in the jurisdiction in which the entity operates allows a tax deduction of the intrinsic value of the options on exercise. The intrinsic value of the share options was $1.20 at 31 December 20X2 and $3.40 at 31 December 20X3 on which date the options were exercised.

Assume a tax rate of 30%.

Required:

Show the deferred tax accounting treatment of the above transaction at 31 December 20X2, 31 December 20X3 (before exercise), and on exercise.

Solution

	31/12/20X2	31/12/20X3 before exercise
Carrying amount of share-based payment expense	0	0
Less: Tax base of share-based payment expense		
$(5{,}000 \times \$1.2 \times \frac{1}{2})/(5{,}000 \times \$3.40)$	(3,000)	(17,000)
Temporary difference	(3,000)	(17,000)
Deferred tax asset @ 30%	900	5,100
Deferred tax (Cr P/L) (5,100 – 900 – (Working) 600)	900	3,600
Deferred tax (Cr Equity) (Working)	0	600

On exercise, the deferred tax asset is replaced by a current tax one. The double entry is:

Debit deferred tax (P/L)	4,500	⎫
Debit deferred tax (equity)	600	⎬ reversal
Credit deferred tax asset	5,100	⎭

Debit current tax asset	5,100
Credit current tax (P/L)	4,500
Credit current tax (equity)	600

Working

Accounting expense recognised $(5{,}000 \times \$3 \times \frac{1}{2})/(5{,}000 \times \$3)$	7,500	15,000
Tax deduction	(3,000)	(17,000)
Excess temporary difference	0	(2,000)
Excess deferred tax asset to equity @ 30%	0	600

2.12 Disclosures

IFRS 2 requires entities to disclose information that enables users of the financial statements to understand the **nature and extent** of share-based payment **arrangements that existed during the period**.

(a) A **description** of each type of share-based payment arrangement that existed at any time during the period, including the general terms and conditions of each arrangement;

(b) The **number and weighted average exercise prices** of share options for each of the following groups of options:

- (i) Outstanding at the beginning of the period
- (ii) Granted during the period
- (iii) Forfeited during the period
- (iv) Exercised during the period
- (v) Expired during the period
- (vi) Outstanding at the end of the period
- (vii) Exercisable at the end of the period

(c) For share options **exercised** during the period, the **weighted average share price** at the date of exercise

(d) For share options outstanding at the end of the period, the range of exercise prices and weighted average remaining contractual life

In addition, IFRS 2 requires disclosure of information that enables users of the financial statements to **understand how the fair value** of the goods or services received, or the fair value of the equity instruments granted, during the period **was determined**.

Entities should also disclose information that enables users of the financial statements to understand the effect of share-based payment transactions on the entity's **profit or loss for the period** and on its **financial position**.

(a) The **total expense recognised for the period** arising from share-based payment transactions, including separate disclosure of that portion of the total expense that arises from transactions accounted for as equity-settled share-based payment transactions;

(b) For **liabilities** arising from share-based payment transactions:

- (i) The **total carrying amount** at the end of the period
- (ii) The **total intrinsic value** at the end of the period of liabilities for which the counterparty's right to cash or other assets had vested by the end of the period

2.13 Section summary

IFRS 2 requires entities to **recognise** the goods or services received as a result of **share-based payment transactions.**

- Equity settled transactions: DEBIT Asset/Expense, CREDIT Equity
- Cash settled transactions: DEBIT Asset/Expense, CREDIT Liability
- Transactions are **recognised when goods/services are obtained/received** (usually over the performance period)
- Transactions are measured at fair value: for equity settled transactions, fair value at grant date. For cash-settled transactions, fair value is at each year end date.
- If there is a choice of settlement: entity has the choice – determine if obligation to settle in cash. If so, treat as cash settled. If the counterparty has the choice, recognise the debt and equity component.
- Deferred tax arises due to timing difference between recognising the expense and the tax implication of the transaction.

Chapter roundup

- **IAS 24** is primarily a disclosure standard. It is concerned to improve the quality of information provided by financial statements.

- **Share-based payment** transactions should be recognised in the financial statements. You need to understand and be able to advise on:
    - Recognition
    - Measurement
    - Disclosure

  of both equity-settled and cash-settled transactions.

Quick quiz

1. What is a related party transaction?
2. A managing director of a company is a related party. True/False?
3. What is a cash-settled share based payment transaction?
4. What is grant date?
5. If an entity has entered into an equity settled share-based payment transaction, what should it recognise in its financial statements?
6. Where an entity has granted share options to its employees in return for services, how is the transaction measured?

Answers to quick quiz

1. A transfer of resources, services or obligations between related parties, regardless of whether a price is charged.

2. True. A member of the key management personnel of an entity is a related party of that entity.

3. A transaction in which the entity receives goods or services in exchange for amounts of cash that are based on the price (or value) of the entity's shares or other equity instruments of the entity.

4. The date at which the entity and another party (including an employee) agree to a share based payment arrangement, being when the entity and the other party have a shared understanding of the terms and conditions of the arrangement.

5. The goods or services received and a corresponding increase in equity.

6. By reference to the fair value of the equity instruments granted, measured at grant date.

End of chapter question

Molar and Canal (AIA May 2011)

(a) Molar, a public limited company, is planning to rationalise its operations over the next three years. As part of the plan, Molar is considering changing a number of employee contracts so that settlement of the amounts payable will be by issuing shares, share options or by basing settlement on the company's share price. As this is a new method, the company's finance officer is seeking guidance on the implications of the new scheme for the company's financial statements. He believes that because there is no cash outflow, no amount should be recognised in profit or loss. The following details relate to one suggested method of settlement.

On 1 June 2011 Molar will grant 250 share options to each of its 2,500 employees. All grants are equal and conditional upon the employee working for Molar until 31 May 2014. At the 1 June 2011 the fair value of each option is expected to be $30.

Molar's business plan for the period up to 31 May 2014 shows that it expects 60 employees will leave during the first year of the plan and that 25% of the remainder will leave before 31 May 2014. Of those expected to leave after the first year, it is estimated that two-thirds will leave during the second year of the plan and one-third in the final year.

Required

Advise Molar's finance director of the appropriate accounting treatment of the share options for each of the three years to 31 May 2014 if the company is correct in its estimates concerning the number of employees leaving its employment. **(10 marks)**

(b) Canal, a public limited company, introduced a cash share appreciation rights (SAR) scheme on 1 June 2007. The scheme granted 200 SARs to each of Canal's 1,000 employees on condition they remain working for the company for the next three years ending on 31 May 2010. The following information relates to the scheme.

During the year ended 31 May:	Number of employees: Leaving during the year	Number of employees: Estimated to leave in future	Fair value of share at year end $	Cash per share actually paid $
2008	70	120	15	
2009	80	55	16	
2010	45		17	16.50
2011				18.00

At 31 May 2010, 300 employees exercised their SARs. The remaining employees exercised their SARs at 31 May 2011.

Required

Advise Canal of the amounts to be recognised in the company's financial statements for each of the four years ended 31 May 2011 and explore the difference between Canal's SAR scheme and the scheme Molar plans to introduce.

(10 marks)

(Total 20 marks)

PART C ACCOUNTING AND REPORTING TECHNIQUES

Revenue recognition and off balance sheet finance

Topic list	Syllabus reference
1 Revenue recognition	LO4
2 Off balance sheet finance	LO4
3 Substance over form	LO4
4 Common forms of off balance sheet finance	LO4

Introduction

IFRS 15 *Revenue from Contracts with Customers* is a relatively new and detailed standard providing guidance on revenue recognition. The concept of substance over form is an important principle in determining how transactions are recognised in the financial statements.

Off balance sheet finance is problematic for accountants as it is inconsistent with the *Conceptual Framework's* fundamental characteristic of faithful representation.

1 Revenue recognition

> **FAST FORWARD**
>
> Revenue recognition is straightforward in most business transactions, but some situations are more complicated.

1.1 Introduction

Revenue is a key performance measure used by companies and analysts. The amount of revenue recognised directly affects profit and key ratios such as profit margin and sales growth. Company managers are often under pressure to achieve a particular revenue figure. This pressure along with the complexity of some revenue transactions can lead to deliberate attempts to manipulate revenue recognised, and therefore you should be aware of the ethical risks around revenue recognition.

Recognising and measuring revenue appropriately requires the exercise of professional judgement and is crucial to ensuring that the fundamental qualitative characteristic of faithful representation is satisfied.

1.2 IFRS 15 *Revenue from Contracts with Customers*

> **FAST FORWARD**
>
> IFRS 15 *Revenue from Contracts with Customers* is concerned with the **recognition of revenues** arising from fairly common transactions.
>
> - The sale of goods
> - The rendering of services
> - The use by others of entity assets yielding interest, royalties and dividends
>
> Generally revenue is recognised when the entity has transferred promised goods or services to the customer. The standard sets out five steps for the recognition process.

The objective of IFRS 15 Revenue from Contracts with Customers is to establish the principles for reporting useful information to users of financial statements about the nature, amount, timing and uncertainty of revenue and cash flows arising from a contract with a customer (IFRS 15, para. 1).

The core principle of IFRS 15 is that an entity **recognises revenue to depict the transfer of promised goods or services to customers**.

For straightforward retail transactions IFRS 15 will have little, if any, effect on the amount and timing of revenue recognition. For contracts such as long-term service contracts and multi-element arrangements, it is likely to result in changes either to the amount or to the timing of revenue recognised.

1.3 Scope

IFRS 15 applies to all contracts with customers except:

- Lease contracts within the scope of IFRS 16
- Insurance contracts within the scope of IFRS 17
- Financial instruments and other contractual rights and obligations within the scope of IFRS 9, IFRS 10, IFRS 11, IAS 27 or IAS 28.
- Non-monetary exchanges between entities in the same line of business

(IFRS 15, para 5)

1.4 Definitions

The following definitions are given in the standard.

Key terms

> **Income** – Increases in economic benefits during the accounting period in the form of inflows or enhancements of assets or decreases of liabilities that result in an increase in equity, other than those relating to contributions from equity participants.
>
> **Revenue** – Income arising in the course of an entity's ordinary activities.
>
> **Contract** – An agreement between two or more parties that creates enforceable rights and obligations.
>
> **Contract asset** – An entity's right to consideration in exchange for goods or services that the entity has transferred to a customer when that right is conditioned on something other than the passage of time (for example the entity's future performance).
>
> **Receivable** – An entity's right to consideration that is unconditional – ie only the passage of time is required before payment is due.
>
> **Contract liability** – An entity's obligation to transfer goods or services to a customer for which the entity has received consideration (or the amount is due) from the customer.
>
> **Customer** – A party that has contracted with an entity to obtain goods or services that are an output of the entity's ordinary activities in exchange for consideration.
>
> **Performance obligation** – A promise in a contract with a customer to transfer to the customer either:
>
> (a) A good or service (or a bundle of goods or services) that is distinct; or
> (b) A series of distinct goods or services that are substantially the same ad that have the same pattern of transfer to the customer.
>
> **Stand-alone selling price** – The price at which an entity would sell a promised good or service separately to a customer.
>
> **Transaction price** – The amount of consideration to which an entity expects to be entitled in exchange for transferring promised goods or services to a customer, excluding amounts collected on behalf of third parties.
>
> (IFRS 15, Appendix A)

Revenue **does not include** sales taxes, value added taxes or goods and service taxes which are only collected for third parties, because these do not represent an economic benefit flowing to the entity.

1.5 Recognition and measurement of revenue

Under IFRS 15 revenue is recognised and measured using a five step model.

1	Identify the contract with the customer
2	Identify the performance obligation(s)
3	Determine the transaction price
4	Allocate the transaction price to the performance obligations
5	Recognise revenue when (or as) the performance obligations are satisfied

1.5.1 Step 1 – Identify the contract with the customer

A contract with a customer is within the scope of IFRS 15 only when:

(a) The parties have approved the contract and are committed to carrying it out.
(b) Each party's rights regarding the goods and services to be transferred can be identified.
(c) The payment terms for the goods and services can be identified
(d) The contract has commercial substance
(e) It is probable that the entity will collect the consideration to which it will be entitled.

The contract can be written, verbal or implied.

1.6 Example: Identify the contract with the customer

Jute is a property developer. On 1 June 20X3, Jute entered into a contract with Munro for the sale of a building for $3 million.

Munro paid Jute a non-refundable deposit of $150,000 on 1 June 20X3 and entered into a long-term financing agreement with Jute for the remaining 95% of the promised consideration. The terms of the financing arrangement are that if Munro defaults, Jute can repossess the building, but cannot seek further compensation from Munro, even if the collateral does not cover the full value of the amount owed. Control of the building was transferred to Munro on 1 June 20X3.

Munro intends to use the building as a fitness centre. The building is located in a city where competition in the fitness industry is high, and many successful fitness centres already exist. Munro's experience to date has been in stores selling health foods, and it has no experience of the fitness industry. Munro intends to use income generated by the fitness centre to repay the loan from Jute.

Required

Discuss whether Jute's contract with Munro is within the scope of IFRS 15.

Solution

To be within the scope of IFRS 15, the contract must meet all of the following criteria:

- Jute and Munro have approved the contract
- Jute can identify its own and Munro's rights under the contract
- Jute can identify payment terms
- The contract has commercial substance
- It is probable that Jute will collect the consideration due

Munro's ability to pay is in doubt and therefore we must question whether it is probably that Jute will collect the consideration due:

(i) Munro's liability under the loan is limited because the loan is non-recourse. If Munro defaults, Jute is not entitled to full compensation for the amount owed, but only has the right to repossess the building.

(ii) Munro intends to repay the loan (which has a significant balance outstanding) from income derived from its fitness centre. This is a business facing significant risks because of high competition in the industry and because of Munro's limited experience.

It is therefore not probable that Jute will collect the consideration to which it is entitled in exchange for the transfer of the building. The contract does not meet the criteria within IFRS 15 and the revenue recognition model cannot be applied.

In situations where the revenue recognition model cannot be applied, IFRS 15 permits amounts received from customers to be recognised as revenue when:

(a) **Substantially all** of the consideration has been received and is not refundable; or
(b) The seller has **terminated the contract**

Neither of these are applicable to Jute, therefore, Jute cannot recognise revenue for any of the consideration received.

Jute must account for the non-refundable $150,000 deposit as a liability at 1 June 20X3.

1.6.1 Step 2 Identify the separate performance obligations

The key point is to identify the distinct goods or services under the contract. A contract includes promises to provide goods or services to a customer. Those promises are called performance obligations. A company would account for each performance obligation separately only if the promised good or service is distinct. A good or service is distinct if it is sold separately or if it could be sold separately because it has a distinct function and a distinct profit margin. Factors for consideration as to whether an entity's promise to transfer the good or service to the customer is separately identifiable include, but are not limited to:

(a) The entity does not provide a significant service of integrating the good or service with other goods or services promised in the contract.

(b) The good or service does not significantly modify or customize another good or service promised in the contract.

(c) The good or service is not highly dependent on or highly interrelated with other goods or services promised in the contract

1.7 Example: Identifying the separate performance obligation

Office Solutions, a limited company, has developed a communications software package called CommSoft. Office Solutions has entered into a contract with Logisticity to supply the following:

(a) Licence to use CommSoft

(b) Installation service. This may require an upgrade to the computer operating system, but the software package does not need to be customized

(c) Technical support for three years

(d) Three years of updates for CommSoft

Office Solutions is not the only company able to install CommSoft, and the technical support can also be provided by other companies. The software can function without the updates and technical support.

Required

Explain whether the goods or services provided to Logisticity are distinct in accordance with IFRS 15 *Revenue from Contracts with Customers.*

Solution

CommSoft was delivered before the other goods or services and remains functional without the updates and the technical support. It may be concluded that Logisticity can benefit from each of the goods and services either on their own or together with the other goods and services that are readily available.

The promises to transfer each good and service to the customer are separately identifiable In particular, the installation service does not significantly modify the software itself and, as such, the software and the installation service are separate outputs promised by Office Solutions rather than inputs used to produce a combined output.

In conclusion, the goods and services are distinct and amount to four performance obligations in the contract under IFRS 15.

1.7.1 Step 3 Determine the transaction price

The transaction price is the amount of consideration a company expects to be entitled to from the customer in exchange for transferring goods or services. The transaction price would reflect the company's probability-weighted estimate of **variable consideration** (including reasonable estimates of contingent amounts) in addition to the **effects of the customer's credit risk** and the **time value of money** (if material).

Variable contingent amounts are only included where it is highly probable that there will not be a reversal of revenue when any uncertainty associated with the variable consideration is resolved. Examples of where a variable consideration can arise include: discounts, rebates, refunds, price concessions, credits and penalties.

1.8 Example: Determining the transaction price

Taplop supplies laptop computers to large businesses. On 1 July 20X5, Taplop entered into a contract with TrillCo, under which TrillCo was to purchase laptops at $500 per unit. The contract states that if TrillCo purchases more than 500 laptops in a year, the price per units is reduced retrospectively to $450 per unit. Taplop's year end is 30 June.

(a) As at 30 September 20X5, TrillCo had bought 70 laptops from Taplop. Taplop therefore estimated that TrillCo's purchases would not exceed 500 in the year to 30 June 20X6, and would therefore not be entitled to the volume discount.

(b) During the quarter ended 31 December 20X5, TrillCo expanded rapidly as a result of a substantial acquisition, and purchased an additional 250 laptops from Taplop. Taplop then estimated that TrillCo's purchases would exceed the threshold for the volume discount in the year to 30 June 20X6.

Required

Calculate the revenue Taplop would recognise in:

(a) The quarter ended 30 September 20X5
(b) The quarter ended 31 December 20X5

Your answer should apply the principles of IFRS 15 *Revenue from Contracts with Customers*.

Solution

(a) Applying the requirements of IFRS 15 to TrillCo's purchasing pattern at 30 September 20X5, Taplop should conclude that it was highly probable that a significant reversal in the cumulative amount of revenue recognised ($500 per laptop) would not occur when the uncertainty was resolved, that is when the total amount of purchases was known. Consequently, Taplop should recognise revenue of 70 × $500 = $35,000 for the first quarter ended 30 September 20X5.

(b) In the quarter ended 31 December 20X5, TrillCo's purchasing pattern changed such that it would be legitimate for Taplop to conclude that TrillCo's purchases would exceed the threshold for the volume discount in the year to 30 June 20X6, and therefore that it was appropriate to reduce the price to $450 per laptop. Taplop should therefore recognise revenue of $109,000 for the quarter ended 31 December 20X5. The amount is calculated as from $112,500 (250 laptops × $450) less the change in transaction price of $3,500 (70 laptops × $50 price reduction) for the reduction of the price of the laptops sold in the quarter ended 30 September 20X5.

1.8.1 Step 4 Allocate the transaction price to the performance obligations

Where a contract contains more than one distinct performance obligation, a company allocates the transaction price to all separate performance obligations in proportion to the stand-alone selling price of the good or service underlying each performance obligation. If the good or service is not sold separately, the company would estimate its stand-alone selling price.

So, if any entity sells a bundle of goods and/or services which it also supplies unbundled, the separate performance obligations in the contract should be priced in the same proportion as the unbundled prices. This would apply to mobile phone contracts where the handset is supplied 'free'. The entity must look at the stand-alone price of such a handset and some of the consideration for the contract should be allocated to the handset.

1.9 Example: Allocating transaction price to performance obligations

Gibson Motor Sales sells a car to a customer for $21,000, including two years' servicing. The car is sold without servicing for $20,520 and the standalone cost of servicing is $540 per year.

Required

Identify the performance obligations in the sale and explain how the transaction price is allocated to each performance obligation.

Solution

There are two performance obligations – the sale of the car and the provision of servicing for the next two years.

The transaction price is allocated to each performance obligation as follows:

Performance obligation	Stand-alone selling price	% of total	Revenue allocated
Car	$20,520	95%	$19,950 (21,000 × 95%)
Servicing ($540 × 2)	$1,080	5%	$1,050 (21,000 × 5%)
Total	$21,600	100%	$21,000

1.9.1 Step 5 Recognise revenue when (or as) a performance obligation is satisfied

The entity satisfies a performance obligation by transferring **control** of a promised good or service to the customer. A performance obligation can be satisfied **at a point in time**, such as when goods are delivered to the customer, or **over time**. An obligation satisfied **over time** will meet one of the following criteria:

(a) The customer simultaneously receives and consumes the benefits as the performance takes place.

(b) The entity's performance creates or enhances an asset that the customer controls as the asset is created or enhanced.

(c) The entity's performance does not create an asset with an alternative use to the entity and the entity has an enforceable right to payment for performance completed to date.

The amount of revenue recognised is the amount allocated to that performance obligation in Step 4.

An entity must be able to **reasonably measure** the outcome of a performance obligation before the related revenue can be recognised. In some circumstances, such as in the early stages of a contract, it may not be possible to reasonably measure the outcome of a performance obligation, but the entity expects to recover the costs incurred. In these circumstances, revenue is recognised only to the extent of costs incurred.

1.10 Contract costs

The incremental costs of **obtaining** a contract (such as sales commission) are **recognised as an asset** if the entity expects to recover those costs.

Costs that would have been incurred regardless of whether the contract was obtained are recognised as an expense as incurred.

Costs incurred in **fulfilling** a contract, unless within the scope of another standard (such as IAS 2 *Inventories*, IAS 16 *Property, Plant and Equipment* or IAS 38 *Intangible Assets*) are recognised as an asset if they meet the following criteria:

(a) The costs relate directly to an identifiable contract (costs such as labour, materials, management costs);

(b) The costs generate or enhance resources of the entity that will be used in satisfying (or continuing to satisfy) performance obligations in the future; and

(c) The costs are expected to be recovered.

Costs recognised as assets are amortised on a systematic basis consistent with the transfer to the customer of the goods or services to which the asset relates.

1.11 Performance obligations satisfied over time

For each performance obligation satisfied over time, revenue should be recognised by measuring progress towards complete satisfaction of that performance obligation (IFRS 15: para. 39).

Methods of measuring the satisfaction of performance obligations completed to date encompass output methods and input methods.

Method	Explanation	Examples
Output	On basis of direct measurements of the **value to the customer** of the goods or services transferred to date relative to the remaining goods or services promised under the contract	• Surveys of performance completed to date • Appraisals of results achieved • Time elapsed • Units produced • Units delivered
Input	On the basis of the **entity's efforts or inputs** to the satisfaction of a performance obligation relative to the total expected inputs	• Resources consumed • Labour hours expended • Costs incurred • Time elapsed • Machine hours used

(IFRS 15, paras 41, B14, B15, B18)

If an entity cannot reasonably measure the outcome of a performance obligation (eg in the early stages of a contract) but the entity expects to recover the costs incurred in satisfying the performance obligation, it should recognise revenue only to the extent of costs incurred. This applies until it can reasonably measure the outcome of the performance obligation (IFRS 15: para. 45).

1.12 Example: Contract where performance obligations are satisfied over time

Building firm Boyle commenced a contract to construct a new warehouse for a customer on 1 January 20X5, with an estimated completion date of 31 December 20X6. The customer gains control over the warehouse as the contract progresses and Boyle has no other use for the warehouse. Boyle has an enforceable right to payment for the work it completes. The final contract price is $1,500,000, and the contract is expected to be profitable. Boyle uses the output method and measures revenue based on work completed to date. Relevant financial information in the first year, to 31 December 20X5 is as follows:

- Costs incurred amounted to $600,000.
- Certificates of work completed have been issued, to the value of $750,000.
- The customer has been invoiced for $800,000 to date and has settled $400,000 of this.

Required

Calculate the contract profit in 20X5.

Solution

This is a contract in which the performance obligation is satisfied **over time**. Boyle is carrying out the construction work for the benefit of the customer rather than creating an asset for its own use and it has an enforceable right to payment for work completed to date.

IFRS 15 states that the amount of payment that the entity is entitled to corresponds to the amount of performance completed to date, which approximates to the costs incurred in satisfying the performance obligation plus a reasonable profit margin.

In this case, the satisfaction of performance obligations is based on the certified work to date. At 31 December 20X5 the entity will recognise revenue of $750,000 and cost of sales of $600,000, leaving profit of $150,000.

1.13 Performance obligations satisfied at a point in time

A performance obligation not satisfied over time will be satisfied at a point in time. This will be the point in time at which the customer obtains control of the promised asset and the entity satisfies a performance obligation.

Some indicators of the transfer of control are:

(a) The entity has a present right to payment for the asset.
(b) The customer has legal title to the asset.
(c) The entity has transferred physical possession of the asset.
(d) The significant risks and rewards of ownership have been transferred to the customer.
(e) The customer has accepted the asset.

1.14 Sale with a right of return

Where goods are sold with a right of return, an entity should not recognise revenue for goods that it expects to be returned. It can calculate the level of returns using the expected value method (the probability-weighted sum of amounts) or simply estimate the most likely amount. This will be shown as a refund liability and a deduction from revenue.

The entity also recognises an asset (adjusted against cost of sales) for its right to recover products from customers on settlement of the refund liability.

Question — Sale with a right to return

On 31 December 20X7, Lansdale sold Product X to a customer for $12,100 payable 24 months after delivery. The customer obtained control of the product at contract inception. However, the contract permits the customer to return the product within 90 days. The product is new and Lansdale has no relevant historical evidence of product returns or other available market evidence.

The cash selling price of Product X is $10,000, which represents the amount that the customer would pay upon delivery of the same product sold under otherwise identical terms and conditions as at contract inception. The cost of the product to Lansdale is $8,000.

Required

Advise Lansdale on how to account for the above transaction.

Answer

Lansdale should **not recognise revenue** on transfer of the product to the customer on 31 December 20X7. This is because the existence of the **right of return** (within 90 days) and the **lack of historical evidence** (since this is a new product) mean that Lansdale **cannot conclude that it is highly probable** that a **significant reversal** in the amount of cumulative revenue recognised **will not occur**. Consequently, revenue may only be recognised when the right of return lapses (provided the customer has not returned the goods).

On 31 December 20X7, an **asset** should be recorded for the **right to recover the product** and the item should be **removed from inventory** at the amount of $8,000 (the cost of the inventory):

DEBIT	Asset for right to recover product to be returned	$8,000	
CREDIT	Inventory		$8,000

A **receivable and revenue of $10,000** will be recognised when the **right of return lapses** on 31 March 20X8 provided the product is not returned. The **'asset for right to recover product to be returned'** will also be **transferred to cost of sales:**

DEBIT	Receivable	$10,000	
CREDIT	Revenue		$10,000
DEBIT	Cost of sales	$8,000	
CREDIT	Asset for right to recover product to be returned		$8,000

The contract also includes a **significant financing component** since there is a **difference** between the amount of the **promised consideration** of $12,100 and the **cash selling price** of $10,000 at the date the goods are transferred to the customer.

During the three-month **right of return period** (1 January 20X8 – 31 March 20X8) **no interest** is recognised because **no contract asset or liability** is recognised.

Interest revenue on the receivable should then be recognised at the **effective interest rate** (based on the remaining contractual term of 21 months) in accordance with IFRS 9 *Financial Instruments*.

1.15 Warranties

If a customer has the option to purchase a warranty separately from the product to which it relates, it constitutes a distinct service and is accounted for as a separate performance obligation. This would apply to a warranty which provides the customer with a service in addition to the assurance that the product complies with agreed-upon specifications.

If the customer does not have the option to purchase the warranty separately, for instance if the warranty is required by law, that does not give rise to a performance obligation and the warranty is accounted for in accordance with IAS 37.

1.16 Principal versus agent

An entity must establish in any transaction whether it is acting as principal or agent.

It is a principal if it controls the promised good or service before it is transferred to the customer. When the performance obligation is satisfied, the entity recognises revenue in the gross amount of the consideration for those goods or services.

It is acting as an agent if its performance obligation is to arrange for the provision of goods or services by another party. Satisfaction of this performance obligation will give rise to the recognition of revenue in the amount of any fee or commission to which it expects to be entitled in exchange for arranging for the other party to provide its goods or services.

Indicators that an entity is an agent rather than a principal include the following:

(a) Another party is primarily responsible for fulfilling the contract.

(b) The entity does not have inventory risk before or after the goods have been ordered by a customer, during shipping or on return.

(c) The entity does not have discretion in establishing prices for the other party's goods or services and, therefore, the benefit that the entity can receive from those goods or services is limited.

(d) The entity's consideration is in the form of a commission.

(e) The entity is not exposed to credit risk for the amount receivable from a customer in exchange for the other party's goods or services.

Example: Principal versus agent

This example is taken from the standard.

An entity operates a website that enables customers to purchase goods from a range of suppliers. The suppliers deliver directly to the customers, who have paid in advance, and the entity receives a commission of 10% of the sales price.

The entity's website also processes payments from the customer to the supplier at prices set by the supplier. The entity has no further obligation to the customer after arranging for the products to be supplied.

Required

Explain whether the entity a principal or an agent?

Solution

The following points are relevant:

- Goods are supplied directly from the supplier to the customer, so the entity does not obtain control of the goods.
- The supplier is primarily responsible for fulfilling the contract.
- The entity's consideration is in the form of commission.
- The entity does not establish prices and bears no credit risk.

The entity would therefore conclude that it is acting as an agent and that the only revenue to be recognised is the amounts received as commission.

1.17 Options for additional goods or services

If an option in the contract grants the customer the right to acquire additional goods or services at a discount which can only be obtained by entering into the contract, that option gives rise to a performance obligation.

Revenue is recognised when the additional future goods or services are transferred, or when the option expires. Revenue will be based on the stand-alone selling price of the goods or services, taking account of the discount.

If the option granted to the customer does not offer a discount, it is treated as a marketing offer and no contract exists until the customer exercises the option to purchase.

1.18 Customers' unexercised rights

When a customer pays in advance for goods or services the prepayment gives rise to a contract liability, which is derecognised when the performance obligation is satisfied.

If, having made a non-refundable prepayment, the customer does not exercise their right to receive the good or service, the unexercised right is often referred to as breakage. A breakage amount can be recognised as revenue if the pattern of rights exercised by the customer gives rise to the expectation that the entity will be entitled to a breakage amount. If this does not apply, it can be recognised as revenue when the likelihood of the customer exercising its rights becomes remote.

1.19 Non-refundable upfront fees

A non-refundable upfront fee is often charged at the beginning of a contract, such as joining fees in health club membership contracts.

In many cases upfront fees do not relate to the transfer of any promised good or service but are simply advance payments for **future** goods or services. In this case revenue is recognised when the future goods or services are provided.

If the fee relates to a good or service the entity should evaluate whether or not it amounts to a separate performance obligation. This depends on whether it results in the transfer of an asset to the customer. The fee may relate to costs incurred in setting up a contract, but these setup activities may not result in the transfer of services to the customer.

1.20 Licensing

A licence establishes a customer's rights to the intellectual property of an entity. Intellectual property can include software, music, franchises, patents, trademarks and copyrights.

The promise to grant a licence may be accompanied by the promise to transfer other goods or services to the customer. If the promise to grant the licence is **not** distinct from the promised goods or services, this is treated as a single performance obligation.

If the promise to grant the licence **is** distinct, it will constitute a separate performance obligation. The entity must establish whether the performance obligation is satisfied 'at a point in time' or 'over time'.

In this respect the entity should consider whether the nature of the entity's promise in granting the licence to a customer is to provide the customer with either:

(a) A **right to access** the entity's intellectual property as it exists throughout the licence period; or

(b) A **right to use** the entity's intellectual property as it exists at the point in time at which the licence is granted.

A **right to access** exists where the entity can make changes to the intellectual property throughout the licence period, the customer is exposed to the effects of these changes and the changes do not constitute the transfer of a good or service to the customer. In this case the promise to grant a licence is treated as a performance obligation satisfied over time and the entity recognises revenue over time by measuring the progress towards complete satisfaction of that performance obligation.

Where this does not apply, the nature of the entity's promise is the **right to use** its intellectual property as it exists at the point in time at which the licence is granted. This means that the customer can direct the use of, and obtain substantially all of the remaining benefits from, the licence at the point at which it is transferred. The point at which revenue can be recognised may be later than the date on which the licence is granted if the customer does not have immediate access to the intellectual property, for instance if it has to wait to be granted an access code.

When **royalties**, based on sales or on usage, are promised by the customer in exchange for a licence of intellectual property, revenue can be recognised at the later of the following occurrences:

(a) The sale or usage occurs; and
(b) The performance obligation to which the royalty has been allocated has been satisfied.

1.21 Repurchase agreements

Under a repurchase agreement an entity sells an asset and promises, or has the option, to repurchase it. Repurchase agreements generally come in three forms:

(a) An entity has an obligation to repurchase the asset (a forward contract).
(b) An entity has the right to repurchase the asset (a call option).
(c) An entity must repurchase the asset if requested to do so by the customer (a put option).

In the case of a forward or a call option the customer does not obtain control of the asset, even if it has physical possession. The entity will account for the contract as:

(a) A lease in accordance with IFRS 16, if the repurchase price is below the original selling price; or

(b) A financing arrangement if the repurchase price is equal to or greater than the original selling price. In this case the entity will recognise both the asset and a corresponding liability.

If the entity is obliged to repurchase at the request of the customer (a put option), it must consider whether or not the customer is likely to exercise that option.

If the repurchase price is lower than the original selling price and it is considered that the customer does not therefore have significant economic incentive to exercise the option, the contract should be accounted for as an outright sale, with a right of return.

If the repurchase price is greater than or equal to the original selling price and is above the expected market value of the option, the contract is treated as a financing arrangement.

1.21.1 Example: Contract with a call option

This example is taken from the standard.

An entity enters into a contract with a customer for the sale of a tangible asset on 1 January 20X7 for $1 million. The contract includes a call option that gives the entity the right to repurchase the asset for $1.1 million on or before 31 December 20X7.

This means that the customer does not obtain control of the asset, because the repurchase option means that it is limited in its ability to use and obtain benefit from the asset.

Solution

As control has not been transferred, the entity accounts for the transaction as a **financing arrangement**, because the exercise price is above the original selling price. The entity continues to recognise the asset and recognises the cash received as a financial liability. The difference of $0.1 million is recognised as interest expense.

If on 31 December 20X7 the option lapses unexercised, the customer now obtains control of the asset. The entity will derecognise the asset and recognise revenue of $1.1 million (the $1 million already received plus the $0.1 million charged to interest).

1.21.2 Example: Contract with a put option

The same contract as above includes instead a put option that obliges the entity to repurchase the asset at the customer's request for $900,000 on or before 31 December 20X7, at which time the market value is expected to be $750,000.

Solution

In this case the customer has a significant economic incentive to exercise the put option because the repurchase price exceeds the market value at the repurchase date. This means that control does not pass to the customer. Since the customer will be exercising the put option, this limits its ability to use or obtain benefit from the asset.

In this situation the entity accounts for the transaction as a lease in accordance with IFRS 16. The asset has been leased to the customer for the period up to the repurchase and the difference of $100,000 will be accounted for as payments received under a lease.

1.22 Consignment arrangements

When a product is delivered to a customer under a consignment arrangement, the customer (dealer) does not obtain control of the product at that point in time, so no revenue is recognised upon delivery.

Indicators of a consignment arrangement include:

(a) The product is controlled by the entity until a specified event occurs, such as the product is sold on, or a specified period expires.

(b) The entity can require the return of the product, or transfer it to another party.

(c) The customer (dealer) does not have an unconditional obligation to pay for the product

1.23 Bill-and-hold arrangements

Under a bill-and-hold arrangement goods are sold but remain in the possession of the seller for a specified period, perhaps because the customer lacks storage facilities.

An entity will need to determine at what point the customer obtains control of the product. For some contracts, control will not be transferred until the goods are delivered to the customer. For others, a customer may obtain control even though the goods remain in the entity's physical possession. In this case the entity would be providing custodial services to the customer over the customer's asset.

For a customer to have obtained control of a product in a bill and hold arrangement, the following criteria must all be met:

(a) The reason for the bill-and-hold must be substantive (for example, requested by the customer).
(b) The product must be separately identified as belonging to the customer.
(c) The product must be ready for physical transfer to the customer.
(d) The entity cannot have the ability to use the product or to transfer it to another customer.

1.23.1 Example: Bill and hold arrangement

This example is taken from the standard.

An entity enters into a contract with a customer on 1 January 20X8 for sale of a machine and spare parts. It takes two years to manufacture these and on 31 December 20X9 the customer pays for both the machine and the spare parts but only takes physical possession of the machine. The customer inspects and accepts the spare parts but requests that they continue to be stored at the entity's warehouse.

Solution

There are now three performance obligations – transfer of the machine, transfer of the spare parts and the custodial services. The transaction price is allocated to the three performance obligations and revenue is recognised when (or as) control passes to the customer.

The machine and the spare parts are both performance obligations satisfied at a point in time, and for both of them that point in time is 31 December 20X9. In the case of the spare parts, the customer has paid for them, the customer has legal title to them and the customer as control of them as they can remove them from storage at any time.

The custodial services are a performance obligation satisfied over time, so revenue will be recognised over the period during which the spare parts are stored.

Question — Applying the five step model

On 1 January 20X4, Angelo enters into a 12-month 'pay monthly' contract for a mobile phone. The contract is with TeleSouth, and terms of the plan are:

(a) Angelo receives a free handset on 1 January 20X4

(b) Angelo pays a monthly fee of $200, which includes unlimited free minutes. Angelo is billed on the last day of the month

Customers may purchase the same handset from TeleSouth for $500 without the payment plan. They may also enter into the payment plan without the handset, in which case the plan costs them $175 per month.

The company's year-end is 31 July 20X4.

Required

Show how TeleSouth should recognise revenue from this plan in accordance with IFRS 15 *Revenue from Contracts with Customers*. Your answer should give journal entries:

(a) On 1 January 20X4
(b) On 31 January 20X4

Answer

IFRS 15 requires application of its five-step process:

(i) **Identify the contract with a customer.** A contract can be written, oral or implied by customary business practices.

(ii) **Identify the separate performance obligations in the contract.** If a promised good or service is not distinct, it can be combined with others.

(iii) **Determine the transaction price.** This is the amount to which the entity expects to be **'entitled'**. For variable consideration, the probability – weighted expected amount is used. The effect of any credit losses shown as a separate line item (just below revenue).

(iv) **Allocate the transaction price to the separate performance obligations in the contract.** For multiple deliverables, the transaction price is allocated to each separate performance obligation in proportion to the **stand-alone selling price** at contract inception of each performance obligation.

(v) **Recognise revenue when (or as) the entity satisfies a performance obligation,** that is when the entity **transfers** a promised good or service to a customer. The good or service is only considered as transferred when the customer obtains **control** of it.

Application of the five-step process to TeleSouth

(i) **Identify the contract with a customer.** This is clear. TeleSouth has a 12-month contract with Angelo.

(ii) **Identify the separate performance obligations in the contract.** In this case there are two distinct performance obligations:

(1) The obligation to deliver a handset
(2) The obligation to provide network services for 12 months

(The obligation to deliver a handset would not be a distinct performance obligation if the handset could not be sold separately, but it is in this case because the handsets are sold separately.)

(iii) **Determine the transaction price.** This is straightforward: it is $2,400, that is 12 months × the monthly fee of $200.

(iv) **Allocate the transaction price to the separate performance obligations in the contract.** The transaction price is allocated to each separate performance obligation in proportion to the **stand-alone selling price** at contract inception of each performance obligation, that is the stand-alone price of the handset ($500 and the stand-alone price of the network services ($175 × 12 = $2,100.00):

Performance obligation	Stand-alone selling price $	% of total	Revenue (=relative selling price = $2,400 × %) $
Handset	500.00	19.2%	460.80
Network services	2,100.00	80.8%	1,939.20
Total	2,600.00	100%	2,400.00

(v) **Recognise revenue when (or as) the entity satisfies a performance obligation,** that is when the entity **transfers** a promised good or service to a customer. This applies to each of the performance obligations:

(1) When TeleSouth gives a handset to Angelo, it needs to recognise the revenue of $460.80.

(2) When TeleSouth provides network services to Angelo, it needs to recognise the total revenue of $1,939.20. It's practical to do it once per month as the billing happens.

Journal entries

On 1 January 20X4

The entries in the books of TeleSouth will be:

| DEBIT | Receivable (unbilled revenue) | $460.80 | |
| CREDIT | Revenue | | $460.80 |

Being recognition of revenue from the sale of the handset

On 31 January 20X4

The monthly payment from Angelo is split between amounts owing for network services and amounts owing for the handset.

DEBIT	Receivable (Angelo)	$200	
CREDIT	Revenue (1,939.20/12)		$161.60
CREDIT	Receivable (unbilled revenue)(460.80/12)		$38.40

Being recognition of revenue from monthly provision of network services and 'repayment' of handset

1.24 Presentation

Contracts with customers will be presented in an entity's statement of financial position as a contract liability, a contract asset or a receivable, depending on the relationship between the entity's performance and the customer's payment.

Receivable	If an entity's **right to consideration is unconditional** (only the passage of time is required before payment is due), it should recognise a receivable(*IFRS 15: para. 108*)
Contract asset	If the **entity transfers goods or services before the customer pays**, it should present the contract as a 'contract asset' if the entity's right to consideration is **conditional** on something other than the passage of time(eg the entity's performance) (*IFRS 15: para. 107*)
Contract liability	If customer **pays consideration** or the entity has a right to an amount of consideration that is unconditional (ie a receivable) **before the entity transfers the goods or services** to the customer, the entity should present the contract as a 'contract liability' when the payment is made or is due (whichever is earlier) (*IFRS 15: para. 106*)

1.25 Example: Satisfaction of performance obligations over time

Pretti Co commenced the construction of a bridge for a local authority on 1 January 20X7. The local authority will gain control of the bridge as it is completed and Pretti Co has no other use for the bridge. Pretti Co has an enforceable right to payment for the work completed to date. Pretti Co measures satisfaction of its performance obligations based on time incurred. It is estimated that it will take 80,000 labour hours to complete the bridge.

Total contract price	$750m
Costs incurred to date	$225m
Hours incurred to date	32,000
Estimated costs to completion	$340m
Amounts invoiced to customer to date	$290m
Amounts received from customer to date	$200m

Required

(i) Calculate the relevant balances relating to the contract for inclusion in the financial statements of Pretti Co for the year ended 31 December 20X7.

(ii) Recalculate the balances assuming the total contract price is $550m rather than $750m. All other information remains the same.

Solution

(i) We will calculate the amounts to be recognised for the contract in the statement of profit or loss and statement of financial position assuming the amount of performance obligation satisfied is calculated using the proportion of costs incurred method.

1 *Estimated profit*

	$m
Total contract price	750
Less costs incurred to date	(225)
Less estimated costs to completion	(340)
Estimated profit	185

If the contract was expected to be loss-making overall, the contract is considered onerous and would be accounted for under IAS 37. As it is expected to be profit making, we account for revenue based on satisfaction of performance obligations to date.

2 *Satisfaction of performance obligations*

Satisfaction of performance obligations is measured by reference to the number of hours incurred as a proportion of the total expected labour hours Costs to date / total estimated costs: 32,000 / 80,000 = 40%

Revenue is recognised based on 40% of the total contract price.

3 *Statement of profit or loss*

	$m
Revenue (40% × $750m)	300
Cost of sales	(225)
Profit	75

4 *Statement of financial position*

Current assets	
Trade receivables ($290m – 200m)	90
Contract asset (W)	10

	$m
Working: Revenue recognised	300
Less receivable	(290)
Contract asset	10

As all amounts billed have been received, there is no receivable.

(ii) If the total contract price was $550m, the contract would be loss making. Loss making contracts are recognised as onerous contracts under IAS 37.

1 *Estimated loss*

	$m
Total contract price	550
Less costs incurred to date	(225)
Less estimated costs to completion	(340)
Estimated loss	(15)

The loss is recognised in full as a provision for an onerous contract. It is accounted for by increasing cost of sales and creating a separate loss provision.

2   *Statement of profit or loss*

	$m
Revenue (40% × $550)	220
Cost of sales (revenue + loss on onerous contract)	(235)
Loss	(15)

3   *Statement of financial position*

	$m
Current assets	
Trade receivables ($290m – $200m)	90
Current liabilities	
Contract liability (W)	70
Provision for onerous contracts	15

Working

Revenue recognised	220
Less receivable	(290)
Contract liability	(70)

1.26 Disclosure

The following amounts should be disclosed unless they have been presented separately in the financial statements in accordance with other standards:

(a)   Revenue recognised from contracts with customers, disclosed separately from other sources of revenue

(b)   Any impairment losses recognised (in accordance with IFRS 9) on any receivables or contract assets arising from an entity's contracts with customers, disclosed separately from other impairment losses

(c)   The opening and closing balances of receivables, contract assets and contract liabilities from contracts with customers

(d)   Revenue recognised in the reporting period that was included in the contract liability balance at the beginning of the period

(e)   Revenue recognised in the reporting period from performance obligations satisfied in previous periods (such as changes in transaction price)

Other information that should be provided;

(a)   An explanation of significant changes in the contract asset and liability balances during the reporting period

(b)   Information regarding the entity's performance obligations, including when they are typically satisfied (upon delivery, upon shipment, as services are rendered etc.), significant payment terms (such as when payment is typically due) and details of any agency transactions, obligations for returns or refunds and warranties granted

(c)   The aggregate amount of the transaction price allocated to the performance obligations that are not fully satisfied at the end of the reporting period and an explanation of when the entity expects to recognise these amounts as revenue

(d)   Judgements, and changes in judgements, made in applying the standard that significantly affect the determination of the amount and timing of revenue from contracts with customers

(e)   Assets recognised from the costs to obtain or fulfil a contract with a customer. This would include pre-contract costs and set-up costs. The method of amortisation should also be disclosed.

1.27 Likely impact on companies

Revenue is generally an entity's most important financial performance indicator, and one extensively scrutinised by analysts and investors. IFRS 15 is likely to impact on **the timing, measurement, recognition and disclosure of revenue**. These impacts will require adjustments **in policies, procedures, internal controls and systems.**

1.27.1 Timing of revenue

By far the most significant change in IFRS 15 is to the **pattern of revenue reporting. Even if the total revenue reported does not change,** the timing will change in many cases.

The example of TeleSouth, our fictitious company above, illustrates this point. Under IAS 18 *Revenue*, the old standard, TeleSouth would **not recognise any revenue from the sale of handset,** on the grounds that TeleSouth has given it to Angelo free. TeleSouth would view the free handset as a cost of acquiring a new customer, and the cost would be recognised in profit or loss immediately.

Revenue from the provision of network services would be recognised on a monthly basis as follows:

DEBIT	Receivable/Cash	$200	
CREDIT	Revenue		$200

TeleSouth's year-end is 31 July 20X4, which means that the contract falls into more than one accounting period. The impact of changing from IAS 18 to IFRS 15 for TeleSouth, for the year ended 31 July 20X4 is as follows:

Performance obligation	Under IAS 18	Under IFRS 15
	$	$
Handset	00.00	460.80
Network services: (200 × 6)/(161.60 × 6)	1,200.00	969.60
Total	1,200.00	1,430.40

The variation in timing has tax implications, and if the tax rate changes, may have an overall effect on profit.

Question — Recognition

Discuss under what circumstances, if any, revenue might be recognised at the following stages of a sale.

(a) Goods are acquired by the business which it confidently expects to resell very quickly.
(b) A customer places a firm order for goods.
(c) Goods are delivered to the customer.
(d) The customer is invoiced for goods.
(e) The customer pays for the goods.
(f) The customer's cheque in payment for the goods has been cleared by the bank.

Answer

(a) A sale must never be recognised before the goods have even been ordered by a customer. There is no certainty about the value of the sale, nor when it will take place, even if it is virtually certain that goods will be sold.

(b) A sale must never be recognised when the customer places an order. No performance obligation has been satisfied at that point. Even though the order will be for a specific quantity of goods at a specific price, control over the goods has not yet been transferred to the customer. The customer may cancel the order, the supplier might be unable to deliver the goods as ordered or it may be decided that the customer is not a good credit risk.

(c) A sale will be recognised when delivery of the goods is made only when:

    (i) The sale is for cash, and so the cash is received at the same time; or
    (ii) The sale is on credit and the customer accepts delivery (eg by signing a delivery note).

(d) The critical event for a credit sale is usually the despatch of an invoice to the customer. At that point the performance obligation has been satisfied. There is then a legally enforceable debt, payable on specified terms, for a completed sale transaction.

(e) The critical event for a cash sale is when delivery takes place and when cash is received; both take place at the same time.

It would be too cautious or 'prudent' to await cash payment for a credit sale transaction before recognising the sale, unless the customer is a high credit risk and there is a serious doubt about his ability or intention to pay.

(f) It would again be over-cautious to wait for clearance of the customer's cheques before recognising sales revenue. Such a precaution would only be justified in cases where there is a very high risk of the bank refusing to honour the cheque.

2 Off balance sheet finance

FAST FORWARD

The subject of **off balance sheet finance** is a complex one which has plagued the accountancy profession. In practice, off balance sheet finance schemes are often very sophisticated and they are beyond the range of this syllabus.

Key term

'**Off balance sheet finance**' is the funding or refinancing of a company's operations in such a way that, under legal requirements and existing accounting conventions, some or all of the finance may not be shown in its statement of financial position.

'Off balance sheet transactions' are transactions which meet the above objective. These transactions may involve the **removal of assets** from the statement of financial position, as well as liabilities, and they are likely to have a significant impact on the profit or loss.

2.1 Why off balance sheet finance exists

Why might company managers wish to enter into such transactions?

(a) In some countries, companies traditionally have a lower level of gearing than companies in other countries. Companies in Germany, for example, tend to have relatively high gearing due to the relationships between companies and their banks. Off balance sheet finance is used to **keep gearing low**, probably because of the views of some analysts and brokers that high gearing is high risk.

(b) A company may need to keep its gearing down in order to stay within the terms of **loan covenants** imposed by lenders.

(c) A quoted company with high borrowings is often expected (by analysts and others) to declare a **rights issue** in order to reduce gearing. This has an adverse effect on a company's share price and so off balance sheet financing is used to reduce gearing **and** the expectation of a rights issue.

(d) Analysts' short term views are a problem for companies **developing assets** which are not producing income during the development stage. Such companies will match the borrowings associated with such developing assets, along with the assets themselves, outside the statement of financial position. They are brought back into statement of financial position once income is being generated by the assets. This process keeps return on capital employed higher than it would have been during the development stage.

(e) Groups of companies have excluded **subsidiaries** from consolidation in an off balance sheet transaction because they carry out completely different types of business and have different characteristics. The usual example is a leasing company (in say a retail group) which has a high level of gearing.

You can see from this brief list of reasons that the overriding motivation is to avoid **misinterpretation**. In other words, the company does not trust the analysts or other users to understand the reasons for a transaction and so avoids any effect such transactions might have by taking them 'off balance sheet'. Unfortunately, the position of the company is then misstated and the user of the financial statements is misled.

You must understand that not all forms of 'off balance sheet finance' are undertaken for cosmetic or accounting reasons. Some transactions are carried out to **limit or isolate risk**, to reduce interest costs and so on. In other words, these transactions are in the best interests of the company, not merely a cosmetic repackaging of figures which would normally appear in the statement of financial position.

2.2 The off balance sheet finance problem

The result of the use of increasingly sophisticated off balance sheet finance transactions is a situation where the users of financial statements do not have a proper or clear view of the **state of the company's affairs**. The disclosures required by national company law and accounting standards did not in the past provide sufficient rules for disclosure of off balance sheet finance transactions and so very little of the true nature of the transaction was exposed.

Whatever the purpose of such transactions, **insufficient disclosure** creates a problem. This problem has been debated over the years by the accountancy profession and other interested parties and some progress has been made (see the later sections of this chapter). Company collapses during recessions have often revealed much higher borrowings than originally thought, because part of the borrowing was not included in the statement of financial position.

The main argument used for disallowing off balance sheet finance is that the true **substance** of the transactions should be shown, not merely the **legal form**, particularly when it is exacerbated by poor disclosure.

3 Substance over form

Substance over form is not defined in accounting standards, however, the Conceptual Framework refers to substance in its description of faithful representation. It states that 'to be useful, financial information must not only represent relevant phenomena, but it must also faithfully represent the substance of the phenomena that it purports to represent.' (Conceptual Framework, para. 2.12)

In many cases, the substance of a transaction and its legal form are the same. However, where that is not the case, the entity must report the substance.

3.1 IAS 24 *Related Party Disclosures*

IAS 24 requires financial statements to disclose fully material transactions undertaken with a related party by the reporting entity, **regardless of any price charged** (see Chapter 20).

3.2 Consolidated financial statements

This is perhaps the most important area of off balance sheet finance which has been prevented by the application of the substance over form concept. The use of **quasi-subsidiaries** was very common in the 1980s. These may be defined as follows.

Key term

> A **quasi-subsidiary** of a reporting entity is a company, trust, partnership or other vehicle that, though not fulfilling the definition of a subsidiary, is directly or indirectly controlled by the reporting entity and gives rise to benefits for that entity that are in substance no different from those that would arise were the vehicle a subsidiary.

The main off balance sheet transactions involving quasi-subsidiaries were as follows.

(a) **Sale of assets.** The sale of assets to a quasi-subsidiary was carried out to remove the associated borrowings from the statement of financial position and so reduce gearing, or perhaps so that the company could credit a profit in such a transaction. The asset could then be rented back to the vendor company under an operating lease (no capitalisation required by the lessee). This can no longer happen since the introduction of IFRS 16.

(b) **Purchase of companies or assets**. One reason for such a purchase through a quasi-subsidiary is if the acquired entity is expected to make losses in the near future. Post-acquisition losses can be avoided by postponing the date of acquisition to the date the holding company acquires the entity from the quasi-subsidiary.

(c) **Business activities conducted outside the group**. Such a subsidiary might have been excluded through a quasi-subsidiary or not consolidated under an excuse of 'dissimilar activities'. Exclusion from consolidation might be undertaken because the activities are high risk and have high gearing.

The current accounting standard applicable to accounting for subsidiaries within the group financial statements is IFRS 10 *Consolidated Financial Statements*. Prior to this, the applicable standard was IAS 27 *Consolidated and Separate Financial Statements*, issued initially in 1989 and revised in 2003 and 2008. This standard introduced a definition of a subsidiary based on **control** rather than just ownership rights, thus substantially reducing the effectiveness of this method of off-balance sheet finance. IAS 27 defined control of another entity as follows.

Key term

> **Control** is the power to govern the financial and operating policies of an entity so as to obtain benefit from its activities. (IAS 27)

IAS 27 stated that control exists when:

(a) The parent has a **majority of the voting rights** in the subsidiary (possibly **by agreement** with other members); or

(b) The parent can appoint or remove a **majority of the** board of the subsidiary; or

(c) The parent can **direct the operating and financial policies** through a statute or agreement; or

(d) The parent can cast the **majority of votes** at a board meeting of directors (or equivalent).

The main effects of this definition on the use of quasi-subsidiaries were as follows.

(a) The use of 'voting rights' rather than 'equity shares' prevented the use of **company structures** which gave the benefits of ownership to one class of shareholder without the appearance of doing so, eg a company has 100 'A' shares with 10 votes each and 900 'B' shares with one vote each.

(b) The use of 'the right to appoint or remove a majority of the board' prevented control through **differential voting rights** at board meetings.

IAS 27 therefore **curtailed drastically** the use of quasi-subsidiaries for off balance sheet finance. More complex schemes are likely to be curtailed by the issue of IFRS 10 *Consolidated Financial Statements* which uses control as the single basis for consolidation (see Chapter 11), the IASB's *Conceptual Framework* and by various other standards (see below).

You may also hear the term **creative accounting** used in the context of reporting the substance of transactions. This can be defined simply as the manipulation of figures for a desired result. Remember, however, that it is very rare for a company, its directors or employees to manipulate results for the purpose of fraud. The major consideration is usually the effect the results will have on the company's share price. Some areas open to abuse (although some of these loopholes have been closed) are given below and you should by now understand how these can distort a company results.

(a) Income recognition and cut-off
(b) Manipulation of reserves
(c) Revaluations and depreciation
(d) Window dressing
(e) Changes in accounting policy

Creative accounting, off balance sheet finance and related matters (in particular how ratio analysis can be used to discover these practices) often come up in articles in the financial press. Find a library, preferably a good technical library, which can provide you with copies of back issues of such newspapers or journals and look for articles on creative accounting.

Question
Manipulation

One of the ways in which financial statements can be manipulated is through the use of extraordinary items.

True or false?

Answer

False, though true in the past. IAS 1 *Presentation of Financial Statements* outlaws extraordinary items.

4 Common forms of off balance sheet finance

FAST FORWARD

We will look at some of the **major types** of off balance sheet finance, including factoring, sale and leaseback and securitisation.

How does the theory of the *Conceptual Framework* **apply in practice**, to real transactions? The rest of this section looks at some complex transactions that occur frequently in practice. We will consider how the principles of the *Conceptual Framework* would be applied to these transactions.

- Factoring of receivables/debts (IFRS 15)
- Securitised assets (IFRS 9)
- Loan transfers (IFRS 9)

Exam focus point

These examples are taken from a UK Standard on reporting the substance of transactions, but that standard uses almost the same definitions for assets, liabilities, recognition, etc as the IASB *Conceptual Framework*, and so these notes are applicable internationally. Note also that, in all the cases discussed, there may be situations somewhere between the two extremes given in each.

4.1 Factoring of receivables/debts

Where debts or receivables are factored, the original supplier **sells the debts to the factor**. The sales price may be fixed at the outset or may be adjusted later. It is also common for the factor to offer a credit facility that allows the seller to draw upon a proportion of the amounts owed.

In order to determine the correct accounting treatment it is necessary to consider whether the significant risks and rewards of ownership of the debts have been passed on to the factor, or whether the factor is, in effect, providing a loan on the security of the debtors. If the seller has to **pay interest** on the difference between the amounts advanced to them and the amounts that the factor has received, and if the seller bears the **risks of non-payment** by the debtor, then the indications would be that the transaction is, in effect, a loan.

4.1.1 Summary of indications of appropriate treatment

The following is a summary of indicators of the appropriate treatment.

Indications the debts are *not an asset* of the seller	Indications that the debts are an *asset* of the seller
Transfer is for **a single non-returnable fixed sum**.	**Finance cost varies** with speed of collection of debts, eg: • By adjustment to consideration for original transfer; or • Subsequent transfers priced to recover costs of earlier transfers.
There is **no recourse** to the seller for losses.	There is **full recourse** to the seller for losses.
Factor is paid **all amounts** received from the factored debts (and no more). Seller has no rights to further sums from the factor.	Seller is required to **repay** amounts received from the factor on or before a set date, regardless of timing or amounts of collections from customers.

4.1.2 Required accounting

Where the seller has retained no significant risks and rewards of ownership relating to the debts and has no obligation to repay amounts received from the factors, the receivables should be derecognised from its statement of financial position and no liability shown in respect of the proceeds received from the factor. A profit or loss should be recognised, calculated as the difference between the carrying amount of the debts and the proceeds received.

Where the seller does retain the significant risks and rewards of ownership, a gross asset (equivalent in amount to the gross amount of the receivables) should be shown in the statement of financial position of the seller within assets, and a corresponding liability in respect of the proceeds received from the factor should be shown within liabilities. The interest element of the factor's charges should be recognised as it accrues and included in profit or loss with other interest charges. Other factoring costs should be similarly accrued and included in profit or loss within the appropriate caption.

4.2 Securitised assets

Securitisation is very common in the financial services industry, and the assets that are most commonly securitised are mortgages and credit card financial statements, although hire purchase loans, trade debts and even property and inventories are sometimes securitised. **Blocks of assets** are thus financed, rather than the company's general business.

The normal procedure is for the assets to be transferred by the person who held them (the originator) to a special purpose company (the issuer) in exchange for cash. The issuer will use the proceeds of an issue of debentures or loan notes to pay for the assets. The shares in the issuer are usually held by a third party so that it does not need to be consolidated. The issuer will usually have a very small share capital, and so most of the risk will be borne by the people who lent it the money through the debentures to pay for the assets. For this reason there is usually some form of insurance taken out on the assets to give some security for the lenders.

4.2.1 Summary of indications as to accounting treatment

The following is a summary of indications of the appropriate treatment.

	Indications that the securitised assets are *not assets* of the seller	Indications that the securitised assets are *assets* of the originator
Originator's individual financial statements	Transaction price is **arm's length price** for an outright sale.	Transaction price is **not arm's length price** for an outright sale.
	Transfer is for a **single, non-returnable fixed sum**.	Proceeds received are **returnable**, or there is a provision whereby the originator may keep the securitised assets on repayment of the loan notes or reacquire them.
	There is **no recourse** to the originator for losses.	There is or may be **full recourse** to the originator for losses, eg: • Originator's directors are unable or unwilling to state that it is not obliged to fund any losses • Noteholders have not agreed in writing that they will seek repayment only from funds generated by the securitised assets
Originator's consolidated financial statements	Issuer is owned by an **independent third party** that made a substantial capital investment, has control of the issuer, and has the benefits and risks of its net assets.	Issuer is a **subsidiary** or quasi-subsidiary of the originator.

4.2.2 Required accounting: Originator's financial statements

Where the originator has retained no significant risks and rewards of ownership relating to the securitised assets and has no obligation to repay the proceeds of the note issue, the asset should be derecognised from its statement of financial position, and no liability shown in respect of the proceeds of the note issue. A profit or loss should be recognised, calculated as the difference between the carrying amount of the assets and the proceeds received.

Where the originator has retained the significant risks and rewards of ownership, a gross asset (equal in amount to the gross amount of the securitised assets) should be shown on the statement of financial position of the originator within assets, and a corresponding liability in respect of the proceeds of the note issue shown within liabilities. No gain or loss should be recognised at the time the securitisation is entered into (unless adjustment to the carrying value of the asset independent of the securitisation is required).

4.2.3 Required accounting: issuer's financial statements

The requirements set out in the paragraphs above for the originator's individual financial statements also apply to the issuer's financial statements. In most cases the issuer will be required to show the gross amounts, in which case the provisions of Section 4.2.2 will apply.

4.3 Loan transfers

These are arrangements where a loan is transferred to a transferee from an original lender. This will usually be done by the **assignment of rights and obligations** by the lender, or the **creation of a new agreement** between the borrower and the transferee. The same principles apply to loan transfers as to debt factoring and securitised assets.

4.3.1 Summary of indications of appropriate treatment

Indications that the loan is *not* a *liability* of the lender	Indications the loan is a *liability* of the lender
Transfer is for a **single, non-returnable fixed sum**.	The proceeds received are **returnable** in the event of losses occurring on the loans.
There is **no recourse** to the lender for losses from any cause.	There is **full recourse** to the lender for losses.
Transferee is paid **all amounts received** from the loans (and no more), as and when received. Lender has no rights to further sums from the loans or the transferee.	Lender is required to **repay amounts received** from the transferee on or before a set date, regardless of the timing or amount of payments by the borrowers.

4.3.2 Required accounting

Where the lender has retained no significant risks and rewards of ownership relating to the loans and has no obligation to repay the transferee, the loans should be derecognised from its statement of financial position and no liability shown in respect of the amounts received from the transferee. A profit or loss may arise for the lender. Where the profit or loss is realised in cash it should be recognised, calculated as the difference between the carrying amount of the loans and the cash proceeds received. Where, however, the lender's profit or loss is not realised in cash and there are doubts as to its amount, full provision should be made for any expected loss but recognition of any gain, to the extent it is in doubt, should be deferred until cash has been received.

Where the lender has retained the significant risks and rewards of ownership, a gross asset (equivalent in amount to the gross amount of the loans) should be shown in the statement of financial position of the lender within assets, and a corresponding liability in respect of the amounts received from the transferee should be shown within creditors. No gain or loss should be recognised at the time of the transfer (unless adjustment to the carrying value of the loan independent of the transfer is required).

Chapter roundup

- Revenue recognition is straightforward in most business transactions, but some situations are more complicated.
- IFRS 15 *Revenue from Contracts with Customers* is concerned with the **recognition of revenues** arising from fairly common transactions.
    - The sale of goods
    - The rendering of services
    - The use by others of entity assets yielding interest, royalties and dividends

    Generally revenue is recognised when the entity has transferred promised goods or services to the customer. The standard sets out five steps for the recognition process.
- The subject of **off balance sheet** finance is a complex one which has plagued the accountancy profession. In practice, off balance sheet finance schemes are often very sophisticated and they are beyond the range of this syllabus.
- We will look at some of the **major types** of off balance sheet finance, including factoring, sale and leaseback and securitisation.

Quick quiz

1. Revenue should include sales tax. True or false?
2. How is revenue from royalties recognised?
3. Why do entities want to use 'off balance sheet' finance?
4. What is a quasi-subsidiary?
5. What are the common features of transactions whose substance is not really apparent?
6. When should a transaction be recognised?

Answers to quick quiz

1. False

2. Royalty revenue is recognised on an accruals basis in accordance with the substance of the relevant agreement.

3. Often off-balance sheet finance is a method of removing assets and liabilities from the statement of financial position to present a better picture of financial position

4. An entity that does not fulfil the definition of a subsidiary but is directly or indirectly controlled by the reporting entity and gives rise to benefits that are in substance no different from those arising if it were a subsidiary.

5. (a) The legal title is separated from the significant risks and rewards of ownership
   (b) The transaction is linked to others so that the commercial effect cannot be understood without reference to the complete series.
   (c) The transaction includes one or more options under such terms that it is likely the option(s) will be exercised.

6. When it is probable that a future inflow or outflow of benefit to the entity will occur and the item can be measured in monetary terms with sufficient reliability.

End of chapter question

IFRS 15

Caravans Deluxe is a retailer of caravans, dormer vans and mobile homes, with a year end of 30 June 20X8. It is having trouble selling one model – the $30,000 Mini-Lux, and so is offering incentives for customers who buy this model before 31 May 20X7:

(a) Customers buying this model before 31 May 20X7 will receive a period of interest free credit, provided they pay a non-refundable deposit of $3,000, an instalment of $15,000 on 1 August 20X7 and the balance of $12,000 on 1 August 20X9.

(b) Equipment for the caravan, normally worth $1,500, is included free in the price of the caravan.

On 1 May 20X7, a customer agrees to buy a Mini-Lux caravan, paying the deposit of $3,000. Delivery is arranged for 1 August 20X7.

As the sale has now been made, the director of Caravans Deluxe wishes to recognise the full sale price of the caravan, $30,000, in the accounts for the year ended 30 June 20X7.

Required

Show how the IFRS 15 five-step plan is applied to this sale. Assume a 10% discount rate. Show the journal entries for this treatment.

IFRS for SMEs

Topic list	Syllabus reference
1 Introduction	LO4
2 Who can use the IFRS for SMEs?	LO4
3 Structure of the IFRS for SMEs	LO4
4 Concepts and pervasive principles	LO4
5 Financial statements	LO4
6 Group financial statements	LO2, LO4
7 Financial instruments	LO4
8 Assets	LO4
9 Liabilities	LO4
10 Other topics	LO4

Introduction

The IFRS for SMEs provides simplified accounting for eligible entities. Local legislative authorities can decide which entities can or must use the IFRS for SMEs within a given jurisdiction.

1 Introduction

> **FAST FORWARD**
>
> The IFRS for SMEs was developed to provide a simpler accounting regime within the IFRS Accounting Standard framework for non-publicly listed entities. IFRS for SMEs is a stand-alone standard.

1.1 Why was the IFRS for SMEs developed?

Full IFRS Accounting Standards cover a wide range of accounting issues, and are specifically designed to meet the needs of investors in, and creditors of, publicly listed companies. The standards are often complex and have extensive disclosure requirements.

In making these standards more relevant to large, listed companies, they have become less relevant to the needs of the users of small and medium-sized entities (SMEs). These users are more focused on cash flows, liquidity and solvency.

The characteristics of SMEs mean that applying full IFRS Accounting Standards to them has the following issues:

Relevance	Some IFRS Accounting Standards are **not relevant** to small and medium-sized company accounts; for example, a company with equity that is not quoted on a stock exchange has no need to comply with IAS 33 *Earnings per Share*.
Cost to prepare	One of the underlying principles of financial reporting is that the **cost and effort** required to prepare financial statements **should not exceed the benefits** to users. This applies to all reporting entities, not just smaller ones. However, smaller entities are more likely to make use of this as a reason not to comply with full IFRS Accounting Standards.
Materiality	IFRS Accounting Standards apply to **material** items. In the case of smaller entities, the amount that is material may be very small in monetary terms. However, the effect of not reporting that item may be material by nature in that it would mislead users of the financial statements. Consider, for example, IAS 24 *Related Party Disclosures*. Smaller entities may well rely on trade with relatives of the directors/shareholders which are relatively small in value, but essential to the operations of the entity and should therefore be disclosed.

The IFRS for SMEs was therefore developed in order to provide a simpler accounting regime which:

- Is relevant to the needs of users of private entity accounts;
- Is understandable across borders; and
- Takes into account cost-benefit considerations.

One particular aim of the IASB in developing the IFRS for SMEs was to provide a standard for entities in countries that have no national GAAP. The IFRS for SMEs makes an international accounting framework accessible to entities that do not have the resources to adopt full IFRS Accounting Standards.

1.2 IFRS for SMEs vs full IFRS Accounting Standards

Although the IFRS for SMEs is based on full IFRS Accounting Standards, a number of aspects of full IFRS Accounting Standards are omitted, whilst others are simplified:

- Certain topics which are not relevant to smaller and private entities are omitted completely (see below).
- Recognition and measurement rules are simplified.
- Where there is a policy choice in full IFRS Accounting Standards, the IFRS for SMEs generally adopts the simpler option.
- Disclosure requirements are significantly reduced (from 3,000 disclosures in full IFRS Accounting Standards to approximately 300).
- Much of the implementation guidance within full IFRS Accounting Standards is omitted.

1.2.1 Omitted topics

Topics which are less relevant to non-publicly accountable entities have been omitted completely. These include:

- The accounting requirements for non-current assets held for sale (IFRS 5)
- Segment reporting (IFRS 8)
- Earnings per share (IAS 33)
- Interim financial reporting (IAS 34)
- Insurance contracts (IFRS 4*)
- Accounting and reporting by retirement benefit plans (IAS 26*)

Exam focus point

*IFRS 4 and IAS 26 are not within the Paper 13 syllabus.

2 Who can use the IFRS for SMEs?

FAST FORWARD

The IFRS for SMEs defines those entities which are eligible to use it as entities which do not have public accountability and which publish general purpose financial statements.

2.1 Eligibility

Despite the name of the standard, eligibility to use the IFRS for SMEs is not dependent on the size of an entity. In the context of the standard, SMEs are defined as entities that:

- Do not have public accountability; and
- Publish general purpose financial statements for external users.

Subsidiaries of a parent company which uses full IFRS may use the IFRS for SMEs as long as they meet the definition given above. The ED states that a parent company may use the IFRS for SMEs in its own separate financial statements if it meets the criteria, even if certain subsidiaries do not.

2.1.1 Public accountability

An entity has public accountability if:

(1) Its debt or equity instruments are traded in a public market, or the entity is in the process of issuing debt or equity instruments which will be traded in a public market; or

(2) It holds assets in a fiduciary capacity for a broad group of outsiders as one of its primary businesses. The ED clarifies that this may be but will not necessarily be the case for banks, mutual funds etc.

2.1.2 General purpose financial statements

General purpose financial statements are financial statements which are directed towards the common needs of a wide range of users.

Question — Public accountability

Give examples of types of companies which are publicly accountable and therefore not permitted to use the IFRS for SMEs.

Answer

Companies may not use the IFRS for SMEs if they are publicly accountable. A company is publicly accountable if:

(1) Its debt or equity instruments are listed in a public market or are in the process of being listed eg in the UK, companies which are listed (or will be listed) on the London Stock Exchange (LSE) or Alternative Investment Market (AIM).

(2) It holds assets in a fiduciary capacity for a broad group of outsiders as one of its primary businesses. Banks, insurance entities, securities brokers and dealers and pension funds are all examples of companies which hold assets in a fiduciary capacity for a range of third parties. However it must also be considered (under the ED) whether these are primary businesses.

2.2 Application of the standard

The decision as to which entities are permitted or required to use the IFRS for SMEs is a matter for the relevant authorities in individual jurisdictions, and changes to local laws are likely to be required before the standard can be adopted in practice. Currently, some countries require the use of IFRS Accounting Standards (including the IFRS for SMEs) for unlisted companies; others allow its use and some prohibit the use of IFRS.

Very few countries currently require the use of the IFRS for SMEs for unlisted companies; these include Antigua and Barbuda.

Countries which allow the use of the IFRS for SMEs for unlisted companies include Barbados, South Africa and the USA.

Countries which currently do not permit the use of IFRS Accounting Standards for unlisted companies include India and Thailand.

2.3 Advantages of adopting the IFRS for SMEs

There are a number of potential advantages to companies of applying the IFRS for SMEs rather than local GAAP. Depending on the requirements of local GAAP, these may include:

- Improvements in the quality of financial reporting
- Less onerous reporting requirements than local GAAP

For the accounting boards of the countries themselves, use of the IFRS for SMEs may remove the need to maintain local GAAP.

In addition, some countries, for example Bahrain and Chile, require all companies to use IFRS Accounting Standards in their financial reporting. In these countries the IFRS for SMEs provides a less onerous option than full IFRS.

The obvious downside of adopting a new GAAP, even where it is simplified, is the management of the transition and associated costs, including new software and training.

3 Structure of the IFRS for SMEs

FAST FORWARD — The standard is organised into 35 sections, each dealing with a specific area of accounting.

The IFRS for SMEs is organised into sections, each relating to a specific area of accounting. It is written clearly and concisely and is significantly easier to read than full IFRS Accounting Standards. The standard is accompanied by a glossary of terms, illustrative financial statements and a disclosure checklist.

The sections of the standard are as follows:

1	Small and medium-sized entities
2	Concepts and pervasive principles
3	Financial statement presentation
4	Statement of financial position
5	Statement of comprehensive income and income statement
6	Statement of changes in equity and statement of income and retained earnings
7	Statement of cash flows
8	Notes to the financial statements
9	Consolidated and separate financial statements
10	Accounting policies, estimates and errors
11	Basic financial instruments
12	Other financial instruments issues
13	Inventories
14	Investments in associates
15	Investments in joint ventures
16	Investment property
17	Property, plant and equipment
18	Intangible assets other than goodwill
19	Business combinations and goodwill
20	Leases
21	Provisions and contingencies
22	Liabilities and equity
23	Revenue
24	Government grants
25	Borrowing costs
26	Share-based payment
27	Impairment of assets
28	Employee benefits
29	Income tax
30	Foreign currency translation
31	Hyperinflation
32	Events after the end of the reporting period
33	Related party disclosures
34	Specialised activities
35	Transition to the IFRS for SMEs

Note that as the standard was last updated in 2015, certain terms do not correspond to those used in full IFRS. For example, IAS 1 has recently amended the name of the income statement to become statement of profit or loss and other comprehensive income, yet the IFRS for SMEs still uses the 'old' terms.

An exposure draft was issued in 2022 for the third edition of IFRS for SMEs. After feedback was received a revised exposure draft was issued in March 2024.

The remainder of this chapter groups related sections of the IFRS for SMEs in order to explain the accounting requirements of the standard. In particular we shall focus on **differences from full IFRS**. The content of the first section of the standard dealing with the definition of small and medium-sized entities was covered in Section 2 above. Section 34 Specialised activities concerns agriculture and extractive industries and is outside the scope of your syllabus.

4 Concepts and pervasive principles

FAST FORWARD

The IFRS for SMEs includes a section on concepts and pervasive principles which is an abbreviated form of the *Conceptual Framework*.

Section 2 of the IFRS for SMEs deals with concepts and pervasive principles. This section is based on the IASB's 2010 *Conceptual Framework,* and there are therefore some inconsistencies with the 2018 version. It includes explanation of the qualitative characteristics of information, defines the elements of the financial statements and provides guidance on their recognition and measurement. In addition this section clarifies that the accruals basis of accounting should be used in preparing financial statements other than the statement of cash flows and that offsetting of assets and liabilities is not allowed other than where specifically required or permitted by the IFRS for SMEs.

4.1 Qualitative characteristics

The qualitative characteristics of financial information are listed as:

- Understandability
- Relevance
- Materiality
- Reliability
- Substance over form
- Prudence
- Completeness
- Comparability
- Timeliness

These characteristics are not identical to those within the *Conceptual Framework*, however they are very similar. The IFRS for SMEs requires that in applying the characteristics, a balance is achieved between benefit and cost.

Question — Qualitative characteristics

Explain what is meant by each of the characteristics of financial information listed in the IFRS for SMEs.

Answer

Understandability	Information should be presented so as to be understandable to users with a reasonable knowledge; information should not be omitted on the grounds that it may be difficult to understand.
Relevance	Information provided should be relevant to the decision-making needs of users.
Materiality	Information is material and so relevant if its omission or misstatement could influence the economic decisions of users.
Reliability	Information must be reliable; this is the case where it is free from material error and bias and represents faithfully what it purports to represent.
Substance over form	Transactions and events should be presented in accordance with their commercial substance and not merely their legal form.
Prudence	Prudence (a degree of caution) should be exercised when making judgements so that assets or income are not overstated and liabilities or expenses are not understated.
Completeness	The information in the financial statements should be complete within the boundaries of materiality and cost.
Comparability	Users must be able to compare the financial statements of an entity through time to identify trends and compare the financial statements of one entity with another. Therefore consistency must be applied in accounting treatment and accounting policies disclosed.
Timeliness	Information should be provided within the decision time frame of the

users of the financial statements.

4.2 Elements of the financial statements, their recognition and measurement

The IFRS for SMEs defines assets, liabilities, equity, income and expenses in accordance with the 2010 *Conceptual Framework*.

Items are recognised when the definition of an element is met and:

(1) It is probable that any future economic benefit associated with the item will flow to or from the entity; and

(2) The item has a cost or value that can be measured reliably.

These recognition criteria are identical to those within full IFRS.

The measurement bases specified by the IFRS for SMEs are historical cost and fair value. In most cases the standard requires items to be measured at historical cost, however in some cases it requires revaluation to fair value where such information is readily available.

5 Financial statements

FAST FORWARD

> The IFRS for SMEs is generally consistent with IAS 1 in respect of requirements for the presentation of financial statements, although there is some relaxation of the full IFRS requirements.

Sections 3–8 of the IFRS for SMEs deal with the content and presentation of a set of financial statements. The requirements of these sections are generally consistent with those of IAS 1 *Presentation of Financial Statements*. Section 10 of the standard deals with accounting policies, estimates and errors; this section is generally consistent with IAS 8 *Accounting Policies, Changes in Accounting Estimates and Errors*.

5.1 Financial statement presentation

Section 3 of the IFRS for SMEs deals with fair presentation, compliance with the IFRS for SMEs, going concern, the frequency of reporting, consistency of presentation, the provision of comparative information, materiality and aggregation and a complete set of financial statements.

In respect of compliance with the IFRS for SMEs, Section 3 allows departure from the requirements of the standard only in very rare circumstances, in which case extra disclosures are required.

A complete set of financial statements as required by the IFRS for SMEs includes:

Statement required by IFRS for SMEs	Difference from IFRS
A statement of financial position	Generally consistent with that set out in IAS 1 with certain items that must be presented on the face of the main statement and others that may be presented instead in notes to the accounts.
A statement of comprehensive income (one or two statements)	The statement of comprehensive income for a company applying the IFRS for SMEs will include (where relevant) only three items of other comprehensive income: • Some foreign exchange gains and losses • Some actuarial gains and losses • Some changes in fair value of hedging instruments Otherwise, the guidance is consistent with IAS 1, with minimum disclosure requirements and analysis of expenses by either nature or function.

Statement required by IFRS for SMEs	Difference from IFRS
A statement of changes in equity	The statement of changes in equity is prepared and presented in line with the requirements of IAS 1. Where a company has no changes to equity other than profit or loss, dividends and retrospective adjustments, it may present a statement of income and retained earnings rather than a statement of comprehensive income and statement of changes in equity
A statement of changes in cash flows	All companies applying the IFRS for SMEs are required to prepare a statement of cash flows, with cash flows organised into operating, investing and financing amounts. Either the direct or indirect method may be applied
Notes to the accounts	Within the notes to the financial statements, a company must state that it has applied the IFRS for SMEs and disclose its accounting policies. Disclosure of significant judgements and sources of estimation uncertainly is also required.

Certain guidance contained within full IFRS is relaxed, in particular:

1. A third statement of financial position at the start of the earliest comparative period is not required when there is a retrospective restatement of items.
2. Where there is no other comprehensive income in any of the periods presented, an entity may present an income statement (statement of profit or loss) rather than a statement of comprehensive income (statement of profit or loss and other comprehensive income).
3. A single statement of income and retained earnings may be presented instead of a statement of comprehensive income and statement of changes in equity where the only changes to equity in a period arise from profit or loss, the payment of dividends and retrospective adjustments (see below).
4. The standard relaxes the requirement under full IFRS to disclose comparatives for the reconciliation of the opening and closing number of shares.

5.2 Accounting policies, estimates and errors

FAST FORWARD

> Where the IFRS for SMEs does not specifically address a transaction, the requirements of the IFRS for SMEs in relation to similar issues or the Concepts and pervasive principles section of the standard are considered.

Section 10 of the IFRS for SMEs specifies that the requirements of the standard should be applied where they specifically address a transaction. Where this is not the case, the following hierarchy should be applied in the development of accounting policies:

(1) The requirements of the IFRS for SMEs in relation to similar issues
(2) Guidance within the Concepts and pervasive principles section of the standard

Guidance within full IFRS may also be considered although this is not mandatory.

The treatment of changes to accounting policies, accounting estimates and errors is in line with that prescribed by IAS 8.

6 Group financial statements

> **FAST FORWARD**
>
> The IFRS for SMEs includes a different definition of control from IFRS 10, however consolidation procedures are largely the same.

Four sections of the IFRS for SMEs deal with group accounting issues: Section 9 deals with consolidated and separate financial statements; Sections 14 and 15 with investments in associates and joint ventures respectively and Section 19 with business combinations and goodwill.

Note that certain group issues dealt with in full IFRS are not referred to in the IFRS for SMEs. These include step acquisitions and the measurement period.

6.1 Consolidated financial statements

The IFRS for SMEs requires that consolidated financial statements are prepared where there is a parent-subsidiary relationship, except where:

- The parent itself is a subsidiary and its ultimate parent prepares consolidated accounts under either full IFRS or the IFRS for SMEs; or
- The subsidiary was acquired with the intention to dispose of it within 12 months.

In the latter case, the subsidiary is held at fair value with changes in fair value recognised in profit or loss unless fair value cannot be measured reliably in which case it is measured at cost less impairment.

6.1.1 Control

In common with IFRS 10 *Consolidated Financial Statements*, a parent-subsidiary relationship is established based on control.

Key term

> **Control** is the power to govern the financial and operating policies of an entity so as to obtain benefits from its activities.

Control is presumed to exist where a parent owns directly, or indirectly, more than half of the voting power of an entity. It also exists where the parent does not have more than half of the voting power itself but does have:

- Power over more than half of the voting power by virtue of an agreement with other investors
- Power to govern the operating and financial policies of the entity under statute or an agreement
- Power to appoint or remove the majority of Board members or other controlling body
- Power to cast the majority of votes at meetings of the Board or other controlling body

The IFRS for SMEs also extends this definition to include special purpose entities (entities created to accomplish a narrow objective) which are controlled by a parent entity.

The standard clarifies that combined financial statements relate to all entities under common control rather than only those under common control by a single investor. The IFRS for SMES does not require preparation of combined financial statements.

6.1.2 Consolidation procedures

The consolidation procedures of the IFRS for SMEs are identical to those within IFRS 10, with one exception: where use of a uniform accounting date is impracticable, the IFRS for SMEs does not require that subsidiary accounts prepared to a date within three months of the parent's reporting date are used. Where use of a uniform accounting date is impracticable, the most recent accounts should be used and adjustments made for transactions occurring between the two dates.

6.2 Separate financial statements

The IFRS for SMEs does not require the presentation of separate financial statements for the parent company. Where they are prepared, the investment in a subsidiary, associate or joint venture is recognised either:

- At cost less impairment; or
- At fair value with changes in fair value recognised in profit or loss.

6.3 Investments in associates and joint ventures

FAST FORWARD

Investments in associates and jointly controlled entities (JCEs) may be accounted for using the cost model, equity accounting or the fair value model.

The definition of significant influence contained within the IFRS for SMEs and applied to establish a parent-associate relationship is equal to that given in IAS 28 *Investments in Associates and Joint Ventures*.

The definition of joint control and types of joint arrangement differ, however to those given in IFRS 11 *Joint Arrangements*. The requirements of the IFRS for SMEs are based on the 'old' joint arrangement rules of IAS 31 *Interests in Joint Ventures*.

6.3.1 Joint ventures

Key term

The definition of **joint control** is provided as:

The contractually agreed sharing of control over an economic activity which exists only when the strategic financial and operating decisions relating to the activity require the unanimous consent of the parties sharing control.

This is a very similar definition to that within IFRS 11, however the IFRS 11 definition refers to 'relevant activities' rather than 'strategic financial and operating decisions', where relevant activities are those activities of the investee which significantly affect the investee's returns.

The IFRS for SMEs differs more significantly in how it classifies joint arrangements. These are:

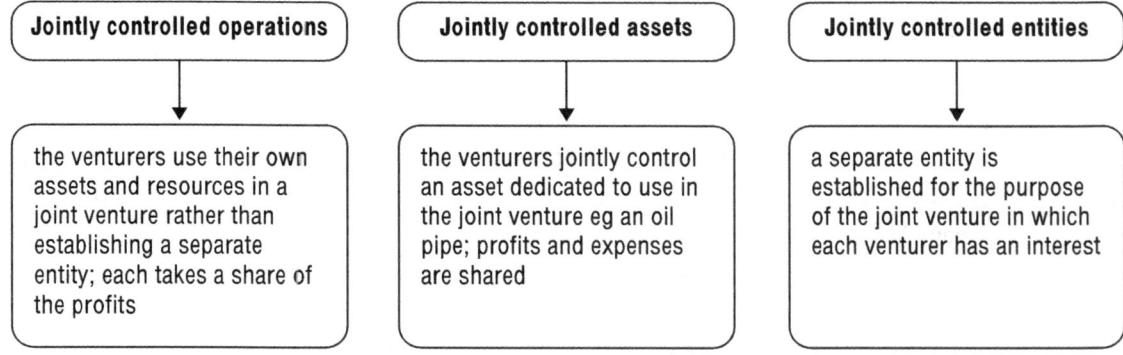

Jointly controlled operations	Jointly controlled assets	Jointly controlled entities
the venturers use their own assets and resources in a joint venture rather than establishing a separate entity; each takes a share of the profits	the venturers jointly control an asset dedicated to use in the joint venture eg an oil pipe; profits and expenses are shared	a separate entity is established for the purpose of the joint venture in which each venturer has an interest

6.3.2 Accounting treatment

In respect of an interest in a **jointly controlled operation**, a venturer recognises in its own financial statements:

(a) The assets which it controls and liabilities which it incurs; and
(b) The expenses which it incurs and its share of income from the joint venture.

In respect of an interest in a **jointly controlled asset**, a venturer recognises in its own financial statements:

(a) Its share of the jointly controlled assets
(b) Any liabilities that it has incurred
(c) Its share of any jointly incurred liabilities
(d) Any income from the sale or use of its share of the output of the joint venture

(e) Its share of any expenses incurred by the joint venture
(f) Any expenses incurred in respect of its interest in the joint venture

The IFRS for SMEs requires that a **jointly controlled entity** is measured in the financial statements in the same way as an **associate**, using:

- The cost model (cost less accumulated impairment losses);
- The equity method as required by IAS 28; or
- The fair value model (fair value with gains and losses recognised in profit or loss).

One model is applied to all associates and one model to all JCEs.

Where a published price quotation is available, the fair value model must be used in preference to the cost model.

This is a simplification of the rules within IAS 28 where the equity method must be applied.

6.4 Business combinations and goodwill

FAST FORWARD

Under the IFRS for SMEs, the NCI is not taken into account in the calculation of goodwill, acquisition costs form part of the cost of the combination and contingent consideration is only included where payment is probable and can be reliably measured.

The IFRS for SMEs requires the application of the purchase method to business combinations. This is very similar to the acquisition method required by IFRS 3 *Business Combinations* with the following notable exceptions:

(1) Contingent consideration is only included within the cost of the combination where it is probable and can be reliably measured.

(2) Directly attributable acquisition costs form part of the cost of the combination (and so increase goodwill).

(3) Goodwill is calculated as the difference between the cost of the combination and the share of the fair value of identifiable net assets acquired.

(4) There is no option to measure the non-controlling interest at fair value at acquisition; it is always measured as a proportion of the net assets of the subsidiary. This means that any non-controlling interest in the acquiree is measured at the non-controlling interest's proportionate share of the recognised amounts of the acquiree's identifiable net assets.

(5) Goodwill is amortised over its useful life; if this cannot be estimated, it is a maximum of 10 years.

Question
Goodwill

Potter Co is an unlisted entity which applies the IFRS for SMEs. On 1 September 20X2 Potter acquired 80% of the ordinary shares in Finch Co, paying $2 million immediately and agreeing to pay a further $2.12 million on 1 September 20X3 if Finch Co achieved a 5% growth in sales revenue in the year after acquisition. The cost of capital of Potter Co is 6%. On the date of acquisition, the fair value of the identifiable net assets in Finch Co was $1.8 million. Directly attributable costs of acquisition amounted to $50,000.

By the group year end of 28 February 20X3, Finch Co had achieved only a 2% growth in sales revenue on an annualised basis. The directors of Potter Co believed that further increase was unlikely given difficult trading conditions.

The directors of Potter Co have been unable to estimate a useful life for the goodwill arising in Finch Co.

At what amount is goodwill reported in the consolidated financial statement of position of Potter Co at 28 February 20X3?

PART C ACCOUNTING AND REPORTING TECHNIQUES

Answer

- The contingent consideration in respect of the combination is unlikely to be received given the growth in sales revenue to date and difficult trading conditions. Therefore it is ignored in the calculation of goodwill.
- Acquisition costs are included as part of the cost of the combination.
- As the directors have been unable to estimate the useful life of goodwill, it is amortised over ten years:

	$
Cash consideration	2,000,000
Acquisition costs	50,000
	2,050,000
Share of FV of identifiable NAs acquired (80% × $1.8m)	(1,440,000)
Goodwill arising at acquisition	610,000
Amortisation $610,000/10 × 6/12	(30,500)
Carrying amount at 28 February 20X3	579,500

Tutorial note

If Potter applied full IFRS, the goodwill calculation would be as follows:

	$
Cash consideration	2,000,000
Deferred consideration (assuming FV = PV)	
2,120,000/1.06	2,000,000
	4,000,000
NCI (assume measured as a proportion of net assets)	
20% × $1.8m	360,000
	4,360,000
FV of identifiable NAs acquired	(1,800,000)
Goodwill arising at acquisition	2,560,000

This goodwill would not be amortised but instead tested for impairment at each period end.

7 Financial instruments

FAST FORWARD

The IFRS for SMEs contains two sections on accounting for financial instruments: basic financial instruments and other financial instruments. Basic financial instruments are normally measured at amortised cost and other financial instruments at fair value.

Sections 11 and 12 of the IFRS for SMEs deal with basic and other financial instruments respectively. Entities which adopt the IFRS for SMEs may elect to follow either:

- the provisions of Sections 11 and 12;
- or IAS 39 *Financial Instruments: Recognition and Measurement* with, the disclosure requirements of Sections 11 and 12

7.1 Basic and other financial instruments

The IFRS for SMEs defines basic and other financial instruments and provides examples of each. **Basic financial instruments** include:

- Cash
- Accounts receivable or payable
- Loans from banks and other third parties (includes foreign currency loans and those with standard loan covenants)
- An investment in non-convertible preference shares and non-puttable ordinary shares or preference shares
- A commitment to receive a loan that cannot be settled net in cash
- Most debt instruments where returns to the holder are fixed or referenced to an observable interest rate

Other financial instruments include:

- An investment in another entity's equity instruments other than those listed above
- Options, rights, warrants, future and forward contracts and swaps
- Investments in convertible debt (because the return can vary with the market price of shares rather than just with interest rates)
- Commitments to receive a loan that can be settled net in cash

7.2 Initial measurement

7.2.1 Basic financial instruments

Basic financial instruments are initially measured at the **transaction price** (including transaction costs other than where the instrument is measured at fair value through profit or loss). However, where an arrangement constitutes a **financing transaction**, the instrument is measured at the present value of future payments discounted at a market rate of interest.

7.2.2 Example: initial measurement of basic financial instruments

- A long-term loan made to another entity (a financial asset) is measured at the present value of cash receivable.
- Amounts receivable from customers (financial assets) are recognised at the undiscounted amount receivable from the customer – normally the invoice price
- A cash purchase of another entity's shares (a financial asset) is recognised at the amount of cash paid to acquire the shares.
- A loan received from a bank (a financial liability) is measured at the present value of cash payable to the bank.
- Amounts owed to suppliers (financial liabilities) are recognised at the undiscounted amount owed to the supplier – normally the invoice price.

7.2.3 Other financial instruments

Other financial instruments are measured at fair value, which is normally the transaction price.

7.3 Subsequent measurement

7.3.1 Basic financial instruments

Basic financial instruments are measured at **amortised cost** using the **effective interest method**, with the following exceptions:

(1) Shares whose fair value can be measured reliably are measured at fair value, with changes recognised in profit or loss

(2) Shares whose fair value cannot be measured reliably are measured at cost less impairment

(3) Commitments to receive a loan that cannot be settled net in cash are measured at cost (which may be $nil) less impairment.

The best evidence of fair value may be a price in a binding sale agreement in an arm's length transaction.

7.3.2 Other financial instruments

Other financial instruments are measured at fair value with changes recognised in profit or loss. Some changes in the value of hedging instruments are recognised initially in other comprehensive income. Where the fair value of equity instruments cannot be measured reliably, cost less impairment is required.

Question — Financial Instruments

On 1 January 20X0, Grey Co acquires a bond for $900,000, incurring transaction costs of $50,000. Interest of $40,000 is receivable annually in arrears from 31 December 20X0 to 31 December 20X4, and the bond will be redeemed for $1.1million on 31 December 20X4. The effective interest rate is 6.96%.

What amounts are recognised in the financial statements at 31 December in each of the years to redemption, assuming that Grey Co applies the IFRS for SMEs including the provisions in respect of financial instruments?

Answer

The bond is a basic financial instrument (financial asset) which is initially measured at $900,000 plus the transaction costs of $50,000:

Year	b/f	Interest income at 6.96%	Cash received	C/f
20X0	950,000	66,120	(40,000)	976,120
20X1	976,120	67,938	(40,000)	1,004,058
20X2	1,004,058	69,882	(40,000)	1,033,940
20X3	1,033,940	71,962	(40,000)	1,065,902
20X4	1,065,902	74,186	(1,140,088)	0

Extracts from the relevant financial statements are:

Statement of financial position at 31 December

	20X0	20X1	20X2	20X3	20X4
Financial asset	976,120	1,004,058	1,033,940	1,065,902	0

Statement of profit or loss and other comprehensive income for the year ended 31 December

	20X0	20X1	20X2	20X3	20X4
Interest receivable	66,120	67,938	69,882	71,962	74,186

7.4 Impairment testing

Basic instruments measured at amortised cost must be assessed for evidence of impairment at the end of each reporting period. Any impairment loss is recognised in profit or loss immediately. An impairment loss may be reversed if the loss is decreased due to an event after recognition of the impairment.

Entities should also apply this guidance on impairment testing to other financial instruments measured at cost less impairment.

7.5 Derecognition

For both basic and other financial instruments the following derecognition rules are applied:

- Financial assets are derecognised when contractual rights to cash flows expire, substantially all risks and rewards are transferred or control is transferred, even where some risks and rewards are retained.
- Financial liabilities are derecognised when the obligation is discharged, cancelled or expires.

7.6 Disclosure

The same disclosure requirements apply to both basic and other financial instruments:

- Carrying value of each category of financial asset/liability (FVTPL, cost less impairment, amortised cost)
- Details of debt instruments such as interest rate and maturity
- The basis for determining fair value where a financial instrument is measured at fair value
- Details of financial assets which have been transferred but not derecognised
- Details of collateral
- Defaults and breaches on loans payable
- Items of income, expense, gains and losses

In this area, the volume of disclosures is significantly less than that required by full IFRS.

8 Assets

FAST FORWARD

> The IFRS for SMEs requires that all PPE is held under the cost model and all investment property is held under the fair value model provided that fair value can be reliably measured without undue cost or effort.

The IFRS for SMEs deals with assets in sections on inventories, investment property, property, plant and equipment, intangible assets other than goodwill, leases, borrowing costs, and impairment of assets.

8.1 Inventories

The requirements of the IFRS for SMEs are consistent with the requirements of IAS 2 *Inventories* in respect of accounting for inventories. In particular:

- Inventories are measured at the lower of cost and net realisable value
- Cost is established using an actual cost basis, FIFO or weighted average cost.

8.2 Investment property

IAS 40 *Investment Property* allows entities to choose whether to apply the cost model or fair value model to their investment properties. The IFRS for SMEs removes this choice, requiring that where reliable measurement of a fair value is available, the fair value model is applied.

Therefore investment properties are carried at fair value in the statement of financial position with gains and losses recognised in profit or loss.

The standard does provide an exemption from the requirement to measure at fair value on the grounds of 'undue cost or effort'. If it is the case that establishing fair values would involve undue cost or effort, investment properties are accounted for in accordance with Section 17 on property, plant and equipment.

Unlike IAS 40, the IFRS for SMEs does not provide extensive guidance on transfers in and out of the investment property category.

8.3 Property, plant and equipment

Although the IFRS for SMEs bases Section 17 on IAS 16 *Property, Plant and Equipment*, there are a number of differences between the requirements of the two:

- As the IFRS for SMEs omits the topic of assets held for sale, these fall within the scope of PPE under Section 17. Therefore, there is no separate presentation of assets held for sale in the statement of financial position.

- A review of residual values, useful lives and depreciation methods is only required where there is a significant change in the asset or how it is used.

- Component depreciation of complex assets is only required where major parts of an asset have 'significantly different patterns of consumption of economic benefits'.

8.4 Intangible assets other than goodwill

FAST FORWARD

> The IFRS for SMEs does not permit internally generated development costs to be capitalised. All intangible assets must be amortised over a finite useful life.

Most of the requirements of the IFRS for SMEs mirror those contained within IAS 38 *Intangible Assets*. There are three notable exceptions:

(1) The IFRS for SMEs requires all internally generated intangible assets, including development costs, to be recognised in profit or loss. Capitalisation of these amounts is not permitted.

(2) The standard requires all intangible assets to be amortised over a finite life, which is a maximum of ten years unless an entity can estimate a different life reliably.

(3) The revaluation model is not available for intangible assets.

8.5 Leases

IFRS 16 has not amended the treatment of leases in the IFRS for SMEs. The requirements of the IFRS for SMEs are broadly in line with those of IAS 17 *Leases*, however, unlike IAS 17, the IFRS for SMEs does not require the straight-line method to be used for operating leases where payments to the lessor are structured to increase with general inflation.

8.5.1 Example: Operating leases

Reindeer Co leases office space from Moose Co for five years under an operating lease. The lease payments are structured to reflect an expected 10% general inflation rate over the term of the lease as follows:

Year 1 $100,000

Year 2 $110,000

Year 3 $121,000

Year 4 $133,000

Year 5 $146,000

A rent expense equal to the amounts shown above is recognised by Reindeer Co in the relevant year. If escalating payments are not structured to reflect general inflation, then an equal amount of $122,000 is recognised in profit or loss each year. This is calculated as the sum of the five payments divided by five years.

8.6 Borrowing costs

> **FAST FORWARD**
>
> All borrowing costs are expensed as incurred under the IFRS for SMEs.

Under IAS 23 *Borrowing Costs*, all eligible borrowing costs incurred in relation to qualifying assets must be capitalised. The IFRS for SMEs, however, requires all borrowing costs to be expensed as incurred.

8.7 Impairment of assets

The IFRS for SMEs states that:

- **Inventories are impaired** when their selling price less costs to complete and sell is less than carrying value;
- **Other assets are impaired** when their recoverable amount is less than their carrying amount.

Guidance on when an impairment may have arisen and how recoverable amount is calculated is generally consistent with IAS 36 *Impairment of Assets*, although unlike full IFRS, the IFRS for SMEs has no requirement to test goodwill and intangible assets not available for use for impairment annually.

Like IAS 36, the IFRS for SMEs requires that goodwill is allocated to the CGUs that are expected to benefit from the synergies of the combination for the purpose of impairment testing. The IFRS for SMEs states that if an allocation is not possible:

- The acquired entity is tested as a whole for impairment where it has not been integrated into the existing business; or
- The entire group is tested where the acquired business has been integrated.

The issue of corporate assets is not dealt with in the IFRS for SMEs.

9 Liabilities

Section 21 of the IFRS for SMEs deals with provisions and contingencies and Section 22 deals with liabilities and equities.

9.1 Provisions and contingencies

The requirements of the IFRS for SMEs on the recognition and measurement of provisions and contingencies are consistent with IAS 37 *Provisions, Contingent Liabilities and Contingent Assets*. This section of the standard also includes an appendix of examples which are similar to those in the full standard.

9.2 Liabilities and equity

This section of the IFRS for SMEs is derived from:

- IAS 1 *Presentation of Financial Statements*
- IAS 32 *Financial Instruments: Presentation*
- IFRIC 2 *Members' Shares in Co-operative Entities and Similar Instruments*
- IFRIC 17 *Distributions of Non-cash Assets to Owners*

Guidance is provided for classifying financial instruments as either equity or liabilities in line with IAS 32, this guidance includes certain puttable instruments as equity.

9.2.1 Accounting for original issue of shares

Section 22 provides guidance on accounting for shares when first issued as follows:

- Amounts owed in respect of shares already issued are presented as an offset to equity rather than as an asset.
- Where cash is received prior to the issue of shares, an increase in equity is reported only where the cash is not repayable.
- An increase in equity is not reported where equity instruments have been subscribed for but not issued and payment has not been received.
- Equity instruments are measured at the fair value of cash or other resources received or receivable net of the direct costs of issue.

These principles are also extended to apply to the sale of options, rights and warrants.

9.2.2 Other issues

This Section of the IFRS for SMEs also:

- Clarifies that bonus issues do not result in any change to total equity.
- Requires a split-accounting approach to compound instruments (as required by IAS 32 with the liability component accounted for in the same way as a similar standalone financial liability.
- Requires that the fair value of consideration provided for treasury shares (equity instruments that have been issued and subsequently reacquired by an entity) is deducted from equity.
- Requires that the fair value of distributions to owners are deducted from equity.
- Requires that the fair value of non-cash distributions declared are recognised as a liability with changes in fair value recognised in equity.
- Mirrors the requirements of IFRS 10 by requiring that changes in a parent's controlling interest in a subsidiary that do not result in a loss of control are treated as transactions with equity holders in their capacity as equity holders.

10 Other topics

The remaining sections of the IFRS for SMEs deal with revenue, government grants, share-based payment, employee benefits, income tax, foreign currency translation and hyperinflation, events after the end of the reporting period, related party disclosures and transition to the IFRS for SMEs.

10.1 Revenue

The guidance contained within Section 23 of the IFRS for SMEs is generally consistent with IAS 18 *Revenue,* recognising revenue when the risks and rewards of ownership are transferred to the third party, rather than when performance obligations are satisfied, which is the approach of the IFRS 15 five-step model. It also incorporates the current requirements based on IAS 11 *Construction Contracts*, which recognises revenue on long term contacts based on stage of completion of the contract. IFRIC 13 *Customer Loyalty Programmes* and an example based on IFRIC 15 *Agreements for the Construction of Real Estate* are also implicit in the standard.

This section of the standard is one of three with an appendix. The appendix contains similar examples of the application of the guidance on accounting for revenue to those contained in the appendix to IAS 18.

10.2 Government grants

FAST FORWARD The IFRS for SMEs simplifies the accounting requirements in respect of government grants.

The IFRS for SMEs simplifies the IAS 20 *Accounting for Government Grants and Disclosure of Government Assistance* requirements with regard to accounting for government grants. In particular:

- Grants are measured at the fair value of the asset received or receivable
- Grants that do not impose future performance conditions are recognised in income when receivable
- Grants that do impose future performance conditions are recognised in income when the performance conditions are met
- Grants received before the revenue recognition criteria are satisfied are recognised as a liability

The IFRS for SMEs does not deal with the issues of government assistance, non-monetary government grants or the repayment of government grants.

10.3 Share-based payments

The accounting guidance provided in the IFRS for SMEs in respect of share-based payments is consistent with IFRS 2 *Share-based Payment*, albeit with simplified rules for measuring the fair value of equity instruments granted.

10.4 Employee benefits

FAST FORWARD The measurement of a defined benefit pension scheme obligation is simplified if measurement using the projected unit credit method involves undue cost or effort.

The IFRS for SMEs, like IAS 19 *Employee Benefits,* provides guidance on accounting for short-term employee benefits, long-term benefits other than pensions, termination benefits and post-employment benefits. The prescribed accounting treatment for the first three types of benefit is consistent with IAS 19. In the case of post-employment benefits, and specifically defined benefit pension schemes, the accounting treatment is simplified.

In particular, in measurement of the defined benefit obligation, the projected unit credit method need only be used where it does not involve undue cost or effort. Otherwise, the measurement of the obligation can be simplified with factors such as estimated future salary increases and expected service of current employees ignored.

10.5 Income tax

FAST FORWARD The IFRS for SMEs is based on IAS 12 with adjustments for consistency with other Sections in the IFRS for SMEs. The 2015 version of the IFRS for SMEs made significant changes to the standard to align it with IAS 12.

Section 29 of the IFRS for SMEs is derived from IAS 12 *Income Taxes*. The guidance within Section 29 in respect of current tax mirrors that of IAS 12, although where the IFRS for SMEs specifically prohibits the discounting of current taxes, IAS 12 is silent.

IFRS for SMEs as originally issued in 2009 contained a number of differences to IAS 12. The revised 2015 version has removed the majority of the differences and can now be considered consistent with IAS 12.

10.6 Foreign currency translation and hyperinflation

Section 30 of the IFRS for SMEs deals with foreign currency translation. It provides guidance on determining functional currency, recording foreign currency transactions and translating foreign currency accounts into the presentation currency. Its requirements are similar to those of IAS 21 *The Effects of Changes in Foreign Exchange Rates*, although the IFRS for SMEs does not allow gains and losses of a net investment in a foreign entity that are initially recognised in other comprehensive income to be reclassified to profit or loss.

Section 31 deals with hyperinflation, and this is a simplified version of the guidance contained within IAS 29 *Financial Reporting in Hyperinflationary Economies*.

10.7 Events after the end of the reporting period

There are no differences between Section 32 of the IFRS for SMEs, which deals with events after the end of the reporting period and the requirements of IAS 10 *Events After the Reporting Period*.

10.8 Related party disclosures

IAS 24 *Related Party Disclosures* is concerned with defining a related party and prescribing the required disclosures in relation to them. Section 33 of the IFRS for SMEs reduces the disclosure requirements of full IFRS, in particular requiring disclosure of the compensation of key management personnel in aggregate only.

10.9 Transition to the IFRS for SMEs

The final section of the IFRS for SMEs is based on IFRS 1 *First-time Adoption of IFRS* and provides guidance for entities who are applying the IFRS for SMEs for the first time.

A number of exemptions are available within the full standard which may be applied when preparing a first set of financial statements under IFRS. The IFRS for SMEs includes all of these exemptions as well as a number of additional exemptions and relaxations. In total there are five mandatory exemptions and 12 optional exemptions. There is also a general exemption from retrospective application where this would be impracticable. In this instance 'impracticable' is defined as being 'when the entity cannot apply it after making every reasonable effort to do so'.

Chapter roundup

- The IFRS for SMEs was developed to provide a simpler accounting regime within the IFRS framework for non-publicly listed entities. IFRS for SMEs is a stand-alone standard.

- The IFRS for SMEs defines those entities which are eligible to use it as entities which do not have public accountability and which publish general purpose financial statements.

- The standard is organised into 35 sections, each dealing with a specific area of accounting.

- The IFRS for SMEs includes a section on concepts and pervasive principles which is an abbreviated form of the *Conceptual Framework*.

- The IFRS for SMEs is generally consistent with IAS 1 in respect of requirements for the presentation of financial statements, although there is some relaxation of the full IFRS requirements.

- Where the IFRS for SMEs does not specifically address a transaction, the requirements of the IFRS for SMEs in relation to similar issues or the Concepts and pervasive principles section of the standard are considered.

- The IFRS for SMEs includes a different definition of control from IFRS 10, however consolidation procedures are largely the same.

- Investments in associates and JCEs may be accounted for using the cost model, equity accounting or the fair value model.

- Under the IFRS for SMEs, the NCI is not taken into account in the calculation of goodwill, acquisition costs form part of the cost of the combination and contingent consideration is only included where it is probable of payment and can be reliably measured.

- The IFRS for SMEs contains two sections on accounting for financial instruments: basic financial instruments and other financial instruments. Basic financial instruments are normally measured at amortised cost and other financial instruments at fair value.

- The IFRS for SMEs requires that all PPE is held under the cost model and all investment property is held under the fair value model provided that fair value can be reliably measured without undue cost or effort.

- The IFRS for SMEs does not permit internally generated development costs to be capitalised. All intangible assets must be amortised over a finite useful life.

- All borrowing costs are expensed as incurred under the IFRS for SMEs.

- The IFRS for SMEs simplifies the accounting requirements in respect of government grants.

- The measurement of a defined benefit pension scheme obligation is simplified if measurement using the projected unit credit method involves undue cost or effort.

- The IFRS for SMEs is based on IAS 12 with adjustments for consistency with other Sections in the IFRS for SMEs. The 2015 version of the IFRS for SMEs made significant changes to the standard to align it with IAS 12.

Quick quiz

1. Which entities can use the IFRS for SMEs?
2. What topics are omitted from the IFRS for SMEs?
3. How many sections is the IFRS for SMEs split into?
4. Under what circumstances may an entity present a statement of income and retained earnings rather than a statement of comprehensive income and statement of changes in equity?
5. How does the cost of a business combination under the IFRS for SMEs differ from that under full IFRS?
6. How are basic financial instruments normally measured?
7. How are investment properties measured under the IFRS for SMEs?
8. What is the treatment of borrowing costs under the IFRS for SMEs?
9. How are the requirements of IAS 19 simplified in the IFRS for SMEs?

Answers to quick quiz

1. Those companies:
   - Which are not publicly accountable (ie not listed on a public market (or in the process of listing) and which do not hold assets for a wide range of third parties in a fiduciary capacity) and
   - Which prepare general purpose financial statements.

2. Complex topics which are not relevant to smaller private entities are omitted. These include segment reporting, interim reporting, earnings per share, assets held for sale and insurance contracts.

3. It is split into 35 sections.

4. When the only changes to equity are profit or loss, the payment of dividends and retrospective adjustments.

5. Acquisition costs form part of the cost of consideration whereas they must be expensed under full IFRS. In addition contingent consideration is only included where it will probably be paid; under full IFRS it is always included at fair value.

6. At amortised cost.

7. At fair value provided that it can be reliably measured and does not involve undue cost or effort.

8. All borrowing costs are expensed as incurred.

9. The projected unit credit method need not be applied if this results in undue cost or effort.

End of chapter question

Tramwell

Tramwell Co is an unlisted, wholly owned subsidiary of Ramses Co. Ramses is listed on a national stock exchange, and is required to apply IFRS in preparing its financial statements.

Tramwell currently prepares its financial statements using local GAAP, however the Finance Director has heard that the IFRS for SMEs has recently been issued and is considering changing from local GAAP to the IFRS for SMEs.

The most recent statement of financial position of Tramwell, is given below:

	$'000	$'000
Non-current assets		
Property, plant and equipment		3,470
Investment properties		1,100
Development costs		220
		4,790
Current assets		
Inventories	321	
Financial assets (cost)	400	
Receivables	245	
Cash	63	
	1,029	
Current liabilities		
Current tax	114	
Payables	321	
	435	
Net current assets		594
Total assets less current liabilities		5,384

	$'000	$'000
Long-term liabilities		
Deferred tax		(256)
Bank loan		(400)
Net assets		4,728
Share capital		500
Retained earnings		2,668
Investment property reserve		360
Revaluation reserve		1,200
Equity and reserves		4,728

Required:

Prepare a briefing note for the Finance Director which includes advice on:

(a) Whether Tramwell can adopt the IFRS for SMEs in preparing its financial statements
(b) How accounting policies may change compared to local GAAP
(c) The practical aspects of adopting the IFRS for SMEs

Your advice should relate specifically to the circumstances of Tramwell.

Note. you are not required to address first-time adoption or the transition provisions of the IFRS for SMEs.

(Total 20 marks)

Ratio and trend analysis

Topic list	Syllabus reference
1 Sources of information and the role of regulation	LO2
2 The broad categories of ratios	LO2
3 Profitability and return on capital	LO2
4 Liquidity and working capital	LO2
5 Long-term solvency: Debt and gearing/leverage	LO2
6 Shareholders' investment ratios	LO2

Introduction

An entity's stakeholders will each have a different interest in its financial statements. Some may wish to track an entity's performance over time to see whether it has improved or declined. Others may wish to compare the performance of one or more entities as the basis to an investment decision. Common accounting ratios, and more importantly the analysis and interpretation of those ratios can help to provide the information that stakeholders need.

1 Sources of information and the role of regulation

The financial statements of a business are designed to provide information about its performance and financial position to its investors, lenders and other creditors to help them to make decisions about providing economic resources to the entity. (Conceptual Framework, para 1.2) The bare figures, however, are not particularly useful and it is only through **comparisons** (usually using ratios) that their significance can be established. Comparisons may be made with previous financial periods, with other similar businesses or with averages for the particular industry. The choice will depend on the purpose for which the comparison is being made and the information that is available.

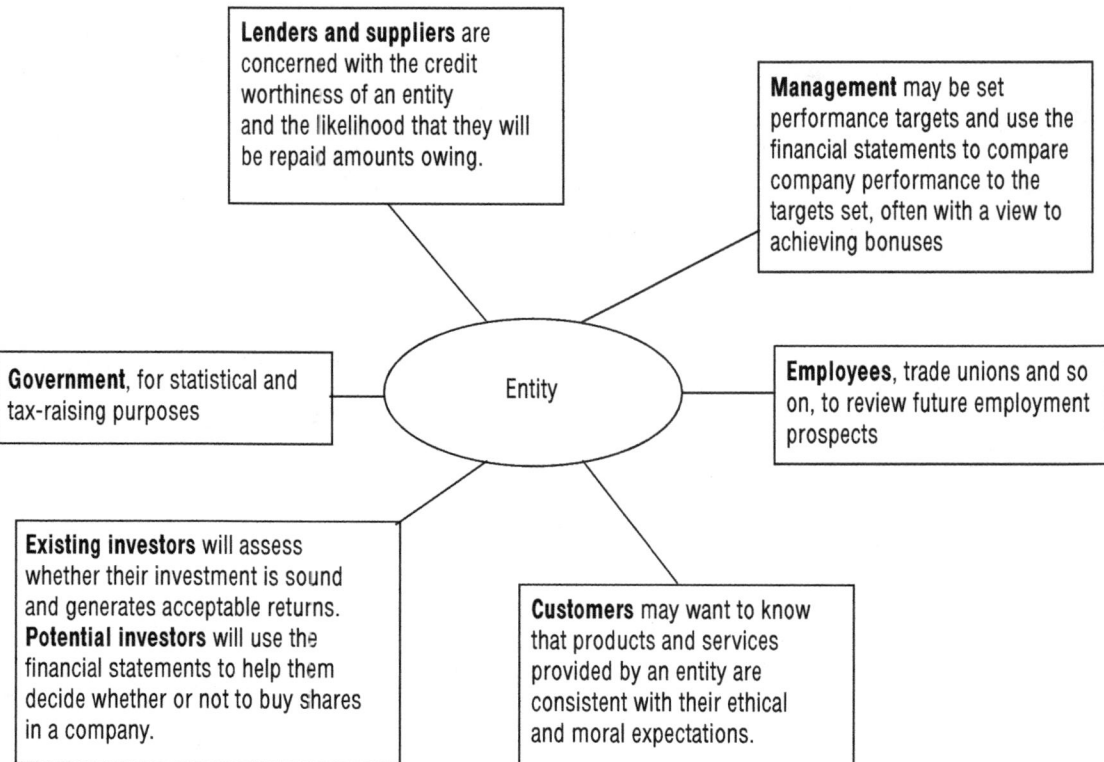

Although we have seen that the *Conceptual Framework* is focused on those who provide economic resources to a company, there are a wide range of stakeholders who are interested in the performance and financial position of a company:

This text is concerned with financial rather than management accounting and the ratios discussed here are therefore likely to be calculated by external users. The following sources of information are readily available to external users.

- Published financial statements and interim statements
- Documents filed as required by company legislation
- Statistics published by the government
- Other published sources eg *Investors Chronicle, The Economist, Wall Street Journal*

1.1 Financial analysis

The **lack of detailed information** available to the outsider is a considerable disadvantage in undertaking ratio analysis. The first difficulty is that there may simply be insufficient data to calculate all of the required ratios. A second concerns the availability of a suitable 'yardstick' with which the calculated ratios may be compared.

1.1.1 Inter-temporal analysis

Looking first at inter-temporal or trend analysis (comparisons for the same business over time), some of the **problems** include the following.

- Changes in the nature of the business
- Unrealistic depreciation rates under historical cost accounting
- The changing value of the functional currency
- Changes in accounting policies
- New accounting standards such as the adoption of IFRS 16 Leases

Other factors will include changes in government incentive packages, changes from purchasing equipment to leasing it, and so on.

1.1.2 Cross-sectoral analysis

When undertaking 'cross-sectoral' analysis (making comparisons with other companies) the position is even more difficult because of the problem of identifying companies that are comparable. **Comparability** between companies may be impaired due to the following reasons.

(a) Different degrees of diversification

(b) Different production and purchasing policies (if an investor was analysing the smaller car manufacturers, he would find that some of them buy in engines from one of the 'majors' whilst others develop and manufacture their own)

(c) Different financing policies (eg leasing as opposed to buying)

(d) Different accounting policies (one of the most serious problems particularly in relation to non-current assets and inventory valuation)

(e) Different effects of government incentives

The major **intragroup comparison organisations** (whose results are intended for the use of participating companies and are not generally available) go to considerable length to adjust financial statements to comparable bases. The external user will rarely be in a position to make such adjustments. Although the position is improved by increases in disclosure requirements, direct comparisons between companies will inevitably, on occasion, continue to give rise to misleading results.

1.2 Social and political considerations

Social considerations tend to be short-lived or 'fashionable' and therefore each set of statements can be affected by a different movement or fad. In recent years, the social aspect much in evidence has been that of environmental and sustainability issues. Companies have gone to great lengths in recent years to demonstrate their commitment to climate change and sustainability, however there is increasing pressure on companies to do more.

Political considerations may be more far reaching. The regulatory regime may be instituted by statutes, but often self-regulation is encouraged through bodies such as a stock exchange.

1.3 Multinational companies

Multinational companies have great difficulties sometimes because of the need to comply with **legislation** in a large number of countries. As well as different reporting requirements, different rules of incorporation exist, as well as different directors' rules, tax legislation and so on. Sometimes the local rules can be so harsh that companies will avoid them altogether. In California, for example, multinational companies with operations there are taxed on their **world wide** profits, not just their US profits. Local tax regimes may also require information about the group as a whole because of the impact of internal transfer pricing on tax.

Different local reporting requirements will also make **consolidation** more difficult. The results of subsidiaries must be translated not only to the company's functional currency but also using the accounting rules used by the parent. The requirement of IFRS is to use 'uniform accounting policies'.

2 The broad categories of ratios

FAST FORWARD

Make sure that you can **define** all the ratios. Look out for variations in definitions of ratios which might appear in questions.

Exam focus point

Questions are unlikely to be of the standard 'ratio calculation and comment' type. Instead, questions are more focused on your interpretation of, for example, the impact of a particular issue with group accounting; such as the impact of reporting discontinued activities, disposing of an investment in a subsidiary or exchange gains/losses on the assessment of the group's overall performance. Questions could also (for example) ask for a comment on the impact on performance (group or individual company) of a change of accounting policy (see Chapter 18).

Ratio calculations involve **comparing one figure against another** to produce a ratio, and assessing whether the ratio indicates a weakness or strength in the company's affairs.

Ratio analysis and interpretation involves using the information available about a company and the industry in which it operates to explain changes in ratios and consider the impact of the change on the company's stakeholders.

At this level, it is important that you can analyse and interpret ratios. Calculating and defining the ratios is only a starting point.

2.1 The broad categories of ratios

Broadly speaking, basic ratios can be grouped into five categories:

- Profitability and return
- Long-term solvency and stability
- Short-term solvency and liquidity
- Efficiency (turnover ratios)
- Shareholders' investment ratios

Calculating ratios on their own is **not sufficient** for interpreting company financial statements; there are other items of information which should be looked at.

(a) The content of any **accompanying commentary** on the financial statements and other statements

(b) The age and nature of the **company's assets**

(c) Current and future **developments** in the company's markets, at home and overseas, recent acquisitions or disposals of subsidiaries by the parent

(d) Any other **noticeable features** of the financial statements, such as events after the reporting period, contingent liabilities, a qualified auditors' report, the company's taxation position

The following sections summarise what you already know about ratio analysis from your earlier studies. You should then perform the comprehensive questions given in this chapter. The following chapters look at more complex areas of analysis and interpretation, which build on the knowledge in this chapter.

3 Profitability and return on capital

One profit figure that should be calculated and compared over time is **PBIT, profit before interest and tax**, the amount of profit which the company earned before having to pay interest to the providers of loan capital. By providers of loan capital, we usually mean longer-term loan capital, such as debentures and medium-term bank loans, which will be shown in the statement of financial position as 'non-current liabilities'. Also, tax is affected by unusual variations which have a distorting effect.

Profit before interest and tax is therefore:

(a) The profit on operating activities before taxation, plus
(b) Interest charges on long-term loan capital.

Published financial statements do not always give sufficient detail on interest payable to determine how much is interest on long-term finance.

3.1 A warning about comments on profit margin and asset turnover

It might be tempting to think that a high profit margin is good, and a low asset turnover means sluggish trading. In broad terms, this is so. But there is **a trade-off** between profit margin and asset turnover, and you cannot look at one without allowing for the other.

(a) A high profit margin means a high profit per $1 of sales, but if this also means that sales prices are high, there is a strong possibility that sales turnover will be depressed, and so asset turnover lower.

(b) A high asset turnover means that the company is generating a lot of sales, but to do this it might have to keep its prices down and so accept a low profit margin per $1 of sales.

> **Knowledge brought forward from earlier studies**
>
> *Profitability*
>
> Return on capital employed
>
> $$\text{ROCE} = \frac{\text{PBIT}}{\text{Capital employed}} = \frac{\text{PBIT}}{\text{Total assets less current liabilities}}$$
>
> When **interpreting** ROCE look for the following.
>
> - How risky is the business?
> - How capital intensive is it?
> - What ROCE do similar businesses have?
>
> The following **considerations** are important.
>
> - Comparison from year to year
> - Comparison to similar companies
> - Comparison with current market borrowing rates
>
> **Problems**: which items to consider to achieve comparability:
>
> - Revaluation surplus – where one company adopts a revaluation policy and another doesn't, ROCE in the company which revalues will be depressed. The capital employed of this company can be normalised by deducting the revaluation reserve and recalculating ROCE based on the new amount.
>
> - Choices, eg measurement of the non-controlling interest at fair value or as a proportion of net assets. Measurement at fair value will increase goodwill and so capital employed and in turn depress ROCE. This choice is made on an acquisition-by-acquisition basis, meaning that one company may have some 'full' goodwill and some 'partial' goodwill in their statement of financial position.
>
> - Investments and related income – investments in associates and joint ventures which are equity accounted and the associated income are easily excluded from consolidated financial statements in order to make results comparable over time and from group to group.
>
> *Return on equity*
>
> $$\text{ROE} = \frac{\text{Profit after tax and pref div}}{\text{Ordinary share capital + reserves}} \%$$
>
> This gives a more **restricted view** of capital than ROCE, but the same principles apply.
>
> *Secondary ratios*
>
> Profit margin × Asset turnover = ROCE
>
> *Profit margin*

PART C ACCOUNTING AND REPORTING TECHNIQUES

Profit margin = $\dfrac{\text{PBIT}}{\text{Revenue}}$ %   Gross profit margin = $\dfrac{\text{Gross profit}}{\text{Revenue}}$ %

It is useful to compare profit margin to gross profit % to investigate movements which do not match. Take into account:

- Gross profit margin
    - Sales prices, sales volume and sales mix
    - Purchase prices and related costs (discount, carriage etc)
    - Production costs, both direct (materials, labour) and indirect (overheads both fixed and variable)
    - Inventory levels and inventory valuation, including errors, cut-off and stock-out costs
- Profit margin
    - Sales expenses in relation to sales levels
    - Administrative expenses, including salary levels
    - Distribution expenses in relation to sales levels

Depreciation should be considered as a separate item for each expense category.

Asset turnover

Asset turnover = $\dfrac{\text{Revenue}}{\text{Total assets less current liabilities}}$

This measures the **efficiency** of the use of assets. Amend to just non-current assets for capital intensive businesses.

4 Liquidity and working capital

Profitability is of course an important aspect of a company's performance and debt or gearing is another. Neither, however, addresses directly the key issue of liquidity in the **short term**.

Liquidity is the amount of cash a company can put its hands on quickly to settle its debts (and possibly to meet other unforeseen demands for cash payments too). Liquid funds consist of the following.

- Cash
- Short-term investments for which there is a ready market (as distinct from shares held in subsidiaries or associated companies)
- Fixed-term deposits with a bank (eg a six-month high-interest deposit)
- Trade receivables (because they will pay what they owe within a short period of time)
- Bills of exchange receivable (because these represent cash due to be received within a relatively short period of time)

A company can obtain liquid assets from sources other than sales, such as the issue of shares for cash, a new loan or the sale of non-current assets. But a company cannot rely on these at all times, and in general obtaining liquid funds depends on making sales and profits. Even so, **profits do not always lead to increases in liquidity**. This is mainly because funds generated from trading may be immediately invested in working capital or non-current assets, or paid out as dividends.

Efficiency ratios indicate how well a business is controlling aspects of its working capital.

> Knowledge brought forward from earlier studies

Liquidity and working capital
Can a company meet its short-term debts?
Current ratio

$$\text{Current ratio} = \frac{\text{Current assets}}{\text{Current liabilities}}$$

Assume assets realised at book value ∴ theoretical. 2:1 acceptable? 1.5:1? It depends on the industry.

Quick ratio

$$\text{Quick ratio (acid test)} = \frac{\text{Current assets - Inventory}}{\text{Current liabilities}}$$

Eliminates illiquid and subjectively valued inventory. Care is needed: it could be high if **overtrading** with receivables, but no cash. Is 1:1 OK? Many supermarkets operate on 0.3.

Collection period

$$\text{Average collection period} = \frac{\text{Trade receivables}}{\text{Credit turnover}} \times 365$$

Is it **consistent** with quick/current ratio? If not, investigate.

Inventory turnover period

$$\text{Inventory turnover} = \frac{\text{Cost of sales}}{\text{Inventory}} \quad \text{Inventory turnover period} = \frac{\text{Inventory}}{\text{Cost of sales}} \times 365$$

Higher the better? But remember:

- Lead times
- Seasonal fluctuations in orders
- Alternative uses of warehouse space
- Bulk buying discounts
- Likelihood of inventory perishing or becoming obsolete

Accounts payable payment period

$$\text{Accounts payable payment period} = \frac{\text{Trade payables}}{\text{Purchases}} \times 365$$

Use **cost of sales** if purchases are not disclosed.

Cash cycle

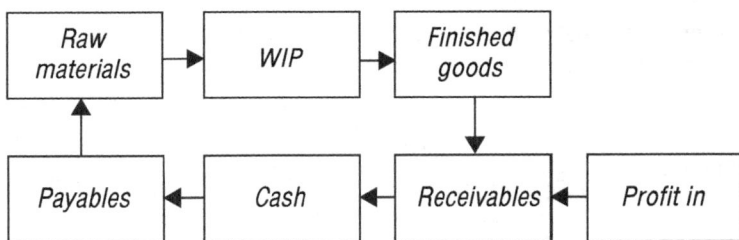

- Cash flow timing does not match sales/cost of sales timing as credit is taken
- Holding inventory delays the time between payments for goods and sales receipts

Reasons for changes in liquidity

- **Credit control** efficiency altered
- Altering **payment period** of creditors as a source of funding
- Reduce **inventory holdings** to maintain liquidity

5 Long-term solvency: Debt and gearing/leverage

Debt and gearing ratios are concerned with a company's **long-term stability**: how much the company owes in relation to its size, whether it is getting into heavier debt or improving its situation, and whether its debt burden seems heavy or light.

(a) When a company is heavily in debt, banks and other potential lenders may be unwilling to advance further funds.

PART C ACCOUNTING AND REPORTING TECHNIQUES

(b) When a company is earning only a modest profit before interest and tax, and has a heavy debt burden, there will be very little profit left (if any) over for shareholders after the interest charges have been paid. And so if interest rates were to go up (on bank overdrafts and so on) or the company were to borrow even more, it might soon be incurring interest charges in excess of PBIT. This might eventually lead to the liquidation of the company.

> **Knowledge brought forward from earlier studies**
>
> *Debt and gearing/leverage*
>
> *Debt/equity*
>
> $$\text{Debt / equity ratio} = \frac{\text{Interest bearing net debt}}{\text{Equity}} \% \quad (>100\% = \text{high})$$
>
> Or
>
> $$\frac{\text{Interest bearing net debt}}{\text{Equity} + \text{interest bearing net debt}} \% \quad (>50\% = \text{high})$$
>
> There is **no definitive answer**; elements included are subjective. The following should be considered
>
> - Convertible loan stock must be split between debt and equity, however fixed interest is paid on the principal until such time as conversion arises. It may therefore be argued that inclusion of the whole amount as debt would give a better indication of gearing levels and capacity to take on more borrowings.
> - Preferred shares should be accounted for as a liability where they are redeemable. Incorrect exclusion of these from debt will improve gearing.
> - Full goodwill based on measurement of the non-controlling interest at fair value will result in a more favourable gearing ratio than partial goodwill based on measurement of the non-controlling interest as a proportion of net assets.
> - The capitalisation of development expenditure will increase equity and so improves the gearing ratio. This is not an accounting choice, however it is fair to say that judgement is employed when applying the recognition criteria.
> - A policy of revaluing property will improve gearing by boosting equity. Where a revaluation exercise has been undertaken recently, the impact on gearing is particularly beneficial (assuming rising values).
>
> *Gearing/leverage*
>
> $$\text{Gearing ratio} = \frac{\text{Prior charge capital}}{\text{Total capital}} \qquad \text{Leverage} = \frac{\text{Total capital}}{\text{Prior charge capital}}$$
>
> *Interest cover*
>
> $$\text{Interest cover} = \frac{\text{PBIT (incl int receivable)}}{\text{Interest payable}}$$
>
> Is this a better way to **measure gearing** or **leverage**? Company must generate enough profit to cover interest. Is a figure of 3+ safe?

5.1 The implications of high or low gearing

Gearing or leverage is, amongst other things, an attempt to quantify the **degree of risk** involved in holding equity shares in a company, both in terms of the company's ability to remain in business and in terms of expected ordinary dividends from the company. The problem with a highly geared company is that, by definition, there is a lot of debt. Debt generally carries a fixed rate of interest (or fixed rate of dividend if in the form of preferred shares), hence there is a given (and large) amount to be paid out from profits to holders of debt before arriving at a residue available for distribution to the holders of equity.

The more highly geared the company, the greater the risk that little (if anything) will be available to distribute by way of dividend to the ordinary shareholders. The more highly geared the company, the greater the percentage change in profit available for ordinary shareholders for any given percentage change in profit before interest and tax. This means that there will be greater **volatility** of amounts available for ordinary shareholders, and presumably therefore greater volatility in dividends paid to those shareholders, where a company is highly geared. That is the risk. You may do extremely well or extremely badly without a particularly large movement in the PBIT of the company.

The risk of a company's ability to remain in business was referred to earlier. Gearing is relevant to this. A highly geared company has a large amount of interest to pay annually. If those borrowings are 'secured' in any way (and debentures in particular are often secured), then the holders of the debt are perfectly entitled to force the company to realise assets to pay their interest if funds are not available from other sources. Clearly, the more highly geared a company, the more likely this is to occur when and if profits fall. Note that problems related to '**off balance sheet' finance** hiding the level of gearing have gradually become rarer, due to standards such as IFRS 16 *Leases*.

Companies will only be able to increase their gearing if they have **suitable assets** to offer for security. Companies with assets which are depreciated rapidly or which are at high risk of obsolescence will be unable to offer sufficient security, eg computer software companies. On the other hand, a property company will have plenty of assets to offer as security whose value is fairly stable (but note the effect of a property slump).

Ideally, the following **gearing profiles** would apply, so that only certain types of company could have higher gearing.

Type of company	Assets	Profits
Highly geared companies	Holding value, long-term	Stable, steady trends
Low geared companies	Rapid depreciation/change	Erratic, volatile

5.2 The effect of accounting policy on gearing/leverage

Variations in accounting policy can have a significant impact on gearing and it will be necessary to consider the individual policies of companies. The main areas which are likely to require consideration area as follows.

(a) Revaluation of non-current assets will have an impact on equity and it will be necessary to consider the frequency of such revaluations.

(b) The structure of group financial statements and methods of consolidation will also have a substantial impact on gearing. For example use of the full goodwill method will improve gearing by including the non-controlling interest within capital.

6 Shareholders' investment ratios

These are the ratios which help equity shareholders and other investors to assess the value and quality of an investment in the **ordinary shares** of a company.

The value of an investment in ordinary shares in a **listed company** is its market value, and so investment ratios must have regard not only to information in the company's financial statements, but also to the current share price.

Earnings per share is a valuable indicator of an ordinary share's performance and you should refer to Chapter 18 to revisit its calculation.

> **Knowledge brought forward from earlier studies**
>
> *Investors' ratios*
>
> *Dividend yield*
>
> Dividend yield $= \dfrac{\text{Div per share}}{\text{Mid-market price}} \%$
>
> - **Low yield**: perhaps the company retains a large proportion of profits to reinvest

PART C ACCOUNTING AND REPORTING TECHNIQUES

- **High yield**: this is a risky company or slow-growing

Dividend cover

$$\text{Dividend cover} = \frac{\text{EPS}}{\text{Dividend per share}}$$

Or $\dfrac{\text{Profit after tax and pref dividend}}{\text{Dividend per ordinary shares}}$

This shows **how safe the dividend is**, or the extent of profit retention. Variations are due to maintaining dividend when profits are declining.

P/E ratio

$$\text{P/E ratio} = \frac{\text{Mid-market price}}{\text{EPS}}$$

The **higher the better** here: it reflects the confidence of the market. A rise in EPS may lead to an increase in P/E ratio (as further rises in EPS are anticipated in the future), but maybe not to same extent: look at the context of the market and industry norms.

Earnings yield

$$\text{Earnings yield} = \frac{\text{EPS}}{\text{Mid-market price}}$$

This shows the dividend yield if there is no retention of profit. It allows you to compare companies with **different dividend payout policies**.

Net assets per share

$$\text{Net assets per share} = \frac{\text{Net assets}}{\text{No of shares}}$$

This is a **crude measure** of value of a company, liable to distortion.

See also **EPS** and **dividend per share**

FAST FORWARD

Always remember that 'profit' and 'net assets' are fairly **arbitrary figures**, affected by different accounting policies and manipulation.

Financial analysis is a vital tool for **auditors**.

Question — Interpretation of financial statements

RST Co is considering purchasing an interest in its competitor XYZ Co. The managing director of RST Co has obtained the three most recent statement of profit or loss and other comprehensive income and statements of financial position of XYZ Co as shown below.

XYZ CO
STATEMENTS OF PROFIT OR LOSS AND OTHER COMPREHENSIVE INCOME FOR YEARS ENDED 31 DECEMBER

	20X6 $'000	20X7 $'000	20X8 $'000
Revenue	18,000	18,900	19,845
Cost of sales	10,440	10,340	11,890
Gross profit	7,560	8,560	7,955
Distribution costs	1,565	1,670	1,405
Administrative expenses	1,409	1,503	1,591
Profit from operations	4,586	5,387	4,959
Interest payable on bank overdraft	104	215	450
Interest payable on 12% debentures	600	600	600

	3,882	4,572	3,909
Profit before taxation			
Income tax	1,380	2,000	1,838
Profit for the period	2,502	2,572	2,071

XYZ CO
STATEMENTS OF FINANCIAL POSITION AS AT 31 DECEMBER

	20X6		20X7		20X8	
	$'000	$'000	$'000	$'000	$'000	$'000
Assets						
Non-current assets						
Land and buildings	11,460		12,121		11,081	
Plant and machinery	8,896		9,020		9,130	
		20,356		21,141		20,211
Current assets						
Inventory	1,775		2,663		3,995	
Trade receivables	1,440		2,260		3,164	
Cash	50		53		55	
		3,265		4,976		7,214
		23,621		26,117		27,425
Equity and liabilities						
Equity						
Share capital	8,000		8,000		8,000	
Retained earnings	6,434		7,313		7,584	
		14,434		15,313		15,584
Non-current liabilities						
12% debentures 20Y1 – 20Y4		5,000		5,000		5,000
Current liabilities						
Trade payables	1,990		2,084		2,246	
Bank	1,300		2,300		3,400	
Taxation	897		1,420		1,195	
		4,187		5,804		6,841
		23,621		26,117		27,425

Required

Prepare a report for the managing director of RST Co commenting on the financial position and performance of XYZ Co and highlighting any areas that require further investigation.

(Marks will be awarded for ratios and other financial statistics where appropriate.)

Answer

To: MD of RST Co
From: An Accountant
Date: XX.XX.XX
Subject: The financial position and performance of XYZ Co

Introduction

This report has been prepared on the basis of the three most recent statements of profit or loss and other comprehensive income and statements of financial position of XYZ Co covering the years 20X6 to 20X8 inclusive. Ratio analysis used in this report is based on the calculations shown in the appendix attached.

Performance

Sales have increased at a steady 5% per annum over the three-year period.

In contrast, the gross profit percentage has increased from 42% in 20X6 to 45% in 20X7 before dropping back to 40% in 20X8. Similarly, operating profit as a percentage of sales was 26% in 20X6, 28.5% in 20X7 and 25% in 20X8. This may indicate some misallocation of costs between 20X7 and 20X8 and should be investigated or it may be indicative of a longer downward trend in profitability.

Return on capital employed, as one would expect, has shown a similar pattern with an increase in 20X7 with a subsequent fall in 20X8 to a level below that of 20X6.

Debt and liquidity

The debt ratio measures the ratio of a company's debt to its equity. Although we have no information as to the norm for the industry as a whole, the debt ratios appear reasonable. However, it should be noted that it has fallen slightly over the three-year period.

When reviewing XYZ Co's liquidity the situation has improved over the period. The current ratio measures a company's ability to meet its current liabilities out of current assets. A ratio of at least 1 should therefore be expected. XYZ Co did not meet this expectation in 20X6 and 20X7.

This ratio can be misleading as inventory is included in current assets. Because inventory can take some time to convert into liquid assets, a second ratio, the quick ratio, is calculated which excludes inventory. As can be seen, the quick ratio, although improving, is low and this shows that current liabilities cannot be met from current assets if inventory is excluded. As a major part of current liabilities is the bank overdraft, the company is obviously relying on the bank's continuing support with short-term funding. It would be useful to find out the terms of the bank funding and the projected cash flow requirements for future funding.

Efficiency ratios

The efficiency ratios, receivables ratio and inventory turnover, give a useful indication of how the company is managing its current assets.

As can be seen from the appendix the receivables collection period has increased over the three years from 29 days to 58 days. This may indicate that the company is failing to follow up its debts efficiently or that it has given increased credit terms to some or all of its customers.

Looking at inventory turnover, this has also risen from 62 days to 122 days. This may be an indication of over-stocking, stocking up on the expectation of a substantial sales increase or the holding of obsolete or slow-moving inventory items which should be written down. More investigation needs to be done on both receivables and inventory.

The financing of additional receivables and inventory has been achieved in the main through the bank overdraft as the trade payables figure has not increased significantly.

Conclusion

The review of the three year financial statements for XYZ Co has given rise to a number of queries which need to be resolved before a useful conclusion can be reached on the financial position and performance of XYZ Co. It may also be useful to compare XYZ Co's ratios to those of other companies in the same industry in order to obtain some idea of the industry norms.

APPENDIX TO MEMORANDUM

	20X6	20X7	20X8
% sales increase ((18,900/18,000) – 1) and (19,845(/18,900) – 1)		5%	5%
Gross profit % (7,560 as % of 18,000), (8,560 as % of 18,900) and (7,955 as % of 19,845)	42%	45%	40%
Operating profit % (4,586 as % of 18,000), (5,387 as % of 18,900) and (4,959 as % of 19,845)	25.5%	28.5%	25%

Return on capital employed

$$= \frac{\text{Profit before interest and tax}}{\text{Capital employed}} \times 100\%$$

	20X6	20X7	20X8
	4,586 – 104 / (14,434 + 5,000)	5,387 – 215 / (15,313 + 5,000)	4,959 – 450 / (15,584 + 5,000)
	= 23%	= 25.5%	= 21.9%

Debt ratio

$$= \frac{\text{Debt}}{\text{Equity}}$$

	20X6	20X7	20X8
	5,000 / 14,434	5,000 / 15,313	5,000 / 15,584

	20X6	20X7	20X8
× 100%	= 34.6%	= 32.7%	= 32.1%

Current ratio

$$= \frac{\text{Current assets}}{\text{Current liabilities}}$$

	20X6	20X7	20X8
	3,265 / 4,187	4,976 / 5,804	7,214 / 6,814
	= 0.78	= 0.86	= 1.06

Quick ratio

$$= \frac{\text{Current assets} - \text{inventory}}{\text{Current liabilities}}$$

	20X6	20X7	20X8
	(3,265 − 1,775) / 4,187	(4,976 − 2,663) / 5,804	(7,214 − 3,995) / 6,814
	= 0.36	= 0.40	= 0.47

Receivables ratio

$$= \frac{\text{Trade receivables}}{\text{Sales}} \times 365 \text{ days}$$

	20X6	20X7	20X8
	1,440 / 18,000	2,260 / 18,900	3,164 / 19,845
	= 29.2 days	= 43.6 days	= 58.2 days

Inventory turnover

$$= \frac{\text{Inventory}}{\text{Cost of sales}} \times 365 \text{ days}$$

	20X6	20X7	20X8
	1,775 / 10,440	2,663 / 10,340	3,995 / 11,890
	= 62 days	= 94 days	= 122.6 days

Question — Interpretation of financial statements 2

You are the management accountant of Fry Co. Laurie Co is a competitor in the same industry and it has been operating for 20 years. Summaries of Laurie Co's statements of profit or loss and other comprehensive income and statements of financial position for the previous three years are given below.

SUMMARISED STATEMENTS OF PROFIT OR LOSS AND OTHER COMPREHENSIVE INCOME
FOR THE YEAR ENDED 31 DECEMBER

	20X6 $m	20X7 $m	20X8 $m
Revenue	840	981	913
Cost of sales	554	645	590
Gross profit	286	336	323
Selling, distribution and administration expenses	186	214	219
Profit before interest	100	122	104
Interest	6	15	19
Profit before taxation	94	107	85
Taxation	45	52	45
Profit for the year	49	55	40

SUMMARISED STATEMENTS OF FINANCIAL POSITION AS AT 31 DECEMBER

	20X6 $m	20X7 $m	20X8 $m
Assets			
Non-current assets			
Intangible assets	36	40	48
Tangible assets	176	206	216
	212	246	264
Current assets			
Inventories	237	303	294
Receivables	105	141	160
Bank	52	58	52
	606	748	770
Equity and liabilities			
Equity			
Ordinary share capital	100	100	100
Retained earnings	299	330	346
	399	430	446
Non-current liabilities			
Non-current loans	74	138	138
Current liabilities			
Trade payables	53	75	75
Other payables	80	105	111
	606	748	770
Dividends paid	24	24	24

You may assume that the index of retail prices has remained constant between 20X0 and 20X2.

Required

Write a report to the finance director of Fry Co in which you:

(a) Assess the performance of Laurie Co, showing any calculations in an appendix to this report.

(b) Recommend five areas which require further investigation, including reference to other pieces of information which would complement your analysis of the performance of Laurie Co.

Answer

(a) To: Finance Director
From: Management accountant
Subject: *Performance of Laurie Co 20X6 to 20X8*

An appendix is attached to this report which shows the ratios calculated as part of the performance review.

Profitability

The gross profit margin has remained relatively static over the three-year period, although it has risen by approximately 1% in 20X8. ROCE, while improving very slightly in 20X7 to 21.5% has dropped dramatically in 20X8 to 17.8%. The profit margin has also fallen in 20X8, in spite of the improvement in the gross profit margin. This marks a rise in expenses which suggests that they are not being well controlled. The utilisation of assets compared to the revenue generated has also declined reflecting the drop in trading activity between 20X7 and 20X8.

Trading levels

It is apparent that there was a dramatic increase in trading activity between 20X7 and 20X8, but then a significant fall in 20X8. Revenue rose by 17% ((981/840) − 1) in 20X7 but fell by 7%

((913/981) – 1) in 20X8. The reasons for this fluctuation are unclear. It may be the effect of some kind of one-off event, or it may be the effect of a change in product mix. Whatever the reason, it appears that improved credit terms granted to customers (receivables payment period up from 46 to 64 days) has not stopped the drop in sales.

Working capital

Both the current ratio and quick ratio demonstrate an adequate working capital situation, although the quick ratio has shown a slight decline. There has been an increased investment over the period in inventories and receivables which has been only partly financed by longer payment periods to trade payables and a rise in other payables (mainly between 20X6 and 20X7).

Capital structure

The level of gearing of the company increased when a further $64m was raised in long-term loans in 20X7 to add to the $74m already in the statement of financial position. Although this does not seem to be a particularly high level of gearing, the debt/equity ratio did rise from 18.5% to 32.0% in 20X7. The interest charge has risen to $19m from $6m in 20X6. The 20X7 charge was $15m, suggesting that either the interest rate on the loan is flexible, or that the full interest charge was not incurred in 20X7. The new long-term loan appears to have funded the expansion in both non-current and current assets in 20X7.

APPENDIX

Ratio	Working	20X6	20X7	20X8
Gross profit margin	(1)	34.0%	34.3%	35.4%
ROCE	(2)	21.1%	21.5%	17.8%
Profit margin	(3)	11.9%	12.4%	11.4%
Assets turnover	(4)	1.78	1.73	1.56
Gearing ratio	(5)	15.6%	24.3%	23.6%
Debt/equity ratio	(6)	18.5%	32.0%	30.9%
Interest cover	(7)	16.7	8.1	5.5
Current ratio	(8)	3.0	2.8	2.7
Quick ratio	(9)	1.2	1.1	1.1
Receivables payment period (days)	(10)	46	52	64
Inventory turnover period (days)	(11)	156	171	182
Payables turnover period	(12)	35	42	46

Workings (all in $m)

		20X6	20X7	20X8
1	Gross profit margin	$\frac{286}{840}$	$\frac{336}{981}$	$\frac{323}{913}$
2	ROCE*	$\frac{100}{473}$	$\frac{122}{568}$	$\frac{104}{584}$
3	Profit margin	$\frac{100}{840}$	$\frac{122}{981}$	$\frac{104}{913}$
4	Assets turnover	$\frac{840}{473}$	$\frac{981}{568}$	$\frac{913}{584}$
5	Gearing ratio	$\frac{74}{74 + 399}$	$\frac{138}{138+430}$	$\frac{138}{138+446}$
6	Debt/equity ratio	$\frac{74}{399}$	$\frac{138}{430}$	$\frac{138}{446}$
7	Interest cover	$\frac{100}{6}$	$\frac{122}{15}$	$\frac{104}{19}$
8	Current ratio	$\frac{394}{133}$	$\frac{502}{180}$	$\frac{506}{186}$

		20X6	20X7	20X8
9	Quick ratio	$\dfrac{157}{133}$	$\dfrac{199}{180}$	$\dfrac{212}{186}$
10	Receivables payment period	$\dfrac{105}{840} \times 365$	$\dfrac{141}{981} \times 365$	$\dfrac{160}{913} \times 365$
11	Inventory turnover period	$\dfrac{237}{554} \times 365$	$\dfrac{303}{645} \times 365$	$\dfrac{294}{590} \times 365$
12	Payables payment period	$\dfrac{53}{554} \times 365$	$\dfrac{75}{645} \times 365$	$\dfrac{75}{590} \times 365$

*ROCE has been calculated here as:

$$\frac{\text{Profit before interest and taxation (PBIT)}}{\text{Capital employed}}$$

where capital employed = equity plus non-current liabilities. It is possible to calculate ROCE using profit after taxation and interest, but this admits variations and distortions into the ratio which are not affected by **trading** activity.

(b) Areas for further investigation include the following:

(i) *Non-current loan*

There is no indication as to why this loan was raised and how it was used to finance the business. Further details are needed of interest rate(s), security given and repayment dates.

(ii) *Trading activity*

The level of sales has fluctuated in quite a strange way and this requires further investigation and explanation. Factors to consider would include pricing policies, product mix, market share and any unique occurrence which would affect sales.

(iii) *Further breakdown*

It would be useful to break down some of the information in the financial statements, perhaps into a management accounting format. Examples would include the following.

(1) Sales by segment, market or geographical area
(2) Cost of sales split, into raw materials, labour and overheads
(3) Inventory broken down into raw materials, work in progress and finished goods
(4) Expenses analysed between administrative expenses, sales and distribution costs

(iv) *Accounting policies*

Accounting policies may have a significant effect on certain items. In particular, it would be useful to know what the accounting policies are in relation to intangible assets (and what these assets consist of), and whether there has been any change in accounting policies.

(v) *Dividend policy*

The company has maintained the level of dividend paid to shareholders (although it has not been raised during the three-year period). Presumably the company would have been able to reduce the amount of long-term debt taken on if it had retained part or all of the dividend during this period. It would be interesting to examine the share price movement during the period and calculate the dividend cover.

Tutorial note. Other matters raised could have included:

1 Working capital problems, particularly inventory turnover and control over receivables

2 EPS (which cannot be calculated here as the number of shares is not given) and other related investor statistics, such as the P/E ratio.

Chapter roundup

- Make sure that you can **define** all the ratios. Look out for variations in definitions of ratios which might appear in questions.
- Always remember that 'profit' and 'net assets' are fairly **arbitrary figures**, affected by different accounting policies and manipulation.
- Financial analysis is a vital tool for **auditors**.

Quick quiz

1. Why might a company's trade creditors be interested in its financial statements?
2. What are the main sources of financial information available to the external users?
3. Apart from ratio analysis, what other information might be helpful in interpreting a company's financial statements?
4. In a period when profits are fluctuating, what effect does a company's level of gearing have on the profits available for ordinary shareholders?
5. Why is it important to consider the accounting policy for non-current assets when analysing return on capital employed?

Answers to quick quiz

1. A company's trade creditors will have three main interests:
   - is the company able to pay the amounts owed?
   - is it likely that the company will continue in operation into the future and will therefore require the products/services provided by the creditor going forward?
   - are they trading with a reputable company?

   Analysis of the financial statements (and the wider annual report) is likely to provide the trade creditors with some information on the above.

2. Published financial statements and interim statements, filed documents, government statistics

3.
   - Other comments in the financial statements eg Directors' Report/Management Commentary/Business review
   - Age and nature of the assets
   - Current and future market developments
   - Recent acquisition or disposal of subsidiaries
   - Notes to the financial statements, auditors' report, events after the reporting period, etc.

4. Profits available for the shareholders will be highly volatile and in some years there may not be earnings cover for an ordinary dividend paid

5. A company that revalues its non-current assets will have a revaluation surplus within equity, and therefore a higher capital employed than a company that holds its assets at historical cost. The ROCE will therefore be lower for a company that adopts a revaluation policy.

End of chapter question

Curia (AIA May 2005)

A client of yours has applied for an executive post with Curia, a limited liability company. He is to be interviewed shortly and is keen to show a good knowledge of the company at the interview. The client has commissioned you to write a report on the recent performance of Curia.

You have obtained the following financial ratios which have been calculated from the financial statements of Curia for the three years ended 31 March 20X3, 20X4 and 20X5.

Financial year ended 31 March	*20X3*	*20X4*	*20X5*
Return on equity	10%	15%	13%
Net income to sales revenue	2.6%	4.3%	4.2%
Sales revenue to total assets	2.11	2.12	1.93
Gross profit to sales revenue	15%	18%	21%
Operating expenses to sales revenue	11%	12%	15%
Current/working capital ratio	1.33	1.42	1.30
Acid test ratio	0.96	1.03	0.95
Credit to customers (months)	1.7	1.5	1.2
Credit from suppliers (months)	1.5	1.5	1.3
Inventory turnover (months)	0.8	0.7	0.6
Earnings per share (cents per share)	14.3	25.2	23.4
Dividend per share (cents per share)	12.5	12.5	12.5
Net assets per share	1.50	1.63	1.74

Required

On the basis of the above information report to your client. Your report should include

- Reviews the performance of Curia as evidenced by the above ratios,
- Makes recommendations as to how the overall performance of Curia could be improved, and
- Indicates any limitations in your analysis.

(25 marks)

PART C ACCOUNTING AND REPORTING TECHNIQUES

Answers to end of chapter questions

IASB

The purpose and status of the IASB's *Conceptual Framework* is included within it, being to:

(a) assist the International Accounting Standards Board (Board) to develop IFRS Standards (Standards) that are based on consistent concepts;

(b) assist preparers to develop consistent accounting policies when no Standard applies to a particular transaction or other event, or when a Standard allows a choice of accounting policy; and

(c) assist all parties to understand and interpret the Standards.

The following points may be made in favour of the *Conceptual Framework*.

(a) Its principles are being used in the formulation of standards, for example its definition of an asset and liability are consistent with new standards, such as IFRS 16 *Leases*. It must be noted, however, that the new definitions provided by the revised *Conceptual Framework* (2018) are now inconsistent with some of the older standards, such as the definition of a liability used in IAS 37 *Provisions, Contingent Liabilities and Contingent Assets*.

(b) The *Conceptual Framework* helps reduce scope for individual judgement and the potential subjectivity that this implies.

(c) Financial statements should be more comparable because, although alternative treatments will still be available, there will be a consistent and coherent framework on which to base one's choice of a particular alternative.

(d) The *Conceptual Framework* puts forward a consistent terminology and consistent objectives, for example in the definitions and the qualitative characteristics.

It could be argued that the *Conceptual Framework* is too theoretical. It is certainly general rather than particular. However, as has been seen with IFRS 15 and IFRS 16, the general principles can be applied to very specific issues in accounting standards. Moreover, in areas not at present covered by accounting standards, the statement can give general guidance. Nevertheless, in the short term, the principles in the *Conceptual Framework*, and the definitions provided, may conflict with some accounting standards which have already been issued before it was revised.

Polymer

POLYMER CO: STATEMENT OF PROFIT OR LOSS FOR THE YEAR ENDED 31 MAY 20X8

	$
Revenue	1,526,750
Cost of sales (W3)	(1,048,000)
Gross profit	478,750
Distribution costs (W4)	(124,300)
Administrative expenses (W5)	(216,200)
Finance costs (W6)	(18,400)
Profit before tax	119,850
Income tax expense	(40,000)
PROFIT FOR THE YEAR	79,850

ANSWERS TO END OF CHAPTER QUESTIONS

POLYMER CO: STATEMENT OF FINANCIAL POSITION AS AT 31 MAY 20X8

	$
ASSETS	
Non-current assets	
Property, plant and equipment (W7)	452,250
Intangible assets	215,500
	667,750
Current assets	
Inventories (W8)	425,750
Receivables (W9)	171,880
Cash and cash equivalents	5,120
	602,750
Total assets	1,270,500
EQUITY AND LIABILITIES	
Equity	
Share capital	300,000
Share premium	100,000
Retained earnings (283,500 + 79,850)	363,350
General reserve	50,000
Revaluation surplus	50,000
	863,350
Non-current liabilities	
10% debentures	100,000
8.4% cumulative redeemable preference shares	100,000
	200,000
Current liabilities	
Trade and other payables (W10)	115,900
Bank overdraft	51,250
Current tax payable	40,000
	207,150
Total equity and liabilities	1,270,500

Workings

1 Depreciation

		$
Cost of sales:	8% × 150,000 plant and equipment	12,000
Administration:	10% × 50,000 furniture and fixtures	5,000
	1/4 × 20% × (75,000 – 25,000) motor vehicles	2,500
		7,500
Distribution:	3/4 × 20% × (75,000 – 25,000) motor vehicles	7,500

2 Depreciation (amortisation) of lease

$75,000 × 1/50   1,500

3 Cost of sales

	$
Opening inventories (108,400 + 32,750 + 184,500)	325,650
Purchases	750,600
Carriage inwards	10,500
Manufacturing wages	250,000
Manufacturing overheads	125,000
Depreciation of plant (W1)	12,000
Closing inventories (W8)	(425,750)
	1,048,000

ANSWERS TO END OF CHAPTER QUESTIONS

4   *Distribution costs*

		$
Per question		116,800
Depreciation (W1)		7,500
		124,300

5   *Administrative expenses*

		$
Per question		158,100
Legal expenses	54,100	
less: solicitors' fees capitalised	(5,000)	
		49,100
Depreciation (W1)		7,500
Amortisation of lease (W2)		1,500
		216,200

6   *Finance costs*

	$
Interest expense on loan notes ($100,000 × 10%)	10,000
Preference dividend	8,400
	18,400

7   *Property, plant and equipment*

	Freehold land $	Leasehold property $	Plant & Equipment $	Furniture & fixtures $	Motor vehicles $	Total $
Carrying amount per TB						
Cost or valuation	250,000	75,000	150,000	50,000	75,000	
Accumulated dep'n	–	(15,000)	(68,500)	(15,750)	(25,000)	
Net carrying amount	250,000	60,000	81,500	34,250	50,000	
Solicitor's fees	5,000					
Depreciation charge	–	(1,500)	(12,000)	(5,000)	(10,000)	
Carrying amount 31 May 20X8	255,000	58,500	69,500	29,250	40,000	452,250

8   *Inventories*

	$
Raw materials	112,600
Work in progress	37,800
Finished goods	275,350
	425,750

9   *Receivables*

	$
Trade receivables (177,630 – 5,750 allowance for receivables)	171,880

10   *Trade and other payables*

	$
Trade payables	97,500
Loan interest payable	10,000
Preference dividend payable	8,400
	115,900

Schrodenfischer

Conventional financial statements do not highlight or specifically disclose sustainability matters. The managing director should consider following one of the sustainability disclosure frameworks.

There are a number of different options including:

- IFRS Sustainability Disclosure Standards
- GRI Standards
- European Sustainability Reporting Standards (ESRS)

IFRS Sustainability Disclosure Standards are issued by the ISSB, which works alongside the IASB. Schrodenfischer already prepares its financial reporting using IFRS Accounting Standards. As an owner-managed business, IFRS Sustainability Disclosure Standards may not be the most appropriate as the disclosures required are aimed at investors, creditors and lenders. These standards also focus on the impact of sustainability matters on the business, rather than the impact of the business on society and the environment.

Both GRI Standards and ESRS are intended for a wider range of stakeholders and have a focus on the impact of the business on the environment. ESRS applies a double materiality approach, looking at both financial and impacts materiality.

Schrodenfischer is not a listed company so probably will not have a mandatory requirement to adopt any of the standards. As a European company, adoption of ESRS might be the most appropriate, particularly if there is any intention to list the company going forward.

Another option if for Schrondenfischer to prepare a sustainability report as part of the corporate report, using the relevant parts of the frameworks and relevant metrics and targets.

Mancroft

Treatment of the sale of inventory

This transaction is known as 'window dressing'. It should not be shown as a sale; the sale must be cancelled and the inventory re-instated at $1m (cost) rather than $3m sales price.

The entries for the cancellation of the sale are:

DEBIT	Sales	$3m	
CREDIT	Cash (current liabilities)		$3m

For the cancellation of the purchase:

DEBIT	Cash (current assets)	$3m	
CREDIT	Purchases		$3m

The above entries have no effect on retained earnings, but the elimination of unrealised profit, reducing inventory from $3m to $1m, will affect it.

DEBIT	Closing inventory/cost of sales (Hungate's books): 3 – 1	$2m	
CREDIT	Inventory (current asset)		$2m

Ethical implications of sale of inventory

Members of the accounting profession enjoy a number of privileges. These include:

(a) Special status and respect within the community.

(b) Self-regulation, that is regulation by the accountants' professional body.

(c) An exclusive right to certain functions. For example, auditors must be members of certain professional bodies.

Like other professions, the accounting profession has **features that distinguish it** from non-professional jobs. The most important of these is specialist knowledge, but also recognition as being committed to the good of society, rather than just commercial gain.

To **earn this status and these privileges**, accountants should, as a minimum:

(a) Be committed to the fair presentation of financial statements.

(b) Show independence and objectivity in applying financial reporting standards.

(c) Be committed to an ethical approach to business, and apply this in the preparation of financial statements.

Ethical behaviour in the preparation of financial statements, and in other areas, is of **paramount importance**. This applies equally to preparers of financial statements, to auditors and to accountants giving advice to directors. Company accountants act unethically if they use 'creative' accounting in financial statements preparation to make the figures look better.

In treating the inventory as sold, Mancroft is indulging in '**window dressing**'. This is not a genuine sale; its purpose is purely **to show Mancroft's subsidiary Hungate in a better financial position** than is truly the case, in order to increase the likelihood of the sale of Hungate. The 'sale' of inventory would increase cash and retained earnings by $2m, boosting the appearance of both profitability and liquidity. This would **mislead a potential buyer**. Nor would this manipulation be a 'one-off'; if the subsidiary is not sold, the transaction would be carried out again in the interim financial statements. Neither the final financial statements for the year, nor the interim financial statements would give a fair presentation of the financial position and performance.

The treatment of the inventory is therefore **unethical**, and should be reversed when preparing the consolidated financial statements.

Small and medium-sized entities

Advantages

Although IFRS were originally designed to be suitable for all types of entity, they have become increasingly complex in recent years. It is often argued that they are now designed primarily to meet the information needs of **institutional investors in large, listed entities**.

Shareholders of SMEs are often also directors. Therefore, through managing the company and maintaining the financial records, they are already aware of the company's financial performance and position and so do not need the level of detail in financial statements required by external institutional investors of larger companies.

The main external **users of SMEs tend to be lenders, trade suppliers and the tax authorities**. They have **different needs** from institutional investors and are more likely to focus on shorter-term cash flows, liquidity and solvency.

Full IFRS covers a wide range of issues, contain a sizeable amount of implementation guidance and include disclosure requirements appropriate for public companies. This can make them **too complex for users of SMEs to understand.**

Many SMEs now feel that following full IFRS places an unacceptable burden on preparers of SME financial statements – a burden that has been growing as IFRS become more detailed and more countries adopt them. The **cost of following full IFRS often appears to outweigh the benefits**.

The **disclosure** requirements of full IFRS are very **extensive** and as such, can result in **information overload** for the users of SME financial statements, reducing the understandability of financial statements.

Some IFRS still offer **choice of accounting treatments**, leading to **lack of comparability** between different companies adopting different accounting standards.

ANSWERS TO END OF CHAPTER QUESTIONS

Disadvantages

If SMEs follow their own simplified IFRS, their financial statements will **no longer be comparable** with larger companies following full IFRS or SMEs choosing to follow full IFRS. This may make it harder to attract investors.

The changeover from full IFRS to the simplified IFRS for SMEs, will require training and possible changes in systems. This will place both a **time and cost** burden on the company.

Full IFRS is now well established and respected and act as a form of **quality control** on financial statements which comply with it. It could be argued therefore that financial statements which no longer comply with full IFRS will **lose their credibility**. This is often called the 'Big GAAP, Little GAAP divide'.

The new IFRS for SMEs proposes to **reduce disclosures** required by full IFRS. Omission of certain key information might actually make the financial statements **harder to understand**.

Conclusion

The advantages for SMEs of having a separate simplified IFRS outweigh the disadvantages. Now that the IASB has issued the IFRS for SMEs, both preparers and users of SME financial statements will benefit.

Akkeal

AKKEAL: CONSOLIDATED STATEMENT OF PROFIT OR LOSS FOR THE YEAR ENDED 31 MARCH 20X4

	$'000
Revenue (16,400 + 8,870 – 1,500 (W1))	23,770
Cost of sales (5,600 + 4,200 – 1,500 (W) + 25 (W1))	(8,325)
Gross profit	15,445
Operating expenses (5,780 + 3,370)	(9,150)
Dividends receivable (W3)	757
Investment income (233 + 97)	330
Finance cost (333 + 240)	(573)
Share of profit of Joint Venture (1,260 × 25%)	
Share of profit of Associate (2,290 × 30%)	687
Profit before tax	7,911
Income tax expense (1,800 – 500)	(2,300)
Profit for the period	5,511
Attributable to:	
Owners of the parent (Bal fig)	5,018
Non-controlling interest (W2)	493
	5,511
Earnings per share (in cents) (5,018 ÷ 20,000)	25.1

Earnings per share is based on group profit after tax, and non-controlling interest ($5,018,000) divided by 20,000,000 ordinary shares issued and ranking for dividends.

Workings:

1

	$'000
Intercompany sales	1,500
Mark-up	20.00%
Profit loading (1,500 × 20/120)	250
Proportion unsold	10.00%
Provision for unrealised profit	25

Here the provision should be made by Belloan

2

	$'000
Non-controlling interest	
Subsidiary's profit after tax	1,257
Provision for unrealised profit	(25)
	1,232
Non-controlling %	40%
Non-controlling interest	492.8

3 Dividends receivable

Akkeal plc	1,247	
Belloan plc	600	
less		
Belloan plc to Akkeal plc	(420)	60% of 700
Curtyn plc to Akkeal plc	(450)	30% of 1,500
Dojin plc to Akkeal plc	(220)	¼ of 880
	757	

Insolo

This question tests the preparation of a consolidated statement of financial position for a vertical group.

Note. An alternative calculation of the goodwill and non-controlling interest in Transbuy is provided at the end of this Answer.

(a) **Calculation of goodwill**

In Vanior

Interest of holding company (1,350 as % of 2,250)	60%	
Consideration transferred (1,350 × $2.85)	3,847,500	(i)
Net assets acquired		
Reserves at acquisition	1,262,500	
Surplus on revaluation	400,000	
	1,662,500	
Ordinary share capital	2,250,000	
	3,912,500	
by	60%	
	2,347,500	(ii)
Goodwill (i less ii)	$1,500,000	

In Transbuy

		$
Insolo's interest in the consideration transferred by Vanior	Ords: (1,260 × $2.15 × 60%)	1,625,400
	Prefs: (60 × $1.25 × 60%)	45,000
		1,670,400
Insolo's effective interest in the fair value of identifiable NA acquired:	Ords: 60% × 70% × 2,462,857 (see below)	(1,034,400)
	Prefs: 60% × 20% × 300,000	(36,000)
Goodwill in respect of Transbuy		600,000
Impairment to date		(220,000)
Carrying amount of goodwill in Transbuy		380,000
Goodwill in respect of Vanior		1,500,000
Total carrying amount of goodwill		1,880,000

ANSWERS TO END OF CHAPTER QUESTIONS

Transbuy: Identifiable net assets acquired

Ordinary share capital	1,800,000
Reserves at acquisition	662,857
	2,462,857

(b) INSOLO
CONSOLIDATED STATEMENT OF FINANCIAL POSITION AS AT 31 OCTOBER 20X7

ASSETS

Non-current assets $
Intangible asset – goodwill (1,500 + 600 per (a) – 220)	1,880,000
Property, plant and equipment (W1)	12,805,600
Other non-current investments, at cost (W2)	73,800
	14,759,400

Current assets $
Inventories, at cost (W3)	801,200
Trade receivables (W4)	1,152,630
Other receivables (W5)	137,590
Cash and cash equivalents	630,530
	2,721,950
Total assets	17,481,350

EQUITY AND LIABILITIES
Equity
Issued share capital:
Ordinary shares of $1	2,000,000
Preference shares of $1	400,000
Retained earnings (W7)	8,054,167
	10,454,167
Non-controlling interest (W8)	4,165,693
	14,619,860
Non-current liabilities (W6)	1,240,800
	1,240,800

Current liabilities
Trade payables (539.08 + 345.62 + 412.09 – 94.4 (W4))	1,202,390
Other payables (66.9 + 18.7 + 14.5)	100,100
Current taxation (164.2 + 88.6 + 65.4)	318,200
	1,620,690
Total equity	14,619,860
Total liabilities	2,861,490
Total equity and liabilities	17,481,350

Other workings

1   Property, Plant and Equipment

In Insolo	4,568,900
In Vanior	3,556,000
In Transbuy	4,280,700
Surplus on revaluation	400,000
	12,805,600

ANSWERS TO END OF CHAPTER QUESTIONS

2 Non-current Asset Investments

The non-current asset investments consist of

	Insolo $	Vanior $	Transbuy $
In Transbuy			
Ordinary shares	3,847,500		
In Transbuy			
Ordinary shares	–	2,709,000	
Preference shares	–	75,000	
	3,847,500	2,784,000	
Therefore other investments =	22,000	17,600	34,200
	3,869,500	2,801,600	34,200

Therefore consolidated non-current asset investments:

Insolo	22,000
Vanior	17,600
Transbuy	34,200
	73,800

3 Inventories

This is the total for the group companies less the total unrealised profit.

Insolo	440,000
Vanior	186,500
Transbuy	230,800
Unrealised profit (100 – 68.2) + (80 – 55.7)	(56,100)
	801,200

4 Trade Receivables

This is the total for the group companies less the total intercompany indebtedness.

Insolo	539,080
Vanior	306,750
Transbuy	401,200
Intragroup (41.2 + 53.2)	(94,400)
	1,152,630

5 Other Receivables

This is the total for the group companies.

Ie	Insolo	87,090
	Vanior	34,000
	Transbuy	16,500
		137,590

6 Non-current Liabilities

This is the total for the companies in the group less intragroup loans.

Ie	Insolo	500,000
	Vanior	420,000
	Transbuy	320,800
		1,240,800

ANSWERS TO END OF CHAPTER QUESTIONS

7 Retained Earnings

Retained profits at consolidation:

	Insolo $	Vanior $	Transbuy $
Per statement of financial position	6,071,090	3,748,230	2,258,140
Goodwill written off		(220,000)	
Surplus on revaluation		400,000	
Unrealised profit in inventory (W3)	(31,800)	(24,300)	
	6,039,290	3,903,930	2,258,140
Retained profits as at acquisition:			
per statements of financial position		1,262,500	662,857
surplus on revaluation		400,000	
		1,662,500	662,857
Post-acquisition retained profits		2,241,430	1,595,283
Interest of holding company		60%	70%
		1,344,858	1,116,698
Share of sub-subsidiary			60%
			670,019
Hence, to non-controlling interest			446,679
So, group retained profits			
Holding company		6,039,290	
Subsidiaries	1,344,858		
	670,019		
		2,014,877	
		8,054,167	

8 Non-controlling Interest

	Vanior $	Transbuy $
Ordinary share capital	2,250,000	1,800,000
Reserves at consolidation (W7)	3,903,930	2,258,140
	6,153,930	4,058,140
Less Vanior investment in Transbuy (W2)	2,784,000	–
	3,369,930	4,058,140
	× 40%	× (100% – (60% × 70%))
	1,347,972	2,353,721
Pref share capital – Vanior = 100%, Transbuy = (100% – (60% × 20%)) × 300,000	200,000	264,000
	1,547,972	2,617,721
		4,165,693

AN ALTERNATIVE CALCULATION OF THE GOODWILL AND NON-CONTROLLING INTEREST IN TRANSBUY

GOODWILL

Interest of holding co	Ord. (1,260 as % of 1,800)		70%	
	Pref. (60 as % of 300)		20%	
Consideration transferred	(1,260 × $2.15) + (60 × $1.25)		2,784,000	(i)
Net assets acquired				
Reserves at acquisition			662,857	
Ordinary share capital			1,800,000	
			2,462,857	
		by	70%	
			1,724,000	

Preference shares		300,000	
	by	20%	
			60,000
			1,784,000 (ii)
Goodwill (i – ii)			$1,000,000
Goodwill in respect of Vanior (unchanged)			$1,500,000
Impairment			($220,000)
Total carrying amount of goodwill			$2,280,000

Higher by 400,000 (2,280,000 – 1,880,000)

NON-CONTROLLING INTEREST

	Vanior	Transbuy
Ordinary share capital	2,250,000	1,800,000
Reserves at consolidation	3,903,930	2,258,140
	6,153,930	4,058,140
Non-controlling interest (W7)	40%	30%
	2,461,572	1,217,442
Preference shares	200,000	300,000
Non-controlling interest	100%	80%
	200,000	240,000

Total non-controlling interest is	
	2,461,572
	1,217,442
	200,000
	240,000
Extra non-controlling interest in sub-subsidiary (1,116,698 × 40%) (W7)	446,679
	$4,565,693

Total non-controlling interest
Higher by 400,000 (4,565,693 – 4,165,693)

Mozart, Constanza and Salzburg

This question tests the application of knowledge and understanding of group financial statements. This case study required the preparation of a consolidated statement of financial position for a group where a controlling interest in a subsidiary has been disposed of but the former subsidiary has been retained as a joint venture. The question also tests the calculation of profit or loss on the disposal of a block of shares and its different treatments in the financial statements of the parent and the group financial statements.

(a) Interest of holding company in Salzburg

- before disposal   60.0% for   6 months
- after disposal   25.0% for   6 months

Interest sold 35.0%

(i) **Calculation of holding company profit/(loss) on disposal**

	$
Fair value of consideration received (2 × 525,000)	1,050,000
Carrying value of investment sold (35/60 × (60% × 1,500,000 × 2.20))	(1,155,000)
	(105,000)
Income tax relief thereon at 30%	31,500
Holding company's loss on sale	(73,500)

ANSWERS TO END OF CHAPTER QUESTIONS

(ii) Calculation of group profit/loss on disposal

		$
Fair value of consideration received (as above)		1,050,000
Fair value of interest retained = proportion of net assets (25% × 2,230,245 (see below))		557,561
		1,607,561
Net assets at date control lost (60% × 2,230,245) (see below)		(1,338,147)
Goodwill at date control lost		–
Group profit on sale		**269,414**

Net assets at date control lost	$	$
Share capital		1,500,000
Reserves at year-end		986,000
Profit for the year	511,511	
Proportion of year	½	
		(255,755)
		2,230,245

(b) Mozart

CONSOLIDATED STATEMENT OF FINANCIAL POSITION AS AT 31 DECEMBER 20X5

	$
Assets	
Non-current assets	
Intangible assets (W1)	207,000
Property, plant and equipment (5,548,450 + 3,370,400)	8,918,850
	621,500
	9,747,350
Current assets (1,133,000 + 724,000)	1,857,000
Total assets	1,604,350
Equity	
Ordinary shares of $1	5,000,000
Retained earnings (W3)	3,969,500
	8,969,500
Non-controlling interests (40% × 3,660,000)	1,464,000
	10,433,500
Liabilities	
Current liabilities (767,950 – 31,500 tax relief + 434,400)	1,170,850
	11,604,350

Workings

1 *Intangible assets*

	$
Calculation of goodwill in Constanza	
Consideration transferred	1,680,000
Non-controlling interests (40% × 2,455,000)	982,000
	2,662,000
Net assets acquired	
Subsidiary's share capital at acquisition	2,000,000
Subsidiary's reserves at acquisition	455,000
	2,455,000
Goodwill	207,000
Calculation of goodwill in Salzburg	
Consideration transferred (60% × 1,500,000) × $2.20	1,980,000
Non-controlling interests (40% × 2,285,000 (see below))	914,000
	2,894,000
Net assets acquired	
Subsidiary's share capital at acquisition	1,500,000

		$
Subsidiary's reserves at acquisition		785,000
		2,285,000
Goodwill		609,000
Less Impairment to date		(609,000)
Carrying amount		Nil

2   Investment in Joint Venture

	$
Fair value of investment retained on date control lost	557,561
Share of post-disposal earnings (511,511 × 6/12 × 25%)	63,939
	621,500

3   Group Retained Earnings

	Mozart	Constanza	Salzburg 25%	Salzburg 35% sold
	$	$	$	$
Per question/at date of disposal	4,573,500	1,660,000	986,000	730,245
Less: proceeds of disposal	(1,050,000)			
Group profit on disposal (part (a))	269,414			
Tax relief on disposal (part (a))	31,500			
Retained earnings at acquisition		(455,000)	(785,000)	(785,000)
		1,205,000	201,000	(54,755)
Constanza: share of post-acqn. earnings (1,205,000 × 60%)	723,000			
Salzburg: share of post-acqn. earnings (201,000 × 25%)	50,250			
Salzburg: share of post-acqn losses ((54,755) × 35%)	(19,164)			
Goodwill impairment	(609,000)			
	3,969,500			

Eufonion

This is a largely discursive question focusing on functional currencies. The small numerical part is not difficult, but other areas need careful consideration. Part (d) may prove difficult – but it is included in the Basis for Conclusions in the standard.

(a)   The currency of the primary economic environment in which the entity operates generating and expending cash will normally be its functional currency. The entity should consider:

- The currency which mainly influences its selling prices for goods and services, and
- The currency which mainly influences its labour, materials and other costs of providing its goods and services,
- The currency which funds the entity's financing activities
- The currency in which the funds from operating activities are normally retained.

If the functional currency is not obvious from the above, management should use its judgement to decide which currency most faithfully represents the economic effects of its transactions and conditions.

(b)   All items in the statement of financial position would be translated at the closing rate of €1 = $1.38074 (1/0.72425).

	€m	Factor	$m
ASSETS			
Non-current assets			
Property, plant and equipment	420	1.38074	580

	€m	Factor	$m
Current assets			
Inventories	26	1.38074	36
Trade and other receivables	42	1.38074	58
Cash and cash equivalents	8	1.38074	11
	76		105
Total assets	496		685
EQUITY AND LIABILITIES			
Equity			
Share capital	200	1.38074	276
Retained earnings	107	1.38074	148
	307		424
Non-current liabilities	85	1.38074	117
Current liabilities			
Trade and other payables	63	1.38074	87
Current taxation	41	1.38074	57
	104		144
Total liabilities	189		261
Total equity and liabilities	496		685

(c) As far as the statement of profit or loss is concerned income and expenses should be translated using exchange rates as at the date of the transactions. If exchange rates have not fluctuated significantly the company may be able to use the average rate as an approximation for the actual rates.

Assets and liabilities should be translated using the closing rate as at the end of the reporting period. IAS 21 does not offer any guidance as to how equity items should be translated. The exposure draft proposed using the closing rate for equity items other than 'those resulting from income and expenditure recognised in the period'. However, IAS 21 is silent. The directors could follow the proposals in the exposure draft. Other authorities recommend using historical rates for equity items.

All exchange differences resulting from the translation from the functional currency to the presentation currency should be separately disclosed in equity.

The directors should also disclose in the financial statements

- That the presentation currency is different from the functional currency
- What the functional currency is
- The reason for using a different presentation currency.

(d) There are strong arguments in favour of allowing a reporting entity to present its financial statements in a currency other than its functional currency.

- It is consistent with the increasing globalisation of economic activity and the capital market.
- It is consistent with removing restrictions in order to increase the efficiency of the international capital markets.
- Many reporting entities do not have a single functional currency, and it may not be clear which one should be the presentation currency.
- Some jurisdictions may require the presentation of financial statements in the local currency which might not be the same as the functional currency. This would mean reporting entities preparing two sets of financial statements for legal rather than economic reasons.
- A company may raise capital in a variety of markets – and therefore should have the right to report to markets in the appropriate currency.
- Management may not use one single currency in managing the activities of a global group – control and monitoring may be done in different currencies as appropriate.

Arguments against include:

- The functional currency is the currency of the primary economic environment in which the reporting entity operates. This should therefore be the currency which most usefully reflects the economic effects of transactions and events on the entity.

- If an entity has a number of functional currencies the functional currency in which top management controls and monitors performance should be the currency used for the financial statements.

- Presentation of the financial statements in more than one currency may be confusing for users. It might be better to present in the functional currency – but, if helpful, present convenience translations outside the scope of international standards.

Porter

PORTER GROUP
STATEMENT OF CASH FLOWS FOR THE YEAR ENDED 31 MAY 20X6

	$m	$m
Cash flows from Operating Activities		
Profit before taxation	112	
Adjustments for:		
Depreciation	44	
Impairment losses on goodwill (W2)	3	
Foreign exchange loss (W8)	2	
Investment income – share of profit of associate	(12)	
Investment income – gains on financial assets measured at fair value	(6)	
Interest expense	16	
	159	
Increase in trade receivables (132 – 112 – 16)	(4)	
Decrease in inventories (154 – 168 – 20)	34	
Decrease in trade payables (110 – 98 – 12 – (W8) 17 PPE payable)	(17)	
Cash generated from operations	172	
Interest paid (W7)	(12)	
Income taxes paid (W6)	(37)	
Net cash from operating activities		123
Cash flows from investing activities		
Acquisition of subsidiary, net of cash acquired (26 – 8)	(18)	
Purchase of property, plant and equipment (W1)	(25)	
Purchase of financial assets (W4)	(10)	
Dividend received from associate (W3)	11	
Net cash used in investing activities		(42)
Cash flows from financing activities		
Proceeds from issue of share capital	18	
(332 + 212 – 300 – 172 – (80 × 60%/2 × $2.25))		
Proceeds from non-current borrowings (380 – 320)	60	
Dividend paid	(45)	
Dividends paid to non-controlling interests (W5)	(4)	
Net cash from financing activities		29
Net decrease in cash and cash equivalents		110
Cash and cash equivalents at the beginning of the year		48
Cash and cash equivalents at the end of the year		158

ANSWERS TO END OF CHAPTER QUESTIONS

Workings

1 *Additions to property, plant and equipment*

PROPERTY, PLANT AND EQUIPMENT

	$m		$m
b/d	812		
Revaluation	58	Depreciation	44
Acquisition of subsidiary	92		
Additions on credit (W8)	15		
∴ Additions for cash	25	c/d	958
	1,002		1,002

2 *Impairment losses on goodwill*

GOODWILL

	$m		$m
b/d	10		
Acq'n of subsidiary		∴ Impairment losses	3
[(80 × 60%/2 × 2.25) + 26 − (120 × 60%)]	8		
		c/d	15
	18		18

3 *Dividends received from associate*

INVESTMENT IN ASSOCIATE

	$m		$m
b/d	39		
P/L	12	∴ Dividends received	11
OCI	8		
		c/d	48
	59		59

4 *Purchase of financial assets*

FINANCIAL ASSETS MEASURED AT FAIR VALUE

	$m		$m
b/d	0		
P/L	6		
∴ Additions	10		
		c/d	16
	16		16

5 *Dividends paid to non-controlling interests*

NON-CONTROLLING INTERESTS

	$m		$m
		b/d	28
∴ Dividends paid	4	TCI	12
c/d	84	Acquisition of subsidiary (120 × 40%)	48
			88
	88		

6 Income taxes paid

INCOME TAX PAYABLE

	$m		$m
		b/d (deferred tax)	26
		b/d (current tax)	22
		P/L	34
∴ Income taxes paid	37	OCI	17
c/d (deferred tax)	38	Acquisition of subsidiary	4
c/d (current tax)	28		
	103		103

7 Interest paid

INTEREST PAYABLE

	$m		$m
		b/d	4
		P/L	16
∴ Interest paid	12		
c/d	8		
	20		20

8 Foreign currency transaction

Transactions recorded on: $m $m

(1) 5 March DEBIT Property, plant and equipment (102m/6.8) 15
              CREDIT Payables   15

(2) 31 May   Payable = 102m/6.0 = $17m

             DEBIT P/L (Admin expenses)   2
             CREDIT Payables (17 – 15)   2

Tollirene

Report

To: Chief Executive Officer
From:
Date:
Subject: Impact of International Standards on Tollirene

IFRS 1 applies to the first financial statements produced using IFRS. In the case of Tollirene that will be both the interim financial statements and the full financial statements for the year ended 31 December 20X5.

The standard allows for what essentially is a form of 'fresh start' accounting. An opening Statement of financial position will be prepared as at the start of the period covered by the financial statements and this defines the date of transition to IFRS. In the case of Tollirene this will be 1 January 20X4. The opening statement of financial position will:

- Recognise all assets and liabilities required by IFRS,

- Not recognise any assets and liabilities not permitted by IFRS,

- If necessary, reclassify any items into the appropriate type of asset, liability or component of equity required by IFRS and

- Measure each asset, liability and component of equity using IFRS.

ANSWERS TO END OF CHAPTER QUESTIONS

When it comes to measuring the opening assets and liabilities there are a number of exemptions which Tollirene may elect to use. These will allow Tollirene to avoid having to apply certain requirements of certain IFRS retrospectively, and include:

- Business combinations, allowing Tollirene not to have to apply IFRS 3 *Business Combinations* retrospectively.

- Fair value or revaluation as deemed cost, allowing Tollirene to measure an item of property, plant and equipment in the opening statement of financial position at fair value or using a previous revaluation.

- Cumulative translation differences, allowing Tollirene to value cumulative translation differences for all foreign operations at zero as at the date of transition to IFRS.

- Compound financial instruments, which would permit Tollirene not to split a compound financial instrument at inception into separate liability and equity components as required by IAS 32.

- Assets and liabilities of subsidiaries, associates and joint ventures, which covers the valuation of assets and liabilities in the separate financial statements of a subsidiary, associate or joint venture which adopts IFRS at a later date than its parent or *vice versa*.

There is supplementary implementation guidance which gives examples of the implementation of each of the above.

IFRS 1 makes it clear that the estimates used by Tollirene to prepare its opening IFRS statement of financial position should be consistent with the estimates made for the same date under local GAAP unless there is objective evidence that the estimates were in error. So any information received about those estimates after the date of transition to IFRS should be treated as a non-adjusting event under IAS 10 and reported in the statement of profit or loss and other comprehensive income for the year ended 31 December 20X4.

After establishing its opening IFRS statement of financial position [ie as at 1 January 20X4] Tollirene will present its financial statements for the year ended 31 December 20X5 along with comparative figures for the year ended 31 December 20X4 under IFRS. It will also present a statement of financial position at 1 January 20X4 (the date of transition to IFRS). These financial statements will also need to include a number of reconciliations required by IFRS 1. Tollirene will need to include the following reconciliations:

(1) A reconciliation of equity as at 1 January 20X4 [the date of transition to IFRS] reported under local GAAP with the figure reported under IFRS.

(2) A similar reconciliation of equity as at 31 December 20X4 reported under local GAAP with the figure reported under IFRS.

(3) A reconciliation of the total comprehensive income reported for the year ended 31 December 20X4 using local GAAP with the total comprehensive income reported for the same period using IFRS.

The implementation guidance gives an example of how Tollirene might present these reconciliations. These adopt a columnar approach. The reconciliation of equity takes the form of a summarised statement of financial position with three columns of figures. In the first column Tollirene would present its local GAAP figures. The third column gives the equivalent figures using IFRS. The middle column identifies the effect of transition to IFRS. Each difference in the figures is explained in a supporting note. The reconciliation of total comprehensive income adopts a similar layout using a summarised statement of profit or loss and other comprehensive income with three columns and supportive notes.

As all the companies in the Tollirene group have adopted IFRS at the same time the above process will be repeated in each of the group companies.

Tollirene might also find it has to publish quarterly reports under the proposed EU Transparency Directive. Depending on when this is implemented, the financial information contained in the first quarter's report and all other interim reports will also have to be based on IFRS.

Summary

- The above shows that the most demanding accounting year for Tollirene will be the current year ie the year ending on December 20X4, when it will need to prepare two sets of financial statements using local GAAP and IFRS respectively.

- If all the companies in the Tollirene group intend converting to IFRS they should continue preparing their 20X3 financial statements using local GAAP. However, Tollirene as the listed holding company should include additional information about the groups plans to convert to IFRS in its Annual Report for 20X3.

- During 20X4 all the companies in the group will need to prepare two sets of financial statements, one using local GAAP and one using IFRS and IFRS 1. The local GAAP financial statements will be published in the Annual Report for 20X4. The IFRS financial statements will enable Tollirene to prepare a set of consolidated financial statements using IFRS and this will allow it to quantify the effect of the transition to IFRS in its Annual Report for 20X4.

- During 20X5 all the companies in the group will prepare their financial statements using IAS/IFRS. This will enable Tollirene to publish its interim financial statements and its Annual Report for 20X5 in accordance with IFRS and IFRS 1.

Please do not hesitate to contact me if I can be of any further help.

Tutorial note: This question was originally set when many EU companies would have been preparing to report under IFRS for the first time. However, the method of making the transition from previous (local) GAAP to IFRS remains the same and the advice given in the answer is still relevant.

It should also be noted that the EU Transparency Directive took effect in January 2007 and therefore quarterly reporting is now relevant to all EU listed entities.

NCH

This is a detailed question on knowledge and understanding of IAS 36 *Impairment of Assets* and its application to a case study about a cash generating unit.

(a)

Year ended 31 March ...	20X7	20X8	20X9
Real cost of capital	8.15%	8.15%	9.20%
Discount factor	0.924641701	0.854962276	0.782932487
Calculation of value in use	20X7	20X8	20X9
Units sold	1,500,000	500,000	500,000
Selling price	17.80	17.80	17.80
Income generated	26,700,000	8,900,000	8,900,000
Scrap proceeds			1,000,000
	26,700,000	8,900,000	9,900,000
Discount factor	0.9246	0.8550	0.7829
PV	24,687,933	7,609,164	7,751,032
Net present value	€40,048,129		
Summary of values			
Carrying amount	€132,350,000		
Value in use	€40,048,129		
Net realisable value	€115,294,500		

(b) The carrying amount should be changed to the unit's fair value less costs of disposal of €115,294,500. This will result in an impairment loss of €17,055,500 [€132,350,000 less €115,144,500]. The impairment loss should be recognised in profit or loss in the year in which the impairment arises – here, in the year ending 31 March 20X6.

ANSWERS TO END OF CHAPTER QUESTIONS

(c) (i) The impairment loss would be recognised in the Revaluation Reserve up to the amount of any previous recognised revaluation gain. Any excess impairment would be charged to profit or loss.

(ii) If the impairment loss cannot be allocated to a particular non-current asset it should be apportioned within the cash generating unit in a way which reduces the most subjective values first, ie

(1) To reduce any goodwill in the cash generating unit;

(2) Any excess should be charged to other assets of the cash generating unit on a pro rata basis.

In making the allocation the carrying amount of an individual asset should not be reduced below the highest of:

- The asset's net selling price (if determinable);
- The asset's value in use (if determinable); and
- Zero.

If the above restricts the amount of the impairment loss allocated to a particular asset the excess should be allocated to other assets on a *pro rata* basis.

Grimsel

This question covers various aspects of accounting for non-current assets. Topics covered include component depreciation, treatment of decommissioning costs, reversal of impairments, calculation of goodwill and the treatment of negative goodwill.

(a) Component depreciation is where various components of a long-lived asset may be depreciated over the appropriate lives for those components rather than the (longer) economic life of the asset. For example, a building may include heating equipment and roofing and these may be depreciated over the appropriate lives for those components. Those lives may be different from each other and shorter than the economic life of the building as a whole. IFRS requires a component approach to depreciation.

(b) If Trin decommissions its machinery and plant, there will be substantial costs incurred. However, it is not legally liable to decommission. It could leave the machinery and plant in place – but this would reduce the value of the premises. Because there is no legal obligation (and presumably no constructive obligation) the decommissioning costs should not be recognised until they are incurred. It would not be possible to make a provision for decommissioning costs.

IAS 37 *Provisions, Contingent Liabilities and Contingent Assets* requires a provision to be recognised only if (1) there is a present obligation as a result of a past event (2) it is probable that an outflow of resources will be required, and (3) a reliable estimate can be made of the outflow. The first condition is not met here.

(c)

	$	
Depreciation for 20X7	15,250	ie 122,000 divided by 8
This would give a carrying amount of	106,750	122,000 less 15,250
Estimate of recoverable amount	125,000	

Carrying amount as it would have been had the previous impairments not been recognised

	$
Cost	240,000
Accumulated depreciation (5/12 of cost)	100,000
	140,000

This is the maximum carrying amount that can be reported as at 31 October 20X7 and thus limits the amount of the impairment that can be reversed.

ANSWERS TO END OF CHAPTER QUESTIONS

Statement of profit or loss and other comprehensive income

So depreciation charge for 20X7 is (140,000 c/f – 122,000 b/f)   (18,000) ie a negative charge to depreciation

Statement of financial position

and the asset is reported as	$
Cost	240,000
Accumulated depreciation	100,000
Carrying amount	140,000

As this asset's recoverable amount of $125,000 is less than its depreciated historical cost, the asset would be written down to $125,000. So the net write off for 20X7 would be a negative charge to depreciation of $3,000 and the asset would be reported as its recoverable amount of $125,000.

(d) **Calculation of goodwill**

	$'000
Property, plant and equipment	8,000
Inventory	2,000
Receivables	3,710
Cash	430
Deferred tax balance	2,200
Patents	1,000
Customer list	1,500
Current liabilities	(3,775)
Non-current liabilities	(12,500)
	2,565
Amount paid	2,000
Gain on bargain purchase	(565)

(e) There is a presumption that in an arm's length transaction negative goodwill should not arise. The first thing to do, therefore, is to ensure that all assets and liabilities have been identified – in particular, all intangible assets. Second, the valuations attached to all assets and liabilities should be reviewed to ensure that they are appropriate ie at fair values. If negative goodwill remains it should be treated as a bargain purchase and reported as part of profit or loss for the year.

Financial instruments

(a) Not all of the costs involved are costs of making the issue. The following costs should be written off to profit or loss as incurred:

- Feasibility study $6,480
- Management time negotiating the issue $8,500

The following costs are issue costs and should be written off against reserves:

- Publicity and printing costs $11,500
- Legal fees and costs $23,400

If there is a share premium account, the issue costs should be written off against this. Otherwise they should be written off against another reserve eg retained earnings.

(b) The finance charge reported in the statement of profit or loss and other comprehensive income for Years 1 to 4 will be $900,000 each year. If the issuer elects to redeem the bonds at the start of the fifth year, there will be a loss on the exercise of the option of $2,500,000. This will be reported in the statement of profit or loss and other comprehensive income for Year 5.

ANSWERS TO END OF CHAPTER QUESTIONS

(c) The cash flow model is:

Year	Balance b/f	Finance cost at 11.37351% of b/f	Cash paid at % of nominal amount	Balance c/f
	$	$	$	$
1	800,000	90,988	44,000 (5.5%)	846,988
2	846,988	96,332	48,000 (6.0%)	895,320
3	895,320	101,829	52,000 (6.5%)	945,150
4	945,150	107,497	56,000 (7.0%)	996,646
5	996,646	113,354	60,000 (7.5%)	1,050,000

If the interest is not paid until after the financial year end, the financial statements will include the following figures for the first two years:

Statement of profit or loss and other comprehensive income	Year 1	Year 2
Interest payable	90,988	96,332
Statement of financial position	Year 1	Year 2
Accrued interest	44,000	48,000
Loans	846,988	895,320

Trench Quarries

(a) (i) IFRS 16 distinguishes between the inception date (when leases are classified) and the lease term commencement date (when recognition takes place) so Trench Quarries could make an initial calculation of the asset and liability at inception but may not recognise these in the financial statements until the commencement date, if later.

> **Tutorial note:** these amounts may in some circumstances be revised.

The inception date is the earlier of the date of the lease agreement and the date of commitment of the parties to its principal provisions, which is 1 October 2009. The lease term commencement date is the date on which Trench Quarries is entitled to exercise its right to use the machine and is the date of initial recognition of the assets, liabilities, income and expenses related to the lease in its financial statements. This is also 1 October 2009. Therefore, despite the postponement of the lease rental payments the asset and liability should be recognised from 1 October 2009.

Trench Quarries should recognise a right–of-use asset and a liability in its statement of financial position at the commencement of the lease term (1 October 2009). The measurement of the right-of-use asset is the sum of the present value of the lease payments (8.1m) and the initial direct costs (0.2m), making the right-of-use asset total $8.3 million. This amount will be depreciated over the lease term of 5 years.

Interest will accrue from 1 October 2009 using the interest rate implicit in the lease. The rental payments from 1 January 2010 must be apportioned as to the payment of this accrued interest and repayment of the lease liability.

(b) IFRS 16 defines a lease as a contract that conveys to the customer ('lessee') the right to use an asset for a period of time in exchange for consideration. A company assesses whether a contract contains a lease on the basis of whether the customer has the right to control the use of an identified asset for a period of time.

The most significant effect of the new requirements in IFRS 16 will be an increase in leased assets and financial liabilities. Accordingly, for companies with material off balance sheet leases, there will be a change to key financial metrics derived from the company's assets and liabilities (for example, leverage ratios).

For companies with material off balance leases, IFRS 16 changes the nature of expenses related to those leases. IFRS 16 replaces the typical straight-line operating lease expense for those leases with a depreciation charge for lease assets (included within operating costs) and an interest expense on lease liabilities (included within finance costs). This change aligns the lease expense treatment for all leases. Although the depreciation charge is typically even, the interest expense reduces over the life of the lease as lease payments are made. This results in a reducing total expense as an individual lease matures.

Leasing provides an important and flexible source of financing for many companies. However, the old lease accounting Standard made it difficult for investors and others to get an accurate picture of a company's lease assets and liabilities, particularly for industries such as the airline, retail and transport sectors.

Listed companies using IFRS Standards or US GAAP are estimated to have around US$3.3 trillion of lease commitments; over 85% of which do not appear on their balance sheets.

This somewhat arbitrary distinction made it difficult for investors to compare companies. It also meant that investors and others had to estimate the effects of a company's off balance sheet lease obligations, which in practice often led to overestimating the liabilities arising from those obligations. IFRS 16 solves this problem by requiring all leases to be reported on a company's balance sheet as assets and liabilities.

The new standard provides increased transparency on companies' lease assets and liabilities and will also improve comparability between companies that lease and those that borrow to buy.

Employee benefits

(i) **Present value of obligation**

	20X8 $K	20X9 $K
Present value of obligation at start of year	20,000	23,000
Interest cost thereon at 8%	1,600	1,840
Current service cost	1,250	1,430
Benefits paid	(987)	(1,100)
Actuarial gain/(loss)	1,137	330
Present value of obligation at end of the year	23,000	25,500

(ii) **Market value of plan assets**

	20X8 $K	20X9 $K
Market value of plan assets at start of year	20,000	21,500
Expected return thereon at 8%	1,600	1,720
Contributions	1,000	1,100
Benefits paid	(987)	(1,100)
Remeasurement of plan assets	(113)	(920)
Market value of plan assets at end of the year	21,500	22,300

(iii) **Amounts recognised in statement of profit or loss and other comprehensive income:**

	20X8 $K	20X9 $K
Recognised in profit or loss:		
Current service cost	(1,250)	(1,430)
Net interest cost on defined benefit liability (asset)	0	(120)
Recognised in other comprehensive income		
Actuarial gain on defined benefit obligation	1,137	330
Remeasurement of plan assets	(113)	(920)

DT

Calculation of deferred tax liability

	Carrying amount $m	Tax base $m	Temporary differences $m
Goodwill (Note 1)	14	–	–
Subsidiary (Note 1)	76	60	16
Inventories (Note 2)	24	30	(6)
Property, plant and equipment (Note 3)	2,600	1,920	680
Other temporary differences			90
Property sold – tax due 30.11.20X4 (165/0.3)		–	550
Liability for health care benefits	100		(100)
Unrelieved tax losses (Note 4)			(100)
Temporary differences			1,130

Deferred tax liability (Note 1)	16	at 25%	4.0
Deferred tax asset (note 2)	(6)	at 25%	(1.5)
Deferred tax asset (100 + 100)	(200)	at 30%	(60.0)
Deferred tax liability (bal fig)	1,320	at 30%	396.0
Total differences	1,130		338.5
Less: Opening deferred tax liability			(280)
Addition to goodwill re deferred tax attributable to subsidiary (Note 1)			(4)
Deferred tax expense for the year			54.5

Notes

1. As no deduction is available for the cost of goodwill in the subsidiary's tax jurisdiction, then the tax base of goodwill is zero. Paragraph 15a of IAS 12, states that DT should not recognise a deferred tax liability in respect of taxable temporary differences arising from the initial recognition of goodwill. Goodwill will be increased by the amount of the deferred tax liability in respect of the remaining taxable temporary differences in the subsidiary, ie 25% × $16m = $4m.

2. Unrealised group profit eliminated on consolidation is 20% × $30m = $6m. Deferred tax is provided for at the receiving company's rate of tax (ie at 25%).

3. The tax that would arise if the properties were disposed of at their revalued amounts which was provided at the beginning of the year will be included in the temporary difference arising on the property, plant and equipment at 30 November 20X1.

4. DT has unrelieved tax losses of ($34m + $56m)/0.3 ie $300m. This will be available for offset against current year's profits ($110m) and against profits for the year ending 30 November 20X2 ($100m). Because of the uncertainty about the availability of taxable profits in 20X3, no deferred tax asset can be recognised for any losses which may be offset against this amount. Therefore a deferred tax asset may be recognised for the losses to be offset against taxable profits in 20X2. That is $100m × 30% ie $30m.

ANSWERS TO END OF CHAPTER QUESTIONS

Comment

The deferred tax liability of DT will rise in total by $335·5 million ($338·5m – $3m), thus reducing net assets, distributable profits, and post-tax earnings. The profit for the period will be reduced by $54·5 million which would probably be substantially more under IAS 12 than the old method of accounting for deferred tax. A prior period adjustment will occur of $280m – $3m as IFRS are being applied for the first time (IFRS 1) ie $277m. The borrowing position of the company may be affected and the directors may decide to cut dividend payments. However, the amount of any unprovided deferred tax, analysed into its major components, was required to be disclosed under the previous standard used. IAS 12 brings this liability onto the statement of financial position but because the bulk of the liability has already been disclosed the impact on the share price should be minimal.

Bartolo

(a) The increase in profit attributable to ordinary equity holders on conversion of potential ordinary shares is:

	Increase in earnings $	Increase in no. of ord. shares	Earnings per incremental share Cents
Number of shares resulting from options	nil	460,000	nil
Deemed to be issued at full market price (460,000 × 0.85/0.99)		(394,949)	
Deemed issued for no consideration		65,051	
Convertible preference shares (800,000 × 6.8%) and (800,000 × 1.25)	54,400	1,000,000	5.44
Convertible bonds (5,500,000 × 12% × (100% – 30% tax) and (5,500,000 × 2.5)	462,000	13,750,000	3.36

The larger the earnings per incremental share the smaller dilutive effect.

So now consider in descending order of dilutive effect.

Calculation of dilutive or antidilutive effect of potential ordinary shares

	Profit: continuing operations $	Ordinary shares	Per share Cents	
Profit from continuing operations	880,000	20,000,000	4.40	
Options	nil	65,051		
	880,000	20,065,051	4.39	dilutive
12% convertible bonds	462,000	13,750,000		
	1,342,000	33,815,051	3.97	dilutive
6.8% convertible preference shares	54,400	1,000,000		
	1,396,400	34,815,051	4.01	antidilutive

The antidilutive effect of the convertible preference shares is ignored.

So, the diluted EPS figure is 3.97 cents.

(b) **Theoretical ex-rights fair value per share**

Initial holding of shares	10	at $1.40 per share	14.0
Rights issue	1	at $1.15 per share	1.15
	11		15.15

Therefore, theoretical ex-rights fair value per share is $1.38 ie 15.15 divided by 11.00

Calculation of adjustment factor for bonus element

Fair value per share before exercise of rights	1.40	
Theoretical ex-rights fair value per share	1.38	
Adjustment factor	1.014492754	

Weighted average number of shares in issue

First 3 months:
Shares in issue	25,000,000	
Adjustment factor	1.014492754	
	25,362,318.84	
Weighting	¼	6,340,580

Last 9 months:
Shares in issue	27,500,000	
Weighting	¾	
		20,625,000
		26,965,580

Calculation of EPS

This year
Profit on ordinary activities after taxation	3,100,000	
Weighted average number of shares in issue	26,965,580	
So, EPS	11.50	cents

Recalculation of previous year's EPS
Profit on ordinary activities after taxation	2,200,000	
Number of shares in issue (after bonus element)	25,362,319	
So, restated EPS	8.67	cents

or

Previous year's EPS	8.80	cents	X	
Adjustment to number of shares for bonus element	1.014492754		Y	
So, restated EPS	8.67	cents	x/y	

(c) **Current year's EPS**

Profit before taxation ($)	2,276,850
Taxation	(1,350,000)
Transfer from deferred taxation	227,600
Profit after tax ($)	1,154,450
So EPS =	23.1 cents
(ie 1,154,450 / 5,000,000)	

Previous year's EPS (restated for comparatives)

As previously stated	22.2 cents
Old number of shares in issue	4,000,000
New number of shares in issue	5,000,000

Restated EPS = previous EPS times old no. of shares divided by new no. of shares

22.2 times 4,000,000 / 5,000,000

= 17.8 cents

ANSWERS TO END OF CHAPTER QUESTIONS

Tine Foods

This question explores a number of aspects of accounting and reporting techniques.

(a) IAS 37 defines a provision as 'a liability of uncertain timing or amount'. What distinguishes a provision from other liabilities is the uncertainty of the liability.

(b) A provision should be recognised when, and only when:

  (i) An entity has a present obligation (legal or constructive) as a result of a past event;

  (ii) It is probable (ie more likely than not) that an outflow of resources embodying economic benefits will be required to settle the obligation; and

  (iii) A reliable estimate can be made of the amount of the obligation. The standard notes that it is only in extremely rare cases that a reliable estimate will not be possible.

(c) Under IAS 37 there is a potential liability depending on the outcome of the appeal – although the probability of the appeal succeeding may be regarded as low given the circumstances. This should therefore be reported as a contingent liability, with the potential amount disclosed. The company might prefer not to disclose an amount on the grounds that it is not possible to estimate it with sufficient reliability. However, the company has just sold the brand name and should be aware of its liability under that contract if the brand name is cancelled. It should also be possible to estimate any further legal costs and damages should the appeal be successful.

(d) Charge to profit or loss would be $494,000 as reorganisation costs; the provision is no longer needed so $500,000 would be written back to profit or loss – making a net addition to profit (reduction in loss) of $6,000. The accrued reorganisation costs would appear as a current liability in the statement of financial position.

Molar and Canal

Tutorial note: this question concerns share-based payment schemes. The starting point with such a question is to identify the type of scheme being examined.

(a) Advice to finance director:

This is an equity-settled share-based payment transaction. In other words, Molar has received employee services in exchange for equity instruments of the company. It is an increasingly common method of settling amounts owed for the payment of goods or services. If Molar had paid for the employees services in cash the amount would be recognised in profit or loss. The finance director is quite typical of those who believe that, as there is no cash outflow, there should not be any charge to profit or loss. However, this would ignore the fact that Molar has entered into a transaction and to ignore it would result in financial statements which did not reflect all economic transactions of the company.

The basic principle behind IFRS 2 *Share-based Payment* is that all transactions are measured at fair value. The fair value of transactions with employees is measured by reference to the fair value of the equity instruments at the grant date, that is, the date that Molar and the employees agree to the arrangement: 1 June 2011.

Molar should recognise a remuneration expense as employees provide their services over the three year vesting period. As employees will leave the scheme at various points during the three years, the number of options that are likely to vest at the end must be recalculated each year.

The accounting entry each year is:
Dr Expense in profit or loss
Cr Other component of equity

The amount to be recognised as an expense each year would be found by calculating the accumulated expense at the end of each year of the scheme and measuring the change, as follows:

- *Year to 31 May 2012*

    Number of employees likely to remain in the scheme as at 31 May 2012:

    2,500 (as at 1 June 2011) – 60 (expected to leave during first year) – 610 (25% of those expected to leave before 31 May 2014; ie 2,500 – 60 = 2,440) = 1,830.

    Expense recognised: 1,830 × 250 (no. of share options) × $30 (fair value at grant date × 1/3 (one year of scheme) = $4.575m

- *Year to 31 May 2013*

    Number of employees likely to remain in the scheme as at 31 May 2013:

    2,440 (as at 1 June 2012) – 407 (2/3 of those expected to leave during second year, that is 610 × 2/3) = 2,033.

    Accumulated expense as at 31 May 2013:

    2,033 × 250 (no. of share options) × $30 (fair value at grant date) × 2/3 (two years of scheme) = $10.165m

    Expense recognised: $10.165 – $4.575 = $5.590m

- *Year to 31 May 2014*

    Number of employees likely to be in the scheme as at 31 May 2014; that is, on vesting day:

    2,033 (as at 1 June 2013) – 203 (1/3 of those expected to leave during final year, that is 610 × 1/3) = 1,830.

    Accumulated expense as at 31 May 2014:

    1,830 × 250 (no. of share options) × $30 (fair value at grant date) × 3/3 (three years of scheme) = $13.725m

    Expense recognised: $13.725m – $10.165 = $3.560m

(b) Advice to Canal:

This is a cash-settled share-based payment transaction. Canal has acquired employees' services in exchange for amounts of cash measured by reference to the company's share price. They are known as 'share appreciation rights' (SARs). Under the scheme Canal's employees will become entitled to future cash payments based on the increase in the company's share price over a specified period of time, that is, three years. Unlike Molar's equity settled scheme, SARs are measured at the fair value of the **liability**; that is, the liability to transfer cash. The liability is therefore re-measured at each year end. This is unlike an equity settled scheme where fair value is measured at the grant date and remains constant.

Any changes in the fair value of the liability are recognised in profit or loss. Similar to Molar's equity settled scheme, the cost of employees' services are recognised over the period such services are provided but unlike an equity settled scheme, the credit is to liabilities that is, the accounting entry each period is:

Dr Expense in profit or loss
Cr Liabilities

The amount to be recognised as an expense each year would be found by calculating the accumulated liability at the end of each year of the scheme and measuring the change, as follows:

- *Year to 31 May 2008*

    Number of SARs likely to vest: 1,000 – 190 = 810.

    Expense for the year and liability as at year end: 810 (employees) × 200 (SARs) × $15 × 1/3 = $0.810m

- *Year to 31 May 2009*

    Number of SARs likely to vest: 1,000 – 70 (left during 2008) – 135 = 795.

    Liability as at year end: 795 (employees) × 200 (SARs) × $16 × 2/3 = $1.696m

    Expense for the year: $1.696m - $0.810m = $0.886m

- *Year to 31 May 2010*

    Liability at year end for SARs not exercised: $1.717m

    1,000 – 195 (left to date) – 300 (exercised during year): 505 (employees) × 200 (SARs) × $17 =

        Expense

    SARs actually exercised during the year: 300 (employees) × 200 (SARs) × $16.50 $0.990m

    Expense for the year: $1.717m - $1.696m = $0.0.021m $0.021m

        $1.011m

- *Year to 31 May 2011*

    Final cash settlement: 505 (employees) × 200 (SARs) × $18 = $1.818m

    Expense for year: $1.818m (final cash settlement) – $1.717m (liability b/f) = $0.101m

IFRS 15

The director wishes to recognise the sale as early as possible. However, following IFRS 15 *Revenue from Contracts with Customers*, revenue from the sale should only be recognised when the performance obligations in the contract have been satisfied.

Performance obligations in the contract

The contract contains a promise to deliver the caravan and a promise to deliver additional goods free of charge. These are distinct promises and therefore the contract contains two performance obligations.

Transaction price

The transaction price is made up of three elements.

A significant financing component must be considered where consideration is received more than 12 months before or after the date on which revenue is recognised (being the delivery date, 1 August 20X7). Therefore the payment on 1 August 20X9 must be discounted to present value at 1 August 20X7.

	K
Deposit	3,000
Payment on 1.8.X7 (the delivery date)	15,000
Payment on 1.8.X9 ($12,000/ 1.1^2)	9,917
	27,917

Allocation to performance obligations

The transaction price is allocated based on standalone selling prices:

Caravan	30,000/31,500 × $30,000	= $28,571
Free equipment	1,500/31,500 × $30,000	= $1,489

Recognition of revenue

The two performance obligations are satisfied simultaneously on 1 August 20X7, and therefore all revenue is recognised on this date.

Journal entries are as follows:

1 May 20X7

The receipt of cash in the form of the $,3000 deposit is recognised on receipt as a contract liability (deferred income) in the statement of financial position by:

DEBIT	Bank	$3,000	
CREDIT	Contract liability (deferred income)		$3,000

1 August 20X7

Revenue is recognised together with payment of the first $15,000. The contract liability is transferred to be revenue:

DEBIT	Bank	$15,000	
DEBIT	Contract liability	$3,000	
DEBIT	Receivable	$9,917	
CREDIT	Revenue		$27,917

Tramwell

Briefing Note
To: Finance Director
From: Accountant
Re: IFRS for SMEs

The purpose of this briefing note is to address the following issues:

(1) Whether Tramwell is eligible to adopt the IFRS for SMEs
(2) How the accounting policies of Tramwell may change under the IFRS for SMEs
(3) The practical considerations of adopting the IFRS for SMEs

Eligibility to adopt

The IFRS for SMEs can be applied by those entities which:

(a) Do not have public accountability;
(b) Publish general purpose financial statements for external users; and
(c) Are permitted to by the legislative authorities of the jurisdiction in which they operate.

An entity with public accountability is an entity whose debt or equity instruments are traded or will be traded in a public market, or an entity which holds assets in a fiduciary capacity for a broad range of third parties. Although Tramwell's parent company Ramses is listed (and so its debt or equity instruments are publicly traded), Tramwell itself is not. The IFRS for SMEs stipulates that in this situation, provided that the subsidiary itself is not publicly accountable, it may apply the standard. The second part of the definition of public accountability refers to holding assets in a fiduciary capacity for third parties as a primary part of the business. It is clear from Tramwell's statement of financial position that Tramwell's business is not primarily concerned with holding assets for others. Therefore Tramwell does not have public accountability.

It is also apparent that Tramwell does publish general purpose financial statements, which are presumed to be for external users. Therefore the second condition is met.

Tramwell therefore meets the eligibility criteria stipulated within the IFRS for SMEs. However, it may only apply the standard if the legislative authorities of the country in which it operates permits application.

Accounting policies

A review of Tramwell's statement of financial position (SOFP) reveals a number of areas in which accounting policies would change on adoption of the IFRS for SMEs:

- In respect of PPE, you should note that the IFRS for SMEs requires a review of residual values, useful lives and depreciation methods only where there is a significant change in an asset or how it is used.

- It is unclear whether items of PPE are self-constructed or adapted after purchase for use by Tramwell. Where this is the case and borrowing costs are incurred in order to meet construction or adaption costs, the IFRS for SMEs is clear that these costs must be recognised in profit or loss and may not be capitalised.

- In respect of investment properties, the IFRS for SMEs requires measurement at fair value, unless this involves undue cost or effort. It appears that investment properties are currently measured at fair value under local GAAP, however the existence of an investment property reserve suggests that fair value gains and losses are currently recognised in equity. Under the IFRS for SMEs these must be recognised in profit or loss, meaning that the profits of Tramwell may become more volatile.

- Tramwell's SOFP includes capitalised development costs of $220,000. The IFRS for SMEs requires that all internally generated intangible assets, including development costs are recognised immediately in profit or loss. If Tramwell is engaged in a number of ongoing development costs, this will result in lower profits after adoption of the IFRS for SMEs.

- Tramwell has recognised $400,000 financial assets at cost. It is unclear what type of financial assets these are. Under the IFRS for SMEs, financial instruments are classified as either 'basic' or 'other'. Basic financial instruments are generally measured at amortised cost using the effective interest method and other financial instruments at fair value with changes recognised in profit or loss. Clarification is required before further advice can be given in this area.

- The IFRS for SMEs includes illustrative financial statements where a suggested format for the statement of financial position is provided. This shows all assets in the 'top half' of the SOFP and all equity, reserves and liabilities in the 'bottom half'. Although the standard does not prescribe this format or sequence of items, it is the format usually adopted by companies applying IFRS therefore Tramwell may wish to change to such a format on adoption of the IFRS for SMEs.

Practical considerations

If Tramwell adopts the IFRS for SMEs, it must consider a number of practical issues as well as the impact on amounts reported in the financial statements.

In the first case, IFRS for SMEs accounting software will be required. This may involve a significant capital outlay. In addition, accounting staff will need to be trained in its operation. Accounting staff will also need training in the requirements of the IFRS for SMEs, and as the standard evolves and is updated, staff knowledge will need to be updated.

Tramwell should also consider whether the IFRS for SMEs is a widely accepted financial reporting framework in the business environment in which it operates. For example, local finance providers may require additional disclosures and statements which may result in a cost-benefit test not being met.

Tramwell's results are consolidated into the Ramses group accounts. As accounting policy differs in some instances between full IFRS and the IFRS for SMEs, the need for GAAP adjustments on consolidation is not removed.

ANSWERS TO END OF CHAPTER QUESTIONS

If local tax law is based on accounting treatment, taxable income and therefore taxes payable could change under the IFRS for SMEs. Other items affected by profits and where policy review may therefore be needed include:

- Distributable reserves and potential dividends
- Management compensation

Curia

The following suggested solution is indicative only.

REPORT
FROM:
TO:
DATE:
SUBJECT: Financial performance of Curia

The following report is based on a series of financial ratios calculated from the financial statements of Curia for the financial years 20X3, 20X4 and 20X5.

The overall performance of Curia as evidenced by its return on equity has fluctuated. There was a significant improvement from 20X3 to 20X4 due to significant improvements in profitability on trading (net income to sales revenue) and a marginal improvement in assets utilisation (sales revenue to total assets).

That improvement in overall efficiency was not maintained in 20X5 and return on equity declined to 13%. This time the decrease was due to a significant decline in assets utilisation which is now at its lowest for the three-year period. There was an accompanying decline in profitability on trading but this may be marginal.

Earnings per share have followed a similar pattern to return on equity. There was a very significant rise in earnings per share for 20X4 – but this was followed by a decline of approximately 10% in 20X5. Dividends per share, however, have been constant over the three-year period suggesting that there may have been relative increases in profits retained within the company in 20X4 and 20X5.

Changes in the profitability on trading over the three-year period seem to be attributable to steadily increasing margins on sales (gross profit to sales revenue). However, progress here seems to have been offset by increases in operating expenses (operating expenses to sales revenue) – particularly in 20X5.

Control of working capital seems efficient. There has been no significant trend in the current and acid test ratios and, while it is not known what business sector Curia operates in, these ratios seem to have been stable for the past three years. All components of working capital seem to be being managed more efficiently with falling trends in the period of credit taken by customers and from suppliers, and increasingly efficient turnover of inventory.

The fall in efficiency in the use of assets to generate sales (sales revenue to total assets) and the increasing net assets per share would therefore appear to signify increasing investment in non-current assets. It may be that some of the inefficiency in the use of these non-current assets may be temporary and may disappear once the assets become fully utilised for a full financial year.

Recommendations for improving the performance of Curia.

The overall performance of Curia could be improved by:

- Better control of operating expenses. Reducing operating expenses would increase profitability on sales and hence overall return on equity.
- Careful monitoring of non-current assets utilisation. Increasing sales revenue to non-current assets would increase sales revenue to total assets and hence overall return on equity.

Limitations

- It has been assumed that all the data is comparable ie that similar accounting policies have been used over the three years.

- It has only been possible to look at trends within Curia over the past three years. It would be useful to compare Curia's performance with its competitors – particularly the leading firms in the same industry sector with a view to knowing what is achievable.

- It would be useful to know more about the sector Curia operates in and general economic conditions. This would help identify what changes are attributable to changes in sector performance and general economic conditions and changes attributable to good or bad management.

- The available information is very limited. It would be useful to have additional information about the quality of Curia's management, its risk exposure and the prospects for the industry sector.

Practice question bank

Question 1

Nedell Corp, a multinational diversified company, is preparing its financial statements for the year ended 31 October 20X6. A number of issues have arisen and the company has asked you for advice.

(a) During its financial year ended on 31 October 20X6 Nedell Corp sold a commercial building to one of its directors, A J Parrish for a selling price of $1.5 million. The sale of the property was approved by the board of directors but A J Parrish did not participate in the discussions and did not vote on the decision and therefore the finance director believes that the transaction does not need to be disclosed. A valuation of $1.6 million was determined by a firm of independent valuers.

Required

Comment on the ethical implications of the sale and advise how it should be dealt with in the financial statements for the year ended 31 October 20X6 **(5 marks)**

(b) Nedell Corp has entered into an agreement to dispose of its activities in Brazil. Competition and monopoly legislation requires the disposal to be scrutinised by a regulatory body. It is expected that the sale will shortly be given clearance and that the disposal will be completed within the next six months.

Required

Advise how this matter should be reported in Nedell Corp's financial statements. **(5 marks)**

(c) Nedell Corp includes in land and buildings a property which was previously owner-occupied but, due to it no longer being required, is now rented out to a third party for the purposes of earing rentals. Nedell Corp has continued to present the property in land and buildings at cost less depreciation and would prefer to continue to account for the property in this way going forward.

Required

Explain how the property should be accounted for in accordance with IFRS Standards. **(6 marks)**

(Total 20 marks)

Question 2 – AIA May 2015

(a) Fere, a public limited company, is considering whether to adopt a revaluation policy under IAS 16 *Property, Plant and Equipment* in the financial statements for the year ended 30 April 2015. The directors require advice on the accounting implications of such an adoption and have provided the following information concerning one of the entity's assets.

The asset was purchased on 1 May 2009 at a cost of $10 million. During the purchase period, Fere incurred additional administration and general overheads of $100,000. The asset has a life of ten years and a residual value of $nil. Depreciation is provided on a straight-line basis. On 30 April 2012, the asset was revalued to $3.5 million. On 30 April 2015 the asset was revalued to $5 million.

The directors would choose to deal with depreciation by eliminating it against the asset's gross carrying amount as allowed by IAS 16.

Upon each revaluation the useful life of the asset did not change.

Required

Fere's directors understand that the *Conceptual Framework* permits a 'mixed measurement approach' which sees a different measurement basis being applied to non-current assets. They are concerned adopting such an approach is inconsistent with the enhancing qualitative characteristic of undestandability.

(i) Advise the directors as to how a mixed measurement approach is consistent with the *Conceptual Framework*. **(4 marks)**

(ii) Advise the directors of the accounting entries necessary had Fere adopted a revaluation policy from 30 April 2012 and of whether any adjustments to prior years would be necessary at 30 April 2015 to comply with IAS 8 *Accounting Policies, Changes in Accounting Estimates and Errors*. **(6 marks)**

Fere has entered into two new lease contracts during the year. One such contract is for the three year lease of five executive cars, the terms of which meet the definition of a lease under IFRS 16. The directors would like to account for the lease costs as a staff cost as the rental costs are incurred.

(b) (i) Explain, with reference to the *Conceptual Framework*, how the lease contract should be accounted for. **(4 marks)**

(ii) On 1 May 2014, Fere entered into a contract to acquire the right to use of a machine under a four year lease. The expected useful life of the machine on commencement of the lease is five years. Under the terms of the contract, a deposit of $700,000 was payable on the commencement of the lease. The present value of the future lease payments was $1,871,100. A further three instalments of $700,000 are payable annually in advance. The interest rate implicit in the lease is 6%.

Required

Advise Fere's directors of the amounts to be included in its statement of profit or loss and statement of financial position for Year 1 under IFRS 16. **(6 marks)**

(Total 20 marks)

Question 3 – AIA Nov 2016

(a) Atab, a public limited company, is preparing group financial statements for the year ended 31 October 2016. The entity has two investments as follows:

(i) Atab owns 100% of the equity of Begi. The equity was originally acquired for $7.5 million when the fair value of Begi's identifiable net assets was $4.5 million. On 31 October 2016 Atab sold 60% of the equity to Cogni for $2 million. On disposal the carrying amount of Begi's net assets in Atab's group financial statements was $1.8 million and the fair value of Atab's remaining 40% interest in Begi was $1.2 million. As a result of the sale, Atab and Cogni have joint control over Begi.

Atab has attempted to follow IAS 28 *Investments in Associates and Joint Ventures*, and has used the equity method to account for the initial carrying amount of the joint venture at cost; ie $3 million, being 40% of the original cost. Atab has recognised a loss on disposal of $2.5 million.

(ii) Atab gained significant influence over Blo by acquiring 25% of Blo's equity shares on 1 November 2015 for $5.1 million. Directly attributable costs were $400,000. The fair value of Blo's identifiable net assets on 1 November 2015 was $16 million.

On 31 October 2016, Atab acquired an additional investment of 20% in Blo at a cost of $6.8 million and incurred directly attributable costs of $200,000. Atab retained significant influence over Blo. In the year to 31 October 2016 Blo's retained earnings increased by $13.5 million and on that date an item of plant and equipment in Blo's financial statements increased in value by $3.5 million.

Required

Advise Atab on how the above investments should be accounted for in its group statement of financial position as at 31 October 2016. You should show the amount to be disclosed for goodwill relating to (ii).

Note. Marks for individual sections are shown above.

(12 marks)

(b) Alac is considering forming an investee for the purpose of developing a new health drink. Two entities, Bin and Cons, have approached Alac each with a view to entering into separate contractual arrangements with Alac concerning the product. The details are as follows:

Bin is proposing an arrangement whereby Bin will develop the drink and obtain regulatory approval for it. Alac would be responsible for manufacturing and marketing the drink once regulatory approval has been received. Both parties would have unilateral ability to make all decisions concerning their own activity.

Cons is proposing an arrangement identical to Bin's with the exception that both Alac and Cons will jointly make decisions over both activities.

Required

Advise Alac on whether, under each proposal, joint control exists in accordance with IFRS 11 *Joint Arrangements*. **(4 marks)**

(c) Exten and Gect have established a joint venture sharing profits in the ratio 60:40 respectively. Exten has contributed inventory with a historical cost of $3.4 million to the venture and has estimated its net realisable value at either $3.7 million or $3 million. Exten is now preparing its group financial statements and has included $3.4 million in revenue.

Required

Advise Exten on how to account for the above transaction should the inventory be valued at
(i) $3.7 million and (ii) $3 million. **(4 marks)**

(Total 20 marks)

Question 4 – AIA Nov 2012 (amended)

Bing is a public limited company and operates in the aerospace industry.

(a) Bing, together with two other public limited companies Ollis and Roy, have established a fourth entity Doe for the purpose of building a new type of passenger aircraft. Ownership and responsibilities with respect to Doe are as follows:

Company	Ownership of Doe	Responsibility
Bing	49%	To build the body of the aircraft
Ollis	32%	To build the aircraft engines
Roy	19%	To design and build the aircraft flight control systems and mechanics.

Bing and Ollis have entered into a contractual arrangement whereby all budgeting, capital expenditure, treasury management, dividend policy, production, marketing, sales and human resource decisions they take in connection with the activities of Doe require the unanimous consent of Bing and Ollis. Roy is not represented on Doe's board of directors although Roy does participate in Doe's policy-making processes.

Required

Advise each company on how to account for their respective interest in Doe, making reference to the IASB *Conceptual Framework* fundamental qualitative characteristics where relevant. **(10 marks)**

(b) Bing, together with Ong and Luft, established a jointly controlled entity Thansa. Each company contributed $10 million in cash in exchange for one-third of the equity of Thansa. Thansa then used $24 million of the contributed cash to acquire a manufacturing plant from Bing. It was agreed between all parties that $24 million represented the plant's fair value. The plant was carried in Bing's financial statements at $15 million.

Required

Prepare journal entries to contrast the treatments if Bing were to account for the transaction using (i) proportional consolidation and (ii) equity accounting. **(8 marks)**

(c) On 1 November 2011 Bing entered into a joint venture arrangement with Carav under which both companies acquired and controlled 50% of the equity of a jointly controlled entity Deecee. Deecee's statement of financial position on 1 November 2011 showed a portfolio of debt instruments with a gross carrying amount of $10 million against which a loss allowance of $0.1 million for 12-month expected credit losses was recognised. The loss allowance was calculated as the present value of the lifetime expected credit losses of $1 million x 10% chance of default within 12 months. The debt matures in five years' time and carries an interest rate of 10%. No cash is received in respect of the debt instruments and a discount factor of 8% has been applied in calculating the loss allowance. Due to a decrease in the credit rating of the assets, Deecee has determined that at 31 October 2012, the debt asset has moved to stage 2 of the IFRS 9 expected credit loss model and the present value of lifetime expected credit losses is calculated as $1.08 million.

Required

Calculate the debt instrument figure that will appear in Deecee's statements of financial position as at 31 October 2012 using the expected loss model in IFRS 9 *Financial Instruments*. **(4 marks)**

(Total 20 marks)

Question 5 – AIA May 2014

(a) The functional currency of Arenta, a public limited company, is the Dollar ($). Two years ago, Arenta established a European-based subsidiary Rima that produces and sells electronic equipment throughout Europe. The sale prices for Rima's goods, labour and materials are determined in Euros (€). Rima has often considered exporting outside Europe but believes that the external market forces and government regulations around the world are too restrictive to make this feasible. Rima is financed predominantly by an inter-company loan from Arenta denominated in dollars and regularly transfers cash flows from its operations to Arenta.

The directors of Arenta are not sure how to determine Rima's functional currency for the purpose of producing its consolidated financial statements.

Required

Advise Arenta's directors of Rima's functional currency. Explain your advice. **(5 marks)**

(b) Rima has produced the following draft financial statements for the year ended 30 April 2014.

Statement of financial position	€m	€m
Non-current assets		831
Current assets		
Inventories	514	
Trade receivables	237	
		751
		1,582
Equity share capital (€1 shares)		267
Retained earnings		776
		1,043
Non-current liabilities		304
Current liabilities		235
		1,582
Statement of profit or loss		
Profit before tax		443
Tax		200
Profit for the year		243

(i) Rima was incorporated during May 2012 when Arenta subscribed $70 million for 100% of the equity share capital. No dividends were paid during the year.

(ii) All transactions occurred evenly throughout the year.

(iii)
Exchange rates:	€ː$
On incorporation	4ː1
30 April 2013	3.5ː1
Average for the year ended 30 April 2014:	3ː1
30 April 2014	2ː1

Required

Translate the above financial statements of Rima for the purpose of the consolidation exercise for the year ended 30 April 2014 showing and describing all movements in the group's equity and retained earnings as a result of the translation exercise. **(10 marks)**

(c) The IASB believes that the purpose of the statement of profit or loss and other comprehensive income is to provide information about the financial performance of an entity that is useful to a wide range of users in making economic decisions. For this purpose, all changes in net assets are regarded as 'performance' in its widest sense. Many entities have responded to this wide definition of performance, by disclosing non-GAAP key performance indicators.

Required

Advise Arenta's directors of how any exchange gains/losses, calculated in (b), will be accounted for and disclosed in the group statement of profit or loss and other comprehensive income and of the impact this will have on the group's non-GAAP key performance indicators (KPIs).

(5 marks)

(Total 20 marks)

Question 6 – AIA May 2014

(a) Several years ago Ezmee, a public limited company, acquired 25% of the equity shares of one of its main competitors, Stoe. The purchase consideration was $4 million. The other 75% of shares have been held ever since by a single investor so that Ezmee had no influence over Stoe's operating activities. Ezmee accounts for such investments at fair value through other comprehensive income.

On 30 April 2013, Ezmee acquired a further 45% of Stoe for $13 million cash and gained control. At that date the carrying amount of Ezmee's initial investment in Stoe was $5 million and the fair value of Stoe's identifiable net assets was $25 million. It has been estimated that, due to the entity gaining control, Stoe had to pay a premium of 8% to acquire the additional 45% shareholding.

Ezmee includes non-controlling interest in its consolidated financial statements at fair value.

Required

Advise the Ezmee's directors of the figures to be included in the entity's consolidated financial statements for goodwill and non-controlling interest and explain how the initial holding of 25% should be accounted for as at 30 April 2013. **(10 marks)**

(b) When measuring the fair values of Stoe's identifiable net assets at 30 April 2013 a number of provisional figures were used. During the year ended 30 April 2014 the following information became available:

– At 30 April 2013 Stoe held a passive investment at a fair value of $2 million in Pan, a mining company. During February 2014, as a result of Pan's discovery of a new deposit of minerals, the fair value of Stoe's investment increased to $3 million.

– Stoe owned a property which was surplus to requirements as at 30 April 2013. Stoe was actively looking for a buyer at that date and included the property in the financial statements at a carrying amount of $1 million. Stoe eventually disposed of the property in July 2013 for $1.4 million.

- At 30 April 2013 Stoe had six months outstanding on a contract to service equipment. On gaining control, Ezmee assumed responsibility for the service contract. The customer had paid an annual fee of $2.4 million and Stoe therefore carried deferred revenue of $1.2 million in its year end financial statements. During June 2013 it was finally agreed that companies similar to Stoe would incur costs of $0.9 million to fulfill the contract and would expect to earn a profit mark-up for that effort of 20%.

- At the date Ezmee gained control of Stoe, one of Stoe's identifiable net assets was a brand name, Diga. As Ezmee owned a similar product, it did not intend to market Diga post-control. Ezmee discontinued sales of the Diga product thereby enhancing sales of its own product and the value of its own brand name. As the future cash flows from sales of Diga were expected to be nil, Ezmee included it as an intangible asset in Stoe's identifiable net assets at a fair value of zero. During the following year it became known to Ezmee that other companies within the industry would have been willing to acquire the name Diga for $1 million at 30 April 2013 and to continue to sell the product.

Required

Advise Ezmee's directors of the effect, if any, the above information will have on the remeasurement of goodwill as at 30 April 2013. Explain your advice. **(10 marks)**

(Total 20 marks)

Question 7 – AIA Specimen exam

Oliver is a qualified accountant who is employed by Zanger, an unquoted company that manufactures electronic components. Zanger operates from a single, large factory that is the largest employer in Corrtown.

Oliver is assisting with the preparation of Zanger's annual report for the year ended 30 September 2017. The company has had a difficult year and it has sustained large losses that have pushed its gearing ratio close to the upper limit imposed by a debt covenant. If the debt covenant is breached then the bank will be entitled to foreclose on the loan, which will put Zanger out of business.

Oliver has conducted an impairment review of the equipment in Zanger's factory. In his opinion, the equipment is impaired and an adjustment should be made. He reported his findings to Zanger's Finance Director, who congratulated him for his thoroughness, but then asked him to destroy all working papers relating to the impairment review and to delete any files on his laptop. The Finance Director said that the impairment adjustment would put Zanger in breach of its debt covenant and would cause the bank to put the company out of business.

The Finance Director reminded Oliver that the local economy in Corrtown relies on Zanger. Apart from those employed in Zanger's factory, many others work for small business that provide Zanger with goods and services. Local retailers depend on Zanger's employees to remain viable. Those who own their own homes will be unable to pay their mortgages and house prices will slump, creating massive financial difficulties.

Required

(a) Evaluate the ethical dilemma faced by Oliver and advise him on how he should respond to the Finance Director's request. **(12 marks)**

(b) Critically analyse the assertion that it is often difficult for accountants to identify the public interest. **(8 marks)**

(Total 20 marks)

Question 8 – AIA Nov 2013

Ravar, a public limited company, operates through a number of foreign subsidiaries. One of its subsidiaries, Krow, operates as an autonomous subsidiary. Krow's functional currency is the Zlotty (Zy). Krow has produced the following draft financial statements for the year ended 31 October 2013:

KROW
STATEMENT OF FINANCIAL POSITION AS AT 31 OCTOBER 2013

	Zy (m)	Zy (m)
Non-current assets		
Property, plant and equipment		83
Current assets		
Inventories	141	
Trade receivables	78	
Cash and cash equivalents	34	
		253
Total assets		336
Equity		
Share capital		23
Retained earnings		239
		262
Current liabilities		74
		336

STATEMENT OF PROFIT OR LOSS AND OTHER COMPREHENSIVE INCOME FOR THE YEAR ENDED 31 OCTOBER 2013

	Zy (m)
Revenue	1,651
Cost of sales	1,318
Gross profit	333
Expenses	99
Profit before tax	234
Income tax expense	80
Profit after tax	154

The following information is relevant to Ravar's investment in Krow:

(i) Krow paid dividends of Zy64 million on 18 July 2013.

(ii) Ravar gained control of Krow on 31 October 2010 by acquiring 75% of its share capital for a cash consideration of $14.3 million. At that date, Krow's retained earnings were Zy49 million.

Group policy is to measure non-controlling interest at the date control is gained at fair value. The fair value of non-controlling interest in Krow at 31 October 2010 was $4.6 million. The fair value of Krow's identifiable net assets was not significantly different to carrying amount at the date control was gained.

(iii) Goodwill is reviewed for impairment each year. These showed no impairment loss provisions have been necessary to date.

(iv) Exchange rates

	Zy to $
31 October 2010	4.51
31 October 2011	4.26
31 October 2012	4.05
31 October 2013	3.75
18 July 2013	3.96
Average for year to 31 October 2013	3.80

PRACTICE QUESTION BANK

Required

(a) Advise Ravar's directors of the translated figures that would be included in Ravar's consolidated financial statements for the year ended 31 October 2013 with reference to Krow's:

   (i) Statement of financial position
   (ii) Statement of profit or loss and other comprehensive income
   (iii) Goodwill
   (iv) Retained earnings
   (v) Non-controlling interest
   (vi) Total foreign currency translation difference for the year. **(16 marks)**

(b) On 1 November 2013, Ravar accepted in principle an unexpected offer for the sale of half its holding in Krow. It is expected the sale will be finalised before the next reporting date; although, as the offer was unexpected, actions to complete the sale have yet to be taken substantially. Ravar believes that acceptance of the offer clearly shows it no longer intends to recover its investment principally through use of the asset and that Krow's results should therefore be presented in accordance with IFRS 5 *Non-current Assets Held for Sale and Discontinued Operations*.

Required

Advise Ravar whether the provisions of IFRS 5 should be applied to the results of Krow in the financial statements for the year ended 31 October 2014. **(4 marks)**

(Total 20 marks)

Question 9 – AIA May 2015 (amended)

Fusaro is a quoted company specialising in digital software solutions. In the year ended 31 March 2018, the directors have entered into several transactions for the first time. The directors are unsure of the accounting treatment of these items, including any deferred tax consequences, and require your advice on the following:

(a) Fusaro granted 1,000 $1 equity share options to each of its 100 staff on 1 April 2017. The share options vest in three years' time, on 31 March 2020, provided that the employees still work for the company. The fair value of each share option at 1 April 2017 is $6 per share.

On 1 April 2017, the directors anticipated that 25% of the relevant employees would leave the company within the three-year vesting period, and would forfeit their rights to the share options. At 31 March 2018, the directors reassessed the expected number of leavers and revised their assumption to 20%.

In the country that Fusaro operates tax relief is given on the intrinsic value of the shares at the date of exercise. At 31 March 2018, the intrinsic value of the share options was calculated at $9 per share.

Required

Advise the directors on the correct accounting treatment for the share options granted to Fusaro's employees. **(7 marks)**

(b) On 1 April 2017, Fusaro introduced a new retirement benefit scheme. Under the terms of the scheme, Fusaro will contribute 7% of the total remuneration expense into the pension scheme on behalf of its employees. Fusaro's obligations are limited to its annual contribution to the fund each year, and the employees' pension will be solely dependent on the performance of pension fund.

Total staff remuneration for the year ended 31 March 2018 was $5 million, and Fusaro had paid $200,000 into the pension fund by 31 March 2018.

Tax relief on pension contributions are deductible on a cash basis.

Required

Advise the directors on the correct accounting treatment for the new retirement benefit scheme operated by Fusaro. **(5 marks)**

(c) Fusaro's management have heard that many companies now publish non-GAAP KPIs in addition to those required by IFRS. The management wish to publish earnings per share (EPS) figures based upon earnings before interest, tax, depreciation and amortisation (EBITDA). Fusaro's finance director, however, has dismissed the idea as she believes that the financial statements prepared using IFRS Standards should provide all the information needed by the users of financial statements.

Required

Critique, with reference to the Conceptual Framework, the finance director's opinion that the financial statements provide all the information needed by the users of financial statements and advise Fusaro's management whether the practice of reporting an EPS figure based upon EBITDA is ethically acceptable and to what extent it complies with IFRS Standards. **(8 marks)**

(Total 20 marks)

Question 10 – AIA Nov 2014

(a) Denz is a public limited company. The company employs fifty people and has an annual turnover of $50 million. Denz's business model is to invest in small private fast growing companies with the aim of disposing of the investment at such time in the future when sale profits can be maximised.

On 1 November 2013 Denz gained control of Zin Limited, an unlisted company, by acquiring 75% of Zin's equity. The fair value of Zin's identifiable net assets was $3 million. Denz paid $3.34 million immediately and agreed to pay a further $3.54 million in one year's time if Zin's sales volumes increased by more than 20% over the year. Accounting and legal fees concerning the acquisition were paid by Denz and amounted to $83,000. Denz estimates its cost of capital at 5%.

The group year end is 31 October 2014. By that date, Zin's sales volume had increased by 12%. Zin believed that future growth in sales volumes would stabilise at 15% per annum due to a competitor entering the market. Due to the increased competition, Zin estimated that goodwill would have a useful life of six years. Zin measures goodwill using the 'full' goodwill approach.

Required

(i) Advise Denz of the goodwill amount to be included in its group statement of financial position for the year ended 31 October 2014 with respect to its investment in Zin.

(5 marks)

(ii) The directors of Denz are considering a delisting of the entity so that its equity or debt would no longer be available to the public; although the entity would still prepare general purpose financial statements.

Advise Denz how your advice in (i) above would have changed had Denz been an unlisted company upon the acquisition of Zin. **(7 marks)**

(b) Deliberations by the directors of Denz concerning whether or not to delist the entity have reached a stalemate. The directors cannot agree on the benefits of adopting the IFRS for SMEs. They also require clarity on the impact of the IFRS for SMEs on one of the entity's main assets, investment properties. Denz currently measures investment property at cost under IAS 40 *Investment Property*. Denz owns an investment property which comprises land and buildings. The land could be sold for redevelopment and the best price it could obtain for doing so is $9 million; although currently Denz has no intention of selling. A reliable market value of the land and buildings as a going concern is $5 million.

Required

(i) Advise the directors of Denz on the benefits to the entity of adopting the IFRS for SMEs.

(5 marks)

(ii) Advise Denz on the impact of adoption on the entity's financial statements with respect to its investment property. **(3 marks)**

(Total 20 marks)

PRACTICE QUESTION BANK

Question 11 – May 2017

Wilton was listed on the stock exchange on 1 May 2016. During the year ended 30 April 2017 the company appointed a number of non-executive directors and established an audit committee. The convener of the audit committee has raised the following issues for discussion with the finance director.

(a) Wilton makes and sells food products. The finance director is concerned that the requirements of IFRS 8 *Operating Segments* will put Wilton at a competitive disadvantage because other manufacturers may discover that Wilton's seafood division is very profitable.

The following analysis relates to the year ended 30 April 2017:

	Revenue $m	Profit $m	Net assets $m
Fresh foods, excluding seafood	100	10	18
Fresh seafood	40	8	9
Tinned vegetables	150	110	23
Frozen vegetables	160	87	26
	450	215	76

The production director has suggested that Wilton could simply claim that it has a single segment, namely food, and that no further analysis is required.

Required

(i) Explain whether it would be acceptable to restrict segmental information on the basis that a full report would harm Wilton's competitive position. **(4 marks)**

(ii) Explain the minimum segmental reporting requirements for Wilton. **(6 marks)**

(b) As at 1 May 2016 the present value of the obligation arising from Wilton's defined benefit pension plan was $650m. At that date the fair value of the plan's assets was $635m.

The discount rate at the start of the year was 7.8%. By the end of the year it had risen to 11.5%.

The following figures were recorded during the year ended 30 April 2017:

	$m
Current service cost	124
Benefits paid	128
Contributions received	70

On 30 April 2017 the present value of the plan's obligation was $730m and the fair value of the plan's assets was $645m.

Required

(i) Calculate the figures that will appear with respect to pensions in Wilton's financial statements for the year ended 30 April 2017. **(5 marks)**

(ii) Evaluate, with reference to the *Conceptual Framework*, the suggestion that the estimate for the value of the plan's obligations is too uncertain to be reflected in the financial statements. **(5 marks)**

(Total 20 marks)

Question 12 – May 2015

(a) Quest, a public limited company, intends to dispose of a group of assets together with a number of associated liabilities. The entity's year end is 30 April. On 1 May 2014 the assets and liabilities associated with this disposal were as follows:

	$m
Goodwill allocated to the disposal group	2.55
Property, plant and equipment (PPE) at a revalued amount	7.82

Property, plant and equipment at cost	9.69
Inventory	4.08
Investment in equity instruments	3.06
	27.20
Liabilities associated with above assets	(4.20)
Other group liabilities to be paid out of disposal proceeds	(8.00)

On 31 October 2014, the disposal group was classified as held-for-sale in accordance with IFRS 5 *Non-current Assets Held for Sale and Discontinued Operations*. At that date it was found that goodwill had not been impaired, the revalued amount for PPE carried at a valuation was $7 million, depreciation on PPE carried at cost during the period was $1 million, there was no change necessary to inventory valuation or the amount for liabilities and the fair value of investments in equity instruments was $2.6 million. The fair value of the disposal group at that date was $15 million.

Required

Advise Quest of the accounting treatment of the above disposal group if Quest was to produce group financial statements as at 31 October 2014. **(12 marks)**

(b) Quest's directors understand that IFRS 5 *Non-current Assets Held for Sale and Discontinued Operations* requires that for an asset to be classified as held for sale it must be available for immediate sale. The entity has committed to a plan to sell a building used as its headquarters. The entity will either move temporarily into alternative accommodation or will wait until construction of a new building is complete.

Required

Advise Quest's directors whether, and if so under what circumstances, the above commitment will qualify the building as being for 'immediate sale' under IFRS 5. **(4 marks)**

(c) Quest's directors are considering a first investment in Tinu, an overseas group entity. Tinu is domiciled in a country which requires IFRS in an entity's financial reporting. However, the directors have heard that international investors need to be cautious when assessing such an entity's financial performance due to (1) the possible impact of changes to International Generally Accepted Accounting Principles (GAAP) and (2) an entity's choice of practices concerning the presentation of information in its financial statements.

Required

Advise Quest's directors how their assessment of Tinu's performance may be affected by the two issues mentioned above. **(4 marks)**

(Total 20 marks)

Question 13 – Nov 2014

(a) Paxdal, a public limited company whose functional currency is the dollar ($), acquired 100% of the equity share capital of Dia upon its incorporation many years ago. The functional currency of Dia, a foreign entity, is the boli (β). The equity shares were acquired when the exchange rate was $1= β2. Paxdal is consolidating the financial statements of the subsidiary for the year ended 31 October 2014 at which point the exchange rate was $1= β4 (2013 comparative $1= β3). The weighted average exchange rate for the year was $1= β3.5. Dia is domiciled and trades in a country whose economic environment provides strong indicators of the existence of hyperinflation.

Dia has produced the following draft financial statements for use by Paxdal in the consolidation exercise:

DIA
STATEMENT OF PROFIT OR LOSS FOR THE YEAR ENDED 31 OCTOBER 2014

	βm
Sales	52.50

Cost of sales		(49.79)
Depreciation		(0.75)
Finance charge		(0.53)
Profit before tax		1.43
Income tax		(0.69)
Profit for the year		0.74

STATEMENT OF FINANCIAL POSITION AS AT 31 OCTOBER 2014

		2014	2013
		βm	βm
Property, plant and equipment		8.25	9.00
Inventories		4.50	4.07
Trade receivables		6.00	7.20
Cash and cash equivalents		0.90	0.30
	Total assets	19.65	20.57
Trade payables		5.76	6.80
Taxation		0.69	1.31
Non-current liabilities		5.40	5.40
	Total liabilities	11.85	13.51
Share capital		1.50	1.50
Retained earnings		6.30	5.56
	Total equity	7.80	7.06

Required

Prepare translated financial statements for Dia for use by Paxdal in its consolidation exercise. Your statement of financial position should show comparative figures. **(12 marks)**

(b) Paxdal is known mainly as a highly successful retailer of mobile technology which it distributes through a chain of High Street shops; whereas Dia develops and manufactures devices which allow people to control appliances in the home by using their smartphones. The directors of Paxdal wish to exclude Dia from Paxdal's consolidated financial statements on the grounds that, not only are Dia's activities too dissimilar but Dia is the only entity within the group to have suffered hyperinflation and that to include the financial results of Dia would mislead users and thereby reduce the usefulness of the group statements.

Required

Advise the directors whether the option to exclude Dia is available to them under IFRS.

(4 marks)

(c) Paxdal's directors have been advocates of historical cost accounting for many years. They are are aware that the Conceptual Framework allows for a mixed measurement approach to be taken, but are concerned as to the reliability of fair values in financial reporting and argue that historical cost accounting provides more objective, verifiable and reliable information which is more useful to users as it is free from bias and is better at restricting managers' ability to manipulate financial reports.

Required

Advise the directors on the benefits that users of Paxdal's financial statements would gain from Paxdal's use of fair value reporting. **(4 marks)**

(Total 20 marks)

PRACTICE QUESTION BANK

Question 14 – Nov 2014

Mendez, a public limited company, is preparing group financial statements for the year ended 31 October 2014. The entity is seeking advice on a number of matters concerning the non-current assets section of the statement of financial position.

(a) Mendez holds less than a majority of the voting rights in a number of investments, as follows:

   (i) 46% of the voting rights of Gon. The remaining 54% of Gon's voting shares is held by widely dispersed independent shareholders. The largest remaining holding by any one shareholder is 1.3%. There is no history of any remaining shareholders acting jointly at the entity's annual general meetings.

   (ii) 45% of the voting rights of Ena. The remaining 55% of Ena's voting rights is held by five shareholders. Two of the remaining shareholders hold 26% each. At a recent AGM these two shareholders combined to vote against a policy change proposed by Mendez. The other three remaining shareholders hold 1% each of the voting rights.

   Required

   Advise Mendez on how the investments in Gon and Ena should be accounted for in its group financial statements. **(5 marks)**

(b) During the year Mendez acquired Orca, a company engaged in oil and gas technology. Mendez is concerned about two issues involved in the acquisition:

   (i) A significant factor in the decision to acquire Orca was the reputation of the company's research staff, many of whom are internationally renowned in the field.

   (ii) Orca has a five-year contract to supply goods to a customer, Jorz. Orca's directors believe that Jorz will renew the agreement at the end of the contract. Orca could not sell the contract without selling the business as a whole.

   Required

   Advise Mendez on whether the above two items could be identified as assets in the group statement of financial position. **(4 marks)**

(c) At 31 October 2014, Mendez employees are working on four research and development projects. The following information refers to each of these projects:

	1	2	3	4
	$000	$000	$000	$000
Expenditure incurred during the year:				
Salaries and wages	156	52	75	91
Indirect overheads	–	8	13	5
Direct overheads	29	10	39	8
Staff training costs	5	–	–	–
Patents	–	–	5	–
Market analysis	5	–	26	–
Carrying amount as at 1 November 2013	–	–	1,170	728
	195	70	1,328	832

Project notes

(1) This two-year project involves the testing of a new oil product. Mendez believes the entity has the technical ability and resources to complete the project before selling it. Market analysis costs were incurred early in the R&D phase and established that there will be a ready market for the product.

(2) Costs refer to an online product database commercially launched some years ago and fully amortised in the previous accounting period. The costs were incurred to ensure that the asset retained its functional capacity to service higher volumes of user contacts.

(3) These costs refer to a project designed to make fuel use more efficient in jet engines. A prototype of the system was successfully tested last year and, as a result, Mendez had

expected the project to be highly profitable. However, development is well behind schedule this year due to a large number of research and development staff leaving their employment to work for a competitor. The staff have not yet been replaced and Mendez now believes that the competitor has gained significant ground in developing a competing technology.

(4) Commercial production began at the start of the year. The asset's recoverable amount is $1.5 million and Mendez expects revenues will be received over an indefinite period.

Required

Advise Mendez on how each project should be accounted for in the financial statements for the year ended 31 October 2014 and of the amount to be included in the group statement of financial position at that date. **(11 marks)**

(Total 20 marks)

Question 15 – May 2017 (amended)

Millennium manufactures steel. The company has a single large site that is situated in a region where there is a great deal of heavy industry.

Millennium's site is divided into several plants, each of which has a defined role. The plants trade with one another, but also with external customers. For example, Millennium's rolling mill makes steel plates from steel supplied by the Millennium's steel works, which operates the furnaces that make the steel. The rolling mill sells 90% of its output to Millennium's pipeworks and the remaining 10% is sold to external customers.

The rolling mill's assets have the following carrying amounts:

	$m
Land	25
Buildings	50
Rolling plant	45
	120

Millennium's board believes that it could sell the rolling mill in its entirety for $80m. They believe that the future cash flows from the mill have a net present value of $55m.

The land occupied by the rolling mill has a fair value of $30m.

If Millennium combines the rolling mill with the pipeworks then the total carrying amount of the assets is $280m, with a combined potential sales value of $300m and a combined net present value of $420m.

Required

(a) Advise whether the rolling mill's assets are impaired. **(4 marks)**

(b) Calculate the carrying amounts of the rolling mill's assets, assuming that they are impaired. **(4 marks)**

Millenium has made a loss in the year in each of the last three financial years and the industry is in decline. It operates in a tax jurisdiction that allows the carry forward of unused tax losses for a five year period. Millenium has recognised a material deferred tax asset in respect of the carry-forward of unused tax losses as the directors believe that recognising the asset is consistent with the definition of an asset per the *Conceptual Framework*.

Millenium breached a covenant attached to a bank loan which is due for repayment in two years' time. The loan agreement terms state that a breach in loan covenants entitles the bank to demand immediate repayment of the loan. Millenium believes that the bank will allow it to pay on the original due date and therefore have decided to present the loan in non-current liabilities on the statement of financial position.. The breach of covenants is not expected to impact on Millenium's ability to operate as a going concern.

(c) Discuss, with reference to the Conceptual Framework, the proposed treatment of Millenium's deferred tax asset and the financial reporting issues raised by its loan covenant breach.

(12 marks)

(Total 20 marks)

Question 16 – Nov 2012

Expan, a public limited company, organises its business into two operating segments: (1) supermarkets and convenience stores and (2) property investment. The following summary has been taken from Expan's most recent draft statement of income. The presentation is based on the directors' belief that certain items recognised in reported profit before tax can vary significantly from year to year and therefore create a volatility in reported earnings which does not reflect Expan's underlying performance. The directors believe that the 'underlying profit before tax' and the 'underlying basic earnings per share' present a clearer and more consistent presentation of the underlying performance of Expan's ongoing business to shareholders.

EXPAN GROUP
EXTRACTS FROM DRAFT GROUP STATEMENT OF INCOME FOR THE YEAR ENDED 31 OCTOBER 2012

	Notes	2012 $m	2011 $m
Profit before tax		24	23
Analysed as:			
Underlying profit before tax		19	18
Profit on disposal of properties		3	1
Investment property fair value movements		1	5
Financing fair value movements	1	1	(1)
		24	23
Income tax expense		6	5
Profit for the year attributable to ordinary shareholders		18	18
Earnings per share	2	cents	cents
Basic		32.14	33.33
Underlying basic		23.21	24.07

Notes

(1) Fair value gains and losses on non-derivative financial assets and liabilities carried at amortised cost.

(2) Basic earnings per share is calculated by dividing the earnings attributable to ordinary shareholders by the weighted average number of ordinary shares in issue during the year.

Required

Advise the directors of Expan on how the following transactions should be dealt with in the entity's financial statements for the year ended 31 October 2012.

(a) (i) On 1 November 2011 Expan introduced a customer loyalty programme for customers purchasing a specialised range of goods. The loyalty points have no expiry date and each point may be exchanged for goods valued at $1. During the year 4 million points were granted on sales of $40m but owing to customers' unfamiliarity with the scheme only 20% of points had been redeemed by 31 October 2012.

However, the directors believe that 75% of the remaining points will be redeemed in the following year and that the remainder will never be redeemed. Expan's directors have not made any adjustments in the financial statements in connection with the new loyalty scheme. The directors believe none are necessary as the scheme closely resembles a 'money off' voucher scheme currently in use. **(5 marks)**

(ii) Expan purchased a 5% non-derivative financial asset in Nap on 1 November 2010 for $10 million. The asset had a term of five years and a maturity value of $13 million. Expan has measured these assets at amortised cost using the effective interest method. The effective interest rate on the asset is 10%. The financial asset has been correctly accounted for in the year to 31 October 2012 but the associated loss allowance has not yet been accounted for. At 1 November 2011 a stage 1 loss allowance of $0.2 million was recognised, based on the present value of lifetime credit losses of $1 million and a 20% change of default in the next 12 months. A discount factor of 8% has been applied when calculating the present value of lifetime credit losses.

On 31 October 2012 Nap went into liquidation and therefore entered stage 3 of the expected credit loss model. The present value of the lifetime expected credit losses is $1.82 million and **(4 marks)**

(b) Recalculate Expan's basic and underlying basic earnings per share figures for the year ended 31 October 2012, following any profit adjustments that are necessary as a result of your answer to part (a). **(4 marks)**

(c) An increasing number of entities have adopted a number of different ways of presenting the earnings that directors believe are sustainable and more transparently and accurately reflect the entity's underlying* financial performance. Although Expan has drawn up the entity's draft statement of profit or loss in a manner which reflects this belief by presenting 'underlying profit before tax' and 'underlying earnings per share', the directors are still unsure whether they are violating IFRS.

*The word 'underlying' refers to a financial reporting metric that does not have an agreed definition but is commonly used by entities to represent performance attributable to continuing operations, that is, before adjustments for, for example, gains or losses from disposal of properties, investment property fair value movements, impairment of goodwill, IAS 19 pension financing gains or losses and any other items that are material and infrequent in nature.

Required

Advise Expan's directors whether the reporting of underlying figures is acceptable practice within the context of IFRS. **(7 marks)**

(Total 20 marks)

Question 17 – Nov 2012

Pera, a public limited company, operates in the mining industry.

(a) (i) During the year ended 31 October 2012 Pera sold inventory to Otion a subsidiary for $20 million. The subsidiary sold 75% of this inventory to external parties before the 31 October 2012 and fully expects the remaining inventory to be sold within the first few months of the following year. Pera made a profit of 30% on the selling price. Both Pera and the subsidiary are subject to the same tax jurisdiction and pay tax on profits of 30%.

(2 marks)

(ii) Pera also controls an overseas subsidiary Kram which, in the year ended 31 October 2012, made a loss adjusted for tax purposes of $10 million. The loss may only be relieved by carrying it forward to be offset against Kram's future taxable profits. Kram expects profits to grow over the forthcoming year. In Kram's jurisdiction taxable profits are subject to tax at 20%. **(2 marks)**

(iii) On 1 November 2011 Pera paid $20 million cash to acquire 100% of the equity of a competitor Ember. The fair value of Ember's identifiable net assets was $16 million. The tax

base of the net assets was $14 million. Ember has not identified any deferred tax asset as part of its identifiable net assets.

Required

Advise Pera on how the above transactions will affect the deferred tax amounts recognised in Pera's group financial statements for the year ended 31 October 2012.

(2 marks)

(b) Pera exerts control over an operating subsidiary Santi. Pera also holds 15% of the equity of another entity Compu. The 15% holding in Compu will allow Santi access to highly specialised mining technology owned by Compu and provided to Santi for use free of charge. This commitment will begin in December 2012. So that Pera can monitor the use of the technology Pera participates in Compu's operating and financial policy decisions.

The Pera directors are unsure about whether a related party situation exists between the three companies.

Required

Advise Pera's directors how the above transaction should be dealt with in the Pera group financial statements for the year ended 31 October 2012 and explain the purpose of any disclosure requirements. **(7 marks)**

(c) Pera is considering the introduction of interim financial reporting during the year ended 31 October 2013. The first report would be for the six months to 30 April 2013. In planning for the introduction of interim reporting Pera wishes to be advised of the appropriate accounting treatment for the following event.

Pera is planning the major overhaul and restructuring of a distribution facility. Work is scheduled to begin in August 2013 although contracts will not be issued until May 2013; at which date Pera is planning to inform the workforce of the plan. The overhaul will take four months and cost $5 million. As a result of the reorganisation retraining costs of $1 million are likely to be incurred in October 2013.

The workforce will receive a year-end bonus of 10% of wages based on profits over the year. Owing to the seasonal nature of work at the distribution facility most of the profits are earned in the second half of the year. It is not possible to measure the monthly profits with any accuracy.

The distribution facility is planning to develop a new computer based distribution system. It is planned to spend $2 million on 1 November 2012 to carry out basic research into the system's feasibility. It is intended that feasibility will be established by 1 May 2013 at which point a further $3 million will be spent to develop the system. Pera plans to have the system fully commissioned by October 2013.

Required

Advise Pera's directors on the appropriate accounting treatment of the above transactions if the entity were to introduce interim financial reporting on 30 April 2013. **(7 marks)**

(Total 20 marks)

Question 18 – Nov 2012

(a) Globalisation involves the close integration of national economies and removal of any obstacles to free trade. Thus, globalisation requires the further integration of world capital markets. The result of such integration is that entities that were once dependent on domestic financial markets for debt and equity capital now have access to financial markets outside of their national borders. To aid the preparers and users of the financial statements of these entities, International Financial Reporting Standards (IFRS) attempt to ensure consistency in the interpretation and application of generally accepted accounting principles (GAAP) from country to country. However, the transition to IFRS often involves significant changes to an entity's financial reporting as IFRS Accounting Standards often introduce new accounting practices that were not required by the entity's domestic GAAP.

Required

Appraise the challenges faced by an entity adopting IFRS for its financial reporting and discuss how amendments to its accounting practices and the availability of alternatives in IFRS could lead to inconsistency between entities in their financial reporting. **(9 marks)**

(b) A public limited company Recto has chosen to adopt IFRS and has a date of transition of 1 November 2012. On 1 November 2010 Recto acquired manufacturing property with an expected remaining useful life of 50 years for $12 million and accounted for it at cost. The property is depreciated systematically over 50 years. Under domestic GAAP the property was revalued to $14 million on 1 November 2011 with any consequent adjustment being recognised in equity. Following initial recognition the property was measured at fair value less subsequent depreciation and any impairment losses.

Upon transition to IFRS and in accordance with IAS 16 *Property, Plant and Equipment,* Recto's directors selected the cost model as the appropriate accounting policy for measurement of the manufacturing property. However, they are unsure which figure to use in the financial statements. The market value of the property at 1 November 2012 is $15 million.

Required

Advise Recto's directors on the options available concerning the initial measurement of the manufacturing property at the date of transition to IFRS and show by use of journal entries the necessary financial statement adjustments which will have to be made under each option.

(11 marks)

(Total 20 marks)

Question 19 – May 2013

Olco, a public limited company, owns and manages hotels. The company uses leasing as a way to finance the business and is seeking advice on how to account for these transactions. The directors have also asked for advice on the impact of IFRS 16 *Leases*.

(i) Olco leases laptops and tablets from an IT supplier for use by management in hotels. The list price of these items is between $200 and $500 and Olco rents machines for a three year period, at the end of which they are returned to the IT supplier for recycling or disposal.

(ii) Olco operates a hotel transport service and is considering the acquisition of a fleet of vehicles. The directors are uncertain about the impact the method of acquisition might have on the company's gearing as shown on its balance sheet. The acquisition alternatives are either to lease the fleet or to buy it via a loan. The fleet would cost $1 million if purchased. Forecasts show the purchase would increase operating profit by 12% per annum. Current operating profit is $400,000, share capital is $2 million and the current debt/equity gearing ratio is 0.5:1.

Olco would negotiate a four-year lease. The annual lease payments would be $286,000 payable in advance. Olco's cost of borrowing is 15% and the rate implicit in the lease would be 9.7%.

The following discount factors are relevant:

Year	Annuity at 15%
1	0.870
2	1.626
3	2.283
4	2.855

Required

Prepare a report for the directors of Olco to advise them on the following:

(a) How the lease of laptops and tablets in (i) will be accounted for under IFRS 16

(5 marks)

PRACTICE QUESTION BANK

(b) The impact on the company's gearing and return on capital employed if the fleet of vehicles in (ii) is acquired both by purchase and leasing, and **(9 marks)**

(c) The reasons why the IASB issued IFRS 16 *Leases*, with reference to the *Conceptual Framework*, and what impact the changes in IFRS 16 changes would have on Olco's accounting. **(6 marks)**

(Total 20 marks)

Question 20 – May 2013

Mondo, a public limited company, is a manufacturer and trades through three distinct business segments which operate in different parts of the world. Operating results are regularly reviewed by the company's chief operating decision maker (CODM). The directors are seeking advice on how the principles and requirements of IFRS 8 *Operating Segments* should apply to the group. The following information has been extracted from the company's records:

Segment	Number of employees	Turnover External $m	Turnover Internal $m	Profit/(loss) before common costs $m	Net assets before common items Assets $m	Net assets before common items Liabilities $m
Tuedo	100	360	20	(26)	510	350
Wedon	200	500	10	176	1,300	480
Thurso	300	840	–	100	3,400	2,300

Common costs include central head office service costs of $17 million, property management costs of $30 million and post-employment service costs of $20 million. Mondo has confirmed that these costs are included in the CODM review but is unsure of how to allocate them to segments.

The Tuedo segment comprises a subsidiary which was recently acquired by Mondo. In return for a guaranteed contract for the sale of goods to Tuedo's former owners, Mondo did not take over Tuedo's post-employment benefit obligations upon acquisition. Tuedo's turnover figure includes sales of $200 million to Tuedo's former owners. All current Tuedo employees belong to a defined contribution scheme. All Wedon and Thurso employees are members of a defined benefit scheme.

The average age of property, plant and equipment in the three segments is: Tuedo 5 years, Wedon 10 years and Thurso 15 years. Property management costs accrue in close proportion to the age of the assets.

Most strategic management decisions are made centrally by head office staff. Mondo estimates that staff time spent on decision making and general management duties is in proportion to the turnover of each segment.

The CODM is provided with amounts for all assets and liabilities, apart from the head office, as part of his review. The head office was valued at $20 million. This was purchased with a 6% loan for the same amount. Neither the loan nor the asset is included in the above asset and liability figures. Loan interest is not included in the segment profit or loss figures although Mondo has indicated that it is a cost reviewed by the CODM.

Mondo attributes $420 million of its external sales and $300 million of its non-current assets to its country of domicile. $260 million of Mondo's external sales are attributed to one foreign country.

Required

Advise the directors of Mondo on how the principles and requirements of IFRS 8 *Operating Segments* would apply to the information given above. In particular, Mondo requires advice on the:

- Allocation of Mondo's common costs, assets and liabilities
- Recognition and reporting of the company's reportable segments
- Reporting of information about Mondo's geographical areas of trading and major customers.

(20 marks)

PRACTICE QUESTION BANK

Question 21 – May 2013 (amended)

You are the financial accountant of Seph, a public limited company. The directors of Seph are aware that one of its competitors as recently changed to apply fair values rather than historical cost where possible. They have asked you to explain more about the relevant accounting standard that deals with fair values

Required

(a) Advise the directors of Seph on the requirements of IFRS 13 Fair Value Measurement, making reference to the *Conceptual Framework* where relevant. **(8 marks)**

(b) Seph has assumed responsibility for a decommissioning liability in a business combination. This involves the dismantling of an offshore oil platform in 10 years' time. Seph would be contractually allowed to transfer the liability to a third party but, due to its unique nature, a quoted price is not available for the amount Seph would be willing to pay to complete the transfer.

Seph assesses long-term liabilities of this nature on a cost-plus basis by taking into account the future cash outflows that a market participant would be expected to incur to fulfil the obligation. Based upon its experience of fulfilling obligations of this type and on its knowledge of the market, Seph has provided the following data relevant to the measurement of the dismantling obligation:

(i) Labour costs have been estimated on the basis of current market rates, adjusted for expected increases. There is a 30% probability they will amount to $20 million, a 40% probability they will amount to $25 million and a 30% probability they will amount to $35 million.

(ii) Industry practice is to allocate overheads and plant operating costs at 90% of expected labour costs.

(iii) The profit mark-up that a third-party contractor would typically require for undertaking the dismantling and assuming the risk associated with the obligation is 20%

(iv) The compensation that a contractor would typically require for the risk that actual cash flows may differ from those expected is 5% of cash flows after inflation.

(v) Based on market and economic forecasts the rate of inflation is estimated to be 4.5% over the ten-year period. The inflation factor to reflect this is 1.553.

(vi) The risk-free rate of interest for a bond maturing in ten years' time is 6%. Seph has estimated that a rate of 3% is appropriate to reflect its own credit risk and risk of non-performance.

The following present value discount factors are relevant:

Period (years)	3%	6%	9%
10	0.744	0.558	0.422

Required

Advise Seph of the amount to be included in the entity's statement of financial position to reflect the above dismantling obligation. Explain the background to the calculations. **(12 marks)**

(Total 20 marks)

Question 22 – Nov 2015

(a) Employee benefits form a significant part of Bee's costs. Bee is a public limited company. The entity has recently appointed a new finance director (FD) who is seeking advice on how this type of cost should be accounted for in the entity's financial statements. The following employee benefit transactions relate to Bee's financial statements for the year ended 31 October 2015.

PRACTICE QUESTION BANK

(i) As part of the entity's terms of employment, Bee began a defined benefit scheme for the FD's benefit. The following information relates to this scheme:

	$'000
As at 1 November 2014	
Fair value of scheme assets	256
Defined benefit obligation	266
Past service cost	20
For the year ended 31 October 2015	
Gross service cost	115
Present value of FD's contributions	106
Remeasurement loss	17
Actual contribution by Bee to the scheme	100

The appropriate discount rate as at 1 November 2014 was 10%

The actual contribution by Bee to the scheme has been included in profit or loss.

Required

Provide calculations to advise Bee on the treatment of the above transactions in the entity's statement of comprehensive income for the year ended 31 October 2015.

(4 marks)

(ii) On 1 November 2012 Bee granted 5,000 share options to each of its 15 main sales staff. Vesting is conditional upon the member of staff working for Bee for the next three years. Bee estimated that the fair value of each option was $20.

During the first year, two staff members left and at the year end Bee estimated that a further four would leave before the end of the vesting period.

During the second year, one further staff member left and Bee estimated that a further two would leave before the end of the vesting period.

During the third and final year of the scheme, no members of staff left.

Required

Provide calculations to advise Bee on the treatment of the above transaction in the entity's financial statements for the year ended 31 October 2015. **(4 marks)**

(iii) On 1 October 2015, Bee announced a plan to close a manufacturing plant on 31 March 2016 and to terminate the employment of all employees at the plant. Bee requires the employees to stay in service until closure of the plant to complete existing orders. The termination plan is as follows: each employee who remains in service until the factory closes will receive a cash payment of $10,000 payable in the following month. Any employee leaving before the factory closes will receive a cash payment of $6,000.

On 1 October 2015, 1,000 employees were in service at the factory. At that time, Bee estimated that 100 employees would leave before the factory closes on 31 March 2016.

At 31 October 2015, none of the employees had left service at the factory.

Required

Provide calculations to advise Bee on the treatment of the above transaction in the entity's financial statements for the year ended 31 October 2015. **(4 marks)**

(b) Sac, a public limited company, is a subsidiary of Bee. Sac has awarded equity shares it holds in Bee to its employees in exchange for services performed. Sac has an obligation as a principal to settle the award with its employees.

PRACTICE QUESTION BANK

Bee's new FD is of the opinion that the group financial statements should simply reflect economic reality and, as such, the award should not be recognised as it is ultimately a cost to the shareholders and not to the entity.

Required

Advise the FD on whether his opinion complies the IASB *Conceptual Framework* on the matter and on how this transaction would be accounted for in (i) the Bee group consolidated financial statements, (ii) the separate financial statements of Bee, and (iii) the separate financial statements of Sac. **(8 marks)**

(Total 20 marks)

Question 23 – May 2014

(a) The Sideel group operates in the oil industry. Occasionally the group's activities cause contamination of rivers and land. The group rectifies this contamination only if it is a legal requirement of the country in which it occurs. This corporate attitude to the environment has been widely criticised. Many commentators have observed that Sideel demonstrates little concern for the impact that the group's business model may have on the environment. As a result of the group's environmental stance Sideel has never produced an environmental report. The group has three long-term contracts to operate in three countries where contamination has become an issue during the year ended 30 April 2014:

Country 1: No law exists requiring clean up of contamination. Industry experts have estimated the costs of clean up to be $13 million.

Country 2: A law requiring clean up exists and the cost has been estimated by industry experts at $10 million.

Country 3: A law requiring clean up of land already contaminated has been passed but it will not come into force until 1 May 2014. The cost of clean up is estimated to be $15 million.

Required

(i) Advise Sideel's directors on how the group should account for the above three events in the group financial statements for the year ended 30 April 2014. You must explain your advice. **(6 marks)**

(ii) Advise Sideel's directors on the benefits to the group of producing a social and environmental report. **(11 marks)**

(b) At 30 April 2014 Sideel is being sued by a customer for damages of $100 million relating to a claim that one of its products was not fit for purpose. The customer has begun legal proceedings although Sideel is disputing any liability for the damage. Sideel's legal team has estimated that Sideel has a 30% chance of losing the case. The team has also estimated that, given the circumstances, there is a 10% chance that actual outflows, if any, will differ from those expected.

Required

Advise Sideel on how the above event would be accounted for in its financial statements for the year ended 30 April 2014. **(3 marks)**

(Total 20 marks)

Question 24

(a) Krz, a public limited company, sells vehicles in three different markets. At various stages in its history, the entity has transacted in all three markets and retains the ability to do so at any time. Krz currently holds one thousand identical vehicles and is reviewing their fair value in accordance with IFRS 13 *Fair Value Measurement*. The following information relates to transactions in the vehicles in the respective markets:

	America	Europe	Asia
Total market volume	20%	70%	10%
Volume of market achieved by Krz	55%	30%	15%
	$'000	$'000	$'000
Price per vehicle	60	50	56
Transaction costs per vehicle (eg commissions)	6	2	1
Costs to transport each vehicle to the market	2	2	2

Required

Advise Krz, showing relevant calculations, how the fair value of the vehicles should be determined.

(8 marks)

(b) On 30 April 2014 Krz owned a vehicle showroom which it rented to Buz and on which Buz owed rent of $1 million. Krz employs professional valuers and the showroom was carried in Krz's financial statements at its fair value of $20 million. On 5 May 2014, before the financial statements were authorised for issue, Buz unexpectedly announced its insolvency and informed Krz that it would be seeking to write off the full amount of its debt.

Required

Advise Krz how the above events should be accounted for in its financial statements for the year ended 30 April 2014. **(5 marks)**

(c) Krz purchased an asset for $10 million on 1 May 2011. Depreciation is calculated on a straight-line basis over the asset's useful life of five years. The local tax jurisdiction allows a tax allowance on such assets over four years on a straight-line basis but does not allow the tax base of such assets to be adjusted for revaluations. On 1 May 2013 the business use of the asset was reviewed. The asset's depreciation method and useful life remained unchanged but the carrying amount of the asset was increased to its fair value of $9 million.

Krz is unsure of the financial reporting implications of the revaluation.
The tax rate for all years is 30%.

Required

Advise Krz of the effect of the revaluation on the deferred tax figures carried in its financial statements for the year ended 30 April 2014. **(7 marks)**

(Total 20 marks)

Question 25

You work for Eurotoc, a limited liability company, which seeks growth through acquisitions. You are a member of a team which is investigating the possible purchase of Choggerell, a limited liability company which manufactures a product which is complementary to the products currently being sold by Eurotoc.

Your team leader wants you to prepare a report for the team evaluating the recent performance of Choggerell and the quality of its management, and has given you the following financial information which has been derived from the financial statements of Choggerell for the three years ended 31 March 20X6, 20X7 and 20X8.

Financial year ended 31 March	20X6	20X7	20X8
Revenue (€million)	2,243	2,355	2,237
Cash and cash equivalents (€million)	(50)	81	(97)
Return on equity	13%	22%	19%
Sales revenue to total assets	2.66	2.66	2.01
Cost of sales to sales revenue	85%	82%	79%
Operating expenses to sales revenue	11%	12%	15%
Net income to sales revenue	2.6%	4.3%	4.2%
Current/Working Capital ratio (to 1)	1.12	1.44	1.06
Acid test ratio (to 1)	0.80	1.03	0.74

PRACTICE QUESTION BANK

Financial year ended 31 March	20X6	20X7	20X8
Inventory turnover (months)	0.6	0.7	1.0
Credit to customers (months)	1.3	1.5	1.7
Credit from suppliers (months)	1.5	1.5	2.0
Net assets per share (cents per share)	0.86	0.92	0.97
Dividend per share (cents per share)	10.0	14.0	14.0
Earnings per share (in cents)	11.5	20.1	18.7

Required

Use the above information to prepare a report for your team leader which:

- Reviews the performance of Choggerell as evidenced by the above ratios,
- Makes recommendations as to how the overall performance of Choggerell could be improved, and
- Indicates any limitations in your analysis.

(20 marks)

Question 26 – May 2016

(a) The draft statement of profit or loss of the Verti Group as at 30 April 2016 shows profit attributable to ordinary shareholders of the parent entity of $12 million and a loss from discontinued operations attributable to the parent entity of $8 million.

Verti has 4 million ordinary equity shares outstanding with a market value of $80 each. There are 400,000 ordinary share options outstanding with an exercise price of $60 each.

Verti has in issue 1.6 million convertible preference shares with a par value of $100 each. The preference shares are entitled to a cumulative dividend of $0.10 per share. Each preference share will convert into 2 ordinary shares.

Verti has $200 million 6% convertible bonds in issue. Each $1,000 bond is convertible into 20 ordinary shares. Interest expense is not affected by amortisation of premium or discount.

The relevant tax rate is 30%.

Required

Advise Verti of the basic and diluted earnings per share figures to be disclosed in the group income statement for the year ended 30 April 2016. **(12 marks)**

(b) Verti operates in the telecommunications industry. The entity's directors are supportive of the International Standards Board's (IASB) attempts to publish Generally Accepted Accounting Principles (GAAP) which govern how entities define their periodic earnings. They believe that GAAP helps to ensure a level of reliability and consistency across firms and over time. The directors have now become concerned about the development of non-GAAP earnings performance measures disclosed by a large number of the entity's competitors in their financial reporting and require advice on whether Verti is at a competitive disadvantage by not disclosing such information.

Required

Advise Verti's directors on whether the disclosure of non-GAAP (also known as 'pro-forma') earnings measures is likely to add valuable information to the entity's annual reporting or whether it would be seen as an example of the entity indulging in earnings management.

(4 marks)

(c) Verti's directors are keen to develop the entity's engagement with capital providers and have been informed of a development in corporate reporting known as The International Integrated Reporting Framework. They were previously unaware of the existence of the framework and would like advice on what impact it may have on the entity's annual reporting, which presently focusses primarily on traditional concepts of historical performance.

Required

Advise Verti's directors on the possible impact of the above 'framework' on the annual reporting of the group as far as its engagement with capital providers and its focus on historical performance are concerned. **(4 marks)**

(Total 20 marks)

Practice answer bank

PRACTICE ANSWER BANK

Question 1

A question of miscellaneous mini case studies involving knowledge and application of IAS 24 *Related Party Disclosures*, including discussion of ethics around such transactions, IFRS 5 *Non-current Assets Held for Sale and Discontinued Operations*, IAS 40 *Investment Property* and IAS 28 *Investments in Associates and Joint Ventures*.

(a) This is a related party transaction under IAS 24 *Related Party Disclosures*. IAS 24 includes within its definition of a related party: a party that has significant influence over an entity and members of the key management personnel of a company and therefore, AJ Parrish, as a director is a related party. Transactions with related parties are not uncommon and there is no legal requirement for a company to sell its assets to a related party at the full fair value. There are however ethical implications in that undertaking the transaction at less than full fair value has resulted in a reduced profit on sale and therefore less distributable profits for the shareholders. IAS 24 requires disclosure of the nature of any related party relationship as well as any information about the transactions and outstanding balances.

The information to be disclosed will include all of the factual information given in the question. IAS 24 requires related party disclosures in order to draw attention to the possibility that an entity's financial position and profit or loss may have been affected by the existence of related parties and by transactions and outstanding balances with such parties. Practice Statement 2 clarifies that if information provided by a disclosure could not reasonably be expected to influence the decisions primary users make based on the financial statements, then that disclosure need not be made. The involvement of related parties is a qualitative factor when assessing materiality. This factor reduces the quantitative threshold and the entity should then go back and re-assess whether the information is material.

The fact that the finance director does not consider that the transaction needs disclosed calls into question their professional competence and due care as they should have a sound understanding of the IFRS Standards.

(b) Applying IFRS 5 *Non-current Assets Held for Sale and Discontinued Operations*, the Brazilian activities should be classified as held-for-sale (para 6). Accordingly, the company should disclose separately in the statement of financial position the assets and liabilities of the Brazilian activities.

IFRS 5 includes in its definition of a discontinued operation, a business that is classified as held-for-sale and represents a separate major line of business or geographical area of operations (paragraph 32). The results of the Brazilian activities should be disclosed separately in the statement of profit or loss and other comprehensive income (paragraph 33(a)). The company should also include in the notes an analysis of revenue, costs, and tax from the discontinued operations and the net cash flows attributable to the operating, investing and financing activities of the discontinued operations (paragraph 33).

(c) As the property is no longer owner occupied and is now held for the purpose of earnings rental income, it meets the definition of an investment property and should be accounted for by applying IAS 40 *Investment Property*. IAS 40 defines an investment property as 'property (any combination of land and buildings) held to earn rentals or for capital appreciation or both rather than being used in the production and supply of goods and services or held for sale in the ordinary course of business.' On the classification of the property as an investment property, the following accounting procedures should be applied:

- The property should be accounted for in accordance with IAS 16 Property, Plant and Equipment to the date of transfer. It should be revalued to its fair value at the date of transfer with any gain or loss accounted for in accordance with IAS 16.

- The property should be derecognised land and buildings and instead should be separately recognised as an investment property. The investment property will be initially measured at its fair value (which will be equal to the fair value assigned at the date of transfer.

PRACTICE ANSWER BANK

The investment property is subsequently measured using either the cost model or the fair value model. If Nedell elects to use the cost model, it will depreciate the investment property across its useful life in the same way as for land and buildings accounted for under IAS 16. If it elects to use the fair value model, it will be required to determine the fair value of the investment property at each reporting date and recognise the gain or loss in profit or loss. No depreciation is charged when the fair value model is adopted.

Question 2

Part (a) concerns the measurement bases permitted by the Conceptual Framework and the adoption by an entity of the revaluation model for property, plant and equipment under IAS 16 and the impact of IAS 8 *Accounting Policies, Changes in Accounting Estimates and Errors*. It also requires a discussion of the accounting treatment under IFRS 16 *Leases*.

(a) (i) A 'mixed measurement' approach means that a company selects a different measurement basis (eg historical cost or current value) for its various assets and liabilities, rather than using a single measurement basis for all items. The measurement basis selected should reflect the type of entity and sector in which it operates and the business model that the entity adopts.

The mixed measurement approach can be criticised as it makes it difficult for the users to understand the carrying amounts included within the financial statement. However, the counter argument is that a single measurement basis may not provide the most relevant information to users. The *Conceptual Framework* confirms that the IASB uses a mixed measurement approach in developing standards. The measurement methods included in standards are those which the IASB believes provide the most relevant information and which most faithfully represent the underlying transaction or event.

In adopting the revaluation method, Fere is applying the current value measurement basis permitted in IFRS Standards. When an IFRS Standard allows a choice of measurement basis such as in IAS 16, the directors must exercise judgement as to which basis will provide the most useful information for its primary users. Furthermore when selecting a measurement basis, the directors should consider measurement uncertainty. The *Conceptual Framework* states that for some estimates, a high level of measurement uncertainty may outweigh other factors to such an extent that the resulting information may have little use.

(ii)

	$m	
Cost 1 May 2009	10.0	
		Company policy would be to
Depn to 30 April 2012 (3yrs × $1m)	3.0	eliminate depn against gross CA
Carrying amount 30 April 2012	7.0	
		This deficit would be written off to
Revaluation deficit 30 April 2012	3.5	profit or loss.
CA 1 May 2012	3.5	
		Company policy would be to
Depn to 30 April 2015 (3 yrs × $0.5m)	1.5	eliminate depn against gross CA
CA at 30 April 2015	2.0	
Revaluation surplus*	3.0	
	5.0	

* $1m of the surplus would be credited to the revaluation surplus in OCI representing the difference between the CA that would have resulted had the asset been held on a cost basis ($4m) and the CA on a revalued basis ($5m). The remaining $2m would be taken through profit or loss.

Although the adoption of a revaluation policy by Frere and changing from a cost model would be a change in accounting policy, it is **not** dealt with as a prior year adjustment under

IAS 8 *Accounting Policies, Changes in Accounting Estimates and Errors*. Therefore comparatives would not have to be amended.

(b) (i) IFRS 16 *Leases* requires a single lessee accounting model to be applied which reduces the number of off-balance sheet leases. Upon lease commencement, provided a contract meets the definition of a lease under IFRS 16, a lessee recognises a right-of-use asset and a lease liability. After lease commencement, a lessee measures the right-of-use asset using a cost model less accumulated depreciation and accumulated impairment. The lease liability is initially measured at the present value of the future lease payments, discounted at the rate implicit in the lease if that can be readily determined. There are optional recognition exemptions available in respect of short term leases, where short term is 12 months or less, and leases of low value assets, where low value is not defined but is intended to cover for example the lease of office equipment and small technology items. The optional recognition exemptions would not apply for the lease of cars and therefore Fere does not have the option to simply recognise the expense within staff costs and must recognise a right of use asset and associated lease liability. The cost of depreciation of the right of use asset could be classified as a staff cost. The interest incurred in respect of the lease liability will be a finance cost.

(ii) Right of use asset and lease liability

On initial recognition, the lease liability would be measured at the present value of the future lease payments of $1,871,100. It will be subsequently measured as:

	$
PV of future lease payments	1,871,100
Interest at 6% (6% × $1,871,100)	112,266 (SPL)
Carrying amount of the lease liability at end Year 1	1,983,366

The right of use asset is initially recognised as the initial measurement of the lease liability plus the deposit paid = $1,871,100 + 700,000 = £2,571,100

The asset is depreciated over four years, which is the shorter of the lease term and its useful life. Depreciation for the year is therefore $642,774

The carrying amount of the asset at the end of Year 1 is $1,928,325.

The lease liability and the carrying amount of the right of use asset will be recognised in the statement of financial position.

The finance charge (interest) and depreciation will be in the statement of profit or loss.

Question 3

Syllabus section: 13.2

This question concerns IFRS 11 *Joint Arrangements* and their accounting using the equity method as set out in IAS 28 *Investments in Associates and Joint Ventures*. Part (a) concerns a subsidiary which becomes a joint venture, part (b) concerns the identification of joint control in a joint arrangement, (c) concerns the accounting treatment of gains, losses and revenue in a joint venture.

(a) (i) **Tutorial note:** Atab's accounting is incorrect. Under IFRS 10, if a parent loses control of an entity, the retained interest must be measured at its fair value and this fair value becomes the cost on initial recognition of an investment in an associate or joint venture (IFRS 10.25). Therefore, Atab's use of historic cost of $3m (and therefore its subsequent measurement of a loss on disposal of $2.5m) is incorrect.

Correct measurement of gain/loss on disposal of 60% of Begi's shares

PRACTICE ANSWER BANK

	$m
Fair value of consideration	7.5
Fair value of Begi's identifiable net assets	4.5
Goodwill on acquisition	3.0
Carrying amount of Begi's net assets	1.8
	4.8

	$m	
Less: sale proceeds of 60%	2.0	
fair value of remaining 40% of Begi	1.2	
		3.2
Loss on disposal of 60% of Begi		1.6

Atab's original (incorrect) accounting will have been as follows in the consolidated accounts:

	$m	$m
DR Cash	2.0	
DR Joint Venture	3.0	
DR Retained earnings	2.5	
CR Net assets		7.5

The correct accounting treatment is shown above. To correct the consolidated accounts Atab must therefore:

	$m	$m
DR Net assets	2.7	
CR Joint Venture		1.8
CR Retained earnings		0.9

(ii) **Tutorial note:** When an investor increases its ownership in an existing joint venture or associate (and control is not acquired) there is no significant change in the nature and economic circumstances of the investment. Therefore there is no justification for re-measurement of the existing interest at the time of the increase (as there would be if **control** was acquired).

The cost of an investment in an associate or joint venture (and each additional acquisition) is allocated between net assets and goodwill for the purpose of disclosure. However, this does not result in any revaluation of the existing and recognised share of net assets (IAS 28.32).

For the purpose of calculating the goodwill to be disclosed in the notes, we must calculate the fair value of the associate's net assets at the year end.

FV of Blo's net assets at 31 October 2016

	$m
FV of INAs at 1 Nov 2015	16.0
Increase in Blo's retained earnings	13.5
Increase in fair value of plant and equipment	3.5
	33.0

	% held	Carrying amount of investment (inc costs IAS 28) $m	Share of net assets $m	Goodwill included in investment (balance) $m
Original investment	25	5.5	4.0 (16m × 25%)	1.5
Additional investment	20	7.0	6.6 (33m × 20%)	0.4
Share of Blo's profit for the year (25% × $13.5m)		3.4	3.4	—
		15.9	14.0	1.9

(b) Bin

'Relevant activities' are the activities of the investee that significantly affect the investee's returns (IFRS 10.10). As each party is able to unilaterally direct their own activity, no joint control exists because Alac and Bin do not collectively direct the relevant activities of the arrangement.

Cons

Because both Alac and Cons make all decisions together throughout the arrangement's life, it is unnecessary to determine which party significantly affects the returns of the arrangement. They are all directed in the same manner. Alac and Cons have joint control over the arrangement.

(c) As this is a joint venture, the inclusion of $3.4m in revenue is unacceptable under IFRS 15 *Revenue from Contracts with Customers*. Under IAS 28 (2011) *Investments in Associates and Joint Ventures*, the consolidated statement of comprehensive income should include the group share of the JV's profit or loss as a one-line entry. When a joint venturer contributes assets to a JV any gain or loss is recognised to the extent that it reflects the substance of the transaction. As a result:

(i) Only the gain attributable to the interests of the other joint venturers should be recognised in the financial statements. Exten would make a gain of $300,000 but only 40% can be considered as realised; ie that proportion attributable to Gect. Exten should therefore include a gain of $120,000 in 'profit or loss attributable to joint ventures'.

(ii) A loss of $400,000 would be made on the inventory. The full amount should be recognised when the transaction shows evidence that the NRV of the asset is less than cost. If it is probable that the loss will be incurred, prudence requires that Exten recognises the full loss in 'profit or loss attributable to joint ventures'.

> **Tutorial Note**: this shows that an asymmetric treatment of gains and losses still exists in corporate reporting.

Question 4

This question concerns the accounting for interest in joint ventures.

(a) Under IFRS 11 a joint venture is a contractual arrangement whereby two or more parties have joint control and have rights to the net assets of the arrangement. Joint control is the contractually agreed sharing of control and exists only when the activity's strategic operating and financial decisions require the unanimous consent of the parties sharing control.

Quite clearly, as Bing and Ollis control 81% of Doe's equity, the two companies share control. As any strategic decisions concerning Doe must be made by the two companies acting in unison, Doe should be accounted for as a joint venture in each of the individual company's financial statements. Doe is therefore a joint venture under IFRS 11.

IFRS 11 requires that venturers account for their interest using the equity method according to IAS 28. Bing and Ollis must therefore use the equity method.

Roy does not have joint control of Doe due to the terms of the contractual agreement between Bing and Ollis and must therefore account for its 19% interest either as a financial asset within the scope of IFRS 9 or as an associate within the scope of IAS 28. Under IAS 28 a holding of less than 20% of the voting power of Doe would be presumed not to give rise to significant influence, and thereby associate status, unless it can be clearly demonstrated that there is in fact significant influence. Although Roy is not represented on Doe's board of directors, Roy does participate in policy-making processes and also provides essential technical information and expertise. Under IAS 28 Roy would therefore account for Doe as an associate.

The different classification of investments as 'normal' financial investments under IFRS 9, associates under IAS 28 or joint ventures under IFRS 11 reflects the Conceptual Framework's fundamental qualitative characteristic of faithful representation as it allows different investments to be accounted for according to the underlying substance of the investment.

(b)

	Proportionate consolidation		*Equity accounting*	
	Dr	Cr	Dr	Cr

PRACTICE ANSWER BANK

		$m	$m	$m	$m
Net cash from Thansa (24m – 10)		14		14	
Share of Thansa cash [(30 – 24)/3]		2			
Gain in sale of plant:					
Fair value	24				
Carrying amount	15				
Gain	9 × 2/3		6		6

Tutorial note: the above entry is similar in concept to the entry made in consolidated accounts to eliminate inter-company profit. Bing cannot make a profit with itself and so its share of the profit must be eliminated.

Share of Thansa manufacturing plant
[(1/3 × 24) carrying amount to Thansa – eliminated profit 3]   5

Tutorial note: the above entry reflects the fact that Bing still controls 1/3 of the plant at its carrying amount to Bing; ie 1/3 × 15.

PPE manufacturing plant (derecognition of plant)			15		15
Investment in Thansa (associated company)				7	
		21	21	21	21

(c) Deecee has assessed that the debt asset was at level 1 of the IFRS 9 expected credit loss model on 1 November 2011 which requires 12 month expected credit losses to be assessed and recognised. At that date, the carrying amount of the debt asset would be $9.9 million ($10 million gross less $0.1 million loss allowance). By 31 October 2012 there had been a significant increase in credit risk associated with the debt assets and the portfolio had moved to level 2 which requires the present value of lifetime expected credit losses to be recognised. The accounting required for the debt assets and the loss allowance in the year to 31 October 2012 are as follows:

Debt asset

	Opening £'000	Finance income @ 10%	Interest received	Closing
2012	10,000	1,000	–	11,000

Loss allowance

	£'000
Opening 12 month ECL allowance	100
Unwind discount @ 8%	8
Increase in loss allowance	972
Closing ECL allowance	1,080

The carrying amount of the debt asset at 31 October 2012 is therefore $9,920 ($11,000 - 1,080). The finance income in the following year is calculated based on the gross carrying amount of the debt asset.

Question 5

This question involves the translation of a subsidiary's financial statements for the purpose of a consolidation exercise.

Foreign currency translation

(a) Rima's functional currency (FC) will be the currency of the primary economic environment in which the entity operates; ie the one in which it primarily generates and expends cash (IAS 21.9). However, it is not obvious from the question whether this is the $ or the €. As there is a lack of clarity, Arenta's directors must use their judgement to determine the FC that most faithfully represents the economic effects of the subsidiary's underlying business circumstances.

Arenta's directors should first give priority to the primary indicators of business circumstances before, if necessary, considering other factors (IAS 21.12). IAS 21 requires the directors to consider two primary factors:

- The currency that mainly influences sales prices for goods and services (ie usually the currency in which sales prices for goods and services are denominated and settled); and
- The currency of the country whose competitive forces and regulations mainly determine the sale prices of its goods and services.

As Rima produces and sells its goods throughout Europe, the € clearly influences the sale prices of its electronic equipment and also its labour and materials. Also, as external market forces and government regulations are too restrictive to foster external exports, Rima's business circumstances are subject only to restrictions from within Europe.

Other factors (ie the currency in which funds from financing activities are generated and the currency in which receipts from operating activities are usually retained [IAS 21.10]) are only to be considered if the FC is not obvious. In this case Rima's FC is obviously the € so other factors do not have to be considered by the directors.

> **Tutorial note:** if Rima was, for instance, purchasing the electronic equipment in dollars rather than producing it in Europe so that its operating costs were mainly in dollars, its FC would no longer be obvious. In this case, the other factors would have to be considered.

(b)

> **Tutorial note:** as Rima's FC is different to the parent company Arenta, its financial statements must be translated to the currency of Arenta; ie dollars. Rima is acting in a semi-autonomous way so any change in the exchange rate will have little or no effect on the group's cash flows. Instead, any change in exchange rates will affect Arenta's net investment and the translation is carried out from this perspective.

It is recommended that the translation exercise is carried out in the sequence shown.

Workings

1 Translate Rima's SoFP as at 30 April 2014

> **Tutorial note:** Arenta acquired 100% of Rima's shares on incorporation therefore the post acquisition retained earnings can be found by deducting the translated share capital figure (effectively the cost to Arenta of the subscribed shares) from the translated shareholders' equity figure.

		€ : $	$m
Non-current assets	(€831)	2 : 1	415.5
Inventories	(€514)	2 : 1	257.0
Trade receivables	(€237)	2 : 1	118.5
Non-current liabilities	(€304)	2 : 1	(152.0)

Current liabilities	(€235)	2 : 1	(117.5)
Translated shareholders' equity as at end of year			521.5
Equity share capital	(historical cost)		70.0
Retained earnings	(balance)		451.5
			521.5

2 *Translate Rima's SoPL*

			$m
Profit after tax	(€243)	3 : 1	81.0

3 *Translate Rima's shareholders' equity at start of year*

		$m
Shareholders' equity at end of year (in euros)	Q	1,043.0
Retained profit after tax (in euros)		243.0
Shareholders' equity at start of year (in euros)		800.0
		$m
Translated opening shareholders' equity	3.5 : 1	228.6

4 *Calculate the exchange difference*

		$m
Shareholders' equity (in dollars): at end of year	W1	521.5
at start of year	W3	228.6
Movement in equity		292.9
Retained profit after tax	W2	81.0
Exchange gain for the year		211.9

(c) IAS 1 requires that exchange differences on translating foreign operations are included in other comprehensive income. Items of other comprehensive income must be grouped into those that will and those that will not be subsequently reclassified into profit or loss. Consequently, the exchange gain of $211.9m will be disclosed under the former group as IAS 21 requires such a reclassification for translation gains or losses upon subsequent disposal of a foreign subsidiary.

Investors commonly analyse an entity's performance by using non-GAAP KPIs such as EBITDA (earnings before interest tax depreciation and amortisation) or 'underlying profits' (EBITDA adjusted for other non-cash movements). EBITDA and 'underlying' figures can be used to analyse and compare profitability between companies and industries because they eliminate the effects of financing and accounting decisions and, with underlying, non-cash adjustments such as gains and losses due to fair value adjustments and foreign subsidiary translation. It is common therefore for translation gains and losses to have no impact on such KPIs. However, they are non-GAAP metrics and as a result allow a greater amount of discretion as to what is (and is not) included in their calculation. This means that companies often change the items included in their calculation from one reporting period to the next. Such flexibility will therefore be afforded to Arenta's directors. However, when considering such changes, the directors must always remember their overriding ethical and accounting responsibilities to act in the best interests of the entity's stakeholders.

Question 6

(a) This question involves a step acquisition in which the initial holding was held as a passive investment – due to the holding company being unable to exert significant influence. It therefore involves consideration of IFRS 3 *Business Combinations* and IFRS 9 *Financial Instruments*.

> **Tutorial note:** Ezmee's initial holding of 25% must be measured at its FV at 30 April 2013 (we know that its carrying amount is $5m but we need to see if this is different to its FV). We are not told what the FV is and so must use the cost of the further acquisition of 45% as a guide. However, the cost includes a premium of 8% because Ezmee is buying a controlling interest. If we are to use the cost as a guide to the price of the initial investment, the premium must be adjusted.

Cost of 45% investment without the premium loading:
$13m (per Q) × 100/108 = $12.04m

	$m
FV of the initial holding of 25%:	
FV of 100% holding using the above figure $12.04 × 100/45 = $26.76	
FV of 25% holding therefore = $26.76 × 25%	6.69

> **Tutorial note:** alternatively this could be calculated as 12.04 × 25/45 = 6.69.

Carrying amount of initial investment of 25% (per Q)	5.00
Gain transferred to profit or loss	1.69

As the initial investment is carried at FV through other comprehensive income Ezmee will have previously included gains of $1m (carrying amount 5 – original cost 4) in other comprehensive income. Under IFRS 9 these previous gains of $1m must also be transferred to profit or loss.

Calculation of goodwill

FV of non-controlling interest $26.76 (see above) × 30%	8.03
FV of consideration (6.69 [see above] + 13)	19.69
	27.72
FV of Stoe's identifiable net assets (per Q)	25.00
Goodwill	2.72

(b) **This question concerns the amounts used to measure identifiable net assets when measuring goodwill on acquisition. It is drawn from syllabus sections 13.3 and 13.4 and is covered by BPP Learning & Practice Workbook chapters:**

13   Intangible non-current assets

Under IFRS 3 the measurement period within which adjustments can be made to provisional amounts used in the measurement of goodwill cannot exceed one year.

Investment in Pan

The facts concerning the new mining deposits came to light within the one year remeasurement period allowed by IFRS 3. However, the increase in fair value is the result of circumstances arising in February 2014 and do not reflect circumstances at 30 April 2013. No change will therefore be allowed to the measurement of goodwill.

Property

As the property was surplus to requirements, Stoe would have included it in the financial statements at its expected net realisable value $1m. The disposal at $1.4m in July 2013 is likely to reflect the fair value at 30 April 2013 and goodwill will therefore be adjusted by the increase of $0.4m.

Deferred revenue

IFRS 3 requires that items are included in the calculation of goodwill at their fair value. The fair value of a liability is defined in IFRS 13 as the price that would be paid to transfer a liability in an orderly transaction between market participants at the measurement date (IFRS 13 App.A). The deferred revenue represents an upfront payment for a service that has not yet been provided by Stoe but for which responsibility has been assumed by Ezmee. Its fair value must therefore be used in the calculation of goodwill. Fair value is $0.9m [incurred cost] × 1.2 [profit loading] = $1.08m. Goodwill must therefore be adjusted by the decrease in liabilities of $0.12m.

Intangible asset Diga

IFRS 3 requires an acquirer to recognise an identifiable asset such as Diga at its fair value determined in accordance with its use by other market participants (IFRS 3 B43). Ezmee's future intentions not to use the asset should only be reflected in determining its fair value if that is what other market participants would do. However, during the year ended 30 April 2014 it became known that other companies within the industry would have acquired the brand name and would have sold the product. Therefore IFRS 3 would require a value of $1m to be attributed to the brand name for the purpose of measuring goodwill.

Adjustments should be made as follows:

	$m
Goodwill (as in (a) above)	2.72
Investment in Pan	–
Property	(0.40)
Deferred revenue	(0.12)
Intangible asset Diga	(1.00)
Revised goodwill figure as at 30 April 2013	1.20

Question 7

(a) The basic ethical dilemma is that Oliver has a duty to the users of the financial statements to report truthfully. However, that duty is in conflict with the fact that a truthful report will lead to the company's failure and the associated impact on the company's employees and the economy of the town in which the company is based. It could be argued that the interests of the employees and the bank are in conflict. If Oliver makes an honest report then the bank will be able to act to withdraw its funds from Zanger while it still can. But a dishonest report will enable Zanger to keep its staff in full employment.

The dilemma is complicated by the fact that the accounting issues that will affect the outcome are a matter of professional judgement. In the event that the impairment problem comes to light, Oliver and the remainder of Zanger's management team could easily deny that they had been aware of the matter.

Oliver has a clear ethical duty to act with integrity, which requires behaviour that is straightforward and honest. The fact that he has been instructed to destroy documents that would otherwise incriminate him and his colleagues clarifies the extent of the dishonesty that is being considered. He should also act with objectivity, which means that the accounting treatment of the asset in question should be considered without regard to the implications of that decision.

Oliver could risk bringing the accountancy profession into disrepute, because he is a qualified accountant and must demonstrate professional behaviour. At best, he will appear negligent if problems arise with the financial statements and, at worst, he will appear fraudulent if the circumstances come to light.

It could be argued that Oliver's dilemma is less complicated than it appears. He could prepare the financial statements correctly and then ask the bank to consider a sympathetic response to the breach of the debt covenant. It is not necessarily a foregone conclusion that the funding will be withdrawn and the bank may be keen to support Zanger rather than go through the disruption of foreclosure proceedings.

(b) There is no single 'public interest' that can be measured or evaluated in the light of different decisions. Society has a variety of needs and those needs may come into conflict. There can be pressing needs at a local level that undoubtedly impact upon the public interest, but they may affect society as a whole in a different manner. For example, keeping these employees in secure jobs is in the public interest. Unfortunately, publishing misleading figures and undermining confidence in the professionalism of accountants is against the wider public interest.

The concern is that there may be conflicting effects that make it difficult to tell whether the public interest has suffered any net gain or loss. For example, suppose Zanger dismissed Oliver and published misleading financial statements. Oliver might feel that it would be against the public interest to remain silent and to leave the bank ignorant of the breach of the breached debt covenant. Having said that, any report will put him in breach of the duty of confidence, which would undermine the accountancy profession's credibility and would harm the public interest in the process. Also, if Oliver makes his concerns known then he will risk undermining the reputation of accountants and the accountancy profession simply by drawing attention to an 'accounting scandal'.

Protecting the public interest may be further complicated by the fact that it is not always clear how interested parties will be affected. For example, misleading the bank about the debt covenant will not necessarily expose it to loss. The bank will almost certainly have other safeguards in place to protect it against default and so the technical breach of the gearing limit may not create any specific risk. Having said that, the discovery of this breach could undermine the banking industry's confidence in accounting numbers and that could damage the wider public interest by making it more difficult for companies to obtain credit.

Overall, deciding how best to protect the public interest often requires a very delicate balance.

Question 8

This question requires the consolidation of a foreign subsidiary. It also requires knowledge of IFRS 5.

(a)

> **Tutorial note:** Krow uses a different functional currency to that of its parent Ravar. This means that despite being controlled by Ravar, Krow conducts financial activities in its own currency and is therefore independent of Ravar. In fact, the question tells us that Krow is autonomous. Changes in currency exchange rates will therefore have little or no effect on the present and future cash flows from operations of either company. Rather, any changes will affect Ravar's net investment in Krow and not Krow's individual monetary and non-monetary items. It is therefore appropriate to translate Krow's financial statements using the closing rate approach; ie 'closing rate' reflects the net investment at the reporting date.
>
> An important point to note is that we are translating from Zy into $ so we **divide** by the exchange rate!

(i) Translation of Krow – statement of financial position

	Zy(m)	Rate	$m
PPE	83	3.75	22.13
Inventories	141	3.75	37.60
Trade receivables	78	3.75	20.80

PRACTICE ANSWER BANK

Cash and cash equivalents	34	3.75	9.07
	336		89.60
Share capital	23	4.51	5.10
Retained earnings:			
Pre-control	49	4.51	10.86
Post-control [Zy239m – Zy49m]	190	bal	53.91
			69.87
Current liabilities	74	3.75	19.73
	336		89.60

(ii) *Translation of Krow – statement of profit or loss and other comprehensive income*

	Zy(m)	Rate	$m
Revenue	1,651	3.80	434.47
Costs of sales	1,318	3.80	346.84
Gross profit	333		87.63
Expenses	99	3.80	26.05
Profit before tax	234		61.58
Income tax expense	80	3.80	21.05
Profit after tax	154		40.53

(iii) *Goodwill in Krow at 31 Oct 2010*

	Zy(m)	Zy(m)	rate	$m
FV of consideration transferred [$14.3m × 4.51]		64.49		
FV of NCI [$4.6m × 4.51]		20.75		
Less: FV of identifiable net assets:				
Share capital	23.00			
Retained earnings	49.00			
		(72.00)		
Goodwill at 31 Oct 2010		13.24	4.51	2.94
Exchange gain for year 2010–2011	bal			0.17
Goodwill at 31 Oct 2011		13.24	4.26	3.11
Exchange gain for year 2011–2012	bal			0.16
Goodwill at 31 Oct 2012		13.24	4.05	3.27
Exchange gain for year 2012–2013	bal			0.26
Goodwill at 31 Oct 2013		13.24	3.75	3.53

> **Tutorial note:** goodwill remains unchanged in Zy as there has been no impairment

(iv) *Group retained earnings re Krow*

Share post control [$53.91 × 75%]	40.43
Share of goodwill exchange differences [(0.17 + 0.16 + 0.26) × 75%]	0.44

(v) *Non-controlling interest*

At date control gained (Q)	4.60
Share of retained earnings post-control [$53.91 (wi) × 25%]	13.48
Share of goodwill exchange differences [(0.17 + 0.16 + 0.26) (wiii) × 25%]	0.15
	18.23

(vi) *Exchange differences for the year ended 31 Oct 2013*

Statement of profit or loss and other comprehensive income
Other comprehensive income

- On translation of Krow's net assets $m

PRACTICE ANSWER BANK

Closing net assets at closing rate (wi)			69.87
Less: opening net assets at opening rate:			
	Zy(m)		
Net assets at 31 Oct 2013 (Q)	262		
Less profit for the year after tax (Q)	(154)		
Add dividends paid (Q)	64		
	172	@4.05	42.47
			27.40
Less: translated retained profit for the year			
[$40.53 (wii) − $16.17 [(dividends paid) Zy64m/3.96]			24.36
			3.04
• On goodwill (wiii)			0.26
Exchange gain for the year			3.30

Tutorial note: the above calculation may be explained as follows: closing net assets = opening net assets + retained profit. If we adjust (translate) all three components of the equation by the appropriate exchange rates, we are left with a balancing figure which is in effect the exchange gain/loss caused by the translation of those net assets.

The foreign currency translation difference of $3.3m will be described in OCI as an item that 'may be reclassified subsequently to profit or loss' under IAS 1.

(b) Ravar is disposing of a controlling interest in Krow whilst retaining an interest; which may, subsequent to the sale, be accounted for either as an associated company or a trade investment (this depends on whether Ravar retains significant influence or not). From the point control is lost, Krow should cease to be accounted for as a subsidiary (ie on a line-by-line basis). However, up to that point, the accounting for Krow will depend upon whether it can be judged that the assets are 'held for sale'.

Under IFRS 5, Ravar would classify Krow as being a disposal group held for sale if its carrying amount will be recovered principally through sale in a single transaction rather than through use. IFRS 5 lays down the following conditions:

(1) The asset is available for immediate sale in its present condition and sale is highly probable.

(2) The asset is currently actively marketed at a price that is reasonable in relation to its fair value.

(3) The sale is expected to be completed within a year of the date of classification.

(4) It is unlikely that the plan to sell the asset will be significantly amended or withdrawn and actions have been substantially taken to complete the sale.

(5) Management is committed to the sale plan.

Not all the conditions laid down in IFRS 5 appear to have yet been met; ie in particular, condition 4 (in that actions have not yet been taken substantially) and condition 5 (in that the offer has only been accepted in principle).

On balance, it could be concluded therefore that until conditions 4 and 5 are satisfied or the sale actually takes place (whichever comes first) there should be no change to the accounting for Krow and it should be fully consolidated on a line-by-line basis.

Question 9

Part (a) concerns a reverse acquisition whereby a listed company acquires shares in a private company in such a way that the private company becomes the acquirer under IFRS 3 *Business Combinations*. It also requires a discussion of the (arguable) demise of proportionate consolidation. It is drawn from syllabus sections 13.1 and 13.3 and requires application of knowledge from the BPP Learning & Practice Workbook Chapter 6 *Revision of basic groups*.

(a) *Share options*

PRACTICE ANSWER BANK

In accordance with IFRS 2 *Share Based Payments* this is an equity settled transaction.

The share options should be recognised at fair value at the date of grant of $6, over the vesting period of three years.

Fusaro should recognise the share based payment expense based on the best available estimate of the number of share options that are expected to vest. The initial leavers estimate of 25% is not relevant, and the calculations for the year ended 31 March 2018 should be based on the revised 20% estimate determined at the year end.

The share based payment expense/equity reserve for the year ended 31 March 2018 is calculated as follows:

	$	
2018: 1,000 options × (100 × 80%) × $6 × 1/3	160,000	[1]

Since the tax relief on the share based payment is not deductible until the share options are exercised, this creates a deferred tax asset as at 31 March 2018.

Tax relief is based on the intrinsic value of the share options (which represents the difference between the market value of the share at exercise less the exercise price). Since the share options vest over time the tax base of the share based payment at 31 March 2018 is calculated as follows:

	$	
2018: 1,000 options × (100 × 80%) × $9 × 1/3	240,000	[1]

This generates a deferred tax asset of $48,000 ($240,000 x 20%) at 31 March 2018. [1]

The deferred tax is credited to the profit or loss account unless the expected tax deduction exceeds the cumulative share based payment expense recognised to date. Here the deferred tax credit on the excess tax deduction is recognised directly in equity. [1]

[4 marks for calculations]
[3 marks for discussion ½ mark per relevant point made]
(max 7 marks)

At 31 March 2018, the expected tax deduction exceeds the share based payment expense by $140,000 ($300,000 - $160,000). Therefore, a tax credit of $16,000 ($80,000 x 20%) should be recognised in profit or loss and a tax credit of $28,000 ($140,000 x 20%) recognised in equity.

(b) *Retirement benefit scheme*

This is a defined contribution scheme since Fusaro's only obligation is to make a fixed contribution into the scheme each year. The pension risk (risk of variable returns) lies with the employee, since the pensions are not guaranteed and are based on the future performance of the pension fund.

Fusaro should account for the contributions made to the pension fund on an accruals basis. Therefore, an expense of $350,000 ($5m x 7%) should be recognised in profit or loss in the year ended 31 March 2018. Since Fusaro has only paid $200,000 into the fund by the year-end, it should accrue for the unpaid contributions of $150,000 in the statement of financial position. [1]

As tax relief for pension contributions is obtained on a cash basis, the corresponding tax base relating to the pension accrual is nil. A deductible temporary difference of $150,000 arises at the year end, which represents a deferred tax asset of $30,000. [1] Since the pension contributions are expensed to profit or loss, the deferred tax credit will also be recognised in profit or loss.

[2 marks for calculations]

Part (c) requires discussion of issues surrounding an entity's publication of KPIs, including an examination of whether financial statements are the only information that the users require.

(c) The *Conceptual Framework* states that the primary users of financial statements are existing and potential lenders, lenders and other creditors who make decisions about providing economic resources to the entity. General purpose financial information should provide useful information (that which is relevant and faithfully represents the underlying reality) to those primary users. This is consistent with the opinion of the finance director that the financial statements, as prepared under IFRS Standards, provide the users with all the information that they need. There is however an increasing trend towards reporting so called 'non-GAAP' alternative performance measures which are presented either alongside the financial statements or in separate press reports. The reporting of an eps figure based upon EBITDA is an alternative performance measure as EBITDA is not a term defined in the IFRS Standards. Reporting EBITDA, and eps based on EBITDA has its roots in 'impression management'. This is the practice whereby entities attempt to control the impressions of corporate performance made by financial statement users by, for instance, reporting a non-GAAP EDITDA eps figure which shows the entity in a better light than that shown by the GAAP-based eps figure (as required by IAS 33 *Earnings Per Share*). It could be that management are acting altruistically and are keen to provide users with more accurate and/or more useful information. This is a virtuous act and can be seen to be ethically acceptable. However, their motivation may be to deliberately make the entity look more profitable because, for instance, their remuneration may be linked to eps growth. If so, the practice cannot be ethically acceptable.

There is no barrier to reporting non-GAAP information and IAS 33 would allow Fusaro to present an eps figure based on EBITDA. However, there are certain rules which must be adhered to:

1. The weighted average number of shares used in the denominator must be the same as that required by IAS 33.

2. A reconciliation must be provided between the numerator (ie earnings) used in the EBITDA eps calculation and the line item (ie the profit figure appearing in the group income statement) used in the IAS 33 eps calculation.

The EBITDA figure must be shown in the notes and not in the statement of profit or loss..

Question 10

This question concerns the IASB's stand-alone standard *IFRS for SMEs* and involves the application of knowledge concerning (a) the differences between accounting practices using full IFRS and those using the SAS and (b) the applicability and usefulness of the SAS in a corporate reporting context.

(a) (i) As Denz is a PLC it must use full IFRS in its financial statements. In this respect, goodwill in Zin would be calculated as follows:

	$m
FV of consideration transferred for 75% investment	3.34
Contingent consideration	3.37
This is estimated using present values ($3.54m/1.05)	
FV of NCI	0.75
Denz uses the full goodwill method. As FV is not given, it must be estimated (using a proportion of net assets approach) $3m × 25%	
	7.46
FV of identifiable net assets	3.00
Goodwill	4.46

If Denz believes that the information concerning Zin's sales targets is reliable and, as a result, contingent consideration will not have to be paid a case could be made for an adjustment to the goodwill on acquisition by excluding the consideration. Following this approach, which is equally acceptable, the goodwill figure as at 31 October 2014 would be $1.09m.

(ii) Had Denz not been a PLC upon the acquisition of Zin then it would not have had public accountability. Also, the entity's business model does not involve the holding of assets in a fiduciary capacity for a broad group of outsiders. This, together with the absence of public accountability, means that Denz would have had the option of adopting the IFRS for SMEs in its financial statements. This would have the following impacts:

- Contingent consideration is only included where it is probable and can be reliably measured: this is not the case here.

- Acquisition costs form part of the cost of acquisition and so increase goodwill.

- NCI is not included in the calculation of goodwill: goodwill is the difference between the cost of the combination and Denz's share of the FV of Zin's identifiable net assets.
- Goodwill is amortised over its useful life, or if this cannot be estimated, 10 years.

Goodwill would have been calculated as follows:

FV of consideration transferred for 75% investment	3.34
Acquisition costs (not allowed under full IFRS)	0.83
	4.17
Denz's share of Zin's identifiable net assets ($3m × 75%)	2.25
	1.92
Goodwill amortisation (1/6)	0.32
Goodwill	1.60

(b) (i) Denz has a turnover of $50m and employs 50 people. It would therefore probably satisfy local criteria as to the size of an SME; although the IFRS for SMEs does not identify SMEs on the basis of size but on the basis of whether they are publicly accountable or not. The main benefit to Denz would therefore be to reduce the cost burden of reporting, which is often much heavier for smaller entities. The cost burden of adopting full IFRS may not be justifiable on the grounds of providing useful information to the users of Denz's financial statements. Much of the present financial reporting framework is based upon the needs of larger entities so full-IFRS based statutory financial statements would be less relevant to the users of Denz's financial statements.

A narrower range of decisions will be made by users based on Denz's financial statements. For instance, as an SME and with a business model which is mainly based on one income stream, Denz is likely to have fewer complex transactions and therefore will have a reduced need for complex analysis by users. The full IFRS disclosure requirements would be inappropriate and for this reason the IFRS for SMEs has much fewer disclosure requirements. Full-IFRS disclosures are more relevant to investment decisions in capital markets and are therefore mainly irrelevant to an unlisted SME. This will result in significant cost savings for Denz.

The IFRS for SMEs is based on the principles contained in the full IFRS programme. Therefore it will be quite straight forward for Denz to adopt new practices if it ever decided to gain a new listing in future.

(ii) The IFRS for SMEs requires that Denz uses fair value to measure investment properties. Fair value generally refers to the property's market value. Market value would be the best possible price reasonably obtainable by the seller. Therefore with the land and buildings cost could not be used. The best possible price is $9m. This should be used to value the land and a value of zero given to the buildings. Gains and losses on adoption would be recognised in profit or loss.

Question 11

The question deals with the issues associated with segmental reporting and the implications of protecting commercial sensitivity.

(a)

> **Tutorial note:** There can be valid commercial considerations associated with protecting business information, but those must be balanced against the need to inform shareholders. The first part of this question requires the expression of an opinion, which must be supported.
>
> A further opinion is required in (b) (ii).
>
> There is no need to agree with the direction taken in the Model Answer, provided the arguments that are offered are properly supported.

(i) Quoted companies must keep their shareholders informed, even if it is costly to do so because of commercial sensitivity. There would be no point in having accounting standards if their requirements can be set aside on the basis that the directors would prefer not to make those disclosures.

The history of segmental reporting has been about change and development in the regulations in order to force companies to publish useful segmental reports. Segmental reports have generally been less helpful than they could have been because directors often aim to meet the minimum reporting requirements set out in terms of the letter of the rules.

(ii) The fact that each of the four elements listed in the analysis being studied by management is an operating division suggests that each has its own separate risk characteristics. A divisional structure implies autonomy and an element of each division having its own risk characteristics.

The analysis being studied by management suggests that each of the four elements is studied separately. IFRS 8 *Operating Segments* states that the fact management tracks the performance of each segment means that all must be disclosed in the segmental information.

The fact that seafood is relatively small may have been sufficient justification to merge it with fresh food, but seafood exceeds the 10% threshold in terms of net assets, which would make it a reportable segment.

The remaining segments all look substantial and it may be necessary for Wilton to break the totals down even further if there are reportable segments within, say, frozen vegetables.

(b) (i)

	$m
Present value of plan obligation at 1 May 2016	650.0
Interest cost	50.7
Current service cost	124.0
Benefits paid	(128.0)
Actuarial (gain)/loss on obligation (balancing figure)	33.3
Present value of plan obligation at 30 April 2017	730.0

	$m
Fair value of assets at 1 May 2016	635.0
Expected return on plan assets	73.0
Contributions received	70.0
Benefits paid	(128.0)
Actuarial gain/(loss) on obligation (balancing figure)	(5.0)
Fair value of assets at 30 April 2017	645.0

(ii) The *Conceptual Framework* requires that information is included in the financial statements if it is useful to the primary users of the financial statements in making decisions about providing resources to an entity. Information is useful if it is relevant and faithfully represents the underlying reality. There is no concession in the Conceptual Framework as regards the certainty of measurement. It does, however, require that prudence, which is related to faithful representation, is exercised when making judgements under conditions of uncertainty. When figures are highly subjective, it could be argued that there is too much doubt as to their accuracy for reporting purposes. The company needs to predict a host of factors into the long-term future, including the longevity of staff, salary levels at the date of retirement and returns on investments, which will almost certainly span a range and will include art and property, which may not have readily observable market prices.

Conversely, there is an actuarial profession that exists to advise members on the management of pension schemes. Those experts are, necessarily, required to make the assumptions described above in order to maintain the solvency of pension schemes. While those predictions will always have a margin for error, they are regarded as sufficiently

Question 12

(a) Parts (a) and (b) concern the accounting for a disposal group and an asset under IFRS 5 *Non-current Assets Held for Sale and Discontinued Operations*.

TNs:

Immediately before classification as held for sale, the carrying amount of the net assets of a disposal group (DG) must be accounted for using the normal group policies for the individual assets and liabilities of the disposal group.

Upon classification as a DG any impairment loss must be allocated, first to any goodwill in the DG and then to other non-current assets (but only those included in the measurement rules of IFRS 5 – which excludes inventory as it's a CA and not an NCA and, specifically, Investments in equity instruments as they re accounted for under IFRS 9). Allocation is on a pro rata basis.

	As at 1 May 2014 $m	CA upon class^n as held for sale 31 Oct 2014 $m	Alloc^n of imp loss $m	CA in group accounts after class^n as held for sale $m
Goodwill	2.55	2.55^1	(2.55)	–
PPE revalued	7.82	7.00^2	(1.41)^7	5.59
PPE cost	9.69	8.69^3	(1.76)^8	6.93
Inventory	4.08	4.08^4	–	4.08
Inv in equity instruments	3.06	2.60^5	–	2.60
Liabilities assoc with above	(4.20)	(4.20)^4		(4.20)
Other liabilities	(8.00)	–^{6}		
		20.72		
FV of DG		15.00		
Impairment loss		5.72	5.72	15.00

No depreciation will be charged on PPE from the date classified as held for sale.

^{1} No impairment to goodwill

^{2} Revalued PPE must be stated at its revalued CA and the impairment loss will be included in profit or loss.

^{3} Normal depreciation will be charged for the period up to classification as held for sale.

^{4} No change per question

^{5} Investment in equity instrument must be stated at FV with the loss shown in other comprehensive income.

^{6} These liabilities are not to be assumed by the purchaser of the DG and are to be settled from the proceeds from disposal and so are not part of the DG's net assets.

^{7} $7 \div 15.69 \, (7 + 8.69) \times 5.72$

^{8} $8.69 \div 15.69 \times 5.72$

(b) Temporary accommodation

If the time taken to vacate the building and move into temporary accommodation is usual and customary for such assets then at the date the entity becomes committed to the plan, it qualifies as being available for immediate sale. IFRS 5 also requires that the sale is highly probable. If vacation would not be complete within one year of the commitment date then the building would not be available for immediate sale unless there are events beyond Quest's control which would extend the date thus.

Wait until construction of a new building is complete

Quest would wait until the new building is complete before vacating its current HQ and transferring it to the buyer. This would demonstrate that the HQ is not available for immediate sale and would not become so until construction of the new building was complete. This would apply even if a firm commitment to transfer the current building to a future buyer has been made.

(c) Part (c) concerns the difficulties of international financial analysis. It is drawn from syllabus sections 13.2 and requires application of knowledge from the FAR 2 Learning & Practice Workbook Chapter 23 *Ratio and trend analysis.*

Changes to GAAP

If the IASB has issued new standards or interpretations or the country in which Tinu is domiciled requires new measures by statute (ie changes to GAAP), there is usually flexibility (albeit restricted) concerning the period over which Tinu may adopt the new pronouncements. Tinu's directors may make a decision concerning whether to adopt the new GAAP based upon its effect on financial performance. The directors may then have difficulty in assessing Tinu's real performance. There may also be an issue concerning the comparability of Tinu's performance with other entities.

Choice of practices concerning presentation

The IASB requires a minimum layout in financial statements, mainly under IAS 1 *Presentation of Financial Statements.* This means in practice that Tinu's directors could produce financial statements following any format or layout it wishes so long as it complies with the 'minimum' requirement. This extends to the titles of financial statements which can be anything the entity wishes so long as the meaning is clear and reflects the purpose of the statement. The 'minimum' requirement also often allows entities to choose between different formats; eg the statement of other comprehensive income can be a separate statement or can be linked to the profit or loss statement; also, detail can often be shown on the face of a statement or in the notes to the accounts. When entities are allowed this freedom they will often choose a presentation policy which serves the purpose of best impressing investors. Quest would need to be wary of this when analysing Tinu's performance. It may be the case that Quest may have to recreate Tinu's accounts into a more recognisable form. Tinu may follow IFRS but this does not mean that differences in GAAP and presentation practice have been eliminated.

Question 13

This question involves (a) the translation of a subsidiary's hyperinflationary functional currency to a non-hyperinflationary presentation currency, (b) the potential to exclude subsidiaries from consolidation and (c) the use of fair value reporting.

(a) Tutorial note: IAS 21 *The Effects of Changes in Foreign Exchange* Rates allows an entity to present its financial statements in any currency. If the functional currency (FC) differs to the presentation currency (PC) a translation is required. A group may contain many individual entities with different FCs so each set of financial statements must be expressed in the common PC so that a common set of group accounts may be prepared. When a hyperinflationary FC is translated into a non-hyperinflationary PC, the basic procedure is (IAS 21.42):

(i) the entity should restate its financial statements in accordance with IAS 29 *Financial Reporting in Hyperinflationary Economics.*

(ii) all amounts are translated at the closing rate, except that

(iii) comparative amounts are those that were presented as current year amounts in the relevant prior year financial statements (ie not adjusted for subsequent changes in price levels or exchange rates).

PRACTICE ANSWER BANK

As there is no mention to the contrary in the question we can ignore step (i).

DIA
STATEMENT OF INCOME FOR THE YEAR ENDED 31 OCTOBER 2014

		$m
Sales	52.50/4	13.13
Cost of sales	49.79/4	(12.45)
Depreciation	0.75/4	(0.19)
Finance charge	0.53/4	(0.13)
Profit before tax		0.36
Income tax	0.69/4	(0.17)
Profit after tax		0.19

DIA
STATEMENT OF FINANCIAL POSITION AS AT 31 OCTOBER 2014

		2014 $m		2013 $m
Property, plant and equipment	8.25/4	2.06	9.00/3	3.00
Inventories	4.50/4	1.13	4.07/3	1.36
Trade receivables	6.00/4	1.50	7.20/3	2.40
Cash and cash equivalents	0.90/4	0.22	0.30/3	0.10
Total assets		4.91		6.86
Trade payables	5.76/4	1.44	6.80/3	2.27
Taxation	0.69/4	0.17	1.31/3	0.44
Non-current liabilities	5.40/4	1.35	5.40/3	1.80
Total liabilities		2.96		4.51
Share capital	1.50/4	0.38	1.50/3	0.50
Retained earnings	W1	1.57	5.56/3	1.85
Total equity		1.95		2.35

W1: 2014 retained earnings

Balance brought forward from 2013		1.85	
Profit after tax for the year		0.19	
Exchange difference (loss):			
Op ret earnings at op rate (5.56/3)	1.85		
Op ret earnings at cl rate (5.56/4)	1.39	(0.46)	
		1.58	(rounding)

(b) IFRS 10 *Consolidated Financial Statements* provides guidance on the procedures to be applied when preparing the combined financial statements of a parent and its subsidiaries.

The rules on exclusion are strict as this is a common method used by entities to manipulate their group financial statements. Dia is quite highly geared (ie non-current liabilities are approx. 27.5% of total assets) and if Paxdal could exclude the subsidiary from its group statements, group gearing would be improved. This is one way of removing liabilities from the balance sheet and is therefore not allowed by IFRS. It is also highly unethical.

Some commentators would agree with Paxdal's directors and would argue that Dia should be excluded on the grounds of dissimilar activities; ie inclusion would result in misleading results. IFRS 10 firmly rejects this argument. The IASB argues that exclusion is not justified on the basis that more relevant results can be provided about subsidiaries by firstly including them in the group statements and then providing additional information about 'dissimilar' activities under IFRS 8 *Operating Segments*.

Hence IFRS 10 requires that consolidated financial statements are prepared to include ALL subsidiaries, both foreign and domestic, other than:

- Those held for sale under IFRS 5

- Those which cannot be controlled due to long-term restrictions imposed eg by the country's government.

As none of the above applies to Paxdal's case, Dia must be included in the consolidation exercise.

(c) IFRS Standards use a mixed measurement approach, which means that different measurement bases are used for different classes of elements. This is opposed to a single measurement basis in which all items are measured using the same basis, eg all items are measured at fair value. The IASB believes that a mixed measurement approach provides the most useful information to primary users of financial statements. The *Conceptual Framework* includes historical cost and current value as its two measurement bases. Fair value is one way of measuring current value. Fair value (FV) reporting (as advocated by IFRS 13 *Fair Value Measurement*) has distinct benefits which would help to overcome these disadvantages. They can be summarised as follows:

Paxdal operates through a chain of High Street shops. If these shops are owned by Paxdal, the use of the cost model under IAS 16 *Property, Plant and Equipment* could seriously understate their value. Such an understatement could produce misleading information to users who may be trying to assess the entity's current and 'real' gearing and earning power potential. The depression of asset value could make Paxdal vulnerable to a takeover. Also, as retail fashions change, the equipment in the shops may become quickly out-of-date and may need replacing at shorter intervals.

The use of FVs has the potential to protect the entity from a takeover and to flag up the need to make provisions for replacement in earlier years.

The same thinking could also apply to Dia's manufacturing and distribution equipment. The mobile smartphone technology field changes rapidly and it is very possible that manufacturing and distribution equipment and networks may have to be updated at frequent intervals.

The technology industry has particular problems when it comes to valuing closing inventory. Technology changes rapidly and any new designs or products coming to the market tend to be marketed at high prices which eventually reduce as the technology becomes more available to buyers. So a company using the standard approach of FIFO may have closing inventory at lower prices than those included in cost of sales. This has the potential to overstate cost of sales and thereby lead to relatively lower profits. This may be the case with Paxdal as it is a highly successful retailer so it is assumed the entity is rarely left with large amounts of old higher priced stock.

Under IFRS entities are now permitted to revalue non-current assets such as property, plant and equipment and to use fair values for items such as investment property and financial instruments. Such developments, and the use of FVs in acquisition accounting to measure goodwill, are becoming more accepted by investors and users who argue that HCA is out-of-date and not relevant to their decision making. It is argued that FV information, based on active market prices, is the best available measure of the future economic benefits (eg cash flows) which an asset can be expected to generate.

Question 14

This is a multi-part question and concerns the accounting for non-current assets.

Part (a) involves the identification of control when dealing with investments where less than a majority of the investee's voting shares are held by the investor.

Part (b) requires a discussion concerning the recognition of intangible assets upon an acquisition.

Part (c) requires calculation and discussion of the amount to be capitalised for R&D expenditure.

(a) Despite holding less than 50% of the voting rights, Mendez might have power to control the investees if its rights are sufficient to give it power when it has the practical ability to direct the investee's activities unilaterally. This is known as *de facto* control (IFRS 10. para B41). Mendez must consider all the facts and circumstances, including:

- The size of its holding relevant to the size and dispersion of other holdings;
- The likely impact of any potential voting rights held by Mendez;
- Any rights arising from other contractual arrangements; and

- Any additional facts and circumstances concerning the directing by Mendez of an investee's activities; such as Mendez's voting patterns at AGMs.

Having considered the above, if it is still not clear that Mendez has power, then Mendez would not control the investee (IFRS 10. para B46)

(i) Mendez would have power to control Gon due to its dominant voting interest. This is based on the fact that it has a 46% interest whereas no other shareholder holds more than 1.3% of the voting shares. The other shareholders are widely dispersed. A large number of them would have to act in unison to outvote Mendez and there is no history of this. Therefore Mendez has de facto control and Gon would be consolidated as a subsidiary.

(ii) Mendez would **not** have power over Ena. The two remaining shareholders with large holdings of 26% each could easily combine to outvote Mendez – as they did when voting against Mendez's proposed change of policy. The size of Mendez's holding and its size relative to other shareholders would not give it power.

(b) Both the research staff and the customer contract are intangible in nature (ie 'an identifiable non-monetary without physical substance') and would be accounted for under IAS 38. IAS 38 defines an asset as 'a resource controlled by an entity from which future economic benefits are expected to flow to the entity' (IAS 38.8).

(i) Orca's research staff would obviously be thought as 'assets' by Mendez as they were a significant factor in the entity's decision to buy the company. However, they could not be recognised as assets in Mendez's group financial statements because they would not meet IAS 38's recognition criteria; namely, in the absence of any other legal rights it would not be possible to show that Mendez could control the economic benefits embodied in the staff; as they could easily leave employment and work elsewhere for another company.

(ii) An intangible asset needs to be identifiable so that it can be distinguished from goodwill. The two elements of identifiability are separability or the existence of contractual or other legal rights. The supply agreement between Orca and Jorz is not separable but it does meet the contractual/legal right criterion for identification as an intangible asset.

It is unlikely that an active market exists for this type of intangible asset. In its absence, the fair value would be measured on a basis that reflects the amounts Mendez would have paid in an arm's length transaction between knowledgeable willing parties (IAS 38.40).

(c) IAS 38 requires that research costs are written off. Development costs are capitalised if, and only if, Mendez can demonstrate all of the following IAS 38.57):

- Technical feasibility of completing the project;
- Its intention to complete the project and its ability to use or sell it;
- How the project will generate future economic benefits;
- The availability of adequate technical, financial and other resources to complete the project; and
- Its ability to reliably measure the project's attributable costs.

The following table applies the above principles to the scenario.

Project		1	2 *	3 **	4 ***
		$'000	$'000	$'000	$'000
Salaries and wages		156	–	–	–
Indirect overheads	Specifically disallowed by IAS 38	–	–	–	–
Direct overheads		29	–	–	–
Staff training costs	Specifically disallowed by IAS 38	–	–	–	–
Patent		–	–	–	–
Market analysis	Effectively disallowed by IAS 38 as it refers to gaining knowledge and is therefore a research cost.	–	–	–	–

Carrying amount at 1 November 2013	–	–	–	728
Carrying amount at 31 October 2014	185	–	–	728

Notes

Project 1: Qualifies as development expenditure and must be capitalised. However, staff training and market analysis must be expensed.

Project 2: Costs incurred in ensuring the database is up-to-date and retains functional capacity would be deemed to be part of a routine process. As it does not involve innovations to the database or new technology, the costs do not meet the definition of 'research' or 'developments' and must be written off as an expense.

Project 3: Although the project was previously capitalised, the IAS 38 criteria for recognition (see above) now no longer apply as Mendez does not appear to have the technical resources to complete the project. The ability to generate future economic benefits must also be called into question. The costs should therefore be written off.

Project 4: Costs incurred after commercial production begins must be written off as they would not pass the recognition criteria to be capitalised. As the asset has an indefinite life it is not amortised but tested for impairment. As recoverable amount ($1.5m) is greater than carrying amount ($0.728m) there is no impairment and it will be carried in the SoFP at $0.728m.

Question 15

The question deals with the issues associated with accounting for impairment of cash generating units, and the wider issue of the roles and responsibilities of the accountant.

(a)

> **Tutorial note:** Questions about impairment often hinge on the identification of cash generating units.

The first question is whether we should be considering the rolling mill in isolation. Arguably, we could argue that the rolling mill is part of the steelmaking site. The site, overall, is not impaired because it has a recoverable amount of $420m, considerably higher than the carrying amount of $280m.

The rolling mill is a cash generating unit. We know that because the output from the mill could be sold separately. It makes little difference that the bulk of the output is actually sold to another division of Millennium.

The rolling mill is impaired because the recoverable amount is $80m, which is less than the carrying amount of $120m.

(b) The impairment loss is $120m – 80m = $40m. This is divided as follows:

	Carrying amount $m	Proportion	Allocation of impairment loss $m	Adjusted carrying amount $m
Land	25	0	(5)	30
Buildings	50	53%	24	26
Rolling plant	45	47%	21	24
	120	100%	40	80

(c) **Deferred tax asset**

The *Conceptual Framework* defines an asset as a right that has the potential to produce economic benefits, so from a *Conceptual Framework* perspective, it is understandable that the directors believe that a deferred tax asset can be recognised as the losses do have the potential to result in a tax reduction in the future. The *Conceptual Framework* does not however override any IFRS Standards and the directors must therefore look to IAS 12 Income Taxes. According to IAS 12, an entity should recognise a deferred tax asset in respect of the carry-forward of unused tax losses to the extent that it is probable that future taxable profit will be available against which the losses can be utilised. IAS 12 therefore, has higher criteria than the Conceptual Framework as it requires that there is a probable benefit rather than just the right to produce benefits. IAS 12 stresses that the existence of unused losses is strong evidence that future taxable profit may not be available. For this reason, convincing evidence is required about the existence of future taxable profits. Millenium has now made losses in three consecutive financial years, and therefore significant doubt exists about the likelihood of future profits being generated. It would therefore seem that Millenium is incorrect to recognise a deferred tax asset in respect of its unused tax losses.

Covenant breach

Millenium is currently presenting the loan as a non-current liability. IAS 1 *Presentation of Financial Statements* states that a liability should be presented as current if the entity:

- Settles it as part of its operating cycle;
- Is due to settle the liability within 12 months of the reporting date; or
- Does not have an unconditional right to defer settlement for at least 12 months after the reporting date.

At the reporting date, Millenium has a current liability as did not have an unconditional right to defer settlement of the loan for at least 12 months - it believes this may be possible, but it does not have the unconditional right. In the statement of financial position, the loan should be reclassified as a current liability. This is consistent with the fundamental qualitative characteristic of faithful representation per the *Conceptual Framework* as the correct presentation of the bank loan is a current liability is needed if the financial statements are to represent the terms of the loan covenant.

Question 16

This question concerns the assessment of an entity's financial performance; in particular: the recent and growing use of 'underlying profit' presentations and the related earnings per share figures as key performance indicators in the statement of profit or loss: and the ethical issues that arise.

(a) (i) Under IFRS 15 the awarding of points to customers is a performance obligation. Expan should allocate the transaction price of $40m to the product and the points on a relative stand-alone basis. The stand-alone selling price of the goods is $40m, as the price is the same regardless of whether the customer accepts the points. The stand-alone price of the points is $3.2m ((20% + (80% × 75%)) × $4m).

The consideration of $40m should be allocated as follows:

	$'000	
Product	37,037	$40m × $40m/$43.2m
Points	2,963	$40m × $3.2m/$43.2m
	40,000	

Since 20% of the points had been redeemed by 31 October 2012, revenue of $592,600 (20% × $2,963k) should be recognised for the points and $37,037,000 for the products. The contract liability will be $2,370,400 ($2,963,000 – $592,600).

(ii) **This part concerns impairment of a financial asset and involves consideration of: IFRS 9 *Financial Instruments*.**

The liquidation of Nap gives objective evidence of impairment and means that a loss allowance must be recognised based on stage 3 of the expected credit loss model under IFRS 9 *Financial Instruments*. The original 12-month ECL must be unwound and the increase required as a result of the move to stage 3 must be accounted for as follows:

	Dr	Cr
	$m	$m

Finance costs in profit or loss ($0.02 + $1.6)	1.62	
Loss allowance		1.62

(b) Weighted average number of shares in issue = 56m as follows:

2012: Basic $18m/32.14p

or

2012: Underlying basic $18m − ($3m + $1m + $1m)/23.21p

Recalculation of eps for year ended 31 Oct 2012:	Basic	Underlying
	$m	$m
Draft profit attributable to ordinary shareholders	18.00	13.00
See (a) (i) above	(2.37)	(2.37)
See (a) (ii) above	(1.62)	(1.62)
Adjusted profit figures	14.01	9.01
Weighted average number of shares (see above)	56m	56m
New eps figures	25.02	16.09

(c) **This part requires a discussion of current developments, in particular whether the *Conceptual Framework*'s objective of useful information is violated by the inclusion of information not subject to current IFRS.**

The *Conceptual Framework* states quite categorically that the objective of financial information is the provision of information which is useful to investors, lenders and other creditors, who are considered the primary users of published financial statements. Although 'underlying' profit and 'underlying' earnings per share is not defined by IFRS and therefore may not be directly comparable with the similarly adjusted figures of other companies, there is a growing belief in business that without such adjustments an entity's true potential and sustainable earnings figures can be hidden from view.

This is partly due to current value accounting (such as the use of fair values), which, due to the recent economic crisis, has forced entities to take significant write-downs in asset values. The impact of these write-downs on statutory profit has led to many entities reporting what they believe are 'sustainable' performance figures.

Of course, there is the possibility that underlying profit as a key indicator of corporate performance may mislead investors. Expan's original draft accounts show earnings per share and profit before tax figures little changed from 2011. As shown above this is due to errors in accounting which, when amended, show significant decreases in both indicators. There is no indication that a desire to present similar indicators to 2011 is what drove Expan to use the incorrect accounting treatments in 2012 but it does highlight the risk of allowing entities the freedom, unrestrained by IFRS, to present information in this way.

An additional problem is that if underlying figures become a prime focus of analysts, shareholders and management, the lack of guidance gives rise to a potential for a lack of consistency in reporting. The lack of an agreed definition gives rise to problems for auditors who will become concerned about inconsistent profit adjustments leading to differences in the amount of disclosure and the impact on the Framework's requirement for comparability across entities.

However, it is incumbent upon directors to act in an ethical manner when producing financial statements. Underlying profit is an important development in the key indicators used to report corporate performance as it provides potentially useful information on the 'normalised' profit of the entity. However, it should not receive greater priority than any other KPI which comments on results and like any other emerging approach to reporting performance, it is critically important that it is transparent and consistently applied year-to-year across both the entity and industry sector.

PRACTICE ANSWER BANK

Question 17

(a) **This part of the question concerns the accounting for deferred taxation in the context of consolidated accounts. It requires a consideration of:**

IAS 12 *Income Taxes*

(i) As Otion has 25% of the inventory still unsold at the year end there will be a provision for unrealised profit of $1.5m ($20m × 30% × 25%) in the group financial statements. However, the fact that Pera has already suffered income tax on the profit gives rise to a timing difference for deferred tax purposes. In the following year when the remaining inventory is sold the provision for unrealised profit will be released but will not be taxed. This gives rise to a deferred tax asset of $0.45m ($1.5m × 30%).

The deferred tax asset is recognised to the extent that it is recoverable. That is, it is more likely than not that sufficient tax profits will arise from which the reversal of the timing difference can be deducted. In this case Otion fully expects the inventory to be sold in the following year and so the asset would be recognised and carried forward on that basis.

(ii) Kram's unrelieved tax loss gives rise to a timing difference because although the loss is recognised in the group financial statements, it can not yet be recognised for tax purposes as it can only be relieved by carrying it forward to be offset against Kram's future profits. Kram expects profits to grow over the forthcoming year so it will generate sufficient profits for the purpose of offsetting this tax loss. A deferred tax asset in the group financial statements will therefore be recognised at $2.5m ($10m × 25%).

As with Otion, the deferred tax asset is recognised to the extent that it is recoverable.

(iii) As the group deferred tax position is viewed from the perspective of the group as a whole, the fair value adjustment made for the purpose of consolidating the financial statements of Ember will affect the deferred tax charge for the year. Ember has not recognised a deferred tax asset as part of its calculation of identifiable net assets. So a provision should be made for the difference between the fair value of identifiable net assets acquired and their carrying amount; that is $0.6m [($16m − $14m) × 30%].

(b) **This part of the question involves a consideration of whether related party transactions exist for the purpose of reporting the results of the Pera group. It involves:**

IAS 24 *Related Party Disclosures*

Santi is a subsidiary of Pera. Whether a related party situation exists with Compu depends upon the nature of the dealings between the entities. A holding of less than 20% of an entity is assumed not to result in significant influence unless it can be shown otherwise. Pera can participate in Compu's operating and financing policies. Therefore Compu will be deemed to be an associate of Pera.

Under IAS 24 Compu and Santi are related parties as Pera has control over Santi and exerts significant influence over Compu.

Tutorial note: control has to exist in Santi and/or Compu for them to be related. If Pera had simply exerted significant influence over both then they would not have been related.

A related party transaction is defined as a 'transfer of resources, services or obligations between related parties, regardless of whether a price is charged' (IAS 24.9). The IFRS therefore applies to gifts of assets. Although the mining technology is to be provided free of charge the fair market value of the transaction will therefore have to be disclosed.

An issue arises because the commitment to use the technology will not become firm until December 2012 after the year end. However, IAS 24.21 specifically includes 'commitments to do something if a particular event occurs' as an example of a qualifying related party transaction. This is a new requirement introduced by IAS 24.

Upon adopting IAS 24 Pera would be required to disclose comparative commitments at the end of the previous reporting period. Also, although IAS 24 does not refer specifically to materiality (as it is covered by IAS 1), the general concept of materiality would have to be applied. The commitment is likely to be material as it refers to 'highly specialised mining technology'. The presence of such a commitment is likely to be of significant interest to investors.

Pera's (and the individual entities') financial statements would be more difficult to understand if related party transactions were to be excluded. In extreme cases, transactions such as the transfer of technology free of charge may be part of a deliberate strategy aimed at manipulating the profitability of entities. If this was to be so then the financial statements would not be showing a true and fair view in that they would not be free from bias and would not therefore be providing useful information to the user.

(c) **This part of the question concerns planning for the introduction of interim financial reporting.**

IAS 34 is not a mandatory standard in that it only provides guidelines for those entities wishing to introduce interim financial reporting. There are sections dealing with minimum components, scope, form and content and explanatory notes. A large part however deals with recognition and measurement principles and provides guideline as to their practical application.

The main principle in IAS 34 is that an entity should adopt the same recognition and measurement principles as it does in its annual financial statements. So, for example, the interim report should not contain provisions for items for which there is no present obligation – just as it would in its annual financial statements. This may of course result in the need to re-measure items in the following interim reports or at the year end. The nature and amount of any significant re-measurements should be reported.

The $5 million cost of the distribution facility overhaul in August 2013 must not therefore be anticipated in the 30 April 2013 interim financial report unless there exists a legal or constructive obligation (IAS 37) at that date. This is unlikely as contracts have not yet been issued and won't be until May 2013; at which time the workforce will be informed.

Similarly, the interim report should not contain an accrual for the year end bonus. Payments are dependent on profits which are seasonal and cannot be measured reliably. Also, there is no constructive obligation to pay bonuses as they are dependent on profits.

IAS 38 requires that costs incurred to generate non-monetary intangible assets, development costs, are expensed unless they form part of an identifiable intangible asset. Under IAS 38 the $2m to be incurred on 1 November 2012 would therefore be classed as a research cost and must be expensed as an identifiable asset is not yet in existence. Once expensed, those costs cannot be subsequently capitalised once development of the system takes place and must therefore remain as expensed items. IAS 34 requires similar treatment in interim financial reports. It would therefore be inappropriate in the interim financial report to 'defer' the initial research costs in the expectation that it will eventually form part of an identifiable intangible asset.

Question 18

(a) **This part of the question specifically concerns the regulation of corporate financial reporting and the implications of changing to IFRS for corporate accounting systems and financial statements.**

Any entity adopting IFRS for its financial reporting faces significant changes as domestic GAAP and IFRS GAAP often differ substantially. This criticism has been levelled against IFRS generally as IFRS tends to introduce far more recognition, measurement and disclosure requirements than required by a country's domestic GAAP. Complexity of this nature can therefore lead to inconsistency in the interpretation of the financial statements.

The presentation of financial statements is governed by IAS 1 which has retained the 'one or two statement' approach to reporting comprehensive income at the option of the entity. To reduce the degree of change necessary, the choice of which to adopt may therefore be made on the basis of which approach corresponds more closely to that required by domestic GAAP. Alternative forms of presentation may therefore lead to inconsistencies in interpretation of performance.

IFRSs are principle-based. It is often claimed that IFRSs provide insufficient guidance on the application of principles. An entity may therefore interpret the principles in an IFRS in different ways, especially in connection with concepts such as 'reliable measurement' and 'probable cash flows'.

Certain IFRS allow alternative accounting practices. For example, IAS 40 *Investment Property* and IAS 16 *Property, Plant and Equipment* both allow a choice of two measurement methods to be used. An entity may again choose a method which corresponds with domestic GAAP which may thereby lead to a lack of comparability between different entities in different countries and inconsistency. The lack of any substantial industry guidance in these areas results in the need to use judgement in the selection of accounting practices.

If the entity in question is adopting IFRS for the first time it will have to consider the requirements of IFRS 1 *First Time Adoption of IFRS* which at the time of adoption allows a number of exemptions from the requirements of IFRS. For example, IFRS 1 permits a first-time adopter not to restate business combinations prior to its date of transition to IFRS. The entity could for example carry forward amortised figures for goodwill. The amortisation method is not allowed by IFRS 3.

Another source of inconsistency between entities could be the IASB's allowance of early-adoption of IFRS. For example any entities adopting IFRS 9 early may have produced figures that were incomparable and inconsistent with entities who decided to use IAS 39 and leave adoption of IFRS 9 until the effective date; although IAS 8 *Accounting Policies, Changes in Accounting Estimates and Errors* does require an entity to report the possible future impact of such an early adoption.

(b) **This part of the question concerns the accounting options available for property, plant and equipment upon transition to IFRS**

Recto may elect to measure the manufacturing property at fair value at the date of transition and use that fair value as the property's deemed cost and then account for the asset prospectively under IAS 16's cost approach or the entity may elect to adopt IAS 16 retrospectively. Alternatively Recto may elect to use previous domestic GAAP if the approach used is comparable to current IFRS requirements – in this case, the appropriate IFRS is IAS 16. Recto has elected to use IAS 16's cost model. There are therefore three options available to Recto upon transition to IFRS on 1 November 2012 to measure cost:

1. Adopt fair value at 1 November 2012 as deemed cost
2. Apply IAS 16's cost approach retrospectively
3. Use domestic GAAP as the basis of cost if acceptable

No adjustments would be necessary under the last option which uses written down revaluations as the carrying amounts under domestic GAAP have been measured using an approach acceptable under IAS 16. That is, the manufacturing property is depreciated systematically over its estimated useful life and the revaluation is measured at fair value less subsequent depreciation and impairment losses.

Options 1 and 2 will require adjustments as follows:

Tutorial note: although not strictly required in answer to the question, to make the adjustments clear, it is best to start such a question with a view of what the brought forward figures would be as at 1 November 2012 under domestic GAAP. The following show the journal entries by way of T accounts to make the entries' impact clearer.

PRACTICE ANSWER BANK

	1 Fair value as deemed cost		2 Applying IAS 16's cost approach	
	Dr	Cr	Dr	Cr
• Manufacturing asset				
As at 1 Nov 2012 under domestic GAAP	14.000		14.000	
1 Nov 2012 acc depn written back		0.286		
Retained earnings [2]	1.286			
1 Nov 2012 initial revaluation surplus w/b				2.000
Balance c/d		15.000		12.000
• Accumulated depreciation				
As at 1 Nov 2012 under domestic GAAP ($14m × 1/49)		0.286		0.286
1 Nov 2012 To asset account	0.286			
1 Nov 2012 Retained earnings w/b			0.286	
1 Nov 2012 Rev surplus Cost based depn w/b				0.240
1 Nov 2012 Ret earnings Cost based depn 2011				0.240
• Revaluation surplus				
As at 1 Nov 2012 under domestic GAAP[1]		2.240		2.240
1 Nov 2012 Trf to retained earnings	2.240			
1 Nov 2012 Revaluation w/b			2.000	
1 Nov 2012 Excess depn w/b			0.240	
• Retained earnings				
1 Nov 2012 increase in FV of asset		1.286		
1 Nov 2012 revaluation surplus trf		2.240		
1 Nov 2012 acc depn Cost based depn 2011			0.240	
1 Nov 2012 acc depn w/b				0.286

[1]		
Asset cost	12.000	
Depreciation year 1 ($12m /50)	0.240	
	11.760	
Revaluation	14.000	
Revaluation surplus	2.240	
[1] Asset cost	12.000	
Depreciation year 1 ($12m /50)	0.240	
	11.760	
Revaluation	14.000	
Revaluation surplus	2.240	

[2] Any gains or losses on adjustment when adopting IFRS 1 must be accounted for in retained earnings.

Tutorial note: the above adjustments may also be shown in journal entry form as follows:

Note. Carrying amount under domestic GAAP:

As at 1 Nov 2011: $12m × 49/50 $11.760m
As at 1 Nov 2012: $14m × 48/49 $13.714m

PRACTICE ANSWER BANK

1 Using fair values at 1 Nov 2012 as deemed cost

	Dr $m	Cr $m
PPE: manufacturing property at CA ($15m – $13.714m)	1.286	
Retained earnings		1.286

Being adjustment of carrying amount to fair value at 1 Nov 2012

	Dr $m	Cr $m
Revaluation surplus ($14m – $11.760m)	2.240	
Retained earnings		2.240

Being reversal of initial revaluation at 1 Nov 2011

2 Applying IAS 16 cost approach retrospectively

	Dr $m	Cr $m
Revaluation surplus (as in note ^{1} above)	2.240	
Manufacturing property ($14m – $12m)		2.000
Accumulated depreciation: depn for 2011 ($12m/50)		0.240

Being reversal of revaluation adjustment at 1 Nov 2011

	Dr $m	Cr $m
Accumulated depreciation ($14m × 1/49)	0.286	
Retained earnings		0.286

Being reversal of depreciation based on initial revaluation at 1 Nov 2011

	Dr $m	Cr $m
Accumulated depreciation		0.240
Retained earnings	0.240	

Being cost based depreciation for y/e 31 Oct 2012

Question 19

This question concerns IFRS 16 *Leases*. It requires a report to be prepared showing how to account for a sale and leaseback, the impact of leases on gearing ratios and discussion of the impact of the new standard.

(a) IFRS 16 *Leases* contains an exemption for low value items. Personal computers and tablets are given as an example of low value items in IFRS 16. They meet the criteria for the exemption because Olco can benefit from use of the assets on their own or together with other resources that are readily available (eg publicly available software).

Rather than applying the usual accounting treatment of recognising right-of-use assets and lease liabilities, Loco can recognise the lease payments in the contract on a straight-line basis over the lease term of three years. (Another systematic basis would also be allowed if it were more representative of the pattern of the consumption of benefits but in this case a straight line basis would seem to be most appropriate.)

Deferred income balance (SoFP)		40.0

Right of use assets	110.7	
Lease obligation		110.7

($27m annual rent × 4.100 [discount factor])

During the year ended 30 April 2013

Lease obligation: rental payments	27.0	
Cash		27.0

Finance cost: profit or loss	7.75	
Lease obligation		7.75

($110.7 × 7%)

Depreciation: profit or loss	22.14		
Lease asset accumulated depreciation		22.14	
($110.7/5)			

(b)

Accounting entries	$m
Opening obligation	1.000
Rental (paid in advance)	(0.286)
Obligation during the year	0.714
Interest at 9.7%	0.069
Closing obligation	0.783

Tutorial note: note use of implicit rate of interest above and not Olco's borrowing cost.

Accounting entries

	Current $000	Buy $000	Lease $000
Operating profit (+ 12% increase)	400	448	448
Finance charge	–	(150)*	(69)**
Depreciation	–	(250)	(250)
Rental			
Adjusted profit	400	48	129

*$1m × 15%
**See calculation above

Share capital	2,000	2,000	2,000
Long term debt	1,000	1,000	1,000
Loan to purchase assets		1,000	
Lease obligation			783
Capital employed	3,000	4,000	3,783
Gearing ratios	0.5:1	1:1	0.89:1
ROCE	13.3%	1.2%	3.4%

(c) Impact of IFRS 16, *Leases*

IFRS 16 was introduced in response to criticism of the previous standard IAS 17 which allowed some lease contracts to be recognised 'off balance sheet', resulted in seemingly similar transactions being accounted for differently and caused difficulty in making comparisons between entities that purchased assets using for example loan finance and those who acquired assets through leasing contracts. IFRS 16 is consistent with the definition of an asset and liability under the *Conceptual Framework*. The *Conceptual Framework* defines an asset as a right that has the potential to product economic benefits. A lease contains the right to use an asset for the period of the lease and the use of that asset is expected to generate benefits in the form of increased returns or reduced costs. The *Conceptual Framework* defines a liability as an obligation to transfer economic resources as a result of a past event. Entering into the lease contract is the past event and the requirement to make payments over the term of the lease represents the transfer of economic resources. IFRS 16 has fundamentally changed the accounting for leases. All leases, with very limited exemptions available for short term leases and leases of assets with a low underlying value, will be recognised in the statement of financial position at lease commencement – this is the 'right-of-use model'. It requires a right of use asset and a corresponding lease liability to be recognised and therefore has eradicated off balance sheet finance in respect of lease transactions.

The requirements of IFRS 16 will increase the carrying amount of an entity's assets, which impacts on ratios such as ROCE, and will increase its liabilities, which impacts on ratios such as gearing. Many entities have had to renegotiate other financing contracts such as bank loans as the impact of leases has had a significant impact on covenants.

PRACTICE ANSWER BANK

Question 20

This question requires the application of knowledge to a scenario concerning segmental reporting and the writing of a report to advise a company's directors. The main issues are to do with the inclusion/exclusion of common costs and assets and liabilities in the segment report and the identification of segments for reporting purposes.

Measurement

There is the potential for a mismatch between the internal information presented to a chief operating decision maker (CODM) for decision making and that presented externally in a company's IFRS-compliant financial statements. There is no requirement in IFRS 8 that the two are similar. Rather, IFRS 8 requires the amounts reported in the segmental reports to be on the same basis as those used by the CODM. It appears that Mondo complies with that requirement. Any significant differences must be reconciled; eg where segment assets are reported, between reported assets and the entity's assets as reported in the statement of financial position.

The IFRS prohibits the segmental reporting of any items unless that measure is used by the CODM for determining resource allocation and for assessing performance. However, the IFRS does not prescribe the reporting treatment of common costs and common assets. Instead – and as such reporting could have a significant effect on segment analysis – the IFRS requires that the allocation is made on a reasonable basis. In this respect:

- *Central head office service costs*: would best be allocated on the basis of turnover as head office staff spend time on strategic duties in proportion to the turnover of each segment.

- *Property management costs*: would be best allocated on the basis of the age of properties as such costs accrue in close proportion to that age.

- *Post employment service costs*: would be best allocated on the basis of pensionable employees in each segment.

- *Loan interest*: IFRS 8 does not require symmetry between revenues and expenses included in segment results and the assets and liabilities allocated to segments. The IFRS simply requires disclosure of the nature and effect of any asymmetrical allocations. Another example would be where depreciation of the head office is included in segment results but the depreciated asset is excluded. In the absence of any indication of how best to allocate interest costs, they have been allocated on the same basis as central head office costs.

Allocation

	Basis	Tuedo $m	Wedon $m	Thurso $m
Profit/(loss)		(26)	176	100
Central head office costs				
(eg Tuedo $380m/$1,730m × $17m)	Turnover	(4)	(5)	(8)
Property management costs				
(eg Wedon 10yrs/30yrs × $30m)	Age of property	(5)	(10)	(15)
Post-employment service costs				
(eg Thurso 300/500 × $20m)	Pensionable employees	–	(8)	(12)
Loan interest				
(eg Tuedo $380m/$1,730m × [$20m × 6%])	Turnover	(0.3)	(0.3)	(0.6)
Adjusted profit/(loss)		(35.3)	152.7	64.4

Recognition and reporting of reportable segments

Qualitative criteria

All three segments meet IFRS 8's qualitative criteria for an operating segment. These are that:

- It engages in a business activity from which it earns revenues and incurs expenses;
- Its operating results are regularly reviewed by a chief operating decision maker with respect to making decisions about resource allocation and performance; **and**
- Discrete financial information is available for the segment (IFRS 8.5)

Quantitative criteria

Once the segments have been identified as above, the IFRS requires the application of quantitative criteria to determine whether each segment should be reported separately. If **any** of the following apply then the segment is reported separately (IFRS 8.13):

- Reported revenue is 10% or more of the combined (internal and external) revenue of all operating segments; or
- The segment's reported profit or loss, in absolute terms, is 10% or more of the greater of:
    - (i) The combined profit of all operating segments that did not report a loss; or
    - (ii) The combined loss of all operating segments that reported a loss; or
- Its assets are 10% or more of the combined assets of all operating segments.

Applying the above quantitative criteria to:	Tuedo	Wedon	Thurso
Reported revenue	√	√	√
Combined profit	√	√	√

Note: combined profit = $217.1m [10% = $21.7m] and combined loss = $35.3m [10% = $3.53m]. so $21.7m is the benchmark

Combined assets	x	√	√

As only one of the criteria has to be satisfied, all segments count to be reported separately

Reporting of information about geographical areas of trading and major customers.

Geographical areas

IFRS 8 requires revenues from external customers and non-current assets (excluding financial assets, deferred tax assets, post-employment benefit assets and rights arising under insurance contracts) to be classified into those attributed to Mondo's own country of domicile and those attributed to all foreign countries (IFRS 8.33).

Therefore, Mondo must disclose the following information:

	External sales $m	Non-current assets*
Attributed to:		
Country of domicile	420	300
All foreign countries	1,310	4,910
	1,730	5,210

*assuming there are none of the assets mentioned above.

In addition, if revenues from external customers or assets attributed to an individual foreign country are material, separate disclosure of that country's revenues or assets is required (IFRS 8.33). The IFRS does not define what is meant by 'material' but given that 10% is used for other purposes, it is reasonable to assume the same percentage can be used for this purpose. Mondo sells $260m of goods to one country. As this is 15% of external sales, Mondo should disclose the name of the country and the amounts involved.

PRACTICE ANSWER BANK

Reporting of information about major customers

IFRS 8 would require Mondo to give information showing the extent of its reliance on major customers (IFRS 8.34). Mondo sold $200m of goods to Tuedo's former owners. As this is more than 10% of total sales, Mondo should disclose:

- The fact
- The amount involved
- The reportable segment involved; ie Tuedo.

Note. Mondo does not have to disclose the name of the customer – although several companies do so!

Question 21

This question concerns the application of fair values.. Part (b) requires application of IFRS 13 to a scenario involving the measurement of a dismantling obligation assumed in a business combination.

(a) **Definition of fair value**

The Conceptual Framework permits historical cost or current value accounting to be applied, or a combination of both, which is known as the mixed measurement approach. Fair value is one of the measurement bases within current value accounting. IFRS 13 defines fair value (FV) as 'the price that would be received to sell an asset or paid to transfer a liability in an orderly transaction between market participants at the measurement date' (IFRS 13 Appendix A).

Measurement of fair value

The FV of an asset or liability is to be a market-based and non entity-specific exit price (IFRS 13.B2). So Seph would only be allowed to use entity-specific prices in very restricted circumstances – as explained below in 'valuation techniques'.

The market-based nature of the price means it takes into account current market conditions when measuring those assets and liabilities. So, for instance, if Seph held a financial asset, the price will be the amount the asset **could** be sold for or, if Seph held an issued bond, the price would be the amount Seph **could** pay to transfer it to someone else.

Due to the market-based nature, the measure of the item (asset or liability) must take into account the characteristics of that item and the assumptions made by market participants. It is assumed that transactions will take place in the **principal market** in which an orderly transaction for the item would take place or, in its absence, the most **advantageous** market.

The principal market is the market with the greatest liquidity (in terms of volume and level of activity for that item). If there is no principal market, the price in the most advantageous market would be used; ie the market in which Seph could achieve the most beneficial price; eg by maximising the amount received or minimising the amount paid. If market activity is in decline, then IFRS 13 recognises that valuation techniques (see below) may have to be used to measure FV; although in such a case it would have to be determined whether this still represented an orderly sale (eg a forced sale would have to be accounted for outside the FV requirements). Although the price may have to be adjusted if costs are incurred to transport an asset to the principal (or most advantageous) market, transaction costs would not be included in fair value because such costs are not a characteristic of the asset or liability.

Non-financial assets

The fair value measurement will consider the use to which the asset can be put. The measurement takes into account the ability of a market participant to generate economic benefits by using the asset in its highest and best use. Unless market factors dictate otherwise, the IFRS envisages that Seph's current use of a non-financial asset reflects its highest and best use. In doing so, Seph must consider whether the asset is used in combination with other assets or on a stand-alone basis and whether the use of the asset is physically possible, legally permissible and financially feasible.

Valuation techniques

When transactions are directly observable in a market, the determination of FV is relatively straightforward, but when they are not, a valuation technique is used. IFRS 13 describes three such valuation techniques:

- The **market approach** uses prices and other relevant information generated by market transactions involving identical or comparable assets or liabilities,
- The **income approach** converts future amounts (eg cash flows or income or expenses) to a single current amount (using present value techniques), and
- The **cost approach** determines a value which reflects the amount that would be required currently to replace the service capacity of an asset (also known as current replacement costs).

The technique chosen should be consistently applied to maximise the use of relevant observable inputs and minimise unobservable inputs. There are three levels of inputs as follows:

Level 1   These are fully observable (eg unadjusted quoted prices in an active market for identical assets and liabilities that Seph can access at the measurement date).

Level 2   These are directly or indirectly observable but exclude level 1 inputs; eg quoted prices for **similar** assets in active markets, prices for similar or identical assets in non-active markets or quoted rates used for valuation purposes.

Level 3   These are unobservable inputs; eg Seph's own assumptions about selling prices.

Disclosures

IFRS 13 requires a number of quantitative and qualitative disclosures about FV measurements. Many are related to the three-level hierarchy shown above on the basis of their input to the valuation techniques adopted. This requirement already exists for financial instruments under IFRS 7, but is extended to other assets and liabilities (within its scope) by IFRS 13.

Disclosure requirements may also depend upon whether the FV measurement is **recurring** (other IFRSs require or permit FV in the SoFP at the end of each reporting period) or non-recurring (other IFRSs require or permit in the SoFP in particular circumstances); eg if an entity is using recurring FV measurements using level 3 unobservable inputs, it must disclose the impact of those measurements on profit or loss or other comprehensive income.

(b) **Background**

The fair value (FV) of a liability is determined on the assumption that the liability would be transferred on the measurement date but would remain outstanding; ie it is a transfer value and not an extinguishment/settlement cost. The FV of the obligation must take into account non-performance risk (the risk that Seph will not fulfil its obligation) and Seph's own credit risk. As a level 1 (observable) price is not available to Seph to assess the liability's transfer value, the entity must measure its FV from the perspective of a market participant that owes the liability, using a valuation technique (IFRS 13.40).

Seph is contractually allowed to transfer the obligation to a market participant but, even if it had not been, IFRS 13 does not allow a separate input into the valuation exercise to reflect this. The effect of the restriction would be either implicitly or explicitly included in other inputs into the FV price (IFRS 13.45–46).

Seph assesses long-term liabilities on a cost-plus basis – hence the need for the calculations to include separately the return for the undertaking and the risk premium. If the assessment had been on a fixed-fee basis, for example, these two inputs would have been indistinguishable.

Calculation		$m
Expected labour cost	$20m × 30% + $25m × 40% + $35m × 30%	26.50
Overheads	$26.50 × 90%	23.90
		50.40
Contractor's profit mark-up	+ 20%	10.08

PRACTICE ANSWER BANK

Calculation			$m
			60.48
Inflation		×	1.553
			93.93
Market risk premium	+ 5%		4.70
			98.63
Discount rate 9%		×	0.422
PV of expected cash flows using discount rate of 9%			41.62

Question 22

This question concerns employee benefits. IFRS devotes considerable attention to them in two standards – IFRS 2 *Share-based Payment* and IAS 19 *Employee Benefits* – which applies to all other employee benefits. Part (a) of the question requires calculations of (i) the amounts to be included in the statement of comprehensive income (SOCI) re a defined benefit scheme, (ii) and (iii) the amounts to be included in the SOCI and statement of financial position re share-based payments and termination benefits respectively. Part (b) requires a discussion of the controversies related to IFRS2 and recognition of an appropriate accounting treatment.

(a) (i)

	$'000
Impact of transactions on statement of comprehensive income (SOCI)	
Actual contribution by Bee to the scheme	–

> **Tutorial note:** Under IAS 19 contributions to defined benefit schemes are a movement between line items in the statement of financial position; ie the reduction in cash for Bee is reflected by an increase in the scheme assets. Hence there is no effect on the SOCI.

Net service cost (115 – 106)	9

> **Tutorial note:** the present value of employees' contributions attributable to the period, reduce the cost of the benefits to the entity (IAS 19.92)

Net interest cost [10% × (266 – 256)]	1
Past service cost	20

> **Tutorial note:** past service costs would have been included in the net scheme obligation as at 1 November 2014 so there is no need to charge an interest cost on them for the current year.

To be recognised in profit or loss	30
Remeasurement loss	
To be recognised in other comprehensive income under the title 'Items that will not be reclassified to profit or loss'.	17

(ii)

	Calculation of cumulative liability	Cum. liability $'000	Expense for the year $'000
Year 1	5,000 options × 9 × $20 × 1/3	300,000	300,000
Year 2	5,000 options × 10 × $20 × 2/3	666,667	366,667
Year 3	5,000 options × 12 × $20	1,200,000	533,333

(iii)

> **Tutorial notes:**
>
> The number of staff members who leave during Years 1 and 2 are not relevant to the calculation of the cumulative liability as it is based upon the number who Bee **expects** to stay for the whole vesting period. However, they are taken into account in estimating the number of options that will finally vest at the end of Year 3.
>
> Total expected cash flows are $9.6m [(1,000 × $6K + 900 × $4K (10 – 6)]
>
> IAS 19 requires that termination benefits, paid regardless of whether the employee stays and renders service, should be provided for as a liability immediately. This should be at the earlier of when the plan is announced and when the entity recognises the relevant restructuring costs. In this question we assume that is 1 October 2015.

Liability to recognise at 31 Oct 2015: 1,000 employees × $6,000   6.0m

> **Tutorial note:** Under IAS 19 that part of the termination plan which relates to benefits received as a result of providing service must be recognised incrementally as short-term benefits (because they are payable within 12 months). No discounting is required.

Liability to recognise at 31 Oct 2015:
900 emp'ees × incremental benefit $4,000 (10 – 6) / 6 months   0.6m

                                                                6.6m

(b) *The FD's opinion on share-based payment (SBP)*

SBP is a very controversial subject as it usually involves the issue of shares and option to employees, most commonly senior management, as remuneration. It is usually undertaken by entities in an attempt to align the employees' economic interests with those of the shareholders.

Usually, the SBP does not entail a cash cost to the entity. However, there is a cost to shareholders (as identified by the FD) through dilution of their shareholdings. There developed a consensus amongst investors therefore that such awards (which amount to remuneration for the employee) should be recognised in the financial statements. There is also an argument that as the SBPs are a reward for employees and those employees provide a service over the duration of the share-based payment agreement, known as the vesting period, an expense should be recognised in the statement of profit or loss to match against the revenue or other income generated by those employees during the same period. Accounting for SBP transactions is therefore an application of accrual accounting, which is required by the Conceptual Framework.

Treatment in the Bee Group financial statements

The award would be accounted for as an equity-settled transaction; ie the cost would be recognised in the group SOCI and in the group SOFP as a movement in equity. This is because the parent **group** receives services as consideration for its own equity.

Treatment in the separate financial statements of Bee

Bee **as a separate entity** does not receive the services of Sac's employees nor does it have an obligation to settle the transaction. It is not therefore within the scope of IFRS 2 and would not be accounted for.

Treatment in the separate financial statements of Sac.

The award is accounted for as a cash-settled transaction because Sac has the obligation to settle the award with assets (ie equity held in Bee) rather than with Sac's own equity.

PRACTICE ANSWER BANK

> **Tutorial note:** Sac is granting the award as a principal (ie not as an agent of Bee). If Sac was granting the award under instructions from Bee (ie as an agent) it is likely that it would be accounted for as an equity-settled transaction.

Question 23

This question concerns environmental and social reporting involving financial reporting and narrative reporting.

(a) (i) Under IAS 37, an entity must recognise a provision if, and only if:

– The amount can be measured reliably

– Cash outflow is probable, and

– A present obligation (legal or constructive) exists which has arisen as a result of a past obligating event.

As industry experts have estimated the clean up costs, it can be assumed that the first criterion is satisfied in all three situations.

In **country 1** no law exists which would require Sideel to rectify any contamination. Also, Sideel's environmental stance would suggest that a constructive obligation does not exist as the entity only rectifies contamination if it has a legal obligation to do so. A provision would therefore be inappropriate.

In **country 2** a law exists requiring a clean up by Sideel. The second two criteria are satisfied and therefore a provision of $10 million is required adjusted, if appropriate, to reflect the time value of money.

Although in many cases it will be impossible to be virtually certain of the enactment of a law until it is actually enacted (IAS 37.22), as a date has been set for enactment by **country 3** it is virtually certain that a law will be enacted which will require clean up of the land already contaminated. The virtual certainty of the new law being enacted means that a cash outflow is probable and that Sideel has a present legal obligation as a result of the past contamination. A provision of $15 million is required adjusted, if appropriate, to reflect the time value of money.

(ii) The benefits to Sideel of producing a separate social and environmental report (SER) concern stakeholder communication and in particular its impact on any stakeholder wishing to make an overall assessment of the group's performance. The process by which an SER is produced would also help to identify inefficiencies in its management systems. These benefits can be outlined as follows:

– Sideel's market share in the oil industry could be increased if it is seen to be a more attractive supplier than its competitors. The publication of more detailed performance information would increase customer confidence. An SER would be attractive to customers as those customers themselves are under increasing pressure by their own stakeholders to deal only with 'environmentally friendly' suppliers. There would be a competitive advantage from disclosure.

– Investors are becoming increasingly concerned about risks to the sustainability of operations in the oil industry. A report produced with sufficient and high quality information about mitigation of those risks by Sideel would make the group more attractive to investors.

– There is a growing international demand for transparency in the reporting of sustainability. If Sideel wishes to continue the development of operations internationally it will have to improve its corporate image. An SER would be just the vehicle to help achieve this.

- Sideel has a very poor reputation as a corporate citizen. Production of a social and environmental report would help foster better relations with local communities and foster better community support for its activities.

- Sideel's environmental stance is bound to annoy regulators. By producing an SER and perhaps identifying ways in which its environmental performance may be improved, the entity's relationship with regulators would be improved.

- The process by which an SER is produced would help Sideel to identify inefficiencies in its operations and thereby improve its management information system. This would have the additional benefit of helping to identify opportunities to reduce costs and use of resources.

(b) Under IAS 37 a contingent liability is a possible obligation or a present obligation that is not recognised. A present obligation would not be recognised if either it is not probable that an outflow of resources will be required to settle it or because the amount of the obligation cannot be measured with sufficient reliability. A contingent liability is disclosed unless the chance of occurrence is remote.

Sideel has a possible obligation only and, as it is not remote (say less than a 5% chance of occurrence), under IAS 37 the amount should be disclosed in the notes to the accounts.

Question 24

(a) This question involves the determination of the fair value of an asset. It requires a decision as to the entity's principal market.

11 Interim reporting, first-time adoption and fair values

IFRS 13's fair value measurement assumes that the transaction to sell the vehicles will take place in Krz's principal market [PM] or (in its absence) in the most advantageous market for that asset. (IFRS 13.16).

While the perspective of the entity is considered when determining the PM, the decision is based upon overall market volume or level of activity for the asset in question. It is not based upon the volume or level of activity of Krz's own transactions in that market. Applying these criteria, the PM is clearly Europe as it has a greater volume of activity for the vehicles in question (70%). This is despite Krz selling more of its vehicles in America and despite its most advantageous market (because of the higher net profit of $53K [see below]) being Asia.

	America $000	Europe $000	Asia $000
Price per vehicle	60	50	56
Transaction costs per vehicle (eg commissions)	6	2	1
Costs to transport each vehicle to the market	2	2	2
Net profit	52	46	53

An entity may have more than one PM for identical assets if for example different units *within* the entity have different exit strategies for the assets. However, this does not appear to be relevant to this question. Therefore, if FV is to be measured on the basis of one principal market it would not be appropriate to value identical assets at different FVs because Krz's management intend to sell them in three different markets. Nor would it be appropriate to use a FV averaged over the three markets. Rather, the vehicles should be measured on the basis of the FV in the market determined to be the entity's PM; ie Europe.

IFRS 13 is clear that transaction costs are not to be included in the determination of fair value (IFRS 13.25–26). The FV of the vehicles will therefore be $48,000 × 1,000 = $48m.

PRACTICE ANSWER BANK

(b) This question involves accounting for events after the reporting period and concerns the valuation of investment property at fair value and the tenant's insolvency.

19 Provisions, contingencies and events after the reporting period

The vehicle showroom would be shown in Krz's SoFP as an investment property. The fair value of investment property reflects, amongst other things, the quality and reliability of the tenant's covenants to meet the rental payments due.

IAS 40 *Investment Property* would require that Krz recognise the property's market conditions when assessing its FV at the 30 April 2014. This would not normally involve hindsight. The insolvency of Buz would not normally therefore be an adjusting event to the carrying amount of the showroom. Unless there are circumstances to the contrary (which does not appear to be the case in this question) the showroom property would still hold a value in the market. IAS 10 states quite clearly that a decline in the market value of investments after the reporting period and before the date on which the financial statements are authorised for issue, is a non-adjusting event as the condition does not normally relate to conditions existing at the end of the reporting period (IAS 10.11–12,22). The showroom would continue to be carried on the SoFP at $20m.

However, the event will be an adjusting one in relation to the amount due from Buz at 30 April 2014. The financial statement should therefore be amended by the write off of the $1m owing by Buz.

(c) This question involves accounting for deferred tax when an asset has been revalued to fair value.

17 Taxation

Year ended	Carrying amount of asset in SoFP	Tax base of asset	Temp timing diff	D tax liability @30%	Movement in D tax liability	D tax charge in SoPL and OCI	D tax impact on revaluation reserve
	$m	$m	$m	$m	$m	$m	$m
30.4.2012[1]	8.00	7.50	0.50	0.15	0.15	0.15	–
30.4.2013	6.00	5.00	1.00	0.30	0.15	0.15	
30.4.2014[2]	9.00	2.50	6.50	1.95	1.65	0.15	1.50

Tutorial note: remaining years for information							
30.4.2015	4.50	–	4.50	1.35	(0.60)	(0.60)	(0.75)
30.4.2016	–	–	–	–	(1.35)	(1.35)	(0.75)

[1] Carrying amount depreciation based on $10m/5 years
Tax base allowance based on $10m/4 years

[2] As at 30 April 2014 the asset will be revalued from $4m to $9m. Therefore $5m in fair value gain will be transferred to revaluation reserve (via SoPL & OCI). The deferred tax impact on the fair value gain will be $5m × 30% = $1.5m.

Question 25

A time series analysis of the results of a potential takeover target using financial ratios.

The following suggested solution is indicative only.

REPORT

FROM:
TO:
DATE:

SUBJECT: Financial performance of Choggerell

The following report is based on a series of financial ratios calculated from the financial statements of Choggerell for the financial years 20X6, 20X7 and 20X8.

The overall performance of Choggerell as evidenced by its return on equity has fluctuated. There was a significant improvement from 20X6 (13%) to 20X7 (22%) due to improvements in profitability on trading (net income to sales revenue).

That improvement in overall efficiency was not maintained in 20X8 and return on equity declined to 19%. This time the decrease was due to a significant decline in asset utilisation which at 2.01 is now at its lowest for the three year period. Profitability on trading was maintained – although there was a marginal decline.

Earnings per share have followed a similar pattern to return on equity. There was a very significant rise in earnings per share for 20X7 – but this was followed by a small decline in 20X8. Dividends per share, however, have been maintained in 20X8 after a significant increase in 20X7.

Changes in the profitability on trading over the three year period seem to be attributable to steadily increasing margins on sales (decreasing cost of sales relative to sales). However, progress here seems to have been offset by increases in operating expenses (operating expenses to sales revenue).

Control of working capital does not seem to have been optimal. The current and acid test ratios have fluctuated but were the lowest for the three years in 20X8. Inventory turnover has been falling for the past three years and the period of credit taken by customers has increased significantly. This suggests possible liquidity problems and there seems to have been a significant overdraft at the end of 20X6 and 20X8. The period of credit taken from suppliers has increased significantly in 20X8 and is now an average of two months which may invite pressure from suppliers for faster payment.

The fall in efficiency in the use of assets to generate sales (sales revenue to total assets) and the increasing net assets per share would therefore appear to be a result of increasing non-current assets and possible poor working capital management.

Recommendations for improving the performance of Choggerell

The overall performance of Choggerell could be improved by:

- Better control of operating expenses. Reducing operating expenses would increase profitability on sales and hence overall return on equity.

- Careful monitoring of non-current asset utilisation. Increasing sales revenue to non-current assets would increase sales revenue to total assets and hence overall return on equity.

- Careful cash flow management to avoid widely fluctuating cash balances and the reliance on bank overdrafts.

Limitations

- It has been assumed that all the data is comparable ie that similar accounting policies have been used over the three years.

- It has only been possible to look at trends within Choggerell over the past three years. It would be useful to compare Choggerell's performance with its competitors – particularly the leading firms in the same industry sector with a view to knowing what is achievable.

PRACTICE ANSWER BANK

- It would be useful to know more about the sector Choggerell operates in and general economic conditions. This would help identify what changes are attributable to changes in sector performance and general economic conditions and what are attributable to good or bad management.
- The available information is very limited. It would be useful to have additional information about the quality of Choggerell's management, its risk exposure and the prospects for the industry sector.

Question 26

(a) This question concerns the calculation of group basic and diluted earnings per share.

> **Tutorial note:** The earnings figure on which basic eps is calculated should be the consolidated net profit or loss for the year after tax non-controlling interests and after adjusting for returns to preference shareholders if necessary (ie if not already included in the income statement). For diluted eps, IAS 33 *Earnings per Share* requires that we start with the basic earnings figure and reflect any changes that would arise if the potential shares outstanding in the period were actually issued. (IAS 33.33).
>
> Potential ordinary shares are only to be treated as dilutive if their conversion to ordinary shares would **decrease** eps (or increase loss per share) from **continuing** operations. In other words, the earnings used in the calculation should be those **before** any profit or loss from discontinued operations.

Step 1: *Judging the cumulative impact of potential shares*

> **Tutorial note:** Where an entity has a variety of **potential** ordinary shares, in deciding whether they are dilutive (ie are included in the calculation) or antidilutive (ie ignored in the calculation), each item must be considered in sequence from the most to the least dilutive. Only those items which produce a cumulative dilution are included in the calculation. We must therefore perform a calculation to show which is the most and which is the least dilutive.

	Increase in earnings $m	Increase in number of ordinary shares m	Earnings per incremental share $
Options			
Increase in earnings	nil		
Increase in shares			
400,000 × ($80 − $60)/$80		0.1	nil
Convertible preference shares			
Increase in earnings			
(1.6m × $0.1)	0.16		
Increase in ordinary shares			
(1.6m × 2)		3.2	0.05
6% convertible bonds			
Increase in earnings			
(200m × 6% × (1 − 0.3 tax)	8.4		
Increase in shares			
(200,000 × 20)		4.0	2.1

The order in which to include the dilutive instruments is therefore:

1. Most dilutive: options
2.   convertible preference shares
3. Least dilutive: convertible bonds

Step 2: *calculation of basic and diluted eps*

	Profit from continuing operations attributable to ordinary equity shareholders of parent entity $m	Ordinary shares m	Per share $	
As per draft accounts ($12m + $8m)	20.0	4.0	5	
Options	–	0.1		
	20.0	4.1	4.88	dilutive
Convertible pref shares	0.16	3.2		
	20.16	7.3	2.76	dilutive
Convertible bonds	8.40	4.0		
	28.56	11.3	2.53	dilutive
Basic group eps			**$5.0**	
Diluted group eps			**$2.53**	

(b) Entities in industries such as telecommunications often have numerous and complex income streams. A one-size-fits-all GAAP approach therefore seems an inappropriate way for management to report performance. For that reason, demand has grown for custom-made performance measures which supplement (rather than replace) the GAAP earnings measure disclosed by management. Typically, a non-GAAP measure would exclude non-cash (eg fair value adjustments) and one-off (eg restructuring provisions) items.

This is not a new phenomenon and has been discussed by regulators (eg the US SEC and UK FRC) for decades; often with dire warnings of the potential confusion for users. The information is not only published in regulated statements but in narrative reports and press briefings. The confusion arises because it is often difficult to discern the motives behind the non-GAAP measures. On the one hand the exclusion of unusual items may actually improve transparency by, for example, making it easier for Verti and its competitors to compare across firms and over time. The non-GAAP information may also be used to provide a link between information in the regulated statements and the actual performance calculations on which users such as investors often typically rely. On the other hand, allowing management free rein over what to publish gives them the opportunity to indulge in earnings management, which is both inappropriate and unethical. It is no coincidence that, typically, the excluded items will be expenses.

In entities such as telecom companies, there is clearly a place for the non-GAAP reporting of those KPIs used by management, possibly in private, to direct and manage the entity. However, there is also a place for regulated information to avoid management acting opportunistically. This is an example of the classic conflict between relevance and reliability.

As investors are likely to concentrate on the (usually) higher non-GAAP KPI of an entity, it is entirely possible that an entity such as Verti, not indulging in non-GAAP reporting, would lose competitive advantage. Perhaps the way forward is for regulators to insist on the publication of reconciliations between non-GAAP and regulated KPIs.

(c) It is argued that capital providers are interested in so much more than simply financial returns on their investment. An integrated report (IR) would set out how Verti's strategy, governance, performance and prospects leads to the creation of value. It will be very different from the entity's present traditional corporate reporting which concentrates primarily on financial performance. The aim of the IR would be to explain to Verti's capital providers how the entity creates value over time. The term 'capital providers' is very wide and would include employees, customers, suppliers, business partners, local communities, legislators, regulators and policymakers; as well as the traditional providers of financial capital.

Verti's historically-based financial statements would still be essential, particularly for compliance purposes, but they are unlikely to provide meaningful information regarding business value. It is argued that users and capital providers need a more forward-looking focus which attempts to present a fuller, more holistic view of the entity's activities. To achieve this, the framework will encourage Verti to prepare a report that shows the entity's performance against targets and strategies, explains how the various capitals are employed and affected by those activities and presents a more long-term view of the entity's organisation and activities.

It is often said that the compliance-led approach under IFRS is 'boilerplate' in execution and that an IR will provide information more business relevant than at present. An IR would not **replace** Verti's present form of reporting but would pull together information already produced to explain, and help users to assess, the key drivers of value creation. Information not material to this assessment would not be reported. It is possible that the IR could be prepared in response to the IASB's non-mandatory IFRS Practice Statement *Management Commentary* (issued in December 2010) which is a non-binding framework for the presentation of narrative reporting to accompany financial statements prepared under IFRS. The IR could be published either as a stand-alone document or included in the entity's financial statements.

The report would include traditional performance information but would also include the following key components: organisational overview and the external environment under which the entity operates, governance structure, business model, risks and opportunities, strategy and resource allocation, achievement of key objectives and outlook and challenges.

Entities such as Verti struggle to communicate value through traditional reporting. The IR could prove to be a useful tool for an entity wishing to shift its reporting focus from traditional annual performance to long-term stakeholder value creation. The IR would be useful to companies such as Verti who wish to develop their engagement with capital providers by developing their narrative reporting around their business model to explain how the business has been developed.

Exam question bank

1 Aguila (November 2021)

The Aguila Group consists of Aguila and its two subsidiary companies, Belmonte and Cabeza. The statements of financial position for the year ended 30 September 2021 are shown below:

	Aguila $000	Belmonte $000	Cabeza Kr000
ASSETS			
Non-current assets			
Property, plant and equipment	23,000	15,000	30,000
Investments			
– In Belmonte (at fair value)	9,200	-	-
– In Cabeza (at cost)	8,000	-	-
	40,200	15,000	30,000
Current assets			
Inventories	15,000	9,100	18,750
Trade and other receivables	20,000	9,000	15,000
Cash and cash equivalents	8,000	4,000	5,000
	43,000	22,100	38,750
Total assets	83,200	37,100	68,750
EQUITY AND LIABILITIES			
Equity			
Equity shares	10,000	5,000	7,500
Retained earnings	20,075	7,100	11,250
Other components of equity	1,125	-	-
	31,200	12,100	18,750
Non-current liabilities	30,000	15,000	30,000
Current liabilities	22,000	10,000	20,000
	83,200	37,100	68,750

The following information is relevant:

1. On 1 October 2019, Aguila purchased 15% of the equity share capital of Belmonte for $1,200,000. Aguila made an irrevocable election to hold the investment at 'fair value through other comprehensive income', and any subsequent fair value gains arising are included in 'other components of equity' in Aguila's own financial statements shown above.

   On 1 April 2021, Aguila acquired an additional 55% of Belmonte's equity share capital for $6,875,000. The fair value of the initial 15% shareholding was $1,875,000 on 1 April 2021. Aguila continues to hold the investment in Belmonte at 'fair value through other comprehensive income' and the combined 70% equity holding in Belmonte had a fair value of $9,200,000 on 30 September 2021.

   On 1 April 2021, the fair value of Belmonte's assets and associated liabilities were equal to their book value with the exception of depreciable plant and equipment, whose fair value exceeded its carrying value by $1,500,000. The plant and equipment had a remaining useful life of 5 years on 1 April 2021, and it is group policy to charge depreciation on a monthly basis.

   Belmonte's profit for the year ended 30 September 2021 was $3,100,000.

   Aguila chose to measure the non-controlling interest in Belmonte at fair value at the date of acquisition. On 1 April 2021, the non-controlling interest in Belmonte had a fair value of $3,750,000.

2 Aguila acquired 80% equity interest in Cabeza, for $8,000,000 on 1 October 2019. Cabeza's functional currency is the Krona (Kr). On 1 October 2019, Cabeza had retained earnings of Kr 6,390,000. Aguila holds the investment in Cabeza at original cost in its own financial statements.

The fair value of the net assets acquired were equal to their book value on 1 October 2019 and no fair value adjustments were required on acquisition of Cabeza.

The fair value of the non-controlling interest was Kr4,000,000 on 1 October 2019.

Cabeza made a profit in the year ended 30 September 2021 of Kr2,760,000 and a profit of Kr2,100,000 in the previous year ended 30 September 2020. Cabeza did not pay dividends in the post-acquisition period.

An impairment test on 30 September 2021, indicated impairment losses of Kr1,058,000 should be written off against the consolidated goodwill of Cabeza. No further impairment losses had been written off previously.

Relevant exchange rates are as follows:

	Kr to $
1 October 2019	2.0
30 September 2020	2.2
30 September 2021	2.5
Average rate for the year ended 30 September 2020	2.1
Average rate for the year ended 30 September 2021	2.3

3 Immediately after the year end, Aguila acquired a further 10% equity shareholding in Belmonte on 1 October 2021 for $1,325,000. The directors would like your advice on how to account for this additional investment in the consolidated statements for the year ended 30 September 2022.

Required

(a) Prepare the consolidated statement of financial position for the Aguila group as at 30 September 2021. **(30 marks)**

(b) Advise, with suitable computations, how the additional 10% investment in Belmonte acquired on the 1 October 2021, should be accounted for in the consolidated financial statements for the year ended 30 September 2022. **(5 marks)**

(c) The IASB's *Conceptual Framework for Financial Reporting* (2018) contains revised criteria for the recognition of liabilities.

Critically evaluate how the recognition criteria for a provision under IAS 37 *Provisions, Contingent Liabilities, and Contingent Assets* differs from the Conceptual Framework's (2018) revised liability recognition criteria. **(5 marks)**

(Total = 40 marks)

2 Diablo (November 2021)

Diablo is a trading group that operates in the retail fashion industry. The directors of Diablo require advice on several impairment related issues in the year ended 30 September 2021.

(a) **Impairment test for CGUs**

On 1 October 2019, Diablo acquired 100% of the equity share capital in Navajo for $100 million. The fair value of Navajo's identifiable assets was $70 million and consolidated goodwill of $30 million was recognised on acquisition.

Navajo consists of three separate cash generating units (CGUs), Division A, Division B and Division C, which operate independently of each other. Diablo allocated the $30 million consolidated goodwill arising on acquisition to the three cash-generated units based on the fair value of net assets in each division on 1 October 2019. The consolidated goodwill was attributed to the separate cash generating units in the ratio of 2:3:1 to A, B and C respectively on 1 October 2019.

Due to poor trading conditions in the year ended 30 September 2021, an impairment test was carried out.

The fair value of the net assets for each division (excluding the goodwill allocation above) at 30 September 2021 is shown below:

	Division A $000	Division B $000	Division C $000
Property, plant and equipment	20,000	45,000	8,000
Net current assets	10,000	12,000	5,000
	30,000	57,000	13,000

The recoverable amount of each division was based on value in use. The recoverable amount of each division on 30 September 2021 is as follows:

	Division A $000	Division B $000	Division C $000
Recoverable amount	34,000	55,000	19,000

Required

Advise the directors, with suitable calculations, on the accounting treatment of the impairment in Diablo's consolidated financial statements for the year ended 30 September 2021. **(6 marks)**

(b) **Revalued property**

Diablo owns a property which was acquired on 1 October 2016 for $5,000,000. The property had an estimated life of 20 years and is being depreciated on a straight-line basis. The property was revalued to $4,800,000 on 30 September 2020 as permitted by IAS 16 *Property, Plant and Equipment*. The property's useful remaining life was unchanged, and Diablo opted to make the annual transfer between the revaluation surplus and retained earnings for the excess depreciation each year.

As a result of a fall in property prices, the property was subject to an impairment test on 30 September 2021. The results of the impairment test indicated that the property had a value in use of $3,200,000, and its fair value less costs to sell was estimated at $3,400,000.

Required

Advise on how any impairment loss will be accounted for in Diablo's own financial statements for the year ended 30 September 2021. **(7 marks)**

(c) **Loan receivable**

Tucson, a key supplier of the Diablo group, experienced cash flow difficulties during 2020. On 1 October 2020, Diablo provided a five-year $10 million loan to Tucson at an effective rate of interest of 5% per annum to protect its supply chain. The loan was repayable in five equal instalments in arrears, starting on 30 September 2021. Diablo's business model was to collect the underlying cash flows of interest and principal only. On 1 October 2020, the present value of expected credit losses over the duration of the loan (based on a 4% discount factor) was $500,000. Diablo estimated the probability of default in the next 12 months was 20%.

During 2021, Tucson's financial difficulties worsened, and the company was unable to pay its first loan instalment due on 30 September 2021. Diablo's directors believe that the default represents objective evidence of impairment. The present value of the lifetime credit losses was revised to $5 million on 30 September 2021.

3 Roca (November 2021)

Roca is an unquoted trading company. The directors require advice on the treatment of share appreciation rights (SARs), other employment benefits, accounting for a lease, and a future network contract.

(a) **Share appreciation rights (SARs)**

On 1 October 2019, Roca granted 500 $1 share appreciation rights (SARs) to each of its 2,000 employees. Employees will be eligible to exercise their rights on 30 September 2022, provided that they remain employed by Roca.

On 30 September 2020, Roca estimated that 10% of employees would leave within the vesting period and forfeit their rights to the SARs. On 30 September 2021, the estimate of total leavers was revised to 25%.

On 1 October 2019, the fair value of each $1 SAR was $5. This fair value of each $1 SAR was $6 on 30 September 2020 and $8 on 30 September 2021.

The SAR liability was correctly calculated in accordance with IFRS 2 *Share-based payments* on 30 September 2020.

Required

Advise the directors of Roca on the accounting treatment of the SARs in the year ended 30 September 2021. **(5 marks)**

(b) **Employee benefits**

Roca has operated a pension scheme for its employees for a number of years. Under the terms of the scheme, Roca is contractually obliged to make an annual contribution each year equal to 7% of total employee remuneration in the year. Roca has no further contractual obligations under the terms of the pension scheme, and the pension paid to former employees is based solely on the future performance of the pension fund.

Roca paid $500,000 into the pension scheme in the year ended 30 September 2021.

In the year ended 30 September 2021, Roca paid wages and salaries of $8 million. In addition, staff are contractually entitled to a profit related bonus each year. A profit based bonus of $3 million for the year ended 30 September 2021, will be paid out to employees on 23 December 2021.

Required

Advise the directors on how the above employment benefits should be accounted for in Roca's financial statements for the year ended 30 September 2021. **(5 mark)**

(c) **Lease of equipment**

On 1 October 2020, Roca signed a contract to lease an item of equipment for four years. Under the terms of the contract, Roca is required to make four annual payments of $500,000 per annum in arrears commencing on 30 September 2021. The present value of the future lease payments on 1 October 2020 is $1,773,000. The rate of interest implicit in the lease is 5% per annum.

Roca received a cash payment of $50,000 from the lessor on 1 October 2020 as an incentive to sign the lease.

Required

Advise the directors on the correct accounting treatment for the lease in the year ended 30 September 2021. **(5 marks)**

(d) **Future contract for network services**

On 1 October 2021, Roca entered into a contract with Paron, a telecommunications company, for the supply of network services for three years. The contract contains details of Roca's technical specifications and quality levels required.

Under the terms of the contract, Paron will provide and install computer servers (hardware) at Roca's head office on 1 October 2021 when the contract commences. Paron determines the quality and speed of data transportation and can reconfigure or replace the servers as required. Paron is solely responsible for the operation and maintenance of the servers.

The directors of Roca are unsure whether the contract contains a lease under IFRS 16 *Leases* and have come to you for advice.

Required

Advise the directors on whether the contract for network services falls within the scope of IAS 16 *Leases*. Briefly consider the appropriate accounting treatment in the year ended 30 September 2022. **(5 marks)**

(Total 20 marks)

4 Gila (November 2021)

The Gila group consists of Gila, a quoted trading company, and several trading subsidiaries and associates. The following extracts have been taken from the consolidated financial statements for the year ended 30 September 2021:

Extracts from the consolidated statement of financial position:

	2021 $000	2020 $000
Non-current assets		
Property, plant and equipment	61,500	51,000
Goodwill	22,000	25,500
Investment in associates	5,600	5,000
Equity		
Equity $1 shares	31,800	30,000
Share premium	16,200	5,000
Retained earnings	29,500	25,000
	77,500	60,000
Non-controlling interest	12,000	9,000
Total equity	89,500	69,000
Non-current liabilities		
Long term borrowings	15,000	10,000

EXAM QUESTION BANK

Extracts from the consolidated statement of profit or loss for the year ended 30 September 2021:

	$000
Share of profit from associates	1,600
Profit for the year attributable to:	
Owners of the parent	7,500
Non-controlling interest	1,500
	9,000

There were no disposals of property, plant and equipment in the year. Depreciation of $7,000,000 was charged to profit and loss in the year ended 30 September 2021.

Gila acquired a 30% significant interest in Huachuca for cash on 1 May 2021. Gila received dividends from associates during the year of $2,000,000.

On 30 September 2021, Gila acquired an 80% equity interest in Laguna. The consideration paid consisted of $3,000,000 in cash and the issue of 1 million $1 shares in Gila, which had a market value of $7.00 each on 30 September 2021.

The fair value of Laguna's assets acquired and liabilities assumed on 30 September 2021 are shown below:

	$000
Property, plant and equipment	2,500
Net current assets (inventories, receivables, payables)	3,000
Cash and cash equivalents	1,000
	6,500
Equity $1 shares	1,000
Retained earnings	5,500
	6,500

It is group policy to measure the non-controlling interest at fair value at the date of acquisition. The fair value of Laguna's non-controlling interest on 30 September 2021 was $2,500,000.

Required

(a) Prepare the following extracts from the consolidated statement of cash flows for the year ended 30 September 2021:

    (i) Cash flows from investing activities
    (ii) Cash flows from financing activities **(10 marks)**

(b) **Disclosures**

During the year ended 30 September 2021, approximately 20% of Gila's purchases came from Tota, a company owned by the finance director's wife. The price paid for the goods was considerably higher than market value.

The finance director feels that it is unnecessary to disclose these transactions in the financial statements for the year ended 30 September 2021. He argues that the goods supplied by Tota were of higher quality to those obtained from other suppliers, and that the transactions took place at an arm's length basis.

Required

Advise whether the transactions with Tota require separate disclosure in Gila's financial statements for the year ended 30 September 2021 and briefly discuss any ethical issues arising.

You should refer to relevant IFRS and IFRS Practice Statement 2 *Making Materiality Judgements* as appropriate .**(10 marks)**

(Total 20 marks)

5 Amyklas (May 2022)

Amyklas is the parent company of the Amyklas group.

Amyklas is a mining company established in 1970. In April 2017, it acquired an 80% controlling interest in Dion, a clothing retailer, to diversify its operations. Despite being a profitable acquisition, the management of Dion took up a disproportionate amount of the directors' time. Therefore, in April 2021 the directors decided to sell its investment in Dion to focus on its core business activities in the mining industry. The sale took place on 30 September 2021.

On 1 April 2021, Amyklas acquired a 75% shareholding in Nabis, a mining company, to strengthen its strategic position within the mining industry.

The statements of financial position for each group member as at 31 March 2022 is shown below:

	Amyklas $000	Dion $000	Nabis $000
ASSETS			
Non-current assets			
Property, plant and equipment	1,800	1,450	1,100
Investments			
– In Dion (notes 1 & 2)	1,760		
– In Nabis (notes 3 & 4)	1,325		
	4,885	1,450	1,100
Current assets			
Inventories	320	260	210
Trade and other receivables	290	240	190
Cash and cash equivalents	3,800	100	50
	4,410	600	450
Total assets	9,295	2,050	1,550
EQUITY AND LIABILITIES			
Equity			
Equity $1 shares	1,000	800	500
Retained earnings	2,945	650	450
	3,945	1,450	950
Non-current liabilities	500	400	350
Current liabilities	1,450	200	250
Suspense account - disposal of Dion (note 2)	3,400	-	-
Total equity and liabilities	9,295	2,050	1,550

The following information is relevant:

1 Amyklas acquired 80% of Dion's $1 equity share capital on 1 April 2017 for $1,760,000. At the date of acquisition Dion's retained earnings were $200,000.

On 1 April 2017, the fair value of Dion's net assets acquired were equal to their book value, with the exception of depreciable property, plant and equipment, whose fair value was $100,000 higher than its book value. The property, plant and equipment had a remaining useful life of 10 years on 1 April 2017. Depreciation is charged on a monthly basis.

It is group policy to measure the non-controlling interest at fair value at the date of acquisition. On 1 April 2017, the fair value of the non-controlling interest in Dion was $440,000.

The consolidated goodwill arising on acquisition of Dion, had previously been impaired by 20% in the year ended 31 March 2020. No further goodwill impairments have been required.

Dion's reported profit for the year ended 31 March 2022 was $300,000. Assume that profits accrue evenly over the year.

2   On 30 September 2021, Amyklas sold its entire 80% investment in Dion for $3,400,000. The directors of Amyklas were unsure how to account for the disposal, and therefore debited cash and credited a suspense account with the sale proceeds.

3   On 1 April 2021, Amyklas acquired a 75% shareholding in Nabis for $1,325,000 in cash which was paid immediately and is correctly accounted for in its statement of financial position shown above. Amyklas is contractually required to pay additional consideration of $242,000 on 31 March 2023. No entries have been made in respect of this additional consideration due. A 10% discount factor should be used where relevant.

On 1 April 2021, Nabis had retained earnings of $350,000 and the fair value of its net assets was $1,150,000. The difference between the book value and fair value of the net assets acquired relates to non-depreciable land.

The fair value of the non-controlling interest in Nabis was $500,000 on 1 April 2021.

4   On 31 March 2022, the recoverable amount of Nabis was $1,725,000. The directors would like you to calculate and account for any necessary impairment loss.

Required

(a) Critically evaluate the extent that the classification and subsequent accounting treatment of discontinued operations under IFRS 5 *Non-current Assets Held for Sale and Discontinued Operations* is consistent with the requirements of the *Conceptual Framework for Financial Reporting* (2018) **.(5 marks)**

(b) Advise the directors on whether the disposal of Dion on 30 September 2021 represents a discontinued operation in accordance with IFRS 5 *Non-current Assets Held for Sale and Discontinued Operations* and explain how this might affect the presentation of the consolidated financial statement of profit or loss and other comprehensive income for the year ended 31 March 2022.

Calculations are not required. **(5 marks)**

(c) Calculate the group profit on disposal of Dion for inclusion in the consolidated statement of profit or loss for the year ended 31 March 2022. **(5 marks)**

(d) Prepare the consolidated statement of financial position for the Amyklas group as at 31 March 2022. **(20 marks)**

(e) On 1 April 2022, Amyklas disposed of 100,000 $1 equity shares in Nabis for $300,000 (a 20% equity shareholding). The directors of Amyklas are unsure of the accounting treatment of this disposal and require your advice on the accounting treatment in the consolidated statements for the year ended 31 March 2023.

Required

Advise, with suitable computations, how the disposal of the 100,000 $1 equity shares in Nabis, should be accounted for in the consolidated financial statements for the year ended 31 March 2023. **(5 marks)**

(Total = 40 marks)

6 Spartan (May 2022)

Spartan is a manufacturer of kitchens and bathrooms. The company has grown rapidly due to a recent increase in demand for home improvements. Spartan mainly sells to trade retailers but has recently begun selling direct to the public. The directors of Spartan are currently finalising the financial statements for the year ended 31 March 2022. They have approached you for advice on matters relating to revenue recognition and the issue of a convertible bond.

(a) **New commercial contracts**

Spartan entered into two new commercial contracts in the year ended 31 March 2022. Due to high competition in the kitchen and bathroom retail sector, Spartan was required to offer each new client bespoke terms to win the contracts.

Contract 1

On 1 October 2021, Spartan entered into a 12-month contract to supply a national retailer with bathroom suites. The sales value of the contract was $2,500,000.

Under the terms of the contract, Spartan was required to make an upfront non-refundable payment to the retailer of $250,000. The payment was required to cover the cost of modifications to the retailer's display areas. Spartan made the payment on 1 October 2021 and immediately expensed the $250,000 to the profit or loss account.

By 31 March 2022, Spartan had sold goods with a market value of $1,250,000 to the client.

Contract 2

On 28 February 2022, Spartan secured a contract with an independent retailer to supply kitchens. Under the terms of the contract, Spartan will supply the kitchens to the client on 90 days approval, during which time the client can return the goods without penalty.

In March 2022, Spartan delivered kitchens with a market value of $400,000 to the client. The kitchens had cost $250,000 to manufacture. The sale has been recorded in the draft financial statements for the year ended 31 March 2022.

This is the first time that Spartan has sold goods on approval. The sales director is confident that the new client will accept the goods but is unable to produce relevant historical evidence in support of this claim.

Required

Advise the directors of Spartan how the above contracts should be accounted for. **(7 marks)**

(b) **Non-refundable deposits**

Spartan has recently started selling its products direct to the public. Customers are required to pay a non-refundable deposit of 10% of the sales price at the time the order is placed. The remainder of the balance is payable on delivery of the goods.

Non-refundable deposits of $300,000 in total were collected from customers in March 2022. Due to supply chain issues, it is expected that the goods will not be available for customer collection until May 2022. The directors have recognised the full $300,000 as revenue in the draft financial statements for the year ended 31 March 2022 as the deposits are non-refundable.

Required

Advise the directors of Spartan on how the non-refundable deposits received from customers should be accounted for. **(3 marks)**

(c) **Convertible loan stock**

On 1 April 2021, Spartan issued 2,000 units of convertible loan stock at par value of $1,000 per unit to fund the expansion of its manufacturing business.

The convertible loan stock pays coupon interest of 3% per annum. Each $1,000 unit of loan stock can either be redeemed at par or converted into 2,000 $1 Spartan shares on 31 March 2024, at the option of the holder. The market rate of interest for similar three-year loan stock with no rights of conversion was 9% on 1 April 2021.

Spartan incurred loan stock issue costs of $100,000 on 1 April 2021.

When preparing the draft accounts for the year ended 31 March 2022, the directors credited an equity reserve with the full $2,000,000 proceeds received, as they felt confident that all loan stockholders would take the equity share option at the redemption/conversion date.

In addition, the directors have expensed both the transaction costs and the 3% coupon interest paid to the profit or loss account in the year.

You have calculated that the effective rate of interest on the financial liability component of the bond (as adjusted for transaction costs) is 11%,

The following discount factors have been provided:

Periods	3%	9%	11%
1	0.971	0.917	0.901
2	0.943	0.842	0.813
3	0.915	0.772	0.731

Required

Advise the directors, with suitable calculations, on the accounting treatment of the convertible loan stock in the financial statements of Spartan for the year ended 31 March 2022. Show the double entry for any corrections you are required to make to the draft financial statements. **(10 marks)**

(Total 20 marks)

7 Mesoa (May 2022)

Mesoa is a quoted trading company. The directors of Mesoa require your advice on accounting for a defined benefit pension plan, equity share options and two deferred tax issues in the year ended 31 March 2022.

(a) **Defined benefit pension plan**

Mesoa operates a defined benefit pension plan (DB plan) for all of its employees. On the 1 April 2021, the DB plan showed a net deficit of $5,000,000 brought forward. This net deficit was presented as a 'net pension liability' under non-current liabilities in Mesoa's own financial statements for the year ended 31 March 2021.

The current service cost for the year ended 31 March 2022 has been estimated at $550,000. During the year ended 31 March 2022, Mesoa made cash contributions into the DB plan of $750,000 and benefits paid to former employees were $400,000.

On 1 April 2021, the rules of the DB plan were amended to provide additional benefits to members. The present value of the increase in the future pension obligation was estimated at $500,000 on 1 April 2021.

The yield on high quality corporate bonds was 6% on 1 April 2021 and this rose to 7% by 31 March 2022.

On 31 March 2022, the actuarial report indicated that the DB plan deficit had increased to $6,100,000 by the year end.

Required

Calculate the amounts to be included in the Mesoa's statement of profit or loss and other comprehensive income for the year ended 31 March 2022 for the DB plan. **(6 marks)**

(b) **Equity share options**

On 1 April 2020, Mesoa granted 500 $1 share options to 1,000 employees on condition that they remain in employment on 31 March 2023. The fair value of each $1 share option on 1 April 2020 was $9.

On 31 March 2021 the directors of Mesoa estimated that 20% of the relevant employees would leave over the vesting period and would forfeit their rights to the shares.

On 31 March 2022, the directors revised their estimate of expected employee departures to 15% over the three-year vesting period.

In the tax jurisdiction in which Mesoa operates, tax relief is available on the intrinsic value of the share option at the date of exercise. The intrinsic value of each $1 share option was estimated at $4.50 on 31 March 2021 and $5.70 on 31 March 2022.

Whilst preparing the financial statements for the year ended 31 March 2022, it was discovered that the deferred tax on the share options had been erroneously omitted from the financial statements for the year ended 31 March 2021. The directors are unsure of how to correct this as the 2021 accounts have been signed off and filed with the relevant authority.

Assume a tax rate of 20% applies.

Required

Advise the directors on the financial accounting treatment of the employee share options for the year ended 31 March 2022 and explain how the deferred tax omission from the 2021 financial statements should be dealt with. **(10 marks)**

(c) **Trading losses**

Mesoa has experienced trading difficulties recently due to the COVID-19 pandemic. In the previous year ended 31 March 2021, Mesoa reported a tax-adjusted trading loss of $100 million. The tax-adjusted trading loss for the year ended 31 March 2022 (after adjustments for items (a) and (b) above) has been calculated at $10 million. The directors expect that the company will break even in the year ended 31 March 2023 and will return to profitability in 2024.

The directors have recognised a deferred tax asset of $22 million [($100m + $10) x 20%] in the statement of financial position as at 31 March 2022.

In the tax jurisdiction in which Mesoa operates trading losses can be carried forward against future profits for a maximum of two years.

Assume a tax rate of 20% applies.

Required

Advise the directors of Mesoa on the financial accounting treatment of the deferred tax asset in the financial statements for the year ended 31 March 2022. **(4 marks)**

(Total 20 marks)

8 Prytanis (May 2022)

The Prytanis group is a retail trading group which consists of a number of wholly owned subsidiaries and one 40% associate. The functional currency of the Prytanis group is the dollar "$".

(a) **Cash flows from operating activities**

The figures shown below have been extracted from the consolidated financial statements for the year ended 31 March 2022:

Extracts from the consolidated statement of profit or loss for the year ended 31 March 2022

	$m
Profit before tax (note 1)	300
Taxation	(55)
Profit for the year	245

Extracts from the consolidated statement of financial position as at 31 March 2022

	2022 $m	2021 $m
Non-current assets		
Property, plant and equipment (note 2)	170	120
Goodwill	130	110
Investment in associate (note 1)	20	50
Current assets		
Inventories	75	60
Trade receivables	90	70
Current liabilities		
Trade and other payables	85	45
Tax payable	15	20

The following information is relevant:

1. The associate reported a total loss of $50 million in the year ended 31 March 2022. The consolidated profit before tax figure above includes the group's share of the associate's loss of $20 million. Due to associate's poor financial performance the directors conducted an impairment review on 31 March 2022. The impairment loss relating to the associate has been debited to the profit or loss account. The associate did not pay out any dividends in the year.

   Depreciation on property, plant and equipment for the year has been correctly calculated and charged to the profit or loss account.

   Finance costs of $30 million were debited to the profit and loss account in the year. This includes finance costs of $5 million charged on a $20 million zero-coupon bond which was held on an amortised cost basis.

2. On 1 September 2021, Prytanis acquired property, plant and equipment for 240 million Francs on credit. The invoice was paid in full on 31 December 2021. The relevant exchange rates are shown as follows:

Exchange rates	$1: Francs
1 September 2021	$1: 6 Francs
31 December 2021	$1: 5 Francs

   Any resulting foreign exchange loss/gain on settlement has been correctly calculated and debited/credited to the profit or loss account.

   There were no disposals of property, plant and equipment in the year.

3   On 1 January 2022, Prytanis acquired 100% of the equity share capital of Gorgo. Consolidated goodwill relating to this acquisition of $20 million has been correctly calculated and included in the extracts above. The fair value of Gorgo's net assets on 1 January 2022 include the following:

	$m
Property, plant and equipment	35
Inventories	25
Trade receivables	15
Trade payables	(30)

Consolidated goodwill was not impaired in the year ended 31 March 2022.

Required

Prepare the "Cash flows from operating activities" section of the consolidated statement of cash flows for the ended 31 March 2022, using the indirect method. **(10 marks)**

(b) **Excessive disclosures**

The directors of the Prytanis group are becoming increasing concerned about the volume of disclosures required in the financial statements. They feel that the cost of producing these disclosures far outweigh the benefits provided to the users of financial statements.

Required

Critically evaluate the directors' comments on the usefulness of comprehensive disclosures in the financial statements. You should consider any benefits from, and barriers to, reduced disclosure in financial statement and refer to relevant IFRS including Practice Statement 2: *Making Materiality Judgements*. **(10 marks)**

(Total 20 marks)

9 Argon (November 2022)

Argon is the parent company of the Argon group, whose functional currency is the dollar ($). Argon acquired controlling interests in two unconnected companies, Cobalt and Zinc, during the year ended 30 September 2022.

Extracts from Argon, Cobalt and Zinc's financial statements for the year ended 30 September 2022 are shown below:

Statements of profit and loss for the year ended 30 September 2022:

	Argon	Cobalt	Zinc
	$000	$000	ZL 000
Revenue	9,400	4,400	37,908
Cost of sales	(4,500)	(1,800)	(11,880)
Gross profit	4,900	2,600	26,028
Distribution costs	(950)	(700)	(4,860)
Administrative expenses	(540)	(520)	(4,320)
Investment income	550		
Profit before tax	3,960	1,380	16,848
Income tax expense	(650)	(280)	(2,160)
Profit for the year	3,310	1,100	14,688

Extract from the statements of financial position as at 30 September 2022:

	Argon $000	Cobalt $000	Zinc ZL 000
EQUITY			
Equity share capital	5,000	1,000	1,000
Retained earnings:			
At 1 October 2021	10,000	3,500	12,500
Profit for the year	3,310	1,100	14,688
Dividends paid on 30 September 2022	(1,000)	(600)	-
At 30 September 2022	12,310	4,000	27,188
	17,310	5,000	28,188

The following information is relevant:

1 On 1 October 2021, Argon acquired 80% of the equity share capital of Zinc, an overseas company, as part of the group's international expansion plan. Zinc is based in Poland, where the domestic currency is the Zloty (ZL). Zinc manufactures goods in Poland and all raw materials, labour and other manufacturing costs are purchased and paid for in Zloty. Approximately two-thirds of all sales are exports abroad to unconnected parties and are invoiced in dollars. The remaining revenue is from domestic sales in Poland which are invoiced in Zloty. Following the acquisition, Zinc continues to operate independently from the rest of the group. All strategic and operational decisions are made by Zinc's board of directors based in Poland. Zinc's profits will continue to be retained in Zloty and are available for future investment as required. It is anticipated the Zinc will not be required to declare any dividends in the foreseeable future.

The directors of Argon require advice on how to determine Zinc's functional currency post acquisition. In addition, the directors would like to know how Zinc's functional currency would affect the preparation of the consolidated statement of financial position and statement of financial position for the year ended 30 September 2022.

2 Argon paid $5,000,000 to acquire 80% of the equity shares in Zinc on 1 October 2021.

At the date of acquisition, the fair value of Zinc's assets and liabilities were ZL 20,250,000 and it had retained earnings of ZL 12,500,000. The difference between the fair value and book value of Zinc's net assets at acquisition relates to depreciable property, plant and equipment with a remaining life of five years on 1 October 2021. Depreciation of property, plant and equipment is charged to cost of sales.

It is group policy to measure the non-controlling interest at fair value at the date of acquisition. The fair value of Zinc's non-controlling interest on 1 October 2021 was ZL 6,250,000.

Zinc was subject to an impairment test on 30 September 2022, and consolidated goodwill should be written down by ZL 2,700,000. Goodwill impairment losses are recognised in administrative expenses.

Relevant exchange rates are as follows:

	ZL: $1
1 October 2021	5
30 September 2022	6
Average rate for the year ended 30 September 2022	5.4

3 Argon acquired 40% of Cobalt's $1 equity shares 1 October 2020 for $2,000,000. From that date, Argon was entitled to appoint four out of ten directors to Cobalt's board and exercised a significant influence over its financial and operating policies. Cobalt's retained earnings were $2,500,000 on 1 October 2020.

On 1 April 2022, Argon acquired an additional 35% of Cobalt's $1 equity shares for $2,800,000 cash.

Cobalt's share price on 1 April 2022 was $8 per share.

The fair value of Cobalt's identifiable assets and liabilities was equal to their book value on 1 April 2022.

Cobalt paid a dividend on 30 September 2022, and Argon correctly included its share of the dividend in its own financial statements.

Assume that profits occur evenly throughout the year.

Required

(a) Advise the directors of Argon on how Zinc's functional currency should be determined and briefly discuss how this would affect the preparation of the consolidated statements for the year ended 30 September 2022. **(10 marks)**

(b) Calculate the goodwill balance for inclusion in the consolidated statement of financial position as at 30 September 2022 arising on the acquisition of Cobalt and Zinc during the year. **(10 marks)**

(c) Calculate the current year translation difference on Zinc's net assets for inclusion in the consolidated statement of profit or loss and other comprehensive income for the year ended 30 September 2022. **(5 marks)**

(d) Prepare Argon's consolidated statement of profit or loss and other comprehensive income for the year ended 30 September 2022. **(15 marks)**

(Total 40 marks)

10 Neon (November 2022)

Neon is a manufacturing company which prepares its accounts to 30 September each year. Neon has entered into three separate leasing transactions for the first time in the year ended 30 September 2022. The directors are unsure how to account for them and have come to you for advice on the correct accounting treatment.

(a) **Sale and lease back**

On 1 October 2021, Neon entered into a sale and leaseback agreement with a bank to sell its head office. Under the terms of the agreement, the property was sold to the bank for $4,000,000 and immediately leased back under a five-year lease. The fair value of the property was $3,600,000 on 1 October 2021. The excess consideration received of $400,000 represents additional loan finance provided by the bank.

Under the terms of the sale Neon is required to pay five annual instalments of $500,000 per annum in arrears commencing on 30 September 2022. On 1 October 2021, the present value of the future payments due was $1,895,000, of which $1,495,000 relates to the lease and $400,000 to the additional loan finance provided.

Neon had initially acquired the property on 1 October 2011 for $1,250,000 and depreciated it on a straight-line basis over its expected useful life of 50 years.

The rate of interest implicit in the lease is 10% per annum.

Required

Advise the directors of Neon on how the sale and lease back transaction should be accounted for in the year ended 30 September 2022. **(10 marks)**

(b) **Investment Property**

On 1 October 2021, Neon acquired an investment property for $8,000,000 which it immediately let out under a five-year lease to Cee. The property had a useful economic life of 50 years on 1 October 2021. Neon acquired the property for its investment potential and will retain legal title to the property throughout its useful life.

Under the terms of the lease, Cee is required to pay rent of $500,000 per annum. To secure the lease, Neon agreed to a six month 'rent free' period at the start of the lease.

This is the first investment property Neon has acquired and the directors are unsure how to account for it.

Required

Advise the directors of Neon on the investment property transactions in the year ended 30 September 2022. **(4 marks)**

(c) **Contract for energy**

On 30 September 2022, Neon signed a 25-year contract with GreenCo, a utility supplier, to purchase all the electricity produced by a new solar power plant with effect from 1 October 2022.

The solar power plant is specifically stated in the contract, and GreenCo has no substitution rights. All electricity produced by the solar power plant will be purchased by Neon and GreenCo cannot provide electricity from an alternative solar power source.

The solar power plant has been purpose built to meet Neon's requirements. Neon previously hired a team of solar experts to design the solar power plant and to determine its location. GreenCo is responsible for the construction, operation, and maintenance of the solar power plant in line with Neon's specific requirements. Legal title of the solar power plant belongs to GreenCo, who will be entitled to claim tax credits on its construction. Neon will be eligible to claim renewable energy tax credits on the electricity purchased each year.

The directors of Neon are unsure whether the contract with GreenCo contains a lease under IFRS 16 *Leases*.

Required

Advise the directors of Neon on whether the above contract with GreenCo contains a lease in accordance with IFRS 16 *Leases*. **(6 marks)**

(Total 20 marks)

11 Krypton (November 2022)

Krypton is a quoted biotech company specialising in the development of new generation technologies for use in the early detection of human diseases and viruses.

On 1 October 2021, Krypton borrowed $10,000,000 from a bank to fund further development work. The loan agreement stipulates that Krypton's gearing ratio (calculated as long-term liabilities/equity) should not exceed 100%. In the event of the gearing ratio exceeding the 100% limit, the loan will be repayable in full immediately.

The following extract is taken from Krypton's draft statement of financial position for the year ended 30 September 2022:

	$
Non-current liabilities	
Bank loan	10,000,000
Equity	
Equity share capital – $1	1,000,000
Retained earnings	7,100,000
Other components of equity	3,000,000

The draft financial statements are due to be presented for approval at the next board meeting, which is scheduled to take place on 1 December 2022.

A member of the finance team has recently raised concerns over the accounting treatment of two specific items (listed below) with the internal audit committee. The finance director has been suspended pending a full investigation. You have been asked to advise on the correct accounting treatment of each issue raised as part of the investigation.

(a) **Biotech plant**

On 1 October 2021, Krypton acquired a new biotech plant for $4,000,000 which has an expected useful life of 15 years. Depreciation is charged on a straight-line basis. The finance director has capitalised the cost of the plant and has correctly calculated and charged one year's worth of straight-line depreciation to profit or loss in the year.

To be awarded a licence to operate the biotech plant, Krypton is contractually obliged to decommission the biotech plant at the end of its useful life. The present value of the decommissioning costs in fifteen years' time has been correctly calculated at $375,000 on 1 October 2021, based on risk-adjusted discount factor of 10%. As per the finance director's specific instructions, no entries have been made relating to the future decommissioning costs in the draft accounts.

Required

Advise on how the decommissioning costs should be accounted for in the financial statements for the year ended 30 September 2022. **(6 marks)**

(b) **Share appreciation rights**

On 1 October 2021, Krypton issued 500 $1 share appreciation rights (SARs) to each of its 1,000 staff. The SARs vest in three years' time when each member of staff will receive a cash payment based on the intrinsic value of each $1 SAR at that date.

The intrinsic value of each $1 SARs is shown below:

1 October 2021	$8.50
30 September 2022	$9.90
30 September 2024 (estimate)	$16.80

It is anticipated that 20% of staff will leave over the three-year vesting period and will forfeit their rights to the SARs.

No entries have been made in the draft accounts in respect of the SARs, despite the finance director being fully aware that this contravenes the requirements of IFRS 2 *Share Based Payments*.

Required

Advise the correct accounting treatment of the share appreciation rights (SARs) in the year ended 30 September 2022. **(4 marks)**

(c) Based on your recommendations in (a) and (b) calculate a revised gearing ratio for the year ended 30 September 2022. **(3 marks)**

(d) Critically discuss any ethical issues arising from the above scenario and the implications for the borrowing covenant. **(7 marks)**

(Total 20 marks)

12 Xenon (November 2022)

(a) The Xenon group comprises of Xenon and its one subsidiary Radon. The group specialises in voice recognition technology that is powered by artificial intelligence (AI).

Xenon acquired 90% of the equity shares in Radon for $11,250,000 on 1 October 2019 when its retained earnings were $4,300,000. The fair value of Radon's net assets were equivalent to their carrying value at that date. Xenon opted to measure the non-controlling interest at fair value of $1,250,000 on 1 October 2019.

The following extracts have been taken from the statements of financial position for the year ended 30 September 2022:

	Xenon $000	Radon $000
Share capital - $1 equity shares	1,000	1,000
Retained earnings		
At 1.10.21	25,000	8,500
Profit for the year ended 30 September 2022	6,000	3,200
Dividends (paid 30 September 2022)	(2,000)	(1,200)
Retained earnings at 30.9.22	29,000	10,500
Total equity	30,000	11,500

The following information is relevant for the year ended 30 September 2022:

1. On 1 April 2022, Xenon disposed of 250,000 shares in Radon for $3,600,000. No entries have been made in respect of this disposal in Xenon's own individual financial statements.

2. Assume profit accrues evenly throughout the year.

Required

Prepare the consolidated statement of changes in equity for the Xenon Group for the year ended 30 September 2022 **(12 marks)**

(b) The Xenon group was founded in 2002, by Teng Li who currently owns 100% of Xenon's $1 equity share capital. The business has grown rapidly due to the demand for AI enabled voice recognition technology. Teng plans to exit the business in the next few years to pursue other interests. He intends to sell his shares in Xenon at a significant premium on exit from the business and is currently looking at ways to attract suitable buyers who are willing to pay a high price.

Teng has recently read an article on how integrated reporting can help communicate value creation within a firm. He is keen to explore the prospect of adopting integrated reporting within the Xenon group and would like to know whether this might help attract a potential buyer.

Required

Critically discuss to what extent the adoption of integrated reporting could help maximise the potential to attract a buyer for Xenon, as part of Teng's exit strategy from the business. **(8 marks)**

(Total = 20 marks)

13 Nysa (May 2023)

Nysa is the parent company of a trading group which operates in the electric vehicle charging market. The Nysa group has built up a strong reputation within the renewable energy sector for its environmental and social policies and practices.

The Nysa group comprises of three entities: Nysa, Xanadu and Eden.

In addition, Nysa acquired a 50% equity investment in Nbu, a newly established joint arrangement for $10 million on 1 April 2022.

The statements of financial position of Nysa, Xanadu and Eden for the year ended 31 March 2023 are shown below:

	Nysa $m	Xanadu $m	Eden $m
ASSETS			
Non-current assets			
Property, plant and equipment	242	30	20
Intangible assets	100	50	25
Investments			
– Xanadu	90	-	-
– Eden	-	50	-
– Nbu	10	-	-
	442	130	45
Current assets	140	50	30
Total assets	582	180	75
EQUITY AND LIABILITIES			
Equity			
Equity shares - $1 shares	100	50	10
Retained earnings	222	56	30
Other components of equity	50	14	-
	372	120	40
Non-current liabilities	100	30	10
Current liabilities	110	30	25
Total equity and liabilities	582	180	75

The following information is relevant:

1 **Acquisition of Nbu**

 On 1 April 2022 Nysa entered into a joint arrangement with Valhalla (an unconnected entity) to operate a new electric charging network. A newly established entity, Nbu, was set up to run the arrangement.

 Nysa and Valhalla each paid $10 million for a 50% share of Nbu's equity share capital.

 Under the terms of the arrangement all decisions require unanimous agreement from both investors. Each investor is entitled to a 50% share of Nbu's net assets on the winding up of Nbu.

 In the year ended 31 March 2023, Nbu's reported profit after taxation was $8 million.

 The directors are unsure of the accounting treatment of the joint arrangement and have asked you for advice on this matter.

2 **Acquisition of Xanadu**

 Nysa acquired a 75% equity interest in Xanadu on 1 April 2020 for $90 million. On 1 April 2020, the balances on Xanadu's retained earnings and other components of equity were $35 million and

$10 million respectively. The fair value of Xanadu's net assets was calculated at $100 million at the date of acquisition.

The difference between the fair value of the net assets acquired and their carrying amounts relates to Xanadu's internally generated intangible assets which had an estimated useful life of five years on 1 April 2020.

It is group policy to measure the non-controlling interest at fair value at the date of acquisition. Xanadu's non-controlling interest had a fair value of $30 million on 1 April 2020.

No impairment losses have been previously recognised in earlier years. On 31 March 2023, Xanadu's recoverable amount was calculated at $132 million.

3 **Acquisition of Eden**

On 1 April 2022, Xanadu acquired an 80% equity interest in Eden for $50 million. The cost of the investment in Eden has been correctly accounted for in Xanadu's own financial statements shown above.

Eden had retained earnings of $25 million on 1 April 2022. At the date of acquisition, Eden's net assets had a fair value of $45 million. The difference between the fair value of Eden's net assets and their carrying amounts is attributed to non-depreciable land.

The fair value of Eden's net assets of $45 million above does not include a contingent liability which Eden had disclosed in its own financial accounts. The contingent liability had a fair value of $5 million on 1 April 2022 and this had reduced to $nil on 31 March 2023.

Eden's non-controlling interest is valued at fair value at the date of acquisition. Eden's $1 equity shares were quoted at $6.25 per share on 1 April 2022.

Required

(a) Advise Nysa's directors on how the investment in Nbu should be accounted for in the consolidated financial statements for the year ended 31 March 2023. **(5 marks)**

(b) Prepare the consolidated statement of financial position for the Nysa group as at the year ended 31 March 2023.

Work to the nearest $0.1 million and show all your workings. **(25 marks)**

(c) The rapidly increasing global focus on sustainability related issues has led to a widespread increase in sustainability reporting. Sustainability reporting integrates an entity's environmental, social and governance (ESG) performance.

ESG performance is becoming increasingly important to investors and more and more investors are choosing to incorporate ESG factors into their decision-making process.

Required

Critically discuss why ESG performance has become increasingly important to investors when making their investment decisions. **(10 marks)**

(Total 40 marks)

14 Nirvana (May 2023)

Nirvana is a manufacturing company whose functional currency is the dollar ($). The following transactions took place in the year ended 31 March 2023.

(a) **Sterling Bonds**

On 1 April 2022, Nirvana issued £10 million 6% five-year sterling bonds and incurred issue costs of £0.2 million (all figures stated in UK pounds sterling).

The sterling bonds are traded on the London Stock Exchange in the UK. Coupon interest is paid annually in arrears, in UK pounds sterling, on 31 March each year.

The sterling bonds will be redeemed in five years' time at a premium. The effective rate of interest is 6.5%.

The following exchange rates have been provided:

	£1:$
1 April 2022	£1 : $1.30
31 March 2023	£1 : $1.20
Average rate for the year ended 31 March 2023	£1 : $1.25

The directors are unsure of how to account for the sterling bonds in the financial statements for the year ended 31 March 2023.

Required

Advise the directors on the accounting treatment of the sterling bonds in the financial statements for the year ended 31 March 2023. **(7 marks)**

(b) **Aluminium forward contract**

On 1 February 2023, Nirvana entered a forward contract to purchase 3,000 tonnes of aluminium for $2,300 per tonne for delivery on 30 June 2023. Under the terms of the forward contract Nirvana can either take delivery of the aluminium on 30 June 2023, or can settle the contract net in cash.

On 31 March 2023, the price of aluminium has risen to $2,500 per tonne.

Required

Advise the directors on the accounting treatment of the aluminium forward contract if:

(i) Nirvana intends to take physical delivery of the aluminium on 30 June 2023 for business use; or

(ii) The forward contract is a speculative contract which Nirvana intends to settle net in cash on 30 June 2023.

(6 marks)

(c) **Defined benefit pension plan**

Nirvana operates a defined benefit pension plan for the benefit of its employees. On retirement, each employee will qualify for an annual pension based on their final salary and the number of years' service with Nirvana.

The following information is relevant for the year ended 31 March 2023:

	$m
Present value of the pension obligation:	
– At 31 March 2022	62
– At 31 March 2023	75
Fair value of the pension plan assets:	
– At 31 March 2022	50
– At 31 March 2023	60

	$m
Current service cost for the year	20

Discount factors
- At 31 March 2022   6%
- At 31 March 2023   7%

Nirvana contributed $20 million cash into the pension plan during the year. Benefits paid to former employees amounted to $12 million in the year ended 31 March 2023.

On 1 April 2022, the terms of the defined benefit plan were amended to enhance the benefits paid to former employees. This amendment resulted in an increase to the present value of the defined benefit obligation of $8 million on 1 April 2022.

Required

Advise the directors on how the defined benefit plan should be accounted for in the year ended 31 March 2023. **(7 marks)**

(Total 20 marks)

15 Nibiru (May 2023)

Nibiru is a quoted trading company. The directors of Nibiru require your advice on the accounting treatment of the following transactions which took place in the year ended 31 March 2023.

(a) **Readily traded asset**

Nibiru has recently started trading in an asset that is readily traded in three separate markets: Europe, the United Kingdom (UK) and the United States of America (USA). The asset is held on a fair value basis in accordance with IFRS 13 *Fair Value Measurement*.

Nibiru currently trades in the asset in the USA market only. The directors of Nibiru are keen to expand into Europe and UK markets as part of their medium term expansion strategy.

The directors are unsure how to determine the fair value per unit of the asset for inclusion in the financial statements for the year ended 31 March 2023.

The following information is relevant for the year ended 31 March 2023:

	Europe	UK	USA
Volume sales in market (in units)	5 million	2 million	3 million
	$	$	$
Sales price (per unit)	150	180	130
Transaction costs (per unit)	15	18	13
Transport costs (per unit)	10	5	8

Required

Advise the directors of Nibiru how the fair value per unit should be determined in accordance with IFRS 13 Fair Value Measurement. **(6 marks)**

(b) **Development land**

Nibiru owns a large plot of land that has previously been used for agricultural purposes. The land is situated in an upcoming residential development area.

Similar plots of agricultural land have been developed into luxury residential accommodation. Nibiru has recently applied for planning permission to develop the land for residential purposes. The directors are confident that planning permission will be granted by mid-summer 2023 and plan to start construction work soon after.

Nibiru paid $2 million for the land several years ago. A valuation exercise was carried out on 31 March 2023 by an independent valuer. The land was valued at $5 million for agricultural purposes and at $10 million for residential use.

Required

Advise the directors of Nibiru how to determine the fair value of the land on 31 March 2023 as per IFRS 13 *Fair Value Measurement*. **(4 marks)**

(c) **Interest free loans**

On 1 April 2022, Nibiru issued $10 million interest free loans to its employees. The loans are repayable in full in three years' time. The current market rate of interest for similar three-year loans is 8%. Nibiru's business model is to collect the underlying cash flows of interest and principal only.

Required

Advise the directors of Nibiru on the correct accounting treatment of the interest free loans in the financial statements for the year ended 31 March 2023. **(5 marks)**

(d) **Share options**

On 1 April 2022, Nibiru issued 500 $1 share options to each of its 1,000 staff. The share options are conditional on staff being employed by Nibiru on 31 March 2025. The fair value of the share option was calculated at $10 per share on 1 April 2022.

The share options cannot be exercised unless Nibiru's share price reaches $25 on 31 March 2025. Provided the share price target is met, the share options can be exercised at any time during the following two years i.e., from 1 April 2025 to 31 March 2027.

On 1 April 2022, the directors estimated that 20% of the staff would leave and forfeit their rights to the shares. This estimate was subsequently revised down to 15% on 31 March 2023.

Nibiru's $1 equity shares were quoted at $20 per share on 1 April 2022 and at $22 on 31 March 2023. The directors are confident that the share price target will be met on 31 March 2025.

Required

Advise the directors on the accounting treatment of the share options in the financial statements for the year ended 31 March 2023. **(5 marks)**

(Total 20 marks)

16 Elysium (May 2023)

The Elysium group comprises of Elysium and its one subsidiary Avalon.

(a) Elysium acquired a 70% equity interest in Avalon for cash consideration of $90 million several years ago. At the date of acquisition, Avalon's retained earnings were $70 million The book value of Avalon's net assets were equal to their fair values at the date of acquisition.

Elysium opted to measure the 30% non-controlling interest in Elysium at its fair value of $45 million at acquisition. Consolidated goodwill was correctly calculated at $55 million at the date of acquisition.

The following extract was taken from Elysium's consolidated statement of financial position as at **31 March 2022**:

	$m
EQUITY	
Equity shares - $1 each	50.0
Retained earnings at 31 March 2022	386.5
	436.5

	$m
Non-controlling interest at 31 March 2022	69.0
Total equity at 31 March 2022	505.5

In addition, the following information has been extracted from individual statements of financial position for Elysium and Avalon as at **31 March 2023**:

	Elysium $m	Avalon $m
EQUITY		
Equity shares - $1 each	50.0	10.0
Retained earnings		
– As at 1 April 2022	330.5	150.0
– Profit for the year ended 31 March 2023	82.0	36.0
Retained earnings as at 31 March 2023	412.5	186.0
Total equity at 31 March 2023	462.5	196.0

On 1 October 2022, Elysium purchased an additional two million $1 Avalon shares at their fair value of $29 per share.

Assume profit accrues evenly throughout the year.

Required:

(i) Advise the directors on the accounting treatment of Avalon in the consolidated statements for the year ended 31 March 2023. **(5 marks)**

(ii) Prepare the consolidated statement of changes in equity for the Elysium Group for the year ended 31 March 2023. **(8 marks)**

(Total 13 marks)

(b) **Bond disclosures**

In 2019 Elysium issued $100 million bonds of which 80% was allocated to investors focused on environmental issues. The bond agreement included a covenant which requires Elysium to reduce its carbon emissions by 75% by 31 March 2024. Elysium will face a significant penalty if the carbon emissions target is not met.

The terms of the bonds and details of the covenant have been disclosed in the notes to the financial statements. In addition, the directors have emphasised their commitment and progress towards reducing Elysium's carbon emissions by 75% in the notes to the financial statements.

Shortly before the consolidated statements for the year ended 31 March 2023 are authorised for issue, the accountant discovered a report from an independent sustainability expert which indicates that the directors have over-exaggerated Elysium's progress towards the carbon emissions target. Based on the data included in the report, it is unlikely that Nysa will achieve the emissions target by 31 March 2024.

On approaching the finance director about this, the accountant was instructed not to tell anyone about the report as a breach of the loan covenant could lead to serious repercussions for the Elysium group. The accountant is a newly qualified AIA accountant and is worried about losing their job.

Required

Critically evaluate the ethical issues arising in part (b) and consider any actions the accountant should take to resolve this matter. **(7 marks)**

(Total 20 marks)

17 Uno (November 2023)

Uno is the parent company of a quoted trading group whose functional currency is the US Dollar ($).

The Uno Group comprises of three companies Uno, Dos and Tres. Uno and Dos prepare their financial statements in dollars ($). Tres is based overseas and its functional currency is the Dinar (D).

The statements of financial position for Uno, Dos and Tres as at 30 September 2023 are shown below:

	Uno $000	Dos $000	Tres $000
ASSETS			
Non-current assets			
Property, plant and equipment	5,700	1,600	12,725
Investments			
– Dos – 30%	1,200		
– Dos – additional 40%	2,020		
– Tres	4,800		
	13,720	1,600	12,725
Current assets	4,250	1,050	9,150
Total assets	17,970	2,650	21,875
EQUITY AND LIABILITIES			
Equity			
Equity shares - $1 shares	1,000	200	1,200
Retained earnings	7,020	800	10,325
	8,020	1,000	11,525
Non-current liabilities	7,200	900	5,800
Current liabilities	2,750	750	4,550
Total equity and liabilities	17,970	2,650	21,875

The following information is relevant:

1 **Acquisition of Dos**

   Uno acquired a 30% equity stake in Dos for $1.2m on 1 October 2021 and exerted a significant influence over its financial and operating policy decisions. Dos had retained earnings of $0.45m on 1 October 2021.

   On 1 April 2023, Uno purchased a further 40% stake in Dos and acquired control from that date. Uno acquired the shares at their full fair value of $25 each. Uno paid dealer's fees of $20,000 on this share purchase and the fees have been capitalised as part of the cost of the acquisition.

   It is group policy to recognise the non-controlling interest at fair value at the date of acquisition.

   Dos reported a profit of $0.3m in the year ended 30 September 2023. Profits accrue evenly overtime.

2 **Tres**

   Uno purchased 80% of the equity share capital of Tres on 1 October 2021 for $4.8 million. At that date Tres has retained earnings of 2.4m Dinars. The fair value of the net assets of Tres were equal to their carrying amount and no fair value adjustments are required on the acquisition.

   The following information has been extracted from the notes to the financial statements of Tres (all amounts are shown in Dinars):

	D000
Profit for the year ended 30 September 2022	4,025
Profit for the year ended 30 September 2023	5,460

	D000
Dividends paid on:	
30 September 2022	560
30 September 2023	1,000

On 1 October 2021, the fair value of the non-controlling interest in Tres was valued at 14.4m Dinars.

Further to an impairment test on 30 September 2023, consolidated goodwill is to be written down by 18.4m Dinars. Goodwill impairment losses are to be translated at closing rate on 30 September 2023 in accordance with group policy. No goodwill impairment losses were recognised in the year ended 30 September 2022.

Exchange rates are as follows:

	Dinars to $1
1 October 2021	12
30 September 2022	11.2
30 September 2023	10
Average rate for the year ended 30 September 2022	11.5
Average rate for the year ended 30 September 2023	10.5

3 **Profit related bonus scheme**

The Uno group operates a bonus scheme for its directors provided that stringent profit targets have been met. Based on the draft consolidated profit for the year ended 30 September 2023, profit targets have not been achieved.

Required

(a) Discuss how the investment in Dos should be accounted for in Uno's consolidated statements for the year ended 30 September 2023. Your answer should include the following calculations:

(i) Gain or loss on the remeasurement of the previously held 30% investment.
(ii) Goodwill arising on the acquisition of Dos. **(10 marks)**

(b) Prepare the consolidated statement of financial position for the Uno group as at 30 September 2023.

Work to the nearest $0.1 million and show all your workings. **(25 marks)**

(c) On review of the draft consolidated statements for the year ended 30 September 2023, the finance director proposes that the gains arising on the translation of Tres (from part b) should be reclassified from other comprehensive income and recognised in profit or loss for the year instead.

The finance director feels that their proposed treatment would be more consistent with the requirements of the *Conceptual Framework for Financial Reporting* which states that the statement of profit or loss is the primary source of information about an entity's performance.

Required

Critically evaluate the finance director's proposals for recognising the gains arising on the translation of Tres in profit or loss in the year ended 30 September 2023. **(5 marks)**

(Total 40 marks)

18 Cuatro (November 2023)

Cuatro is a quoted company specialising in the design and development of environmentally friendly construction equipment. The directors of Cuatro require your advice on the accounting treatment of the following transactions which took place in the year ended 30 September 2023.

In the tax jurisdiction in which Cuatro operates income tax is charged at 25%.

(a) **Lease contract**

On 1 October 2022, Cuatro signed a contract to lease a machine for four years. Under the terms of the lease, Cuatro is required to make four annual lease payments of $240,000 per annum, payable in arrears, on 30 September each year. On 1 October 2022, the present value of the future lease payments was $831,625 based on the rate of interest implicit in the lease of 6% pa.

Cuatro paid direct costs associated with the lease of $8,375 on 1 October 2022.

At the end of the lease term the machine is to be returned to the lessor. The useful life of the machine is ten years.

In the tax jurisdiction in which Cuatro operates lease payments and direct costs are tax deductible when paid.

Required

Advise the directors on the accounting treatment of the lease contract, including any deferred tax consequences, in the year ended 30 September 2023. **(7 marks)**

(b) **Share options**

On 1 October 2021, Cuatro granted 1,000,000 $1 equity share options to its senior management team on condition that they remain in employment for three years. The fair value of each $1 equity share was $10.50 on 1 October 2021.

Tax relief is available on the intrinsic value of the shares when the share options are exercised. The share options had an intrinsic value of $9 per share on 30 September 2022. On 30 September 2023, the intrinsic value had increased to $18 per share.

Required

Advise the directors on the accounting treatment of the equity share options, including any deferred tax implications, in the financial statements for the year ended 30 September 2023.

(8 marks)

(c) **Specialised equipment**

On 1 September 2023, Cuatro signed a contract with a customer to design and build specialised equipment at an agreed price of cost plus 30%. Cuartro will invoice the customer for the equipment in full on delivery with 30-day payment terms.

Under the terms of the contract, Cuatro will work closely with the customer on the design and development of the equipment. The equipment will be manufactured by a third-party supplier who will build the equipment based on Cuartro's exact specifications.

The supplier will deliver the equipment to the customer's premises. Cuatro will pay the supplier directly for the cost of the equipment.

The contract specifies that the supplier is responsible for the correction of any manufacturing defects. Cuatro is responsible for the correction of any defects linked to the design specifications of the equipment.

Required

Advise the directors on whether Cuatro is acting as principal or agent in the above contract in accordance with IFRS 15 *Revenue from Contracts with Customers*. **(5 marks)**

(Total 20 marks)

19 Cinco (November 2023)

Cinco is a property investment company which holds a portfolio of commercial properties let out under short- and long-term operating leases. Cinco has adopted the fair value model basis for its investment properties in accordance with IAS 40 *Investment Properties*. The fair value of investment property is highly dependent on interest rates.

(a) **Office building**

On 1 October 2017 Cinco acquired a new office building for $8 million and immediately began using it as its head office. Cinco depreciated the office building on a straight line basis over its expected useful life of 50 years under the cost model basis. (Assume the cost of the land is neglibible.)

On 1 October 2022, Cinco relocated to larger premises and the office building was reclassifed as an investment property and rented out to a third party on a ten year operating lease.

The fair value of the office building was $10 million on 1 October 2022. By 30 September 2023 the building's fair value had increased to $12 million.

The directors of Cinco are unsure how the change of use of the office building will affect the financial statements in the year ended 30 September 2023.

Required

Advise the directors of Cinco on how the office building should be accounted for in the financial statements for the year ended 30 September 2023. **(4 marks)**

(b) **$10 million loan**

On 30 September 2023, Cinco secured a ten-year $10 million bank loan. Interest will be charged on the loan at a fixed rate of 8% per annum payable in arrears on 30 September each year. Cinco paid loan arrangement fees of $200,000 on 30 September 2023.

The loan has been specifically obtained to finance the purchase of some additional commercial properties for investment purposes.

The finance director understands that IFRS 9 *Financial Instruments* permits financial liabilities to be held either at amortised cost or at fair value through profit or loss. However, the finance director is undecided on which alternative would be most appropriate for Cinco and has come to you for advice on both alternatives.

Required

Advise the finance director on how the $10 million bank loan should be accounted for on 30 September 2023 under both alternatives. You should also consider how the choice of accounting treatment will impact on Cinco's reported profit in future periods. **(7 marks)**

(c) **Investment in bonds**

Cinco invests its surplus cash in short and medium-term investments. Cinco intends to collect any contractual cash flows arising on its investments but will sell the investments prior to their redemption date should a better investment opportunity arise.

On 1 October 2022, Cinco acquired bonds with a par value of $1,000,000 at a 10% discount. The bonds are redeemable on 30 September 2027 at par value. The bonds pay a coupon rate of 5% per annum in arrears on 30 September each year. Cinco incurred transaction costs of $20,000. The effective rate of interest has been correctly calculated at 7% per annum.

On 30 September 2023, the bonds had a fair value of $980,000.

Required

Advise the directors on how the investment in bonds will be accounted for in Cinco's financial statements for the year ended 30 September 2023. **(6 marks)**

(d) **Speculative futures contract**

On 1 August 2023, Cinco entered a speculative futures contract with a financial institution to buy 500 tonnes of cocoa for $3,000 tonne for delivery on 31 March 2024. The contract will be settled net in cash.

Cinco paid transaction costs of $400 on 1 August 2023 and these have been capitalised as part of the initial cost of the contract.

On 30 September 2023, the fair value of an equivalent cocoa futures contract for delivery on 31 March 2024, was $3,250 per tonne.

Required

Advise the directors how the speculative forward contract will be accounted for in Cinco's financial statements for the year ended 30 September 2023. **(3 marks)**

(Total 20 marks)

20 Ocho (November 2023)

The Ocho group consists of the parent company Ocho and several trading subsidiaries and joint ventures. The group operates in the mining industry.

The following information has been extracted from the consolidated statement of financial position as at 30 September:

	2023 $000	2022 $000
Non-current assets		
Property, plant and equipment	50,300	40,000
Investment in joint ventures	10,200	5,000
Equity		
Equity $1 shares	12,000	10,000
Share premium	6,500	5,000
Retained earnings	35,250	9,000
	53,750	24,000
Non-controlling interest	6,840	4,500
Total equity	60,590	28,500
Non-current liabilities		
Long term borrowings	14,000	9,000

In addition, the following extracts are taken from the consolidated statement of profit or loss for the year ended 30 September 2023:

	$000
Profit or loss:	
Share of profit from joint ventures	5,500
Profit for the year attributable to:	
Owners of the parent	27,500
Non-controlling interest	3,600
	31,100

Depreciation of $3.5 million was expensed to the consolidated profit or loss account in the year ended 30 September 2023. There were no disposals of property, plant and equipment in the year.

On 1 October 2022, Ocho acquired a 50% equity stake in Nueve, a joint venture with a national government. Ocho paid cash of $1.2 million to acquire these equity shares. The joint venture has been correctly accounted for in accordance with IAS 28 *Investments in Associates and Joint Ventures*.

On 30 September 2023, Ocho disposed of a 70% equity interest in Diez. The group profit on disposal of $720,000 has been correctly calculated and included in consolidated profit or loss for the year, as shown below:

Group profit on disposal of Diez

	$000	$000	$000
Proceeds (all cash)			2,000
Net assets of Diez at 30 September 2023:			
Property, plant and equipment	1,200		
Inventories	400		
Trade receivables	500		
Overdraft	(200)		
Trade payables	(750)		
		1,150	
Goodwill at 30.9.23		850	
NCI at 30.9.23		(720)	
			(1,280)
Group profit on disposal of Diez			720

There were no other acquisitions or disposals of subsidiaries or joint ventures in the year ended 30 September 2023. No impairment losses have been recognised in the year.

Required

(a) Prepare the following extracts from the consolidated statement of cash flows for the year ended 30 September 2023:

    (i)   Cash flows from investing activities
    (ii)   Cash flows from financing activities   **(10 marks)**

(b) **SMEs and sustainability reporting**

The 2022 KPMG Survey of Sustainability Reporting found that 96% of the world's largest companies report on sustainability matters. Whilst sustainability reporting has been embraced by large global firms, the practice of sustainability reporting is not widespread amongst small and medium sized companies (SMEs).

Recent studies have identified several specific challenges SMEs face which might prevent them from voluntarily engaging with sustainability reporting.

Required

Critically evaluate the main challenges sustainability reporting presents to SMEs and consider how these challenges might be overcome.   **(10 marks)**

(Total 20 marks)

Exam answer bank

1 Aguila

Parts (a) and (b) require the preparation of the consolidated statement of financial position including a piece-meal acquisition and an overseas subsidiary and a discussion on the accounting treatment of the purchase of an additional 10% shareholding post year-end. (Syllabus area 2).

The following chapters from the AIA Financial Accounting and Reporting 2 study text are relevant:

Chapter 6: Revision of basic groups
Chapter 8: Changes in group structure
Chapter 9: Foreign currency translation

(a) Aguila: Consolidated statement of financial position as at 30 September 2021

	$'000
ASSETS	
Non-current assets	
Property, plant, and equipment 23,000 + 15,000 + 1,350 (W2 (iii)) + 12,000 (W3)	51,350.0
Goodwill 450 (W2 (ii)) + 2,020.8 (W4)	2,470.8
	53,820.8
Current assets	
Inventories 15,000 + 9,100 + 7,500 (W3)	31,600.0
Trade and other receivables 20,000 + 9,000 + 6,000 (W3)	35,000.0
Cash and cash equivalents 8,000 + 4,000 + 2,000 (W3)	14,000.0
	80,600.0
Total assets	134,420.8
EQUITY AND LIABILITIES	
Equity	
Equity shares	10,000.0
Retained earnings (W5)	22,447.0
Other components of equity (W2 (i))	675.0
Translation reserve (W6)	(1,775.4)
	31,346.6
Non-controlling interest 4,170 (W7) + 1,904.2 (W8)	6,074.2
	37,420.8
Non-current liabilities 30,000 + 15,000 + 12,000 (W3)	57,000.0
Current liabilities 22,000 + 10,000 + 8,000 (W3)	40,000.0
	134,420.8

Workings

1   Group structure

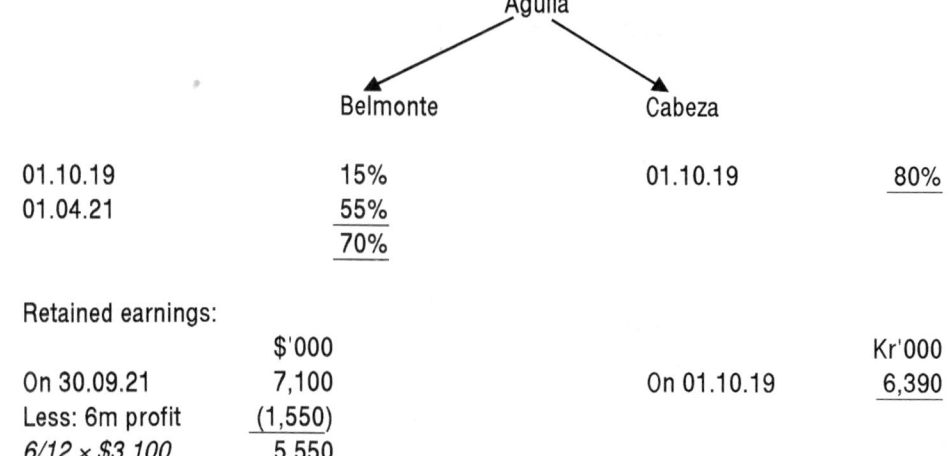

Retained earnings:

	$'000		Kr'000
On 30.09.21	7,100	On 01.10.19	6,390
Less: 6m profit	(1,550)		
6/12 × $3,100	5,550		

EXAM ANSWER BANK

2 Step acquisition: Belmonte

> **Tutorial note:**
>
> Consolidate the investment in Belmonte from the date control is achieved (1 April 2021).
>
> Restate value of original 15% holding to fair value on 1 April 2021.
>
> − As the 15% equity investment is 'held at fair value through other comprehensive income', the change in fair value will be shown as 'other comprehensive income' (OCI) in the consolidated statement of profit or loss and other comprehensive income and in consolidated 'other components of equity' (OCE).

(i) Restate cost of 15% investment to fair value at 01.04.21

	$000
Fair value at 01.04.21	1,875
Cost	(1,200)
To consolidated OCI/OCE	675

(ii) Goodwill at acquisition

	$000	$000
Consideration (55%)		6,875
Fair value (15%)		1,875
Non-controlling interest (30%)		3,750
Fair value of net assets acquired:		
Equity shares	5,000	
Retained earnings (W1)	5,550	
Fair value adjustment	1,500	
		(12,050)
Goodwill		450

(iii) Fair value adjustment

	At 01.04.21 $000	Movement $000	At 30.09.21 $000
Depreciable plant and equipment	1,500	(150)	1,350

Depreciation: $1,500/5 years × 6/12 = 150

3 Translation of Cabeza

	Kr000	Rate	$000
ASSETS			
Property, plant and equipment	30,000	2.5	12,000
Inventories	18,750	2.5	7,500
Trade and other receivables	15,000	2.5	6,000
Cash and cash equivalents	5,000	2.5	2,000
	68,750		27,500
EQUITY & LIABILITIES			
Equity shares	7,500	2.0	3,750
Retained earnings:			
− At 01.10.19	6,390	2.0	3,195
− Profit for year ended 30.09.20	2,100	2.1	1,000
− Profit for year ended 30.09.21	2,760	2.3	1,200
Translation difference (balance)			(1,645)
Non-current liabilities	30,000	2.5	12,000
Current liabilities	20,000	2.5	8,000
	68,750		27,500

4 Goodwill: Cabeza

	Kr000	Rate	$000
Consideration paid $8,000 × 2	16,000	2	8,000.0
Non-controlling interest	4,000	2	2,000.0
Fair value of net assets acquired			
Equity shares	(7,500)	2	(3,750.0)
Retained earnings (W1)	(6,390)	2	(3,195.0)
Goodwill at 01.10.19	6,110	2	3,055.0
Translation loss (balance)	–		(277.7)
At 30.09.20	6,110	2.2	2777.3
Impairment	(1,058)	2.3	(460.0)
Translation loss (balance)	–		(296.5)
Goodwill at 30.09.21	5,052	2.5	2,020.8

5 Retained earnings

	Aguila $000	Belmonte $000	Cabeza $000
	20,075	7,100	5,395
		(150)	
		(5,550)	(3,195)
		1,400	2,200
Group share:			
Belmonte: 1,400 × 70%	980		
Cabeza: 2,200 × 80%	1,760		
Less: group share goodwill impairment loss 460 (W4) × 80%	(368)		
	22,447		

6 Translation reserve

	$000
Group share translation differences on net assets: (1,645) × 80%	(1,316.0)
Group share translation differences on goodwill: ((277.7) + (296.5)) × 80%	(459.4)
	(1,775.4)

7 Non-controlling interest (NCI): Belmonte

	$000
NCI at acquisition (W2)	3,750.0
NCI's share of post-acquisition retained earnings 1,400 (W5) × 30%	420.0
	4,170.0

8 Non-controlling interest (NCI): Cabeza

	$000
NCI at acquisition (W4)	2,000.0
NCI's share of post-acquisition retained earnings: 2,200 (W5) × 20%	440.0
NCI's share goodwill impairment loss: 460 (W4) × 20% (92.0)	(92.0)
NCI's share of translation loss on net assets (1,645) (W3) × 20%	(329.0)
NCI's share of translation loss on goodwill: ((277.7) + (296.5)) (W4) × 20%	(114.8)
	1,904.2

(b) **Purchase of an additional 10% equity shareholding 1 October 2021**

Belmonte becomes an 80% subsidiary on 1 October 2021, following Aguila's acquisition of an additional 10% of its equity shares. As Aguila had already achieved control of Belmonte on 1 April

2021 (when it first acquired a 70% stake), in substance no new acquisition has taken place on 1 October 2021.

Instead, the transaction is accounted for as transaction between two existing parties i.e., the group and the non-controlling interest. Group share of Belmonte increases from 70% to 80%, and the non-controlling interest reduces from 30% to 20%. The adjustment is made in equity, being the difference between the consideration paid for the new 10% shareholding and the proportionate decrease in the non-controlling interest.

The non-controlling interest has reduced by $1,390,000 (10/30 × $4,170,000). Since Aguila paid $1,325,000 for the additional 10% shareholding, a gain of $65,000 will be recognised in Aguila's retained earnings

Consolidated goodwill remains unchanged at $450,000 since the acquisition is treated as a transaction between two existing ownership parties rather than as a new acquisition.

The double entry to record the transaction is as follows:

	Dr $000	Cr $000
Non-controlling interest 4,170 (W7) × 10/30		
Cash		1,325
Aguila's retained earnings (balance)		

Additional areas where credit might be given, note this is not an exhaustive list:

- Own figure rule applies throughout.
- Candidates will obtain marks for workings even if the figures are not transferred onto the consolidated statement of financial position.
- Double entry is not required to achieve full marks for part (c).

(c) **Recognition Criteria: Conceptual Framework (2018) vs IAS 37 *Provisions, Contingent Liabilities and Contingent Assets*.**

Part (c) requires a critical evaluation of the recognition criteria for liabilities under the Conceptual Framework (2018) and IAS 37 *Provisions, Contingent Liabilities and Contingent Assets* (Syllabus areas 1 & 3).

The following chapters from the AIA Financial Accounting and Reporting 2 study text are relevant:

Chapter 1: Current thought and practice
Chapter 19: Provisions, contingencies and events after the reporting period

The IASB's Conceptual Framework (2018) defines a liability as "A present obligation of the entity to transfer an economic resource as a result of past events." (Conceptual Framework: para. 4.29).

Under the Conceptual Framework's (2018) revised recognition criteria, a liability will be recognised provided that:

- The item meets the definition of a liability; and
- Recognition provides users with useful information that is relevant and/or provides a faithful representation of the liability.

IAS 37 *Provisions, Contingent Liabilities and Contingent Assets* defines a provision as "a liability of uncertain timing or amount" (IAS 37: para. 10) which is recognised when:

- A present obligation exists as a result of a past event; and
- It is probable that an outflow of resources embodying economic benefits will be requires to settle the obligation; and
- A reliable estimate can be made

(IAS 37: para. 14)

The amended Conceptual Framework (2018) recognition criteria removes both the probability and reliably measured criteria and instead, focuses on providing users with relevant information that faithfully represents the liability. The Conceptual Framework's (2018) revised recognition criteria focuses on the qualitative characteristics of useful financial information. The IASB believe that the revised recognition criteria provides a coherent set of concepts enabling standard setters to develop standards that better meet the needs of users of financial statements.

In contrast, the recognition criteria thresholds of IAS 37 *Provisions, Contingent Liabilities and Contingent Assets* are set higher than per the *Conceptual Framework* (2018). A provision can only be recognised where an outflow of economic resources is probable i.e., the outflow of resources is more likely than not to occur (or in other words greater than a 50% chance of occurring). IAS 37 *Provisions, Contingent Liabilities and Contingent Assets* higher recognition criteria threshold is intended to prevent significant profit manipulation through the misuse of provisions.

While a conflict exists between the *Conceptual Framework* (2018) and the standard, it is unlikely that either the probability or reliability criteria will be removed from IAS 37 *Provisions, Contingent Liabilities and Contingent Assets* any time soon.

> **Additional areas where credit might be given, note this is not an exhaustive list:**
> - Discussion of previous Conceptual Framework (2010) definition of a liability.
> - Any additional points relating to either Conceptual Framework (2018) and IAS 37 *Provisions, Contingent Liabilities and Contingent Assets*.

2 Diablo

This question required candidates to consider various impairment issues arising in the year including the impairment of individual cash generating units (CGUs), a previously revalued property and a financial asset (Syllabus area: 3).

The following chapters from the AIA Financial Accounting and Reporting 2 study text are relevant:

Chapter 12: Tangible non-current assets and inventory
Chapter 14: Financial instruments

(a) **Impairment of cash generating units**

Navajo consists of three separate cash generating units (CGUs), and each CGU should be considered separately for the purposes of the impairment test. According to IAS 36 *Impairments*, a CGU represents "the smallest group of assets… that generates cash-flows that are largely independent of each other" (IAS 36; para. 68). As divisions A, B and C operate independently of each other, each division qualifies as a separate CGU.

As the CGU's were acquired as part of a business combination (IFRS 3 *Business Combinations*), the goodwill arising on acquisition should be allocated to the individual CGUs for the purposes of impairment testing. This is because goodwill is not capable of generating its own cash flows independent of other assets within the CGU.

Where possible the goodwill should be allocated to each individual CGU on some arbitrary basis. Diablo has done this based on the fair value of each CGU's net assets at the date of acquisition, but other methods are permissible. The consolidated goodwill of $30 million has been allocated in the ratio of 2:3:1 to divisions A, B, C.

The carrying value of each division, including the allocated goodwill, is compared to the recoverable amount of the unit to determine whether an impairment loss is required. Where the CGU's carrying value is higher than its recoverable amount, an impairment has occurred, and the net assets should be written down to their recoverable amount.

	Division A $000	Division B $000	Division C $000
Allocated goodwill (2:3:1)	10,000	15,000	5,000
Property, plant and equipment	20,000	45,000	8,000
Net current assets	10,000	12,000	5,000
Carrying value of CGU on 30.9.21	40,000	72,000	18,000
Recoverable amount	34,000	55,000	19,000
Impairment loss	6,000	17,000	n/a

As shown above, Divisions A & B require impairment and the net assets will be written down to their recoverable amounts of $34 million and $55 million respectively. The impairment losses arising will be written off against goodwill first, with any balance being allocated against other assets within the scope of IAS 36 *Impairments* (i.e., property, plant and equipment) on a pro rata basis. Net current assets do not fall within the scope of IAS 36 *Impairments* and are ignored for the purposes of allocating the impairment loss.

Division A's impairment loss of $6 million would be written off against its allocation of consolidated goodwill only. The $17 million impairment loss arising in Division B will be firstly written off against the $15 million allocated goodwill of the unit, with the remaining $2 million being written off against its property plant and equipment. The total impairment loss of $23 million ($6m + $17m) will be written off against the profit or loss account in the year ended 30 September 2021.

Division C does not require impairment and would remain at its carrying value of $18 million in the consolidated statement of financial position.

Following the impairment, the carrying value of the net assets of the three divisions to be incorporated into the Diablo group consolidated statement of financial position as at 30 September 2021 are shown below:

	Division A $000	Division B $000	Division B $000	Consolidated Statements $000
Goodwill	4,000	-	5,000	9,000
Property, plant and equipment	20,000	43,000	8,000	71,000
Net current assets	10,000	12,000	5,000	27,000
	34,000	55,000	18,000	107,000

(b) **Revalued Property**

An impairment loss occurs when the carrying value of the property exceeds the recoverable amount. The recoverable amount is the higher of the asset's value in use or its fair value less costs to sell. IAS 36 *Impairments* defines value in use as "the present value of the future cash flow expected to be derived from an asset" and fair value less costs to sell as "the price that would be received to sell an asset or paid transfer a liability in an orderly transaction" less transaction costs (IAS 36: para 6). The property's recoverable amount is $3.4 million (being the higher of value in use of $3.4 million and fair value less costs to sell of $3.2 million).

The carrying value of the property on 30 September 2021 prior to the impairment test is $4.5 million (W1).

An impairment loss of $1.1 million has occurred on 30 September 2021 ($3.4 million – $4.5 million). When a previously revalued asset has been impaired the impairment loss is first written off against any related balance on the revaluation surplus account, with any excess being charged to profit or loss.

Since Diablo has opted to make the annual transfer of excess depreciation from revaluation surplus to retained earnings each year, the remining balance on the revaluation surplus before the impairment write off is $750,000 (W2). Therefore, the first $750,000 of the impairment loss is written off in 'other comprehensive income' with the remaining $350,000 being written off to profit or loss in the year.

The asset will be shown in the Diablo's statement of financial position at its recoverable amount of $3.4 million. Subsequently, depreciation will be charged on the revised carrying amount in future periods.

Workings

1 Property, plant and equipment

			$'000
01.10.16	Cost		5,000
30.09.17	Depreciation $5,000/20 years		(250)
30.09.18	Depreciation		(250)
30.09.19	Depreciation		(250)
30.09.20	Depreciation		(250)
30.09.20	Carrying amount		4,000
	To revaluation surplus (balance)		800
30.09.20	Revalued amount		4,800
30.09.21	Depreciation $4,800/16 years		(300)
30.09.21	Carrying amount		4,500
	Impairment (balance)		(1,100)
30.09.21	Recoverable amount (fair value less cost to sell)		3,400

2 Revaluation surplus

		$000
30.09.20	Revaluation surplus (W1)	800
30.09.21	Reserve transfer (excess depreciation) $800/16	(50)
30.09.21		750
30.09.21	Impairment	(750)
		–

(c) **Loan receivable**

The impairment of the loan receivable falls within the scope of IFRS 9 *Financial Instruments* under the projected unit credit method. The loan receivable represents an investment in debt. Since Diablo's business model is to collect the underlying cash flows of interest and principal, the loan receivable is held on an amortised cost basis. The loan receivable is initially recorded at its fair value of $10 million and finance income of $500,000 is subsequently recognised in profit or loss at the effective rate of interest of 5%.

The gross carrying value of the loan receivable is $10.5m prior to the impairment test.

Loan receivable		$'000
01.10.20	Fair value	10,000
30.09.21	Interest income 5,000 × 5%	500
30.09.21	Amortised cost	10,500

On 1 October 2020, Diablo should also recognise an allowance for credit losses of $100,000 being 12 months expected credit losses. This is calculated by applying the expected probability of default in the next 12 months by the lifetime expected credit losses at the inception of the loan i.e.,

$500,000 × 20%. The $100,000 will be expensed to profit or loss and the allowance will be netted off against the gross value of the loan receivable on 1 October 2020.

At the year end, $4,000 finance costs should be expensed to profit or loss and credited to the allowance, representing the unwinding of the discount factor at 4%.

The default of the first loan instalment on 30 September 2021, is objective evidence of impairment. Since the risk of default has significantly increased during the year, the allowance for expected credit losses has moved from a stage 1 adjustment into stage 3. Therefore, the revised lifetime expected credit losses of $5,000,000 is recognised in full. A further $4,896,000 is credited to the allowance and expensed to profit or loss.

Allowance for expected credit losses		$'000
01.10.20	12 months expected credit loss	100
30.09.21	Finance cost @ 4%	4
30.09.21		104
30.09.21	Impairment (balance)	4,896
30.09.21	Revised lifetime expected credit losses	5,000

The loan receivable will be presented in Diablo's statement of financial position at 30 September 2021 as follows:

	$000
Loan receivable	10,500
Less: allowance for expected credit losses	(5,000)
Net carrying amount	5,500

Additional areas where credit might be given, note this is not an exhaustive list:

- Any further discussion relevant to the scenario.
- Follow through marks available.

---

3 Roca

This question examines the accounting treatment of share appreciation rights, employee benefits, lease of an asset, and advice on accounting for a network contract

The following chapters from the AIA Financial Accounting and Reporting 2 study text are relevant:

Chapter 15: Leasing contracts
Chapter 16: Employee benefits
Chapter 20: Related parties and share-based payment

(a) **Share appreciation rights (SARs)**

The SARs represent a cash settled share-based payment in accordance with IFRS 2 *Share Based Payments*. This is because qualifying employees will receive a cash payment based on the value of Roca's shares when the SARs vest on 30 September 2022.

The exercise of the SARs is conditional on being employed by Roca on 30 September 2022, therefore the SARs are expensed to profit or loss over the three-year vesting period. A corresponding SAR liability will be recognised, as an obligation to settle in cash exists.

The SARs are initially measured at fair value at the date of grant, and then subsequently remeasured to fair value at the end of the accounting period each year. In addition, the expected number of qualifying employees is amended each year. The increase in the liability each year is expensed to profit or loss.

At 30 September 2020, Roca would have recognised a SAR liability/P/L expense of $1,800,000 (W2).

On 30 September 2021, the cumulative share-based payment expense/SAR liability was $4,000,000 (W2). This would be recognised as a current liability in Roca's statement of financial position as it is due for payment within one year on 30 September 2022.

Roca would also recognise an expense of $2,200,000 (W2) in profit or loss in the year.

(W2) SAR liability and P/L expense:

	$
Y/e 30 September 2020	
SAR liability/ P/L expense [500 × (2,000 × (100 – 10%))] × $6 1/3	1,800,000
Y/e 30 September 2021	
SAR liability b/d	1,800,000
Profit or loss expense (Balance)	2,200,000
SAR liability c/d [500 × (2,000 × (100-25%))] × $8 × 2/3	4,000,000

(b) **Employee benefits**

Defined contribution scheme

Roca operates a defined contribution scheme because:

- Roca is contractually obliged to make annual payments into the scheme on behalf of its employees;
- It has no further obligations under the terms of the fund;
- The value of the pension plan depends on the future performance of the fund; and
- The pension risk (risk of variable pension payments) is borne by the employees.

Since Roca has no additional obligations under the pension scheme, it will expense the pension contribution to profit or loss in the accounting period in which the employee services were rendered. Roca will expense the employer contributions of $770,000 to profit and loss [7% × ($8m + $3m)]. [1]

The unpaid employer contributions of $270,000 [$770,000 – $500,000] [½] will be recognised as an accrual in Roca's statement of financial position as at 30 September 2021.

Bonus

The bonus represents a payment in exchange for employee services provided in the year ended 30 September 2021. This short-term employment benefit is recognised on an accruals basis in the period in which the service was rendered.

Under IAS 19 *Employee Benefits*, the expected cost of the bonus payment can only be recognised provided that:

- A contractual or constructive obligation exists to make the bonus payment; and
- The bonus can be reliably estimated

(IAS 19: para. 19)

Both conditions have been satisfied since the employees are contractually entitled to the bonus and Roca has determined a reliable estimate of the expected cost. Therefore, Roca will expense the $3,000,000 bonus to profit or loss and will accrue for the bonus liability in its statement of financial position as at 30 September 2021.

(c) **Lease of equipment**

In accordance with IFRS 16 *Leases*, a right of use asset and a lease liability should be recognised on commencement of the lease on 1 October 2020.

Lease liability

The initial lease liability on 1 October 2020 will be recognised at the present value of the future lease payments i.e. $1,773,000.

Subsequently, the lease liability will be held on an amortised cost basis. Finance costs of $88,650 (W1) are recognised in profit or loss at the rate of interest in the lease of 5%, which are added to the lease liability. The lease liability is reduced by the first instalment on 30 September 2021.

The lease liability at 30 September 2021, will be disclosed between the amount falling due within one year (the 'current liability' component) and the amount falling due after more than one year (the 'non-current liability' component). Roca will recognise a current liability of $431,917 ($1,361,650 – $929,733)(W1) and a non-current liability of $929,733(W1) in the statement of financial position for the year ended 30 September 2021.

Year ended 30 September	B/f	Finance costs @ 5%	Annual instalment	C/f
	$	$	$	$
2021	1,773,000	88,650	(500,000)	1,361,650
2022	1,361,650	68,083	(500,000)	929,733

Right of use asset

On 1 October 2020, a right of use asset is recognised at the present value of the future lease payments minus the lease incentive i.e., $1,723,000 ($1,773,000 – $50,000). [$^1/_2$] The right of use asset will be depreciated over the shorter of the lease term or the useful life of the asset.

A depreciation charge of $430,750 ($1,723,000 / 4 years) is recognised in profit or loss. [$^1/_2$] The right of use asset will be shown at its carrying amount of $1,292,250 in the statement of financial position ($1,723,000 – $430,000).

(d) **Future contract for network services**

IFRS 16 *Leases* stipulates that a contract includes a lease if it conveys the right to control the use of an identified asset for a period of time, in exchange for consideration.

An identified asset is explicitly identifiable in the contract.

The right to control the use of an asset throughout the duration of the contract arises when the customer has:

- The right to substantially all the economic benefits from the use of the asset; and
- The right to direct the asset's use.

The network contract does not contain a lease. This is because Roca does not have the right to control the use of the servers. Roca's decision-making rights are limited to determining the level of service required at the start of the contract only. Paron is the only party that can make decisions about the use of the servers during the period of use: they have sole responsibility for their operation and maintenance and are entitled to reconfigure or substitute the servers throughout the duration of the contract. Paron therefore controls the servers that provide network services to Roca.

The contract should be accounted for as service contract, whereby the costs are expensed to profit or loss over the period of use.

There is no need to consider whether an identifiable asset exists as this would not affect the decision as Roca does not control the servers.

> **Additional areas where credit might be given, note this is not an exhaustive list:**
> - Any further discussion relevant to the scenario.
> - Follow through marks available.
> - Part (d) further discussion on whether an identifiable asset exists.

4 Gila

Part (a) required candidates to prepare extracts from the consolidated statement of cash flows (Syllabus area: 2).

The following chapter from the AIA Financial Accounting and Reporting 2 study text is relevant:

Chapter 10: Group statement of cash flows

(a) **Extracts from consolidated statement of cash flows for the year ended 30 September 2021**

(i) Cash flow from investing activities

	$'000
Acquisition of subsidiary, net of cash acquired (3000) + 1,000	(2,000)
Acquisition of associate (W2)	(1,000)
Purchase of property, plant and equipment (W1)	(15,000)
Dividends received	2,000
Net cash used in investing activities	(16,000)

(ii) Cash flows from financing activities

	$'000
Proceeds from the issue of share capital	6,000
Proceeds from long term borrowings (15,000 – 10,000)	5,000
Dividends paid by parent (W3)	(3,000)
Dividends paid to non-controlling interest (W4)	(1,000)
Net cash used in financing activities	7,000

Workings

1 **Property, plant and equipment**

	$'000
Balance b/d	51,000
On acquisition of Laguna	2,500
Depreciation	(7,000)
Additions in year (balance)	15,000
Balance c/d	61,500

2 **Investment in associates**

	$'000
Balance b/d	5,000
Share of profit of associates (P/L)	1,600
Dividends received	(2,000)
Purchase of Huachuca in year (balance)	1,000
	5,600

3 **Equity shares (share capital/share premium)**

	$'000
Balance b/d (30,000 + 5,000)	35,000
Issued on acquisition of subsidiary (1m × $7)	7,000
Cash issue of shares (balance)	(6,000)
Balance c/d (31,800 + 16,200)	48,000

4 **Non-controlling interest**

	$'000
Balance b/d	9,000
NCI's share of profit for the year (P/L)	1,500
NCI acquired on acquisition of subsidiary	2,500
Dividend paid	(1,000)
Balance c/d	12,000

(b) **Related party disclosures**

Part (b) required candidates to consider whether related party disclosures were required taking into account IAS 24 *Related Party Disclosures* and Practice Statement 2 *Making Materiality Judgements* (Syllabus area: 3). Candidates were also required to consider any ethical issues of non-disclosure (Syllabus area: 1).

The following chapters from the AIA Financial Accounting and Reporting 2 study text are relevant:

Chapter 2: Presentation of published financial statements
Chapter 4: Ethics and regulation of corporate financial reporting
Chapter 20: Related parties and share-based payment

The purchase of goods from Tota represents a related party transaction in accordance with IAS 24 *Related Party Disclosures*. Tota is a related party because it is owned by a close family member of Gila's key management personnel i.e. Tota is owned by the finance director's wife.

Disclosures should include details of the nature of the related party relationship (but no requirement to identify Tota by name), the value of the transactions and any outstanding balances at the year end and details of any guarantees or commitments. References to 'arm's length' transactions may only be made if these claims can be substantiated.

Related party disclosures highlight the prospect that an entity's profit or loss or financial position may have been affected by related party relationships or transactions. To ensure that the financial statements are fairly presented, directors must apply the correct accounting treatment in accordance IFRS and ensure that all material transactions are adequately disclosed.

A key issue here is whether the purchases from Tota are considered material to the users of Gila's financial statements. Practice Statement 2 *Making Materiality Judgements* asserts that even when disclosures are required by IFRS, disclosures are not required where the information provided is not material. Information is considered to be material if its omission or misstatement influences the decisions made by the users of the financial statements.

Materiality is assessed both quantitatively and qualitatively. From a quantitative perspective, 25% of Gila's purchases came from Tota which may have considerably impacted profits if the price paid for the goods was set artificially high. Based on the high volume of transactions in the year, it is highly likely that these would be considered material from a quantitative perspective. However, even if the transactions were not considered quantitatively material, other qualitative factors should be considered to determine whether relevant related party disclosures are required. Users are likely to be interested in any transactions between the finance director and his close family members, given a perceived opportunity for abuse exists. Based on the volume of the transactions and the nature of the related party relationship, it is highly likely that related party disclosures would be beneficial for users of the financial statements.

The omission of material related party disclosures contravenes IAS 24 *Related Party Disclosures* and may be construed as a deliberate attempt to downplay the significance of the transactions with Tota in the year. The finance director's reluctance to disclose the transactions may be motivated by financial gain (via his wife's company). In putting his own self-interest first, the finance director is behaving unethically, by deliberately omitting key information from the financial statements which would be useful for users of its financial statements.

Additional areas where credit might be given, note this is not an exhaustive list:

- Part (a): Follow through marks apply throughout. Credit given for workings not transferred to extracts.
- Part (b): Further discussion of related party disclosures and/or the concept of materiality.

5 Amyklas

Parts (a) and (b) require the critical evaluation and application of discontinued operations in accordance with IFR5 *Non-current Assets Held for Sale and Discontinued Operations* and the 2018 Conceptual Framework (Syllabus areas 1 & 2).

The following chapters from the AIA Financial Accounting and Reporting 2 study text are relevant:

Chapter 1: Current thought and practice
Chapter 18: Reporting financial performance

(a) **IFRS 5 and the 2018 *Conceptual Framework***

In accordance with IFRS 5 *Non-current Assets Held for Sale and Discontinued Operations* (IFRS 5) results of a discontinued operation are shown separately in the statement of profit or loss and other comprehensive income. The rationale for this approach is to ensure that users are provided with relevant information about the on-going and discontinued operations of the business. This enables users to distinguish between profits and cash flows from ongoing activities separately from activities that have ceased.

The 2018 *Conceptual Framework* states that the objective of general-purpose financial reporting is to provide information to the primary users of financial statements (existing and potential investors and lenders). Information is considered useful if it is relevant and faithfully represents economic substance of transactions.

The accounting treatment of a discontinued operation in accordance with IFRS 5, enhances the usefulness of the financial information presented in the statement of profit or loss by presenting relevant information to users. Information is considered relevant if "it is capable of making a difference in the decisions made by users.... Financial information is capable of making a difference in decisions if it has a predictive value, confirmatory value or both" (*2018 Conceptual Framework*: paras.2.6-2.7).

Users require the information presented in the financial statements to confirm what has happened in the past and to predict (forecast) what might happen in the future. Presenting the results of the discontinued operation separately in the statement of profit or loss enables users to either look back on the historic financial performance to date and/or base any future predictions on the entity's continuing operations.

However, whilst the treatment of IFRS 5 discontinued operations is, in theory, consistent with the requirements of the *Conceptual Framework* (2018), in practice problems may exist in how the standard is applied. The IASB has formally acknowledged that what might qualify as "a separate major line of business or geographical area of operations" is open to interpretation. Therefore what might be considered discontinued operation by one entity may not be considered discontinued by another leading to inconsistency in its application. The differences in approach will, to a certain extent, be dependent on how the entity determines its operating segments under IFRS 8 *Operating Segments*. This inconsistency in the application of the IFRS 5 discontinued operation definition may therefore lead to difficulties for users when interpreting the financial information presented to inform their economic decisions.

(b) **IFRS 5 Discontinued operation**

IFRS 5 *Non-current Assets Held for Sale and Discontinued Operations* (IFRS 5) defines a discontinued operation as:

"a component of an entity which either has been disposed of or classified as held for sale, and:

(i) Represents a separate major line of business or geographical area of operations; or
(ii) Is a single co-ordinated plan to dispose of a separate major line or area or operations; or
(iii) Is a subsidiary acquired exclusively for resale."

[IFRS 5: para. 32]

EXAM ANSWER BANK

The disposal of Dion appears to meet the IFRS 5 discontinued operation criteria because:

- Dion represents a separate component of the group as its operations and cashflows are clearly distinguishable from the rest of the group. Dion would qualify as a separate cash-generating unit (CGU); and
- The disposal took place within the year ended 31 March 2022; and
- Represents the disposal of a separate major line of business, since the group have decided to withdraw from the clothing retail business in order to focus on its core mining business.

The discontinued operation would be presented separately in the consolidation statement of profit or loss and other comprehensive income for the year ended 31 March 2021, usually as a single line item consisting of:

- Dion's post tax profit in 6 months to 30 September 2021;
- Any post-tax gains/losses on reclassification as 'held for sale disposal group' or on disposal of Dion's assets prior to the group disposal of equity shares.
- The post tax group profit or loss on disposal of Dion

Parts (c), (d) and (e) require the calculation of the group profit on disposal of a subsidiary, the preparation of the consolidated statement of financial position and a discussion on the accounting treatment of the disposal of a 10% interest in a subsidiary post year end (Syllabus area 2).

The following chapters from the AIA Financial Accounting and Reporting 2 study text are relevant:

Chapter 6: Revision of basic groups
Chapter 8: Changes in group structure

(c) **Group profit on disposal of Dion**

	$000	$000
Sale proceeds		3,400
Less: Net assets at 30.9.21		
Share capital	800	
Retained earnings (W1)	500	
Remaining fair value adjustment (W3)	55	
	1,355	
Goodwill (W2)	880	
Less: NCI @ 30.9.21 (W4)	(447)	(1,788)
		1,612

(d) **Amyklas: Consolidated statement of financial position as at 31 March 2022**

	$000
ASSETS	
Non-current assets	
Property, plant and equipment 1,800 + 1,100 + 300 (W5)	3,200
Goodwill	475
	3,675
Current assets	
Inventories 320 + 210	530
Trade and other receivables 290 + 190	480
Cash and cash equivalents 3,800 + 50	3,850
	4,860
Total assets	8,535

EQUITY AND LIABILITIES
Equity

Equity $1 shares	1,000
Retained earnings (W7)	4,340
	5,340
Non-controlling interest (W8)	425
	5,765
Non-current liabilities 500 + 350	850
Current liabilities 1,450 + 250 + 220 (W5)	1,920
Total equity and liabilities	8,535

(e) **Disposal of shares in Nabis on 1 April 2022**

Amyklas sold 100,000 shares i.e., a 20% stake in Nabis to the non-controlling interest. The group shareholding therefore reduces from 75% investment to 55% and the non-controlling interest's share increases from 25% to 45%.

Amyklas still retains control of Nabis following the disposal of shares. In substance no disposal has taken place and no profit or loss on disposal should be recognised in the consolidated profit or loss account. Instead, the transaction should be recorded as a reallocation of equity interests between the group and the non-controlling interest. This is calculated by comparing the proceeds of sale to the proportionate increase in the non-controlling interest and is shown as an adjustment in equity.

Adjustment to equity:

	$000
Proceeds from sale	300
Increase in the NCI (W9)	(336)
	(36)

	Debit $000	Credit $000
Bank	300	
Amyklas' retained earnings	36	
Non-controlling interest		336

> **Additional areas where credit might be given, note this is not an exhaustive list:**
>
> - Discussion of other relevant points relating to IFRS 5 *Non-current Assets Held for sale* and *Discontinued Operations or the Conceptual Framework* (2018).
> - Own figure rule applies throughout.
> - Candidates will obtain marks for workings even if the figures are not transferred onto the consolidated statement of financial position.
> - Double entry is not required to achieve full marks for part (e).

Workings

1   **Group structure**

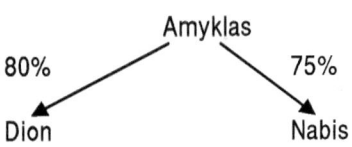

Acquired 1 April 2017: RE = $200,000   Acquired 1 April 2021: RE = $350,000

Disposal 30.9.21		
RE on 31.3.22	650,000	
Less: 6m profit (6/12 × $300k)	(150,000)	
RE at 30.9.21	500,000	

2   **Goodwill: Dion**

	$'000	$'000
Consideration paid		1,760
Non-controlling interest (fair value)		440
Less: fair value of net assets acquired		
Share capital	800	
Retained earnings (W1)	200	
Fair value	100	
		(1,100)
Goodwill at 1 April 2017		1,100
Impairment: 20% × 1,100		(220)
		880

3   **Fair value adjustment: Dion**

	At 1.4.17 $'000	Change $'000	At 30.9.21 $'000
Property, plant and equipment	100	(45)	55
100/10 × 4.5 years			

4   **Non-controlling interest on 30.9.21: Dion**

		$000
NCI at acquisition (W2)		440
NCI share of post-acquisition reserves		
At 30.9.21 (W1)	500	
Less: FV depreciation (W3)	(45)	
RE at 1.4.17 (W1)	(200)	
	255	
	× 20%	51
Less: NCI share of goodwill impairment (W2) 220 × 20%		(44)
NCI @ 30.9.21		447

5   **Goodwill: Nabis**

	$'000	$'000
Consideration		
Cash		1,325
Deferred cash $242,000/ 1.10^2		200
Non-controlling interest (fair value)		500

EXAM ANSWER BANK

	$'000	$'000
Fair value of net assets acquired		
Share capital	500	
Retained earnings	350	
Fair value adjustment - land (balance)	300	
	1,150	(1,150)
Goodwill at 01.04.21		875
Impairment (W6)		(400)
Goodwill at 31.03.21		475

Deferred cash: unwind discount factor on 31.03.22
Finance cost = 200 × 10% = $20k
Deferred cash liability at year-end = $220 ($200k + $20k)

6 Impairment: Nabis

	$'000	$'000
Net assets at 31.03.22		
Equity shares	500	
Retained earnings	450	
Fair value adjustment - land	300	1,250
Goodwill (W5)		875
Carrying value at 31.03.22		2,125
Impairment		(400)
Recoverable amount		1,725

7 Group retained earnings

	Amykias $000	Deon $000	Nabis $000
At year end / disposal date (W1)	2,945	500	450
Fair value depreciation (W3)		(45)	
Profit on disposal Dion (part a)	1,612		
Unwinding of discount factor (W5)	(20)		
Pre-acquisition retained earnings (W1)		(200)	(350)
		255	100
Group share post-acquisition retained earnings			
Dion: 80% × 255	204		
Nabis: 75% × 100	75		
Less: Goodwill impairments			
Dion: 80% × 220 (W2)	(176)		
Nabis: 75% × 400 (W6)	(300)		
	4,340		

8 Non-controlling interest: Nabis

	$000
NCI at acquisition (W5)	500
NCI % post-acquisition retained earnings (W7) 100 × 25%	25
Less: NCI % of impairment loss (W6) 400 × 25%	(100)
	425

9 Disposal of Nabis: increase in the NCI

	$
25% NCI b/f at 01.04.22 (W2)	420
Increase in NCI 20/25 × 420	336
45% NCI at 01.04.22	756

6 Spartan

This question required candidates to consider revenue recognition issues relating to the acquisition of three new contracts in the year and the treatment of convertible loan stock (Syllabus area: 3).

The following chapters from the AIA Financial Accounting and Reporting 2 study text are relevant:

Chapter 14: Financial instruments
Chapter 21: Revenue recognition and off-balance sheet

(a) **New commercial contracts**

Contract 1

The $250,000 upfront payment made was not in exchange for goods or services from the client. Instead, the $250,000 represents a reduction in the selling price of the bathroom suites sold. The $250,000 up-front payment represents a 10% discount ($250,000/$2,500,000) on the agreed contract price of $2,500,000.

On 1 October 2021, Spartan should have recognised a contract asset of $250,000 in its statement of financial position. Subsequently, the contract asset will be shown as a 10% reduction in revenue in line with how revenue is recognised on the transfer of the bathroom suites.

As goods with a value of $1,250,000 have been transferred to the client by 31 March 2022, revenue of $1,125,000 will be recognised in the profit or loss account i.e., $1,250,000 invoiced less $125,000 contract asset released in the year. As of 31 March 2022, the remaining contract asset of $125,000 will be presented under current assets in the statement of financial position.

Contract 2

Spartan should not recognise revenue on the transfer of goods to the client in the year ended 31 March 2022. This is the first time that Spartan has sold goods on approval and the client is still within the 90-day return period. In addition, Spartan has no previous historical evidence to support the sales director assertions that the sale is highly probable.

Revenue from the transaction should be recognised at the earlier of:

(i) The date Spartan receives formal confirmation that the client has accepted the goods; or

(ii) At the end of the 90-day period.

Revenue of $400,000 should be reversed out of the profit or loss account. In addition, Spartan should record a 'right to recover asset' of $250,000 (i.e., cost of goods transferred) in its statement of financial position at the year end. The right to recover asset should be transferred from cost of sales and presented under current assets, separately from inventories, in the statement of financial position as at 31 March 2022.

Revenue will be recognised at the end of the 90-day approval period (provided that the customer has not formally accepted the goods earlier or returned the goods). At that point, Spartan should recognise revenue and a corresponding trade receivable of $400,000. The 'right to recover asset' of $250,000 will be debited to Spartan's cost of sales in its profit or loss at the same time.

(b) **Non-refundable deposits**

In accordance with IFRS *15 Revenue from Contracts with Customers*, revenue from the sale of goods is recognised at a specific point in time when the customer obtains control of the goods and Spartan has satisfied its performance obligation. The following factors provide evidence that control of the goods have passed to the customer:

- Spartan has a present right to payment for the goods;
- Legal title of the goods has transferred to the customer

- Spartan has transferred physical possession of the goods to the customer
- The customer assumes the risks and rewards of ownership of the goods
- The customer has accepted the asset.

Due to supply chain issues the goods have not been transferred to the customer by the year-end and therefore the customer does not yet control the promised goods. The non-refundable deposit is therefore an advance payment for goods yet to be received and should be recognised as a liability (deferred income) in the statement of financial position at the year end.

There are limited circumstances where non-refundable consideration may be recognised as revenue immediately. However, these exceptions only apply where the entity is unable to identify a contract with the customer (step 1 of the 5-step model). This is not the case in this situation as a contract clearly exists between Spartan and the customer and 'step 1' of the revenue recognition model is met.

(c) **Convertible loan stock**

The convertible loan stock represents a compound instrument because the loan stock issued displays the characteristics of both a financial liability and an equity instrument.

According to IAS 32 *Financial Instruments* a financial liability includes an "obligation to deliver cash to another entity" (IAS 32: para. 11). The obligation to pay an annual coupon interest of 3% and potentially the prospect of repaying the $2,000,000 in cash to the loan stock holders on the redemption date, would indicate that the loan stock, in part, satisfies the definition of a financial liability.

In addition, the right to convert the loan stock into a fixed number of equity shares in the future represents an equity option, which needs to be separately recognised in the statement of financial position.

Firstly, the loan stock needs to be separated into its financial liability and equity components at the date of issue i.e., 1 April 2021. This is calculated as follows:

1 The financial liability component is calculated first and is based on the present value of the future cash flows relating to the loan discounted at the market rate of interest for similar non-convertible loan stock.

2 The equity component represents the balance between the $2,000,000 proceeds and the initial value of the financial liability component.

At 1 April 2021:

Financial liability component:		Cash flow $	Discount factor @ 9%	Present Value $
31.3.22	Coupon $2m × 3%	60,000	0.917	55,020
31.3.23	Coupon	60,000	0.842	50,520
31.3.24	Coupon + Principal	2,060,000	0.772	1,590,320
				1,695,860

Equity component: ($2,000,000 – 1,695,860) 304,140

Secondly, the transaction costs associated with the issue of loan stock will be deducted from the financial liability/equity instruments. The issue costs are allocated in proportion to the value of the financial liability and equity components are as follows:

	Total $	Financial liability $	Equity $
As allocated on 1.1.21	2,000,000	1,695,860	304,140
Transaction costs: 1,695,860:304,140	(100,000)	(84,793)	(15,207)
	1,900,000	1,611,067	288,933

Subsequently, the loan stock is held on an amortised cost basis and the equity component remains fixed at $288,933 until the redemption/conversion date.

The directors' expectation that all loan stockholders will choose the equity share option at the redemption/conversion date is irrelevant and is specifically prohibited by IAS 32: *Financial Instruments: Presentation*. Eurotas has an obligation to pay the annual coupon and/or principal to the loan-stock holders throughout the three-year period of issue and this obligation will only be extinguished when the loan stock is converted/redeemed in three years' time.

The directors have incorrectly recognised an equity reserve of $2,000,000 and expensed the transaction costs to the profit or loss account. The double entry to record this is:

	Debit $	Credit $
Equity reserve (2,000,000 – 288,933)	1,711,067	
P/L – transaction costs		100,000
Financial liability		1,611,067

Finance costs on the financial liability component are recognised in profit or loss based on the effective rate of interest (as adjusted for transaction costs) of 11%.

Year ended	B/f $	Finance costs @ 11% $	Coupon paid $	C/f $
31.03.22	1,611,067	177,217	(60,000)	1,728,284

Finance costs of $177,217 should be recognised in profit or loss and the financial liability should be stated at its carrying amount of $1,728,284 in the financial statements for the year ended 31 March 2022.

The directors have incorrectly expensed the coupon interest of $60,000 to profit or loss. The following double entry is required to correct this:

	Debit $	Credit $
Finance costs – P/L ($177,217 – $60,000)	117,217	
Financial liability		117,217

> **Additional areas where credit might be given, note this is not an exhaustive list:**
> - Any further discussion relevant to the scenario.
> - Follow through marks are available throughout.

7 Mesoa

This question examines the accounting treatment of a defined benefit pension plan, accounting for equity share options, the deferred tax treatment of share options and trading losses and accounting for a prior period error.

The following chapters from the AIA Financial Accounting and Reporting 2 study text are relevant:

Chapter 16: Employee benefits
Chapter 17: Taxation
Chapter 18: Reporting financial performance
Chapter 20: Related parties and share-based payment

(a) **Defined benefit pension plan**

Extracts from statement of profit or loss and other comprehensive income for the year ended 31 March 2022.

Profit or loss $'000
Current service costs 550
Past service cost 500
Net interest cost (W1) 330

Other comprehensive income
Remeasurement loss on DB obligation (W1) 470

1 **Defined benefit obligation**

	$'000
B/f deficit	5,000
Interest cost (5,000 + 500) × 6%	330
Current service cost	550
Past service cost	500
Cash contributions	(750)
Benefits paid to former employees	-
	5,630
Remeasurement loss on DB obligation	470
C/f deficit	6,100

(b) **Equity share options**

The equity settled transactions represent an equity-settled share-based payment under IFRS 2 *Share-based Payments*.

The share-based payment expense is recognised over the three-year conditional (vesting period) based on their fair value at the date of grant of $9 per option. The directors are required to reassess their estimate of total employee departures over the three-year period and factor this into the year-end calculations.

At 31 March 2021 the share based payment expense/reserve was calculated as follows:

	$'000
C/f: (1,000 × 80%) × 500 options × $9 × 1/3	1,200

At 31 March 2022, the share based payment reserve is calculated as

	$000
B/f: (1,000 × 80%) × 500 options × $9 × 1/3	1,200
P/l expense (balance)	1,350
C/f: (1000 × 85%) × 500 options × $9 × 2/3	2,550

A share-based payment expense of $1,350,000 would be recognised in profit or loss and the cumulative share-based payment reserve has a value of $2,550,000 in the statement of financial position.

As tax relief is available on the exercise of the share options on 31 March 2023, a deferred tax asset should be recognised on this deductible temporary difference. As tax relief is given on the intrinsic value of the shares the tax base is calculated on the cumulative proportion of the intrinsic value to date.

In the year ended 31 March 2021, a deferred tax asset of $120,000 should have been recognised in the statement of financial position, as calculated below:

	$'000
Intrinsic value (1,000 × 80%) × 500 options × $4.50 × 1/3	600
Deferred tax asset @20%	120

Since this has been omitted from the 2021 financial statements in error, this should be corrected in the current year as a prior period error in accordance with IAS 8 *Accounting Policies, Changes in Accounting Estimates and Errors*. This requires the retrospective restatement of the prior year comparatives to correct the error and the financial impact of the error is recognised in equity (retained earnings) rather than in this year's profit or loss.

The double entry to correct the error is as follows:

	Debit $'000	Credit $'000
Deferred tax asset (SOFP)	120	
Tax P/L (adjusted for in retained earnings)		120

At 31 March 2022, the deferred tax asset is calculated as follows;

	$'000
Deferred tax asset b/f	120
Tax – P/L	203
Deferred tax asset c/f	
20% × [(1,000 × 85%) × 500 options × $5.7 × 2/3]	323

This is recorded as:

	Debit $'000	Credit $'000
Deferred tax asset (SOFP)	203	
Tax P/L (adjusted for in retained earnings)		203

Since the intrinsic value of each equity option is lower than its fair value of $9 per option, the increase in the deferred tax asset is recognised as a tax credit in profit or loss.

(c) **Trading losses**

The unrelieved trading losses represent a deductible temporary difference. A deferred tax asset is usually recognised, in recognition of the future tax savings available when the tax losses are relieved against future taxable profits.

IAS 12 *Income Taxes* only permits the recognition of deferred tax assets to the extent that they are recoverable i.e., it is expected that sufficient future profits exist to utilise the benefit of the tax losses. In the tax jurisdiction in which Mesoa operates, tax losses can be carried forward for a maximum of two years.

The tax adjusted loss of $100 million relating to the year ended 31 March 2021, would only be available for tax relief in the years ended 31 March 2022 and 2023. Given that Mesoa's loss making in the year ended 31 March 2022, and is only expected to break even in 2023, the entire tax benefit of the loss is likely to be wasted. Mesoa has incorrectly recognised a deferred tax asset of $20 million ($100m × 20%) in relation to this loss which requires reversal.

The tax adjusted loss of $20 million in the year ended 31 March 2022 is eligible for tax relief in the years ended 31 March 2023 and 2024. Given that it is unlikely that any tax relief will be available in the year ended 31 March 2023, Mesoa needs to generate $10 million of tax adjusted trading profits in the year ended 31 March 2024 to obtain full tax relief on the loss. The directors are hopeful that Mesoa will return to profitability in the year ended 31 March 2024, however this is dependent on the accuracy of the budgets and forecasts presented. A maximum deferred tax asset of $2 million ($10m × 20%) can be recognised in respect of the 2022 tax adjusted loss provided that the assumptions relating to the recoverability of the tax loss are valid.

> **Additional areas where credit might be given, note this is not an exhaustive list:**
> - Any further discussion relevant to the scenario.
> - Follow through marks available.

8 Prytanis

Part (a) required candidates to prepare extracts from the consolidated statement of cash flows (Syllabus area: 2).

The following chapter from the AIA Financial Accounting and Reporting 2 study text is relevant:

Chapter 10: Group statement of cash flows

(a) **Cash flows from operating activities**

	$'000
Cash generated from operations	
Profit before tax - P/L	300
Group share of associate's loss	20
Impairment of associate (W1)	10
Depreciation (W1)	25
Finance costs - P/L	30
Foreign exchange loss on PPE (W4)	8
	393
Decrease in inventories (W2)	10
Increase in trade receivables (W2)	(5)
Increase in trade payables (W2)	10
	408
Interest paid (30 – 5)	(25)
Tax paid (W3)	(60)
	323

Workings

1 **Non-current assets**

	PPE $'000	Goodwill $'000	Investment in Associate $'000
B/f	120	110	50
Group share of associate's loss			(20)
Addition - overseas PPE (W4)	40		
Acquisition of subsidiary	35	20	
Depreciation - P/L (balance)	(25)		
Impairment - P/L (balance)			(10)
C/f	170	130	20

2 **Working capital**

	Inventory $'000	Trade receivables $'000	Trade payables $'000
B/f	60	70	45
Acquisition of subsidiary	25	15	30
Increase/decrease in the year	(10)	5	10
C/f	75	90	85

3 **Tax**

	$'000
B/f	20
P/L charge for year	55
Tax paid (balance)	(60)
C/f	15

4 **Purchase of overseas property, plant & equipment**

	$'000
At 1.09.21	
Record at spot rate - 240m Francs/6 (W1)	40
At 31.12.21	
Settled at - 240m Francs/5	48
Foreign exchange loss - P/L (balance)	8

(b) **Disclosures**

Part (b) required candidates to consider the benefits of and barriers to reduced financing accounting disclosures in the financial statements considering recent amendments to IAS 1 *Presentation of Financial Statements* and Practice Statement 2 *Making Materiality Judgements* (Syllabus areas: 1 & 3).

The following chapters from the AIA Financial Accounting and Reporting 2 study text are relevant:

Chapter 2: Presentation of published financial statements
Chapter 18: Reporting financial performance

IAS 1 *Presentation of Financial Statements* requires entities to fairly present their financial statements. Fair presentation is achieved through compliance with IFRS along with sufficient disclosure to provide users with relevant information for decision making purposes. Disclosures are intended to provide additional information, both quantitative and qualitative, on the content of the financial statements for the benefit of its primary users. IAS 1 *Presentation of Financial Statements* also requires entities to make additional disclosures on items not presented in the financial statements such as contingent liabilities, events after the reporting period end and capital commitments. Entities may also need to provide additional disclosures for stock exchange and other regulatory requirements. These additional requirements add a further layer of complexity and duplication of information presented.

The increasing burden of providing financial accounting disclosures to investors and regulators is time consuming and costly for the business. From the entity's perspective the costs of providing the information may far outweigh the benefits obtained from providing the information to users. However, the problems of excess disclosure extend beyond costs associated with their preparation. Arguably primary users may also benefit from a reduction in the amount of unnecessary disclosure in the financial statements.

IFRS has been developed with the world's capital markets in mind and the disclosure requirements have been shaped around this. Financial markets require extensive disclosures to enable institutional investors make relevant investment decisions.

However, the provision of extensive information could lead to unnecessarily long and indigestible reports being presented. Excess disclosures could potentially obscure relevant information required by users, preventing them from identifying the key issues relating to the entity's current financial performance and prospects for the future.

In response to the concerns of preparers and users of financial statements the IASB launched its Disclosure Initiative in 2013, to address the problem of 'excess baggage' within the financial statements. The following problems were identified with the then current disclosures:

- Entities failed to provide sufficient relevant information.

- The disclosures made contained too much irrelevant information which could lead to important information being obscured; and

- Entities frequently adopted a 'checklist' approach to IFRS disclosure requirements, making all disclosures listed irrespective of whether they were material or not.

Materiality was considered a key contributory factor of the disclosure problem and as a direct result the definition of material was amended as follows:

"Information is material if omitting, misstating or **obscuring it** could reasonably be expected to influence decisions that the primary users... make on the basis of those reports.... In other words, materiality is an entity-specific aspect of relevance based on the nature or magnitude, or both, of the items to which the information relates in the context of an individual entity's financial report" (IAS 1: para. 7).

The revised definition of 'material' highlights the fact that providing too much information is as problematic as omission or misstatement. The IASB's Practice Statement 2: *Making Materiality* Judgements was developed to assist entities when moving away from standardised 'checklist' based disclosures towards more relevant entity specific accounting information. Whilst the move towards fewer, more relevant, disclosures is welcomed in principle there are several behavioural barriers that need to be overcome.

Determining what is considered material to users requires a high level of professional judgement. Entities will need to carefully consider whether information contained in their accounting disclosures represents material information or whether it needs to be removed. Arguably this process may be just as costly and/or time consuming as the current 'checklist' approach.

Entities may be reluctant to pre-empt what information users consider relevant for decision making purposes for fear of repercussions. A reduction in the number of disclosures in the annual report could be construed as a deliberate attempt to hide information from users. Entities might also fear the risk of challenge from auditors or regulators which may lead to sanctions and fines/penalties being imposed. The risk of reputational damage may well outweigh the cost and effort of providing the additional disclosures.

Given that the provisions of Practice Statement 2: *Making Materiality* Judgements are non-mandatory there is a danger that entities will remain cautious when considering making changes to the current disclosures for fear of repercussions.

> **Additional areas where credit might be given, note this is not an exhaustive list:**
>
> - Part (a): Follow through marks apply throughout. Credit given for workings not transferred to extracts.
>
> - Part (b): Further discussion of the benefits/barriers to reduced disclosure and/or the definition of materiality/ IFRS Practice Statement 2: *Making Materiality Disclosures*.

9 Argon

Part (a) requires candidates to determine the functional currency of a newly acquired overseas entity in the year in accordance with IAS 21 *The Effects of Changes in Foreign Exchange Rates*. Parts (b) – (d) require the calculation of several items for inclusion in the consolidated statements including goodwill, current year translation differences of the overseas operation and the preparation of the consolidated statement of profit or loss and other comprehensive income (LO:2).

The following chapters from the AIA Financial Accounting and Reporting 2 study text are relevant:

Chapter 6: Revision of basic groups
Chapter 8: Changes in group structures
Chapter 9: Foreign currency translation

(a) **Functional currency of Zinc**

According to IAS 21 *The Effects of Changes in Foreign Exchange Rates* the functional currency is "*the currency of the primary economic environment in which the entity operates*" (IAS 21: para. 8).

The primary economic environment is usually linked to where the entity generates and spends cash.

IAS 21 *The Effects of Changes in Foreign Exchange Rates* sets out several factors to consider when determining an entity's functional currency, including:

(i) the currency that mainly influences the sales price of good and services. Zinc sells in both dollars and zloty. Two-thirds of Zinc's sales are in dollars, suggesting that the functional currency should be the dollar.

(ii) the currency that mainly influences labour, material and other costs. All Zinc's raw material, labour and other costs are settled in zloty, which indicates that the functional currency should be the zloty.

(iii) whether the activities of the foreign operation represent an extension of the parent's operations or of an autonomous unit. Given that Zinc continues to operate as an autonomous unit, with all board decisions being made in Poland, Zinc is sufficiently independent from the rest of the group.

(iv) to what extent the level of transactions between group members represents a high/low proportion of the overseas entity's operations. All of Zinc's sales are with unconnected third parties and all of its costs are incurred in Poland. The absence of intra-group transactions is further evidence of Zinc's autonomy which would suggest the zloty is the most appropriate functional currency.

(v) Whether the cash flows generated from overseas activities are readily available for distribution to the parent. Zinc's profits are retained in zloty and are available for reinvestment rather than remitted back to the parent as a dividend. This suggests that the zloty should be Zinc's functional currency.

Considering all the above factors, the zloty is the most appropriate functional currency for Zinc, even after it joins the Argon group on 1 October 2021.

For the purposes of consolidation, Zinc's financial statements will be translated into dollars at the year end. Its assets and liabilities would be translated into dollars at the year-end closing rate of 6 ZL: $1 and its income and expenses in profit or loss are translated at the average rate for the year of 5.4 ZL: $1 (actual rate is also permitted).

Goodwill and fair value adjustments are treated as separate assets of Zinc. Therefore, the goodwill/fair value adjustments will be calculated in zloty and then translated into dollars at closing rate each year end.

Any exchange differences arising on the translation of net assets and goodwill are be recognised in other comprehensive income (OCI) and attributed to the group and non-controlling interest proportionately.

(b) **Goodwill: Zinc**

	ZL 000	ZL 000	Ex. rate	$'000
Consideration paid: $5m × 5		25,000.0		
Non-controlling interest		6,250.0		
Net assets acquired				
Share capital	1,000.0			
Retained earnings	12,500.0			
Fair value adjustment	6,750.0			
		(20,250.0)		
At 1 October 2021		11,000.0	5	2,200.0
Impairment		(2,700.0)	5.4	(500.0)
Translation loss (Balance)		–		(316.7)
At 30 September 2022		8,300.0	6	1,383.3

Goodwill in Cobalt

		$'000
Consideration paid (new 35%)		2,800.0
Fair value (40% holding) 1,000 × 40% × $8		3,200.0
Non-controlling interest 1,000 × 25% × $8		2,000.0
Net assets acquired		
Share capital	1,000.0	
Retained earnings		
A1 1 October 2021	3,500.0	
Profit to 31 March 2022: 6/12 × 1,110	550.0	
		(5,050.0)
Goodwill at 1 April 2022		2,950.0

(c) **Current year translation difference: Zinc**

	ZL 000	Ex. rate	$000
Opening net assets (part b) at CR	20,250.0	6	3,375.0
Opening net assets (part b) at OR	20,250.0	5	4,050.0
			-675.0
Retained profit for the year			
Profit for the year (per Q)	14,688.0		
Less: fair value depreciation 6,750/5	-1,350.0		
At CR	13,338.0	6	2,223.0
At AR	13,338.0	5.4	2,470.0
			-247.0
CY exchange loss – to OCI			-922.0

Alternative working

	ZL 000	Ex. rate	$000
Closing net assets at CR			
At 1.10.21	20,250.0		
Add: profit for the year	14,688.0		
Less: fair value depreciation	-1,350.0		
	33,588.0	6	5,598.0
Opening net assets at OR	20,250.0	5	4,050.0
			1,548.0
Less: retained profit for year (as above)	13,338.0	5.4	2,470.0
CY exchange loss to OCI			-922.0

(d) **Argon: Consolidated statement of profit or loss and other comprehensive income for the year ended 30 September 2022**

		$'000
Revenue	9,400 + (6/12 × 4,400) + 7,020 (W2)	18,620.0
Cost of sales	4,500 + (6/12 × 1,800) + 2,200 (W2) + 250 (W3)	(7,850.0)
Gross profit		10,770.0
Distribution costs	950 + (6/12 × 700) + 900 (W2)	(2,200.0)
Administrative expenses	540 + (6/12 × 520) + 800 (W2) + 500 (1b)	(2,100.0)
Investment income	550 – (600 × 75%)	100.0
Remeasurement gain (W4)		580.0
Share of profit of associate	1,100 × 6/12 × 40%	220.0
Profit before taxation		7,370.0
Income tax	650 + (6/12 × 280) + 400 (W2)	(1,190.0)
Profit for the year		6,180.0
Other comprehensive income		
Exchange differences on translating foreign operation (316.7) (1b) + (922.0) (1c)		(1,238.7)
Total comprehensive income for the year		4,941.3
Profit attributable to:		
Owners of the parent		5,648.5
Non-controlling interest (W5) 394.0 + 137.5		531.5
		6,180.0
Total comprehensive income attributable to:		
Owners of the parent		4,657.6
Non-controlling interest (W5) 146.3 + 137.5		283.8
		4,941.3

Workings

1 **Group Structure**

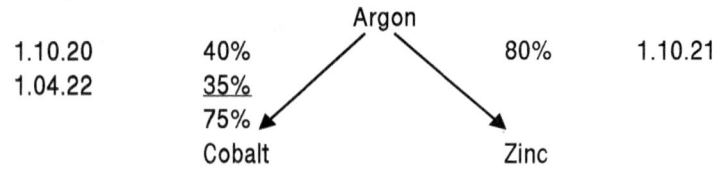

1.10.20	40%	80%	1.10.21
1.04.22	35%		
	75%		
	Cobalt	Zinc	

2 **Translation of Zinc**

	ZL 000	Ex.rate	$'000
Revenue	37,908	5.4	7,020
Cost of sales	(11,880)	5.4	(2,200)
Gross profit	26,028	5.4	4,820
Distribution costs	(4,860)	5.4	(900)
Administrative expenses	(4,320)	5.4	(800)
Profit before tax	16,848	5.4	3,120
Income tax expense	(2,160)	5.4	(400)
Profit for the year	14,688	5.4	2,720

EXAM ANSWER BANK

3 **Zinc fair value depreciation for the year**

	ZL 000	Ex.rate	$'000
Revenue	37,908	5.4	7,020
Fair value adjustment (1b)	6750.0		
Depreciation / 5 years	1,350.0	5.4	250.0

4 **Remeasurement gain on achieving control: Cobalt**

		$000
Fair value of 40% retained 1,000 × 40% × $8		3,200.0
Less: Equity valuation of associate on 1 April 2022		
Cost	2,000.0	
% Post-acquisition profits		
[(3,500 + 6/12 x1,100) – 2,500] × 40%	620.0	
		(2,620.0)
Remeasurement gain in P/L		580.0

5 **Non-controlling interest – SPLOCI**

	Zinc PFY $'000	Zinc TCI $'000	Cobalt PFY/TCI × 6/12 $'000
Profit/TCI			
– Zinc: as translated (W2)	2,720.0	2,720.0	
– Cobalt: 1,100 × 6/12			550.0
Goodwill impairment (1b)	(500.0)	(500.0)	-
Fair value depreciation (W3)	(250.0)	(250.0)	-
Translation of foreign operation			
– Goodwill	-	(316.7)	-
– On net assets	-	(922.0)	-
	1,970.0	731.3	550.0
NCI %	20%	20%	25%
	394.0	146.3	137.5

Additional areas where credit might be given, note this list is not exhaustive:

- Additional relevant discussion points in part (a).
- Full marks awarded if goodwill impairment is translated at closing rate in part (b) (as permitted per IAS 21).
- The use of own figures applies throughout.
- Credit will be given for alternative workings presented.
- Marks are available for workings even if the figures are not transferred to the consolidated statement of profit or loss and other comprehensive income.

EXAM ANSWER BANK

10 Neon

This question required candidates to consider three separate leasing transactions in the year including a sale and leaseback arrangement, the treatment of an operating lease under lessor accounting, and determining whether a contract contained a lease (LO: 3).

The following chapters from the AIA Financial Accounting and Reporting 2 study text are relevant:

Chapter 15: Leases
Chapter 12: Non-current assets and inventory

(a) **Sale and leaseback**

Per IFRS 16 *Leases*, the accounting treatment of a sale and lease back transaction depends on whether in substance a sale has occurred. This will be dependent on whether a performance obligation has been satisfied in accordance with IFRS 15 *Revenue from Contracts with Customers*.

A performance obligation has been satisfied as Neon has transferred the main risks and rewards of ownership associated with the property to the bank. The leaseback period is for five years out of the property's remaining useful life of 40 years and legal title of the property remains with the bank throughout. The leaseback element of the contract meets the definition of a lease under IFRS 16 *Leases* as Neon has the right to use the property for five years and has an obligation to make lease payments over the lease term.

On 1 October 2021, the property's carrying amount of $1,000,000 ($1,250,000 × 40/50) should be derecognised and replaced with a right of use asset arising from the sale and leaseback. The right of use asset is initially measured at the proportion of the previous carrying amount of the property that relates to the right of use retained by Neon.

A right of use asset of $415,277 is recognised on 1 October 2021 calculated as $1,000,000 (carrying amount) × $1,495,000/$3,600,000 (present value of future lease payments/fair value).

In addition, because in substance a disposal has occurred Neon should recognise a gain on the disposal of the property. The gain on the sale of the building amounts to $2,600,000 of which:

(i) $1,079,722 relating to the right of use property retained ($2,600,000 × $1,495,000/$3,600,000); and

(ii) $1,520,278 ($2,600,000 – $1,079,722) relating to the rights transferred to the buyer.

The gain on the rights transferred to the buyer of $1,520,278 is recognised in profit or loss in the year.

A financial liability of $1,895,000 (equal to the present value of the future lease payments plus the additional loan finance) is recognised at the inception of the lease.

On 1 October 2021, Neon accounts for the transaction as follows:

	Dr $	Cr $
Cash	4,000,000	
Right of use asset	415,278	
Property, plant and equipment		1,000,000
Financial liability		1,895,000
Gain on rights transferred (P/L)		1,520,278

Subsequently, the right of use asset will be depreciated over the shorter of the lease term and the remaining useful life of the asset. Therefore, the right of use asset is depreciated over five years. Depreciation of $83,056 ($415,278/5 years) will be charged to profit or loss in the year. The right of use asset will be shown in the statement of financial position at a carrying amount of $322,222 ($415,278 – $83,056).

The financial liability will be held on an amortised cost basis, with finance costs being recognised in profit or loss at the implicit rate of interest of 10%. Finance costs of $189,500 will be expensed to profit or loss in the year ended 30 September 2022. The year-end lease liability of $1,584,000, should be split into its current and non-current liability components. Non-current liabilities are $1,242,950 and current liabilities at $341,550 ($1,584,500 – $1,242,950)

Year ended	B/f	Interest @ 10%	Instalment	C/f
	$	$	$	$
30.09.22	1,895,000	189,500	(500,000)	1,584,500
30.09.23	1,584,500	158,450	(500,000)	1,242,950

(b) **Lease of investment property**

The lease of the investment property would qualify as an operating lease under IFRS 16 *Leases* since substantially all of the risks and rewards of ownership have been retained by Neon evidenced by:

(i) The lease term is only for five years out of the property's total useful life of 50 years. The lease term does not therefore represent the majority of the property's useful life.

(ii) Neon retains legal title to the property throughout the lease period and intends to hold onto the property throughout its useful life.

The lease rental should be recognised in profit or loss on an accruals basis over the five year lease term. As the first six-months of the are 'rent free' the total lease payments received are $2,250,000 ($250,000 + (4 × $500,000). Neon should therefore recognise rental income of $450,000 per annum in profit or loss.

At 30 September 2022, a receivable of $150,000 ($450,000 – $250,000 cash received) should be recognised in Neon's statement of financial position.

Neon should continue to recognise the investment property in its statement of financial position under the cost or fair value model in accordance with IAS 40 *Investment Properties.* Under the cost model, depreciation of $160,000 ($8,000,000/ 50 years) would be charged to profit or loss and the investment property would be shown at a carrying amount of $7,840,000 in the statement of financial position on 30 September 2022.

Under the fair value model, the property value would be restated to fair value at the year end and the resulting fair value gain/loss would be recognised in the profit or loss account for the year. No depreciation is charged if the fair value model is adopted.

(c) **Contract for energy**

On 30 September 2022, the directors of Neon are required to assess whether the contract with GreenCo contains a lease in accordance with IFRS 16 *Leases. A* contract is deemed to contain a lease if the contract specifies a right to control the use of an identified asset, for a period of time, for consideration.

The solar power facility satisfies the criteria as an identified asset because it is explicitly identified in the contract, and GreenCo has no rights of substitution.

The contract gives Neon the right to control the identified asset over the 25-year contract term because:

(i) Neon has the right to substantially all of the economic benefits from the use of the facility over contract term. Neon has exclusive use of the solar power facility as it will purchase all the electricity produced and is entitled to renewable energy tax credits each year from when it buys the electricity.

GreenCo does has legal title to the asset and is also eligible to claim tax credits on the construction of the facility. However, these economic benefits are linked to the ownership of

EXAM ANSWER BANK

the facility, rather than the use of the facility, and therefore are not relevant when determining whether the contract contains a lease.

(ii) Neon has the right to direct the use of the solar power facility over the period of use. Despite the fact that Neon is not responsible for the day-to-day operation of the fact, the facility is purpose built to meet Neon's specific requirements. The use of the facility is therefore pre-determined based on Neon's design specifications. Effectively, the design of the facility has pre-determined how and what the asset is used for over the 25 year contract period.

The contract with GreenCo contains a lease as Neon has the exclusive right to use the solar power facility for 25 years.

The contract contains multiple components: the lease component (linked to the exclusive use of the right of use asset) and the non-lease component (the supply of electricity).

IFRS 16 *Leases* requires the lease component to be accounted for separately from the non-lease component. The lease component is accounted for under IFRS 16 *Leases* and the non-lease component is accounted for as a separate expense in profit or loss in line with how the electricity is supplied.

The consideration in the contract is allocated to the lease/non-lease components based on the stand-alone prices of the lease/non-lease components.

> **Additional areas where credit might be given, note this is not an exhaustive list:**
> - Any further relevant discussion points relevant to the scenario
> - Own figure rule applies throughout

11 Krypton

The question required the identify the correct accounting treatment of decommissioning costs and a cash-settled share-based payment. Candidates were then asked to recalculate the gearing ratio following the amendments to the financial statements and consider any ethical considerations identified (LOs: 1 & 3).

The following chapters from the AIA Financial Accounting and Reporting 2 study text are relevant:

Chapter 4: Ethics and regulation of corporate financial reporting
Chapter 19: Provisions, contingencies and events after the reporting period
Chapter 20: Related parties and share-based payment
Chapter 23: Ratio and trend analysis

(a) **Decommissioning costs**

A provision for decommissioning costs should be recognised if the following IAS 37 *Provisions, Contingent Liabilities and Continent Assets* recognition criteria has been met:

- present obligation as a result of a past event exists;
- leading to a probable outflow of resources; and
- the amount of the provision can be reliably measured.

The decommissioning costs satisfy the IAS 37 *Provisions, Contingent Liabilities and Continent Assets* recognition criteria because:

- A present obligation exists, since Krypton is required to decommission the plant as part of the conditions of the operating licence being granted which arose from a past event (when the operating licence was granted);

- It is probable that a future outflow of economic will occur in 15 years' time when the decommissioning work takes place; and
- A reliable estimate exists of the resources of $375,000

A decommissioning provision should be recognised on 1 October 2021, at the present value of $375,000, and this amount will be added to the initial cost of the asset.

Additional depreciation of $25,000 ($375,000/15 years) should be charged to profit or loss account relating to the additional capitalised costs.

Furthermore, since the provision is held on a present value basis, a finance charge of $37,500 is charged to profit or loss in the year and added to the initial provision. This represents the unwinding of the discount factor on the provision at 10%.

The decommissioning provision will be presented in non-current liabilities in the statement of financial position at $412,500 ($375,000 + $37,500). In addition, retained earnings will reduce by $62,500 ($25,000 + $37,500) in respect of reduction in profit for the year due to the additional depreciation and finance costs.

(b) **Share Appreciation Rights (SARs)**

The share appreciation rights represent a cash settled share-based payment under IFRS 2 *Share Based Payments*. The relevant share-based payment expense should be recognised over the three-year vesting period in line with the conditions of the scheme. In addition, since Krypton has an obligation to settle the SARs in cash, a liability is recorded based on the proportion of the vesting period to date.

The expense is based on the fair value of the SARs. As the amount of cash required to settle the liability will change in line with share price movements, the SARs should be valued at their fair value at each year end during the vesting period. In the year ended 30 September 2022 the SARs will be valued at $9.90 each. In addition, the liability will be based on the expected number of qualifying employees. At 30 September 2022, it is expected that 20% of staff will leave and will forfeit their rights to the SARs and an estimate of total leavers is factored into the year-end computation.

At 30 September 2022, the fair value of the SAR liability is $1,320,000 (500 × 1,000 × $9.90 × 1/3 × 80%). As this is the first year of the vesting period, the full $1,320,000 is expensed to profit or loss in the year.

As the obligation to settle the SAR occurs in two years' time, the obligation is presented under non-current liabilities in the statement of financial position for the year ended 30 September 2022.

(c) **Revised gearing ratio**

	Per draft accounts $	Provision $	SAR $	Amended $
Long term liabilities				
Loan	10,000,000			10,000,000
Provision		412,500		412,500
SAR		—	1,320,000	1,320,000
	10,000,000			11,732,500
Equity				
S'capital	1,000,000			1,000,000
R'earnings	7,100,000	(25,000)	(1,320,000)	5,717,500
		(37,500)		
OCE	3,000,000			3,000,000
	11,100,000			9,717,500
Gearing	90%			120.7,%

(d) **Ethics**

Both items have been incorrectly accounted for in the financial statements for the year ended 30 September 2022. Based on the draft accounts Krypton has achieved a gearing ratio of 90%, which satisfies the bank covenant limit set.

Following the correction of the financial statements for the year ended 30 September 2022, the revised gearing ratio is 120.7% which is significantly above the gearing covenant threshold. All the amendments required have negatively impacted the gearing ratio by either increasing the level of non-current liabilities and/or reducing total equity.

Whilst the errors may be genuine mistakes, it is more likely that they are deliberate attempt to reduce gearing to the required level. The finance director was ultimately responsible for ensuring that the financial statements are prepared in accordance with International Financial Reporting Standards and the evidence collected suggests that this has not been the case.

In both cases the correct IFRS treatment has not been followed which suggests either a lack of professional competence or (more likely) a deliberate attempt to manipulate the financial statements to satisfy the gearing covenant. It is likely that the finance director was unduly influenced by a self-interest threat (job security) linked to the consequences associated with breaking the loan covenant which compromised his integrity and objectivity. The audit committee should ensure that the relevant disciplinary procedures are actioned which may lead to criminal prosecution if the finance director is found to have fraudulently misstated the financial statements.

Since the loan covenant has been breached, the loan is repayable immediately. This may lead to going concern issues, particularly if Krypton does not have the funds available to repay the loan and therefore may not be able to operate into the foreseeable future.

Following the results of the inquiry, the financial statements should be amended in line with the relevant IFRS. In addition, a representative of Krypton should contact the bank with a view to renegotiating the terms of the loan to avoid it being withdrawn or alternatively, look for alternative sources of long-term finance to cover any shortfall.

> **Additional areas where credit might be given, note this is not an exhaustive list:**
> - Further discussion points linked to the scenario, including additional ethical issues/actions to be taken in part d.
> - Own figure rule applies to revised gearing ratio in part (d).

12 Xenon

Part (a) examined the consolidated statement of changes in equity for a group including the treatment of the disposal of shares in a subsidiary (with no loss of control) (LO:2).

Part (b) required candidates to consider how the adoption of the Integrated Report could benefit a prospective buyer (LO's: 1&3).

The following chapters from the AIA Financial Accounting and Reporting 2 study text are relevant:

Chapter 2: Presentation of published financial statements
Chapter 3: Environmental and social reporting
Chapter 6: Revision of basic groups
Chapter 8: Changes in group structures

(a) **Xenon: Consolidated statement of changes in equity for the year ended 30 September 2022**

	Share capital $'000	Retained earnings $'000	Non-controlling interest $'000	Total $'000
At 1.10.21 (W2)/(W3)	1,000	28,780	1,670	31,450
Total comprehensive income (W4)		7,700	720	8,420
Adjustment to parent's equity (W6)		(975)	4,575	3,600
Dividends paid (W5)		(2,000)	(420)	(2,420)
At 30.09.22 (W7)/(W8)	1,000	33,505	6,545	41,050

Workings

1 **Group structure**

Retained earnings at 1.10.19: $4,300

Retained earnings at 1.4.22
B/f 1.10.21   8,500
6m to 30.4.22
(3,200 × 6/12)   1,600
    10,100

2 **Group retained earnings at 1.10.21**

	Xenon $'000	Radon 90% $'000
Retained earnings at 30.9.21	25,000	8,500
Pre-acquisition retained earnings (W1)		(4,300)
		4,200
Group share:		
90% × 4,200	3,780	
	28,780	

3 **Non-controlling interest at 1.10.21**

90% × 4,200   3,780

	$'000
NCI at acquisition	1,250
NCI % post-acquisition profits (4,200 × 10%)	420
	1,670

4 **Total comprehensive income**

	Xenon $'000	Radon $'000	Consolidated $'000
Profit for the year	6,000	3,200	9,200
Less: intra-company dividend (W5)	(780)	-	(780)
	5,520	3,200	8,420

Attributable to:
Owners of the parent (balance) ... 7,700
Non-controlling interest
(3,200 × 10% × 6/12) + (3,200 × 35% × 6/12) ... 720
8,420

5 **Intra-company dividends: Radon**

- Dividend of $1,200,000 on 30 September 2022.
- Group share: $780,000 ($1,200,000 × 65%) is eliminated from TCI on consolidation
- Non-controlling interest share: $420,000 ($1,200,000 × 35%) included in the consolidated statement of changes in equity.

6 **Group retained earnings at 30.9.22 (proof)**

	Xenon	Radon 90% to 1.4.22	Radon 65% from 1.4.22
	$'000	$'000	$'000
Retained earnings at 30.9.22 / disposal (W1)	29,000	10,100	10,500
Adjustment to parent's equity (W8)	(975)		
Pre-acquisition retained earnings		(4,300)	(10,100)
		5,800	400
Group share:			
90% × 5,800	5,220		
65% × 400	260		
	33,505		

7 **Non-controlling interest at 30.9.22 (proof)**

	$'000
At acquisition	1,250
NCI % post-acquisition profit to 1.4.22: 5,800 × 10%	580
10% NCI at 1.4.22	1,830
Increase in NCI (balance)	4,575
35% NCI at 1.4.22 (1,830 × 35/10)	6,405
NCI% post-acquisition profit from 1.4.22: 400 × 35%	140
35% NCI at 30.9.22	6,545

8 **Part disposal: adjustment to parent's equity**

	$'000
Proceeds	3,600
Increase in non-controlling interest (W7)	(4,575)
Adjustment to parent's equity	(975)

Additional areas where credit might be given, note this is not an exhaustive list:

- The use of own figures applies throughout.
- Credit will be given for alternative workings presented.
- Marks will be awarded for relevant workings even if these have not been included on the face of statement of changes in equity.

(b) **Integrated Reporting**

Integrated Reporting is concerned with how the business creates value through the use of six capitals: financial, manufactured, intellectual, human, social and natural capitals over the longer term. Integrated reporting will enable Xenon to present a holistic view of how its value is created over time by utilising the both the financial and non-financial resources available to it.

Since the shares are likely to be marketed at a substantial premium, any prospective buyer will pay close attention to the Xenon's future prospects, including its future profitability and cash generating ability. Xenon's value creation narrative, both in terms of how value has been created and the mechanisms in place to ensure future value creation will be of paramount importance.

Xenon's value creation narrative will help explain the how each of the following six capitals contribute to the value created within the firm:

- **Financial capital:** the financial resources available to fund Xenon's operations and future growth ambitions.
- **Manufactured capital**: the tangible assets available for production e.g. land and buildings, plant and equipment etc.
- **Intellectual capital**: the processes and knowledge based intellectual capital available within the business including licences, trademarks, and patents.
- **Human capital:** the technical skills, competencies and expertise of Xenon's staff and management team.
- **Social capital:** the nature of relationships between Xenon and its customers, suppliers and other key stakeholders.
- **Natural capital:** the access and proximity to natural resources such as power, water, infrastructure etc.

The capitals are inter-connected, and a trade-off exists between short term profit maximisation and longer-term strategic aims. This longer-term strategic focus on long term value creation will enable Xenon to present a comprehensive picture of the business and its prospects for future growth.

Given the technological nature of the business, the majority of the value created by Xenon will be attributable to its knowledge based intangible assets and human capital i.e., its intellectual property and staff expertise, which conventional financial reporting does not capture.

IAS *38 Intangible Assets* permits the recognition of intangible assets only if it is probable that future economic benefits will flow to the entity and the cost of the asset can be reliably measured. Consequently, only a small proportion of intangible assets are recognised in the financial statements, typically those acquired from third parties.

Potential buyers need to understand of how both internally generated and externally acquired intangible assets create value for the business. The integrated report offers an opportunity to communicate the significance of intangible assets to the value creation process.

If Teng is looking to sell his shares for the highest possible price, then the integrated report will facilitate the communication of information beyond the financial statements focusing on the other key drivers of value within the business.

> **Additional areas where credit might be given, note this is not an exhaustive list:**
> - Further discussion relating to the benefits of integrated reporting from an investor perspective
> - Recognition and evaluation of other benefits to Xenon

EXAM ANSWER BANK

13 Nysa

Part (a) (i) requires candidates to classify and account for a newly acquired joint venture using the equity accounting method (Syllabus area 2: LO 2, 3, and 4).

Part (a) (ii) requires the preparation of the consolidated statement of financial position for a vertical group (Syllabus area 2: LO 2, 3, and 4).

Part (b) (iii) requires a discussion on the importance of sustainability reporting (ESG reporting) to investor (Syllabus area 1: LO1).

The following chapters of the BPP Financial Accounting and Reporting study text are relevant:

Chapter 3: Environmental and social reporting
Chapter 6: Revision of basic groups
Chapter 8: Changes in group structures

(a) **Investment in Nbu**

IFRS 11 *Joint Arrangements* defines a joint arrangement as "an arrangement in which two or more parties have joint control" (IFRS 11: para 4). In addition, a joint arrangement has the following characteristics (IFRs 11: para 5):

- "the parties are bound by a contractual arrangement
- The contractual arrangement gives two or more of those parties joint control over the arrangement"

A joint arrangement exits because both Nysa and Valhalla are bound by a contractual agreement. In addition, there is evidence of joint control within the agreement as decision making requires unanimous consent.

IFRS 11 *Joint Arrangements* identifies two different types of joint arrangement:

Joint operation: A joint operation exists where each venturer has rights to their share of the assets and liabilities of the arrangement.

Joint venture: This is where each venturer is entitled to their share of the net assets of the arrangement.

Under the terms of the agreement, Nysa is entitled to a 50% share in the net assets of Nbu.

Therefore, the investment should be accounted for as a joint venture.

IAS 27 *Separate Financial Statements* permits the investment in Nbu to be held in Nysa's own separate financial statements at either:

- Cost; or
- Fair value in accordance with IFRS 9 Financial Instruments; or
- Under equity accounting under IAS 28 *Investments in Associates and Joint ventures*

In Nysa's consolidated statements, the joint venture should be accounted for using equity accounting as specified in IAS 28 *Investments in Associates and Joint Ventures*.

In Nysa's consolidated statement of financial position, the investment in the joint venture will be initially recorded at cost of $10 million. The joint ventures carrying amount will subsequently increase by Nysa's share of Nbu's post-acquisition profits, as shown below:

Investment in joint venture.

	$m
Cost of 50% investment	10.0
Share of post-acquisition profits ($8m × 50%)	4.0
	14.0

In the consolidated statement of profit or loss and other comprehensive income, Nysa's share of Nbu's profit will be presented as a separate line item (immediately before the group profit before taxation line item), as follows:

	$m
Share of profit of joint venture ($8m × 50%)	4.0

(b) **Nysa: Consolidated statement of financial position as at 31 March 2023.**

	$m
ASSETS	
Non-current assets	
Property, plant and equipment 242 + 30 + 20 + 10 (W6)	302.0
Intangible assets 100 + 50 + 25 + 2 (W3)	177.0
Goodwill 10 (W2)/(W4) + 22.5 (W5)	32.5
Investment in joint venture (part a)	14.0
	525.5
Current assets 140 + 50 + 30	220.0
Total assets	**745.5**
EQUITY AND LIABILITIES	
Equity	
Equity shares - $1 shares	100.0
Retained earnings	238.0
Other components of equity	53.0
	391.0
Non-controlling interest 20.5 + 29 9 (W9)	49.5
	440.5
Non-current liabilities 100 + 30 + 10	140.0
Current liabilities 110 + 30 + 25	165.0
Total equity and liabilities	**745.5**

Workings

1 Group structure

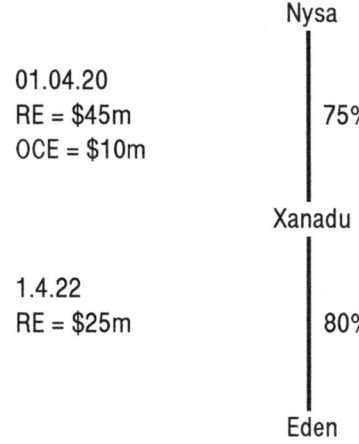

Eden Effective interest = 75% × 80% = 60%
Eden NCI = 40%

> **Tutorial note:**
>
> Nysa must consolidate all companies under its control, either directly (Xanadu) or indirectly (Eden).
>
> Eden's assets and liabilities are consolidated on a line-by-line basis as these are controlled by Nysa
>
> Ownership interest is reflected in equity based on the effective interest percentages. Group retained earnings includes the group's 60% share of Eden's post-acquisition profits and the non-controlling interest is allocated the remaining 40% share.

2 **Goodwill: Xanadu**

	$m	$m
Consideration paid		90.0
Non-controlling interest (fair value)		30.0
Fair value of net assets acquired at 01.04.2020		
Share capital	50.0	
Retained earnings (per question)	45.0	
Fair value adjustment - intangible assets (balance)	5.0	
Fair value of net assets at acquisition (per question)	100.0	(100.0)
Goodwill at 01.04.2020		20.0
Impairment		(10.0)
Goodwill at 31.03.2023		10.0

3 **Fair value Adjustment: Xanadu**

	At 01.04.2020 $m	Movement $m	At 31.03.2023 $m
Intangible assets	5.0	(3.0)	2.0

Fair value amortisation:
$5m / 5 years × 3 years = $3m

4 **Impairment: Xanadu**

	$m
Net assets: carrying amount at 31.03.2023 per SOFP	120.0
Remaining FV adjustment at 31.03.2023 (W3)	2.0
Goodwill (W2)	20.0
	142.0
Recoverable amount (per question)	132.0
Impairment loss	10.0

5 **Goodwill: Eden**

	$m
Consideration paid: $50m × 75%	37.5
Non-controlling interest: 10m × 40% × $6.25	25.0

Fair value of net assets acquired on 01.04.2022	$m	$m
Share capital	10.0	
Retained earnings (per question)	25.0	
Fair value adjustment - land (balance)	10.0	
Fair value of net assets (excluding contingent liability)	45.0	
Less: fair value of contingent liability	(5.0)	(40.0)
Goodwill at 01.04.2022 & 31.03.2023		22.5

> **Tutorial note:**
>
> **Eden's goodwill**
>
> The consolidation is prepared from Nysa's perspective. As Nysa owns 75% of Xanadu, it should recognise only 75% of the consideration paid by Xanadu to acquire Eden in the goodwill working.
>
> The remaining 25% of the consideration paid by Xanadu, will be adjusted for in Xanadu's non-controlling interest working.

6 Fair value adjustments: Eden

	At 01.04.2022 $m	Movement $m	At 31.03.2023 $m
Land (non-depreciable)	10.0	-	10.0
Contingent liability	(5.0)	5.0	-

7 Retained earnings

	Nysa $m	Xanadu $m	Eden $m
Per question	222.0	56.0	30.0
Fair value amortisation: Xanadu (W3)		(3.0)	
Contingent liability: Eden			5.0
At acquisition (W1)		(35.0)	(25.0)
		18.0	10.0
Group share:			
Xanadu: 18 × 75%	13.5		
Eden: 10 × 60%	6.0		
Share of joint ventures profit for the year (part a)	4.0		
Group % goodwill impairment:			
Xanadu: 10 (W4) × 75%	(7.5)		
	238.0		

8 Other components of equity

	Xanadu $m	Nysa $m
At year end	50.0	14.0
At acquisition (W1)		(10.0)
		4.0
Group share:		
Xanadu: 4 × 75%	3.0	
	53.0	

9 Non-controlling interest

	Xanadu $m	Nysa $m
NCI at acquisition	30.0	25.0
NCI share post-acquisition retained earnings:		
Xanadu: 18(W7) × 25%	4.5	
Eden: 10 × 40%		4.0
NCI % post-acquisition other components of equity (W8)		
Xanadu: 4(W8) × 25%	1.0	
Less: NCI share of cost of Eden: $50m × 25%	(12.5)	
NCI share of goodwill impairment	(2.5)	
Xanadu: 10 (W4) × 25%	20.5	29.0

(c) **Sustainability (ESG) reporting**

Investors have become increasingly interested in sustainability related activity when making investment decisions. This has been driven by an increased awareness and understanding of climate change and other sustainability-related issues from a broad range of stakeholder groups including national governments, consumers, suppliers, activists and investors.

Investors require assurances that the firms they are investing in are engaging in ethical and sustainable practices. This requires a better understanding of how the business operates in terms of environmental and social performance and how its governance structure enables it to recognise and respond to sustainability related risks and opportunities.

Sustainability reporting provides key information on an entity's environmental, social and corporate governance (ESG) performance. The ESG report includes both qualitative and quantitative information to facilitate a better understanding of the major risks and opportunities related to the entity.

In recent years investors have become more aware of ESG related issues and are actively avoiding investing in companies with poor ESG reputations linked to high pollution levels or poor working conditions etc. Investors may also seek to disinvest due to the perceived risks of operating in a non-ESG compliant environment. Investors can incorporate ESG information into the investment decision-making processes to ensure that investments are aligned to their own values and beliefs.

More importantly, a growing number of institutional investors are realigning their investment portfolios towards firms with better ESG propositions more broadly. This fundamental shift in investor sentiment demonstrates the significance of ESG performance in investment appraisal.

ESG information provides a comprehensive view of an entity's performance which supports better investment decisions. Integrating ESG factors into the decision-making process reduces risk and creates value for investors.

Firms with strong ESG propositions are considered less risky and better prepared for the long term and arguably better positioned to cope with uncertainty. In contrast, firms with poor ESG performance are considered riskier in terms of potential legal and regulatory interventions, reputational damage and threats to future operations. Investors are keen to understand the risks associated with their investments, and the risk management strategies in place to deal with those risks.

In addition, investors are keen to understand the long-term value creation prospects of their investments. Firms with strong ESG propositions are generally considered to offer better long-term growth potential and superior financial returns due to:

- Higher turnover growth: A strong ESG profile may provide opportunities for growth by access to new markets and expansion in existing ones.

- Cost savings: Environmental initiatives such as reducing energy consumption and waste have the potential to reduce costs for the business and therefore increasing the profitability of the firm.

- Lower cost of capital: Research suggests that firms with strong ESG reputations have access to cheaper finance and have lower costs of capital.

- Access to talent: A strong ESG reputation can help to attract and retain talent.

14 Nirvana

This question examined the financial accounting treatment of an issue of overseas bonds, an aluminium forward contract and a defined benefit plan (Syllabus area 3: LO 2, 3 & 4).

The following chapters of the BPP Financial Accounting 2 and Reporting study text are relevant:

Chapter 9: Foreign currency translation
Chapter 14: Financial Instruments
Chapter 16: Employee benefits

(a) **Sterling Bonds**

The £10 million 6% sterling bonds are classified as a financial liability in accordance with IFRS 9 *Financial Instruments* as two separate obligations exist under the terms of the bond i.e., to pay an annual coupon rate and to redeem the bonds in five years' time.

As the bonds are denominated in UK pounds sterling, the financial liability will be first calculated in sterling, and then translated into dollars (Nirvana's functional currency) at the appropriate rate in accordance with IAS *19 The Effects of Changes in Foreign Currency Rates* for inclusion in the financial statements for the year ended 31 March 2023.

On the 1 April 2022, the bonds should be recognised at their fair value of £10 million less the £0.2 million transaction costs of issue. The net cash received of £9.80 million will be translated at spot rate of £1:$1.30 at the transaction date. Nirvana will initially record a bond liability of $12.74 million in its accounts.

The bonds are subsequently held on an amortised cost basis at an effective rate of interest of 6.5% per annum. A finance cost of £0.64 million arises which is translated at average rate for the year of £1:$1.25. Nirvana will expense the translated finance cost of $0.80 million to the profit or loss for the year ended 31 March 2023.

The £0.6 million coupon interest paid on 31 March 2023 will be translated at the exchange rate at the payment date i.e., at £1: $1.20. The coupon paid is translated at $0.72 million which reduces the liability and credited to cash.

On 31 March 2023, the bond liability of £9.84 million is translated at closing rate at the year end of £1:$1.20. The bonds will be included in Nirvana's statement of financial position at a carrying amount of $11.81 million.

A foreign exchange gain of $1.01 million arises on the translation of the sterling bonds into dollars. This foreign exchange gain will be expensed to profit or loss for the year ended 31 March 2023.

IAS 19 *The Effects of Changes in Foreign Currency Rates* is silent on where in profit or loss the foreign exchange gain should be recorded. However, as the foreign exchange gain relates to a financing transaction, it would be appropriate to include this as part of finance income.

Workings

1 *Sterling Bonds*

Date		£m	Rate	$m
01.04.2022	Cash raised on issue less transaction costs	9.80	1.30	12.74
	Finance costs @ 6.5%	0.64	1.25	0.80
31.03.2023	Coupon paid £10m × 6%	(0.60)	1.20	(0.72)
				12.82
31.03.2023	Foreign exchange gain		(Balance)	1.01
31.03.2023	Balance c/f	9.84	1.20	11.81

(b) **Aluminium forward contract**

The aluminium forward contract is a derivative contract because (IFRS 9: Appendix A):

- Its value changes in response to an underlying variable i.e., its fair value changes in response to changes in price of aluminium;
- It requires no initial investment. Nirvana paid nothing on 1 February 2023 to enter into the contact; and
- It will be settled at a future date i.e., 30 June 2023.

The accounting treatment of the aluminium contract depends on whether the contract is classified as a financial contract or an executory contract. FRS 9 *Financial Instruments* only applies to financial contracts.

IFRS 9 *Financial Instruments* applies to "those contracts to buy or sell a non-financial item that can be settled net in cash or another financial instrument, or by exchanging financial instruments, as if the contracts were financial instruments" (IFRS 9: para. 2.4). These are treated as financial contracts.

Contracts that lead to "the receipt or delivery of a non-financial item in accordance with the entity's expected purchase, sale or usage" (IFRS 9: para. 2.4) are considered as executory contracts which are outside of the scope of IFRS 9 *Financial Instruments*.

(i) **If Nirvana intends to take physical delivery of the aluminium for business use.**

The contract would be treated as an executory contract as Nirvana intends to take delivery of the aluminium at the end of the contract. The purchase of the aluminium is not accounted for until Nirvana obtains control of the asset i.e., when the aluminium is delivered on 30 June 2023.

(ii) **If the contract is a speculative contract that Nirvana intends to settle net in cash.**

In contrast, if Nirvana intends to settle the contract net in cash, this would be classified as a financial contract and therefore would fall under the scope of IFRS 9 *Financial Instruments*. The financial derivative contract would be classified as held at fair value through profit or loss.

On 1 February 2023, the derivative contract will be recorded at its fair value of $nil, as no cash was exchanged on signing the contract.

On 31 March 2023, the derivative is stated at its fair value at the year-end as follows:

		$m
1 February 2023	3,000 tonnes @ $2,300	6.9
31 March 2023	3,000 tonnes × $2,500	7.5
Gain on forward contract		0.6

As the fair value of the aluminium forward contract is rising, this results in a fair value gain of $0.6 million on the contract which will be credited in profit or loss. Nirvana will recognise a financial asset of $0.6million in its statement of financial position as at 31 March 2023.

(c) **Defined benefit pension plan**

Extracts from profit or loss and other comprehensive income:

Profit or loss	$m
Current service cost	(20.0)
Past service cost	(8.0)
Net interest cost (4.2 - 3.0)	(1.2)
	(29.2)
Other comprehensive income	
Remeasurement loss on plan assets	(1.0)
Remeasurement gain on pension obligation	7.2
	6.2

Extracts from the statement of financial position:

	$m
Non-current liabilities	
Net pension obligation (75.0 - 60.0)	15.0

	FV plan assets $m	PV obligation $m
At 1 April 2022	50.0	62.0
Interest @ 6%		
50m × 6% / (62m + 8m) × 6%	3.0	4.2
Current service cost		20.0
Past service cost 1 April 2022		8.0
Contributions	20.0	
Benefits paid to former employees	(12.0)	(12.0)
	61.0	82.2
Remeasurement loss on plan assets (balance)	(1.0)	
Remeasurement gain on obligation (balance)	–	(7.2)
At 31 March 2023	60.0	75.0

15 Nibiru

This question examined the accounting treatment of a readily traded asset and development land in accordance with IFRS 13 Fair Value Measurement; an interest free loan to employees and an equity settled share-based payment. (Syllabus area 3: LO 2, 3 & 4).

The following chapters of the BPP Financial Accounting 2 and Reporting study text are relevant:

Chapter 14: Financial Instruments
Chapter 18: Reporting financial performance
Chapter 20: Related parties and share based payments

(a) **Readily traded asset**

In accordance with IFRS 13 *Fair Value Measurement*, fair value is defined as "the price that would be received to sell an asset or paid to transfer a liability in an orderly transaction between participants at the measurement date" (IFRS 13: Appendix A).

IFRS 13 Fair Value Measurement assumes that the transaction takes place in the principal market or "the market with the greatest volume and level of activity." (IFRS 13: Appendix A). Provided Nibiru can access all three markets, the European market is the principal market for the asset because it has the highest total number of sales of 5 million units.

In computing the assets fair value in the European market, transport costs are included but transaction costs are ignored. Therefore, the asset will be valued at $140 per unit [$150 – $10].

In the absence of a principal market, the fair value is determined in the most advantageous market which is defined as "the market that maximises the amount that would be received to sell the asset, after taking into account transaction costs and transport costs." (IFRS 13: Appendix A) as shown below:

	Europe $	UK $	USA $
Sales price (per unit)	150	180	130
Transaction costs (per unit)	(15)	(18)	(13)
Transport costs (per unit)	(10)	(5)	(8)
	125	157	108

The UK market is the most advantageous market as Nibiru would maximise its net revenue (after all costs) in the UK. Based on the most advantageous market the fair value of the asset would be calculated at $175 [$180 – $5] per unit.

(b) **Development land**

The land is a non-financial asset whose fair value is determined using the "highest and best use" basis (IFRS 13: para 27). The fair value is determined from a market participants perspective and alternative uses are considered in the fair valuation process.

The highest and best use takes into consideration all alternative uses which are "physically possible, legally permissible and financially feasible" (IFRS 13: para. 28) as follows:

- Physically possible: this takes into account the physical characteristics of the asset that market participants would consider when pricing the asset e.g., location and size.
- Legally permissible: this considers any legal restrictions on the assets use.
- Financially feasible: considers any financial constraints associated with any alternative use.

The land is situated in an upcoming residential development area and similar plots have already been developed into luxury residential accommodation. Therefore, the physically possible criterion is met.

Nibiru requires planning permission before development work can commence. Planning permission has been applied for and is expected to be granted soon. Once granted the planning permission will enable Nibiru to legally develop the land for residential purposes.

In addition, the development project appears financially feasible. The market value of residential land exceeds its agricultural value. Therefore, the change of use will enable Nibiru to maximise the economic benefits associated with the land.

The fair value of the land will be calculated as the higher of:

- The fair value of the land based on its current agricultural use of $5 million:
- The fair value of the land if used for residential purposes of $10 million.

Based on the information provided the fair value of the development land on 31 March 2023 is $10 million.

(c) **Interest free loans**

The interest free loans will qualify as a financial asset under IFRS 9 *Financial Instruments* since Nibiru has a contractual right to the repayment of the loans in three years' time. In accordance with IFRS 9 *Financial Instruments*, financial assets are initially measured at fair value at initial recognition.

Usually, the fair value of the loan receivable would be equal to the $10 million cash value of the loans. However, as the loans are provided on an 'interest free' basis, the fair value of the loan receivable is the present value of its cash flows discounted at market rates of interest of 8%.

The present value of the $10 million loan discounted using the three-year 8% discount factor is $7.9 million [$10m × 1/1.08^3) on 1 April 2022. The $2.1 million difference between the $10 million cash value and its fair value at inception on 1 April 2022 is treated as employee compensation under IAS 19 *Employee Benefits*. This employee compensation will be expensed to profit or loss over the three-year loan period.

As Nibiru's business model is to collect the underlying cash flows on the loan, the loan receivable will be held on an amortised cost basis at an effective rate of interest of 8%.

Finance income $0.6million [$7.9m × 8%] will be credited to profit or loss in the year ended 31 March 2023. At the year-end the loan receivable will be shown in Nibiru's statement of financial position at a carrying amount of $8.5million [$7.9m + $0.6m].

Employee compensation of $0.6million (i.e., the equivalent of finance income) will be expensed to profit or loss in the year. This prevents an accounting mismatch between the amounts of finance income and employee compensation recognised in profit or loss. The remaining $1.5million [$2.1m – $0.6m] employee compensation will be expensed to profit or loss over the next two years.

(d) **Share options**

The share options represent an equity settled transaction in accordance with IFRS 2 *Share-Based Payments*.

The share options will be valued at their fair value at the date of grant of $10 per option. The fair value of $10 remains fixed in all subsequent calculations and is not updated for any future changes in fair value.

The equity settled transaction is recognised in profit or loss over the vesting period. Under the terms of the share options two conditions must be met before the share options can be exercised.

Firstly, employees must remain in Nibiru's employment for three years until 31 March 2025. This performance related condition should be considered when calculating the relevant share-based payment expense each year.

The second condition is a market-based condition i.e., the share price must reach $25 per share on 31 March 2025. Market conditions are not taken into consideration in computing the relevant share-based payment expense. This is because market conditions have already been incorporated into the fair value of the share-based payment at the date of grant.

The equity settled share-based payment should therefore be spread over a three-year vesting period irrespective of whether the share price target has been achieved.

In addition, the directors need to reassess the number of expected qualifying employee at each year end.

The share-based payment expense of $1.42 million is expensed to profit or loss and credited to equity, calculated as follows:

	$m
Share based payment expense	
500 options × (1,000 × 85%) × $10 × 1/3	1.42

16 Elysium

Part (a)(i) required a discussion of a step acquisition of shares in a subsidiary (70% to 90% shareholding). Part (a) (ii) examined the consolidated statement of changes in equity for the Elysium group. (Syllabus area 2: LO 2, 3 and 4).

Part (b) required candidates to consider the ethical considerations relating to overexaggerated claims in the notes to the accounts. (Syllabus area 1: LO1).

The following chapters from the AIA Financial Accounting and Reporting 2 study text are relevant:

Chapter 2: Presentation of published financial statements
Chapter 4: Ethics and regulation of corporate financial reporting
Chapter 6: Revision of basic groups
Chapter 8: Changes in group structures

(a) (i) Accounting treatment of Avalon.

Elysium obtained control of Avalon when it acquired its initial 70% shareholding in the company. Prior to the acquisition of the additional 20% shareholding, Avalon would be fully consolidated in the consolidated financial statements on a line-by-line basis.

The purchase of an additional 20% shareholding would not constitute an acquisition as Elysium continues to have a controlling interest in Avalon. The additional share purchase is treated as transaction between two existing parties i.e., the parent and the non-controlling interest (the parent's controlling interest has increased from 70% to 90% and the non-controlling interest has decreased from 30% to 10%).

The reallocation between the group and the non-controlling interest is recognised in equity. This is calculated as the difference between the consideration paid and the proportionate decrease in the non-controlling interest on the date of the change.

Consolidated goodwill is calculated at the date the parent first acquired control of the subsidiary i.e., when Elysium first acquired a 70% controlling interest. The purchase of the additional 20% shareholding in Avalon does not affect the goodwill calculation. Since consolidated goodwill has not been impaired in the post-acquisition period, consolidated goodwill will continue to be included in the financial statement of financial position at its original value of $55 million.

A 10% non-controlling interest will be recognised in the consolidated statement of financial position as at 31 March 2023.

Avalon's income and expenses will be consolidated in full on a line-by-line basis in the consolidated statement of profit or loss and other comprehensive income for the year. As the acquisition took place part way through the year, the non-controlling interests share of profit and total comprehensive income will be calculated based a 30% share for the first six months and 10% for the last six months of the year.

(ii) Elysium: Consolidated statement of changes in equity for the year ended 31 March 2023.

	Share capital $m	Retained earnings $m	Non-controlling interest $m	Total $m
At 1 April 2022 (per Q)	50.0	386.5	69.0	505.5
Total comprehensive income (W2)		110.8	7.2	118.0
Adjustment to parent's equity (W3)/(W4)		(8.4)	(49.6)	(58)
At 31 March 2023	50.0	488.9	26.6	565.5

Workings

1 **Group structure**

Retained earnings at 1.10.2022
B/f 1.04.2022   150.0
6m to 30.9.22 (36 × 6/12)   18.0
                                                 168.0

2 Total comprehensive income

	Elysium $m	Avalon $m	Consolidated $m
Profit for the year	82.0	36.0	118.0

	$m
Attributable to:	
Owners of the parent (balance)	110.8
Non-controlling interest	7.2
($36m × 6/12 × 30%) + ($36m × 6/12 × 10%)	
	118.0

3 Step acquisition: purchase of 2m shares

	$m
Consideration paid	58.0
Decrease in non-controlling interest (W3)	(49.6)
Adjustment to parent's equity	8.4

4 Non-controlling interest

	$m
At acquisition	45.0
NCI % post-acquisition profit to 1.10.22: (168 (W1) – 70) × 30%	29.4
30% NCI at 1.10.22	74.4
Decrease in NCI (balance)	**(49.6)**
10% NCI at 1.10.22 (74.4 × 10/30)	24.8
Not required for question	
NCI% post-acquisition profit from 1.10.22: 36m × 6/12 × 10%	1.8
10% NCI at 31.3.23 (proof)	26.6

5 Group retained earnings at 31.3.22 (proof)

	Elysium $m	Avalon 70% to 01.10.2022 $m	Avalon 90% from 01.04.2022 $m
Retained earnings at 1.10.22 / disposal (W1)	412.5	168.0	186.0
Adjustment to parent's equity (W8)	(8.4)		
Pre-acquisition retained earnings		(70.0)	(168.0)
		98.0	18.0
Group share:			
70% × 98	68.6		
90% × 18	16.2		
	488.9		

Additional areas where credit might be given, note this is not an exhaustive list:

- The use of own figures applies throughout.
- Credit will be given for alternative workings presented.
- Marks will be awarded for relevant workings even if these have not been included on the face of statement of changes in equity.

(b) **Bond disclosures**

When preparing the financial statements for the year ended 31 March 2023, the directors of Elysium need to ensure that:

- The financial statements have been prepared in accordance with International Financial Reporting Standards (IFRS); and
- The transactions and events included faithfully represent the economic phenomena that they purport to represent; and
- Adequate disclosure is provided to assist users with the proper understanding of transactions and events occurring in the period.

The $100 million bonds should be accounted for as a financial liability on an amortised cost basis in accordance with IFRS 9 *Financial Instruments*. There is nothing in the scenario to suggest that the bonds have been incorrectly accounted for. Furthermore, the associated terms and conditions (including details of the loan covenant) have been disclosed in the notes to the accounts.

The bonds include a covenant based on a reduction in carbon emissions and Elysium will incur a significant penalty if the target is not met. The finance director has behaved unethically by over exaggerating Elysium's progress towards the emissions target in a deliberate attempt mislead users. This contravenes the ethical principles of integrity and professional behaviour.

On discovering the report from the independent sustainability expert, the accountant has already approached the finance director to discuss this issue further. The finance director's subsequent behaviour constitutes an intimidation threat which contravenes all ethical principles. In addition, the accountant's objectivity may be under threat due to the fear of losing their job (a self-interest threat). Despite these ethical dilemmas the accountant must ensure that their objectivity is uncompromised without fear of repercussions.

Based on conversations to date It is unlikely that the finance director will amend the disclosures. The accountant should therefore escalate this issue to other board members or to Elysium's audit committee. The accountant may also wish to contact the AIA's ethical helpline or take legal advice before taking any further action.

It is also advisable to document all communications with the finance director in relation to this matter.

17 Uno

Parts (a) and (b) require the preparation of the consolidated statement of financial position including a step-acquisition and an overseas subsidiary [Syllabus area 2]. In part (c) candidates were required to consider the ethical implications surrounding the reclassification of the translation gains arising on a foreign subsidiary to profit or loss. [Syllabus area 1: LO2 & LO3].

The following chapters from the AIA Financial Accounting and Reporting 2 study text are relevant:

Chapter 4: Ethics and regulation of corporate financial reporting
Chapter 6: Revision of basic groups
Chapter 8: Changes in group structure
Chapter 9: Foreign currency translation

(a) Uno had a significant influence over Dos from 1 October 2021 until 1 April 2023, and therefore would have equity accounted for its 30% shareholding in Dos. When Uno acquired an additional 40% shareholding in Dos on 1 April 2023, it obtained control over Dos when it became a 70% subsidiary. Dos will therefore be consolidated on a line-by-line basis from 1 April 2023.

In the consolidated statement of profit or loss and other comprehensive income the income and expenses of Dos will be time apportioned so that only six months of post-acquisition amounts are

EXAM ANSWER BANK

recognised. The assets and liabilities of Dos are included in the consolidated statement of financial position at their year-end value (and no time apportionment is necessary).

Since control of Dos has been achieved in stages, in substance Uno has 'disposed' of its original 30% associate investment and replaced this with a new 70% subsidiary.

The carrying amount of the 30% associate is uplifted to fair value on 1 April 2023, and the resulting gain of $240,000 is recognised in the consolidated statement of profit or loss and in consolidated retained earnings in the statement of financial position, as shown below:

(i) **Restate cost of 30% associate to fair value at 01.04.2023.**

	$'000	$'000
Fair value at 01.04.23: 200 (SC) × 30% × $25		1,500.0
Carrying value of associate on 01.04.23		
Cost	1,200.0	
Share of post-acquisition profits		
30% × [650 (W1) – 450]	60.0	-1,260.0
Gain on remeasurement	1,200.0	240.0

Goodwill is calculated when control is first achieved on 1 April 2023. The consideration paid consists of the cash paid to acquire the additional 40% equity stake plus the fair value of the original 30% shareholding on 1 April 2023. The finance director has incorrectly capitalised acquisition costs (dealers fees) on the purchase of the additional 40% shareholding. In accordance with IFRS 3 *Business Combinations*, acquisition costs should be expensed to the profit or loss account as incurred and not treated as part of the cost of the investment. The cost of the additional 40% shareholding should be amended to $2 million in Uno's statement of financial position.

The 30% non-controlling interest should be measured fair value of $1.5 million on 1 April 2023 (200,000 shares × 30% × $25) in accordance with Uno's accounting policy.

Consolidated goodwill has been calculated as follows:

(ii) **Goodwill when control first achieved 01.04.2023.**

	$'000	$'000
Consideration (40%): 200 (SC) × 40% × $25		2,000.0
Fair value (30%)		1,500.0
Non-controlling interest (30%)- as above		1,500.0
Fair value of net assets acquired:		
Equity shares	200.0	
Retained earnings (W1)	650.0	
		-850.0
Goodwill		4,150.0

(b) **Consolidated statement of financial position as at 30 September 2023.**

	$'000
ASSETS	
Non-current assets	
Property, plant, and equipment 5,700 + 1,600 + 1,272.5 (W2)	8,572.5
Goodwill 4,150(part a) + 5,000 (W3)	9,150.0
	17,722.5
Current assets 4,250 + 1,050 + 915(W2)	6,215.0
Total assets	23,937.5

EXAM ANSWER BANK

	$'000
EQUITY AND LIABILITIES	
Equity	
Equity shares	1,000.0
Retained earnings (W4)	6,509.0
Translation reserve (W5)	1,018.0
	8,527.0
Non-controlling interest 1,545.0 (W6) + 1,230.5 (W7)	2,775.5
	11,302.5
Non-current liabilities 7,200 + 900 + 580 (W2)	8,680.0
Current liabilities 2,750 + 750 + 455 (W2)	3,955.0
	23,937.5

Workings.

1 **Group structure.**

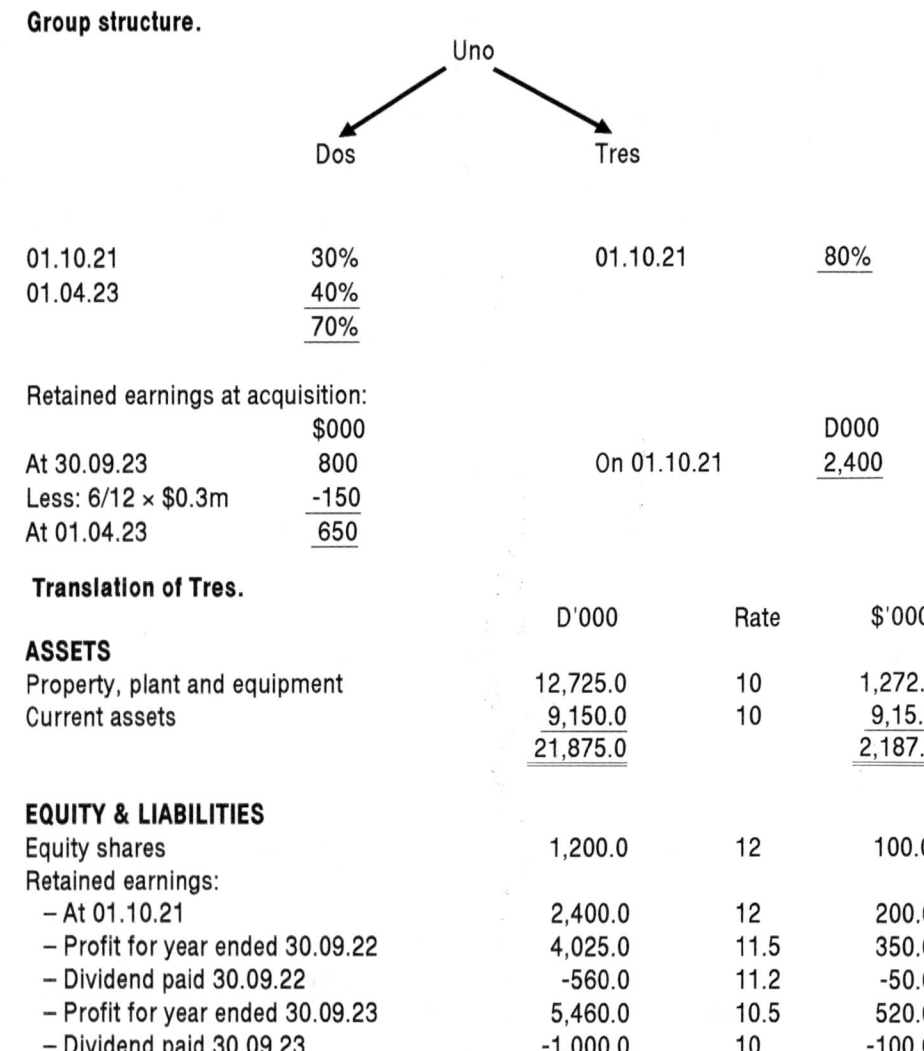

	Dos		Tres	
01.10.21	30%	01.10.21	80%
01.04.23	40%		
	70%		

Retained earnings at acquisition:

	$000		D000
At 30.09.23	800	On 01.10.21	2,400
Less: 6/12 × $0.3m	-150		
At 01.04.23	650		

2 **Translation of Tres.**

	D'000	Rate	$'000
ASSETS			
Property, plant and equipment	12,725.0	10	1,272.5
Current assets	9,150.0	10	9,15.0
	21,875.0		2,187.5
EQUITY & LIABILITIES			
Equity shares	1,200.0	12	100.0
Retained earnings:			
– At 01.10.21	2,400.0	12	200.0
– Profit for year ended 30.09.22	4,025.0	11.5	350.0
– Dividend paid 30.09.22	-560.0	11.2	-50.0
– Profit for year ended 30.09.23	5,460.0	10.5	520.0
– Dividend paid 30.09.23	-1,000.0	10	-100.0
Translation difference		Balance	132.5
Non-current liabilities	5,800.0	10	580.0
Current liabilities	4,550.0	10	455.0
	21,875.0		2,187.5

3 Goodwill: Tres.

	D000	Rate	$'000
Consideration paid 4,800 × 12	57,600.0		
Non-controlling interest (to W7)	14,400.0	12	1,200.0
Fair value of net assets acquired			
Equity shares	-1,200.0		
Retained earnings (W1)	-2,400.0		
Goodwill at 01.10.22	68,400.0	12	5,700.0
Translation gain	-	Balance	407.1
At 30.09.22	68,400.0	11.2	6,107.1
Impairment	-18,400.0	10	-1,840.0
Translation gain	-	Balance	732.9
Goodwill at 30.09.23	50,000.0	10	5,000.0

4 Retained earnings

	Uno $000	Dos (30%) $000	Dos (70%) $000	Tres $000
Per SOFP/(W1)/(W2)	7,020.0	650.0	800.0	920
Share dealing fees (part a)	-20.0			
Gain on remeasurement (part a)	240.0			
Less: pre-acquisition (W1)		-450.0	-650.0	-200.0
		200.0	150.0	720.0
Group share:				
Dos: 200 × 30%	60.0			
Dos: 150 × 70%	105.0			
Tres: 720 × 80%	576.0			
Less: goodwill impairment loss				
1,840 (W) × 80%	-1,472.0			
	6,509.0			

5 Translation reserve.

	$'000
Group share translation differences on net assets:	
132.5 (W2) × 80%	106.0
Group share translation differences on goodwill:	912.0
[407.1 + 732.9](W3) × 80%	
	1,018.0

6 Non-controlling interest (NCI): Dos.

	$'000
NCI at acquisition (part a)	1,500.0
NCI's share of post-acquisition retained earnings 150 (W4) × 30%	45.0
	1,545.0

7 Non-controlling interest (NCI): Tres.

	$'000
NCI at acquisition (W3)	1,200.0
NCI's share of post-acquisition retained earnings: 720 (W4) × 20%	144.0
NCI's share goodwill impairment loss: 1,840 (W4) × 20%	-368.0
NCI's share of translation gain on net assets 132.5 (W2) × 20%	26.5
NCI's share of translation gain on goodwill: [407.1+ 732.9] (W3) × 20%	228.0
	1,230.5

(c) **Reclassification of translation gains to profit or loss.**

According to the *Conceptual Framework for Financial Reporting (Conceptual Framework)* the statement of profit or loss is the primary source of information of an entity's financial performance. In principle all income and expenses should be included in profit or loss.

However, this principle was designed to assist the International Accounting Standards Board (IASB) when developing new financial reporting standards and was not intended for general application.

The *Conceptual Framework* further states that the IASB may decide that income and expenses relating to the change in value of an asset or liability may be classified as other comprehensive income (OCI). This would be appropriate where it provides more relevant information or more faithful representation. In addition, the *Conceptual Framework* recommends, but does not require, any income or expenses classified in OCI should be reclassified to profit or loss in a future period.

IAS 21 *The Effects of Changes in Foreign Exchange Rates* requires all gains or losses on the translation of a foreign operation to be recognised in OCI. The current year exchange gains arising on the translation of Tres should be reported in OCI and allocated between the group and the non-controlling interest proportionately in the statement of profit or loss and other comprehensive income.

Where a conflict exists between the *Conceptual Framework* and the requirements of a financial reporting standard (IFRS/IAS), the requirements of the IFRS/IAS prevail over those of the *Conceptual Framework*. The finance director's proposal to reclassify the current year translation gains from OCI to profit or loss is therefore incorrect and should not be actioned.

The finance director's motivation for the reclassification is questionable. The proposal is most likely driven by a need to increase the reported profit figure for the year to achieve the bonus target. The finance director has an ethical duty to ensure that the financial statements are prepared in accordance with International Financial Reporting Standards which are fairly presented in accordance with IAS 1 *Presentation of Financial Statements.*

The finance director's proposal could well be a genuine error based on the misinterpretation of the guidance in the *Conceptual Framework* which would bring their professional competence into question. However, given the sophisticated rationale put forward for the proposal, this is more likely to represent a deliberate attempt to manipulate the reported profit figure for the year which breaches of the ethical principles of integrity and objectivity.

> **Additional areas where credit might be given, note this is not an exhaustive list:**
>
> - Any additional points relating to either Conceptual Framework (2018) and IAS 21 *The Effects of Changes in Foreign Exchange Rates.*

18 Cuarto

This question required candidates to consider various impairment issues arising in the year including the deferred tax implications of a lease (part a) and an equity settled share-based payment scheme (part b) and revenue recognition (part c). [Syllabus area: 3: LO3].

The following chapters from the AIA Financial Accounting and Reporting 2 study text are relevant:

Chapter 15: Leasing contracts
Chapter 17: Taxation
Chapter 20: Related parties and share-based payment
Chapter 21: Revenue recognition

(a) **Lease contract**

On 1 October 2022, Cuatro will recognise a right of use asset and a lease liability in accordance with IFRS 16 *Leases*. A right of use asset of $840,000 is recognised at initial recognition, which is equal to the present value of the minimum lease payments of $831,625 plus the direct costs associated with the lease of $8,375.

The right of use asset is subsequently depreciated over the shorter of the lease term (4 years) or the useful life of the asset (10 years). Depreciation of $210,000 ($840,000/4 years) is expensed to profit or loss. The carrying amount of the machine is $630,000 on 30 September 2023.

On 1 October 2022, the initial value of the lease liability is equal to the present value of the future lease payments of $831,625. Subsequently the lease liability is held on an amortised cost basis at the rate of interest implicit in the lease of 6%. A finance cost of $49,898 is expensed to profit or loss in the year, and this will increase the value of the lease liability. The lease liability is reduced by the first instalment of $240,000 paid on 30 September 2023.

The carrying amount of the lease liability of $641,523 at 30 September 2023 should be sub-divided into the current liability and non-current liability components: current liability = $201,509 ($641,523 − $440,014) and non-current liability = $440,014 as shown below:

Year ended 30 September	B/f	Finance cost @ 6%	Instalment	C/f
	$	$	$	$
2023	831,625	49,898	(240,000)	641,523
2024	641,523	38,491	(240,000)	440,014

For deferred tax purposes the carrying values of the lease liability and the right of use assets are netted off against each other to produce a net liability of $11,523 (W1)

Cuarto can claim tax relief on the lease instalment and the direct lease costs paid in the year. The tax base is therefore nil as no further tax relief is available.

A deductible temporary difference arises because the lease instalment and the direct lease costs are lower than the depreciation expense and the finance cost charged to profit or loss in the year.

A deferred tax asset of $2,881 (W1) is recognised in Cuarto's statement of financial position for the year ended 30 September 2023. This amount is credited in full to the tax charge for the year in profit or loss.

Workings

1   **Deferred tax asset**

	$
Carrying amount at 30 September 2023:	
Right of use asset	630,000
Lease liability	-641,523
	11,523
Tax base	0
Deductible temporary difference	-11,523
Deferred tax asset @ 25%	2,881

(b) **Share options**

The 1,000,000 $1 equity share options granted on 1 October 2021 are classified as an equity settled share-based payment in accordance with IFRS 2 *Share Based Payments*. The share-based payment is recognised over the vesting period of three years based on their fair value at the date of grant of $10.50 per equity share option.

On 1 October 2022, a share-based payment reserve of $3,500,000 (1,000,000 options × $10.50 × 1/3) is recognised in equity. By 30 September 2023, the cumulative value of share-based payment reserve has increased to $7,000,000 (1,000,000 options × $10.50 × 2/3). A share-based payment expense of $3,500,000 ($7,000,000 − $3,500,000) is recognised in profit or loss for the year ended 30 September 2023.

Cuatro can claim tax relief on exercise of the equity share options at the end of the three-year vesting period on 30 September 2024. A deductible temporary difference occurs on which a deferred tax asset should be recognised in Cuatro's statement of financial position.

Tax relief is available on the intrinsic value of the share options at the date of exercise. During the vesting period this is estimated as based on the intrinsic value at 30 September each year. The fair value of the equity share options at grant is disregarded in the deferred tax calculations since this amount is not eligible for tax relief.

On 30 September 2022, the intrinsic value of the share options is $9 per share. A deductible temporary difference of $3,000,000 (1,000,000 × $9 × 1/3) occurs which creates a deferred tax asset of $750,000 (W2). Since the cumulative share-based payment expense of $3,500,000 exceeds the deductible temporary difference of $3,000,000, the deferred tax benefit is credited in full to profit or loss.

On 30 September 2023, the deductible temporary difference increases to $12,000,000 (1,000,000 × $18 × 2/3). The carrying amount of the deferred tax asset should be increased to $3,000,000 (W2) on 30 September 2023.

As the cumulative deductible temporary difference now exceeds the cumulative share-based payment expense to date by $5,000,000 ($12,000,000 – $7,000,000), the deferred tax benefit arising on this excess should be recognised directly in equity. A tax benefit of $1,250,000 (W2) is credited to equity and a tax benefit of $1,000,000 (W2) is credited to profit or loss in the year ended 30 September 2023 as shown below:

2 Deferred tax asset

		$
Deferred tax asset at 30.9.22	1,000,000 × $9 × 1/3 × 25%	750,000
Credited to:		
– Equity	($12,000,000 – $7,000,000) × 2/3 × 25%	1,250,000
– Tax in P/L	Balance	1,000,000
Deferred tax asset at 30.9.23	1,000,000 × $18 × 2/3 × 25%	3,000,000

(c) Specialised equipment

In accordance with IFRS 15 *Revenue from Contracts* with Customer, Cuatro will be treated as the principal in this arrangement provided that it controls the specialised equipment before it is transferred to the customer. The following factors should be considered when determining if Cuatro controls the specialised equipment prior to its transfer to the customer:

The company has primary responsibility for the fulfilment of the contract. Despite subcontracting the manufacture of the equipment to a supplier, ultimately a single performance obligation exists to provide the equipment to the customer which Cuarto is wholly responsible for. Cuarto is responsible for the design of the equipment and instructs the supplier to build the equipment to its exact specifications. If the design specifications are incorrect, Cuatro is responsible for the correction of any design defects. The supplier cannot direct the use of the equipment and any future responsibilities are limited to the correction of any manufacturing defaults only. Cuatro therefore is primary responsibility for the fulfilment of the contract.

Inventory risk lies with the entity. Cuarto has responsibility to correct any design defects that may occur, which suggests that Cuatro bears the inventory risk of the contract.

The entity has discretion in establishing the sales price. Cuatro has negotiated an agreed sales price of cost plus 30% with the customer. The supplier plays no part in the sales price recognition with the customer.

Based on the above evidence, Cuatro controls the specialised equipment before it is transferred to the customer and should be treated as principal in this arrangement. Cuarto will recognise the revenue from the sale of the specialised equipment when the customer assumes control of the machine i.e., on delivery to the customer.

> **Additional areas where credit might be given, note this is not an exhaustive list:**
> - Any further discussion relevant to the scenario.
> - Follow through marks available.

19 Cinco

This question examines the accounting treatment of investment property (part a), the issue of $10 million bonds (part b), a financial asset held at fair value through other comprehensive income (part c) and a speculative futures contract (part d). [Syllabus area c: LO3].

The following chapters from the AIA Financial Accounting and Reporting 2 study text are relevant:

Chapter 12: Tangible non-current assets and inventory
Chapter 14: Financial instruments

(a) **Office building**

Whilst the building was used as Cinco's head office it would have been accounted for in accordance with IAS 16 *Property, Plant and Equipment* under the cost model basis in accordance with Cinco's accounting policy. On 30 September 2022, the office building had a carrying amount of $7,200,000 ($8,000,000 × 45/ 50 years).

On 1 October 2022, the office building will be recognised as an investment property due its change of use and subsequently will be accounted for under the provisions of IAS 40 *Investment Properties*. Immediately prior to the change of use, the office building should be revalued to its fair value of $10,000,000 and the increase in fair value is recognised in accordance with IAS 16 *Property, Plant and Equipment*. A revaluation surplus of $2,800,000 ($10,000,000 – $7,200,000) should be accumulated in equity and recognised as other comprehensive income.

Subsequently the office building is accounted for at fair value under IAS 40 *Investment Properties* in accordance with Cinco's accounting policy. On 30 September 2023, the office building is remeasured to its fair value of $12,000,000 and the fair value gain of $2,000,000 ($12,000,000 – $10,000,000) [1] is recognised in profit or loss. No depreciation is charged under the fair value model of IAS 40 *Investment Properties*.

(b) **$10 million Loan**

The $10 million bank loan would be classified as a financial liability on 30 September 2023.

Most financial liabilities are held on an amortised cost basis in the statement of financial position. On that basis, Cinco should recognise the bank loan initially at fair value minus transaction costs on 30 September 2023, which would result in a financial liability of $9,800,000 ($10,000,000 – $200,000).

In subsequent periods the bank loan would be held on an amortised costs basis. Finance costs would be recognised in profit or loss at the effective rate of interest each year and added to the financial liability. The effective rate of interest is based on the loan's internal rate of return and incorporates both the 8% per annum interest rate plus the initial transaction costs of $200,000. Bank interest charged of $800,000 ($10,000,000 × 8%) will be deducted from the financial liability on 30 September each year.

Whilst most financial liabilities are held on an amortised cost basis, IFRS 9 *Financial Instruments* does permit the use of the "fair value through profit or loss" classification at initial recognition to eliminate or significantly reduce and accounting mismatch. IFRS 9 *Financial Instruments* defines an accounting mismatch as "a measurement recognition inconsistency….that would otherwise arise from measuring assets or liabilities or recognising the gains or losses on them on different bases (IFRS 9: 4.2.2 (a)).

This option would be available to Cinco as the bank loan is used to fund the purchase additional investment properties which are held on the fair value model basis of IAS 40 *Investment Properties*. The investment properties would be revalued to their fair value each year with any fair value gains or losses being recognised in profit or loss. An accounting mismatch exists under the amortised cost model since the fair value changes arising on the investment property will not agree with the profit or loss impact of the bonds.

Cinco may opt to eliminate this accounting mismatch by classifying the bank loan as "fair value through profit or loss" on 30 September 2023. This would mean that the bank loan is initially recorded at its fair value of $10,000,000 and the $200,000 transaction costs would be immediately expensed to profit or loss. Subsequently, the bank loan would be restated to fair value each year and the fair value gains or losses would be reported directly in profit or loss. The fair value gains/losses arising on the loan would offset the fair value losses/gains on the investment properties. This would either eliminate or significantly reduce the accounting mismatch arising on the two connected items.

(c) **Investment in bonds**

In accordance with IFRS 9 *Financial Instruments* the investment in bonds would be classified as an investment in debt which would either be accounted for on an amortised cost basis or at fair value through other comprehensive income depending upon an entity's business model. Cinco intends to collect the underlying cash flows (of coupon interest and principal) and to sell the financial assets should the opportunity arise. The investment will therefore be accounted for at fair value through other comprehensive income.

On 1 October 2022, the bonds will be recorded at fair value plus transaction costs. Cinco purchased the bonds at a 10% discount to par value which means that the bonds should be initially measured at $920,000 (($1,000,000 × 90%) + $20,000).

Subsequently, the bonds will be measured at fair value through other comprehensive. However, finance income is recognised in profit or loss each year at the effective rate of interest of 7% as shown below:

	$
Fair value on 1 October 2022 (($1,000,000 × 90%) + $20,000)	920,000
Finance income ($920,000 × 7%)	64,400
Coupon received ($1,000,000 × 5%)	-50,000
	934,400
Fair value gain to OCI (balance)	45,600
Fair value at 30 September 2023	980,000

Finance income of $64,400 is recognised in profit or loss. Coupon interest of $50,000, based on the par value of the bond, will be credited to the financial asset on 30 September 2023.

The financial asset is restated to its fair value of $980,000 on 30 September 2023. The resulting fair value gain of $45,600 is recognised in other comprehensive income in the year ended 30 September 2023.

(d) **Speculative futures contract**

IFRS 9 *Financial Instruments* applies to derivative contracts to buy or sell non-financial items settled net in cash. The speculative futures contract is a financial derivative as it is due to be settled net in cash on 31 March 2024. The derivative would be classified as held at fair value through profit or loss.

On 1 August 2023, the fair value of the contract is $nil. The $400 transaction costs have been incorrectly capitalised, and these should be expensed to profit or loss.

On 30 September 2023, the derivative contract will be restated to its fair value as calculated below:

	$
Fair value at 30.9.23 ($3,250 × 500 tonnes)	1,625,000
Fair value at 01.08.23 ($3,000 × 500 tonnes)	1,500,000
Gain	125,000

Cinco will recognise a financial asset of $125,000 and the corresponding gain of $125,000 is credited to profit or loss.

> **Additional areas where credit might be given, note this is not an exhaustive list:**
> - Any further discussion relevant to the scenario.
> - Follow through marks available.

20 Ocho

Part (a) required candidates to prepare extracts from the consolidated statement of cash flows [Syllabus area: 2:LO2].

The following chapter from the AIA Financial Accounting and Reporting 2 study text is relevant:

Chapter 10: Group statement of cash flows

(a) Extracts from consolidated statement of cash flows for the year ended 30 September 2022

(i) **Cash flow from investing activities.**

	$'000
Sale of subsidiary, net of cash 2,000 + 200 (overdraft)	2,200
Acquisition of joint venture (Nueve)	-1,200
Purchase of property, plant and equipment (W1)	-15,000
Dividends received (W2)	1,500
Net cash used in investing activities	-12,500

(ii) **Cash flows from financing activities**

	$'000
Proceeds from the issue of share capital	3,500
Proceeds from long term borrowings (14,000 – 9,000)	5,000
Dividends paid by parent (W3)	-1,250
Dividends paid to non-controlling interest (W4)	-540
Net cash used in financing activities	6,710

Workings

1 **Property, plant and equipment**

	$'000
Balance b/d	40,000
Depreciation	-3,500
Disposal of Diez	-1,200
Additions in year (balance)	15,000
Balance c/d	50,300

2 **Investment in joint ventures.**

	$000
Balance b/d	5,000
Share of profit of joint ventures (P/L)	5,500
Purchase of Nueve in the year	1,200
Dividends received (balance)	-1,500
Balance c/d	10,200

3 Equity shares (share capital/share premium)

	$'000
Balance b/d (10,000 + 5,000)	15,000
Cash issue of shares (balance)	3,500
Balance c/d (12,000 + 6,500)	18,500

4 Retained earnings

	$'000
Balance b/d	9,000
Profit for the year (group share)	27,500
Dividend paid (balance)	-1,250
Balance c/d	35,250

5 Non-controlling interest

	$'000
Balance b/d	4,500
NCI's share of profit for the year (P/L)	3,600
Disposal of subsidiary (Nueve)	- 720
Dividend paid (balance)	-540
Balance c/d	6,840

(b) Part (b) required candidates to critically evaluate the main challenges sustainability reporting presents to SMEs and to consider how these challenges might be overcome. [Syllabus area: 1:LO1].

The following chapter from the AIA Financial Accounting and Reporting 2 study text are relevant:

Chapter 3: Environmental and social reporting

Sustainability reporting: challenges for SMEs

SMEs may have various reasons for not fully embracing sustainability reporting, including:

- **Lack of resources:** SMEs have limited financial and human resources available to them compared to large multinational corporations. Recent pressures linked to rising costs and the cost-of-living crisis may further prevent SMEs from investing in areas such as sustainability reporting.

- **Prioritisation:** SMEs juggle multiple priorities e.g., sales growth, cash flow, business survival etc., and sustainability reporting is unlikely to be of high priority. SMEs may lack awareness of the benefits of sustainability reporting to them or may struggle to understand how sustainability reporting aligns with their own core business objectives.

- **Data collection:** Sustainability reporting requires the capture and analysis of sustainability related data. This might prove problematic for SMEs lacking the relevant data capture systems and processes in place to achieve this.

- **Lack of expertise:** SMEs are unlikely to have the relevant expertise in sustainability reporting. This can lead to difficulties when trying to navigate and implement the complexities of sustainability reporting without proper support or guidance from sustainability experts.

- **Complexity:** The various sustainability frameworks in place can be complex and difficult for SMEs to understand and implement. SMEs might perceive the process of sustainability reporting as time consuming and challenging, which discourages their engagement.

- **Low stakeholder pressure:** SMEs may perceive their stakeholders (customers, suppliers, employees) are less demanding and are unlikely to require detailed sustainability reporting information from them. In the absence of stakeholder pressure, SMEs are unlikely to prioritise sustainability reporting.

EXAM ANSWER BANK

Strategies to overcome the challenges associated with sustainability reporting.

There are several strategies available to SMEs to overcome some if these challenges:

- **Start small:** SMEs can start by focusing on a small number of sustainability metrics that are most relevant to their business. Over time SMEs can gradually add to the sustainability metrics it has identified.

- **External support:** SMEs may wish to partner with local industry associations or business support networks that can provide support and expertise in sustainability reporting. This support is often provided free of charge or at a nominal cost to the business.

- **Collaboration with other SMEs:** SMEs may wish to collaborate with other SMEs in their area to collectively overcome their challenges through the sharing best practices, experiences, and expertise

- **Technology:** Several sustainability reporting software packages exist that can simplify the data collection, analysis, and reporting process. The adoption of sustainability reporting software may be a cost-effective way of streamlining the sustainability reporting process.

- **Communicate and engage:** SMEs should engage with their key stakeholders including customers, suppliers and employees to understand what sustainability topics are important to them and to help to identify areas to prioritise and work on.

> **Additional areas where credit might be given, note this is not an exhaustive list:**
>
> - Part (a): Follow through marks apply throughout. Credit given for workings not transferred to extracts.
>
> - Part (b): Further relevant discussion on sustainability reporting for SMEs.

Mock exam questions and answers

FINANCIAL ACCOUNTING AND REPORTING 2

PROFESSIONAL LEVEL 2

FINANCIAL ACCOUNTING and REPORTING 2

Mock Exam

Time allowed - 3 hours

Answer ALL Questions

**Clear workings should be submitted with all your answers.
All calculations should be made to the nearest $ (or $000) as appropriate.**

You are allowed an additional 15 minutes reading time before the exam begins.

CREATING WORLD CLASS ACCOUNTANTS

1 Arvo

Arvo is a quoted company that has grown significantly in recent years due to its acquisition strategy. The individual statements of financial position for the members of the Arvo group are shown below as at 31 March 2025:

	Arvo $m	Becco $m	Como $m	Disueri $m
ASSETS				
Non-current assets				
Property, plant and equipment	165	36	30	40
Investments (at fair value):				
Becco	90	–	–	–
Como	–	24	–	–
Disueri	15	–	–	–
	270	60	30	40
Current assets	70	20	15	15
Total assets	340	80	45	55
EQUITY AND LIABILITIES				
Equity				
Share capital – $1 equity shares	50	10	5	5
Retained earnings	95	25	15	12
Other components of equity	40	10	–	5
Total equity	185	45	20	22
Non-current liabilities	100	20	15	16
Current liabilities	55	15	10	17
Total equity and liabilities	340	80	45	55

The following information is relevant:

1. Arvo acquired 90% of the equity shares in Becco on 1 April 2023 for $72 million in cash. The fair value of Becco's net assets at 1 April 2023 was $50 million, which included retained earnings of $18 million and other components of equity of $2 million. The difference between the fair value of the net assets acquired and their carrying amounts relates to property which had a remaining useful life of 20 years at 1 April 2023.

   It is group policy to measure the non-controlling interest at fair value at the date of acquisition. The fair value of the 10% non-controlling interest in Becco was $8 million at 1 April 2023.

2. On 1 April 2024, Becco acquired an 80% stake in Como for $20 million. The fair value of the net assets acquired was $20 million, which included retained earnings of $10 million (Como had no other components of equity). The difference between the fair value of the net assets acquired and their carrying amounts relates to non-depreciable land. The fair value of the non-controlling interest was valued at $5 per share at the date of acquisition.

3. Arvo acquired 10% of the equity in Disueri on 1 April 2024 for $2 million. On 31 March 2025, Arvo acquired an additional 50% stake in Disueri for $12.5 million. At 31 March 2025, the fair value of Disueri's net assets were equal to their carrying amounts and no fair value adjustments were required. The fair value of the 40% non-controlling interest in Disueri on 31 March 2025 was $10 million.

4. It is group policy to record all investments at fair value through other comprehensive income in accordance with IFRS 9 *Financial Instruments*. The investments shown in the above statements of financial position were correctly recorded at fair value at 31 March 2025, and the resulting fair value gain has been included in other comprehensive income.

On 31 March 2025, the fair value of each $1 equity share was:

	Market value per $1 equity share $
Becco	10
Como	6
Disueri	5

5 During the year ended 31 March 2025, Como sold goods for $10 million and $5 million to Arvo and Becco respectively at a 25% mark up. As at 31 March 2025, half of these goods remained unsold and have been included in the closing inventory of Arvo and Becco.

6 On 2 January 2025, Como acquired inventory from an overseas supplier for €5 million and the invoice remained unpaid at the year end. Como had correctly recorded the transaction on 2 January 2025, but no further entries have been made.

The following exchange rates are relevant:

| 02.01.2025 | €1 = $1.20 |
| 31.03.2025 | €1 = $1.30 |

7 On 1 April 2024, Arvo issued 20 million $1 zero coupon redeemable bonds at par value and included the $20 million cash raised in non-current liabilities. The bonds are redeemable in five years' time at a 20% premium.

Issue costs of $1 million were incurred and these have been written off to profit or loss in the year. No further entries have been made in the year in respect of these bonds. The effective rate of interest for the bonds has been calculated at 4.8% per annum.

8 An impairment review was conducted on 31 March 2025, and it was decided that the goodwill arising in Becco and Como should be impaired by $10 million and $2 million respectively. The goodwill created on the acquisition of Disueri remains unchanged.

Required

(a) Prepare the consolidated statement of financial position for the Arvo group as at 31 March 2025.

All calculations should be shown to the nearest $0.1 million. Ignore any deferred tax consequences of consolidation. **(35 marks)**

(b) Discuss how the accounting treatment of the redeemable bonds in item 7 above provides useful information to users of financial statements. Your answer should discuss the application of the fundamental qualitative characteristics of useful information as described in the IASB's *Conceptual Framework for Financial Reporting*.

(5 marks)

(Total 40 marks)

2 Wax

The directors of Wax have asked for your advice on the use of fair values in the preparation of their financial statements.

The company owns a piece of land in the town where its head office is located. That land was purchased by Wax for $50,000 in 1970, when the company's founder wished to celebrate the company's first ten years in business. The land was landscaped and set aside as a public park for all of the townspeople to enjoy.

Since 1970 Wax has become a public company and has been quoted on the stock exchange. Despite that, it still retains the piece of land.

Wax's directors have been debating the application of fair value accounting to the land.

- Similar plots of land in similar locations can be purchased on the open market for $2 million.
- When Wax was negotiating a bank loan recently, the bank offered to accept the land as collateral against which to secure the full value of the loan, which was for $5 million.
- A local property expert believes that the land could be sold on the open market for $6 million.
- Wax's board believes that if the company spent $10 million on development, the land could be converted to a shopping centre worth $30 million.

Wax's directors have found the concept of fair values difficult ever since IFRS 2 *Share-based Payment* required Wax to recognise the fair value of the instruments issued under the company's executive share options scheme.

Required

(a) Discuss the difficulties associated with determining the fair value of this land to Wax, taking account of the requirements of IFRS 13 *Fair Value Measurement*. **(10 marks)**

(b) Discuss the difficulties associated with determining the fair value of executive share options under IFRS 2. **(10 marks)**

(Total 20 marks)

3 Liscia

Liscia is a manufacturer and supplier of transit vans used for business purposes. The directors of Liscia are currently preparing the accounts for the year ended 31 March 2025, and require your advice on the following matters:

(1) On 1 October 2024 Liscia entered into a 12-month contract with Marcio, a new customer, to supply vans at $10,000 each. Under the terms of the contract, if Marcio purchases more than 1,000 vans in the year, the purchase price of each van will be retrospectively reduced to $9,500 per van. Liscia invoices Marcio on a quarterly basis starting on 31 December 2024 and Marcio is required to settle the invoice in full in 30 days. Following successful credit checks the contract was issued and signed by both parties.

In the quarter ended 31 December 2024, Marcio purchased 100 vans. At this point Liscia estimated that it was unlikely that Marcio would buy 1,000 vans in the year to qualify for the volume discount. In the quarter ended 31 March 2025, Marcio purchased 600 vans and placed a firm order for delivery of a further 500 vans in the quarter ended 30 June 2025. **(6 marks)**

(2) On 1 April 2024, Liscia issued 20,000 $1,000 2% convertible bonds at par. Each $1,000 bond is convertible in three years' time into 500 $1 equity shares at the option of the bond holder. The market rate of interest for similar $1,000 bonds without conversion rights is 5%. Liscia incurred issue costs of $1 million. The effective rate of interest for the liability component of the convertible bonds is 6.8% due to the allocation of the issue costs.

The following discount factors are applicable:

Year	2%	5%	6.8%
1	0.980	0.952	0.936
2	0.961	0.907	0.877
3	0.942	0.864	0.821

(8 marks)

(3) On 1 February 2025, Liscia signed a contract to buy a machine from an overseas supplier for 10 million dinars on 31 July 2025. The machine is custom built, based on Liscia's specifications, and will be ready for delivery and installation on 31 July 2025. To hedge against adverse foreign currency movements, Liscia enters into a forward contract to buy 10 million dinars on 31 July

2025 at an exchange rate of $1 to 2.5 Dinars. The directors wish to use hedge accounting in accordance with IFRS 9 *Financial Instruments*.

The spot rates and forward exchange rates are:

	Spot rate	Forward contract for delivery on 31.7.18
01.02.2025	$1 : 2.45D	$1 : 2.50D
31.03.2025	$1 : 2.20D	$1 : 2.25D

(6 marks)

Required

Advise the directors of the correct accounting treatment of the above transactions for the year ended 31 March 2025.

(Total 20 marks)

4 Randall

Randall is a privately-owned furniture design and manufacturing company which prepares its accounts in accordance with International Financial Reporting Standards. Randall manufactures and installs high quality office furniture for a wide range of corporate clients. The company was founded 30 years ago and is still 100% owned by its founder who is also the Managing Director of the company.

At the planning meeting for the next accounting period, the Managing Director suggested to the Finance Director (a qualified accountant) that a number of changes be made to Randall's accounting policies and estimates. The proposed changes are outlined below.

Randall's manufacturing machinery is currently being depreciated on a straight-line basis over five years. The Managing Director would like to extend the useful life of this plant to 10 years. Historically, profits or losses on disposal of machinery have been minimal.

Randall has two main revenue streams. Firstly, the company earns revenue from the sale of office furniture to corporate clients. Secondly, the company offers an installation service in exchange for a fee. The Managing Director would like to revise the revenue recognition policy so that revenue is recognised when the customer signs the contract rather than on delivery and over the period of installation of the furniture respectively.

Finally, the Managing Director has noticed that in the past year, there has been a decrease in the percentage of furniture returned by customers for repair under warranty. He would like to reduce the provision for warranties in the forthcoming year.

As the Managing Director was leaving the meeting, he mentioned to the Finance Director that now he had reached the age of 65, he would like to retire and sell the business in one year's time.

Required

Discuss the ethical and accounting implications of the above situations from the perspective of the Finance Director.

(20 marks)

[End of question paper]

AIA PROFESSIONAL QUALIFICATION

PROFESSIONAL LEVEL 2

FINANCIAL ACCOUNTING AND REPORTING 2

MODEL ANSWERS

> Valid alternative points, whether or not they are shown in the Model Answers, will be given credit where appropriate.

CREATING WORLD CLASS ACCOUNTANTS

MOCK EXAM 2 ANSWERS

1 Arvo

(a) Consolidated statement of financial position for the year ended 31 March 2025.

	$m
ASSETS	
Non-current assets	
Property, plant and equipment 165 + 36 + 30 + 40 + 18 (W2c) + 5 (W3c)	294.0
Goodwill 20 (W2b) + 3 (W3b) + 3 (W4b)	26.0
	320.0
Current assets 70 + 20 + 15 + 15 – 1.5 (W8)	118.5
Total assets	438.5
EQUITY AND LIABILITIES	
Equity	
Share capital – $1 equity shares	50.0
Retained earnings (W5)	91.4
Other components of equity (W6)	25.6
	167.0
Non-controlling interest (W7)	23.1
	190.1
Non-current liabilities 100 + 20 + 15 + 16 – 1 (W10) + 0.9 (W10)	150.9
Current liabilities 55 + 15 + 10 + 17 + 0.5 (W9)	97.5
Total equity and liabilities	438.5

W1 Group structure

```
                              Arvo
01.04.2023                   /    \
RE = $18m          90%      /      \
OCE = $2m                  /        \
                        Becco      Disueri
01.04.2024                         01.04.2024    31.03.2025
RE = $10m          80%             10%           + 50% = 60%
OCE = $0m
                                                 RE = $12m
                        Como                     OCE = $5m
```

Como Effective interest = 90% × 80% = 72%
Como NCI = 28%

Tutorial note:

Becco & Como

Arvo must consolidate any entity that it controls, either directly (Becco) or indirectly (Como). Como's assets and liabilities are consolidated on a line by line basis since Arvo controls these. When recognising Arvo's share of post-acquisition reserves, Arvo's 72% effective interest must be used (with the remaining 28% being allocated to Como's non-controlling interest).

Disueri

Disueri should be recognised in the consolidated statement of financial position from date control is achieved ie 31.03.2025.

W2 Acquisition of Becco

(a) Restate fair value of investment to original cost

	$m
Investment per Arvo's statement of financial position	90.0
Original cost (per question)	72.0
Increase in fair value (included in OCE)	18.0

Adjustment	Dr $m	Cr $m
Arvo's OCE	18.0	
Investment in Becco		18.0

> **Tutorial note:**
>
> **Investment in Becco**
>
> The investment in Becco is currently stated at fair value in Arvo's own financial statements. On consolidation this uplift in fair value is removed in order to restate the investment to its original cost, ie the consideration paid in the goodwill working in W2(b).

(b) Goodwill

	$m	$m
Consideration paid (original cost)		72.0
Non-controlling interest (fair value)		8.0
Fair value of net assets acquired at 01.04.2023		
Share capital	10.0	
Retained earnings (per question)	18.0	
Other components of equity (per question)	2.0	
Fair value adjustment – property (balance)	20.0	
Fair value of net assets at acquisition (per question)	50.0	(50.0)
Goodwill at 01.04.2023		30.0
Impairment		(10.0)
Goodwill at 31.03.2025		20.0

(c) Fair value adjustment

	At 01.04.2023 $m	Movement $m	At 31.03.2025 $m
Property	20.0	(2.0)	18.0

Fair value amortisation: $20m/20 years × 2 years = $2m

W3 Acquisition of Como

(a) Restate fair value of investment to original cost

	$m
Investment per Becco's statement of financial position	24.0
Original cost (per question)	20.0
Increase in fair value (included in OCE)	4.0

Adjustment	Dr $m	Cr $m
Becco's OCE	4.0	
Investment in Como		4.0

> **Tutorial note:**
>
> **Investment in Como**
>
> The investment in Como is currently stated at fair value in Arvo's own financial statements. On consolidation this uplift in fair value is removed in order to restate the investment to its original cost, ie the consideration paid in the goodwill working in W3(b).

(b) Goodwill

	$m	$m
Consideration paid (original cost) $20m × 90%		18.0
Non-controlling interest (fair value)		7.0
5m shares × 28% (effective interest) × $5 (fair value at acquisition)		
Fair value of net assets acquired at 01.04.2024		
Share capital	5.0	
Retained earnings (per question)	10.0	
Other components of equity (per question)	–	
Fair value adjustment – land (balance)	5.0	
Fair value of net assets at acquisition (per question)	20.0	(20.0)
Goodwill at 01.04.2024		5.0
Impairment		(2.0)
Goodwill at 31.03.2025		3.0

> **Tutorial note:**
>
> **Como's goodwill**
>
> The consolidation is prepared from Arvo's point of view. Therefore, since Arvo owns 90% of Becco, it should recognise only 90% of the consideration paid by Becco to acquire Como in the goodwill working.
>
> The remaining 10% of the consideration paid by Becco, will be adjusted for in Becco's non-controlling interest working (W7).

(c) Fair value adjustment

	At 01.04.2024 $m	Movement $m	At 31.03.2025 $m
Land (non-depreciable)	5.0	–	5.0

W4 Acquisition of Disueri

(a) **Restate original 10% holding to fair value when control is achieved on 31.03.2025**

- Normally, the carrying amount of the original 10% investment would be uplifted to fair value at the date control was achieved. However, this is not necessary since the original 10% investment has already been restated to fair value on 31.03.2025 in accordance with group policy.
- Fair value of the original 10% stake is $2.5 million (5m shares × 10% × $5) at 31.03.2025.

(b) **Goodwill**

	$m	$m
Fair value of original 10% holding (as above)		2.5
Consideration paid for additional 50% shareholding (per question)		12.5
Non-controlling interest (fair value)		10.0
Fair value of net assets acquired at 31.03.2025		
Share capital	5.0	
Retained earnings (as per statement of financial position)	12.0	
Other components of equity (as per statement of financial position)	5.0	
Fair value adjustment (per question)	–	
Fair value of net assets at acquisition (per question)	22.0	(22.0)
Goodwill at 31.03.2025		3.0

W5 Retained earnings

	Arvo $m	Becco $m	Como $m	Disueri $m
Per question	95.0	25.0	15.0	12.0
Fair value amortisation (W2c)		(2.0)		
Unrealised profit (W8)			(1.5)	
Foreign exchange loss (W9)			(0.5)	
Redeemable bonds (W10)				
Issue costs	1.0			
Finance costs	(0.9)			
At acquisition (W1)		(18.0)	(10.0)	(12.0)
		5.0	3.0	–
Group % retained earnings:				
Becco: 90% × 5m	4.5			
Como: 72% × 3m	2.2			
Group % goodwill impairment:				
Becco: 90% × 10m	(9.0)			
Como: 72% × 2m	(1.4)			
	91.4			

W6 Other components of equity

	Arvo $m	Becco $m	Como $m	Disueri $m
Per question	40.0	10.0	–	5.0
Cancel fair value uplift				
• Becco shares (W2a)	(18.0)			
• Como shares (W3a)		(4.0)		

At acquisition (W1)	(2.0)	–	(5.0)
	4.0	–	–
Group % post acquisition:			
Becco: 90% × 4m	3.6		
	25.7		

W7 Non-controlling interest

	Becco $m	Como $m	Disueri $m
NCI at acquisition (from goodwill W2b/3b/4b)	8.0	7.0	10.0
NCI % retained earnings (W5)			
Becco: 10% × 5m	0.5		
Como: 28% × 3m (W5)		0.8	
NCI % other components of equity (W6)			
Becco: 10% × 4m	0.4		
NCI % goodwill impairment:			
Becco: 10% × 10m	(1.0)		
Como: 28% × 2m		(0.6)	
Less: Becco's NCI's % cost of Como:			
$20m × 10%	(2.0)		
	5.9	7.2	10.0

Total NCI: 5.9 + 7.2 + 10.0 = $23.1m

W8 Unrealised profit

	$m
Como → Arvo: $10m × 25/125 × ½	1.0
Como → Becco: $5m × 25/125 × ½	0.5
Total unrealised profit	1.5

	Dr $m	Cr $m
Como's retained earnings (W5)	1.5	
Inventory (current assets)		1.5

W9 Foreign transaction

	$m
02.01.2025 – Record at spot rate: €5m × $1.20	6.0
31.03.2025 – Translate at year-end closing rate: €5m × $1.30	6.5
Foreign exchange loss	0.5

	Dr $m	Cr $m
Como's P/L (retained earnings)	0.5	
Como's current liabilities		0.5

W10 Zero coupon bonds

Issue costs should have been deducted from opening liability balance and not debited to profit or loss.

Correction:	Dr $m	Cr $m
Non-current liabilities	1.0	

Arvo's retained earnings (W5)   1.0

Recognise finance costs in profit or loss at the effective rate of interest of 4.8%

	$m
01.04.2024 Cash raised	20.0
Less: issue costs	(1.0)
	19.0
31.03.2025 Finance costs: $19m × 4.8%	0.9
At 31.03.2025	19.9

	Dr $m	Cr $m
Arvo's retained earnings (W5)	0.9	
Non-current liabilities		0.9

> **Additional areas where credit might be given, note this is not an exhaustive list:**
> - Own figure rules apply throughout.
> - Candidates will obtain marks for workings even if the figures are not transferred onto the consolidated statement of financial position.

(b) According to the IASB's Conceptual Framework, there are two fundamental qualitative characteristics of useful information: relevance and faithful representation.

Information is relevant if it is capable of making a difference in the decisions made by users, which means the information has predictive value and/or confirmatory value.

To be a faithful representation, information must accurately reflect the transaction it purports to represent. Faithful representation encompasses the concept of 'substance over form', whereby the economic reality of a situation should be presented, rather than only its strict legal form.

Arvo has issued zero coupon redeemable bonds thereby raising net cash of $19 million. The bonds are zero coupon, which means Arvo does not have to pay any annual interest to the bond holders, which means that on a strict legal basis, they are 'interest free'. However, in substance, the bonds are not cost free, as Arvo has to pay a premium of 20% on redemption. To reflect the substance of the arrangement, IFRS 9 *Financial Instruments: Recognition and Measurement*, requires that the bonds are measured using amortised cost.

The technique of amortised cost recognises that in reality, even though the bonds have a zero interest rate, they are not 'cost free' to Arvo. By applying the effective interest rate to the outstanding liability each year, an effective amount of interest is calculated and charged to profit or loss. This spreads the effective cost of the bonds over the period in which the funds raised are expected to be used to generate economic benefits. This treatment therefore reflects the substance of the arrangement and so provides a faithful representation of it.

It could be argued that it would be better to only recognise the premium on redemption when the bond is redeemed. However, this would provide less relevant information because not all costs associated with generating economic benefits in current periods will have been reflected. This will therefore limit the confirmatory and predictive value of the information.

2 Wax

(a) The basic problem is that Wax has permitted the land to be used as a public park for more than 40 years. Presumably, it yields little economic value to the company, other than as a source of positive publicity. As a public park it does not, in itself, yield any revenues and so the land's fair value would be close to zero as long as it remains in that role.

Presumably, the land remains Wax's property and must be available for redevelopment for business purposes, otherwise the bank would be unwilling to accept it as collateral. The valuation is probably on the conservative side because lenders are usually keen to value assets on the understanding that they can be realised quickly at that price.

IFRS 13 asks for the fair value to be determined in terms of the principal market for that asset. We have at least two possibilities because similar plots can be purchased for $2 million, but a higher value has been suggested for this specific property. Presumably, the $2 million valuation is for plots of a similar size in either the same or a similar town. The principal market for Wax's land should be the market for this specific plot, taking into account such factors as proximity to transport links, suitability for development and so on.

There is the further question of whether the value of the land should take into account the possibility of redevelopment as a retail site. IFRS 13 requires that it be valued at its highest and best use. Spending $10 million on the land would increase its value to $30 million, which suggests that it could be valued at the $20 million net. The only real condition would be that this basis would depend on the land being suitable for such development and there would have to be a realistic belief that redevelopment would be permissible.

> **Tutorial note:** Fair values can often only be fully understood when put in the particular context in which the question has been raised.

> **Additional areas where credit might be given, note this is not an exhaustive list:**
> - Credit will be awarded for any valid discussion that relates to the requirement. Candidates could, for example, discuss the disparity between the various values attached to the land according to the scenario. There could also be issues concerning the objectivity of specific values (eg sales of similar plots in the area have observable selling prices whereas valuation reports are matters of opinion).

(b) IFRS 2 requires that shares issued as payment should be valued in terms of the fair value of the goods or services received. Unfortunately, when the shares are used to reward employees as a part of a remuneration scheme then there is no realistic way to measure the value of the services received in return for the shares. The skills applied by the directors cannot be evaluated apart from the assets and other resources that they use to generate wealth. There is no objective way to measure the value of the work done by the directors, even by looking at the going rates offered for similar work by other companies.

The requirements of IFRS 2 impose a duty to report an estimated value, even though that estimate may be unreliable and open to challenge. The financial statements must, however, still present fairly.

The biggest problem with determining the fair value of executive share options (ESOPs) is that they tend to have a number of specific features that means they differ from the options that are commonly traded on the open market. For example, there is usually a vesting period during which the right to the ESOPs might lapse. For example, a director may lose all rights to ESOPs that have been granted but not yet vested in the event of termination of employment. Further complications include the possibility that an ESOP can often only be exercised on a specific date at the end of the vesting period, which makes them even less comparable to traded options.

There are valuation models that can be used to give at least a defensible valuation for an option. For example, the Black Scholes model is frequently applied in order to estimate the value of the options. Unfortunately, there is no objective basis on which to evaluate the accuracy of the resulting prices. Indeed, IFRS 2 sets out a number of bases that are to be applied in the event that there is no directly comparable market price.

> **Tutorial note:** The basis for a critique of any accounting standard boils down to basic questions, such as the potential conflict between relevance and reliability.

> **Additional areas where credit might be given, note this is not an exhaustive list:**
> - Credit will be granted for additional points or expansion. For example, the applicability of Black Scholes to ESOPs is open to doubt because the conditions attached to ESOPs differ materially from those attached to traded options. There could also be motivational issues, such as board members being keen to undervalue ESOPs for the sake of making their remuneration appear less generous.

3 Liscia

The contract with Marcio will be accounted for in accordance with IFRS 15 *Revenue from Contracts with Customers* five step model.

A written contract exists between Liscia and Marcio which has commercial substance from which each party's rights and payment terms can be identified. The successful credit checks would suggest that it is probable that Liscia will be able to collect the amounts due from Marcio (step 1).

Under the terms of the contract Liscia's single performance obligation can be easily identified. Liscia is obliged to provide vans to Marcio over the 12-month contract term (step 2).

Liscia must then determine the transaction price (step 3). The transaction price is the amount of consideration that Liscia expects to be entitled to in exchange for transferring vans to Marcio.

In the quarter ended 31 December 2024, Marcio's buying patterns to date indicated that the volume discount would not apply and therefore Liscia should recognise revenue of $1,000,000 (100 × $1,000). In the quarter ended 31 March 2025, the purchase of an additional 600 vans and the firm order of a further 500 vans, provides sufficient evidence that Marcio qualifies for the volume discount and that this will need to be applied retrospectively to reduce the purchase price to $9,500 per van. In the quarter ended 31 March 2025, Liscia should recognise revenue of $5,650,000 [(600 × $9,500) − (100 × $500)], which represents the revenue from the quarter 2 sales less the $500 reduction for quarter 1 sales.

As a single performance obligation exists there is no requirement to allocate the transaction price to the separate performance obligations (step 4).

Liscia will recognise the revenue as the performance obligation is satisfied (step 5). Liscia will satisfy its performance obligation when Marcio receives control of the vans (this is normally at the point of delivery). In the year ended 31 March 2025, Liscia will recognise total revenue of $6,650,000 (700 × $9,500) as shown above. Revenue relating to the firm order of 500 vans will be recognised in the quarter ended 30 June 2025 when the vans are made available to Marcio.

$20 million convertible bonds

The convertible bonds will be accounted for as a compound instrument in accordance with IAS 32 *Financial Instruments: Presentation*. A compound instrument contains two components: a financial liability component (a contractual obligation to deliver cash to another entity) and an option over the entity's shares (the equity component). For Liscia, the economic effect of issuing the convertible bonds is substantially the same as simultaneously issuing a debt instrument and an option to the bond holders to acquire equity shares in three years' time.

IAS 32 *Financial Instruments: Presentation* requires the debt and equity components to be presented separately in the statement of financial position to reflect the economic substance of the arrangement and in accordance with the definitions of financial liabilities and equity instruments.

The $20 million cash raised will be separated into the debt and equity components on 1 April 2024. The fair value of the financial liability is established first and this is usually done using a discounted cash flow approach. The relevant discount rate is 5% ie the market rate of interest for similar bonds without conversion rights. The equity component represents the residual value after deducting the fair value of the liability from the $20 million cash proceeds raised.

				$
Cash raised				20,000,000
Less:				
Financial liability component				
(Coupon interest $20m × 2% = $400,000 pa)				

	Cash flow $	5% Discount factor	Present value $	
31.03.2025 Interest paid	400,000	0.952	380,800	
31.03.2019 Interest paid	400,000	0.907	362,800	
31.03.2020 Interest paid	400,000	0.864	345,600	
31.03.2020 Principal	20,000,000	0.864	17,280,000	
				18,369,200
Equity component (balance)				1,630,800

The issue costs of $1 million are then allocated against the initial value of the debt and equity components on a pro-rata basis as follows:

	Total $	Financial liability $	Debt $
Initial debt/equity split	20,000,000	18,369,200	1,630,800
Issue costs	(1,000,000)	(918,460)	(81,540)
	19,000,000	17,450,740	1,549,260

$1,000,000 × 18,369,200/20,000,000 = $918,460
$1,000,000 × 1,630,800/20,000,000 = $81,540

On 1 April 2024, the financial liability component will be recorded at $17,450,740 and the equity component at $1,549,260. The value of the equity component will remain fixed at $1,549,260 for the three years until conversion. The financial liability component will subsequently be held on an amortised cost basis at the revised effective rate of interest of 6.8% due to the allocation of the issue costs above.

	At 01.04.2024 $	Finance cost at 6.8% $	Interest paid $	At 31.03.2025 $
Financial liability	17,450,740	1,186,650	(400,000)	18,237,390

Finance costs of $1,186,650 will be expensed to profit or loss in the year. The financial liability will be carried at $18,237,390 in the statement of financial position at 31 March 2025

Forward contract

The forward contract is a derivative contract in accordance with IFRS 9 *Financial Instruments* which Liscia should recognise in its financial statements from 1 February 2025 when it became party to the contractual provisions of the contract.

As at the 1 February 2025 the fair value of the forward contract is nil. As 31 March 2025 the derivative is restated to fair value as follows

		$
Fair value at 31.03.2025	10,000,000 Dinars/2.25	4,444,444
Fair value at 01.02.2025	10,000,000 Dinars/2.50	4,000,000
Gain on forward contract		444,444

Liscia will recognise a financial asset of $444,444 at 31 March 2025. The fair value gain would normally be credited to profit or loss immediately unless the conditions for hedge accounting have been met in accordance with IFRS 9 *Financial Instruments*.

The following conditions must be satisfied for hedge accounting to apply:

MOCK EXAM 2 ANSWERS

(a) The hedging relationship must consist of relevant hedging instruments and eligible hedged items. A forward foreign currency contract would qualify as a relevant hedging instrument and the future purchase of the machine would qualify as a highly probable forecast transaction.

(b) The hedge must be properly documented at inception, including details of the hedged item and the hedging instrument, the type of hedge and how the hedge effectiveness will be calculated. It is unclear from the scenario presented whether the relevant documentation has been prepared and this requires further investigation.

(c) The hedge effectiveness requirements are met. In summary, this requires ensuring that there is an economic relationship between the hedged item and the hedging instrument; the effect of credit risk does not dominate changes in value and the hedge ratio of the hedging relationship falls within acceptable parameters (IFRS 9 *Financial Instruments*, para. 6.4.1).

> **Tutorial note:**
>
> Candidates are expected to have a general awareness of the IFRS 9 *Financial Instruments* hedging criteria and how it may apply to the scenario.

On the basis that the above criteria have been met, Liscia would account for this transaction as a cash flow hedge. This is because Liscia is hedging the risk in the changes of future cash flows in respect of a highly probable forecast transaction (the purchase of a machine in dinars on 31 July 2025).

The cash flow hedge will be accounted for as follows:

The portion of the gain on the forward contract that is deemed to be effective is recognised in other comprehensive income and in a corresponding cash flow hedge reserve in the statement of financial position. Any excess gain will be credited to profit or loss account immediately.

The effective portion is measured by comparing the gain to the unrecognised movement in the value of the asset calculated at the relevant spot rate as shown below:

		$
Value of asset at 31.03.2025	10,000,000 Dinars/2.20	4,545,455
Value of asset at 01.02.2025	10,000,000 Dinars/2.45	4,081,632
Increase in cost of the asset (unrecognised)		463,823

Since the gain on the forward is less that the increase in the cost of the asset at 31 March 2025, the hedge is deemed to be fully effective at this point and full gain of $444,444 is recognised in other comprehensive income.

> **Tutorial note (double entry not required)**
>
> | | Dr $ | Cr $ |
> |---|---|---|
> | **Cash flow hedge** | | |
> | Financial asset | 444,444 | |
> | Other comprehensive income/cash flow reserve | | 444,444 |

> **Additional areas where credit might be given, note this is not an exhaustive list:**
> - The use of own figures applies throughout.
> - Credit will be given for all reasonable assumptions made.
> - Marks will be awarded for any other relevant discussion points made.

4 Randall

As an qualified accountant, the Finance Director (FD) should act in accordance with the fundamental ethical principles as described in the IESBA Code is the fundamental principle of professional competence requires the FD to ensure the accounts comply with IFRS Standards. Therefore, the FD should only accept the proposed changes if they comply with IFRS Standards.

The FD should also be aware of threats to the fundamental principles. Here there is a self-interest threat as the Managing Director (MD) wishes to retire and sell his shares in one year's time which may incentivise him to increase profit in order to maximise his exit price from the business.

Accounting implications

Changes in accounting policies and estimates

IAS 8 *Accounting Policies, Changes in Accounting Estimates and Errors* only permits a change in accounting policy if the change:

- Is required by an IFRS; and
1. Results in information that is more relevant and reliable.

    A change in accounting estimate is only required when changes occur in the circumstances on which the estimate was based or as a result of new information or more experience.

    Changing an accounting policy or estimate purely to boost profits and share price would contravene IAS 8 and be considered unethical.

Extending the useful life of manufacturing machinery

IAS 16 *Property, Plant and Equipment* requires the useful life of an asset to be reviewed at least each financial year end, and, if expectations differ from previous estimates, the change should be accounted for prospectively as a change in accounting estimate.

The MD wishes to double the useful life of the machinery. This would reduce the amount of depreciation charged each year on machinery significantly, thereby increasing profit.

However, there does not appear to be any evidence that the useful life of machinery should be increased given there have been minimal profits or losses on disposal in the past which suggests that the current useful life of five years is appropriate. If the useful life of the machinery were underestimated to the extent the MD is suggesting, this would have resulted in substantial profits on disposal.

The useful life of the machinery should remain at five years in the absence of any evidence to suggest that its utility to Randall will increase to 10 years.

Recognising revenue when the customer signs the contract

IFRS 15 *Revenue from Contracts with Customers* requires the entity to identify the performance obligations in a contract.

Here, there appear to be two performance obligations in a typical contract with a customer. Firstly, the promise to transfer goods in the form of office furniture, and secondly, the promise to transfer a service in the form of installation of the office furniture. The MD's proposal to revise the revenue recognition policy fails to split the performance obligations as both revenue streams would be recognised when the customer signs the contract.

Revenue should be recognised when each performance obligation is satisfied. This occurs when the promised good or service is transferred to a customer. The sale of office furniture results in satisfaction of a performance obligation at a point in time. IFRS 15 indicators of the transfer of control include transfer of physical possession of the asset and the customer having the significant risks and rewards of ownership. In the case of Randall's office furniture, the transfer of control appears to take place at the point of delivery of the furniture to the customer rather than when the customer signs the contract. Therefore, the existing revenue recognition policy is correct and the MD's proposed change would contravene IFRS 15.

The installation service results in satisfaction of a performance obligation over time. IFRS 15 requires revenue to be recognised by measuring progress towards complete satisfaction of the performance obligation. Therefore the current policy of recognising revenue over the period of installation is correct and the MD's proposed change to recognise it when the customer signs the contract would contravene IFRS 15 and not be permitted.

It is worth noting that the MD's proposed changes would both result in earlier recognition of revenue and therefore profit.

Reducing the warranty provision

Under IAS 37 *Provisions, Contingent Liabilities and Contingent Assets,* where there is a present obligation, probable outflow and a reliable estimate, a provision should be made for the best estimate of the expenditure required to settle the obligation.

Here, there seems to be evidence to suggest that expected expenditure has fallen as fewer customers are returning furniture under warranty. Therefore, there may be some justification in reducing the provision which would result in a decrease in expenses and increase in profit.

This would be a change in accounting estimate given that the proportion of returns and likely repair costs involve management judgement. As such, it should be accounted for prospectively.

Ethical implications

The proposed increase of the machinery's useful life appears to be unjustified because the evidence indicates that the current useful life is still appropriate.

The change to revenue recognition is not permitted because it would contravene IFRS 15.

There are possible advocacy and intimidation threats here if the FD feels pressured to act in the MD's best interests. There is also a familiarity threat if the FD were inclined to accept the changes out of friendship. Either way, if the FD were to accept the change to the useful life of the machinery and the change in revenue recognition, this would be a breach of the fundamental ethical principle of professional competence (due to non-compliance with IFRS), objectivity (giving in to pressure from the FD) and integrity (if they did so knowingly, with the sole motivation of maximising the exit price for the MD).

The proposed decrease in the warranty provision appears potentially justifiable due to the decrease in furniture returned under warranty. However, if on further investigation there is insufficient evidence to justify the decrease in provision and the sole motivation is to boost profits and maximise the MD's exit price, this change would not be permitted.

The FD should explain to the MD why the proposed changes to the useful life of the machinery and revenue recognition are not permitted. If the MD refuses to accept this, as the MD is the founder, sole shareholder and most senior director, external advice would be required. It would be appropriate to seek professional advice, including considering whether legal advice is required. Finally, resignation should be considered if the matters cannot be resolved.

MOCK EXAM 2 ANSWERS

Index

INDEX

Note: **Key Terms** and their page references are given in **bold**

12-month expected credit losses
credit losses, 353

Accounting concepts, 4
Accounting mismatch, 346
Accounting policies, 77, **462**
Accounting profit, 422
Accounting records, 30
Accounting standards, 4
Accrual accounting, 458
Accrual basis of accounting, 458
Acquiree, 107
Acquirer, 107
Active market, 270
Actuarial gains and losses, 401
Advantages of global harmonisation, 21
Amortised cost, 352
Analysis of exchange differences, 217
Antidilution, 476
Asset, 16, 280, 400
Asset ceiling, 400
Asset turnover, 585
Assets held for sale, 466
Associate, 106, 108, 109, 446
Associates and joint ventures, 240

Barriers to harmonisation, 21
Basis of provision of deferred tax, 438
Big GAAP/little GAAP, 96
Bonus issues, 200
Borrowing costs, 287
BS 7750 Environmental Management System, 58
Business combination, 107

Capital, 20
Capital reductions, 200
Capitalisation/bonus issue, 478
Carrying amount, 282, 289, 303
Cash, 231
Cash equivalents, 231
Cash flow hedge, 360
Cash flows, 230, **231**
Cash generating unit, 294
CERES Principles, 57
Change in accounting estimate, 462

Change in functional currency, 220
Changes in accounting policy, 77, 78
Changes in equity, 44
Close members of the family of an individual, 509
Closing rate, 208
Comparative accounting systems, 21
Comparative information, 461
Competence, 81
Component of an entity, 468
Compound financial instruments, 339
Conceptual Framework, 12, 335
Conceptual nature of employee benefit costs, 398
Confidentiality, 81
Conflict of interest, 84
Consistency of presentation, 458
Consolidated financial statements, 106
Consolidated income statement, 135
Consolidated Statement Of Financial Position, 136
Consolidating sub-subsidiaries, 155
Constructive obligation, 406, **495**
Contingent asset, 501
Contingent consideration, 107, 110
Contingent liability, 501
Contingent share agreement, 476
Contingently issuable ordinary shares, 476
Contract, 335, 531
Contract asset, 531
Contract liability, 531
Control, 106, 550, 565
Conversion, 206
Cost, 281, 303
Costs to sell, 467
Credit loss, 352
Cross-sectional analysis, 583
Current asset, 38
Current asset, 38
Current cost of a liability, 19
Current cost of an asset, 19
Current liability, 39
Current service cost, 400
Current tax, 422
Current value, 17
Customer, 531

INDEX

Date of effective control, 154
Date of transition to IFRS, 264
Debt ratios, 588
Deductible temporary differences, 425, 432, 445
Deemed cost, 264
Deferred consideration, 110
Deferred tax, 424
Deferred tax assets, 424
Deferred tax liabilities, 424
Deferred taxation and business combinations, 443
Deficit or surplus, 400
Defined benefit liability, 408
Defined benefit plans, 399, 404, 405
Defined contribution plans, 399, 404
Demographic assumptions, 407
Depreciation, 263
Derivative, 335
Determining functional currency, 210
Diluted eps, 480
Dilution, 476
Dilutive potential ordinary shares, 484
Direct holdings in sub-subsidiaries, 167
Direct method, 233
Disclosure of financial instruments, 365
Discontinued operation, 468
Discount rate, 408
Disposal group, 465
Disposal of foreign entity, 220
Disposals, 180
Due care, 81

Eco-audit, 58
Eco-labelling, 58
Economic life, 386
Economies ceasing to be hyperinflation economies, 224
Effect of GAAP on gearing, 589
Effective date of disposal, 181
Elements of financial statements, 16
Embedded derivative, 357
Employee benefits, 399
Entity, 335
Entry price, 270
Environmental audit, 58
Environmental Impact Assessments (EIAs), 58
Environmental Quality Management (EQM), 58
Environmental SWOT analysis, 58
Equity, 16
Equity instrument, 335, 514
Equity instrument granted, 514

Equity method, 107, 108, 134
Ethical framework, 81
European Commission (EC), 5, 22
Exchange difference, 208
Exchange rate, 208
Exemption from preparing group accounts, 115
Exit price, 270
Expected credit losses
  credit losses, **352**, 354
Expenses, 16

Fair presentation and compliance with IASs, 457
Fair value, 18, 107, 127, 264, 281, 303, 308, 335, 387, 400, 467, 515
Fair value adjustments, 129
Fair value hedge, 360
Fair value of a liability, 273
Finance lease, 386
Financial Accounting Standards Board (FASB), 13
Financial analysis, 582
Financial asset, 334
Financial assumptions, 407
Financial instrument, 334, 352
Financial liability, 335
Financing activities, 231, 232
First IFRS financial statements, 264
Fixed assets, 281
Fixed production overheads, 309
Foreign associates, 220
Foreign currency, 208, 263
Foreign operation, 210
Forgivable loans, 285
Fulfilment value, 18
Functional currency, 208
Fundamental principles, 80

Generally Accepted Accounting Principles (GAAP), 5, 13
Going concern, 457
Goodwill, 134, 326, **327**
Goodwill and fair value adjustments, 219
Government grants, 285
Grant date, 515
Grants related to assets, 285
Grants related to income, 285
Gross investment in the lease, 387
Group, 106
Guaranteed residual value, 387

Harmonisation and international differences, 21
Hedge effectiveness, 358
Hedge of a net investment in a foreign operation, 360
Hedged item, 358
Hedging, 358
Hedging instrument, 358
Held for sale, 466
Historical cost, 17
HKFRS 11, 141, 142
Hyperinflation, 221

IAS 1 *Presentation of financial statements*, 31, 341
IAS 10 Events after the reporting period, 494
IAS 16 Property, plant and equipment, 281
IAS 18 Revenue, 560, 577
IAS 19 Employee benefits, 398
IAS 2 *Inventories*, 308
IAS 21 The effects of changes in foreign exchange rates, 208
IAS 22 Business combinations, 446
IAS 23 Borrowing costs, 287
IAS 24 Related party disclosures, 508
IAS 24 Related Party Disclosures, 549
IAS 25 Accounting for investments, 109
IAS 28 Investments in associates, 133
IAS 33 Earnings per share, 476
IAS 34 Interim financial reporting, 258
IAS 37 Provisions, contingent liabilities and contingent assets, 495
IAS 39, 343
IAS 7 Statements of cash flows, 230
IAS 8 Accounting policies, changes in accounting estimates and errors, 462
IAS 8 Accounting policies, changes in accounting estimates and errors, 133, 423
IASB Conceptual Framework, 14
IASB
 structure, 11
IFAC Code of Ethics, 80
IFRS 1 first time adoption of international financial reporting standards, 264
IFRS 10, 115
IFRS 15, 531
IFRS 15 Revenue from contracts with customers, 530, 555
IFRS 15 Revenue from Contracts with Customers, 530
IFRS 18 Presentation and Disclosure of Financial Statement, 49
IFRS 3 Business combinations, 126, 316, 327, 446

IFRS 5
 Non-current Assets Held for Sale and Discontinued Operations, 465
IFRS 5 Non-current assets held for sale and discontinued operations., 289
IFRS 5 Non-current Assets HELD FOR SALE AND Discontinued Operations, 465
IFRS for small and medium-sized entities, 96
IFRS Practice Statement Management Commentary, 487
Impaired asset, 290
Impairment, 289
Implications of high or low gearing, 589
Impracticable, 463
Inception of the lease, 386
Income, 16, 531
Incremental costs, 386
Independent, 80
Indirect method, 233
Indirect versus direct, 234
Initial direct costs, 386
Inputs, 270
Intangible asset, 316
Intangible non-current asset, 327
Integrated reporting, 65
Interest, dividends, losses and gains, 340
Interest cost, 401
Interest rate implicit in the lease, 381, 386
Interim financial report, 258
Interim period, 258
International Accounting Standards Committee (IASC), 6
International Ethics Standards Board for Accountants (IESBA), 80
International Federation of Accountants (IFAC), 5
International Financial Reporting Standards, 4
International Integrated Reporting Council, 65
Inter-temporal analysis, 583
Intrinsic value, 515
Inventories, 308
Investing activities, 231, 232
Investment, 109
Investment Entities, 115
Investment property, 303
Investments in debt instruments, 352

Joint arrangement, 106
Joint control, 106, 566
Joint operation, 107
Joint venture, **107**, 108, 446

INDEX

Key management personnel, 509

Lease, 376, 381
Lease payments, 381
Lease term, 382, 386
Lessee's incremental borrowing rate of interest, 381, 387
Leverage, 589
Liability, 16, 495
Lifetime expected credit losses, 353, 355
Limited liability, 30
Liquidity, 586
Loan transfers, 553
Loss allowance, 352

Management Commentary, 487, 488
Market participants, 270
Material, 458, 462
Materiality, 260, 458
Measurement date, 515
Measurement of revenue, 531
Measuring unit current at the balance sheet date, 222
Minimum lease payments, 381, 386
Minority interests, 156, 157, 159
Mintzberg, 69
Monetary items, 208
Most advantageous market, 270
Multi-employer plans, 399
Multinational companies, 583

Nature of profit, 78
Net defined benefit liability, 400
Net interest on the net defined benefit liability, 401
Net investment in a foreign operation, 210
Net investment in the lease, 387
Net realisable value, 308, 310
Non-cancellable lease, 386
Non-controlling interest, 107, 218, 240, 299
Non-current asset, 281

Off balance sheet finance, 548
Offsetting, 461
Offsetting a financial asset and a financial liability, 341
Onerous contract, 498
Opening IFRS statement of financial position, 264

Operating activities, 231
Operating cycle, 38
Operating lease, 381, 386
Operating segment, 471
Options, 482, 487
Options, warrants and their equivalents, 476
Ordinary share, 476
Other comprehensive income, 42
Other long-term employee benefits, 399
Owner-occupied property, 303

Parent, 106
Past service cost, 401
PBIT, profit before interest and tax, 584
Pension schemes, 403
Performance obligation, 531
Piecemeal acquisitions, 191
Plan assets, 400
Post-employment benefit plans, 399
Post-employment benefits, 399
Potential ordinary share, 476
Power, 106
Present value of a defined benefit, 400
Presentation and disclosure of taxation, 441
Presentation currency, 208
Presentation of accounting policies, 461
Presentation of financial instruments, 337
Previous GAAP, 264
Principal market, 270
Prior period errors, 462
Professional behaviour, 81
Profit, 21
Profit margin, 585
Profitability, 584
Progress with harmonisation, 22
Property, plant and equipment, 281
Prospective application, 462
Provisions, 495
Purchased goodwill, 327
Purpose of financial statements, 456

Qualifying asset, 287
Qualifying insurance policy, 400
Quasi-subsidiary, 549

Ratios, 584
Receivable, 531
Recognition, 16, 287
Recoverable amount, 467
Related party, 509

Related party transaction, 508, **509**
Relevant activities, **106**
Remeasurements of the net defined benefit liability, **401**
Reporting date, **264**
Reporting period, 35
Residual value, **281**
Restructuring, **499**
Retrospective application, **462**
Retrospective restatement, **462**
Return on plan assets, **401**
Revalued assets, 429
Revenue, **531**
Reversal of an impairment loss, 301
Right-of-use asset, **381**
Rights issue, 479

Sale and leaseback transactions, 390
Sare split/reverse share split, 478
Seasonal fluctuations, 79
Securitised assets, 552
Segment reporting, 470
Service cost, **400**
Settlement, **401**, 410
Share option, **514**
Share-based payment arrangement, **514**
Share-based payment transaction, **514**
Shareholders' investment ratios, 589
Short-term employee benefits, **399**, 401
Significant influence, **106**, 108, **510**
Small Business Enterprise and Employment Act, 96
Social and political considerations, 583
Spot exchange rate, **208**
SSAP 1, 550
Stand-alone selling price, **531**
Statement of comprehensive income, 40
Statement of financial position, 35
Subsidiaries, 110
Subsidiary, **106**, 109

Substance over form, 549
Sub-subsidiaries, 153
Supplier audits, 58

Tax, 263
Tax base, **425**, 443
Tax expense (tax income), **422**
Tax planning opportunities, 437
Taxable profit (tax loss), **422**
Taxable temporary differences, **425**, 427, 445
Temporary differences, **425**
Termination benefits, **399**, 418
Transaction costs, **270**
Transaction price, **531**
Translation, 207
Treasury shares, 340
Trend analysis, 583
True and fair view, 6

Underlying asset, **381**
Unearned finance income, **387**
Unguaranteed residual value, **381**, **387**
United Nations (UN), 5
Unprofessional behaviour, 84
Useful life, **387**

Value in use, 18, **291**, 467
Value of purchased goodwill, 327
Variable lease payments, **387**
Variable production overheads, **309**
Vest, **515**
Vesting conditions, **515**
Vesting period, **515**

Window dressing, 80
Working capital, 39

INDEX